Lecture Notes in Control and Information Sciences

Edited by A. V. Balakrishnan and M. Thoma

Vol. 1: Modelling and Identification of Distributed Parameter Systems
Proceedings, IFIP Working Conference, Rome, Italy, June 21–26, 1976
Edited by A. Ruberti
Approx. 500 pages. 1977

Vol. 2: New Trends in Systems Analysis
International Symposium, Versailles, December 13–17, 1976
Edited by A. Bensoussan and J. L. Lions
VII, 768 pages. 1977

Vol. 3: Differential Games and Applications
Proceedings of a Workshop, Enschede, Netherlands, March 16–25, 1977
Edited by P. Hagedorn, H. W. Knobloch, and G. J. Olsder
XII, 236 pages. 1977

Vol. 4: M. A. Crane, A. J. Lemoine
An Introduction to the Regenerative Method for Simulation Analysis
VII, 111 pages, 1977

Lecture Notes in
Control and
Information Sciences

Edited by A.V. Balakrishnan and M.Thoma

2

New Trends in Systems Analysis

International Symposium, Versailles, December 13–17, 1976

IRIA LABORIA
Institut de Recherche d'Informatique et d'Automatique
Rocquencourt - France

Edited by A. Bensoussan and J. L. Lions

Springer-Verlag
Berlin Heidelberg GmbH 1977

Editors
Prof. A. Bensoussan
Prof. J. L. Lions

IRIA LABORIA
Domaine de Voluceau – Rocquencourt
F–78150 Le Chesnay/France

With 104 Figures

ISBN 978-3-540-08406-8 ISBN 978-3-540-37193-9 (eBook)
DOI 10.1007/978-3-540-37193-9

Originally published by Springer-Verlag Berlin Heidelberg New York in 1977

2061/3020-543210

This symposium is organized by the Institut de Recherche d'Informatique et d'Automatique under the sponsorship of :

- *Association Française pour la Cybernétique Economique et Technique (AFCET)*
- *International Institute for Applied Systems Analysis (IIASA)*
- *International Federation of Automatic Control (IFAC) :*
  - *Technical Committee of Systems Engineering*
  - *Technical Committee of Theory*

Ce colloque est organisé par l'Institut de Recherche d'Informatique et d'Automatique IRIA sous le patronage de :

- Association Française pour la Cybernétique Economique et Technique (AFCET)
- International Institute for Applied Systems Analysis (IIASA)
- International Federation of Automatic Control (IFAC) :
  - Technical Committee of Systems Engineering
  - Technical Committee of Theory

ORGANIZATION COMMITTEE
COMITÉ D'ORGANISATION

A. Bensoussan (IRIA-LABORIA - Université Paris IX-Dauphine)
J. Casti (IIASA)
P. FAURRE (AFCET-IRIA/LABORIA)
H.K. Kwakernaak (IFAC-Twente University)
J.L. LIONS (Collège de France - IRIA/LABORIA)
Y. Sawaragi (Kyoto University)

SCIENTIFIC SECRETARY
SECRÉTAIRE SCIENTIFIQUE

M. ROBIN (IRIA/LABORIA)

ORGANISATION
SYMPOSIUM SECRETARIAT

Th. Bricheteau (IRIA/External Relations Department)

Table of Contents — Table des matieres

CONTROL OF DISTRIBUTED PARAMETER SYSTEMS
CONTROLE DES SYSTÈMES DISTRIBUÉS

INDUSTRIAL ROBOTICS AND APPLICATIONS OF MICROPROCESSORS
ROBOTIQUE INDUSTRIELLE ET APPLICATIONS DES MICROPROCESSEURS

SYSTEMS ANALYSIS IN PROBLEMS OF ENERGY
APPLICATION DE L'ANALYSE DE SYSTÈMES AUX PROBLÈMES DE L'ENERGIE

APPLICATIONS OF CONTROL THEORY
APPLICATIONS DE LA THÈORIE DU CONTROLE

ENVIRONMENT AND POLLUTION
ENVIRONNEMENT ET POLLUTION

CONTROL OF DISTRIBUTED PARAMETERS

CONTROLE DES SYSTÈMES DISTRIBUÉS

OPTIMAL EXPLOITATION OF A SPATIALLY DISTRIBUTED FISHERY

Frank C. Hoppensteadt
Courant Institute of Mathematical Sciences
New York University
251 Mercer Street
New York, NY 10012

Abstract

Exploitation of a fish population distributed in a habitat bounded on one side by a breeding ground and on the other by an unfavorable environment is studied. The population's dynamics on the breeding grounds are assumed to be described by a simple depensatory function. The effects on this population of harvesting by a fishing fleet are determined as maximum effort and harvesting quotas are varied. In particular, threshold values for these parameters are derived beyond which an open access fishery collapses. Competition with an external fleet and dynamic optimization are discussed briefly.

This work was performed at the University of British Columbia in a Workshop on Mathematical Problems in Ecology, organized by Professor Donald A. Ludwig, July, 1976. The author gratefully acknowledges his hospitality and that of the University of British Columbia.

1. Biological Structure of the Fishery.

A hypothetical fishery is analyzed here in which there is harvesting in an adult stock habitat bounded on one side by a breeding ground and on the other by an environment unfavorable to the fish. Two configurations of this kind are described in Figure 1.

Harvesting effort is focussed on the adult habitat. In this region, dispersal of the fish, natural mortality, removal to the breeding grounds and harvesting will be accounted for. No fish cross over into the unfavorable region, however there is a flux into the adult habitat from the breeding ground. This influx is due to production of adults in the breeding grounds. Production is modelled simply by assuming that no new adults are recruited if the total population in the adult habitat is below a threshold level T, but that new recruits arise at a constant rate, independent of adult population size, provided that the total adult population size exceeds T. T may be interpreted as a threshold of predator satiation, and the fact that production is independent of population size can be interpreted as the breeding grounds having a limited capacity which is easily exceeded by the fish. The reproduction curve is described in Figure 2.

2. Economic Structure of the Fishery.

Management of the fishery to optimize various revenue schemes will be described. To fix ideas, we consider a fishery like that described in Figure 1a, and introduce a variable x to measure distance from the breeding into the adult habitat. Thus, the position $x = 0$ corresponds to a location on the boundary between the breeding ground and the adult habitat, and the position $x = X$ corresponds to the boundary between the adult habitat and the unfavorable environment.

At each position, there will be a cost per unit effort of harvesting which is denoted by $c(x)$. Thus, if an effort $E(x)$ is exerted at x, the net expense at x will be $c(x)E(x)$. On the other hand, if a harvest $h(x)$ results from E at x, then the income realized with price p per unit harvest will be $ph(x)$, so the net revenue at x is

$$\rho(x) = ph(x) - c(x)E(x) = \text{revenue density} .$$

We suppose that p, the price per unit harvest, and $c(x)$, the cost per unit effort density, are fixed. c is assumed here to be a non-decreasing function of x, although in general, it might have any profile.

The first problems to be studied pertain to discovering an optimum strategy for allocating harvesting effort in the fishery subject to the constraint of limited harvest or limited effort. This is done in the next section by means of a mathematical formulation of the problem.

3. Mathematical Analysis of a Management Problem.

The population of adults distributed in the habitat bounded by the breeding ground and by an unfavorable environment will be described in terms of the population density, $u(x,t)$, at time t. Thus, the number in the population a distance x from the breeding ground is $u(x,t)$ at time t. Within the habitat, fish are dispersed and removed from the population by natural mortality, breeding and harvesting. To begin with, no fish pass through the boundary $x = X$. This is expressed mathematically by the flux condition $(\partial u/\partial x)(X,t) = 0$ for all $t > 0$. There is a flux through the boundary at $x = 0$ from the breeding ground. This is described by a constant A if the total population in the adult habitat exceeds the threshold value T (that is, if $\int_0^X u(x,t)dx \geq T$), but the flux from the breeding ground is zero if $\int_0^X u(x,t)dx < T$. This is summarized by

$$\begin{pmatrix}\text{reproduction}\\ \text{model}\end{pmatrix} \qquad (\partial u/\partial x)(0,t) = -\tilde{A}(u) = \begin{cases} -A & \text{if } \int_0^X u(x,t)dx \geq T \\ 0 & \text{if } \int_0^X u(x,t)dx < T \,. \end{cases}$$

Note that the positive constant A is independent of the total populations' excess over T.

These assumptions are summarized in the mathematical model:

(1) $\partial u/\partial t = \sigma^2 \partial^2 u/\partial x^2 - \alpha u - h$ (dynamic equation in adult habitat)

(2) $(\partial u/\partial x)(0,t) = -\tilde{A}(u)$ (flux into adult habitat from breeding ground)

(3) $(\partial u/\partial x)(X,t) = 0$ (no fish cross to the unfavorable environment)

(4) $u(x,0)$ = given (initial population distribution is prescribed) .

Here σ^2 measures the dispersal rate of the fish (its dimensions are area/time), α is the combined removal rate (incorporating loss through natural mortality and to breeding), and h is the harvesting rate density.

3.1 Population Equilibrium with No Harvesting.

The system (1-4) is studied first for an equilibrium distribution ($\partial u/\partial t = 0$) when no harvesting effort is exerted ($h = 0$). Thus, we consider the problem

$$\partial^2 u^o/\partial x^2 - \mu^2 u^o = 0 \,, \tag{5}$$

where $\mu^2 = \alpha/\sigma^2$. The solution of this problem is easily found to be

(6) $$u^o = [A \cosh \mu(x-X)]/[\mu \sinh(\mu X)]$$

unless $\int_0^X u^o(x)dx < T$, when $u^o \equiv 0$. To ensure that the population is viable, we must specify that

(7) $$\int_0^X u^o(x)dx \equiv A/\mu^2 \geq T \, .$$

If the condition (7) is satisfied, then the population can maintain itself, and its equilibrium distribution is given by (6). This is described in Figure 3.

Next, the effects of exploitation on a viable population are considered.

3.2 Fishery at Equilibrium Managed by Harvest Quota.

Usually some assumption is made about the relation between effort and harvest. A typical one is $h = qEu$ where q is called the coefficient of catchability. In this case, the unit revenue at x is given by

$$\rho/h = p - (c(x)/qu) \, ,$$

where again p is the unit price and $c(x)/qu$ is the cost of harvesting one unit at position x from a population of size u. Although more general effort-harvest relations can be analyzed using the methods derived here, we will consider only this simple one. Note that the expression $\rho/h = 0$ can be solved for u as a non-decreasing function of x (recall that c is assumed to be a non-decreasing function of x). This is shown in Figure 4. It will be shown that this curve plays an important role in the economics of the fishery.

The total revenue obtained with a harvesting distribution h(x) is

$$\mathcal{R}(u,h) = \int_0^X (p - c(x,u))h(x)dx^{\dagger} . \tag{8}$$

It is this functional which we wish to maximize with several constraints imposed. The first of these is that at each site the revenue density $(p-c)h(x)$ is non-negative. Next, we suppose that the harvesting density is bounded

$$0 \leq h \leq h_{max} \tag{9}$$

where h_{max} is a constant. Moreover, the total harvest is to be bounded

$$\int_0^X h(x)dx \leq H \qquad \text{(harvest quota)} . \tag{10}$$

h_{max} and H are the critical parameters in the following analysis.

With harvesting, the population equilibrium is determined by the problem

$$d^2u/dx^2 - \mu^2 u = (h(x)/\sigma^2) , \qquad (du/dx)(0) = -A , \qquad (du/dx)(X) = 0 , \tag{11}$$

where $h(x)$ specifies the distribution of harvesting.

The problem is to determine a harvesting strategy $h(x)$ in such a way as to maximize $\mathcal{R}$ in (8) subject to the constraints (9,10,11).

This is easily done. As a first step, at points where $p - c(x,u) > 0$, maximum harvesting should be applied, but where $p - c(x,u) < 0$, no harvesting should be done. Therefore, $h = h_{max}$ is applied on an interval $0 \leq x \leq s$, and $h = 0$ for $s \leq x \leq X$. We refer to s as the stop-harvest point. This reduces the equilibrium problem to one for u and s:

---

† Here and below we write $c(x,u)$ for $c(x)/qu$, and to fix ideas we take $c(x) = mx$ where m might be steaming cost/distance.

(12) $d^2u/dx^2 - \mu^2 u = h_{max}/\sigma^2$, $0 \leq x \leq s$,

(13) $d^2u/dx^2 - \mu^2 u = 0$, $s \leq x \leq X$,

(14) $(du/dx)(0) = -A$, u and du/dx continuous at $x = s$,
$du/dx(X) = 0$,

(15) $\rho(x) \geq 0$, $0 \leq x \leq s$,

(16) $h_{max}\, s \leq H$ (harvest quota) .

This problem must be solved for the population density u and the stop-harvest position s.

Let us first suppose that

$$h_{max}\, X < H ,$$

so the harvest quota imposes no real constraint. While some technical details about the explicit solution arise here, the problem is easily solved. (See Appendix A.) The result is obvious. Let $u^*(x)$ denote the population distribution and let s^* denote the stop-harvest position in this unconstrained case. We first consider the case where $T = 0$. The harvest in this case is $h_{max}\, s^*$. The solution is described in Figure 5. If h_{max} is small, $s^* = X$, and as h_{max} increases, s^* decreases. In mathematical terminology, as $h_{max} \uparrow \infty$, the harvesting density approaches a delta function supported at $x = 0$ having strength A. Thus, in the limit all harvesting is focussed on the boundary of the breeding ground, and all incoming fish are collected. h_{max} is a measure of the fleet's technological capacity; the higher h_{max}, the more fishing can be focussed where fish are not exposed to mortality risk. However, if $h_{max} > h_{max}(T)$, then the control $h = h_{max}$ for $0 \leq x \leq s$ and $h = 0$ for $s < x < X$ is no longer the optimal one. This singular solution will not be derived here.

If $T > 0$, then h_{max} cannot exceed a certain bound $h^*_{max}(T)$. For beyond this value, the fishery collapses. The value $h^*_{max}(T)$ can be determined from the equation $\int_0^X u^*(x,h_{max})dx = T$, where u^* is given in the Appendix. This value is depicted in Figure 7(b).

Next, the effect of the harvest quota must be investigated. We again consider first the case where $T = 0$. For a value $H < s^*h_{max}(s^*)$, the stop harvest position must lie to the left of s^*. This is shown in Figure 6. In this case, the stop harvest point is given by $s = H/h_{max}$, and the population's distribution is easily found as in Appendix A. As $h_{max} \uparrow \infty$ the harvest density again approaches a delta function with support at $x = 0$ and strength H. In this limit, we see that the total population is

$$U = (A-H)/\mu^2 .$$

Therefore, if $H > A - \mu^2 T$ and h_{max} is large, the fishery collapses. The results of this discussion are summarized in Figure 7.

3.3 Fishery Controlled by Constraint on Fishing Effort.

The equilibrium problem (12-16) can be rewritten in terms of effort:

(17) $$d^2u/dx^2 - \mu^2 u - qE_{max}u = 0 , \qquad 0 \le x \le s^*$$

(18) $$d^2u/dx^2 - \mu^2 u = 0 , \qquad s^* \le x \le X$$

(19) $$(du/dx)(0) = -A , \qquad u \text{ and } du/dx \text{ continuous at } x = s^*,$$

$$(du/dx)(X) = 0 ,$$

(20) $$\rho(x) \ge 0 , \qquad 0 \le x \le s^*.$$

The solution of this problem proceeds as in 3.2. As E_{max} increases, $s^* \downarrow 0$ and so the effort is focussed at $x = 0$. Again there is a threshold value for E_{max}; when E_{max} exceeds this threshold, the fishery collapses. The details of the calculation are not presented here.

3.4 Equilibrium Problem When There is a Minimum Cost: $c(x) = I + mx$.

When a minimum cost of fishing is significant, then harvesting may drive the population to a state where $s = 0$, even though the population is viable. In this case, the fishery population survives, but all revenue is dissipated. Initial costs may be due to taxation, and this shows that such measures can effectively protect a resource.

3.5 Equilibrium Problem When There is Offshore Competition.

An offshore fishery drains stock from the adult habitat, and can be modelled by either 12-16 or 17-20 with the boundary condition at $x = X$ (no flux) replaced by

(21) $$(du/dx)(X) = -B.$$

Clearly, in the examples treated earlier, this drain on the adult stock lowers the collapse thresholds of harvest and effort.

3.6 The Dynamic Control Problem.

The adult fishery described by model (1-4) should equilibrate under the conditions discussed earlier in this section. The solutions to those equilibrium problems suggest that the solution of the dynamic problem has the form

$$\begin{aligned} h(x,t) &= h_{max}, \qquad 0 \le x \le s(t), \\ &= 0, \qquad s(t) \le x \le X, \end{aligned}$$

where the stop-harvest boundary $x = s(t)$ must be determined. Now the problem corresponding to the unconstrained maximum current revenue problem is

(22) $\partial u/\partial t = \sigma^2 \partial^2 u/\partial x^2 - \alpha u - h_{max}$, $0 \le x \le s(t)$,

(23) $\partial u/\partial t = \sigma^2 \partial^2 u/\partial x^2 - \alpha u$, $s(t) \le x \le X$,

(24) $(\partial u/\partial x)(0,t) = -\tilde{A}[u]$, $(\partial u/\partial x)(X,t) = 0$,

(25) $u(x,0)$ given

(26) $\rho(s(t)) = 0$.

This must be solved for $u(x,t)$ and $s(t)$. This free boundary problem is reminiscent of the Stefan problem which arises in various physical and economic problems. This problem provides a way of testing the equilibrium solutions found in the earlier sections. The dynamics of this system and the stability of the equilibria are discussed in [1].

3.7 Dynamic Control Problem with Future Revenues as a Performance Index.

The problems described here fit into a setting in which an economic performance index more realistic than current revenue is used. This is the present value of a harvesting policy, and it is given by

$$PV[h] = \int_0^\infty e^{-rt} \int_0^X \rho(x,t)\,dx\,dt ,$$

where r is the discount rate. This functional of the harvesting policy, $h(x,t)$, is to be maximized subject to equations (1-4). Dynamic programming methods have been used [1] to construct solutions of finite horizon approximations to this problem. However, these preliminary results are incomplete.

4. Open Access Fishery.

In unmanaged fisheries, it frequently happens that if any revenue can be generated, someone will exert the effort to do it. This is referred to as an open access fishery. In this case all revenue is dissipated, and the results are often catastrophic to the resource. The mathematical formulation of the open access fishery (at equilibrium) is

$$\begin{Bmatrix}\text{open}\\ \text{access}\\ \text{fishery}\end{Bmatrix} \qquad \begin{aligned} &0 = \sigma^2\left(\frac{\partial^2 u}{\partial x^2}\right) - \alpha u - h\ , \qquad 0 \le x \le X\ ,\\ &\frac{\partial u}{\partial x}(0) = -\tilde{A}(u)\ , \qquad \frac{\partial u}{\partial x}(X) = 0\ ,\\ &\int_0^X \left[p - \frac{c(x)}{qu(x)}\right] h(x)\,dx = 0\ . \end{aligned}$$

We begin with $T = 0$ and $c(x) = mx$. h cannot be positive over an interval, since over such an interval $u = c(x)/pq$ and so $h(x) = -mx/pq < 0$. Therefore, $h(x)$ must be a delta function with support at some point $\bar{s}$ and with strength h_{max}. $\bar{s}$ can be determined in the following way: Let $h(x) = h_{max}\delta(x-\bar{s})$ and

$$u(\bar{s}) = c(\bar{s})/pq\ , \qquad \sigma^2\frac{\partial^2 u}{\partial x^2} - u = h_{max}\delta(x-\bar{s})\ ,$$

$$\frac{\partial u}{\partial x}(0) = -A\ , \qquad \frac{\partial u}{\partial x}(X) = 0\ .$$

Thus, if $G(x,\bar{s})$ is Green's function for this problem, we have

$$G(\bar{s},\bar{s}) = c(\bar{s})\sigma^2/h_{max}pq\ .$$

This is the determining equation for $\bar{s}$.

As before, if $T > 0$, then sufficiently large h_{max} will result in collapse of the fishery.

5. Summary.

A model is formulated here for a spatially distributed fishery. This incorporates several desirable features such as a depensatory reproduction function, dispersal of adults, and mortality. At the same time the model is sufficiently simple to provide straightforward answers to several questions pertaining to control of the fishery.

In the case of an open access fishery, increased technical capability eventually leads to collapse of the adult breeding stock. Means of preventing this are imposition of harvest quotas or restrictions on effort allocation. Under various management policies (that is, constraints), allocation of harvest and effort were determined that optimize the sustained (equilibrium) current revenue generated by the fishery.

A more realistic economic performance index to optimize is the present value of all future harvest allocations

$$PV[h] = \int_0^\infty e^{-rt} \int_0^X \rho(x)dxdt \ .$$

This is a more difficult problem to analyze (for example, it entails a dynamic optimization problem). However, the case where the discount rate is near zero should approximate the bionomic equilibrium case (that is, the maximum sustained current revenue problem), and the case of large discount rate should be near the open access fishery [1].

Optimization of spatially distributed fisheries have evidently not been treated in the literature. Details of some results given here are presented in [1]. There are also some results presented in [2] where a slowly dispersing species ($\sigma << 1$) is described by approximation methods.

Appendix A: General Solution of (12,13,14).

The problem (12,13,14) can be solved for any choice of s: The general solution of

$$d^2u/dx^2 - \mu^2 u = h_{max}/\sigma^2 , \qquad (du/dx)(0) = -A ,$$

is

$$u = -(A/\mu)\sinh(\mu x) + C_1\cosh(\mu x) - h_{max}/\sigma^2\mu^2 ,$$

and the general solution of

$$d^2u/dx^2 - \mu^2 u = 0 , \qquad (du/dx)(X) = 0 ,$$

is

$$u = C_2\cosh\mu(x-X) .$$

The two constants C_1 and C_2 can be determined from the smoothness condition (14):

$$-(A/\mu)\sinh(\mu s) + C_1\cosh(\mu s) - (h_{max}/\sigma^2\mu^2) = C_2\cosh[\mu(s-X)] ,$$

$$-A\cosh(\mu s) + \mu C_1\sinh(\mu s) = \mu C_2\sinh[\mu(s-x)] .$$

The solutions are

$$C_1 = \{(A/\mu)\cosh(\mu X) - (h/\mu^2\sigma^2)\sinh[u(s-X)]\}/\sinh(\mu X) ,$$

$$C_2 = \{(A/\mu) - (h/\mu^2\sigma^2)\sinh(\mu s)\}/\sinh(\mu X) .$$

Unconstrained Solution, (u*,s*).

In the unconstrained case, the stop-harvest point s is determined by the position at which the revenue density vanishes: $\rho(s^*) = 0$. This occurs when

$$p = (I + ms^*)/u(s^*) \qquad \text{or} \qquad u(s^*) = \frac{I}{p} + \frac{m}{p} s^* .$$

Since $u(s^*) = C_2\cosh[\mu(s^*-X)]$, we see that the equation for s^* becomes

$$[(A/\mu) - h_{max}/\sigma^2\mu^2)\sinh(\mu s^*)]\cosh[\mu(s^*-X)]/\sinh\mu X$$

$$= \frac{I}{p} + \frac{ms^*}{p} .$$

The solution for s^* depends on the sizes of the various parameters. In the cases of interest, there is either a unique solution satisfying $0 < s^* < X$ or one greater than X in which case we take $s^* = X$.

The unconstrained solution is denoted by $u = u^*(x)$, or by $u = u^*(x,h_{max})$ if the value of h_{max} is not clear from the context.

Bibliography

[1] F. C. Hoppensteadt, Math. Meth. of Pop. Biol., (in press).

[2] C. W. Clark, Math. Bio-Econ., J. Wiley, (in press).

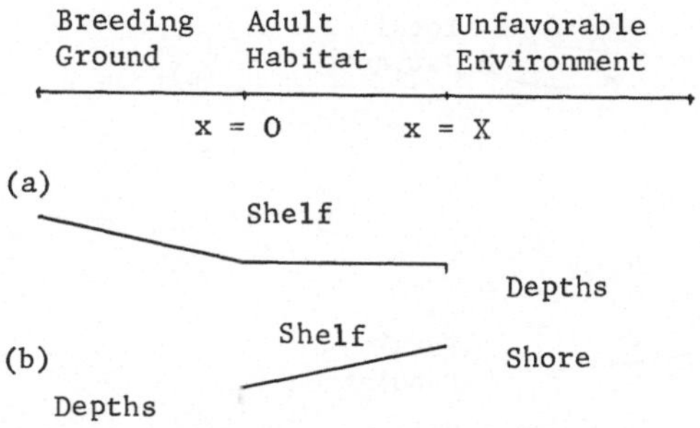

Figure 1. a. Spawning. b. Scallop

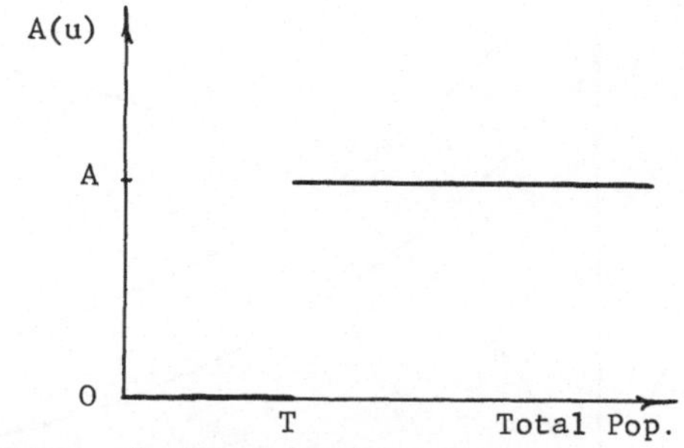

Figure 2. Reproduction curve.

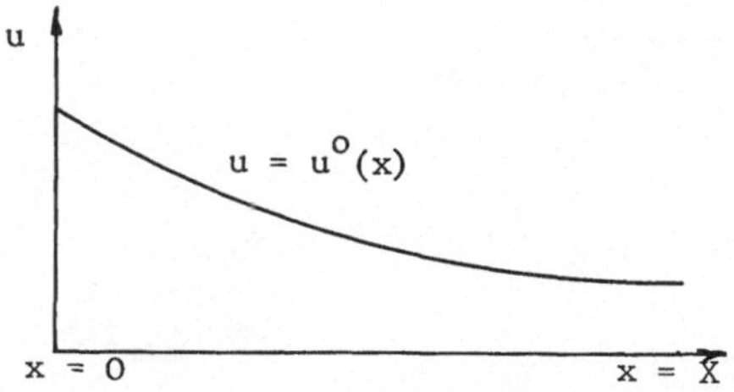

Figure 3. Equilibrium distribution of fish, with no harvesting.

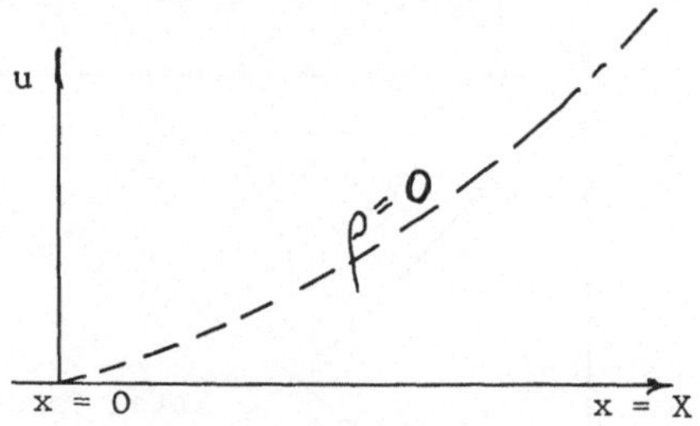

Figure 4. "Break-even" population level for an open access fishery.

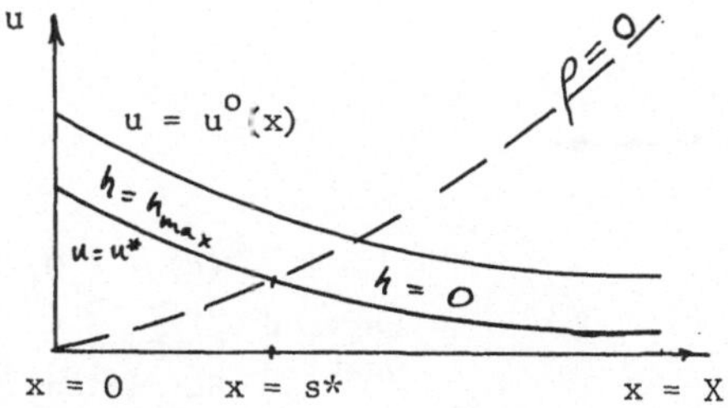

Figure 5. The curve labelled u* describes the equilibrium population distribution for the maximum sustained current revenue (Bio-economic equilibrium)

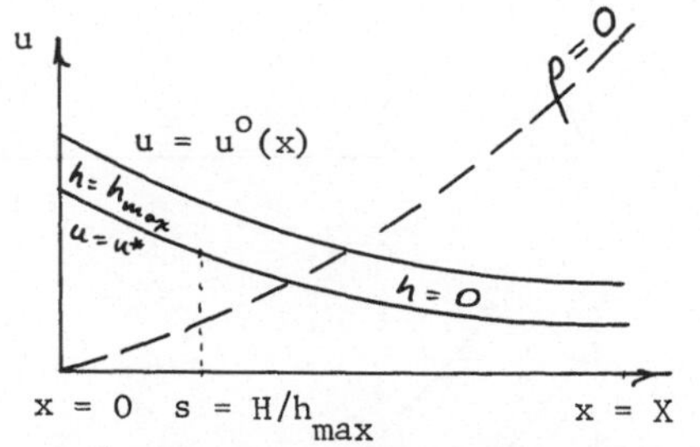

Figure 6. This depicts the population distribution ($u = u^*$) when the harvest quota H is imposed ($H < s^* h_{max}$).

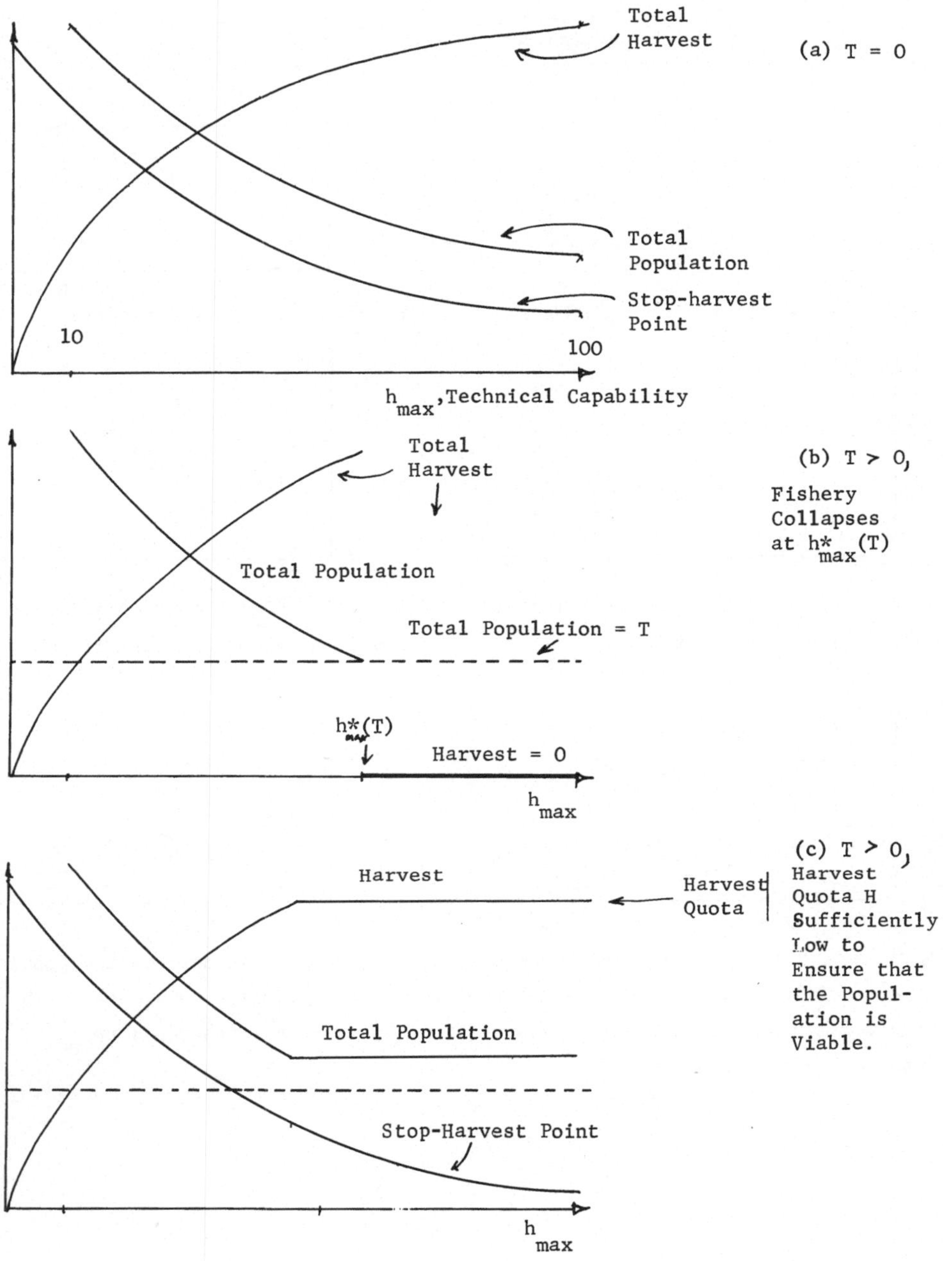

Figure 7. Bionomic Equilibria. A sample calculation of the stop-harvest point, the harvest size and the total population size as functions of the technical capability h_{max} of the fleet. For these calculations, $\mu = 1$, $A = .9$, and $\sigma = X = m = p = 1$. The vertical scale in these figures is different for each of the three parameters plotted, and these scales are not indicated here.

DISTRIBUTED-PARAMETER NUCLEAR REACTOR OPTIMAL CONTROL

SPYROS TZAFESTAS*
Department of REACTORS
NRC "Demokritos", Athens, Greece

ABSTRACT

A survey of the distributed-parameter optimal control methods, applied to nuclear reactors, is presented. Specifically, after a brief introduction to the derivation of the nuclear reactor distributed-parameter differential and integral models, the formulation of the linear-quadratic, the bilinear, the eigenvalue assignment, and the stochastic control problems is given, and the main existing solution methods are outlined. A set of simple but representative examples is provided to illustrate the theoretical results. Much further work is required for designing and implementing practical finite dimensional optimal (suboptimal) controllers based on distributed-parameter models of complete power reactor systems.

1. INTRODUCTION

Our purpose in this communication is to provide an up to date survey of the recent advances in distributed-parameter (DP) nuclear reactor control. From a theoretic point of view DP optimum control is presently at a well advanced stage. Some books and survey papers already existing in the field are given in {1}-{6} where one may find most of the theory and bibliography today available. Concerning the optimum control of nuclear reactors the effort was mainly concentrated to solving poing-reactor problems {7}-{26} and fewer works, e.g. {27}-{31} deal with space-dependent reactor models. This seems to be somehow natural, since even in the pure control theory there was a certain delay between lumped-parameter control results and corresponding DP ones. Here we wish to emphasize that, except a number of particular points which are due to the nature of the phenomena occuring in nuclear reactors and require special care, most of the available DP control results can be readily applied to nuclear reactors. This will be seen from the discussion of the problems to be studied in the sequel.

Some of the most important nuclear reactor control problems are: i) Start-up control, ii) Shut-down control, iii) spatial (xenon) oscillation control, and iv) load change regulation.

All these problems have been studied by several workers. For example,

---

*Also with the Control Systems Laboratory, Patras University, Patras, Greece.

Shen and Haag {7} studied a core-start-up system using a one-equation-kinetics model, and Ruiz {8} solved the same problem using a two-equations-kinetics model. Ash {9} treats the shutdown control problem, Rosztoczy et.al.{10} consider and solve the nuclear power control by the Pontryagin principle for minimmum control rod displacement. Duncombe and Rathbone {11} consider a complete PWR power system consisted from nine equations. Two performance indexes were studied, namely: i) power error and "power x reactivity" penalty, and ii) power error and reactivity penalty: The resulting feedback system provides continuous load-following in the sense that control rod action is reoptimized continuously as the load demand varies. We feel that this load change compensation problem can also be solved for DP nuclear power models. Kliger {12} solves the problem of moving the power level from one equilibrium level to another in minimum time,invoking the Banach space approach and the generalized Hölder's inequality. Tzafestas and Chrysochoides {13} solve the problem of input-output decoupling and eigenvalue control of multivariable (e.g. multi-core) reactors, and Reddy and Sannuti {14} apply the singular perturbation technique for finding the optimal power controller for a two-core coupled nuclear reactor system.

The above works are representative of the achievements in the point reactor control field but they are not exhaustive.

Two other aspects basic in DP nuclear reactor control analysis and design are "simulation" and "stability". These aspects have also been studied very deeply and a variety of useful results is available.

Due to space limitations these results will not be reviewed here. The interested reader may refer to {33}-{38}.

The present survey is organized as follows. Section 2 provides the differential and integral equation models of space-dependent nuclear reactors, which include the main phenomena occuring in them. In section 3 we formulate the linear quadratic optimum control problem of nuclear reactors and review three methods of solution, namely the modal expansion technique (based on a DP TPBVP or Riccatti equation), the direct variational synthesis approach, the discrete-time solution method, and the adjoint space technique. Section 4 deals with the nonlinear reactor control problem and studies the variational technique and the Hölder's inequality approach to the bilinear control. Section 5 gives a brief exposition of the eigenvalue control problem, and section 6 gives some comments on the control of stochastic nuclear reactors, and on the special topic of selecting the measurement and control spatial points for better performance. Finally in section 7 we collect some indicative numerical examples which support many of the theoretical results.

2. DISTRIBUTED-PARAMETER NUCLEAR REACTOR MODELS

2.1. Differential model

Distributed-parameter nuclear reactor models were studied in{27}-{32}. Details of the derivations may be found in {28}. Consider a power reactor with stationary fuel. The neutron balance is described by the Boltzmann, or transport theory, model which, when there are no steep gradients in neutron flux, is approximated by the following multigroup space-time state-space model {39}-{40}:

$$A(X,x,t)X_t(x,t)=F[X,x,t],x\varepsilon D;\ \beta[X,x,t)]=0,\ x\varepsilon\partial D \tag{1}$$

where $X(x,t)$ is the state vector function, $A(X,x,t)$ is a matrix-valued function of its arguments of appropriate dimensions, $F[...]$ is a spatial operator over D, D and ∂D are the spatial domain of interest and its boundary surface, and $\beta[...]$ is a spatial operator over ∂D, compatible with $F[...]$.

The nonlinear DP state-space model (1) is quite general and can embrace all phenomena occuring in a reactor system. The model is also valid for "multi-region" reactors which have some parameters with step discontinuities on the interfaces of the various regions.

For a reactor with one fast, one slow, and one delayed group the model (1) has $A=\mathrm{diag}[\upsilon_F^{-1},\upsilon_s^{-1},1]$, $X=[\Phi_F,\Phi_s,C]$, $\beta(X,x,t)=X$, and

$$F(X,x,t)=\begin{bmatrix}\{\nabla.D_F\nabla-(\Sigma_{aF}+\Sigma_R)+(1-\beta)\nu\Sigma_{fF}\}\Phi_F+(1-\beta)\nu\Sigma_{fs}\Phi_s+\lambda_c C\\ \Sigma_R\Phi_F+(\nabla.D_s\nabla-\Sigma_{as})\Phi_s\\ \beta\nu\Sigma_{fF}\Phi_F+\beta\nu\Sigma_{fs}+\Phi_s-\lambda_c C\end{bmatrix} \tag{2}$$

where Φ_F=fast neutron flux, Φ_s= slow neutron flux, and C=precursor concentration. Here $\Phi_F,\Phi_s,D_F\nabla\Phi_F$ and $D_s\nabla\Phi_s$ are continuous at all region interfaces, and X vanishes at the extrapolated boundaries.

Clearly, the diffusion model (1) is not valid near a control rod due to the sharp flux gradient. For small control rod displacements the effect of the discontinuity will remain essentially constant, and so it is possible to express the control rod movement as a movement of the interface. The usual approximation is that Σ_{as}, the thermal absorption cross-section, is given by

$$\Sigma_{as}(x,t)=\Sigma_{aso}(x)+\sum_{k=1}^{N}u_k(t)\delta(x-x_k) \tag{3}$$

where $\Sigma_{aso}(x)$ is some average value, and $u_k(t)$ is the strength of a thermal abasoption source or sink at the end x_k of the kth control rod (measured experimentally). Equation (3) represents the effect of slightly displacing the control rods. By an appropriate sort of gearing $u_k(t)$ can be realized as a linear function of the control signal.

An other phenomenon which affects Σ_{as} is the xenon poisoning process. In general the total thermal absorption cross-section Σ_{as} is equal to

$$\Sigma_{as}=\Sigma_{aso}(x)+\sigma_{as,Xe}N_{Xe}(x,t) \tag{4}$$

where N_{Xe} is the concentration of Xe, and all control rods are assumed at their average position (i.e. all $u_k=0$ so that $\Sigma_{as}=\Sigma_{aso}$,"clean reactor"). The dynamic evolution of N_{Xe} is governed by

$$(N_{Xe})_t=\lambda_I N_I(x,t)+\gamma_{Xe}\Sigma_{fF}(x)\Phi_F(x,t)+\gamma_{Xe}\Sigma_{fs}(x)\Phi_s(x,t)$$

$$-\lambda_{Xe}N_{Xe}(x,t)-\sigma_{as,Xe}N_{Xe}(x,t)\Phi_s(x,t) \tag{5}$$

where the iodine concentration N_I is described by

$$(N_I)_t=\gamma_I\Sigma_{fF}(x,t)\Phi_F(x,t)+\gamma_I\Sigma_{fs}(x,t)\Phi_s(x,t)-\lambda_I N_I(x,t) \tag{6}$$

Analogous equations hold for the samarium as well. Consideration of the decay chains of Xe^{135} and Sm^{149} sufficiently approximates the total fission product poisoning process (see {41}).

Concerning the temperature effects, a positive temperature feedback coefficient may lead to an unstable nuclear reactor, whereas a large negative feedback temperature coefficient may stabilize the system by balancing other existing destabilizing effects.

To take into account the temperature effects we use first-order Taylor expansions about a mean temperature $\bar{T}(x)$ of the type

$$\Sigma_{fs}(x,\bar{T})=\Sigma_{fs}(x,\bar{T})+\{\partial\Sigma_{fs}(x,T)/\partial T\}_{\bar{T}}(T-\bar{T}) \tag{7}$$

In reactor calculations it is usually assumed that all heat generated is removed by the cooling system , and so equating the rate of change of internal energy to that gained from fission less the heat removed, we arrive at the equation

$$\rho(x)c_T(x)T_t(x,t)=\nabla.k(x)\nabla T(x,t)+\varepsilon\Sigma_{fF}(x,T)\Phi_F(x,t)+\varepsilon\Sigma_{fs}(x,t)\Phi_s(x,t) \tag{8}$$

with boundary conditions similar to those for the neutron flux. A process that is very often neglected is fuel burn-up since this takes place in a number of months. Adjoining (1) and (3)-(8) we obtain the overall DP nuclear reactor state-space model which is nonlinear and extremely complex. This overall model can also be put in the form (1) by appropriate definitions of A,F, β and X.

Usually, we use linearized models by considering small deviations of the state variables from their nominal (operating-point) ones. In this case the controller (optimal etc) is designed such that the operating-point performance is optimal and also to keep the deviations as smaller as possible. We assume that the "operating-point" is the "steady -state" which means that the control rods at the steady-state position keep the reactor exactly critical in the presence of poisons etc. The steady-state $\bar{X}(x)$ is determined by setting $X_t(x,t)=0$, i.e. by solving the algebraic equation

$$F(\bar{X}(x),x)=0 \tag{9}$$

Defining by $\tilde{X}(x,t)$ the deviation of the state vector from its steady state $\bar{X}(x,t)$, i.e. $\tilde{X}(x,t)=X(x,t)-\bar{X}(x,t)$, inserting it in (1), and neglecting higher-order terms (i.e. products of $\tilde{X}$ components etc) yields the linear model $\tilde{A}(x,t)\tilde{X}_t(x,t)=\tilde{\mathcal{L}}(x,t)\tilde{X}(x,t)+\tilde{B}(x,t)u(t)$, which if premultiplied by $\tilde{A}^{-1}(x,t)$($\tilde{A}(x,t)$ must be nonsigular for all $x\varepsilon D$ and t of interest) can be written as

$$X_t(x,t)=\mathcal{L}(x,t)X(x,t)+B(x,t)u(t),\ x\varepsilon D, t\geqslant t_o \tag{10}$$

where we used again the symbol $X(x,t)$ for $\tilde{X}(x,t)$. Here $\mathcal{L}(x)$ is a linear spatial differential operator and $B(x)$ is a known matrix.

This is the linear DP nuclear reactor model which is to be studied here, and holds only for small control rod movements about some steady-state operating point $\bar{X}(x,t)$. The linearized boundary conditions associated to (10) have the linear form

$$a(x)X(x,t)=0,\ x\varepsilon\partial D,\ t\geqslant t_o \tag{11}$$

where $a(x)$ is a spatial operator over ∂D compatible with $\mathcal{L}(x)$.

2.2. Integral model

The linear integral equation model of a DP nuclear reactor corresponding to (10)-(11) has the form

$$X(x,t)=\int_D K(x,t;x',t_o)X_o(x')dx'+\int_{t_o}^{t}\int_D K(x,t;x',\tau)B(x',\tau)U(x',\tau)d\tau dx \tag{12}$$

where $X_o(x), x\varepsilon D$ is the state function at $t=t_o$, $K(x,t;x',t_o)$ is the Green's matrix function, and $U(x',\tau)$ is of the form {see (3)}:

$$U(x',\tau)=\sum_{k=1}^{N} u_k(\tau)\delta(x'-x_k) \tag{13}$$

Introducing (13) into (12) yields the model

$$X(x,t)=X_o(x,t)+L(t_o,t)u(t),\text{where } X_o(x,t)=\int_D K(x,t;x',t_o)X_o(x')dx' \tag{14}$$

$$L(t_o,t)=\int_{t_o}^{t}\tilde{K}(x,t;\tau)d\tau,\ u(t)=[u_1(t),u_2(t),\dots,u_N(t)]^T$$
$$\tilde{K}(x,t,\tau)=[K(x,t;x_1,\tau)B(x_1,\tau),\dots,K(x,t;x_N,\tau)B(x_N,\tau)] \tag{15}$$

Equation (14) constitutes the integral DP nuclear reactor model which will be under study in the present paper. Details about it and the properties of the Green's function may be found in several books and papers (e.g.{42}-{44}). Both models (10) and (14) are "deterministic", i.e. they do not take into account possible stochastic effects on the operation of the nuclear reactors. Some comments concerning the control of stochastic reactors will be given in section 6.

3. LINEAR-QUADRATIC NUCLEAR REACTOR CONTROL

As in most engineering areas the linear-quadratic optimum control of DP nuclear reactors constitutes the basis of the whole control design theory. Very broadly the DP linear-quadratic control problem (LQP) can be stated as follows: Given a linear DP nuclear reactor system in the form (10) or (14) choose the control input $u(t)$ such that to minimize a quadratic cost functional of the type

$$J=\int_{t_o}^{t_f} g(\tau)d\tau,\quad g(\tau)=\int_D G(x,\tau)dx$$
$$G(x,\tau)=\frac{1}{2}\{X^T(x,\tau)Q(x,\tau)X(x,\tau)+U^T(x,\tau)R(x,\tau)U(x,\tau)\} \tag{16}$$

Using the expression (13) of $U(x',\tau)$, $g(\tau)$ takes the form

$$g(\tau)=\frac{1}{2}\{\int_D X^T(x,\tau)Q(x,\tau)X(x,\tau)dx+u^T(\tau)\underline{R}(\tau)u(\tau)\} \tag{17}$$

where $u(\tau)$ is as shown in (15), and $\underline{R}(\tau)=\mathrm{diag}[R(x_1,\tau)\ldots.,R(x_N,\tau)]$.

This problem has been treated by many authors both for general DP systems and nuclear systems by several techniques as e.g. dynamic programming {3},{45},{46}, indirect variational methods {47},{48}, direct variational methods {32},{49},{50}, maximum principle {2},{30} etc. Here we shall review: i) the indirect variational modal expansion technique {27},{28}, ii) the direct approach which is based on the integral model {32},{50}, the discrete-time solution {51}, and iv) the adjoint space technique {52}-{53}.

3.1. Modal expansion technique

In this technique the state variable $X(x,t)$ is expanded into a series of either the so called "clean reactor modes $\theta_k(x)$" or the "Kaplan modes $\Psi_m(x)$". To illustrate the method consider the linear model (10) corresponding to the case where all neutron flux groups and delayed neutrons are lumped and averaged into one variable $\Phi(t)$, in which case we have the equations

$$\begin{bmatrix}1 & 0 & 0\\ 0 & 1 & 0\\ 0 & 0 & 1/\upsilon\end{bmatrix}\begin{bmatrix}N_I\\ N_{Xe}\\ \Phi\end{bmatrix}_t=\begin{bmatrix}-\lambda_I & 0 & \gamma_I\varepsilon\Sigma_f\\ \lambda_I & -(\lambda_{Xe}+\sigma_{a,Xe}\bar{\Phi}) & -\sigma_{a,Xe}\bar{N}_{Xe}+\gamma_{Xe}\varepsilon\Sigma_f\\ 0 & -\sigma_{a,Xe}\bar{\Phi} & \nabla.D\nabla+\nu\varepsilon\Sigma_f-\Sigma_a-\sigma_{a,Xe}\bar{N}_{Xe}\end{bmatrix}\begin{bmatrix}N_I\\ N_{Xe}\\ \Phi\end{bmatrix}$$
$$+\begin{bmatrix}0 & 0\ldots\ldots\ldots\ldots & 0\\ 0 & 0\ldots\ldots\ldots\ldots & 0\\ -\bar{\Phi}\delta(x-x_1) & -\bar{\Phi}\delta(x-x_2)\ldots\ldots\ldots & -\bar{\Phi}\delta(x-x_N)\end{bmatrix}\begin{bmatrix}u_1\\ u_2\\ \vdots\\ u_N\end{bmatrix} \tag{18}$$

The "clean reactor" model is obtained by putting $\bar{N}_{Xe}=N_{Xe}=u_k=0$ i.e.

$$\frac{1}{\upsilon}\Phi_t=\{\nabla.D\nabla+(\nu\varepsilon\Sigma_f-\Sigma_a)\}\Phi \tag{19}$$

while the full model (18) is defined to be the "Kaplan" model. Clearly, the eigenvalues λ_i and the orthonormal eigenfunctions $\theta_k(x)$ of (19) are determined by

$$\{\nabla.D\nabla+(\nu\varepsilon\Sigma_f-\Sigma_a)\}\theta_k(x)=\lambda_k\theta_k(x),\ x\varepsilon D \tag{20}$$

Expanding Φ, N_{Xe}, N_I as

$$\Phi(x,t)=\sum_{k=0}^{\infty}C_{\Phi,k}(t)\theta_k(x),\ N_{Xe}(x,t)=\sum_{k=0}^{\infty}C_{Xe,k}(t)\theta_k(x),N_I(x,t)=\sum_{k=0}^{\infty}C_{I,k}(t)\theta_k(k)$$

and introducing into the model (18) yields the modal equations, but unless $\Sigma_f,\bar{\Phi}$ and $\bar{N}_{Xe}$ are spatially flat these equations involve all modes i.e. we have full mode coupling. Actually this mode coupling is the principal disadvantage of the clean reactor modal expansion method, and does not exist when expanding in terms of the Kaplan eigenfunctions $\Psi_m(x)$ being determined by the overall operator in (18), i.e. by

$$\omega_m\tilde{A}(x)\Psi_m(x)=\tilde{\mathcal{L}}(x)\Psi_m(x)\ ,x\varepsilon D \tag{21}$$

where ω_m is the eigenvalue corresponding to $\Psi_m(x)$. The adjoint eigenfunctions $\Psi_j^*(x)$ are determined by the adjoint equation

$$\omega_j\tilde{A}^*(x)\Psi_j^*(x)=\tilde{\mathcal{L}}^*(x)\Psi_j^*(x),\ x\varepsilon D \tag{22}$$

and satisfy the biorthogonality relation

$$<\Psi_j^*,\tilde{A}\Psi_m>=\int_D\Psi_j^*(x)\tilde{A}(x)\Psi_m(x)dx=\delta_{jm}\quad \text{(Kronecker delta)}$$

Expanding the whole state vector as

$$X(x,t)=\sum_{m=0}^{\infty}\xi_m(t)\Psi_m(x),\ \xi_m(t)=<\Psi_k^*,X(x,t)> \tag{23}$$

and introducing into (18) yields for m=0,1,2,....,

$$d\xi_m(t)/dt=\omega_m\xi_m(t)+<\Psi_m^*,\tilde{B}u>,\ \xi_m(t_o)=<\Psi_m^*,X(x,t_o)> \tag{24}$$

Clean modes are proved to be complete whereas Kaplan modes are not guarranteed to be complete. The main question of clean modal expansions is the convergence which has to be checked individually. In practice one assumes existence, uniqueness and completeness of the Kaplan modal expansion and proceeds as in the clean reactor expansion. In this way by using Kaplan modes one has guarranteed mode decoupling so that controlling the one mode does not affect the others. However calculation of Kaplan modes is more involved than that of the clean reactor modes.

The main result derived by Wiberg concerns controllability and can be stated as follows. "Any finite number of modes of the linear reactor model (18) can be returned to the zero state by an appropriate control

if i) the reactor is equipped with a minimum number of control rods equal to the maximum multiplicity of the spatial operator $\mathcal{L}(x)$ in (18), and ii) all control rods are not on any possible modes of a combination of modes corresponding to the same eigenvalue". Of course using more control rods may lead to improved response.

Let us distinguish the "spatial control" problem, in which we wish to drive all spatial deviations to a steady state (regulator problem), from the "power control" problem, in which it is desired to follow the changes of the desired steady-state (servomenchanism problem). Assuming that the high modes are to be controlled by the spatial controller, the power controller has to control only the fundamental mode.

Thus, denoting by $X_s(x,t)$ the state vector of the spatial (or harmonic) control system we have, by eqn. (23):

$$X_s(x,t)=X(x,t)-\xi_o(t)\Psi_o(x) \tag{25}$$

where $\xi_o(t)$ is to be controlled by the power controller. Then we choose the action $u_N(t)$ of the Nth control rod such that to balance the effect of all other rods on the fundamental mode, and find

$$u_N(t)=-\{\sum_{k=1}^{N-1}\Psi_o^{*(2)}(x_k)\bar{\Phi}(x_k)u_k\}/\{\Psi_o^{*(2)}(x_N)\bar{\Phi}(x_N)\} \tag{26}$$

where $\Psi_o^{(i)}$ denotes the ith component of the vector function Ψ_o.

Introducing (25) and (26) into (18) { or (10)} yields the spatial reactor model

$$X_s(x,t)_t=\mathcal{L}(x)X_s(x,t)+B_{N-1}(x)u^{N-1}(t)+C(x,t) \tag{26a}$$

where $u^{N-1}(t)$ is the vector u(t) without the last component $u_N(t)$, and C(x,t) is a known function arizing by this procedure. Now since the measured quantity (output) Y(x,t), which is actually to be fed back for closing the loop, is the flux deviation $\Phi(x,t)$ we put

$$Y(x,t)=M(x)X(x,t)=\begin{bmatrix}0 & 0 & 1\end{bmatrix}\begin{bmatrix}N_I\\ N_{Xe}\\ \Phi\end{bmatrix}$$

Also the power control system must be able to follow the commands of the operators and so the deviation of the fundamental is not present in the cost functional, i.e. $g(\tau)$ of eqn. (17) now takes the form

$$g(\tau)=\frac{1}{2}\{\int_D X_s^T(x,\tau)M^T(x)Q(x,\tau)M(x)X_s(x,\tau)dx+u_{N-1}^T(\tau)\underline{R}(\tau)u_{N-1}(\tau)\}$$

Applying the DP linear quadratic control theory {3},{47} one finds that the optimal control is given by

$$u_{N-1}^o(t) = -\underline{R}^{-1}(t)\int_D B_{N-1}^T(x)\lambda_s(x,t)dx \tag{27}$$

where $X_s(x,t)$ and its adjoint vector $\lambda_s(x,t)$ satisfy the DP canonical equations

$$\partial X_s(x,t)/\partial t=\mathcal{L}X_s-B_{N-1}\underline{R}^{-1}\int_D B_{N-1}^T\lambda_s dx+C \ , \ x\varepsilon D \tag{28a}$$

$$-\partial\lambda_s(x,t)/\partial t=\mathcal{L}^*\lambda_s+M^TQMX_s+C, \ x\varepsilon D \tag{28b}$$

$$aX_s(x,t)=0, \ a^*\lambda_s(x,t)=0, \ x\varepsilon\partial D \tag{28c}$$

$$X_s(x,t_o)=X_{so}(x), \ \lambda_s(x,t_f)=0 \ , \ x\varepsilon D \tag{28d}$$

Equations (28a-d) constitute a DP two-point boundary-value problem (TPBVP). One way of solving them is to use Kaplan mode expansion, i.e. to set

$$X_s(x,t)=\sum_{m=0}^{\infty}\xi_{s,m}(t)\Psi_m(x),\lambda_s(x,t)=\sum_{m=0}^{\infty}n_{s,m}(t)\Psi_m^*(x) \tag{29}$$

in which case, by truncating the infinite summations to the nth term, we obtain

$$\begin{aligned}&\dot{\underline{\xi}}_s=\Omega\underline{\xi}_s-G\underline{R}^{-1}G^T\underline{n}_s+\gamma \quad , \ \underline{\xi}_s(t_o)=\underline{\xi}_{s,0}\\ &-\dot{\underline{n}}_s=\Omega^T n_s+E\xi_s+\gamma \quad , \ \underline{n}_s(t_f)=0\end{aligned} \tag{30}$$

where (for i,j=1,2,...,n):

$$G_{ij}=\langle\Psi_i^*,B_j\rangle \qquad \underline{\xi}_s=\begin{bmatrix}\xi_{s,1}\\ \vdots\\ \xi_{s,n}\end{bmatrix} \ , \ \underline{n}_s=\begin{bmatrix}n_{s,1}\\ \vdots\\ n_{s,n}\end{bmatrix}$$

$$E_{ij}=\langle\Psi_i,M^TQM\Psi_j\rangle$$

The TPBVP (28a-d) or (30) can be converted to a Riccati type equation by setting

$$\lambda_s(x,t)=\int_D P(x,x',t)X_s(x,t)dx \quad \text{or} \quad \underline{n}_s(t)=P(t)\underline{\xi}_s(t)$$

as described in {28},{47} etc. The finite mode controller is obtained by using the truncated series (29) for $\lambda_s(x,t)$ in (27), i.e.

$$u_{N-1}^o(t)=-\sum_{m=0}^{n}\underline{R}^{-1}\int_D B_{N-1}^T(x)n_{s,m}(t)\Psi_m^*(x)dx \tag{31}$$

This is the result of controlling a finite number of modes. Its practicality is due to the fact that if the control system does not interact with the uncontrolled modes we need to control only a few modes of the reactor. Actually an infinite setof modes affect the cost function, despite the fact that they are stable. Hence one must not try to improve the optimality by controlling more than a certain number of modes.

3.2. Direct variational synthesis approach

In this approach, which is also called the "parametrization" approach we use the integral model (14) of the reactor, and express the control vector function in terms of a finite number of coordinate functions not necessarily orthogonal to each other {32} ,{49}-{50}. Some immediate advandages of the direct approach are that the TPBVP encountered above is avoided and also that existence and uniqueness of the optimal control can be established in a natural manner.

We start by expanding u(t) of model (14) in terms of a finite number of elements taken from a complete set of orthonormal basis $\{w_j(t), j=1,2,\ldots, t\epsilon[t_o,t_f]\}$ with $\int_{t_o}^{t_f}\Psi_j(t)\Psi_i(t)dt=\delta_{ij}$

Usually $w_j(t)$ are Legendre or Chebychev polynomials. Here we take the opportunity to propose the Walsh function family which is a family of two-valued discrete-time functions with nice properties {50},{77}-{80}. Thus we write

$$u(t)=\begin{bmatrix}u_1\\ \vdots\\ u_N\end{bmatrix}=\begin{bmatrix}\sum_{i=1}^{m} a_{1i}w_i(t)\\ \vdots\\ \sum_{i=1}^{m} a_{Ni}w_i(t)\end{bmatrix}=W(t)\underline{a} \tag{32}$$

where

$$W(t)=\begin{bmatrix}\underline{w}^T(t) & & 0\\ & \ddots & \\ 0 & & \underline{w}^T(t)\end{bmatrix}, \underline{a}=\begin{bmatrix}\underline{a}_1\\ \vdots\\ \underline{a}_N\end{bmatrix},\ \underline{a}_j=\begin{bmatrix}a_{j1}\\ \vdots\\ a_{jm}\end{bmatrix}, \underline{w}(t)=\begin{bmatrix}w_1(t)\\ \vdots\\ w_m(t)\end{bmatrix}$$

Introducing (32) into (14) yields

$$X(x,t)=X_o(x,t)+\Xi(x,t)\underline{a},\quad \Xi(x,t)=\int_{t_o}^{t}\tilde{K}(x,t;\tau)W(\tau)d\tau \tag{33}$$

Similarly the function g(τ) in (17) takes the form

$$g(\tau)=\frac{1}{2}\{\int_D X^T(x,\tau)Q(x,\tau)X(x,\tau)dx+\underline{a}^T\underline{\tilde{R}}(\tau)\underline{a}\} \tag{34}$$

where $\underline{\tilde{R}}(\tau)=W^T(\tau)\underline{R}(\tau)W(\tau)$. Introducing (33) in (34) and evaluating the first and second partial derivatives of

$$J=\int_t^{t_f} g(\tau)d\tau \text{ with respect to } \underline{a} \text{ we find}$$

$$\frac{\vartheta J}{\vartheta \underline{a}}=\int_t^{t_f}\int_D \Xi^T(x,\tau)Q(x,\tau)X_o(x,\tau)dxd\tau+S(t)\underline{a}$$

$$\frac{\vartheta^2 J}{\vartheta a^2}=S(t),\quad S(t)=\int_t^{t_f}\{\underline{\tilde{R}}(\tau)+\underline{\tilde{Q}}(\tau)\}d\tau$$

where

$$X_o(x,\tau)=\int_D K(x,\tau;x',t)X(x,t)dx',\quad \underline{\tilde{Q}}(\tau)=\int_D \Xi^T(x,\tau)Q(x,\tau)\Xi(x,\tau)dx$$

Equating to zero $\vartheta J/\vartheta\underline{a}$ yields the optimal coefficient vector $\underline{a}$, i.e.

$$\underline{a}^o=-S^{-1}(t)\int_t^{t_f}\int_D \Xi(x,\tau)Q(x,\tau)X_o(x,\tau)dxd\tau$$

$$=-S^{-1}(t)\int_t^{t_f}\int_D\int_D \Xi(x,\tau)Q(x,\tau)K(x,\tau,x',t)X(x,t)dxdx'd\tau \tag{35}$$

under the condition that $S(t)>0$ for all t of interest. The optimal control is then found by introducing a^o in the expression (32).

When it is desired the state X(x,t) to follow a desired trajectory $X_d(x,t)$, $g(\tau)$ in (34) must be assumed of the form

$$g(\tau)=\frac{1}{2}\{\int_D \tilde{X}^T(x,\tau)Q(x,\tau)\tilde{X}(x,\tau)dx+\underline{a}^T\underline{\tilde{R}}(\tau)\underline{a}\}$$

where $\tilde{X}(x,\tau)=X(x,\tau)-X_d(x,t)$, and $\underline{a}^o$ is found to be

$$\underline{a}^o=-S^{-1}(t)\int_t^{t_f}\int_D \Xi(x,\tau)Q(x,\tau)\tilde{X}(x,\tau)dxd\tau \tag{36}$$

3.3. Discrete-time nuclear reactor control

The discrete-time solution of the LQP is directly useful for computer control and is derived by means of the principle of optimality {51}. Discretizing in time the integral nuclear reactor model (14) we find:

$$X_{k+1}(x)=\int_D G_k(x,x')X_k(x')dx'+B_k(x)u_k \tag{37}$$

$$G_k(x,x')=K(x,\overline{k+1}\Delta t,x',k\Delta t),B_k(x)\int_{k\Delta t}^{(k+1)\Delta t}\tilde{K}(x,\overline{k+1}\Delta t;\tau)d\tau \tag{37a}$$

The problem is to choose u_k so as to minimize

$$J_N=\sum_{k=1}^{N}\{\int_D\int_D X_k^T(x)Q(x,x')X_k(x')dxdx'+u_{k-1}^T R u_{k-1}\}$$

where Q,R are symmetric positive definite of appropriate dimensions. Let $J_N^o(X_k(x))$ be the optimal value of J_N. Then for the last N-k stages

$$J_{N-k}^o(X_k(x))=\min_{u_k}\{\int_D\int_D X_{k+1}^T(x)Q(x,x')X_{k+1}(x)dxdx'+u_k^T R u_k+J_{N-(k+1}^o(X_{k+1}(x))\} \tag{38}$$

Assume that J_{N-k}^o can be written in the quadratic form

$$J_{N-k}^o(X_k(x))=\int_D\int_D X_k^T(x)P_{N-k}(x,x')X_k(x')dxdx' \tag{39}$$

and define the matrix $C_{N-k}(x,x')$ as

$$C_{N-k}(x,x')=P_{N-k}(x,x')+Q(x,x') \tag{40}$$

Then introducing (37), (39) and (40) into (38), equating to zero the partial derivative of the result with respect to u_k, and solving for u_k yields the optimum state feedback control

$$u_k=-T_k^{-1}\int_D S_k(x)X_k(x)dx \tag{41}$$

where

$$T_k=\int_D\int_D B_k^T(x')C_{N-(k+1)}(x',x'')B_k(x'')dx'dx''+R \tag{41a}$$

$$S_k(x)=\int_D\int_D B_k^T(x')C_{N-(k+1)}(x',x'')G_k(x'',x)dx'dx'' \tag{41b}$$

Using (41), and equating the kernels of the quadratic terms of both sides of (38), yields the following recursive DP Riccatti equation for $C_{N-k}(x,x');k=N,N-1,\ldots,0$:

$$C_{N-k}(x,x')=Q(x,x')+\iint_{DD} G_k^T(x'',x)C_{N-(k+1)}(x'',x''')G_k(x''',x')dx''dx'''$$

$$-S_k^T(x)T_k^{-1}S_k(x'),\quad C_o(x,x')=Q(x,x') \tag{42}$$

One approach for solving (42) is to reduce it to an algebraic equation using finite-dimensional orthogonal expansions. Thus consider the complete family of orthonormal functions $\{v_i(x),\ x\varepsilon D,\ i=1,2,\ldots.\}$ and expand $C_k^{ij}(x,x')$ as

$$C_k^{ij}(x,x')=\sum_{q,r=0}^{n} c_k^{ij} v_q(x)v_r(x')=\underline{v}^T(x)C_{*,k}^{ij}\underline{v}(x')$$

or in matrix form $C_k(x,x')=V^T(x)C_{*,k}V(x')$. Similarly $G_k(x,x')=V^T(x)G_{*,k}V(x')$ where the matrices $C_{*,k}$, $G_{*,k}$, $v(x)$ and $V(x)$ are appropriately defined. Now, using the orthonormality property of the function $v_i(x)$ we find

a) $\iint_{DD} G_k^T(x'',x)C_{N-(k+1)}(x'',x''')G_k(x''',x')dx''dx'''=\Omega_k^T(x)C_{*,N-(k+1)}\Omega_k(x')$

where

$$\Omega_k(x')=\int_D V(x)V^T(x)G_{*,k}V(x')dx=F_kV(x')$$

b) $\iint_{DD} B_k^T(x)C_{N-(k+1)}(x,x')B_k(x')dxdx'=H_k^TC_{*,N-(k+1)}H_k$

where

$$H_k=\int_D V(x')\int_{k\Delta t}^{(k+1)\Delta t} V^T(x')G_{*,k}(\tau)V(x')dx'd\tau$$

c) $\iint_{DD} G_k^T(x',x)C_{N-(k+1)}(x',x'')B_k(x'')dx'dx''=\Omega_k^T(x)C_{*,N-(k+1)}H_k$

d) $C_{N-k}(x,x')=V^T(x)C_{*,N-k}V(x')$, e) $Q(x,x')=V^T(x)Q_*V(x')$

and so the DP Riccatti equation (42) reduces to the conventional algebraic one

$$C_{*,N-k}=Q_*+F_k^TC_{*,N-(k+1)}\{F_k^T-H_k(H_k^TC_{*,N-(k+1)}H_k+R)^{-1}\ H_k^TC_{*,N-(k+1)}F_k\} \tag{43}$$

which can be solved backwards through algebraic operations only. An equation of the same form could be obtained by first expanding the spatial operator in terms of its eigen functions (i.e. convert the DP model to a LP one), and then discretize in time and apply discrete LP optimal control theory. This approach suffers from the necessity to find or compute the eigenfunctions which is a difficult task. Expanding in terms of general orthonormal sets overcomes this necessity and saves much computing effort. The actual choise of the retained number of functions depends on the accuracy (which increases if we take more terms) and computational effort (which recommends less terms).

3.4. Adjoint space technique

This technique is useful when the control function is of dimensionality greater than that of the final state. Suppose that the admissible control $U(x,t)$, $x\varepsilon D$ belongs to a Hilbert space H with inner product and norm:

$$<U_1,U_2>_H=\int_{t_o}^{t_f}\int_D U_1^T(x,t)U_2(x,t)dxdt,||U||_H=\{<U,U>\}^{1/2}$$

and that at a specific time t_f, $X(x,t_f)$ belongs to a Hilbert space $\mathfrak{X}_f$ defined by

$$<X_1,X_2>_{\mathfrak{X}_f}=\int_D X^T(x,t_f)X(x,t_f)dx,\ ||X(x,t_f||_{\mathfrak{X}_f}=\{<X,X>_{\mathfrak{X}_f}\}^{1/2}$$

The space $\mathfrak{X}_f$ is in general of lower dimensionality than H. The problem to be treated here is to minimize

$J=||X(x,t_f)-X_d(x)||_{\mathfrak{X}_f}$ subject to $||U||_H^2\leqslant L^2$

where $\{X_d(x),\ x\varepsilon D\}\varepsilon\mathfrak{X}_f$ is a desired final state, and the system is described by {see (12) or (14)}

$$X(x,t)=X_o(x,t)+L(x,t)U(x,t)$$

where the operator $L(x,t)$ is assumed to be bounded and compact.

For existence theorems see {52}-{53}. To find the solution we equate to zero the functional derivative with respect to $U(x,t)$ of $J(U)=||L(x,t_f)U(x,t)-X_d(x)||_{\mathfrak{X}_f}$, $\tilde{X}_d(x)=X_d(x)-X^o(x,t_f)$ and obtain the operator equation

$$A(x,t_f)U(x,t)=L^*(x,t_f)\tilde{X}_d(x) \tag{44}$$

where the operator $A(x,t_f)=L^*(x,t_f)L(x,t_f)$ is selfadjoint, compact and nonnegative and hence it has at most a countable number of eigenvalues λ_i and orthonormalized eigenfunctions $\{\Psi_i\}$. This solution is globally optimum as it can be easily verified.

By the adjoint space technique the problem is reduced entirely into $\mathfrak{X}_f$ which by assumption has less dimensionality than H.

Define the control space $=\{U\varepsilon H,||U||_H\leqslant L^2\}$. Since $A(x,t_f)$ is nonnegative, the operator $\{A(x,t_f)+\mu I\}$, $\mu>0$ has a bounded inverse, and so the solution of (44) is given by the limit as $\mu\to 0$ of

$$U_\mu(x,t)=\{A(x,t_f)+\mu I\}^{-1}L^*(x,t_f)\tilde{X}_d(x) \tag{45}$$

Now, suppose first that

$\sup_{\mu>0}||U_\mu||_H^2\leqslant L^2$ and expand $L^*(x,t_f)\tilde{X}_d(x)$ as

$$L^*(x,t_f)X_d(x)=\sum_{i=1}^{\infty}<L^*(x,t_f)\tilde{X}_d(x),\Phi_i>_H\Phi_i(x,t)$$

where $\Phi_i(x,t)$, $i=1,2,\ldots$ are the orthonormalized eigenfunctions of $A(x,t_f)\Phi_i(x,t)=\lambda_i\Phi_i(x,t)$. Then setting $U_\mu(x,t)=\sum_{i=1}^{\infty}c_i(\mu)\Phi_i(x,t)$ and introducing it in (45) gives

$$c_i(\mu)=\frac{1}{\lambda_i+\mu}<L^*(x,t_f)\tilde{X}_d(x),\Phi_i(x,t)>_H$$

Thus finally

$$U^o(x,t)=\sum_{i=1}^{\infty}\frac{1}{\lambda_i}<L^*(x,t_f)\tilde{X}_d(x),\Phi_i(x,t)>_H\Phi_i(x,t) \qquad (46)$$

When $\sup_{\mu>0}||U_\mu||_H^2>L^2$ the optimal control $U^o(x,t)$ is simply given by $U^o(x,t)=U_{\mu_o}(x,t)$ where $U_{\mu_o}(x,t)$ is determined from the relation $||U_{\mu_o}||_H^2=L^2$.

We now wish to express the optimal control $U^o(x,t)$ in terms of the eigenfunctions $\Psi_i(x)$ of $L(x,t_f)L^*(x,t_f)$ which are determined by

$$L(x,t_f)L^*(x,t_f)\Psi_i(x)=\lambda_i\Psi_i(x) \qquad (47)$$

and belong to $\mathfrak{X}_f$. Clearly, the solution of the eigenvalue-eigenfunction problem (47) is much easier than that corresponding to (44) since $\Psi_i(x)$ has less dimensions than $\Phi_i(x,t)$. From the relation

$$L^*(x,t)L(x,t)\Phi_i(x,t)=L^*(x,t)L(x,t)\{\frac{1}{\sqrt{\lambda_i}}L^*(x,t)\Psi_i(x)\}$$

$$=\frac{1}{\sqrt{\lambda_i}}L^*(x,t)\lambda_i\Psi_i=\lambda_i\{\frac{1}{\sqrt{\lambda_i}}L^*(x,t)\Psi_i\}$$

it follows $\Phi_i(x,t)=(1/\sqrt{\lambda_i})L^*(x,t)\Psi_i(x)$. Hence (46) gives

$$U^o(x,t)=\sum_{i=1}^{\infty}\frac{1}{\lambda_i}<\tilde{X}_d(x),\frac{1}{\sqrt{\lambda_i}}L^*\Psi_i>_H\frac{1}{\sqrt{\lambda_i}}L^*\Psi_i$$

$$=L^*(x,t_f)\{\sum_{\substack{i=1\\ \lambda_i\neq 0}}^{\infty}\frac{1}{\lambda_i}<\tilde{X}_d(x),\Psi_i(x)>_{\mathfrak{X}_f}\Psi_i(x)\} \qquad (47)$$

Equations (46) and (47) show that we can work either in space H or in space $\mathfrak{X}_f$. If it is desired to avoid finding the eigenvalues and eigenfunctions of LL*, equation (44) must be solved by computational techniques {53}-{54}.

4. BILINEAR NUCLEAR REACTOR CONTROL

Actually the nuclear reactor system is of the bilinear type, i.e. it contains the product of the control input and the controlled output, but it is linear in the input and output separately. Here we shall outline two methods of controlling a bilinear nuclear reactor system the one being derived through normal variational theory {29}, and the other by means of a generalized version of Hölder's inequality for the case of more than two elements and Banach spaces {12},{53}-{54}.

4.1. Variational technique

Consider a nuclear reactor model with one fast, one slow, and one delayed neutron group of the type (2), namely

$$\upsilon_F^{-1}\partial\Phi_F/\partial t=(\nabla.D_F\nabla-\Sigma_R)\Phi_F+(1-\beta)\nu\Sigma_{fs}\Phi_s+\lambda C$$
$$\upsilon_s^{-1}\partial\Phi_s/\partial t=(\nabla.D_s\nabla-\Sigma_a)\Phi_s+\Sigma_R\Phi_F,\quad \partial C/\partial t=\beta\nu\Sigma_{fF}\Phi_s-\lambda C \qquad (48)$$

where D_F and D_s are the fast and slow (thermal) diffusion coefficients, Σ_R and Σ_a are the removal and absorption cross-sections, and $\Sigma_{fs}\simeq\Sigma_{fF}=\Sigma_f$ is the fission cross-section (a constant).

In the case of a reactor used in nuclear rockets the fuel loading density is relatively large and so the thermal leakage term $\nabla.D_s\nabla\Phi_s$ is negligible compared to the thermal absorption rate. Also due to the high velocity of fast neutrons, the term $\upsilon_F^{-1}\partial\Phi_F/\partial t$ can be neglected. Hence the model (48) simplifies to

$$\nabla.D_F\nabla\Phi_F-\Sigma_R\Phi_F+(1-\beta)\nu\Sigma_f\Phi_s+\lambda C=0$$
$$\Phi_F=(\Sigma_a/\Sigma_R)(1+\ell_o/T)\Phi_s,\quad \partial C/\partial t=\beta\nu\Sigma_f\Phi_s-\lambda C \qquad (49)$$

where $\ell_o=\upsilon_s^{-1}\Sigma_a^{-1}$ is the mean life time, and $T=\Phi_s/(\partial\Phi_s/\partial t)$ is the reactor period.

Now, since ℓ_o/T is much smaller than unity, the second equation (49) gives $\Phi_F=(\Sigma_a/\Sigma_R)\Phi_s$ and so the first equation (49) becomes

$$\nabla^2(\tau\Sigma_a\Phi_s)-\Sigma_a\Phi_s+(1-\beta)\nu\Sigma_f\Phi_s+\lambda C=0$$

where $\tau=D_F/\Sigma_R$. Finally taking into account the fact that in a nuclear rocket the disturbances occur mainly along the axial direction z we can assume that $\Phi_s=\Phi_s(z,t)$ and $C=C(z,t)$, in which case our reactor model becomes

$$(1-b\partial^2/\partial z^2)\{u(z,t)X_1(z,t)\}=a_{11}X_1(z,t)+a_{12}X_2(z,t)$$
$$\partial X_2(z,t)/\partial t=a_{21}X_1(z,t)+a_{22}X_2(z,t) \qquad (50)$$

for $0<z<\ell$ where $b=\tau$ is the average value of Fermi age, $X_1(z,t)=\Phi_s(z,t)$, $X_2(z,t)=C(z,t)$, $u(z,t)=\Sigma_a(z,t)$ (the control variable), $a_{11}=(1-\beta)\nu\Sigma_f$, $a_{12}=-a_{22}=\lambda$, and $a_{21}=\beta\nu\Sigma_f$.

The boundary conditions are

$$X_1(0,t)=X_1(\ell,t)=0,\quad X_2(0,t)=X_2(\ell,t)=0 \qquad (51)$$

where ℓ is the extrapolated length of the reactor.

At start-up the power of the reactor must increase from a small value ($\approx$10kW) to a large one ($\approx 10^6$kW) at a minimum time, so as the thrust of the rocket is generated as quickly as possible. The required controller is found to be of the bang-bang type which results in dinscontinuities in one of the output. To overcome this discontinuity a second optimization is necessary.

The first optimization concerns the design of the reference control system. Due to the spatial boundary conditions the fundamental mode of the state variables X_1 and X_2 can be assumed sinusoidal in z, i.e.

$$X_i(z,t)=Y_i(t)\sin(\pi z/\ell),\ i=1,2 \tag{52}$$

The control variable is found to be a function of time only i.e. $u(z,t)=u_R(t)$. Using these facts the model (50) gives

$$Y_1(t)=A_{12}Y_2(t),\ d\ell nY_2(t)/dt=\gamma(t),\gamma(t)=a_{12}A_{21}+a_{22} \tag{53}$$

where $A_{12}=a_{12}/[(1+b\pi^2/\ell^2)u_R(t)-a_{11}]$, $A_{21}=a_{21}/[(1+b\pi^2/\ell^2)u_R(t)-a_{22}]$.

The variable $\gamma(t)$ in (53) can be written as

$$\gamma(t)=\lambda\rho(1-\rho),\ \rho=(k-1)/\beta k=\text{reactivity in dollars} \tag{53}$$

where $k=\nu\Sigma_f/u_R(t)(1+b\pi^2/\ell^2)$ is the multiplication factor. Clearly,$\gamma(t)$, which is equivalent to the reciprocal of the stable reactor period, must be bounded for avoiding prompt criticality (i.e.ρ = 1 dollar) which implies that $u_R(t)$ must be bounded too, i.e.

$$u_{R2}\leqslant u_R(t)\leqslant u_{R1} \tag{54}$$

By the maximum principle $u_R(t)$ must operate at its extreme values (bang-bang)and so for i=1,2:

$$X_{R,i}(z,t)=\begin{cases} Y^1_{oi}e^{\gamma t}\ \sin(\pi z/\ell),t_o\leqslant t\leqslant t_1 \\ Y^2_{oi}e^{\gamma t_1}\ \sin(\pi z/\ell),t_1\leqslant t\leqslant t_f \end{cases} \tag{55}$$

where the constants Y^j_{oi} must be calculated from the reactor power level and the superscripts of Y_{oi} correspond to the intervals $[t_o,t_1]$ and $[t_1,t_f]$.

From (53) and (55) it is clear that if $X_{R,2}(z,t)$ has to be continous at $t=t_1$ (i.e. $Y^1_{o2}=Y^2_{o2}$), then $X_{R,1}$ must have a discontinuity at $t=t_1$ (i.e. $Y^1_{o1}\neq Y^2_{o1}$).

The second optimization concerns the design of the control correction $\Delta u(z,t)$ such that to reduce the power variations due to inexact initial conditions and/or arbitrary disturbances. To this end,the system equations are linearized about the reference ones by neglecting the higher order terms as indicated in (10). In the present case the linearized (or perturbed) reactor model for $t_o\leqslant t\leqslant t_1$ has the form

$$(1-b\partial^2/\partial z^2)\{u^1_R\delta X^1_1\}=a_{11}\delta X^1_1+a_{12}(Y^1_{20}/Y^1_{10})\delta X^1_2-u^1$$

$$\partial(\delta X^1_2)/\partial t=a_{21}(Y^1_{10}/Y^1_{20})\delta X^1_1+(a_{22}-\gamma)X^1_2$$

where $\delta X^1_i=\Delta X_i/Y^1_{io}e^{\gamma t}$ (i=1,2), $u^1_R=\nu\Sigma_f(1-\beta\gamma/(\lambda+\gamma))/(1+\tau\pi^2/\ell^2)$, and

$$u^1(z,t)=(1/Y^1_{10}e^{\gamma t})(1-b\partial^2/\partial z^2)\{X_{R1}\Delta u(z,t)\} \tag{56}$$

with ΔX_i and Δu being the variations of X_i,u about the reference (operating point) values.

Analogous equations hold for the time interval $t_1\leqslant t\leqslant t_f$ with the only difference that we must set $\gamma=0$, and $\delta X^2_i=\Delta X_i/Y^2_{io}e^{\gamma t_1}$.

The exponential weighting is usel to obtain more uniform distribution of errors at t_1 and t_f, and also to increace the range where the linearized equations hold. Solving (56) for $\Delta u(z,t)$ gives

$$\Delta u(z,t)=(Y_{10}^{1}e^{\gamma t}/bX_{R1})\int_{o}^{\ell}G(z,\zeta)u^{1}(\zeta,t)d\zeta,\quad t_o\leqslant t\leqslant t_1$$

Similarly

$$\Delta u(z,t)=(Y_{10}^{2}e^{\gamma t_1}/bX_{R1})\int_{o}^{\ell}G(z,\zeta)u^{2}(\zeta,t)d\zeta,\quad t_1\leqslant t\leqslant t_f$$

Hence the second optimization problem reduces to that of choosing $u^i(\zeta,t)$, i=1,2 such that to minimize a quadratic cost functional of the type (16) and (17), namely:

$$J^i=\frac{1}{2}\int_{t_o}^{t_f}\int_{o}^{\ell}\{Q_1(\vartheta X_1^i)^2+Q_2(\delta X_2^i)^2+R(u^i)^2\}dzdt\quad ,i=1,2$$

This minimization can be carried out by conventional DP variational theory {47} and leads to a DP TPBVP which for both intervals $t_o\leqslant t\leqslant t_1$ and $t_1\leqslant t\leqslant t_f$ has the same form. Let $\xi_{jk}^i(t)$, $n_{jk}^i(t)$, and $v_k^i(t)$ the Fourier coefficients of ϑX_j^i, λ_j^i (the adjoint variable of δX_j^i) and $u^i(z,t)$, i.e. $\xi_{jk}^i(t)=\int_o^{\ell}\vartheta X_j^i(z,t)\sin(k\pi z/\ell)dz$, i,j=1,2, etc. The TPBVP for the Fourier coefficients has the form

$$\dot{\xi}_{2k}^1=(\gamma-a_{22})\xi_{1k}^1-(\gamma-a_{22})\xi_{2k}^1,-A_k^1\ \xi_{1k}^1+A_1^1\xi_{2k}^1-v_k^1=0$$

$$\dot{n}_{2k}^1=-A_1^1n_{1k}^1+(\gamma-a_{22})n_{2k}^1-2Q_2\xi_{2k}^1,2Rv_k^1-n_{1k}^1=0$$

$$2Q_1\xi_{1k}^1-A_k^1n_{1k}^1+(\gamma-a_{22})n_{2k}^1=0$$

The optimal controls $u^1(z,t)$ and $u^2(z,t)$ are synthesized by a finite number of terms of the series

$$u^i(z,t)=\frac{2}{\ell}\sum_{k=1}^{\infty}v_k^i(t)\sin(k\frac{\pi z}{\ell}),\quad i=1,2 \tag{56a}$$

For more details refer to {29}. We remark that actually this technique is similar to that described in sec. 3.1.

4.2. Hölder's inequality technique

This technique, essentially due to Sarachik and Kranc {55}, was used for linear point reactors by Gyftopoulos and Kyong {23}, for bilinear point reactors by Kliger {12}, and for general DP systems by Pethsuwan {54} and Tzafestas {53}. Here we follow the lines of Kliger for applying the method to a one-delayed group DP nuclear reactor model of the type:

$$\frac{\vartheta}{\vartheta t}\begin{bmatrix}n(x,t)\\ C(x,t)\end{bmatrix}=\begin{bmatrix}\frac{m^2\nabla-\beta}{\ell} & \lambda\\ \frac{\beta}{\ell} & -\lambda\end{bmatrix}\begin{bmatrix}n(x,t)\\ C(x,t)\end{bmatrix}+\begin{bmatrix}(1-\beta)/\ell\\ \beta/\ell\end{bmatrix}n(x,t)\delta k(x,t)$$

where $n(x,t)$ is the neutron level, $C(x,t)$ is the concentration of precursors, and $\delta k(x,t)$ is the space-time varying reactivity input.

The integral representation of this model is

$$\begin{bmatrix} n \\ C \end{bmatrix} = \int_D G(x,t;\xi,t_o) \begin{bmatrix} n_o(\xi) \\ C_o(\xi) \end{bmatrix} d\xi + \int_{t_o}^{t} \int_D G(x,t;\xi,\tau) \begin{bmatrix} (1-\beta)/\ell \\ \beta/\ell \end{bmatrix} n(\xi,\tau)\delta k(\xi,\tau) d\xi d\tau \quad (57)$$

Assuming one dimensional spatial domain D the control can be succesfully effected by one control rod at the point x_o in which case we write as usual $\delta k(x,t) = \delta k(t)\,\delta(x-x_o)$ and the above model reduces to:

$$\tilde{n}(x,t) = \int_{t_o}^{t} g_1(x,t;x_o,\tau)n(x_o,\tau)\delta k(\tau)d\tau \quad (58a)$$

$$\tilde{C}(x,t) = \int_{t_o}^{t} g_2(x,t;x_o,\tau)n(x_o,\tau)\delta k(\tau)d\tau \quad (58b)$$

where

$$G = \begin{bmatrix} g_{11} & g_{12} \\ g_{21} & g_{22} \end{bmatrix}, \quad \begin{matrix} g_1 = g_{11}(1-\beta)/\ell + g_{12}\beta/\ell \\ g_2 = g_{21}(1-\beta)/\ell + g_{22}\beta/\ell \end{matrix}$$

$$\tilde{n}(x,t) = n(x,t) - \int_D [g_{11}n_o(\xi) + g_{12}C_o(\xi)]d\xi$$

$$\tilde{C}(x,t) = C(x,t) - \int_D [g_{21}n_o(\xi) + g_{22}C_o(\xi)]d\xi$$

The problem is to find that reactivity input $\delta k(t), t_o \leqslant t \leqslant t_f$ which satisfies, the constraint

$$\lim_{p_1\to\infty} ||\delta k(t)||_{p_1} = \lim_{p_1\to\infty} \{\int_{t_o}^{t_f} |\delta k(t)|^{p_1} dt\}^{1/p_1} < \delta k_{max} \quad (59)$$

and drives the state from its initial state $n(x,t_o)=n_o(x)$, $C(x,t_o) = C_o(x)$ to a desired final state $n(x,t_f)=n_d$, $C(x,t_f)=C_d$ at $t=t_f$*.

The solution of this problem can be found in two steps, namely:

Step 1: Solve the final value (minimum norm) control problem for t_f fixed, i.e. the problem of driving the initial state to the desired one with minimum norm $\lim_{p_1\to\infty} ||\delta k(t)||_{p_1}$.

Step 2: Solve the minimum time problem by simply determining the smallest time for which the state at first is driven in the desired final value, i.e. find the minimum t_f which satisfies the equation $\lim_{p_1\to\infty} ||\delta k(t)||_{p_1} = \delta k_{max}$.

The input $\delta k(t)$ that satisfies (58a-b), must obey the following equation for any $\lambda_1(x)$ and $\lambda_2(x)$, $x\varepsilon D$:

$\lambda_1(x)\tilde{n}(x,t_f) + \lambda_2(x)\tilde{C}(x,t_f)$

---

*In the DP case it should be more realistic if one assumes that the system is ε-controllable and finds that $\delta k(t)$ which drives the state to within a sphere of the desired final state {53}-{54}.

$$= \int_{t_o}^{t_f} \{ \lambda_1(x) g_1(x,t_f;x_o,\tau) + \lambda_2(x) g_2(x,t_f;x_o,\tau)\} n(x_o,\tau)\delta k(\tau) d\tau \qquad (60)$$

Applying the generalized Hölder's inequality to (60) gives

$$|\lambda_1\tilde{n}+\lambda_2\tilde{C}|_D \le ||\lambda_1 g_1+\lambda_2 g_2||_{p_3}\,||n||_{p_2}\,||\delta k||_{p_1} \qquad (61)$$

where $1/p_1+1/p_2+1/p_3=1$, $p_1>1, p_2>1, p_3>1$, and

$$|f(x)|_D = |\int_D f(x)dx| \,,\; ||n||_{p_2} = \{\int_{t_o}^{t_f} |n(x_o,\tau)|^{p_2} d\tau\}^{1/p_2}$$

$$||\delta k(\tau)||_{p_1} = \{\int_{t_o}^{t_f} |\delta k(\tau)|^{p_1} d\tau\}^{1/p_1} \,,\; ||g(x,t;x_o,\tau)||_{p_3} = \{\int_{t_o}^{t_f}\int_D |g(x,t;x_o,\tau)|^{p_3} dx d\tau\}^{1/p_3}$$

Equivalently (61) can be written as

$$||\delta k||_{p_1} > |\lambda_1\tilde{n}+\lambda_2\tilde{C}|_D / ||\,n\,||_{p_2}\,||\lambda_1 g_1+\lambda_2 g_2||_{p_3}$$

for any λ_1 and λ_2, and so the minimum possible norm $||\delta k||_{p_1}$ is given by

$$||\delta k||_{p_1,\min} = \max_{\{\lambda_1,\lambda_2;p_2,p_3\}} |\lambda_1\tilde{n}+\lambda_2\tilde{C}|_D / ||\,n\,||_{p_2}\,||\lambda_1 g_1+\lambda_2 g_2||_{p_3} \qquad (62)$$

The equality sign in (62) holds only when

$$|\delta k|^{p_1} = A|n|^{p_2} = B|\lambda_1(x) g_1(x,t_f,x_o,\tau)+\lambda_2(x) g_2(x,t_f,x_o,\tau)|_D^{p_3}$$

or $A|n(x_o,\tau)|^{p_2/p_1} = B|\lambda_1 g_1+\lambda_2 g_2|^{p_3/p_1}$, and the sign of

$\delta k(\tau) n(x_o,\tau)\int_D \{\lambda_1(x) g_1(x,t_f,x_o,\tau)+\lambda_2(x) g_2(x,t_f;x_o,\tau)dx$ is constant.

Now since in the constraint (59), $p_1 \to \infty$, it follows that A=B, and hence

$$|n(x_o,\tau)|^{p_2} = |\lambda_1 g_1+\lambda_2 g_2|^{p_3} \,,\; 1/p_2+1/p_3=0 \qquad (63)$$

Introducing (63) into (62) yields

$$||\delta k||_{\infty,\min} = 1 / \min_{\{|\lambda_1\tilde{n}+\lambda_2\tilde{C}|_D=1,p_3\}} \int_{t_o}^{t_f}\int_D |\lambda_1(x) g_1(x,t_f,x_o,\tau)+\lambda_2(x) g_2(x,t_f,x_o,\tau)|^{p_3} dx d\tau \qquad (64)$$

The optimal $\delta k(t)$ is determined by the equality sign of the Hölders inequality, i.e:

$$\delta k^o(t) = A\,\mathrm{sgn}\{n(x_o,t)\int_D [\lambda_1^o(x) g_1(x,t_f;x_o,t)+\lambda_2^o(x) g_2(x,t_f;x_o,t)]dx\} \qquad (65)$$

where $\lambda_1^o(x), \lambda_2^o(x)$ are the optimal values of $\lambda_1(x)$ and $\lambda_2(x)$. The constant A is chosen such that (64) is satisfied, i.e. $A=||\delta k||_{\infty,\min}$. Now, since the neutron power $n(x_o,t)$ never becomes negative $\delta k^o(t)$ in (65) is simplified to

$$\delta k^o(t) = ||\delta k||_{\infty,\min}\,\mathrm{sgn}\int_D \{\lambda_1^o(x) g_1(x,t_f;x_o,t)+\lambda_2^o(x) g_2(x,t_f;x_o,t)\}dx \qquad (66)$$

The solution of the minimum time problem is determined as follows.

a) Replace $||\delta k||_{\infty,\min}$ in (66) by the maximum allowed reactivity value δk_{max} and solve the equation $||\delta k||_{\infty,min}=\delta k_{max}$, namely {see (64)}:

$$1/\int_o^{t_f}\int_D |\lambda_1^o g_1+\lambda_2^o g_2|^{p_3^o} dxd\tau=\delta k_{max} \qquad (67)$$

where λ_1^o,λ_2^o, p_3^o are the optimal values of λ_1,λ_2 and p_3, with respect to t_f.

b) The minimum value of t_f for which (67) holds is the optimum time t_f^o, and so (66) gives

$$\delta k^o(t)=\delta k_{max} \text{ sgn } \int_D\{\lambda_1^o(x)g_1(x,t_f^o,x_o,t)+\lambda_2^o(x)g_2(x,t_f^o;x_o,t)\}dx \qquad (68)$$

Clearly the controller (68) is of the "bang-bang" type i.e. the control input consists of the full amount of the allowed reactivity and its polarity changes at the roots of $\text{sgn}\int_D(\lambda_1^o g_1+\lambda_2^o g_2)dx$.

A possible computational implementation is {53}:

i) At each time t determine the conjugate functions $\lambda_1^o(x)$, $\lambda_2(x)^o$, $x\varepsilon D$, and p_3^o which minimize $\int_{t_o}^{t_f}\int_D|\lambda_1 g_1+\lambda_2 g_2|^{p_3}dxd\tau$ {see(64)} under the constraint $|\lambda_1\tilde{n}(x,t_f)+\lambda_2^o\tilde{C}(x,t_f)|_D=1$.

ii) Find the smallest time t_f^o at which (67) is satisfied.

The following algorithm can be used

i) Start with the initial time and increase t by small increments Δt until (67) is satisfied.

ii) At each time compute the conjugate functions. The problem of finding $\lambda_1^o(x)$ and $\lambda_2^o(x)$ can be reduced to that of solving a set of integral equations. In fact from (64) we obtain the unconstrained minimization of

$$J=\int_{t_o}^{t_f}\int|\lambda_1 g_1+\lambda_2 g_2|^{p_3}dxd\tau+\mu|\int_D\lambda_1\tilde{n}(x,t_f)+\lambda_2\tilde{C}(x,t_f)dx|$$

where μ is a new Lagrange multiplier.

The main drawback of the controller (68) is that it is of the open-loop type and so it is insensitive to the system parameter variations and/or disturbances. A way of determining a closed-loop implementation, i.e.

$\delta k(t)=\delta k_{max}$ sgn $Z(n(x,t),C(x,t),n_d(x),C_d(x))$ is provided in {12}.

5. NUCLEAR REACTOR EIGENVALUE CONTROL

Eigenvalue control theory has found applications in many areas as e.g. aircraft and helicopter autostabilization, cascade vehicle systems, economic systems etc. {56}. Here the results of {57}-{61} will be applied to a time-invariant DP nuclear reactor model of the type (10)-(11), i.e. to

$$X_t(x,t)=\mathcal{L}(x)X(x,t)+B(x)u(t),\ x\varepsilon D,\ a(x)X(x,t)=0,\ x\varepsilon\partial D \qquad (69)$$

The state vector function $X(x,t)$ is expanded in terms of the Kaplan eigenfunctions $\Psi_m(x)$ as shown in (23). The result is the Kaplan modal model, i.e.

$$\dot{\xi}_k=\omega_k\xi_k+\langle\Psi_k^*,Bu\rangle,\xi_k(t_o)=\langle\Psi_k^*,X(x,t_o)\rangle \tag{70}$$

The problem is to find a linear feedback control law u(t) which moves a certain set of eigenvalues $\omega_1,\omega_2,\ldots,\omega_m$ to a set of desired values $\rho_1,\rho_2,\ldots,\rho_m$.

To solve the problem consider first the case where u(t) is scalar. Then assuming that the input u(t) is sought in the linear feedback form

$$u(t)=K_1\xi_1(t)+K_2\xi_2(t)+\ldots+K_m\xi_m(t) \tag{71}$$

and introducing in (70) yields the closed-loop Kaplan modal system

$$\dot{\underline{\xi}}(t)=A_o\underline{\xi}(t),\ A_o=\begin{bmatrix} A & 0 \\ \tilde{A} & \Omega \end{bmatrix},\underline{\xi}^T=[\xi_1,\xi_2,\ldots,\xi_m,\xi_{m+1},\ldots]$$

where $\Omega=\mathrm{diag}\,(\omega_{m+1},\omega_{m+2},\ldots)$, $\mu_i=\int_D\Psi_i^*(x)B(x)dx$, and

$$A=\begin{bmatrix} \omega_1+\mu_1K_1 & \mu_1K_2\cdots\cdots\mu_1K_m \\ \mu_2K_1 & \omega_2+\mu_2K_2\cdots\mu_2K_m \\ \cdots\cdots & \cdots\cdots \\ \mu_mK_1 & \mu_mK_2\cdots\omega_m+\mu_mK_m \end{bmatrix},\ \tilde{A}=\begin{bmatrix} \mu_{m+1}K_1\cdots\cdots\mu_{m+1}K_m \\ \mu_{m+2}K_1\cdots\cdots\mu_{m+2}K_m \\ \cdots\cdots\cdots \\ \cdots\cdots\cdots \end{bmatrix} \tag{72b}$$

The eigenvalues ρ_i, $i=1,2,\ldots m,m+1,\ldots$ are given by the solution of the characteristic equation $\det(\rho_iI-A_o)=0$ which splits in two equations, namely $\det(\rho_iI-A)=0$, $i=1,2,\ldots,m$, and $\det(\rho_iI-\Omega)=0$, $i=m+1,m+2,\ldots\ldots$ The second equation gives $\rho_i=\omega_i$ which means that the eigenvalues $\omega_{m+1},\omega_{m+2},\ldots$ remain unaltered by a feedback law of the type (71). Solving the first gives the required gains $K_j(j=1,2,\ldots,m)$ as

$$K_j=\prod_{k=1}^{m}(\rho_k-\omega_j)/\{\mu_j\prod_{\substack{k=1\\k\neq j}}^{m}(\omega_k-\omega_j)\},\ j=1,2,\ldots,m \tag{73}$$

which through (71) make the first m closed-loop eigenvalues equal to ρ_1, $\rho_2,\ldots,\rho_m$. Clearly, the condition under which $\omega_1,\omega_2,\ldots,\omega_m$ are controllable from u(t) is $\mu_j\neq0$ for all $j=1,2,\ldots,m$. The gains K_j, $j=1,2,\ldots,m$ will be real only if μ_j,ω_j and ρ_j, $j=1,2,\ldots,m$ are real or occur in complex conjugate pairs. In terms of the reactor state X(x,t) the control law (71) is expressed as

$$u(t)=\sum_{j=1}^{m}K_j\langle\Psi_j^*(x)X(x,t)\rangle \tag{74}$$

Now consider the case where u(t) is the vector $u(t)=[u_1,u_2,\ldots,u_N]^T$. Then writing the forcing term B(x)u(t) of (69) as

$$B(x)u(t)=\sum_{s=1}^{N}b_s(x)u_s(t) \tag{75}$$

where $b_s(x)$ is the sth column of B(x), (73) is replaced by

$$\sum_{s=1}^{N}\mu_{js}K_{js}=\prod_{k=1}^{m}(\rho_k-\lambda_j)/\prod_{\substack{k=1\\k\neq j}}^{m}(\lambda_k-\lambda_j),j=1,2,\ldots,m \tag{76}$$

where $\mu_{js}=\int_D \Psi_j^*(x)b_s(x)dx$. Equation (76) shows that we now have some degrees of freedom to select the K_{js}'s so as to satisfy, simultaneously with the eigenvalue shifting, other control design requirements.

When some components of the state vector function X(x,t) are not available to be used in the feedback law (74) one can use the measured output function Y(x,t), $x\varepsilon D$, $t\geqslant t_o$ for constructing an estimate of X(x,t), $x\varepsilon D$, $t\geqslant t_o$, i.e. use output feedback through a DP observer. One way of doing this may be found in {59}. Some other studies of DP observers are provided in {62}-{64}.

6. STOCHASTIC NUCLEAR REACTOR CONTROL

The models studied so far are deterministic, i.e. they do not take into account the stochastic nature of the processes occuring in a reactor, and the external disturbances and measurement inaccuracies. Actually one can reformulate the optimal control theory within the frames of stochastic analysis and statistics by using appropriate stochastic models.

The stochastic counterpart of model (10) is {66}:

$$X_t(x,t)=\mathcal{L}X(x,t)+B(x,t)u(t)+W(x,t),\ x\varepsilon D$$

$$Z(x,t)=MX(x,t)+V(x,t),\ x\varepsilon D;\quad a(x)X(x,t)=0,\ x\varepsilon\partial D \qquad t\geqslant t_o \qquad (77)$$

where Z(x,t) is the measured output process, and W(x,t), V(x,t), $x\varepsilon D$ are regular stochastic processes with zero mean values and covariance matrices given by

$$E\{W(x,t)W^T(y,\tau)\}=C_W(x,y,t)\delta(t-\tau),\quad E\{W(x,t)V^T(y,\tau)\}=0$$

$$E\{V(x,t)V^T(y,\tau)\}=C_V(x,t)\delta(x-y)\delta(t-\tau)\quad x,y\varepsilon D,\ t,\tau\geqslant t_o \qquad (78)$$

where $C_W(x,y,t)$ is a symmetric nonnegative matrix function, and $C_V(x,t)$ is symmetric positive definite for all $x\varepsilon D$. The relations in (78) indicate that W(x,t) is a DP stochastic process white in t, V(x,t) is a process white in both x and t, and the two processes are mutually independent.

The stochastic counterpart of model (14) is {49}:

$$X(x,t)=X_o(x,t)+L(t_o,t)u(t)+L_o(t_o,t)W(x,t),\ x\varepsilon D$$

$$Z(x,t)=MX(x,t)+V(x,t),\ x\varepsilon D \qquad t\geqslant t_o \qquad (79)$$

where $L_o(t_o,t)\ \int_{t_o}^{t}\int_D K(x,t,y,\tau)[\cdot]dyd\tau$, and W(x,t), V(x,t) have the same properties as above

The problem is to determine the feedback control u(t) which minimizes an average quadratic cost functional of the type

$$J=E\{\int_{t_o}^{t_f} g(\tau)d\tau\}$$

where g(t) is given by (17).

Since here the state X(x,t) is not precisely known, in order to be used in the feedback law one must determine an on-line estimate $\hat{X}(x,t)$ by employing the available data $Z(x,t), x\varepsilon D$, to $t_0 \leqslant \tau \leqslant t$ as t increases, and use it in place of $X(x,t)$.

This is based on the well-known separation principle {66} {67}, and $\hat{X}(x,t)$ is provided by a DP optimal filter {68},{69}.

The resulting feedback controller for the model (77) has again the form (27), with the only difference that now $\lambda_s(x,t)$ is replaced by

$$\lambda_s(x,t)=\int_D P(x,y,t)\hat{X}_s(x,t)dx \tag{80}$$

where $P(x,y,t)$ satisfies the DP Riccati equation and $\hat{X}_s(x,t)$ is the filtered estimate of $X(x,t)$ provided by the DP filter. Similarly, the solution of the problem for the integral model (79), as determined by the direct approach, has again the form (32) and (35), i.e.

$$u(t)=-W(t)S^{-1}(t)\int_t^{t_f}\int_D\int_D \Xi(x,\tau)Q(x,\tau)K(x,\tau,x',t)\hat{X}(x,t)dxdx'd\tau \tag{81}$$

Optimal filters providing $\hat{X}(x,t)$, either in continuous time, or discrete time are given in {49},{68}-{69} and will not be written here.

A problem which is worthwhile to be mentioned at this point is that when the measurements of $Z(x,t)$ in (77) and (79) are available at only a finite number of spatial points namely $x_j, j=1,2,...,q$, one can select the location of these points to improve the filter performance as much as possible. Works discussing the optimal location problem of measurement points include {70}-{75}. Also, when applying pointwise control to a DP system, it is possible to choose the spatial points at which control is applied (e.g. the position of the control rods in a reactor) such that to improve the optimality of the controller as much as possible {76}.

7. APPLICATION EXAMPLES

The application examples which are collected here illustrate many aspects of the DP reactor control theory outlined in the previous sections. Although the reactor models considered are the simplest ones, and the mumerical results come from computer simulation rather than real nuclear process operation, the examples provide a useful guide for handling the mathematical part of real nuclear reactor control design problems. Further examples can be found in the references.

Example 1 {27},{28}

Consider a homogeneous slab nuclear reactor described by the scalar equation $(1/\upsilon)d\Phi/dt=D\vartheta^2\Phi/\vartheta x^2+(\nu\varepsilon\Sigma_f-\Sigma_a)\Phi-\Sigma\Phi u_k\delta(x-x_k)$. In this model all energy groups of flux and all the delayed neutron groups are collected in one averaged variable, and all other effects are neglected. The steady state $\bar{\Phi}(x)$ {see (9)} is given by the solution of $Dd^2\bar{\Phi}/dx^2+(\nu\varepsilon+\Sigma_f-\Sigma_a)\bar{\Phi}=0$, which for a slab of length h is equal to

$\bar{\Phi}=\bar{\Phi}_{max}\sin(\pi x/h)$. The criticality condition is $-D(\pi/h)^2+(\nu\varepsilon\Sigma_f-\Sigma_a)=0$.

The linearized model about the steady state is

$$X_t(x,t)=\upsilon(D\vartheta^2/\vartheta x^2+\nu\varepsilon\Sigma_f-\Sigma_a)X-\upsilon\bar{\Phi}\sum_{k=1}^{N}u_k^{\cdot}(t)\delta(x-x_k) \tag{82}$$

with boundary conditions $X(0,t)=X(h,t)=0$ for all t.

Here $X=\delta\Phi$ is the variation of Φ about the steady state.

The analytic solution of this model (Kaplan expansion form) is

$$X(x,t)=\sqrt{2\upsilon/h}\sum_{m=0}^{\infty}\xi_m(t)\sin(m+1)\frac{\pi x}{h}$$

and so the state of the spatial (harmonic) system is {see (25)}:

$$X_s(x,t)=\sqrt{2\upsilon/h}\sum_{m=1}^{\infty}\xi_m(t)\sin(m+1)\frac{\pi x}{h} \tag{83}$$

and the action $u_N(t)$ of the Nth control rod which eliminates the effect of all other rods on the fundamental mode is {see (26)}:

$$u_N=-\{\sum_{m=1}^{N-1}u_k\bar{\Phi}_{max}\sin^2\frac{\pi x_k}{h}\}/\bar{\Phi}_{max}\sin^2\frac{\pi x_N}{h} \tag{84}$$

Introducing (83) and (84) into (82) we find the spatial reactor model {see (26a)}:

$$\frac{1}{\upsilon}\frac{\vartheta X_s}{\vartheta t}=(D\frac{\vartheta^2}{\vartheta x^2}+\nu\varepsilon\Sigma_f-\Sigma_a)X_s-\sum_{k=1}^{N-1}b_k(x)u_k$$

$$b_k(x)=\bar{\Phi}_{max}\sin(\frac{\pi x}{h})\sum_{k=1}^{N-1}\{\delta(x-x_k)-(\sin^2\frac{\pi x_k}{h}/\sin^2\frac{\pi x_N}{h})\delta(x-x_N)\}u_k$$

The problem is to choose the u_k's such that to reduce the deviation $X_s(x,t)$ to zero.

According to Wiberg's controllability result this can be done with at least one control rod in addition to that used to control the steady-state (i.e. the power system).

Wiberg {28} has used this minimum number of control rods (N=2) and derived the canonical equations (30) for the first two harmonics. These equations were solved for a realistic set of parameter values, the final result being {see (31)}:

$$u_1(t)=u^o_{N-1}(t)=\frac{\Sigma_a h}{\bar{\Phi}_{max}}[-0.000483,-0.000173]\begin{bmatrix}\xi_1(t)\\ \xi_2(t)\end{bmatrix}$$

$$u^o_2(t)=u^o_N(t)=\frac{\Sigma_{aso}h}{\bar{\Phi}_{max}}[0.000267,\ 0.0000956]\begin{bmatrix}\xi_1(t)\\ \xi_2(t)\end{bmatrix}$$

In practice the Kaplan modes $\xi_1(t)$ and $\xi_2(t)$ are constructed by using the spatial profile $\Phi(x,t)$ measured by the detection system {65}.

Thus if $\Phi(x,t)$ is detected at the points $x=z_i (i=1,2,\dots,L+1)$ the modes $\xi_o,\xi_1,\dots,\xi_L$ are found by solving the L+1 algebraic equations

$$X_s(z_i,t)=\Phi(z_i,t)-\bar{\Phi}(z_i)=\sqrt{\frac{2\upsilon}{h}}\sum_{m=0}^{L}\{\sin\frac{(m+1)\pi x}{h}\}\xi_m(t)$$

Of course the location of the detectors has to be chosen properly such that the coefficient matrix of this system to be not ill-conditioned.

Example 2{51}

The system under study is the same as that of example 1 with a total of three control rods. By linearizing it about the steady state, and using (84), we again arrive at the spatial (harmonic) reactor model

$$\partial X/\partial t=a^2\partial^2X/\partial x^2+cX+\sum_{j=1}^{2} b_j\delta(x^j-x)u^j \tag{85}$$

$$X_o(0,t)=X(h,t)=0$$

where for notation simplicity X is used here in place of X_s.
The problem is to minimize the cost function

$$J_N=\sum_{k=1}^{N}\{\int_o^h X_k^2(x)dx+u_{k-1}^T Ru_{k-1}\},\quad u_k=\begin{bmatrix}u_k^1\\ u_k^2\end{bmatrix}$$

with parameter values $a^2=1600$, $c=0.252$, $h=250$ cm, $\tau=0.1$ sec, $b_k=-10\cdot\sin\pi x^j$, $x^1=0.25$, $x^2=0.6$, $R=\mathrm{diag}\{56,56\}$.
The discrete-time form of system (85) is

$$X_{k+1}(x)=\int_o^h G(x,x')X_k(x')dx'+B(x)u_k \tag{86}$$

The problem was solved by two policies. Policy 1 is based on (43) for computing C_* corresponding to approximation degrees n=1,4 and 5. Policy 2 is based on a conversion of the DP system to a lumped-parameter model, consisting of four ordinary differential equations corresponding to four modes, and an application of conventional lumped optimal control theory. The orthonormal set of functions used in policy 1 is $v_i(x)=\sqrt{2/h}\,\sin(k\pi x/h)$, i=1,2,3,.... The function $C_k(x,x')$ is approximated by the series of the four first functions $v_i(x)$.
The results are plotted in Fig 1 with an initial disturbance at t=0 of the form shown.

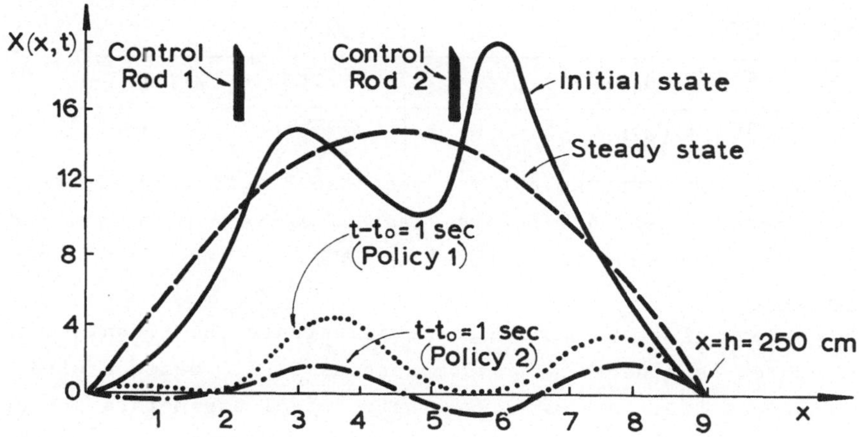

Fig.1: Optimal state after 1 sec for policies 1 and 2.

The figure shows the shape of the steady-state at t=1 sec for both policy 1 (n=4) and policy 2. The values of the optimal cost J for policy 1 are in general found to be smaller than those for policy 2. Although the value of J in policy 1 decreases with increase in n, use of low values of n is recommended since this reduction is small.

Example 3 {48}

This example illustrates the effectiveness of the direct variational synthesis method (sec. 3.2.) and concerns the stochastic system {see (77)}:

$$X_t(x,t)=a^2\partial^2 X(x,t)/\partial x^2+U(x,t)+W(x,t),\quad X(x,t_o)=X_o(x),\quad X(0,t)=X(1,t)=0$$

and the cost functional

$$J=E\{\int_{t_o}^{t_f}\int_0^1[\{X(x,t)-X_d(x,t)\}^2+RU^2(x,t)]dxdt$$

with parameter values $a^2=0.0033$, $T=t_f-t_o=15$sec, and R=5.
The stochastic disturbance covariance is assumed to be

$E\{W(x,t)W(y,\tau)\}=C_w(x)\delta(x-y)\delta(t-\tau)$ with $C_w(x)=0.5(\sin\pi x+0.5\sin 3\pi x)$ and the state function is supposed fully and exactly measured in which case no filter is required to provide X(x,t).

The optimal control $U^o(x,t)$ is found in the form of a double series expansion in terms of a time orthonormaltime function base $\{w_i(t),\ i=1,2,\dots,\infty,\ t\varepsilon[t_o,t_f]\}$ and a space function base $\{\Psi_j(x),\ j=1,2,\dots,\infty,\ x\varepsilon[0,1]\}$, i.e.

$$U(x,t)=\sum_{i,j=1}^{m} a_{ij}\Psi_j(x)w_i(t) \tag{87}$$

where $\Psi_j(x)=\sqrt{2}\sin(j\pi x)$, and the w's are chosen as the shifted Chebychev or Legendre polynomials shown below.

Basis	Chebychev	Legendre
$w_1(t)$	$\sqrt{1/T}$	$\sqrt{1/T}$
$w_2(t)$	$\sqrt{3/T}(2\theta-1)$	$\sqrt{3/T}(2\theta-1)$
$w_3(t)$	$\sqrt{15/7T}(8\theta^2-8\theta+1)$	$\sqrt{5/T}(6\theta^2-6\theta+1)$
$w_4(t)$	$\sqrt{35/17T}(32\theta^3-48\theta^2+18\theta-1)$	$\sqrt{7/T}(20\theta^3-30\theta^2+12\theta-1)$

Figure 2 shows the computed optimal response X(x,t) at different times within the control period T for the case of symmetric initial and desired conditions, and four terms (m=4) in (87).

Example 4 {29}

The purpose of this example is to illustrate the technique of sec. 4.1. The system considered is an homogeneous C-U^{235} reactor with the atom ratio about 500, in which case the physical parameters are approximately equal to $\beta=0.0075$, $\upsilon=2.5$, $\lambda=0.1\ \text{sec}^{-1}$, $\Sigma_f=0.09\text{cm}^{-1}$, $\upsilon=325\text{cm}^2$, and ℓ=3ft, with $\gamma_{max}(t)=0.23$ and $t_1-t_o=50$ sec for initial power level 10^6kW.

We choose t_f-t_1 60 sec, i.e. t_f-t_o =110 sec., and $Q_1=1$, $Q_2=0$ and $R=3\times10^4$ cm^2.

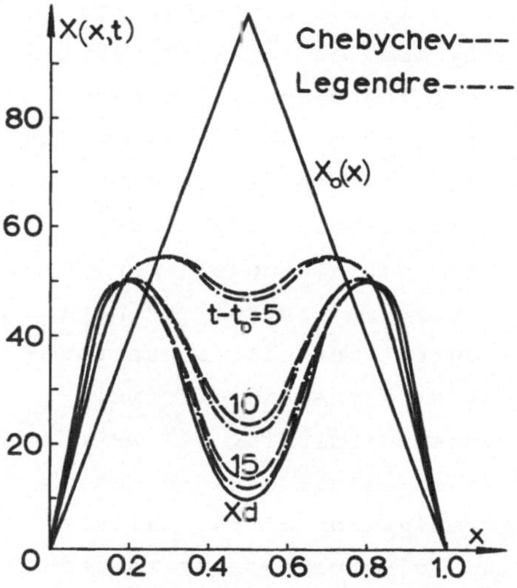

Fig 2. Optimal state after 5,10, and 15 sec.

The optimum control for the fundamental frequency is found to be {see (56a)}:

$$v_1^1(t)=\frac{A_1^1}{a_1^1}\{2\xi_1^1(t)+\frac{\gamma\ell}{2(\lambda+\gamma)}e^{-(\lambda+\gamma)(t_1-t)}\} \qquad t_o\leq t<t_1$$

$$v_1^2(t)=\frac{A_1^2}{a_1^2}\{1+tgh\omega_1^2(t_2-t)\}\xi_1^2(t) \quad t_1\leq t<t_f$$

where

$A_1^1=u_{R1}(b\pi^2/\ell^2+1)-a_{11}=5.7\times10^{-4}$cm^{-1},

$A_1^2=u_{R2}(b\pi^2/\ell^2+1)-a_{11}=1.875\times10^{-3}$ cm^{-1}

$a_1^1=0.01, a_1^2=0.1, \omega_1^2=-a_{22}=\lambda$.

Example 5 {53}

The adjoint space technique is applied to the following diffusion model.

$$\partial X/\partial t=\partial^2X/\partial x^2+U(x,t),\ 0<x<1;\ X(0,t)=X(1,t)=0,\ X(x,0)=X_o(x)$$

which has the integral representation

$$X(x,t)=X_o(x,t)+\int_o^{t}\int_o^{1}K(x,t;x',\tau)U(x',\tau)dx'd\tau \tag{88}$$

$$K(x,t,x',\tau)=\sum_{i=1}^{\infty}2\exp\{-i^2\pi^2(t-\tau)\}\sin(i\pi x)\sin(i\pi x')$$

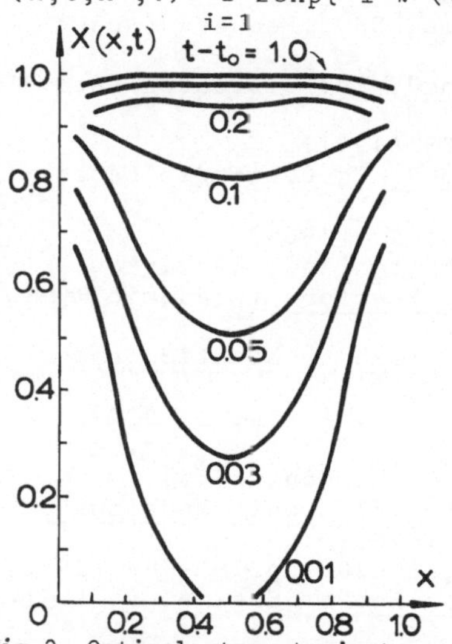

Fig.3. Optimal state trajectory with the final-value control

We assume that $X_o(x)=0$, $0\leq x\leq1$ and $X_d(x)=1$, $0\leq x\leq1$, so that $X_d(x)=1$, $0\leq x\leq1$. Here $\langle\tilde{X}_d(x),\Psi_i(x)\rangle_{\mathcal{X}_f}\int_o^1\sqrt{2}\sin(i\pi x)dx=\sqrt{2\{1+(-1)^{i+1}\}/i\pi}$

and so the optimal control is found to be {see (47)}

$$U^o(x,t)=\sum_{k=1}^{\infty}\frac{\sqrt{2}ak}{\lambda_k}\exp\{-k^2\pi^2(1-t)\}\sin(k\pi x) \tag{89}$$

Using (89), (88) gives the optimal trajectory which is shown in Fig. 3.

8. CONCLUDING REMARKS

Nuclear reactors with spatial effects belong to the general class of DP dynamic systems which are modelled by partial differential equations. In the present survey paper we attempted to collect the existing results concerning the methodology of optimally controlling DP nuclear reactors and present them in a unified form such that to make clear their key points, similarities and differences. Actually much of the work carried out in this area is of the classified type, but the results included here seem to be sufficient to show the significance of designing nuclear power plants on the basis of DP models and control methods. Some points which are promising for further study are i) formulation and study, both theoretically and experimentally, of more complete models for the control rod behaviour such that to incorporate large control rod movements, ii) application of other existing DP control methods to nuclear systems and comparison of their effectiveness with the aid of simulation, iii) study of complete power reactor systems including all existing subsystems and phenomena (e.g.heat tranfer, time delays etc) as has been done in {11} for point reactors, iv) investigation of the validity of stochastic models and controllers, v) study of more aspects concerning the pointwise control (using control rods), vi) investigation of the applicability of identification methods for estimating nuclear reactor parameters using input-output measurements, and vii) further study of point wise control and selection of the positions of the points where control is exerted.

REFERENCES

1. BUTKOVSKII, A.G., Distributed Control Systems (American Elsevier, 1968)
2. LIONS, J.L., Control Problems in Systems described by PDE: Mathematical Theory of Control (Academic Press, 1967)
3. WANG,P.K.C., in "Advances in Control Systems, Ed.C.Leondes (Academic Press, 1964),pp.75-172.
4. BROGAN,W.L., in "Advances in Control Systems", Ed. C.Leondes (Academic Press, 1968),pp.221-316.
5. ROBINSON,A.C., Automatica, Vol.7, pp.371-388 (1971)
6. AXELBAND,E., in "Advances in Control Systems", Ed.C.Leondes (Academic Press, 1969), pp.258-308
7. SHEN,C.and HAAG,F., IEEE Trans. Vol. NS-11,p.1. (1964)
8. RUIZ,A., Proc. 1963 Electro-Nuclear Conf. (Ritchland, Washigton)
9. ASH,M., Optimal Shutdown Control of Nuclear Reactors (Academic Press, 1966)
10. ROSTOCZY, Z. et. al., Proc AEC 2nd Symp. on Reactor Kinetics and Control, 1963 (TID 7662 AEC Symp . Series 2, 1964)
11. DUNCOMBE, E. and RATHBONE, D., IEEE Trans.: Vol. AC-14, pp.277-283 (1969)
12. KLIGER,I., Proc 3rd IFAC Congress, paper 26C (London, 1966)
13. TZAFESTAS, S. and CHRYSOCHOIDES,N., Proc 6th IFIP Conf: Modeling and Optimization in the Service of Man. (Nice, 1975)
14. REDDY, P. and SANNUTI, P., IEEE Trans. Vol, AC-20, pp.766-769 (1975)
15. SMITH,H.Jr., Dynamics and Control of Nuclear Rocket Engine, Ph.D Thesis, MIT (1960)
16. STACEY,W.M., Nucl. Sci. Engrg. Vol. 34, pp. 257-260 (1968).

17. MOHLER, R., LAMS 3068 (1964) and Trans. ANS, Vol 7, pp.58 (1964)
18. LIPINSKI, W. and VACROUX, IEEE Trans, Vol NS-17, pp.510-516 (1970)
19. SALO,S., Nucl. Sci. Engrg. Vol. 50, pp. 46-52 (1973)
20. KLIGER,I., Proc.Univ. of Arizona Symp:Neutron Dynamics and Control, (1965)
21. RAJU,G. and STELZER,M., IEEE Trans. Vol. NS-17, pp.541-548 (1970)
22. WEAVER,L., Reactor Dynamics and Control: State Space Techniques, (American Elsevier, 1968)
23. KYONG, S. and GYFTOPOULOS,E., Trans. ANS, Vol.8, p.479 (1965)
24. CIECHANOWICS:W. and SOLBERG,K., Proc. ENEA-OECD Symp. Appl. of On-line Computers to Nuclear Reactors (Sand fiord, Noway, 1968)
25. SECKER,P.A. and WEAVER,E., Trans. ANS, Vol.8, p.234 (1965)
26. WOODCOCK,G. and BABB,A., Trans. ANS, Vol.8, p.235 (1965)
27. WIBERG, D., Trans. ANS, Vol. 7, p.219 (1964)
28. WIBERG,D., in "Advances in Control Systems", Ed. C.Leondes (Academic Press, 1967).
29. SHEN, C.N. and LIU, T.C., Proc 3rd IFAC Congress, Paper 26B (london 1966)
30. USU,C. and BAILEY,R., Trans.ANS, Vol. 10, p.253 (1967)
31. KLIGER,I., Trans.ANS. Vol.8, p.233 (1964)
32. KYONG,S., Nucl. Sci. Engrg, Vol.32, pp.146-149 (1968)
33. VICHNEVETSKY,R.V., Simulation, pp.269-281 (Dec. 1968)
34. VICHNEVETSKY,R.V., Simulation, pp.169-180 (Apr. 1971)
35. ANTONIADES,J., Nuclear Reactor Simulation: A Literature Survey, Demo 75/12, GAEC-NRC Demokritos (Athens, 1975).
36. KASTENBERG,W., in "Advances in NS and Technol". Ed.E.Kennelly, Vol. 5 (Academic Press, 1969).
37. KASTENBERG, W., Nucl. Sci. Engrg., Vol. 37, pp.19-29 (1969)
38. KASTENBERG,W., Automatic Control Theory and Appl., pp.16-23 (1974)
39. WILKINS,J.E.Jr., Proc. Symp.Appl.Math., Vol. 11.p.105,Am.Math.Soc. N.Y. (1961)
40. ERLICH,R., Proc. Symp.Appl. Math., Vol.11,p.151,Am.Math.Soc.N.Y. (1961).
41. GLASSTONE, S. and EDLUND, M., "The Elements of Nuclear Reactor Theory", (Van Nostrand, 1952).
42. COURANT, R. and HILBERT,D.,"Methods of Math. Physics" (Wiley, 1962)
43. GARABEDIAN, R., Partial Differential Equations (J.Wiley, 1964)
44. TZAFESTAS,S., "Optimal Estimation and Control of DPS", Ph.D. Thesis, Southampton Univ. (1969).
45. TZAFESTAS, S. and NIGHTINGALE, J.,Proc. IEE, Vol. 116, pp.79-1015 (1969)
46. ERZBERGER, H. and KIM,M., Information and Control, Vol.9, pp.265-278 (1966)
47. TZAFESTAS,S., Int.J. Control, Vol. 12,pp.593-608 (1970)
48. KIM,M. and GAJWANI,S., IEEE Trans Vol, AC-13, pp.191-193 (1968)
49. AIDAROUS, S. and GHONAIMY,M., Automatica, Vol.11, pp.203-207 (1975)
50. TZAFESTAS,S. and CHRYSOCHOIDES, N., Nucl. Sci. Engrg., Vol. (1977) in press.
51. HASSAN, M. and SOLBERG, K., Automatica, Vol.6, pp.408-417 (1970)
52. BALAKRISHNAN,A., J.SIAM Contr., Ser.A, Vol. 1, pp.109-127 (1963)
53. TZAFESTAS,S., J.Franklin Inst., Vol. 295, pp.317-342 (1973)
54. PETHSUWAN, K., "The Optimal Control of linear DPS" Ph.D. Thesis Imperial College, London (1967).
55. SARASHIK, P. and KRANC, G., 2nd IFAC Congress, Basle, Switzerland, pp.306-314, Butterworths, London (1963)
56. PORTER, B.and CROSSLEY, R., "Modal Control Theory and Applications". (Taylor and Francis, 1972).
57. PORTER, B. and BRADSHAW, A., Int.J. Control, Vol. 15, p.673 (1972)
58. BRADSHAW, A. and PORTER,B., Int. J.Control, Vol. 16, p.277 (1972)
59. TZAFESTAS,S., Proc. Int. Conf.Syst.Control, PSG College of Techno-

logy,Coimbatore , India (1973).
60. TZAFESTAS, S., IEEE Trans. Vol. AC-19, pp.455-457 (1974).
61. KÖHNE, M. and ZEITZ, M., IEEE Trans, Vol. AC-20, pp.303-304 (1975)
62. KÖHNE. M., DP State Observers (in German), Beitragzum VDI/VEE-Aussprachetag "Filter ver fahren und Beobach tungssysteme inder Meß- und-Reglungstechnik", Frankfurt/M., 17(1975)
63. KÖHNE,M., Proc. IFIP Conf. on DPS Modeling and Identification, Rome (June, 1966).
64. KITAMURA,S. et.al., Electr. Engrg. in Japan, Vol. 92, pp.142-149 (1972).
65. GOULD,L. and MURRAY-LASSO,M., IEEE Trans. , Vol. AC-11, pp.729-757 (1966)
66. TZAFESTAS, S. and NIGHTINGALE, J. Proc.IEE,Vol.115,pp.1213-1220(1968).
67. BENSOUSSAN, A., Proc. IFAC Symp. on Control of DPS, Banffo, Canada (1971).
68. BENSOUSSAN, A., "Filtrage Optimal des Systemes Lineaires" (Dunod, 1971).
69. TZAFESTAS, S., in " Identification, Estimation, and Control of DPS", Ed: W.Ray and D. Lainiotis (Marcel Dekker, 1976)
70. BENSOUSSAN,A., Proc. Intern. Symp. on Stability of Stochastic Dynamical Systems, Coventry, England (Springer Verlag, 1972)
71. YU., T.K. and SEINFELD,J.H., Int.J. Control, Vol. 18,p.785 (1973)
72. CHEN, W.H. and SEINFELD,J.H., Int.J.Control, Vol.21,p.1003 (1975)
73. AIDAROUS, S. et.al., Int. J. Control, Vol. 22, p.197 (1975)
74. AMOUROUX,et. al., Proc IFIP Conf.on DPS Modeling and Identification, Rome (June, 1976).
75. AIDAROUS, S. et.al., Proc. IFIP Conf. on DPS Modeling and Identification, Rome (June, 1976).
76. AIDAROUS, S. et. al., Int. J. Control (1976) in press.
77. WALSH, J.L., Am. J. Math, Vol. 45, pp. 5-24 (1923)
78. PICHER,F., Proc. of the Walsh functions Symp, Washington D.C., pp. 17-22 (1970).
79. CORRINGTON,M.S., IEEE Trans., Vol. CT-20, pp. 470-475 (1973).
80. STAVROULAKIS, P.and TZAFESTAS, S., Int.J.Control (1977), in press.

ON A CLASS OF OPTIMIZATION PROBLEMS INVOLVING DOMAIN VARIATIONS

P.K.C.Wang
Department of System Science
University of California
Los Angeles,California
U.S.A.

1. INTRODUCTION

Recently, a number of studies have been made on the optimal control and identification of distributed systems in which the geometric domain is the control variable or the object to be identified [1]-[3]. Here, we consider a class of optimization problems involving geometric domain variations. Certain specialized versions of these problems are motivated from the problem of confining a plasma in a closed bounded spatial domain by means of external electromagnetic fields [4],[5]. In the development of this paper, we begin with the simplest optimization problems in which the geometric domain is to be chosen so that a given functional is minimized or maximized. Then, we treat more complex problems in which the geometric domain is related to a control or manipulatable variable by a set-valued mapping. Also, problems involving domain motions are discussed briefly. Here, discussions are limited to simple results. A more complete treatment of these problems will be given elsewhere [6].

2. SIMPLEST OPTIMIZATION PROBLEM

To fix ideas, we begin with a simple example. Let $f=f(x_1,x_2)$ be a real-valued nonnegative function defined on $\mathbb{R}^2$ representing the intensity of sunlight (or rainfall) at a point (x_1,x_2) on a flat land. A farmer wishes to allocate his farmland $\omega \subset \mathbb{R}^2$ with a given area ($\text{meas}(\omega)=\alpha$) such that a minimum or maximum amount of sunlight is collected. Mathematically, this problem corresponds to choosing a geometrical domain ω from a specified class Ω such that the functional

$$J(\omega) = \int_\omega f(x_1,x_2)dx_1dx_2 \tag{1}$$

takes on its minimum or maximum value. There are many possibilities for specifying Ω. For example, a possible Ω is the set of all bounded connected subsets of $\mathbb{R}^2$ each having total measure α. Another possible Ω is the set of all subsets of $\mathbb{R}^2$ generated by translating a given set ω_o with $\text{meas}(\omega_o)=\alpha<\infty$. A variation of the foregoing problem is to allow f to be dependent on time t. Given a time interval [0,T], and a class Ω_T of set-valued functions $\omega(\cdot)$ with $\omega(t) \subset \mathbb{R}^2$ and $\text{meas}(\omega(t))=\alpha$, we wish to find a $\omega^o(\cdot)\in \Omega_T$ such that the functional J_T takes on its minimum value, where

$$J_T(\omega(\cdot)) = \int_0^T dt \int_{\omega(t)} f(t,x_1,x_2)dx_1dx_2. \tag{2}$$

Now, a generalized version of the simplest optimization problem can be stated as follows:

Problem (P1): Let Γ be a subset of the Euclidean n-space $\mathbb{R}^n$ with meas$(\Gamma)>\alpha$, a specified positive number, and Ω be the set of all subsets ω of Γ with meas$(\omega)=\alpha$. Let f be a real-valued function defined and integrable on Γ. Find an optimal domain $\omega^o\in\Omega$ such that $J(\omega^o)\leqslant J(\omega)$ for all $\omega\in\Omega$, where

$$J(\omega) = \int_\omega f(x)dx \tag{3}$$

in which $x=(x_1,\ldots,x_n)$ denotes a point in $\mathbb{R}^n$ and $dx=dx_1\cdots dx_n$.

To facilitate the discussion of the foregoing problem, we introduce a few notations and definitions similar to those given in [2].

Let ω_i and ω_j be two admissible elements in Ω. We define the increment $\delta\omega_{ij}$ (see Fig.1) by:

$$\omega_j = \omega_i+\delta\omega_{ij} \triangleq \{x\in\Gamma: "x\in\delta\omega^+_{ij}" \text{ or } "x\in\omega_i \text{ and } x\notin\delta\omega^-_{ij}"\}, \tag{4}$$

where $\delta\omega^+_{ij}$ and $\delta\omega^-_{ij}$ are subsets of Γ defined by

$$\delta\omega^+_{ij}=\{x\in\omega_j : x\notin\omega_i\}, \qquad \delta\omega^-_{ij}=\{x\in\omega_i : x\notin\omega_j\}. \tag{5}$$

Note that if $\omega_i\cap\omega_j=\phi$, then $\delta\omega^+_{ij}=\omega_j$ and $\delta\omega^-_{ij}=\omega_i$. As in [2], we shall also use the notations

$$\omega_i+\delta\omega_{ij} = \omega_i+\delta\omega^+_{ij}-\delta\omega^-_{ij}, \quad |\delta\omega_{ij}|=\delta\omega^+_{ij}\cup\delta\omega^-_{ij}, \tag{6}$$

and $\omega_i+\delta\omega_{ij}\to\omega_i$ if meas$(|\delta\omega_{ij}|)\to 0$.

Let ω^o and $\omega^o+\delta\omega$ be elements in Ω. Then the increment of the functional J is given by

$$\Delta J(\omega^o,\delta\omega) \triangleq J(\omega^o+\delta\omega)-J(\omega^o) = \int_{\omega^o+\delta\omega} f(x)dx - \int_{\omega^o} f(x)dx$$

$$= \int_{\delta\omega^+} f(x)dx - \int_{\delta\omega^-} f(x)dx. \tag{7}$$

For ω^o to be a solution to problem (P1), it is necessary and sufficient that $\Delta J(\omega^o,\delta\omega)\geqslant 0$ for all $\delta\omega$ such that $\omega^o+\delta\omega\in\Omega$. Since $\delta\omega^-\subset\omega^o$ and $\delta\omega^+\subset\complement\omega^o$ (the complement of ω^o), a trivial sufficient (but not necessary) condition for ω^o to be optimal is that $f(x)\geqslant 0$ for all $x\in\omega^o$ and $f(x)\leqslant 0$ for all $x\in\complement\omega^o$.

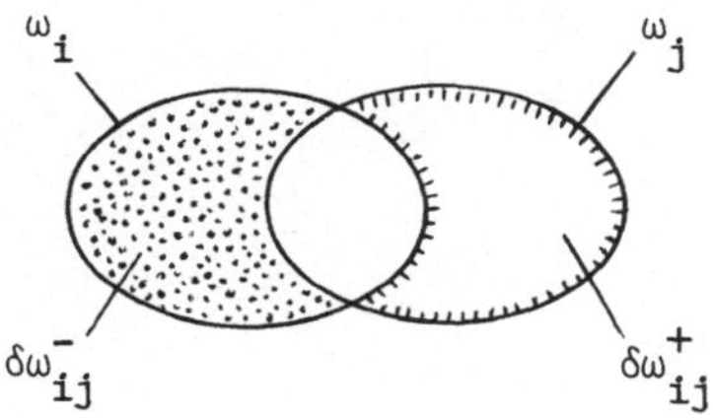

Fig.1

Now, we give a result for problem (P1).

<u>Theorem 1</u>: Let f be a real-valued continuous function defined on a compact set Γ, and $S_c \overset{\Delta}{=} \{x \in \Gamma : f(x) < c\}$, where c is a real number. Then problem (P1) has a solution given by $\omega^o = S_{c^o}$ for some real number c^o with $\text{meas}(S_{c^o}) = \alpha$.

<u>Proof</u>: Since f is continuous on a compact set Γ, by Weierstrass theorem, there exist two real numbers $\hat{c}$ and $\check{c}$ such that $-\infty < \check{c} \leq f(x) \leq \hat{c} < \infty$ for all $x \in \Gamma$. Evidently, for any $c \in [\check{c}, \hat{c}]$, the set S_c is nonempty. Moreover, $\overline{S}_c$, the closure of S_c, is compact, since Γ is compact. To show that S_{c^o} with $\text{meas}(S_{c^o}) = \alpha$ is a solution to problem (P1), we consider the increment of J from $J(S_{c^o})$ due to an admissible domain perturbation δS_{c^o} (i.e. $(S_{c^o} + \delta S_{c^o}) \subset \Gamma$ and $\text{meas}(S_{c^o} + \delta S_{c^o}) = \alpha$):

$$\Delta J(S_{c^o}, \delta S_{c^o}) = J(S_{c^o} + \delta S_{c^o}) - J(S_{c^o})$$

$$= \int_{\delta S^+_{c^o}} f(x)dx - \int_{\delta S^-_{c^o}} f(x)dx. \tag{8}$$

Since $\text{meas}(S_{c^o}) = \text{meas}(S_{c^o} + \delta S_{c^o}) = \alpha$, we have $\text{meas}(\delta S^+_{c^o}) = \text{meas}(\delta S^-_{c^o}) = \beta < \alpha$. It follows from (8) that

$$\Delta J(S_{c^o}, \delta S_{c^o}) \geq \beta\{\min_{\overline{\delta S^+_{c^o}}} f(x) - \max_{\overline{\delta S^-_{c^o}}} f(x)\}. \tag{9}$$

From the definitions of S_{c^o} and $\delta S^{\pm}_{c^o}$, $f(x) \geq c^o$ uniformly on $\delta S^+_{c^o}$ and $f(x) \leq c^o$ uniformly on $\delta S^-_{c^o}$. Consequently, $\{\min_{\overline{\delta S^+_{c^o}}} f(x) - \max_{\overline{\delta S^-_{c^o}}} f(x)\} \geq 0$. Thus, $\Delta J(S_{c^o}, \delta S_{c^o}) \geq 0$ for all admissible δS_{c^o} implying that S_{c^o} is a solution to problem (P1).||

<u>Remarks</u>:

(R2.1) In general, S_{c^o} could be consisted of the union of disconnected subsets $S_{c^o,i}$ of Γ. In this case, we can write $S_{c^o} = \bigcup_i S_{c^o,i}$ and

$$\Delta J(S_{c^o},\delta S_{c^o}) = \sum_i \left\{ \int_{\delta S^+_{c^o,i}} f(x)dx - \int_{\delta S^-_{c^o,i}} f(x)dx \right\}, \tag{10}$$

where

$$\delta S_{c^o} = \bigcup_i \delta S_{c^o,i} . \tag{11}$$

The proof given for Theorem 1 remains valid in this case.

(R2.2) The solutions to problem (P1) with f being continuous on a compact Γ remain essentially identical to those given in Theorem 1 when Ω is changed to the set of all nonempty connected subsets ω of Γ with $meas(\omega)=\alpha<\infty$. Here, if $S_{c^o}=\bigcup_i S_{c^o,i}$ is a solution as given by Theorem 1 with $S_{c^o,i}$ being disconnected subsets of $\Gamma\subset \mathbb{R}^n$ with $n>1$, then the connected domain S_{c^o} formed by any arcwise connection of all $S_{c^o,i}$'s (or connections made by (n-1)-dimensional surfaces lying in Γ) is a solution to the modified problem (P1). This observation is invalid for n=1.

(R2.3) The result given in Theorem 1 and remarks (R1) and (R2) remain valid when $\Gamma = \mathbb{R}^n$, but f is continuous and uniformly bounded below on $\mathbb{R}^n$.

The result given in Theorem 1 is consistent with intuition that in order to minimize $J(\omega)$, the domain ω should be distributed so that it contains as much as possible the regions in Γ where f takes on relatively small values. This suggests that the optimal domain ω^o may be determined by first locating the global minimum points x^i of f in Γ, and then constructing a sequence of sets $S_{c_j}=\{x\in\Gamma:f(x)<c_j\}, j=1,2,\ldots,$ each containing every x^i, and with $c_1<c_2<c_3<\cdots$. An optimal domain ω^o is obtained when $meas(S_{c_j})=\alpha$ for some c_j.

Now, we give a sufficient condition for the uniqueness of the optimal domain ω^o. First, we note that if ω^o is an optimal domain for problem (P1), then a set formed by the union of ω^o with any subset of Γ with zero Lebesgue n-measure is also optimal. Therefore, to obtain a uniqueness result, we require that the admissible domains to be open subsets of $\mathbb{R}^n$.

<u>Theorem 2</u>: Let f be a strictly convex function defined on Γ, a compact convex subset of $\mathbb{R}^n$ with $meas(\Gamma)=\beta>0$. Let Ω be the set of all open subsets ω of Γ with $meas(\omega)=\alpha<\beta$, where α is a specified positive number. Then, there exists a unique $\omega^o\in\Omega$ such that $J(\omega^o)\leqslant J(\omega)$ for all $\omega\in\Omega$. Moreover, $\omega^o=\{x\in\Gamma:f(x)<c^o\}$ for some real number c^o.

<u>Proof</u>: The existence of an optimal ω^o can be established in the same way as in Theorem 1, since the convexity of f on Γ implies its continuity on Γ. To show uniqueness of ω^o, assume there exist two distinct ω^o_1 and ω^o_2 such that $meas(\omega^o_1)=meas(\omega^o_2)=\alpha$. Obviously, since ω^o_1 and ω^o_2 are open subsets of $\mathbb{R}^n$ having the same total measure, it is impossible to have $\omega^o_1\subset\omega^o_2$ or $\omega^o_1\supset\omega^o_2$. So the remaining possibility is that the

subsets $\delta\omega_{12}^{+}=\{x\in\omega_2^o : x\notin\omega_1\}$ and $\delta\omega_{12}^{-}=\{x\in\omega_1^o : x\notin\omega_2\}$ are nonempty. But this case is ruled out by the fact that $f(x)\geqslant c^o$ on the complements of ω_1^o and ω_2^o when f is strictly convex on Γ. Thus, we have $\omega_1^o=\omega_2^o$.||

Results similar to Theorems 1 and 2 can be established for the case where the functional

$$J_T(\omega(\cdot)) = \int_0^T dt \int_{\omega(t)} f(t,x)dx \tag{12}$$

is minimized over the set Ω_T consisting of all set-valued functions $\omega(\cdot)$ which are continuous on $]0,T[$ with respect to the Hausdorff metric, with $\omega(t)\subset\Gamma$ and $\text{meas}(\omega(t)) =\alpha<\infty$ for each $t\in]0,T[$, where Γ is a given compact set in $\mathbb{R}^n$ with $\text{meas}(\Gamma)>\alpha$. In particular, if f is a real-valued continuous function defined on $[0,T]\times\Gamma$, then the optimal domain $\omega^o(t)$ for each fixed $t\in]0,T[$ is given by $\omega^o(t)=\{x\in\Gamma: f(t,x)\leqslant c(t)\}$ such that $\text{meas}(\omega^o(t))=\alpha$.

3. MORE COMPLEX OPTIMIZATION PROBLEMS

Now, we consider optimization problems in which the geometric domain is related to a control or manipulatable variable by a set-valued mapping. Let f be a specified function on $\mathbb{R}^n$ into $\mathbb{R}^1$, and u denote the control variable taking its values in a control set $\mathcal{U}$. We are given a mapping $\mathcal{F}$ from $\mathcal{U}$ into the space of all nonempty compact subsets of $\mathbb{R}^n$ (i.e. $\mathcal{F}(u)\subset\mathbb{R}^n$). An optimization problem can be stated as follows:

<u>Problem (P2)</u>: Find a $u^o\in\mathcal{U}$ such that $J(u^o)\leqslant J(u)$ for all $u\in\mathcal{U}$, where

$$J(u) = \int_{\mathcal{F}(u)} f(x)dx. \tag{13}$$

To establish the existence of solutions to problem (P2), we introduce the following assumptions:

(a1) $\mathcal{U}$ is a compact subset of a normed linear space U.

(a2) The mapping $\mathcal{F}:\mathcal{U}\to 2^{\mathbb{R}^n}$ (the space of all nonempty compact subsets of $\mathbb{R}^n$) is continuous with respect to the norm of U and the Hausdorff metric on $2^{\mathbb{R}^n}$ induced by the Euclidean norm for $\mathbb{R}^n$. Moreover, $\text{meas}(\mathcal{F}(u))>0$ for any $u\in\mathcal{U}$.

(a3) $f\in L^\infty(\mathbb{R}^n)\cap L^1_{\ell oc}(\mathbb{R}^n)$.

Under the foregoing assumptions, we verify that the functional $J:\mathcal{U}\to\mathbb{R}^1$ is continuous. Let u and u' be two admissible controls in $\mathcal{U}$. Then, we have

$$|J(u)-J(u')| = \left|\int_{\mathcal{F}(u)} f(x)dx - \int_{\mathcal{F}(u')} f(x)dx\right|$$

$$= \left|\int_{\delta\mathcal{F}(u)^+} f(x)dx - \int_{\delta\mathcal{F}(u)^-} f(x)dx\right|$$

$$\leq \|f\|_{L^\infty(\mathbb{R}^n)} \{\text{meas}(\delta F(u)^+) + \text{meas}(\delta F(u)^-)\}, \tag{14}$$

where $\delta F(u)^+ = F(u) \cap CF(u')$ and $\delta F(u)^- = F(u') \cap CF(u)$. Under assumption (a2), $\|u-u'\|_U \to 0$ implies that the Hausdorff distance $d(F(u), F(u')) \to 0$, which in turn implies $\text{meas}(\delta F(u)^+ \cup \delta F(u)^-) \to 0$ or J is continuous on $\mathcal{U}$. By Weierstrass theorem, we have the following result:

Theorem 3: Under assumptions (a1)-(a3), problem (P2) has a solution.

It will be seen later that the existence of a unique optimal element u^o for problem (P2) requires stringent conditions on f and F. Similar to problem (P1), a necessary and sufficient condition for u^o to be optimal is that

$$\begin{aligned} \Delta J(u^o, \delta u) &= \int_{F(u^o+\delta u)} f(x)dx - \int_{F(u^o)} f(x)dx \\ &= \int_{\delta F(u^o)^+} f(x)dx - \int_{\delta F(u^o)^-} f(x)dx \geq 0 \end{aligned} \tag{15}$$

for all admissible perturbations δu such that $(u^o+\delta u) \in \mathcal{U}$, where $\delta F(u^o)^+ = F(u^o) \cap CF(u^o + \delta u)$ and $\delta F(u^o)^- = F(u^o+\delta u) \cap CF(u^o)$.

As in the case of the simplest problem, we may develop similar results for the time-dependent version of problem (P2), namely, given a finite time interval $I =]0,T[$, find a $u^o(\cdot) \in \mathcal{U}(I)$ (a specified set of all admissible control functions) such that the functional

$$J_T(u) = \int_0^T dt \int_{F(u(t))} f(t,x)dx \tag{16}$$

takes on its minimum value, where f is a given function of t and x. Also, if f is continuous on $\mathbb{R}^n$, and $\bigcup_{u \in \mathcal{U}} F(u) = \mathbb{R}^n$ with $0 < \text{meas}(F(u)) = \alpha < \infty$ for all $u \in \mathcal{U}$, then we expect that the optimal control u^o for problem (P2) has the property that $F(u^o)$ contains a global minimum point x of f in $\mathbb{R}^n$ as in the case of problem (P1). However, u^o may not have this property if we remove the requirement that $\text{meas}(F(u)) = \alpha$ for all $u \in \mathcal{U}$, since for a $u \in \mathcal{U}$ such that $x \in F(u)$, $\text{meas}(F(u))$ may be large to give a nonminimum value of J.

Let ω_α be a given open subset of $\mathbb{R}^n$ with $\text{meas}(\omega_\alpha) \doteq \alpha < \infty$, and u denote the pair $(\underline{a}, A)$, where $\underline{a}$ is a vector in $\mathbb{R}^n$ and A is a linear map on $\mathbb{R}^n$ into $\mathbb{R}^n$. We associate each u with an affine mapping $A_u(\cdot) = \underline{a} + A(\cdot)$ on $\mathbb{R}^n$ into $\mathbb{R}^n$. Let u be elements of a given nonempty set $\mathcal{U}$. We introduce a set-valued mapping F from $\mathcal{U}$ into $2^{\mathbb{R}^n}$ defined by

$$F(u) = \underline{a} + A(\omega_\alpha). \tag{17}$$

Thus, problem (P2) corresponds to finding a $u^o=(\underline{a}^o,A^o)\in U$ such that the functional J given by (13) takes on its minimum value.

To give a complete formulation of the foregoing problem, we imbed U in the normed linear space $U=\mathbb{R}^n\times L$, where L is the space of all linear transformations on $\mathbb{R}^n$ into $\mathbb{R}^n$ with a norm defined by $\|u\|=\|\underline{a}\|_{\mathbb{R}^n}+|A|$, where $|A|$ is the norm of A induced by the Euclidean norm for $\mathbb{R}^n$. Since $\text{meas}(A(\omega_\alpha))=0$ when A is singular, we only need to consider the case where U consists of pairs $(\underline{a},A)$ with A being nonsingular. Evidently, a mapping F of the form (17) satisfies assumption (a2). From Theorem 3, if U is compact and $f\in L^\infty(\mathbb{R}^n)\cap L^1_{loc}(\mathbb{R}^n)$, then an optimal $u^o=(\underline{a}^o,A^o)$ exists. Now, for a $u^o\in U$ to be optimal, it is necessary and sufficient that

$$\Delta J(u^o,\delta u) = \int_{\underline{a}^o+\delta\underline{a}+(A^o+\delta A)(\omega_\alpha)} f(x)dx - \int_{\underline{a}^o+A^o(\omega_\alpha)} f(x)dx$$

$$= \int_{(A^o+\delta A)(\omega_\alpha)} f(x-\underline{a}^o-\delta\underline{a})dx - \int_{A^o(\omega_\alpha)} f(x-\underline{a}^o)dx \geqslant 0 \qquad (18)$$

for all admissible perturbations $\delta u=(\delta\underline{a},\delta A)$. For those perturbations δu with $\delta A=0$, (17) reduces to

$$\Delta J(u^o,\delta\underline{a}) = \int_{A^o(\omega_\alpha)} \{f(x-\underline{a}^o-\delta\underline{a})-f(x-\underline{a}^o)\}dx \geqslant 0 \qquad (19)$$

for all admissible $\delta\underline{a}$. If f is continuously differentiable on $\mathbb{R}^n$ and $\underline{a}$ belongs to a compact convex subset of $\mathbb{R}^n$, then we deduce from (19) that a necessary condition for u^o to be optimal is that

$$J'(u^o)\cdot\delta\underline{a} = \int_{A^o(\omega_\alpha)} \nabla_x f(x-\underline{a}^o)\cdot(\underline{a}-\underline{a}^o)dx \geqslant 0 \qquad (20)$$

for all $(\underline{a},A^o)\in U$. If ω_α has a sufficiently smooth boundary $\partial A^o(\omega_\alpha)$ so that Green's theorem holds on $A^o(\omega_\alpha)$, then (20) can be rewritten as

$$\left\{\int_{\partial A^o(\omega_\alpha)} f(x-\underline{a}^o)\eta(x)d(\partial A^o(\omega_\alpha))\right\}\cdot(\underline{a}-\underline{a}^o) \geqslant 0 \qquad (21)$$

for all admissible $\underline{a}$, where $\eta(x)$ is the outward unit normal at $x\in\partial A^o(\omega_\alpha)$. When the set of all admissible $\underline{a}$'s is $\mathbb{R}^n$, then (21) reduces to

$$\int_{\partial A^o(\omega_\alpha)} f(x-\underline{a}^o)\eta(x)d(\partial A^o(\omega_\alpha)) = 0, \qquad (22)$$

which implies that for $(\underline{a}^o,A^o)$ to be optimal, the average of each component of $f(\cdot-\underline{a}^o)\eta(\cdot)$ over the boundary of $A^o(\omega_\alpha)$ must vanish.

For those perturbations δu with $\delta\underline{a}=0$, we have from (17) the following necessary condition for optimality:

$$\int_{(A^o+\delta A)(\omega_\alpha)} f(x-\underline{a}^o)dx \geqslant \int_{A^o(\omega_\alpha)} f(x-\underline{a}^o)dx \tag{23}$$

for all admissible δA.

Remarks:

(R3.1) A special case of problem (P2) with F in the form of (17) is the one where the A's are restricted to measure preserving transformations such as unitary transformations. In this case, (13) can be rewritten as

$$J(u) = \int_{\omega_\alpha} f(A^{-1}(x-\underline{a}))dx. \tag{24}$$

Thus, the problem reduces to a simpler one with a fixed spatial domain ω_α.

(R3.2) Consider the problem of minimizing

$$J(A) = \int_{A(\omega_\alpha)} (x_1^2+x_2^2)dx_1dx_2 \tag{25}$$

over the set $\mathcal{U}$ of all rotational transformations A, where $\omega_\alpha=\{(x_1,x_2)\in\mathbb{R}^2:x_1^2/a_1^2 + x_2^2/a_2^2\leqslant 1\}$ with $a_1,a_2>0$. Evidently, any $A\in\mathcal{U}$ is optimal. This simple example shows that the strict convexity of f is insufficient to ensure the uniqueness of solution to problem (P2). Note that the uniqueness of the optimal A for the above problem may be obtained by modifying f such that the level sets $\{x\in\mathbb{R}^2:f(x)<c\}$ are nonsymmtrical about the origin. But for J(A) given by (25), the optimal A may not be unique even with ω_α being symmetrical about the origin.

4. OPTIMIZATION PROBLEMS INVOLVING DYNAMICS

So far, we have discussed only optimization problems involving geometric domain variations without dynamics. Now, we consider a simple optimization problem in which the motion of the geometric domain is governed by an ordinary differential equation.

Let $I=]0,T[$ be a given finite time interval. For any fixed $t\in[0,T]$, we consider set-valued mappings F_t induced by translations of a given open subset $\omega(t)$ of $\mathbb{R}^n$ with $0<\text{meas}(\omega(t))=\alpha(t)<\infty$, and

$$F_t(u) = (\underline{a}(t;\underline{a}_o,u) + \omega(t))\subset\mathbb{R}^n, \tag{26}$$

where $\underline{a}(t;\underline{a}_o,u)$ is a solution of the differential equation:

$$d\underline{a}/dt = h(t,\underline{a},u) \tag{27}$$

with given initial condition $\underline{a}(0)=\underline{a}_o\in\mathbb{R}^n$ and some $u\in\mathcal{U}([0,t])$. Here, we take the set $\mathcal{U}(I)$ of all admissible controls u to be measurable functions defined on I and taking values in Δ, a compact subset of $\mathbb{R}^m$. The optimization problem can be stated as follows:

Problem (P3): Find a $u^o \in \mathcal{U}(I)$ such that $J(u^o) \leqslant J(u)$ for all $u \in \mathcal{U}(I)$, where

$$J(u) = \int_0^T dt \int_{\underline{a}(t;\underline{a}_o,u)+\omega(t)} f(t,x)dx, \tag{28}$$

and $\underline{a}(t;\underline{a}_o,u)$ is a solution of (27).

It is apparent that if for any $t \in I$, the attainable set $A(t;\underline{a}_o) \triangleq \{\underline{a}(t;\underline{a}_o,u) : u \in \mathcal{U}([0,t]\}$ is compact; $\omega(t)$ is continuous in t with respect to the Hausdorff metric, and f is continuous on $[0,T] \times \bigcup_{0\leqslant t\leqslant T} \overline{(A(t;\underline{a}_o)+\omega(t))}$, then problem (P3) has a solution.

In the particular case where (27) has the form:

$$d\underline{a}/dt = A(t)\underline{a} + \psi(t,u), \tag{29}$$

where A(t) is an n×n matrix whose elements are continuous on [0,T], and ψ is continuous on $[0,T]\times\Delta$, then the attainable set at t from $\underline{a}_o$ is given by

$$A(t;\underline{a}_o) = \left\{\underline{a}(t;\underline{a}_o,u) = \Phi(t,0)\underline{a}_o + \int_0^t \Phi(t,\tau)\psi(\tau,u(\tau))d\tau : u \in \mathcal{U}([0,t])\right\}, \tag{30}$$

where $\Phi(t,\tau)$ is the state transition matrix of the system $d\underline{a}/dt = A(t)\underline{a}$. It is known that if Δ is compact, then $A(t;\underline{a}_o)$ is compact and convex [7]. Let $\underline{a}^o(t;\underline{a}_o,u^o)$ denote the solution of (29) at t with $\underline{a}(0)=\underline{a}_o$ and an optimal control u^o. Since $A(t;\underline{a}_o)$ is convex, we have the following necessary condition for optimality [8]:

$$J'(\underline{a}^o)\cdot(\underline{a}-\underline{a}^o) = \int_0^T dt \int_{\omega(t)} \nabla f(t,x-\underline{a}^o(t;\underline{a}_o,u^o))\cdot(\underline{a}(t;\underline{a}_o,u)-\underline{a}^o(t;\underline{a}_o,u^o))dx \geqslant 0 \tag{31}$$

for all admissible $\underline{a}(\cdot;\underline{a}_o,u)$. The above variational inequality can be rewritten as

$$\int_0^T dt \left\{\int_{\omega(t)} \nabla f(t,x-\underline{a}^o(t;\underline{a}_o,u^o))dx\right\}\cdot\left\{\int_0^t \Phi(t,\tau)(\psi(\tau,u(\tau))-\psi(\tau,u^o(\tau)))d\tau\right\}$$

$$= \int_0^T d\tau \left\{\int_\tau^T \Phi(t,\tau)^T\left(\int_{\omega(t)} \nabla f(t,x-\underline{a}^o(t;\underline{a}_o,u^o))dx\right)dt\right\}\cdot(\psi(\tau,u(\tau))-\psi(\tau,u^o(\tau))) \geqslant 0 \tag{32}$$

for all $u \in \mathcal{U}(I)$, where $(\cdot)^T$ denotes transposition. If for any $t \in [0,T]$, $\omega(t)$ has a sufficiently smooth boundary $\partial\omega(t)$, we may apply Green's theorem to (32) to obtain

$$\int_0^T d\tau \left\{\int_\tau^T \Phi(t,\tau)^T\left(\int_{\partial\omega(t)} f(t,x-\underline{a}^o(t;\underline{a}_o,u^o))\eta(x)d(\partial\omega(t))\right)dt\right\}\cdot$$

$$(\psi(\tau,u(\tau))-\psi(\tau,u^o(\tau))) \geqslant 0 \tag{33}$$

for all $u \in \mathcal{U}(I)$. By introducing the adjoint system:

$$\frac{dp(t;u^o)}{dt} = -A(t)^T p(t;u^o) - \int_{\omega(t)} \Delta f(t,x-\underline{a}^o(t;\underline{a}_o,u^o))dx, \quad (34)$$

$$p(T;u^o) = 0,$$

condition (32) can be reduced to

$$\int_0^T p(t;u^o)\cdot(\psi(t,u(t))-\psi(t,u^o(t)))dt \geq 0 \quad (35)$$

for all $u \in \mathcal{U}(I)$.

The foregoing problem is motivated from that of confining a plasma by means of external time-varying electromagnetic fields. Assuming an electron-ion collisionless plasma, the evolution of the particle number densities in the position-velocity space with time is governed by the Vlasov equation:

$$\partial f_j/\partial t + v\cdot\nabla_r f_j + \alpha_j(E+v\times B)\cdot\nabla_v f_j = 0, \quad (36)$$

with initial data at t=0 given by

$$f_j(0,r,v) = f_{jo}(r,v) \geq 0, \quad (37)$$

where j=e for electrons and j=i for ions; ∇_r and ∇_v denote the gradient operators with respect to the position vector $r \in \mathbb{R}^3$ and velocity vector $v \in \mathbb{R}^3$ respectively; α_j is the charge-mass ratio of a particle of the j-th species; E and B denote respectively the total electric and magnetic fields due to external sources and the plasma. For the case where the control corresponds to an external uniform time-varying electric field $E_c(t)$ and a static external magnetic field $B_{ext}=(0,0,B_{o3})$, we have, under the assumption of quasi-neutrality,

$$E(t,r) \simeq E_c(t), \quad B(t,r) = B_{ext}. \quad (38)$$

In physical situations, the functions f_{jo} have compact support in the x=(r,v) space. It is of interest to choose a control $u=E_c$ in an admissible class $\mathcal{U}(I)$ such that the time-averaged total number of ions in a given compact spatial domain Θ in the position space given by

$$J(u) = \int_0^T dt \int_{\Theta\times\mathbb{R}^3} f_i(t,r,v;u)drdv \quad (39)$$

is maximized. Using the method of characteristics, we can rewrite (39) as

$$J(u) = \int_0^T dt \int_{\Theta\times\mathbb{R}^3} f_{io}(X_i(0;x,t,u))dx, \quad (40)$$

where X_i is the solution of

$$dX_i/d\tau = A_i X_i + B_i u \tag{41}$$

with initial condition

$$X_i(\tau;x,\tau,u) = x, \tag{42}$$

where

$$A_i = \left[\begin{array}{c|ccc} O_3 & & I_3 & \\ \hline & 0 & \omega_i & 0 \\ O_3 & -\omega_i & 0 & 0 \\ & 0 & 0 & 0 \end{array}\right] \quad ; \quad B_i = \left[\begin{array}{c} O_3 \\ \hline \alpha_i I_3 \end{array}\right] \tag{43}$$

with $\omega_i = \alpha_i B_{o3}$; O_3 and I_3 being 3×3 zero and identity matrices respectively. A more explicit form for (40) is given by

$$J(u) = \int_0^T dt \int_{F_t(u)} f_{io}(x)dx, \tag{44}$$

where F_t is a set-valued mapping defined by

$$F_t(u) = \alpha_i\left(-\int_0^t \phi_i(\tau)u(\tau)d\tau, \int_0^t \dot{\phi}_i(\tau)u(\tau)d\tau\right) + \mathcal{Q}_t((\Theta\times \mathbb{R}^3)\cap \text{supp}(f_{io})), \tag{45}$$

where $\mathcal{Q}_t$ is a linear transformation given by

$$\mathcal{Q}_t((r,v)) = (r + \phi_i(t)v, -\dot{\phi}_i(t)v), \tag{46}$$

where

$$\phi_i(t) = \omega_i^{-1}\begin{bmatrix} -\sin\omega_i t & -\cos\omega_i t & 0 \\ \cos\omega_i t & -\sin\omega_i t & 0 \\ 0 & 0 & -\omega_i t \end{bmatrix}, \quad \dot{\phi}_i(t) = d\phi_i(t)/dt. \tag{47}$$

Evidently, the optimal ion-confinement problem reduces to the form of problem (P3). A more detailed discussion of the optimal plasma confinement problems is given in references [4] and [5].

In this paper, we have considered serveral optimization problems involving variations of the geometric domain. Only simple cases are presented to facilitate the discussion. A more complete treatment including the computational aspects of these problems will be given in a forthcoming paper [6].

ACKNOWLEDGMENT

This work was supported by an AFOSR grant No.74-2662.

REFERENCES

[1] J.L.Lions, Some Aspect of the Optimal Control of Distributed Parameter Systems, Regional Conf. Series in Appl. Math. No.6, S.I.A.M. Philadelphia,1972.

[2] J.Cea,A.Gioan and J.Michel,"Quelques Resultats sur l'Identification de Domains", Calcolo,Vol.X,1973,pp.207-232.

[3] D.Chenais,"On the Existence of a Solution in a Domain Identification Problem", J.Math.Anal.Appl.,Vol.52,No.2,1975,pp.189-219.

[4] P.K.C.Wang,"Optimal Control of a Class of Linear Symmetric Hyperbolic Systems with Applications to Plasma Confinement",J.Math.Anal.Appl.,Vol.28,No.3,1969, pp.594-608.

[5] P.K.C.Wang and W.A.Janos,"A Control-Theoretic Approach to the Plasma Confinement Problem",J.Optimization Theory and Applications,Vol.5,No.4,1970,pp.313-329.

[6] P.K.C.Wang,"Optimization Problems Involving Geometric Domain Variations", in preparation.

[7] L.W.Neustadt,"The existence of Optimal Controls in the Absence of Convexity Conditions",J.Math.Anal.Appl.,Vol.7,1963,pp.110-117.

[8] J.L.Lions, Contrôle Optimal de Systèmes Gouvernés par des Equations aux Dérivés Partielles, Dunod,Paris,1968.

PARAMETER ESTIMATION IN DISTRIBUTED CHEMICAL SYSTEMS

Bruno Van den Bosch
Instituut voor Chemie-ingenieurstechniek
Katholieke Universiteit te Leuven
de Croylaan 2, B3030 Heverlee, Belgium

Abstract

The problem of estimating constant and spatially varying parameters in distributed chemical systems is considered. Constant parameters are identified by a classical approach illustrated for a problem concerning deactivation of a fixed bed catalytic reactor. An alternative procedure based upon the equation errors proves very efficient. For the estimation of spatially varying parameters the techniques developed in optimal control theory are available. This approach is applied upon an elementary example of two-phase flow in oil reservoirs.

INTRODUCTION

A large number of papers have been published in recent years, dealing with various aspects of system identification problems and showing applications on this subject in the most widely differing fields. Actually this domain of research has grown so fast that a review only of the surveys published over the last decade forms a considerable challenge. The extension to distributed systems, although a rather recent development made possible by the introduction of modern high-speed computers, does not escape from the same problem of diversity. The wide range of topics to be considered in identification problems of distributed systems is discussed in a survey by Goodson and Polis [9].

The present paper restricts its scope to the identification of parameters in some specific distributed systems belonging to the chemical engineering field. The applications to be discussed will be tackled along the roads paved by previous research within this domain. First, a problem of estimating kinetic parameters of a reaction carried out in a fixed bed catalytic reactor is considered. A major fraction of the production output of the chemical industry deals at one or more stages with such reactors, indicating the importance of correctly modeling these processes. The experimental and theoretical aspects of parameter identification in heterogeneous catalysis have been reviewed by Froment [8]. When modeling industrial reactors the distributive nature has to be taken into account, since temperature and concentrations vary with position as well as in time. The time dependence often may be attributed to catalyst deactivation. This phenomenon of catalyst mortality, typical of many industrial reactors, and its relation to the prediction of catalyst properties have been discussed by Butt [3]. Usually deactivation is incorporated into the reactor model by using phenomenological or empirical rate expressions. A set of constant kinetic and deactivation parameters needs to be estimated from the model consisting of differential equations reflecting the distributive nature of the system. The general treatment of such problems will be discussed, followed by a method based upon the use of equation errors. The latter procedure will then be illustrated for a specific example.

When no deactivation rate expressions are available, the identification is performed by updating the catalyst activity profiles. This is a problem of estimating spatially varying parameters. Parameterization is a possible approach, reducing the problem to estimating a set of constant parameters. Optimal control theory, however, has provided the techniques for identifying such variable parameters. The optimal control analogy was first employed by Chen and Seinfeld [6]. An important domain for application of these techniques is the estimation of subsurface properties occurring in petroleum reservoirs. The principles of this method will be discussed and illustrated in the present paper for an elementary case of two-phase flow in oil reservoirs.

IDENTIFICATION IN DISTRIBUTED SYSTEMS

Identification consists in the selection of a system equivalent to the system considered. This general definition involves a wide variety of aspects, as discussed in the excellent review by Åström and Eykhoff [1]. A fortiori the same holds true for distributed systems [9]. In order to classify identification problems several criteria are possible, some of which are mentioned in Table 1. This allows a more precise description of the examples of the present paper within the framework of identification theory.

With respect to the a priori knowledge one distinguishes between black box problems requiring the complete determination of a model and grey box problems, where the model is presumed, leaving a set of parameters to be determined. The mathematical

Table 1. Possible Subdivisions of Identification Problems [1,9].

Criterion		
A priori knowledge	black box	grey box
Purpose	control	diagnostic
Model	linear	nonlinear
Errors	measurement	equation
Methods	direct	indirect

models can be either linear or nonlinear, the linear case allowing the use of ad hoc techniques. Most commonly systems are identified with the intention of implementing a control strategy. In many situations, however, the primary purpose is the analysis of a system with the determination of the system parameters as a final goal. The present paper will deal with the latter case, called "diagnostic" [1], for distributed "grey box" systems modeled by nonlinear equations.

The model equations specified from basic conservation principles can be written as

$$\underline{L}(\underline{x},\underline{t},\underline{a}) = \underline{0} \quad \text{in } \Omega \tag{1}$$

where $\underline{L}$ is a vector of n differential equations relating the n state variables $\underline{x}$ to the independent variables $\underline{t}$ and the parameters $\underline{a}$. In addition a set of initial and boundary conditions is given. Equivalence of systems is decided upon in terms of a criterion based upon errors related to the model in such a way that minimization of the criterion results in a reduction of the errors. Most commonly the measurement errors are considered. This output error criterion is depicted in Figure 1. The observation equations are

$$\underline{y} = \underline{h}(\underline{x},\underline{t}) + \underline{n} \quad \text{at } \underline{t} = \underline{t}_r,\ r = 1,2,\ldots, R \tag{2}$$

relating the m observation variables $\underline{y}$ to $\underline{x}$ and $\underline{t}$ at the observation points $\underline{t}_r$, where the disturbances $\underline{n}$ are caused by noise. An objective function J can now be determined from the residuals $\underline{e}$ between the calculated output of the system for some estimated values $\underline{\alpha}$ of the parameters and the observed outputs

$$\underline{e} = \underline{y} - \underline{h}[\underline{x}(\underline{\alpha}),\underline{t}] \quad \text{at } \underline{t} = \underline{t}_r,\ r = 1,2,\ldots, R \tag{3}$$

The most common objective function is the least squares function

$$J = \sum_{r=1}^{R} \underline{e}_r^T \underline{e}_r \tag{4}$$

but other functions can be considered when combining the maximum likelihood principle with statistical knowledge [1]. Restricting the discussion to the objective function

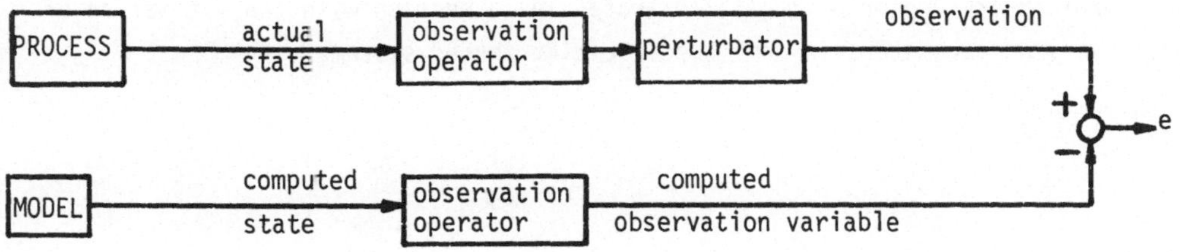

Figure 1. Output error criterion

of Eq. 4, the problem becomes an optimization problem where the performance index J has to be minimized with respect to the parameters. As in optimal control theory this can be done by directly minimizing J using first-order or second-order algorithms. First-order methods make use of the gradient

$$\frac{\partial J}{\partial \underline{a}} = 2 \sum_{r=1}^{R} \underline{e}_r^T \frac{\partial \underline{e}_r}{\partial \underline{a}} \tag{5}$$

The derivatives in Eq. 5 involve the sensitivity coefficients $\frac{\partial \underline{x}}{\partial \underline{a}}$. For each parameter a_j the sensitivity coefficients are the solution of a set of n coupled sensitivity equations obtained by differentiation of Eq. 1 with respect to a_j[10]. Second-order methods also employ the second derivatives

$$\frac{\partial^2 J}{\partial \underline{a}^2} = 2 \sum_{r=1}^{R} \frac{\partial \underline{e}_r^T}{\partial \underline{a}} \frac{\partial \underline{e}_r}{\partial \underline{a}} + 2 \sum_{r=1}^{R} \underline{e}_r^T \frac{\partial^2 \underline{e}_r}{\partial \underline{a}^2} \tag{6}$$

When neglecting the second term on the r.h.s. of Eq. 6, because the residuals $\underline{e}_r$ are small, second-order methods like first-order methods only require the solution of the sensitivity equations.

The above procedure is simply an extension of an existing method to distributed systems. It has the disadvantage of requiring to solve sets of differential equations for the state variables as well as for the sensitivity coefficients at each iteration of the minimization algorithm. This may become very time consuming for distributed systems and one may want to consider alternative methods. A possible procedure based upon the use of the equation error will be discussed for a problem of identifying constant parameters in a distributed system.

When spatially varying parameters are to be estimated a straightforward approach consists in parameterization by a fixed number of constant parameters, followed by the above procedure. The same disadvantages, however, will hold even more now because of the large number of sensitivity equations involved. Moreover one may prefer to leave the nature of the parameters untouched and develop a general approach, not restricting the parameters a priori to some specific functions. A possible way towards the solution of the latter problems is provided by the direct methods of optimal control theory, which will be illustrated in connection with the estimation of spatially varying parameters in some specific distributed systems.

ESTIMATION OF CONSTANT PARAMETERS

Use of the equation errors

If one uses the technique of numerical differentiation for the derivatives occurring in the model equations, the differential equations are reduced into algebraic equations. After introducing an objective function based upon the equation errors, minimization techniques can be used as before, but now the sensitivity coefficients can be calculated from algebraic equations. A simple way for implementing this principle exists when the state variables are observed directly at a series of points. Straightforward polynomial interpolation formulas can be used and substitution into the model equations gives the desired algebraic equations. Because of the oscillatory character of interpolation formulas large errors may arise for the derivatives in the observation points, restricting the applicability to sufficiently smooth functions. It seems, however, that this simple method has been discarded too easily in many instances, since a few straightforward improvements are possible. A first observation concerns the fact that errors on derivatives obtained through numerical differentiation can be reduced significantly by selecting the interpolation nodes as the zero's of orthogonal polynomials, as shown in detail by Villadsen and Michelsen [14]. Second, it was shown that through integration of the equation errors over the observation domain, positive and negative errors cancel each other, leading to very accurate parameter estimates [12]. The approach can best be illustrated by a simple example.

Consider the one-variable one-parameter model

$$\frac{\partial x}{\partial t_1} = a \frac{\partial^2 x}{\partial t_2^2} \qquad (7)$$

with boundary conditions

$$x(t_1,0) = x(t_1,1) = 0 \qquad 0 \leq t_1 \leq 0.2 \qquad (8)$$

and initial condition

$$x(0,t_2) = \sin \pi t_2 \qquad 0 \leq t_2 \leq 1 \qquad (9)$$

Eq. 7 is the dimensionless heat equation modeling the transient temperature in a wall with the surroundings at a given constant temperature [11]. For a parameter value a = 1 and for the initial condition of Eq. 9 the transient temperature is

$$x = \exp(-a\pi^2 t_1) \sin \pi t_2 \qquad (10)$$

If the temperature is given at a series of N points $t_{2,j}$ at M discrete times $t_{1,i}$ one gets the interpolation formula

$$x' = \sum_{j=1}^{N+2} \sum_{i=1}^{M+1} \ell_j^{II}(t_2)\ell_i^{I}(t_1)\, y_{i,j} \tag{11}$$

where ℓ_j^{II} and ℓ_i^{I} are Lagrange-interpolation polynomials [14] with respect to t_2 and t_1 respectively, and $y_{i,j}$ is the given value of x at point $t_{2,j}$ and at time $t_{1,i}$. The Lagrange polynomials satisfy the conditions

$$\ell_i^{I}(t_{1,k}) = \delta_{i,k} \qquad i,k = 1,2,\ldots, M + 1 \tag{12a}$$

$$\ell_j^{II}(t_{2,k}) = \delta_{j,k} \qquad j,k = 1,2,\ldots, N + 2 \tag{12b}$$

showing that x' equals $y_{i,j}$ at each observation point. Substitution of Eq. 11 into Eq. 7 gives the equation error

$$e = \frac{\partial x'}{\partial t_1} - a\,\frac{\partial^2 x'}{\partial t_2^2} \tag{13}$$

and the parameter a can now be estimated by minimizing the objective function

$$J = \int_0^{0.2}\int_0^{1} e^2\, dt_2 dt_1 \tag{14}$$

The minimum of J is obtained when

$$\frac{\partial J}{\partial a} = 0 \tag{15}$$

resulting in the parameter estimate

$$\alpha = \frac{\displaystyle\int_0^{0.2}\int_0^{1} \left(\frac{\partial x'}{\partial t_1}\right)\left(\frac{\partial^2 x'}{\partial t_2^2}\right) dt_2 dt_1}{\displaystyle\int_0^{0.2}\int_0^{1} \left(\frac{\partial^2 x'}{\partial t_2^2}\right)^2 dt_2 dt_1} \tag{16}$$

Since all expressions in Eq. 16 are polynomials, the integrations involved can be performed exactly by the use of Lobatto-quadrature formulas [12]. Table 2 shows results for α for variable N and M, where the interpolation nodes were preselected as the zeros of orthogonal polynomials and noisefree data were presumed. The possibility of obtaining high accuracy with little computational requirements follows from the table. A simultaneous increase of N and M actually results in as high an accuracy

Table 2. Value of $|\alpha-1|$ for Variable N and M

N \ M	2	3	4	5	6
2	2×10^{-1}	2×10^{-1}	2×10^{-1}	2×10^{-1}	2×10^{-1}
3	6×10^{-2}	3×10^{-3}	2×10^{-3}	1×10^{-3}	1×10^{-3}
4	5×10^{-2}	3×10^{-3}	1×10^{-3}	1×10^{-3}	1×10^{-3}
5	5×10^{-2}	2×10^{-3}	3×10^{-5}	1×10^{-6}	1×10^{-6}
6	5×10^{-2}	2×10^{-3}	3×10^{-5}	8×10^{-7}	5×10^{-7}

as desired, showing the efficiency of this procedure in the theoretical case of accurate measurements. A more realistic application will be dealt with in the next section.

Catalyst deactivation problem

Fixed bed reactors subject to catalyst deactivation typify the distributed nature of chemical engineering systems. Figure 2 gives a schematic picture of these reactors, consisting of long cylindrical tubes filled with a porous granular material supporting the catalyst. The reactants enter the tube at one side, flow over the bed where they react in order to leave the reactor at the other side. The central device on Figure 2 depicts a tube used for measuring the concentrations in the particular example discussed further.

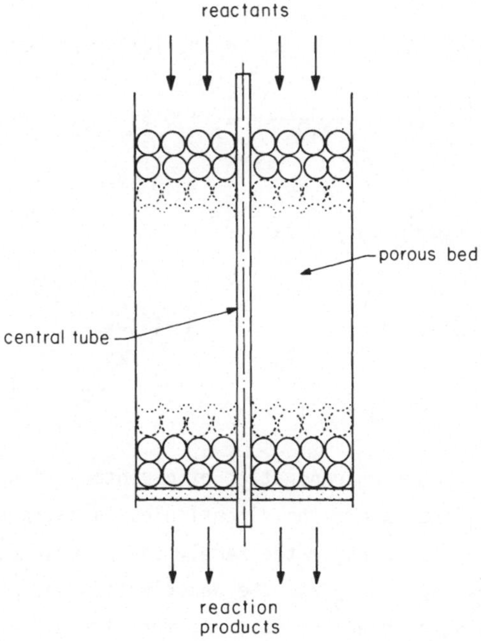

Figure 2. Schematic picture of fixed bed reactor

Many industrial reactions suffer from catalyst deactivation attributable to several causes [3]. Poisoning of the catalyst through chemisorption of impurities or sintering through agglomeration of the support are relatively slow processes, the kinetics of which can be described by

$$\frac{\partial s}{\partial t} = r_1(\underline{C})r_2(T)r_3(s) \tag{17}$$

Eq. 17 relates the activity s to the concentrations $\underline{C}$ and temperature T through phenomenological or empirical rate expressions. If no deactivation model is available the quasi-steady state assumption can be used. It requires updating of the catalyst activity profile, which is a problem of estimating spatially varying parameters to be discussed further. A third cause for deactivation is coking or fouling by deposition of carbonaceous residues on the catalyst surface. This is a rather rapid phenomenon requiring empirical correlations. A complete investigation of such a problem was performed by De Pauw and Froment [7] for the case of deactivation of a platinum catalyst used for the isothermal isomerization of n.pentane. The following reaction scheme was proposed

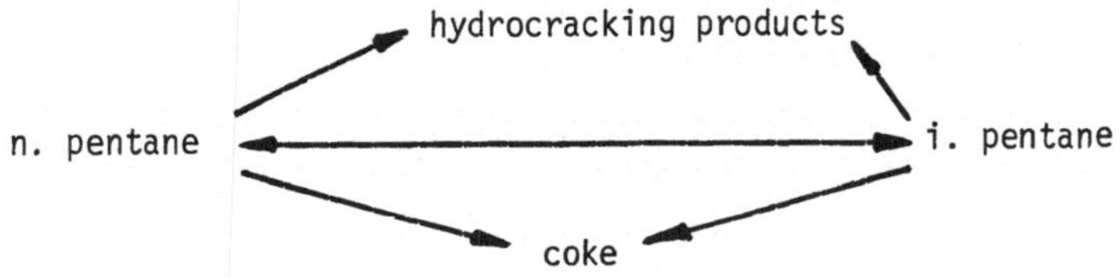

(18)

At an intermediate stage of the investigation the following model was accepted

$$e^{a_7 x_4}\frac{\partial x_1}{\partial t_1} = -41.84\left[\left(\frac{x_1 - x_2/2.133}{.431 - x_3/2 + 10x_2}\right) a_1 + 0.5\left(\frac{x_1}{.431 - x_3/2}\right)^{a_5} a_2\right] \tag{19a}$$

$$e^{a_7 x_4}\frac{\partial x_3}{\partial t_1} = 41.84\left(\frac{x_1}{.431 - x_3/2}\right)^{a_5} a_2 \tag{19b}$$

$$e^{a_7 x_4}\frac{x_4}{t_2} = 9\left[\frac{\left(\frac{x_1}{.431 - x_3/2}\right)^{a_6}}{1 + 10\,\frac{x_2}{.431 - x_3/2}}\, a_3 + \frac{\left(\frac{x_2}{.431 - x_3/2}\right)^{a_6}}{\left(10 + \frac{.431 - x_3/2}{x_2}\right)}\, a_4\right] \tag{19c}$$

where x_1, x_2, x_3 and x_4 are the concentration of n.pentane, i.pentane, hydrocracking products and coke, and t_1 and t_2 are the dimensionless axial position and time. There are seven parameters to be estimated namely the kinetic constants a_1, a_2, a_3 and a_4, the reaction order a_5 and a_6 and the deactivation parameter a_7. Data are available for x_1, x_2 and x_3 at nine values of t_1 for nine different values of time, whereas data for x_4 are given only at the final time $t_2 = 1$.

The principle of polynomial approximations introduced in the previous section has been used to solve this problem. The data were approximated by polynomials of fifth degree with respect to both t_1 and t_2. The results obtained by this method are compared in Table 3 with results obtained for the output error criterion. The agreement is obvious and the values are close to results obtained from experiments not subjected to deactivation. Most important, however, is the significant gain in computation time.

Table 3. Comparison of Results for Two Different Methods

Objective function	a_1	a_2	a_3	a_4	a_5	a_6	a_7	computation time(seconds)
Measurement errors	419×10^{-4}	866×10^{-6}	588×10^{-6}	522×10^{-5}	1.43	2.37	333	5000
Equation errors	452×10^{-4}	1000×10^{-6}	654×10^{-6}	577×10^{-5}	2.21	2.74	405	10

ESTIMATION OF SPATIALLY VARYING PARAMETERS

Indirect methods

In a previous section the minimization of an objective function J by direct methods has been discussed. Both first-order and second-order methods were shown to require the solutions of the sensitivity equations. Second-order methods, however, are superior from the point of view of convergence of the minimization algorithm [2] and have become the classical tools for solving identification problems. Especially the very efficient Marquardt method can be mentioned in this connection.

Because of the considerable computation times involved in solving the sensitivity equations - one set of n equations for each parameter a_j - one may consider the use of indirect methods. This is especially true for distributed systems containing a large number of parameters, as is the case after parameterization of spatially varying parameters. The indirect methods are often referred to as the optimal control approach. They require the solution of only one set of n adjoint equations in addition to the n state equations as will be shown further. Moreover, a general treatment is possible for problems containing spatially varying parameters. The principle will be first discussed here for a model consisting of algebraic equations containing constant parameters. Extension to differential equations with spatially varying parameters will be illustrated in the application to follow.

One can define a new performance index

$$\bar{J} = J + \sum_{r=1}^{R} \underline{\lambda}_r^T \underline{L}_r \qquad (20)$$

where $\underline{\lambda}_r$ is an arbitrary vector of dimension n. Introducing a perturbation $\delta\underline{a}$ in $\underline{a}$ induces a perturbation $\delta\bar{J}$ in $\bar{J}$,

$$\delta\bar{J} = \sum_{r=1}^{R} \left(\frac{\partial J}{\partial \underline{x}_r} + \underline{\lambda}_r^T \frac{\partial \underline{L}_r}{\partial \underline{x}_r} \right) \delta\underline{x}_r + \left(\sum_{r=1}^{R} \underline{\lambda}_r^T \frac{\partial \underline{L}_r}{\partial \underline{a}} \right) \delta\underline{a} \tag{21}$$

When solving Eq. 4 for $\underline{x}$, $\bar{J}$ equals J, and choosing $\underline{\lambda}_r$ to satisfy

$$\left(\frac{\partial \underline{L}_r}{\partial \underline{x}_r} \right)^T \underline{\lambda}_r = - \left(\frac{\partial J}{\partial \underline{x}_r} \right)^T \qquad r = 1,2,\ldots, R\ . \tag{22}$$

one obtains

$$\frac{\partial J}{\partial \underline{a}} = \sum_{r=1}^{R} \underline{\lambda}_r^T \frac{\partial \underline{L}_r}{\partial \underline{a}} \tag{23}$$

One now has an expression for the gradient of J based upon the n adjoint variables $\underline{\lambda}$, the values of which have to be calculated at R points from Eq. 22. This allows the use of first-order algorithms for minimizing J. Table 4 presents schematically the different possibilities with respect to the minimization of J as well as with respect to the calculation of the gradients. It follows that one has to compromise between the optimal control approach with slow convergence but restricted computational requirements and the classical approach, allowing faster converging algorithms at the cost of increasing computational efforts at each step.

Table 4. Comparison of Identification Methods

	First-order techniques	Second-order techniques
Direct methods	Inefficient	Classical approach
Indirect methods	Optimal control approach	Not available

Petroleum reservoir history matching

The estimation of oil reservoir properties on the basis of well production data is called history matching. It consists in the determination of rock porosity and directional permeabilities on the basis of data for pressure and production rates at the well. The treatment of such problems using the optimal control approach for models considering single phase flow has been discussed [4,5]. It was shown that ill-conditioning was a major obstacle towards solution of these problems.

Recently history matching has been extended to an elementary example of two-phase flow [13] and the problem will be discussed here for illustrating the estimation of a spatially varying parameter occurring in a differential equation. The circular oil reservoir depicted in Figure 3 is considered. Oil is produced at the

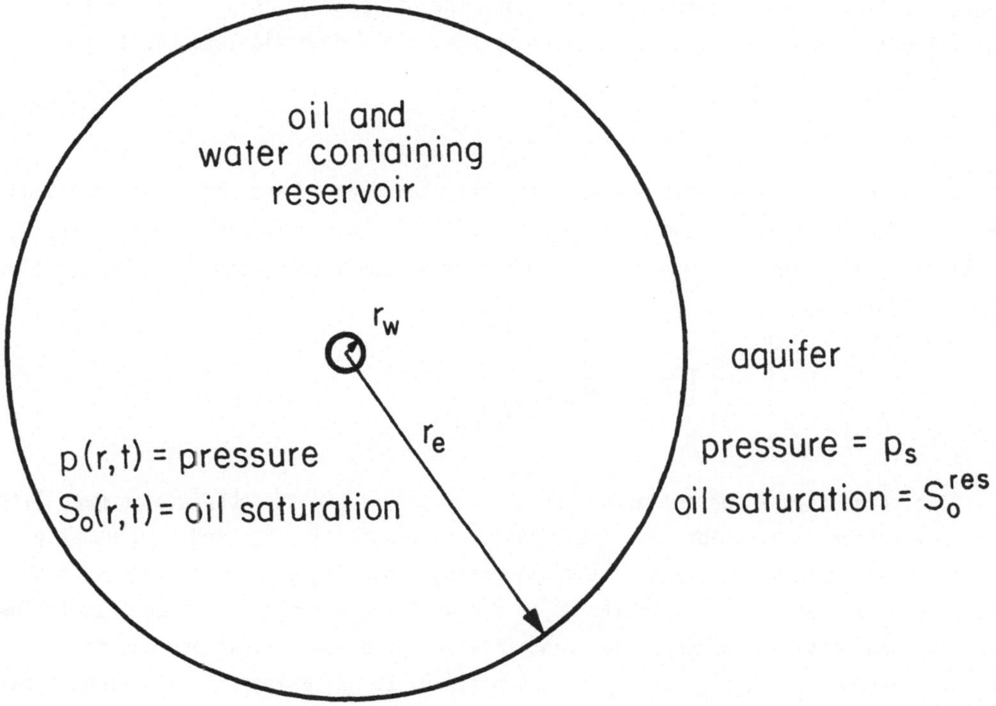

Figure 3. Circular oil reservoir with central well

centrally located well, while water enters through the exterior boundary of the formation.

Assuming incompressible rock and fluids the oil saturation S_o and the pressure p follow from [13]

$$\int_{z_o}^{z} \phi(\zeta)(\zeta+U)\, d\zeta = - \frac{h(K)}{(r_e-r_w)^2}\, r_w\, q\, t \tag{24}$$

$$(z + U)\left(\frac{k_{ro}}{\mu_o} + \frac{k_{rw}}{\mu_w}\right) k(z)\, \frac{\partial p}{\partial z} = r_w\, q \tag{25}$$

with initial condition

$$S_o(r,0) = S_o^0(r) \qquad r_w \le r \le r_e \tag{26}$$

and boundary condition

$$p(r_e,t) = p_s \qquad t > 0 \tag{27}$$

These equations determine the pressure p and the oil saturation S_o, K being the initial value of S_o at z_o, as a function of time t and dimensionless position

$$z = \frac{r - r_w}{r_e - r_w} \tag{28}$$

The radial coordinate r varies between the well boundary r_w and the exterior boundary r_e. The constants in the model are the dimensionless well radius $U = r_w/(r_e-r_w)$, the velocity q at the well and the oil and water viscosities μ_o and μ_w. The function h(K) is defined as

$$h = \left[\frac{\partial}{\partial S_o}\left(\frac{k_{ro}/\mu_o}{k_{ro}/\mu_o+k_{rw}/\mu_w}\right)\right]_{S_o=K} \tag{29}$$

The parameters to be estimated are the porosity ϕ and the obsolute permeability k as a function of position, and the relative permeabilities k_{ro} and k_{rw}, usually specifies as cubic polynomials of the saturation. Available data are values of the pressure p_w and of the oil velocity q_o at the well for a number of times. It follows that one can consider two separate identification problems. First one has to estimate the parameters ϕ, k_{ro} and k_{rw} on the basis of Eq. 24 using the oil velocity data. Second the parameter k has to be determined on the basis of Eq. 25 using the well pressure data. The latter problem is of particular interest in this context.

The objective function to be minimized is

$$J = \frac{1}{2}\sum_{r=1}^{R}[p_r^o - p(0,t_r)]^2 \tag{30}$$

From Eq. 25 the following relation between perturbations in k and p exists

$$\delta k\,\frac{\partial p}{\partial x} + k\,\frac{\partial \delta p}{\partial x} = 0 \tag{31}$$

The corresponding perturbation of J is

$$\delta J = -\sum_{r=1}^{R}[p_r^o - p(0,t_r)]\;\delta p(0,t_r) \tag{32}$$

Multiplication of Eq. 34 at each t_r by a variable λ_r followed by integration over the z-domain and addition to Eq. 35 gives

$$\delta J = \sum_{r=1}^{R}\int_o^1 \lambda_r\left(\frac{\partial p}{\partial z}\bigg|_{t_r}\right)\delta k\;dx \tag{33}$$

where λ_r is the solution of the adjoint equation

$$\frac{\partial}{\partial z}(\lambda_r k) = 0 \qquad r = 1,2,\ldots, R \tag{34}$$

with initial condition

$$\lambda_r k + [p_r^o - p(0,t_r)] = 0 \quad \text{at } z = 0; \quad r = 1,2,\ldots, R \tag{35}$$

The pressure profiles for a particular simulation are shown in Figure 4. The estimation of k(z) from the pressure equation turns out to be ill-conditioned, as can be expected from the time behavior shown in Figure 4. Only the value of k(z) at the well can be identified from the data, whereas values in the interior of the reservoir cannot be estimated allowing an infinite number of solutions. This result is an indication of the ill-conditioned nature of the general history-matching problem.

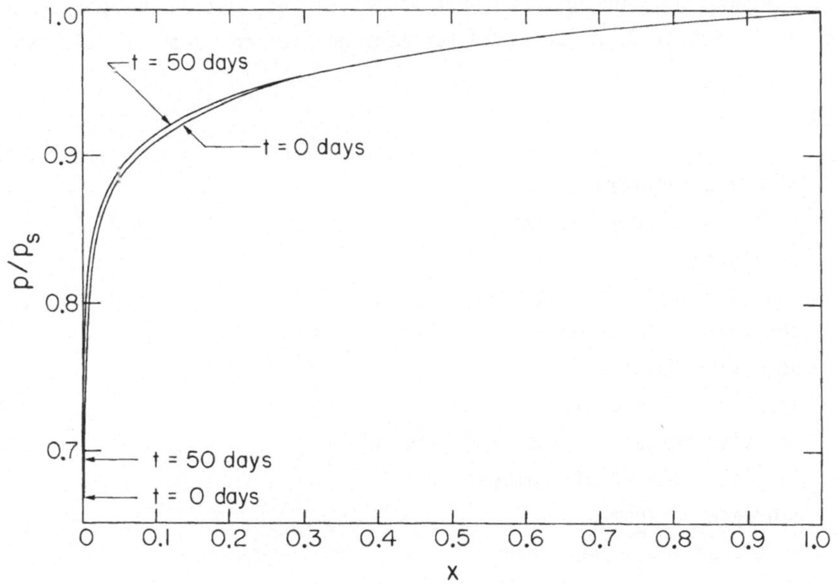

Figure 4. Pressure distributions in the reservoir

CONCLUSIONS

The identification of constant and spatially varying parameters in mathematical models for distributed systems has been studied. The procedure for solving these problems mainly amounts to a choice between direct minimization methods using second-order optimization algorithms and indirect methods employing first-order minimization techniques, a method widely used in optimal control theory. The first procedure is useful when estimating constant parameters, as illustrated for the case of identifying kinetic parameters in a fixed bed reactor model. An alternative and efficient approach, however, consists in the use of an objective function based upon equation errors. This procedure gives accurate estimates with an important gain in computation time.

When the number of parameters is large or for spatially varying parameters, the indirect methods prove interesting. They allow general treatment of the problem, requiring only the solution of a set of adjoint equations the number of which equals the number of state equations. The example of two-phase flow in circular petroleum reservoirs illustrates the procedure, at the same time revealing the ill-conditioned nature of history-matching problems.

ACKNOWLEDGMENT

I am grateful to N.A.T.O. for a research fellowship for a stay at the California Institute of Technology, during which part of this investigation was performed. I am indebted to Professor J. H. Seinfeld for many helpful comments and discussions.

NOMENCLATURE

$\underline{a}$	set of parameters
$\underline{C}$	vector of concentrations
$\underline{e}$	residues
h	function defined in Eq. 29
$\underline{h}$	observation functions
J	objective function
k	absolute permeability
k_{ro}, k_{rw}	relative permeabilities of oil and water
K	initial value of oil saturation
ℓ	Lagrange polynomial
$\underline{L}$	vector of model equations
m	number of observation variables
M	observation points in t_1-direction
n	number of state variables
N	observation points in t_2-direction
p	pressure
q	velocity
r	radial coordinate
R	number of observation points
s	catalyst activity
S_o	oil saturation

$\underline{t}$	independent variables
T	temperature
U	dimensionless well radius
$\underline{x}$	vector of state variables
$\underline{y}$	observation variables
z	dimensionless radial coordinate
$\underline{\alpha}$	vector of parameter values
$\delta_{i,k}$	Kronecker delta
$\underline{\eta}$	noise vector
$\underline{\lambda}$	adjoint variables
μ_o, μ_w	oil and water viscosities
ϕ	porosity

Subscripts

e	exterior boundary
i	point in t_1-direction
j	point in t_2-direction
r	observation point
w	well

Superscripts

I	polynomials for t_1
II	polynomials for t_2

REFERENCES

1. Åström, K. J., and Eykhoff, P.: System Identification - A Survey. Automatica, 7 (1971) 123-162.
2. Bard, Y.: Comparison of Gradient Methods for the Solution of Nonlinear Parameter Estimation Problems. SIAM J. Numer. Anal., 7 (1970) 157-186.
3. Butt, J. B.: Progress Towards the A Priori Determination of Catalytic Properties. AIChE Jl., 22 (1976) 1-26.
4. Chavent, G., Dupuy, M., and Lemonnier, P.: History Matching by Use of Optimal Theory. Soc. Pet. Eng. J., 258 (1975) 74-86.
5. Chen, W. H., Gavalas, G. R., Seinfeld, J. H., and Wasserman, M. L.: A New Algorithm for Automatic History Matching. Soc. Pet. Eng. J., 257 (1974) 593-608.
6. Chen, W. H., and Seinfeld, J. H.: Estimation of Spatially Varying Parameters in Partial Differential Equations. Int. J. Control, 15 (1972) 487-495.
7. DePauw, R. P., and Froment, G. F.: Deactivation of a Platinum Reforming Catalyst in a Tubular Reactor. Chem. Eng. Sci., 30 (1975) 789-801.
8. Froment, G. F.: Model Discrimination and Parameter Estimation in Heterogeneous Catalysis. AIChE Jl., 21 (1975) 1041-1057.
9. Goodson, R. E., and Polis, M. P.,: A Survey of Parameter Identification in Distributed Systems. Proceedings of the 6th IFAC World Congress, Boston (Mass.) 8.2 (1975) 1-12.
10. Seinfeld, J. H.: Identification of Parameters in Partial Differential Equations, Chem. Eng. Sci. 24 (1969) 65-74.

11. Seinfeld, J. H., and Chen, W. H.: Estimation of Parameters in Partial Differential Equations from Noisy Experimental Data, Chem. Eng. Sci., 26 (1971) 753-766.
12. Van den Bosch, B., and Hellinckx, L. J.: A New Method for the Estimation of Parameters in Differential Equations, AIChE Jl. 20 (1974) 250-255.
13. Van den Bosch, B., and Seinfeld, J. H.: History Matching in Two-Phase Petroleum Reservoirs. Soc. Pet. Eng. J., submitted.
14. Villadsen, J. V., and Michelsen, M. L.: Solution of Differential Equation Models by Polynomial Approximation. Prentice-Hall Inc., New Jersey, to be published.

On-line Estimation and Identification of a Nonlinear, Distributed-parameter Process: The Dehydrogenation of Ethylbenzene to Form Styrene in a Tubular, Fixed-bed, Catalytic Reactor

W. Fred Ramirez
David E. Clough

Department of Chemical Engineering
University of Colorado
Boulder, Colorado 80309 USA

ABSTRACT

The industrial production of styrene monomer is achieved via the dehydrogenation of ethylbenzene in the presence of steam over a metal oxide catalyst at a temperature around 600°C. The goal of this investigation was to develop and demonstrate an on-line scheme for estimation of process variables and identification of the dehydrogenation reaction parameters using a distributed-parameter, Kalman filter. This technique was first tested by computer simulation and accurately estimated the process states. Reaction parameters were identified well also, although they proved to be more sensitive to process noise than the state variables. A pilot plant and digital computer system were constructed in order to investigate experimentally the on-line identification scheme. The filter proved effective in estimating process variables. As the simulation predicted, the experimental identification of dehydrogenation reaction parameters was sensitive to process noise; however, the identified parameters are shown to be of potential use in optimization of the reactor operating conditions.

INTRODUCTION

A dilemma which occurs frequently in the practice of chemical engineering arises from the conflict between the theoretician and the practitioner. This is that the theoretician presents an elegant mathematical model of a chemical phenomenon or process based on fundamental principles; whereas, the practitioner arms himself with reams of logs and chart paper, that is, raw data. It is certain that each has valuable information; therefore, how do we combine the two resources to yield an improved estimate of process behavior?

The field of applied statistics has provided many tools which are useful in reduction of data and derivation of simple models; however, difficulty usually arises when these techniques are faced with a complex mathematical model such as that which describes the dehydrogenation of ethylbenzene to form styrene [6]. Two approaches to this problem have been developed. The first can be described as regression analysis or non-sequential estimation and consists of adjusting model parameters in order to maximize the agreement between model and collected data. This is done in an off-line mode; that is, data are gathered over a period of time and then are processed in batch fashion. Computational difficulty is still high for complicated models which involve a number of differential equations, either ordinary or partial. The nonlinear regression schemes often employed require numerous solutions of the model with different parameter values.

A second approach to reconciling model and data is that of sequential estimation. Although it is not essential that this be an on-line operation, the burden of continual transport of data from the process to an off-line computational facility often justifies direct handling. Sequential estimation techniques do not require large amounts of historical data: as each set of process measurements is acquired, it is combined with the last estimate of process variables and parameters to produce an updated estimate. The method of combination, commonly called a filter, uses the mathematical model and must account for the stochastic nature of the measurement information. On-line sequential estimation involving a complex mathematical model requires a process digital computer to carry out the filter calculations.

DERIVATION OF THE ON-LINE FILTER

The mathematical model for the ethylbenzene dehydrogenation reactor presented by Clough and Ramirez [6] is represented by a series of nonlinear partial differential equations and supporting algebraic relationships. A first step in the derivation of an optimal estimation scheme for such a model is to define a performance index by which the estimation is judged. The classic performance criterion is that of weighted least squares which is defined as

$$J = \frac{1}{2}\int_0^\theta\int_\Omega \{(\underline{y} - \underline{h}(\underline{u}))^T \underline{\underline{Q}}^{-1} (\underline{y} - \underline{h}(\underline{u})) + (\underline{u} - \hat{\underline{u}})^T \underline{\underline{R}}^{-1} (\underline{u} - \hat{\underline{u}})\}\, dzdt \quad (1)$$

where

$\underline{y}$ = measurement vector,
$\underline{h}$ = model output transformation,
$\underline{u}$ = true state variable vector,
$\hat{\underline{u}}$ = estimate of state variables,
$\underline{\underline{Q}}^{-1}$ = measurement error weighting matrix, and
$\underline{\underline{R}}^{-1}$ = state error weighting matrix.

The first term of the above equation represents error associated with measurements, and the second term accounts for error in the system model. It is desired to derive a manner by which to obtain values $\hat{\underline{u}}$ which continually minimize J. The difficulty of this derivation depends on the complexity of the model. If the weighting values above are specified from covariance matrices:

$$\begin{aligned}\underline{\underline{Q}} &= E\{(\underline{y} - \underline{h}(\underline{u}))^T(\underline{y} - \underline{h}(\underline{u}))\}, \text{ and}\\ \underline{\underline{R}} &= E\{(\underline{u} - \hat{\underline{u}})^T(\underline{u} - \hat{\underline{u}})\}\end{aligned} \quad (2)$$

where

$E(\cdot)$ is the expected value operator,

then minimization of J will yield a maximum-likelihood estimate of $\hat{\underline{u}}$.

For a process model consisting of linear, ordinary differential equations, the filter derivation was described by Kalman and Bucy [11]. Wiener [19] earlier had derived the steady state version of this filter. Estimation equations for a process described by nonlinear ordinary differential equations have been derived by Detchmendy and Sridhar [7]. The extension of the optimal filter to linear partial differential equations was presented by Balakrishnan and Lions [4] and Falb [8]. These derivations required measurement information to be available at every point in the spatial domain, an unrealistic stipulation. Thau [18] and later Sakawa [14] treated the case of point measurements. The conversion of the continuous measurement filter to the case of discrete measurements can be accomplished by introduction of the Dirac measure [10,12].

Seinfeld [14] derived estimation equations for the case of nonlinear partial differential equations with point measurements by transformation of the estimation problem into the solution of an equation of the Hamilton-Jacobi type. In a later note, Seinfeld and Hwang [16] modified this derivation and also presented a separate result obtained by extending the work of Pell and Aris [13]. A more general result has been presented by Hwang, et al. [10]. If measurement information is available only at discrete time intervals, estimation equations may be further modified by inclusion of additional Dirac measure terms [3].

The applications of sequential estimation to processes which are best modeled by nonlinear partial differential equations are indeed few. One experimental application of a distributed-parameter filter has been reported to this time. Ajinkya, et al. [1], used such a filter to estimate the transient temperature profile in an aluminum slab subject to heating and cooling. This process was modeled by a single, linear, partial differential equation. Their filter was tested both in open-loop and closed-loop control configurations. Ajinkya, et al. [2], applied such a filter to data previously gathered from a packed-bed reactor in order to estimate catalyst decay. They simulated on-line estimation by processing the data in sequential fashion on an off-line computer, and, in estimating carbon deposition, they inferred measurement points and using gas phase composition measurements.

It is desired to derive a scheme by which the temperature and compositions along the styrene reactor can be estimated. Also, identification of the parameters of the main dehydrogenation reaction is advantageous. Measurements along the reactor are available only at four discrete points, and these are temperatures. At the exit of the reactor, and after transport delay and separator capacitance, periodic measurements of composition are available via gas chromatography.

The mathematical model for the styrene reactor can be reduced to the following general form:

$$\frac{\partial \underline{u}}{\partial t} = \underline{f}(t,z,\underline{u}, \frac{\partial \underline{u}}{\partial z}) + \underline{\psi}\ (t,z) \qquad (3)$$

where

$\underline{u}$ = state variable vector of temperature, nine compositions, and dehydrogenation rate parameter,

$\underline{f}$ = a set of nonlinear differential expressions corresponding to a deterministic model of the process, and

$\underline{\psi}$ = model noise vector.

The states of the actual system have been augmented by a catalyst decay parameter which is directly related to the rate of dehydrogenation of ethylbenzene. In the deterministic model the rate is defined by the typical Arrhenius expression as

$$k = \exp(F_1 - E_1/F_g\, T) \tag{4}$$

The augmented state variable of the long-term decay of the rate is postulated to be given by

$$\frac{\partial k(t,z)}{\partial t} = - \frac{k(t,z)}{\tau} \tag{5}$$

where

τ = decay time constant

Boundary conditions for Equation 3 can be specified from the model in the form

$$\underline{g}(t,\underline{u}) = \underline{0} \text{ for } z = 0 \tag{6}$$

and a set of initial conditions must be given as

$$\underline{u}(0,x) = \underline{u}^{\circ}(z) \text{ for } z = 0 \text{ to } L. \tag{7}$$

Measurements made along the reactor and at the exit can be described by

$$\underline{y}_i = \underline{h}_i(t,z_i,\underline{u}(t,z_i)) + \underline{\nu}(t,z_i) \tag{8}$$

where

$\underline{\nu}(t,z_i)$ = measurment noise vector, and

z_i = axial locations of measurements.

For this system, the functions $\underline{h}_i$ are:

for i = 1 to 4,

$$h_i = \underline{H}_i^T \underline{u} \tag{9}$$

where

$\underline{H}_i^T = (1\ 0\ 0\ \ldots 0)$, and

for i = 5,

$$\underline{h}_5 = \underline{u}(t,L). \tag{10}$$

The continuous filter equations derived by Seinfeld and Hwang [16] may be written for the above model equations as follows

$$\frac{\partial \hat{\underline{u}}}{\partial t} = \underline{f}\,(t,z,\hat{\underline{u}}, \frac{\partial \hat{\underline{u}}}{\partial z}) + \underline{\underline{P}}(t,z)(\frac{\partial h}{\partial \underline{u}})^T_{\hat{\underline{u}}}\, \underline{\underline{Q}}^{-1} \times \sum_{i=1}^{5} (\underline{y}_i - \underline{h}_i(t,z_i,\hat{\underline{u}}_i))\delta(z - z_i)$$

and

$$\frac{\partial \underline{\underline{P}}(t,z)}{\partial t} = (\frac{\partial \underline{f}}{\partial \underline{u}})_{\hat{\underline{u}}} \underline{\underline{P}}(t,z) + \underline{\underline{P}}(t,z) (\frac{\partial \underline{f}}{\partial \underline{u}})^T_{\hat{\underline{u}}} + \frac{\partial}{\partial z} (\frac{\partial \underline{f}}{\partial \underline{u}})_{\hat{\underline{u}}} \frac{\partial \underline{\underline{P}}(t,z)}{\partial z} + \frac{\partial \underline{\underline{P}}(t,z)}{\partial z} \frac{\partial}{\partial z} (\frac{\partial \underline{f}}{\partial \underline{u}})^T_{\hat{\underline{u}}}$$

$$+ \underline{\underline{P}}(t,z) \frac{\partial}{\partial \underline{u}} [(\frac{\partial \underline{h}}{\partial \underline{u}})^T_{\hat{\underline{u}}} \underline{\underline{Q}}^{-1} \{ \sum_{i=1}^{5} (\underline{y}_i - \underline{h}_i(t,z_i,\hat{\underline{u}}_i))\delta(z - z_i)\}] \underline{\underline{P}}(t,z) + \underline{\underline{R}} \qquad (12)$$

An important approximation in the derivation of Equations 11 and 12 is that correlation of estimate errors at different spatial locations is negligible. This assumption is adopted here following the work of Pell and Aris [13] since the number of axial measurement points are few. This and a further approximation that the terms in Equation 12 involving the axial partial derivative of $\underline{\underline{P}}(t,z)$ are small allow reformulation of the equation in terms of a set of ordinary differential equations at the measurement points. The filter equations then become

$$\frac{\partial \hat{\underline{u}}}{\partial t} = \underline{f}(t,z,\hat{\underline{u}}, \frac{\partial \hat{\underline{u}}}{\partial z}) + \sum_{i=1}^{5} \underline{\underline{P}}_i(t) (\frac{\partial \underline{h}_i}{\partial \underline{u}})^T_{\hat{\underline{u}}_i} \underline{\underline{Q}}^{-1} (\underline{y}_i - \underline{h}_i(t,z_i,\hat{\underline{u}}_i))\delta(z - z_i) \qquad (13)$$

and, for i = 1 to 5,

$$\frac{d\underline{\underline{P}}_i(t)}{dt} = (\frac{\partial \underline{f}}{\partial \underline{u}})_{\hat{\underline{u}}_i} \underline{\underline{P}}_i(t) + \underline{\underline{P}}_i(t) (\frac{\partial \underline{f}}{\partial \underline{u}})^T_{\hat{\underline{u}}_i} - \underline{\underline{P}}_i(t)[(\frac{\partial \underline{h}_i}{\partial \underline{u}})^T_{\hat{\underline{u}}_i} \underline{\underline{Q}}^{-1}(\frac{\partial \underline{h}_i}{\partial \underline{u}})_{\hat{\underline{u}}_i}]\underline{\underline{P}}_i(t) + \underline{\underline{R}} \quad (14)$$

The last equation is computed only at the measurement points since $\underline{\underline{P}}$ enters into Equation 13 only at those locations. A complete numerical solution of Equations 13 and 14 would require real time integration of eleven partial and sixty-six ordinary differential equations since $\hat{\underline{u}}$ is of dimension eleven and $\underline{\underline{P}}$ is symmetric and eleven-by-eleven. This task is not feasible; in fact, this computation cannot be justified even on a large, off-line digital computer.

At this point a series of judgments are set forth which simplify the filter equations so that they may be computed in real time. The goal is a workable scheme which will retain the desirable properties of estimation of process states and identification of the main reaction rate parameter. The first simplification made is to avoid evaluation of Equation 14 on-line. This can be achieved by computing the steady state values of $\underline{\underline{P}}_i$. In order to accomplish this, a nominal steady state for the process must be specified for $\underline{u}$ so that the Jacobian matrix

$(\frac{\partial \underline{f}}{\partial \underline{u}})_{\underline{u}_{ss}}$ can be evaluated.

The filter matrix will then have lost its dynamic character; however, the time scale of those dynamics must be compared to the process dynamics of interest in order to judge the loss. Reactor dynamics occur on a scale of one second, and, yet, decay in reaction rate is known to occur over hours, days, even months. If attention is focused on the latter time scale, the model equations take on a quasi-steady-state form ; that is, steady state solution is established rapidly for each new value of the rate parameter as it gradually decays.

It is then sufficient to compute

$$\underline{f}'(z,\underline{\hat{u}}_j, \frac{d\underline{\hat{u}}_j}{dz}) = \underline{0} \tag{15}$$

to yield an estimate of $\underline{\hat{u}}_j$ and to apply the step corrections at the measurement points, z_i, as

$$\frac{\partial \underline{\hat{u}}_i}{\partial t} \simeq \frac{\underline{\hat{u}}_{i_{j+1}} - \underline{\hat{u}}_{i_j}}{\Delta t} = \underline{\underline{P}}_i' \left(\frac{\partial \underline{h}_i}{\partial \underline{u}}\right)^T_{\underline{\hat{u}}_{i_j}} \underline{\underline{Q}}^{-1}(\underline{y}_{i_j} - \underline{h}_i(t_j, z_i, \underline{\hat{u}}_{i_j})) \tag{16}$$

for i = 1 to 5.

Since the rate parameter dynamics are slow, its dynamics enters the estimate,

$$\frac{\partial \hat{k}}{\partial t} \simeq \frac{\hat{k}_{j+1} - \hat{k}_j}{\Delta t} = -\frac{\hat{k}_j}{\tau} + \sum_{i=1}^{5} P_i \left(\frac{\partial \underline{h}_i}{\partial \underline{u}}\right)^T_{\underline{\hat{u}}_{i_j}} \underline{\underline{Q}}^{-1}(\underline{y}_{i_j} - \underline{h}_i(t_j; z_i \underline{\hat{u}}_{i_j}))\delta(z - z_i) \tag{17}$$

To carry out the solution of Equation 15, one solves the equation for the spatial derivatives so that a conventional numerical integration may be used. These is then the requirement that values of k be available at each spatial step of this integration. This creates a problem since Equation 17 will yield parameter estimates only at the measurements points. It is proposed that estimates of rate parameter and temperature (from Equation 16) at the measurement points be used to determine values of the activation energy, E_1, and frequency factor, F_1, via least squares regression on Equation 4. The form of Equation 4 may then be used with the computed values of E_1 and F_1 for the solution of the steady state, $\underline{\hat{u}}'$.

The algorithm proposed for on-line state estimation and parameter identification is as follows :

1. Compute a model estimate by solving the steady state equations $\underline{f}'(z,\underline{u},\frac{d\hat{u}}{dz}) = \underline{0}$ using present values of E_1 and F_1.
2. Obtain measurements of temperature along the reactor and compositions of the reactor effluent.
3. Estimate values of the temperature and compositions at measurement points using Equation 16.
4. Estimate values of the rate parameter at measurement points using Equation 17.
5. Determine new values of activation energy and frequency factor by least squares regression on Equation 4 using the latest pair estimates (T_{i_j}, k_{i_j}), i = 1 to 5.
6. Return to step 1.

The above is seen as a workable scheme; in fact, one which has been implemented on a styrene pilot plant using a small process computer to carry out the estimation calculations. First, however, the steady state filter matrix had to be computed off-line for typical process conditions. Also, to gain confidence in the estimation algorithm, it was simulated off-line.

COMPUTATION OF THE FILTER MATRIX

In order to arrive at numerical values for the filter matrix $\underline{\underline{P}}_i$ at steady state, it is necessary to determine those values which will satisfy Equation 14 with left-hand-side set equal to zero. This computation could seemingly be handled using some type of iterative scheme for the solution of nonlinear algebraic equations. In this case, that would amount to solution of sixty-six simultaneous nonlinear algebraic equations. The steady state solution is most readily attained by simultaneous numerical integration of the equations until all elements of $\underline{\underline{P}}_i$ cease to change appreciably. This approach has been used successfully here.

As a prelude to the numerical solution, the Jacobian matrix must be evaluated for typical values of process parameters. Two approaches were used. The first required a lengthy analytical derivation of the elements of the Jacobian matrix followed by computation. In the second, the states $\underline{u}$ were perturbed a small amount, and the elements of the matrix were computed by the approximate formula

$$\frac{\Delta f_n}{\Delta u_m} .$$

Agreement of the results of the two approaches to within one percent served as a check. A different Jacobian matrix was computed for each measurement point.

Numerical integration of Equation 14 was attempted using a variety of methods. It became apparent that the system of equations was extremely "stiff", that is, the dynamics of the coupled equations covered a wide time scale as would occur with a system of linear equations with widely separated eigenvalues. An integration scheme was implemented based on work of Gear [9]. This k-step implicit variable-step, variable-order algorithm is reported to be expecially useful for the numerical solution of stiff equations. Although this technique succeeded in integrating the equations several orders of magnitude farther ahead in time than previous attempts, it still did not produce the desired steady state result within the computational time limit.

At this point, an important decision was made to further simplify the estimation scheme to make it workable. The number of process variables to be directly estimated was reduced from ten to four, retaining temperature and concentrations of the three major components, ethylbenzene, styrene and hydrogen. These four, when augmented by the rate parameter require the solution of a filter matrix of dimension five-by-five. Those components which were removed from the estimation scheme are still computed by the solution of the steady state process model.

Given the reduced size of the filter matrix, numerical solution is feasible. For the five filter matrices computed, the process time for solution was on the order of several hundred seconds and computer time required was seventy-five to one hundred seconds on the CDC 6400 computer. The first columns of the filter matrices for measurement points along the reactor are presented in Table I. Other matrix elements do not enter in the estimation calculations. All elements of the filter matrix for the reactor exit are also presented in Table I.

One of the simplifications of the filter equations, (11) and (12), was to drop the terms in Equation 12 involving axial partial derivatives of $\underline{\underline{P}}(t,z)$. The magnitude of those terms have been estimated by simple difference formulas using the values of Table I. It was found that for diagonal elements of $\underline{\underline{P}}$, the axial derivative terms are five orders of magnitude smaller than other terms of Equation 12, and, for off-diagonal terms, the relative significance is at most one hundred times smaller than other terms. Based on this evidence, it can be concluded that neglecting the axial partial derivative terms in Equation 12 was justified.

SIMULATION OF ON-LINE FILTER

The implementation of the on-line filter on the actual pilot plant and process computer system was preceded by testing the filter on a simulated process. In this manner, errors in computer programming were eliminated and, in general, confidence was gained in the algorithm. Simulation of process measurements was achieved by solving the steady state model with a rate parameter unknown to the estimator, adding noise content to solution values, and supplying these as measurements to the estimator algorithm.

Several simulations were carried out for various conditions of noise and initial estimates. The merit of the estimator can be judged by how well it predicts the hidden process states as well as its ability to estimate the true activation energy and frequency factor of the dehydrogenation reaction.

A critical test of the estimator was carried out by simulation with an initial guess of rate parameter intentionally set with an error of one hundred percent. Results of this simulation are presented in Figure 1 as a plot of one of the reactor intermediate temperatures' true value, measurement, and estimated value versus the estimator iteration. The initial excursion of the estimate is due to the error in rate parameter. Also, the path of estimates of activation energy versus frequency factor with iteration as a running parameter is shown in Figure 2. It is evident that the estimator functions properly; in fact, it shows potential for the identification of the kinetic parameters. It should be noted that, as the figure shows, those parameters are extremely sensitive to noise in temperature and rate. The linear estimation path is due to a statistical interaction between the parameters of the Arrhenius expression. As shown by Shimulis [17], identification will yield results distributed about a line of slope

$$R_g \, T_{hm}$$

where

R_g : gas law constant

T_{hm}: harmonic mean of experimental temperatures.

ON-LINE ESTIMATION AND IDENTIFICATION

In order to demonstrate the on-line operation of the estimation and identification algorithms, a pilot plant was designed and constructed [6]. The process minicomputer used for automated operation of the pilot plant is described by Clough [5]. It is based around a Data General Nova 1210 minicomputer with 24K of magnetic core memory. In designing the system special emphasis was placed on the process and operator interfaces as opposed to programmer-oriented peripheral devices. An extension of BASIC, a high-level interpreter computer language, was used as the programming language. Although the extended BASIC language provides the programming tools necessary for monitoring and control of the pilot plant, the necessity to carry out many asynchronous tasks complicates the problem. In order to facilitate multiple-task programming, an executive routine has been developed. This framework allows implementation of several program segments, each of which executes at a specified time interval and at a particular level of priority. When the executive routine has control, it selects the task of highest priority which needs to be executed, then jumps to that program segment. Once the task is completed, it returns control to the executive routine. If the program segment requires too much time for completion, it must be segmented and successively re-entered.

The on-line implementation of the filter as a BASIC program segment was accomplished by subdividing the estimation scheme since the entire computation could not be handled at one time without interfering with other program segments. The estimation calculations of Equations 16 and 17 are computed at one time, then upon subsequent entry into the program, the least squares regression is carried out to determine new values. A series of one hundred entries into the program is necessary in order to integrate the steady state model across the reactor spatial domain. As the model is being computed, a check is made to see if the spatial position of the integration is a measurement point. If so, the variables used in the estimation step are transferred to that part of the program.

Due to higher-than-expected noise levels encountered experimentally, the on-line implementation of the estimator was occasionally unstable. Reduction of all filter gains by one-half, however, provided for an effective estimator. Figure 3 shows the estimates of activation energy and frequency factor with estimator iteration as a running parameter. The first estimate of the plot is substantially in error; however, subsequent values approach rapidly a reasonable value and then show the effects of process noise. The linear path again represents a statistical phenomenon. Such an iteration path is also exhibited by the filter simulation (see Figure 2).

On-line model estimates of temperature and conversion at one particular iteration are shown in Figure 4 along with the measurement points versus the reactor spatial position. Measurement of conversion is only available at the reactor exit.

As a part of off-line optimization studies [6], the relationship between the kinetic parameters and optimal steam-to-ethylbenzene feed ratio was determined and is presented here in Figure 5. An important result is drawn from the superimposition of this Figure with Figure 4. This result is that the lines of constant optimal steam-to-ethylbenzene feed ratio (SOR) align with the identification linear path as shown in Figure 6. The implication of this alignment is that an accurate estimate can be made of the optimal feed ratio even though the identification reflects a high sensitivity to process noise.

From one point of optimal SOR it is desired to determine the effect of a small variation in frequency factor and activation energy which would preserve constant reactor performance. This change would therefore be such that the main reaction rate constant, k, would change minimally along the reactor. A general form for this variation is the line

$$E_1 = aF_1 + b \tag{18}$$

and it is tangent to the optimal contour at the point of interest. Introducing Equation 18 into Equation 4, by eliminating F_1,

$$k = \exp\left(E_1\left(\frac{1}{a} - \frac{1}{R_g T}\right) - \frac{b}{a}\right) \tag{19}$$

In this last equation, it is noted that the rate constant, k, will vary as E_1 is changed. This variation is minimized by choosing the constant, a, such that

$$a = R_g\, T_{hm}, \tag{20}$$

which is the slope of the linear estimation path. Therefore, the optimal steam-to-ethylbenzene ratio (SOR) is given by the contour of constant optimal SOR which has as its tangent the observed linear estimation path.

CONCLUSIONS

The on-line operation of a styrene pilot plant under computer control has been demonstrated. Theoretical and experimental investigations of this catalytic dehydrogenation of ethylbenzene indicate that an improvement in process operation is achieved by on-line optimization of the steam-to-ethylbenzene feed ratio. This parameter should be changed due to the slow deactivation of the catalyst activity. Identification of reaction parameters is facilitated via use of an on-line, distributed parameter Kalman Filter.

Even though the two parameter estimates are quite sensitive to process noise, they are linearly interrelated, due to a statistical phenomenon associated with the Arrhenius expression. The resulting linear estimation path is tangent to the optimal constant steam-to-ethylbenzene ratio contour. The noise sensitivity of the estimator does not therefore limit its usefulness in optimization.

ACKNOWLEDGMENTS

The authors acknowledge major financial support for this project from the National Science Foundation (GK35861). An additional NSF grant (GK34234) provided the basic process computer system. Dow Chemical Company contributed sound technical advice on the construction and operation of the pilot plant. A private communication from Russell Krug provided valuable insight on the statistical behavior of the Arrhenius expression.

NOTATION

a	slope of estimation line
b	intercept of estimation line
E_1	activation energy of dehydrogenation reaction
$E(\cdot)$	expected value operator
F_1	frequency factor of dehydrogenation reaction
$\underline{f}$	vector of nonlinear, ordinary differential equations forming steady state model
$\underline{g}$	vector of boundary condition function
$\underline{H}$	output transformation constant vector
$\underline{h}$	output transformation vector function
J	estimation performance criterion
k	dehydrogenation rate parameter
L	length of reactor
$\underline{\underline{P}}$	Kalman filter gain matrix
$\underline{P}$	Kalman filter gain vector
$\underline{\underline{Q}}$	variance matrix of measurement error
$\underline{\underline{R}}$	covariance matrix of model error
R_g	ideal gas law constant
T	temperature
t	time
$\underline{u}$	state vector
$\underline{y}$	measurement vector
$\underline{z}$	spatial independent variable

Greek Letters

$\delta(\cdot)$	Dirac measure operator
$\underline{\nu}$	measurement noise vector
$\underline{\psi}$	model noise vector
θ	an arbitrary time value
τ	catalyst decay time constant

Subscripts

hm	harmonic mean
i	measurement location i

j discrete time point j

m,n indices

ss steady state

Superscripts

o initial condition

T transpose

' partition excluding elements relating to k

^ estimated quantity

REFERENCES

[1] Ajinkya, M.B., M. Kohne, H. Mader, and W.H. Ray, Automatica (Nov. 1975).

[2] Ajinkya, M.B., W.H. Ray, and G.F. Froment, I&EC Proc. Des. Dev. 13, No. 2, p. 107 (April 1974).

[3] Ajinkya, M.B., W.H. Ray, T.K. Yu, and J.H. Seinfeld, Int. J. Systems Sci. 6, No. 4, p. 313 (1975).

[4] Balakrishnan, A.V., and J.L. Lions, J. Comput. Sci. 1, p. 391 (1967).

[5] Clough, D.E., Ph.D. Dissertation, University of Colorado (1975).

[6] Clough, D.E., and W.F. Ramirez, submitted for publication to AIChE Journal.

[7] Detchmendy, D.M., and R.S. Sridhar, J. Bas. Eng. 88D, p. 362 (1966).

[8] Falb, P.L., Inf. Control 11, p. 102 (1967).

[9] Gear, C.W., Communications of ACM, Vol. 14, p. 176 (March 1971).

[10] Hwang, M., J.H. Seinfeld, and G.R. Gavalas, J. Math. Anal. Appl. 34, No. 1, p. 49 (1972).

[11] Kalman, R.E., and R.S. Bucy, J. Bas. Eng. 83, p. 95 (1961).

[12] Meditch, J.S., Automatica 7, p. 315 (1971).

[13] Pell, T.M., and R. Aris, Ind. Eng. Chem. Fund. 9, No. 1, p. 15 (1970).

[14] Sakawa, Y., Int. J. Control 16, No. 1, p. 115 (1972).

[15] Seinfeld, J.H., Chem. Eng. Sci. 24, p. 75 (1969).

[16] Seinfeld, J.H., and M. Hwang, Chem. Eng. Sci. 25, p. 741 (1970).

[17] Shimulis, V.I., Kinetics and Catalysis 10, p. 837 (1968).

[18] Thau, F.E., Proc. 1968 JACC, (Michigan, Ann Arbor) p. 610 (1968).

[19] Wiener, N., The Interpolation and Smoothing of Stationary Time Series, MIT Press (1949).

TABLE I

FILTER MATRIX

REACTOR POSITION

1	2	3	4
1.119	1.006	1.037	1.017
-1.492×10^{-7}	-1.179×10^{-7}	-8.602×10^{-8}	-6.087×10^{-8}
3.132×10^{-7}	2.596×10^{-7}	2.016×10^{-7}	1.493×10^{-7}
7.071×10^{-8}	7.779×10^{-8}	7.308×10^{-8}	6.266×10^{-8}
4.182×10^{-7}	4.181×10^{-7}	4.180×10^{-7}	4.178×10^{-7}

EXIT

9.889×10^{-1}	-3.069×10^{-10}	-5.389×10^{-10}	1.375×10^{-9}	-4.478×10^{-8}
-3.069×10^{-10}	2.405×10^{-16}	-1.136×10^{-16}	-1.186×10^{-16}	-2.984×10^{-15}
-5.389×10^{-10}	-1.136×10^{-16}	2.566×10^{-16}	1.160×10^{-16}	2.820×10^{-15}
1.375×10^{-9}	-1.186×10^{-16}	1.160×10^{-16}	2.485×10^{-16}	2.712×10^{-15}
-4.478×10^{-8}	-2.984×10^{-15}	2.820×10^{-15}	2.712×10^{-15}	8.760×10^{-14}

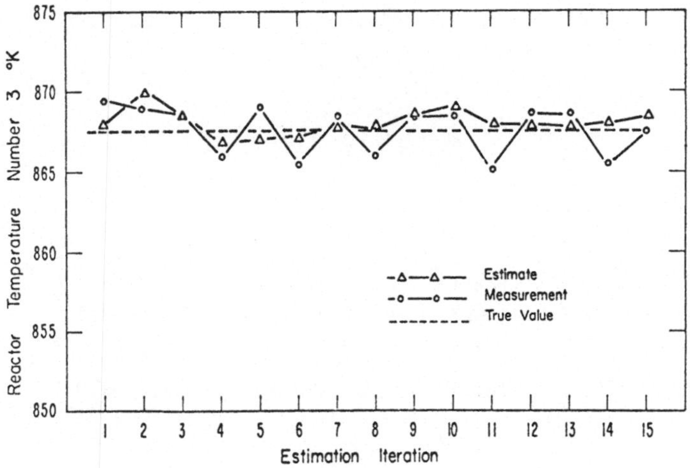

Figure 1. Simulated Temperature Estimation

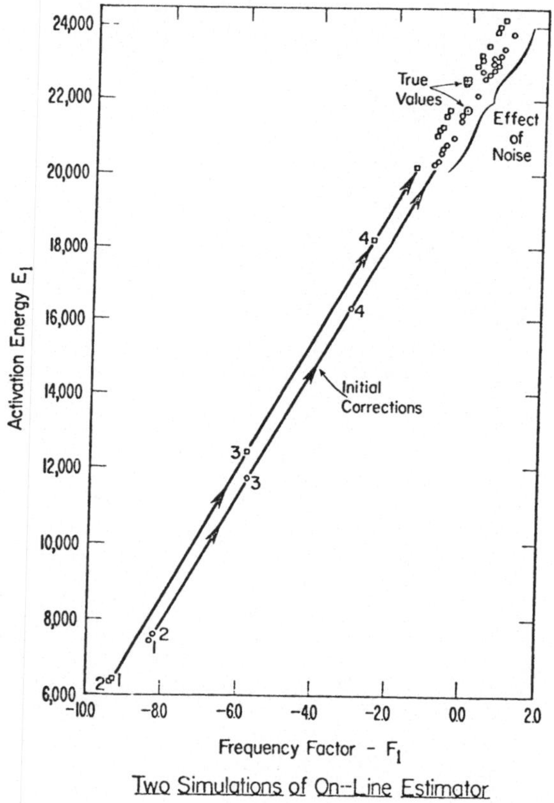

Figure 2. Simulated Identification of Kinetic Parameters

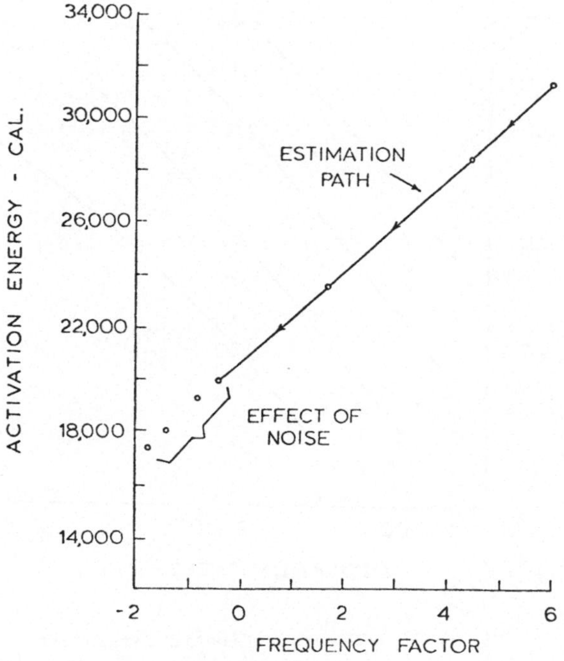

Figure 3. On-line Identification of Kinetic Parameters

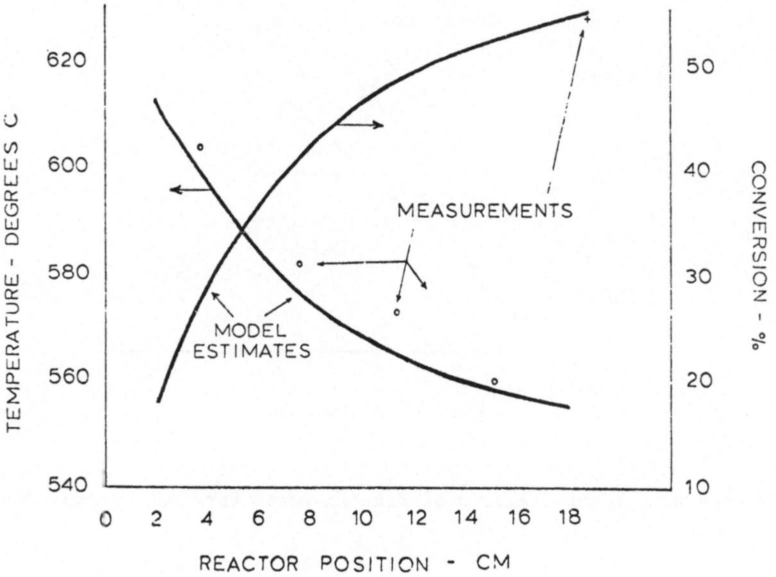

Figure 4. On-line Estimation

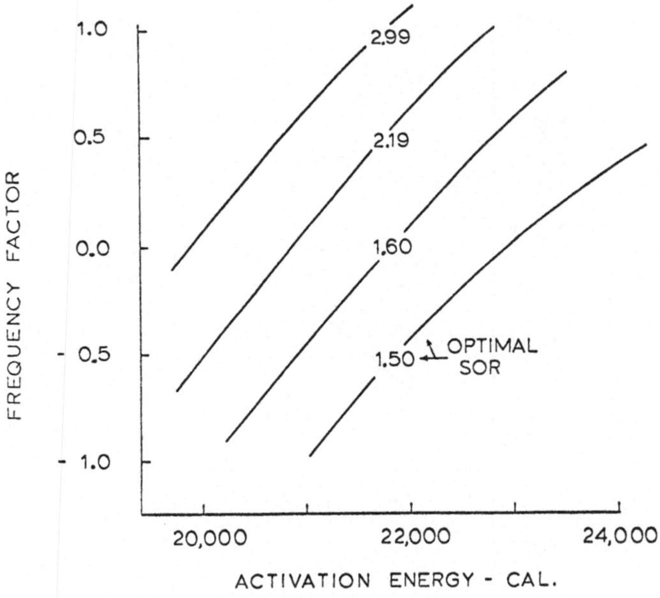

Figure 5. SOR versus Kinetic Parameters

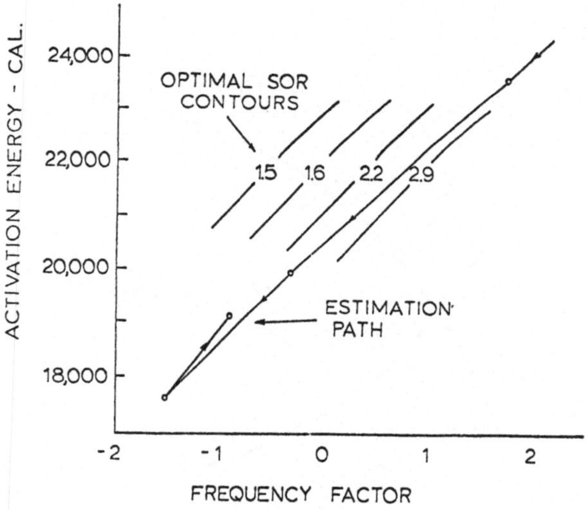

Figure 6. Identification of Kinetic Parameters and Optimal SOR

SOME PROBLEM ARISING IN DISTRIBUTED PARAMETER REACTOR SYSTEMS

Y. Kuroda and A. Makino
Department of Nuclear Engineering
Tokai University, Japan

1. INTRODUCTION.

In nuclear reactors with large sized core, spacially dependent, dynamical models should be considered for investigating the stability, control and identification problems. The main characteristics of such distributed parameter models are on one hand presented by their coupled structures which may be somewhat similar with those of chemical reactor systems or biological systems, and on the other hand by a pointwise control and pointwise observation scheme.

When the problem is limited to the optimal control, many studies have been so far made by using the modal expansion and nodal expansion methods [1], [2] and furthermore function analysis techniques [3], [4], [5]. However, in obtaining optimal solutions , attention has been not so much paid on the feasibility of pointwise control and pointwise observation. So the purpose of this paper is to make clear the situations on this point by using an optimal terminal control problem based on the coupled neutronic system [6], [7].

2. REACTOR CORE MODEL.

Assuming
- one energy group
- one delayed neutron group
- one spatial domain
- no feedback effects,

we have an original reactor core model in terms of the neutron flux Y_1 (x,t) and the precursor concentration $Y_2(x,t)$ by

$$\frac{\partial Y_1}{\partial t} - v \sum_{i,j}^{n} \frac{\partial}{\partial x_i} D(x,t) \frac{\partial}{\partial x_j} Y_1 + v[\Sigma_a(x,t)-(1-\beta)\nu\Sigma_f(x,t)]Y_1 + v\Sigma_{co}(x,t)Y_1 - v\lambda Y_2 = 0 \quad (1)$$

$$\frac{\partial Y_2}{\partial t} - \beta\nu\Sigma_f(x,t)Y_1 + \lambda Y_2 = 0 \quad (2)$$

$$Y_1(x,t)=0 \ , \ Y_2(x,t)=0 \qquad \text{on } \Gamma \quad (3)$$

$$Y_1(x,o) = Y_{10} \ , \ Y_2(x,o) = Y_{20} \qquad \text{in } \Omega \tag{4}$$

where :

- control action is introduced through $\Sigma_{co}(x,t)$, i.e., macroscopic absorption cross-section in terms of the control rods ;
- $Y_1(x,t)$ is the only observable state variable ;
- parameters appeared in Eq. (1) and Eq. (2) are assumed as positive constants, except for $D(x,t)$, $\Sigma_a(x,t)$ and $\Sigma_f(x,t)$, i.e. diffusion constant, macroscopic absorption cross-section with respect to incore materials not including $\Sigma_{co}(x,t)$, and macroscopic fission cross-section ; $D(\cdot,t)$, $\Sigma_a(\cdot,t)$ and $\Sigma_f(\cdot,t) \in L^\infty(\Omega)$; $D(x,t) > d_1 > 0$, $\Sigma_a(x,t) > d_2 > 0$ and $\Sigma_f(x,t) > d_3 > 0$
- Ω is a bounded open domain (reactor core) in $\mathbb{R}^n$ $(n \leq 3)$; Γ is its sufficiently smooth extrapolation boundary.

Linearizing the original model around the stationary state distributions, i.e. $\overline{Y}_{10}(x)$, $\overline{Y}_{20}(x)$ and $\overline{\Sigma}_{co}$ which are assumed as independent of space and time as follows :

$$Y_1(x,t) = \overline{Y}_{10}(x)+y_1(x,t), \ Y_2(x,t) = \overline{Y}_{20}(x)+y_2(x,t), \ \Sigma_{co}(x,t) = \overline{\Sigma}_{co}+\Sigma'_{co}(x,t)$$

We have :

$$\frac{\partial y_1}{\partial t} - v \sum_{i,j}^{n} \frac{\partial}{\partial x_i} D(x,t) \frac{\partial}{\partial x_j} y_1+v[\Sigma_a(x,t)-(1-\beta)\nu\Sigma_f(x,t)+\overline{\Sigma}_{co}]y_1-v\lambda y_2 = -v\overline{Y}_{10}(x)\Sigma'_{co}(x,t) \tag{5}$$

$$\frac{\partial y_2}{\partial t} -\beta\nu\Sigma_f(x,t)y_1 + \lambda y_2 = 0 \tag{6}$$

$$y_1(x,t) = 0 \ , \ y_2(x,t) = 0 \qquad \text{on } \Gamma \tag{7}$$

$$y_1(x,o) = y_{10} \ , \ y_2(x,o) = y_{20} \qquad \text{in } \Omega \tag{8}$$

In the sequel, dicussions will be made on the above linearized reactor core model. Concerning the original model, a comment will be given later.

Remark 1 : When any feedback effect, for example, temperature feedback effect is considered, $\Sigma_a(y_3(x,t))$, where y_3 means temperature distribution , should be linearly approximated around the stationary temperature distribution.

3. SOLUTION OF THE LINEARIZED REACTOR CORE MODEL.

Let V and H be two real Hilbert spaces with $V \subset H$, V dense in H with continuous injection. Let V' be the dual of V ; we identify H with its dual so that $V \subset H \subset V'$. Let V be $H_o^1(\Omega) \times L^2(\Omega)$ and H be $L^2(\Omega) \times L^2(\Omega)$.

In order that the reactor core model given by (5), (6), (7), (8) assures the unique solution in

$$W(0,T) = \{y \in L^2(0,T;V) \ , \ \frac{dy}{dt} \in L^2(0,T;V')\} \quad [6],$$

it is necessary to show that :

a) $\forall \underline{\phi},\underline{\psi} \in V$, the function $t \to a(t;\underline{\phi},\underline{\psi})$ is measurable and $|a(t;\underline{\phi},\underline{\psi})| \leq C\|\underline{\phi}\|_V\|\underline{\psi}\|_V$, where C is independent of $t,\underline{\phi},\underline{\psi}$; $\underline{\phi},\underline{\psi}$ are test functions in V :

$$\underline{\phi} = (\phi_1,\phi_2)^T \ , \ \underline{\psi} = (\psi_1,\psi_2)^T \ ; \|\underline{\phi}\|_V^2 = \|\phi_1\|^2_{H_o^1(\Omega)} + \|\phi_2\|^2_{L^2(\Omega)}$$

b) There exists $\mu, \alpha > 0$ such that $a(t;\underline{\phi},\underline{\phi}) + \mu\|\underline{\phi}\|_H^2 \geq \alpha\|\underline{\phi}\|_V^2$, $\forall \underline{\phi} \in V$, where

$$\|\underline{\phi}\|_H^2 = \|\phi_1\|^2_{L^2(\Omega)} + \|\phi_2\|^2_{L^2(\Omega)}$$

3.1. Proof of (a).

It is evident from the assumptions that function $t \to a(t;\underline{\phi},\underline{\psi})$ is measurable ; we move to the proof of the latter part.

$$\begin{aligned} a(t,\underline{\phi},\underline{\psi}) = &\int_\Omega \{-v \sum_{i,j}^n \frac{\partial}{\partial x_i} D(x,t) \frac{\partial}{\partial x_j} \phi_1 + v[\Sigma_a(x,t) - (1-\beta)\nu\Sigma_f(x,t) + \Sigma_{co}]\phi_1 - v\lambda\phi_2\}\psi_1 d\Omega \\ &+ \int_\Omega [-\beta\nu\Sigma_f(x,t)\phi_1 + \lambda\phi_2]\psi_2 \, d\Omega \end{aligned} \tag{9}$$

Putting

$$\sup_{\substack{x\in\Omega \\ t\in]0,T[}} D(x,t) = D_o \ , \ \sup_{\substack{x\in\Omega \\ t\in]0,T[}} \Sigma_a(x,t) = \Sigma_{ao} \ , \ \inf_{\substack{x\in\Omega \\ t\in]0,T[}} \Sigma_f(x,t) = \Sigma_{fo} \ , \text{ and}$$

considering $\phi_1(x,t)|_\Gamma = 0$ and $1-\beta > 0$ (from the physical reason), then we have

$$\left.\begin{aligned} |a(t;\underline{\phi},\underline{\psi})| \leq |&vD_o \sum_{i,j}^n (\frac{\partial\phi_1}{\partial x_i},\frac{\partial\psi_1}{\partial x_j})_{L^2(\Omega)} + v[\Sigma_{ao} - (1-\beta)\nu\Sigma_{fo} + \overline{\Sigma}_{co}](\phi_1,\psi_1)_{L^2(\Omega)} - \\ &- v\lambda(\phi_2,\psi_1)_{L^2(\Omega)} - \beta\nu\Sigma_{fo}(\phi_1,\psi_2)_{L^2(\Omega)} + \lambda(\phi_2,\psi_2)_{L^2(\Omega)}| \end{aligned}\right\} \tag{10}$$

Putting

$$a_1 = vD_o \ , \ a_2 = v[\Sigma_{ao} - (1-\beta)\nu\Sigma_{fo} + \overline{\Sigma}_{co}] \ , \ a_3 = -v\lambda \ , \ a_4 = -\beta\nu\Sigma_{fo} \ ,$$

$$a_5 = \lambda \ , \ S = \text{Max}\{|a_1|,|a_2|,|a_3|,|a_4|,|a_5|\}$$

we have from the Schwartz inequality and $(\sum_i^5 |a_i|)^2 \leq 6 \sum_i^5 |a_i|^2$

$$|a(t;\underline{\phi},\underline{\psi})|^2 \le S^2\Big[\sum_{i,j}^{n}\|\frac{\partial\phi_1}{\partial x_i}\|_{L^2(\Omega)}\|\frac{\partial\psi_1}{\partial x_j}\|_{L^2(\Omega)} + \|\phi_1\|_{L^2(\Omega)}\|\psi_1\|_{L^2(\Omega)} + \|\phi_2\|_{L^2(\Omega)}\times$$

$$\times\|\psi_1\|_{L^2(\Omega)} + \|\phi_1\|_{L^2(\Omega)}\|\psi_2\|_{L^2(\Omega)} + \|\phi_2\|_{L^2(\Omega)}\|\psi_2\|_{L^2(\Omega)}\Big]^2$$

$$\le bS^2(\|\phi_1\|^2_{L^2(\Omega)} + \|\phi_2\|^2_{L^2(\Omega)} + \sum_{i=1}^{n}\|\frac{\partial\phi_1}{\partial x_i}\|^2_{L^2(\Omega)})(\|\psi_1\|^2_{L^2(\Omega)} + \|\psi_2\|^2_{L^2(\Omega)} \qquad (11)$$

$$+ \sum_{j=1}^{n}\|\frac{\partial\psi_1}{\partial x_j}\|^2_{L^2(\Omega)}) \le c^2\|\underline{\phi}\|^2_V\|\underline{\psi}\|^2_V \ \blacksquare$$

3.2. Proof of (b).

Putting $a'_1 = vD_o$, $a'_2 = v[\Sigma_{ao}-(1-\beta)\nu\Sigma_{fo}+\Sigma_{co}]$, $a'_3 = -(v\lambda+\beta\nu\Sigma_{fo})$ and making use of inequality $(\phi_1,\phi_2)_{L^2(\Omega)} \le \frac{1}{2}(\|\phi_1\|^2_{L^2(\Omega)} + \|\phi_2\|^2_{L^2(\Omega)})$, we have

$$a(t;\underline{\phi},\underline{\phi}) \ge a'_1\sum_{i}^{n}\|\frac{\partial\phi_1}{\partial x_i}\|^2_{L^2(\Omega)} + (a'_2 + \frac{a'_3}{2})\|\phi_1\|^2_{L^2(\Omega)} + (\lambda+\frac{a'_3}{2})\|\phi_2\|^2_{L^2(\Omega)} + \qquad (12)$$

$$+ \lambda\|\phi_2\|^2_{L^2(\Omega)}$$

Assuming $a'_2 + \frac{a'_3}{2} \le 0$ and $\lambda + \frac{a'_3}{2} \le 0$, there exists ℓ, $m > 0$ such that $\ell+a'_2 + \frac{a'_3}{2} > 0$ and $m + \frac{a'_3}{2} + \lambda > 0$.

Putting $\mu = \mathrm{Max}\{\ell,m\}$ and $b_1=a'_1$, $b_2=a'_2 + \frac{a'_3}{2}$, $b_3= \frac{a'_3}{2} +2\lambda$, the inequality (12) becomes

$$a(t;\underline{\phi},\underline{\phi})+\mu\|\underline{\phi}\|^2_H \ge b_1\sum_{i=1}^{n}\|\frac{\partial\phi_1}{\partial x_i}\|^2_{L^2(\Omega)} + (b_2+\mu)\|\phi_1\|^2_{L^2(\Omega)} + (b_3+\mu)\|\phi_2\|^2_{L^2(\Omega)}$$

$$\ge \mathrm{Min}\{b_1,b_2+\mu,\ b_3+\mu\}\|\underline{\phi}\|^2_V \qquad (13)$$

$$= \alpha\|\underline{\phi}\|^2_V \ . \ \blacksquare$$

3.3. Unique Existence of the Solution of the reactor Core Model.

From the results from 2.2 and 2.3, the problem given by (5), (6), (7), (8) becomes equivalent to the variational form

$$\left.\begin{aligned}&(\frac{d\underline{y}}{dt},\underline{\phi}) + (A(t)\underline{y},\underline{\phi}) = (\underline{f},\underline{\phi}) , \quad \forall\,\underline{\phi}\in V\\ &\frac{d\underline{y}}{dt} \in L^2(0,T,V') , \ \underline{y}(o) = \underline{y}_o\end{aligned}\right\} \qquad (14)$$

where

$$\underline{y} = [y_1, y_2]^T, \quad \underline{y}_o = [y_{10}, y_{20}]^T$$

$$\underline{f} = D\underline{u} = [-v\bar{Y}_{10}(x)\Sigma'_{co}(x,t), 0]^T \in L^2(0,T;V')$$

$$A(t) = \begin{bmatrix} \sum_{i,j}^{n} \frac{\partial}{\partial x_i} D(x,t) \frac{\partial}{\partial x_j} + v[\Sigma_a(x,t) - (1-\beta)\nu\Sigma_f(x,t) + \Sigma_{co}] & -v\lambda \\ -\beta\nu\Sigma_f(x,t) & \lambda \end{bmatrix}$$

Since the variational form (14) assures the unique solution [7], it follows that the linearized reactor core dynamics has the unique solution $\underline{y}$ in $L^2(0,T;H_o^1(\Omega) \times L^2(\Omega))$, given $\underline{y}_o \in L^2(0,T;H^2(\Omega) \times H^2(\Omega))$.

4. POINTWISE CONTROL AND OBSERVATION.

In the linearized reactor core model, pointwise control is defined by

$$D\underline{u} = [v \sum_{i=1}^{N} \bar{Y}_{10}(x_i) u_i(t) \otimes \delta(x - x_i), \; 0] \tag{15}$$

where $D = \mathcal{L}(\mathbb{R}^N; V')$.

Namely reactor control is applied at the N's positions of control rods in Ω which are constrained by the reactor core geometry.

4.1. In case of $\Omega \subset \mathbb{R}$ - Pointwise Control and Pointwise Observation.

The Dirac measure δ representing the pointwise control belongs to the function space $H^{-[\frac{n}{2}]-1}$, so that in this case (n=1) $u(t) \otimes \delta(\cdot)$ belongs to $L^2(0,T;H^{-1}(\Omega))$, from where it follows that the linearized reactor core model assures the unique solution $y(\cdot)$ in $L^2(0,T;(H_o^1(\Omega) \times L^2(\Omega))$. Therefore pointwise observation becomes meaningful, since $H_o^1(\Omega) \subset H^1(\Omega) \subset C^o(\bar{\Omega})$.

Here pointwise observation is defined by

$$\left.\begin{aligned} & Z(x_j,t) = y_1(x_j,t) = C\underline{y} \qquad (j=1,\ldots,M) \\ & C \in \mathcal{L}(H_o^1(\Omega); \mathbb{R}^M) \\ & Z(x_j,\cdot) \in L^2(0,T) \end{aligned}\right\} \tag{16}$$

Namely neutron flux measurements are made at the M's points in Ω.

4.2. In case of $\Omega \subset \mathbb{R}^{2,3}$ - Pointwise Control and Local Average Observation.

In this case $u_i(t) \otimes \delta(\cdot)$ belongs to $L^2(0,T;H^{-2}(\Omega))$, so that in order to obtain the pointwise observation, it is required that the solution $\underline{y}$ does exist in $L^2(0,T;H^2(\Omega) \times L^2(\Omega))$. But since 2(b), i.e., "V-elliptic" property does not hold in this case, it follows that pointwise control is not meaningful in the case of $\Omega \subset R^{2,3}$.
On the other hand, the unique solution $\underline{y}(\cdot)$ is obtained in $L^2(0,T;L^2(\Omega))$ by means of transposition [7], so that the pointwise observation in a sense of local average observation becomes meaningful. Here, local average observation is defined in terms of small observation domains $\{\Omega_K\}$, where $\Omega_K \cap \Omega_\ell = \emptyset$, $\Omega_K \subset \Omega (K=1,\dots,M)$ by

$$Z(\Omega_K,\cdot) = \int_{\Omega_K} |\underline{y}(x,\cdot)|\, dx \in L^2(0,T) \tag{17}$$

Remark 2 : Introduction of the Dirac Measure for pointwise control should be more precisely given by the following :

Since for $S > \frac{n}{2}$, $H^S(\Omega) \subset C^o(\bar{\Omega})$ and the injection from $H^S(\Omega)$ into $C^o(\bar{\Omega})$ is continuous, it follows that

$$H^{1/2+\epsilon}(\Omega) \subset C^o(\bar{\Omega}) \Longrightarrow \delta(\cdot) \in (H^{1/2+\epsilon}(\Omega))' \qquad n=1$$
$$H^{1+\epsilon}(\Omega) \subset C^o(\bar{\Omega}) \Longrightarrow \delta(\cdot) \in (H^{1+\epsilon}(\Omega))' \qquad n=2$$
$$H^{3/2+\epsilon}(\Omega) \subset C^o(\bar{\Omega}) \Longrightarrow \delta(\cdot) \in (H^{3/2+\epsilon}(\Omega))' \qquad n=3$$

Therefore the solution $\underline{y}(\cdot)$ should be assured in

$$L^2(0,T,\ H^{1/2+\epsilon}(\Omega)\times L^2(\Omega)),\ L^2(0,T;\ H^{1+\epsilon}(\Omega)\times L^2(\Omega)) \text{ and } L^2(0,T;\ H^{3/2+\epsilon}(\Omega)\times L^2(\Omega))$$

depending on n [7], [5].

Remark 3 : When the control belongs to $L^2(\Omega)$ and the parameters appeared in the linearized reactor core model are sufficiently smooth in terms of the coordinates space, the solution $\underline{y}(\cdot)$ is meaningful in $L^2(0,T;(H^2(\Omega)\times L^2(\Omega))$. So the strict pointwise observation is meaningful.

Remark 4 : When the spacially differential operator A in the linearized reactor core model is the infinitesimal generator of a semi-group operators and pointwise control is introduced by characteristic functions in $L^2(\Omega)$, then the local average observation is meaningful, independently of the dimensionality of the coordinates space [8], [9].

5. OPTIMAL TERMINAL CONTROL OF THE LINEARIZED REACTOR CORE MODEL.

The process of obtaining the optimal terminal control is here formally given

Cost functional

$$J(\underline{u}) = \|C\underline{y}(\underline{u}) - Zd\|^2_{(L^2(0,T))^M} + (N\underline{u},\underline{u})_{(L^2(0,T))^N} \tag{18}$$

Pointwise control

$$\{u_1,\dots,u_N\} \in (L^2(0,T))^N \tag{19}$$

Observation

$$\left.\begin{aligned} C\underline{y} &= \{y_1(x_1\cdot),\dots,y_1(x_M\cdot)\} \in (L^2(0,T))^M \qquad \Omega \in \mathbb{R} \\ C\underline{y} &= \{\int_{\Omega_1} y_1(x_1\cdot)dx_1,\dots,\int_{\Omega_M} y_1(x_1\cdot)dx\} \in (L^2(0,T))^M \qquad \Omega \in R^{2,3} \end{aligned}\right\} \tag{20}$$

Making use of the results as above stated and the theorem [6], the optimal terminal control $\hat{u}_r \in \mathcal{U}ad$ is uniquely determined as the solution of the two points boundary value problem which may be given in terms of the cases of $\Omega \subset \mathbb{R}^{2,3}$:

$$\left.\begin{aligned} &\frac{\partial y_1}{\partial t} - v \sum_{i,j}^{2,3} \frac{\partial}{\partial x_i} D(x,t) \frac{\partial}{\partial x_j} y_1 + v[\Sigma_a(x,t) - (1-\beta)\ \Sigma_f(x,t) + \overline{\Sigma}_{co}]y_1 - v\lambda y_2 \\ &\quad = -v \sum_{r=1}^{N} y_o(x_r)\hat{u}_r(t) \otimes \delta(x-x_r) \end{aligned}\right\} \tag{21}$$

$$\frac{\partial y_2}{\partial t} - \beta v \Sigma_f(x,t)y_1 + \lambda y_2 = 0 \tag{22}$$

$$y_1(x,t)=0\ ,\ y_2(x,t)=0 \quad \text{on } \Gamma \tag{23}$$

$$y_2(x,o) = y_{10}\ ,\ y_2(x,o) = 0 \quad \text{in } \Omega \tag{24}$$

$$\left.\begin{aligned} &-\frac{\partial p_1}{\partial t} - v \sum_{i,j}^{2,3} \frac{\partial}{\partial x_j} D(x,t) \frac{\partial}{\partial x_i} p_1 + v[\Sigma_a(x,t) - (1-\beta)\ \Sigma_f(x,t) + \overline{\Sigma}_{co}]p_1 - \beta v \Sigma_f(x,t)y_1 \\ &\quad = \sum_{\ell}^{M} \chi_\ell(x)(y_\ell(\hat{u}) - Zd) \end{aligned}\right\} \tag{25}$$

$$-\frac{\partial p_2}{\partial t} - v\lambda p_1 + \lambda p_2 = 0 \tag{26}$$

$$p_1(x,t) = 0,\ p_2(x,t) = 0 \quad \text{on } \Gamma \tag{27}$$

$$p_1(x,T) = 0,\ p_2(x,T) = 0 \quad \text{in } \Omega \tag{28}$$

where p_i means adjoint state variable and χ_ℓ characteristic function in terms of small observation region $\Omega_\ell \subset \Omega$.

Remark 5 : If the relative rate of change in the reactor power in terms of a mean prompt generation time is very small, a sudden change in the reactor power follows from a rapid change in reactivity. This is called prompt jump approximation. In this case the neutron flux, namely reactor power may be considered as in equilibrium at any instant, and reactor core dynamics is under the same boundary and initial conditions reduced to

$$\left.\begin{aligned} & - v \sum_{i=1}^{n} \frac{\partial}{\partial x_i} D(x,t) \frac{\partial}{\partial x_j} y_1 + v(\Sigma_a(x,t) - (1-\beta)\nu\Sigma_f(x,t) + \Sigma_{co}) y_1 - v\lambda y_2 = \\ & = - v \sum_{r=1}^{N} \bar{Y}_{10}(x_r) u_r(t) \quad \delta(x - x_r) \end{aligned}\right\} \tag{29}$$

$$\frac{\partial y_2}{\partial t} - \beta\nu\Sigma_f(x,t) y_1 + \lambda y_2 = 0 \tag{30}$$

Although Eq. (29) is not an evolution equation, the optimal control problem is dealt with in the frame of the formulation in this section.

Remark 6 : The problem of initial state determination for D.P.S. is not generally well-posed, in the sense that the initial state depends continuously on the observation data [10]. Therefore it is not reasonable to make use of the cost functional in terms of not measurable state variables (in our case the precursor concentration) without any improvements even if the unique existence of the observability is asserted. This remark is also applicable to the feedback control problem.

6. COMMENT ON THE BILINEAR CONTROL OF REACTOR CORE MODEL.

We shall give a comment on the original problem governed by Eq. (1) $\sim$ (4). In case of distributed control where $\Sigma_{co}(\cdot t)$ belongs to $L^\infty(\Omega)$, the unique solution may be asserted in $L^2(0,T;\ H_o^1(\Omega)\times L^2(\Omega))$. In case of pointwise control, the control term in Eq.(1) is represented by

$$D\underline{u} = [-v \sum_{r=1}^{N} y_1(x_r,t) U_r(t) \otimes \delta(x-x_r),\quad 0]^T \tag{31}$$

Putting $V(x_r,t) = y_1(x_r,t)U_r(t)$, the problem becomes a bilinear control in terms of time at each location of control rods. Assuming $U_r(t) \in L^2(0,T)$ as an apparent control and also $y_1(x_r,t) \in L^2(0,T)\ (T < \infty)$, the existence of the optimal control may be discussed in the same frame with the linearized case, although the solving process is technically different from the latter.

7. CONCLUSIONS.

In this paper we study the feasibility of pointwise control in a simple reactor core model by means of the spacially differential operator method. Results obtained indicate that in the pointwise control in nuclear reactor core models local average observation is meaningful under milder conditions. The same philosophy will be readily applicable to the case with feedback effects, provided the feedback effect concerned is linearized. However, feedback effects may be generally nonlinearly coupled with the macroscopic absorption cross-section through multi-region structures. Therefore, in order to investigate in a more realistic and strict sense the optimal control or identification problem on the nuclear reactor systems, it is above all needed to establish physically as well as mathematically reasonable models thereof. Furthermore, the problems on the allocation and the number of detectors should be solved.

REFERENCES.

[1] W.M. STACEY IR. : Space Time Nuclear Reactor Kinetics (Book) Academic Press (1969)

[2] T. IWAZUMI, R. KOGA : Optimal Feedback Control of a Nuclear Reactor as a Distributed Parameter System.
J. NUCL. SCI. TECH. Vol. 1, (1973).

[3] S.H. KYONG : An Optimal Control of a Distributed Parameter Reactor
NUCL. SCI. ENG. 32 (1968).

[4] Y. KURODA, A. MAKINO : Optimal Control for a Class of Nuclear Reactor Systems with Distributed Parameter System.
Proc. of IFAC Symposium on the Control of Distributed Parameter System, 1972.

[5] C. SAGUEZ : Contrôle Ponctuel et Contrôle en Nombres Entiers de Systèmes Distribués, Rapport Laboria N° 82 (1974).

[6] J.L. LIONS : Contrôle Optimal de Systèmes Gouvernés par des Equations aux Dérivées Partielles, Dunod, Paris (1968).

[7] J.L. LIONS and E. MAGENES : Non homogeneous boundary value problems and applications, Vol. 1, 2 , Springer (1972).

[8] S.G. GREENBERG : Pointwise Regulation of Distributed Parameter Systems,
IBM Scientific Center, Rep. 320-2052, Nov. (1969).

[9] S.G. GREENBERG : On Quadratic Optimization and Distributed Parameter Systems,
IEEE Trans., on AC 16, April 1971.

[10] J. KOBAYASKI : Initial state determination for Distributed Parameter Systems,
SIAM J. Control and Optimization Vol. 14, N° 5, August 1976.

Likelihood Ratios for Time-Continuous Data Models: The White Noise Approach

A. V. Balakrishnan
System Science Department
University of California

Paper presented at the IRIA International Symposium on New Trends in Systems Analysis, December 1976, Versailles, France.

Abstract We develop a formula for likelihood functionals for signals in additive noise in the time-continuous case using a white noise approach. It is shown that the formula differs from the well-known formula in the Wiener process version by the appearance of an additional term corresponding to the conditional mean square filtering error.

1. Introduction. In much of engineering literature on identification (too voluminous to be referred to individually. See the several volumes of proceedings of IFAC Symposia on System Identification and Parameter Estimation, 1970, 1973 and 1976) it is customary to consider the observed data as sampled periodically in time -- even when the basic phenomena are modelled by time-continuous differential equations. The usual 'hand-waving' argument is then made that the 'limiting' continuous-time case is no more than a mathematical detail; and that anyhow in digital computer processing, conversion to sampled data is a basic step. This is indeed true; but the authors almost invariably proceed to use the model:

$$y_n = S_n + N_n$$

where $\{S_n\}$ is the information-bearing time series and $\{N_n\}$ the observation noise series, and (this is the crucial point) take $\{N_n\}$ as a sequence of independent variables. But this requires that the sampling rate be not more than twice the noise bandwidth, itself unknown. Of course, to answer this objection, one can allow $\{N_n\}$ to be correlated; but then the correlation function must be known. Now it is very unrealistic to require the correlation function of instrument noise; and even when known, it adds a lot to the complication but little to the performance. We maintain that it is much better to use a time-continuous model

$$y(t) = S(t) + N(t) \tag{2}$$

and allow the sampling rate to be as high as the A-D converter wants to use. But in the time-continuous model we are faced with another problem; the basic tool in identification is the likelihood ratio (for fixed parameters): the Radon-Nikodym derivative of the probability measure induced by the process $y(\cdot)$ to that induced by $N(\cdot)$. But this likelihood ratio is difficult to implement even when the spectrum of $N(\cdot)$ is known, which it is not. What we can say for sure is that the bandwidth of the (instrument) noise is large compared with that of the process $S(\cdot)$. At this point the earlier engineering literature used the notion of "white noise" a process with constant spectral density over all frequencies in a formal way. In the sixties it became fashionable to replace this by the "Wiener process" model as "more rigorous". Thus we replace (2) by

$$Y(t) = \int_0^t S(\sigma)d\sigma + W(t) \tag{3}$$

where $W(t)$ is a Wiener process. We have then, to be sure, the advantage of the powerful machinery of Martingales and Ito integrals. In fact the likelihood functional (for the case where signal and noise are independent which we assume thruout) can then be written down as: [see [1]]:

$$\text{Exp} - 1/2\left\{\int_0^T ||\hat{S}(t)||^2 dt - 2 \int_0^T [\hat{S}(t), dY(t)]\right\} \tag{4}$$

where $\hat{S}(t)$ is the best mean square estimate of $S(t)$ given the observation $Y(s)$ upto time t. But the hooker is that the second term is an Ito integral:

$$\int_0^T [\hat{S}(t), dY(t)]$$

This integral is defined on the basis that $Y(t)$ is of unbounded variation with probability one. On the other hand no physical instrument can produce such a wave form! Indeed, we must now go back to (2) where it came from and thus replace

$$dY(t) \text{ by } y(t)dt$$

This is all right if $S(t)$ is deterministic; if not, we no longer obtain the value prescribed by the Ito formula! In particular, any algorithm based on it leads to erroneous results. Most authors of papers on the subject probably have never bothered to calculate anything based on actual data; and of course in any digital computer simulation it is possible to mask this completely. Indeed, almost all simulation models employ the discrete version (1).

Faced with this difficulty we have to examine more precisely the model again. Thus what we want to exploit is the fact that the bandwidth of the noise is large compared to that of the process $S(\cdot)$. Hence what is really needed is the 'asymptotic form' of the likelihood functional as the bandwidth goes to infinity in an arbitrary manner.

Such a theory has been developed by the author using a precise notion of white noise. See [2] for details. We take the 'sample points' to be in a Hilbert Space with Gauss measure theorem. Thus in (2) we consider $N(t)$ $0 < t < T$ as path-wise square integrable in $[0,T]$; as elements in the L_2-space $L_2(R_n; (0,T))$, (the observation having its range in R_n, n-dimensional Euclidean Space). Corresponding to white noise with 'unit' spectral density, we define the Gauss measure by:

$$E[e^{i\int_0^T [N(t),\, h(t)]dt}] = \text{Exp} - 1/2 \int_0^T [h(t),\, h(t)]dt$$

for each $h(\cdot)$ in $L_2[R_n; (0,T)]$, defining thus the characteristic function of the Gauss measure.

The difference between this set-up and the Wiener-process set-up is simply this. Let $\{\phi_n(\cdot)\}$ denote a complete orthornormal system in $L_2[R_n, (0,T)]$. Then

$$\int_0^T [\phi_n(t), N(t)]dt = \zeta_n$$

yield a sequence of zero-mean, unit variance Gaussians. The sample-space for the sequence is ℓ_2, since

$$\sum_1^\infty \zeta_n^2 = \int_0^T N(t)^2 dt < \infty$$

On the other hand, given such a sequence it is standard practice to take R^∞ as the sample space and via the Kolmogorov theory, construct a countably additive measure on the Borel sets of R^∞. [This is also the countably additive extension to Nuclear Spaces via the Minlos theorem]. This is in fact the Wiener process theory, in which of course, all of ℓ_2 has zero measure. Both set ups of course agree on the measures of cylinder sets. What is rendered difficult by using ℓ_2 as the sample space is the notion of a random variable. Whereas this is trivial in the R^∞ model -- any Borel-measurable function being a random variable -- it is the central issue in the ℓ_2 - set-up. In other words, given any functional $f(\cdot)$ on $L_2[R_n; (0,T)]$, even continuous thereon, it need not define a random variable. We define it as a random variable if and only if for any sequence P_n of finite dimensional projections converging strongly to the identity, the sequence $\{f(P_n(\cdot)\}$ is Cauchy in probability, and all such sequences are equivalent. Thus we have a smaller class of random variables; the implication being that the Ito integrals in the Wiener process theory may not correspond to random-variables on ℓ_2. Moreover the 'limiting' notion corresponds to the 'bandwidth expanding' notion.

2. Likelihood Ratio: White Noise Theory.

Let us now examine likelihood ratios (Radon Nikodym derivatives) in terms of the white noise theory. Let

$$y(t) = S(t) + N(t) \quad 0 \leq t \leq T < \infty \tag{2.1}$$

where $S(\cdot)$ and $N(\cdot)$ are independent processes. We shall assume that the signal $S(\cdot)$ has finite energy:

$$\int_0^T E(||S(t)||^2)dt < \infty \tag{2.2}$$

For each t, $0 < t \leq T$, let

$$W(t) = L_2[R_n; (0,t)]$$

We shall shorten W(T) to simply W. Under condition (2.2), the process $S(\cdot)$ induces a countably additivie measure on W (and hence on W(t) for each t). [The cylinder measure on W can be extended to be countably additive, in other words; this is a consequence of the Sazonov theorem, see [2]]. Thus (2.1) defines a weak distribution on W defined by the characteristic function:

$$E[e^{i[y,h]}] = C_s(h) \ \ \text{Exp} - 1/2 \ ||h||^2 \tag{2.3}$$

where

$$C_s(h) = E[e^{i[S,h]}] \tag{2.4}$$

where we have used the inner-product notation:

$$[S,h] = \int_0^T [S(t), h(t)]dt, \ h \in W.$$

Then the cylinder measure μ_y induced by $y(\cdot)$ is absolutely continuous with respect to Gauss measure μ_G and the Radon-Nikodym derivative is defined by the function:

$$f(\omega) = \int_W \text{Exp} - 1/2 \ \{||S||^2 - 2 \ [S,\omega)\} \ d\mu_s \tag{2.5}$$

Thus for any cylinder set C,

$$\mu_y(C) = \lim_{n\to\infty} \int_C f(P_n\omega)\, d\mu_G$$

where P_n is any sequence of finite dimensional projections strongly convergent to the identity. This result has been proved in [3].

Let $\{\phi_n\}$ be an orthonormal basis in W and let L denote the mapping of W into ℓ_2:

$$Lx = a;\ a_n = \int_0^T [x(\sigma),\ \phi_n(\sigma)]d\sigma.$$

Let

$$LS = \zeta$$

Let μ_ζ denote the measure induced on ℓ_2 by this mapping. Then we can rewrite (2.5) in the form

$$f(\omega) = \int_{\ell_2} \text{Exp} - 1/2\ \{[\zeta,\zeta] - 2\ [\zeta,\ L\omega]\}\ d\mu_\zeta \tag{2.6}$$

It must be emphasised that (2.6) is defined for every element ω in W. Note also that (2.6) can be defined with respect to any orthonormal system $\{\phi_n\}$.

The likelihood functional f(y) where y(·) is the observation, will now be expressed in a form similar to (4). For this purpose, let (2.6) be defined with respect to the orthonormal system $\{\phi_n\}$. For each t, $0 < t \leq T$, define the operators $\Lambda(t)$, mapping W into ℓ_2 by:

$$\Lambda(t)x = a;\ a_n = \int_0^t [\phi_n(\sigma),\ x(\sigma)]d\sigma \tag{2.7}$$

Let

$$R(t) = \Lambda(t)\ \ \Lambda(t)^*. \tag{2.8}$$

Then the Radon-Nikodym derivative of the measure induced by the process y(·) over [0,t] with respect to Gauss measure on W(t) is given by:

$$f(t,\omega) = \int_{\ell} \text{Exp} - 1/2 \ \{[R(t)\ \zeta,\zeta] - 2\ [\zeta,\ \Lambda(t)\omega]\}\ d\mu_{\zeta} \tag{2.9}$$

Note that (T) = L. Let P_n denote the projection operator corresponding to the first n basis functions $\{\phi_1\}$, i = 1,...n. Then we define

$$\hat{\zeta}(t) = \lim_{n} E[\zeta | \Lambda(t)\ P_n y] \tag{2.10}$$

As shown in [3], we have (Bayes Formula) that

$$(t) = \frac{\int_{\ell_2} \zeta \ \text{Exp} - 1/2 \ \{[R(t)\zeta,\zeta] - 2\ [\zeta,\ \Lambda(t)y]\}\ d\mu_{\zeta}}{\int_{\ell_2} \text{Exp} - 1/2 \ \{[R(t)\zeta,\zeta] - 2\ [\zeta,\ \Lambda(t)y]\}\ d\mu_{\zeta}} \tag{2.11}$$

Note that, by Schwartz Inequality

$$||\hat{\zeta}(t)||^2 \leq \frac{\int_{\ell_2} ||\zeta||^2 \ \text{Exp} - 1/2 \ \{[R(t)\zeta,\zeta] - 2\ [\zeta,\ \Lambda(t)y]\}\ d\mu_{\zeta}}{\int_{\ell_2} \text{Exp} - 1/2 \ \{[R(t)\zeta,\zeta] - 2\ [\zeta,\ \Lambda(t)y]\}\ d\mu_{\zeta}}$$

$$= \frac{\int_{\ell_2} ||\zeta||^2 \ \text{Exp} - 1/2 \ ||\ R(t)\zeta - \Lambda(t)y||^2 \ d\mu_{\zeta}}{\int_{\ell_2} \text{Exp} - 1/2 \ ||\ R(t)\zeta - \Lambda(t)y||^2 \ d\mu_{\zeta}}$$

$$\leq c\ E[||\zeta||^2]\ \text{Exp} + 1/2\ (||\ \Lambda(t)y|| + k)^2,\ 0 < c,\ k < \infty \tag{2.12}$$

It should be noted that such an estimate is not available in the Wiener process version. Moreover we shall show that (2.9) is actually absolutely continuous in t with an L_2-derivative. Let $\phi(t)$ be infinitely differentiable with compact support in (0,T). Then

$$\int_0^T [f(t,\omega)\ \phi'(t)]dt$$

$$= \int_{\ell_2} \int_0^T [\text{Exp} - 1/2 \ \{[R(t)\zeta,\zeta] - 2\ [\zeta,\ \Lambda(t)\omega]\}\ \phi'(t)dt]\}\ d\mu_{\zeta}$$

$$= \int_{\ell_2} \left(\int_0^T - 1/2 \; ||\sum_1^\infty \phi_i(t)\zeta_i||^2 + \; [\sum_1^\infty \phi_i(t)\zeta_i, \; \omega(t)] \right) \left(\text{Exp} - 1/2 \; \{[R(t)\zeta,\zeta] \right.$$

$$\left. - 2 \; [\zeta, \; \Lambda(t)\omega]\} \quad \phi(t)dt \right) \; d\mu_\zeta \tag{2.13}$$

where we note that both

$$||\sum_1^\infty \phi_i(t)\zeta_i||^2 \quad \text{and} \quad [\sum_1^\infty \phi_i(t)\zeta_i, \; \omega(t)]$$

are in L_2 [0,T] for each ζ in ℓ_2. Hence the derivative is (defined a.e. $0 < t < T$):

$$\int_{\ell_2} (-\tfrac{1}{2}||\sum_1^\infty \phi_i(t)\zeta_i||^2 + [\sum_1^\infty \phi_i(t)\zeta_i, \; \omega(t)]) \;\; \text{Exp} - 1/2 \; \{[R(t)\zeta,\zeta] - 2 \; [\zeta, \; \Lambda(t)\omega]\} \; d\mu_\zeta$$

we shall next prove that

$$g_N(t) = \sum_1^N \phi_i(t)\hat{\zeta}_i(t) \qquad 0 \le t \le T$$

converges in the norm of W. But this is immediate from the fact that, analogous to (2.12):

$$||g_N(t)||^2 \le E[||\sum_1^N \phi_i(t)\zeta_i||^2] \; \text{Exp} + 1/2 \; ||\Lambda(t)y||^2 \qquad \text{a.e.} \quad 0 < t < T$$

Let

$$\hat{S}(t) = \sum_1^\infty \phi_i(t)\hat{\zeta}_i(t)$$

and

$$\widehat{||S(t)||^2} = \frac{\int_{\ell_2} ||\sum_1^\infty \phi_i(t)\zeta_i||^2 \; \text{Exp} - 1/2 \; \{[R(t)\zeta,\zeta] - 2 \; [\zeta, \; \Lambda(t)y]\} \; d\mu_\zeta}{\int_{\ell_2} \text{Exp} - 1/2 \; \{[R(t)\zeta,\zeta] - 2 \; [\zeta, \; \Lambda(t)y]\} \; d\mu_\zeta}$$

Then from (2.13) we can write:

$$\frac{d}{dt} \; \text{Log} \; f(t, \; y) = - 1/2 \; \{||\hat{S}(t)||^2 - 2 \; [\hat{S}(t), \; y(t)2 + \widehat{||S(t)||^2} - ||\hat{S}(t)||^2\}$$

and hence finally, for the log likelihood functional:

Log f(y)

$$= -1/2\left\{\int_0^T ||\hat{S}(t)||^2 dt - 2\int_0^T [\hat{S}(t), y(t)]dt + \int_0^T [\widehat{||S(t)||^2} - ||\hat{S}(t)||^2]\, dt\right\} \tag{2.13}$$

we note that the third term can also be expressed as

$$\underset{n\to\infty}{\text{limit}}\; E[||S(t) - \hat{S}(t)||^2 \mid \Lambda(t)P_n y] \tag{2.14}$$

The formula (2.13) differs from the Wiener process version in the appearance of the third term; in the case where S(t) is Gaussian, we know that (2.14) reduces to

$$E[||S(t) - \hat{S}(t)||^2]$$

which is then also independent of the observation $y(\cdot)$; see [3]. Note that (2.14) can be large in the case where the noise level is large. Formula (2.13) was derived in [3] for a seemingly less general case by a different method. Finally we remark that (2.13) is consistent with the 'circle differential' formalism of Ito [4].

References

1. Y. Liptser and A. Shiryayev: Statistics of Random Processes, Nanka 1974.
2. A. V. Balakrishnan: Applied Functional Analysis, Springer-Verlag, 1976.
3. A. V. Balakrishnan: Radon-Nikodym Derivatives of a class of weak distributions on Hilbert Spaces, Journal of Applied Mathematics and Optimization, 1977 (to be published).
4. K. Ito: Stochastic Differentials, Journal of Applied Mathematics and Optimization Vol. 1, No. 4, 1975.

ESTIMATES FOR SEQUENCES BIORTHOGONAL TO CERTAIN COMPLEX EXPONENTIALS AND BOUNDARY CONTROL OF THE WAVE EQUATION

H.O. Fattorini
University of California
Departments of Mathematics and System Science
Los Angeles, CA 90024/USA

§1. Introduction. Let Ω be a bounded domain in m-dimensional Euclidean space R^m with piecewise C^∞ boundary Γ, and let Γ_0 be a subset of Γ.

The following boundary control problem was studied by RUSSELL in [12]. Consider a control process whose states are described by the wave equation

$$u_{tt}(x,t) = c^2 \Delta u(x,t) \quad (x \in \Omega, \quad t \geq 0) . \tag{1.1}$$

Both the initial state of the system

$$u(x,0) = u_0(x) \quad u_t(x,0) = u_1(x) \quad (x \in \Omega) \tag{1.2}$$

and its final state at some time $T > 0$

$$u(x,T) = v_0(x) \quad u_t(x,T) = v_1(x) \quad (x \in \Omega) \tag{1.3}$$

are given in advance. The solution is required to satisfy a boundary condition of the following type, where $\partial/\partial\eta$ indicates outer normal derivative:

$$\begin{aligned} \alpha u(x,t) + \beta \frac{\partial u}{\partial \eta}(x,t) &= f(x,t) \quad (x \in \Gamma_0, \quad t \geq 0) \\ \alpha u(x,t) + \beta \frac{\partial u}{\partial \eta}(x,t) &= 0 \qquad\quad (x \in \Gamma \setminus \Gamma_0, \quad t \geq 0) \end{aligned} \tag{1.4}$$

$(\alpha^2 + \beta^2 > 0, \ \alpha\beta \geq 0)$ where f is a control function. We formulate the problem as follows:

CONTROL PROBLEM. Let $\mathcal{E}$, $\mathcal{F}$ be spaces of functions defined in Ω, and let $u_0, v_0 \in \mathcal{E}$, $u_1, v_1 \in \mathcal{F}$. Does there exist a control function f (say, in $L^2(\Gamma_0)$) such that the solution of (1.1), (1.2), (1.4) satisfies (1.3) for some $T > 0$?

A solution to the problem was given by RUSSELL in [12] for the case where $\mathcal{E}$ is the SOBOLEV space $H_0^1(\Omega)$ of all functions with first partials in $L^2(\Omega)$ which vanish in Γ, $\mathcal{F} = L^2(\Omega)$ and the boundary condition in (1.4) is the DIRICHLET boundary condition $(\beta = 0)$ under the condition that the pair (Ω, Γ) should be star-complemented. Leaving aside some technical requirements (to be found in [12]) this means that there must exist a region Ω^*, star-shaped with respect to one of its points x^* such that

$$\Omega \subseteq C(\overline{\Omega^*}) \tag{1.5}$$

$$\Gamma \setminus \Gamma_0 \subseteq \partial\Omega^* \tag{1.6}$$

where C indicates complement, $\overline{}$ indicates closure and $\partial\Omega^*$ is the boundary of Ω^*.

We consider here the case where Ω is a parallelepipedon $P = \{x;\ 0 < x_j < X_j\ (1 \leq j \leq m)\}$, where $x = (x_1,\ldots,x_m)$, $X_1,\ldots,X_m > 0$ and Γ_0 is one of the 2n faces that make up the boundary of P. This case is especially interesting because Γ_0 "just misses" to be star-complemented; more precisely, although Γ_0 is not star-complemented it becomes so after an arbitrarily small deformation of P.

FIGURE 1

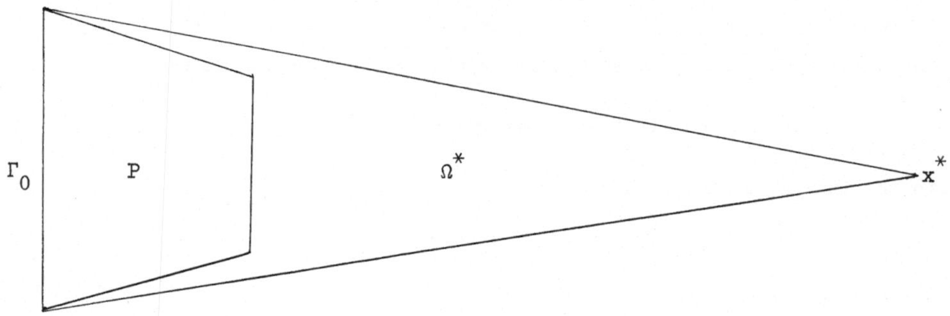

It was conjectured by RUSSELL in [12] that his results on the solution of the control problem above do not extend to the present case. We prove here this conjecture. More precisely, we prove (Theorem 4.1) that the control problem has no solution unless the spaces $\mathcal{E}$, $\mathfrak{F}$ contain only extremely smooth functions (these functions must, in particular, admit an extension to all of R^m which is real analytic there). On the other hand, there are also results in the opposite direction: conditions of the same type (but somewhat stronger) guarantee that the problem has a solution (Theorem 4.2).

Both the necessary and the sufficient conditions are obtained (following RUSSELL) by reducing the controllability problem to a sequence of moment problems, which is done in Section 2, writing formal series solutions of these problems by means of biorthogonal sequences and then proving existence or nonexistence of solutions (Theorems 4.1 and 4.2) by using certain estimates on these sequences. These estimates are obtained in Section 3.

The necessary results on solution of initial-boundary value problems can be found in LIONS-MAGENES [9], [10]. We note that, since solutions of the wave equation are reversible in time we do not lose generality by replacing the final condition (1.3) by

$$u(x,T) = u_t(x,T) = 0 \quad (x \in \Omega) \tag{1.7}$$

which will be done consistently in what follows.

§2. Controllability and moment problems. Let A be the Laplace operator in P with NEUMANN boundary conditions,

$$\frac{\partial u}{\partial \eta}(x) = 0 \quad (x \in \Gamma)$$

It is well known that A is self adjoint and has pure point spectrum; its eigenvalues are $\{-\lambda_\alpha\}$ where

$$\lambda_\alpha = c_1^2\alpha_1^2 + c_2^2\alpha_2^2 + \cdots + c_m^2\alpha_m^2 \tag{2.1}$$

where $\alpha = (\alpha_1,\ldots,\alpha_m)$ is an arbitrary vector of nonnegative integers and $c_j = \pi/X_j$, $1 \leq j \leq m$. The (normalized) eigenfunction corresponding to λ_α is

$$\varphi_\alpha(x) = 2^{m/2}(X_1X_2 \cdots X_m)^{-1/2} \cos c_1\alpha_1x_1 \cdots \cos c_m\alpha_m x_m \ .$$

Let now $u(x,t)$ be a sufficiently smooth solution of (1.1), (1.2), (1.4), (1.7) in $P \times [0,T]$; as pointed out in the previous section we may restrict ourselves to the case where the final data are zero. Develop the initial data u_0, u_1 in Fourier series with respect to the eigenfunctions $\{\varphi_\alpha\}$,

$$u_0(x) = \sum_\alpha \mu_{\alpha,0}\varphi_\alpha(x) \ , \quad u_1(x) = \sum_\alpha \mu_{\alpha,1}\varphi_\alpha(x)$$

Let $\omega_\alpha = \lambda_\alpha^{1/2}$. Define

$$w_{\alpha,0}(x,t) = \varphi_\alpha(x)\cos \omega_\alpha t$$

$$w_{\alpha,1}(x,t) = \varphi_\alpha(x) \frac{\sin \omega_\alpha t}{\omega_\alpha} \qquad \text{if } |\alpha| \neq 0$$

$$w_{\alpha,1}(x,t) = \varphi_\alpha(x)t \qquad \text{if } \alpha = 0$$

Then $w_{\alpha,0}$, $w_{\alpha,1}$ are solutions of the wave equation (1.1) in $P \times [0,T]$. Integrating now $0 = u(w_{tt} - \Delta w)$ over $P \times [0,T]$ with $w = w_{\alpha,0}$, $w = w_{\alpha,1}$ we obtain after application of the divergence theorem that

$$\int_{\Gamma\times[0,T]} f(x,t)\varphi_\alpha(x)\cos \omega_\alpha t \, d\sigma \, dt = -\mu_{\alpha,1} \tag{2.2}$$

$$\int_{\Gamma\times[0,T]} f(x,t)\varphi_\alpha(x) \frac{\sin \omega_\alpha t}{\omega_\alpha} d\sigma \, dt = \mu_{\alpha,0} \qquad (|\alpha| > 0) \tag{2.3}$$

$$\int_{\Gamma\times[0,T]} f(x,t)\varphi_\alpha(x)t \, d\sigma \, dt = \mu_{\alpha,0} \quad \text{for } \alpha = 0 \tag{2.4}$$

where $d\sigma$ denotes the element of area of Γ. We assume from now on that f vanishes outside of

$$\Gamma_0 = \{x \in \Gamma \ ; \ x_m = 0\} \ .$$

In Γ_0 we have

$$\varphi_\alpha(x) = (2/X_m)^{1/2}2^{(m-1)/2}(X_1\cdots X_m)^{-1/2}\cos c_1\alpha_1x_1\cdots\cos c_{m-1}\alpha_{m-1}x_{m-1}$$

$$= (2/X_m)^{1/2}\eta_{\tilde\alpha}(\tilde x)$$

where we have set $\tilde\alpha = (\alpha_1,\ldots,\alpha_{m-1})$, $\tilde x = (x_1,\ldots,x_{m-1})$. Clearly $\{\eta_{\tilde\alpha}\}$ ($\tilde\alpha$ ranging over all $(m-1)$-dimensional vectors with nonnegative integer components) is a complete orthonormal system in $L^2(\Gamma_0)$.

We interpret now, as in [4] the set of equalities (2.2), (2.3), (2.4) as a sequence of moment problems. To this end, define

$$f_{\tilde{\alpha}}(t) = \int_{\Gamma_0} f(\tilde{x},t)\eta_{\tilde{\alpha}}(\tilde{x})d\tilde{x} \tag{2.5}$$

Then, for every fixed $\tilde{\alpha}$, $f_{\tilde{\alpha}}$ is a solution of the moment problem

$$\int_0^T f_{\tilde{\alpha}}(t)\cos \omega_\alpha t\ dt = -(X_m/2)^{1/2}\ \mu_{\alpha,1} \qquad (\alpha_m \geq 0) \tag{2.6}$$

$$\int_0^T f_{\tilde{\alpha}}(t)\sin \omega_\alpha t\ dt = \omega_\alpha (X_m/2)^{1/2}\ \mu_{\alpha,0} \qquad (|\tilde{\alpha}| > 0 \text{ or } \alpha_m > 0) \tag{2.7}$$

$$\int_0^T f_{\tilde{\alpha}}(t)t\ dt = (X_m/2)^{1/2}\ \mu_{\alpha,0} \qquad (|\tilde{\alpha}| = \alpha_m = 0) \tag{2.8}$$

and, conversely, if, for each $\tilde{\alpha}$, $f_{\tilde{\alpha}}$ is a solution of the above moment problem and the series

$$f(\tilde{x},t) = \sum_{\tilde{\alpha}} f_{\tilde{\alpha}}(t)\eta_{\tilde{\alpha}}(\tilde{x})$$

is convergent in $L^2(\Gamma_0)$, then f is a solution of the controllability problem in Section 1.

For reasons of symmetry we transform the problem as follows. Let α_m be now an arbitrary (positive or negative) integer. We write again $\alpha = (\tilde{\alpha},\alpha_m) = (\alpha_1,\ldots,\alpha_{m-1},\alpha_m)$ (still requiring that $\alpha_1,\ldots,\alpha_{m-1}$ be nonnegative) and adopt the following convention: <u>when α is used as a subindex, we consider the values $\alpha_m = -0$ and $\alpha_m = +0$ different</u>: also, we set $\operatorname{sgn}(0) = 1$, $\operatorname{sgn}(-0) = -1$ whether or not α appears as a subindex. We can then condense (2.6) and (2.7) as

$$\int_{-T/2}^{T/2} g_{\tilde{\alpha}}(t)e^{i(\operatorname{sgn}\alpha_m)\omega_\alpha t}\ dt = \nu_\alpha \qquad (-\infty < \alpha_m < \infty) \tag{2.9}$$

where

$$\nu_\alpha = -(X_m/2)^{1/2}\ e^{-i(\operatorname{sgn}\alpha_m)\omega_\alpha T/2}\ (\mu_{\alpha,1} - i(\operatorname{sgn}\alpha_m)\omega_\alpha\mu_{\alpha,0})\ ,$$

$$g_{\tilde{\alpha}}(t) = f_{\tilde{\alpha}}(t + T/2)$$

when $\tilde{\alpha} \neq 0$. When $\tilde{\alpha} = 0$ the equations (2.9) are the same for $|\alpha_m| > 0$ (note that in this case $\omega_\alpha = c_m\alpha_m$) and the two remaining equations are replaced by

$$\int_{-T/2}^{T/2} g_{\tilde{\alpha}}(t)dt = -(X_m/2)^{1/2}\ \mu_{\alpha,1} = \nu_{\tilde{\alpha},+0} \tag{2.10}$$

$$\int_{-T/2}^{T/2} g_{\tilde{\alpha}}(t)t\ dt = (X_m/2)^{1/2}(\mu_{\alpha,0} + (T/2)\mu_{\alpha,1}) = \nu_{\tilde{\alpha},-0} \tag{2.11}$$

We attempt to solve these problems in the following way. Assume that, for every $\tilde{\alpha}$ we can find in $L^2(\Gamma_0)$ a sequence $\{\psi_\alpha\ ;\ -\infty < \alpha_m < \infty\}$ biorthogonal to $\{e^{i(\operatorname{sgn}\alpha_m)\omega_\alpha t}\}$, that is, such that

$$\int_{-T/2}^{T/2} \psi_\alpha(t) e^{i(\operatorname{sgn} \alpha'_m)\omega_{\alpha'} t}\, dt = \delta_{\alpha_m,\alpha'_m} \tag{2.12}$$

(here δ is the KRONECKER delta and $\alpha = (\alpha_1,\ldots,\alpha_{m-1},\alpha'_m)$ where α'_m is another arbitrary integer, the distinction between -0 and $+0$ being always observed). Then we can write formally a solution of (2.9), (2.10), (2.11) as follows:

$$f(\tilde{x},t) = g(\tilde{x},t - T/2) \qquad (\tilde{x} \in \Gamma_0,\ \ 0 \le t \le T)$$

where

$$g(\tilde{x},t) = \sum_{\tilde{\alpha}} g_{\tilde{\alpha}}(t)\eta_{\tilde{\alpha}}(\tilde{x}) \qquad (\tilde{x} \in \Gamma_0,\ \ |t| \le T/2), \tag{2.13}$$

and

$$g_{\tilde{\alpha}}(t) = \sum_{\alpha_n=-\infty}^{\infty} \nu_\alpha \psi_\alpha(t) .$$

Accordingly, if good estimates can be obtained for the L^2 norms of the $\psi_{\tilde{\alpha}}$ there is hope that the series (2.13) will be convergent under modest requirements on the FOURIER coefficients of u_0, u_1. We shall go, however, in the opposite direction: making use of the fact (proved in the next section) that the norm of any orthonormal sequence grows exponentially with $|\tilde{\alpha}|$, we show that the moment problem (2.9),(2.10),(2.11) -- thus the control problem in Section 1 -- has no solution unless extremely stringent conditions are forced upon the initial data u_0, u_1. To this end, we establish the following result. (Here and afterwards $C, C', C_1, c, \ldots$ etc. are constants, not necessarily the same for different inequalities.)

2.1. THEOREM. <u>For every</u> α <u>let</u> M_α <u>be a positive constant. Assume that for every multisequence</u> $\nu = \{\nu_\alpha\}$ <u>such that</u>

$$|\nu_\alpha| \le CM_\alpha \tag{2.14}$$

<u>there exists a solution</u> $g(\tilde{x},t)$ <u>of</u> (2.9), (2.10), (2.11), in $L^2(\Gamma_0 \times (-T/2,T/2))$. <u>Then, for arbitrary</u> $\tilde{\alpha}$ <u>there exists a biorthogonal sequence</u> $\{\psi_\alpha\ ;\ -\infty < \alpha_n < \infty\}$ <u>such that</u>

$$\|\psi_\alpha\| \le CM_\alpha^{-1} \tag{2.15}$$

<u>Proof</u>: Let E be the Banach space of all multisequences $\nu = \{\nu_\alpha\}$ that satisfy (2.14) (norm: $\|\nu\| = \sup\{|\nu_\alpha|M_\alpha^{-1}\}$). Let F be the closed subspace of all g in $L^2(\Gamma_0 \times (-T/2,T/2))$ that satisfy the equalities (2.13), (2.9), (2.10), (2.11) with $\nu = 0$ and consider the operator $G : E \to L^2(\Gamma_0 \times (-T/2,T/2))/F$ defined by $G\nu = g + F$, where $g + F$ denotes the equivalence class of g in $L^2(\Gamma_0 \times (-T/2,T/2))$. It is easy to see that G is closed; it then follows from the closed graph theorem that for any $\nu \in E$ there exists a solution g of (2.9) - (2.13) with

$$\|g\|_{L^2(\Gamma_0\times(-T/2,T/2))} \le C\|\nu\| \tag{2.16}$$

where C does not depend on ν. Take now $\alpha = (\alpha_0,\ldots,\alpha_{m-1},\alpha_m)$ fixed and

$\gamma = (\gamma_0, \dots, \gamma_{m-1}, \gamma_m)$ another multi-index. Define $\nu_\gamma^{(\alpha)} = \delta_{\alpha_1,\gamma_1}\delta_{\alpha_2,\gamma_2} \cdots \delta_{\alpha_m,\gamma_m}$. Let $g^{(\alpha)}$ be the solution of (2.9) - (2.12) corresponding to $\{\nu_\gamma^{(\alpha)}\}$ that satisfies (2.16). It is clear that $\{g_{\tilde{\alpha}}^{(\alpha)} ; -\infty < \alpha_n < \infty\}$ satisfies (2.16). But

$$g_{\tilde{\alpha}}^{(\alpha)}(t) = \int_{\Gamma_0} g^{(\alpha)}(\tilde{x},t)\eta_{\tilde{\alpha}}(\tilde{x})\, d\tilde{x}$$

and $\|\nu_\gamma^{(\alpha)}\| = M(\alpha)^{-1}$ so that (2.15) follows immediately.

§3. Estimates for biorthogonal sequences. To simplify the notation we take here $X_n = \pi$ and set $c_1^2\alpha_1^2 + \cdots + c_{m-1}^2\alpha_{m-1}^2 = \mu$. We study then sequences biorthogonal to

$$\{e^{i\omega_n(\mu)t} ; -\infty < n < \infty\} \tag{3.1}$$

in an arbitrary interval $|t| \leq T/2$, where

$$\omega_n(\mu) = (\mu^2 + n^2)^{1/2} \operatorname{sgn} n \qquad (|n| \geq 0) ,$$

$$\omega_0(\mu) = \mu , \quad \omega_{-0}(\mu) = -\mu$$

μ a parameter. Obviously the relevant range for μ is either $\mu = 0$ (in which case the function $e(t) = t$ is to be added to (3.1)) or μ bounded away from zero ($\mu \geq \mu_0 = \inf(c_1, \dots, c_{n-1})$). Since we are mainly interested in asymptotic estimations as $\mu \to \infty$, we will consider the second range most of the time. In view of

$$\omega_n(\mu) = n + 0(\mu^2/2n) \qquad \text{as} \quad |n| \to \infty$$

it follows from Theorem II in LEVINSON [8] that if $T \leq 2\pi$ not only the sequence (3.1) is total in $L^2(-T/2,T/2)$ but the same is true if we amputate any of its elements (any finite number of its elements if $T < 2\pi$). It results then that all of the elements of (3.1) belong to the subspace generated by the others, which precludes existence of a biorthogonal sequence.

If $T > 2\pi$ biorthogonal sequences exist: however, we leave the question of existence for the end of the section and try first to obtain estimates from below valid for any biorthogonal sequence.

Let then $T > 2\pi$ and let $\psi_{\mu,n}$ $(\mu \geq \mu_0)$ be a sequence in $L^2(-T/2,T/2)$ biorthogonal to (3.1). The FOURIER transforms

$$\Psi_{\mu,n}(\zeta) = \int_{-T/2}^{T/2} e^{i\zeta t}\, \psi_{\mu,n}(t)\, dt \tag{3.2}$$

are entire functions of exponential type $\leq T/2$ which belong to L^2 over the real axis; moreover, by the PLANCHEREL theorem

$$\|\Psi_{\mu,n}\|_{L^2(-\infty,\infty)} = 2\pi\|\psi_{\mu,n}\|_{L^2(-T/2,T/2)} \tag{3.3}$$

It is clear that $\Psi_{\mu,n}(\omega_m(\mu)) = \delta_{mn}$. Then, since the function

$$\Theta_{\mu,n}(\zeta) = \frac{(\mu^2 - \zeta^2)^{1/2}}{\zeta - \omega_n(\mu)} \sinh \pi(\mu^2 - \zeta^2)^{1/2}$$

is entire and vanishes for $\zeta = \omega_m(\mu)$ $(m \neq n)$ we can write

$$\Psi_{\mu,n}(\zeta) = \Theta_{\mu,n}(\zeta)\Phi_{\mu,n}(\zeta)$$

where Φ is as well entire. We freeze now n and study the μ-dependence of $\Phi_{\mu,n}$ as $\mu \to \infty$; we assume, by reasons of convenience, that $n \geq 1$.

3.1. LEMMA. (a) <u>For each</u> $\mu \geq \mu_0$, $\Phi_{\mu,n}$ <u>is an entire function of exponential type</u> $\leq T/2$. (b) $\Phi_{\mu,n}$ <u>belongs to</u> L^2 <u>on the real axis and</u>

$$\|\Phi_{\mu,n}\|_{L^2(-\infty,\infty)} \leq C\|\Psi_{\mu,n}\|_{L^2(-T/2,T/2)} \qquad (\mu \geq \mu_0) \tag{3.4}$$

<u>Proof</u>: It follows from elementary properties of $\sin z$ for z complex that if $0 < \varphi \leq |\arg \zeta| \leq \pi - \varphi$ there exists a constant $\delta > 0$ such that $|\Theta_{\mu,n}(\zeta)| \geq \delta$. Then

$$|\Phi_{\mu,n}(\zeta)| \leq Ce^{T|\zeta|/2} \qquad (\varphi \leq |\arg \zeta| \leq \pi - \varphi) \tag{3.5}$$

Estimation of $\Phi_{\mu,n}(\zeta)$ inside the two angles is somewhat less simple. We observe first that, since $\Psi_{\mu,n}$ is entire of exponential type, by virtue of the HADAMARD factorization theorem (BOAS [2]) it can be written as a canonical product

$$\Psi_{\mu,n}(\zeta) = a\zeta^p e^{b\zeta} \prod_{k=1}^{\infty} \left(1 - \frac{\zeta}{\zeta_k}\right) e^{\zeta/\zeta_k}$$

where $\zeta_1, \zeta_2, \ldots$ are the non-null zeros of $\Psi_{\mu,n}$ (clearly $\{\omega_m(\mu)\ ;\ m \neq n\}$ is a subset of $\{\zeta_k\}$ but the latter set may contain much more elements than the first). Dividing by the factors corresponding to the $\omega_m(\mu)$, $m \neq n$ we see that $\Phi_{\mu,n}$ itself can be written as a canonical product,

$$\Phi_{\mu,n}(\zeta) = a\zeta^p e^{b\zeta} \prod \left(1 - \frac{\zeta}{\tilde{\zeta}_k}\right) e^{\zeta/\tilde{\zeta}_k}$$

where the $\{\tilde{\zeta}_k\}$ are a part of the $\{\zeta_k\}$. We observe next that since $\Psi_{\mu,n}$ is of exponential type -- a fortiori of order one --, if $\rho > 1$

$$\sum_{k=1}^{\infty} |\zeta_k|^{-\rho} < \infty \tag{3.6}$$

(BOAS [2], p. 17). Accordingly the same condition holds for the $\{\tilde{\zeta}_k\}$ and, by virtue of a well-known estimation for canonical products (BOAS [2], p. 19) $\Phi_{\mu,n}$ must be of order 1, that is, for any $\varepsilon > 0$,

$$|\Phi_{\mu,n}(\zeta)| \leq C_\varepsilon e^{|\zeta|^\varepsilon} \tag{3.7}$$

Combining this inequality with (3.5) and one of the PHRAGMÉN-LINDELÖF theorems we see that $\Phi_{\mu,n}$ is of exponential type $\leq T/2$.

We need now the following auxiliary result:

3.2. LEMMA. Let $k > 0$, $\delta \leq k/2$, $\mathcal{I} = \{I_n\}$ a family of disjoint open intervals, each one of them of length $\leq \delta$. Then there exists a sequence of real numbers $\{\nu_n\}, \ldots < \nu_n < \nu_{n+1} < \cdots$ such that

$$|\nu_n - kn| \leq \delta, \quad |\nu_{n+1} - \nu_n| \geq \delta \qquad (-\infty < n < \infty) \tag{3.8}$$

and such that no ν_n lies in an interval of $\mathcal{I}$.

The proof is immediate: we start with the sequence $\nu_n = kn$. If any of the elements of this sequence lies in one of the I_n we push it (say, to the right) until we reach the endpoint of I_n; since we do not move it more than δ, (3.8) follows.

We use now Lemma 3.2 in the following way: given $\mu \geq \mu_0$, $\rho > 0$ consider the family of intervals $\mathcal{I}(\mu,\rho) = \{I_n(\mu,\rho)\ ;\ -\infty < n < \infty\}$ (we observe again the distinction of $+0$ and -0 as subindices and the rule $\operatorname{sign}(+0) = 1$, $\operatorname{sign}(-0) = -1$) defined as follows:

$$I_n(\mu,\rho) = \{\xi\ ;\ \xi \geq 0,\ \ |(\xi^2 - \mu^2)^{1/2} - n| < \rho\}$$

$$= ((\mu^2 + (n - \rho)^2)^{1/2},\ (\mu^2 + (n + \rho)^2)^{1/2}) \qquad (n \geq 0)\ ,$$

$$I_n(\mu,\rho) = -I_{-n}(\mu,\rho) \qquad (n \leq -0)\ .$$

It is easy to see that these intervals are pairwise disjoint if $\rho < \min(1/2,\mu_0)$. Assume ρ is fixed and ξ does not belong to any of the $I_n(\mu,\rho)$. It follows that $|\sin \pi(\xi^2 - \mu^2)^{1/2}|$ is bounded away from zero uniformly in $\mu \geq \mu_0$, while $|(\xi - \omega_n(\mu))/(\xi^2 - \mu^2)^{1/2}|$ is bounded outside of I_0, I_{-0}, also independently of μ. Then

$$|\Theta_{\mu,n}(\xi)| \geq c > 0\ , \tag{3.9}$$

where c does not depend on μ, if $\xi \notin \cup\, I_n(\mu,\rho)$. We take now $k = 2\pi/(T + 1)$, $\delta = k/2$, $\rho = \min(1/4,\mu_0)$. Applying Lemma 3.2 we see that, for each $\mu \geq \mu_0$ there exists a sequence $\{\nu_n(\mu)\}$ satisfying (3.8) none of whose elements belong to $\cup_n I_n(\mu,\rho)$. Making use of the second condition (3.8) only and of a theorem of PLANCHEREL and POLYA (BOAS, p. 101) we obtain, keeping in mind that $\Psi_{\mu,n}$ has exponential type $\leq T/2$ and inequality (3.9),

$$\sum_{m=-\infty}^{\infty} |\Phi_{\mu,n}(\nu_m(\mu))|^2 \leq C \sum_{m=-\infty}^{\infty} |\Psi_{\mu,n}(\nu_m(\mu))|^2 \leq C' \int_{-\infty}^{\infty} |\Psi_{\mu,n}(\xi)|^2\, d\xi \tag{3.10}$$

where the constant C' is only a function of δ (and thus does not depend on μ). We bring now into play a theorem of DUFFIN and SCHAEFFER [3] (see also BOAS [1]). According to it the two conditions (3.8) guarantee the existence of a constant C dependent only on δ and such that

$$\int_{-\infty}^{\infty} |\Phi_{\mu,n}(\xi)|^2 \, d\xi \le C \sum_{m=-\infty}^{\infty} |\Phi_{\mu,n}(\nu_m(\mu))| \; .$$

This inequality, together with (3.10) and (3.3) implies the desired result.

REMARK. It is possible to show that $\Phi_{\mu,n}$ is actually of type $\le (T - \pi)/2$. We do not need this fact.

It is a consequence of (3.2) that

$$|\Psi_{\mu,n}(\xi)| = |\Theta_{\mu,n}(\xi)\Phi_{\mu,n}(\xi)| \le T^{1/2} \|\psi_{\mu,n}\|_{L^2(-T/2,T/2)} \qquad (-\infty < \xi < \infty) \tag{3.11}$$

Using now (3.9) and the elementary inequality $(\sinh x)/x \ge e^x/(2x+1)$ $(x \ge 0)$ we easily obtain that

$$|\Theta_{\mu,n}(\xi)| \ge c e^{\pi\mu/2} \qquad (|\xi| \le (3/4)^{1/2} \mu)$$

so that, combining this inequality with (3.11) we obtain

$$|\Phi_{\mu,n}(\xi)| \le C T^{1/2} e^{-\pi\mu/2} \beta_{\mu,n} \qquad (|\xi| \le (3/4)^{1/2} \mu) \tag{3.12}$$

where C does not depend on μ and we have set $\|\psi_{\mu,n}\| = \beta_{\mu,n}$. Our argument ends now by applying a version of the heuristic principle that "a nonzero holomorphic function which is too small in too large a set must be quite large somewhere else." In other words, we shall show that inequalities (3.4) and (3.12) clash unless the right-hand side of (3.4) grows quite fast when $\mu \to \infty$, which is precisely what we seek to prove. In order to precise this argument, we begin by obtaining suitable bounds for $\Phi_{\mu,n}$ in the complex plane. This is easy, for in view of Lemma 3.1 (a) and the PALEY-WIENER theorem

$$\Phi_{\mu,n}(\zeta) = \int_{-T/2}^{T/2} e^{i\zeta t} \varphi_{\mu,n}(t) dt$$

where $\varphi_{\mu,n}$ belongs to $L^2(-T/2,T/2)$ and its norm equals $(2\pi)^{-1}$ times the norm of $\Phi_{\mu,n}$ in $L^2(-\infty,\infty)$. Accordingly, if $|\text{Im}\,\zeta| \le \gamma$

$$|\Phi_{\mu,n}(\zeta)| \le C T^{1/2} e^{T|\text{Im}\,\zeta|/2} \beta_{\mu,n} \; . \tag{3.13}$$

We recall now that the function $z = \text{tgh}\,\zeta = (e^{\zeta} - e^{-\zeta})/(e^{\zeta} + e^{-\zeta})$ maps conformally the horizontal strip $|\text{Im}\,\zeta| \le \pi/4$ into the unit circle $|z| < 1$.

FIGURE 2

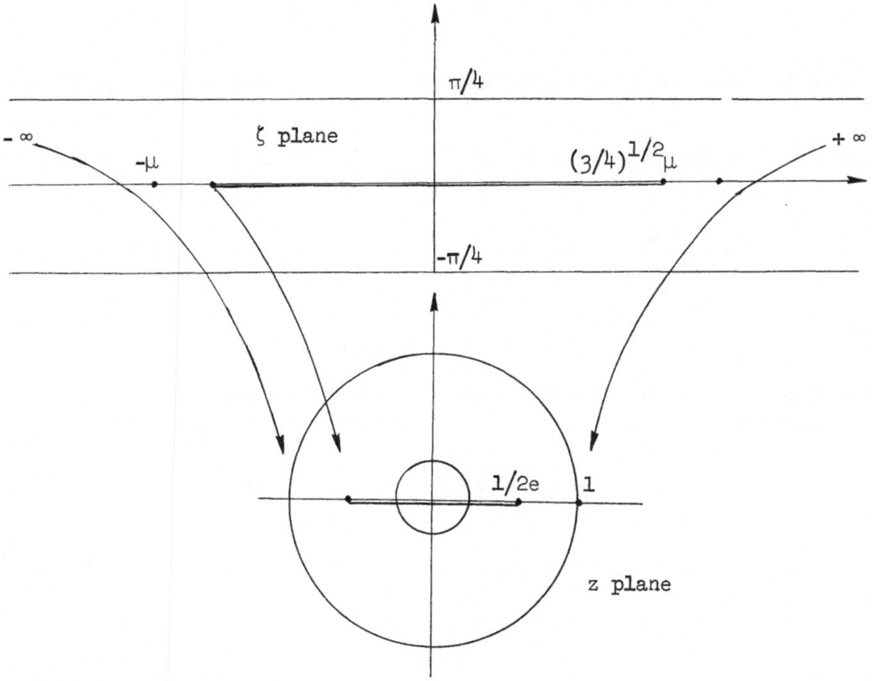

Then the function

$$f_{\mu,n}(z) = \alpha_{\mu,n}\Phi_{\mu,n}(\text{arg tgh } z)\,,$$

where $\alpha_{\mu,n}$ is a constant as yet to be determined, is analytic in $|z| \leq 1$ except at $z = 1,-1$ but it is anyway continuous there. Since $\Psi_{\mu,n}(\omega_n(\mu)) = 1$, if we choose

$$\alpha_{\mu,n} = \Theta(\omega_n(\mu)) = (-1)^n\ \pi(\mu^2 + n^2)^{1/2}$$

we shall also have

$$f_{\mu,n}(0) = 1$$

so that we are in the right setting to apply the theorem in LEVIN [7], p. 21 to the effect that for any $\eta \leq 3e/2$ we must have

$$|f_{\mu,n}(z)| \geq \exp\left(-\left(2 + \log\frac{3e}{2\eta}\right)\ \log m_{\mu,n}\right) \tag{3.14}$$

in the circle $|z| \leq 1/2e$ outside a set of circles $C_k = \{z\ ;\ |z - z_k| \leq r_k\}$ with $\Sigma\, r_k \leq 2\eta/e$, where $m_{\mu,n}$ denotes the maximum modulus of $f_{\mu,n}$ in the unit circle. If we now take $\eta = 1/5$ it is plain that the sum of the radii of the exceptional circles will not surpass $2/5e$. Selecting μ so large that the image of the segment $(-(3/4)^{1/2}\mu,(3/4)^{1/2}\mu)$ through the map $\zeta \to z$ contains $I = (-1/2e,1/2e)$ it is clear that there exists a $z \in I$ for which, by virtue of (3.12)

$$|f_{\mu,n}(z)| \le C\mu T^{1/2} e^{-\pi\mu/2}\, \beta_{\mu,n} \tag{3.15}$$

and for which inequality (3.14) will also be satisfied. To take profit of this, we note that by virtue of (3.13)

$$m_{\mu,n} \le C' T^{1/2}\, \beta_{\mu,n} .$$

Replacing this in (3.14), combining with (3.15) and taking logarithms we easily obtain

$$\log \beta_{\mu,n} \ge C_1\mu - C_2 \log T - \log \mu - C_3$$

where C_1, C_2, C_3 are constants $(C_1, C_2 > 0)$ independent of μ.

We can now state our main result.

3.3. THEOREM. Let $\mu \ge \mu_0 > 0$. For each μ let $\{\psi_{\mu,n} ; -\infty < n < \infty\}$ be a sequence biorthogonal to (3.1) in $L^2(-T/2,T/2)$ (in order that such a sequence should exist it is necessary that $T > 2\pi$). Then for every integer n there exist constants $c, C, k > 0$ such that

$$\|\psi_{\mu,n}\|_{L^2(-T/2,T/2)} \ge C T^{-k} e^{c\mu} \qquad (\mu \ge \mu_0) \tag{3.16}$$

where all the constants are independent of μ, T.

On the positive side we have the following result:

3.4. THEOREM. Let $\mu = 0$ or $\mu \ge \mu_0$, $T > 2\pi$. Then, for each μ there exists a sequence $\{\psi_{\mu,n} ; -\infty < n < \infty\}$ biorthogonal to (3.1) in $L^2(-T/2,T/2)$ such that

$$\|\psi_{\mu,n}\|_{L^2(-T/2,T/2)} \le C e^{\pi\mu} \tag{3.17}$$

Proof: We define, as in KAHANE [6]

$$H_{\mu,n}(\zeta) = \Theta_{\mu,n}(\zeta) \cdot \frac{\sin \eta(\zeta - \omega_n(\mu))}{\eta(\zeta - \omega_n(\mu))} \tag{3.18}$$

where $\eta < (T - 2\pi)/2$. Obviously $H_{\mu,n}$ is an entire function of exponential type $\le T/2$. We estimate now the integral of $|H_{\mu,n}|^2$ in the real axis. Making use of the inequality $(\sinh x)/x \le e^x/2$ we easily obtain that

$$|\Theta_{\mu,n}(\xi)| \le C\mu e^{\pi\mu} \qquad (|\xi| \le \mu). \tag{3.19}$$

In the range $|\xi| > \mu$ we estimate with the help of the inequality $|(\sin \pi x)/(x-n)| \le 1$ in $\{\xi ; |(\xi^2 - \mu^2)^{1/2} - n| \le 1\}$ and of the inequality $|\sin x| \le 1$ elsewhere. We obtain

$$|\Theta_{\mu,n}(\xi)| \le C(\mu + |n|) \qquad (|\xi| > \mu) \tag{3.20}$$

The orthonormal sequence is obtained by setting

$$\psi_{\mu,n}(t) = \frac{1}{2\pi\alpha_{\mu,n}} \int_{-\infty}^{\infty} e^{-i\xi t} H_{\mu,n}(\xi) d\xi$$

where $\alpha_{\mu,n} = H_{\mu,n}(\omega_n(\mu)) = \Theta_{\mu,n}(\omega_n(\mu)) = (-1)^n \pi(\mu^2 + n^2)^{1/2}$. The estimate (3.17) then follows from (3.19), (3.20) and the PLANCHEREL theorem.

§4. Interpretation of the results. We use here the estimations in Section 3 to show that the control problem in Section 1 has no solution even for very smooth initial data u_0, v_0.

4.1. THEOREM. There exist functions u_0, v_0 infinitely differentiable in P and satisfying the NEUMANN boundary condition in Γ such that the control problem in Section 1 has no solution $f \in L^2(\Gamma_0 \times (0,T))$ for any $T > 0$.

Proof: Let T be fixed. In the notation of Section 2, consider the space $\mathcal{E}$ of all functions u defined in P that admit a FOURIER development.

$$u(x) = \sum_{\alpha} \mu_\alpha \varphi_\alpha(x) \tag{4.1}$$

such that

$$|\mu_\alpha| \leq Ce^{-\delta|\alpha|} \tag{4.2}$$

where $|\alpha| = \alpha_1 + \cdots + \alpha_m$ and δ is a positive constant to be determined later. It is plain that all functions in $\mathcal{E}$ satisfy the NEUMANN boundary condition and are infinitely differentiable (differentiation under the summation sign any number of times is clearly permissible). In fact, it is even true that any function in $\mathcal{E}$, extended to R^m by (4.1) can be analytically extended to a neighborhood of R^m in unitary space C^m. Observe next (as we see through a simple change of variables) that, if $a > 0$ and $\{\psi^a_{\mu,n}(t)\}$ is a sequence biorthogonal to $\exp(\pm i(\mu^2 + a^2n^2)^{1/2}t)$ in $(-T/2,T/2)$ then $\{a^{-1}\psi^a_{\mu,n}(t/a)\}$ is biorthogonal to $\exp(\pm i((\mu/a)^2 + n^2)t)$ in $(-aT/2,aT/2)$. Hence,

$$\|\psi^a_{\mu,n}\| \geq Ce^{(c/a)\mu} \tag{4.3}$$

where c is the constant in the exponent of (3.16) and we subsume in C the T-dependence of the right-hand side. With this information in hand, we can make our choice of δ in (4.2) now: if, as in Section 2, we set $c_j = \pi/X_j$ $(1 \leq j \leq m)$ and $\mu^2 = c_1^2\alpha_1^2 + \cdots + c_{m-1}^2\alpha_{m-1}^2$ then we take $\delta < c \max(c_1/c_m, \ldots, c_{m-1}/c_m) = c\max(X_m/X_1, \ldots, X_m/X_{m-1})$.

Assume then that the control problem in Section 1 has a solution in $L^2(\Gamma_0 \times (0,T))$ for every $u_0, v_0 \in \mathcal{E}$. Then the moment problem (2.9), (2.10), (2.11), (2.13) has a solution $g \in L^2(\Gamma_0 \times (0,T))$ for every multisequence $\{\nu_\alpha\}$ that satisfies (4.2). It follows from Theorem 2.1 that there exists a sequence $\{\psi_\alpha\}$ biorthogonal to

$\{\exp(\pm i(\mu^2 + c_m^2 n^2)^{1/2} t)\}$ in $|t| \leq T/2$ such that

$$\|\psi_\alpha\|_{L^2(-T/2,T/2)} \leq Ce^{\delta|\alpha|} \tag{4.4}$$

It is obvious that inequalities (4.4) and (4.3) (with $a = c_m$) may not coexist. Thus there exist $u_0, v_0 \in \mathcal{E}$ such that the control problem has no solution for the T previously fixed. A category argument shows now that there are as well $u_0, v_0 \in \mathcal{E}$ such that the control problem has no solution for any $T > 0$. In fact, it follows from one of the well known footnotes to the closed graph theorem that the set $\mathfrak{n}_T$ of all $(u_0, v_0) \in \mathcal{E} \times \mathcal{E}$ such that the control problem has a solution for a given $T > 0$ must be of the first category. It suffices then to take a sequence $T_n \to \infty$ and (u_0, v_0) in the intersection of the complements of the $\mathfrak{n}_{T_n}$. A positive result for the control problem can be obtained using Theorem 3.4 and manipulations of the type performed before and after (4.3). We leave these manipulations to the reader and limit ourselves to stating the result.

4.2. THEOREM. *Let* u_0, u_1 *be given by*

$$u_0(x) = \sum_\alpha \mu_{\alpha,0}\varphi_\alpha(x) \ , \quad u_1(x) = \sum_\alpha \mu_{\alpha,1}\varphi_\alpha(x)$$

with

$$\sum_\alpha (|\lambda_\alpha \mu_{\alpha,0}|^2 + |\mu_{\alpha,1}|^2)\gamma(\tilde{\alpha})^2 = \tau(u_0,u_1)^2 < \infty$$

where

$$\log \gamma(\tilde{\alpha}) = \pi((X_m/X_1)^2\alpha_1^2 + \cdots + (X_m/X_{m-1})^2\alpha_{m-1}^2)^{1/2} .$$

Then the control problem has a solution f *in* $L^2(\Gamma_0 \times (0,T))$; *moreover,*

$$\|f\|_{L^2(\Gamma_0\times(0,T))} \leq C\tau(u_0,u_1) .$$

It is interesting to compare the present results for the wave equation with those in [4]. It is shown there that systems governed by the heat equation in a parallelepipedon are quite impervious to whether control is applied on the whole boundary or in just one face, a situation that contrasts sharply with the present one. Another result of the "one face is not enough" type can be found in QUINN and RUSSELL [13]; the objective is to obtain uniform exponential rates of decay for the wave equation in a parallelepipedon by boundary damping, and it is shown that this is not possible if damping is applied at only one face.

REFERENCES

[1] R. P. BOAS, JR., Integrability along a line for a class of entire functions, Trans. Amer. Math. Soc. 73 (1952), 191-197.

[2] R. P. BOAS, JR., Entire functions, Academic Press, New York, 1954.

[3] R. J. DUFFIN and A. C. SCHAEFFER, A class of nonharmonic Fourier series, Trans. Amer. Math. Soc. 72 (1952), 341-366.

[4] H. O. FATTORINI, Boundary control of temperature distributions in a parallelepipedon, SIAM J. Control 13 (1975), 1-13.

[5] K. D. GRAHAM and D. L. RUSSELL, Boundary value control of the wave equation in a spherical region, SIAM J. Control 13 (1975), 174-195.

[6] J. P. KAHANE, Sur les fonctions moyenne-périodiques bornées, Ann. Inst. Fourier VII (1957), 293-314.

[7] B. Ja. LEVIN, Distribution of zeros of entire functions (Russian) Goztekhizdat, Moscow, 1956. English translation: Amer. Math. Soc., Translations of Mathematical Monographs, vol. 5, Providence, R.I., 1964.

[8] N. LEVINSON, Gap and Density Theorems, Amer. Math. Soc. Colloquium Publications, vol. XXVI, New York, 1940.

[9] J. L. LIONS and E. MAGENES, Problèmes aux limites non homogènes et applications, vol. 1, Dunod, Paris, 1968.

[10] J. L. LIONS and E. MAGENES, Problèmes aux limites non homogènes et applications, vol. 2, Dunod, Paris, 1968.

[11] D. L. RUSSELL, A unified boundary controllability theory for hyperbolic and parabolic partial differential equations, Studies in Appl. Math. LII (1973), 189-211.

[12] D. L. RUSSELL, Exact boundary value controllability theorems for wave and heat processes in star-complemented regions, Differential Games and Control Theory, ed. Roxin, Liu, Sternberg, Marcel Dekker, New York, 1974.

[13] J. P. QUINN and D. L. RUSSELL, Asymptotic stability and energy decay rates for solutions of hyperbolic equations with boundary damping, Math. Research Center Technical Summary Report #1575, University of Wisconsin, 1975.

[14] T. I. SEIDMAN, Observation and prediction for the heat equation IV: Path observability and controllability, Math. Research Report 76-4, University of Maryland Baltimore County, 1976.

[15] T. I. SEIDMAN, Boundary observation and control for the heat equation, Calculus of Variations and Optimal Control, 321-351, Academic Press, New York, 1976.

This work was partly supported by the National Science Foundation under grant MP71-02656 A04.

THE APPLICATION OF DISTRIBUTED PARAMETER STATE ESTIMATION THEORY TO A METALLURGICAL CASTING OPERATION

by

F. K. Greiss and W. H. Ray
Department of Chemical Engineering
University of Wisconsin
Madison, Wisconsin 53706
USA

Abstract

A mathematical model for the continuous casting of mild steel was developed and compared with experimental data. This model was then used as a basis for a nonlinear state estimation algorithm which provides on-line estimates of the solidified crust thickness and solid temperature distribution based only on noisy steel surface measurements. The computational algorithm, which makes use of eigenfunction decomposition methods, was found to be computationally efficient, and the filter performed well under simulation, even in the face of large temperature measurement errors.

INTRODUCTION

Among the more interesting problems arising from distributed parameter processes are the on-line estimation and control of the position of a moving boundary. These problems occur in a wide range of applications, including:

- (i) the continuous casting of steel.
- (ii) the spreading of crude oil spills.
- (iii) the narrow zone combustion of coal in underground gasification, of coke in the regeneration of coked packed bed reactors, and of trees, grass, and shrubs during wildland forest fires.
- (iv) the estimation of the position of the water-oil front during the secondary recovery of oil.

In all of these applications, only a limited number of sensors are available and yet a reliable estimate of the moving boundary is required in real time in order to allow feedback control action.

Some first theoretical results in developing state estimators for this class of problems have already appeared [1,2]. In addition, basic results are available for the feedback control of this class of problems [3-6]. However, there remains the problem of testing the performance of the state estimator in the face of sensor errors and the development of on-line algorithms which are computationally efficient and which may be implemented in real time.

In the present paper we apply the state estimation results developed earlier [1,2] to the problem of estimating the solid crust thickness and the temperature profiles inside the mould region of a continuous casting unit. We make use of an eigenfunction decomposition of the resulting filter and covariance equations to develop an algorithm capable of solving the equations efficiently in real time. The model, which forms the basis of the filter, is compared with experimental data and then is used in this feasibility study of the filter.

THE CONTINUOUS CASTING PROCESS

The continuous casting of steel is an increasingly important part of modern steelmaking because it is a much more efficient route to steel slabs and billets than the conventional ingot casting-re-heating-slab rolling operation. The process, sketched in Figure 1, involves pouring molten steel at the top of a water cooled mould and continuously drawing out a thin walled steel slab or billet at the bottom. If the solid steel crust is too thin when leaving the mould, either due to some process upset or because the withdrawal rates are too high, the molten steel core will "breakout" and the casting machine must be shut down. By employing a distributed parameter filter to estimate the steel shell thickness in real time, one could operate at high average withdrawal rates while detecting potential breakouts before they occur and thus take appropriate control action.

A number of workers have studied the steady state modelling of the continuous casting machine (e.g., [7-16]), but only Soliman [17] seems to have studied the dynamic behaviour of the process. Unfortunately, his model is too complex for on-line computation; thus we have developed an alternate model of the process.

The Mathematical Model

As may be seen in Figure 1, which represents the mould region in a typical continuous casting process, there are three distinct zones present, the solid, liquid + solid (freezing zone), and liquid

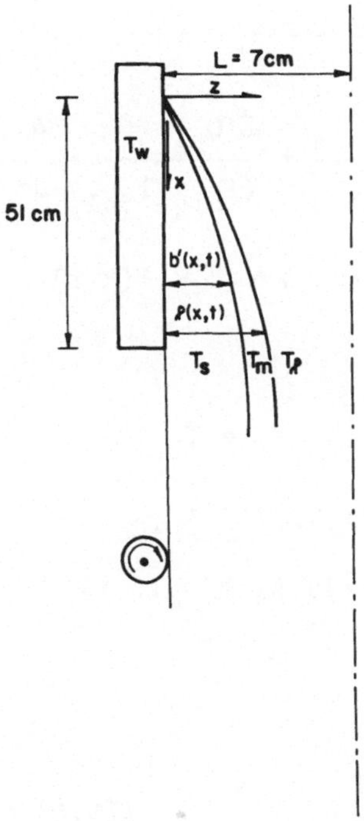

Figure 1 The mould region of a continuous casting operation

zones. The modelling equations for these respective zones are as follows:

(i) the solid region

$$\frac{\partial T_S}{\partial t} + u_c \frac{\partial T_S}{\partial x} = \alpha_s \frac{\partial^2 T_S}{\partial z^2} \qquad \begin{array}{c} 0 < z < b'(x,t) \\ x > 0 \end{array} \tag{1}$$

with boundary conditions

$$x = 0, \quad T_S(z,0,t) = \psi_S(z,t) \tag{2}$$

$$z = 0, \quad k_S \frac{\partial T_S}{\partial z} = h(x)(T_S(0,x,t) - T_w) \tag{3}$$

$$z = b'(x,t), \quad T_S(b',x,t) = T_{Sol} \tag{4}$$

(ii) <u>the freezing region (mushy zone)</u>

$$\frac{\partial T_m}{\partial t} + u_c \frac{\partial T_m}{\partial x} = \alpha_m \frac{\partial^2 T_m}{\partial z^2} + \frac{\mathcal{L}/C_{p_m}}{(T_{Liq}-T_{Sol})} \frac{d}{dt} \left\{ \frac{\ell(x,t)-z}{\ell(x,t)-b'(x,t)} \right\} \tag{5}$$

$$b'(x,t) < z < \ell(x,t)$$

with boundary conditions

$$z = b'(x,t), \qquad T_m(z,x,t) = T_{Sol} \tag{6}$$

$$z = \ell(x,t), \qquad T_m(z,x,t) = T_{Liq} \tag{7}$$

$$x = 0, \qquad T_m(z,0,t) = \psi_m(z,t) \tag{8}$$

(iii) <u>the liquid region</u>

$$\frac{\partial T_\ell}{\partial t} + u_c \frac{\partial T_\ell}{\partial x} = \alpha_\ell \frac{\partial^2 T_\ell}{\partial z^2} \qquad \ell(x,t) < z < L \tag{9}$$

with the boundary conditions

$$z = \ell(x,t), \qquad T_\ell(z,x,t) = T_{Liq} \tag{10}$$

$$z = L, \qquad \frac{\partial T_\ell}{\partial z} = 0 \tag{11}$$

$$x = 0, \qquad T_\ell(z,0,t) = \psi_\ell(z,t) \tag{12}$$

In addition, at the two moving boundaries we have

$$k_S \left. \frac{\partial T_S}{\partial z} \right|_{z=b'(x,t)} = k_m \left. \frac{\partial T_m}{\partial z} \right|_{z=b'(x,t)} \tag{13}$$

$$k_m \left. \frac{\partial T_m}{\partial z} \right|_{z=\ell(x,t)} = k_\ell \left. \frac{\partial T_\ell}{\partial z} \right|_{z=\ell(x,t)} \tag{14}$$

The meaning of the symbols is given in the Appendix.

Calculations with this model show that temperature gradients in the solid region are very much larger (~600°C temperature drop across the solid zone) than those in the liquid or freezing zone (~30°C across both zones). In addition, the thickness of the solid region was found to be very much larger than that of the freezing zone. For these reasons, it would seem that a good approximation to this present model would be to assume that the liquid is well mixed and the temperature is uniform across the liquid zone. In addition, one could approximate the freezing zone by an interface so that the complex model (1-14) reduces to Eqns (1-4) for the solid region with the solidifying boundary described by

$$\frac{\partial b'(x,t)}{\partial t} = \frac{k_S}{\mathcal{L}\rho_S} \left.\frac{\partial T_S}{\partial z}\right|_{z=b'(x,t)} + \frac{h_\ell}{\mathcal{L}\rho_\ell}(T_S(b',x,t) - T_\ell(x,t)) \tag{15}$$

The well mixed liquid zone temperature T_ℓ may be modelled separately if desired. However in this study we shall assume that T_ℓ is a specified function.

It is possible to eliminate the variable x from the partial differential equations (1-4,15) by noting that the vertical flow in the mould is along the characteristic lines

$$\frac{dx}{dt} = u_c \qquad x(0) = x_0 \tag{16}$$

Thus the solution along these characteristic lines may be determined from:

$$\frac{\partial T_S}{\partial t} = \alpha_S \frac{\partial^2 T_S}{\partial z^2} \qquad 0 < z < b'(t) \tag{17}$$

$$z = 0, \quad k_S \frac{\partial T_S}{\partial z} = h(T_S(0,t) - T_w) \tag{18}$$

$$z = b'(t), \quad T_S = T_{Sol} \tag{19}$$

$$t = 0 \quad , \quad T_S(z,0) = \psi_S(z) \tag{20}$$

$$\frac{db'(t)}{dt} = \frac{k_S}{\mathcal{L}\rho_S} \left.\frac{\partial T_S}{\partial z}\right|_{z=b'(t)} + \frac{h_\ell}{\mathcal{L}\rho_\ell}(T_S(b',t) - T_\ell(t)) \tag{21}$$

These equations are nonlinear due to the moving boundary; thus we shall make some transformations which will convert the equations to a fixed boundary problem. Let us define the variables

$$u_S = \frac{T_S - T_{Sol}}{T_{Sol}} \;, \quad r = \frac{z}{b'(t)} \;, \quad b(t) = b'(t)/L \;,$$
$$u_W = \frac{T_W - T_{Sol}}{T_{Sol}} \;, \quad H = \frac{hL}{k_S} \;, \quad \eta = \frac{k_S \; T_{Sol}}{\rho_S \mathcal{L} \alpha_S} \tag{22}$$
$$u_\ell = \frac{T_\ell - T_{Sol}}{T_{Sol}} \;, \quad K = \frac{h_\ell L}{\alpha_S \mathcal{L} \rho_\ell} T_{Sol} \;, \quad \tau = \int_0^t \frac{\alpha_S}{b'(t')^2} dt'$$

By substituting (22) into Eqns (17-21) and making the boundary conditions homogeneous through the use of a Dirac delta function, the model becomes

$$\frac{\partial u_S(r,\tau)}{\partial \tau} = \frac{\partial^2 u_S(r,\tau)}{\partial r^2} + r \frac{d \ln b(\tau)}{d\tau} \frac{\partial u_S(r,\tau)}{\partial r} - b(\tau) H(u_S(0,\tau) - u_W) \delta(r) \tag{23}$$

$$0 < r < 1$$

$$\frac{d \ln b(\tau)}{d\tau} = \eta \left. \frac{\partial u_S}{\partial r} \right|_{r=1} - K b(\tau) u_\ell(\tau) \tag{24}$$

$$r = 0 \;, \quad \frac{\partial u_S}{\partial r} = 0 \tag{25}$$

$$r = 1 \;, \quad u_S = 0 \tag{26}$$

Even though these equations are nonlinear, one may find their solution exactly through an orthonormal eigenfunction expansion of the form

$$u_S(r,\tau) = \sum_{n=1}^{\infty} A_n(\tau) \phi_n(r) \tag{27}$$

where the nonlinear term

$$F(r,\tau) = r \frac{d \ln b(\tau)}{d\tau} \frac{\partial u_S(r,\tau)}{\partial r} - b(\tau) H(u_S(0,\tau) - u_W) \delta(r) \tag{28}$$

may also be expanded as

$$F(r,\tau) = \sum_{n=1}^{\infty} c_n(\tau)\, \phi_n(r) \tag{29}$$

The eigenfunctions, $\phi_n(r)$, are those associated with the linear part of (23-26) and are the solution of

$$\ddot{\phi}(r) + \lambda_n^2\, \phi_n(r) = 0 \qquad 0 < r < 1 \tag{30}$$

$$\left.\begin{aligned} \dot{\phi}_n(0) &= 0 \\ \phi_n(1) &= 0 \end{aligned}\right\} \quad n = 1,2,\ \ldots \tag{31}$$

which yields

$$\left.\begin{aligned} \phi_n(r) &= \sqrt{2}\ \cos \lambda_n r \\ \lambda_n &= (2n-1)\ \pi/2 \end{aligned}\right\} \quad n = 1,2,\ \ldots \tag{32}$$

The mathematical model may then be reduced to the Fourier coefficients

$$\frac{dA_n(\tau)}{d\tau} = -\lambda_n^2\, A_n(\tau) + c_n(\tau) \tag{33}$$

where

$$\begin{aligned} c_n(\tau) &= \int_0^1 F(r,\tau)\, \phi_n(r)\, dr \\ &= -\left\{2\, \frac{d \ln b(\tau)}{d\tau} \sum_{m=1}^{\infty} A_m(\tau)\, \lambda_m\, I_{nm} \right. \\ &\qquad \left. + \sqrt{2}\ b(\tau)\, H(u_S(0,\tau) - u_W) \right\} \end{aligned} \tag{34}$$

and

$$I_{nm} = \begin{cases} \dfrac{2m-1}{2(m+n-1)(m-n)\pi} & n \neq m \\ \dfrac{1}{2(2m-1)\pi} & n=m \end{cases} \quad (35)$$

The moving boundary equation (24) then becomes

$$\frac{d \ln b(\tau)}{d\tau} = \sqrt{2} \;\; \eta \sum_{k=1}^{\infty} (-1)^k \lambda_k A_k(\tau)$$

$$-Kb(\tau) \; u_\ell(\tau) \quad (36)$$

By truncating the eigenfunction expansion after an appropriate number of terms, N, one need only solve Eqns (33) and (36) and substitute the results into (27) to obtain the desired dynamic temperature profiles and boundary position. This involves the numerical solution of $N+1$ ordinary differential equations.

In order to test the validity of our model, simulations were carried out for the conditions shown in Table 1 and compared with the experimental data of Weinberg et al. [15,16] for the same operating conditions. The model predictions for solid crust thickness versus time (or axial position), shown in Figure 2, are in excellent agreement with the data; thus it appears that our model is representative of actual experimental operations, and we may proceed in confidence with the state estimation study.

TABLE 1

Property values used in the computation

$T_{Sol} = 1495°C$
$T_{Liq} = 1523°C$
$C_{p_S} = C_{p_\ell} = 0.16$ cal/gm°C
$k_S = k_\ell = 7.02 \times 10^{-3}$ cal/cm sec°C
$T_\ell = 1525°C$
$h_\ell = 0.01355$ cal/cm^{2}sec°C
$u_c = 2.34$ cm/sec
$T_c = 21°C$
$h = 0.044 \left[\dfrac{1-0.98\,x}{100}\right]^*$ (x is in cms) cal/cm^{2}sec°C
$\rho_S = \rho_\ell = 7.4$ gm/cm^3
$L = 7$ cm

*ref. [9,16]

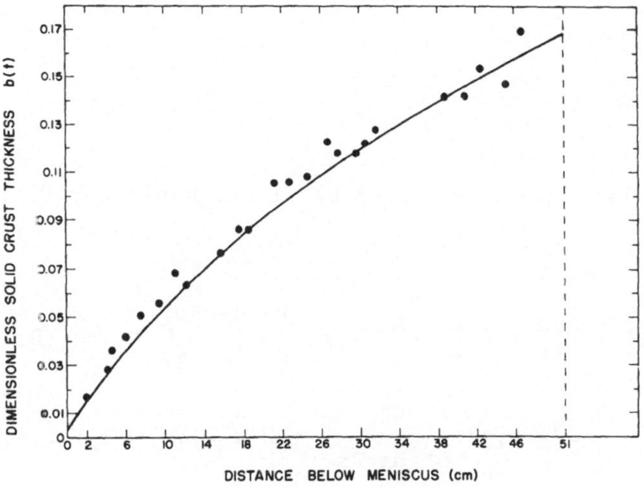

Figure 2 A comparison of our model predictions with the experimental data of Weinberg et al. [15,16].

THE STATE ESTIMATION ALGORITHM

State estimation equations for nonlinear distributed systems having moving boundaries were developed in [1,2], so that the derivation shall not be repeated here. For the case of continuous surface temperature measurements

$$y(\tau) = u_S(0,\tau) + \varepsilon(\tau) \tag{37}$$

where $\varepsilon(\tau)$ is a random measurement error, the least squares state estimator for the continuous casting problem takes the form

$$\frac{\partial \hat{u}_S}{\partial \tau} = \frac{\partial^2 \hat{u}}{\partial r^2} + r \frac{d \ln \hat{b}(\tau)}{d\tau} \frac{\partial \hat{u}}{\partial r} - b(\tau)\, H(\hat{u}_S(0,\tau) - u_W)\, \delta(r) + P^{uu}(r,0,\tau)\, Q(\tau)\, (y - \hat{u}_S(0, \tau)) \tag{38}$$

$$\frac{d\hat{b}(\tau)}{d\tau} = \eta\, \hat{b} \left.\frac{\partial \hat{u}_S}{\partial r}\right|_{r=1} - K\, \hat{b}^2\, u_\ell(\tau) + P^{ub}(0,\tau)\, Q(\tau)\, (y - \hat{u}_S(0, \tau)) \tag{39}$$

$$\hat{u}(1,\tau) = 0 \tag{40}$$

$$\frac{\partial \hat{u}(0,\tau)}{\partial r} = 0 \tag{41}$$

The relevant differential sensitivity (i.e., nonlinear "covariance") equations are

$$\begin{aligned} P_\tau^{uu}(r,s,\tau) = {} & P_{rr}^{uu} + P_{ss}^{uu} - P^{bu}(s,\tau)\,\frac{r}{\hat{b}^2}\,\frac{d\hat{b}}{d\tau}\,\frac{\partial \hat{u}_S}{\partial r} + H(\hat{u}_S(0,\tau) - u_w)\,\delta(r) \\ & - P^{ub}(r,\tau)\,\frac{s}{\hat{b}^2}\,\frac{d\hat{b}}{d\tau}\,\frac{\partial \hat{u}_S}{\partial s} + H(\hat{u}_S(0,\tau) - u_w)\,\delta(s) \\ & - P^{uu}(r,0,\tau)\,Q(\tau)\,P^{uu}(0,s,\tau) \\ & + P_s^{uu}(r,s,\tau)\,\frac{s}{\hat{b}^2}\,\frac{d\hat{b}}{d\tau} \\ & + P_r^{uu}(r,s,\tau)\,\frac{r}{\hat{b}^2}\,\frac{d\hat{b}}{d\tau} + R^{+}(r,s,\tau) \end{aligned} \tag{42}$$

$$\begin{aligned} P_\tau^{ub}(r,\tau) = {} & \left[\eta \left.\frac{\partial \hat{u}}{\partial r}\right|_{r=1} - 2\hat{b}\; u_\ell(\tau)\; K\right] P^{ub}(r,\tau) \\ & - P^{bb}(\tau)\left[\frac{r}{\hat{b}^2}\,\frac{d\hat{b}}{d\tau}\,\frac{\partial \hat{u}}{\partial r} + H(\hat{u}_S(0,\tau) - u_w)\,\delta(r)\right] \\ & + P_{rr}^{ub}(r,\tau) + P_s^{uu}(r,1,\tau)\,\eta\,\hat{b}(\tau) + \\ & P_r^{ub}(r,\tau)\,\frac{r}{\hat{b}}\,\frac{d\hat{b}}{d\tau} - P^{uu}(r,0,\tau)\,Q(\tau)\,P^{ub}(0,\tau) \end{aligned} \tag{43}$$

$$\begin{aligned} \frac{dP^{bb}}{d\tau} = {} & 2\left[\eta \left.\frac{\partial \hat{u}_S}{\partial r}\right|_{r=1} - 2\hat{b}u_\ell(\tau)\; K\right] P^{bb}(\tau) \\ & + \eta\hat{b}(\tau)\; P_r^{ub}(1,\tau) - P^{bu}(0,\tau)\,Q(\tau)\,P^{ub}(0,\tau) \\ & + \eta\hat{b}(\tau)\; P_s^{bu}(1,\tau) + R^{-1}(\tau) \end{aligned} \tag{44}$$

with the symmetry condition

$$P^{ub}(r,\tau) = P^{bu}(r,\tau) \tag{45}$$

The boundary conditions are

$$\left.\begin{aligned} &P_s^{uu}(r,s,\tau) + R_0^{-1}(\tau)\,\delta(r) = 0 \\ &P_s^{bu}(s,\tau) = 0 \end{aligned}\right\} \; s = 0 \tag{46}$$

$$\left.\begin{aligned} &P_r^{uu}(r,s,\tau) + R_0^{-1}(\tau)\,\delta(s) = 0 \\ &P_r^{ub}(r,\tau) = 0 \end{aligned}\right\} \; r = 0 \tag{47}$$

$$\left.\begin{aligned} &P^{uu}(r,s,\tau) = 0 \\ &P^{bu}(s,\tau) = 0 \end{aligned}\right\} \; s = 1 \tag{48}$$

$$\left.\begin{aligned} &P^{uu}(r,s,\tau) = 0 \\ &P^{ub}(r,\tau) = 0 \end{aligned}\right\} \; r = 1 \tag{49}$$

where $R(r,s,\tau)$, $R(\tau)$, $Q(\tau)$, $R_0(\tau)$ are positive weighting factors. The entire filter is summarized in Table 2. In the column of initial conditions, $\hat{b}(0)$ and $\hat{u}_S(r,0)$ represent our best initial guesses of $b(0)$ and $u_S(r,0)$. The initial values of $P^{bb}(0)$, $P^{bu}(s,0)$, $P^{ub}(r,0)$ and $P^{uu}(r,s,0)$ are basically arbitrary but the initial errors in b and u may be used as a guide to their selection.

TABLE 2

Summary of the Filter Equations

	Equations	Initial Conditions	Boundary Conditions
Estimates			
$\hat{b}(\tau)$	(39)	$\hat{b}(0)$	none
$\hat{u}_S(r,\tau)$	(38)	$\hat{u}_S(r,0)$	(40,41)
Differential sensitivities			
$P^{bb}(\tau)$	(44)	$P^{bb}(0)$	none
$P^{ub}(r,\tau)$	(43)	$P^{ub}(r,0)$	(46-49)
$P^{uu}(r,s,\tau)$	(42)	$P^{uu}(r,s,0)$	(46-49)

To solve the filter and covariance equations, we used an eigenfunction expansion technique in the form

$$\hat{u}(r,\tau) = \sum_{n=1}^{\infty} A_n(\tau)\, \phi_n(r) \tag{50}$$

$$P^{uu}(r,s,\tau) = \sum_{n=1}^{\infty} \sum_{m=1}^{\infty} a_{nm}(\tau)\, \phi_n(r)\, \phi_m(s) \tag{51}$$

$$P^{ub}(r,\tau) = \sum_{n=1}^{\infty} B_n(\tau)\, \phi_n(r) \tag{52}$$

where the nonlinear source terms may be defined by

$$\begin{aligned} F(r,\tau) &= r \frac{d \ln \hat{b}}{d\tau} \frac{\partial \hat{u}_S}{\partial r} - \hat{b}(\tau)\, H(\hat{u}_S(0,\tau) - u_W)\, \delta(r) \\ &\quad + P^{uu}(r,0,\tau)\, Q(\tau)\, (y - \hat{u}_S(0,\tau)) \\ &= \sum_{n=1}^{\infty} c_n(\tau)\, \phi_n(r) \end{aligned} \tag{53}$$

$$\begin{aligned} F^{uu}(r,s,\tau) &= -P^{bu}(s,\tau) \left[\frac{r}{\hat{b}^2} \frac{d\hat{b}}{d\tau} \frac{\partial \hat{u}_S}{\partial r} + H(\hat{u}_S(0,\tau) - u_W)\, \delta(r) \right] \\ &\quad - P^{ub}(r,\tau) \left[\frac{s}{\hat{b}^2} \frac{d\hat{b}}{d\tau} \frac{\partial \hat{u}_S}{\partial s} + H(\hat{u}_S(0,\tau) - u_W)\, \delta(s) \right] \\ &\quad - P^{uu}(r,0,\tau)\, Q(\tau)\, P^{uu}(0,s,\tau) \\ &\quad + P^{uu}_s(r,s,\tau) \frac{s}{\hat{b}^2} \frac{d\hat{b}}{d\tau} \\ &\quad + P^{uu}_r(r,s,\tau) \frac{r}{\hat{b}^2} \frac{d\hat{b}}{d\tau} + R^+(r,s,\tau) \\ &= \sum_{n=1}^{\infty} \sum_{m=1}^{\infty} D_{nm}(\tau)\, \phi_n(r)\, \phi_m(s) \end{aligned} \tag{54}$$

$$F^{ub}(r,\tau) = \left[\eta \left.\frac{\partial \hat{u}_S}{\partial r}\right|_{r=1} - 2K\hat{b}\, u_\ell\right] P^{ub}(r,\tau)$$

$$-P^{bb}(\tau)\left[\frac{r}{\hat{b}^2}\frac{d\hat{b}}{d\tau}\frac{\partial \hat{u}_S}{\partial r} + H(\hat{u}_S(0,\tau) - u_w)\,\delta(r)\right]$$

$$+P_S^{uu}(r,1,\tau)\,\eta\,\hat{b} + P_r^{ub}(r,\tau)\,\frac{r}{\hat{b}}\frac{d\hat{b}}{d\tau}$$

$$-P^{uu}(r,0,\tau)\;Q(\tau)\;P^{ub}(0,\tau)$$

$$= \sum_{n=1}^{\infty} E_n(\tau)\;\phi_n(r) \tag{55}$$

The quantities $\phi_n(r)$ and λ_n are defined by Eqn (32) and

$$\lambda_{nm} = \sqrt{\lambda_n^2 + \lambda_m^2} \tag{56}$$

Thus the eigen-coefficient equations become

$$\dot{A}_n(\tau) = -\lambda_n^2\, A_n(\tau) + c_n(\tau) \tag{57}$$

$$\dot{a}_{nm}(\tau) = -\lambda_{nm}^2\, a_{nm}(\tau) + D_{nm}(\tau) \tag{58}$$

$$\dot{B}_n(\tau) = -\lambda_n^2\, B_n(\tau) + E_n(\tau) \tag{59}$$

where c_n, D_{nm}, and E_n are given by

$$c_n(\tau) = -\sqrt{2}\;\; H\hat{b}(\hat{u}_S(0,\tau) - u_w) - 2\,\frac{d\,\ln\hat{b}}{d\tau}\sum_{m=1}^{N} A_m(\tau)\,\lambda_m I_{nm}$$

$$+\sqrt{2}\;\; Q(\tau)(y - \hat{u}(0,\tau))\sum_{m=1}^{N_c} a_{nm} \tag{60}$$

$$D_{nm}(\tau) = B_n\left(-2\sqrt{2}\ \ H(\hat{u}_S(0,\tau) - u_w) + \frac{2}{\hat{b}^2}\frac{d\hat{b}}{d\tau}\left(\sum_{j=1}^{N} \lambda_j A_j I_{jm}\right)\right)$$

$$+B_m\left[-2\sqrt{2}\ \ H(\hat{u}_S(0,\tau) - u_w) + \frac{2}{\hat{b}^2}\frac{d\hat{b}}{d\tau}\left(\sum_{k=1}^{N} \lambda_k A_k I_{kn}\right)\right]$$

$$-2\,\frac{d\ \ln\ \hat{b}}{d\tau}\left(\sum_{k=1}^{N_c} a_{km}\lambda_k I_{mk} + \sum_{j=1}^{N_c} a_{nj}\lambda_j I_{nj}\right)$$

$$-2Q(\tau)\sum_{k=1}^{N_c} a_{nk}\sum_{j=1}^{N_c} a_{jm} + \frac{2R^+(-1)^{m+1}(-1)^{n+1}}{\lambda_m\lambda_n}$$

$$+R_0^{-1}\left(\frac{(-1)^{n+1}}{\lambda_n} + \frac{(-1)^{m+1}}{\lambda_m}\right) \tag{61}$$

$$E_n(\tau) = \frac{2}{\hat{b}^2}P^{bb}(\tau)\frac{d\hat{b}}{d\tau}\sum_{j=1}^{N} A_j\lambda_j I_{jn} - \sqrt{2}\ \ P^{bb}\ H(\hat{u}_S(0,\tau) - u_w)$$

$$-2\,\frac{d\ \ln\ \hat{b}}{d\tau}\sum_{k=1}^{N_c}\lambda_k B_k I_{kn} - \left(\sqrt{2}\ \ \eta\sum_{m=1}^{N}\lambda_m A_m(-1)^{m+1}\right.$$

$$\left.+2\hat{b}\,u_\ell\,K\right)B_n\ -2Q(\tau)\sum_{k=1}^{N_c} B_k\sum_{m=1}^{N_c} a_{nm} \tag{62}$$

The variables $\hat{b}(\tau)$ and $P^{bb}(\tau)$ may be determined from

$$\frac{d\hat{b}}{d\tau} = -\eta\ \hat{b}\ \sqrt{2}\ \sum_{m=1}^{N}(-1)^{m+1}\ \lambda_m A_m(\tau)$$

$$-\hat{b}^2 K u_\ell + \sqrt{2}\left(\sum_{k=1}^{N_c} B_k\right) Q(\tau)(y - \hat{u}_S(0,\tau)) \tag{63}$$

$$\frac{dP^{bb}}{d\tau} = -2P^{bb}\left[\eta\ \sqrt{2}\ \sum_{m=1}^{N}\ (-1)^{m+1}\ \lambda_m A_m(\tau)\ +2\hat{b}u_\ell K\right]$$

$$+2\sqrt{2}\ \ \eta\ \hat{b}\sum_{k=1}^{N_c}\ (-1)^{k+1}\ \lambda_k B_k(\tau)$$

$$-\left(\sum_{i=1}^{N_c} B_i(\tau)\right) Q(\tau)\left(\sum_{j=1}^{N_c} B_j(\tau)\right) + R^{-1}(\tau) \tag{64}$$

The state estimation algorithm then consists of coupled filter and differential sensitivity equations (i.e., Eqns (38-49)). Through eigenfunction decomposition, one may reduce this set of 5 ordinary and partial differential equations to an equivalent set of $N+1$ ordinary differential equations for the filter and $\left(1 + N_c + \frac{N_c^2 + N_c}{2}\right)$ ordinary differential equations for the differential sensitivities. Here N is the number of eigenfunctions retained for the filter estimates, and N_c is the number of eigenfunctions used to represent the differential sensitivities.

Although it would be possible to solve both the filter and sensitivity equations in real time, it would probably be more practical in practice to solve the sensitivity equations in an approximate way off-line for a nominal state trajectory so that only $N+1$ equations need be integrated in real time. In this way our state estimator could be easily implemented in real time on presently available process control computers.

COMPUTATIONAL RESULTS

In the present study, it was found (after some adjustments in the computational procedure [2]), that $N = 4$ was sufficient to provide a good solution to the filter equations and $N_c = 3$ sufficed for adequate filter performance. Thus the filter simulation required the solution of 15 ordinary differential equations. In order to provide a test of the observability of both the temperature profile and the boundary position as well as to give an indication of the robustness of the filter in the face of large measurement errors, a number of simulations were performed. The steel surface temperature measurement "data" were provided by a simulation of the model in which the resulting surface temperatures, $u_S(0,\tau)$ were corrupted by adding zero mean white Gaussian noise from a random number generator having a specified standard deviation σ.

A selection of results may be seen in Figures 3-6 for the filter parameters given in Table 3. As can be seen, this nonlinear filter performs well, converging from extremely poor initial guesses in a very short time even in the face of 100°C standard deviation measurement error. The filter + differential sensitivity calculations were carried out on the Univac 1110 computer of the University of Wisconsin computer center and required approximately 28 seconds for a complete simulation.

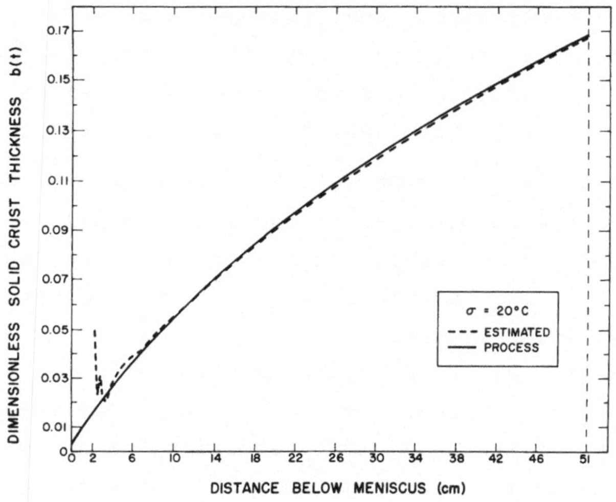

Figure 3 Filter estimates and process behaviour for the solid crust thickness, $\sigma = 20°C$

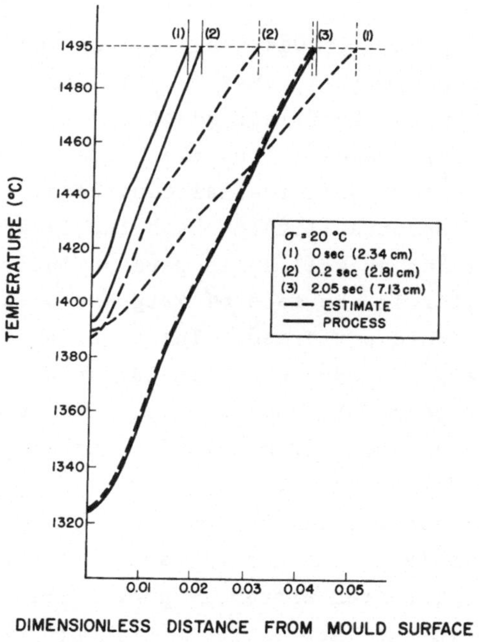

Figure 4 Filter estimates and process behaviour for the temperature profile in the solid crust, $\sigma = 20°C$.

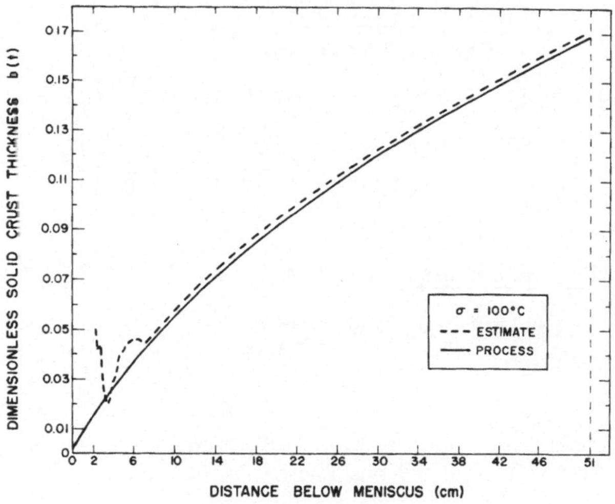

Figure 5 Filter estimates and process behaviour for the solid crust thickness, σ = 100°C.

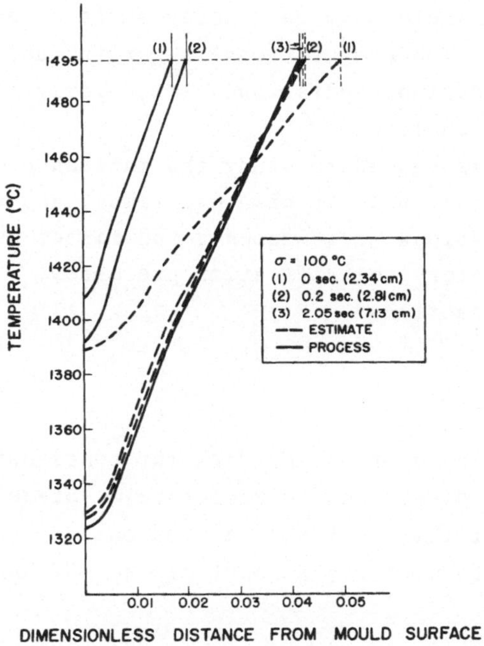

Figure 6 Filter estimates and process behaviour for the temperature profile in the solid crust, σ = 100°C.

TABLE 3
Filter Parameters

Figure No.	σ	$Q(\tau)$	$P^{bb}(0)$
3,4	20°C	1.96	0.001
5,6	100°C	0.0784	0.007

For all runs: $\hat{b}(0) = 0.05$, $R^{-1} = R_0^{-1} = R^{+} = 0$,
$B_n(0) = 0$, $D_{nm}(0) = \frac{1.02}{\lambda_n \lambda_m}$

CONCLUSIONS

In this study we have applied nonlinear state estimation theory to a model of the continuous casting process. We have shown that our mathematical model is in good agreement with experimental data. In addition simulation testing of the filter with artificially generated random measurement errors indicates that the filter should perform well in applications where only very noisy surface temperature measurements are available. The computational algorithm developed seems quite adequate for real time implementation, particularly if only the filter equations are solved on-line.

Further work is needed to study the influence of having temperature measurements only at discrete times, and to determine the real time computational requirements and filter performance when implemented on laboratory solidification processes. Work is in progress in these directions.

ACKNOWLEDGEMENTS

We are indebted to Dr. W. H. Park for contributions to the early part of this project, and to Professor J. Szekely for helpful discussions. Part of this work was carried out at the State University of New York at Buffalo with the support of the NSF RANN program.

REFERENCES

1. W. H. Ray and J. H. Seinfeld, Automatica, 11, 509 (1975).
2. F. K. Greiss, MS Thesis, State University of N.Y. at Buffalo, Buffalo, New York (1976).
3. P. K. C. Wang, Adv. Control Systems, 1, 75 (1964).

4. P. K. C. Wang, Int. J. Control, 5, 317 (1967).

5. N. N. Golub, Proceedings First IFAC Symp. on Control of Dist. Parameter Systems, paper 12.2 Banff (1971).

6. J. L. Lions, ibid review paper No. 2, Banff (1971).

7. A. W. D. Hills, JISI, 203, 18 (1965).

8. E. A. Mizikar, Trans. Met. Soc. AIME, 239, 1747 (1967).

9. A. W. D. Hills, Trans. Met. Soc. AIME, 245, 1471 (1969).

10. J. Szekely and V. Stanek, Met. Trans., 1, 119 (1970).

11. J. Szekely and R. T. Yadoya, Met. Trans., 3, 2673 (1972).

12. J. Szekely and R. T. Yadoya, Met. Trans., 4, 1379 (1973).

13. A. A. Tzavaras, Symposium on Continuous Casting, Chicago, A.I.M.E., p. 197 (1973).

14. L. Nemethy et al., "Continuous Casting", ed. D. L. McBride and T. E. Dancy, proceedings of a conference sponsored by the Phys. Chem. of Steel Making Comm. TSAIME, 130 (1961).

15. S. K. Morton and F. Weinberg, JISI, 211, 13 (1973).

16. J. K. Brimacombe and F. Weinberg, JISI, 211, 24 (1973).

17. M. A. Soliman, private communication (1974).

NOMENCLATURE

A,B,c,E,D,a	Eigen-coefficients
b'	Solid crust thickness
b	Dimensionless solid crust thickness
h	Heat transfer coefficient at mould wall
h_ℓ	Heat transfer coefficient at liquid surface
H	Dimensionless heat transfer coefficient
k	Thermal conductivity
$\mathcal{L}$	Latent heat of solidification
ℓ	Distance from mould surface to liquidus line
L	Distance from the mould surface to its center
$P^{uu}, P^{ub}, P^{bu}, P^{bb}$	Differential sensitivities
$R^{-1}, R^{+}, R_0^{-1}, Q$	Weighting factors
r	Normalized distance from the mould surface

t	Time
T	Temperature
u_S	Dimensionless temperature
u_c	Casting speed
x	Distance below meniscus
z	Distance from the mould surface

<u>Greek</u>

α	Thermal diffusivity
λ	Eigenvalue
ϕ	Eigenfunction
ρ	Density
τ	Scaled time
ψ	Initial condition

<u>Subscripts</u>

ℓ	Liquid region
m	Mushy region
Liq	Liquidus line
S	Solid region
Sol	Solidus line

BOUCLE OUVERTE ET BOUCLE FERMEE ADAPTEE POUR LES SYSTEMES DISTRIBUES. UN EXEMPLE D'APPLICATION A LA COMMANDE EN TEMPS REEL D'UN PROCESSUS

M. SORINE

IRIA-LABORIA
78150 - Rocquencourt (France)

Résumé.

La méthode dite de la "boucle ouverte adaptée" a été présentée par YVON [1], nous la rappelons brièvement. Le principal obstacle à l'utilisation des méthodes de boucle fermée adaptée est la résolution, en temps réel, d'équations de Riccati. Nous donnons un algorithme de résolution de cette équation (algorithme du type Chandrasekhar) suffisamment rapide pour permettre d'envisager des applications temps réel. Enfin nous présentons une expérience de commande d'un processus (régi par l'équation de la chaleur non linéaire) à l'aide de la méthode de boucle ouverte adaptée.

1. Introduction.

Nous commençons par rappeler la formulation du problème de contrôle linéaire quadratique de LIONS [1] et quelques résultats.

Soient V, H, E, F, des espaces de Hilbert, V dense dans H avec injection continue. En identifiant H à son dual on a :

(1.1) $$V \subset H \subset V'$$

Soient les opérateurs suivants :

(1.2) $$A \in \mathcal{L}(V,V') \quad , \quad V\text{-coercif}$$

(1.3) $$B \in \mathcal{L}(E,V')$$

(1.4) $$C \in \mathcal{L}(V,F)$$

(1.5) $$N \in \mathcal{L}(E,E) \quad , \quad E\text{-coercif et symétrique .}$$

L'état du système est donné par :

(1.6) $$\begin{cases} \frac{d}{dt} y + Ay = f + Bv \quad \text{sur }]0,T[\ , \quad 0 < T < +\infty \\ y(o) = y_o \end{cases}$$

où

(1.7) $$\begin{cases} f \in L^2(0,T;V') \\ v \in L^2(0,T;E) \\ y_o \in H \end{cases}$$

v étant le contrôle. Le coût à minimiser est :

(1.8) $$J(v) = \int_o^T |Cy(t;v) - zd(t)|_F^2 \, dt + \int_o^T (Nv(t),v(t))_E \, dt$$

où $zd \in L^2(0,T;F)$.

On a alors les résultats suivants (LIONS [1]) :

Théorème 1.1. i) Sous les hypothèses (1.1)...(1.7), (1.6) a une solution unique y(v) vérifiant :

(1.9) $$y \in W(0,T)$$

ii) E_{ad} étant un convexe fermé de E, il existe un contrôle unique u tel que :

$$(1.10) \qquad \begin{cases} u \in L^2(0,T;E_{ad}) \\ J(u) \leq J(v) \qquad \forall\, v \in L^2(0,T;E_{ad}) \end{cases}$$

iii) Dans le cas $E_{ad} = E$, il existe $P(t) \in \mathcal{L}(H,H)$ et $r(t) \in H$, $t \in]0,T[$ tels que le contrôle optimal u s'écrive :

$$(1.11) \qquad u(t) = -N^{-1}\Lambda_E^{-1} B^*(P(t)y(t;u) + r(t)) \quad (1)$$

■

Notons K(t) le gain de la loi de feedback optimal (1.11) :

$$(1.12) \qquad K(t) = N^{-1} \Lambda_E^{-1} B^* P(t)$$

Les résultats qui suivent caractérisent sous certaines conditions P(t), K(t), r(t), permettant la synthèse du feedback optimal.

Théorème 1.2. avec les hypothèses supplémentaires :

(1.13) $B \in \mathcal{L}(E,H)$; $f \in L^2(0,T;H)$

l'injection de V dans H est compacte

posons ;

$$(1.14) \qquad \begin{cases} D_1 = BN^{-1} \Lambda_E^{-1} B^* \\ D_2 = C^* \Lambda_F C \\ g = -C^* \Lambda_F zd \end{cases}$$

alors P et r sont solutions des équations suivantes :

$$(1.15) \qquad \begin{cases} -\frac{dr}{dt} + A^*r + PD_1r = Pf + g \qquad \text{sur }]0,T[\\ r(T) = 0 \ , \quad r \in W(0,T) \end{cases}$$

$$(1.16) \qquad \begin{cases} (-\frac{dP}{dt}(t))\eta + PA\eta + A^*P\eta + PD_1P\eta = D_2\eta \qquad \text{sur }]0,T[\\ P(T) = 0 \\ \forall\, \eta \in W(0,T) \text{ tel que } A\eta \in L^2(0,T;H),\ \eta' \in L^2(0,T;H). \end{cases}$$

P et r sont ainsi définis de façon unique.

■

(1) Λ_X désigne l'isomorphisme canonique de l'espace de Hilbert X sur son dual X'.

Notons enfin le résultat suivant (CASTI - LJUNG [1], BARAS - LAINIOTIS [1]) dont on démontre un analogue discret et qui s'écrit formellement ainsi :

<u>Théorème 1.3.</u> P est aussi l'unique solution du système :

$$(1.17)\qquad \begin{cases} \frac{dP}{dt}(t) = - L^*(t)\ \Lambda_F L(t) & \text{sur }]0,T[\\ - \frac{dL}{dt}(t) + L(t)A + L(t)D_1\ P(t) = 0 \\ P(T) = 0\ ,\quad L(T) = C \end{cases}$$

dont la variante suivante permet de caractériser directement K(t) :

$$(1.18)\qquad \begin{cases} \frac{dK}{dt}(t) = - N^{-1}\ \Lambda_E^{-1}\ B^*\ L^*(t)\ \Lambda_F\ L(t) \\ - \frac{dL}{dt}(t) + L(t)A + L(t)BK(t) = 0 \\ K(T) = 0\ ,\quad L(T) = C \end{cases}$$

■

(1.17) est un système d'équations du type Chandrasekhar, l'analogue discret de (1.18) présente comme on le verra des avantages numériques importants.

2. Principe de la méthode d'adaptation.

Nous rappelons ici la méthode de boucle ouverte adaptée de YVON [1] qui est utilisée dans l'expérience temps réel présentée au paragraphe suivant. Nous donnons enfin un schéma stable et convergent de calcul de P(t), K(t), particulièrement économique en temps, ce qui permet d'envisager une méthode de boucle fermée adaptée.

2.1. La méthode de boucle ouverte adaptée.

Soit (t_i) i=0,...,N une subdivision de l'intervalle [0,T] avec $t_o=0$, $t_N=T$, $t_{i+1} > t_i$.
Posons :

$$(2.1)\qquad \eta = \sup_{i=1,\dots,N} (t_i - t_{i-1})$$

L'état du système et le coût à minimiser sont donnés respectivement par (1.6) et (1.8). f est le terme de perturbation, la seule hypothèse faite dessus est : $f \in L^2(0,T;V')$.
Le principe de la méthode est le suivant :

i) On mesure l'état du système à l'instant t_{i-1}

ii) Durant l'intervalle de temps $[t_{i-1}, t_i[$ on applique au système le contrôle calculé pendant l'intervalle précédent $[t_{i-2}, t_{i-1}[$ (calculé hors ligne pour i=1) et on calcule le contrôle qui sera appliqué sur $[t_i , t_{i+1}[$.

Plus précisément notons u_η le contrôle réellement appliqué au système et y_η l'état de ce système. Nous avons :

$$(2.2)\qquad \begin{cases} \frac{d}{dt}y_\eta(t) + Ay_\eta(t) = f + Bu_\eta(t) & \text{sur }]0,T[\\ y_\eta(o) = y_o \end{cases}$$

Introduisons enfin la famille de problèmes de contrôle suivante :

Problème P_{t_i} :

$$(2.3)\qquad \begin{cases} \frac{d}{dt}\varphi + A\varphi = B\,v & \text{sur }]t_i, T[\\ \varphi(t_i) = z_\eta(t_i) \end{cases}$$

$$(2.4)\qquad J_{t_i}(v) = \int_{t_i}^{T} |C\varphi(t;v) - zd(t)|_F^2\, dt + \int_{t_i}^{T} (Nv(t),v(t))_E\, dt$$

$$(2.5)\qquad u(t_i;t) = \operatorname{Arg}\min_{v\in L^2(t_i,T;E_{ad})} J_{t_i}(v) \in L^2(t_i,T;E_{ad})$$

où

$$(2.6)\qquad z_\eta(o) = y_o$$

et $z_\eta(t_i)$, pour $i \geq 1$ est une extrapolation de la mesure $y_\eta(t_{i-1})$ donnée par :

$$(2.7)\qquad \begin{cases} \frac{d}{dt}z(t) + Az(t) = B\,u_\eta(t) & \text{sur }]t_{i-1},t_i[. \\ z(t_{i-1}) = y_\eta(t_{i-1}) \end{cases}$$

$$(2.8)\qquad z_\eta(t_i) = z(t_i)$$

P_{t_i}, $i \geq 1$, a une solution unique qui ne dépend que des valeurs $u_\eta(t)$ pour $t < t_i$, la solution de P_o ne dépend pas de u_η, de sorte que nous pouvons poser :

$$(2.9)\qquad u_\eta(t) = u(t_i;t) \quad \text{pour} \quad t \in [t_i, t_{i+1}[.$$

où $u(t_i;t)$, solution de P_{t_i}, est calculé sur $[t_{i-1},t_i[$.

Notons $K(t,s)$ l'application de H dans E définie pour $0 \leq s \leq t \leq T$ par :

(2.10)
$$\begin{cases} K(t,s)h = u(s;t) \text{ solution du problème } P_s \\ \text{avec comme condition initiale } \varphi(s) = h. \end{cases}$$

nous avons alors le résultat suivant : (BAMBERGER - SAGUEZ - YVON [1])

Théorème 2.1. Sous l'hypothèse $B \in \mathcal{L}(E,H)$ et l'une des hypothèses suivantes :

(2.11) $E_{ad} = E$

(2.12)
$$\begin{cases} E_{ad} \neq E \\ \text{l'injection de } V \text{ dans } H \text{ est compacte} \\ C \in \mathcal{L}(H;F) \end{cases}$$

on a lorsque $\eta \to 0$

(2.13)
$$\begin{cases} y_\eta \to \bar{y} \quad \text{dans } W(0,T) \text{ faible} \\ u_\eta \to \bar{u} \quad \text{dans } L^\infty(0,T;E) \text{ faible } * \end{cases}$$

où u_η et y_η sont définies par (2.9) et (2.2) et où $\bar{y}$ est défini de manière unique comme solution de :

(2.14)
$$\begin{cases} \frac{d}{dt}\bar{y}(t) + A\bar{y}(t) - BK(t,t)\,\bar{y}(t) = f \\ \bar{y}(o) = y_o \end{cases}$$

$\bar{u}$ étant alors donné par :

(2.15) $\bar{u}(t) = K(t,t)\,\bar{y}(t).$

■

Reamrque 2.1 : Dans le cas d'un contrôle frontière ($B \in \mathcal{L}(E,V')$), on peut, sur des exemples, étendre les résultats de ce théorème.

Remarque 2.2. : Dans le cas $E_{ad} = E$ le feedback (2.15) coïncide avec le feedback optimal (calculable hors ligne via la résolution d'une équation de Riccati), associé au problème P_o.

Remarque 2.3 : Dans les résultats précédents on a "prédit" f par 0 au cours de l'adaptation. Toute autre prédiction aurait convenu. En pratique on choisira une prédiction "raisonnable" (C si la perturbation est "petite" par exemple).

2.2. Equations de Chandrasekhar et esquisse d'une méthode de boucle fermée adaptée.

Introduisons les éléments de la discrétisation du problème de contrôle (1.6), (1.8). (voir NEDELEC [1]) dans le cas $E_{ad} = E$.

Nous noterons $(.,.)_X$, $|.|_X$, le produit scalaire et la norme dans l'espace de Hilbert X.

Considérons les approximations internes $(V_\alpha, r_\alpha, q_\alpha)$, $(E_\beta, r_\beta, q_\beta)$, $(F_\gamma, r_\gamma, q_\gamma)$ des espaces V, E, F, toutes stables et convergentes (1) avec :

$$(2.16) \qquad \begin{cases} r_\alpha \in \mathcal{L}(V,V_\alpha), & q_\alpha \in \mathcal{L}(V_\alpha,V) \\ r_\beta \in \mathcal{L}(E,E_\beta), & q_\beta \in \mathcal{L}(E_\beta,E) \\ r_\gamma \in \mathcal{L}(F,F_\gamma), & q_\gamma \in \mathcal{L}(F_\gamma,F) \end{cases}$$

où V_α, E_β, F_γ sont des espaces de dimensions respectives N, m, p et où q_α, q_β, q_γ sont injectifs.

Posons $k = \frac{T}{M}$, M entier > 0 et $\xi = (\alpha,\beta,\gamma,k)$ paramètre de l'approximation destiné à tendre vers 0.

Dans la suite $\xi \to 0$ signifiera α, β, γ, $k \to 0$ indépendamment. Munissons les espaces des produits scalaires suivants (et des normes associées) :

$$((.,.))_{V_\alpha} = (q_\alpha.,q_\alpha.)_V \; ; \; (.,.)_{V_\alpha} = (q_\alpha.,q_\alpha.)_H$$

$$(.,.)_{E_\beta} = (q_\beta.,q_\beta.)_E \; ; \; (.,.)_{F_\gamma} = (q_\gamma.,q_\gamma.)_F$$

les normes associées étant notées $\|.\|_{V_\alpha}$, $|.|_{V_\alpha}$, $|.|_{E_\beta}$, $|.|_{F_\gamma}$.

Définissons alors les opérateurs :

$$(2.17) \qquad \begin{cases} A_\xi \in \mathcal{L}(V_\alpha) \text{ tel que : } (A_\xi \varphi_\alpha,\Psi_\alpha)_{V_\alpha} = \langle Aq_\alpha\varphi_\alpha,q_\alpha\Psi_\alpha \rangle_{VV'} \\ B_\xi \in \mathcal{L}(E_\beta,V_\alpha) \text{ tel que : } (B_\xi u_\beta,\varphi_\alpha)_{V_\alpha} = \langle Bq_\beta u_\beta,q_\alpha\varphi_\alpha \rangle_{VV'} \\ C_\xi \in \mathcal{L}(V_\alpha,F_\gamma) \text{ tel que : } (C_\xi\varphi_\alpha,z_\gamma)_{F_\gamma} = (Cq_\alpha\varphi_\alpha,q_\gamma z_\gamma)_F \\ N_\xi \in \mathcal{L}(E_\beta) \text{ tel que : } (N_\xi u_\beta,V_\beta)_{E_\beta} = (Nq_\beta u_\beta,q_\beta V_\beta)_E \end{cases}$$

(1) Pour $(V_\alpha,r_\alpha,q_\alpha)$, par exemple, cela signifie que les normes des opérateurs r_α et q_α sont majorées indépendamment de α et que $\lim_{\alpha\to 0} q_\alpha r_\alpha h = h$ dans V fort. $\forall h \in V$.

et les éléments suivants :

$$(2.18)\quad \begin{cases} f_\xi^n \in V_\alpha \text{ tel que } (f_\xi^n,\varphi_\alpha)_{V_\alpha} = \frac{1}{k}\int_{nk}^{(n+1)k} < f(t),q_\alpha\varphi_\alpha >_{VV'} dt \\ zd_\xi^n \in F_\gamma \text{ tel que } (zd_\xi^n,z_\gamma)_{F_\gamma} = \frac{1}{k}\int_{nk}^{(n+1)k} (zd(t),q_\gamma z_\gamma)_F\, dt \end{cases}$$

$\forall\ \varphi_\alpha,\ \Psi_\alpha \in V_\alpha$, $\forall\ u_\beta,\ V_\beta \in E_\beta$, $\forall\ z_\gamma \in F_\gamma$; $n=0,\dots,M-1$

Posons :

$$(2.19)\quad \begin{cases} D_{1\xi} = B_\xi\ N_\xi^{-1}\ B_\xi^* \\ D_{2\xi} = C_\xi^*\ C_\xi \\ g_\xi^n = -\ C_\xi\ zd_\xi^n \end{cases}$$

nous noterons I_N l'identité de V_α.

L'analogue discret du problème (1.6), (1.8) est alors, pour un schéma de discrétisation implicite en temps et dans le cas sans contrainte :

$$(2.20)\quad \begin{cases} \dfrac{y_\xi^{n+1}-y_\xi^n}{k} + A_\xi\ y_\xi^{n+1} = f_\xi^n + B_\xi\ v_\xi^n \\ y_\xi^o = y_{o\xi} = r_\alpha y_o \end{cases}$$

où $v_\xi^n \in E_\beta$ et $y_\xi^n \in V_\alpha$, $n = 0,\dots, -1$.

Le critère à minimiser est :

$$(2.21)\quad J_\xi(v_\xi) = k \sum_{n=0}^{n=M-1} \{|C_\xi y_\xi^{n+1} - zd_\xi^{n+1}|_{F_\gamma}^2 + (N_\xi v_\xi^n, v_\xi^n)_{E_\beta}\}$$

où $v_\xi = (v_\xi^o,\dots,v_\xi^{M-1})$ parcourt $(E_\beta)^M$.
il s'agit de trouver $u_\xi \in (E_\beta)^M$ tel que

$$(2.22)\quad J_\xi(u_\xi) = \operatorname*{Inf}_{v_\xi \in (E_\beta)^M} J_\xi(v_\xi)$$

Nous avons le résultat suivant (NEDELEC [1]) :

<u>Théorème 2.2.</u> Sous les hypothèses (1.1),...(1.7) et (2.17), (2.18) et avec les hypothèses faites sur les approximations, le problème (2.20),...,(2.22) a une solution unique donnée par :

(2.23) $$u_\xi^n = - N_\xi^{-1} B_\xi^* (P_\xi^n y_\xi^n + r_\xi^n) \qquad n=0,\dots,M-1$$

où $P_\xi^n \in \mathcal{L}(V_\alpha)$ est l'unique solution de l'équation :

(2.24) $$\begin{cases} -\dfrac{P_\xi^{n+1}-P_\xi^n}{k} + A_\xi^* P_\xi^n + P_\xi^{n+1} A_\xi + P_\xi^{n+1} D_{1\xi} P_\xi^n + k(D_{2\xi}-P_\xi^{n+1}A_\xi)(I_N+kA_\xi)^{-1} \\ \qquad\qquad (A_\xi + D_{1\xi}P_\xi^n) = D_{2\xi} \\ P_\xi^M = 0 \qquad n=0,\dots,M-1 \end{cases}$$

avec de plus :

(2.25) $$P_\xi^n = P_\xi^{n*} \text{ et } P_\xi^n \geq 0 \qquad n=0,\dots,M-1$$

et où $r_\xi^n \in V_\alpha$ est l'unique solution de l'équation :

(2.26) $$\begin{cases} -\dfrac{r_\xi^{n+1}-r_\xi^n}{k} + A_\xi^* r_\xi^n + P_\xi^{n+1} D_{1\xi} r_\xi^n = P_\xi^{n+1} f_\xi^n + g_\xi^{n+1} + k(P_\xi^{n+1}A_\xi - D_{2\xi}) \\ \qquad\qquad (I_N+kA_\xi)^{-1}(D_{1\xi}r_\xi^n - f_\xi^n) \\ r_\xi^M = 0 \quad , \quad n=0,\dots,M-1 \end{cases}$$

■

Dans la résolution de l'équation de Riccati discrète (2.24) le calcul de P_ξ^n connaissant P_ξ^{n-1} nécessite la détermination de $N(N+1)/2$ variables (en tenant compte de la symétrie). Le schéma qui suit est l'analogue discret de (1.17), (1.18) (On trouvera une démonstration des équations (2.24), (2.26) et des résultats à venir dans SORINE [1]).

<u>Théorème 2.3.</u> Avec les mêmes hypothèses qu'au théorème 2.2, P_ξ^n est aussi l'unique solution du système suivant (Equations de Chandrasekhar discrètes) :

(2.27) $$\begin{cases} \dfrac{P_\xi^{n+1}-P_\xi^n}{k} = - L_\xi^{n+1*}\, \tilde{L}_\xi^n \\ -\dfrac{L_\xi^{n+1}-L_\xi^n}{k} + L_\xi^n[A_\xi + D_{1\xi}P_\xi^{n+1}] + kL_\xi^n D_{1\xi}(I_N+kA_\xi^*)^{-1}(D_{2\xi}-A_\xi^* P_\xi^{n+1}) = 0 \\ -\dfrac{\tilde{L}_\xi^{n+1}-\tilde{L}_\xi^n}{k} + \tilde{L}_\xi^n[A_\xi + D_{1\xi}P_\xi^{n+1}] + k\tilde{L}_\xi^n D_{1\xi}(I_N+kA_\xi^*)^{-1}(D_{2\xi}-A_\xi^* P_\xi^{n+1}) = 0 \\ P_\xi^M = 0 \ , \quad L_\xi^M = C_\xi(I_N+kA_\xi)^{-1} \ , \quad \tilde{L}_\xi^M = C_\xi \quad ; \quad n=0,\dots,M-1 \end{cases}$$

■

Connaissant P_ξ^{n+1}, L_ξ^{n+1}, $\tilde{L}_\xi^{n+1}$; L_ξ^n et $\tilde{L}_\xi^n$ s'obtiennent par la résolution de 2 p systèmes linéaires d'ordre N (2 Np variables à déterminer) et P_ξ^n est donné explicitement par la première relation (2.27).

Si on ne s'intéresse qu'au gain de la loi de feedback discrète (2.23)

$$K_\xi^n = N_\xi^{-1} B_\xi^* P_\xi^n , \qquad n=0,\dots,M \tag{2.28}$$

le système approché suivant donne de bons résultats numériquement (LEROY - SORINE [1])

$$\begin{cases} \dfrac{K^{n+1} - K^n}{k} = - N_\xi^{-1} B_\xi^* L^{n+1*} L^n \\ -\dfrac{L^{n+1} - L^n}{k} + L^n[A_\xi + B_\xi K^n] = 0 \\ K^M = 0 , \quad L^M = C_\xi ; \qquad n=0,\dots,M-1 \end{cases} \tag{2.29}$$

Il y a alors N(m+p) variables à déterminer à chaque pas de temps. Lorsque m et p sont petits devant N (cas des contrôles et observations frontières par exemple) la résolution de (2.27) est plus rapide que celle de (2.24), le gain en temps est de l'ordre de N/(2m+2p). Le résultat qui suit précise les propriétés numériques du schéma (2.27), (2.28).

<u>Théorème 2.4.</u> Avec les hypothèses du théorème 2.2. la solution P_ξ^n, K_ξ^n du système (2.27), (2.28) vérifie :

i) (Stabilité) a) $|P_\xi^n h_\xi|_{V_\alpha} \leq c|h_\xi|_{V_\alpha}$

b) si de plus $B \in \mathcal{L}(E,H)$, on a : $|K_\xi^n h_\xi|_{E_\beta} \leq c|h_\xi|_{V_\alpha}$

où c est une constante indépendante de ξ.

ii) (Convergence) a) $\lim\limits_{\xi\to 0} q_\alpha P_\xi^n h_\xi = P(s)h$ dans H fort.

b) si de plus $B \in \mathcal{L}(E,H)$, on a : $\lim\limits_{\xi\to 0} q_\beta K_\xi^n h_\xi = K(s)h$ dans E fort

quand $\lim\limits_{\xi\to 0} h_\xi = h$ dans H fort et $nk \leq s < (n+1)k$. $\forall s \in [0,T]$.

■

<u>Remarque 2.4.</u> Les théorèmes (2.2), (2.3), (2.4) se généralisent au cas où les opérateurs A, B, C, N dépendent du temps (les équations (1.15),...(1.18) aussi, voir LIONS [1]; BARAS - LAINIOTIS [1]). Les équations de Chandrasekhar dicrètes se parallèlisent et conduisent (au moins théoriquement, car il faut posséder un M-pro-

cesseur!) à un gain en temps de calcul analogue à celui du cas étudié ici. (SORINE [1]).

Remarque 2.5. On trouvera des résultats de comparaison plus précis des schémas (2.24) et (2.27) dans LEROY - SORINE [1].

Remarque 2.6. La résolution des systèmes (2.27), (2.29) est possible en temps réel ce qui permet d'envisager la méthode de boucle fermée adaptée suivante pour les systèmes non linéaires sans contraintes avec coût quadratique.

Après avoir mesuré l'état du système à l'instant t_{i-1} et calculé le contrôle optimal $u(t_i,t)$, $t \in [t_i,T[$ et l'état optimal $y(u(t_i;t);t)$, on linéarise le système des équations d'état autour de cet état optimal et on calcule le feedback optimal associé au système linéarisé et au coût quadratique. Ces calculs se passent pendant $[t_{i-1},t_i[$ et le système physique est soumis sur cet intervalle au feedback précédemment calculé.

Cette méthode n'est évidemment pas optimale (la méthode de boucle ouverte adaptée ne l'est pas non plus) et on se heurte à une difficulté : La solution $u(t_i;t)$, lorsqu'elle existe, n'est pas unique en général.

3. Un exemple d'implémentation de la méthode de boucle ouverte adaptée.

3.1. Le système physique et la boucle de commande.

Nous nous proposons de contrôler un système dont l'état $y(v)$ est solution de l'équation suivante :

$$(3.1)\quad \begin{cases} \dfrac{\partial}{\partial t} y(x,t) - \dfrac{\partial^2}{\partial x^2} y(x,t) = f(x,t) \quad 0 < x < 1 \quad , \quad 0 < t < T \\ -\dfrac{\partial}{\partial x} y(0,t) + \sigma|y(0,t)|^3\, y(0,t) = v(0,t) \\ \dfrac{\partial}{\partial x} y(1,t) + \sigma|y(1,t)|^3\, y(1,t) = v(1,t) \\ y(x,0) = y_0(x) \end{cases}$$

qui représente, par exemple, l'évolution de la température dans un barreau que l'on chauffe et qui rayonne par ses extrémités.

Actuellement le système qui admet ce modèle est un montage électronique. La partie linéaire (1ère équation (3.1)) modélise le comportement d'une série de cellules Résistance-capacité. Les deux équations suivantes de (3.1) modélisent un montage effectué sur un calculateur anaologique EAI 380. Un schéma simplifié de l'ensemble est montré figure 1 (La description détaillée du matériel, du software et des résultats expérimentaux se trouve dans SORINE [1]).

Une caractéristique importante du système, en vue de l'expérience qui suit, est sa "constante de temps".

Pour fixer le idées, partant de $y_0(x) = 0$ et maintenant $v(1,t)$ à zéro, si $v(0,t)$ est pris égal à un échelon unité, $y(1,t)$ atteint 90% de sa valeur asymptotique en environ 1 heure.

Enfin notons qu'une comparaison des réponses numériques du modèle et analogiques du système à diverses entrées fait apparaître une erreur de modélisation toujours inférieure à 10% .

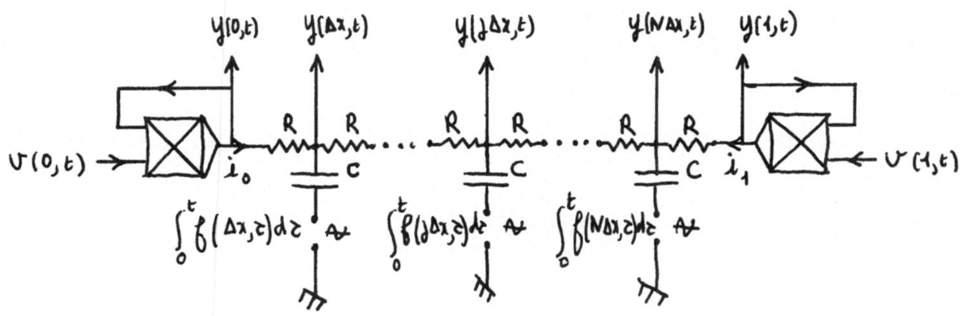

$i_0 = \sigma|y(o,t)|^3\, y(o,t) - v(o,t)$ $\qquad \Delta x = 1/N+1$

$i_1 = \sigma|y(1,t)|^3\, y(1,t) - v(1,t)$ $\qquad RC = (\Delta x)^2$

Figure 1 : le système à commander : schéma de principe.

La boucle de commande se compose des éléments suivants :

- une chaine de mesure capable de mesurer la tension en divers points du circuit et de convertir le résultat sous forme digitale. Elle permet de déterminer l'état discret associé à y(v) (soit 16 composantes dans la configuration actuelle) en moins de 2.10^{-3}s. Elle est constituée de capteurs, d'un multiplexeur, d'un convertisseur analogique-numérique.

- un calculateur T 2000 de TELEMECANIQUE.
Sa mémoire comporte 16 Kmots de 19 bits. Le cycle mémoire est de 1µs l'addition et la multiplication en virgule fixe durent respectivement 3µs et 10 µs.
Les programmes sont écrits en assembleur.

- Une chaine d'action capable de convertir les résultats en tensions ou courants selon le cas et de les maintenir. Elle est constituée d'un convertisseur numérique-analogique, de bloqueurs et de générateurs de courant.

L'ensemble du système et de la boucle de commande est représenté figure 2.

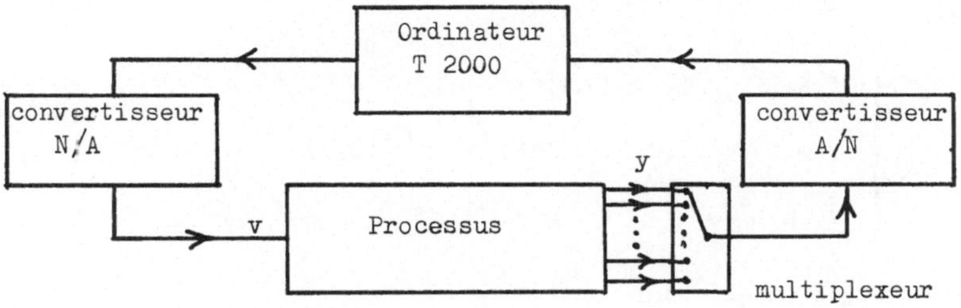

Figure 2. Le système et sa boucle de commande.

Les mesures effectuées sur le système sont mémorisées durant l'expérience et visualisées à la fin sous forme de surfaces de R^3 qui représentent donc l'évolution du profil de température du "barreau" dans le temps. Le système de visualisation "temps réel" permet de choisir la perspective la plus représentative et de la photographier (unité de visualisation TEKTRONIX). Les figures qui suivent ont été obtenues de cette façon.

Les axes représentent le temps (t) l'abcisse sur la barre (x) l'état (y). Des réseaux [x = constante] et [t = constante] relient les points de mesure. L'écart entre deux lignes consécutives t_{i-1}, t_i du réseau [t = constante] représente donc le temps de résolution du problème P_{t_i}.

3.2. Implémentation de la méthode et résultats.

Nous nous intéresserons à la minimisation de l'un des deux critères suivants :

$$(3.2) \qquad J_1(v) = \int_0^T \{|y(0,t)-zd(0,t)|^2 + |y(1,t)-zd(1,t)|^2\}\, dt + \nu \int_0^T \{v(0,t)^2 + v(1,t)^2\}\, dt.$$

$$(3.3) \qquad J_2(v) = \int_0^1 |y(T,x)-zd_T(x)|^2 dx + \nu \int_0^T [v(0,t)^2 + v(1,t)^2]\, dt.$$

Les contraintes à respecter (d'ordre technologique) portent sur le contrôle et sont du type :

$$(3.4) \qquad |v(0,t)| \leq M\,, \quad |v(1,t)| \leq M$$

Nous avons le résultat (LIONS [1]; [2]) :

Théorème 3.1. en prenant dans (3.1)

$$(3.5)\qquad \begin{cases} f \in L^2(]0,T[\times]0,1[) \\ v(0,t) \in L^2(0,T) , \quad v(1,t) \in L^2(0,T) \\ y_o \in L^2(0,1) \end{cases}$$

(3.1) a une solution unique vérifiant

$$(3.6)\qquad \begin{cases} y \in L^2(0,T;H^1(0,1)), \quad y' \in L^2(0,T;H^{-1}(0,1)) \\ y \in C([0,T], L^2(0,1)) \end{cases}$$

Si nous prenons alors :

$$(3.7)\qquad zd(0,t) , \ zd(1,t) \in L^2(0,T) \ . \quad zd_T(x) \in L^2(0,1) , \quad \nu > 0$$

les problèmes de contrôle (3.1), (3.2), (3.4) ou (3.1), (3.3), (3.4) ont au moins une solution.

■

Remarque 3.1. Si on fait $\sigma = 0$ dans (3.1) les résultats du §. 2 s'appliquent. Nous prenons ici $\sigma > 0$ de sorte que ces résultats ne sont plus justifiés (essentiellement parcequ'on ne sait pas montrer l'unicité de la solution des problèmes de contrôle du théorème 3.1).

Les résultats pratiques sont malgré cela satisfaisants.

■

Les principales caractéristiques du programme sont les suivantes :
Les nombres de points de discrétisation en temps et en espace sont respectivement 50 et 16.

Les équations d'état sont résolues par une méthode de Newton, le problème de contrôle est résolu par une méthode de gradient projeté ou conjugué.

La durée $t_i - t_{i-1}$, que l'on doit connaître à t_{i-1} pour pouvoir extrapoler la mesure, est une estimation du temps de résolution du problème P_{t_i} au vu de $y(t_{i-1})$ et de l'état que l'on aurait dû avoir à t_{i-1} si le système n'avait pas été perturbé.

L'expérience montre qu'il est préférable de surestimer ce temps de calcul (donc d'appliquer peut-être plus longtemps que nécessaire l'ancien contrôle) et de prévoir les effets, éventuellement plus importants, de la perturbation constatée. En effet, on remarque que le nouveau contrôle dans le cas où il diffère de l'ancien en diffère (partie corrective du contrôle) dans les instants qui suivent t_i. Il est donc essentiel que le contrôle soit effectivement calculé avant t_i, date prévue de fin du calcul.

Les expériences dont on présente les résultats ont toutes duré 1 heure (T = 1h). Les perturbations (involontaires) étaient toujours présentes pendant ces expériences, mais de faible amplitude.

Les perturbations volontaires sont toujours de grande amplitude et repérables sur les figures.

4. Remarques finales.

Remarque 4.1. Pour que l'adaptation du contrôle soit efficace il faut que l'algorithme de résolution des problèmes P_{t_i} soit rapide. On pourrait penser que des algorithmes simplifiés conviennent mieux à ce type d'expérience temps réel. Les faits ont montré ici que des algorithmes relativement sophistiqués (par exemple au niveau du choix de la direction et du pas de descente) sont préférables : Les programmes sont longs à écrire et à mettre au point mais les temps de résolution sont plus courts.

Remarque 4.2. La méthode présentée s'est avérée particulièrement robuste vis à vis des perturbations, même de forte amplitude, de faible durée. Cela est lié au fait que lorsqu'on constate une perturbation sur l'état on suppose implicitement dans l'algorithme que la cause a disparu dès l'instant de mesure (car on écrit f=0 par exemple).

Remarque 4.3. Dans cette expérience on pouvait mesurer l'état discret complet ce qui veut dire que l'on utilise un grand nombre de sondes (16 ici). Dans SORINE [1] à l'aide des mesures faites au bord (2 sondes) sur un intervalle de temps, on estime l'état à un instant, l'étape "contrôle" de l'algorithme suivant cette estimation est la même qu'ici.

Références.

A. BAMBERGER - C. SAGUEZ - J.P. YVON [1] ; Contrôle en boucle ouverte adaptée de systèmes distribués. Rapport Laboria N° 128 (Juin 1975).

J. BARAS - D.G. LAINIOTIS [1] ; Chandrasekhar algorithms for linear time varying distributed systems. Conference on Information Sciences and Systems. (1976).

J. CASTI - L. LJUNG [1] ; Reduction of the Operator Riccati Equation. Siam J. Control Vol. 13 n° 4 July 1975.

D. LEROY - M. SORINE [1] ; Résolution numérique de l'équation de Riccati et algorithmes de Chandrasekhar. Rapport Laboria à paraître.

J.L. LIONS [1] ; Contrôle optimal de systèmes gouvernés par des équations aux dérivées partielles. DUNOD Paris 1968.

[2] ; Quelques méthodes de résolution des problèmes aux limites non linéaires. DUNOD Paris 1969.

M. NEDELEC [1] ; Thèse, Paris 1970.

M. SORINE [1] ; Thèse de Docteur-Ingénieur, à paraître.

J.P. YVON [1] ; Etude de la méthode de boucle ouverte adaptée pour le contrôle de systèmes distribués. International Conference on Control theory, Numerical Methods and Computer Systems Modelling, Rocquencourt, June 1974.

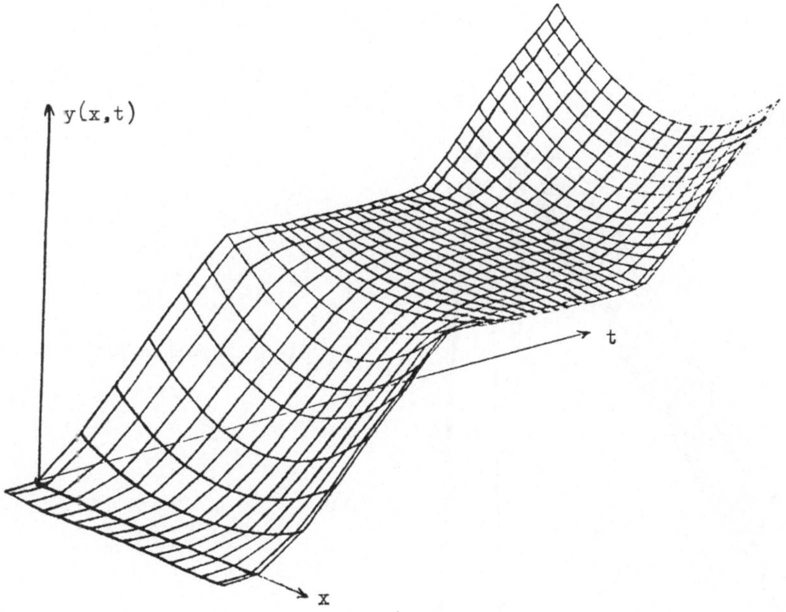

Critère $J_1(v)$: $zd(0,t) = zd(1,t) = \begin{cases} \alpha t & ; \ 0 \leq t \leq T/3 \\ \alpha T/3 & ; \ T/3 \leq t \leq 2T/3 \\ \alpha(t - T/3) & ; \ 2T/3 \leq t \leq T \end{cases}$

Ci-dessus : système non perturbé, ci-dessous : système perturbé.

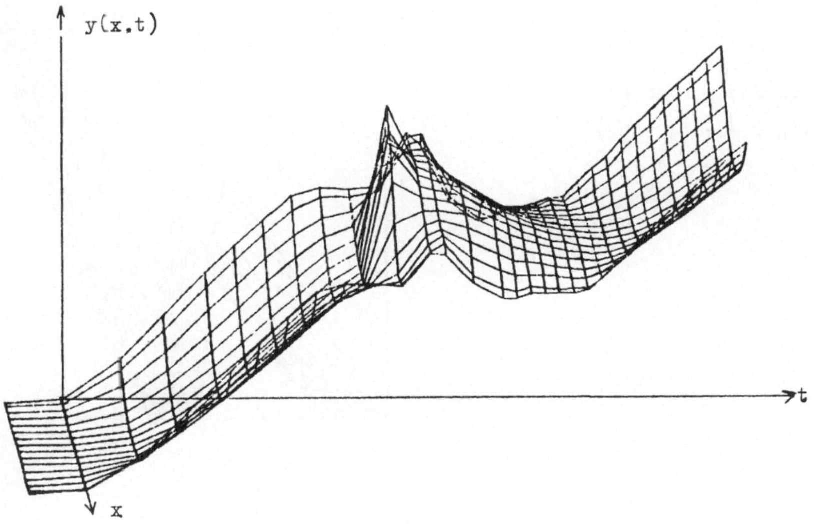

Critère $J_2(v)$ $zd_T(x) = \alpha x(1-x)$

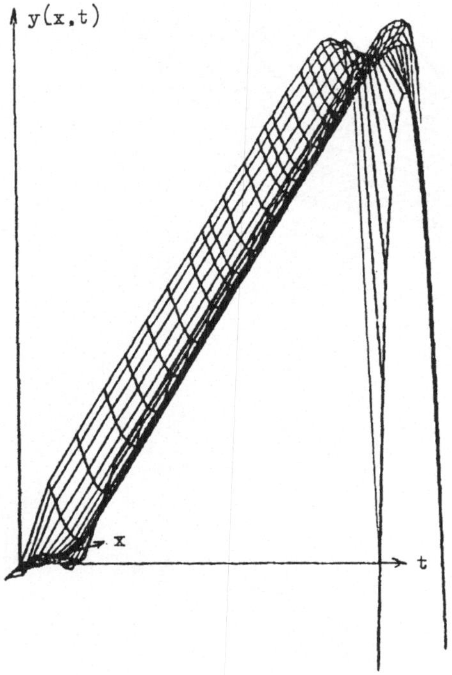

Système non perturbé

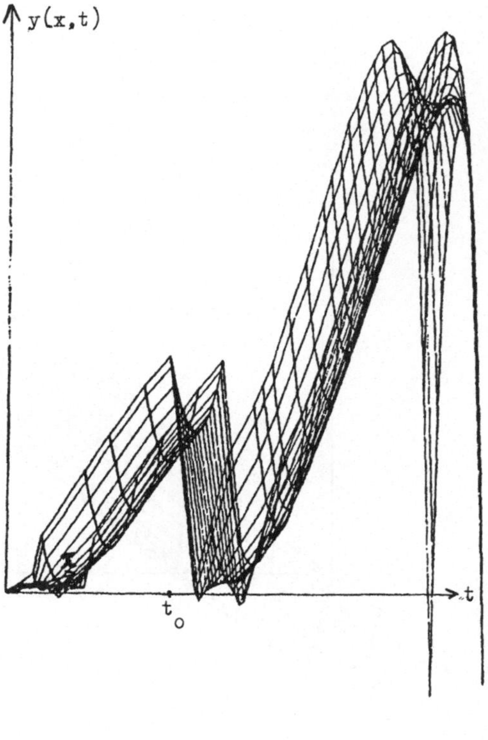

Système perturbé
(remis à zéro à t_o)

Critère $J_2(v)$ $zd_T(x) = \alpha \sin 3\Pi x$

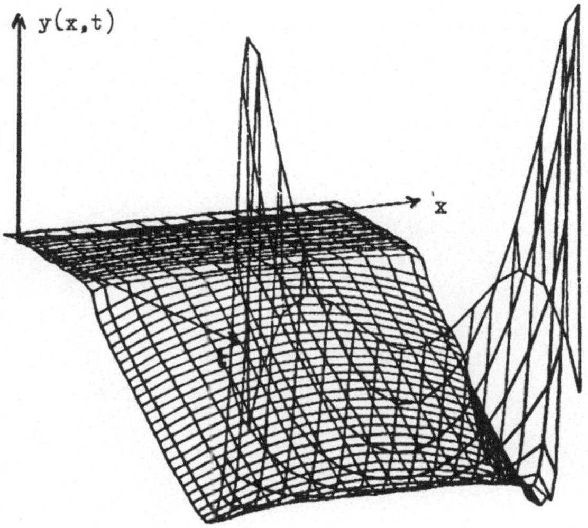

Système non perturbé

Système perturbé

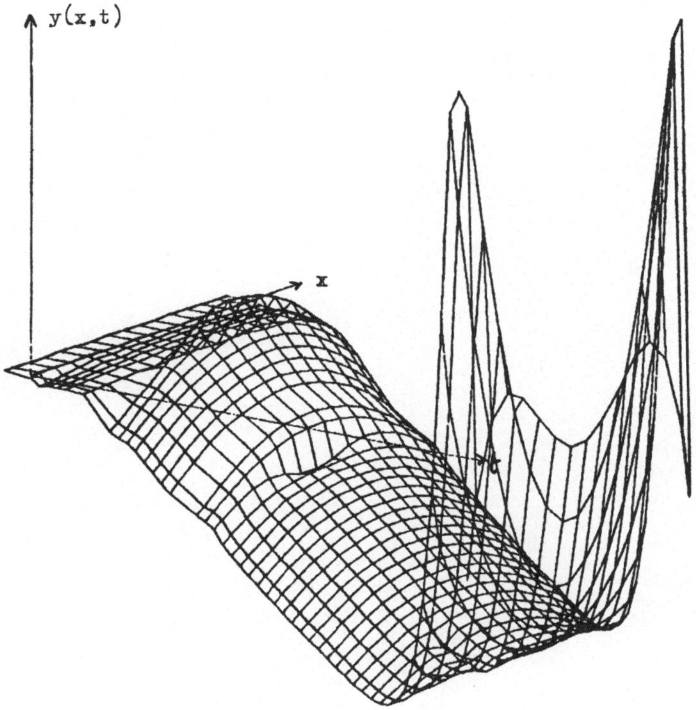

INDUSTRIAL ROBOTICS AND APPLICATIONS OF MICROPROCESSORS

ROBOTIQUE INDUSTRIELLE ET APPLICATIONS DES MICROPROCESSEURS

Control of Industrial Robots by Means of Microprocessors

E. Freund and M. Syrbe

Institut für Informationsverarbeitung in Technik und Biologie der Fraunhofer-Gesellschaft, Sebastian-Kneipp-Str. 12 - 14, 7500 Karlsruhe 1, West-Germany

Abstract

The paper deals with the investigation and simulation of various control concepts for industrial robots. The nonlinear and the linearized model of a robot with three degrees of freedom of the arm is given and the control laws for the linearized and nonlinear version are compared.

As a new approach a nonlinear control concept is presented which gains high accuracy for rapid motion of the robot and requires low computational effort. For an advanced type of robot, the actual realization of the data handling problems with microprocessors is discussed.

1. Introduction

Industrial robots are gaining an increasing attention nowadays. Many questions are of high interest in this context, for example the development of sensors, the problem of pattern recognition, the development of languages, etc. In this paper, the attention is focused to the control problems and the realisation of the data handling problems with microprocessors.

Various control concepts have been studied and partially realized in actual systems, e. g. at Stanford University [1] and MIT [2] to mention some among many others. However, there are important goals which have not been reached so far: These are the development of control concepts for high accuracy and rapid motion with low computional effort in order to create a very flexible and also from the economical point of view interesting system.

In this paper, various control concepts are investigated and realized in application to the nonlinear model of a robot with three degrees of freedom of the arm by a digital simulation. Among the considered methods is the conventional PD-controller which is used in generally available robots as well as the time-optimal controller which is realized in more advanced systems [1]. Contrary to previous work, a nonlinear control concept with nonlinear decoupling is presented here as a new approach to the solution of this problem. The results of the simulation allow a discussion about the usefulness of the various control concepts. The realisation of these concepts with microprocessors as well as the general data handling problem is considered in the last part of the paper for an advanced type of industrial robots.

2. Principal configuration and model

For the principal investigation of control strategies for an industrial robot as shown in fig. 10 (section 6) a basic configuration with three degrees of freedom of the arm is considered. The control concepts developed for this system must be of general nature to assure that they can be extended to systems with more degrees of freedom, especially to the type of robot in fig. 10. The basic system to be investigated for this purpose has one rotational and two translational joints and is shown in the (x,y)-plane in fig. 1.

This arm can be lifted along the vertical z-axis which is the third degree of freedom. This basic system itself is also of high interest because more than 70 % of all industrial robots available are of this design. The problem to be solved is the control of movement of the hand along a desired trajectory. The control of the hand itself is unrelated to this motion and is not considered in this context. The solution of the control problem mentioned above for rapid motion and high accuracy requires the exact mathematical model of the arm.

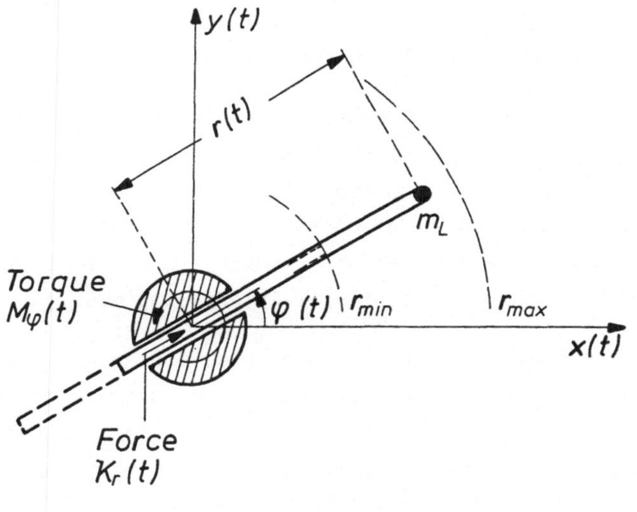

Fig. 1: Principal configuration

The most suitable coordinate system for the modelling is a cylindric system with the coordinates r(t), φ(t) and z(t). The kinetic equations of the configuration which is shown in fig. 1 with z as additional degree of freedom can be derived using the Lagrange equations. For this purpose the following notations are introduced:

The state variables are:

$$x_1(t) = r(t) \quad x_3(t) = \varphi(t) \quad x_5(t) = z(t)$$
$$x_2(t) = \dot{r}(t) \quad x_4(t) = \dot{\varphi}(t) \quad x_6(t) = \dot{z}(t) \tag{1}$$

with $r(t)$ and $z(t)$ as translational motions and $\varphi(t)$ as the angle of rotation (see fig. 1), the dot means the derivation with respect to t. The inputs are

$$u_1(t) = K_r(t) \qquad u_2(t) = M_\varphi(t)$$
$$u_3(t) = K_z^*(t) = -(m + m_L)\, g + K_z(t) \tag{2}$$

where $K_r(t)$, $M_\varphi(t)$ and $K_z(t)$ are the drives corresponding to $r(t)$, $\varphi(t)$ and $z(t)$, g is the gravity coefficient, m and m_L are the masses of the arm and the load (including the mass of the hand), respectively.

Denoting the mass and the radius of upright column (rotating with $\varphi(t)$, see fig. 1) as m^* and r^*, respectively, and the length of the arm as l, the following abbreviation is used

$$k = \frac{m^* r^{*2}}{2} + \frac{ml^2}{3}$$

Then, the system can be described by a state space representation of the form:

$$\begin{bmatrix} \dot{x}_1 \\ \dot{x}_2 \\ \dot{x}_3 \\ \dot{x}_4 \\ \dot{x}_5 \\ \dot{x}_6 \end{bmatrix} = \begin{bmatrix} x_2 \\ x_1 \cdot x_L^2 - \frac{m \cdot l}{2(m+m_L)} \cdot x_4^2 \\ x_4 \\ \frac{-2[(m+m_L)x_1 - m\frac{l}{2}]}{k - ml \cdot x_1 + (m+m_L)x_1^2} \cdot x_2 \cdot x_4 \\ x_6 \\ 0 \end{bmatrix} + \begin{bmatrix} 0 & 0 & 0 \\ \frac{1}{m+m_L} & 0 & 0 \\ 0 & 0 & 0 \\ 0 & \frac{1}{k - ml \cdot x_1 + (m+m_L) \cdot x_1^2} & 0 \\ 0 & 0 & 0 \\ 0 & 0 & \frac{1}{m+m_L} \end{bmatrix} \cdot \begin{bmatrix} u_1 \\ u_2 \\ u_3 \end{bmatrix} \tag{3a}$$

$$y_1 = x_1 \quad y_2 = x_3 \quad y_3 = x_5 \tag{3b}$$

Fig. 2 gives the physical interpretation of the model (3) together with the control which is considered later. The nonlinear term in the second row of (3a) represents the centrifugal force which couples the rotational movement with the dynamic of the translation. The torque due to the coriolis force couples the radial (translational) movement of the arm with the dynamic of the rotation while the dynamic of the translation in z-direction is uncoupled (fig. 2). The influence of the coriolis force is described by the nonlinear term in the 4th row of the state equation in (3a). For robots which are designed for re-

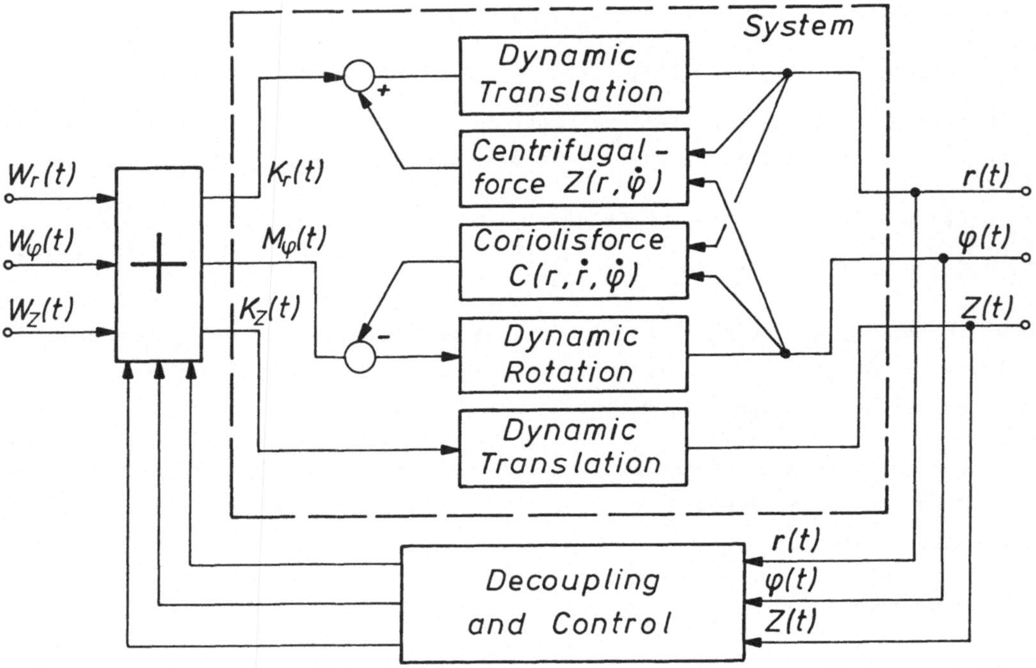

Fig. 2: Principle model structure and control

latively slow motions, these coupling terms can be neglected to some extend so that conventional controllers (like PID) lead to fairly satisfactory results. However, if the motions of the robot come to the range of human speed of motion, these terms cannot be neglected anymore which means that the nonlinear model (3) is the apropriate system representation. The nonlinear equation of motion (3) have never been used for the design of control systems for industrial robots so far. The equations employed for this purpose were usually of relatively simple nature and always linear. The linearized equations of motion can be obtained from (3) if the state variables (1) are considered with respect to a trajectory characterized by a mean radius R, a mean translational velocity V_r and a mean angular velocity V_φ which correspond to r(t), $\dot{r}$(t) and $\dot{\varphi}$(t), respectively. Then, new state variables of the linearized system are

$$\bar{x}_1(t) = r(t)-R, \quad \bar{x}_3(t) = \varphi(t), \quad \bar{x}_5(t) = z(t)$$
$$\bar{x}_2(t) = \dot{r}(t)-V_r, \quad \bar{x}_4(t) = \dot{\varphi}(t)-V_\varphi, \quad \bar{x}_6(t) = \dot{z}(t) \qquad (4)$$

This leads to the linearized equations given in (5), where $\underline{\bar{x}}(t)$ contains the state variables $\bar{x}_1(t)$ to $\bar{x}_6(t)$:

$$\dot{\underline{\bar{x}}} = \begin{bmatrix} 0 & 1 & 0 & 0 & 0 & 0 \\ a_{21} & 0 & 0 & a_{24} & 0 & 0 \\ 0 & 0 & 0 & 1 & 0 & 0 \\ a_{41} & a_{42} & 0 & a_{44} & 0 & 0 \\ 0 & 0 & 0 & 0 & 0 & 1 \\ 0 & 0 & 0 & 0 & 0 & 0 \end{bmatrix} \underline{\bar{x}} + \begin{bmatrix} 0 & 0 & 0 \\ b_{21} & 0 & 0 \\ 0 & 0 & 0 \\ 0 & b_{42} & 0 \\ 0 & 0 & 0 \\ 0 & 0 & b_{63} \end{bmatrix} \cdot \begin{bmatrix} u_1 \\ u_2 \\ u_3 \end{bmatrix} \tag{5a}$$

$$y_1 = \bar{x}_1, \quad y_2 = \bar{x}_3, \quad y_4 = \bar{x}_5 \tag{5b}$$

where: $a_{21} = V_\varphi^2 \qquad a_{24} = \frac{2V_\varphi}{(m+m_L)}[(m+m_L)R - m\frac{l}{2}]$

$$a_{41} = -2(m+m_L)V_r V_\varphi \frac{k+mlR-(m+m_L)R^2 - \frac{m^2 l^2}{2(m+m_L)}}{[k-mlR+(m+m_L)R^2]^2}$$

$$a_{42} = -\frac{2V_\varphi[(m+m_L)R-m\frac{l}{2}]}{k-mlR+(m+m_L)R^2} \qquad a_{44} = -\frac{2V_r[(m+m_L)R-m\frac{l}{2}]}{k-mlR+(m+m_L)R^2}$$

$$b_{21} = b_{63} = \frac{1}{m+m_L} \qquad b_{42} = \frac{1}{k-mlR+(m+m_L)R^2}$$

3. Design based on the linearized equations

If for the arm of the robot rapid motion (e. g. comparable to human motion) and high accuracy is required, a decoupling of the outputs $r(t)$, $\varphi(t)$ and $z(t)$ cannot be avoided anymore. A decoupling of the linearized equations of motion of a robotic arm was presented in [1] for the Stanford Arm with 3 degrees of freedom. This was done by transforming the system into Luenbergers controllability canonical form and compensation of the coupling terms via state feedback. This is, however, in general a relatively complicated approach. Due to the direct approach with the most suitable coordinate system, the equations for the decoupling of the linearized system (5) or other systems can be given without any state transformations applying e. g. [3] in the frequency domain or [4] in the time domain.

For the design of the control system, the input vector $\underline{u}(t)$ of the linearized system that contains $u_1(t)$, $u_2(t)$ and $u_3(t)$ is split into two vector where the first one related to decoupling called $\underline{u}_d(t)$ and the second one represents the control itself denoted $\underline{u}_c(t)$. This means

$$\underline{u}(t) = \underline{u}_c(t) + \underline{u}_d(t) \tag{6}$$

with $u_c = [u_{c_1}\ u_{c_2}\ u_{c_3}]'$ and $u_d = [u_{d_1}\ u_{d_2}\ u_{d_3}]'$

Introducing the new inputs of the overall system

$$\underline{w}(t) = [w_r\ \ w_\varphi\ \ w_z]' \tag{7}$$

which are the desired values or trajectories of $r(t)$, $\varphi(t)$ and $z(t)$, decoupling means that $r(t)$ effects only $w_r(t)$, $\varphi(t)$ only $w_\varphi(t)$ and $z(t)$ only $w_z(t)$. This context is shown in fig. 2 together with the physical model of the basic system. Application of wellknown decoupling theory for linear systems (e. g. [3] in the frequency domain or [4] in the time domain) leads to the following law that decouples system (5)

$$\begin{aligned}
u_{d_1}(t) &= -2V_\varphi[(m+m_L)R-m\tfrac{l}{2}]\cdot\bar{x}_4 \\
u_{d_2}(t) &= 2(m+m_L)V_rV_\varphi\frac{k+mlR-(m+m_L)R^2-\frac{m^2l^2}{2(m+m_L)}}{k-mlR+(m+m_L)R^2}\cdot\bar{x}_1 + 2V_\varphi[(m+m_L)R-m\tfrac{l}{2}]\cdot\bar{x}_2 \\
u_{d_3}(t) &= 0
\end{aligned} \tag{8}$$

There are several possibilities to design the controller for the decoupled linearized system. Pole assignement in the state space using state feedback is equivalent to the use of PD-controllers in this case as far as the characteristic equation of the overall system is concerned because there are 3 PD-controller for 6 Poles in 3 subsystems. Therefore, from both possibilities only the PD-controller is considered here. If the characteristic equations have the form

$$\begin{aligned}
\ddot{r}(t) + \alpha_{1_r}\dot{r}(t) + \alpha_{o_r}r(t) &= 0 \\
\ddot{\varphi}(t) + \alpha_{1_\varphi}\dot{\varphi}(t) + \alpha_{o_\varphi}\varphi(t) &= 0 \\
\ddot{z}(t) + \alpha_{1_z}\dot{z}(t) + \alpha_{o_z}z(t) &= 0
\end{aligned} \tag{9}$$

the PD-controllers are represented by the following equations that can be directly programmed on the computer:

$$\begin{aligned}
u_{c_1}(t) &= [(m+m_L)(\alpha_{o_r}+V_\varphi^2)](w_r-y_1)+\alpha_{1_r}(w_r-y_1)^{\bullet} \\
u_{c_2}(t) &= [k-mlR+(m+m_L)R^2]\alpha_{o_\varphi}(w_\varphi-y_2)+(\alpha_{1_\varphi}-\frac{2V_r[(m+m_L)R-m\frac{l}{2}]}{k-mlR+(m+m_L)R^2})(w_\varphi-y_2)^{\bullet} \\
u_{c_2}(t) &= (m+m_L)\alpha_{o_z}(w_z-y_3)+\alpha_{1_z}(w_z-y_3)^{\bullet}
\end{aligned} \tag{10}$$

This completes with (8) the control and decoupling of system (5) in view of (6). The actual physical system, however, is governed by the nonlinear equations (3). In practice this causes severe consequences for changing conditions: If for working procedures of the arm of the robot the movement deviates from the trajectory defined by R, V_r and V_φ in (4), then the control laws (8) and (10) loose effectiveness. This is due to the fact that in these cases decoupling is not complete anymore and the desired dynamic of the characteristic equation (9) is not reached anymore which can easily be seen from (8) and (10). Therefore, an effective control for high accuracy would require readjustment of the parameters in (8) and (10) for different working trajectories. This is a severe disadvantage of this design which is (in most cases even without decoupling) the most common form of control of robots. The simulation in section 5 demonstrates this problem.

The alternative to the PD-controller is a time-optimal controller in combination with the decoupled system (decoupling laws in (8)). For the system considered here, the time-optimal controller is a bang-bang controller which has in view of (6) with $\underline{u}_d$ from (8) the form [5]:

$$\begin{aligned} u_{c_1}(t) &= - U_r \operatorname{sgn}\left[U_r(\bar{x}_1 - w_r) + \tfrac{1}{2}|\bar{x}_2|\cdot\bar{x}_2\right] \\ u_{c_2}(t) &= - U_\varphi \operatorname{sgn}\left[U_\varphi(\bar{x}_3 - w_\varphi) + \tfrac{1}{2}|\bar{x}_4|\cdot\bar{x}_4\right] \qquad (11) \\ u_{c_3}(t) &= - U_z \operatorname{sgn}\left[U_z(\bar{x}_5 - w_z) + \tfrac{1}{2}|\bar{x}_6|\cdot\bar{x}_6\right] \end{aligned}$$

where U_r, U_φ and U_z are the applied torques of the motors. On the computer, these equations have to be programmed together with (8).

This type of control was used for the control system of the Stanford Arm [1]. However, it still contains the disadvantages of the decoupling of the linearized system (5) for changing working conditions which were described before. The time behaviour of the system itself is essentially determined by the amount of disturbances due to uncomplete decoupling. The simulation of the time-optimal controller is shown in section 5.

4. Design based on the nonlinear system representation

The disadvantages of the control concepts in section 3 which where based on the linearized system, can be avoided by application of nonlinear control theory. This was not yet used for the design of control systems for industrial robots, however, it leads to very satisfactory results.

Before application to the actual nonlinear system (3), the method is introduced without proof [6, 7].

The procedure presented is a general one and is not restricted to the application investigated here.

The nonlinear system to be considered here has the state space description

$$\underline{\dot{x}}(t) = \underline{A}(\underline{x},t) + \underline{B}(\underline{x},t)\underline{u}(t) \qquad (12a)$$

$$\underline{y}(t) = \underline{C}(\underline{x},t) + \underline{D}(\underline{x},t)\underline{u}(t) \qquad (12b)$$

where $\underline{x}(t)$ is the n-dimensional state vector, $\underline{u}(t)$ and $\underline{y}(t)$ are the m-dimensional input and output vectors, respectively, $\underline{A}(\underline{x},t)$, $\underline{B}(\underline{x},t)$, $\underline{C}(\underline{x},t)$ and $\underline{D}(\underline{x},t)$ are of compatible order. The goal of the control method is to decouple the nonlinear system and to allow arbitrary pole assignment. For this purpose a nonlinear feedback of the type

$$\underline{u}(t) = \underline{F}(x,t) + \underline{G}(\underline{x},t)\underline{w}(t) \qquad (13)$$

with $\underline{F}(x,t)$ as a m x 1 matrix and $\underline{G}(x,t)$ as a nonsingular m x m matrix and $\underline{w}(t)$ as new m-dimenisonal input vector is applied to system (12). With respect to system (12) a nonlinear operator can be defined for k = 1,2...

$$N_A^k\, C_i(\underline{x},t) = \frac{\partial}{\partial t} N_A^{k-1}\, C_i(\underline{x},t) + \left\{\frac{\partial}{\partial \underline{x}} N_A^{k-1} C_i(\underline{x},t)\right\} \underline{A}(\underline{x},t) \qquad (14)$$

where $N_A^0\, C_i(\underline{x},t) = C_i(\underline{x},t)$ and $C_i(\underline{x},t)$ is the i-th component of the vector $\underline{C}$ (i = 1,2,...,m). Another basic definition is the differential order ($\underline{D}_i$ is the i-th row vector of $\underline{D}(\underline{x},t)$)

$$d_i = 0 \quad \text{if} \quad D_i(\underline{x},t) \neq \underline{0}$$

and for $\underline{D}_i(\underline{x},t) = 0$ (15)

$$d_i = \min\left\{j: \left[\frac{\partial}{\partial \underline{x}} N_A^{j-1} C_i(\underline{x},t)\right] \underline{B}(\underline{x},t) \neq \underline{0},\ j = 1,2,\ldots n\right\}$$

System (12) is decoupled, i. e. $y_i(t)$ is only effected by $w_i(t)$ (i = 1,2,...m) if (13) is chosen in the form

$$\underline{F}(\underline{x},t) = \underline{F}^*(\underline{x},t) = -\underline{D}^{*-1}(\underline{x},t)\left[\underline{C}^*(\underline{x},t) + \underline{M}^*(\underline{x},t)\right] \qquad (16)$$

$$\underline{G}(\underline{x},t) = \underline{G}^*(\underline{x},t) = \underline{D}^{*-1}(\underline{x},t)\ \underline{\Lambda} \qquad (17)$$

The matrices in (11) are given as follows [6, 7]: $\underline{D}^*(\underline{x},t)$ is an m x m matrix with the i-th row (i = 1,2,...m)

$$\underline{D}_i(\underline{x},t) = \begin{cases} \underline{D}_i(\underline{x},t) & \text{for } d_i = 0 \\ \left[\frac{\partial}{\partial \underline{x}} N_A^{d_i-1} C_i(\underline{x},t)\right] \underline{B}(\underline{x},t) & \text{for } d_i \neq 0 \end{cases} \qquad (18)$$

$\underline{C}^*(\underline{x},t)$ is an m-dimensional vector with the i-th component (i = 1,2,...m)

$$C_i^*(\underline{x},t) = N_A^{d_i}\, C_i(\underline{x},t) \qquad (19)$$

The i-th component of $\underline{M}^*(\underline{x},t)$ has the form

$$M_i(\underline{x},t) = \begin{cases} 0 & \text{for } d_i = 0 \\ \sum\limits_{k=i}^{d_i-1} \alpha_{k,i} \, N_A^k C_i(\underline{x},t) & \text{for } d_i \neq 0 \end{cases} \tag{20}$$

The m x m matric $\underline{\Lambda}$ is a diagonal matrix with the elements λ_i (i = 1,2,...m). Application of (13) with (16) and (17) to (12) leads to the overall behaviour of all input-output pairs $y_i(t)$, $w_i(t)$ (i = 1,2,...m)

$$y_i^{(d_i)} + \alpha_{d_i-1,i} y_i^{(d_i-1)} + \ldots + \alpha_{o,i} y_i = \lambda_i \, w_i \tag{21}$$

where the $\alpha_{k,i}$ and λ_i are constants that can be arbitrarily chosen in $\underline{M}^*$ and $\underline{\Lambda}$. The decoupling itself is achieved by (17) in connection with the first part of the feedback (16) which is

$$\underline{F}_1^*(\underline{x},t) = -\underline{D}^{*-1}(\underline{x},t) \cdot \underline{C}^*(\underline{x},t) \tag{22}$$

while the pole assignment of the decoupled system is obtained by the second part

$$\underline{F}_2^*(\underline{x},t) = -\underline{D}^{*-1}(\underline{x},t) \cdot \underline{M}^*(\underline{x},t) \tag{23}$$

Application of this nonlinear decoupling theory to a nonlinear system as represented in (3), gives the following control laws which include decoupling as well as pole assigrement:

$$\begin{aligned} u_1(t) &= -\left[(m+m_L)\cdot x_1 - m\tfrac{l}{2}\right]\cdot x_4^2 + (m+m_L)\left[-\alpha_{1_r}\cdot x_2 - \alpha_{o_r}\cdot x_1 + \lambda_r \cdot w_r\right] \\ u_2(t) &= \left\{\left[2(m+m_L)\cdot x_1 - ml\right]\cdot x_2 - \alpha_{1_\varphi}\left[k - ml\cdot x_1 + (m+m_L)\cdot x_1^2\right]\right\}\cdot x_4 + \left[k - ml\cdot x_1 + (m+m_L)\cdot x_1^2\right] \\ &\qquad \left[-\alpha_{o_\varphi}\cdot x_3 + \lambda_\varphi \cdot w_\varphi\right] \\ u_3(t) &= (m+m_L)\left[-\alpha_{1_z}\cdot x_6 - \alpha_{o_z}\cdot x_5 + \lambda_z \cdot w_z\right] \end{aligned} \tag{24}$$

This yields the overall behaviour:

$$\begin{aligned} \ddot{r}(t) + \alpha_{1_r}\,\dot{r}(t) + \alpha_{o_r}\,r(t) &= \lambda_r\,w_r(t) \\ \ddot{\varphi}(t) + \alpha_{1_\varphi}\,\dot{\varphi}(t) + \alpha_{o_\varphi}\,\varphi(t) &= \lambda_\varphi\,w_\varphi(t) \\ \ddot{z}(t) + \alpha_{1_z}\,\dot{z}(t) + \alpha_{o_z}\,z(t) &= \lambda_z\,w_z(t) \end{aligned} \tag{25}$$

The nonlinear control laws (24) can be programmed on the computer without any additional difficulties in comparison to the programming of the linear control

laws given in section 3. The actual computer time for the processing of the nonlinear control law (24) is only 30 % higher than the computer time needed for the PD-controller plus linear decoupling (eqns. (10) and (8)) or for the time-optimal controller plus linear decoupling (eqns. (11) and (8)). The nonlinear control presented here avoids the disadvantages of the PD-controller and the time-optimal controller with linear decoupling which were discussed in section 3. Contrary to these control systems the nonlinear control law (24) guarantees complete decoupling and invariance of the desired dynamics of the overall system for all trajectories in various working processes. This nonlinear approach is a general one and can be applied to other configurations and robots with more degrees of freedom.
The simulation of the results is shown in section 5.

5. Digital Simulation

For the digital simulation of the various control concepts (section 3 and 4) in connection with the nonlinear system (3), the block-oriented language DISKOS for the simulation of continuous systems was used on the Siemens 4004 computer. As basic system an actual design of a robot was simulated that is described by equations (3) with the parameters $m = 20$ kg, $l = 1,5$ m, $m^* = 40$ kg, $r^* = 0,2$ m. The load applied to the arm was $m_L = 15$ kg.

For the display of the different behaviour of the various control concepts, the movement of the arm in the (x,y)-plane (fig. 1) was selected while the value of the third degree of freedom, the lifting along the vertical z-axis, was kept constant. The figures 3 to 9 present the results of the digital simulation, which were produced from the original hardcopies of the graphic display. Fig. 3 shows the desired trajectory in the (x,y)-plane, which gives via a transformation the input values $w_r(t)$ and $w_\varphi(t)$, while w_z is kept constant. The hand point goes from the beginning of the trajectory to the end in 17,5 sec (the rational movement needs 8,5 sec) which means that the translational and rotational speed are in a quite normal range with respect to working procedures. The response of the nonlinear system (3) in combination with various controllers and linear and nonlinear decoupling is displayed in figures 4 to 9. These responses to the desired trajectory in fig. 3 represent the actual values of $r(t)$ and $\varphi(t)$ which are plotted via a transformation in the (x,y)-plane (see fig. 1) while z is constant. To show the deviations between the desired and the actual values, all figures 4 to 9 contain the desired trajectory.

The plots in figures 4, 6 and 8 are based on the various controllers in connection with linear decoupling (control laws $\underline{u}_d(t)$ (8), always in application to the nonlinear model (3)), while figures 5, 7 and 9 show the behaviour to nonlinear decoupling (in the nonlinear feedback (13) the part (17) in connection with (22)).

From fig. 4 it can be seen that the PD-controller (10) together with linear decoupling is not very satisfactory because of the big deviations and the strong overshooting. The overshooting happens in spite of the fact that the PD-controller was adjusted to aperiodic behaviour for a similar but somewhat simpler trajectory. The aperiodic behaviour itself is extremly important for industrial robots because by overshooting (as shown in fig. 4) the arm of the robot may be demaged by hitting obstacles, or the assembling parts or tools may be kicked away. Fig. 5 shows that this behaviour can be extremly improved by application of nonlinear decoupling. This is due to the reduction of disturbances which was explained in the discussion of the control concepts in sections 3 and 4.

The behaviour of the time-optimal controller in fig. 6 and fig. 7 reveals this improvement to some extend as well, especially in the last phase of the trajectory, because the nonlinear decoupling (fig. 7) avoids the very frequent switching and the oscillation at the endpoint.

Because of the most efficient use of the available torques of the motors, the time-optimal controller with nonlinear feedback proves as good solution for transportation tasks (for instance) with medium requirement on accuracy.

Fig. 8 shows the response of the system by application of the nonlinear controller (in the nonlinear feedback (13) the part (23)) and linear decoupling. Here, the effects of linear decoupling can be seen very clearly, because there is no overshooting at the endpoint but strong deviations along the trajectory. Fig. 9 demonstrates the efficiency of the nonlinear controller with nonlinear feedback (eqns. (16) and (17)) which led to the control laws (24). The actual movement of the arm of the robot is perfectly matched with the desired trajectory. This behaviour as shown in the simulation can also be reached for faster motions and other forms of trajectories without any readjustement of the controller. This was pointed out in the discussion of section 4. It seems that this new nonlinear control strategy and the combination of the time-optimal controller with nonlinear decoupling is a very useful concept for highly advanced robots. The approach itself is a general one and is also applicable to other configurations than the considered one, where it is of special advantage for robotic systems with a relatively high number of joints.

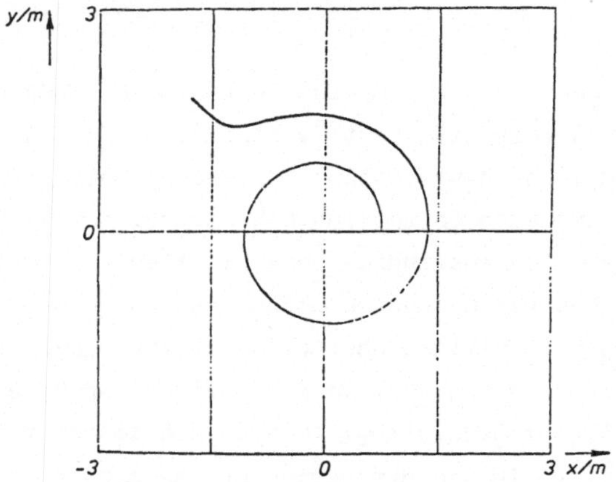

Fig. 3: Desired trajectory

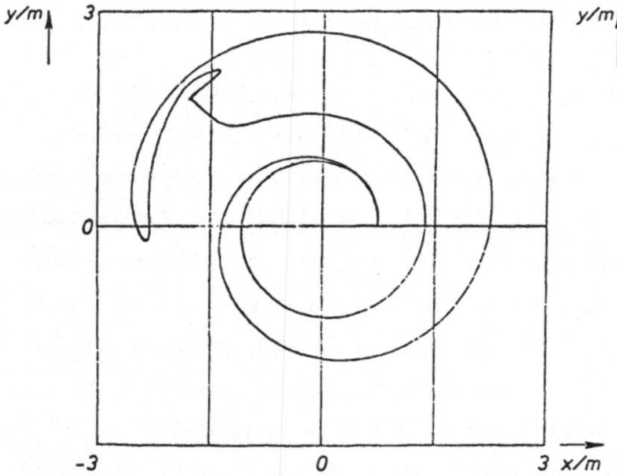

Fig. 4: Response for the PD-controller and linear decoupling

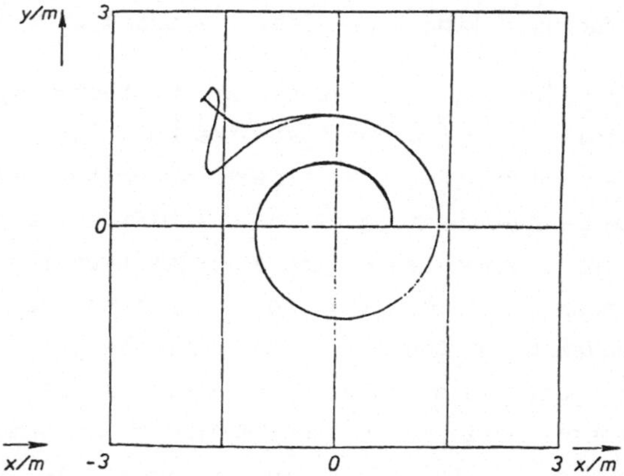

Fig. 5: Response for the PD-controller and nonlinear decoupling

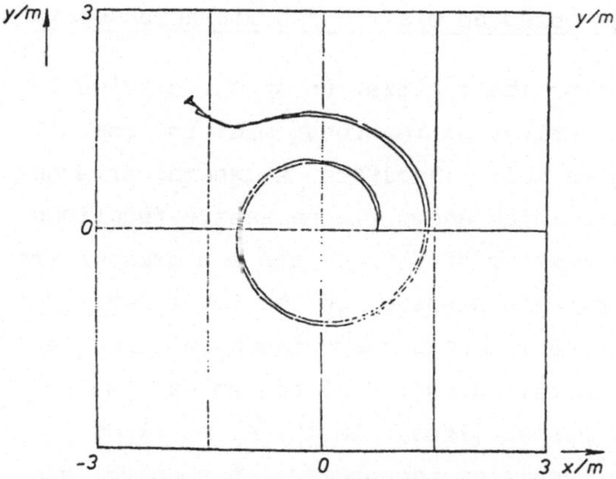

Fig. 6: Response for the time-optimal controller and linear decoupling

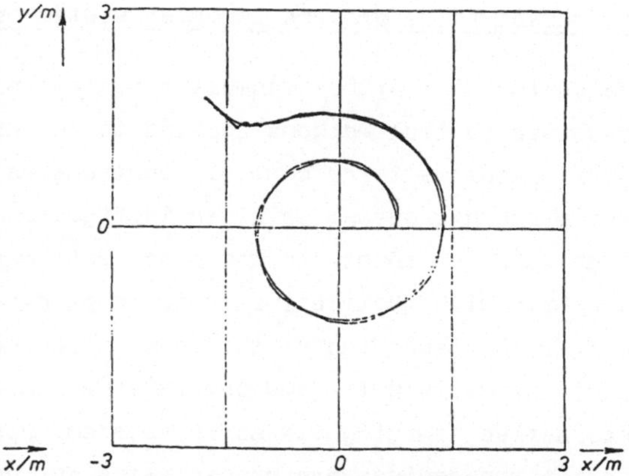

Fig. 7: Response for the time-optimal controller and nonlinear decoupling

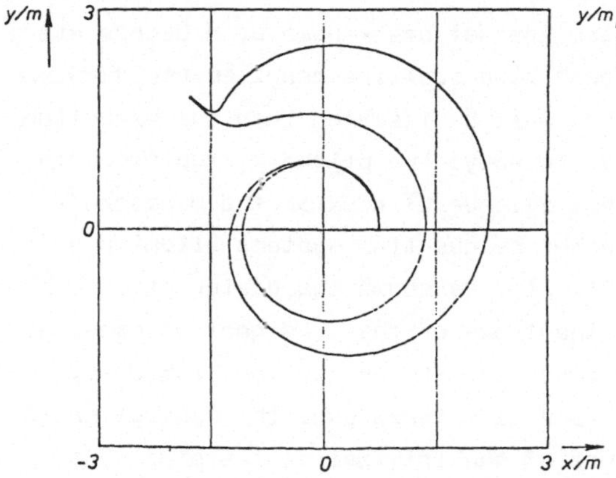

Fig. 8: Response for the nonlinear controller and linear decoupling

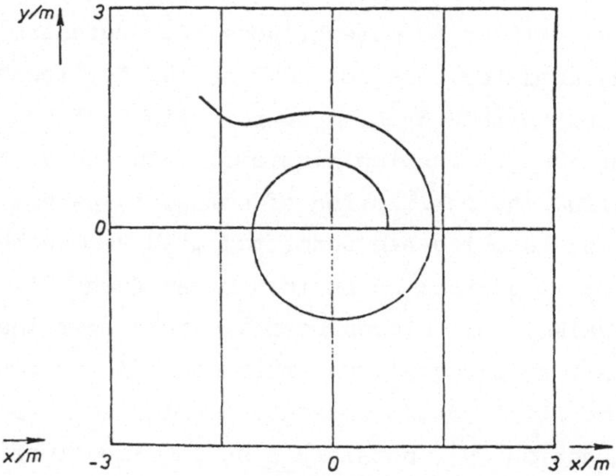

Fig. 9: Response for the nonlinear controller and nonlinear decoupling

6. Concept for a process computer system based on distributed microprocessors

The design of a process computer system for the realization of the previously described control methods applied to the drives of the robot must include all other measurement and control functions as well. Therefore, a general arrangement of such a system is given in fig. 10 which shows all necessary functions of an advanced robot. In the upper left quarter of fig. 10, arm and gripper are presented with their drive controls as described above. In the lower left quarter the recording of the working procedure is shown with teach-in and subsequent automatic path- and parameter optimization (solid lines) as well as interactive learning via screen-system (dashed lines). In the upper right quarter the devices are concentrated for position measurement, for coordinate transformation of picture cells and pattern as well as for the subsequent preprocessing. The TV-cameras are adjustable with respect to position and focal distance via drives and position controllers. These position signals are fed into the coordinate transformation automatically. In the lower right quarter of fig. 10, the tool- and obstacle recognition is shown following the preprocessing. These extensive signal processing problems which all set high standards with respect to on-line data processing, require an adequately adjusted design of the computer system.

Centralized computers, possibly protected against break-down by a second stand-by computer, are not well suited for these high realtime requirements, because considerable program coordination efforts must be inserted into the execution of the application programs, compulsory. Nowadays low priced microprocessors allow the realization of computer systems by several distributed microprocessors which are connected with each other by bus line systems allowing a mutual protection against break-down [8]. Fig. 11 shows the design of such a system. Four microprocessors take over the tasks of the TV-signal processing, pattern recognition, drive control and recording of the working procedure. The fifth system presented on the left hand side takes over the control panel function [9], possibly also the functions of the interactive learning. The sixth system presented at the right hand side permits on-line dialog programming language. This system, which is possibly connected only during the installation period and afterwards removed, serves for the economical programming of the distributed microprocessors. Here, for various system states the distribution of the required program modules must be determined by language elements during the design process. This yields reconfiguration properties of the computer system. The same applies to the replacement of not accessible signals (corresponding to program variables). Concerning this problem an investigation of existing program languages proved that the easiest approach is an extension of the program language PEARL [10]. This language separates each program into a "system devision"(for determination of supply of the program variables via I - O devices) and a "problem division"(for determination of the operation) [11]. The mentioned requirements can be fulfilled by adding preferably a "station division" for the determination of the station characteristic (fig. 12, STATION...STAEND) and a "load division" for the determination of loading and reconfiguration strategy (fig. 12, LOAD...LODEND). Further details would be beyond the scope of this paper, the person concerned with this subject is refered to [10].

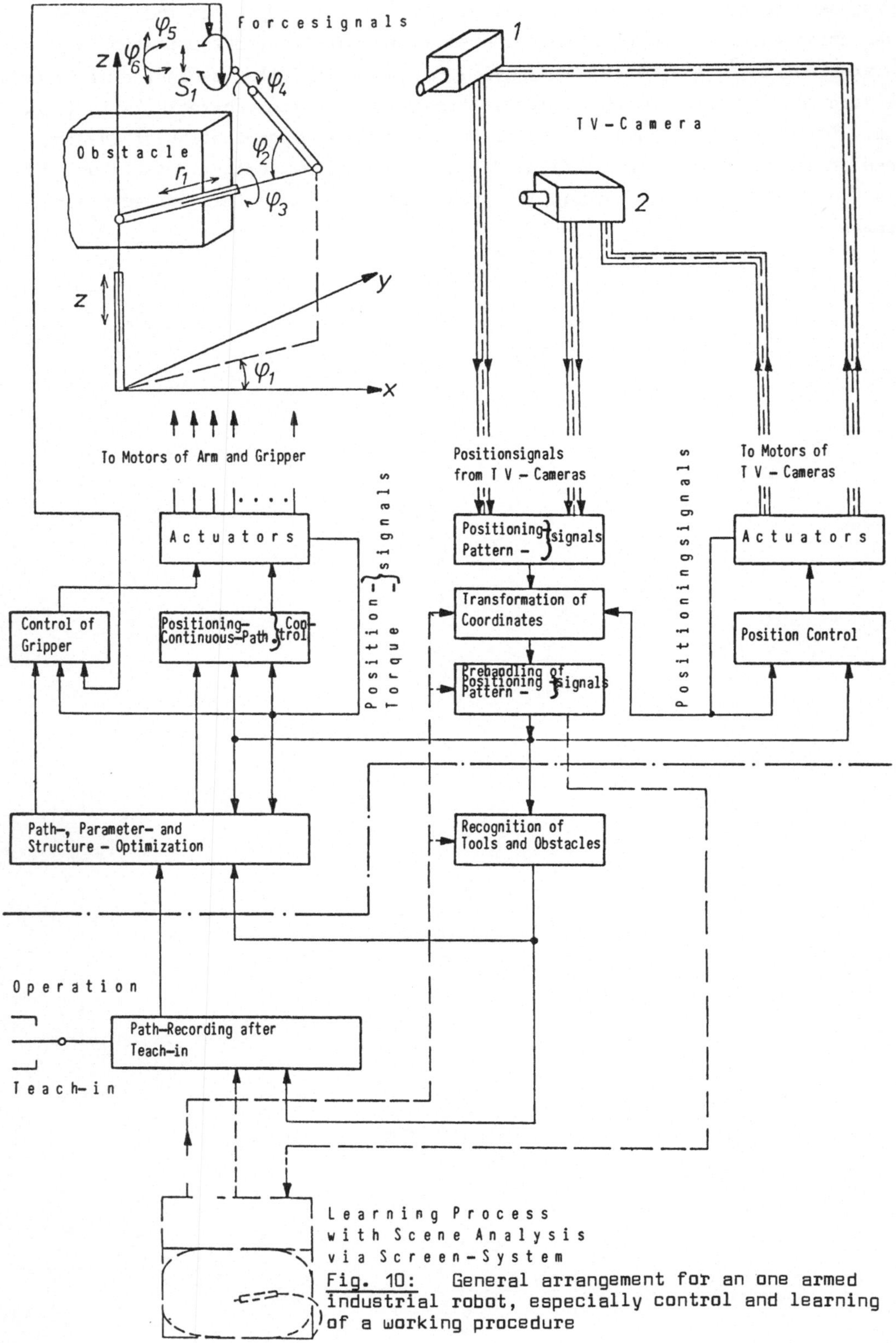

Fig. 10: General arrangement for an one armed industrial robot, especially control and learning of a working procedure

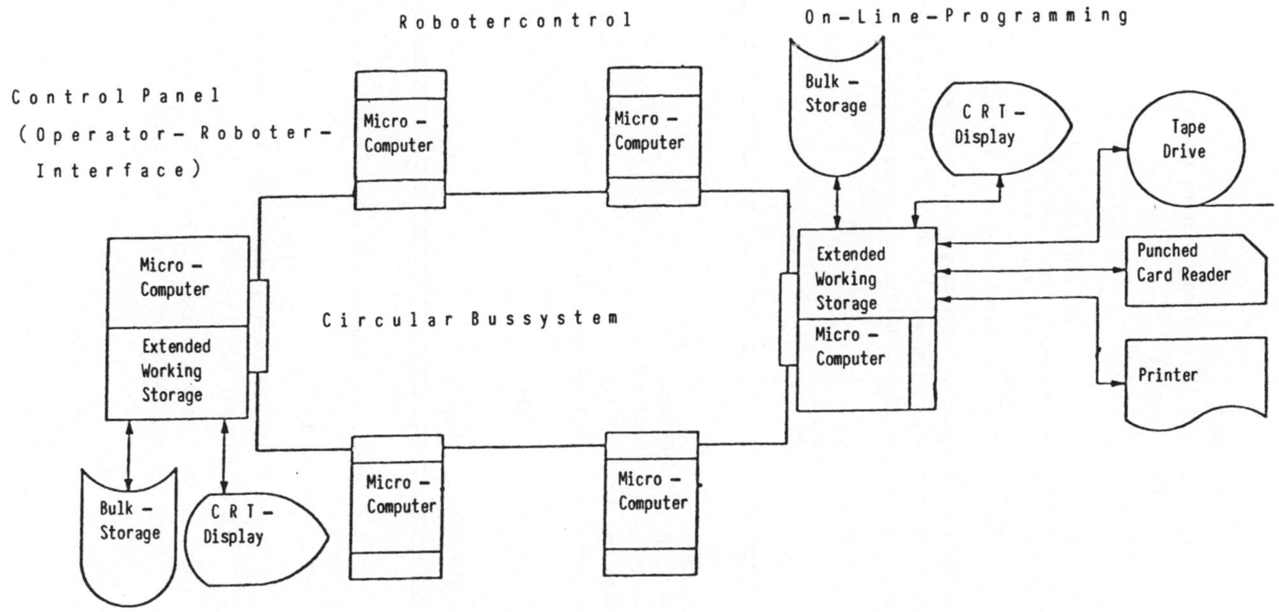

Fig. 11: Structure of a distributed real time computer system

```
STATION;

     NAME = station identifier (name);
     KEY = lower global address limit, upper global address limit;
     TYPE = type identifier (e. g. number)
     STATE = status identifier (name)
     DEVICEn = name,
               DEVADDR: (global addresses of the device registers),
               DRIVER: (external references of the driver program),
               CHANID: identifiers (names) for the process
               BITID : signal connections,
               MODE  : identifiers for the operating mode of the device;

     OSRES = specification of the resident operating system functions;
     OSMIC = specification of the microprogrammed operating system functions;
     OSPROC = operating system functions available as procedures;

     NAME = ... further stations ...

STAEND;
```

STATION-Division

```
MODULE LIBRARY name;
LOAD;
     NORMAL TO station name PRIO number,
            :/* MULTIPLE LINES ALLOWED */
            TO station name PRIO number;
     STATE = status identifier TO station name PRIO number [RESIDENT];
                          :
     /* MULTIPLE"STATE"-LINES ALLOWED*/
LODEND;
```

LOAD-Division ([...] = option)

```
SYSTEM;
name for          { - >  }
process variable: { < - >} device name, connection identifier, MODE = mode identifier,
                  { < -  }
                  /*1ST ALTERNATIVE*/

                  { - >  } device name, connection identifier, MOD = mode identifier,
                  { < - >} [CORR = adjusting expression],
                  { < -  }
                  /*FURTHER ALTERNATIVES IF EFFICIENT*/
                       REP = {value/PROCEDURE: name/ TASK: name} ;

SYSEND;

{....} : one of the alternatives must be used,

[....] : brackets include optional specifications
```

SYSTEM-Division

Fig. 12: Extensions of a higher level language for programming distributed computer systems

Acknowledgement

We thank Dipl.-Ing. H. Hoyer for performing most of the digital simulation and for some extension of the model- and control equations.

References

[1] Kahn, M.E.; Roth, B., "The Near-Minimum-Time Control of Open-Loop Articulated Kinematic Chains." Transaction of the ASME, Journal of Dynamic Systems, Measurement, and Control, September 1971, pp. 164 - 172.

[2] Whitney, D.E., "Resolved Motion Rate Control of Manipulators and Human Prostheses." IEEE-Transactions, Vol. MMS-10, June 1969, pp. 47 - 53.

[3] Mesarović, M.D., "The Control of Multivariable Systems", John Wiley & Sons, Inc., New York · London, 1960.

[4] Falb, P.L.; Wolovich, W.A., "Decoupling in the Design and Synthesis of Multivariable Control Systems." IEEE Transactions, Vol. AC-12, December 1967, pp. 651 - 659.

[5] Hsu, J.C.; Meyer, A.U., "Modern Control Principles and Applications." Mc-Graw-Hill, New York, 1968.

[6] Freund, E., "Decoupling and Pole Assignment in Nonlinear Systems." Electronics Letters, Vol. 9, No. 16, 9th August 1973, pp. 373 - 374.

[7] Freund, E., "The Structure of Decoupled Nonlinear Systems." INT. J. CONTROL, Vol. 21, No. 3, 1975, pp. 443 - 450.

[8] Syrbe, M., "Höhere Zuverlässigkeit von Prozeßrechensystemen und niedrigere Peripheriekosten durch verteilte Mikroprozessoren." Regelungstechnik, 1974, Heft 9, S. 264 - 268.

[9] Grimm, R., "Autonomous I/O-Colour-Screen-System for Process-Control with Virtual Keyboards Adapted to the Actual Task." Proceedings of the International Symposium "Monitoring Behaviour and Supervisory Control." NATO Scientific Affairs Division, Berchtesgaden, März 1976.

[10] Steusloff, H., "Hardware Structures and Software for Distributed Computer Control Systems." Proceedings of the Third Annual Advanced Control Conf., Purdue University, 1976, Control Engineering, S. 19 - 48.

[11] Eichenauer, B., et al., "PEARL, eine prozeß- und experimentorientierte Programmiersprache." Angew. Informatik 9/73, S. 363 - 372.

CATEGORIZATION AND STATUS OF ASSEMBLY RESEARCH*

J.L. Nevins, D.E. Whitney, et. al.
The Charles Stark Draper Laboratory, Inc.

INTRODUCTION

The advancement and application of any manufacturing technique requires two research issues to be resolved. First, the technique must be understood. That is, there must exist mathematical models of the technique's performance which have been experimentally verified. Second, the relation between the technique and other manufacturing processes with which it will work must be understood so that the new technique can be integrated with the rest of the factory. As these steps are accomplished for more processes, there will emerge integrated factories of a new kind.

Industrial assembly research is currently wrestling with the first set of issues--obtaining basic understanding of the process. This contrasts sharply with the status of material processing techniques: cutting, forming and molding. Here there is a large body of theory and verification, so that the research issues today focus on a.) organizing individual material processing machines into what are called flexible manufacturing cells, b.) controlling the flow of work in these cells, and c.) integrating the cells' operations into the larger factory. This includes study of computer-aided-design of complex parts, automatic reduction of these designs into work plans, schedules and routing sheets, and automatic supervision of the work flow. Assembly research is still in its infancy and is not ready for the integration effort, although the outlines of the research issues are emerging (Reference 1).

At present there are two ways of assembling things--by people or by special purpose machines. A special machine consists of a number of workstations arranged in a line or circle, and is typically a one-of-a-kind device built to assemble one product or subassembly for its entire productive life. The workstations represent the extreme of specialization: Each station performs exactly one function (feed, attach, check, etc.) on exactly one part. The stations' motions are simple and are fixed to a pattern determined by driving cams and linkages. It is therefore difficult to change the machine to accommodate changes in the product or to recover much value if the product goes out of production and the machine must be scrapped. On newer machines it is possible to assemble different models of the same product as long as the differences between models can be kept transparent to the machine.

Assembly is a positioning problem and these machines accomplish assembly by getting the parts to the right positions the first time. Great time and effort are expended in constructing these machines to the accuracy required to do this. Ironically, this effort is not sufficient: the parts themselves are too variable to allow perfectly repeatable machine operation to occur, and no machine can be built

*This work is supported by National Science Foundation Grant no. APR74-18173-A02

without errors. The design of a machine is based on the manufacturer's description of the parts to be assembled. When complete, the machine is first operated with real parts and usually it does not work correctly. There ensures a lengthy period of debugging while the machine and the parts are studied to locate the cause of the failures, which are usually due to differences between real parts and the original specification or design changes in the parts. Even when the machine is finally tuned it will still not function 20% to 35% of the time mainaly due to jams caused by faulty parts.

Poeple represent the opposite extreme in flexibility. They can easily adapt to changes in product, product design, or model mixes, and require much less in the amount and accuracy of the tools and fixtures which aid them. Too much variety in model mix, too much tedium or specialization in the work, or fatigue can cause people to make assembly errors: using the wrong part, leaving a fastener too loose, scratching a fine surface, and so on. Much effort thus is currently being put into redesign of jobs and working conditions to improve what might be called the psychological environment of the workplace.

One should not be trapped by the simple notion that research into assembly machines can result in elimination of people from the workplace. Rather this kind of research seeks to develop a scientific base for the field of assembly and to define and explore the new manufacturing options posed by these systems. It simply is not possible to replace people totally with technological devices at this time or for a number of decades. Designers ill-conceive many systems on the premise that people are doing a fairly simple assembly task only to later find that they were not only assembling but also inspecting or reworking the pieces during the very short time they had them under their control. New assembly systems are merely the first step on the way to understanding the very complex processes of manufacturing and promise to be an alternative to present systems. Like present systems, they will have their regions (volume, batch size, piece part tolerances, size, etc.) where they will be economically viable and regions where they will not!

The goals of assembly research are to better understand the process of putting pieces together (applicable to manual assembly and special purpose machines as well as to new approaches) and to explore ways of creating machines which overcome existing techniques' shortcomings. Such machines would share, to some degree, people's flexibility, tolerance of error in parts and fixtures, and speed of "training", and would share special machines' reproducibility. If equipped with sensors to monitor the interactions between parts and extra motion capability to alter the parts' relative position during attachment, these machines could protect delicate parts, compensate for errors in parts and jigs, and keep track of their own performance. Thus we are talking about quite a new kind of machine: it will be <u>adaptable</u>, capable of sensing and responsing to changes in the parts, jigs and work environment, and programmable, that is, capable of being taught different tasks.

The principal research issues fall into two areas:

a. part mating phenomena: this involves systematic modelling and experimental verification of the events which occur as parts interact during assembly;it requires identification of the essential variables which govern the process so that economical machines capable of mating parts reliably can be specified in an engineering sense.

b. programmability: here the requirement is to understand how to design workstations specialized enough to be economical but not so specialized as to be inflexible, how to arrange such stations into systems complete with equipment which feeds the parts to the stations, transports work from station to station, and controls the actions of stations and system; these actions will be complex, perhaps computer controlled in contrast to the rigid linkage and cam arrangement of special machines.

It is programmability which gives these new machines the ability to learn new tasks and permits their workstations to perform several assembly actions on the same product, as people do and as special machines cannot. The number of stations can therefore be tailored to the required production volume. This makes programmable assembly machines both technologically and economically different from special machines; thus new economic models must be developed to describe them and allow them to be compared with present assembly methods.

RESEARCH STATUS

A. Parts Mating Phenomena

Parts mating phenomena is a name for all the events which occur as pieces are assembled to each other. The pieces do not go together by themselves, of course, which means that any assembly machine (people, too, for that matter) must execute some engineered strategy which is designed to put the pieces together.

Effective assembly strategies must enable the piece-parts to move slightly relative to each other as they slide together or permit their relative motions to be divided into stages marked by changes in direction of motion or applied force. During relative motion, the pieces typically touch one another, setting up contact forces. It has been concluded that any technique which provides for specific relative part motion in response to contact forces should be regarded as an adaptive assembly strategy. Some strategies can be implemented merely by spring-loading the parts within their jigs, while others can be implemented by sensing the contact forces and torques and actively moving the parts in response to the sensory inputs so as to guide the pieces through the various stages of the assembly motion. The former is called the passive strategy approach while the latter is called the active strategy approach.

The main determinant of which type of strategy will succeed is presumed to be the relative error between the parts just as the assembly action begins. Further, it is reasonable to expect that more sensing and active control will be necessary if the initial relative errors are larger. If the cost and inflexibility of jigging can be tolerated, then a passive strategy is likely to be the fastest in execution, if it will work at all. Active strategies appear, at this writing, to be slower, althouth research underway could change that.

To determine how to resolve the speed-jigging-flexibility cost tradeoff requires an economic evaluation because, in principle, an assembly machine designer can spend money for jigs and fixtures to reduce the likely relative error. Further, this tendency toward what might be called task structuring is in large part responsible for industrial efficiency, although it makes restructuring more difficult. Thus, as we discuss part mating strategies, we must keep the economic factors in mind. They will be discussed later in the paper.

To attack the part mating problem scientifically involves analyzing the geometry of idealized task situations and determining what contact forces, moments and friction forces will occur in response to specific relative part positions. As an example of this analytical process, consider the range of situations shown in Figure 1, describing the common "peg in hole" problem. In this figure the amount of relative error increases from left to right and the difficulty of the task depends on the presence or absence of chamfers as well as other variables to be explained. At the left, the relative error is so small that the pieces go together with no sensing or compliance required. The success of the insertion can be predicted from a geometric analysis of the shapes of the pieces which will be given later. To reduce the initial error to this narrow range requires a rigid workstation constructed specifically for this purpose and carefully adjusted on site-the special machine approach.

The next two cases presume that the error is large enough so that the peg will encounter a two point contact (i.e., the peg touches both sides of the hole) part way down or the peg may strike the chamfer on the hole. Holding the peg compliantly may suffice here. The necessary analysis now extends beyond geometry to include friction effects. If a system can be implemented for these errors a system designer would have the options available to him of assembling workpieces which are difficult to jig accurately or of creating workstations which need not be dedicated for life to one part.

Undoubtedly, there are errors so large that spring loading is not enough. Active control becomes necessary. Either the peg misses the chamfer or there is no chamfer. (In absolute terms the error may nevertheless be rather small, a few thousandths of an inch. What matters is the relative error in relation to the parts' geometry.) For these cases geometric and friction analyses must be supplemented by dynamic considerations of sensors and servomechanisms.

Two major classes of active strategies have been recognized (Reference 2). One is called "logic branching" and the other "information". Logic branching consists of enumerating the cases of relative position which could occur and programming a sequence of test moves to determine which case is in effect. The tests are a series of move-and-bump cycles often requiring only binary sensing but typically taking time. Not only have many Artificial Intelligence laboratory experiments used move-and-bump (e.g., the Stanford University water pump demonstration (ref. 11) and the University of Edinburgh Machine Intelligence work (ref. 12)), but the Hitachi Hi-Ti hand does also (refs. 13 and 14). Each of these typically takes three to five seconds to accomplish a chamfered peg-hole insertion, although the details of the strategies and the amounts of initial error are different.

The information strategy concept strives to use force-torque data from the assembly action itself to direct the fine motions, and to eliminate test motions where possible. Detailed analysis of the interactions between parts is necessary so that error conditions can be recognized directly without test detours. The goal is to accomplish insertion in about one second, a time which economic analysis has indicated is necessary (reference 15).

To implement active fine motion strategies for cases of larger error (two point contact, hitting chamfer) or more complex tasks (screw thread mating, push and twist) we have developed an analytically-based strategy for linking force-torque measurements to fine motions. This strategy is called Accommodation (References 6,7,8). It consists of measuring the forces and torques in an end point or hand-oriented coordinate frame and prescribing fine motion velocities in this same frame on the basis of those measurements (Figure 2). A technique called Resolved Motion Rate Control is then used to convert the hand coordinate velocities to commands to the "arm" joints (References 9 and 10). The core of the RMRC technique is that the coordinate frames of interest are task related, not arm dependent.

The importance of the accommodation idea is that it poses the force-torque assembly method in terms of an analytical description of how the gripped part will move when forces act on it. Initially we though that all assembly tasks required active accommodation. Now we know that there is a whole range of techniques for passively or actively providing limited types of force-motion relationships. For technical and economic reasons, it is of interest to know when the simpler strategy will suffice and when it will not. When it does not suffice, active accommodation is the next simplest thing to try, but it may be sufficient to actively control only one or two degrees of freedom, if they are correctly oriented. Friction forces, however, may mask the forces needed to be measured and, if friction is severe enough, the pieces may stop sliding together and jam instead.

The basis for a detailed geometric analysis of insertion is the realization that the peg can wobble back and forth inside the hole. Figure 3 defines the necessary variables: insertion depth ℓ, peg diameter d, hole diameter D, and wobble angle θ. Figure 4 plots the resulting relations between these variables in terms of the dimensionless clearance ratio c, while data from typical parts is shown in Figure 5. In addition this analysis can be applied to real parts based on their design specifications and allows an assembly machine designer to determine the amount of initial error he can tolerate in the assembly of specific parts.

Regardless of how a designer approaches the error control problem, there remain cases where two point contact is unavoidable. What will happen then? If the pieces can continue sliding together and if in so doing they do not damage each other, then the limits on allowable error can be relaxed.

If two point contact can be tolerated then it is clear from Figure 1 that the top of the peg must be allowed to reposition itself passively or must be actively repositioned in order to conform to the hole's geometry. In addition, we must analyze the force-friction behavior of the pieces to better understand the assembly process. Force friction theory will be discussed first, followed by an analysis of passive compliance strategies and experimental investigation of these items.

Figure 6 defines the variables in the force-friction theory in terms of the forces applied to the peg, the friction reaction forces and the basic geometry. Applied forces F_x, F_y, and M are shown at the tip of the peg but can be restated in terms of the gripped end. The theory predicts two types of phenomena. If two point contact occurs for very small ℓ/D, it is possible that force vector T_2, when extended, will pass through the opposite side of the peg between the opposite contact point and the tip. In this case, the peg can become "wedged" in the hole, requiring rather large forces to free it. A geometric and force analysis shows that wedging can occur if, at two point contact, $\ell/D < \mu$ where μ is the coefficient of friction. If two point contact occurs for larger ℓ/D, the peg may stop moving into the hole (i.e., may "jam") but will not wedge: the peg is still free in the hole but the applied forces are pointing the wrong way. The theory shows the avoidance of jamming requires that certain ratios be maintained between the applied forces and moments (Figure 6). These conditions might be fulfilled by a set of springs or by actively sensing these forces and moving the top of the peg so as to satisfy these ratios. Reference 5 contains the derivations of these conditions.

Even if jamming does not occur, we need to know if the parts will be damaged during two point contact. We have done no investigations of this ourselves and know only of Reference 16 which is of limited value. It reports experiments relating normal contact force to the resulting stresses in the materials using an approximate formula for stress in relation to size of contact region. From these preliminary results one can conclude that θ is not a strong determinant of stress but details of chamfer corner shape are: a "rounded" edge can result in 95% reduction in stress compared to a "sharp" edge. Exact definitions of these shapes and the identification of the material used in the experiments are not given, limiting the conclusions one can draw.

Experiments

To verify the above theories two series of experiments have been carried out. One series, reported in Reference 5, attempted to verify the ratio of applied forces and moments indicated by Figure 6. Limited success was achieved because the large pedestal force sensor used could not resolve the moment data finely enough. It was shown, however, that pegs and holes could be wedged together if they were held rigidly enough. Once they were wedged, no sensible force-torque data could be obtained to aid in unwedging them.

Since that time a smaller wrist force sensor has been built (References 2 and 17). See Figure 7. Table 1 gives the performance specifications. It has been mated to a first generation passive compliance device by Drake* which allows the gripper to rotate and translate slightly about a center located approximately at the center of the sensor. It is shown schematically in Figure 8. A series of chamfered steel test pegs has been made yielding various clearance ratios when mated to a chamfered test hole in a cast iron block 2.5cm (1") thick.

This apparatus has been mounted on a milling machine and a series of tests has been run imposing various values of lateral error and angular misalignment.

The goals of these tests were to determine

a) the validity of the geometric analyses for the one-point-contact case.

b) whether "wedging" and "jamming" occur as predicted.

c) whether one can obtain clear data relating lateral error and angular misalignment to measured forces and moments.

*Unpublished design by S. Drake,MIT PhD student.

d) whether such a device can serve as a passive compliance or as the measuring instrument for an active compliance strategy.

Considerable care was taken to ensure documentable initial conditions so that as errors were introduced, their effects could be properly traced.

For example, Figure 8 shows two cases. The first case is for a lateral error only and the second case is with both a lateral error and an angular error.

From the experimental results to date a number of conclusions can be drawn. The following are the foremost:

a) The data are extremely clean, consistent, and repeatable.

b) The separate phases of chamfer crossing, one point contact, and two point contact are clearly distinquishable.

c) In the absence of angular error, the lateral force during one point contact is directly proprotional to the lateral error (to be expected of a linear compliance.)

d) In the presence of angular error, the sign of lateral force during one point contact depends on the signs of lateral and angular error together, so that neither the direction nor the magnitude of lateral or angular error can be predicted during one point contact (geometric analysis predicted this ambiguity). An example of this is shown in Figure 8. (Note the differences in behavior of the lateral force in the two cases shown.)

e) Two point contact is a smooth event in these tests and "jamming" does not occur; the "violent interlocking" often referred to by Japanese researchers does not occur either-at least on the parts that have been tested to date.

f) Unambiguous moment data (proportional to the lateral force data) exist once two point contact begins. A manually closed loop has been successfully demonstrated for a two-axis (X and Y) active compliance strategy to remove the lateral error and recognize the sign of angular error.

Although these conclusions are based on test pieces and need to be extended to other materials and surface conditions, they represent significant results which should give much impetus for more extensive explorations of the sensor-based, minimum parameter description technique for assembly. Not discussed here is the mechanization of these results by real time system where careful integration of the sensor and the associated servo is required. References 6,8,18 and 19 describe the requirements in detail. The combination of geometric and friction analyses, plus the stimulus of the data (Figure 8) gave rise to the invention of a totally new device for accomplishing assembly, the remote center compliance (RCC) (Reference 20) This device* (Fig. 9) accomplishes mechanically what active accommodation does with sensors and servos and allows chamfered peg-hole insertions with 0.0003 clearance ratio (actual clearance = 0.0005") with 1 mm (0.04") or larger initial position errors and a few degrees of angular misalignment. The error tolerance of this passive compliance device is must larger than was originally thought possible for passive devices. At present this device is being used to assemble the pieces of an automobile alternator. What has been found to date indicated that the RCC device accommodates both at the interface where pieces interact during assembly and also has to accommodate to the inaccuracies of the parts feeders in order to pick up the pieces from the various feeding devices.

B. Programmable Assembly Systems

The previous sections analyzed the microstructure of assembly: geometry, sensors, friction, control, and so on. Here we discuss the macrostructure: assembly system configuration and economic analysis.

1. System Configuration

Programmable assembly systems will consist of arrangements of workstations containing programmable assembler "arms", part feeding equipment, tools and jigs. To determine the requirements for such workstations, one needs to know what assembly tasks are likely to occur, so that the needs for tools and sensors can be assessed. Second, the geometry of products must be analyzed. Since one assembly station will typically add several parts to a product unit, the station may need to be able to move the parts in quite general paths and directions of approach. Table 2 lists the assembly actions required by ten sample products (Table 3). Their frequency of occurrence and the approach directions along which they occur are shown in Figure 10. It can be concluded that single peg-hole insertions dominate overall, and dominate the primary direction. Screw insertions are second overall and either dominate or are prominent in the secondary directions. Push-twist tasks are third, indicating a need for a twist axis aligned along a major arm motion axis.

From this it may be concluded that "arms" with three or four degrees of freedom of arm motion can assemble many subassemblies and some complete products. Since the first four directions are defined to be normal or antiparallel to each other, this implies rectangular or cylindrical coordinate arm geometries, with axes aligned to the directions as much as possible. Arms with this type of geometry can be made modular--extra axes can easily be added or removed. This is not as easily done with arms that have elbows. The sufficiency of relatively simple arms is econocally very significant, in terms of both their cost and speed.

* U.S. Patents have been applied for the force sensor and the remote center compliance.

2. Economic Modeling

Now we have all the technological tools we need to describe programmable assembly systems. We now must unify these tools and choose intelligently among the options they offer so that we can place programmable assembly in context with existing techniques.

To do so requires a comparision that can be done on a fairly simple level. What is needed are functions that describe the general shapes of the economic areas and the equations that define boundaries so that economic and technology sensitivity analyses can be done for specific applications.*

Thus only simple, uniform products need be considered, not product families. For this level of modeling it can be shown that the most economic method of assembly is a function of the annual production volume of a product. An illustrative model for programmable assembly is derived in Table 4 and models for transfer lines and manual assembly are derived in Tables 5 and 6. Table 7 contains the basic cost assumptions which will be used later to graphically compare the three methods.

Programmable assembly systems models shown here are assumed to consist of programmable assembly stations and parts feeding tooling where the total amount of parts feeding tooling needed is a function only of the number of parts. The number of assembly stations in the system can vary depending on the number of parts assembled at each station. Thus, a system for assembling ten parts into a product will need to have ten sets of parts feeding tooling, each set specific to a particular part. The system can have ten stations if one part is assembled at each station, yielding the highest production volume, five stations if two parts are assembled at each station, yielding half as much production volume, or two stations if five parts are assembled at each station, yielding one-fifth the volume. The assumptions for the models are listed in the tables.

The principal conclusion of this analysis is that programmable system's unit assembly cost depends on the product of station price and what amounts to the station's cycle time. Cycle time can be reduced by, for example, increasing the speed of the "arm", but nothing will be gained overall if the arm's price rises proportionately. This important result allows the following conclusions to be drawn which bear on assembly system design and research:

1. Assuming the other parameters, such as parts feeding tooling costs, are held constant, design of assembly stations for minimum assembly cost per unit is achieved by minimizing the product of the station price and the part assembly time, not price or time individually.

---

*The details of this analysis can be found in a PhD thesis by M. Lynch, Reference 15

2. Programmable assembler station designs with different prices and assembly times but the same price-time product will result in systems having the same assembly cost per unit, on the average.

3. The sensitivities of the cost of assembly to fractional changes in price and part assembly time are equal in the following sense: reducing the price of the programmable station by a certain fraction will result in the same cost savings as reducing the part assembly time by the same fraction.

The most illustrative way of comparing the economic relationships between programmable assembly, manual assembly and transfer line assembly is graphical. It should be noted that the manual cost per unit (Table 7) is proportional to the number of parts as is the programmable and transfer machine cost per unit. This means that the number of parts in a product does not affect the relative cost of assembly between the three methods. The important variable is the annual volume.

Figure 11 illustrates the region of economic importance for programmable assembly based on the assumptions listed in Table 7 as well as for different payback periods and different hourly labor costs based on the basic cost assumptions listed in Table 7. Two points are to be noted. First, a general region for programmable assembly exists controlled by the yearly volume, the product of assembly station cost and assembly station time, and the payback period. Second, the boundary value between the various regions can be quantitatively examined by sensitivity analysis for specific applications both for economic constraints, technology constraints, and to indicate research directions and the priority for carrying them out. For example, one can study substitutions like electric actuators vs. hydraulic, or six degrees-of-freedom vs. 3, and so on.

In summary, the specific numerical boundaries indicated by the illustration are not important. What is important is that the regions can be defined quantitatively and that the boundaries can be explored by sensitivity analysis for specific applications. The latter is most important for an emerging technology where one is concerned about research issues and methods of prioritizing the areas to be explored.

What is not analyzed here is the economic relationship between jigging and the use of sensors to reduce their cost. These analyses must wait until implementation devices of the adaptable techniques are more mature. However, by technology sensitivity analysis the important research issues can be delineated.

3. Other Considerations

The economic modeling coupled with the kind of manufacturing statistics shown earlier-e.g., the degrees-of-freedom required to accomplish assembly-indicate the manner in which options can be developed to study configurations for economic programmable assembly systems. However, some of the important research issues not illuminated by this kind of analysis need to be mentioned because at present they are not being explored.

These issues are concerned with the computer and software architecture/organization of a multi-station system. Specific issues are the methods of teaching or reprogramming the system, the amount of computation needed at each station, and the division (both hardware and software) between the station processing and the system processing. On first examination it appears that the principal burden will be on the assembly station processor, but this point needs further analysis before this conclusion can be confirmed.

SUMMARY AND CONCLUSIONS

The overall goal of research for assembly therefore is to study the concept of a programmable, adaptable system for industrial assembly. Programmable implies a machine which can be taught different tasks, while adaptability means that the machine is equipped with sensors, controls and strategies which allow it to respond to changes in the parts or the relative part positions during assembly. To advance this field requires establishing a scientific base by identifying the basic issues and defining theoretical and experimental approaches to resolving them. These issues fall into technical and economic groups with heavy mutual influences. The groups are the general approach (i.e., recognition that assembly is primarily a positioning problem), assembly strategies, the relation between technical and economic issues, geometric analysis of insertion tasks, force-friction behavior during insertion, carefully designed reproducible experiments for verifying the analyses, manufacturing task and product statistics, and economic models of new assembly systems.

In conclusion the research described herein tends to suggest that research in automation will have its greatest yield in the near future (3-10 yrs) if the focus is information and control. I.e., careful analysis of the problems to determine minimum parameter methods for describing the process of concern, specification of the information available and the methods of extracting it, coupled with efficient high speed dynamic implementations with appropriate developments in computer and software systems.

REFERENCES

1. Nevins, J.L., Whitney, D.E., et.al."Exploratory Research in Industrial Modular Assembly," Fourth Report, for the period of 1 September 1975 to 31 August 1976, Charles Stark Draper Laboratory, Report No. R-996, September 1976.

2. Nevins, J.L.,Whitney, D.E., et.al., "Exploratory Research In Industrial Modular Assembly" Third Report, for the period 1 December 1974 to 31 August 1975, Charles Stark Draper Laboratory Report No. R-921, October 1975.

3. Kondoleon, A., "Application of a Technological-Economic Model of Assembly Techniques to Programmable Assembly Machine Configuration," S.M. Thesis, MIT Dept. of Mechanical Engineering, May 1976.

4. Simunovic, S., "Task Descriptors for Automatic Assembly," CSDL Report No. T-624, April 1976.

5. Simunovic, S., "Force Information in Assembly Processes," presented at the 5th International Symposium on Industrial Robots, Chicago, September 1975. Proceedings published by Society of Manufacturing Enginners.

6. Nevins, J.L. and Whitney, D.E., "The Force Vector Assembler Concept," C.S. Draper Lab Report No. E-2754, March 1973, presented at First International Symposium on Robot and Manipulator Systems, Udine, Italy, September 1973.

7. Nevins, J.L., Whitney, D.E. and Simunovic, S.N., "System Architecture for Assembly Machines", C.S. Draper Lab Report No. R-764, November 1973.

8. Whitney, D.E., "Force Feedback Control of Manipulator Fine Motions" to appear in proceedings of JACC 1976, Purdue University, July 27-30, 1976.

9. Whitney, D.E., "Resolved Motion Rate Control of Manipulators and Human Prostheses,"IEEE Transactions on Man-Machine Systems, Vol. MMS-10, June, 1969, pp. 47-53.

10.Whitney, D.E., "The Mathematics of Coordinated Control of Prosthetic Arms and Manipulators," ASME Journal of Dynamic Systems, Measurement and Control, December 1972, pp 303-309.

11.Paul, R., "Modeling, Trajectory Calculation and Servoing of a Computer Controlled Arm," Stanford Artificial Intelligence Laboratory Memo AIM-177, Stanford University, Nov. 1972.

12. Popplestone, R.J., "Freddy in Toyland,Machine Intelligence",Vol. 4 (Edinburgh University Press).

13. Goto, T., Inoyama, T. and Takeyasu, K., "Precise Insert Operation by Tactile Controlled Robot," Proceedings of the 2nd Conference on Industrial Robot Technology, March 1974, pp. C1.1-C1.8.

14. Goto, T., Inoyama, T., and Takeyasu,K.,"Precise Insert Operation by Tactile Controlled Robot"HI-T-HAND" Expert 2, "Proceedings of the 4th International Symposium on Industrial Robots," Nov. 1974, pp. 209-218.

15. Lynch, P.M., "Economic-Technological Modeling and Design Criteria for Programmable Assembly Machines," Ph.D. Thesis, MIT Mech. Eng. Dept.,June, 1976 and published as CSDL Report No. T-625.

16. Andreev, G. Ya., Laktionov, N.M., "Problem in the Assembly of Large Parts," Rus. Eng. Jnl., 1966, Vol. XLVI, No. 1, 60-61.

17. Watson, P.C., and Drake, S.H., "Pedestal and Wrist Force Sensors for Automatic Assembly," a paper presented at the 5th International Symposium on Industrial Robots, Chicago, Sept., 1975 and also published as CSDL Report No. P-176, June 1975.

18. Doherty, H. "Fine Motion Stability of a Manipulator," S.M. Thesis, MIT Mechanical Engineering Department, 1974.

19. Jilani, M.A., "Force Feedback Hydraulic Servo for Advanced Automation Machines", S.M. Thesis, MIT Mechanical Engineering Dept., November 1974.

20. Watson, P.C., "A Multidimensional System Analysis of the Assembly Process as Performed by a Manipulator," a paper presented at the 1st North American Industrial Robot Conference and Exposition, Chicago, Ill., Oct. 22-26, 1976.

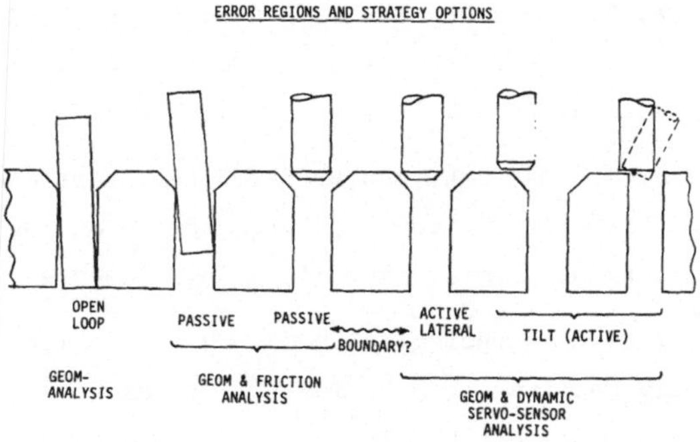

Figuere 1. Error Regions and Strategy Options

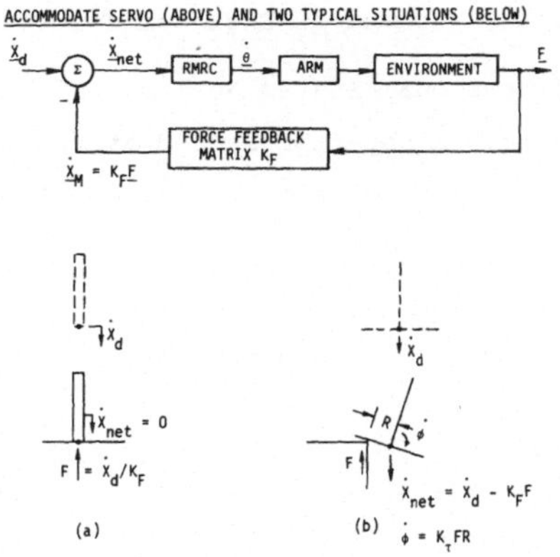

Figuere 2. Accomodation Servo (above) and Two Typical Situations (below)

PEG IN HOLE GEOMETRY

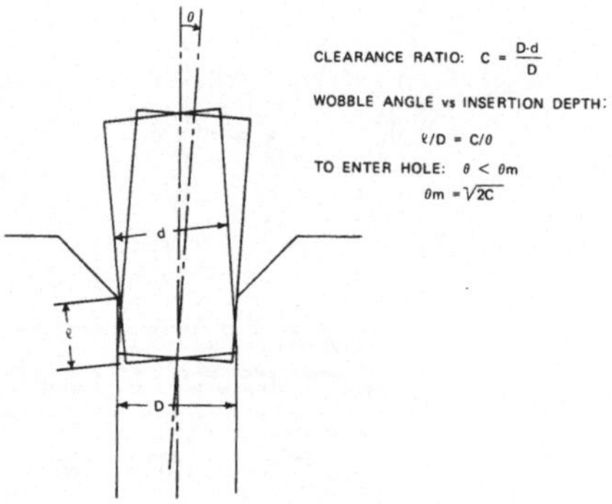

Figuere 3

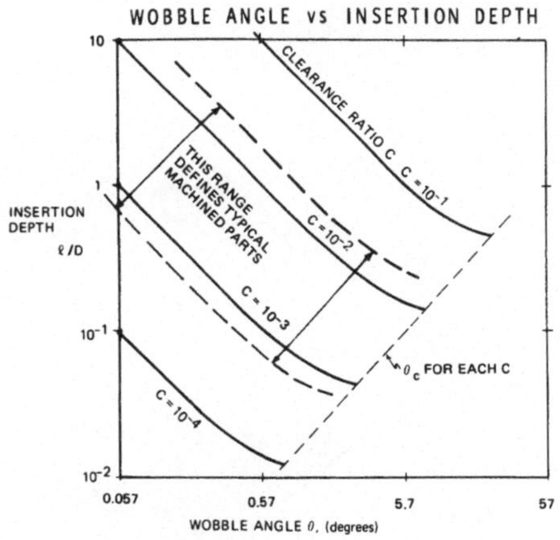

Figuere 4

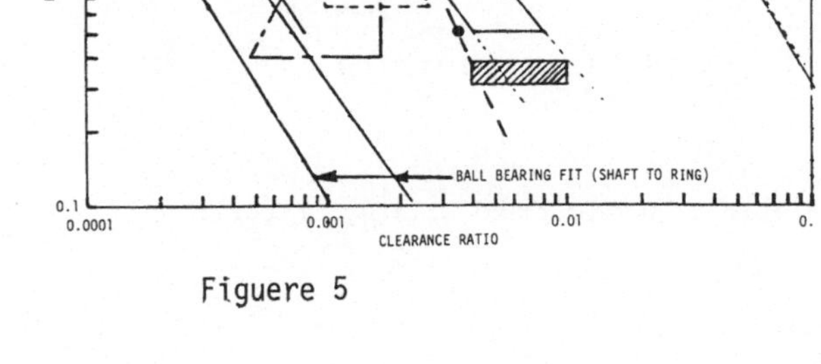

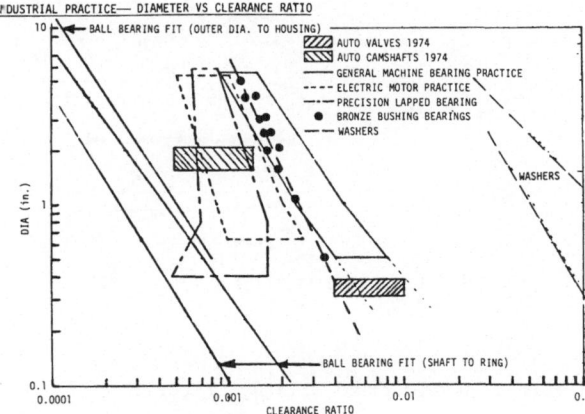

Figuere 5

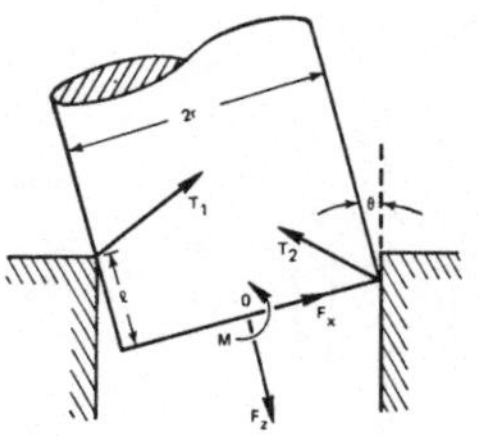

WHERE

F_x, F_z, M – APPLIED FORCES AND MOMENT RESOLVED AROUND LOCATION (0)

T_1, T_2 – REACTION FORCES AT THE CONTACT POINTS

ℓ – PENETRATION DEPTH

θ – MISALIGNMENT ANGLE

μ – COEFFICIENT OF FRICTION

ASSUMPTIONS

- LOW SPEED. QUASI STATIC ANALYSIS, INERTIA FORCES ARE CONSIDERED TO BE SMALL.
- STATIC AND DYNAMIC COEFFICIENT OF FRICTION ARE ASSUMED EQUAL. THIS RESTRICTION CAN EASILY BE REMOVED.
- RIGID PEG AND HOLE. THE DEFORMATION OF THEIR GEOMETRY IS ASSUMED SMALL.
- PERFECT CONTROL OF APPLIED FORCES. THIS REQUIRES A PERFECT READING OF FORCES AND MOMENTS, MEASURED AT THE TIP OF THE PEG, AND AN INFINITE RESOLUTION IN THE POSITION CONTROL. THESE CONSTRAINTS CAN BE MODIFIED FOR DESIGN PURPOSES.

7605C389-3

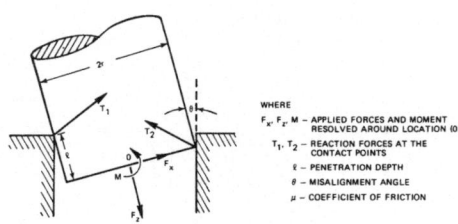

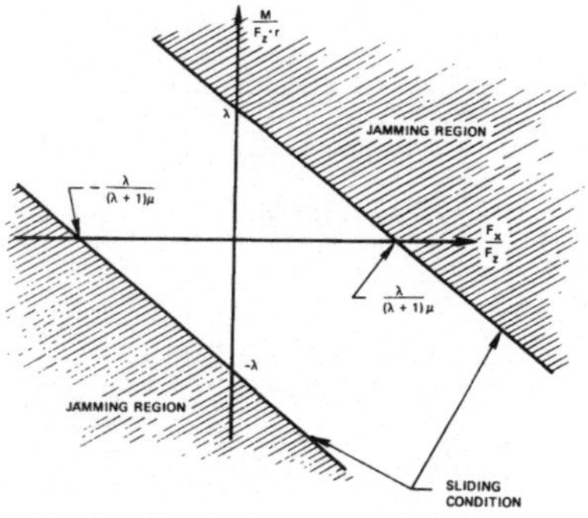

SLIDING CRITERIA FOR THE REGION $\lambda > 1$ OR $\frac{\ell}{D}$

$$\frac{\frac{M}{F_z r}}{\lambda \operatorname{sign}(\theta)} + \frac{\frac{F_x}{F_z}}{\frac{\lambda}{(\lambda+1)\mu} \operatorname{sign}(\theta)} \leq 1$$

WHERE $\lambda = \frac{\ell}{2r\mu}$

7605C389-2

Figure 6. Jamming and Sliding Criteria

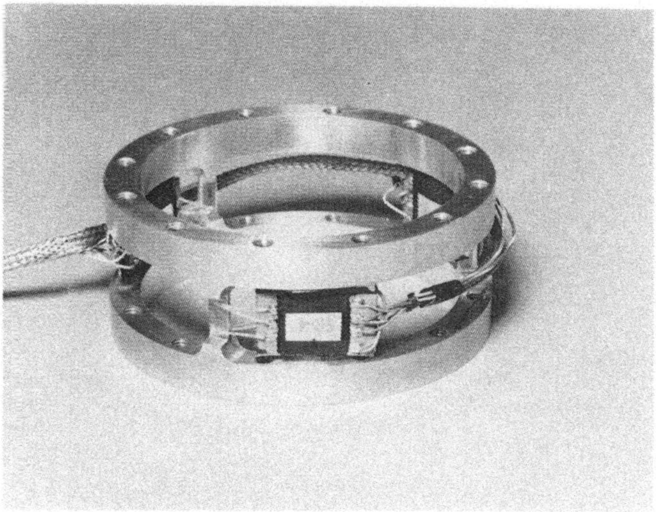

Figure 7. Wrist Force Sensor

Number of channels	6
Effective radius	55 mm
Full scale force per channel	890 newtons (200#)
Overload force per channel	1780 n (400#)
Full scale axial force	2668 n (600#)
Full scale axial moment	134 n-m (99 ft-#)
Full scale transverse force	1540 n (346#)
Full scale transverse moment	89 n-m (65 ft-#)
Resolution of digitizing	One part in 4000 (2.4 oz axially)

Condition	Strain Gage Bridge Output Millivolts	Amplifier Output, Volts	Digitizer Output (Octal)
+Full Scale	10	10	+3777
Zero	0	0	0
-Full Scale	-10	-10	-3777
Each bit of digitizer Output	0.00488	0.00488	0001

Table 1. Wrist Force Sensor Performance

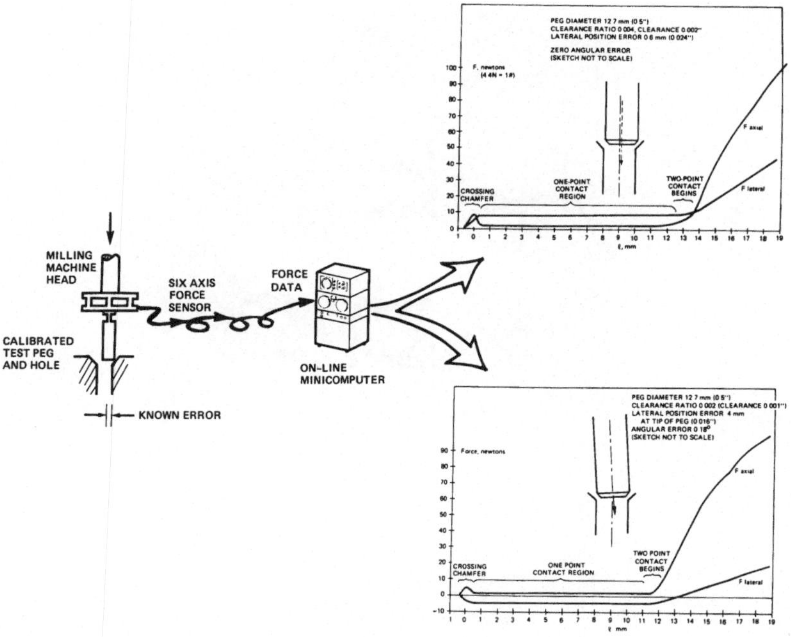

Figure 8. First Definitive Part Mating Experiment

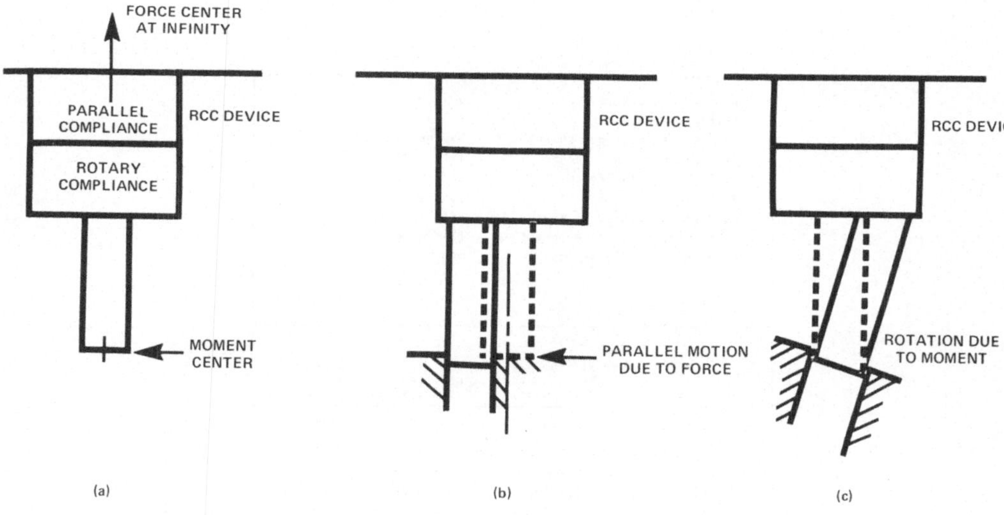

Figure 9. Remote Center Compliance-Concept Mechanization

OPERATION IDENTIFICATION	OPERATION DESCRIPTION
a	simple insertion or placement of part
b	stage insertion or push and twist
c	multiple insertion or alignment
d	perpendicular insertion
e	screw insertion
f	interference insertion
g	part removal
h	test operation
i	flip operation
j	part placement and hold
k	crimp operation
l	release hold
m	weld or solder

Table 2. Assembly Tasks Encountered in Ten Product Items

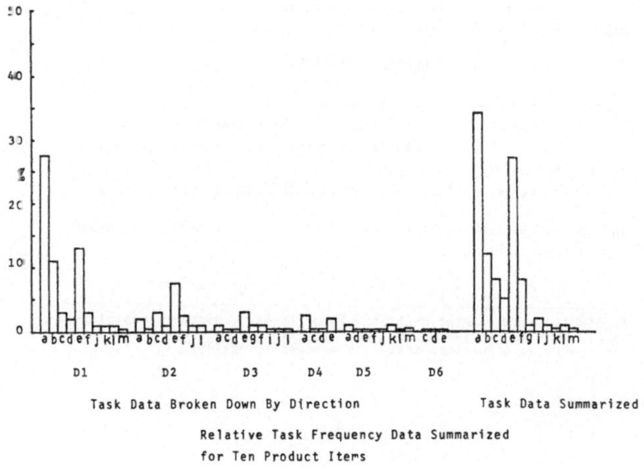

Figure 10.Manufacturing Task and Direction of Operation Statistics

Product	Number of Parts	Longest Dimension of the Largest Family Member
Electric Timer Cover Subassembly*	7	4.5"
Electric Timer Case and Final Assembly*	18	4.5"
Refrigerator Compressor Family	26	10"
Bicycle Coaster Brake	15	6"
Transformer Electric Bushing Family	6 to 8	10"
End Cap Subassemblies for Small Induction Motors	29	7"
Induction Motor Main Body Subassembly and Final Assembly	21	15"
Electric Jigsaw	58	12"
Toaster Oven	41	15"
Automobile Alternator Family**	17	8"

*Currently assembled automatically.
**Currently assembled by a mixture of manual and automatic workstations.

Products Analyzed for Task Statistics

Table 3. Products Analyzed For Task Statistics

Programmable system cost:

$$PSCST = NSTA * STAP + NPART * TOLPP$$

where PSCST = programmable system cost
NSTA = number of assembly stations
STAP = single station price
*TOLPP = tooling price per part

The number of stations required is

$$NSTA = \frac{VOL * NPART * PARTTIME}{NSPY}$$

where PARTTIME = assembly time per part, sec
$NSPY = 1.152 \times 10^7$ sec/yr for an uptime fraction of 0.8, a 250 day year and a 2 shift, 16 hour day.

The assembly system cost is then

$$PSCST = \frac{STAP * VOL * NPART * PARTTIME}{NSPY} + NPART * TOLPP$$

and, using the same payback period model as in eq(II-27), the assembly cost per unit is

$$PCPU = \frac{NPART}{PAYPER}\left[\frac{STAP * PARTTIME}{NSPY} + \frac{TOLPP}{VOL}\right] \longleftarrow$$

*Includes basic feeding mechanism (bowl feeders, hoppers, magazines, etc), feed tracks and chutes, and placement or escapement devices or conveying mechanisms that link the parts together.

Table 4. Programmable Assembly System Economic Model

Manual assembly cost:

MCPU = MATP * LABCST * NPART ←

where MCPU = manual assembly cost per unit

MATP = manual assembly time per part, sec

LABCST = cost rate of labor, $/sec

NPART = number of parts in the product

Fixed automation (transfer machine) assembly cost:

$$TCPU = \frac{TSCST}{PAYPER * VOL}$$

where TCPU = transfer machine assembly cost per unit

TSCST = transfer machine total cost

PAYPER = payback period in years

Next, TSCST = NPART * TMCPP

where TMCPP = transfer machine cost per part

Therefore

$$TCPU = \frac{NPART * TMCPP}{PAYPER * VOL} \leftarrow$$

This model is based on the payback period method rather than discounted cash flow for simplicity. Any particular case can be worked out using the more accurate method.

Table 5 & 6. Economic Models For Manual Assembly and Fixed Automation

ASSUMPTIONS

NUMBER OF PARTS	=	10
PROGRAMMABLE STATION PRICE	=	$30,000
TOOLING PER PART	=	$7500
TRANSFER MACHINE COST PER PART	=	$30,000
PART STATION TIME	=	3 s
PAYBACK PERIOD	=	2 years to 4 years
LABOR COST	=	$7.50/hr to $10.00/hr
MANUAL ASSEMBLY STATION TIME	=	7 s
NUMBER OF SECONDS PER YEAR	=	1.152×10^7

Table 7. Assumptions Used To Compare Economic Models.

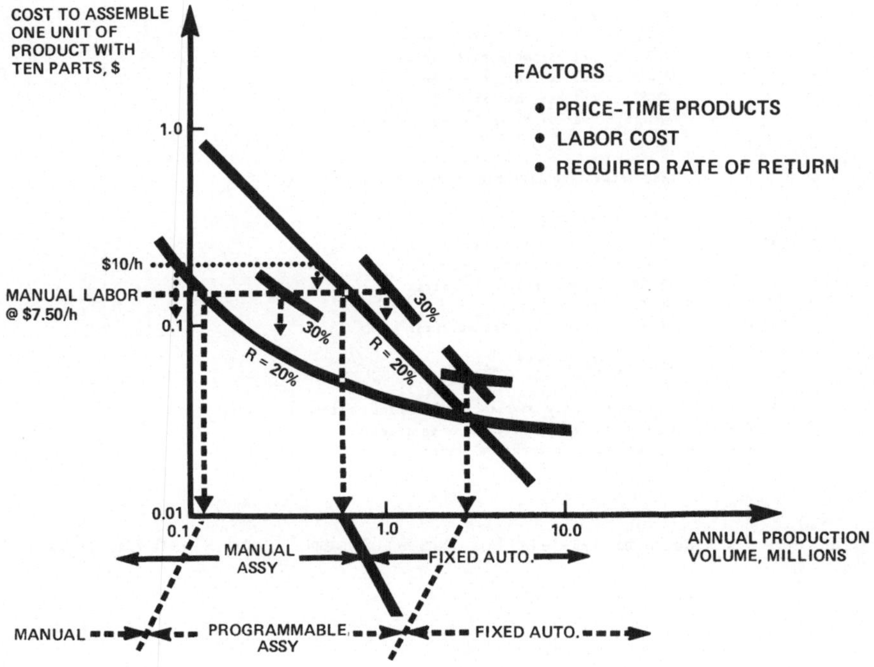

Figure 11. Regions of Economic Advantage for Three Assembly Methods

TACTILE IMAGING FOR COMPONENT RECOGNITION

*C.J.Page, † A.Pugh, § W.B.Heginbotham (U.K)

Summary

A simple, parallel-mode tactile transducer for extracting three-dimensional digital representations of complex engineering components is proposed. In addition, algorithms for computer processing of the tactile information to produce a compact structural description of the scrutinised object are evolved. The possibility exists that these techniques might be applied to future generations of automatic assembly machines with sensory feedback.

1. Introduction

The work described in this publication falls into the general area of scene analysis, which in turn can be thought of as a subset of pattern recognition. Scene analysis also forms a major part of studies on Artificial Intelligence (A.I.). Commercial, but more simplified uses of these techniques have, in recent years, been incorporated in industrial robots. The techniques to be described are specifically intended for this application, or more particularly for imaging three-dimensional engineering components for subsequent handling and assembly.

Much of the research on scene analysis and picture processing up to the present has focussed on visual imaging using monochromatic television cameras. These techniques convert the television picture into a two-dimensional array of discrete picture points or elements. The intensity of each point is in turn quantised into as many coded shades of grey as required. The simplest of these quantisation schemes is the interpretation of an image as a silhouette, i.e. a binary-valued picture. Scene analysis techniques are then used to infer the three-dimensional structure of the imaged scene from the relative intensities of the component picture points. (Ref 4). However, this is a complicated procedure as an attempt is being made to extract three-dimensional structure from two-dimensional information. In addition, perspective distortion and the effects of shadows cause problems.

To overcome some of these difficulties, transducers with "three-dimensional capability" have been used in some experiments; the simplest of these being an optical rangefinder. (Refs.7,9). However, the rangefinder's main deficiency is that it must function in an essentially serial manner; that is, sampling one point after another. It is therefore relatively slow in operation. Tactile techniques have been given only limited attention for scene analysis work, despite the fact that they are capable of providing three-dimensional information. Most previous work has focussed on intelligent research techniques with sets of probes; much in the manner of a blind man using a cane (Refs.6,8,10,11).

The combination of the merits of both visual and tactile imaging techniques can provide easily obtainable, unambiguous three-dimensional data which is acquired by parallel rather than serial sampling. The following discussion will show that this proposal is physically realisable and that the resultant data can be processsed by a set of simple heuristic algorithms. A more extensive treatment has already been published.(Ref.1).

2. A Simple Tactile Sensor

Tactile techniques are attractive in this context for two reasons. Firstly, they do not suffer from perspective distortion and most of the other difficulties associated with visual scene analysis. Secondly, they can be easily adapted to extract three-dimensional information. Fig.1. shows in schematic form the device used. It basically consists of a thick, rigid mount with a square matrix of circular holes drilled in it orthogonally to the plane of the mount. A thin ferrous rod is inserted into each hole with its top end flush with the upper surface of the mount, the tolerances being sufficiently small to ensure that each rod is a sliding fit. When this assembly is lowered over an object, with the plane of the mount parallel to that of the working area; the rods move axially in their respective guides according to the contours of the specimen. The protrusions of the rods above the upper surface of the mount provide a measure of the relative heights of the contours of the object.

If the height of the base of the tactile sensor probe matrix above the ground plane is continually monitored as it is being lowered on to an object, then the height registered when any probe first moves by more than some small threshold displacement from its rest position defines the height of the component at the co-ordinates specified by that particular probe. Position sensing is then simplified as the information required from the probes themselves becomes purely binary, namely "displacement" or "no displacement" from the rest position.

* Instem Ltd.,Stone,Staffs.
† Dept. of Electrical and Electronic Engineering,University of Nottingham.
§ Dept.of Production Engineering and Production Management,University of Nottingham.

The operation of the tactile sensor can be broken down into three sub processes: the lowering of the device on to a component and the continuous monitoring of height, the sampling of the probe states, and the correlation of these two sets of results to form a table of height values for the part. Practical realisation of this system presupposes the availability of a memory (for storing the results of sensing) and some means of lowering the tactile sensor vertically on to a component in small, precise and repeatable increments. At the start of a sensing cycle, the sensor probes are pushed down flush with the body of the device and the data store allocated for the retention of the height of the probe tips above the work surface is initialised. The tactile sensor is them lowered until the tips of the probes are at a distance from the ground plane equal to the length of the probe protruding downwards from the sensor body. Interrogation of probe states is now initiated. When a probe has moved with the corresponding location in the data store still initialised, then that probe has moved for the first time; that is, it has touched the component under examination. The height of the base of the probe matrix at this instant is loaded into the memory location corresponding to the displaced probe. When the state is reached where the last remaining initialised location in the memory has been loaded, no more information can be gained, downward movement is halted and the sensing cycle terminated.

A tactile sensor utilising these principles has been specifically designed to be mounted on an existing research rig, (Ref.1,2). This is a computer-controlled industrial robot which possesses manipulative and sensory capabilities. The tactile sensor is monitored by a relatively simple electronic control system which is itself under the supervision of the executive processor.

Sensing the displacement of each probe is achieved by associating with each probe a co-ordinate winding similar to that used for magnetic core interrogation. This is illustrated in Fig.2. Each 'Read' winding is energised sequentially with a suitable current. 'Sense' windings, in the orthogonal direction, monitor the magnitude of induced e.m.f. of the row of probes under interrogation. If a probe is displaced into the intersecting winding, the mutual coupling between the windings is increased and a higher e.m.f. will be induced in the corresponding sense winding. The displacement of each discrete probe is interrogated after each increment of downward motion. Consequently, it is possible to assemble data appropriate to the progressive motion of each and every probe in the matrix.

The read and sense windings form a matrix of wires with what is effectively a low-voltage differential transformer (LVDT) at each probe position. The matrix is positioned on the top surface of the tactile sensor body and is excited by a sinusoidal current of frequency 500 kHz. The electronic drive system is supplied by a master oscillator. This energises the read windings via an amplifier and also clocks a counter which switches the amplifier output to the read windings of the sensor matrix in a sequential fashion via a group of analogue switches. Another set of analogue switches, again operated sequentially by the counter, directs the outputs on the sense windings to amplification and thresholding circuitry. The counter also controls the addressing circuitry of a random access memory (RAM) used to hold the height values for the probe matrix. The supervisory computer controls this sytem (via suitable interfacing logic) by triggering either an initialising cycle to set up the contents of the RAM, a monitoring cycle to scan the probe states while the tactile sensor is being lowered on to a component, or a read cycle to read the results of this operation from the RAM into computer memory.

3. Algorithms for Processing the Tactile Data

The tactile sensor described above extracts from the scrutinised component a set of height values sampled over a square matrix in the X-Y plane. Some method must now be found of processing these parameters and forming a compact, unambiguous description of the object. The tactile sensor, because of its relatively low resolution, (e.g. 16 x 16), produces a representation of a component which in effect partitions it into a set of horizontal "slices" or "laminations". This is illustrated in Fig.3 (a). Any representation of the part must effectively describe it in terms of the relationship between its component laminations as seen by the tactile sensor. In turn, each lamination must be uniquely described by one or more definitive properties.

3.1. Basic Techniques

The most commonly used method for expressing spatial relationships in scene analysis uses the so-called "relational graph". This is in effect a hierarchial tree structure which expresses one or more symbolic relationships, such as "inside"; "above"; "to the left of"; between component parts of the scene.(Ref.5). Fig.3(b) shows a possible relational graph describing the object shown in Fig.3(a). Each dot or "node" represents a lamination, and each arrow or "directional arc" expresses some relationship between the node at either end. In this case, each arc specifies that the lamination represented by the node at its "tail end" is physically above that represented by the node at its "point end".

The main advantages of this type of structural description for the computer representation of spatial relationships is that it provides a simple and unambiguous method of linking sets of parameters in such a way as to define the underlying structure.

The structural description to be used here describes each lamination in terms of its peripheral contour and its maximum and minimum height values. The relational graph, or "connection tree", relates the laminations, or rather their peripheral contours, in terms of the enclosure of one lamination by another. A directional arc 'between' two nodes means that the peripheral contour at the tail of the arc encloses that at its head. Representing regions of the object by peripheral contours rather than by "laminations" makes it easy to cater for internal depressions and holes in the surface of the examined component. This is because the "hole", while not producing another lamination, nevertheless has a peripheral contour and can be considered as a separate region. The fact that some laminations are essentially "virtual" or "imaginary"; that is, they represent holes or depressions in the surface of the component, can be added to the connection tree by expanding the definition of the tree nodes to include the maximum and minimum heights of the lamination as well as its peripheral contour. The maximum and minimum heights of the parent lamination are appended to the connection-tree node representing the peripheral contour of the lamination. A simple convention to distinguish between "real" and "imaginary" laminations can be adopted as follows.

Where the lamination is real, the maximum height value precedes the minimum height value when appended to the appropriate node. Where the lamination is imaginary, the order is reversed, i.e., the minimum value comes first. An additional feature of the tactile-sensor representation which can be put to good use is that for some components two or more of the laminations may share common segments of their peripheral contours. By inserting extra linkages between the appropriate contours in the connection tree to specify this relationship, the structural description can be further strengthened.

Fig.4. shows examples of some tactile representations of simple components and their corresponding structural descriptions. In all cases the tactile parameters have been reduced to a set of laminations for clarity. In addition, the plan view of each component is identical, and has been reproduced only once as a set of three regions of height, h_1,h_2, and h_3 on a ground place of h_0. The connection trees of three different objects are obtained by varying the relative values of these heights to give three different interpretations of the basic structure. As explained above, the trees relate the component laminations of the part (as defined by their peripheral contours and maximum and minimum height values) by means of the enclosure of one contour by another when viewed from above. The sharing of a common segment by two contours is shown by appending an "s" to the arc linking the two when one is immediately enclosed by the other. When this is not the case, the appropriate nodes are linked by a dotted line with an "s" appended. The simplicity of the overall tree structure arises from two axioms. These can be stated as follows:

a) a contour may enclose many other contours,but it can itself be enclosed by only one other contour

b) the enclosure of contours obeys an associative law (for example, if contour A encloses contour B, which in turn encloses contour C, then A also encloses C).

However, neither of them apply to the sharing of contours, as shown by the connection trees of Fig.4. In addition, Fig. 4(c) shows that two contours which have common segments are not necessarily positioned one inside the other as might be suggested from the other examples.

Processing of the tactile data can conveniently be split into two separate operations: extracting the component contours of an object, together with all necessary quantitative information; and the linking of these contours into a coherent structural description..

A possible complicating factor is that there may be more than one component in the "scene"; that is, the tactile sensor may be lowered on to a group of objects instead of just one. Therefore, the algorithms must partition the regions of the scene into discrete objects during one or the other of the operations.

3.2. Contour Extraction

It is evident that the contours must be obtained by tracing out the boundaries between the regions of the object with due reference to the heights of those regions. The first rule to be adopted for contour extraction is that boundaries are always traced with the region of greater height on the left of an imaginery observer travelling with the contour follower. If this rule is adhered to, the contours of internal holes or depressions can be easily distinguished as they are traced in a clockwise direction rather than in the normal anticlockwise sense. The basic philosophy of the contour-extraction algorithms lies in the fact that the contours of any lamination with a specified upper-height value can be correctly extracted by tracing the boundary between regions of height greater than or equal to the set value and those of lower height than the set value. Fig.5. illustrates this principle for a simple component composed of two laminations of heights h_2 and h_1 respectively, on a ground plane of height h_0. By applying the aforementioned rule twice in succession with the set value at h_2 and h_1 in turn, the contours of the two laminations are correctly traced out as shown in the diagram.

Fig.6. describes the overall operation of contour following in flow-chart form. One complete "scan" of the matrix is performed for every discrete height value represented so as to extract all contours of that height which are present. To ensure correct operation, the tracing of each contour must start at a point where the set height is actually represented, and has not therefore been previously encountered, rather than being set to the "already used" value. When implementing a scheme such as this, it is necessary to ensure that no contour is traced more than once. In addition, contours with shared segments must be noted. Contour points are marked as they are found by setting their height values to a pre-determined out-of-range value. At the same time, the point is marked with the number of the contour and the numbers of all previously traced contours traversing this point are noted. It can be seen that by extracting the contours in descending order of height, a "marked" point encountered during the following of a contour must have been marked on a previous scan. It must therefore have originally been of greater value than the present set height and is treated accordingly. The particular form of the contour follower used prevents any point being traversed twice on the same scan.

While the contours are being extracted checks are made to ensure, for example, that the contour has not been followed to the edge of the "frame", in which case tracing of this particular contour is terminated. This can occur frequently in a practical situation because of the limited size of the sensor. The contour is stored point-by-point as it is being traced. The digitised curve is stored in so-called "chain code" as a pair of starting co-ordinates and a difference sequence of direction vectors (ref 12). Concurrently with tracing, calculations of the enclosed area, perimeter length, centroid co-ordinates and maximum and minimum excursions of the contour in directions parallel to the co-ordinate axes are updated. These parameters will provide quantitative information about the parent object which can be used in conjunction with the final structural description.

Because of the nature of their operation, the contour following algorithms rearrange a scene consisting of several discrete objects into sets of contours, each set containing all contours with a particular maximum height. Re-allocation of contours to specific components must therefore be performed at some later stage. The next stage of processing must also identify those contours which form part of a component not completely covered by the tactile sensor. These can be assembled into "incomplete" connection trees which are then either discarded in the hope that the complete object will be imaged during a subsequent application of the sensor at a different position, or are matched up with connection trees obtained from this later sensor application.

Table 1 defines in condensed form the contour follower used. The crosses and dots represent two height values, with that of the cross being greater than that of the dot. "Tactile points" are examined in blocks of four by the contour follower. When contour following has been initiated, by finding one of the specified block formats during a row-by-row scan of the frame, the follower traces the contour until it either goes off the edge of the frame or arrives back at its starting point. In all but two block permutations the particular format defines both the incoming and outgoing contour directions. This simplicity is a direct result of constraining the follower to trace contours with the point of greater heights on its left. The exceptions are the blocks of two crosses positioned diagonally opposite each other. In these cases, the outgoing contour direction also depends on its incoming direction. It is for this reason that contour following never commences on one of these so-called "diagonal" blocks.

The contour follower is a very simple one: its main feature is that it produces a single, continuous closed curve which includes every point of the contour. Fig.7. shows the follower applied to two adjacent, digitised regions which also illustrates another feature in that it can distinguish between two regions which are almost touching.

3.3. Connection Tree Synthesis

Fig.8(a) shows a scene which, although hardly typical, is not outside the realms of possibility. The suffixed letters refer to the heights of the enclosed regions, the arrows to the directions in which the enclosing contours are traced, and the numbers to the order in which the contours are extracted. Three parts are present, one of which is positioned inside an internal perforation of another. The component contours of this "scene" must be classified into three separate connection trees, as illustrated in Fig.8 (b). In addition, the situation where one of the parts overlaps the edge of the tactile sensor must be detected as it results in some of the contours being incomplete and subsequent rejection by the following algorithms. Table 2 shows the format of the list used to represent contour enclosure in the connection tree. The overall table representing the connection tree consists of a total of three parallel lists; that shown in table 2, one which holds the height values associated with each contour, and one which lists the linkages between shared contours.

Tree synthesis is broken down into three sequential stages as an aid to simplicity and ease of implementation. These are the formation of the basic tree structures (but without shared contour information), the elimination of those contours whose presence can be attributed to the effect of the poor resolution of the tactile sensor and finally, the addition of shared contour information.

Fig.9. shows a flow chart for the formation of the basic connection tree. The practical implementation of this consists of allocating an entry to each contour in a list on the basis of one list for each individual part. Each entry is composed of two parts, one denoting the number of the contour, and one denoting the number of the enclosing contour. Table 2 illustrates the lists describing the connection trees of Fig.8.(b). It can be seen that this representation is simple and easy to process with a computer. In addition to the axioms quoted previously, there is another simple observation which aids the formation of these part lists. This is that a contour which encloses another must enclose a greater area than that of the contour being enclosed. All of these simple axioms are put to good use as can be seen from the flow chart. The initial ordering of all contours in descending order of enclosed area means that the search for the enclosing contour for any particular candidate can be limited to those positioned above it in the list. The algorithm uses two other subsidiary observations: the peripheral contour of the component must be at the top of its respective contour list, and the contour of a depression or internal hole in a component can only enclose the peripheral contour of another part. A consequence of the former is that if a contour is encountered which is not enclosed by another but which is not a "periphery", then it is part of an "incomplete" component caused by partial overlapping of the tactile sensor boundary by the original part. In this case, the contour is allocated to the head of a new part list and the list is marked as incomplete.

At this point, there exists a basic structural description of the scene which, though simple, is adequate for the application of criteria to differentiate between contours which represent significant features of the scene and those caused by the effects of tolerances in the tactile sensor. The simplest method of eliminating extraneous regions is to merge them with adjacent "significant" regions, or in other words to delete the entry for the corresponding contour from the part list. The criterion applied here is that if two adjacent regions differ in height by less than a fixed threshold, they are merged. The adjacency condition is satisfied by stipulating that two regions can only be candidates for merging if one of the contours immediately encloses the other. "Immediately encloses" in this context means that there are no intervening contours. The height of the resultant region is taken to be that of the enclosing contour rather than the average of the two; this prevents erroneous propagation of the merging process through a set of concentric regions of gradually increasing or decreasing height.

In practice, each region is represented by its contours and a set of quantitative parameters. Each part list is examined contour by contour from the periphery downwards, or in physical terms, from the component's periphery inwards. Each entry in the list is regarded in turn as the contour into which suitable, immediately enclosed contours are absorbed. All lower contours in the list are examined in this respect, and when found the corresponding entries are deleted. The entries relating to all regions enclosed by the merged region are then modified. Fig.10 illustrates the effect of merging on a set of concentric regions of heights, 2, 3, 4, 3 and 4 respectively (Fig.10 (a)). The threshold here is one, the minimum possible. The result of the merging process is shown in Fig.10 (b). It can be seen that some of the regions have been selectively absorbed, effecting a reduction of data without masking the significant features.

The final operation to be performed is that of allocating to the connection tree the links between pairs of contours which share portions of their length. This is done by examining the list of numbers of the contours sharing part of their length with each contour traced by the 'follower' algorithms. For every pair of contours which are linked in this fashion, the number of the other contour is written into the part-list entry of the contour with the smaller enclosed area. Therefore, each entry eventually consists of the contour number, the number of the contour which immediately encloses it, the associated maximum and minimum height values, and the numbers of all larger contours which share part of their length with this particular contour.

4. Concluding Remarks

It has been mentioned previously that the algorithms described here are intended for use in artificial intelligence work. This is indeed so. They arose as an indirect result of the shortcomings of visual techniques when applied to practical three-dimensional components. For the past several years, research into automatic handling and assembly has been in progress in the departments of Electrical Engineering and Production Engineering at the University of Nottingham. Visual feedback employing a vertically mounted television camera producing a binary-valued two-dimensional image has been used to control an assembly machine with movable manipulators. This machine can in turn perform simple sorting, assembly, and manipulative tasks on selections of small engineering components, none of which have previously been specified to the machine.

In the first projected application of the techniques described in this paper, the tactile sensor will take the place of one of the manipulators presently mounted on the existing assembly machine. It is the intention that it will function as a low-resolution adjunct to the visual sense, enabling features of the scrutinised component to be imaged in a three-dimensional fashion.

The algorithms which have been outlined here are not necessarily restricted to operating on tactile data: they can obviously work equally well with data from any transducer capable of providing three-dimensional information. A suitable, though slow, device in this context would be the optical rangefinder mentioned previously. The algorithms owe their simplicity without loss of power to one particular constraint upon the application environment, namely that every "scene" consists of a flat "ground plane" upon which rest one or more objects. The tactile sensor is then applied with its axis normal to this ground plane. If an optical range-finder, for example, is used to image some part of what could be called a conventional three-dimensional scene, say a table in a small room, then in the absence of a physical ground plane normal to the axis of the transducer, a hypothetical plane must be constructed at the furthest point of the scene, for the purposes of subsequent analysis.

In conclusion, the tactile sensor and associated software algorithms presented in this paper, although purpose-designed for the imaging three-dimensional components resting on a flat ground plane can nevertheless provide great improvements over conventional imaging techniques.

5. Acknowledgements

The authors are grateful for the design facilities provided through the management of Mr. D.W.Gatehouse. The visually interactive machine referred to in this paper was funded by the Science Research Council,London,England.

6. References

1. Page,C.J. : "Visual and tactile feedback for the automatic manipulation of engineering parts". Ph.D. thesis,Nottingham University,U.K. (1974)
2. Heginbotham, W.B., Gatehouse, D.W., Pugh,A., Kitchin, P.W. and Page, C.J.: "The Nottingham "SIRCH" assembly robot". Proc.1st. Conf. on Industrial Robot Technology, Nottingham University, U.K. (1973).
3. Heginbotham, W.B., Page, C.J. and Pugh, A.: "Robot Research at Nottingham University". Proc. Symposium on Industrial Robots and Robot Exhibition, Tokyo, Japan (November 1974)
4. Roberts, L.G.: "Machine perception of three-dimensional solids", Optical and electro-optical information processing, MIT press (1965).
5. Barrow, H.G. and Popplestone, R.J.: "Relational descriptions in picture processing", Machine Intelligence 6, Ed.Meltzer and Michie,EUP,(1971).
6. Inoue, H.: "Tactile pattern recognition for manipulating objects", Electro-technical Lab.A.I & R. Group Technical Note No.2,Tokyo,Japan (Feb 1973)
7. Shirai, Y.: "Recognition of polyhedra with a rangefinder", Bulletin of the Electro-technical Lab. Vol.35, No.3, pp.96-102 (March 1971).
8. Larcombe, M.:"Tactile perception for robot devices", Proc.1st.Conference on Industrial Robot Technology, Nottingham University, U.K.(1973).
9. Okada, T. and Twuchiya, S.: "Three-dimensional pattern recognition with an artificial hand", Bulletin of the Electrotechnical Laboratory, Vol.35, No.3, pp.334-45 (1971).
10. Kinoshita et al: "Pattern recognition by an artificial tactile sense",Proc. 1st. Int.Jnt. Conf. on Artificial Intelligence, London (1971).
11. Kakikura et al: "On the control of an industrial robot with tactile sensors" Transactions of the Society of Instrumentation and Control (Japan) No.7.p.31 (1971).
12. Freeman, H.: "Techniques for the digital-computer analysis of chain-encoded arbitrary plane curves," Proc.National Electronics Cong.,Vol.17.Chicago,1961.

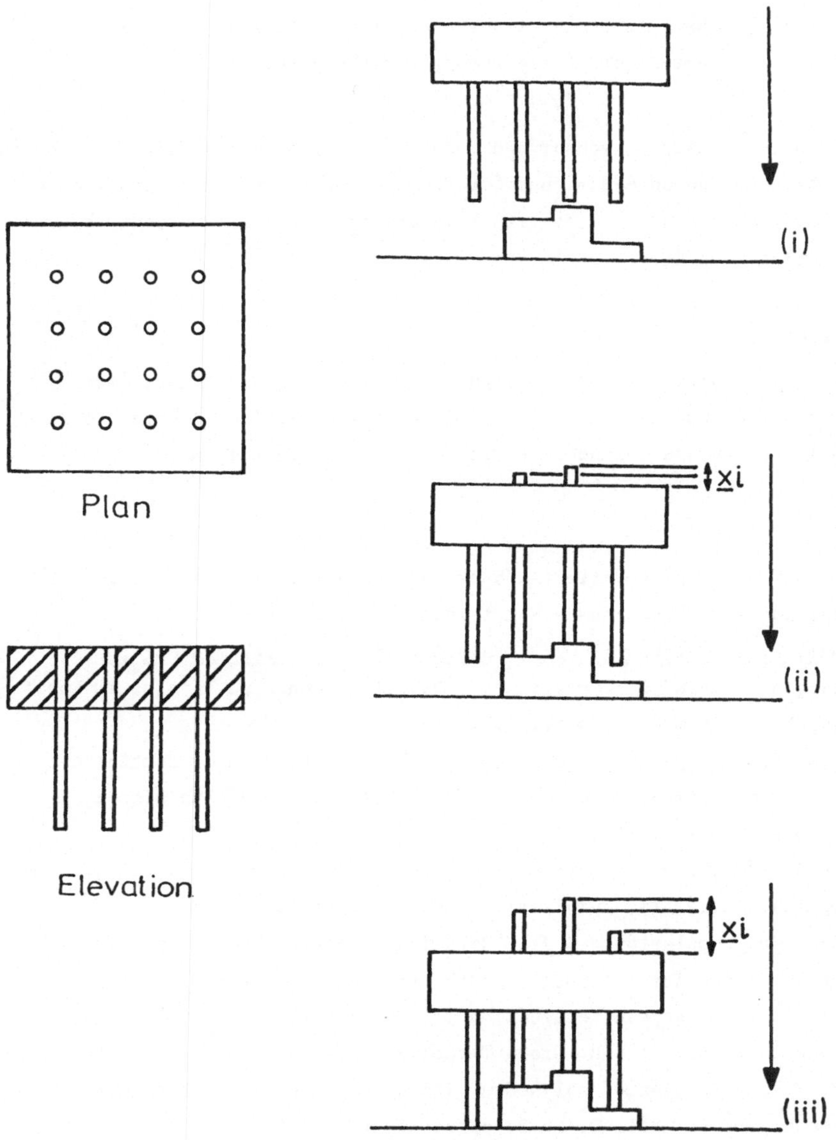

Fig.1. Schematic Representation of Proposed Tactile Sensors

(i), (ii) and (iii) taken in sequence illustrate the operation of the sensor when used to image a three-dimensional component on a flatground-plane. At the point when the base of the sensor touches the ground plane, projections xi of the rods provide a simplified representation of the part's shape.

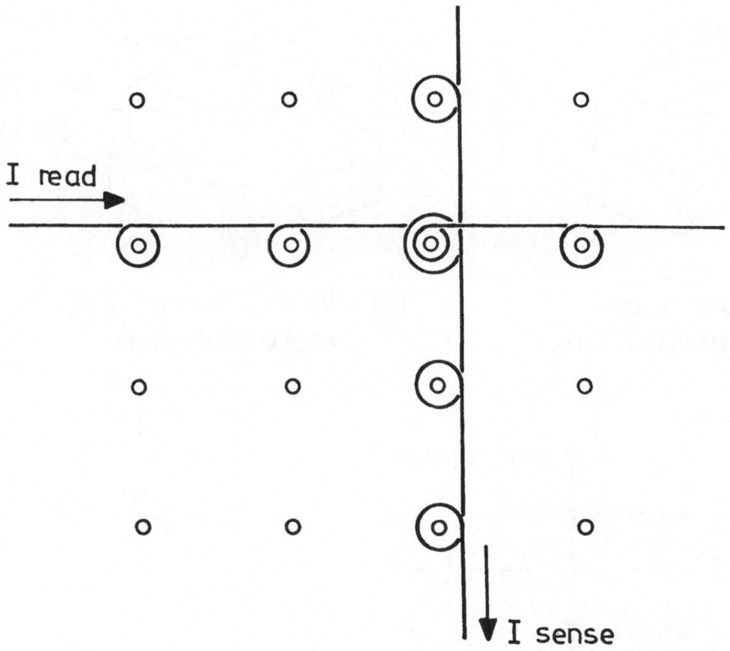

Fig.2. Schematic Illustration of Method used to sense Probe Displacement

The matrix of small circles represents the probes when viewed from vertically above. Each "read" winding (of which only one is shown) forms a series-connected set of transformer windings along a row of the probe matrix. Sense windings form a similar set of transformer secondaries down each column of the matrix, thereby enabling simple X-Y addressing to be used.

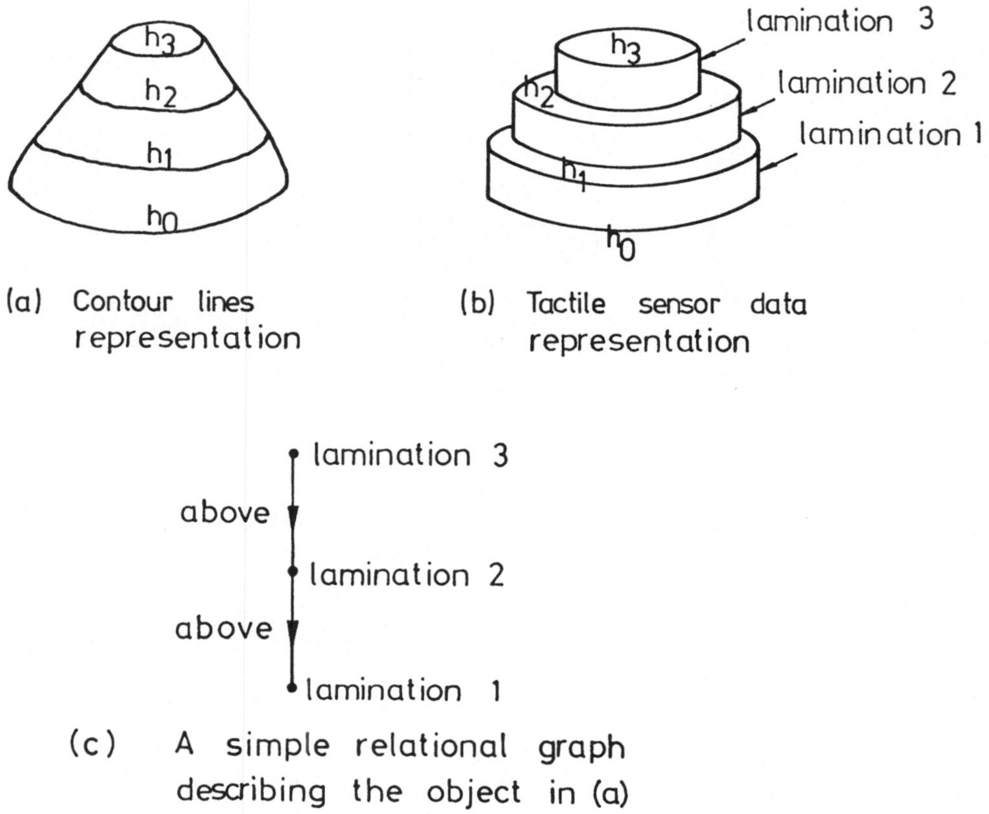

Fig.3. Tactile Sensor and Relational Graph Representations of a Simple Object

(a) shows an object represented by the contour-line technique used in relief maps.

(b) illustrates the tactile-sensor representation of the object.

(c) is a possible relational-graph interpretation of the information contained in (b). The relationship expressed by the tree is that of one "slice" or "lamination" being physically above another.

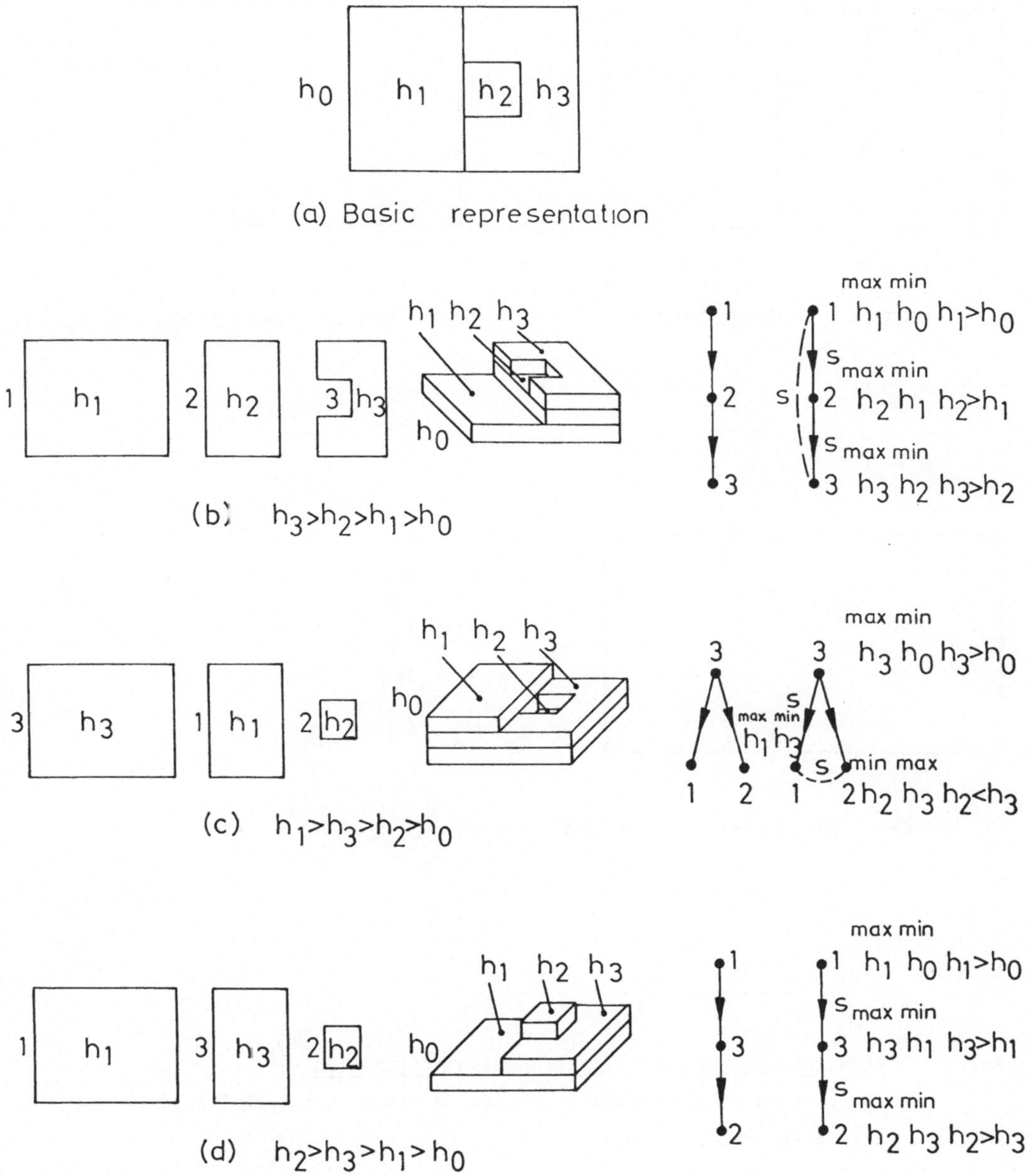

Fig.4. <u>Connection Tree Representations of some Simple Components</u>

The plan views of all the parts are identical (shown in (a)). Each of (b), (c), and (d) shows the peripheral contours of the component laminations, a three-dimensional view of the object, the basic connection tree, and the tree with height and shared-contour data added. Note that contour 2 in (c) encloses a depression and the order of the appended height values is reversed. Note also from (c) that enclosure is not necessary for contour sharing.

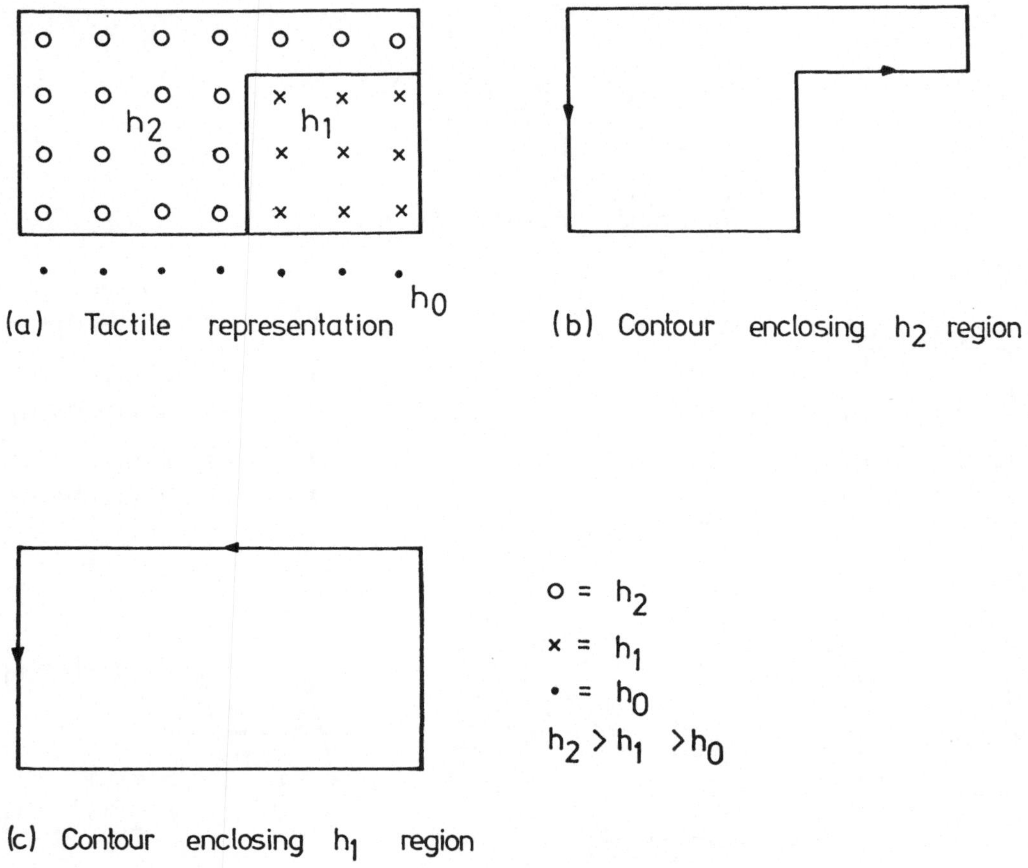

Fig.5. Illustrating the Operation of Contour Extraction

The contour enclosing the h_2 region is traced first, followed by that enclosing the h_1 region.

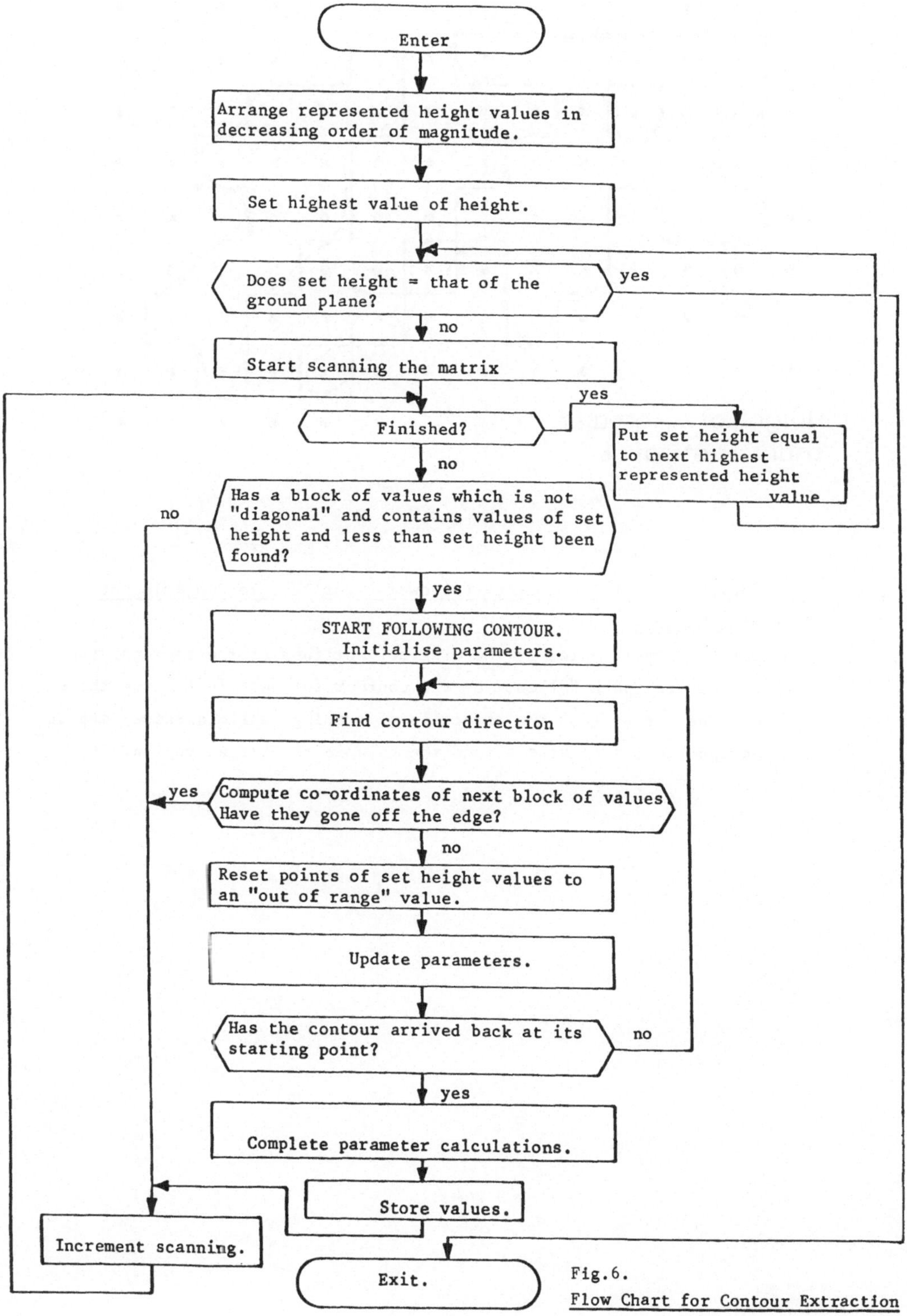

Fig.6.

Flow Chart for Contour Extraction

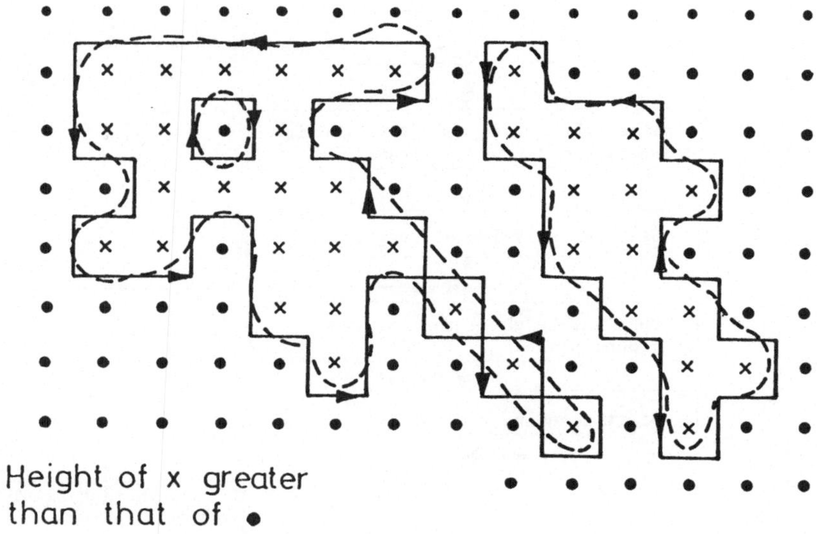

Fig.7. <u>The Application of the Contour-Follower Algorithms to Two Adjacent Disjoint Regions</u>.

The dashed curves represent the original outlines of the regions. The solid curves show the path followed by the contour follower in tracing these curves. The arrows show the direction of tracing (anticlockwise) around the peripheries, clockwise around the hole in the larger region).

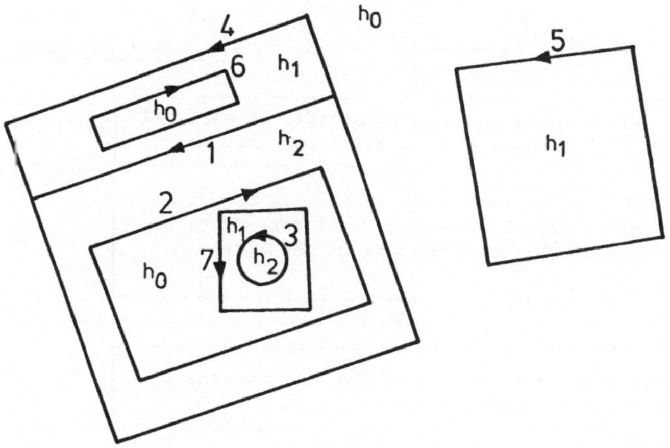

(a) $h_2 > h_1 > h_0$

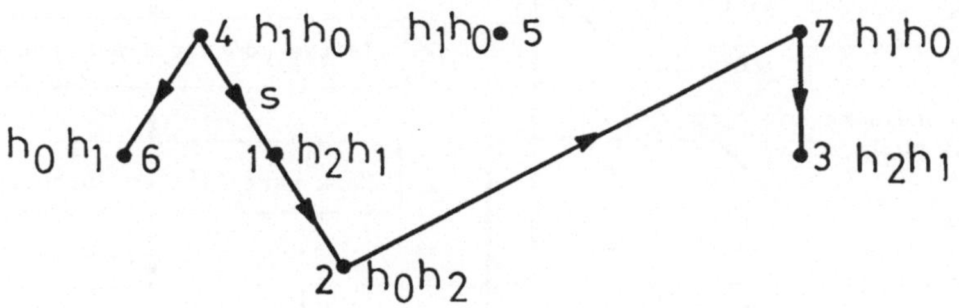

(b)

Fig.8. <u>A Possible Scene as Imaged by the Tactile Sensor</u>

(a) shows the scene with all the contours numbered and each region labelled with its height.

(b) shows the complete connection trees. Note that two separate trees can be linked as shown by the arc joining contour 2 and 7.

Table 2 illustrates one of the three lists used in building up the connection tree; that describing contour enclosure. Note that the enclosing contour number of a peripheral contour is set to zero.

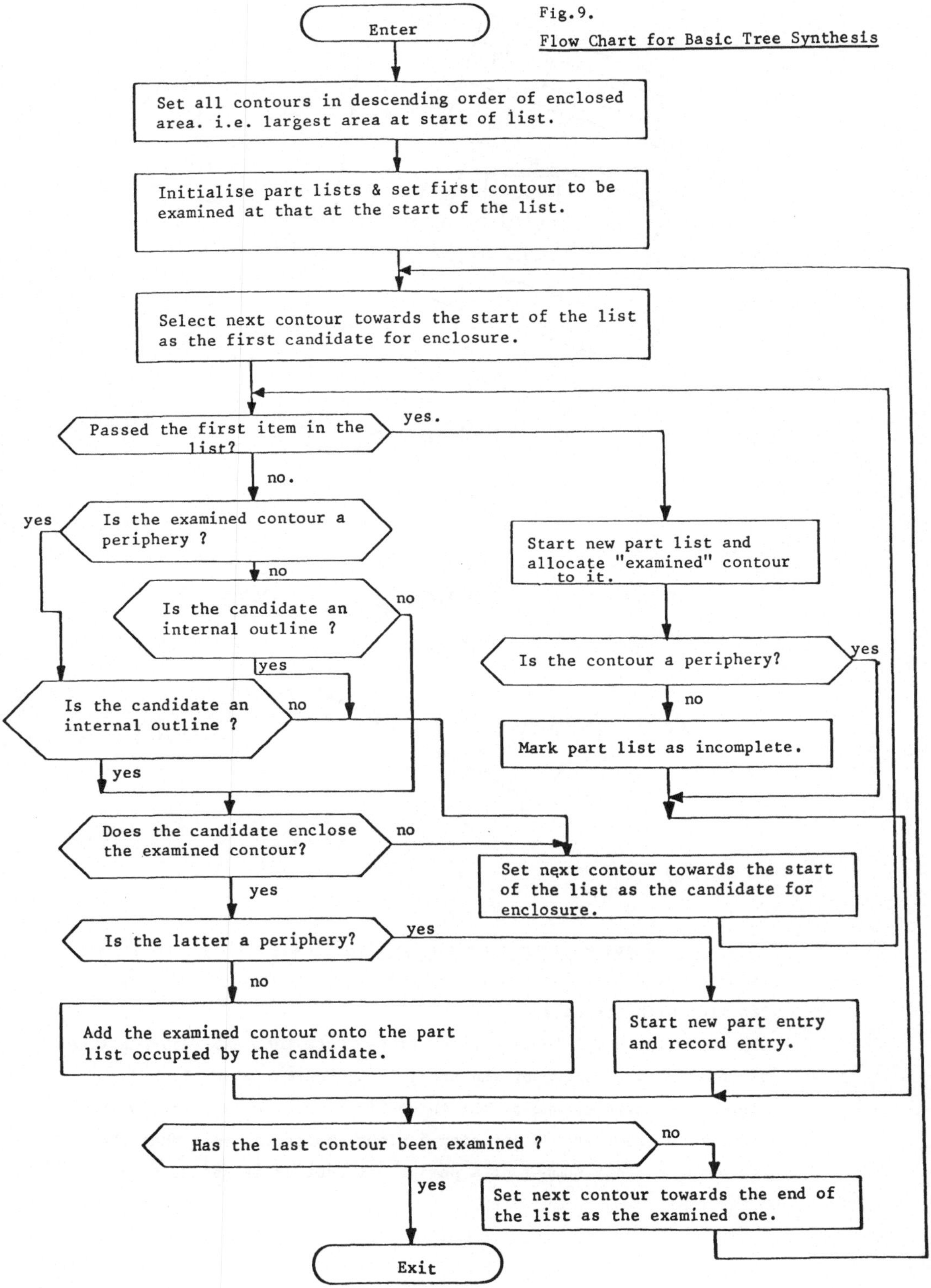

Fig.9.

Flow Chart for Basic Tree Synthesis

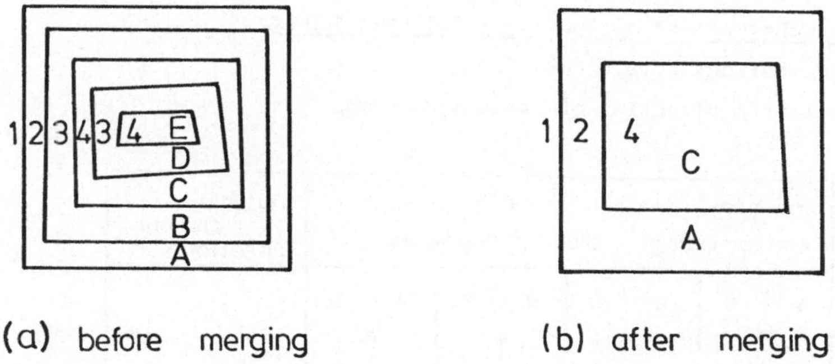

Fig.10. The Merging of Contours

Table 1. A Coherent Set of Contour - Follower Rules.

Convention: X is higher than ·

→ is the direction of contour tracing.

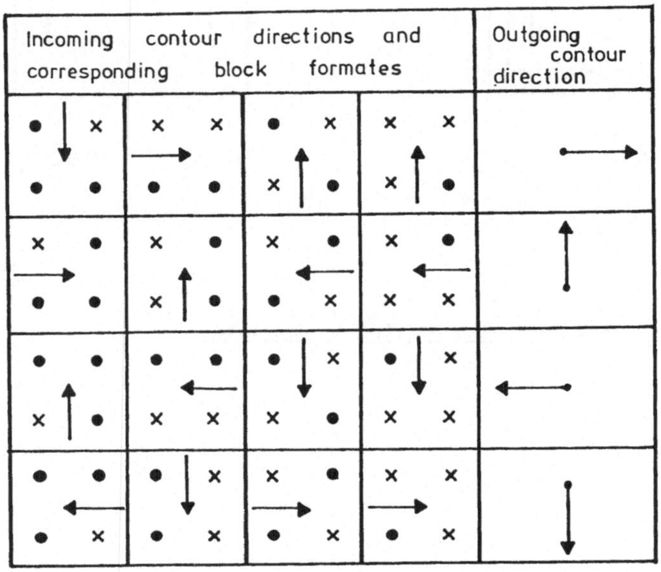

Table 2. List Representation of Contour Enclosure for Fig.8.

Part 1		Part 2		Part 3	
Contour Number	Enclosing Contour Number	Contour Number	Enclosing Contour Number	Contour Number	Enclosing Contour Number
4	0	5	0	7	2
1	4			3	7
2	1				
6	4				

ACKNOWLEDGEMENT

This paper reports some of the results of a research program which has been primarily sponsored by FIAT S.p.A. The authors wish to thank all individuals at FIAT who have participated in this work for their many direct contributions as well as for many stimulating discussions. The authors are also indebted to many colleagues at the C. S. Draper Laboratory who have made substantial contributions to the development of the various systems.

ABSTRACT

The analysis of manufacturing processes from a more formalized point of view allows the utilization of computers and computer techniques for improving process performance. The paper presents some results of a broad program of study and application conducted on mass manufacturing of mechanical parts. An analysis of the process forms the basis for discussing specific potential improvements and their practical realization. The problems and computer-based solutions associated with three specific areas are discussed more in depth as examples of the benefits associated with computer mechanizations in manufacturing. The work contributes also to long range integrated approaches and will be specifically useful in the design of flexible machining systems.

DESIGN AND ANALYSIS OF MASS PRODUCTION OF AUTOMOTIVE PARTS

Louis J. Quagliata
Tze-Thong Chien
Albert L. Hopkins, Jr.
J. Scott Rhodes

The Charles Stark Draper Laboratory, Inc.
Cambridge, Massachusetts 02139
U.S.A.

1.0 Introduction

In years to come, the basic manufacturing processes and the problems with which they are associated may provide a great deal of subject matter for studies in control and information processing, in a manner analogous to what occurred in the fifties and sixties in the search for solutions to problems such as gun-pointing, radar tracking or vehicle trajectory optimization. In order for this field to grow as a useful discipline, it will be necessary to analyze several of the basic industrial processes in depth from a new, more scientific viewpoint*. The hope is that as each of these processes is addressed stage by stage, more formalized understanding of manufacturing problems will emerge, fundamental problems which are common to most or all manufacturing situations will be recognized, and representations, models or abstractions useful in analysis and synthesis will be developed. Traditional manufacturing consists largely of a body of experience which has grown around the fabrication machinery characteristic of each of the basic industries (e.g., rolling mills, machine tools, textile machines, paper machines, etc.) and which is implicitly understood, rather than explicitly formulated today.

The purpose of this paper is to provide an overview of a substantial program of study and application which has been carried out in relation to the process of mass-manufacturing of mechanical parts. The work was primarily sponsored by FIAT S.p.A. of Torino, Italy, and performed in collaboration with different divisions within this organization. It is believed that the effort described is relatively unique in scope as an organized attempt to apply approaches and technology which are usually associated with the aerospace world to more traditional manufacturing areas.

---

* To date, applications of control have been restricted to certain aspects of continuous process control. Continuous processes provided a natural basis for the application of available control and optimization approaches to the extent that they could be modeled as dynamic processes and benefit by the great similarity with other dynamic problems handled successfully by frequency domain and state space methods.

The original stimulus for the work was the simple notion that adopting a systematic viewpoint in the analysis of a large manufacturing process would pave the way for the exploitation of computer-based technology. The introduction of this technology would, in turn, lead to performance improvements and reduction of costs in different stages of the manufacturing process. Being able to improve the performance of processes which have been undergoing development and refinment for decades or even centuries is not a small undertaking. The hope for success stems from the observation that information processing adds new dimensions and capabilities to manufacturing which were not available at the time in which the basic fabrication techniques were originally crystallized.

The study has confirmed that there is broad potential for innovation in manufacturing through the development of explicit procedures and their mechanization with computers. More specifically:

a. Important production issues and parameters have been identified and formalized at certain stages of the process and technical approaches best suited to the structure of each problem have been applied. This lays the foundation for a more formal, "scientific" understanding of the areas addressed.

b. The knowledge gained was translated into specific hardware/software systems. These have achieved explicit improvements in each selected area of production. Many of the most effective applications are not in the direct control of the machinery but involve other areas in the production cycle just as important (e.g., product design, production planning, design standardization, documentation, etc.).

A second objective, which will benefit manufacturing in the future, can be brought closer by introducing computerized models and representation at each stage of the production cycle: activities which, for practical reasons have been kept separate, will be linked to each other and interact much more closely through information processing. For example, the notion that part design and the production engineering required to make the parts should, in principle, work together is well accepted; nevertheless, in most processes this is not possible because of the difficulties of transmitting complex information back and forth between these two functions in a timely way.

2.0 Industrial Production of Metal Parts

In this section, we will attempt to provide an idea of the industrial process which is used for fabricating metal parts as a basis for a discussion of potential areas of improvement and of the methods to achieve this goal.

There are two basic types of metal-cutting machines: general-purpose tools, with which we are all familiar, and which make any part "by hand" on a custom basis, and transfer machines, which make one part type, always the same, in a continuous stream as required, typically, by the automotive industry. The attention of the study has been focused primarily on this latter process, i.e., fabrication of metal parts under mass production conditions.

2.1 Transfer Machine Fabrication

Transfer machines are special machines which comprise many working units (typically, twenty-thirty) located along both sides of a transfer mechanism. This mechanism has the purpose of moving parts automatically from one station to the next of the transfer machine at the completion of each working cycle. At each station, the parts are secured by appropriate clamps and fixtures and are worked on, on opposite faces, by the working units. The synchronized movements of working, clamping and transfer elements are governed by an appropriate sequential controller. Basically, a transfer machine mechanizes the production line concept for metal-cutting machines.

Parts of relative complexity (e.g., engine block, gearbox housing) require a series of transfer machines, i.e., a transfer line, to complete all required metal-cutting operations. The various machines within a transfer line are normally separated by storage elements which are manually or automatically operated. This is to allow separate sections of the production line to stop operation temporarily for maintenance or failure reasons without "bringing down" the entire sequentially organized operation. A typical transfer line for a relatively complex part occupies an area equivalent to half a football field and comprises hundreds of machining stations.

Some of the characterizing features of transfer machines are:

a. Partitioning of the entire work content of the part being manufactured into many elementary subtasks, each of which is assigned to a dedicated tool located in one of the many stations of the transfer line. Typically, we may have 500 tools distributed into 100 stations which are grouped in five transfer machines.

b. Grouping of several tools into multiple tool clusters at each station to allow the machining of an entire hole pattern with a single stroke of a tool-holding fixture. This feature makes each metal-cutting unit into a special machine-tool dedicated to the single part type being manufactured. The metal removal rate and productivity of a special machine-tool, which keeps cutting the same hole pattern over and over again, is extremely high.

c. Very low labor requirement. Typically, one operator for an entire transfer machine which machines complex parts at the rate of two or so a minute.

The high degree of metal-cutting efficiency, the specialization, the simplicity and low cost of "back and forth" metal-cutting units which constitute a transfer machine, and the low incidence of labor costs make the entire transfer machine process extremely efficient at high production rates as compared to general-purpose tool machining. As a result, the cost of fabricating a part such as an engine block under mass production production conditions is dramatically lower, on the order of $25, as compared to as much as $2,500 for manufacturing the same engine "by hand" using general-purpose tools. The other side of the coin is that fabrication by transfer machines is one of the most rigid processes to be found in the traditional manufacturing world in that, once a transfer line is ordered and installed, it can only be utilized for fabricating a single part type at the preassigned production rate.

The mechanics of transfer machine operation have been briefly summarized. Nonwithstanding the efficiency of the basic concept, the process displays many weaknesses, in practice, from the standpoint of reliability and control over its operation. For instance, transfer machines are very vulnerable to failures in the sequencing control chain. In the area of operating costs, variables which would help operators in making decisions affecting costs (tool wear, piece counts, etc.) are practically unobservable. In order to discuss this finer structure of transfer machine operation and approaches for resolving some of the problems, it is helpful, conceptually, to think of transfer machines as being characterized by a "state" as shown in Figure 1. The definition of state is not intended to be exact or complete at this stage, but categories of "state variables" can be identified which relate to the different aspects of transfer machine operation which need to be approached. More specifically:

a. Binary state variables associated with the sequential operation of the machine. Sensors and actuators are ON/OFF devices (microswitches, solenoid valves, motors, etc.). The sensors describe machine condition to the sequential controller; the controller sends out commands to the actuators according to the logic with which it was programmed. We can, therefore, think of a vector of binary variables as characterizing the state of the machine from a sequential control standpoint, at every time.

c. Cumulative variables. A number of such variables (piece counts, number of cycles of usage of each tool, length of stoppages) are very relevant for making correct operating decisions in the management of the machines. Almost no mechanizations exist today for gathering, storing, processing and displaying this type of data for aiding machine operators.

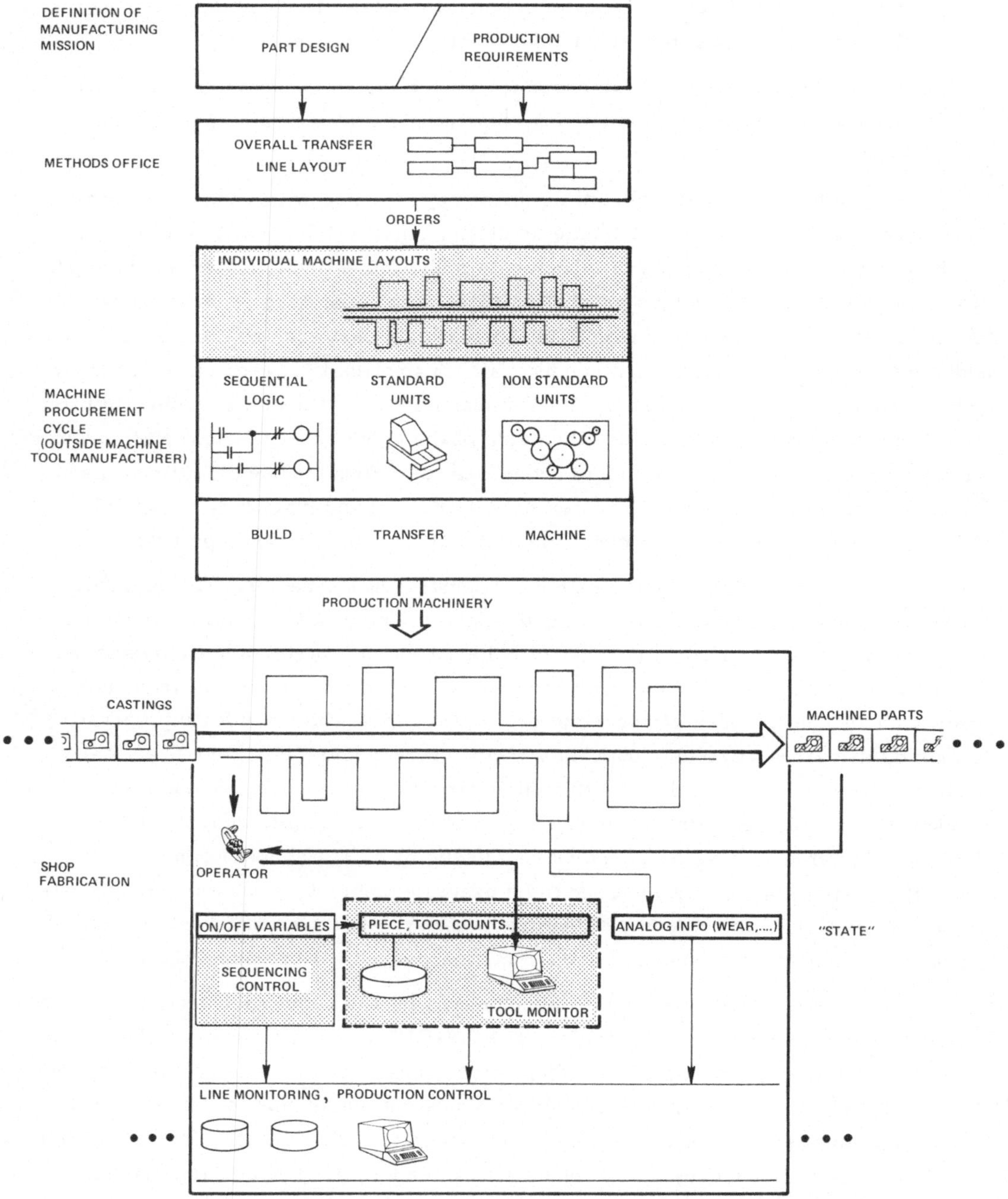

Figure 1 Mechanical Part Manufacture Using Transfer Machines

c. Analog variables. As pieces proceed through a transfer machine, "quality" is attributed to them by all the metal-cutting tools which interact with each part. The state of wear of each tool can be thought of as a monotonically increasing analog function and modeled as a random variable. Conceptually, the vector comprising all such variables in a machine determines the quality of parts being produced. Tool wear information is very difficult and costly to measure in practice. On-line estimates of tool wear would allow maximum utilization of cutting tools, by replacing them only when necessary, and excellent control of the quality of manufactured parts.

Looked at from this point of view, the basic process provides opportunities for the creation of both useful, conceptual models and practical implementations of monitoring and control. Diagnosis of transfer machine failures, more precise methods for specifying sequential controllers, more powerful hardware to build them with, the gathering and processing of data related to machine management, the measurement and estimation of tool wear are some of the areas that need serious rethinking and which have been approached in this study. Two of these areas will be discussed in more depth in sections to follow.

2.2 Upstream Production Functions

Actual fabrication of parts on the shop sloor is only the last stage within a larger production cycle. Upstream of fabrication are found complex activities which are just as important and contribute dramatically to the cost of the parts which are ultimately produced. A full characterization of all production-related functions in the cycle with their different objectives and time frames would be difficult to provide and falls outside of the scope of this paper. Figure 1 simply displays, in schematic form, the main stages in the manufacturing chain which must be considered to form an idea of the scope, cost structure and dynamics of the overall process. In these different functional areas, which do not involve direct control of process or machinery, are also found sizeable opportunities for streamlining and organizing the production environment utilizing computer aids.

Product design (mechanical part design in this specific case) and the setting of the desired levels of hourly production are fundamental functions in the production cycle and among the most complex. These functions will not be discussed further, however, since a general familiarity is assumed on the part of the reader. Attention is only brought on the complexity of the information content which characterizes the entities which are manipulated at this stage (primarily, geometry of parts). Computer representations of these entities for automatic processing or documentation are a natural development*.

---

* A large activity aimed at representing parts synthetically with a computer for purposes of manipulation and engineering verifications is presently ongoing at the C. S. Draper Laboratory (SHAPES). A distinct, but conceptually related activity is directed at digitizing, storing, and editing line drawings (Automated Mechanical Drafting).

Once the geometry, material and tolerances for a given part type have been specified, together with a desired production rate, the next important step in the production cycle is the generation of the special machines which will manufacture that part. This step is normally carried out on the outside by special machine tool manufacturers so that it can aptly be characterized as a "production cycle within a production cycle". The machine procurement cycle (see Figure 1) may take as long as one year or more to complete.

Preliminary to building each machine, a first-pass layout of the entire transfer line is performed by the user organization's Methods Office (see Figure 1). Subsequently, each machine is ordered and the actual design and build cycle is initiated. For simplicity, we have subdivided this cycle into three main stages:

1. The detailed layout of the transfer machine. This can be viewed as a combinatorial problem of assigning all elementary machining operations, which typically number in the hundreds, to one of the stations of the transfer machine. The designer must not only balance the working load on each station, but take into account geometric constraints dictated by the location of the surfaces, sequencing constraints and other technological considerations. Machine layout is a key activity carried out by specialists with many years of experience. Its successful performance determines the initial cost of the machine as well as its expandability.

2. The design of machine subsystems. These can be thought of as falling into the categories of standard and non-standard units. For example, the slide beds, columns, fixture supporting units are "off-the-shelf" and are brought together by special machine manufacturers erector-set style. Non-standard units include the multiple tool-holding fixtures (which comprise relatively complex gear trains) and the transfer and clamping jigs for handling and holding each part. In a different category, we have the design of the sequential controller which will cause the different working units to carry out their assigned tasks in the required sequence (see Figure 1).

3. The building of the transfer machine. This stage comprises the actual building of the subsystems from the detailed drawings, assembly of these into the complete machine, and shakedown of the machine to check that it performs its assigned metal-cutting tasks within the required tolerances.

The layout/design of transfer machines is more of an art than a science today and is characterized by certain massive, bottle-necking design tasks which require the capability for handling a lot of data, for examining a large number of possibilities and tradeoffs, or both. Some such tasks, which we could term "cognitive tasks" are: organizing the many operations into stations in order to minimize the initial cost of the machine; once the mechanical design is complete, performing the logic design of the sequential controller which will implement the specified sequencing of all working, clamping and transfer units; the design of the complex gear trains required to drive all spindles in each multiple-spindle head from a single prime mover.

Some of the most interesting possibilities for streamlining and organizing in the overall cycle of production are related to cognitive tasks such as the few mentioned above. These tasks usually display inherent structure and logic which are quite complex. If the structure can be captured and formalized, however, the difficulty of performing these tasks can be greatly alleviated through computer aids.One outstanding example (computer-aided layout of the process) will be discussed and will illustrate this point effectively. It has already been pointed out that special machine design, the "production cycle within the production cycle", is one of the most logistically complex and costly steps in the overall manufacturing cycle.

In summary, even this simplified discussion of mass-manufacturing of mechanical parts is sufficient to provide a glimpse of challenging technical opportunities both in the area of direct control of the process and in the areas upstream involving product design and process layout. Sections 3, 4 and 5 will deal with specific problems and their associated solutions. The corresponding areas of the overall cycle have been shaded for easy reader reference.

2.3 Production with General-Purpose Tools

Before leaving the general subject of metal part fabrication, it is interesting to compare mass manufacturing with the "normal" manufacturing technique, i.e., the employment of general-purpose machine tools (see Figure 2). The part design function is quite analogous to the one for mass manufacturing, the amount of design effort being proportional to the importance of the parts to be produced (the automotive case is, of course, a special case where great consideration is paid to the needs of mass production). The fundamental difference with respect to the mass production process resides in the fact that the process layout function takes on a completely different character with general-purpose tools and that the machine design design stage is completely lacking.

Fabrication is conducted in machine shopes which contain an ensemble of general-purpose tools of all basic types. The machinery, therefore, is independent of part design, very flexible and capable of responding to the manufacture of "any part type" on a custom basis. The process layout function consists simply of scheduling the part through the various machines within the shop or, in the case of N/C machines, of the part programming which is required*. Except for very small lot

---

* N/C machines are a special case of general-purpose machines where certain functions have been automated and made repeatable.

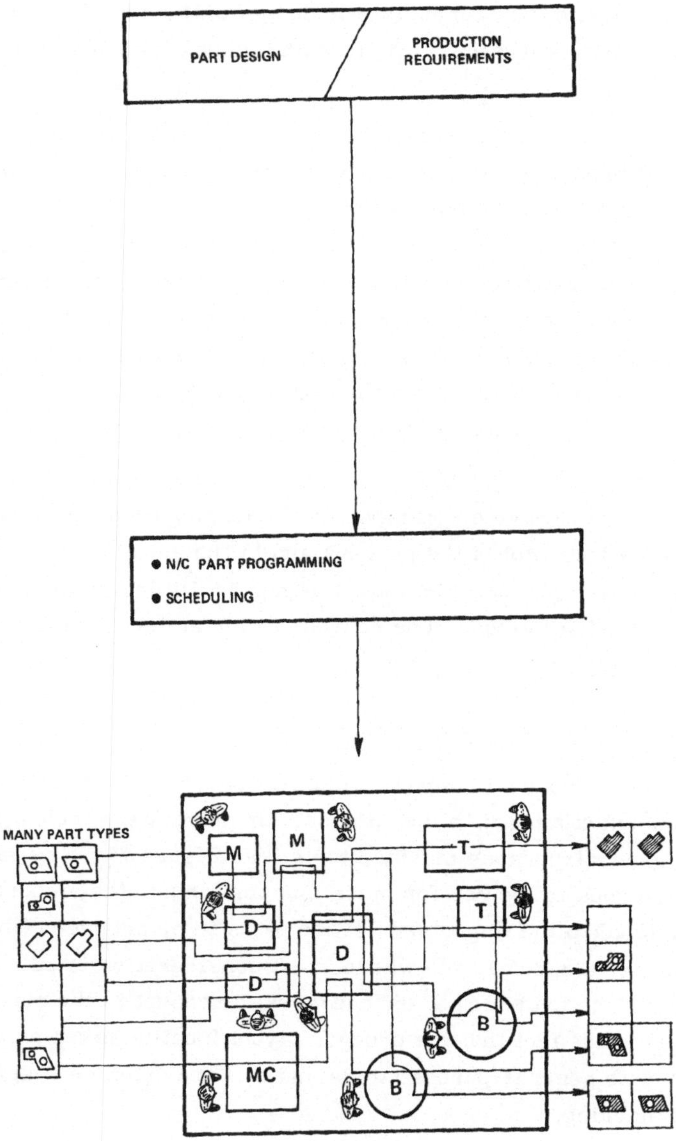

Figure 2 Mechanical Part Manufacturing Using General-Purpose Machine Tools

sizes which take maximum advantage of the flexibility of the machinery, the use of general-purpose tools may lead to low efficiencies and relatively high cost per part. Some of the reasons are the high cost of the machine tool themselves, the high labor content associated with machine shops (at least one man per machining station), the low fraction of the time which each machine spends actually cutting metal, the single-spindle character of general-purpose machines, and the transient and ad hoc character of job shop operation (see Figure 2) which prevents the establishment of a single production stream as in the case of transfer machines.

In considering these two vastly different approaches for manufacturing metal parts, we notice that their points of strength are completely opposite: the effectiveness of mass manufacturing resides in the inherent efficiency of the fabrication process itself. This requires, however, a long and costly secondary production cycle for designing and building special machinery. The flexibility of the machinery practically eliminates this need in the other process, which is its great advantage, but the fabrication process itself is singularly inefficient and costly except at very low production volume.

Today's users is forced to choose between two processes which display markedly different economic performance and are effective respectively only at the very high and the very low ends of the production spectrum. This suggests that it would be highly desirable to develop completely new machining systems or processes to radically modify the economics of fabricating metal parts, particularly in the "medium" production range.

3.0 Computer-Aided Layout Design of Transfer Machines[1]

In order for a transfer machine to achieve high productivity at minimum cost, machining operations must be carefully grouped at each work station to perform the maximum number of operations on both sides of the part. Layout design is the assignment of operations to work stations so that the initial cost of the transfer machine is minimized. Today, this is an operation which is very costly in engineering time. It involves calculating the cutting parameters of every elementary cutting operation and finding the "best" grouping of compatible operations into stations. In present-day design practice, given the very large numbers of solutions to be evaluated and the limited time available, it is impossible for engineers to search exhaustively over all feasible designs to select an optimum scheme which minimizes the initial cost of a production machine (transfer line or rotary indexing machine). The availability of a computer model of the transfer machine layout design creates the possibility of generating alternative machine layouts within the allotted time. That is, the model can be used to provide a preview of many different optimum layouts related to potential modifications in the design of the product, in production methods, and, most importantly, in the production rate. This provides essential information for a sensitivity analysis of the machine cost.

Figure 3 presents the basic functional flow diagram of the inputs to the model which consist of the identification of the machining operations and of the various constraints present in the metal-working process. The basic inputs of the program are divided into two categories: user's inputs and stored data banks. A user must input part specific information from the working drawing of the part to be machined. Data which is common to the design of all transfer machines is stored as data banks to reduce inputs and to enforce general standards. Inputs and Data Banks shown in Figure 3 are self-explanatory:

1. User Inputs

   a. Identification of the operation which consists of the surface number, operation type, tool characteristics, surface dimensions, side of operations, etc.

   b. Precedence relations.

   c. Geometric constraints specifying operations which cannot be grouped within the same station or which must be grouped within the same station.

2. Stored Data Banks

   a. Machinability data.

   b. Compatibility conditions which may be related to surface quality considerations or to kinematic motion of cutting tools.

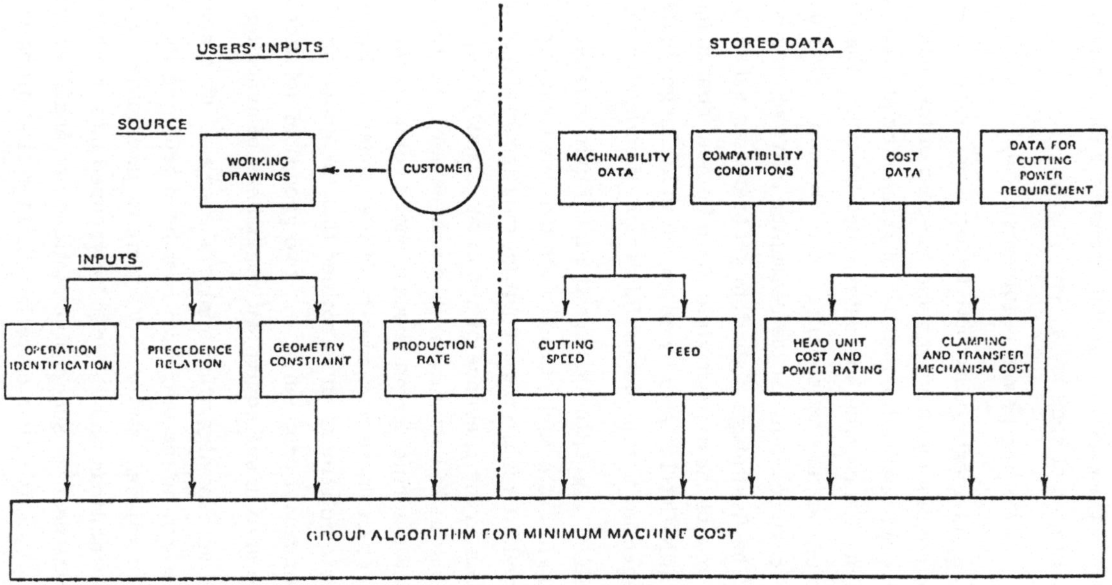

Figure 3. Functional Flow Diagram of Input Data.

c. Cost data regarding transfer and clamping mechanisms, various types of head units, etc.

d. Cutting power requirement data.

Two primary elements contribute to forming the machine cost: the cost of the transfer and clamping mechanisms and the cost of the machine head units. The former cost is proportional to the number of machining stations and is large relative to that of the head units which is determined by either the required power/thrust rating or the size of the gearbox specified at each head. This observation suggests that the minimum cost problem can be decoupled into two stages called MINISTAT and MINICOST. The first stage algorithm generates an exhaustive set of minimum station solutions; one of these must yield the minimum cost machine which is found by application of MINICOST. As is well known in all large-scale systems, such decomposition is essential to the successful design of computer algorithms.

The MINISTAT algorithm groups the maximum number of operations in sequence and/or parallel into each station such that the total number of stations required is minimized. Because the algorithm must generate an intelligent, exhaustive list of solutions in the presence of numerous constraints, dynamic programming is the natural technique to be applied. The presence of constraints, which tends to render the transfer machine design process more complicated, on the contrary causes a simplification of the computation of the model by diminishing the number of feasible candidate solutions. It is noticed that the grouping of operations at each station is a combinational problem, i.e., two groups of solutions with identical operations at the same station are equivalent regardless of ordering.

The minimum cost algorithm analyzes every solution derived in the minimum station stage to determine the minimum cost head grouping for that solution. The algorithm tests two adjacent stations at a time to determine whether they can satisfy the compatibility conditions and also can be grouped into one head more economically than into separate heads. Successive stations are analyzed until two stations are found which cannot satisfy either criteria. Strings of stations which can be grouped constitute a decoupled subsection. The MINICOST solution for a particular MINISTAT solution consists of the optimum cost of each subsection. The minimum cost machine layout design is the solution with the least cost among all the minimum cost head groupings from each MINISTAT solution.

An example for the design of a transfer machine to fabricate cylinder blocks is presented for illustration. There are seventy-nine operations on seventeen surfaces on the left side of the cylinder block and ninety-six operations on twenty-two surfaces on the right side. The MINISTAT algorithm uses a total of 1.60 minutes (Univac 1110) to generate the minimum station solutions with thirteen stations. The exhaustive list consists of twelve solutions on the right side and thirty solutions on the left side. The MINICOST algorithm uses a total of 0.3 minute to generate an optimum head configuration of nine heads for the left side and seven heads for the right side. It is interesting to note that the thirty MINISTAT solutions on the left side generated six head configurations with different costs, while two head configurations with different costs are generated for the twelve MINISTAT solutions on the right side. The complete program uses 60K of storage composed of 36-bit words.

Figure 4 illustrates the computer graphic layout of this transfer machine design. The layout displays a sketch of each head unit size to be used. At each head, the grouped operations on their respective side are identified by their corresponding numbers indicated on the part working drawing and the types of operations. In addition, the program outputs a detailed printout of the transfer machine specification. This includes, besides the information on graphic layout, the power, thrust ratings and the feed rate values at each head unit, the cost data, and the capacity for future production expansion.

The program described, which is termed CALL/1 (Computer-Aided Line Layout), is currently being used by the Machine Tool Division of FIAT S.p.A. Additionally, it has been successfully tried on layout problems and parts provided by American machine tool manufacturers with dramatic reductions in engineering design time (4-5 to 1) plus great improvements in the standardization and exhaustiveness of the output provided. CALL/1 represents an excellent example of how a certain class of "cognitive tasks", i.e., tasks requiring complex skills possessed only by experienced personnel, can be systematically laid down and organized algorithmically within carefully designed computer programs. This result requires substantial effort and very close collaboration between user organizations and systems analysts.

45			ALES. 22, LAMAT. 32, SMUSS. 72										
46								ALES. 22, ALES. 22					
72 - 77				CENTR. 52	FORAT. 53					CONTR. 99	MASCH. 91		CONTR. 99
78				CENTR. 52	FORAT. 53	FORAT. 53			FORAT. 53	CONTR. 99	MASCH. 91		CONTR. 99
79							ALES. 22, ALES. 22						
80 , 81				ALLAR. 61, SMUSS. 71	FORAT. 53					CONTR. 99	MASCH. 91		CONTR. 99
82 - 85							CENTR. 52	FORAT. 53		CONTR. 99		MASCH. 91	CONTR. 99
91		FRESA. 11											

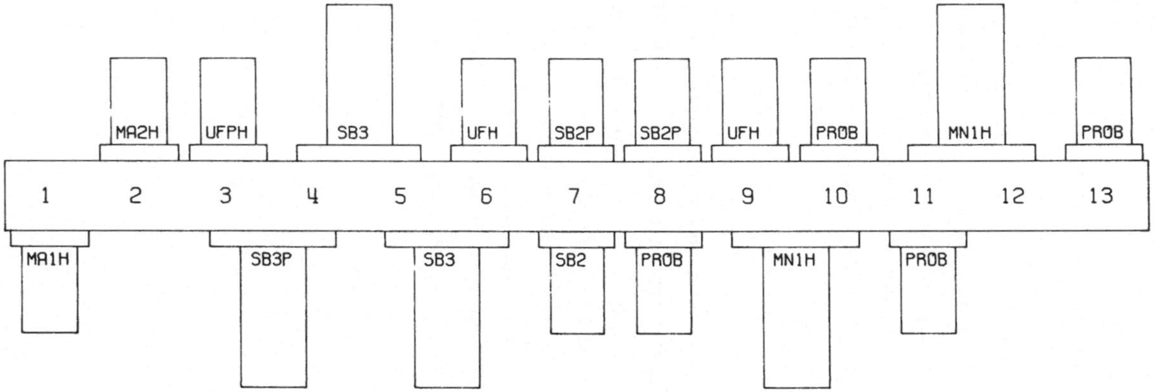

45			ALES. 22, SMUSS. 72										
46				ALES. 22, SMUSS. 72									
47 , 48				CENTR. 52			FORAT. 53	CONTR. 99					
49 , 50					CENTR. 52	FORAT. 53		CONTR. 99	MASCH. 91		CONTR. 99		
52 - 60					CENTR. 52	FORAT. 53		CONTR. 99		MASCH. 91	CONTR. 99		
61 - 66				CENTR. 52			FORAT. 53	CONTR. 99	MASCH. 91		CONTR. 99		
92	FRESA. 11												

Figure 4 Graphical Layout of Transfer Machine for Cylinder Block

4.0 Management of Machines for Minimum Operating Cost

A problem which is completely unresolved in today's operation of high-volume metal-working lines is how to control and minimize the variable costs related to operating the automated equipment. The most important variable costs incurred in operating a transfer machine are attributed to the cutting tools and are the costs of the tools themselves (including resharpening costs), the downtime cost related to lost production while tools are being changed, and the costs of making bad parts. As an indication, the cost of perishable tooling on a transfer machine exceeds the cost of labor and is comparable to the amortization of the machine. Two specific problems in metal-cutting which are principal contributors to high costs and which have been attacked under this program are:

a. Choice of cutting conditions.

b. Tool change strategies.

Optimization of cutting conditions, cutting speed and feed, has been considered for nearly seventy years. An empirical relation between cutting conditions and tool life is used to balance the increased productivity of higher speeds against the higher tool costs and tool change downtime resulting from shorter tool lives. Unfortunately, the tool life relation varies not only with cutting conditions, but with tool and workpiece materials, geometry, static and dynamic stiffness and other properties. As a result, optimization requires extensive tests to determine this relation for each specific application. Although such optimization has been found to often reduce operating costs by factors of two or more, the procedure itself is expensive and, in our experience, not widely used.

A related problem is that of an optimum tool change policy: early changes increase tool usage and tool change downtime while late changes risk costly damage to both tool and workpiece. Tool life in production situations is quite random with standard deviations rarely less than 10% of the average and often exceeding 50% of the average. Such variation makes tool changes at fixed intervals costly. Human operators can often do quite well on the basis of intuition but can also do badly at indicating the proper time for changes. In any case, good operators are becoming rarer as automation increases. Automatic tool wear indicators have not been widely successful as yet, except perhaps in finishing operations where workpiece measurements can be used.

Modeling has been used extensively in analyzing both these problems. It was found, however, that the key impediment to handling the problems systematically was the impossibility of building a log or data base containing accurate and detailed histories of tool changes over statistically significant intervals of time (weeks, months). In other words, we need information on state and state history (see Figure 1). A history of the state would allow to derive statistics on tool lives and related costs under different conditions of operation.

To study possibilities for reducing tool costs in a production environment, CSDL and FIAT have developed the Tool Monitor[2], a computerized system which can be temporarily attached to a transfer machine to monitor tool usage (see Figure 5). A transfer machine normally has between 25 and 200 individual cutting tools. The system automatically detects and times machine stops. The machine operator makes inputs on the input unit shown in Figure 5. Entries, on a ten-digit keyboard, are prompted and echoed on a CRT screen. Operators enter stop reason and, for tool stops, identify the tools changed. Entries of tool condition (broken or not) and measurements before and after resharpening can be used to more accurately measure tool costs. A series of output reports provides detailed information on productivity, tool lives, tool costs, and a full breakdown of value added to the part.

The Tool Monitor provides the tool analysts with an array of exact quantitative information which far exceeds anything that has been available in the past. The information on tool life average and standard deviation and tool breakage and consumption has allowed specification of correct tool change intervals yielding immediate reductions in operating costs of over 10%. Reports are also generated which provide a full breakdown of the contribution of each tool to the value added to the part in the machine under examination. This allows the identification of costly tool positions so that efforts at improvement can be directed where potential gains are greatest. The cost analysis provides a quantitative basis for evaluating any changes in operating policy. Significant additional cost reductions are anticipated through selective application of cutting speed changes and perhaps automatic tool wear indicators.

In terms of the Block Diagram of Figure 1, the Tool Monitor instruments the measurement of that portion of the state labeled "tool counts, piece counts", etc. The gathering of more detailed analog information related to wear of individual tools has also been instrumented for purposes of experimentation ("Head Monitoring"). Both the Tool Monitor and Head Monitor are physically realized in a way that allows them to run under a higher level task called "Line Monitoring", presently under development (see Figure 1). Line Monitoring is aimed at more aggregate Production Control and Information Display functions for an entire transfer line. If we note that computer-based sequential controllers will increasingly be used, we are moving in a direction in which all categories of the "state" identified earlier, are being mechanized and made available for the required control purposes. The mechanization of the state which is emerging takes the form of a comprehensive network of compatible minicomputers or microprocessors organized in a hierarchical fashion.

The importance of the creation of this network of information in the shop, which augments today's fabrication process should not be underestimated. Today, decisions regarding the management of machines are severely limited by the lack of timely information, appropriately processed. Information on machine state is not only largely unobservable, but it is diffuse in location and spread out in time, as typified by the sharp deterioration of information which occurs at the time of a shift change.

Correct information is the key to reorganization and large improvements in the performance of the "uncontrollable" shop environment.

Figure 5 The Tool Monitor

5.0 Sequential Control of Discrete Machines

The repetitive movements of most automatic machinery employed in high-volume production are commanded by logic units which perform sequential control of such movements. Sequential controllers constitute a major cause of problems on the shop floor, primarily as a result of their responses to failures in the sensors and actuators with which they interact. Such component failures result in costly and unpredictable stoppages of the machinery, are difficult to diagnose and, most importantly, may cause the machinery to enter anomalous configurations which result in jamming and severe damage to the machine itself and possible danger to operating personnel.

The primary responsibility for such occurrences lies with present day design techniques which do not guarantee predictable or safe behavior in the face of failures. It is left to the designer to specify interlocks against those failures which he is in a position to predict. These failures, on the other hand, constitute such a common occurrence that it makes sense to devise new ways of designing sequential controllers in order to ensure correct performance for all possible failure modes. A related reason for a second look at sequential controller design is to learn how to specify controllers appropriately for implementation on small control computers. Digital computers by their very nature are very well suited to the control of sequential processes, but this inherent capability has remained unexploited in the absence of modern sequential controller design methods especially intended for computer implementation.

It is interesting to note that sequential controllers have been the subject of limited theoretical work as compared to the closely allied areas of continuous control and sequential switching circuit theory. The primary reason for this void can be found in the fact that intuitive notions are sufficient for designing simple controllers for small or medium systems. As indicated earlier, however, existing methods of synthesis are inadequate for the larger systems. Specifically, the resulting controllers are difficult to verify with respect to the parasitic or anomalous operation which results as a consequence of a failure.

A schematic diagram of a system under sequential control is shown as Figure 6. As the members of a machine are actuated, appropriate ON/OFF sensors (primarily limit switches in the case of manufacturing machines) notify the logic that certain discrete positions have been reached. With this knowledge, the logic generates the appropriate output sequence commands to the actuators (motors, solenoid valves, etc.). It should be noted that the inputs to the controller characterize the state or position of the controlled plant; the outputs of the controller, conversely, characterize the state of control logic.

It is useful to define a state for the entire system as consisting of the array of two-valued discrete variables formed by the outputs of sensors of controlled

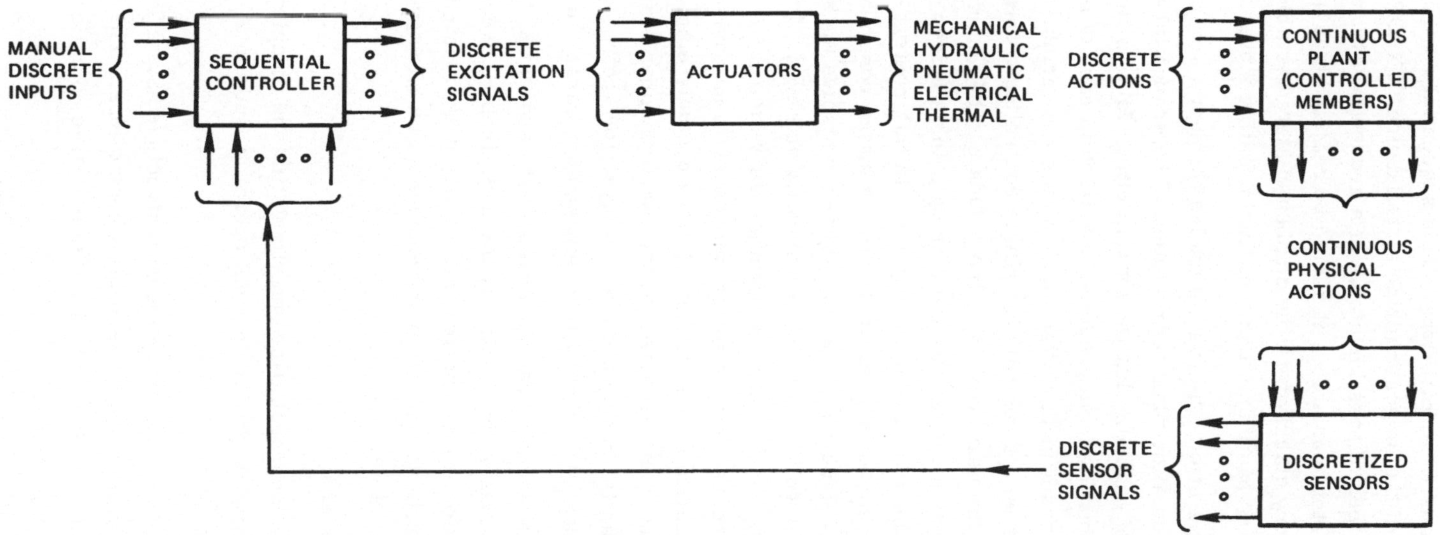

Fig. 6 Sequential System.

members and the outputs of the controllers. This sequential control system state corresponds to the part of the larger machine state labeled "ON/OFF variables" in Figure 1. Since the number of possible states of a sequential system is 2^n, where n is the number of total state variables, it should be realized that the number of possible states increases very quickly with the number of state variables. A system with twenty state variables has more than a million possible states.

During normal operation, the system cycles through a subset of all possible states which constitute the allowed or legal states. The sequential control design problem is simply that of ensuring that the system either follows the prescribed cycle or behaves in a controlled and predictable fashion in case of failure. For several reasons, however, traditional design focuses on state variables rather than complete states. Each step defines only the single controller output or state variable which will command the next desired action. This can be accomplished either by writing a Boolean expression for that variable or by using a ladder diagram equivalent. The statement of the design of the controller, in this context, consists simply of a list of Boolean expressions corresponding to the output commands. Such expressions contain cross references between selected variables in the form of interlocks but knowledge of the entire state is not normally achieved. It should be realized of course that specifying the entire system at every step is, in general, a cumbersome process; this process is impractical moreover in an environment where cost dictates the minimization of the number of relay contacts employed. It can be anticipated at this juncture that the stated restriction in number of storage elements no longer applies when digital computers are employed for control since a large number of binary variables can be stored with no appreciable impact on cost.

It is not difficult to comprehend the reasons why sequential controllers which are designed on a state variable basis display the undesirable behavior pinpointed at the beginning of this section. Two approaches, conceptually related, have been employed to resolve these difficulties. Both approaches make effective use of the concept of sequential system state.

These approaches are:

a. An analytic approach based on simulating the complete behavior of a given sequential system during nominal operation and for all possible single component failures.

b. A synthetic approach which uses a structured State Transition Diagram (STD) approach to design sequential controllers. The STD also represents a source language from which an interpretive compiler generates code for the central minicomputer.

The analytic approach was the source through which the sequential control problem was originally approached. An ambitious event simulator, which is capable of describing both nominal and anomalous behavior, was built. The simulator finds all "static-states" or terminal conditions into which the machine is lead as a result of all possible failures of any of the ON/OFF components. A list of static states is stored on the on-board computer and allows diagnosis of failures. More than one machine at FIAT have been equipped with this diagnostic system, which is capable of pinpointing the failure of hundreds of components.

The synthetic approach is the primary subject of the remainder of this section.

5.1 Sequential Controller Synthesis

It has been stated that the most effective way of specifying the behavior of a sequential system is by laying down an ordered sequence of complete states. A structured State Transition Diagram approach is offered as an effective means of accomplishing this goal while at the same time providing the designer with a tool which is more intuitively related to the actuations and movements of the controlled plant than any of the methods currently in use.

A simple example represents the best way to introduce the methods. Shown in Figure 7(a) is a tank which is filled by turning on a pump-motor (M) and emptied by opening a drain valve (D). It is desired to establish a repetitive cycle which starts filling the tank when the liquid level reaches below L_0 and commences drainage when the level is greater than L_1. Assume that at the beginning of the cycle the system is in state 1 (Figure 7(b)) with the liquid level below L_0 (and L_1) and both actuators off. A START signal enables the first transition to state 2 where M has been turned on. No further actuator activity will occur until the liquid level passes through state 3 ($> L_0$, $< L_1$) and reaches state 4 where the liquid has passed L_1. The motor is automatically shut off (state 5) and the drain valve opened (state 6). Subsequently, the level goes below L_1 again (state 7), below L_0 (state 8) and finally D is closed and the system goes back to state 1.

The figure shows all sixteen (16) possible states of the sequential system of which only eight are legal. The trajectory completely determines the evolution of the state of the system and hence represents a complete statement of desired behavior. Great order and visibility into sequential behavior characterisize the method.

The foregoing example illustrates some interesting characteristics of the State Transition Diagram method.

1. The STD is an effective way of specifying all the bits or state variables of the complete state and of visualizing these effectively.

2. Horizontal movements within an STD denote change in the state of the controller. Vertical movements indicate changes in the state of the sensors. The state of the entire sequential system has been defined earlier to include both inputs and outputs to the controller so that it is natural that a two-dimensional diagram is required for describing the full behavior of the sequential

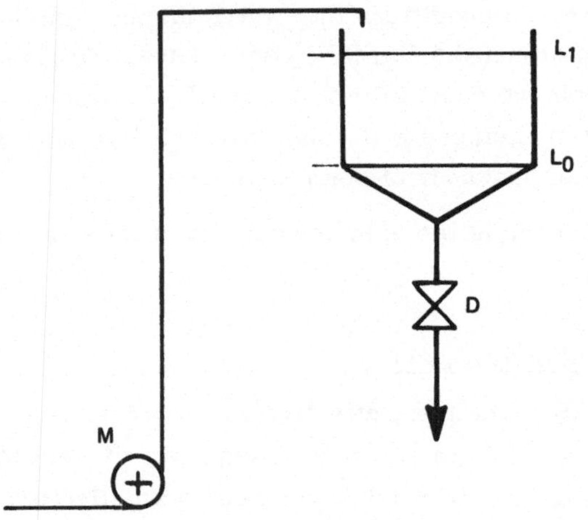

(a)

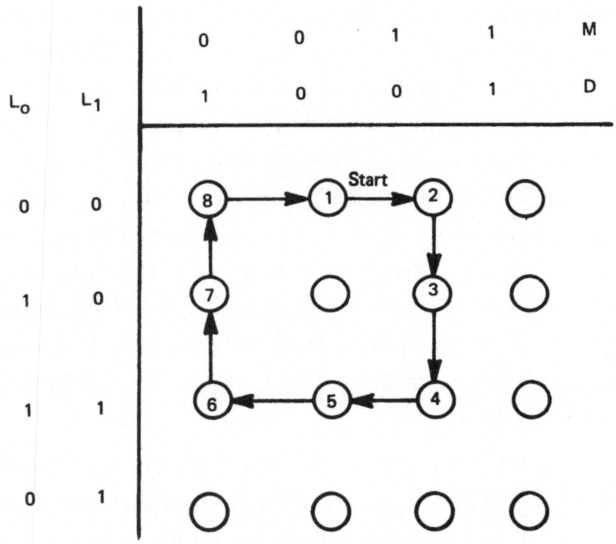

(b)

Fig. 7 Sequential control of repetitive cycle to fill and empty a liquid tank.

system. For reference, the reader is reminded that when we are dealing with the state of a sequential circuit alone, a one-dimensional representation suffices (recall, for example, the State Transition Diagram for a ring counter).

3. A STD is meant to allow a functional representation of the process itself to generate the control logic directly. The approach adopted is conceptual rather than Boolean. This is made possible by the fact that existing software aids allow to go essentially from a STD to the program for the control minicomputer.

4. It is not difficult to augment a State Transition Diagram with additional bits corresponding to variables not explicitly included in the diagram. Moreover, if the system enters one of the illegal states through a failure, alarming functions or other actions can be explicitly specified. The method, in other words, includes dynamic error diagnostics as an intimate part of the logic specification.

5.2 Computer Implementation of State Transition Diagrams

Digital computers are intrinsically capable of controlling sequential processes by their very nature. The approach which is being recommended here is a sequential control language based on the State Transition Diagram. The STD can be readily transferred to a tabular form that serves as a medium level interpretive language for a control computer. This is done as follows:

a. The sequential control specification represented as a set of STD's is copied into a format suitable for automatic processing and then translated by off-line computer into a compact tabular format.

b. The tabular format is stored in a read-only memory attached to the control computer. Also in the ROM is a program called an interpreter which serves the function of scanning both the input variables and the stored tabular information to find the correct values for the output variables.

It is hoped that the strong resemblence of the control language to sequential control behavior will help to produce cost savings in programming and debugging. Once the process is understood by the programmer, he can specify the control without having to make a mental or written translation to Boolean equations. "What you see is what you get."

One of the important purposes of the language is to reduce the impact of system failures through detection and diagnosis. This is implemented through translations to alarm and safety states which are specified either explicitly or implicitly.

The discussion up to this point has asserted that the STD language can allow digital computers to be used as sequential controllers with potential advantages in programming and in performance over controllers utilized today. As indicated, a program in the STD language consists essentially of a list of states, each of which has its own table of other states to which it is allowed to make transitions. The table includes the stimulus for each transition. The STD language is, in reality, a language type and any number of specific languages of this type can be defined. One such language, called TRASC, has been defined by Wolfe[3] and includes several features which make it useful in certain specific sequential control applications. Among such features are some that are concerned with system partitioning, a problem which has been outlined in the previous section.

The computer control method briefly outlined in this section has two main thrusts:

a. High sophistication of control and diagnosis made possible by the use of memory and processing facilities which are lacking in relay controllers or programmable controllers.

b. The ability to use an STD diagram as a source language yielding a modular, simple and straightforward program for the control computer, together with great visibility into the sequential behavior of the system.

5.3 Practical Implementation of Sequential Controllers

We have seen how the relay ladder diagram, long an industry standard, is now in a position to be displaced by a new generation of languages that are oriented toward functional level specification rather than the obsolete microscropic control level. A functional language has been defined at the Draper Laboratory, the associated software developed, and this has been used for pilot implementations which employ minicomputers and microprocessors rather than programmable controllers. The use of specialized translators and interpreters makes this possible without undue proliferation of software.

Perhaps the most notable development in sequential control is the movement towards a separation and strenghtening of the various required functions which has been made possible by the introduction of microprocessors linked within a distributed control architecture. The movement control loop should appropriately be the inner loop. The diagnostic function has taken place as an outer loop heretofore, largely because it was not possible to train programmed controllers to do their own diagnosing. Monitoring is appropriately a higher level function which has little meaning at the inner loop level. The introduction of microprocessors in industrial control along with standard data interfaces has provided a means of combining and enhancing control and diagnosing functions at the inner loop level and for doing the data acquisition and transmission which are required to support monitoring at the outer level. Data communication allows to go from a single machine to embracing an entire transfer line, but also allows to partition the control problem below as is required for the correct synthesis of sequencing controllers for the different working units, employing new functional specification languages. With a distributed control structure which places a great deal of computational power at the local level for control and diagnostic functions, it is also possible to synthesize and aggregate information as required above the level of the control box. Distributed control, long a subject of theoretical control considerations, is now economical as a practical solution. Some of its advantages, as applied to controlling mass production transfer machines, are:

a. Reduced wiring requirements.

b. Utilization of dedicated software.

c. Addition of powerful, localized diagnosis function.

d. Limited authority/hierarchically organized delegation.

A pilot transfer machine which embodies these concepts has been implemented, using a distributed system of microprocessors connected to each other and to a central unit by a data transmission link (see Figure 8). The pilot implementation, the logic of which was designed using the STD approach and the associated software, is not only important because it represents the first high-volume machine control which utilizes microprocessors and distributed control, but also because it represents a key building block for more advanced machining systems in the future.

Figure 8 Sequential Control of a Transfer Machine Made by M.S.T. Using Distributed Microprocessors

6.0 Conclusions

The foregoing examples of computer applications illustrate effectively the direct benefits which can be gained through a type of systematic attack on selected areas which is relatively new to the manufacturing world. Aspects of manufacturing are addressed such as cost control on the shop floor, automated process layout or new techniques for designing and implementing sequential controllers which could not be successfully resolved without the help of computer-based solutions. More rigorous definition of production problems and the laying out of procedures which lend themselves to computer implementation, representing a new viewpoing in considering manufacturing processes, will have a deep influence on the character and efficiency of production.

The problems which have been presented in this paper are very different in nature, but are typical of classes of problems which are found in relation to manufacturing. These are respectively: the class of cognitive tasks (e.g., process layout), the class of activities which relates broadly to instrumenting the "state" of the machine and establishing an information network which complements direct fabrication activities, and the class of design problems related to the specification and implementation of sequential controllers. Other important areas within the production cycle have been addressed in the context of the study. These are the areas of computer aided design of mechanical parts, automated mechanical drafting, computer-aided generation of the specification of gear trains for multiple-spindle heads, the interface between the specification of mechanical movements and that of the sequential controller which will implement such movements. The area of automated warehousing is also under study. It is interesting to note that some of the areas which have been looked at (e.g., computer-aided line layout, logic design, computer-aided gear train layout) are closely related within the production cycle, suggesting the possibility of useful, automatic links between the data structures, associated with each problem.

The studies and implementations above, as they have been described, are aimed at influencing an existing, complex production process in an evolutionary way. These same activities, however, are also key building blocks in the design of new generation or "revolutionaly" machining systems. It was remarked in Section 2 that today's user is limited to a choice between machining solutions which are best matched to the extremes of the production spectrum of mechanical parts. Accordingly, a substantial amount of work has been performed in the definition of new "flexible machining systems" which are aimed at drastically reducing costs in the medium production range. The central idea in the realization of flexible systems is to utilize in the medium range some of the key characteristics which make mass manufacturing so inexpensive (e.g., clustering of tools, automated transfer of parts from one station to the next). The transfer machine organization is the starting point, therefore: the implementation of a flexible system is as a machining system which resembles a transfer machine but is capable of reconfiguring itself to adapt to machining a bounded set of different parts.

In considering the design of such a system, two technical issues become immediately evident in addition to the mechanical design of the individual modules:

a. The necessity to perform a process layout design for a single system to manufacture many part types. This involves analyzing and grouping thousands of elementary operations as opposed to hundreds for the case of a single part which has been discussed. It is unthinkable to be able to perform the layout effectively without the aid of automatic processing in the style of CALL/1.

b. The need for a complex, real-time control system to govern the asychronous movements of the different parts, the dispatching of the required tooling, and part programs to individual stations. The architecture of the sequencing and control system which is most appropriate is that of a distributed system of microprocessors in the style of the realization cited in Section 5.

REFERENCES

1. "A Computer-Aided Minimum Cost Transfer Machine Layout Design", Tze-Thong Chien, Saul Serben, William A. Taylor, and Paolo Rolando, Proceedings of 12th Design Automation Conference, June 1975, IEEE Catalog No. 75-CHO-980-3C.

2. "On-Line Tool Data for Improving Transfer Machine Operation", J. Scott Rhodes, Society of Manufacturing Engineers, Paper No. MR75-193.

3. "A Computer Language for Control of Autonomout Industrial Equipment", P.Wolfe, MIT/Draper Report T-579, FR44700-32, June, 1973.

SYSTEM ANALYSIS IN PROBLEMS OF ENERGY

APPLICATION DE L'ANALYSE DES SYSTÈMES AUX PROBLÈMES DE L'ENERGIE

MACRO-ECONOMIC MODELS, DIFFERENTIAL TOPOLOGY AND ENERGY STRATEGIES*

W. Häfele, R. Bürk, M. Breitenecker, C. Riedel
International Institute for Applied Systems Analysis
A-2361 Laxenburg, Austria

1. Introduction

It is worthwhile to realize that the energy problem has three distinct time phases [1]. The present situation is characterized by the fact that the world's energy consumption is at 7.5 TW years per year, or in short 7.5 TW (1 TW = 10^{12} Watt), out of which 5.5 TW are coming from oil and gas. Oil and gas permit for low capital costs of related infrastructure and their uses are versatile and convenient, be it in the private sector, in industry or in the transportation sector. Prior to the oil crisis also the fuel costs were low. A typical figure was 50 $/million BTU, or 3 $/barrel at the user's end. More than that, the high energy density of oil, per volume and per weight, permitted long range transportation. Shipment from the Persian Gulf amounts to 1.7 TW and the distances bridged are at 10,000 km, which is of global dimensions. Developed and developing countries, therefore, do increasingly rely on such kind of primary energy supply. Unfortunately, the resources of oil and gas are limited. More detailed analyses indicate that oil and gas resources will last only for the next 50 years, the decline of such supply will be felt already after the next 20 years [2].

In the very long run, which is the asymptotic phase of the energy problem, there are a number of options for the practically unlimited supply of primary energy:

- Nuclear fission by breeding (use of U238);
- Nuclear fusion (use of lithium and deuterium);
- Solar energy;
- Dry geothermal energy from the earth's crust.

Although its ultimate recoverable resources are limited, also the large scale uses of coal by advanced technologies might be sufficient in that context. One, therefore, faces the problem of transition from today's first phase to the asymptotic third phase of the energy problem. This

* Invited paper, International Symposium on New Trends in Systems Analysis, 13-17 December 1976, Versailles, France.

transitional phase then constitutes the second phase. More detailed analysis indicates that its time characteristic is at 50 years [3]. We, therefore, have a coincidence: oil and gas probably last for something like 50 years, and it takes such a time period to make a transition into a different energy infrastructure. One, therefore, must start now to analyze the conditions and features of such long range transitions, or in other words, to conceive appropriate energy strategies for the next fifty years.

Such a long range planning horizon is beyond the domain of market forces which are characterized by rates of return; accordingly, it is also beyond the time horizon of related models of economics as such economy models usually have a different purpose. They are meant to understand in greater detail yearly changes of investments, taxes, prices, etc. By contrast, the concept of energy strategies for the next 50 years concentrates much more on trends, on safety margins for appropriate transitions and, above all, on stability and resilience of such strategies. The notion of resilience was developed by C.S. Holling [4] when he studied ecological systems and their evolutions. His fundamental observation is that ecological systems can usually be described by a set of *nonlinear* differential equations of state variables. Such state variables constitute a phase space whose portrait is governed by the singularities of the underlying differential equations. There are separating manifolds that subdivide the phase space into various basins and, usually within such basins, there are trajectories that represent the time evolution of the considered system and attractors that attract the trajectories of a basin. According to Holling,

> "resilience is the ability of a system to absorb and even benefit by unexpected finite changes in system variables and parameters, without deteriorating irreversibly. In contrast, stability describes the ability of a system to absorb very small perturbations about a system of equilibrium."[5]

It should be noted then that resilience is a topological feature. H.-R. Grümm will elaborate on this notion of resilience in greater detail [6].

While resilience is certainly a major orientation for the kind of studies reported in this paper it is not the only one. Catastrophe theory and other topological considerations are equally in mind when long range strategies are to be conceived. What we are driving at, therefore, is a differential topological approach to macroeconomic models and their use beyond traditional schemes of numerical integrations and interpretations.

2. A Conceptualization Aid

To start the above explained new brand of systems analysis it is necessary to conceive a set of equations that permits this. A beginning was made by W. Häfele in 1975 [7] in considering what was called societal equations. The purpose of the exercise was more to pave the way for such studies than to already present an economically meaningful model. The equations were, therefore, as simple as possible. Considered was a national product G that accounts for energy E, labor (which was equated to population P) and expenses K for safety of power stations that are interpreted to be non-productive. We then have

$$G = A \cdot E^{\frac{1}{2}} P^{\frac{1}{2}} - K \quad , \tag{1}$$

with A being a constant.

A Cobb Douglas type production function was used and the elasticities were ad hoc assumed to be $\frac{1}{2}$.

It was further assumed that the installed risk level r of power stations varies inversely with the specific capital costs k per kW installed:

$$r = r_o \frac{k_o}{k} \quad ; \tag{2}$$

$$k = \frac{k}{E} \quad . \tag{3}$$

Quantities indexed by $_o$ refer to a reference state. The per capita consumption of energy e then simply follows this relation:

$$E = e \cdot P \quad . \tag{4}$$

r is the risk level accepted by the society under consideration. It was assumed that society expresses a certain risk acceptance such that the acceptance of risks is the lower the higher the anxieties about risks are, and we assumed that the anxieties about risks vary inversely proportionally to the square of per capita consumption. We, therefore, have:

$$\frac{r}{r_o} = \left(\frac{e_o}{e}\right)^2 . \tag{5}$$

To be here considered artificial model investments can be made only in energy. The share μ of G is meant for that and we have

$$\frac{dD}{dt} = \mu G . \tag{6}$$

Finally, an assumption was made for the growth of population P:

$$\frac{dP}{dt} = \sigma P - \kappa e . \tag{7}$$

The higher the personal well-being, expressed by the per capita consumption, the lower the growth rate was the idea of equation (7). The analysis was indeed made with equation (7) while after a while it was realized that the appropriate equation should have been as follows:

$$\frac{dP}{dt} = P(\sigma - \kappa e) . \tag{7a}$$

In view of the any way artificial nature of the model considered here and in view of the only conceptual and learning purposes of this exercise it may be interesting to present the result of the analysis of equations (1) - (7). The following values for the various parameters were assumed:

$$A = 0.25 \cdot 10^4 \frac{\$}{\text{year} \cdot \text{kW}^{1/2} \cdot \text{capita}^{1/2}} ;$$

$$\frac{E_o}{K_o} = 10 \frac{\$}{\text{kW year}} ;$$

$$e_o = 3 \text{ kW/capita} ;$$

$$\mu = 24 \cdot 10^{-6} \frac{\text{kW}}{\$} ;$$

$$\sigma = 2 \cdot 10^{-2} \frac{1}{\text{year}} ;$$

$$\kappa = 0.25 \cdot 10^6 \frac{(\text{capita})^2}{\text{kW year}} .$$

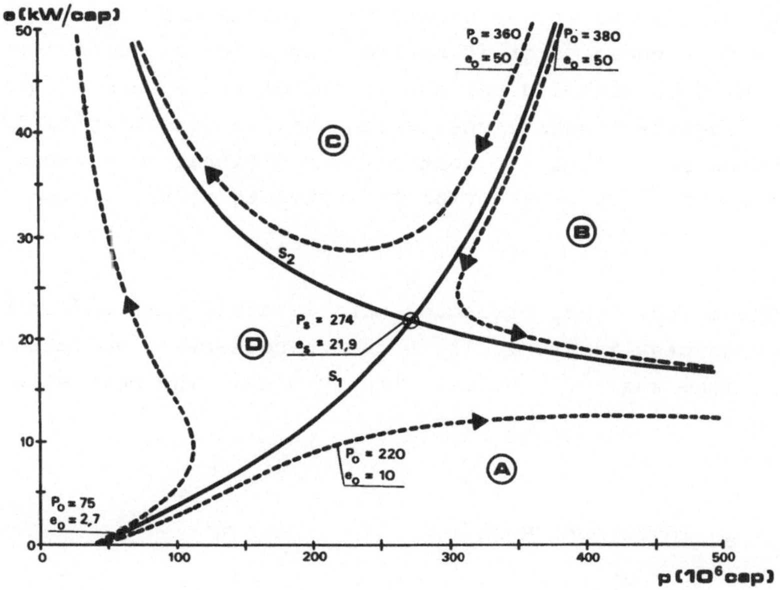

Fig. 1. Solutions in the [e,p] field.

The phase portrait of the model is given in Fig. 1. It is governed by the singular point in the middle of the first quadrant. The singular point is a saddle point, whose permitted only derivatives identify separatrices that thereby constitute four basins of the phase portrait. Extensions of the model to more than two state variables reveal the fact that only the separatrix that goes through the origin e=0, p=0 is a true separatrix. On the left-hand side, the trajectory coming out of the saddle point is an attractor. It characterizes a trend where ever fewer people have an ever increasing per capita consumption, and in the end the population is extinct. On the right-hand side, the trajectory coming out of the saddle point is also an attractor. It characterizes an opposite trend. An evolving population stabilizes at a constant per capita consumption--indeed a radically different fate.

Let us now consider a given initial state and the exogeneous value judgment to aim for the asymptotic evolution where the per capita consumption stabilizes. It is then important to make sure that the starting point is in the right basin. But there is principally no way to do that when only some neighborhood of the initial state is explored: the separatrix is principally indistinguishable from any other trajectory as long as only such neighborhood is considered. Only the saddle point identifies the separatrix that separates the two basins. The generally important point is now this: States of the considered systems that relate to singular points of a phase portrait reflect pathological conditions. It is, therefore, such pathological conditions of the system in question that permit to identify separatrices, which then in turn permits for an appropriate choice of policy. By contrast, traditional macroeconomic modeling usually considers only normal constituents of the system in question.

Let us repeat, the model presented here is artificial and is meant as an aid for conceptualization. It is then necessary to go further and to conceive more realistic models step by step. The next step is described below.

3. A Consumption/Investment Model

When conceiving a more realistic model it is important to identify the salient feature for which the model is meant. The technological options of the asymptotic phase of the energy problem seem to have one thing in common: they are capital intensive, and the question must be raised whether an economy can afford the necessary investments. Indeed, the capital investment for handling 1 kWh of oil power used to be at 100 $, while the capital investment for electricity coming from nuclear fission and covering production, transmission and distribution is between 2000 and 3000 $ per kW_e and 600 - 1000 per kW_{th}. Higher figures must be expected for bulk solar power and probably also for fusion and geothermal. It is not the purpose of this paper to go into numerical details. Instead, the subject of high capital costs will be looked at only generally. This is sufficient as the topological approach concentrates on structures, not on numbers.

The structure of our model can be described qualitatively as follows: We start with the three economic variables E, K and L denoting the total energy consumption per year (measured in kilowatt-hours per year, kWh/y), total capital stock (dollars, $) and total labor force per year (man-hours per year, Ph/y). E and K are decomposed into the sectors of investment goods production, consumer goods production and private use (heating of private homes, private construction, etc.), i.e.

$$E = E_{in} + E_C + E_P \quad , \tag{8}$$

and

$$K = K_{in} + K_C + K_P \quad , \tag{9}$$

whereas L is split into two sectors

$$L = L_{in} + L_C \quad . \tag{10}$$

Hence E_C, for instance, denotes the energy per year going into consumer goods production, K_P the private capital stock and L_{in} the labor force per year going into investment goods production.

With the definitions

$$\alpha_E = E_C/E \qquad 0 < \alpha_E < 1 \tag{11a}$$

$$\alpha_K = K_C/K \qquad 0 < \alpha_K < 1 \tag{11b}$$

$$\alpha_L = L_C/L \qquad 0 < \alpha_L < 1 \tag{11c}$$

$$b_E = E_P/L \qquad 0 < b_E \tag{11d}$$

$$b_K = K_P/L \qquad 0 < b_K \tag{11e}$$

we have

$$\begin{aligned} E_{in} &= (1 - \alpha_E)E - b_E L \\ K_{in} &= (1 - \alpha_K)K - b_K L \\ L_{in} &= (1 - \alpha_L)L \quad . \end{aligned} \tag{12}$$

We now couple (12) to the *changes* of E and K per year, i.e.

$$\begin{aligned} E_{in} &= a_{EE}\,\dot{E} + a_{EK}\,\dot{K} \\ K_{in} &= a_{KE}\,\dot{E} + a_{KK}\,\dot{K} \\ L_{in} &= a_{LE}\,\dot{E} + a_{LK}\,\dot{K} \end{aligned} \tag{13}$$

by means of the positive "technological" coefficients $a_{EE}, \dots a_{LK}$. We hesitate to conceive the analogous column for $\dot{L}_{tot}$ in (13); in many countries the potential for labor is exhausted and more than capital and energy seems to be necessary to increase L. By assuming (13) we imply inelastic investment schemes, capital cannot automatically substitute energy in the considered investments and vice versa. This may be felt to be a drawback, but it is the purpose of the model to play with the coefficients a_{pq} and to study thereby impacts of various technological strategies. It is, therefore, rather an advantage, not a drawback.

Assuming the invertibility of the matrix

$$T = \begin{pmatrix} a_{EE} & a_{EK} \\ a_{KE} & a_{KK} \end{pmatrix} , \qquad (14)$$

we may express $\dot{E}$, $\dot{K}$ by E_{in}, K_{in} using the first two equations (13), and then after substitution into the third equation (13) obtain L_{in} in terms of E_{in}, K_{in}. Combining this with (12) we end up with the following two-dimensional system of differential equations:

$$\begin{pmatrix} \dot{E} \\ \dot{K} \end{pmatrix} = T^{-1}\left(I - (1 + \bar{a}T^{-1}\bar{b} - \alpha_L)^{-1}\bar{b} \otimes \bar{a}\, T^{-1}\right)(I - \bar{\alpha})\begin{pmatrix} E \\ K \end{pmatrix} , \qquad (15)$$

and

$$L = (1 + aT^{-1}\bar{b} - \alpha_L)^{-1}\, aT^{-1}(I - \bar{\alpha})\begin{pmatrix} E \\ K \end{pmatrix} . \qquad (16)$$

Here we have used matrix notation and the definitions

$$\bar{a} = (a_{LE}, a_{LK}), \quad \bar{b} = (b_E, b_K), \quad \bar{\alpha} = \begin{pmatrix} \alpha_E & 0 \\ 0 & \alpha_K \end{pmatrix} ,$$

$$\bar{b} \otimes \bar{a} = \begin{pmatrix} b_1a_1 & b_1a_2 \\ b_2a_1 & b_2a_2 \end{pmatrix} \quad \text{and} \quad I = \begin{pmatrix} 1 & 0 \\ 0 & 1 \end{pmatrix} .$$

We may fix the α's, solve (15) and obtain the phase portrait of the trajectories (E,K) in the E-K-phase space.

Now we introduce the second essential element of the model imposing a constraint on the phase portrait; this turns the model into a highly non-linear problem.

We assume substitutability of E, K and L in the total consumption G_C, expressing it by a Cobb-Douglas function, and couple the consumption linearly to the labor force:

$$C = d \cdot L \tag{17}$$

and

$$C = A \cdot E_C^{\alpha} K_C^{\beta} L_C^{1-\alpha-\beta} \quad . \tag{18}$$

Here α, β and $1-\alpha-\beta$ denote the substitution elasticities; A is a constant.

Before proceeding further a few observations must be made: The model allows for growth and along with it goes a growth of L. The model assumes that there is a reservoir for that growth which can be used without investments of energy, capital and labor. This is a weak point of the present version of the model which asks for later improvement.

Also, the relation between labor, total population and specifically population growth must be taken into account in a later stage of the analysis.

The model allows for optimization; there are more variables than equations. That also will be part of later improvements.

More important, the finite resources that go along with old technologies must be properly taken into account when improvements are made.

Combining (17) and (18) with (11a-c), we obtain after some straightforward steps

$$L = \left[\frac{A}{D} \alpha_E^{\alpha} \alpha_K^{\beta} \alpha_L^{1-\alpha-\beta} E^{\alpha} K^{\beta}\right]^{1/\alpha+\beta}$$

which we insert into (16):

$$\left[\frac{A}{d} \alpha_E^{\alpha} \alpha_K^{\beta} \alpha_L^{1-\alpha-\beta} E^{\alpha} K^{\beta}\right]^{1/\alpha+\beta} = (1 + \bar{a}T^{-1}\bar{b} - \alpha_L)^{-1} \bar{a}T^{-1}(I - \bar{\alpha}) \begin{pmatrix} E \\ K \end{pmatrix} \quad . \tag{20}$$

We introduce as a new variable the ratio between energy and capital

$$\mu = E/K \quad , \tag{21}$$

divide (20) by K, and end up with a transcendental equation relating α_L to μ. $\left(\text{We call } \bar{a}T^{-1} = \bar{c} \equiv (c_1, c_2)\right)$.

$$\alpha_L^{\frac{1}{\alpha+\beta}-1}(1+\bar{c}\bar{b}-\alpha_L) = \left[\frac{A}{d}\,\alpha_E^{\alpha}\,\alpha_K^{\beta}\right]^{1/\alpha+\beta}\left[c_1(1-\alpha_E)\mu^{\beta/\alpha+\beta} + \right.$$

$$\left. + \; c_2(1-\alpha_K)\mu^{-\alpha/\alpha+\beta}\right] \quad . \tag{22}$$

Likewise we introduce the new variable μ in (15) and obtain the two equations

$$\dot{\mu} = D_{12}(1-\alpha_K) + \mu\big(D_{11}(1-\alpha_E) - D_{22}(1-\alpha_K)\big) - \mu^2 D_{21}(1-\alpha_E) \tag{23}$$

and

$$\dot{K}/K \equiv (\log K)^{\cdot} = D_{22}(1-\alpha_K) + \mu D_{21}(1-\alpha_E) \quad , \tag{24}$$

where D_{ik} are the elements of the matrix

$$D = T^{-1}\big(I - (1+\bar{c}\bar{b}-\alpha_L)^{-1}\;\bar{b}\otimes\bar{c}\big) \quad ; \tag{25}$$

they all depend on μ via α_L.

Straightforward calculation yields also

$$\frac{\dot{E}}{E} \equiv (\log E)^{\cdot} = \frac{\dot{\mu}\mu}{\mu} + \frac{\dot{K}}{K} \quad , \tag{26}$$

and

$$\frac{dE}{dK} = \mu + \frac{\dot{\mu}}{(\log K)^{\cdot}} \quad . \tag{27}$$

Let us now analyze the content of (22) and to this end denote the left-hand side by $g(\alpha_L)$ and the right-hand side by $f(\mu)$. We note that g is independent of α_E,α_K and is, therefore, always the same curve once the technological coefficients are chosen, whereas f depends on α_E,α_K. It can be made arbitrarily small in modulus in any interval excluding the origin by a proper choice of α_E,α_K.

The explicit shape of g and f will, of course, depend on the coefficients c_1,c_2 and $1+\bar{c}\bar{b}$ and in particular on their sign. We show g qualitatively in Fig. 2 and indicate the various possibilities of the relative position of α_L^{max} to $\alpha_L = 1$ by case 1 and case 2 respectively. (We omit the possible case $1 + \bar{c}\bar{b} < 1$ since it is not realized by our explicit numbers.)

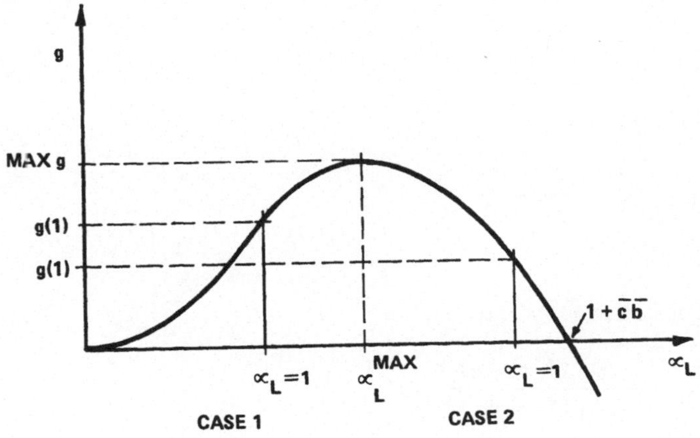

Fig. 2. Left-hand side of transcendental consistency condition.

In Fig. 3 we show two possibilities for f (which we encounter below), namely $c_1, c_2 > 0$ (case I) and $c_1 < 0, c_2 > 0$ (case II).

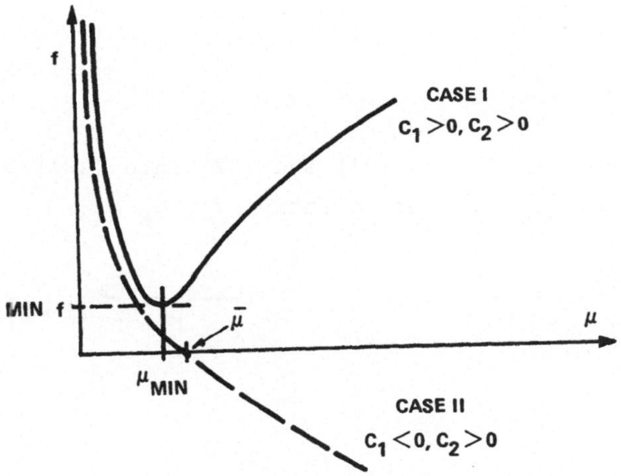

Fig. 3. Right-hand side of transcendental consistency condition.

An obvious condition for the consistency of our model is the solubility of (22), i.e. the range of f must have a non-void intersection with the range of g for $\alpha_L \in (0,1)$.

Hence in case 1I this condition may be expressed by

$$\min f \leq g(1) \quad , \tag{28}$$

and in case 2I by

$$\min f \leq \max g \quad . \tag{28'}$$

Some calculations yield

$$\mu_{\min} = \frac{c_2(1-\alpha_K)\alpha}{c_1(1-\alpha_E)\beta} \quad , \tag{29}$$

$$\alpha_L^{\max} = (1+\bar{c}\bar{b})(1-\alpha-\beta) \quad , \tag{30}$$

$$\min f \equiv f(\mu_{\min}) = \left[\left(\frac{A}{d}\right)^{-1}(\alpha+\beta)^{\alpha+\beta}\alpha^{-\alpha}\beta^{-\beta}c_1^{\alpha}c_2^{\beta}\left(\frac{1-\alpha_E}{\alpha_E}\right)^{\alpha}\left(\frac{1-\alpha_K}{\alpha_K}\right)^{\beta}\right]^{1/\alpha+\beta} \tag{31}$$

$$\max g \equiv g(\alpha_L^{\max}) = \left[(\alpha+\beta)^{\alpha+\beta}(1-\alpha-\beta)^{1-\alpha-\beta}(1+\bar{c}\bar{b})\right]^{1/\alpha+\beta} \tag{32}$$

and

$$g(1) = \bar{c}\bar{b} \quad . \tag{32'}$$

In case 2I, the substitution of (31) and (32) into (28') gives a condition for the allowed region of variation for α_E, α_K:

$$\left(\frac{1-\alpha_E}{\alpha_E}\right)^{\alpha}\left(\frac{1-\alpha_K}{\alpha_K}\right)^{\beta} \leq G \equiv \alpha^{\alpha}\beta^{\beta}(1-\alpha-\beta)^{1-\alpha-\beta}c_1^{-\alpha}c_2^{-\beta}(1+\bar{c}\bar{b})\frac{A}{d} \tag{33}$$

or

$$\alpha_K = \left[1 + G^{1/\beta}\left(\frac{\alpha_E}{1-\alpha_E}\right)^{\alpha/\beta}\right]^{-1} \quad . \tag{34}$$

Analogously, in case 1I we substitute (31) and (32') into (28) and again obtain (33) and (34) but G is replaced by

$$G' \equiv \alpha^{\alpha}\beta^{\beta}(\alpha+\beta)^{-(\alpha+\beta)}c_1^{-\alpha}c_2^{-\beta}(\bar{c}\bar{b})^{\alpha+\beta}A/d \quad . \qquad (33')$$

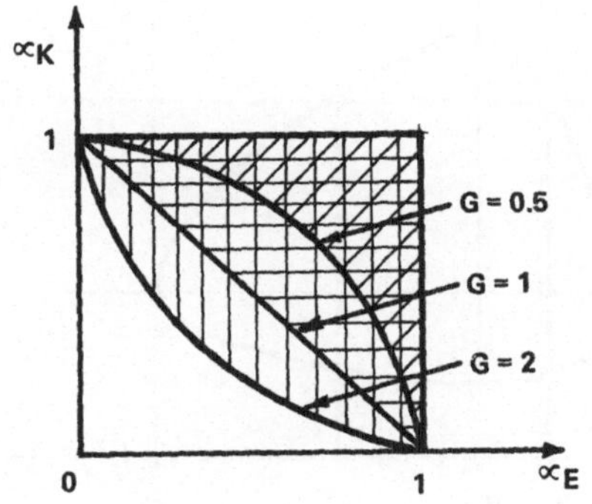

Fig. 4. Domain of consistency for α_E and α_K.

Fig. 4 shows the allowed regions of α_E, α_K for some values of G.

The allowed range of μ is now determined by the requirement that $f(\mu)$ be in the range of g for $\alpha_L \in (0,1)$.

As shown in Fig. 5, the solution of

$$f(\mu) = \max g \qquad (35)$$

yields two values of μ, $\mu^<$ and $\mu^>$, which serve as boundaries in the E-K phase space in situation 2I.

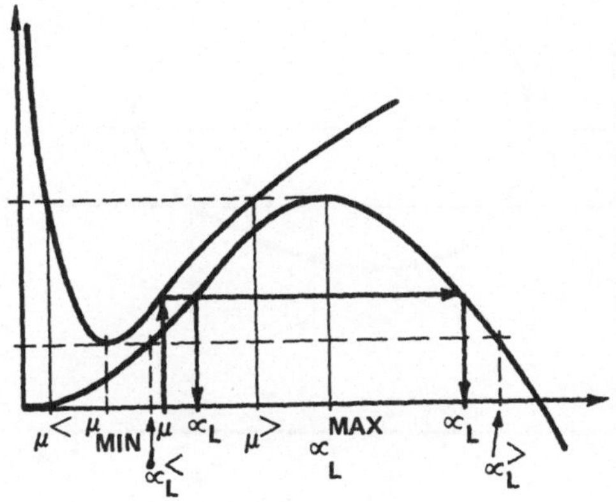

Fig. 5. Range of consistency for the ratio E/K = μ.

If min f $\geq$ g(1) each μ yields two α_L and we obtain two branches for α_L, an upper and a lower branch, which join at $\mu^{\gtrless}$ at the value α_L^{max} (Fig. 6).

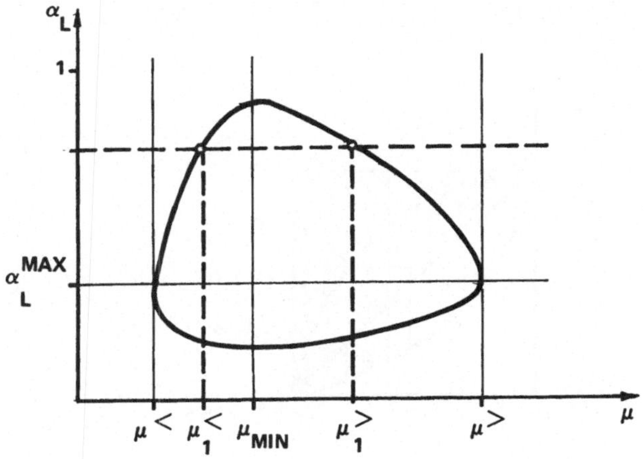

Fig. 6. Dependence of α_L on μ for $\alpha_L^{max} < 1$. Case 1.

If we change α_E, α_K (within their allowed domain, of course) α_L^{max} remains fixed, but $\mu_{min}, \mu^{\gtrless}$ and the shape of the closed curve vary.

If min f < g(1) (indicated by the dotted line in Fig. 5), the upper branch is interrupted since for $\mu \in (\mu^<, \mu^>)$ α_L would attain values greater than one.

In case 1I, the upper branch vanishes completely and, as shown in Fig. 7, the boundaries for μ are now the solutions of

$$f(\mu) = g(1) \qquad (36)$$

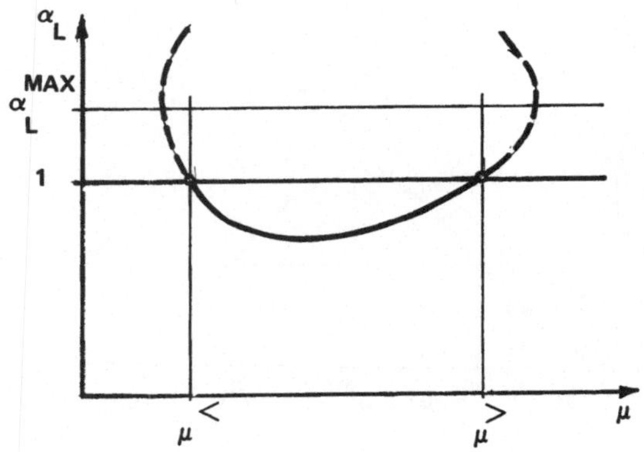

Fig. 7. Dependence of α_L on μ for $\alpha_L^{max} > 1$. Case 2.

The discussion for situation II goes along the same lines and we plot the result in Fig. 8.

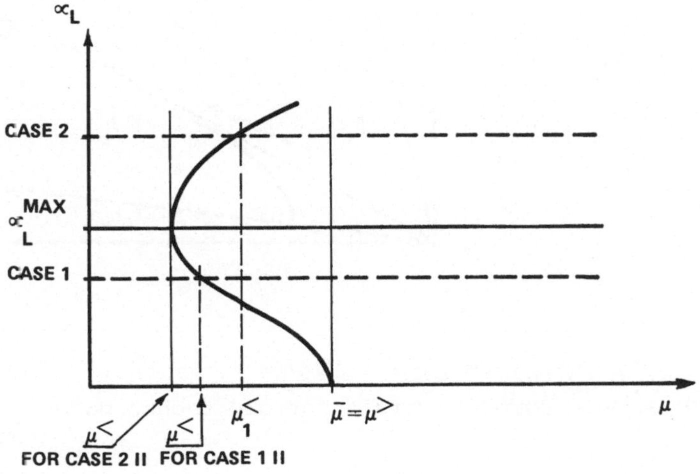

Fig. 8. Dependence of α_L on μ for case II.

Once we have established the correct range for μ and the function $\alpha_L(\mu)$, $\dot{\mu}$ can be calculated point by point from (23).

In all explicit situations discussed later we have one zero for $\dot{\mu}$. The corresponding μ_o is a fixed point for (23) and, therefore, in the E-K-phase space the ray $E/K = \mu_o$ is an invariant manifold. Since we were able to introduce $\dot{\mu}$ and to decouple the original system (15), the phase portrait has the particular property that the slopes of all trajectories are constant along each ray $E/K = \text{const}$.

Let us summarize the qualitative situation. The phase space for E-K is a cone in the positive quadrant of the E-K-plane, bounded by the rays $E/K = \mu^{\gtrless}$. For each branch of $\alpha_L(\mu)$ (with obvious modifications if the upper branch is truncated) we have a fixed ray μ_o which serves as an attractor for all trajectories emerging from below or from above (Fig. 9) in cases 1I and 2I and as a repeller in case 1II (Fig. 10).

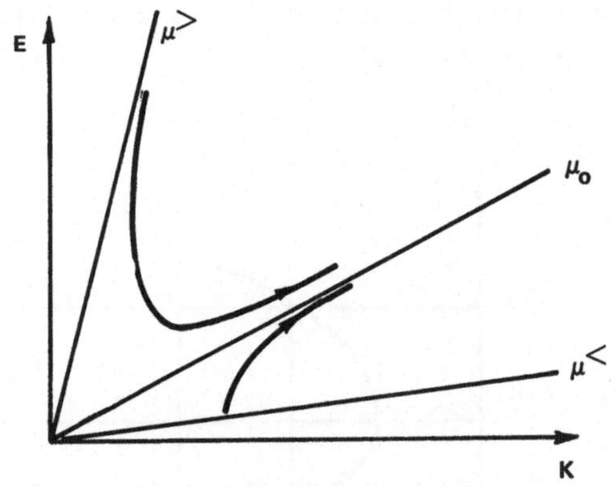

Fig. 9. Phase portrait for old technologies.

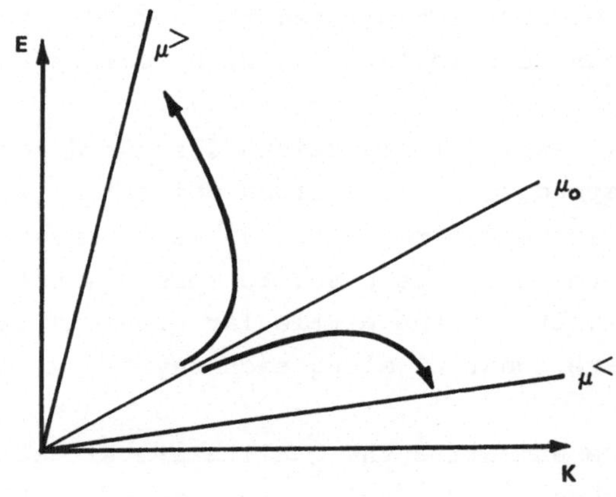

Fig. 10. Phase portrait for new technologies.

4. Choice of Parameters

To make the point of energy strategies it is now crucial to choose the parameters such that real problems are reflected as much as possible by the model which is still somewhat artificial. We consider three cases:

a) old technologies;
b) old technologies plus energy conservation;
c) new technologies.

a_{EE} describes the energy involvement per energy production capacity. It has the dimension year and is, in fact, the time required to produce the energy that is invested. We assume:

$$a_{EE} = \begin{cases} 0.04 \text{ years for cases a) and b)} \\ 3 \text{ years for case c).} \end{cases}$$

Indeed, the harvesting of shale oil, the enrichment of uranium and the large-scale installation of solar absorbers require significant energy investments. No reference is made to any one specific case, the point being the contrast between 0.04 and 3 years.

a_{EK} describes the number of kWh required for increasing the capital stock by one dollar. We assume:

$$a_{EK} = \begin{cases} 7 \text{ kWh/\$} & \text{for cases a) and c)} \\ 4.9 \text{ kWh/\$} & \text{for case b).} \end{cases}$$

Energy conservation is meant to save 30% of the amount originally required.

a_{KE} describes the capital investment for energy production facilities having the dimension $\$\cdot year^2/kWh$. We assume 7500h per year and, in case of old technologies, 300 \$ per kW of production capacity and twice as much, i.e. 600 \$, per kW of delivered capacity (production, transmission and distribution). For new technologies we assume 2000 \$ per kW of production capacity and twice as much for the delivered kW. We, therefore, have

$$a_{KE} = \begin{cases} 0.08 \dfrac{\$ \text{ year}^2}{\text{kWh}} & \text{for cases a) and b)} \\ 0.5 \dfrac{\$ \text{ year}^2}{\text{kWh}} & \text{for case c).} \end{cases}$$

a_{KK} describes the capital investment in the capital stock. It has the dimension year and is, in fact, the rate of return of the considered economy. In case of energy conservation the time required for returning invested capital is assumed to be slightly higher than otherwise. We, therefore, have:

$$a_{KK} = \begin{cases} 1.5 \text{ years} & \text{for cases a) and c)} \\ 1.575 \text{ years} & \text{for case b).} \end{cases}$$

a_{LE} describes the labor investments for energy investments. We assume:

$$a_{LE} = 3 \cdot 10^{-6} \frac{\text{man} \cdot \text{year}^2}{\text{kWh}} .$$

a_{LK} describes the labor investments for capital stock increases. We assume:

$$a_{LK} = 1.6 \cdot 10^{-4} \frac{\text{man} \cdot \text{year}}{\$} .$$

b_E is the private energy consumption per laborer. Assuming 2 kW per laborer under normal conditions and 1.4 kW under the regime of energy conservation, we, therefore, have

$$b_E = \begin{cases} 17{,}000 \frac{\text{kWh}}{\text{year}} & \text{for cases a) and c)} \\ 12{,}000 \frac{\text{kWh}}{\text{year}} & \text{for case b).} \end{cases}$$

b_K describes the private capital stock per laborer. We simply assume:

$$b_K = \begin{cases} 10{,}000 \text{ \$/man} & \text{for cases a) and c)} \\ 10{,}500 \text{ \$/man} & \text{for case b).} \end{cases}$$

d_K describes the consumption per capita. We put:

$$d = 8400 \text{ \$/man} \quad \text{for all cases.}$$

The parameters of the Cobb Douglas function we assume as follows (see (18)):

$$A = 400 \quad \text{(in the units used here)}$$
$$\alpha = 0.15$$
$$\beta = 0.15$$
$$1-\alpha-\beta \equiv \gamma = 0.7$$

In all cases we have assumed $\alpha_E = 0.84$ and $\alpha_K = 0.8$.

5. Results

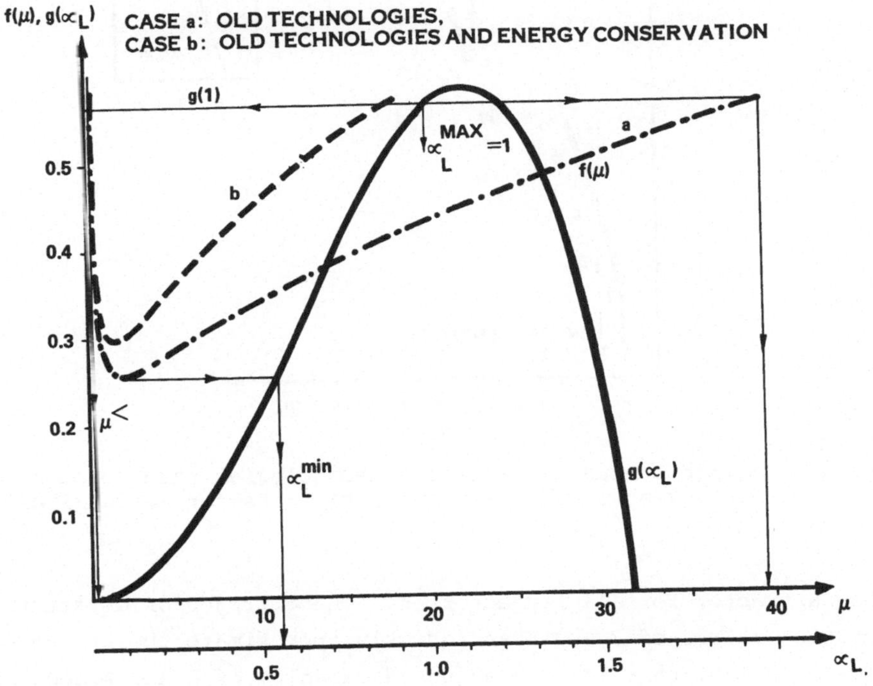

Fig. 11. Determining lower and upper bounds for the labor share α_L and the energy to capital ratio μ on the condition $f(\mu) = g(\alpha_L)$.

Fig. 11 shows the results for case a), that is the old technologies. The ratio μ between E and K must be between $\mu^< = 0.12$ (with a corresponding $\alpha_L = 1$) and $\mu^> = 39.5$ (with $\alpha_L = 1$).

For increasing μ and $\mu^< < \mu < \mu^>$, the share of labor α_L decreases until $\alpha_L^{min} = 0.55$ (for $\mu_{min} = 2.2$) and then increases to its maximum $\alpha_L^{max} = 1$ at $\mu = \mu^>$. As is shown in Fig. 12, the ratio $\mu_o = 3.08$ acts

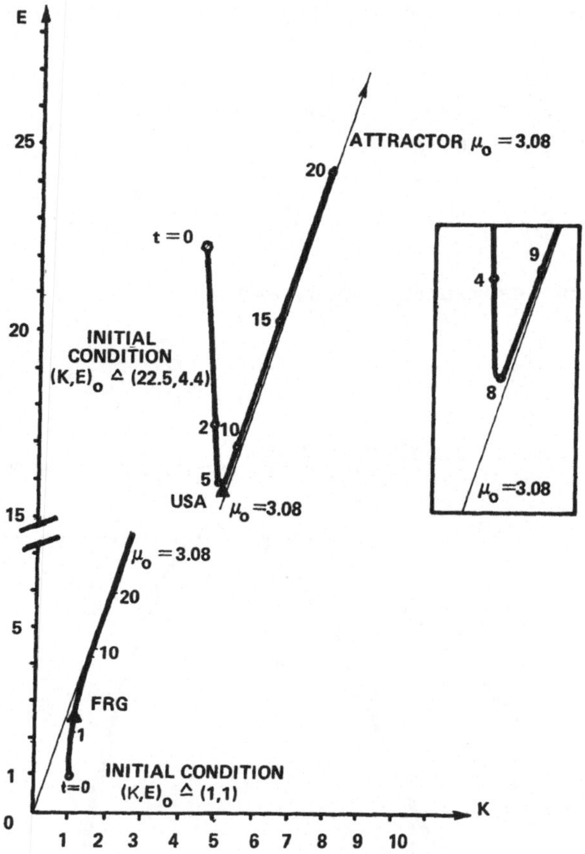

Fig. 12. Phase portrait of the old technologies case (case a); t in years; arbitrary absolute units for energy E and capital K.

as an attractor for all trajectories. These trajectories start at any permitted values of E and K and quickly approximate the attractor from above or below, that is, non-adjusted capacity of E and K becomes adjusted. The points on the trajectories give the evolution of the time parameter. We realize that typical adjustment periods are about 15 years. Actual figures from the US seem to indicate that the state of the economy is above the attractor, that is, too much energy capacity seems to be there. For the Federal Republic of Germany the opposite seems to hold. Another relevant observation seems to be the following. For long-range considerations within the model considered here, it seems to be sufficient simply to consider the attractor $\mu_o = 3.08$ and to forget about all other trajectories. This may permit for quick analysis. Fig. 13 shows how the position μ_0 of the attractor is changed for various allowed shares α_E and α_K.

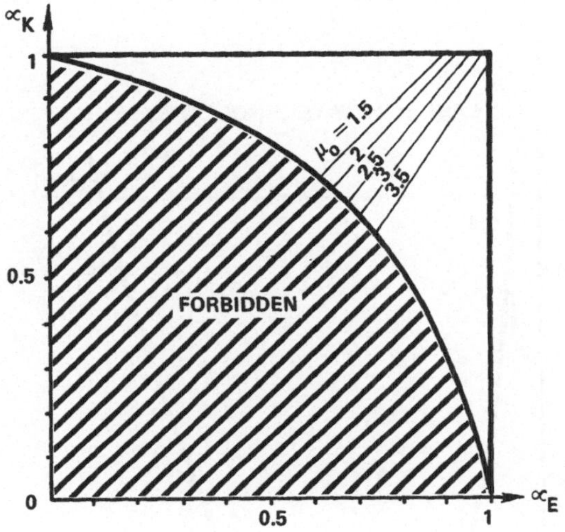

Fig. 13. Dependence of attractors μ_0 on energy and capital shares α_E and α_K. case a): old technologies

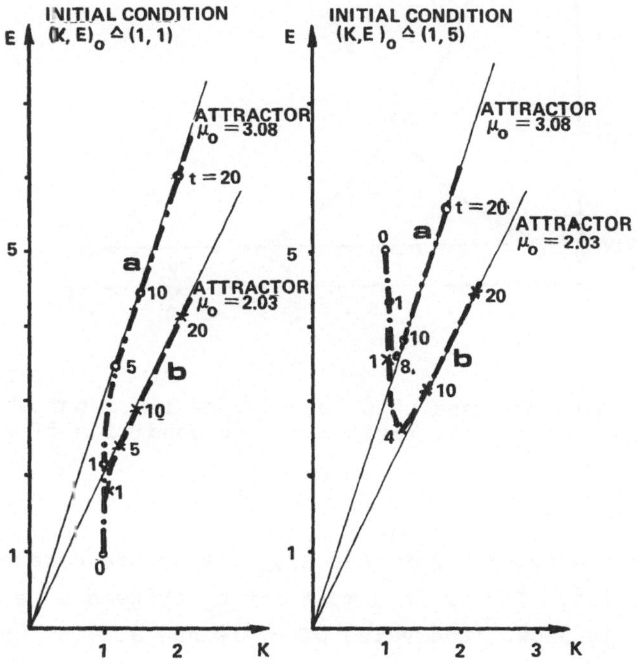

Fig. 14. Phase portraits for the cases of old technologies (case a) and old technologies and energy conservation (case b): t in years; arbitrary absolute units for energy E and capital K.

Fig. 14 shows the results for case b), that is old technologies and energy conservation, compared to case a). The ratio μ must now be between $\mu^{<} = 0.10$ and $\mu^{>} = 16.5$ (see Fig. 11) and the attractor is at $\mu_o = 2.03$. The ratio between energy and capital is smaller than in case a).

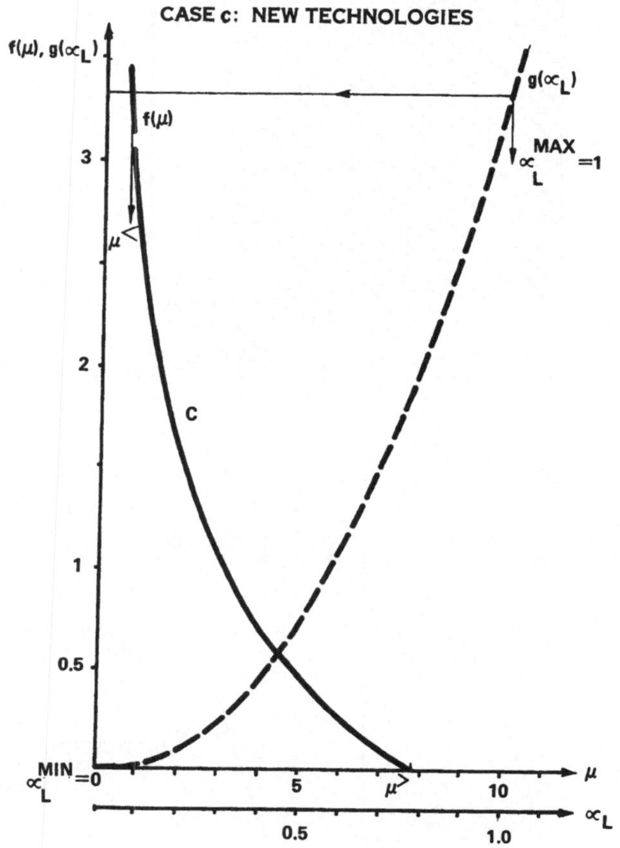

Fig. 15. Determining lower and upper bounds for the labor share α_L and the energy to capital ratio μ on the condition $f(\mu) = g(\alpha_L)$.

Fig. 15 shows the results for case c), that is the case of capital-intensive technologies. The ratio μ must now be between $\mu^{<} = 0.7$ and $\mu^{>} = 7.6$. As Fig. 16 shows, the value of μ_o is now at 4.8. But the phase portrait is qualitatively different: μ_o is no longer an attractor, it becomes a separatrix. Trajectories evolve away from μ_o and approach either the lower or the upper limit of μ. On the lower limits α_L becomes

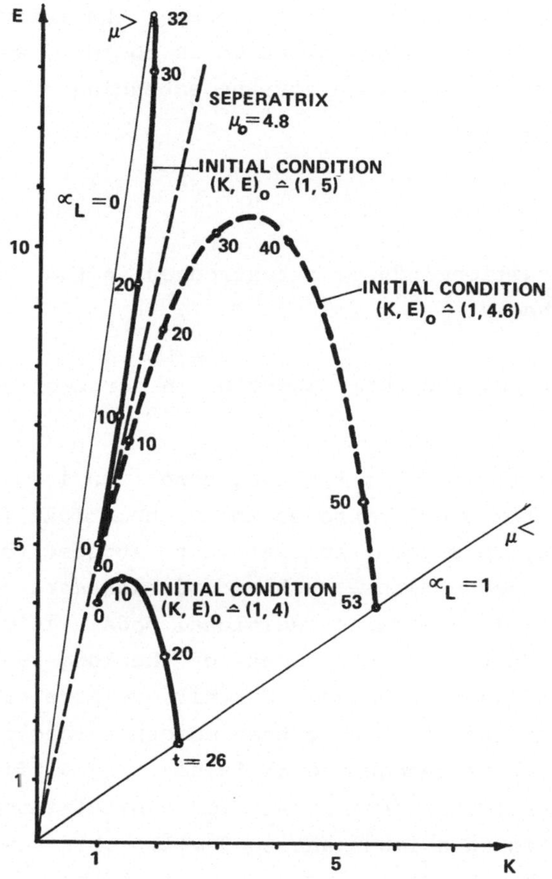

Fig. 16. Phase portrait of the new technologies case (case c); t in years; arbitrary absolute units for energy E and capital K.

unity. No growth can take place any more as all laborers work for consumption and nobody for investments. On the upper limit α_L equals zero, all laborers work for investments. Within the mechanism of the model here considered the new technologies are not consistent with growth. Analytical hints and numerical evidence indicate that the collapse of the phase portrait happens when the Jacobian of the matrix a_{pq} changes its sign. Specifically for the cases considered here we have:

$$a_{pq} = \begin{cases} -0.5 & \text{for case a)} \\ -0.33 & \text{for case b)} \\ +1.0 & \text{for case c)} \end{cases}$$

As work progresses an explicit proof of such indication is expected.

Given the exogeneously given value judgment that growth is desired, and given that the proof of such indication is to come, we are then in a position to formulate a condition for the embedding of new technologies in an economy. We must have

$$a_{EE} \cdot a_{KK} - a_{EK} \cdot a_{KE} < 0 . \qquad (37)$$

Violation of such condition induces catastrophes in the sense of the formal catastrophe theory.

A few words that put the whole exercise in perspective must be added now.

Our point is *not* to say that the real condition is exactly the one expressed above. As the model improves the mathematical form of the condition will change. Our point is instead to suggest that probably, under a wide range of assumptions, such a condition *does exist*. Straightforward integration of large-scale traditional models is probably not the way to make sure that such conditions for the long-range feasibility of energy strategies is not violated. Further, we have *no specific statement* on the viability of this or that modern technology in mind. Once the condition (37) is recognized it is not very difficult to design for a parameter scenario that *does* permit for capital-intensive technologies and growth. It is then imnortant to develop this new trend in systems analysis further by employing proper algorithms for the evaluation of multi-dimensional phase portraits. This new tool should then be used *together* with other tools such as, for instance, the use of traditional large-scale economic models. This may help to establish a richer background for the conception of long-range strategies.

Our future work will concentrate on the following points:

(a) Differentiation between labor and population and the inclusion of population growth;

(b) Optimizations;

(c) Modeling of finite resources and the transition from one technology to another;

(d) Differentiation between the cases for developed and developing countries;

(e) Coupling the economies of different countries through trade and/or foreign aid.

References

[1] Häfele, W., "Energy Systems: Global Options and Strategies," in *IIASA Conference '76*, Vol. 1, 57-91 (International Institute for Applied Systems Analysis, Laxenburg, Austria, 1976).

[2] Wilson, C., *Energy Demand Studies: Major Consuming Countries* (The MIT Press, Cambridge, Massachusetts, and London, England, 1976).

[3] Marchetti, C., "On Strategies and Fate," in W. Häfele et al., *Second Status Report of the IIASA Project on Energy Systems*, RR-76-1, 203-218, (International Institute for Applied Systems Analysis, Laxenburg, Austria, 1976).

[4] Holling, C.S., *Resilience and Stability of Ecological Systems*, RR-73-3 (International Institute for Applied Systems Analysis, Laxenburg, Austria, 1973).

[5] Holling, C.S., in U.S. National Academy of Sciences, *Science, Technology, and Society--A Prospective Look--Summary and Conclusions of the Bellagio Conference*, June 20-27, 1976, Bellagio, Italy.

[6] Grümm, H.-R., "Resilience and Its Application to Energy Systems," International Symposium on New Trends in Systems Analysis, Versailles, December 13-17, 1976.

[7] Häfele, W., "Zielfunktionen," in Kernforschungszentrum Karlsruhe (ed.), *Beiträge zur Kerntechnik*, KFK-2200 and JÜL-1178 (Gesellschaft für Kernforschung, Karlsruhe, 1975), and W. Häfele, "Objective Functions," internal paper (International Institute for Applied Systems Analysis, Laxenburg, Austria, 1975).

SYSTEMS ASPECTS OF LARGE-SCALE SOLAR ENERGY CONVERSION

Jerome M. Weingart
Energy Systems Program
International Institute For Applied Systems Analysis
A-2361 Laxenburg, Austria

PREFACE

In examining the potential role of solar energy conversion as a global energy option, I have been led to issues which ultimately require the tools of systems analysis in their clarification and resolution. Such issues are not only technical in nature; they impinge on both economic and policy-related matters. In particular, much more needs to be known about the behavior of very large integrated solar energy conversion systems in order to insure appropriate and timely policy for the development and use of these important options. In this paper I therefore have attempted to present a new set of challenges, and the rationale for taking up these challenges, to the systems analysis community.

INTRODUCTION

On November 20, 1959 the General Assembly of the United Nations unanimously approved the Declaration of the Rights of the Child, a statement affirming international recognition of and growing committment to the concept of a "birthright" for all humans. Among other things, the Declaration affirms:

> "The child shall enjoy special protection, and shall be given opportunities and facilities ... to enable him to develop physically, mentally, morally, spiritually and socially in a healthy and normal manner and in conditions of freedom and dignity."

One could add that such conditions ought to prevail for the entirety of a human lifetime, not just for childhood. Global development goals that do not include provision of such a birthright to all humans are inconsistent with any concept of a decent world.

Achieving such goals will under the best of circumstances be very difficult and almost certainly require several generations at the least.

Although it is not by itself a sufficient guarantee for a livable world for all inhabitants, a minimum per capita energy level higher than the present one is nevertheless a prerequisite. Present per capita energy use is at the rate of 2 kw(th), a statistic which obscures the fact that much of the world population is living at a subsistence level of a few hundred watts. It is the non-uniform distribution of energy use coupled with the wide variance in efficiency of use which accounts in part for the misery of much of the present world population.

While it can be argued that the industrialized countries could become more efficient in energy use by a factor of two or more over a three decade period, it is inevitable that a decent world will require more energy in the future, not less. There are several factors which make this so. First, the momentum in growth of world population will lead to approximately six billion people shortly after the turn of the century, and this would almost certainly become ten billion or more within the coming century. In addition, the industrialized nations will continue to grow in their demand for energy, although perhaps at a somewhat lower rate than in the past. Finally, the needs of the emerging regions of the world for energy will dictate a rapid growth in demand if prosperity in even modest terms is to be achieved.

Present world energy use (of primary sources) is at the rate of 7.5 Tw(th). A world of ten billion people (10^{10}) living at the 5 kw(th) per capita standard of Western Europe would correspond to an almost order of magnitude increase to 50 Tw(th), and could result from an average rate of growth in the product of population and per-capita energy use of two percent per year over the next century. ($1.02^{100} = 7.24$). An increase by a factor of 2.5 in per capita energy use over this period could occur through a dramatic continuous reduction in the population growth rate; increased affluence will also come from very large increases in the end use efficiency in the developing regions. At the same time, human settlement patterns will continue to move in the direction of increased urbanization and high density settlements (1) and energy use will be increasingly dominated by the consumption of secondary energy carriers (pressurized hot water, electricity and fuels).

The transition over a century or so to such a level of global affluence and stabilized population would be extremely difficult in a world in which oil and gas were both unlimited and cheap. But if the enormous problem of improving the conditions of life for much of the present and future world population seems difficult, it is compounded by the pressures of the inevitable (?) trends towards higher population and higher urban populations, with accompanying non-linear increases in the difficulties of production and delivery of adequate food, energy, housing, health care and education. In addition we face the certain prospect of exhaustion of most of the world's most useful, and until recently least expensive sources of energy - oil and natural gas. This will take place over the coming four to five decades, along with the problems the high prices for these increasingly scarce commodities will create.

Hence, as we attempt to confront the increasingly urgent problems of world human needs, we must also initiate and carry out a world-wide transition from primary reliance on fossil fuels to some mix of long-term sources for the production of heat, electricity and synthetic fuels. While the rate and scale of such a transition will certainly vary from place to place, depending on patterns of needs, resources, wealth, industrialization, and so forth, this transition will ultimately be global and it will be essentially complete within a century. Although there is some argument regarding the extent of recoverable resources of coal, oil and gas, the available resources appear to be in the range of 1500 to 3000 Tw-years, sufficient for world energy needs growing at 2 percent per year for roughly one century. Oil and gas would of course be exhausted much sooner, perhaps in forty to fifty years. What is therefore required is a smooth transition to reliance on the long-term global options. There are exactly four in number.

These primary energy sources, sufficient to provide a livable world of ten billion people for hundreds of centuries at the least, and essentially forever in principle, are the fission sources (via the breeder reactor), the fusion sources (lithium and deuterium), geothermal energy and the sun. Unfortunately we must rule out fusion as an option we can count on, since scientific feasibility has not yet been established, although many experts are convinced that this will be achieved. Geothermal energy is sufficient for world energy needs only in the form of heat in dry rocks and magma. Moreover estimates indicate a technically feasible steady state secondary energy production rate of less than 1 terawatt thermal from such sources if the presently unresolved technical problems can be solved.

Sunlight and fission are all that remain. Certainly the lion's share of attention has been, in terms of science, industry and policy, directed towards the development of large scale nuclear electricity and ultimately, as suggested by Haefele (2) and others, for provision of synthetic fuels as well. While in purely technical terms we are more or less assured of being able to develop fission systems for deployment at the global level, the institutional issues are by no means resolved. New approaches to potential problems related to reactor safety, radioactive waste management and protection from terrorism will be required in order to deploy fission systems at the global level. Possible approaches have been indicated by Haefele(3) and Marchetti(4) to decoupling society and the technologies which will serve society with secondary energy forms.

Both direct and indirect forms of solar energy can be used to produce secondary energy carriers. However the use of the indirect sources (wind, waves, thermal gradients in the oceans, hydraulic potential and the osmotic potential of fresh water flowing into the oceans) appears limited to something on the order of 5 Tw. Only the direct use of the solar irradiance is capable of providing upwards of 50 Tw(th) continuously. Tables 1 & 2 indicate the scale of the problem. Furthermore, as discussed below, provision of energy at the level of many tens of terawatts is possible only through a global deployment of solar conversion facilities in the sunny parts of the world, connected with the demand centers through transmission over long distances of fuels and electricity. Requirements for dedicated land will be on the order of a million square kilometers of sunny (arid wasteland and deserts) regions distributed around the world.

An important aspect of the transition to a world in which non-fossil options provide the majority of energy needs will be the <u>timing</u> of this shift. We know that it requires roughly five decades for a major source of energy to be developed and used on a truly significant scale. Hence the initiation of large scale development and deployment of the long-term alternatives must begin perhaps fifty years or more in advance of the ultimate depletion of the fossil resources. We are perhaps two decades at most into this for fission systems, and only a few years into the development of large-scale solar systems. Even if we <u>could</u> count on fusion, initiation of large scale commercial systems is unlikely, in the most optimistic of scenarios, to begin before the early part of the next century. Therefore we must consider the global deployment of solar conversion systems at the same level of concern as we consider the fission option.

The potential consequences of such large scale use are of special concern. From experience in the field of fission power we know that in the beginning of the technological development period, the large scale aspects of the technology are often not thoroughly examined (or even perceived. Only when large-scale activity commences do such considerations become visible and important. From hindsight we realize that the development of a strong, systems-oriented technology assessment of the fission option might have made a substantial contribution to the recognition and resolution of problems which are now inhibiting the use of such technologies.

Solar energy conversion systems will be no exception to the rule that the large scale use of any new technology bears unexpected and often undesired consequences. Although there appears to be a popular mythology that the use of sunlight is completely "clean", this mythology will fall as large areas of desert lands are covered with machines and valleys are flooded to provide needed hydroelectric storage facilities to permit full use of solar generated electricity. Even the possibilities of climatic modification appear when we consider covering upwards of a million square kilometers of sunny land with solar conversion machines. (5)

In considering the possible use of solar conversion on this scale, a number of questions come to mind. For example, it has been only recently that the production of electricity from large (100 Mwe) solar power plants and the production of synthetic fuels from both fission and solar facilities has been examined. Even less attention has been paid to how a mix of non-fossil energy sources could be integrated into large thermal (district heating), electrical and fuel networks. Yet, without such a systems perspective, it is not easy to see how such options fit into an overall long term energy strategy. This is particularly true of solar energy conversion where we cannot control the energy input to the conversion machines. At the present we do not have a clear idea of how an integrated electrical utility would operate when a substantial portion of installed capacity is in the form of solar power plants, nor do we understand the tradeoffs involved among various solar plant siting strategies (and the effects of dispersion) and the requirements for energy storage and backup generation capacity to guarantee a specified level of overall system reliability. A similar lack of systems understanding applies to the impact of large numbers of solar heated buildings on the demand profile of electric and gas utilities.

These and other issues must be better understood if appropriate public support as well as industrial development and commercialization programs are to be initiated and supported for the necessary decades. In particular, we must concern ourselves with the following classes of issues in which systems considerations will be important, and where new methodologies may have to be developed:

1) Operation and optimization of integrated energy systems in which solar conversion elements are embedded. (This is especially important for electrical utility systems).

2) The complimentary problem of embedding such facilities in the landscape, and the effect of alternative siting strategies on systems operation and economics. (Important since disperssed but interconnected solar systems require

reduced backup and storage capacity relative to single site strategies.)

3) Market penetration dynamics - assessment of the maximum rate and scale at which new energy systems technologies, including solar, can penetrate the energy marketplace.

4) Technology Assessment in the broadest sense, including an examination of environmental and social consequences of alternative energy strategies.

5) Establishment of a rational basis for intercomparison of large scale energy systems options (not to take the place of public or private debate but to provide an explicit framework within which decisions and debate can take place).

6) Determination of the "resilience" of alternative energy strategies to uncertainty, disruption, geopolitical shifts, and so forth.

Each of these will be discussed in turn, after a brief review of the solar resource, technological options for solar energy conversion and some possibilities for global use of these options. It is fair to say that at this point in time, many questions will be raised and few will be immediately answered. However, finding the right questions will be the hardest part of the task for future analyses.

SOLAR ENERGY AS A RESOURCE

The solar resource is unique in that it is a power resource. It is available at a rate determined by the surface temperature (5900 deg. K) and angular size of the sun, the properties of the atmosphere and the earth/sun geometry as seen from a specific place on the globe at a given time. Due to the presence of the atmosphere - a turbulent scattering medium - the maximum power density at the surface of the earth is approximately 1.0 kw/m^2 and is composed of both diffuse (scattered) and direct (focusable) radiation whose ratio depends on the state of the atmosphere. Under very clear sky conditions, direct beam radiation will constitute as much as 90 percent of the total irradiance; under conditions typical of central Europe in the Winter the direct component will often be negligible. The annual average solar energy on the ground will vary from 2 to 6 kwh/m^2-day over the world, the former figure typical of Northern Europe, the latter typical for sunny arid and desert regions. In clear sky environments the direct beam radiation can average 7 - 8 kwh/m^2-day on a surface continuously oriented towards the sun, and it is this resource which will be so important in any true global solar energy scheme.

The statistics of the insolation time series will vary as a function of location and time of year and will reflect the product of a geometrically determined incident radiation and the stochastic filtering effects of the atmosphere. The combination of the diurnal and seasonal cycles and these stochastic fluctuations make it imperative that energy storage elements and possibly long-distance interconnection of solar electric facilities be used to meet systems constraints of economics and reliability.[Further details of the solar resource appear in standard references (6).] Table 3 indicates that solar derived fuels (H_2) and electricity can be produced at a thermal equivalent rate of about 50 w/m^2 (dedicated land area) in the sunny, clear sky regions of the world.

SOLAR ENERGY CONVERSION SYSTEMS OPTIONS

Solar energy must first be converted into other forms of energy prior to use by society. The indirect forms of solar energy, such as wind and waves, will be converted initially to mechanical energy (shaft horsepower) and then to electricity or possibly, via refrigeration cycles, to liquid air. As discussed earlier, the total potential of the indirect solar options is on the order of perhaps 5 Tw(th). The direct use of solar energy is possible via a number of thermodynamic pathways, as illustrated in Figure 1. Once sunlight is converted directly to heat, electricity or a chemical fuel, it can then be used in an energy system such as that indicated schematically in Figure 2 . All energy systems, whether they are bears, breeder reactors or Masseratis are composed of four basic building blocks. These are energy conversion, energy storage, energy transport and power conditioning. The final element refers to the hardware for control of flows, frequency stabilization, AC/DC conversion, voltage control, pressure control, etc. in various parts of an energy system, and to the software (the brains) for operation of the system. Hence a solar energy system is one in which the "front end" conversion element is one in which sunlight is converted to some other form of energy such as heat, electricity or chemical energy.

The very high thermodynamic quality of sunlight, even after passing through a clear atmosphere, permits generation of heat at temperatures in excess of 3000 deg. C (as demonstrated in the magnificent French solar furnace at Odeillo). In fact, with a suitable absorbing cavity it is possible to generate higher temperatures using a plastic fresnel lens available for a few dollars than is possible with the most advanced designs of high temperature reactors. Hence sunlight is a suitable source of thermal energy over the temperature range likely to be of interest for considerable time, and is suitable for operation of Rankine cycle (steam) and Brayton cycle (gas or air) turbines for the generation of electricity or the thermochemical production of hydrogen and oxygen from water. A particular technological format for such conversion is the "central receiver" system in which tracking mirrors or heliostats concentrate solar radiation on an absorber atop a tower to generate steam or hot air to operate a turbine. A 100 Mw(e) sun-following plant would require roughly 15,000 such heliostats, each about 40 m^2 in area with an absorber atop a 200 to 250 meter high tower. Such a system(Fig. 3) would generate power at the rated capacity for 8 to 10 hours per day in sunny regions, with a small amount of storage to buffer the turbine against rapid changes in steam or hot gas conditions. Such systems are under development in the United States (7); a 10 Mw_e plant will be on line at the end of this decade and a 100 Mw_e system should be in operation in the mid-eighties. A similar effort is now being considered in France. Some of the possible systems configurations are shown in Figure 4 . A second conversion approach involves direct conversion of sunlight to electricity via photovoltaic elements or "solar cells". Such units respond to sunlight independent of whether it is direct or diffuse and are therefore suitable for siting in regions of low direct beam insolation. Their development as economically interesting options is being pursued actively in a number of coutries including the U.S. and the Federal Republic of Germany. Finally, for the purposes of this paper, solar fuel production can proceed either via photochemical/biological routes or by conversion of either electricity (via electrolysis) or heat (thermochemical). Interestingly enough, the production of hydrogen from sunlight in sunny regions remote from Europe (perhaps 5000 km distant) may result in a more economic approach to heating of buildings in Europe than on-site use of solar collectors and associated storage, transport and control elements. Although a detailed review of the systems options is inappropriate here, the range of expected costs for solar generated hydrogen transported to Europe is shown for electrolytic and thermochemical processes in Tables 4 and 5.

SOLAR ENERGY CONVERSION - A GLOBAL SYSTEMS SCENARIO

The world is evolving towards a system in which most of the energy-related needs will eventually be provided through the distribution of electricity and fuels. As oil and gas are depleted, other globally transportable fuels must take their place. Hydrogen, methane, alcohols, ammonia and liquid air (the last not strictly a fuel but a negentropy carrier) have all been proposed as the interface between the large scale primary energy sources and the evolving pattern of end uses. Even at the 50 Tw(th) level of a world of 10^{10} people and 5 kw(th) per person, it is possible to supply this demand (forever) from direct use of solar energy. The structure of a global solar energy system would involve hierarchies, but it would depend on the availability of long distance electricity transport and global fuel transport. The present average distance for bulk electricity transport is 100 km but the trends, through high voltage DC transmission, are towards distances on the order of 1000 km or more, and longer distance transmission may be a reality at the time needed (after the year 2000). Transmission of liquid fuels is now a global operation, and the oil business is the largest activity in the world economy. Pipeline transmission of synthetic fuels such as hydrogen will be possible for distances up to perhaps 5000 km. Hence a global solar scenario would include the following features:

1) Local use of solar heating where economics and environmental conditions permits.

2) Solar electric power generation units located throughout the world, primarily in sunny regions, interconnected over distances of perhaps 1000 to 2000 km. and more.

3) Solar fuel (hydrogen?) production units in the sunny parts of the world providing hydrogen and other energy carriers via pipeline and perhaps cryotanker to the entire world.

By making using of the arid and desert wastelands, we can limit the total area required to roughly 20 m^2/kw(th) for the produced secondary energy, corresponding to 10^6 km^2 to provide a world at an order of magnitude greater total demand than today. This picture has a certain internal consistency. In order for the solar option to be a global option, it has to provide primarily fuels and electricity. By virtue of the increasing capacity for economic and reliable long distance transport of these carriers, sunny regions are possible for siting the bulk of the facilities. In addition, global development patterns will require land for settlements and agriculture as well as recreation, forestry and ecological diversity. However, even in a scheme of 40 billion people on the planet, Doxiadis (1) has pointed out that the arid and desert lands will remain essentially uninhabited and unproductive. A global solar option is consistent with this view.

Of course, within such a system solar conversion elements may be embedded locally, and many countries may want to have some fraction of the production capacity within their boundaries.

Such a scenario would have the following attributes, which to some should appear attractive (but further analysis is really required to examine these in detail) :

1) Dispersion of solar fuel and electricity sources over much of the world, minimizing the possibility of embargo (the world would have to embargo itself!).

2) Dispersion of electric production would significantly reduce the need for backup generation capacity and storage requirements as well as permit the minimum solar electricity production costs compatible with the technology at a given time.

3) Production of hydrogen or other fuels would permit storage underground in natural structures (eg depleted oil and gas fields, aquifers) permitting creation of reserves to buffer against political and technical disruption of production units.

4) Such a system would virtually bypass the hazards ascribed to a global nuclear fission system. Disruption of the solar units would have no environmental consequences, no wastes are produced, and the systems would have no military uses in the direct sense (which may, in part, account for the relative lack of interest in solar energy systems for the past several decades).

5) The resource is totally non-depletable; hence true stability in secondary energy production would be assured. (These systems would be the equivalent of giant, non-depletable fuel fields with a production rate limited to 50 watts per square meter of dedicated land).

There are other aspects worth mentioning. It appears (8) that the large solar electric and fuel systems will require primarily concrete, steel and sand in their construction. Although a detailed examination of the materials requirements for the high temperature portion of the system is required, it appears that there will be no fundamental materials problems with such systems. Hence, in constant costs, the cost of such systems should continue to decrease over time, approaching some asymptotic limit. This is thought to be about \$ 500/kw_e for solar thermal electric plants. Finally, the conversion of sunlight and water into hydrogen and oxygen, with subsequent recombination into pure water is in principle a highly attractive global energy system, although the consequences of operation of such a system remain to be evaluated.

We should also realize that the development, construction and operation of such a system would constitute the <u>largest technial, engineering and economic venture of the world</u>. It would dwarf anything undertaken to date, and it would clearly require and perhaps forge new alliances among nations and new institutions to manage this system. But it should be pointed out that the alternative - a global fission system to provide these same 50 Tw to the world, would require investments and engineering and institutional activities just as large. In other words, we are stuck (probably) with the need to create such a giant energy infrstructure; the relation of solar and non-solar options within such a structure is still not well understood.

Of course, such a system would not be created from the top down. It would evolve in stages of development. The initial stage, lasting into the 1990's, would include the construction of hundreds of thousands of buildings with solar thermal equipment, and the embedding of small amounts of solar electric generation capacity in the electrical grids of the industrialized nations (those which had suitable high insolation sites) to perhaps three percent of total capacity. From the mid-Nineties into the first decade(s) of the next century, regional interconnections of solar electric power generation would occur, and solar buildings might be sufficiently abundant to constitute an important modification of the electrical and fuel systems in which they were embedded. Solar fuel production facilities would be increasingly used, with truly large scale solar fuel production occuring in the second decade of the next century. In the first decade of the next century and beyond, continental dimensions would be involved in transport of electricity, permitting the linking of solar power plants over large distances, and to regions not suitable for siting of such facilities.

This is of course only the barest of sketches, but it suggests something of the evolutionary process which such a system, if developed, would proceed through. Since local and regional applications would come first, it will be necessary to precede such developments with appropriate methodologies which permit the evaluation of the potential use for such technologies on a region by region basis. Variations in virtually every parameter determining the economic and production potential of solar options will occur at the regional level. The parameters include meteorological conditions, quality and extent of available land, the technical, economic and institutional structure of the local and regional utility systems, price and availability of other sources of energy, and an array of social and political priorities. No such methodology exists and until it does, it is unlikely that we will be able to assess how the evolution to a global level of use could occur, nor where the important early prospects for solar energy conversion will be.

Because of the need for such methodologies, and the need to assess the significance of a global solar option in advance of having it, a number of systems issues require further investigation. These are discussed in the subsequent sections .

EMBEDDING OF STOCHASTIC ENERGY SOURCES IN INTEGRATED ENERGY SYSTEMS

Solar conversion elements will be embedded in the larger integrated energy systems of society. Because of the possibility of continental and global transport of solar derived fuels, coupled with the feasibility of long term storage (several years), the behavior of large fuel systems will not be affected by short term (daily, hourly, minute to minute) variations in available sunlight. However, the siting of solar electric facilities will involve regions in which there are large stochastic variations in available sunlight, and in which bulk transport of electricity will be below 1000 km for several decades. Hence one extremely important unsolved problem is the development of models which can permit simulation and optimization of the operation of electric utility systems containing solar power plants. In addition, models are required to guide investment decisions when capacity additions are required in response to demand forecasts. Such modeling would permit the following:

1) Determination of storage and/or backup generation capacity for a given utility system as a function of solar capacity on-line and of geographic deployment or siting strategies.

2) Clarification of systems reliability issues involving stochastic sources (direct solar, wind)

3) Determination of the degree to which accurate measurements of insolation in a region are required. (I.e., what is the economic worth of various degrees of detail in insolation data?)

4) Establishment of a common methodological basis for intercomparison of electric generation methods region by region or utility by utility, including detailed determination of the economics of each option.

5) Permits assessment of the costs of solar electric power generation as a function of installed solar capacity in a particular grid.

6) All of this, in turn, permits a more quantitative framework for public, political and industry discussion and decision-making regarding energy options.

Recently the Aerospace Corporation (9) has undertaken pioneering work to establish the characteristics of integrated electric utility systems containing solar conversion elements. However, in their most recent report (10) for the Electric Power Research Institute, they point out that "there is no known analytical method for establishing the optimum distribution of solar capacity between multiple sites"

In addition, they note that :

"Another area which appears to merit further study is the method of dispatching all of the plants in a network which contains both solar and conventional capacity. Dispatching methodology needs to be developed which is suitable for use by a utility, and which minimizes both the total fossil fuel used and the amount of solar energy discarded when demand is low and storage is filled. This dispatching methodology should also permit other constraints (such as limits on pollutant emission) to be imposed on selected plants."

Figure 5 demonstrates the results obtained by Aerospace indicating the extent to which backup generation capacity is required as a function of solar capacity within a given utility system, but with alternate sites used for the plants. The dispersed system requires in the best case only half the backup generation (and associated costs) of the single site cases. A similar observation has been made by Soviet scientists (11) in which the amount of solar radiation available at a given confidence level was found to increase dramtically when many sites were "linked" together , as opposed to the conditions for the best single site investigated. Figure 6 illustrates an additional concern; that is the inter-relationship among solar and hydro units in systems which contain both. Such systems could be of special importance in those countries in Europe (Austria, France for example) in which high costs of fossil fuel make the possibility of coupled solar and hydro systems of some interest (12).

It appears that the development of suitable models for integrated electric systems incorporating solar generation units is a major systems problem yet to be solved, and one whose solution will be required to determine the potential use of this option on a region by region basis.

EMBEDDING OF SOLAR FACILITIES IN THE LANDSCAPE

In principle solar energy conversion over three to five percent of the land could provide each nation in Europe with its total current energy needs; smaller fractions arise when considering sunnier parts (Fig.7) of the world, including emerging nations even in a highly developed future state. However, siting of solar facilities will be a complex process (schematically indicated in Figure 8) and will require formal techniques to carry out efficiently and economically.

For example, formal procedures will be required to permit an assessment of the tradeoffs involved in competition for land resources in regions of the world where such resources are under extreme pressure. Such procedures would permit a formalized guide (not necessarily a rule) for site selection when large numbers of solar facilities are contemplated, and would permit evaluation of alternative siting strategies when these alternative strategies had different costs associated.

This will clearly be related to the results of analyses in which the effects of coupling the output of dispersed sites have been determined. In addition, such techniques will determine the extent to which land use is a real constraint. A recent study in Austria (12) indicates that it is feasible, in terms of available land, to consider a strategy in which four times the present electricity production of Austria is provided through a combination of solar electric power plants and hydro-storage units. This somewhat counterintuitive result arose from a systems perspective in which the entire Austrian electric system could be used for embedding of solar electric facilities.

In addition, an organized siting procedure would permit advance designation of certain areas as potential sites, to permit keeping the solar option "open" in a region. As an example of the effect of distributing solar generation capacity, sunlight for two cities in Austria less than 50 km apart is shown in Figures 9 &10 . The summing of the sunlight in the two regions "smoothes" the variation hour to hour, and suggests how a more detailed examination of multiple site combinations could considerably increase the predictability of available sunlight.

As public concern over the environmental and social aspects of the siting of large industrial facilities grows, it will be increasingly important to provide a framework within which public and political discussion can take place. Again, a formalized procedure for characterizing and ranking various sites for solar facilities would be an important step towards resolving possible future conflicts over the siting of solar and related (i.e. storage) facilities. This "open planning" approach, to be successful, requires the underpinning of a systems analytic framework.

MARKET PENETRATION DYNAMICS FOR NEW ENERGY SYSTEMS

A very important policy issue centers on the rate, scale and ultimate level of production we can expect from a new technological option, including new energy options including fission and solar systems. To have some well-founded sense of the maximum rate at which solar thermal, electric and fuel production options could be useful in various regions would be of enormous consequence in the present debate over solar and nuclear energy. In the United States some opponents of nuclear power have argued that solar energy conversion is an alternative; others proposing a nuclear dominated future have argued that the solar option can not be important for a very long time. We must quantify this discussion if anything useful concerning the relative market position of new energy options in the future is to be said.

Figure 11 demonstrates the present range of disagreement over both total energy demand and the possible role of solar energy conversion in the coming half century or so in the United States. The upper part of the total demand range corresponds to three percent per year growth; the lowest projection corresponds to a recent scenario by Lovins (13,14). Similarly the projections for the maximum possible contribution from solar energy use (both direct and indirect uses) range from essentially no contribution to the maximum curve corresponding to a number of enthusiastic projections by Lovins (13), the MITRE Corporation (15) and others. The large number of projections have been made by various individuals and institutions using a variety of techniques. In some cases the projections are actually formal program goals , such as those of ERDA (16); in others they are the results of various types of model calculations such as those presented by the Stanford Research Institute (17); in yet others they appear to be produced by intuition.

We need something better. The dynamics of large, complex, highly interconnected systems (national economies) constrain the rate at which some new option can enter the marketplace, including the energy market. Fischer and Pry (18) discovered that the process of technological substitution, in which one product or process displaces its more traditional competitor, invariably occurs with a smooth and simple behavior. They found that the substitution of synthetic rubber for natural rubber, water-based for petroleum-based paints, electric for open hearth steel making, and many other examples, all occured in a logistic fashion, in which the penetration or market fraction captured by the "intruder" was given by

$$\ln (f/1-f) = K (t - t_o)$$

where f = fraction of the total market captured by the new competition, t_o = the date at which f = 0.5, and K is a rate constant. Marchetti (19) has extended this approach to that of the energy marketplace, and has discovered that the rate of entrance and departure of various energy sources into and out of the energy marketplace is essentially logistic. This relationship appears to hold rather well over a period of a century or more worldwide, for the United States, and (for shorter periods, due to lack of long term data) for many other countries as well. This remarkable behavior is shown in Figure 12 in which the market shares for wood, coal, oil and natural gas are shown with their logistic counterpart. The growth projection for fission is based on optimistic projections but is probably not inconsistent with purely technological capabilities. The projection for solar energy is based on the assumption that a variety of large scale solar technologies can enter the U.S. energy market in the early 1980's and before, and grow to displace twenty-five percent of the total primary energy demand by the year 2030. This would correspond to solar energy displacing other primary sources (of secondary energy) at a fractional rate exceeding that with which oil and natural gas entered the market. Such a scenario in itself is optimistic and assumes technical, economic and institutional success for large-scale solar technologies within the coming decade to two decades. Such a projection, when overlaid on any reasonable scenario for total energy demand, indicates that it is highly unlikely that any new energy technology entering the marketplace in the 1980's can have a substantial contribution until some four decades later. (Such a scenario for total demand and the fractional solar share developed by Weingart and Nakicenovic(20) is shown in Figure 13.) Yet many scenarios, including those of ERDA, Lovins, the MITRE Corporation (which preshadowed the major U.S. effort in solar energy conversion) are all far more optimistic than this. If indeed the properties of national economies are "smooth" due to their size and complexity, we need to understand the implications of ahistoric departures from what have been well-behaved patterns of change in the past. We do not say that the more optimistic scenarios are "wrong" or impossible; we do point out that they are sufficiently inconsistent with previous behavior to provoke us to inquire into the reasons (the "hidden variables" if you will) behind the smooth external behavior of the economic system. The entire area of the dynamics of the penetration of new technologies into traditional markets is a very rich one for systems analysis and a necessary one for the development of realistic policy for the development and widespread use of new technologies.

TECHNOLOGY ASSESSMENT AND THE INTERCOMPARISON OF ENERGY OPTIONS

In addition to arguments over the rate at which some new energy technology can be made available, there are fundamental disagreements over how the attributes of alternative energy futures can be compared. How, for example, does one weigh the perceived risks of reactor safety, radioactive waste management and the possibility for terrorist disruption of a nuclear energy system (and society) against the perhaps higher direct costs, larger requirements for land and materials, and requirements for remote siting (in the asymptotic phase of deployment) of a solar conversion system? Acknowledging the considerable disagreement in the magnitude of such attributes as reactor safety, it is nevertheless clear that we have no widely accepted or used formal procedure for intercomparing qualitatively different energy systems options, even if agreement on these other issues were possible. There is a need to bring some formal systems techniques, such as decision analysis, into the larger debate over future energy strategies, if only to clarify what it is we are disagreeing about, and perhaps to facilitate conscensus when a decision to initiate new energy production systems is required. We should be prepared, however, for situations in which conscensus will be impossible and in which there will be little chance of widespread agreement or even compromise on the use of a specific technological option. This now appears to be the case in the nuclear debate in the United States, and it is probably true in much of Western Europe where the overall energy situation is much more critical. In the absence of a clear strategy for transition from fossil to non-fossil energy sources, and in the face of the inevitable need to initiate and carry out that transition (and the hour is growing late) we will have to develop strategies which can absorb the disagreement and problems and permit the transition to occur. This brings us to the final consideration of this paper, that of the "resilience" of future energy strategies.

RESILIENT ENERGY STRATEGIES

Biologists have known for decades that complexity and diversity in natural ecosystems are in some way closely linked to the ability of such systems to persist in the face of unexpected and sometimes previously unexperienced assaults. Rene Dubos has often noted that there is an analogy for human ecosystems - that societies which have developed a multiplicity of options for achieving social goals appear to persist longer than societies which are dependent on a single mode of accomplishing a central activity of society.

In the case of the human species there can be little doubt that the species itself will survice, even after the most terrible holocasts. As the biologist Fredrick Smith has said (21): "the problem is that we are doomed to survive". What we are clearly after is not the survival of mankind as a species, but mankind as a dynamic, polycultural system in which the quality of the human experience is continuously improved.

It therefore is desirable and probably necessary to design our technological systems, including energy, in such a way that inevitable fluctuations in personal and social behavior, as well as natural disasters, do not seriously impair the functioning of a vital human society. We would like to somehow insure our ability to make progress in spite of ourselves. That is, we need to design our future strategies to be "resilient".

Holling (22) has defined "resilience" as "the ability of a system to absorb external forces and persist". Such systems can change in such a way that permits the assimilation of shocks without destruction, unlike "brittle" systems which have a threshold for assault, after which they collapse completely. Military strategists have long used John von Neumann's concept of "functional redundancy" in the design of weapons systems in which a specific function is carried out in parallel by a number of functionally identical but physically very different subsystems. A specific example would be coupling inertial guidance, fluidic, and electronic subsystems into the guidance system of a missle. Destruction of the electronic components by a nearbye intense radiation field would not damage the purely mechanical components, permitting the function to continue. Although this example is not a happy one to contemplate, it demonstrates where systems are considered by their designers to have to succeed in the face of multiple assaults, techniques for creating a high degree of resilience have been used.

Such considerations are directly relevant to future energy strategies. If we extend the analogy, there should be intense effort at the parallel development of a multiplicity of physically different, functionally identical energy systems options. This means, in short, the use of the remaining fossil fuels (notably coal) along with fission, fusion, geothermal and solar sources to produce identical secondary energy vectors (heated fluids on a small scale, electricity and synthetic fuels on a larger scale). Failure to develop one or two (or even three) of the long term options would still permit large scale energy production. However, the successful development of several of these options would provide a high degree of resilience in a world energy system.

We would like to create a world energy system in which, for example, large scale embargo was structurally impossible, in which synthetic fuels could be stored sufficiently to permit a smooth response to both man-made and natural disasters, and one in which there were no continual possibly destructive impact on natural ecosystems and climate. We would like to have, once and for all, an assured and adequate source of energy so that the really important human issues could be addressed at the global scale.

As discussed earlier, a global solar energy system would appear to have all the important attributes of a highly resilient global energy system, including the quality of being "safe-fail" rather than "fail-safe". A solar power plant could be destroyed with no direct effect on society, unlike the case of a power reactor catastrophe. Nuclear systems must be fail-safe, since their failure, given present siting strategies, would in many cases be catastrophic.

A combined solar/nuclear(fission) system, evolving from the regional and national to the global scale, might be even more resilient than the solar system alone, at least for the next half century. The market penetration analysis indicates that under the best of circumstances fission systems will be required if the use of fossil fuels is to be substantially moderated; only after some four decades could the solar options really take over. In any case, the development of a multiplicity of energy system options which can function together would appear to buy us an insurance policy against the inevitable large uncertainties of the future.

At IIASA there has been a strong interest in somehow formalizing the concept of resilience (23). Here an extremely important policy issue emerges and again serves to challenge the systems analysis community. How can we somehow quantify the concept(s) of resilience and measure the characteristics of a multi-source energy system against one in which only a single source is dominant? How can we evaluate the benefits of a clearly very expensive policy of developing solar, fission, fusion and geothermal options in parallel? Can such an evaluation be made in a satisfactory formal way and can the results be translated into the polocy area? Can we develop techniques to help us design resilient strategies for the future to help us deal with the unknown. This may be far superior than attempting to predict the future by mandate. After all, "making predictions is very difficult" observed Niels Bohr, "especially about the future".

NOTES AND REFERENCES

1. C. A. Doxiadis and J. G. Papaioannou, Ecumenopolis - The Inevitable City of the Future, Center for Ekistiks, Athens (1974)
2. W. Haefele et al, "Second Status Report of the IIASA Project on Energy Systems", IIASA RR-76-1 (1976)
3. W. Haefele and W. Sassin, "The Global Energy System", Annual Review of Energy, Vol. 2, Annual Reviews, Inc. Palo Alto, Calif. (in press)
4. C. Marchetti, "Transport and Storage of Energy", IIASA Research Report RR-75-38 (1975) and

   C. Marchetti, "From the Primeval Soup to World Government: An Essay on Comparative Evolution", IIASA Research Report RR-76-9 (1976)
5. J. Weingart, J. Williams and G. Kroemer (eds), Procedings of the International Workshop on Climate and Solar Energy Conversion, IIASA (publication expected Spring, 1977)
6. J. Duffie and W. Beckman, Solar Energy Thermal Processes, John Wiley and Sons, New York (1975)
7. "Definition Report - National Solar Energy Research, Development and Demonstration Program", Energy Research and Development Agency, Division of Solar Energy, Washington, D.C. Report No. ERDA-49 (1975)
8. J. Weingart, "Solar Energy as a Global Energy Option", IIASA Research Report (in preparation, publication Spring, 1977)
9. The Aerospace Corporation, "Solar Thermal Conversion Mission Analysis", Vol IV. The Aerospace Corporation, Report ATR-74(7417-16)-1 (1974).
10. Electric Power Research Institute "Penetration Analysis and Margin Requirements Associated with Large-Scale Utilization of Solar Power Plants". EPRI Report ER-198. Prepared by the Aerospace Corporation. (August, 1976)

Note - References 9 and 10 constitute a landmark in the development of a systems approach to large scale solar energy conversion.

11. B. V. Tarnizhevskii and A. N. Smirnova, "Generation of Electric Power at High Reliability Levels Using a Group of Solar Power Plants in an Energy System". Geliotekhnika, Vol. 10, No. 5, pp. 36-43 (1974)

12. N. Weyss in Ref. 2

13. A. B. Lovins, "Energy Strategy: The Road Not Taken?", Foreign Affairs 55, 1, 65-96 (October, 1976)

14. A. B. Lovins, "Scale, Centralization, and Electrification in Energy Systems", Procedings of the Symposium FUTURE STRATEGIES OF ENERGY DEVELOPMENT, Oak Ridge Associated Universities. (In preparation)

Note - References 13 and 14 constitute some of the most thoughtful and stimulating alternative views of future energy systems possibilities and challenge some of the notions associated with the merits of ever-increasing electrical and fuel systems. The entire Procedings (Ref. 14) constitutes an unusual attempt to examine the significance of the energy strategy alternatives we have available to us.

15. The MITRE Corporation, "Systems Analysis of Solar Energy Programs" MTR-6513, 1973 (Available from NTIS)

16. See ref. 7

17. "A Preliminary Social and Environmental Assessment of the ERDA Solar Energy Program 1975-2020" Stanford Research Institute report to the Environmental and Resources Study Branch, Division of Solar Energy, Energy Research and Development Administration, Washington, D.C. 20545 (In press)

18. J. C. Fisher and R. H. Pry, "A Single Substitution Model of Technological Change." Technical Information Series, Report 70-C-215, General Electric Company, Corporate Research and Development, Schenectady, New York (1970)

19. C. Marchetti, "On Strategies and Fate", in Ref. 2

20. J. Weingart and N. Nakicenovic, "Market Penetration Dynamics and the Large Scale Use of Solar Energy", IIASA Technical Report (in preparation) Spring, 1977

21. Fredrick Smith, remarks made at a conference on the human environment, California Institute of Technology, 1971.

22. C.S. Holling, "Resilience and Stability of Ecological Systems", IIASA Report RR-73-3 (1973); see also

    C. S. Holling, "Myths of Ecology and Energy", Ref. 14

23. H. R. Grumm, (Ed.) "Analysis and Computation of Equilibria and Regions of Stability, with Applications in Chemistry, Climatology, Ecology and Economics" (Record of a Workshop). IIASA CP-75-8. (1975); see also

    H. R. Grumm, "Definitions of Resilience", IIASA RR-76-5 (1976)

USES	REGION	10^6 km^2	% TOTAL
Used Fully	Human Settlements Arable Land	0.4 13.0	0.3 8.8
Partial Use	Pastures Forests	21.3 35.3	14.3 23.8
Usable	(not practical)	3.9	2.6
Unused	Wasteland, desert, mountains	62.1	41.8
	Uninhabited islands & Polar	12.5	8.4
TOTAL	Global Land Area	148.5	100.0
Solar (50 w/m^2)	7.5 Tw 50.0 400.0	0.15 1.0 8.0	0.1 0.7 5.4

Table 1 Present Patterns of Land Use and Potential Solar Energy Conversion Area Requirements

DATE	POPULATION 10^9	ENERGY/CAP. kw(th)	WORLD ENERGY Tw(th)	SOLAR AREA 10^6 km^2
NOW	4	2	7.5	0.15
2076	10	5	50.0	1.0
???	20	20	400.0	8.0

Table 2 - Area requirements for solar energy conversion for various combinations of population and per capita energy demand.

SOLAR RESOURCE	TECHNOLOGY	EFFICIENCY	NET OUTPUT (w/m^2)
250 - 300 w/m^2 Direct Beam	STEC	0.2 - 0.35	20 - 50 (elec.) 60 - 150 (th. equiv.)
	SOLAR TH. H_2	0.2 - 0.6	20 - 90 (th.)
80 - 250 w/m^2 Global Rad.	PHOTOVOLTAIC	0.1 - 0.25	6 - 50 (elec.) 18 - 150 (th. equiv.)
	BIOCONVERSION	0.1	6 - 20 (th.)
	LOW TEMP. HEAT	0.3 - 0.5	25 - 125 (th.)

Table 3 - Net production of secondary energy forms (and thermal equivalent) from solar energy conversion. Ground cover ratio of 0.4 to 0.5 assumed for STEC, solar thermal hydrogen; o.8 for PV.

ELECTROLYTIC HYDROGEN FROM SUNLIGHT

	Case 1	Case 2	Case 0
STEC ($/$kw_e$)	700	1400	500
Electrolysis ($/$kw_H$)	400	500	100
System load factor	0.40	0.25	0.4
H_2 cost ($/BBL eq.)	55*	211*	30*

* 0.10 FCR

Table 4 - Estimates using best available data and cost projections for the cost of producing hydrogen by a combination of solar thermal electricity and electrolysis. A ten percent fixed charge rate is assumed.

THERMOCHEMICAL HYDROGEN FROM SUNLIGHT

	Case 1	Case 2	Case 3
Net Efficiency	0.10	0.25	0.64
System Load Fact.	0.25	0.35	0.40
$/kw($H_2$)			
Heliostats	750	240	75
BOP	100	75	45
Thermochem.	400	200	100
Total Cap. Cost	1250	515	220
$/BBL equivalent i = 0.10 (0.15)	100 (150)	30 (45)	11 (17)

Table 5 - Estimates of the likely range of costs for the production of hydrogen by solar thermo-chemical processes using current estimates of almost certain (Case 1), highly likely (Case 2) and possible but optimistic (Case 3) costs of the system elements.

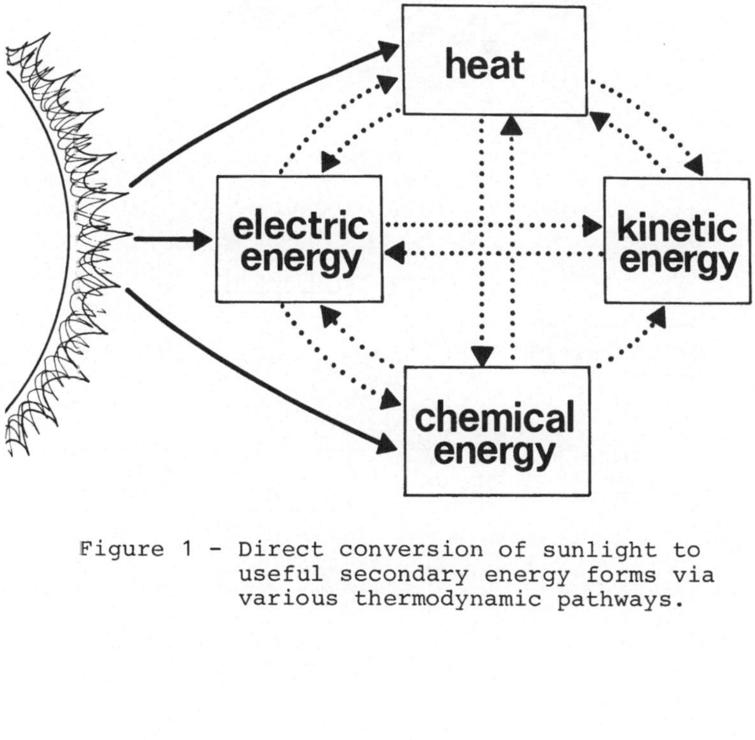

Figure 1 - Direct conversion of sunlight to useful secondary energy forms via various thermodynamic pathways.

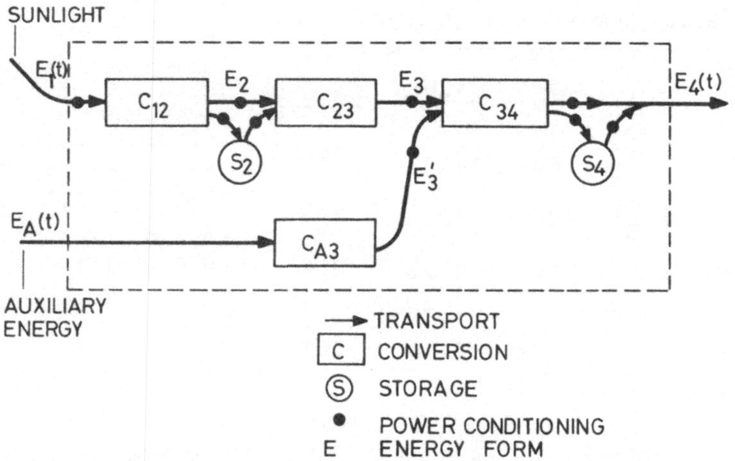

Figure 2 - Generalized schematic of a solar energy conversion system

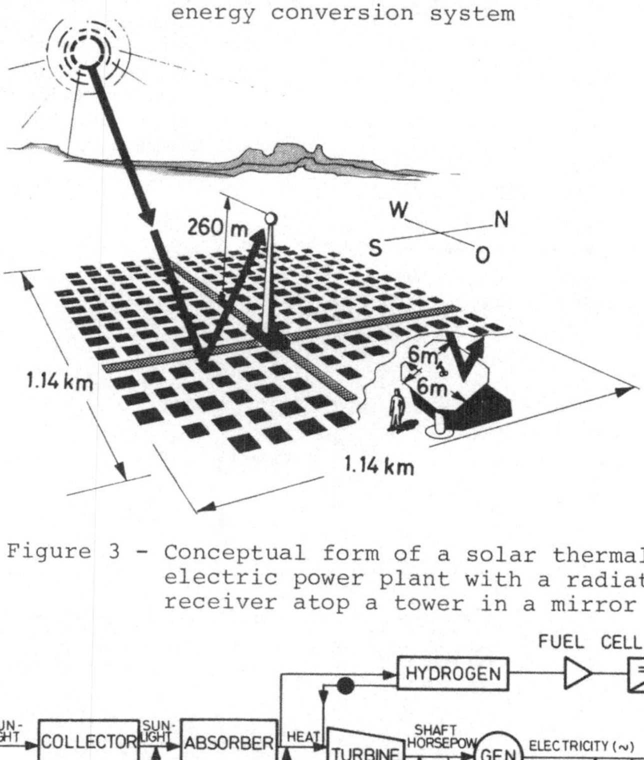

Figure 3 - Conceptual form of a solar thermal electric power plant with a radiation receiver atop a tower in a mirror field.

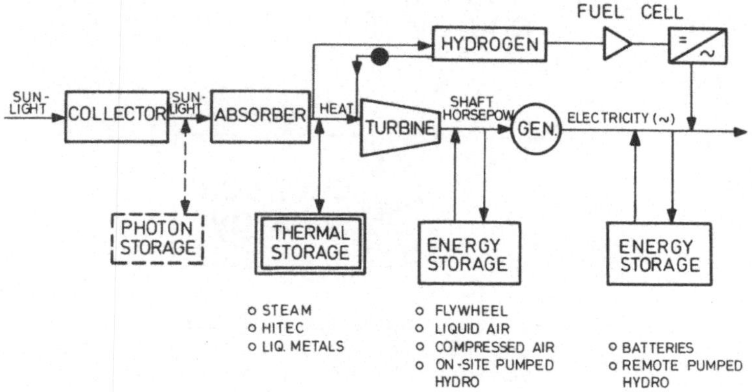

Figure 4 - Possible Combinations of solar thermal energy conversion to electricity and fuel.

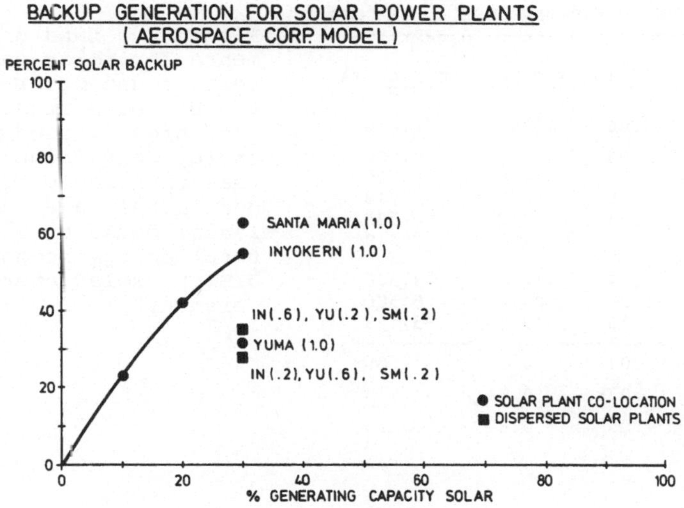

Figure 5 - Backup generation capacity for solar power plants as a function of the percentage of total generation capacity in the form of solar power plants, for a specific utility model for the Southwestern United States. Backup requirements decrease when solar power plants are located in dispersed sites, rather than all in one location.

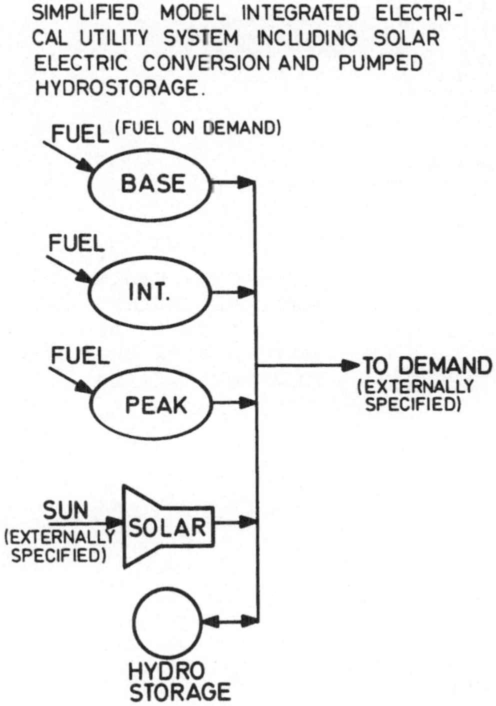

Figure 6 - Schematic of an integrated electric utility system combining solar power plants and hydroelectric storage with conventional generating units. The general problem of modeling and optimizing such a system remains to be solved.

SOLAR ENERGY CONVERSION AND LAND USE IN THE USA

REGION	$10^6 km^2$	% TOTAL	m^2/CAPITA
CONTINENTAL	5.86	1000	26,600
Cropland	.95	17.0	4,500
Grassland Pasture	1.40	24.0	6,380
Woodland Pasture	.16	2.7	718
Other woodland	.13	2.2	585
Farmsteads, roads	.07	1.2	319
Grazing land	.74	12.7	3,378
Forests	1.23	21.0	5,586
All other land	1.13	19.3	5,133
SOLAR ELECTRIC	.012	0.2	55
SOLAR FUELS	.038	0.64	170
TOTAL SOLAR	.05	0.84	225

Figure 7 - Land area requirements for solar energy conversion and other uses in the United States. Half the land area is used for solar energy conversion to food. Less than one percent in additional land (arid wastelands) could provide the total energy needs of the U.S. by solar energy conversion.

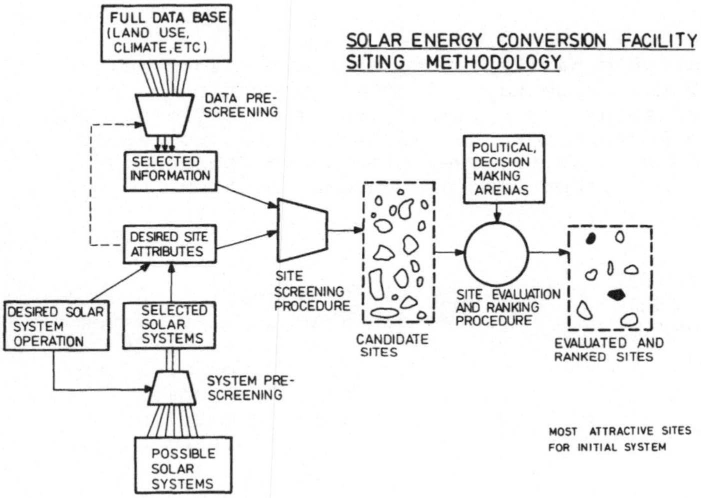

Figure 8 - A schematic of the process required for identification and ranking of suitable sites for solar energy conversion facilities.

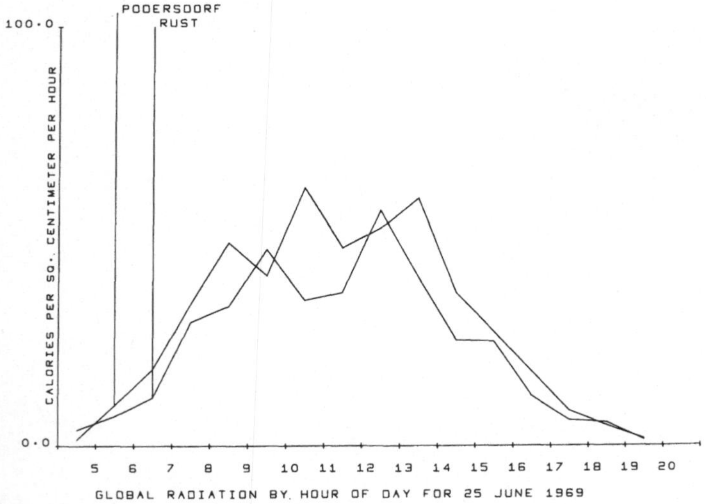

Figure 9 - Hourly sunshine pattern for two cities in the same general region in lower Austria.

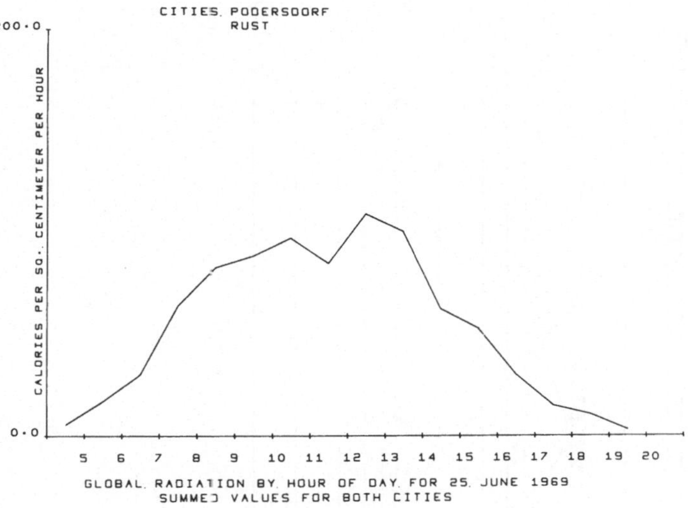

Figure 10 - Solar radiation at two sites (Rust and Podersdorf) in Austria, summed to simulate the interconnection of solar power plants at the two locations.

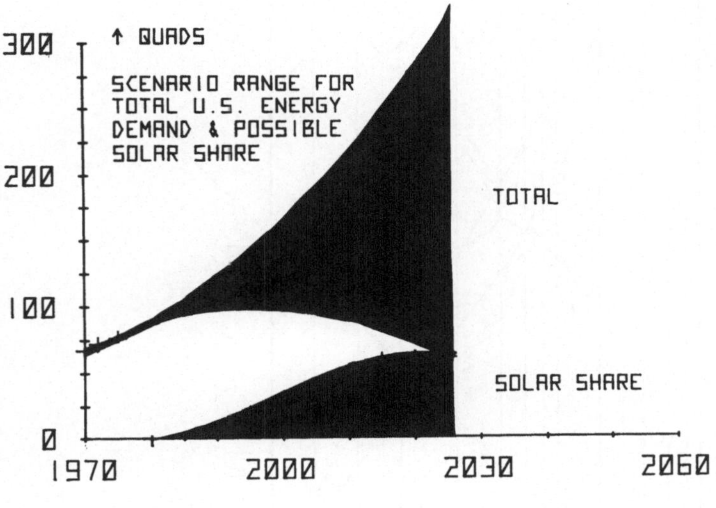

Figure 11 - Scenario range for total U.S. energy demand and the possible contributions from solar energy.

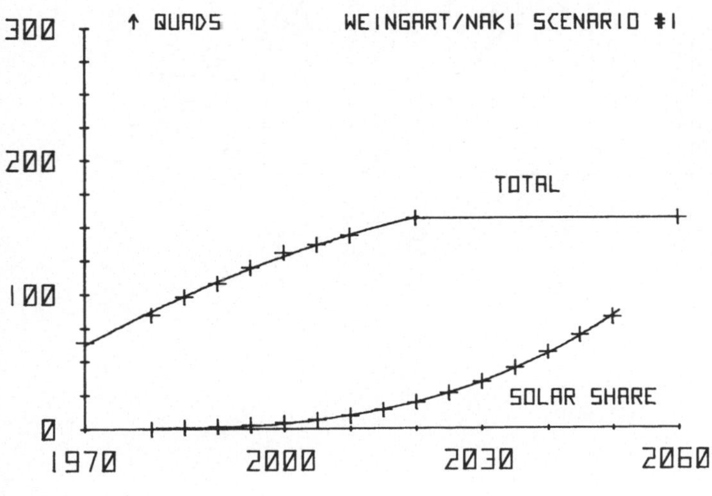

Figure 12 - Logistic scenario for the use of solar energy in the United States to displace other sources of energy, developed by Weingart and Nakicenovic, IIASA.

Figure 13 Logistic fit and projections for primary energy use in the United States, 1850 - 2100. Based on work of Marchetti and Nakicenovic at IIASA.

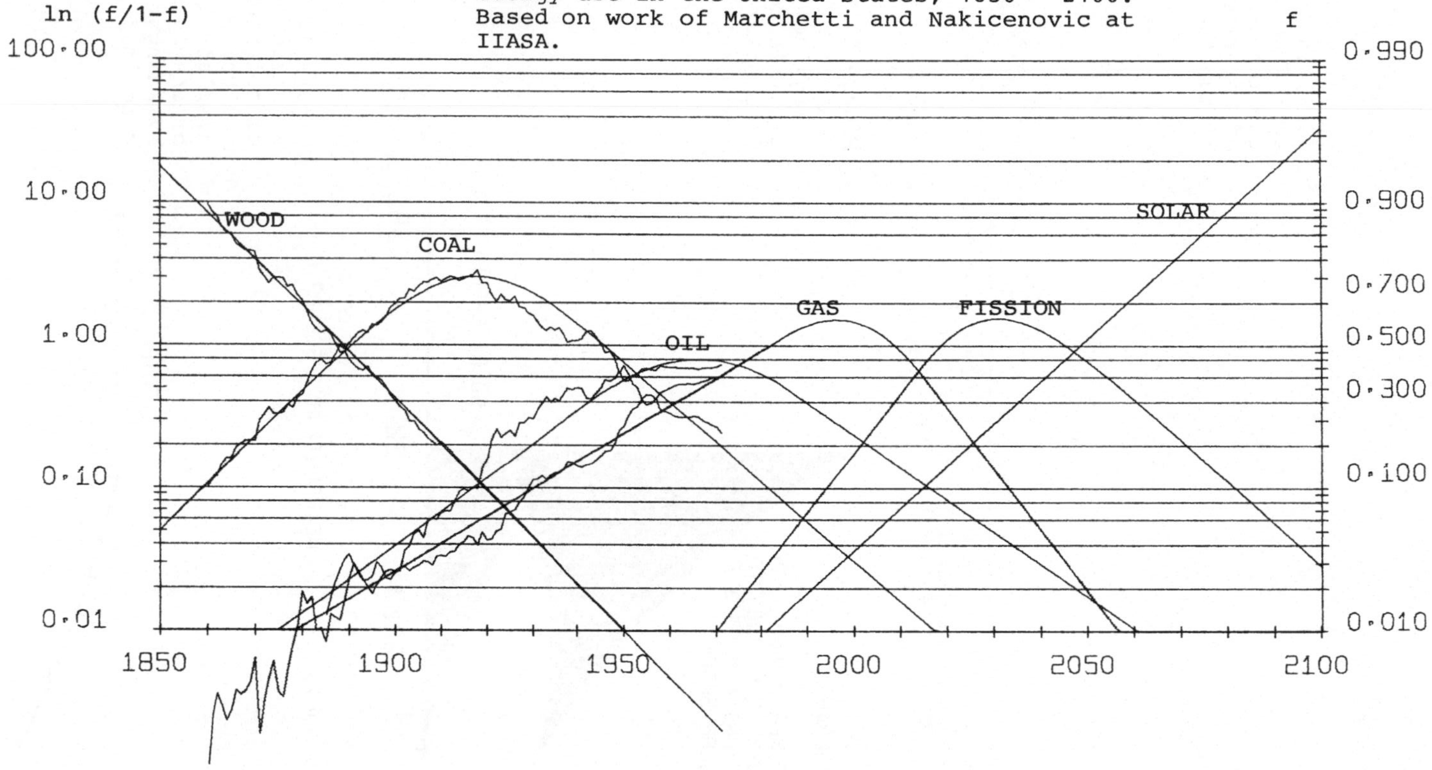

ANALYSE DE SYSTEMES ET PROBLEMES POSES PAR L'ENERGIE SOLAIRE

J.L. Abatut
Laboratoire d'Automatique et d'Analyse des Systèmes
du Centre National de la Recherche Scientifique
7, Avenue du Colonel Roche
31400 TOULOUSE
France

INTRODUCTION

Les recherches sur le développement de sources énergétiques nouvelles sont de plus en plus une nécessité compte tenu notamment des problèmes de disponibilité des sources fossiles d'énergie (sur le plan technique et économique) et des problèmes d'environnement de plus en plus importants.

Dans le cadre du développement en France de filières "énergies nouvelles", le Centre National de la Recherche Scientifique a mis en place en 1975 le Programme Interdisciplinaire de Recherches pour le Développement de l'Energie Solaire, (PIRDES). Ce programme, mené en collaboration étroite avec de nombreux organismes français, publics ou privés (EDF, CNES, CEA, ...) comprend 5 thèmes principaux de recherches :

- Centrales thermo-hélio-électriques
- Conversion photovoltaïque
- Habitat solaire
- Photosynthèse et bio-conversion
- Thermochimie solaire.

A ces thèmes de recherches viennent s'adjoindre des travaux d'intérêt général :

- Etudes climatiques et écologiques
- Etudes économiques et analyse de systèmes.

L'analyse de systèmes, que l'on ne doit pas considérer comme une nouvelle science mais plutôt comme une nouvelle approche d'un problème complexe, a pour objectif essentiel de rechercher le rôle potentiel et la place de l'énergie solaire dans le contexte énergétique, économique, écologique, social d'une région ou d'un pays.

Le secteur de l'énergie ne peut pas être considéré comme une simple juxtaposition de sources, sytèmes de conversion, usages, mais comme un véritable système. Ceci implique qu'une analyse de systèmes sur l'énergie solaire n'est qu'une analyse partielle qui doit être reliée à l'ensemble du secteur énergétique, puis aux domaines économique, écologique et social (figure 1).

L'objectif essentiel de cette communication est de donner quelques idées sur les problèmes d'analyse qui se posent au niveau d'une seule filière de conversion de l'énergie solaire : la conversion hélio-thermo-dynamo-électrique (centrales HTDE de grande puissance).

Après description rapide d'une centrale HTDE seront décrits un certain nombre d'études dont les résultats doivent permettre d'inclure ce type de conversion dans un modèle du secteur solaire, puis du secteur énergétique, enfin dans des modèles plus globaux.

I - FILIERES DE CONVERSION DE L'ENERGIE SOLAIRE

Au dessus de la couche atmosphérique la terre reçoit, le jour, environ 1,35 kw/m^2. La puissance totale interceptée par la terre est de 170.10^{12} kw dont 30% environ est réfléchi par l'atmosphère. L'énergie reçue annuellement à la surface de la terre correspond alors à plusieurs milliers de fois l'énergie consommée dans le monde. Ce type de calculs, effectué par de nombreux auteurs, donne des résultats extrèmement impressionnants et font souvent considérer l'énergie solaire comme une source inépuisable d'énergie. En fait pour évaluer cette source d'énergie il ne faut pas oublier qu'on doit la convertir en énergie utilisable par l'homme et c'est dans ce contexte que se pose tout le problème de l'évaluation des possibilités de l'énergie solaire.

Un autre calcul amusant est celui de la surface au sol qui serait nécessaire pour produire en France les 180 TWh d'électricité produite en 1974 et 1975 :

Schématiquement une centrale HTDE produit une puissance en méga-watts égale à :

$$P_e = \eta\, w(t)\, N\, S_h\, 10^{-3} \text{ MW}$$

η rendement de conversion, évalué à 15 %
N nombre d'héliostats du système de concentration
S_h surface d'un héliostat en m^2
w(t) flux solaire incident en kw/m^2

En supposant un taux de couverture au sol de 20% et de 1200 heures de fonctionnement par an avec un flux solaire direct de 0,850 kw/m^2 la surface au sol nécessaire pour produire les 180 TWh serait de :

$$\text{Sol} = \frac{180\ 10^9\ \ 10^{-6}}{1200 \times 0,15 \times 0,2 \times 0,85} = 5\ 882 \text{ km}^2$$

soit 1 % du territoire métropolitain, ou la superficie moyenne d'une département français, en encore 10 % des 11 départements de la bordure méditerranéenne convenablement ensoleillés (figure 2). Encore faut-il analyser très finement ce système de conversion afin d'évaluer la compétitivité avec les autres ressources énergétiques dans le futur.

Sur la base des technologies actuelles (ou en développement), on peut classer les différentes solutions envisageables pour l'utilisation de l'énergie solaire à partir d'un schéma commun à toutes les sources d'énergie :

"gisement" → "extraction" → "transport" → transformation" → produit fini"

On a alors le schéma de la figure 3. Chaque filière donne un produit fini dont la valeur est fondamentalement liée à la technologie utilisée au contraire d'autres ressources énergétiques.

L'exposé qui suit sera limité au cas des systèmes de conversion hélio-thermo-dynamo-électriques de grande puissance (quelques méga-watts électriques) et donnera une brève description de problèmes relevant de l'analyse des systèmes.

II - CENTRALES HELIO-THERMO-DYNAMO-ELECTRIQUES (HTDE)

En liaison avec les travaux menés par le PIRDES en vue de développer des centrales HTDE du type "champ d'héliostats plus tour" dans la gamme 1-25 MW_e, nous décrivons ici le système 10 MW_e dont les études sont les plus avancées.

Le schéma général de ce type de centrale est donné sur la figure 4. On y distingue quatre parties essentielles :

- le système de concentration et la tour
- la chaudière (récepteur)
- la conversion thermo dynamique, turbine
- l'alternateur.

Les deux dernières parties, turbine et alternateur, peuvent être considérées comme des éléments classiques de centrales thermiques, à l'exception du système de stockage.

Le récepteur qui reçoit le rayonnement solaire concentré, est destiné à chauffer le fluide caloporteur et doit donc posséder un coefficient élevé d'absorption de ce rayonnement.

Enfin le système de concentration du rayonnement solaire est constitué d'environ 1800 miroirs carrés de 49 m^2 de surface chacun, dont le rôle est d'envoyer le rayonnement solaire à l'entrée de la chaudière. Compte tenu du mouvement apparent du soleil, la position de la normale au centre de chacun des miroirs doit se déplacer de telle manière que les rayons réfléchis soient toujours dans l'axe de la chaudière. Un tel type de miroir automatisé (héliostat) est représenté sur la figure 5. Le système de concentration apparaît comme la partie la plus fondamentale de la centrale tant au point de vue technique qu'économique.

III - PROBLEMATIQUE RETENUE ET OPTIMISATION

Schématiquement, figure 6, on peut considérer le problème de développement d'une centrale HTDE comme une combinaison de décisions et d'optimisations, les décisions provenant d'analyses à un niveau supérieur et les optimisations étant pour la plupart " internes".

Les décisions portent sur :

- le choix de la puissance nominale du turbo-alternateur P_e
- la nature et la température du cycle thermo-dynamique, et le type de stockage (nature et durée)
- la durée moyenne journalière de fonctionnement, par ciel clair, y ou bien le seuil w_{smin} du flux solaire incident à partir duquel la centrale fonctionne.

Ces décisions étant fixées, on peut écrire l'expression de la puissance électrique fournie d'une manière simplifiée :

$$P_e(t) = \eta_1 \cdot \eta_2 \cdot \eta_3(t) \cdot w(t) \cdot N.S_h \cdot 10^{-3} \text{ MW}$$

avec :

$w(t)$ le flux solaire incident en kw/m^2

η_1 le rendement du cycle thermo-dynamique et de stockage et le rendement du turbo-alternateur

η_2 le rendement du récepteur

$\eta_3(t)$ le rendement du champ d'héliostats, que l'on peut décomposer :

$$\eta_3(t) = \eta_{c0}(t) \cdot \eta_\rho \cdot \eta_p \cdot \eta_s \cdot \eta_c$$

η_s influence des déformations de structure des héliostats

η_{co} influence du facteur cosinus et des ombres

η_ρ coefficient de réflexion de la surface réfléchissante

η_p influence de la planéité de la surface réfléchissante

η_c influence des erreurs du système de guidage.

N : nombre d'héliostats de surface S_h m^2.

Les optimisations (stockage, récepteur, héliostats,...), permettent d'analyser les différents paramètres η, chaque optimisation étant à double objectif : maximiser individuellement chaque η tout en minimisant le coût global (kw installé).

Dans une deuxième phase, l'adaptation à une courbe de charge donnée (c'est ici un objectif) permet d'évaluer le prix de revient du kwh produit pour les décisions prises.

En faisant varier les décisions dans un ensemble de décisions possibles on doit pouvoir définir la structure optimale de la centrale compte tenu de contraintes données (courbe de charge et lieu d'implantation).

Cette problématique a été initialement choisie au LAAS en vue d'évaluer les possibilités des centrales HTDE. La phase "optimisation" a porté sur les héliostats et leur implantation optimale sur un site donné. Il n'est pas question de développer ici ces travaux mais pour fixer les idées je donne quelques résultats qui montrent que les méthodes d'approche pour chaque optimisation peuvent être de natures très différentes.

Optimisation d'héliostats :

Compte tenu d'un certain nombre de spécifications physiques (précision de pointage, dépense minimale d'énergie de commande, ...), l'objectif est de réaliser un héliostat ayant le prix de revient minimum. Des études de mécanique, de matériaux, de techniques de fabrication, d'automatisation, ... donc des études d'ingénieur de conception et de fabrication, ont permis de définir un héliostat automatisé dont le coût ne dépasse pas 650 F/m^2. C'est encore un coût relativement élevé et un grand nombre d'études techniques sont encore à faire pour diminuer ce coût.

Implantation optimale des héliostats sur un site donné :

Dans ce cas c'est par l'intermédiaire d'une simulation sur calculateur numérique d'un champ d'héliostats qu'a pu se faire cette optimisation. Le problème qui est posé est de placer un nombre maximal d'héliostats sur une surface limitée (essentiellement distance maximale héliostat-tour), tout en maximisant le coefficient η_{co} , c'est-à-dire tout en minimisant les phénomènes d'ombres entre héliostats voisins. L'optimisation a été faite en fixant à priori un pourcentage maximal de pertes énergétiques annuelles dues aux effets d'ombres, par exemple pour un système 1MW_e avec des héliostats de 3,5 m de côté. La figure 7 donne une telle implantation pour des pertes de 3 % et 10 %. Il faut remarquer que pour 3 % le taux de couverture au sol est de 22 % et pour 10 % ce taux est de 30 %, alors que les valeurs moyennes de η_{co} varient de 85 % à 79 %. Ceci met en évidence certaines intéractions entre les différentes optimisations.

Pour l'évaluation du prix de revient du kwh produit c'est par l'intermédiaire de scénarios plaçant ce type de centrales dans des conditions de production bien définies que l'on compte faire cette évaluation. Un premier scénario (étudié avec le service Etudes Economiques Générales d'EDF) consiste à étudier le problème de la gestion optimale du parc de production français en présence de centrales solaires sans stockage (production fatale). A partir d'une courbe de charge donnée, il s'agit de placer au mieux la production des centrales HTDE en vue de la valoriser par rapport aux autres composantes du parc de production. Un deuxième scénario considère des centrales HTDE avec stockage, et une analyse de la gestion optimale du parc doit aider au dimensionnement du stockage. Cette première approche (kw installé et kwh produit) tout en ayant l'avantage de permettre une évaluation rapide des possibilités des centrales solaires, a cependant le défaut essentiel de figer un certain nombre de paramètres (type de centrale, d'héliostats,...) et donc laisse peu de liberté dans le choix des solutions techniques pour la conversion HTDE. Dans ce qui suit est proposée une deuxième approche qui devrait permettre une évaluation simultanée des différentes solutions technologiques.

IV - ANALYSE MORPHOLOGIQUE ET AIDE A LA CONCEPTION

Le problème est maintenant posé de la manière suivante :

"pour produire de l'électricité par un système THDE, quelles sont les "formes" possibles de centrales et comment peut-on évaluer l'intérêt respectif de chaque solution"?

Pour résoudre ce problème on procède en deux étapes :

i) recherche de toutes les solutions possibles par analyse morphologique (aide à la conception)

ii) évaluation de chaque solution par un bilan de toutes les ressources primaires nécessaires à sa construction et son fonctionnement (eau, énergie, terrain, minerais, main d'oeuvre).

Ce type d'approche est actuellement utilisé pour le système de conversion hélio-thermique d'une centrale HTDE (système de concentration et chaudière). Le premier travail consiste à élaborer le tableau morphologique de ce système :

1ère réflexion :	héliostat	cylindroparabolique	conoïde
2ème réflexion :	oui	non	
struture mécanique :	fixe	mobile	
tour :	oui	non	
récepteur :	tronconique	orienté	
récepteur :	fixe	mobile	

L'analyse des incompatibilités de ce tableau permet de dégager les formes possibles, par exemple :

"héliostats, tour, récepteur orienté, récepteur fixe".

Ensuite, tenant compte du fait que chaque constituant premier est en fait une forme à laquelle on peut associer plusieurs états, on construit un deuxième tableau faisant apparaître les états correspondants aux formes déjà déterminées, exemple :

"héliostat focalisation, tour hors du champ, commandes individuelles des héliostats ,...."

Ayant ainsi dressé un catalogue des solutions admissibles, il s'agit de valuer chaque état constituant les différentes formes. Pour cela il est proposé d'associer à chaque état une quantité, sous la forme d'un vecteur, qui représente les consommations en eau, énergie, sols, minerais, main d'oeuvre nécessaires à la construction et au fonctionnement de chaque "état". Ceci permet de construire un vecteur pour chaque solution admissible et ainsi de fournir des éléments quantitatifs d'aide à la décision. Les premiers travaux dans ce sens portent sur l'évaluation des différents types d'héliostats en collaboration avec l'I.I.A.S.A.

CONCLUSION

En guise de conclusion, ce bref exposé, ayant pour but de présenter quel peut être le rôle de l'analyse des systèmes dans les études de développement de nouvelles technologies, a je pense montré que :

1) l'analyse des systèmes fait appel à de nombreuses spécialités d'horizons divers, technique, méthodologie (simulation, optimisation),... et le problème essentiel de l'analyse des systèmes est de définir une PROBLEMATIQUE très claire faisant ressortir les principaux objectifs poursuivis.

2) Pour le cas de l'énergie solaire, en particulier le cas de centrales HTDE, l'analyse des systèmes ne peut que jouer un rôle primodial comme pour toutes les technologies nouvelles.

Dans ces problèmes ce sont des éléments d'aide à la décision qu'il faut fournir, tâche d'autant plus difficile que le secteur énergétique mondial est en pleine évolution et que nos conceptions sur les ressources énergétiques ont été grandement modifiées par des aspects tels que la prise en compte de l'environnement.

3) Deux voies pour aborder le problème de l'évaluation des centrales HTDE ont été présentées. La première relativement traditionnelle cherche des résultats à travers des modèles d'optimisation (gestion de parc de production) alors que la seconde cherche à développer une méthodologie d'aide à la décision faisant abstraction des conditions actuelles technico-économiques. Cette deuxième voie nous semble la plus prometteuse pour évaluer l'impact à très long terme des sources "nouvelles" d'énergie.

Pour terminer, je dois remercier les membres de l'équipe Systèmes Energétiques, Energie Solaire, dont les travaux et résultats ont servi de support à cet exposé, ainsi que le Service d'Etudes Economiques Générales de l'EDF et le Groupe Energie de l'International Institute for Applied Systems Analysis.

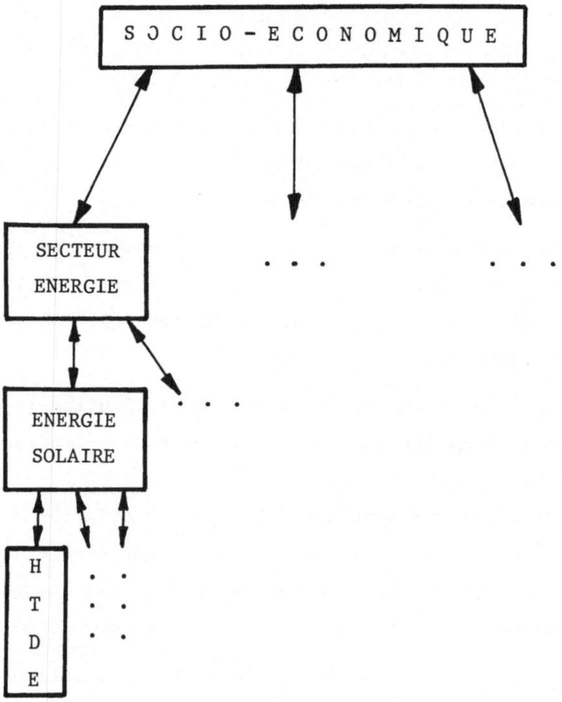

Figure 1

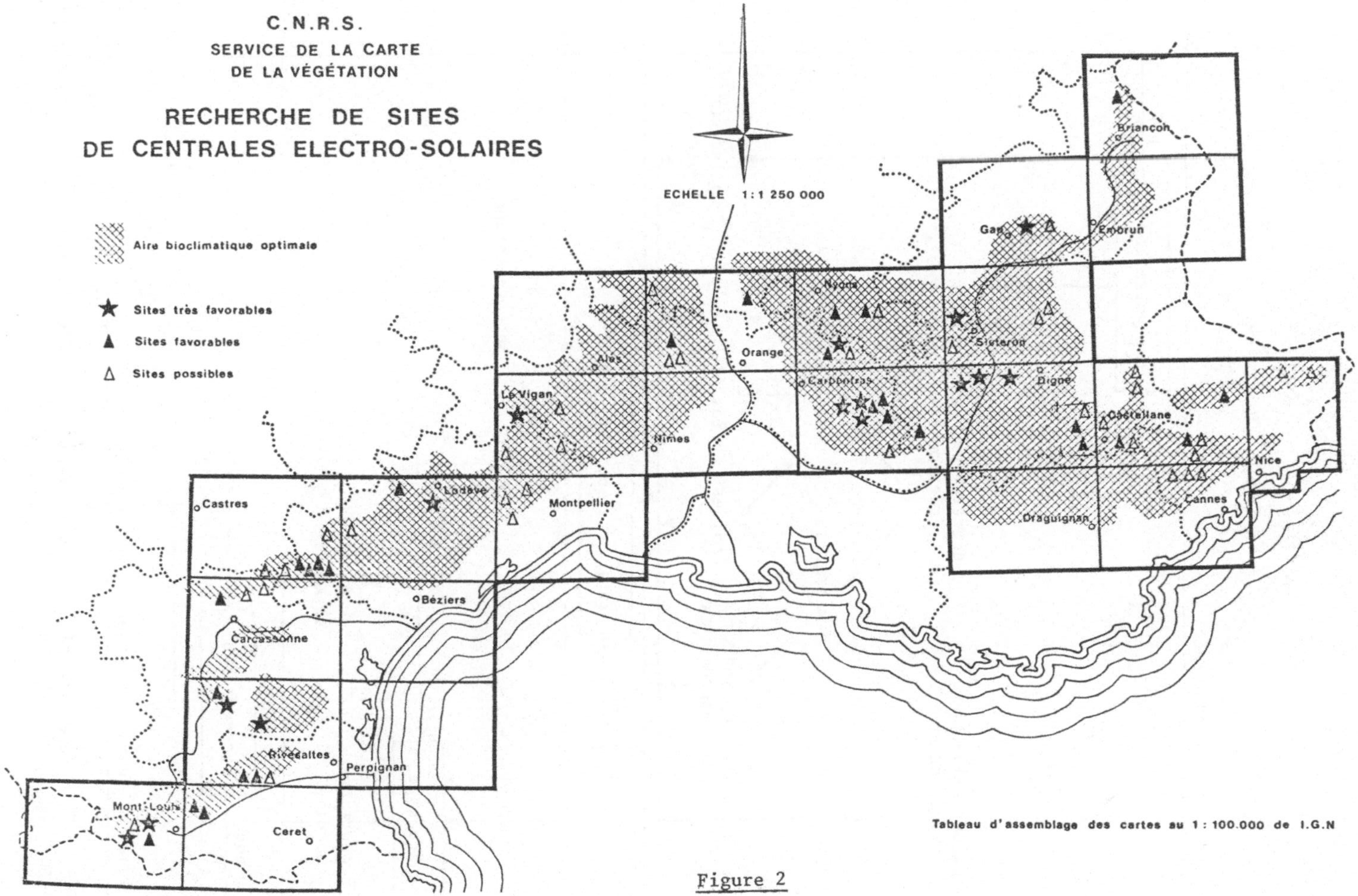
C.N.R.S.
SERVICE DE LA CARTE
DE LA VÉGÉTATION
RECHERCHE DE SITES
DE CENTRALES ELECTRO-SOLAIRES
ECHELLE 1:1 250 000
Aire bioclimatique optimale
Sites très favorables
Sites favorables
Sites possibles
Briançon
Embrun
Gap
Nyons
Sisteron
Orange
Ales
Carpentras
Digne
Le Vigan
Castellane
Nimes
Nice
Lodève
Castres
Montpellier
Cannes
Draguignan
Béziers
Carcassonne
Rivesaltes
Perpignan
Mont-Louis
Ceret
Tableau d'assemblage des cartes au 1 : 100.000 de I.G.N

Figure 2

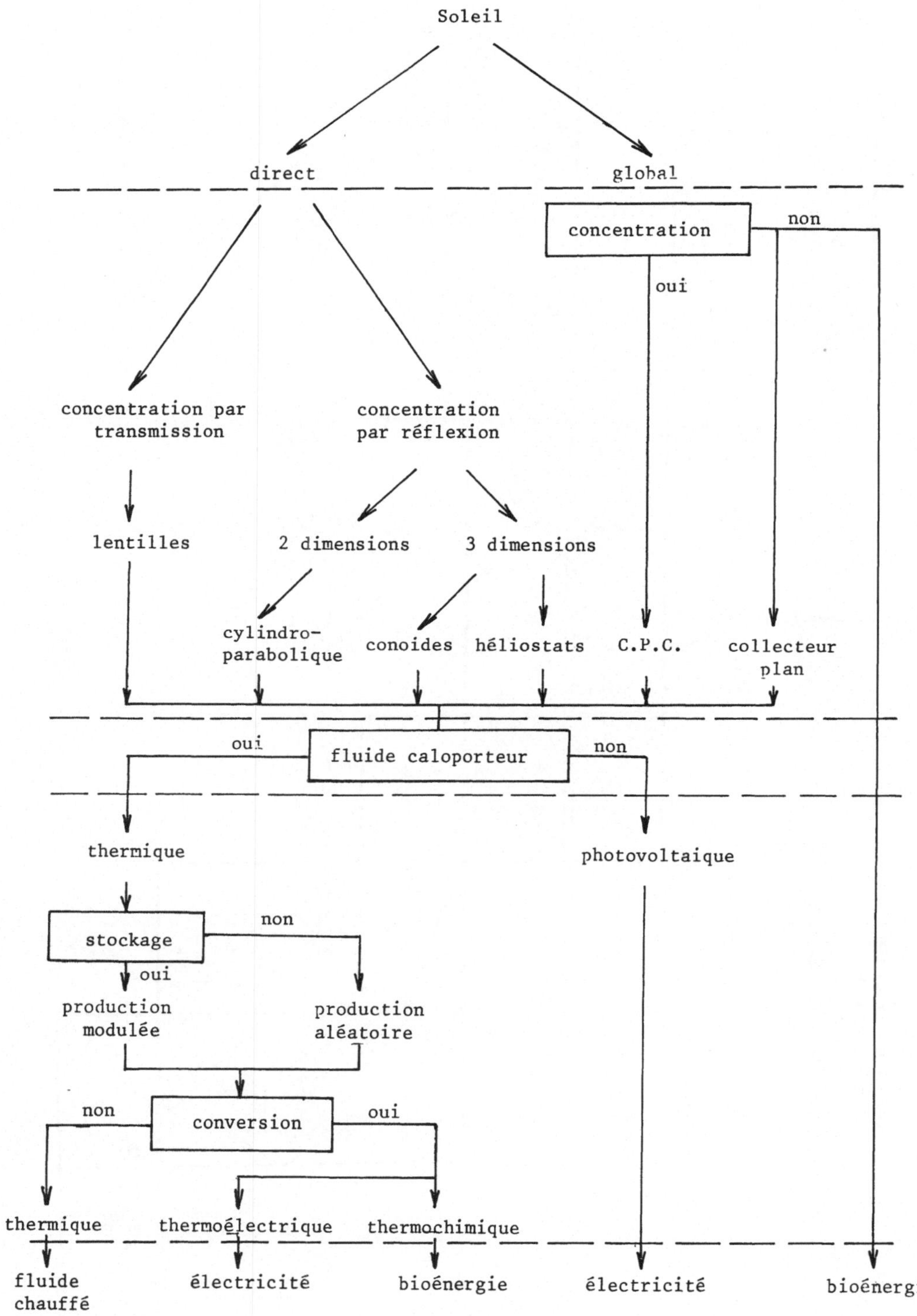
Soleil
direct
global
concentration
non
oui
concentration par transmission
concentration par réflexion
lentilles
2 dimensions
3 dimensions
cylindro-parabolique
conoides
héliostats
C.P.C.
collecteur plan
oui
fluide caloporteur
non
thermique
photovoltaique
stockage
non
oui
production modulée
production aléatoire
non
conversion
oui
thermique
thermoélectrique
thermochimique
fluide chauffé
électricité
bioénergie
électricité
bioénergie

Figure 3

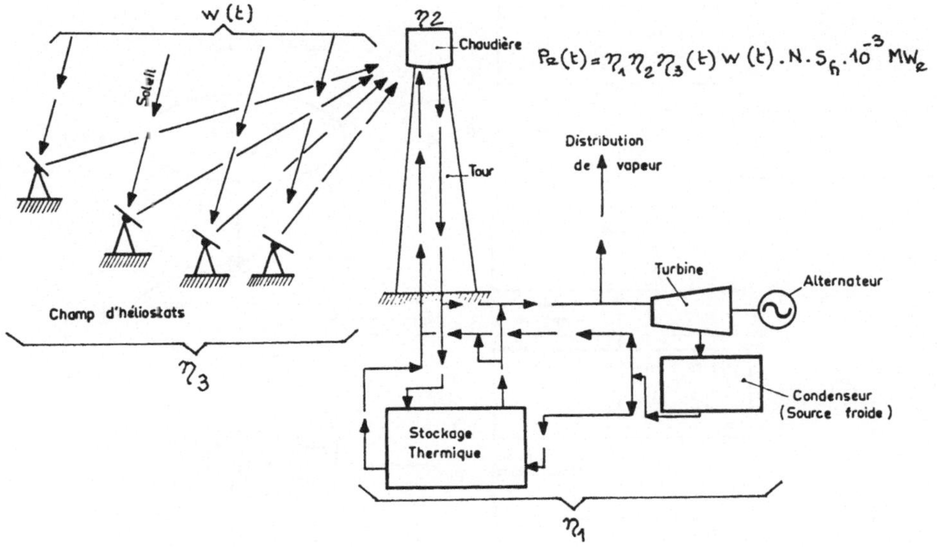

Schéma de principe d'une centrale HTDE

Figure 4

Prototype de l'héliostat (LAAS-SOTEREM) fonctionnant au LAAS (Brevet ANVAR)

Figure 5

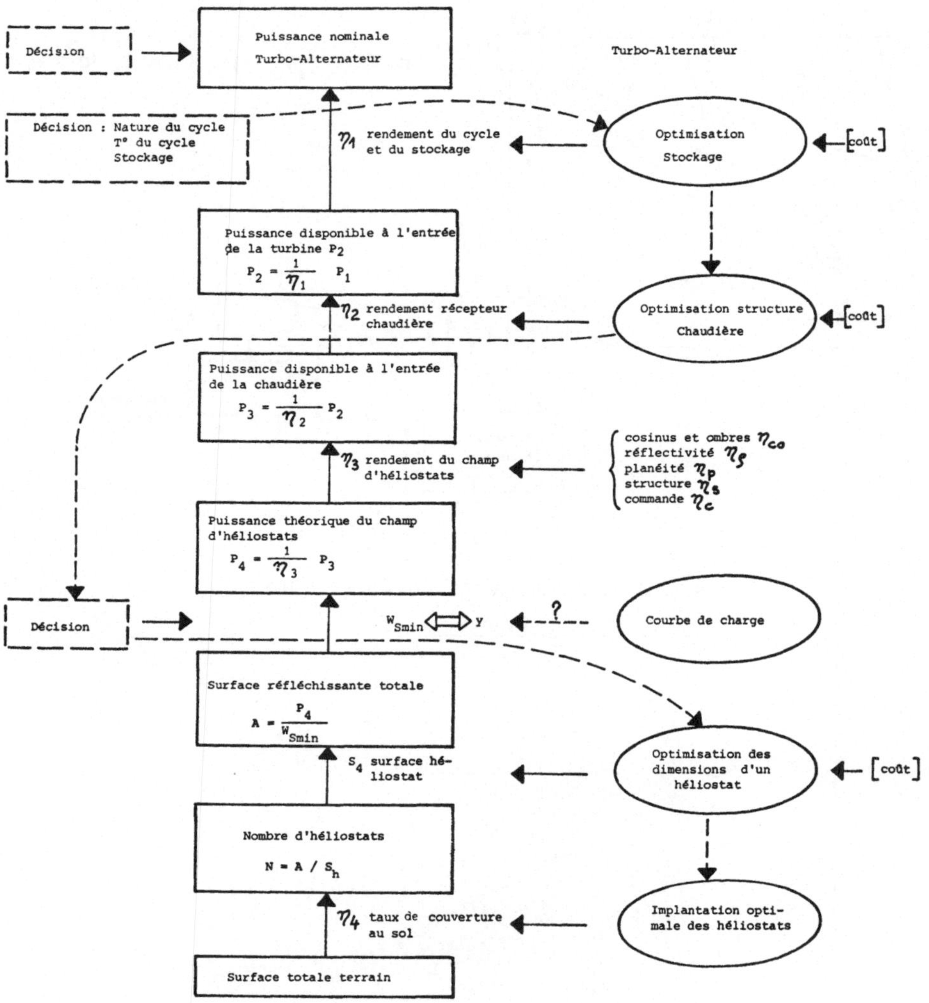

Décision
Puissance nominale
Turbo-Alternateur
Turbo-Alternateur
Décision : Nature du cycle
T° du cycle
Stockage
η1 rendement du cycle
et du stockage
Optimisation
Stockage
coût
Puissance disponible à l'entrée de la turbine P2
P2 = 1/η1 P1
η2 rendement récepteur
chaudière
Optimisation structure
Chaudière
coût
Puissance disponible à l'entrée de la chaudière
P3 = 1/η2 P2
η3 rendement du champ
d'héliostats
cosinus et ombres ηco
réflectivité ηρ
planéité ηp
structure ηs
commande ηc
Puissance théorique du champ d'héliostats
P4 = 1/η3 P3
Décision
WSmin ⇔ y
?
Courbe de charge
Surface réfléchissante totale
A = P4/WSmin
S4 surface hé-
liostat
Optimisation des
dimensions d'un
héliostat
coût
Nombre d'héliostats
N = A / Sh
η4 taux de couverture
au sol
Implantation opti-
male des héliostats
Surface totale terrain

Figure 6

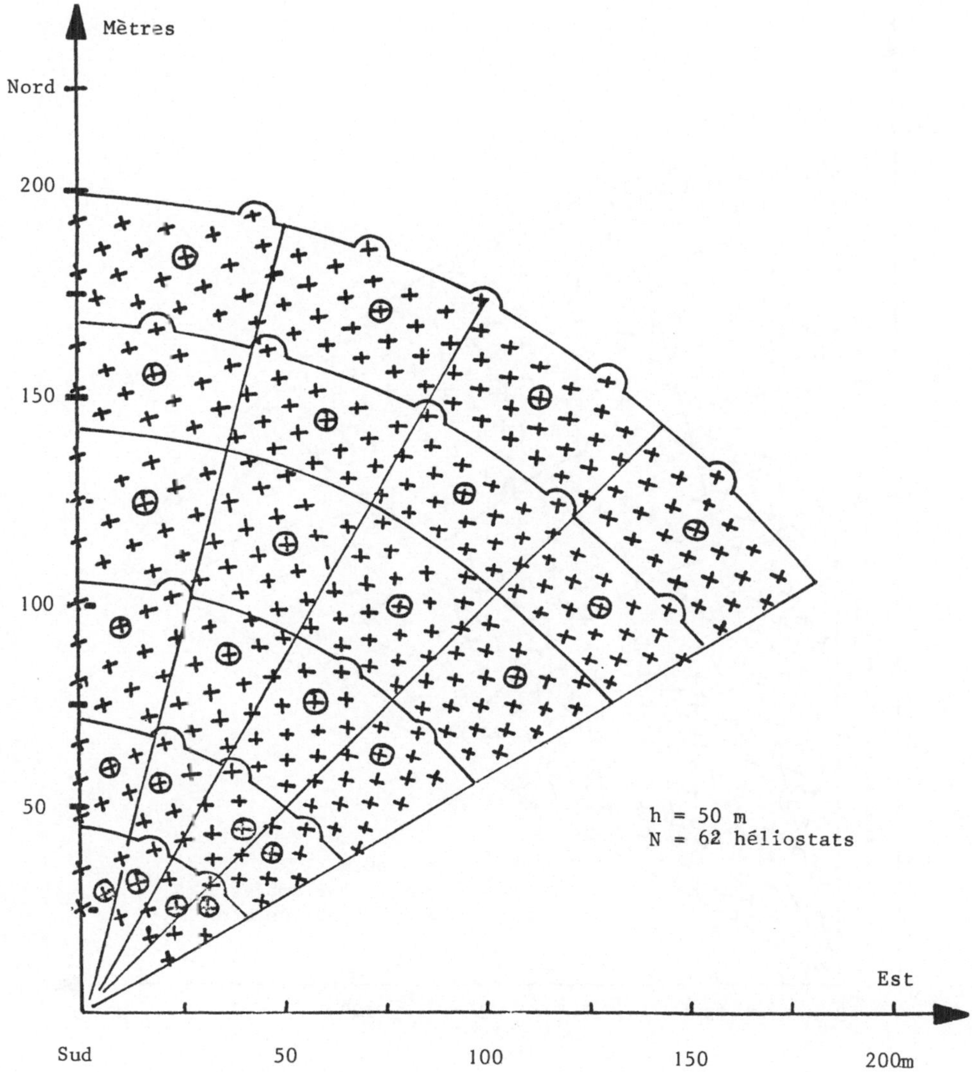

Figure 7a - 3% de pertes énergétiques annuelle

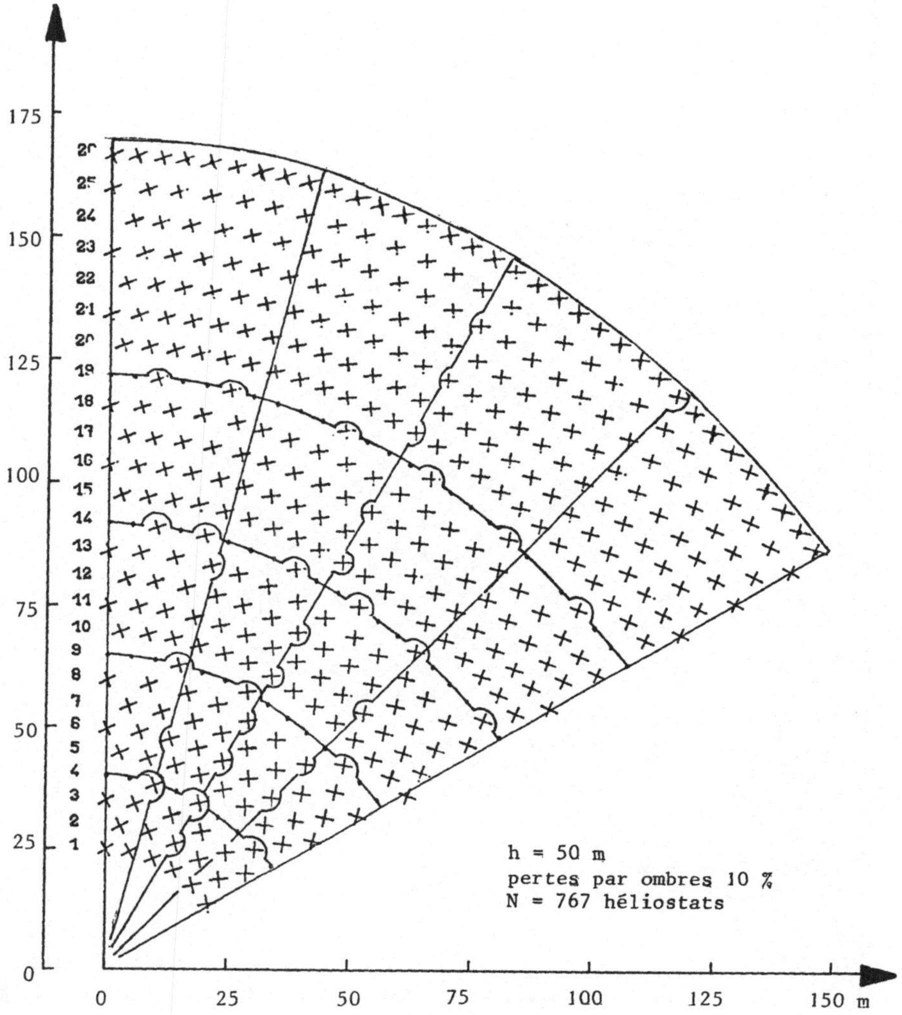

Figure 7 b - 10 % de pertes énergétiques annuelle

Resilience and its Application to Energy Systems
(condensed version)

H.R. Gruemm
IIASA - Loxenburg, Austria

I. Introduction.

The application of concepts and methods from the theories of diffential topology and diffential dynamical systems to model systems occuring in real nature has become of growing interest to scientists working in many different disciplines; I will quote only two instructive examples. R.Thom[1] proposed a geometrical framework for morphogenesis - the evolution of structures - in his works about Catastrophic Theory and was among the first to argue for genericity and structural stability of models. Ecologists started to study the phase-plan of their simple prey-predator models for a structural analysis. In 1973, C.S. Holling[2] in a fundamental paper summarized this new approach to mathematical ecology and introduced the new concept of "resilience". This concept was intended, in Holling's words, to describe "the ability of systems to absorb changes in parameters and state variables and still persist". It was soon recognized that the appropriate mathematical language for the expression of these ideas was, again, the theory of dynamical systems.

At IIASA, the resilience concept was studied in two ways which will be described in this paper: precise mathematical definitions of several "facets" of this concept were given, and as a test of its usefulness, resilience was applied to small schematic models of energy production within an economy (among other problems). This last program is still in progress; a more realistic version, developed from the models mentioned in this talk, has been presented by W. Haefele at this Symposium.

II. The Attractor-Basin Structure and the Resilience Concept.

We assume that the system has been described by a differential equation on its state space. Under genericity assumptions, the state space can then be subdivided into basins, each one with its particular attractor. For purposes of interpretation, one could say that one attractor corresponds to a stable long-term mode of behavior of the system. The basins are separated by basin boundaries which can be calculated either directly or by a Ljopunov-friction type technique.

The resilience concept can be fully expressed in this "language". The whole concept cannot be formalized by a simple mathematical definition, but every single "facet" of it can. An essential distinction must be made between "changes of variables" and "changes of parameter"[3]; we introduced the terms "resilience in state space" (RISP) and "resilience of the state space" (ROSP). RISP expresses the idea that, after an external perturbation of the state variables, the system should still lie in the same basin and thus should tend to the same attractor. It is thus connected to reachability problems. ROSP distinguishes two cases: the changes in parameters can occur on a short time-scale ("suddenly") or on a long one ("adiabatically") when compared with the typical time-scale of the system. In the "sudden" case, the system could well be in a different basin after perturbation because the basin boundaries have shifted. In the "adiabatic" case - as in catastrophic theory - only the changes of the attractors are relevant.*

For various applications, a quantitative measure of resilience (a "resilience number") is useful. The presupposes additional notion on the state space: a distance or, in some cases, a measure. The choice of this distance involves further information about the nature of the perturbations to be taken into account. Various resilience numbers have been proposed[(3)]: for RISP, they involve the distance from the point in state space describing the system to the next basin boundary. The minimum of this distance over a single trajectory can be taken, or this distance can be averaged over a trajectory or over the whole basin, according to the nature of the specific application. For ROSP, the distance to the next morphology** in parameter space - in the sense of Thom[(1)]- can be used as above, or sensitivity of the location of basins and attractors with respect to parameter changes is taken as the resilience number.

III. The Energy Models.

During the investigation of the resilience concept, the Energy group at IIASA constructed some small and highly aggregated models of an abstract society; those models, together with their properties, have been collected in (4)++. These models were explicitely designed to illustrate the basin-attractors approach and the application of the resilience concept. The make no claim to deduction from basic principles or to numerical prediction; they are phenomenological views of how an economy could behave and they intend to show possible, qualitative trends++. In short, they - in Holling's words - use "myths".

All models start with a production function including energy as a production factor. They then add assumptions about population development - dependent on standards of living - , the distribution of GNP between net investment, depreciation and consumption, and the distribution of net investment among the production sectors. With the help of additional hypotheses of a phenomenological character, a deterministic system is obtained.

*Further motivation for the definitions of RISP and ROSP and their mathematical form can be found in (3).

**The parameter values for which the phase portrait of the system changes.

+A realistic version evolved from those simple models is the subject of W.Haefele's presentation (5).

++It has been suggested that such small, qualitative models could be very useful in formulating questions and problems for the large, detailed "global models"((6)).

Full information was obtained about the following questions(4): location and nature of the attractors, location of the basin boundaries, morphologies in parameter space and the corresponding changes of the phase portrait; comparison of different resilience numbers. For one model, a resilience number was included in the objective function of a dynamic optimitation program, obtained by introducing a control variable(7) (the ratio between nuclear and fossile energy production).

References.

(1) Thom, R., Theorie de la morphogenese, Paris.

(2) Holling, C.S., Resilience and Stability in Ecological Systems. Ann. Rev. Ecol. and Systems, 4, 1-23 (1973).

(3) Gruemm, H.R., Definitions of Resilience, IIASA Research Report, RR-76-3.

(4) Gruemm, H.R. and L. Schrattenholzer, Societal Phase Portraits, IIASA Research Memorandum, 1976.

(5) Haefele, W., these Proceedings.

(6) Discussion with M. Mesarovich.

(7) Avenhaus, R. et al, New Societal Equations, IIASA WP-75-67.

Stochastic Modeling of Natural Resource Discovery - The Case of Oil and Gas*

Eytan Barouch, Clarkson College of Technology

and

Gordon Kaufman, Massachusetts Institute of Technology

Introduction

Along with the Arab oil embargo of 1973, came a new awareness of how important it is to understand the effects of alternative strategies for discovery and exploitation of exhaustible energy resources.

While current events poignantly motivate studies of exhaustible resource strategies, such studies in fact have a rather long history. Harold Hotelling, an economist, in a seminal paper written in 1931, addressed the problem of how "best" to exploit an exhaustible resource. Among the questions he asked were, "Suppose (a) mine is publicly owned. How should exploitation take place for the greatest general good, and how does a course having such an objective compare with that of the profit seeking entrepreneur?" Two basic premises he adopted were, first, that the size of the resource base available for exploitation is known with certainty, and second, that the resource base is infinitely divisible with respect to extraction. Similar assumptions are made by many economists in studies that followed. To first order, these assumptions are not unrealistic if the object to be studied is an individual mineral deposit *after it has been discovered.*

If, however, the scope of analysis is enlarged to include the process of discovery, then these two assumptions are less reasonable. For example, application of exploratory effort to a petroleum basin (in the form of pre-drilling geological and geophysical reconaissance, followed by exploratory drilling) yields a sequence of discoveries of deposits of finite size at irregularly spaced points in time. Uncertainty plays a key role.

We shall briefly review some examples of how economists have studied the problem of optimal resource exploitation in order to give the flavor of their analyses and follow with results of our study of the oil and gas exploration process. Our view is probabilistic and built upon assumptions about the "physics" of petroleum exploration derived from examination of observables. The model we have built describes one part of the evolution of the discovery process. How it is best interfaced with positive economic models of individual firm behavior or with a normative social optimality criterion and then used to study optimal patterns of allocation of exploratory effort is an open question.

---

*A talk for Colloque International Sur L'Analyse de Systemes et ses Orientations Nouvelles. December 22, 1976

This work was supported by NSF Grant Nos. ENG75-08403 and SIA74-22773; and ERDA Grant No. E(49-18)-2295.

Models Assuming A Known Resource Base

Recent work by Koopmans (1973) [11], Uhler (1975) [17], and Pindyck (1976) [14] is illustrative of ways in which Hotelling's original model can be generalized.

They are elaborations of the following rather sparse model: let S be the size of the resource base, and assume S is known with certainty. The "social discount rate" r is constant with respect to time and the value (utility) of consumption rate C(t) of S at t is U(C(t)). Then the optimal path of consumption must satisfy

$$\max_{C(t)} \int_0^\infty e^{-rt} u(C(t))dt$$

subject to $\int_0^\infty C(t)dt \leq S$ and $C(t) \geq 0$ for $t \varepsilon [0,\infty)$. If u is increasing, concave, and $u(0) = 0$, then necessary conditions for $C^*(t)$, $t \varepsilon [0,\infty)$ to be optimal give $\int_0^\infty C^*(t)dt = S$ and $e^{-rt}u'(C^*(t)) = \lambda > 0$, λ constant. Consequently, $C^*(t) > 0$ and S is used up as $t \to \infty$.

Koopman's extension of this model is to require $C(t) \geq C$, C a minimum level of consumption required to sustain life. Thus the rate of consumption determines a time T at which the resource is exhausted; clearly $T \leq S/C$. He shows that an optimal consumption path $C^*(t)$ together with an optimal time of exhaustion T^* exist and fulfill $e^{-rt}u'(C^*(t)) = \lambda > 0$ for $t \varepsilon [0,T^*]$ and $u(C^*(T))/C^*(T) = u'(C^*(T))$ at $T = T^*$.

Uhler formulated a model of the petroleum exploration process that is conceptually similar to those sketched above, but which is tailored to reflect specific attributes of petroleum exploration. He argues that exploratory effort has three effects: it results in additions to reserves, geological knowledge is increased, and the resource base S is depleted. Defining x(t) as the cumulative exploration effort in [0,t], $\rho(t) = dx(t)/dt$, $q(x(t),\rho(t))$ as the time rate of additions to reserves from the resource base, and y(t) as the size of reservoir or pool being exploited at time t, he posits $q(x(t),\rho(t)) = Ay(t)[\rho(t)]^\alpha \exp\{-\beta(x(t)-k)^2\}$, A, α, β, and k fixed parameters, so that for given fixed rate of effort $\rho(t)$, q rises for $x(t)<k$ and then declines for $x(t)>k$.

Given a cost of effort function $c(\rho(t)) = a\rho(t) + b(\rho(t))^2$, constant price p, and $y(t) = \exp\{-\gamma x(t)\}$ his objective is to find a function $\rho^*(t)$, $t \varepsilon [0,\infty)$ which satisfies

$$\max_{\rho(t)} \int_0^\infty [pq(x(t),\rho(t)) - c(\rho(t))]e^{-rt}dt.$$

Assuming $\alpha=1$, and that parameters A, α, β, and k have specific numerical values derived from a statistical analysis of reservoir deposition and discovery in Alberta province (Canada), he computes $\rho^*(t)$ numerically and shows that in this particular case there is a meaningful equilibrium solution.

Notice that the size of the resource base plays no essential role. The function

$y(t) = \exp\{-\gamma x(t)\}$ is used as an imperfect surrogate for it.

Pindyck goes further and studies the simultaneous interaction of exploration effort and production given a variety of assumptions about costs, prices, and additions to reserves from exploration and production. His basic model is of the following form: a producer faces a price path $p(t)$ and must choose a rate of production $q(t)$ from a known reserve base R. Additions to the proved reserve base may accrue from exploratory effort $\dot{x}(t) \equiv \rho(t)$ as well, and the rate of addition to the proved reserve base $\dot{a}(t)$ is assumed to be a function of both $\rho(t)$ and cumulative additions to reserves $a(t)$; i.e., $\dot{a}(t) = f(\rho(t), a(t))$ with $\partial f/\partial\rho > 0$ and $\partial f/\partial a < 0$. The proved reserve base at time t is $R(t)$ and at time $t > 0$, $R(t) = R(0) + a(t) - \int_0^t q(t)dt$. Exploration cost $K(\rho(t))$ increases with increasing argument and is assumed convex; similarly for the average cost $C(R(t))$ of production.

The producer wishes to find a simultaneous production and exploration time path $(q^*(t),\rho^*(t))$ that achieves

$$\max_{q(t),\rho(t)} \int_0^\infty [q(t)p(t) - q(t)C(R(t)) - K(\rho(t))]e^{-rt}dt$$

subject to

$$\dot{R}(t) = \dot{a}(t) - q(t), \quad R(t),q(t),a(t),\rho(t) \geq 0$$

and

$$\dot{a}(t) = f(\rho(t),a(t)).$$

Price is endogenous and is determined by market clearing conditions.

Models Under Uncertainty

The effects of introducing uncertainty about the resource base on the optimal extraction path has been studied by Loury (1976) [12] and by Gilbert (1976) [7]. A key feature of both studies is that the *aggregate size* of the resource base is regarded as uncertain a priori. Their models are patterned after the first mentioned model of the previous section.

Gilbert begins with a model in which marginal extraction costs are a constant, K, the social utility or value of a rate of extraction $q(t)$ at t is $u(q(t))$ less $Kq(t)$. Discounting is continuous at a constant rate r. The extraction process begins at time t=0 and the amount of reserves $\tilde{S}(t_0)$ remaining at $t_0 \geq 0$ is a random variable with cumulative distribution function (cdf) $F(S|t_0)$. This cdf $F(\cdot|t_0)$ depends on the "state of information" about the size of the resource case; i.e. an initial distribution $F(\cdot|t_0)$ at t=0 is "updated" as extraction reveals that the resource base is depleted or not. In particular, he assumes that $F(S|t_0) = F(S|\tilde{S}(t_0) \geq a(t_0))$ where $a(t_0)$ is the amount extracted over the time interval $[0,t]$.

The optimal extraction path $q^*(t)$ over the time interval $[t_0,\infty)$ is a path that achieves

$$\max_{q(t)} \int_{t_0}^{\infty} \{ \int_{t_0}^{t} [u(q(w))-Kq(w)]e^{-rw}dw\} dF(a(t)|\tilde{S}(t_0) \geq a(t_0)).$$

He studies this model under a variety of assumptions about the functions u and F.

Loury (1976) [12] examines an almost identical model.

Das Gupta and Stiglitz (1976) [6] investigate models similar to those mentioned thus far, allowing for introduction of a "back-stop" or substitute technology at an uncertain time.

We have approached the process of exploration (for oil and gas) from a somewhat different vantage point.

A Closer Look At Exploration

If a model of resource exhaustion is to mirror essential features of the exploration process, it must incorporate certain geological facts.

Petroleum exploration is random in character (cf. [9]). A program of exploration in a petroleum basin begins with a sequence of information gathering activities such as geological basinal analysis, geophysical reconnaissance surveying, detailed geophysical surveying, and well data analysis when available. The purpose of these activities is to identify *prospects*. A prospect is a geological configuration perceived by the geologist to have trapped hydrocarbons that form a target for drilling. Given the current state of technology, the only way to know for certain whether or not a prospect contains hydrocarbons is to drill a well into it. If an exploratory well is successful, it discovers a pool or field of finite size. On a scale of time, a realization may be schematically viewed as shown in Figure 1, in which Y_j denotes the size of the jth discovery and solid dots on the horizontal axis at t_i denotes a "dry hole" drilled at time t_i. A typical realization of the Y_js is shown in Figure 2, a plot of discovery sizes for Jurassic Central age fields in the North Sea.

Discovery sizes $Y_1,\dots,Y_j,\dots$ possess certain fundamental statistical regularities that to first order are captured by two assumptions. We visualize a sequence of Y_js as being a realization of a sampling process that unfolds in two stages: first, Nature generates a finite number N of pools or fields of sizes $A_1,\dots,A_N$ and deposes them underground. Our first assumption is

> I (Lognormal Size Distribution) $A_1,\dots,A_N$ are values of mutually independent identically distributed lognormal random variables.

This process of deposition is distinct from that of discovery. Discovery may be viewed as sampling without replacement and proportional to size. That is,

> II (Sampling Without Replacement and Proportional to Size) Given $A_1,\dots,A_N$ the probability of observing $A_1,\dots,A_n$ in that order is
>
> $$\prod_{j=1}^{n} A_j/(A_j+\dots+A_N)$$

Empirical justification for the first of the assumptions may be found in, for example, McCrossan (1969) [13], Arps and Roberts (1959) [1] and many other sources. The second is discussed in (1975) [9] and (1976) [2] by the authors.

Juxtaposition of I and II leads to an interesting sampling density for discovery sizes, one rich in mathematical structure. Let Y_j denote the observed value of the jth observation, define $\underline{Y} = (\underline{Y}_1,\dots,\underline{Y}_n)$ as the vector of observations in a sample of size $n \le N$, and assume that f is a member of a class of densities (all of whose members are concentrated on $[0,\infty)$) indexed by a parameter $\underline{\theta} \in \Theta$ so that $\tilde{A}_i$ has density $f(\cdot|\underline{\theta})$. Then given $\underline{\theta}$, N, and infinitesimal intervals $dY_1,\ldots,dY_n$, and defining $b_j = Y_j+\ldots+Y_n$, the probability of observing $\tilde{Y}_1 \in dY_1,\ldots,\tilde{Y}_n \in dY_n$ in that order (or equivalently, of observing $\underline{\tilde{Y}} \in d\underline{Y}$) is

$$P\{\underline{\tilde{Y}} \in d\underline{Y}|\underline{\theta},N\} =$$

$$\frac{\Gamma(N+1)}{\Gamma(N-n+1)} \prod_{j=1}^{n} Y_j f(Y_j|\underline{\theta})dY_j \int_0^\infty \cdots \int_0^\infty \prod_{j=1}^{n} [b_j+A_{n+1}+\ldots+A_N]^{-1} \prod_{k=n+1}^{N} f(A_k|\underline{\theta})dA_k$$

Letting $b_j = Y_j+\ldots+Y_n$ and defining

$$I_{N,n}(\underline{Y}) = \frac{\Gamma(N+1)}{\Gamma(N-n+1)} \int_0^\infty \cdots \int_0^\infty \prod_{j=1}^{n} [b_j+A_{n+1}+\ldots+A_N]^{-1} \prod_{k=n+1}^{N} f(A_k|\underline{\theta})dA_k,$$

the density of $\underline{\tilde{Y}}$ may be written as

$$I_{N,n}(\underline{Y}) \prod_{j=1}^{n} Y_j f(Y_j|\underline{\theta}).$$

Only in the simplest cases does $I_{N,n}(\underline{Y})$ possess a simple representation. Two integral representations of it expressed in terms of the characteristic function

$$G(y) = \int_0^\infty \exp\{-iyx\} f(x|\underline{\theta})dx$$

of f are given in (1976) [4], one useful for computing uniform and non-uniform asymptotic expansions of the density and the other useful for numerical computation. Defining $L(\lambda) = G(-i\lambda)$, and $Z(\lambda) = \sum_{j=1}^{n} p_j \exp\{-\lambda b_j\}$ with

$$p_j = \prod_{\substack{i=1 \\ j\neq i}}^{n} [b_i-b_j]^{-1},$$

we have

$$I_{N,n}(\underline{Y}) = \frac{\Gamma(N+1)}{\Gamma(N-n+1)} \int_0^\infty Z(\lambda)[L(\lambda)]^{N-n} d\lambda.$$

At $\lambda=0$, the first n-2 derivatives of $Z(\lambda)$ are zero, the (n-1)st derivative is one, and so for small λ, $Z(\lambda) \simeq [\lambda^{n-1}/(n-1)!] + O(\lambda^n)$.

Marginal and conditional moments of discovery sizes have reasonably simple integral representations in terms of the Laplace transform $L(\lambda)$ of f: the kth marginal moment of $\tilde{Y}_n$ is

$$n\binom{N}{n}\int_0^\infty \left[\frac{\partial^{k+1}}{\partial^{k+1}\lambda} L(\lambda)\right]^{N-n} [1-L(\lambda)]^{n-1} d\lambda.$$

Figure 3 shows graphs of $E(\tilde{Y}_n)$ for $f(A|\underline{\theta})$ lognormal with $E(\log_e\tilde{A}) \equiv \mu = 6.0$ and $\mathrm{Var}(\log_e\tilde{A}) \equiv \sigma^2 = 3.0$; i.e. $\underline{\theta} = (\mu,\sigma^2) = (6.0,3.0)$. Perhaps the most interesting feature of $E(\tilde{Y}_n)$ is that, regarded as a function of n, it has a turning point at roughly $n \sim \sqrt{N}$. We have computed asymptotic expansions of $I_{N,n}(\underline{Y})$ for $p \equiv N-n$ large in three cases:

(i) n and $\exp\{\sigma^2\}$ fixed

(ii) $\exp\{\sigma^2\}$ fixed and $n = O(\sqrt{p})$ or equivalently n fixed and $\exp\{\sigma^2\} = O(\sqrt{p})$,

(iii) $n\exp\{\sigma^2\}/p = O(1)$.

Cases (ii) and (iii) have been done by the method of steepest descent with two distinct steepest descent points that coalesce when $n\exp\{\sigma^2\}/p = O(1)$.

More particularly, for fixed μ,

$$M_1 = \exp\{\mu + \tfrac{1}{2}\sigma^2\} = O(p^{1/4})$$

$$K = \frac{1}{n}\sum_{j=1}^{n} b_j = O(p^{5/4})$$

$$V = M_1{}^2(\exp\{\sigma^2\}-1) = O(p)$$

$$e^{\sigma^2} = O(\sqrt{p})$$

upon approximating the characteristic function

$$G(y) = \frac{1}{\sigma\sqrt{2\pi}}\int_0^\infty \exp\{-iyx - \frac{1}{2\sigma^2}\log^2 x\}\frac{dx}{x}$$

of the lognormal density by the first three terms in a moment expansion of it*, the density of $\underline{\tilde{Y}}$ is approximated by

$$i^n nQ^n\binom{p+n}{n}\prod_{j=1}^{n} Y_j f(Y_j|\mu,\sigma^2)/[b_j + pM_1]$$

$$\times \int_0^\infty \exp\{Q[\delta\log z - iz - \tfrac{1}{2}z^2]\}dz$$

with

$$Q = \frac{(K+pM_1)^2}{pV} = O(\sqrt{p}) \quad \text{and} \quad \delta = n-1/Q = O(1)$$

---

*The parameter μ plays no essential role so we set it equal to zero.

Case (iii) corresponds to Q large and fixed δ of order one. As δ approaches 1/4, we have two coinciding saddle points and consequently a turning point at $\delta = 1/4$. When the two saddle points are close ($\delta \cong 1/4$) the contribution from both must be taken into account. The usual method of steepest descent is not then applicable and we employ a more sophisticated scheme for asymptotic computation designed by Chester, Friedman, and Ursell (1956) [5].

Viewing the North Sea as the basic sampling unit, and sizes (measured in 10^9 recoverable barrels of oil equivalent) of the 60 fields found by late 1975 in the North Sea, we have studied the likelihood function for parameters μ and σ^2 of $f(\cdot|\underline{\theta})$ and N. Figure 4 is an iso-contour plot in the (μ,σ^2) half-plane for N fixed at 120. It was computed using a uniform expansion for the density of $\underline{\tilde{Y}}$. With n=60, N=120, and σ^2=.98, a conditional maximum likelihood value for σ^2, $n\exp\{\sigma^2\}/N-n = 2.66 = O(1)$, so the uniform expansion is valid. Figure 5 displays the likelihood function for N given μ, σ^2, and the data. These calculations were done using two systems: the TROLL system at the National Bureau of Economic Research Cambridge Computation Center and M.I.T. Project MAC MACSYMA. For a more complete discussion of these calculations, see [3].

In order to make probabilistic predictions of discovery sizes $\tilde{Y}_{n+1}, \tilde{Y}_{n+2}, \ldots$ given $\tilde{Y}_1 \varepsilon dY_1, \ldots, \tilde{Y}_n \varepsilon dY_n$ (given $\underline{\tilde{Y}} \varepsilon d\underline{Y}$), we have computed integral representations for the density of $(\tilde{Y}_{n+1}, \ldots, \tilde{Y}_{n+q})$ given $\underline{\tilde{Y}} \varepsilon d\underline{Y}$ and for the moments $\tilde{Y}^k_{n+m}$ and cross-product moments $\tilde{Y}_{n+q}\tilde{Y}_{n+q+m}$ given $\underline{\tilde{Y}} \varepsilon d\underline{Y}$. For example, defining

$$Z(\xi) = \sum_{j=1}^{n} p_j \exp\{-\xi b_j\}, \quad \text{and} \quad p_j = \prod_{\substack{i=1 \\ j \neq i}}^{n} [b_i - b_j]^{-1},$$

the expectation of $\tilde{Y}_{n+m}$ for m=1,2,.... given $\underline{\tilde{Y}} \varepsilon d\underline{Y}$ is

$$E(\tilde{Y}_{n+m}|\underline{\tilde{Y}} \varepsilon d\underline{Y}) = m \binom{N-n}{m} \{\int_0^\infty [L(\lambda)]^{N-n} Z(\lambda) d\lambda\}^{-1}$$

$$\times \int_0^\infty [L(\lambda)]^{N-(n+m)} L''(\lambda) \int_0^\lambda Z(\xi) [L(\xi) - L(\lambda)]^{m-1} d\xi d\lambda$$

A numerical computation of $E(\tilde{Y}_{n+m}|\underline{\tilde{Y}} \varepsilon d\underline{Y})$ done using the North Sea data appears in [3]. Similar integral representations for cross product moments can be used to compute the marginal (and conditional) correlation structure of $\underline{\tilde{Y}}$.

Drilling Successes and Failures

The random process generating discovery sizes $\tilde{Y}_j$, j=1,2,...,N is imbedded in another random process -- that of drilling successes and failures. Given current technology, the only way to prove or disprove the presence of petroleum in a prospect is by drilling it. Taking into account drilling and defining

$$x_i = \begin{cases} 1 & \text{if the ith wildcat well is successful} \\ 0 & \text{if the ith wildcat well is a dry hole} \end{cases},$$

$$B_i = \begin{cases} Y_i & \text{if } x_i=1 \\ 0 & \text{if } x_i=0 \end{cases},$$

we may view the exploratory process as one generating a sequence $(x_1,B_1),\ldots,(x_i,B_i)$, ... of values of random variables $(\tilde{x}_1,\tilde{B}_1),\ldots,(\tilde{x}_i,B_i)\ldots.$ The most parsimonious view of exploration history, then, is to view the *state* of the physical attributes (as opposed to economic attributes) of the exploration process at a given time as fully described at time t by a vector

$$((x_1,B_1,t_1),\ldots,(x_i,B_i,t_i),\ldots,(x_n,B_n,t_n)) \equiv z_t,$$

where t_i is the time at which (x_i,B_i) is observed and n is the number of wildcat wells drilled in the time interval [0,t].

The probability that a particular wildcat well to be drilled in a given petroleum basin will be successful depends in particular on the amount of geological knowledge garnered from the exploration history of the basin at the time it is to be drilled; only a portion of this knowledge is reflected by z_t. In what follows, we assume that observable physical data consists solely of values of the x_is and B_is, together with the times at which they occur.

The probabilistic character of the drilling process deserves as full a treatment as that of discovery sizes, and we are currently studying it. Discussions of econometric modeling of drilling successes and failures can be found in Pindyck and MacAvoy (1973) [15], Spann and Erickson (1971) [16], and Khazzoom (1971) [10].

Interfacing

How might a model composed of assumptions I and II for discovery sizes and a characterization of the drilling process in terms of successes and failures be used to study the problem of optimal resource exploitation? Here is an intuitive sketch of a simple model that ties our description of discovery sizes to the normative behavior of a firm engaged exclusively in oil and gas exploration.

Consider an exploration firm with sole operating rights in a given petroleum basin containing N fields whose sizes $\tilde{A}_1,\ldots,\tilde{A}_N$ are generated according to assumption I; i.e. $\tilde{A}_1,\ldots,\tilde{A}_N$ are mutually independent with common density $f(\cdot|\underline{\theta})$. Discovery takes place in accordance with assumption II. It is always true that N and $\underline{\theta}$ are not known with certainty. However, to avoid problems of simultaneous parameter estimation and decision, assume initially that the firm knows $\underline{\theta}$ and N. The firm faces a price path p(t) per barrel of oil in place; i.e. there is a market for oil that has been discovered but not produced. It will sell discovered oil in place at the time of discovery (this eliminates the problem of producing a known reserve optimally over time).

The firm makes drilling decisions sequentially, one by one, at discrete points in time spaced h apart; i.e. beginning at t=0, decisions are made at times 0, h, 2h,...,kh, ... At time $t\varepsilon((k-1)h,kh)$, the state z_t is $((x_1,B_1,t_1),\ldots,(x_m,B_m,t_m))$ with $\sum_{j=1}^{m} x_j=n$ if m wells have been drilled in the time interval [0,t] and n discoveries made. A generic drilling decision problem is displayed in the form of a decision tree in Figure 6. The cost of drilling a wildcat well at time t is c(t). The outcome of drilling unfolds in the interval t to t+h. If a discovery is made the firm receives a reward of p(t) times $B_{m+1} = Y_{m+1}$, the amount discovered at time t less c(t). If it is a dry hole, $B_m = 0$ and he suffers cost c(t). The probability that the well will be a success is $q(z_t)$, and it is understood to be a function of z_t, as is the probability law for $\tilde{Y}_{n+1}$. The discount rate r is assumed to be a constant function of time.

If the firm's objective is to maximize the expectation of discounted dollar flow, and we define $V(t,z_t)$ as the expected value of pursuing an optimal policy from time t=kh onwards, then for h small,

$$V(t,z_t) = \max \begin{cases} (1-rh)\, V(t+h,z_t), \\ \hline \{q(z_t)p(t)E_{y|z_t}(\tilde{Y}_{n+1}) - c(t) \\ \quad + \ (1-rh)[q(z_t)E_{y|z_t}V(t+h,(z_t,(1,\tilde{Y}_{n+1},t+h)) \\ \quad + (1-q(z_t))\, V(t+h,(z_t,(0,0,t+h))]\} \end{cases}$$

where $E_{y|z_t}$ denotes expectation with respect to the probability distribution of $\tilde{Y}_{n+1}$

given z_t. If at $t^o, z_{t^o} = ((x_1,B_1,t_1),\ldots,(x_m,B_m,t_m))$ and $\sum_{j=1}^{m} x_j = N$, then $V(t^o,z_t) = 0$ for $t \geq t^o$. That is, once all fields have been discovered, the optimal policy is to cease drilling. Since N is finite and $E(\tilde{Y}_n)$ is finite for $n = 1,2,\ldots,N$, provided that $p(t) < \infty$ for $0 \leq t < \infty$, $V(t,z_t)$ is less than some positive V. Consequently, if the firm is at time t, $e^{-r\tau}V(t+\tau,z_t)$ approaches zero as $\tau \to \infty$.

This prescriptive model is a simple example of how the probabilistic version of the discovery process described earlier might be brought into play. A bit more could be said about its properties by rendering the functional forms of q, p, and c more specific. However, we stop here. It is only meant to be suggestive of one line of attack.

While suffering from an oversimplified description of choices available in an exploration program and from not being incorporated in a competitive environment, this model does describe how the most important observables generated by exploration-drilling successes and failures and discovery sizes -- behaves, and accounts explicitly for the effect of information (z_t) on future expectations ($q(z_t)$ and $E_{y|z_t}$)) even when the number N of fields and the parameter $\underline{\theta}$ of the "superpopulation" density $f(\cdot|\underline{\theta})$ are both known with certainty.

Numerous elaborations deserve consideration: Make the probability of discovery an explicit function of exploratory effort and include the level of exploratory effort in the choice set. Allow more than one wildcat to be drilled at each decision point and consider production over time from known discoveries simultaneously with exploration. And, finally, as it is in reality, regard the parameters N, $\underline{\theta}$, and those indexing $q(z_t)$ as not known with certainty, updating an a priori probability distribution assigned to parameter set via Bayes' theorem as successes, failures, and discovery sizes are observed.

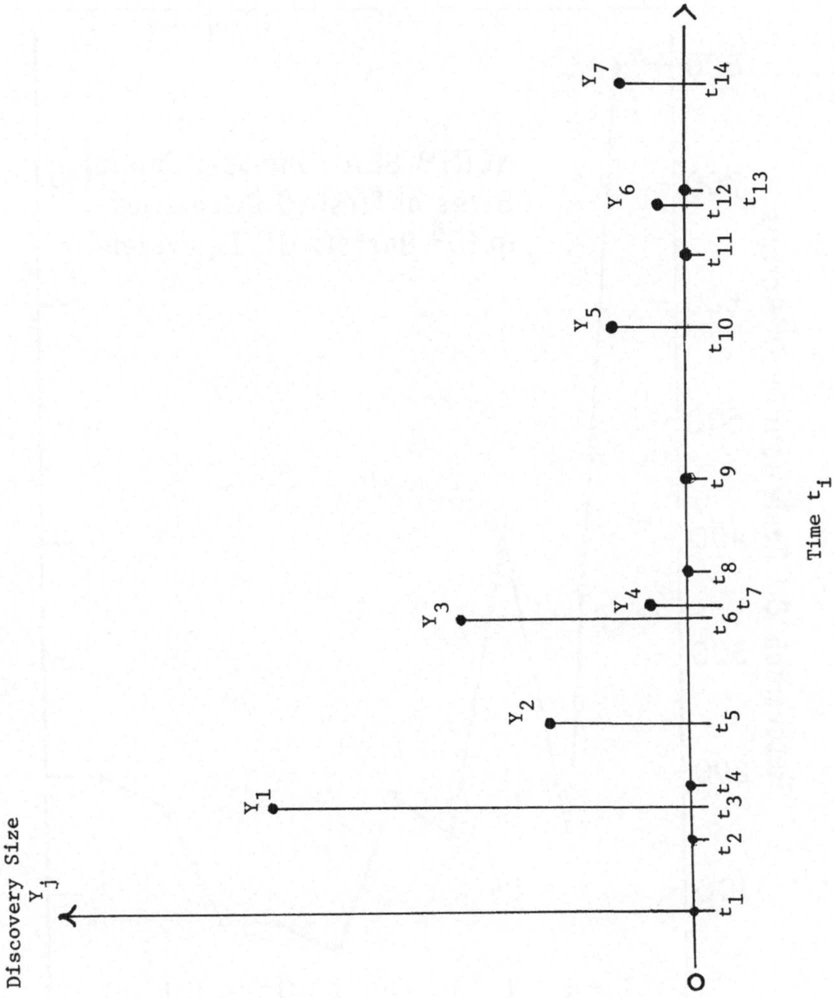
Discovery Size
Y_j
Time t_i
O
Y_1
Y_2
Y_3
Y_4
Y_5
Y_6
Y_7
t_1
t_2
t_3
t_4
t_5
t_6
t_7
t_8
t_9
t_10
t_11
t_12
t_13
t_14

FIGURE 1

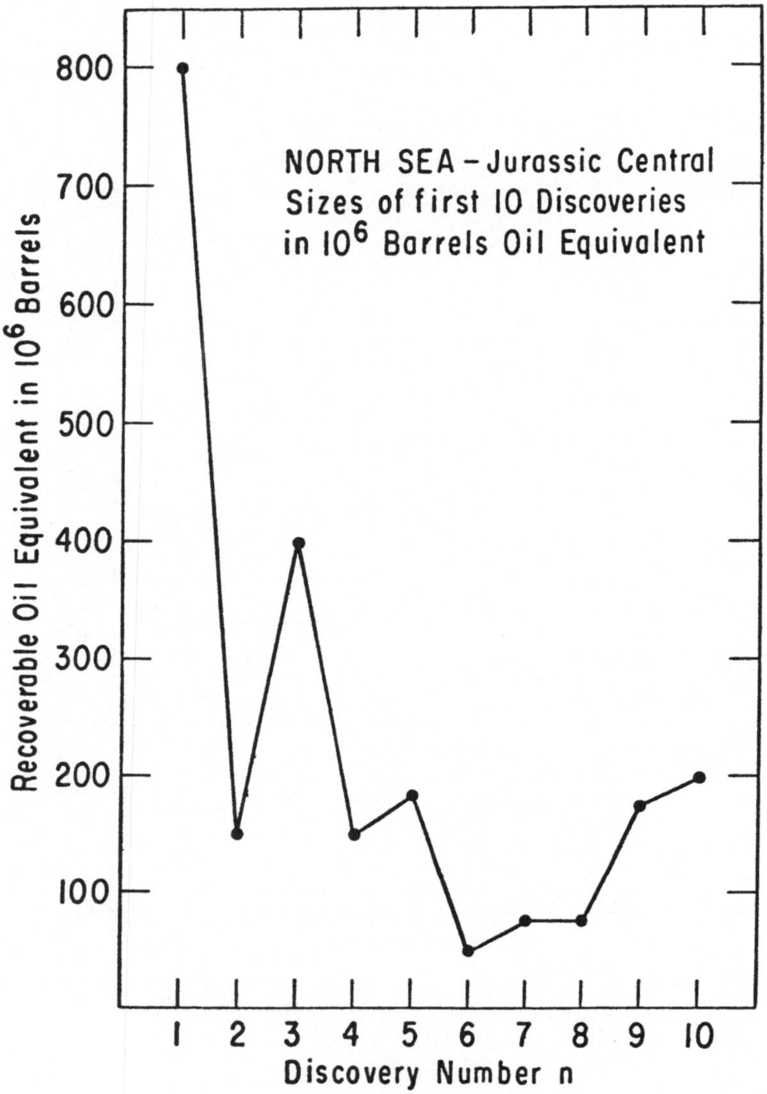
NORTH SEA – Jurassic Central
Sizes of first 10 Discoveries
in 10^6 Barrels Oil Equivalent
Recoverable Oil Equivalent in 10^6 Barrels
800
700
600
500
400
300
200
100
1
2
3
4
5
6
7
8
9
10
Discovery Number n

FIGURE 2

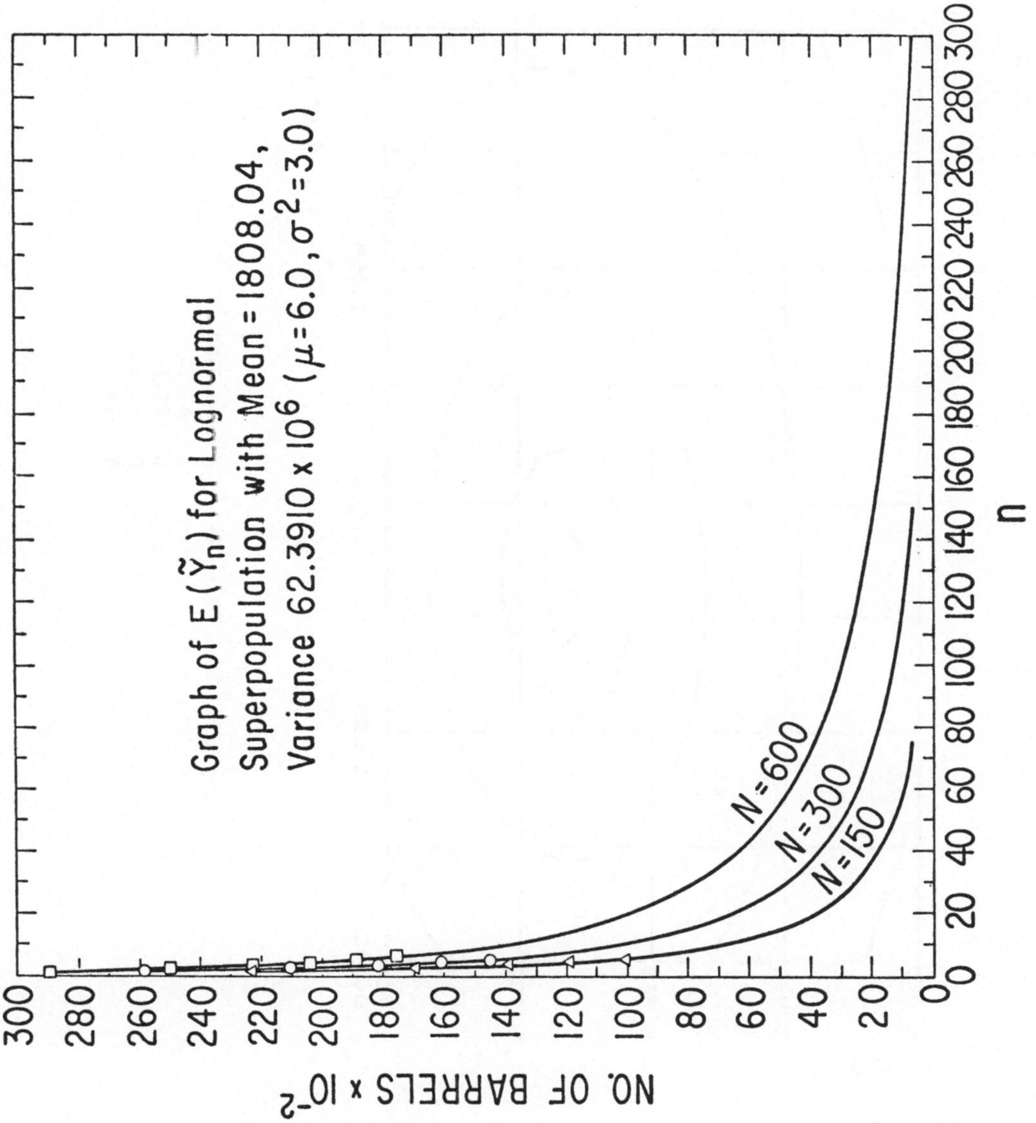

Graph of E ($\tilde{Y}_n$) for Lognormal
Superpopulation with Mean = 1808.04,
Variance 62.3910 x 10^6 (μ=6.0, σ^2=3.0)
N=600
N=300
N=150
NO. OF BARRELS x 10^{-2}
n
0
20
40
60
80
100
120
140
160
180
200
220
240
260
280
300

FIGURE 3

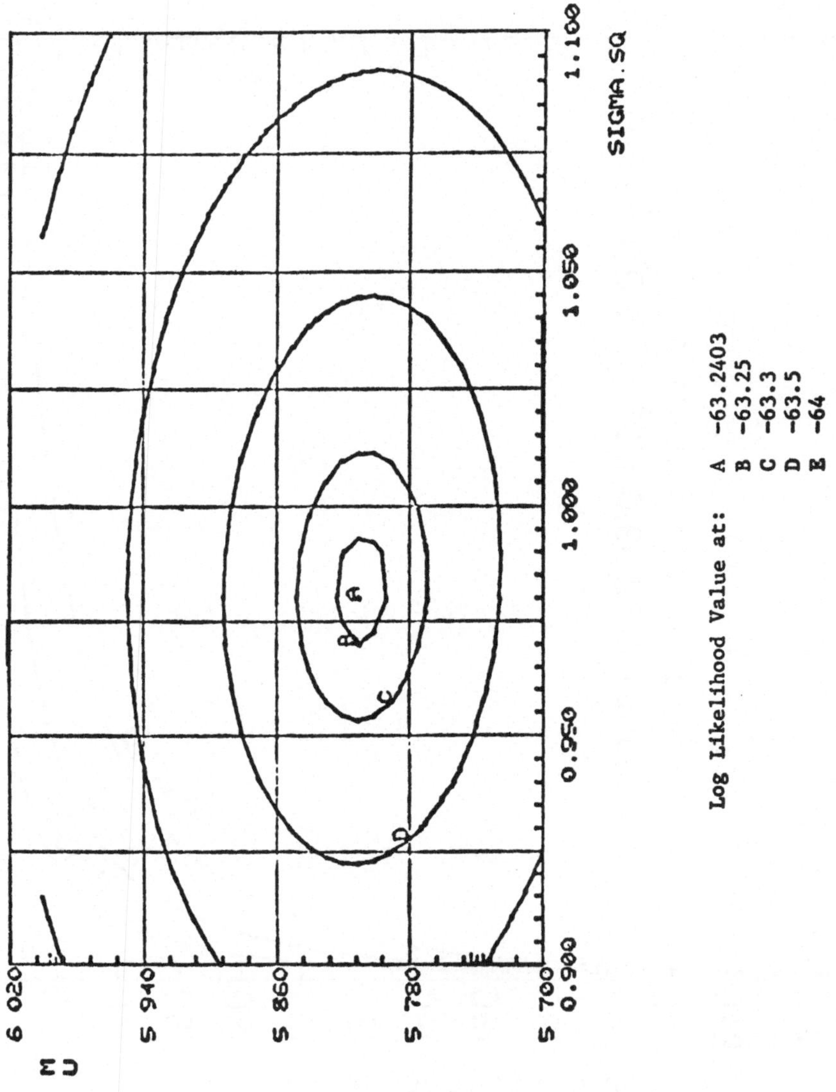

FIGURE 4

North Sea

Isocontours of Likelihood Function
For (μ,σ^2) with N=120 Fixed, n=60
Computed Using Uniform Expansion (4.7)

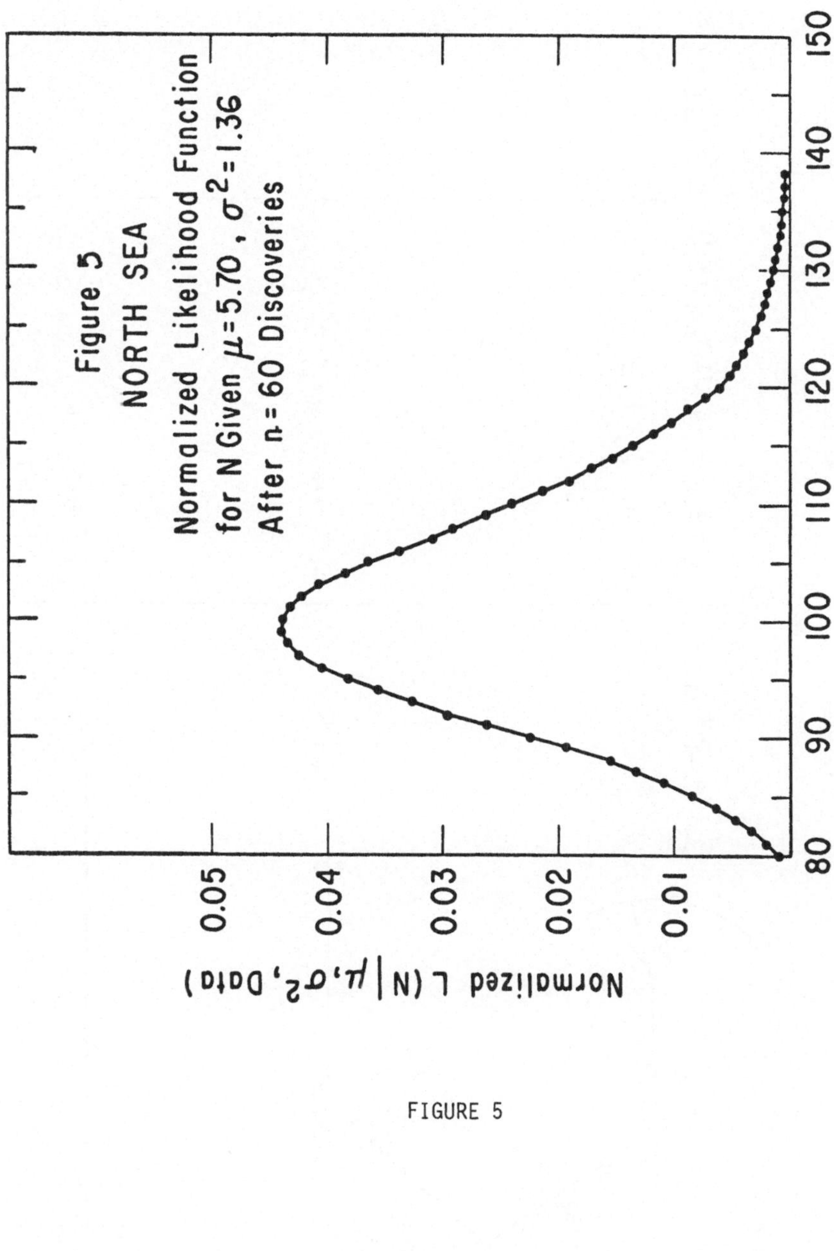
Figure 5
NORTH SEA
Normalized Likelihood Function
for N Given μ=5.70, σ²=1.36
After n=60 Discoveries
Normalized L (N | μ, σ², Data)
0.05
0.04
0.03
0.02
0.01
N
80
90
100
110
120
130
140
150

FIGURE 5

Generic Drilling Decision

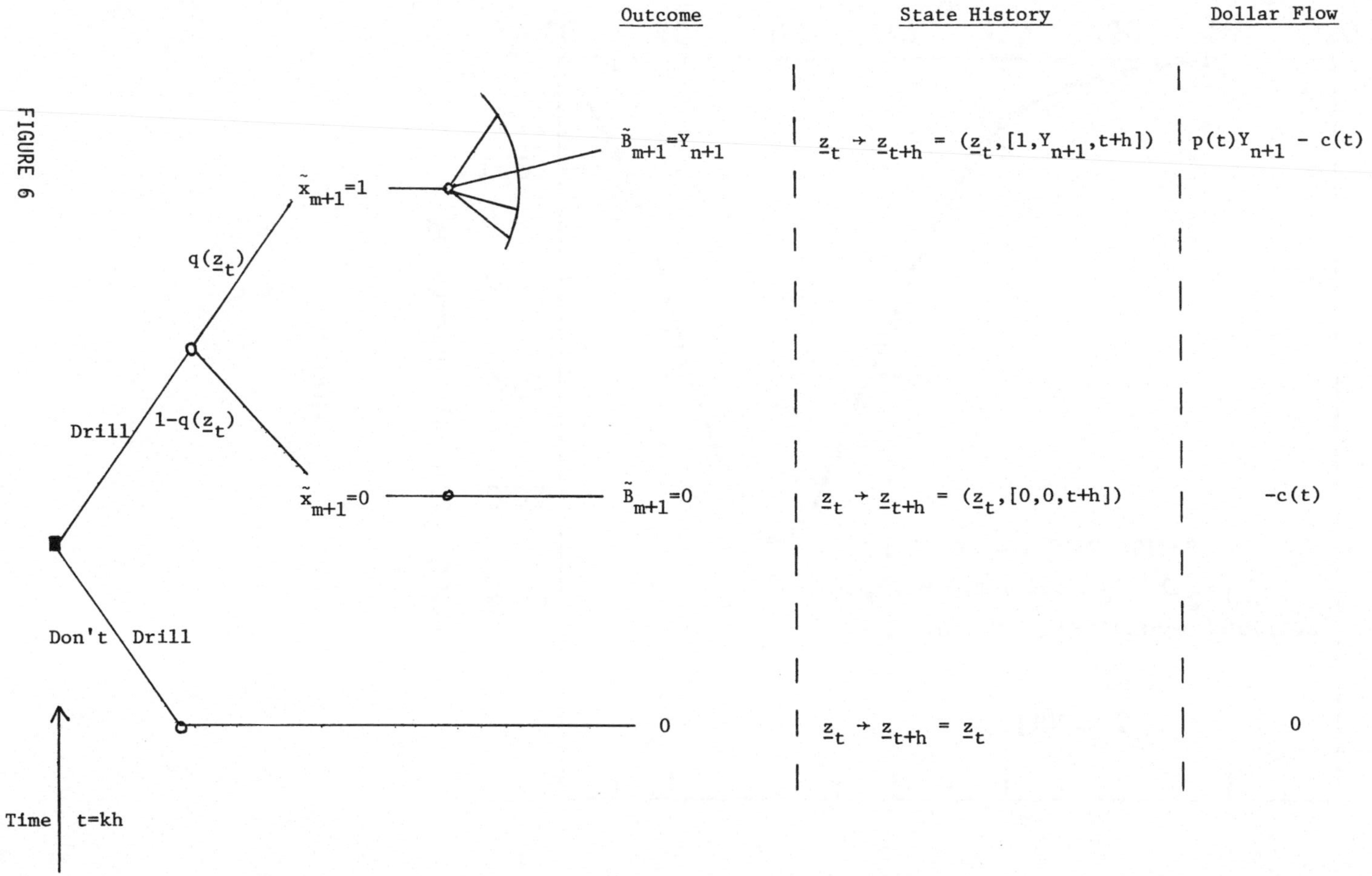

FIGURE 6

References

[1] Arps, J.J. and T.G. Roberts (1958), "Economics of Drilling for Cretaceous Oil Production on the East Flank of the Denver-Julesberg Basin", Bull. AAPG, Vol. 42, No. 11, pp. 2549-2566.

[2] Barouch, E. and G. Kaufman (1976), "Estimation of Undiscovered Oil and Gas", Proceedings of Symposia in Applied Mathematics, Vol. 21, American Mathematical Society (forthcoming, 1977), 15 pages.

[3] Barouch, E. and G. Kaufman (1976), "Oil and Gas Discovery Modelled As Sampling Proportional to Random Size", MIT Working Paper No. 888-76, 63 pages.

[4] Barouch, E. and G.M. Kaufman (1976), "On Sums of Lognormal Random Variables", MIT Sloan School Working Paper No. 831-76, 22 pages.

[5] Chester, E., B. Friedman, and F. Ursell (1956), "An Extension of The Method of Steepest Descents", Proc. Camb. Phil. Soc., Vol. 53, pp. 599-611.

[6] Dasgupta, P. and J. Stiglitz (1976), "Uncertainty and the Rate of Extraction Under Alternative Institutional Arrangements", Technical Report No. 179, Institute for Mathematical Studies in the Social Sciences, Stanford University.

[7] Gilbert, R.J. (1976), "Optimal Depletion of an Unknown Stock", Institute for Mathematical Studies in the Social Sciences, Technical Report No. 207, May, 1976, Stanford University, 46 pages.

[8] Hotelling, H. (1931), "The Economics of Exhaustible Resources", The Journal of Political Economy, Vol. 39, No. 2, April, 1931, pp. 137-175.

[9] Kaufman, G., Y. Balcer, and D. Kruyt (1975), "A Probabilistic Model of Oil and Gas Discovery", Studies in Geology No. 1 - Methods of Estimating the Volume of Undiscovered Oil and Gas Resources, The American Association of Petroleum Geologists.

[10] Khazzoom, J.D., "The FPC Staff's Econometric Model of Natural Gas Supply in the United States." The Bell Journal of Economics and Management Science, Vol. 2, No. 1 (Spring 1971), pp. 51-93.

[11] Koopmans, T. (1973), "Some Observations on 'Optimal' Economic Growth and Exhaustible Resources", in Economic Structure and Development, Ros, Linneman and de Wolff (eds.), pp. 239-255.

[12] Loury, G. (1976), The Optimum Exploitation of an Unknown Reserve, unpublished.

[13] McCrossan, R.G. (1969), "An Analysis of Size Frequency Distribution of Oil and Gas Reserves of Western Canada", Canadian Journal of Earth Sciences, Vol. 6, No. 2, pp. 201-211.

[14] Pindyck, R. (1976), Optimal Exploration and Production of a Nonrenewable Resource, unpublished.

[15] Pindyck, R. and P. MacAvoy, "Alternative Regulatory Policies for Dealing with The Natural Gas Shortage", The Bell Journal of Economics and Management Science, Vol. 4, No. 2 (Autumn 1973), pp. 454-498.

[16] Spann, R. and E. Erickson, "Supply Response in a Regulated Industry: The Case of Natural Gas", The Bell Journal of Economics and Management Science, Vol. 2, No. 1 (Spring 1971), pp. 94-121.

[17] Uhler, R. (1975), "Petroleum Exploration Dynamics", University of British Columbia Economics Department Working Paper.

OPTIMISATION DU CHAMP DE MIROIRS D'UNE CENTRALE SOLAIRE A CONCENTRATION PONCTUELLE

Philippe COURREGE et Jean-Michel LASRY

1.- DESCRIPTION SUCCINCTE D'UNE CENTRALE SOLAIRE A CONCENTRATION PONCTUELLE

Une centrale solaire à concentration ponctuelle est un système destiné à convertir le rayonnement solaire direct (flux de 1 Kw par m^2 environ) en énergie thermique à moyenne ou haute température (300°C à 1000°C selon les prototypes). Cette énergie thermique peut être utilisée directement dans un processus industriel, par exemple chimique, ou transformée en électricité.

On s'intéresse ici à une centrale du type de celle que projette le C.N.R.S. qui comporte les installations et mécanismes suivants :

a) Un ensemble (ou champ) d'héliostats tous identiques entre eux et répartis en des points fixes du sol. Chaque héliostat est constitué par
- un miroir plan ou légèrement focalisant de quelques dizaines de mètres carrés,
- un bâti supportant le miroir
- un mécanisme permettant d'orienter convenablement le miroir suivant la position du soleil.

b) une tour portant à son sommet une chaudière. Cette tour est disposée en un point convenable du champ d'héliostats (voir 2). La chaudière est pourvue d'un capteur qui absorbe le rayonnement renvoyé vers elle par les miroirs, ce qui réalise une concentration ponctuelle de puissance solaire (si l'on assimile la chaudière et son capteur à un point).

c) un système de guidage qui fait que chacun des miroirs du champ d'héliostats suit le soleil dans sa trajectoire - grâce au mécanisme dont il est pourvu - de manière à renvoyer en permanence l'image du soleil sur le capteur de la chaudière.

d) un système de conversion de la puissance thermique recueillie par le capteur : conversion thermodynamique pour produire de l'électricité via un turbo-alternateur, conversion thermo-chimique pour fabriquer un carburant ou d'autres produits chimiques, etc...

e) un système de stockage de l'énergie, sous forme thermique, destiné à régulariser la puissance incidente au système de conversion.
(voir par exemple [1], sessions G, H et J).

On ne dispose pas, de façon opérationnelle, d'un modèle global permettant de clarifier et d'optimiser les choix au niveau de la construction de la centrale, et ultérieurement au niveau de sa gestion. On se contente pour le moment d'approfondir la réflexion sur certaines parties du système : optimisation du champ d'héliostats (voir ci-dessous), étude du stockage (voir [2] et [3]),étude du contrôle de la chaudière (voir [4] et [5])... On néglige ainsi les corrélations importantes qui existent entre ces différents problèmes. Il y a donc là un champ d'application neuf pour la théorie des systèmes.

2.- OPTIMISATION DU CHAMP D'HELIOSTATS

a) Le modèle

Le champ d'héliostats d'une centrale du type étudié ici comporte plusieurs centaines à plusieurs milliers d'héliosats disposés sur un terrain Y que l'on suppose ici plan. Pour décrire la disposition des miroirs (c'est-à-dire des héliostats) sur Y, on se donne un réseau curviligne $\mathfrak{R}$ tel que le centre de chaque maille coïncide avec le centre d'un miroir. On découple le problème de l'optimisation de la disposition $\mathfrak{R}$ des miroirs de l'étude du reste de la centrale en se donnant deux critères particuliers : le prix $\mathbb{P}(\mathfrak{R})$ du champ d'héliostats disposé selon le réseau $\mathfrak{R}$ et l'énergie lumineuse $\mathbb{E}_{\mathfrak{T}}(\mathfrak{R})$ renvoyée sur la chaudière par le champ $\mathfrak{R}$ durant une période donnée ($\mathfrak{T}$ = une journée type, $\mathfrak{T}$ = une année,...).

Il s'agit naturellement de maximiser $\mathbb{E}$ et de minimiser $\mathbb{P}$, donc de décrire l'ensemble de Pareto $\mathcal{P}$ associé à $(\mathbb{E},-\mathbb{P})$. (Un réseau $\mathfrak{R}$ appartient à $\mathcal{P}$ si et seulement si : $\mathbb{E}(\mathfrak{R}') \geqslant E(\mathfrak{R})$ implique $\mathbb{P}(\mathfrak{R}') \geqslant \mathbb{P}(\mathfrak{R})$). On dispose en outre d'un critère de sélection sur $\mathcal{P}$ qui consiste à minimiser le prix moyen $\mathbb{P}(\mathfrak{R})/\mathbb{E}(\mathfrak{R})$ de l'énergie lumineuse renvoyée sur la chaudière.

b) Calcul de l'énergie $\mathbb{E}(\mathfrak{R})$

Pour chaque maille μ du réseau $\mathfrak{R}$, on définit la densité de verre installé par le quotient :

$$d_\mu = \frac{\text{surface du miroir placé dans la maille } \mu}{\text{surface de la maille } \mu} .$$

On considère une fonction M vérifiant $M(y_\mu) = d_\mu$ pour toute maille μ, où y_μ est le centre de la maille μ, et prolongée à tout Y par une interpolation convenable. Notamment, on pose $M = 0$ en dehors du champ de miroir . Ainsi M(y) constitue une notion de densité de verre installé au voisinage du point $y \in Y$. Le support de la fonction M indique la localisation du champ de miroir : on peut donc prendre pour Y le plan tout entier. Comme le problème est invariant par translation, on peut se donner arbitrairement la position $y_o \in Y$ du pied de la tour portant la chaudière.

La remarque fondamentale pour la suite du calcul est que l'énergie lumineuse renvoyée sur la chaudière ne dépend (en première approximation) du réseau $\mathcal{R}$ que via la densité de verre installé (voir [6]). Plus précisément le flux d'énergie renvoyé sur la chaudière à l'instant t est :

$$(1)\qquad W(t) = \int_Y \varphi(t) \min[S^t . V, T_y . V, M(y)\ S^t . N_y^t]dy$$

où V est le vecteur unitaire normal à Y et dirigé vers le haut ; où S^t est le vecteur unitaire pointé à l'instant t vers le soleil ; où T_y est le vecteur unitaire dirigé au point y vers la chaudière ; où N_y^t est la normale au miroir situé en y, supposé convenablement orienté, i.e.,

$$N_y^t = \frac{S^t + T_y}{\|S^t + T_y\|} \quad ;$$

et où $\varphi(t)$ est le flux solaire (direct) incident à l'instant t.

On renvoie le lecteur à [6] pour une approche détaillée de (1).

On a donc $\mathbb{E}_{\mathcal{T}}(\mathcal{R}) = \int_{\mathcal{T}} W(t)dt$, soit :

$$(2)\qquad \mathbb{E}_{\mathcal{T}}(\mathcal{R}) = \int_{\mathcal{T}} \int_Y \varphi(t) \min(S^t . V, T_y . V, M(y)\ S^t . N_y^t)dy\,dt .$$

Posons, pour $y \in Y$ et $a \geqslant 0$:

$$f(y,a) = \int_{\mathcal{T}} \varphi(t) \min(S^t . V, T_y . V, a\,S^t . N_y^t)dt .$$

L'astronomie élémentaire fournit S^t ; la météorologie donne la valeur moyenne statistique de $\varphi(t)$. La fonction f est donc disponible au niveau du calcul effectif.

On a d'après (2) :

$$(4)\qquad \mathbb{E}_{\mathcal{T}}(\mathcal{R}) = \mathbb{F}(M) \quad \text{avec}$$

$$(5)\qquad \mathbb{F}(M) = \int_Y f(y,M(y))dy.$$

c) <u>Calcul du prix $\mathbb{P}(\mathcal{R})$</u>

On a :

$$(6)\qquad \mathbb{P}(\mathcal{R}) = G(M) \quad \text{avec}$$

$$(7)\qquad G(M) = c_o + \int_Y p(y)\,M(y)dy \quad ,$$

où c_o représente des coûts fixes indépendants du champ de miroir, et où p(y) représente le prix du mètre carré de verre installé au voisinage de y : ce prix dépend de la distance $\|y - y_o\|$ de y au pied de la tour y_o, car, par exemple, les héliostats éloignés exigent des réglages plus précis.

d) <u>Optimisation</u>

D'après (4) et (6) on est ramené à chercher l'ensemble de Pareto associé à (F,-G). D'après (3) la fonction $a \to f(y,a)$ est concave pour tout y ;

donc d'après (5) la fonction F est concave. D'après (7) la fonction G est linéaire. On introduit un paramètre de Lagrange $\lambda > 0$ et on cherche la (ou les) solution(s) du problème,

$$(8_\lambda) \qquad \underset{M \geqslant 0}{\text{maximiser}}\ F(M) - \lambda G(M) .$$

Lorsque $\lambda > 0$ varie, M_λ décrit l'ensemble de Pareto cherché. Or, d'après (5) et (7) M_λ est une solution du problème (8_λ) si et seulement si pour tout $y \in Y$, $M_\lambda(y)$ vérifie :

$$(9_\lambda) \qquad f(y, M_\lambda(y)) - \lambda p(y) M_\lambda(y) = \max_{a \geqslant 0} [f(y,a) - \lambda p(y) a] .$$

Et, en notant $\partial f(y,a)$ le sous-différentiel au point a de la fonction $a \to f(y,a)$, l'équation (9_λ) est équivalente à :

$$(10_\lambda) \qquad \lambda p(y) \in \partial f(y, M_\lambda(y)) .$$

Ces équations permettent de déterminer $M_\lambda(y)$ pour chaque y.

<u>Remarque 1</u>.- On peut calculer facilement la dérivée à droite $f'^d(y,a)$ pour $a = 0$ d'après (3) :

$$f'^d(y,0) = \int_{\mathcal{G}} \varphi(t)\, S^t . N_y^t \, dt .$$

Et la zone occupée par les miroirs est donnée par :

$$\text{support } M_\lambda = \{ y \in Y \mid f_a'^d(y,0) \geqslant \lambda p(y) \} .$$

<u>Remarque 2</u>.- Supposons que f(y,a) soit dérivable par rapport à a. Le quotient,

$$r(y,a) = f'(y,a)/p(y)$$

désigne l'augmentation marginale de puissance captée que l'on obtient en installant une unité (de coût) de verre supplémentaire au point y. Un champ de miroir M appartient alors à l'ensemble de Pareto si et seulement si

$$(11) \qquad r(y, M(y)) = \text{constante} \quad (\text{indépendant de } y).$$

<u>Résultats numériques</u>.- Un calcul numérique a été effectué avec les données correspondant au projet de centrale du C.N.R.S. La détermination complète de l'ensemble de Pareto a demandé environ dix minutes sur IRIS 80. La densité de verre installé du champ de miroirs envisagé dans le projet du C.N.R.S. est comparable à l'un des points de l'ensemble de Pareto calculé. D'autre part, il est apparu que (au moins dans ce cas particulier) le critère "minimiser $\mathbb{P}/\mathbb{E}$" est peu sélectif sur l'ensemble de Pareto, en ce sens que dans l'ensemble $\{M \mid G(M)/F(M) \leqslant 1{,}1 \times \min G/F\}$ on trouve des densités M_o et M_1 telles que $F(M_1) = 2F(M_o)$.

REFERENCES

[1] Comptes rendus du Colloque international "Electricité solaire", Toulouse 1-5/3/1976.

[2] M.M. ETIEVANT, PENKE, VIALARON, ALLARD, BONNIN, PHARABOD : Problèmes liés au stockage thermique, p.595 de la référence [1].

[3] J.P. ALLARD, Ph. COURREGE et F. VALETTE : Stockage thermique par chaleur de fusion : modèle simplifié de la dynamique du destockage et application au dimensionnement d'une installation. Rapport interne C.N.R.S.-E.D.F., projet THEM (11/1976).

[4] J.L. ABATUT, B. DESSUS, C. MERSIER, F. PHARABOD: Interaction entre le champ d'héliostats et le système thermodynamique d'une centrale solaire. p. 559 de la référence [1].

[5] Ph. COURREGE : Calcul des flux radiatifs d'une centrale solaire à concentration : (1) Eléments de la théorie du transfert radiatif. Rapport interne C.N.R.S.-E.D.F., projet THEM (9/1976).

[6] Ph. COURREGE : Une évaluation de l'aire efficace d'un champ de miroirs en termes de répartition du verre installé. p. 831 de la référence [1].

* * *

APPLICATIONS OF CONTROL THEORY

APPLICATIONS DE LA THÉORIE DU CONTROLE

APPLICATION OF CONTROL THEORY TO POPULATION POLICY

Huibert Kwakernaak
Department of Applied Mathematics
Twente University of Technology
Enschede, The Netherlands

Summary

Population policy for a single nation is considered as an optimal control problem. It is studied how the population of a country like The Netherlands could be reduced from its present size and age distribution to a prescribed, stationary size and age distribution in the shortest time possible. The control variable is the annual number of live births. Two constraints are taken into account: a socio-psychological constraint consisting of a (time-dependent) lower bound on fertility, and an economic constraint in the form of an upper bound on the demographic burden. The possible effects of emigration are also studied. The problem is solved by linear programming. Numerical results that apply to The Netherlands are shown and extensively discussed.

Introduction

During recent years questions of long-term population policy on national and global scales have been extensively discussed in the popular and scientific press. Much emphasis has been placed on the need to stop unlimited population growth, and, indeed, to reverse the trend. A notable event was the appearance in Great-Britain in 1972 of the report "A Blueprint for Survival" [1]. This publication closely associates the quality of life with population density. In the report, the desirable population density is among other things derived from the food production capacity of any given area. It is concluded that the ideal population size for Great-Britain is about 30 million (as compared to a present population size of about 56 million). The Dutch version of the report [2] quotes an ideal population size of about 5 million or less for The Netherlands (as compared to a present population size of about 13.5 million). This ideal population size should be reached in the next 150 to 200 years.

A peak in the discussions around population problems was reached in 1974, when the World Population Conference took place in Bucharest. In the same year, Mesarovic and Pestel published the Second Report of the Club of Rome [3]. In this report, various scenarios for the future of the world are analyzed. An assumption of several of these scenarios is that the fertility of all regions in the model under consideration reaches a steady-state value within 35 years and remains constant thereafter. If this process would start in 1975, a steady-state condition would be reached after about 75 years, with constant population sizes and age distributions.

It is the purpose of the present investigation to study the question how much time is minimally needed for the population of a given country (in this case The Netherlands) to reach a stationary population of prescribed size. The question is formulated as an optimal control problem. To ensure that the solutions found are reasonably realistic, various constraints are imposed. The first constraint, termed the socio-psychological constraint, imposes a bound on the rate and extent to which the fertility of the population is allowed to decrease. The second constraint, referred to as the economic constraint, prevents the so-called demographic burden (also called the dependence) of the population from exceeding a prescribed bound. The demographic burden is given by the ratio of the number of individuals not of working age (in the age groups 0 to 20, and 65 and over) to the remaining individuals (in the age group 20 to 65). The demographic burden is a rough indication of the economic load imposed on the working population by the dependent part of the population.

A simple discrete-time model for the population process is developed. The control variable is the annual number of births. The method of solution is linear programming. The effects of migration (both emigration and temporary labor) will be considered. A modest sensitivity study is included as well. An extensive discussion of the results of the computations, which have all been done for The Netherlands, concludes the paper.
The present paper is a follow-up of a sequence of research reports [4], [5], [6], and a publication in Dutch [7]. The previous publication does not contain the more detailed mathematical information given in the present paper, and moreover lacks the computations and discussions of the effects of migration. A related publication considers the problem as an optimal control problem for a distributed-parameter system [8].

The demographic model

The basic demographic model is very simple. Because of the specific function woman has in the human reproductive process, we only account for the female population, which is not unusual in demographic studies. If in the sequel the total population is mentioned, it is assumed for simplicity that there are equally many men as women. Strictly speaking this is not entirely correct: in 1973 there were 993 men per 1000 women in The Netherlands [9].

We define the quantity $p(i,j)$ as the number of women in the age group from $(i-1)h$ to ih at the instant t_o+jh, where $i = 1,2,\ldots,\frac{100}{h}$, and $j = 0,1,2,\ldots\ldots$ Here h is a basic time interval, which in demographic calculations usually is 1 year. In the present calculations h has been taken 5 years, to reduce the computational load. For the instant t_o we chose January 1, 1972, 0 hours.

The basic equation of the demographic model is

$$p(i+1,j+1) = p(i,j) - \mu(i,j)p(i,j), \tag{1}$$

with $i = 1,2,\ldots,\frac{100}{h}-1$, and $j = 0,1,2,\ldots$. The first term on the right-hand side expresses that the population ages by h years during a time period of h years. The second term represents the decrease by death of the number of women in the age group from $(i-1)h$ to ih during a period of h years; $\mu(i,j)$ is a mortality coefficient, which depends both on the age group i and the time period j. The values of the mortality coefficients were determined from projections for The Netherlands for the period 1980-1999 [10], [11]. For simplicity it has been assumed that the mortality coefficients do not depend on time (hence are independent of j) for the entire time periods involved in the computations.

The equation (1) has to be supplemented with the equation

$$p(1,j+1) = u(j), \tag{2}$$

for $j = 0,1,\ldots$. Here $u(j)$ is the number of girls born during the period from t_o+jh to $t_o+(j+1)h$ and surviving at the end of this period. We shall consider $u(j)$, $j = 0,1,\ldots$, as the control variable for the problem.

It is very easy to solve the equations (1) and (2). It follows by repeated substitution

$$p(i,j) = \begin{cases} \beta(i,j)p(i-j,0), & j = 0,1,\ldots,i-1, \\ \beta(i,j)u(j-i), & j = i, i+1,\ldots, \end{cases} \tag{3}$$

for $i = 1,2,\ldots,n$, with $n = \frac{100}{h}$, and

$$\beta(i,j) = \prod_{k=1}^{\min(j,i-1)} [1-\mu(i-k,j-k)], \tag{4}$$

for $i = 1,2,\ldots,n$, and $j = 0,1,\ldots$. Here we adopt the convention that a repeated product equals 1 if the lower limit exceeds the upper limit.

Stationary population

If the mortality coefficients $\mu(i,j)$ are assumed to be independent of the time period j, and are therefore replaced with $\mu(i)$, it follows from (3) and (4) that for $j = n+1, n+2, \ldots,$

$$p(i,j) = \bar{\beta}(i)u(j-i), \qquad i = 1,2,\ldots,n, \tag{5}$$

where

$$\bar{\beta}(i) = \prod_{k=1}^{i-1} [1-\mu(i-k)], \qquad i = 1,2,\ldots,n. \tag{6}$$

The coefficient $\bar{\beta}(i)$ has a simple interpretation: it indicates the fraction of the girls born in any time period that survives after ih years. Eq. (5) shows that if the birth volumes $u(j-n)$, $u(j-n+1),\ldots,u(j-1)$ are constant, say equal to the constant $\bar{u}$, the age distribution at time t_o+jh is given by

$$p(i,j) = \bar{\beta}(i)\bar{u}, \qquad i = 1,2,\ldots,n. \tag{7}$$

This age distribution is independent of time, and is called a stationary age distribution. Its shape is entirely determined by the coefficients $\bar{\beta}(i)$, $i = 1,2,\ldots,n$. The corresponding total size of the female population $\bar{P}$ is also independent of j; it is given by

$$\bar{P} = [\sum_{i=1}^{n} \bar{\beta}(i)]\bar{u}. \tag{8}$$

For a given total stationary population size $\bar{P}$, the corresponding stationary birth volume $\bar{u}$ may be found from (8).

Figure 1 gives a comparison of the age distribution of the female population of The Netherlands on January 1, 1972 [11], and the stationary age distribution corresponding to a total female population of 5 million. The obvious differences are accentuated by the data summarized in Table 1. In the stationary situation, the percentage of the young (age group 0 to 20) is much smaller than at present, whereas the percentage of the old (over 65) is considerably higher. The average age shifts from about 34 at present to 41 for the stationary population. These numbers illustrate that a society with a stationary age distribution will be quite different from the present.

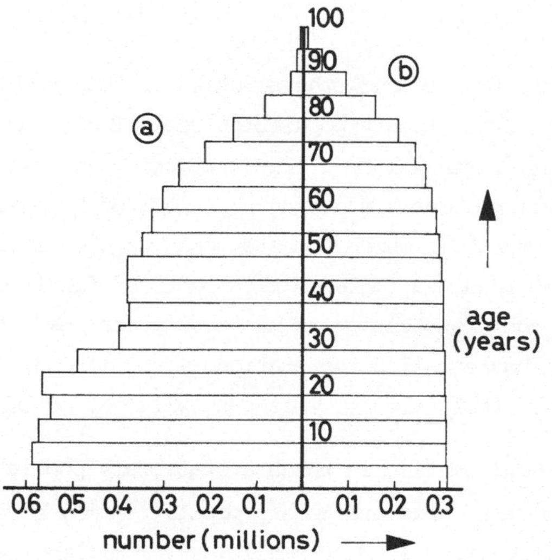

Fig. 1. (a) Age distribution of the Dutch female population on Januari 1, 1972.
(b) Stationary age distribution of the female Dutch population corresponding to a total female population size of 5 million.

TABLE 1: COMPARISON OF SOME DATA CONCERNING THE AGE DISTRIBUTION OF THE DUTCH POPULATION ON JANUARI 1, 1972, AND THE STATIONARY DISTRIBUTION

	1972	stationary
percentage women 0-20 years (%)	34.5	25.1
percentage women 20-65 years (%)	53.9	54.4
percentage women 65+ (%)	11.6	20.5
average age of women (years)	33.7	41.0

Population policy as an optimal control problem

In this section we describe how population policy may be approached as an optimal control problem. It is assumed that a population policy is to be designed that has as its goal to achieve a stationary population, of specified size, in the shortest time possible.

If no additional constraints are imposed, the solution to this problem is easily found. Suppose that $\bar{P}$ is the desired stationary population size. Then from (8) we can obtain the corresponding stationary birth volume $\bar{u}$. The stationary age distribution is reached if and only if the birth volume equals $\bar{u}$ during n periods of h years, i.e., during 100 years, preceding the instant at which the stationary age distribution is achieved. Therefore, the minimum time required to reach the specified final age distribution from an arbitrary initial age distribution is nh = 100 years, except in the unlikely case that the birth volume has equalled the stationary volume $\bar{u}$ during a certain length of time before the initial time t_o. This case will not be considered.

We thus conclude that the minimum time in which a stationary population may be reached is 100 years.The size of this stationary population may be arbitrarily specified. If the target population size is very small (say, 3 million as compared to the present 6.6 million women), the transition from the present age distribution to the terminal distribution will show various undesirable phenomena. First of all, it is to be expected that the birth rate, defined here as the annual number of female births per 1000 females in the fertile age, will temporarily drop to extremely low values during the first decades. Secondly, there will be a period (later than the first-mentioned period).during which the population in the age group 65+ has a very large size as compared to the working population (age group 20 to 65), thus imposing an unadmissible large economic burden on the working population.

To prevent these effects, constraints will be imposed on the solution, which will be discussed in the next sections. The purpose of these constraints is to find more realistic population planning programs,which have some chance of being implementable.

<u>Socio-psychological constraint</u>

An important element in projections of population growth is the so-called <u>fertility</u> pattern. The fertility pattern describes the age specific fertility of women. Figure 2 represents the fertility pattern that was observed in The Netherlands in 1969. The plot shows for each five-year age group (10 to 15, 15 to 20, etc.) the average annual number of surviving girls born during a future period of 5 years from 1000 women in the relevant age group.

We shall assume - in common with the Second Report to the Club of Rome [3] - that the shape of the fertility pattern does not vary with time, but that the pattern may decrease or increase as a whole. We shall furthermore assume that for each projected time period there exists a fertility pattern that imposes a <u>lower bound</u> on the birth

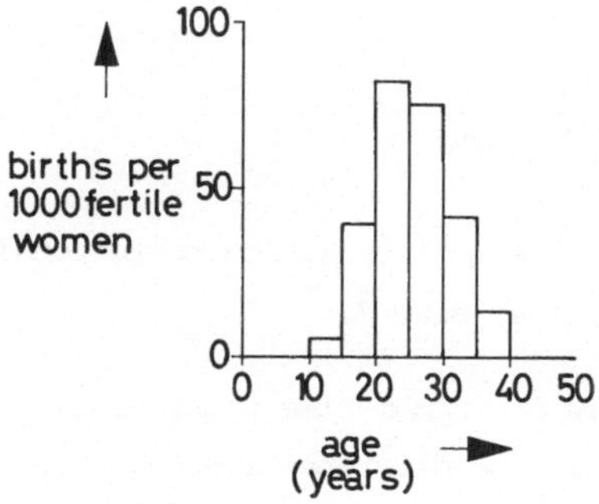

Fig. 2. Fertility pattern observed in The Netherlands in 1969.

volumes. This means that the actual fertility pattern always has to exceed the assumed minimum pattern. Thus we suppose that during the time period from $t_o+(j-1)h$ to t_o+jh the annual number of female births per 1000 women in the age group from $(i-1)h$ will at least have to equal $m(i,j)$. This number is considered as the least socially acceptable number for the relevant time period. Since the total number of births is obtained by summing the numbers of births from women in the various age groups, this socio-psychological constraint imposes the following restriction on the number of births:

$$u(j) > \sum_{i=1}^{n} hm(i,j)p(i,j)/1000 \qquad (9)$$

for $j = 0,1,2,\ldots\ldots$

In the context of this study a certain choice was made for the behavior of the minimal fertility pattern. We assume an exponential decrease from the initial pattern. The initial pattern is taken to be 5% below the pattern observed in 1969. The dependence of the pattern on time is given by

$$m(i,j) = [r + (1-r)e^{-jh/\theta}]m(i,0), \qquad (10)$$

$j = 0,1,2,\ldots.$, where θ is a time constant, and r the fraction of the initial pattern to which the pattern is eventually reduced. In the calculations, unless stated otherwise, we have taken $r = 0.6$, and $\theta = 20$ years. This means that minimum fertility is reduced to 60% of the initial value over a time period of about 40 years.

It is to be expected that the sensitivity of the solution to variations in r and θ is relatively great. A simple sensitivity study is presented in a later section.

With the introduction of the side-condition (9), we have to consider the problem of finding $u(j)$, $j = 0,1,2,\ldots,N-1$, as well as N, such that N is minimal, while (9) is satisfied for $j = 0,1,\ldots,N-1$, and

$$p(i,N) = \bar{p}(i), \qquad i = 1,2,\ldots,n. \tag{11}$$

Here $\bar{p}(i)$, $i = 1,2,\ldots,n$, is the age distribution corresponding to the desired stationary population, with prescribed size $\bar{P}$.

This optimal control problem is a minimum-time problem. Since the solution of minimum-time problems, especially in the discrete-time case, involves certain complications, we prefer to solve a related problem, whose solution yields the answer to the original problem. Therefore, we consider the problem of finding, for given N, the minimum size of the stationary population that may be reached at time N, while satisfying the socio-psychological constraint. Thus we have to find $u(j)$, $j = 0,1,2,\ldots,N-1$, with N given, such that (9) is satisfied for $j = 0,1,\ldots,N-1$, such that $p(i,N)$, $i = 1,2,\ldots,n$, is a stationary age distribution, and such that

$$P = \sum_{i=1}^{n} p(i,N) \tag{12}$$

is minimal. Suppose that this problem has been solved, and let $P_{min}(N)$ indicate the minimum stationary population size reachable within N time periods. It will be seen, and indeed is very plausible, that P_{min} is a strictly decreasing function of N. Therefore, once we have a plot of P_{min} as a function of N, it is very easy to determine the minimum number of time periods N necessary to reach a given stationary population size $\bar{P}$.

We now discuss the solution of the second problem described. The age distribution at time $N \geq n$ is stationary if and only if $u(j) = \bar{u}$, with $\bar{u}$ a constant to be determined, for $j = N-n, N-n+1,\ldots,N-1$. Then we have

$$p(i,N) = \bar{\beta}(i)\bar{u}, \qquad \sum_{i=1}^{n} p(i,N) = [\sum_{i=1}^{n} \bar{\beta}(i)]\bar{u}. \tag{13}$$

Hence, (12) is minimized if $\bar{u}$ is minimized. Substitution of (3) into the constraint (9) yields

$$u(j) \geq \sum_{i=1}^{\min(j,n)} 1000hm(i,j)\beta(i,j)u(j-i) + \sum_{i=j+1}^{n} 1000hm(i,j)\beta(i,j)p(i-j,0),$$

$$j = 0,1,\ldots,N-1. \tag{14}$$

We adopt the convention that a summation cancels if the lower limit exceeds the upper limit.

Thus we have to solve the following problem: minimize $\bar{u}$ with respect to the independent variables u(j) ⩾ 0, j = 0,1,...,N-1, subject to u(N-n) = u(N-n+1) = ...= u(N-1) = $\bar{u}$ and subject to (14). This is a straightforward linear programming problem, which is easily solved numerically once a standard code is available.

Fig. 3 gives some of the numerical results. The solid curve represents the minimal stationary female population size as a function of the time needed to reach it. The plot shows that the minimum female population size reachable in 100 years - the minimal time needed to reach a stationary population of any size - is 9.47 million, corresponding to a total population size of about 18.9 million. The curve also shows that the time needed to reach a stationary total population size of 5 million (2.5 million women) - the ideal population size quoted in the Dutch version of "A Blueprint for Survival" [2] - is about 220 years.

Fig. 3 also indicates - with dashed lines - the time histories of the total population sizes eventually reaching stationary female population sizes of respectively 9.47 million, 5.90 million, and 3.21 million. The time periods required successively are 100, 150, and 200 years.

Fig. 4 shows how the birth volumes would have to behave to reach stationary female populations of respectively 9.47 million, 5.90 million and 3.21 million. The following pattern emerges. Initially the birth volume precisely equals the minimum value allowed by the psycho-sociological constraint. This continues until the instant at which the psycho-sociological minimum value equals the stationary birth volume corresponding to the desired stationary population size. From this instant on it takes 100 years until the stationary situation is reached.

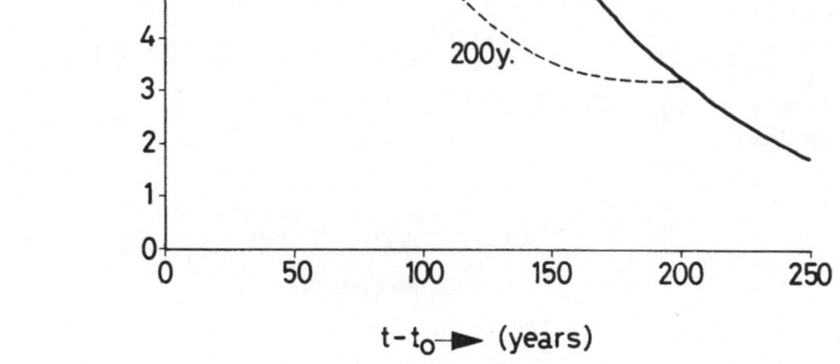

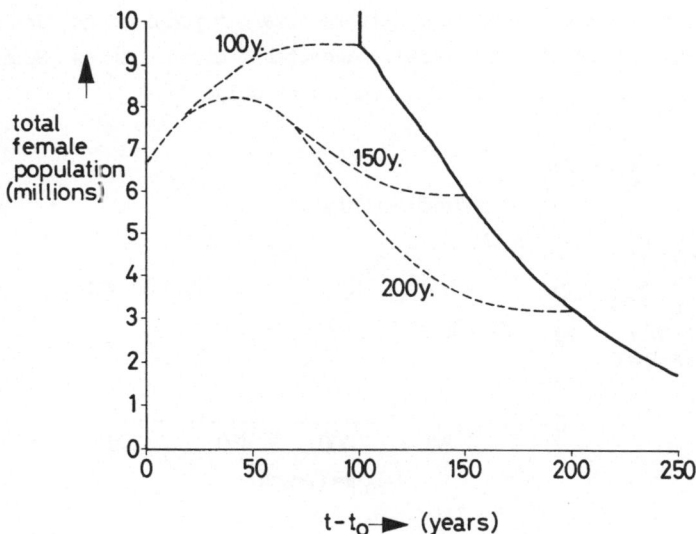

Fig. 3. Total population size as a function of time; socio-psychological constraint only.

Additional clarification is provided in Fig. 5. Here we show for each of the three cases considered how fertility behaves with time. Fertility was defined as the annual number of female births per 1000 fertile women. Fertile women by definition are women in the age group 15 to 40. In each case fertility eventually stabilizes at the value of 40.6, which is the value needed to maintain a stationary population. To achieve an eventual reduction in population size (5.90 million respectively 3.21 million as compared to the initial 6.6 million), fertility temporarily has to assume values below the equilibrium fertility.

A guideline for a practical population policy that has as its goal to achieve a stationary population of prescribed size evidently is first to reduce fertility as quickly as socially possible, and then slowly let it increase again to the equilibrium value.

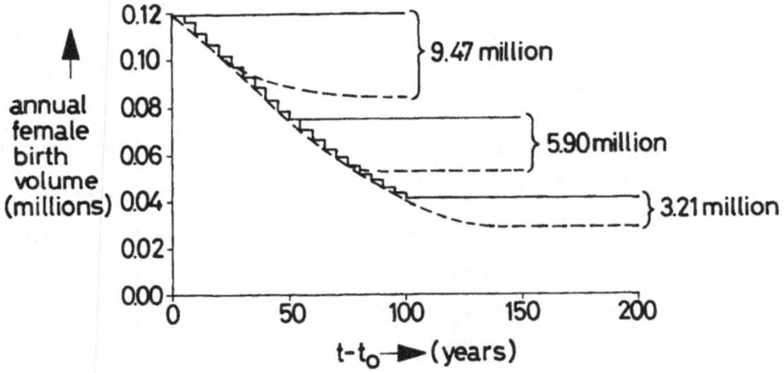

Fig. 4. Annual female birth volumes for different target populations. The dashed lines indicate the minimal socially acceptable birth volumes. Socio-psychological constraint only.

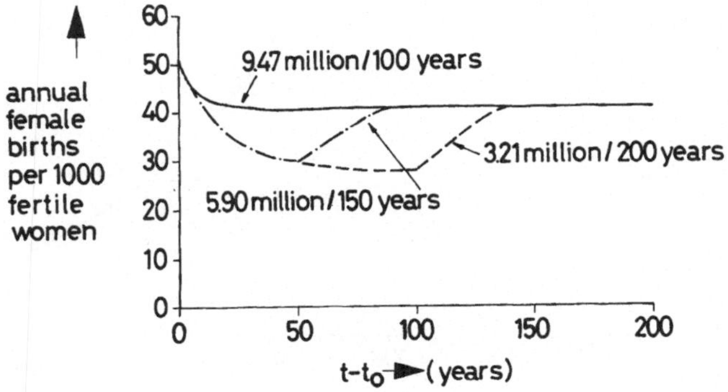

Fig. 5. Fertility as a function of time, for three different target populations. Socio-psychological constraint only.

Demographic burden; economic constraint

An important indicator for demographic processes is the demographic burden as defined in the Introduction. The demographic burden gives a rough indication of the economic effort the working part of the population has to make for the dependent, non-working part. On January 1, 1972, the demographic burden for the female Dutch population [9] was 0.856; for the total population it was 0.841. This last number means that each person in the age group from 20 to 65 has to take care of 0.841 person in the dependent age groups, as well as of himself.

Fig. 6 exhibits plots of the time histories of the demographic burden for each of the three cases considered in the previous section. These time histories typically show three periods. In the first period the demographic burden decreases considerably due to the diminishing juvenile part of the population. This trend reverses soon, until the demographic burden reaches a relatively high value in the second period, which may be attributed to the relative increase of the size of the age group over 65. Following this, the demographic burden settles at its stationary value of 0.837 for the female population.

The peak value that is reached by the demographic burden is about 0.95 for the third time history. Although it is not clear whether this value is insupportably high, it is of some interest to see what happens if the demographic burden is constrained not to exceed a given maximum value. The demographic burden of the female population during the time period j is given by

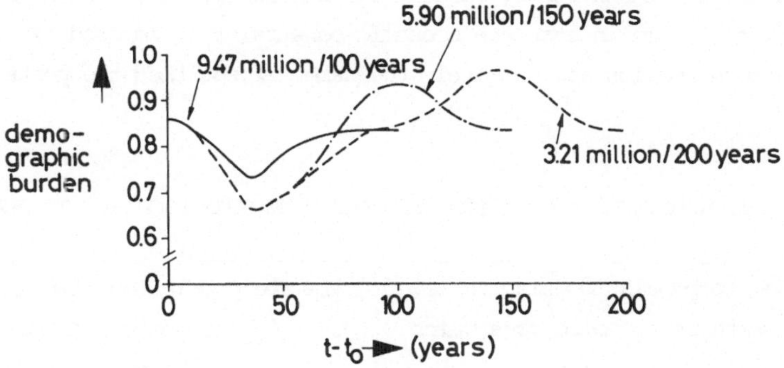

Fig. 6. Demographic burden as a function of time, for three different target populations. Socio-psychological constraint only.

$$d(j) = \frac{\sum_{i \in W^c} p(i,j)}{\sum_{i \in W} p(i,j)}, \tag{15}$$

where $W = \{\frac{20}{h}+1, \frac{20}{h}+2, \ldots, \frac{65}{h}\}$, and W^c is the complement of W in $\{1,2,\ldots,n\}$.

We now add the economic constraint

$$d(j) \leq \alpha \quad , \quad j = 0,1,\ldots,N, \tag{16}$$

where α is a prescribed maximum value. Using (15), this can be rewritten as

$$\sum_{i \in W^c} p(i,j) \leq \alpha \sum_{i \in W} p(i,j), \qquad j = 0,1,\ldots,N. \tag{17}$$

Substitution of $p(i,j)$ as given by (3) adds another set of inequality constraints to the linear constraints of the linear program described in the previous section. Again, numerical solution is straightforward if a linear programming code is available.

Table 2 gives some of the results, where the maximum demographic pressure α is rather arbitrarily taken to be 0.9, slightly higher than the present value of 0.856. The minimal population achievable in a given time span is slightly higher than in the case without economic constraint, but the differences are not alarming. The plots of Fig. 7 indicate the time histories of the birth volumes in comparison with the corresponding cases without economic constraint. It turns out that the time histories only undergo modifications around the time that the birth volume makes its transition from the minimum value to the stationary value. Fig. 8 shows plots of the demographic burden as a function of time in case the economic constraint is imposed. It is seen that the general pattern remains approximately the same, except that the peaks over 0.9 are cut off.

TABLE 2: RELATION BETWEEN POPULATION SIZE AND TIME SPAN REQUIRED TO REACH IT

time span (years)	female population size achieved without economic constraint (millions)	female population size achieved with economic constraint (millions)
100	9.47	9.47
150	5.90	6.30
200	3.21	3.77

On the whole, the effect of the economic constraint is minor. Moreover, it is to be expected that the problems caused by a demographic burden that is temporarily too high can be eased by temporary immigration (guest workers). We shall therefore omit the economic constraint in the remaining discussions.

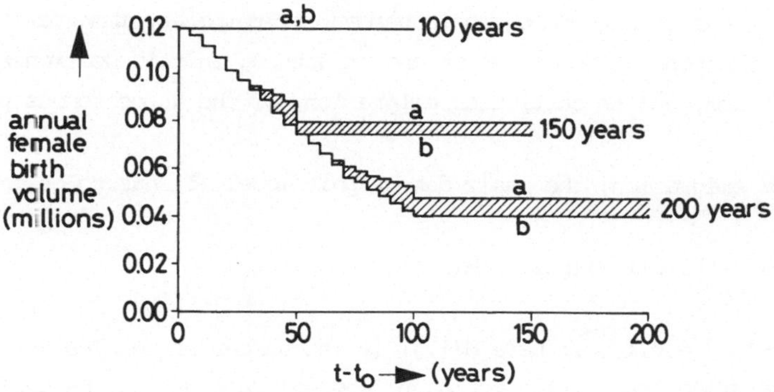

Fig. 7. Annual female birth volumes for three different time spans. a: economic and socio-psychological constraint; b: psycho-sociological constraint only.

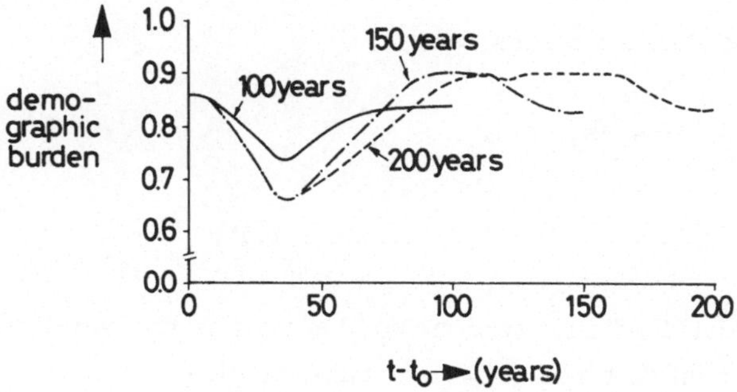

Fig. 8. Demographic burden as a function of time with economic constraint for three different time spans.

Migration

Up to this point we have totally ignored the possible effects of migration. It is clear that if the population size is to be reduced, emigration may play a useful role. At the end of the preceding section we have noted that temporary immigration may help to overcome periods of high demographic burden. As temporary immigration has no lasting effect on the population evolution and structure, in this section we shall only consider migration, and in particular emigration, of the autochtonous population.

To account for emigration, the basic demographic model (1) has to be modified to

$$p(i+1,j+1) = [1-\mu(i,j)]p(i,j)-M(i,j), \tag{18}$$

$i = 1,2,\ldots,n-1$; $j = 0,1,\ldots$. Here $M(i,j)$ is the number of females who at time t_o+jh are in the age group from $(i-1)h$ to ih and who emigrate during the period from t_o+jh to $t_o+(j+1)h$. Solution of these equations together with (2) yields

$$p(i,j) = \begin{cases} \beta(i,j)p(i-j,0)-\sum\limits_{k=1}^{\min(i-1,j)} \beta_k(i,j)M(i-k,j-k), & j = 0,1,\ldots,i-1, \\ \beta(i,j)u(j-i) - \sum\limits_{k=1}^{\min(i-1,j)} \beta_k(i,j)M(i-k,j-k), & j = i,\ i+1,\ldots, \end{cases} \tag{19}$$

where $\beta(i,j)$ is as defined before, and

$$\beta_k(i,j) = \prod_{s=1}^{k-1} [1-\mu(i-s,j-s)], \tag{20}$$

$i = 1,2,\ldots n$; $j = 0,1,2,\ldots$; $k = 1,2,\ldots,\min(i-1,j)$.

For lack of more detailed information, we assume that the age distribution of the emigrating population does not vary with time, so that

$$M(i,j) = q(i)e(j), \quad i = 1,2,\ldots,n,\ j = 0,1,\ldots. \tag{21}$$

Here $q(i)$ is the fraction of emigrating women in the age group from $(i-1)h$ to ih, $i = 1,2,\ldots n$, while $e(j)$ represents the total number of women emigrating during the period t_o+jh to $t_o+(j+1)h$.

The choice of the age distribution $q(i)$, $i = 1,2,\ldots n$, was made on the basis of emigration data for The Netherlands during the period 1950 to 1953 [12]. This was a period of high emigration. The distribution is graphically presented in Fig. 9.

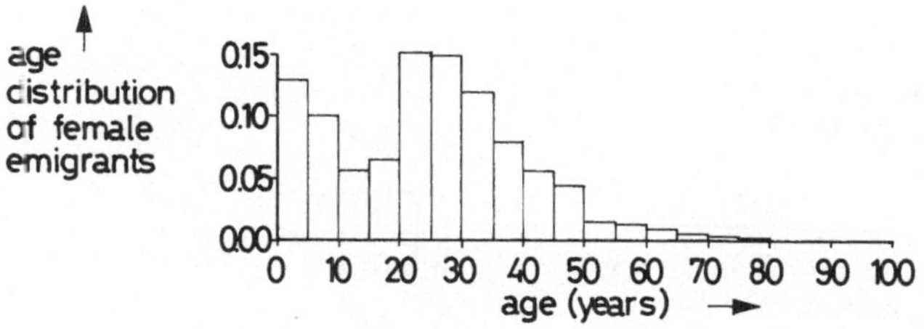

Fig. 9. Age distribution of female emigrants. Fraction of female emigrants in each age group.

The emigration volumes e(j), j = 0,1,...,N-1, are control variables, in addition to the birth volumes u(j), j = 0,1,...,N-1. In order to achieve a stationary situation - without emigration - at the final time N, emigration has to be stopped during the n time periods before the final instant. We therefore set e(N-n) = e(N-n+1) = ... = e(N-1) = 0, which leaves e(j), j = 0,1,...,N-n-1, as control variables. An additional benefit of this is that there is no emigration during periods of high demographic burden (see the plots of Fig. 6), which appears very reasonable.

Emigration is constrained by the requirement

$$0 \leq e(j) \leq \xi(j)h \sum_{i=1}^{n} p(i,j), \quad j = 0,1,\ldots,N-n-1. \tag{22}$$

Here ξ(j) is the maximal fraction of the total female population annually emigrating during the period from t_o+jh to $t_o+(j+1)h$.

We can now consider the problem of minimizing the final stationary population size, including the contribution of emigration, while taking into account the socio-psychological constraint, the economic constraint, or both. Since the economic constraint was seen to be of minor importance, first only the socio-psychological constraint is included. Substitution of p(i,j) as given by (19) into (9) and (22) leads to another linear programming problem, with a number of inequality constraints, and with u(j), j = 0,1,...,N-n-1, $\bar{u}$, and m(j), j = 0,1,...,N-n-1, as independent variables. Also this problem can be solved using a standard linear programming code together with an input program to set up the initial tableau.

Numerical results were obtained for ξ(j) = 0.05, j = 0,1,...,N-n-1, i.e. a maximal emigration of 0.5% annually. This figure corresponds to the highest percentage observed in the fifties. Figure 10 gives some of the results for a total period of 150 years. Emigration is always at its maximal value. The annual birth volume steadily decreases until after about 35 years, when it exhibits a steep rise before falling off to its steady-state value. The peak may be explained by the interference of the social and the emigration constraint: in order to allow emigration to assume its maximal

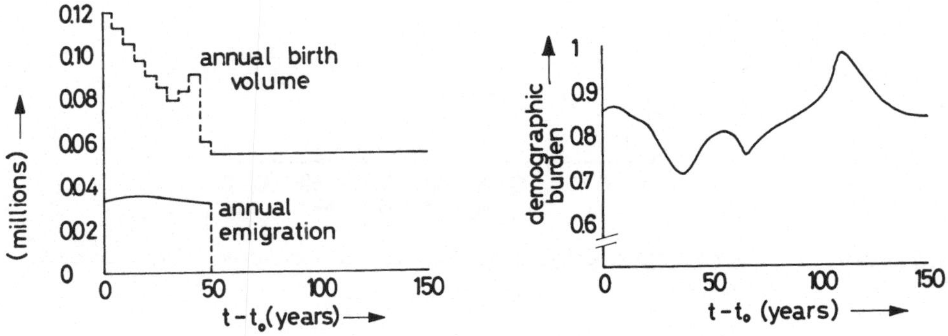

Fig. 10. Annual female births, emigration and demographic burden for a time span of 150 years. Socio-psychological and emigration constraints only.

value, the birth volume temporarily has to rise.

The right-hand side of Fig. 10 shows the time behavior of the demographic burden corresponding to the left-hand side. The irregular behavior may be attributed to the strongly varying behavior of the birth volume. The peak value of 0.98 is higher than in the case without emigration.

The total stationary female population size that is reached after 150 years is 4.30 million, as compared to 5.90 million without emigration. This shows that the potential effect of emigration is considerable.

In a subsequent computation, of which no graphs are shown, the demographic burden was constrained not to exceed the value 0.9. The solution features maximal emigration, a less irregular behavior of the birth volume, and a final stationary female population size of 4.59 million.

Sensitivity study

A simple sensitivity study has been performed by repeating some of the calculations while varying the most critical parameters. In the computations involving the socio-psychological constraint, the parameters r (the eventual maximal reduction in fertility) and θ (the time constant corresponding to which fertility decreases) were initially rather arbitrarily chosen and therefore open to question. Table 3 shows results of computations for a total period of 150 years and different values of r and θ. It is seen that the differences in eventual population sizes are considerable, which is not unexpected.

TABLE 3. CALCULATIONS WITH SOCIO-PSYCHOLOGICAL CONSTRAINT FOR A TIME PERIOD OF 150 YEARS. EVENTUAL FEMALE POPULATION SIZES FOR DIFFERENT VALUES OF r AND θ (MILLIONS).

θ (years)	r 0.5	r 0.6	r 0.7
10	3.53	4.91	6.52
20	4.58	5.90	7.38
30	5.60	6.81	8.14

Discussion

The results of the computations that have been made in the context of this study lead to a number of conclusions. First of all we may conclude that if the goal of a population policy for The Netherlands is to reduce the present size of 13.5 million to a stationary size of 5 million or less - the objective of the Dutch version of "A Blueprint for Survival" [2] - this goal cannot be reached within 200 years (without emigration). Furthermore, it is found that the minimum time to reach a more or less stationary population - no matter what size - is about 80 years; the resulting total population size would be about 19 million.

The computations also show that (without emigration) the social constraint essentially determines the time needed to reach a desired population size. The economic constraint, included to prevent anomalies in the age distribution, turns out to play a minor role. Emigration may be a helpful factor in reducing the eventual population size.

It may be furthermore be seen from the numerical results that the <u>long-term</u> goal of reaching a stationary population of reduced size for the next decades may be translated into <u>short-term</u> tactics consisting of reducing fertility as quickly as socially acceptable - not a very surprising result. The time period over which this short-term policy is to be continued depends on the desired eventual population size and may vary from 50 to 150 years. This means that a decision concerning the desired population size may be postponed for some time.

There is no need to discuss extensively the means that are available for the implementation of a population policy as outlined. Important instruments are: information about birth control, education of the public, social security policy, tax measures, and abortion legislature. The use of an active emigration policy is also evident.

There is no question that the transition as studied in this paper, from the present society to a society with a stationary age distribution and a reduced size, will have major effects. The sweeping changes in age distribution and population size will have far-reaching consequences for the economic activity, education, health care, housing and social security [13]. To illustrate this, Figure 11 shows the time behavior of two indicators for the transition requiring 150 years (without economic constraint and without emigration). The figure presents the time history of the numbers of women in the age groups 0-20 and 65+, in absolute magnitudes and as percentages of the total female population. It is seen that the age group 0-20 after an initial slight increase steadily decreases in size, to stabilize after about 70 years at a constant value. This phenomenon will of course sharply affect the requirements for educational facilities.

The age group 65+ on the other hand increases to more than double its present size. The maximum is reached in about 75 years, after which this population group starts decreasing again. This effect will have important consequences for the need for all sorts of provisions for the aged.

Of course the credibility of the results of the computations strongly depends on the explicit and implicit assumptions. In the sensitivity analysis of the preceding section the effects of changing certain assumptions are pointed out. All of the qualitative conclusions, as presented in the preceding paragraphs, remain unaffected, however.

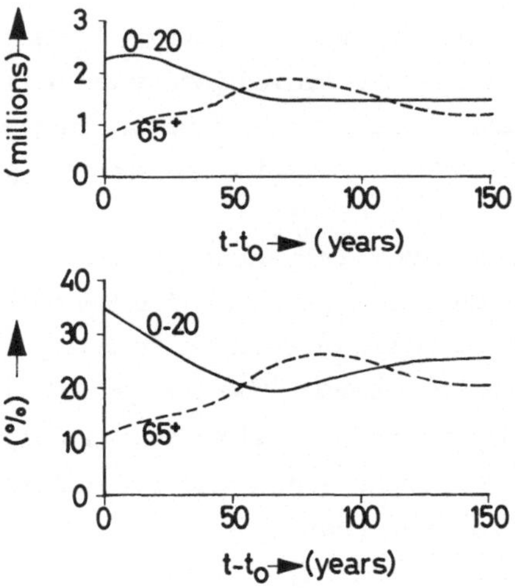

Fig. 11. Time histories of the sizes of the age groups 0-20 and 65+. Socio-psychological constraint only; time span 150 years.

Conclusion

The purpose of the study reported in this paper was to investigate whether considering population policy as an optimal control problem could help determining the possibilities and impossibilities of practical population policy. It is seen that interesting conclusions can be reached, both quantitatively and qualitatively.

Acknowledgement

The author gratefully acknowledges the contribution of J. Jeuring, A. Bosch-de Boer, B.H. Hoeksma and E.A.W. Bolle to the work described in this paper. He is also very grateful to H. Posthumus for completing and running a rather complicated computer program under a high pressure of time.

References

[1] E. Goldsmith, ed., A Blueprint for Survival. Hammondsworth: Penguin Books (1972), 1975. Reprint from The Ecologist vol. 2, no. 1.

[2] Blauwdruk voor Overleving. Amsterdam: Contact, 1973.

[3] M. Mesarovic and E. Pestel, Mankind at the Turning Point: The Second Report to the Club of Rome. New York, 1974.

[4] J. Jeuring, "Bevolkingspolitiek als optimaal besturingsprobleem" (Population policy as an optimal control problem: in Dutch). Student project report, Department of Applied Mathematics, Twente University of Technology, December, 1972.

[5] A. Bosch-de Boer, "Bevolkingspolitiek als optimaal besturingsprobleem II" (Population policy as an optimal control problem II: in Dutch). Student project report, Department of Applied Mathematics, Twente University of Technology, January, 1974.

[6] B.H. Hoeksma, "Bevolkingspolitiek als optimaal besturingsprobleem IV" (Population policy as an optimal control problem IV: in Dutch). Student project report, Department of Applied Mathematics, Twente University of Technology, March, 1975.

[7] H. Kwakernaak, "Bevolkingspolitiek als optimaal besturingsprobleem" (Population policy as an optimal control problem: in Dutch). De Ingenieur, vol. 87, no. 46, pp. 911-917 (November 13, 1975).

[8] G.J. Olsder, R.C.W. Strijbos, "Population planning: a distributed time optimal control problem". Proc. 7th IFIP Conference on Optimization Techniques, Lecture Notes in Computer Science no. 40, p. 721-735. Berlin: Springer, 1976.

[9] Centraal Bureau voor Statistiek (Central Bureau of Statistics), Statistisch Zakboek 1974 (Statistical Pocket Book 1974: in Dutch). Den Haag: Staatsuitgeverij, 1974.

[10] Centraal Bureau voor de Statistiek (Central Bureau of Statistics), "Berekeningen omtrent de toekomstige bevolkingsgroei in Nederland in de periode 1970-2000" ("Computations regarding the future population growth in The Netherlands in the period 1970-2000": in Dutch), CBS-publication nr. B-2. Den Haag: Staatsuitgeverij, 1971.

[11] Centraal Bureau voor de Statistiek (Central Bureau of Statistics), "Toekomstige Nederlandse bevolkingsontwikkeling na 1972" ("Future population development in The Netherlands after 1972": in Dutch), CBS-publication nr. B-13. Den Haag: Staatsuitgeverij, 1973.

[12] Centraal Bureau voor de Statistiek (Central Bureau of Statistics), "Statistiek van de buitenlandse migratie" (Statistics of foreign migration : in Dutch), CBS-publication nr. B-3. Den Haag: Staatsuitgeverij, appears annually.

[13] P. van der Hoek, "De maatschappelijke gevolgen van veranderingen van de leeftijdsstruktuur van de bevolking" (Social effects of changes of the age structure of the population: in Dutch). Student project report no. SII-110, Department of Mechanical Engineering, Delft University of Technology, March 1975.

SOME ASPECTS ON THE CONTROL OF LARGE TANKERS

K.J. Åström
Department of Automatic Control
Lund Institute of Technology
S-220 07 LUND 7, Sweden.

ABSTRACT

This paper reviews models for ship-steering dynamics and for disturbances due to wind and waves. Criteria for ship steering and autopilot design are discussed. The performance of fixed gain autopilots under different operating conditions is analysed. It is shown that there is a good incentive to use adaptive autopilots.

1. INTRODUCTION

Control problems associated with steering of large tankers are discussed in this paper. Many of the arguments can be applied to ship-steering in general. A particular problem with large tankers is, however, that they may be directionally unstable in certain operating conditions. This gives rise to special problems.

The paper is organized as follows. A review of ship-dynamics is given in section 2. The characterization of disturbances due to winds, waves and currents is the topic of section 3. Section 4 deals with criteria. It is shown that normal course-keeping fits nicely into the linear-quadratic-gaussian formulation of the control problem. The control design is thus straightforward. For turning it is, however, important to take the nonlinear effects into account. The processdynamics and the characteristics of the disturbances will change with the operating conditions. The consequences of this for the control system design are discussed in section 5. Analysis based on a simple model gives the order of magnitudes involved. It is shown that it is indeed possible to find a constant gain controller which gives a closed loop system which is reasonably damped. There is, however, a substantial loss in performance with a controller having fixed gains and consequently a gain by having an adaptive controller.

2. SHIP-STEERING DYNAMICS

The equations describing the motion of a ship are well known. They are obtained from conservation of momentum and angular momentum. See Norrbin (1960) and Abkowitz (1964). It is customary to write the equations using a coordinate frame fixed to the ship. See Fig. 1. If the ship is considered as a rigid body it has 6 degrees of freedom. The translational motions are called surge, sway and heave, and the rotational motions are called roll, pitch and yaw. For a ship like a tanker there is little coupling between the different modes and the steering dynamics can therefore be described by considering the surge, sway and yaw motions separately. Introduce coordinates and variables as shown in Fig. 1. The equations of motion can be written as

$$
\begin{aligned}
&m(\dot{u} - vr - x_G r) = X \\
&m(\dot{v} + ur + x_G \dot{r}) = Y \qquad (2.1) \\
&I_z \dot{r} + m x_G (\dot{v} + ru) = N
\end{aligned}
$$

where u and v are the x- and y-coordinates of the velocity and x_G denotes the x-coordinate of the center of mass. The right hand sides of (2.1) are the hydrodynamic forces and moments. These are complicated functions of the motion which are often expressed as functions of acceleration, velocity and helm angle. The main difficulty in modeling shipdynamics is to find suitable expressions for the hydrodynamic forces. The first equation in (2.1) is often neglected when analysing steering because the forward speed u can often be regarded as being a constant.

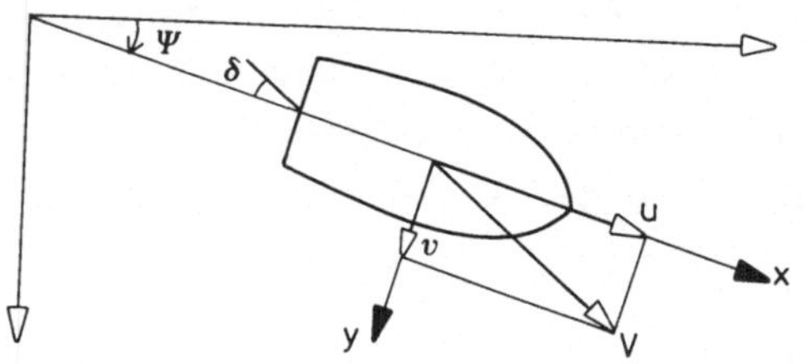

Fig. 1 - Coordinates and variables used for the equation of motion.

Stationary Mctions

Assuming that the rudder is kept in a fixed position the steady state solutions to the equations of motion are obtained by setting time derivatives in (2.1) equal to zero. For slender ships which are directionally stable there is only one stationary solution. For large tankers it can frequently happen that there are three steady state solutions. For example when the rudder is held at center position a directionally stable ship will have a solution corresponding to a straight line motion. For a large tanker this motion can be unstable. Instead there are two stable stationary motions corresponding to turning port or starboard with constant yaw rate. It is common practice to represent the stationary motions with a graph of yaw rate against rudder angle as shown by the curve in Fig. 2. The curve can be determined experimentally by controlling the ship for a constant turning rate and measuring the mean value of the rudder angle.

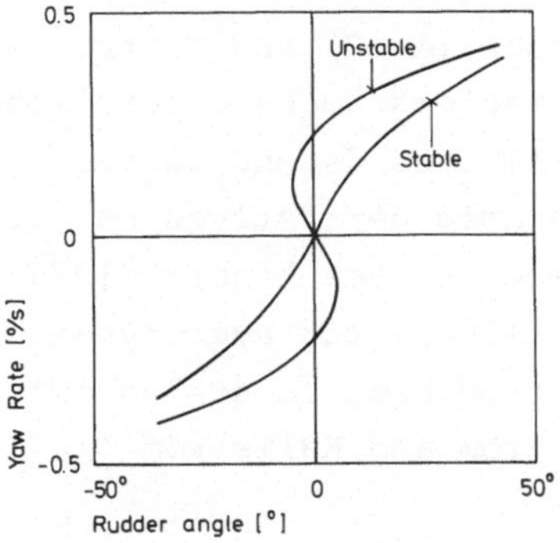

Fig. 2 - Steady state yaw rate as a function of rudder angle.

Linearization

To linearize the equations of motion it is necessary to introduce the partial derivatives of the hydrodynamic forces and moments. The partial derivatives are called 'hydrodynamic derivatives'. They are denoted as follows

$$Y_v = \frac{\partial Y}{\partial v}$$

Using this notation the equations of motion (2.1) can be linearized around the stationary solution v = 0, r = 0 and u = u_0 to give

$$\begin{bmatrix} m-Y_{\dot{v}} & mx_G-Y_{\dot{r}} \\ mx_G-N_{\dot{v}} & I_z-N_{\dot{r}} \end{bmatrix} \begin{bmatrix} \dot{v} \\ \dot{r} \end{bmatrix} = \begin{bmatrix} Y_v & Y_r-mu_0 \\ N_v & N_r-mx_Gu_0 \end{bmatrix} \begin{bmatrix} v \\ r \end{bmatrix} + \begin{bmatrix} Y_\delta \\ N_\delta \end{bmatrix} \delta \qquad (2.2)$$

The derivatives $Y_{\dot{v}}$ and $N_{\dot{r}}$ are negative. They appear in the linearized equations in the same way as mass and inertia, and are therefore called 'added mass' and 'added inertia'. In more accurate representations these terms will depend on the frequency of excitation. The equations of motion are customary rewritten using dimension-free variables by introducing the length of a ship as unit of length and the time it takes to travel a shiplength as the time unit.

The hydrodynamic derivatives can be determined approximatively from hydrodynamic theory. See Comstock (1967) and Norrbin (1971). The derivatives will depend on many factors among others loading, trim and waterdepth..The derivatives will thus depend on the operating conditions of the ship. The hydrodynamic derivatives can also be determined from experiments using scale models. See Motora (1973), Comstock (1967) and Strøm-Tejsen and Chislett (1966). The hydrodynamic derivatives have recently been determined from experiments on ships using system identification methods. See Åström and Källström (1973, 1976) and Åström et al (1974).

State Equations

The linearized equations of motion (2.2) are easily converted to state space form by solving for the derivatives $\dot{v}$ and $\dot{r}$. This gives the following model for the yaw motion of the ship

$$\frac{d}{dt}\begin{bmatrix} v \\ r \\ \psi \end{bmatrix} = \begin{bmatrix} a_{11} & a_{12} & 0 \\ a_{21} & a_{22} & 0 \\ 0 & 1 & 0 \end{bmatrix} \begin{bmatrix} v \\ r \\ \psi \end{bmatrix} + \begin{bmatrix} b_{11} \\ b_{21} \\ 0 \end{bmatrix} \delta \qquad (2.3)$$

where the heading ψ has been introduced as a state variable.

The linearized ship-steering dynamics can thus be described as a third order dynamical system. It was shown in Åström and Källström (1976) that the numerical values of the parameters of the model (2.3) are remarkably similar for many different ships. The parameters will, however, depend on loading, trim and depth.

Transfer Function Models

It follows from (2.3) that the input-output relation between the rudder angle δ and the heading ψ can be represented by the transfer function

$$G(s) = \frac{b_1 s + b_2}{s(s^2 + a_1 s + a_2)} = \frac{K(1 + sT_3)}{s(1 + sT_1)(1 + sT_2)} \tag{2.4}$$

where

$$a_1 = -a_{11} - a_{22}$$

$$a_2 = a_{11}a_{22} - a_{12}a_{21}$$

$$b_1 = b_{21}$$

$$b_2 = a_{21}b_{11} - a_{11}b_{21}$$

The model (2.4) is commonly used for analysing steering and autopilots. The form (2.4) suggest the approximation

$$G_2(s) = \frac{K}{s(1 + sT_N)} \tag{2.5}$$

which was originally proposed by Nomoto (1957).

Nonlinear Models

The linearized models can adequately describe the motion of a ship on straight line course. For tankers the linearized models are, however, inadequate for turning. The nonlinear terms in the equations of motion become important even at moderate yaw rates. Compare Fig. 2. The nonlinear models are obtained by Taylor series expansions of the hydrodynamic forces and moments. Beck and Smitt (1969) have proposed the following approximative model

$$T_1T_2\frac{d^2r}{dt^2} + (T_1+T_2)\frac{dr}{dt} + KH(r) = K(\delta+T_3\frac{d\delta}{dt}) \tag{2.6}$$

where H is the nonlinear function which gives the steady-state relation between δ and r. See Fig. 2.

3. DISTURBANCES

The motion of a ship is influenced by wind, waves and current. Since the purpose of the autopilot is to counteract the influences of the disturbances it is of interest to characterize the disturbances. The currents will not influence the hydrodynamic forces. They will, however, influence the inertial velocity of the ship. There will be a considerable influence of the motion due to wind and waves. In a simplified analysis this is handled by introducing the forces and the moments generated by wind and waves. The equations of motion (2.1) are then changed to

$$\begin{aligned}
m[\dot{u}-(v+v_c)r-x_G r] &= X + X_{wind} + X_{waves} \\
m[\dot{v}+(u+u_c)r+x_G\dot{r}] &= Y + Y_{wind} + Y_{waves} \\
I_z\dot{r}+mx_G[\dot{v}+r(u+u_c)] &= N + N_{wind} + N_{waves}
\end{aligned} \tag{3.1}$$

where v_c and u_c are the velocity components of the current. X_{wind}, Y_{wind} and N_{wind} are the forces and moments generated by the wind and X_{waves}, Y_{waves} and N_{waves} are the forces and moments generated by the waves. Equation (3.1) is only an approximation because the superposition principle is not necessarily valid for large motion. There may also be couplings to the other motions due to wind and waves. For example a pitching motion can change the area exposed to the wind considerably. The moment N_{waves} may thus depend on the pitch angle. Similarly the airflow around the ship may be significantly influenced by the waves which also indicates that it is not always correct to separate the forces due to wind and waves. Under many operating conditions equation (3.1) is, however, a reasonable approximation.

Currents

The influence of currents will now be discussed. In the X-equation v_c appears in the product $v_c r$ which is neglected in the linearized equation. In the Y- and N-equations the current u_c appears in the combination $u+u_c$. The influence of u_c will not be very large unless the currents are comparable to the forward velocity. Since the components of the current u_c and v_c will depend on the heading the currents will also introduce a coupling between yaw angle and the Y- and N-equations.

Windgenerated Disturbances

The windforces X_{wind}, Y_{wind} and the wind moment N_{wind} depend on the shape of the ship above the waterline and the relative windforce as seen from the ship. The windgenerated disturbances will thus also depend on the motion of the ship because this will influence the relative windspeed. The windforces have been investigated both theoretically and experimentally by Wagner (1976) and van Berlekom et al (1975). Wagner (1967) gives the following models for the windforces

$$X_{wind} = \frac{1}{2} C_X(\upsilon) \rho V^2 A_\ell$$

$$Y_{wind} = \frac{1}{2} C_Y(\upsilon) \rho V^2 A_\ell$$

$$N_{wind} = \frac{1}{2} C_N(\upsilon) \rho V^2 A_\ell$$

where ρ and V are air-density and relative wind velocity. The area A_ℓ is the area above the waterline of the ships projection on the x, y-plane. The angle υ is the angle between the relative air velocity and the x-axis. See Fig. 3.

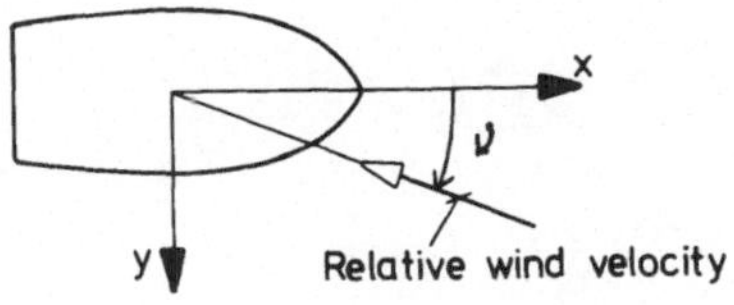

Fig. 3

For a symmetrical ship the functions C_x, C_y and C_N have the following form

$$C_x(\upsilon) = C_x \cos\upsilon$$

$$C_y(\upsilon) = C_y \sin\upsilon$$

$$C_N(\upsilon) = C_N \sin 2\upsilon$$

The paper van Berlekom et al (1975) gives the functions C_x, C_y and C_N for typical tanker configurations based on wind tunnel tests. The wind velocity is modeled as the sum of a constant term and a stochastic term which characterizes the turbulence. Turbulence data is presented in Lumley and Panofsky (1964). The turbulence scale L is approximatively proportional to altitude $L \approx 0.9h$. For typical tankers the turbulence scale is thus smaller than the length of the ship. This means that it is not unreasonable to consider the random fluctuations as white noise. Introducing the expression (3.2) for the windforces into the equation of motion gives the following linearized equations

$$\frac{d}{dt}\begin{bmatrix} v \\ r \\ \psi \end{bmatrix} = \begin{bmatrix} a_{11} & a_{12} & a_{13} \\ a_{21} & a_{22} & a_{23} \\ 0 & 1 & 0 \end{bmatrix} \begin{bmatrix} v \\ r \\ \psi \end{bmatrix} + \begin{bmatrix} b_{11} \\ b_{21} \\ 0 \end{bmatrix} \delta + \begin{bmatrix} e_1 \\ e_2 \\ 0 \end{bmatrix} \qquad (3.3)$$

Compare with (2.3). The effect of the wind in the linearized equations is thus that the coupling terms a_{13} and a_{23} and the disturbances e_1 and e_2 are added. The numerical values of a_{13} and a_{23} will depend on the angle υ. The parameters a_{13} and a_{23} may well change sign. The transfer function corresponding to (3.3) is

$$G(s) = \frac{b_2 s + b_3}{s^3 + a_1 s^2 + a_2 s + a_3} \qquad (3.4)$$

where

$$a_1 = -a_{11} - a_{22} \qquad b_2 = b_{21}$$

$$a_2 = a_{11}a_{22} - a_{12}a_{21} - a_{23} \qquad b_3 = a_{21}b_{11} - a_{11}b_{21}$$

$$a_3 = a_{11}a_{23} - a_{13}a_{21}$$

Compare with (2.4). Notice that in the presence of winds the transfer function relating heading to rudder angle will not necessarily contain an integrator. Experimental evidence of this is given in Åström and Källström (1976).

Wavegenerated Disturbances

There will be substantial forces and moments on a ship due to the motion of the sea. Several attempts have been made to model those forces. Zuidweg (1970) has made the simplifying assumption that the seawaves can be described as a plane sinusoidal wave. The forces and moments can be approximatively described as

$$\begin{aligned} Y_{waves} &= \hat{Y}(\mu)\ \sin\omega t \\ N_{waves} &= \hat{N}(\mu)\ \cos\omega t \end{aligned} \tag{3.5}$$

where μ is the angle between the x-axis and the direction of wave propagation. See Fig. 4. Zuidweg also gives explicit expressions for the functions $\hat{Y}$ and $\hat{N}$. Introducing (3.5) into the equations of motion and linearizing, we find that the linearized equations have the form (3.3) where the elements a_{13} and a_{23} are sine- and cosinefunctions of time. There will also be sinusoidal driving functions in the right hand side of the linearized equation. Zuidweg's model will thus lead to a linear system with periodically varying parameters.

Fig. 4

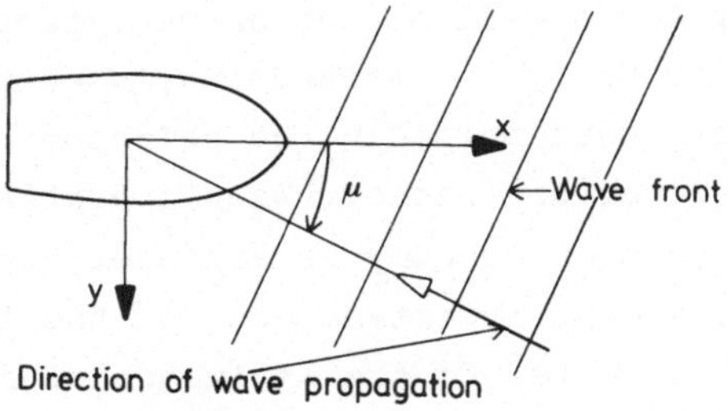

It is an oversimplification to assume that the waves in the ocean can be described as a plane sinusoidal wave. A more fruitful approach is to assume that the level of the sea is a stochastic process in space and time. The spectral density of this stochastic process has been determined both theoretically and empirically under many different conditions. The spectral density will vary significantly depending on wave height. An expository presentation is given by Price and Bishop (1974). The measured spectral densities indicate that the major contribution is from frequencies in the range 0.2 to 0.6 rad/s. Keeping in mind that the dominating time constants of a tanker are of the order of 100 s or more it is reasonable to consider the disturbances as white noise. Assuming that the sealevel is a random process the forces and moments can then be calculated in the same way as Zuidweg treated sinusoidal waves. This would lead to a linear system of the form (3.3) where a_{13}, a_{23}, e_1 and e_2 are random variables.

Summary

The influences of wind, waves and current are thus difficult to model. The disturbances will introduce couplings (a_{13} and a_{23}) from the heading to the sway and yaw equations as well as forcing terms (e_1 and e_2) in the linearized equations. The coupling are small at least for moderate disturbance levels and therefore often neglected. The forcing terms can be considered as the sum of constant and random components. Because of the long time constants of tankers it is reasonable to approximate the random components by white noise both for wind- and wave-generated forces. There is support for such assumptions in results from system identification applied to data from real tankers. See Åström and Källström (1976) and Åström et al (1974).

4. CRITERIA

The criteria to be used in the evaluation and design of autopilots will now be discussed. The criteria will depend on many factors like safety, propulsion economy and accuracy in pathkeeping. When steering in confined waters with several other ships in the neighborhood precision in pathkeeping is the most important factor. When operating in open sea far from other ships propulsion economy is of major concern. For large tankers this factor is the most important one and the following discussion will therefore be limited to the influence of steering on propulsion efficiency. Deviations from the desired heading will give a loss due to a longer distance travelled. The rudder deflections introduced to counteract deviations in heading will, however, give retarding forces. There will also be retarding forces caused by deviations in sway velocity and yaw rate. The x-component of the equation of motion (2.1) can be written as

$$m[\dot{u} - rv - r^2 x_g] = X(u, v, r, \psi, \delta, \dot{u})$$

It was shown by Norrbin (1972) that the most important contribution to the increase of resistance due to course deviations comes from the term vr which represents the Corioli's acceleration due to the coupling of yaw and sway velocity. Assuming small perturbations around a straight line course Norrbin also showed that the average increase in resistance due to steering could be approximatively described by

$$\frac{\Delta R}{R} = \alpha[\overline{\psi}^2 + \lambda \overline{\delta}^2] \tag{4.1}$$

where R is the drag ΔR the increase in drag due to steering $\overline{\psi}^2$ and $\overline{\delta}^2$ are the averages of the squared heading and rudder deviations respectively. Norrbin (1972) gives the values k = 0.014 and λ = 0.08 - 0.10 for a typical tanker. The earlier analysis by Nomoto (1966) which only included rudder losses and the loss due to the increased path gave λ = 8. When designing and evaluating autopilots for steering of tankers in open sea it therefore seems natural to use the following criterion

$$J = \frac{1}{T} \int_0^T [\psi^2(t) + \lambda \delta^2(t)] dt \tag{4.2}$$

We thus have one of the rare occasions when a quadratic performance criterion is physically well motivated and in particular when the weighing between state variable deviations and control actions is given a priori. The value of the lossfunction also corresponds directly to the relative increase in resistance. In a typical case one unit of the lossfunction corresponds to 1.4 % in the resistance.

Recalling that the deviations of the state variables that occur during normal steering are so small that the dynamics can be described by linearized models and that there are good reasons to characterize the disturbances due to wind and waves as random processes we find that the design of autopilots fits the framework of linear-quadratic-gaussian control theory. The design of a regulator for course keeping is therefore straightforward. For design of the turning regulator it is necessary to take the nonlinearities into account. The optimal course keeping regulator based on the model (2.3) and the criterion (4.2) consists of a state feedback from heading, yaw rate and sway velocity while a regulator based on the simple Nomoto model is a state feedback from heading and yaw rate only, i.e. a PD-regulator. It is necessary to include a model of the disturbances, and the regulator will then also contain feedback from the disturbance states. A simple case is to model the disturbances as a constant but unknown moment. Together with the simple Nomoto model this leads to an ordinary PID-regulator which is the basis for most commercial autopilots. The regulators obtained using the more complete model (2.3) and a more detailed disturbance model will be more complex because it includes more statevariables. It is then convenient to use a Kalman filter to provide reliable estimates of the statevariables.

5. VARIATIONS IN PROCESS DYNAMICS AND DISTURBANCE

It has been demonstrated in the previous sections that the problem of controlling a large tanker in normal course keeping is a control problem that fits nicely into the linear-quadratic formulation. The design of a regulator composed of a state-feedback and a Kalman filter is therefore straightforward Such regulators have been determined by Zuidweg (1970). The process dynamics will, however, vary depending on operating conditions such as trim, loading and ocean depth. The characteristics of the disturbances will also vary depending on changing winds and waves. The consequences of these changes will be investigated in this section. In particular, the consequences of using a regulator with fixed feedback gains will be explored. The purpose of the analysis is to develop an understanding for the different effects and to provide order of magnitude estimates. Simple models will therefore be used. The problem of selecting a fixed gain autopilot which gives a closed loop system with good properties for a ship with changing dynamics will first be investigated. This analysis is done purely based on deterministic arguments. The problem of selecting optimal autopilot parameters will next be investigated. This requires stochastic models.

Deterministic Analysis

The linearized steering motion of a tanker can be approximatively described by the transfer function (2.4).

$$G(s) = \frac{K(1+sT_3)}{s(1+sT_1)(1+sT_2)} \approx \frac{K}{s(1+sT_N)} = \frac{K_1}{s(s+a)} \qquad (5.1)$$

which relates heading angle ψ to rudder angle δ. Typical values of the transfer function parameters for a tanker under different operating conditions are given in Table 1.

Table 1 - Parameters of the transfer function (5.1) for a tanker under different operating conditions.

Operating Conditions	T_1	T_2	T_3	K	T_N	a	$K_1 x10^6$
OC1 Ballast	80	15	40	-0.013	50	0.020	250
OC2 Delivery test	160	20	30	-0.040	150	0.007	275
OC3 Fully loaded	1000	25	60	-0.130	1000	0.001	130
OC4 Fully loaded	-300	30	65	0.040	-400	0.003	100

The transfer function parameters will thus change considerably depending on the operating conditions. The ship is stable in operating conditions 1, 2 and 3 but unstable in 4. Also, notice that it is advantageous to use the parameters K_1 and a rather than K and T because K_1 varies less than K. The parameter K_1 changes only by a factor of 3 over the operating conditions shown in Table 1.

To analyse the consequences of the parameter variations for controller design it will be assumed that the ship is controlled by a PD-regulator having the input-output relation

$$\delta(t) = -k_1[\psi - \psi_0] - k_2\frac{d\psi}{dt} \qquad (5.2)$$

where the controller gains k_1 and k_2 are bounded by

$$|k_1| \leq 10$$

$$|k_2| \leq 100 \text{ s} \qquad (5.3)$$

Notice that this regulator is identical to a state-feedback when the system is described by the simple Nomoto model. The bounds mean that a rudder deflection of 20° is obtained either by a heading error of 2° or a yaw rate error of 0.2°/s. In the analysis it will be assumed that the dynamics of the tanker can be described by the transfer function (5.1). The parameter K_1 is assumed constant and equal to -2×10^{-4} s^{-2}. The parameter a is assumed to vary in the range $-0.01 \leq a \leq 0.01$. This will represent the changes in dynamics due to changing operating conditions. Compare with the numbers given in Table 1. It is easy to show that the closed loop poles that are obtained with the regulator (5.2) whose parameters are constrained by (5.3) are those shown in Fig. 5.

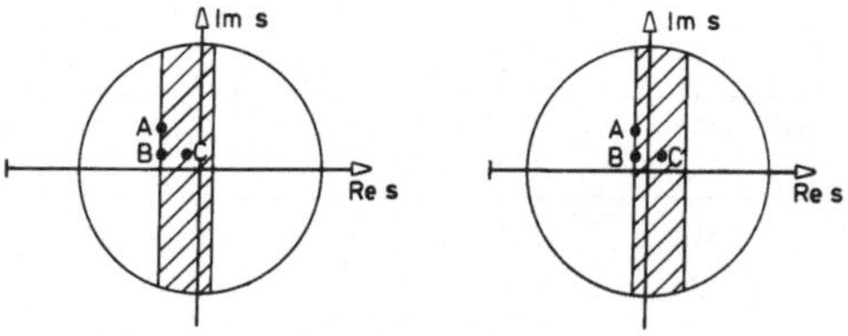

Fig. 5 - The shaded areas show possible positions of the closed loop poles obtained by a regulator (5.2) whose parameters are constrained by (5.1). The different dots correspond to the following gains, A: k_1=2.25, k_2=100, B: k_1=0.25, k_2=0 and C: k_1=0.25, k_2=100.

It is clear from Fig. 5 that the main difficulty in controlling a ship that may be both stable and unstable is to provide sufficient damping. The analysis also show that the essential limitation is due to the limited control authority (5.3). To further the selection of the parameters in an autopilot having fixed gains we will consider a system described by the transfer function where K_1 = -0.0002 and the parameter a can take any value in the interval (-0.01, 0.01). Fig. 6 shows the root loci for the closed loop system poles obtained for different regulator settings.

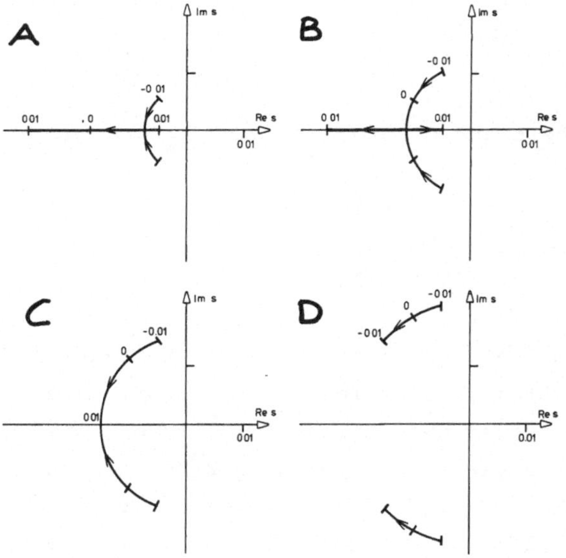

Fig. 6 - Root loci with respect to the parameter a for a closed loop system with regulators
A:k_1=0.25, k_2=100
B:k_1=0.625, k_2=100
C:k_1=1.125, k_2=100
D:k_1=2.125, k_2=100

Fig. 6 clearly shows the advantage of using high values of the controller gains. The figure also shows that it is not possible to get an entirely satisfactory solution with the constraints given by (5.3). The controller having $K_1 = 2.125$ and $K_2 = 100$ is acceptable for $0 \leq a \leq 0.01$ but it gives a poorly damped system for $a = -0.01$.

The purely deterministic analysis indicates that it is possible to choose a fixed gain regulator that will perform acceptably over the whole range of parameter values. The analysis also indicates that the feedback gains k_1 and k_2 should be chosen as high as possible. In the particular case discussed here the effective constraint on the rate feedback is due to the limited control authority (5.3) and the effective constraint on the proportional gain k_1 is due to the requirement on damping.

Stochastic Analysis

The heading signal is normally taken from the gyrocompass. There will be disturbances in this singal due to limited resolution and measurement noise. The rate feedback is obtained by taking the derivative of the heading or from a rate gyro. In both cases there will be disturbances in the measured signal. The disturbances acting on the ship will also vary considerably due to changing wind, waves and currents. A simplified case will again be analysed to provide the qualitative aspects of the trade-off required. Using the simple Nomoto model, the closed loop system can be represented by the blockdiagram shown in Fig. 7.

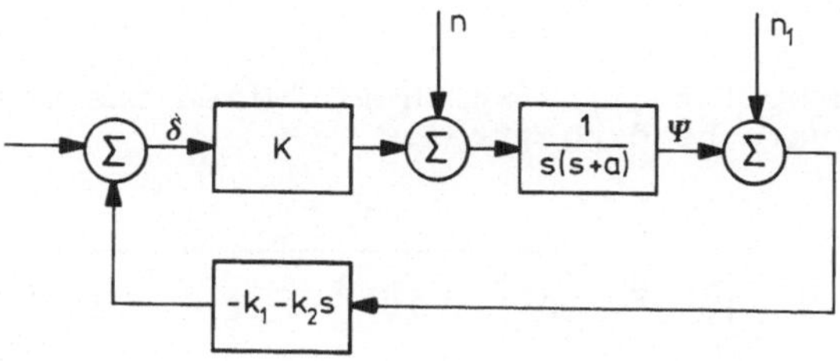

Fig. 7 - Blockdiagram of ship with autopilot.

Assuming small perturbations the relation between the heading and the disturbances can be described by the equation

$$\theta(s) = \frac{N(s) - K_1(k_1+k_2s)N_1(s)}{s^2+s(a+K_1k_2)+K_1k_1} \qquad (5.4)$$

where θ, N and N_1 are the Laplace transforms of heading angle, disturbance torque acting on the ship and noise in the heading measurement. The important factor is the relative magnitudes of the torque disturbance and the measurement noise. In a simplified analysis it is not unreasonable to model n and n_1 as white noises with spectral densities $2\pi\phi$ and $2\pi\phi_1$ respectively. It is easy to show that the mean square heading error is

$$E\psi^2 = \frac{\phi+(K_1^3k_1k_2^2+K_1^2k_1)\phi_1}{2K_1k_1(a+K_1k_2)} \tag{5.5}$$

Minimization of the heading error gives the following optimal controller settings

$$\begin{aligned} K_1k_1 &= \sqrt{\phi/\phi_1} \\ K_1k_2 &= -a + \sqrt{a^2+2\sqrt{\phi/\phi_1}} \end{aligned} \tag{5.6}$$

Notice that the optimal gains only depend on the ratio ϕ/ϕ_1. The minimum value of the lossfunction is

$$E\psi^2 = \phi_1[\sqrt{a+2\sqrt{\phi/\phi_1}}-a] \tag{5.7}$$

The optimal controller settings for different signal to noise ratios are given in Table 2.

Table 2 - Autopilot gains which minimizes the mean square heading error.

ϕ/ϕ_1		10^{-10}	10^{-9}	10^{-8}	10^{-7}	10^{-6}
k_1		0.05	0.16	0.50	1.6	5
k_2	a = 0.01	5	14	37	85	180
	a = 0	22	40	70	126	225
	a = -0.01	105	114	137	185	280

The ratio ϕ/ϕ_1 expresses the relation between the disturbances from wind and waves and those due to measurement errors. The ratio will depend on sea conditions in a fairly complicated way. The general tendency is, however, that ϕ/ϕ_1 increases with increasing wind and waves. It thus follows from Table 2 that low values of controller gains are optimal under nice weather conditions and that the gains should be increased in bad weather. The Table also indicates that the proportional gain k_1 is changed most and that the variations in k_2 are smaller. It also follows from Table 2 that the value of the proportional gain does not depend on a. This gain is thus the same for a stable (a = 0.01) and an unstable (a = -0.01) ship. The rate gain will, however, depend on a. The variation in k_2 with a is larger for small ϕ/ϕ_1 i.e. nice sea conditions.

The minimum values of the variance of the heading error are shown in Table 3. It is seen from the Table that the heading error will vary significantly with the operating conditions. Notice in particular that under fair operating conditions ($\phi/\phi_1 = 10^{-10}$) there is a significant difference between the minimal lossfunctions for a stable and an unstable ship. Notice that the differences between the stable and the unstable ship are less for operating conditions which correspond to heavier seas ($\phi/\phi_1 = 10^{-6}$).

Table 3 - Normalized variances of heading errors for optimal regulators under different operating conditions. In brackets are also shown the errors obtained for two regulators having fixed gain.

a \ ϕ/ϕ_1	10^{-10}	10^{-8}	10^{-6}
0.01	1.0(6.2, 31.3)	7.3(8.2, 31.4)	35.8(214.5, 38.9)
0	4.5(10.6, 36.9)	14.1(14.1, 37.0)	44.7(368, 45.9)
-0.01	20.9(37.1, 45)	27.3(49.5, 45.1)	55.8(1287, 55.8)

In Table 3 are also shown the lossfunctions obtained for controllers having fixed gain. One regulator chosen is optimal for a = 0 (i.e. a marginally stable ship) and $\phi/\phi_1 = 10^{-8}$. This regulator gives substantially higher losses than the optimal controller for nice sea conditions ($\phi/\phi_1 = 10^{-10}$). For bad sea conditions the controller gives a poor performance in particular for an unstable tanker. This agrees with the empirical observation that an autopilot which is well tuned for nice sea conditions frequently is switched off in favour for manual control when the sea conditions get worse. The explanation is that the gains are too low to give good performance in bad sea conditions.

In Table 3 are also shown the performance of a fixed gain controller which is optimal for $\phi/\phi_1 = 10^{-6}$ and $a = -0.01$. This regulator has high gains and its performance changes only a little with different operating conditions. Notice, however, that the regulator gives a very poor performance for the stable ship under nice sea conditions. The lossfunction has the value 31.3 which should be compared with 1 for the optimal regulator. The heading errors are thus more than five times larger than necessary. The reason for this is that the errors in the rate measurement are feedback through the high gain thereby creating unnecessary large rudder motions.

It follows from (5.7) that the lossfunction is proportional to the spectral density of the measurement noise. This shows that it is beneficial to provide careful filtering of the measured signals. The analysis is admittedly based on a simplified model. This has the advantage that the influence of changing ship dynamics and changes in the environment can easily be investigated analytically. The simple model gives the main properties of the problem. To provide reliable quantitative information it is necessary to use more complicated models of the ship and its environment. Such studies based on simulation of more complete models and experiments on full-scale ships shows that the simple model given here gives the correct qualitative features.

6. CONCLUSIONS

Models for the steering dynamics of tankers, for disturbances due to wind and waves and for the performance have been given. It has been concluded that the course-keeping can be formulated as a linear quadratic control problem. For turning even at moderate rates it is, however, necessary to use nonlinear models of the tanker steering dynamics. The influences of parameter variations have been investigated. It has been shown based on an analysis of a simple model that a tanker which may be both stable and unstable depending on the operating conditions can be controlled by a PID-controller. It is possible to use a regulator with fixed gains to provide a reasonable damping over a wide operating range. Such a fixed gain regulator will, however, have a very poor performance in many of the operating conditions. The performance criterion can be improved significantly by tuning the controller parameters. There is a trade-off between elimination of disturbances due to wind and waves and elimination of effects of measurement errors. The general characteristics of the optimal controllers is that both proportional gain and rate gain are increased with increasing force disturbances. The changes in proportional gain are larger than the changes in the rate gain.

The minimum value of the performance index changes considerably with the operating conditions. The mean square heading error is substantially larger under bad weather conditions. There are also large differences in heading error in fair weather when the loading conditions are changed so that the ship changes from being stable to being unstable.

There is a good incentive to decrease the measurement noise by careful filtering. An adaptive autopilot which automatically tunes its parameters for optimum performance as defined by minimum propulsion resistance can be designed using the concept of self-tuning regulators discussed in Åström and Wittenmark (1972, 1973) and Åström, Borisson, Ljung and Wittenmark (1975). Such a regulator has been designed by Källström (1976). The regulator has been tested on several different tankers and it has been in continous operation on one tanker for more than a year.

7. ACKNOWLEDGEMENTS

Over the past years I have learned much about ship dynamics and control from discussions with Dr N.H. Norrbin of the Swedish State Shiptesting Experimental Tank (SSPA) in Gothenburg. I have also had the pleasure of working on a joint project on adaptive ship control with the Kockums Mekaniska Verkstads AB i Malmö, Sweden. The stimulation derived from working with Messrs J. Eriksson, L. Sten and N.E. Thorell of Kockums is gratefully acknowledged. This project was supported by the Swedish Board for Technical Development under contract 734187. I have also benefitted much from a close interaction with my student, Claes Källström, who has designed adaptive autopilots for tankers and done many experiments with them.

8. REFERENCES

Abkowitz, M.A. (1964): Lectures on Ship Hydrodynamics - Steering and Manoeuvrability. Report Hy-5, Hydro- and Aerodynamics Laboratory, Lyngby, Denmark.

Åström, K.J. and Wittenmark, B.(1972): On the Control of Constant but Unknown Systems. Paper 37.5, Proc. of the IFAC 5th World Congress, Paris, France. Distributed by Instrument Society of America, Pittsburgh, Penn., USA.

Åström, K.J. and Källström, C. (1973): Application of System Identification Techniques to the Determination of Shipdynamics. Proc 3rd IFAC Symposium on Identification and System Parameter Estimation, the Hague/Delft, The Netherlands.

Åström, K.J. and Wittenmark, B. (1973): On Self Tuning Regulators. Automatica 9, 185-199.

Åström, K.J. and Källström, C. (1976): Identification of Ship-steering Dynamics. Automatica 12, 9-22.

Åström, K.J., Norrbin, N.H., Källström, C. and Byström, L. (1974): The Identification of Linear Ship-steering Dynamics using Maximum Likelihood Parameter Estimation. Report 1920-1, SSPA, Gotenburg, Sweden.

Beck, M. and Smitt, L.W. (1969): Analogue Simulation of Ship Manoeuvres based on Full Scale Trials on Free-Sailing Model Tests. Report Hy-14, Hydro- and Aerodynamics Laboratory, Lyngby, Denmark.

Comstock, P.J. (1967): Principles of Naval Architecture. The Society of Naval Architects and Marine Engineers, New York.

Källström, C. (1976): Private communication.

Lumley, J.L. and Panofsky, H.A. (1964): The Structure of Atmospheric Turbulence. Wiley, New York.

Motora, S. (1973): Maneuverability, State of the Art. Proc International Jubilee Meeting on the Occasion of the 40th Anniversary of the Netherlands Ship Model Basin, August 30 - September 1, 1972. Netherlands Ship Model Basin, Wageningen, the Netherlands.

Nomoto, K. (1957): On the Steering Qualities of Ships. Int Shipbuilding Progr. Vol 4, No 35.

Norrbin, N.H. (1960): A Study of Course Keeping and Manoeuvring Performance. Publication 45, SSPA, Gotenburg, Sweden. Also available in Proc. First Symposium on Ship Manoeuvrability, Washington D.C., 1960, (DTMB Report 1461).

Norrbin, N.H. (1970): Theory and Observations on the Use of a Mathematical Model for Ship Manoeuvring in Deep And Confined Waters. Publication 68, SSPA, Gothenburg, Sweden. Aslo in Proc 8th Symp. on Naval Hydrodynamics, Pasadena, California, USA.

Norrbin, N.H. (1972): On the Added Resistance due to Steering on a Straight Course. 13th Int Towing Tank Conference, Berlin/Hamburg.

Price, W.G. and Bishop, R.E.D. (1974): Probabilistic Theory of Ship Dynamics. Chapman and Hall, London.

Strøm-Tejsen, J. and Chislett, M.S. (1966): A Model Testing Technique and Method of Analysis for the Prediction of Steering and Manoeuvring Qualities of Surface Vessels. Report Hy-7, Hydro- and Aerodynamics Laboratory, Lyngby, Denmark.

Wagner, B. (1967): Windkräfte an Überwasserschiffen. Schiff und Hafen, 19, 226-250.

van Berlekom, W.B., Trägårdh, P. and Dellhag, A. (1975): Large Tankers-Wind Coefficients and Speed Loss Due to Wind and Sea. Trans. Roy. Inst. of Naval Arch, 117, 41-58.

Zuidweg, J.K. (1970): Automatic Guidance of Ships as a Control Problem. Thesis Technische Hogeschool Delft, the Netherlands.

SYSTEM THEORY AND SOME OF ITS APPLICATIONS IN ECOLOGY, WATER RESOURCES AND ENERGY

by

J. Casti*
International Institute for Applied Systems Analysis
Laxenburg, Austria

* Current Address: Department of Computer Applications and Information Systems and Department of Quantitative Analysis, New York University, 90 Trinity Place, New York, New York 10006.

1. Introduction

One of the characteristics of any intellectual field during the course of its development from an art to a science is an increasing use of precise language and quantitative methodology to replace the often vague, subjective personal opinions which passed for analysis in the early days of the subject. Such a transition took place in physics by the early 1800s and much of the modern work being presented in economics, psychology, and biology gives evidence that such a "hardening" principle will not be confined to the physical sciences. The reason behind such a trend is clear: each developing field gradually reaches a stage beyond which progress is impossible without organized knowledge, because the implications of existing knowledge are too complex to digest without abstractions, that is, without mathematics.

In this paper we wish to explore the evolution of the foregoing trend in applied systems analysis. In particular, we address the question: how can mathematics contribute to applied systems analysis? "Mathematics" in this paper will mean exactly the same thing as it does to the contemporary professional mathematician, namely theorems, proof techniques, rational constructions, etc. We will not examine questions involving data analysis, statistics, numerical formulas, and other pedestrian (although often useful) matters which, to the layman, are also "mathematics".

As a first step in answering the above question, it is necessary to formalize one's intuitive idea of a dynamical system. For present purposes, we regard a system Σ as being a mechanism which transforms element from a given set U of admissible inputs (decisions) into a set Γ of observable outputs (consequences). Mathematically, the above external description of Σ is given by a map

$$f: \quad U \Rightarrow \Gamma$$

A reductionist viewpoint of the foregoing situation is provided by so-called "state variable" models of a dynamical process. Letting $U = R^m$, $\Gamma = R^p$, we introduce a n-dimensional vector function $x(t) \in R^n$ and generate the input/output map f by the relations

$$x(t+1) = g(x(t),u(t),t) \qquad x(t_o) = x_o$$
$$y(t) = h(x(t)),$$

where g and h are suitable functions. Given the above internal description of Σ, generation of the external description f is trivial.

As a consequence of the foregoing set-up, we see that the principal notions needed for a mathematical description of a dynamical process are the ideas of input, output and state. These concepts form the raw material for the construction of a mathematical theory of systems.

In view of the multidisciplinary nature of the present symposium, it seems appropriate to broadly motivate the results to follow. Thus, let us briefly review the primary subject matter of mathematical system theory, referring to the texts [5,6,22] for elaborations. The basic issues addressed by mathematical system theorists seem conveniently to fall into the following categories:

A. Modelling - the basic problem faced by all system analysts is the generation of an internal description of a process from a given external description. However, the external description corresponds to the results of physical measurements and laboratory tests, while the internal model "explains" or "realizes" the data. Usually many realizations will explain the data, so additional criteria must be employed to find good models. Often the requirement that the system state be of minimal dimension is used, justification being supplied by an appeal to Occam's razor. A systematic realization theory for arbitrary processes seems a remote dream, at present. However, very impressive results have been obtained for some broad classes of systems [2,10] and a virtually complete theory, along with numerical algorithms, is now available for processes whose input/output behavior is linear.

B. Reachability - Given an admissible set of decisions, it is of great interest in many cases to determine precisely what system behavior is possible within the constraints imposed upon the inputs. In other words, what can inputs do to alter system behavior? The limitations imposed upon a system's behavior by constraints on the decisions and/or allowable data paths between the decisions and the states are essential pieces of information for any decisionmaker. Such issues comprise the topic of reachability.

C. Observability - The mathematical counterpart of the reachability problem is the question of observability. Focusing now upon the measurable system outputs, we inquire as to precisely how much information concerning the true state of the system is provided by such outputs. Note that this question is independent of any considerations regarding noise and uncertainty in the measurements or system parameters. Rather, what is involved here is the determination of how the data paths from the system state to the output affect the amount of information contained in the measured output. This is clearly a vital question, particularly for those processes in which feedback decisionmaking based upon measurable output is being employed (i.e., almost all realistic decisionmaking situations).

D. Stability - a basic problem of science for centuries has been the analysis of the effect of perturbations upon the dynamical behavior of physical processes. Parameters entering into mathematical models of reality are seldom known exactly; consequently, one must view with suspicion models whose behavior changes radically with small changes in system parameters (global modellers please take note!) Similarly, physical apparatus for measuring various systems outputs and generating system inputs never produce their effects with infinite precision. Thus, we must consider problems of stability as an essential feature of any thorough systems analysis.

E. Optimality - having disposed of the more or less qualitative topics A-D, it is finally reasonable to superimpose a quality criterion upon a given process and speak of an optimal decision rule. It is of utmost importance to note that considerations of optimality come at the end of the analytical process not, as is often observed, at the beginning. Given a particular input/output process, or experimental set-up with data, it makes very little methodological sense to begin speaking of optimal (feedback) decision policies until it is clear that appropriate reachability, observability and stability properties are present. In addition, it goes without saying that a reasonable internal model of the given data must be generated before superimposing a quality criterion. The basic point is that a good number of questions that the analyst wishes to answer concerning the behavior of a process have little, if anything, to do with optimality. Consequently, the tool should be chosen to suit the task and techniques and methods of optimization theory should not be invoked to deal with questions whose basic essence does not relate to optimality.

A great deal has already been presented in the systems analysis literature on topics A (philosophically) and D,E (mathematically). As a result, in this paper we shall focus attention upon some of the structural questions inherent in B omitting, due to space considerations, the equally neglected area C.

2. Survey of Methodology

In a brief paper such as this, it is clearly impossible to do justice to the vast literature on reachability and to present even a small fraction of the useful and important results. Thus, what follows represents a somewhat eclectic selection of basic results which are either particularly simple, useful, and/or indispensable for dealing with the basic issues involved. We separate the class of systems into three groups: linear, bilinear (or multilinear), and nonlinear. As one might suspect, the only case which may be considered to be under more or less complete control is the linear situation, although substantial results are available also for the bilinear case. For these reasons, we have felt it desirable to progress from the state of rather complete knowledge to almost total ignorance in our survey of the current state of this branch of mathematical system theory.

For the purpose of basic definitions, we consider the system Σ described by the equations

$$\Sigma: \quad \dot{x} = f(x,u,t) \quad , \quad x(t_0) = x_0 \quad , \tag{2}$$
$$y(t) = h(x,t) \quad . \tag{3}$$

For simplicity, we assume that $f(0,0,t) = 0$, $h(0,t) = 0$, for all $t \geq t_0$, and that f and h are continuous functions of their arguments. We let $\Phi(t;\tau,x,u)$ denote the solution of (2) corresponding to an initial state x at time τ under application of the input function $u(s)$, $\tau \leq s \leq t$.

Definition 1. An event (τ,x^*) is controllable if and only if there exists an $\bar{t} > \tau$, and an admissible input $u \in \Omega$, (both $\bar{t}$ and u may depend on (τ,x^*) such that

$$\Phi(\bar{t};\tau,x^*,u) = 0.$$

Σ is completely controllable if it is controllable for every event (τ,x^*).

In other words, an event is controllable if and only if it can be transferred to the origin in finite time by application of some admissible input function u.

Definition 2. An event (τ,x^*) is reachable if and only if there is an $\bar{s} < \tau$, and a $u \in \Omega$ (both $\bar{s}$ and u may depend upon (τ,x^*)), such that

$$x^* = \Phi(\tau;\bar{s},0,u) \quad .$$

Σ is completely reachable if and only if it is reachable for every event (τ,x^*).

Graphically, controllability and reachability are as in Figure 1.

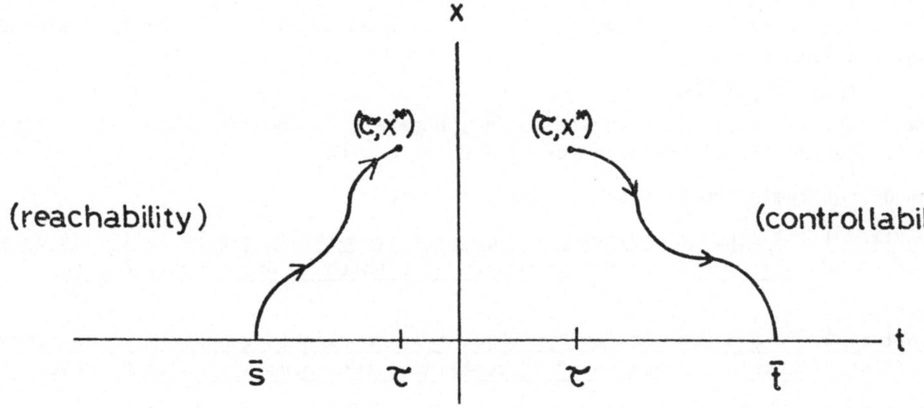

Figure 1. Controllability and Reachability

It is important to note that controllability and reachability are entirely different concepts. They coincide only in special cases, one of which is when Σ is a constant, continuous time, linear system. Caution! Even if a linear system is completely reachable and completely controllable, it does not follow that any event (τ, x) may be transferred to any other event (τ_1, x_1), $\tau_1 \geq \tau$, by suitable choice of input.

A. Linear Systems

We consider the constant, linear version of Σ in which

$$f(x,u,t) = Fx + Gu \quad , \qquad x(0) = 0 \ , \tag{4}$$
$$h(x,t) = Hx \quad ,$$

where F, G, H are constant n×n, n×m, p×n matrices, respectively. In this case, the notions of reachability and controllability coincide. Due to the pioneering efforts of Kalman and others, we have at our disposal a very detailed description of the set of reachable states. The most important result in this direction is the following re-statement of a result first presented in [4].

Theorem 1. Define the n×nm controllability matrix $\mathcal{C}$ as

$$\mathcal{C} = [G \mid FG \mid \ldots \mid F^{n-1}G] \quad .$$

Let Ω be the set of piecewise continuous functions on $[0,\infty]$. Further, let $\mathcal{B} = \{c^{(1)}, c^{(2)}, \ldots, c^{(r)}\}$ be a maximal linearly independent set of vectors from the columns of $\mathcal{C}$. Then the set $\mathcal{R}$ of reachable (or controllable states of Σ coincides with the subspace of R^n spanned by the set $\mathcal{B}$.

Remarks:

(1) The fact that the reachable set is a subspace insures that it is convex.

(2) In general, the set $\mathcal{B}$ is not unique. All that is needed to characterize the reachable set is any maximal linearly independent subset from the columns of $\mathcal{C}$.

(3) Given a particular (τ, x^*), which lies in $\mathcal{R}$, Theorem 1 gives no information as to what control $u(t) \in \Omega$ would lead from the origin to x^*. In general, one would have to solve the following Fredhom integral equation of the first kind for such an input

$$x^*(\tau) = \int_0^\tau e^{F(\tau - s)} Gu(s) ds \quad .$$

An alternate prescription involving generalized inverses is described in [19].

(4) Theorem 1 remains partially valid if the continuous system (4) is replaced by the discrete-time system

$$x_{k+1} = Fx_k + Gu_k \quad .$$

The reachable set is still given by the set $\mathcal{R}$, however, the controllable set is given by $\mathcal{R}$ only if the additional condition $\det F \neq 0$ is imposed.

Some of the useful corollaries of Theorem 1 are

Corollary 1. A constant system $\Sigma = (F,G,-)$ is completely reachable if and only if there is no nontrivial characteristic vector of F which is orthogonal to every column of G.

Corollary 2. A constant system $\Sigma = (F,G,-)$ is completely reachable if and only if the smallest F-invariant subspace of R^n containing the columns of G is R^n itself.

Corollary 3. The state space of Σ may be decomposed into the direct sum

$$R^n = X_1 \oplus X_2 \quad ,$$

which decomposes the system dynamics as

$$\frac{dx_1}{dt} = F_{11}x_1 + F_{12}x_2 + G_1u(t) \quad ,$$

$$\frac{dx_2}{dt} = F_{22}x_2 \quad .$$

The subsystem $(F_{11}, G_1, -)$ is completely reachable.

Remark:

In a problem in which control enters, only the space X_1 has meaning. Thus, it is essential to isolate the space X_1 at the outset as it may be of much lower dimension than the entire space R^n.

Example:

To illustrate Theorem 1 and its corollaries, we consider the simple linear system

$$\begin{aligned}
\dot{x}_1 &= 2x_1 + 4x_2 + x_3 - x_4 + u_2 \quad , \\
\dot{x}_2 &= -x_2 + x_4 + u_1 + u_2 \quad , \\
\dot{x}_3 &= -3x_3 - 2x_4 \quad , \\
\dot{x}_4 &= x_4 \quad .
\end{aligned}$$

The relevant matrices for this system are

$$F = \begin{bmatrix} 2 & 4 & 1 & -1 \\ 0 & -1 & 0 & 1 \\ 0 & 0 & -3 & -2 \\ 0 & 0 & 0 & 1 \end{bmatrix} \quad , \quad G = \begin{bmatrix} 0 & 1 \\ 1 & 1 \\ 0 & 0 \\ 0 & 0 \end{bmatrix} \quad .$$

Computing the controllability matrix , we have

$$\mathscr{C} = \left[\begin{array}{cc|cc|cc|cc} 0 & 1 & 4 & 6 & 4 & 8 & 12 & 20 \\ 1 & 1 & -1 & -1 & 1 & 1 & -1 & -1 \\ 0 & 0 & 0 & 0 & 0 & 0 & 0 & 0 \\ 0 & 0 & 0 & 0 & 0 & 0 & 0 & 0 \end{array}\right] \quad .$$

Since $\mathscr{C}$ is of rank 2, any two linearly independent vectors will suffice to form $\mathscr{L}$. For example,

$$\mathscr{L} = \left\{ \begin{pmatrix} 0 \\ 1 \\ 0 \\ 0 \end{pmatrix}, \begin{pmatrix} 1 \\ 1 \\ 0 \\ 0 \end{pmatrix} \right\} \quad .$$

The subspace of R^4 generated by these vectors is the reachable set for the system. It is characterized as

$$\mathscr{R} = \{x \in R^4 : x_3 = x_4 = 0\} \quad ,$$

i.e., $\mathcal{R}$ is the two-dimensional set of vectors lying in the hyperplane $x_3 = x_4 = 0$.

The case of time-varying F and G is somewhat more complex. The basic result is

Theorem 2. *Let the matrices F(t), G(t) be bounded on every finite interval $t_0 \le t < \infty$. Then an event (τ, x^*) is reachable if and only if $x^* \in$ range $[W(s,\tau)]$, for some $s < \tau$, where*

$$W(s,\tau) = \int_s^\tau \Phi_F(\tau,\sigma)G(\sigma)G'(\sigma)\Phi_F'(\tau,\sigma)d\sigma \quad ,$$

with $\Phi_F(\tau,s)$ being the transition matrix of F(t), i.e.

$$\frac{\partial}{\partial t}\Phi_F(t,s) = F(t)\Phi_F(t,s) \quad , \qquad \Phi_F(s,s) = I \quad .$$

Remarks:

(1) The reachable set $\mathcal{R}$ now depends upon τ and we have

$$\mathcal{R}(\tau) = \text{range } W(t_1,\tau) \quad ,$$

where t_1 is any value of t for which $W(t,\tau)$ has maximal rank.

(2) If $G(\cdot)$ is zero on $(-\infty,\tau)$, we cannot have reachability of (τ,x^*).

(3) Making the substitution $\tau \to t$, $s \to 2\tau - t$, we define a new matrix $W(\tau,t)$ which gives the analogue of Theorem 2 for controllability.

Since the rank conditions implied by remark (1) may not be easy to verify in practice, we give a simpler condition for "analytic" systems, i.e., those systems for which F(t), G(t) are (real) analytic functions of t.

Theorem 3. *Let F(t), G(t) be (real) analytic functions on $t_0 \le t < \infty$. Define the sequence of matrix functions $Q_i(t)$ by*

$$Q_0(t) = G(t) \quad ,$$

$$Q_{i+1}(t) = F(t)Q_i(t) - \dot{Q}_i(t) \quad , \qquad i = 0,1,\ldots,n-1 \quad .$$

Then the linear system $\Sigma = (F(t),G(t),-)$ is completely reachable at time τ if and only if the rank of matrix

$$\mathcal{C}(t) = [Q_0(t)|Q_1(t)| \ldots |Q_{n-1}(t)] = n \quad ,$$

for some time $t \le \tau$.

In analogy with Theorem 1, the reachable set for analytic systems is obtained from the matrix $\mathcal{C}(t)$ by finding the subspace spanned by a maximal set of linearly independent columns.

B. Linearized Systems

Armed with the above results concerning the reachability of linear dynamical systems, it is possible to begin to tackle various nonlinear problems. The most direct approach is to linearize the nonlinear system about a nominal control-state pair and to then apply the above linear theory for a *local* analysis. The problem here, of course, is that the results obtained pertain only to a local region in the neighborhood of the nominal trajectory and control.

Briefly, the procedure is the following: we begin with the nonlinear system

$$x = f(x,u,t) \quad , \tag{5}$$

$$y(t) = h(x,t) \quad . \tag{6}$$

Let $u^*(t)$ be an admissible input and let $x^*(t)$ be the associated trajectory generated by Eq. (5). The dynamics and observations (5) - (6) are then linearized about (x^*,u^*). This yields the linearized system

$$\dot{x} = F_{(x^*,u^*)}(t)x + G_{(x^*,u^*)}(t)\, u$$

$$y(t) = H_{(x^*,u^*)}(t)x \quad ,$$

where

$$F_{(x^*,u^*)}(t) = \frac{\partial f}{\partial x}(x,u,t)\Bigg|_{\substack{x = x^*(t)\\ u = u^*(t)}} \quad ,$$

$$G_{(x^*,u^*)}(t) = \frac{\partial f}{\partial u}(x,u,t)\Bigg|_{\substack{x = x^*(t)\\ u = u^*(t)}} \quad ,$$

$$H_{(x^*,u^*)}(t) = \frac{\partial h}{\partial x}\Bigg|_{x = x^*(t)}$$

Clearly, the results obtained from such an analysis make sense only if i) the functions f and h are sufficiently smooth to justify the linearization and ii) we confine our attention to sufficiently small neighborhoods of the nominal trajectory and control. Here "sufficiently small" must be interpreted in terms of the analytic properties of f and h, i.e., how close they are to being linear and their degree of smoothness.

To illustrate the above ideas, we begin with

Definition 3. Consider the process

$$\dot{x} = f(x,u,t) = Fx + Gu + \ldots$$

$$y = h(x,t) = Hx + \ldots \tag{*}$$

near $x^* = 0$, $u^* = 0$ (here we use the hypotheses $f(0,0,t) = h(0,t) = 0$).

The process is locally controllable if for each $\bar{x}$ in some neighborhood of origin, there exists a piecewise continuous control $u(t)$, $0 \leq t \leq \tau$, such that the system may be transferred to the state $\bar{x}$ from the origin in time τ, τ sufficiently small.

The process is locally observable if for each sufficiently small piecewise-continuous control $u(t)$ on $0 \leq t \leq \tau$, the equality

$$h(x_1(t),t) = h(x_2(t),t)$$

implies

$$x_1(t) = x_2(t) \quad , \quad 0 \leq t \leq \tau \quad , \quad \tau \text{ sufficiently small.}$$

The basic result on local controllability and observability is that the global linear results are sufficient for the local nonlinear results, i.e.,

Theorem 4. The process (*) is locally controllable if

$$\text{rank } [G|FG|\ldots|F^{n-1}G] = n \quad ;$$

<u>it is locally observable if</u>

$$\text{rank}\ [H'|F'H'|\dots|\ (F')^{n-1}H'] = n \quad .$$

C. <u>Bilinear (Multilinear) Systems</u>

The simplest class of nontrivial nonlinear systems, and the only one for which substantial analytic advances have been made, are systems which are linear in the state and control separately, but not jointly, i.e., bilinear systems. A simple scalar example of a system of this sort is

$$\dot{x} = ax + bu + cxu \quad . \tag{7}$$

Obvious extensions to the case when the system is multilinear in the state and/or control will be pursued briefly later.

In view of the relationship between the solution of a bilinear system such as (7), and a time-varying linear system of the form $\dot{x} = A(t)x + B(t)u$, together with the well known connections of the latter type of system with the Lie-algebraic methods of Wei and Norman [20], one would conjecture that the controllability/observability properties of bilinear processes will be essentially algebraic in nature. Thus, the algebraic flavor so evident for linear problems seems also to be an intrinsic feature of the few totally nonlinear problems that have been studied and, as a result, it seems likely that substantial progress in analyzing reachability properties of nonlinear systems will rely upon a thorough study of the algebraic structures involved.

For ease of exposition, but without loss of generality, for the most part we shall consider homogeneous-in-the-state bilinear systems of the type

$$\dot{x} = Fx + Nxu \quad , \qquad x(0) = x_0 \quad , \tag{8}$$

where x and u are n, m-dimensional vectors, respectively and we use the shorthand notation

$$Nxu \triangleq \sum_{i=1}^{m} N_i x u_i(t) \quad ,$$

where $u_i(t)$ is the ith component of the vector u. The matrices F, N_i are assumed constant. It is easily seen that the solution of (8) is given in the form

$$x(t) = \Gamma(t)x_0 \quad , \tag{9}$$

where $\Gamma(t) \in \mathcal{S}_n$, the set of real, nonsingular $n \times n$ matrices, $t \geq 0$. To see that the vector system (8) also includes systems of the form

$$\dot{z} = Az + Bv + Czv \quad ,$$

let F and N_i be defined by adding a single extra row and column to A and C_i, respectively

$$F = \begin{bmatrix} 0 & 0 \\ 0 & A \end{bmatrix} \quad , \qquad N_i = \begin{bmatrix} 0 & 0 \\ B^{(i)} & C_i \end{bmatrix}$$

where $B^{(i)}$ is the ith column of B. Now define

$$x = \begin{bmatrix} 1 \\ z \end{bmatrix} \quad , \qquad u = v \quad .$$

From (9), the first intrinsic property of homogeneous-in-the-state bilinear systems appears: the origin is never controllable! Thus, a more convenient state space for this type of problem is the "punctured" space $R^n - \{0\}$.

Another consequence of (9) is that reachability and controllability properties of (8) are directly connected to the analogous properties of the matrix system

$$\dot{X} = FX + NXu, \qquad (10)$$

where the state space is taken to be $\mathcal{G}_n$ and

$$NXu \triangleq \sum_{i=1}^{m} N_i X u_i(t) \quad .$$

It suffices to study system (10) under the condition that $X(0) = I$, since if we consider any other $X_0 \in \mathcal{G}_n$, then the reachable set at time T equals

$$\{X \in \mathcal{G}_n \; : X = \Gamma X_0, \text{ with } \Gamma \in \text{reachable set of (10) at } T\}.$$

If we let $\mathcal{R}(I)$ denote the set of points reachable from the identity at any time $t \geq 0$, then it can be shown that if $\mathcal{R}(I)$ is a transitive group for (11) on $R^n - \{0\}$, i.e., if $\mathcal{R}(I)$ is such that for all $x, \bar{x} \in R^n - \{0\}$, there exists a $\Gamma \in \mathcal{R}(I)$ such that $x = \Gamma\bar{x}$, then (8) is completely controllable on $R^n - \{0\}$. This result establishes the connection between studying (10) in order to obtain results on the controllability/reachability of (8).

Some additional definitions will be needed to concisely state the results to follow.

Definition 4. Given two $n\times n$ matrices A, B, their Lie product is defined as

$$[A,B] \triangleq AB - BA \quad .$$

Definition 5. A Lie algebra $\mathcal{L}$ in the space of $n\times n$ matrices is a linear subspace of $n\times n$ matrices which is closed under the Lie product operation.

Definition 6. Given a subset $\mathcal{S}$ of the set of $n\times n$ matrices, the Lie algebra generated by $\mathcal{S}$ is the smallest Lie algebra containing $\mathcal{S}$.

Definition 7. Given a Lie algebra $\mathcal{L}$ in the set of $n\times n$ matrices, we define

$$\mathcal{G}_n(\mathcal{L}) \triangleq \left\{\Gamma \; : \; \Gamma = e^{\Lambda_1} e^{\Lambda_2} \cdots e^{\Lambda_r}, \; \Lambda_i \in (\mathcal{L}), \; i = 1,\ldots,r; \; r = 1,2,\ldots \right\} \quad .$$

$\mathcal{G}_n(\mathcal{L})$ is called the connected Lie group associated with $\mathcal{L}$.

Notation:

We let $\mathcal{L}_1$ = the Lie algebra generated by $\{F, N_1, \ldots, N_m\}$.

The principal result concerning controllability (or reachability) of the homogeneous system (10) is

Theorem 5. If $\mathcal{G}_n(\mathcal{L}_1)$ is compact, then $\mathcal{R}(I) = \mathcal{G}_n(\mathcal{L}_1)$, i.e.,

$$\mathcal{R}(I) = \left\{\Gamma : \Gamma = e^{\Lambda_1} e^{\Lambda_2} \cdots e^{\Lambda_r}, \; \Lambda_1 \in \mathcal{L}_1, \; i = 1,\ldots,r; \; r = 1,2,\ldots \right\} \quad .$$

A much simpler form of this result is valid for vector systems of the form

$$\dot{x} = (F + \sum_{i=1}^{m} N_i v_i(t))x(t) + \sum_{i=1}^{r} u_i(t) \, G^{(i)} \quad . \qquad (11)$$

Here the control has been separated into two parts: one part (the vector v(t)) is associated with the purely bilinear part of the system, while the other part (the vector u(t)) is associated with the purely linear part. The elements $G^{(i)}$ are the columns of the linear input matrix G, i = 1,...,r. The principle result is

Theorem 6. The reachable set for the system (11) starting at x = 0 at time t = 0 is the vector space generated by the set $\mathcal{S} = \{L_i^k G^{(i)}\}$, where the L_i are a basis for the Lie algebra $\mathcal{L}_1$, k = 0,1,... .

Theorem 6 is the natural generalization of Theorem 1 as is easily seen by setting all $N_i = 0$, i = 1,...,m. In this event the Lie algebra generated by $\{F,N_1,\ldots,N_m\}$ is just F itself, hence a basis is also F. Thus, the reachable set is the vector space generated by the set $\mathcal{S} = \{F^k G^{(i)}\}$, k = 0,1,..., i = 1,...,r. But, by the Hamilton-Cayley theorem it suffices to restrict k to the range k = 0,1,...,n-1. Hence, the vectors of the set $\mathcal{S}$ coincide with those of the controllability matrix $\mathcal{C}$ of Theorem 1.

The foregoing results regarding bilinear systems may be interpreted as statements concerning the class of "physically interesting" multilinear systems by virtue of the following fundamental result:

Theorem 7 [10]. The conditions under which the canonical state set of a given multilinear input-output function can be constructed in a finite number of steps (i.e., is finite-dimensional) are identical to those under which the same function may be realized by a dynamical system with a bilinear internal structure.

As a consequence of this remarkable result, there is no added generality in assuming that a given experimental set-up is described by a multilinear, rather than bilinear system. If the given experimental data can be explained by any finite-dimensional multilinear state space model, then it can be explained by a bilinear model. Of course, this does not mean that a totally nonlinear model is equivalent to a bilinear one but it does substantially restrict the cases which need be considered. As an example, by introduction of a sufficient number of new variables, a polynomial model be replaced by a multilinear structure which, by Theorem 7, must then be mathematically equivalent (modulo the finiteness restriction) to a bilinear system.

D. Nonlinear Systems

As one might conjecture from the results on multilinear systems, the reachability problem for general nonlinear systems of the form

$$\dot{x} = f(x,u) \quad ,$$

may be studied by examining the Lie algebra generated by the vector field f. Unfortunately, in the general case this problem cannot be reduced to matrix computations as was done above; however, in principle the same techniques apply and once some structure is imposed upon f various computational approaches may be employed. A detailed discussion of these matters requires a degree of mathematical sophistication beyond the bounds of this elementary survey, so we shall refer the reader to [11] for further information. It is of some interest to note, however, that the observability problem for nonlinear systems has received very little attention in the literature with the exception of the brief discussion in [3].

On the above note, we conclude this all too brief survey of methodology and return to the question of its relevance to applied systems analysis - IIASA-style.

3. System-Theoretic Problems at IIASA

This section examines several problems that have been described in earlier IIASA publications from the viewpoint of the methodology discussed above. It is not intended that any of these examples be extensively pursued in the future nor is it of particular interest that these problems represent the "state-of-the-art" in the areas they model. What is important, though, is that they have been seriously proposed as such models. Our aim is only to point out that there have been in the past (and presumably there will continue to be) problems of IIASA interest which possess definite system-theoretic overtones, regardless of whether or not these aspects have been recognized. Ideally, this brief survey of "hometown" problems will be sufficient motivation for future work.

Many of the problems that follow were originally presented within the context of an optimization process. In accordance with the general principle that system structure is more or less independent of externally imposed criteria, we abstract here only those features which do not relate to the particular objective function initially chosen.

A. Renewable Resources Management [12]

A major ecological problem is to develop strategies for the development of resources. The real issue here, as pointed out in [12], is to devise sensible (and implementable) harvesting policies in the face of uncertainties regarding the dynamics of the process and within the context of an ever-changing political and economic environment. This question properly belongs within the domain of adaptive control theory; however, various versions of it may be considered as reachability/constructibility questions for which the above methodology may yield some insight.

Suppose we have a resource system whose state at time t may be described by a vector $x(t)$. A simplified version of the dynamics of this system as adapted from [12] is

$$\dot{x}(t) = Sx(t) + Bx(t-\tau) - Cx(t)E(t) \quad ,$$

where S is a matrix of survival rates, C is a matrix of "catchability coefficients", B is a matrix describing the growth of current population which is dependent upon the state of the system τ units in the past, and $E(t)$ is a vector of total harvesting effort (control) or some other measure of exploitation intensity.

With the exception of the time-lag term involving $x(t-\tau)$, the above problem is seen to be a bilinear control process of the type studied in Section 2. If we assume that the time-lag τ is small compared with the value of t (i.e., the system has been in operation for a large time interval), then we may approximate $x(t-\tau)$ as

$$x(t-\tau) \cong x(t) - \tau\dot{x}(t) + \frac{\tau^2}{2} \ddot{x}(t) \ldots \quad .$$

Keeping only terms up to order τ^2, the above system may be approximated by a modified bilinear process.

Some of the questions which one could attack with the techniques given in Section 2 include:

i) description of the reachable state space at time t, given constraints on the admissible catch effort $E(t)$, i.e., $E(t) \in \mathcal{S}(t)$;

ii) sensitivity of the reachable set to changes in system parameters;

iii) if it is assumed that $E(t)$ is related in some way to taxation and investment rates, a description of the reachable set in terms of these "auxiliary" controls.

In many instances, some or all of the components of the system matrices S, B, and C may be subject to stochastic perturbations having known or unknown distribution functions. In the first case, the preceding methodology may be used in an expected value sense; in the latter case, one is faced with an adaptive process whose methodological treatment transcends the limitations and modest aims of this report. The key point, however, is that the introduction of randomness into the process may complicate the computational aspects of the situation but it presents no new conceptual hurdles. Thus, a thorough understanding of the deterministic methodology will, with sufficient computing power, enable one to deal also with the stochastic case. This is a point that has been repeatedly emphasized in earlier IIASA deliberations.

A somewhat more complicated version of the above problem is given in [13] for the determination of harvesting strategies for salmon. In this problem, the linear time-lag term $Bx(t-\tau)$ is replaced by a nonlinear curve, the so-called Ricker model, without a time-lag and S is taken to be zero, i.e., we have the dynamics (after some algegraic re-arrangement)

$$S_{t+1} = e^{-\alpha(1-S_t)} S_t z_t \quad ,$$

where S_t is the salmon stock level at time t, α is a parameter reflecting the net stock productivity, and $z_t = 1/(1-u_t)$, with u_t representing the net exploitation rate.

By expanding the exponential term as

$$e^{-\alpha(1-S_t)} \cong 1 - \alpha(1-S_t) + \frac{\alpha^2}{2} (1-S_t)^2 + \ldots \quad ,$$

and truncating at some appropriate point, the salmon model becomes a polynomial system with control entering linearly. The reachability structure of such systems may be studied by several means: linearization, conversion to a multilinear problem by introduction of additional state variables, or directly by Lie-algebraic methods.

B. Water Reservoir Regulation [14]

A problem that arises in most water basin networks throughout the world is that of regulating the flow through various dams in the network in order that the entire system behave in some prescribed fashion. Generally, this problem is complicated by the presence of stochastic inflows to the network due to rainfall and underground water run-off. In addition, the conflicting objectives of the various water users must be taken into account. Here we shall consider only the reachability/constructibility questions involving the physical water basin network itself.

A simple example of a problem of this genre is depicted in Figure 2.

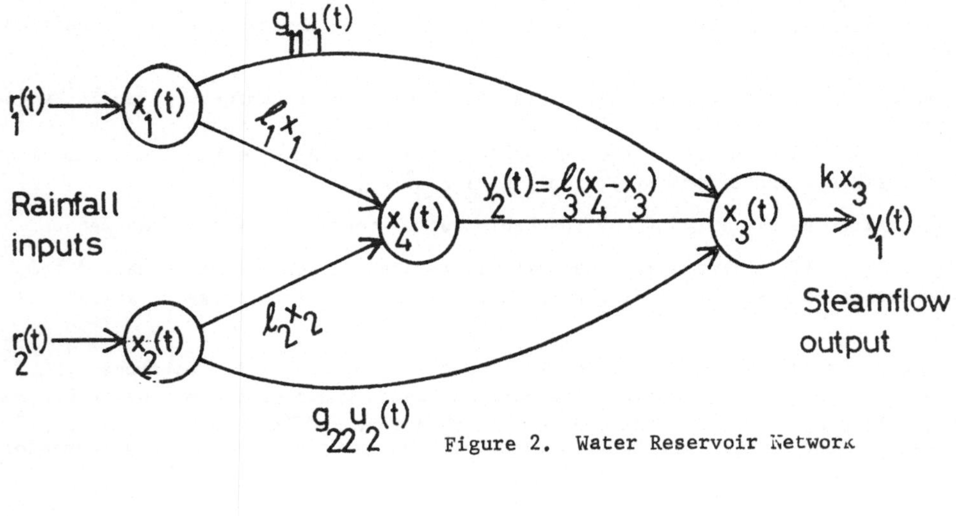

Figure 2. Water Reservoir Network

In Figure 2, $r_1(t)$ and $r_2(t)$ are the rainfall inputs, the states of surface storage at locations 1-3 are $x_1(t)$, $x_2(t)$, $x_3(t)$, respectively, while the state of groundwater storage (including infiltration) is $x_4(t)$. The constants ℓ_1 and ℓ_2 are for infiltration. The expression $\ell_3(x_4-x_3)$ signifies the exchange between the river and groundwater. The system outputs y_1, y_2 are the streamflow output and the contribution of groundwater, respectively.

The continuity equations for this problem are

$$\dot{x}_1 = -\ell_1 x_1 + r_1 - g_{11}u_1 \quad ,$$

$$\dot{x}_2 = -\ell_2 x_2 + r_2 - g_{22}u_2 \quad ,$$

$$\dot{x}_3 = \ell_3(x_4-x_3) - kx_3 + g_{11}u_1 + g_{22}u_2 \quad ,$$

$$\dot{x}_4 = \ell_1 x_1 + \ell_2 x_2 - \ell_3(x_4-x_3) \quad .$$

The outputs are

$$y_1 = kx_3 \quad ,$$

$$y_2 = \ell_3(x_4-x_3) \quad .$$

In vector-matrix form, we have

$$\dot{x}(t) = Fx + Gu + r(t) \quad , \qquad x(0) = c \quad ,$$

$$y(t) = Hx \quad ,$$

where

$$F = \begin{bmatrix} -\ell_1 & 0 & 0 & 0 \\ 0 & -\ell_2 & 0 & 0 \\ 0 & 0 & -(\ell_3+k) & \ell_3 \\ \ell_1 & \ell_2 & \ell_3 & -\ell_3 \end{bmatrix}$$

$$G = \begin{bmatrix} -g_{11} & 0 \\ 0 & -g_{22} \\ g_{11} & g_{22} \\ 0 & 0 \end{bmatrix} \quad , \qquad r(t) = \begin{bmatrix} r_1(t) \\ r_2(t) \\ 0 \\ 0 \end{bmatrix} \quad , \qquad H = \begin{bmatrix} 0 & 0 & k & 0 \\ 0 & 0 & -\ell_3 & \ell_3 \end{bmatrix}$$

By virtue of the closed form expression

$$x(t) = e^{Ft}c + \int_0^t e^{F(t-s)}[Gu(s) + r(s)]ds \quad ,$$

we see that the reachability/constructibility features of the above process are independent* of the rainfall input $r(t)$. Thus, for purposes of analysis, there is no

* independent in the sense that results for the case $r(t) \neq 0$ may be obtained from the $r = 0$ case simply by adding the known vector function $-\int_0^t e^{F(t-s)}r(s)ds$ to x.

loss of generality in assuming $r(t) \equiv 0$. (Intuitively, this is due to the tacit assumption that u(t) can be made arbitrarily large. In the more realistic case where $0 \leq u_i(t) \leq U$, a more refined analysis is required.)

It is an amusing exercise to apply the techniques of Part II to the above system to discover what is already evident from Figure 2; namely, that the system is completely reachable as long as $g_{11} \neq 0$, $g_{22} \neq 0$.

Other water resource problems of a similar nature may be found in the IIASA reports [15] and [16].

C. National Settlement Planning [17]

A number of IIASA urbanologists have been concerned with the question of developing national settlement strategies subject to constraints on resources, immigration quotas, and the like. Several different approaches have been proposed for dealing with this sort of problem, some of them falling into the basic framework considered in this paper. We describe one of these "system-theoretic" approaches, first presented in [17]. The essential aspect of this model is to promote a desired migratory process by differential stimulation of the employment market on the part of the government.

The state equations for the model are

$$\begin{aligned} x(t+1) &= Kx(t) + (I-M)v(t) \quad , \\ v(t+1) &= Mv(t) + u(t) + z(t) \quad , \end{aligned}$$

where the vector $x(t) \in R^n$ represents the population distribution at time t, $v(t) \in R^n$ is the distribution of job vacancies at time t, $u(t) \in R^n$ is the distribution of government stimulated job vacancies and $z(t) \in R^n$ is the distribution of spontaneously occurring vacancies. The matrix K is a diagonal matrix whose elements reflect the natural population growth rates within a region, while M is a migration matrix with elements m_{ij} being the probability that a job vacancy in region j will be filled by someone living in region i, i, j = 1,...,n. The problem, of course, is to choose u(t) so that x(t) (and possible v(t)) follows some desired course.

The budgetary and fixed immigration constraints on the choice of u(t) are given by

i) $u(t) \geq 0$,

ii) $(u(t), r(t)) \leq b$,

iii) $||u(t)|| \leq u$, $\qquad t = 1,2,\ldots,T$.

Here (,) denotes the vector inner product, while $||\cdot||$ is some appropriate norm (e.g., ℓ_1), with r(t) being a function giving the total financial resource available to be offered regionally by the government at period t, b being the total budget available.

By introducing the new vectors

$$s(t) = \left[\frac{0}{u(t)}\right] , \qquad w(t) = \left[\frac{x(t)}{v(t)}\right] , \qquad y(t) = \left[\frac{0}{z(t)}\right] ,$$

$$s,w,y \in R^{2n} ,$$

it is possible to rewrite the above model in the form

$$w(t+1) = Fw(t) + Gs(t) + y(t) \quad ,$$

where

$$F = \left[\begin{array}{c|c} K & I-M \\ \hline 0 & M \end{array}\right] , \qquad G = \left[\begin{array}{c|c} 0 & 0 \\ \hline 0 & I \end{array}\right] .$$

The above constraints restrict the region of admissible inputs s(t). Actually, on the basis of more detailed analysis, for purposes of determining reachable sets it suffices to replace inequalities ii) and iii) by the corresponding equality. (Physically, this fact is fairly obvious but requires a surprising amount of analysis to prove.)

The usual questions surrounding reachability may now be studied with the above "standard" model. As with the previous water example, the forcing term y(t), corresponding to the spontaneously arising jobs, plays no structural role in the reachability analysis.

D. Transportation Systems [18]

Problems involving the regulation of automative traffic flow in urban areas seem tailormade for the type of methodology we have been discussing. Many, if not most, of the mathematical models surveyed in [18] involve systems in which the dynamics of the traffic flow are linear, with the primary question being whether or not it is possible to reach a state of "undersaturation" (normal flow), from a state of "over-saturation" (rush-hour congestion) within a specified time period utilizing various regulation policies (usually control of freeway on-off ramps by traffic lights.) Obviously, this is a reachability problem. Here we present one of the examples from [18] to illustrate the main ideas:

Consider the rectangular traffic network depicted in Figure 3.

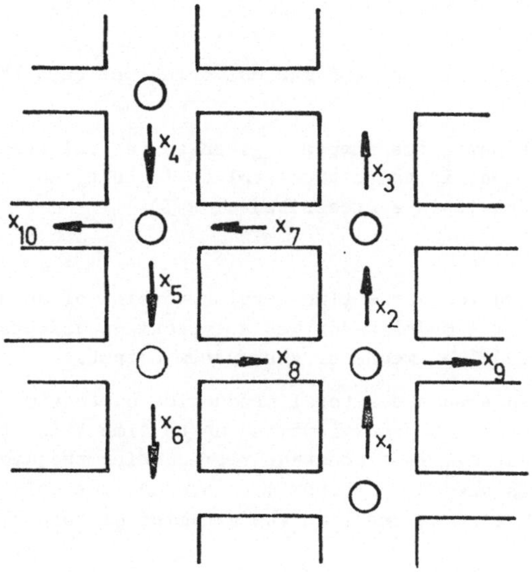

Figure 3. Urban Traffic Network

We assume that the network is over-saturated, i.e., at one or more intersections traffic demand exceeds capacity. Let $x_i(t)$ be the number of cars waiting at intersection i, and let $u_i(t)$ denote the number of cars leaving intersection i during the green light. If we assume that the travel time between two intersections is small compared to the waiting time, then the dynamics of the process are reasonably well described by the equations

$$x(t+1) = x(t) + Gu(t) + q(t) \quad ,$$

where the vector q(t) has components $q_i(t)$ representing the external traffic arriving at intersection i during period t. It is clear from Figure 3 that the flows u_3, u_6,

u_9, and u_{10} are flows out of the network.

The control matrix G takes the form

$$G = \begin{bmatrix} -1 & 0 & 0 & 0 & 0 & 0 & 0 & 0 & 0 & 0 \\ s_1 & -1 & 0 & 0 & 0 & 0 & 0 & r_8 & 0 & 0 \\ 0 & s_2 & -1 & 0 & 0 & 0 & 0 & 0 & 0 & 0 \\ 0 & 0 & 0 & -1 & 0 & 0 & 0 & 0 & 0 & 0 \\ 0 & 0 & 0 & s_4 & -1 & 0 & r_7 & 0 & 0 & 0 \\ 0 & 0 & 0 & 0 & s_5 & -1 & 0 & 0 & 0 & 0 \\ 0 & r_2 & 0 & 0 & 0 & 0 & -1 & 0 & 0 & 0 \\ 0 & 0 & 0 & 0 & r_5 & 0 & 0 & -1 & 0 & 0 \\ r_1 & 0 & 0 & 0 & 0 & 0 & 0 & s_8 & -1 & 0 \\ 0 & 0 & 0 & r_4 & 0 & 0 & s_7 & 0 & 0 & -1 \end{bmatrix}$$

The elements r_i and s_i denote the percentage of cars turning right or left (r_i) and going straight ahead (s_i).

On psychological grounds, it is reasonable to impose the control contraints

$$M_i \leq u_i(t) \leq U_i \quad , \qquad i = 1,\ldots,10 \quad ,$$

where M_i and U_i represent the minimal and maximal number of cars that are acceptable during a given green time.

The basic problem is now quite simple: given an initial state $x(0)$, assumed to be an oversaturated condition, is there a control policy $u(t)$ which transfers $x(t)$ to an undersaturated region within a prescribed time T?

E. Energy Systems [21]

As a final example, we look at a time-varying version of an energy supply-demand process surveyed in [21]. The model describes a typical input/output economy with energy considerations included by means of the system output.

Assume that $x_i(t)$ represents the total production up to time t of economic sector i, while we let $u_i(t)$ denote the total demand up to time t for the output of sector i. Further, we suppose that a_{ij} is a constant representing the amount of production output of sector i which is needed by sector j to produce one unit of production, i, j = 1,...,n. It is fairly easy to see that the dynamics of this elementary model are

$$x_i(t+1) = \sum_{j=1}^{n} a_{ij} x_j(t) + u_i(t) \quad , \qquad i = 1,\ldots,n \quad .$$

Now suppose that we introduce energy considerations into the picture. Let E_i represent the total energy output of sector i, and assume that a known fraction e_{ik} of the total energy output of sector i is sold to sector k, i, k = 1,...,n. Then

$$E_i(t) = \sum_{k=1}^{n} e_{ik} x_k(t) \quad , \qquad i = 1,\ldots,n \quad .$$

The above problem is in standard form for reachability analyses. For instance, we could analyze the question of how to regulate consumer demands in order to stay within capacity constraints imposed upon the production process energy considerations.

It should by now be evident that the above model could be extended to incorporate time-varying coefficients $a_{ij} = a_{ij}(t)$, $e_{ik} = e_{ik}(t)$, to nonlinear dynamics, and constraints on demands (positivity), and still be within the methodological bounds prescribed in this report.

References

1. McFadden, D. "On the Controllability of Decentralized Macroeconomic Systems: The Assignment Problem," in Math. Systems Theory and Economics-I, H. Kuhn, Ed., Springer Lecture Notes in OR & Math. Economics, Vol. 11, New York, 1969.

2. Kalman, R., P. Falb, and M. Arbib, Topics in Mathematical Systems Theory, McGraw-Hill Co., New York, 1969.

3. Kalman, R. Lectures on Controllability and Observability, Proc. CIME Summer School, Edizioni Cremonese, Rome, 1969.

4. Kalman, R. "On the General Theory of Control Systems," Proc. 1st IFAC Congress, Moscow, 1960.

5. Gabasov, R., and F. Kirillova, The Qualitative Theory of Optimal Processes, Nauka, Moscow, 1969 (Russian).

6. Brockett, R. Finite-Dimensional Linear Systems, John Wiley, & Sons, New York, 1970.

7. Markus, L. "Dynamic Keynesian Economic Systems: Control and Identification," in Math. System Theory and Economics-I, H. Kuhn, Ed., Springer Lecture Notes in OR & Math. Economics, Vol. 11, New York, 1969.

8. Bruni, C., G. DiPillo, and G. Koch, "Bilinear Systems: An Appealing Class of 'Nearly Linear' Systems in Theory and Application," IEEE Tran. Auto. Cont. AC-19 (1974), 334-348.

9. Brockett, R. "Lie Algebras and Lie Groups in Control Theory," in Proc. NATO Advanced Study Institute on Geometric and Algebraic Methods for Nonlinear Systems, London, 1973.

10. Isidori, A. "New Results on the Abstract Realization Theory of Nonlinear Input-Output Functions," Ricerche di Automatica 5 (1974), 52-61

11. Lobry, C. "Dynamical Polysystems and Control Theory," Proc. NATO Advanced Study Institute on Geometric and Algebraic Methods for Nonlinear Systems, London, 1973.

12. Walters, C. "Adaptive Control Problems in Renewable Resource Development," Internal Paper, IIASA, 1975.

13. Walters, C. "Optimal Harvest Strategies for Salmon in Relation to Environmental Variability and Uncertainty About Production Parameters," Internal Paper, IIASA, 1975.

14. Sz. Nagy, A. "State-Space Approach to Hydrology," Symposium on Math. Modelling in Hydrology, University College, Galway, Ireland, April 1974.

15. Casti, J. "Algorithms for the Stochastic Inflow-Nonlinear Objective Water Reservoir Control Problem," IIASA Workshop on Vistula and Tisza River Basins, IIASA February 1975.

16. Sz. Nagy, A. "On the Optimal Stochastic Control of Water Resource Systems," Internal Paper, IIASA, 1975.

17. Mehra, R. "An Optimal Control Approach to National Settlement System Planning," IIASA RM-75-58, IIASA, 1975.

18. Strobel, H. "Transportation, Automation, and the Quality of Urban Living," IIASA RR-75-34, IIASA, 1975.

19. Kalman, R., B. Ho, and K. Narendra, "Controllability of Linear Dynamical Systems," Contr. to Diff. Eqs. 1 (1963), 189-213.

20. Wei, J., and E. Norman, "On the Global Representation of the Solutions of Linear Differential Equations as a Product of Exponentials," Proc. Amer. Math. Soc. 15 (1964), 327-334.

21. Charpentier, J. P. "Overview on Techniques and Models Used in the Energy Field," IIASA RM-75-8, IIASA, 1975.

22. Casti, J. Dynamical Systems and Their Applications: Linear Theory, Academic Press, New York (to appear Spring 1977).

CONTROL SYSTEMS WITH DELAYS*: AREAS OF APPLICATIONS AND PRESENT STATUS OF THE LINEAR THEORY

M.C. DELFOUR A. MANITIUS
Centre de Recherches Mathématiques
Université de Montréal
Montréal, Qué. H3C 3J7, Canada

Abstract. This paper surveys several areas of applications of models of hereditary type and summarizes the present status of linear control theory in the autonomous case. By treating hereditary differential systems (HDS) in the Hilbert space M^2 using evolution equations, we show that most system theoretic concepts can be put together in a unified framework. There an important role is played by a certain "hereditary operator" F which permits to achieve substantial simplifications of the existing theory. By using this operator, the spectral theory along with controllability and observability related concepts are reviewed. It is shown that the use of that operator permits to construct notions of controllability and observability which are directly related to feedback stabilization and solvability of the algebraic operator Riccati equation, thus making the whole theory complete.

1. Introduction. The interest in delay and hereditary systems in control theory resulted originally from a known fact that many technological processes include transportation delay which makes them more difficult to control. Systems of such type are frequently encountered in chemical processes where the delays are transportation lags in various pipelines connecting tanks, reactors and other parts of the plant. In many other technological problems delays were used to approximate slow responses of processes involving heat and mass transfers.

In recent years, with the area of applications of the control theory growing to encompass biological, ecological, economical and social problems, it was realized that in many situations the dynamical processes involved were of hereditary nature. Consequently one can observe in the literature a growing trend to model such processes by differential-difference, or by functional differential equations. This in turn results in an increased interest of mathematicians and control theorists in models of hereditary type.

1.1. Models of control systems with delays. A description of several examples of models involving delays, or a more general hereditary dependence on the past can be found in A. MANITIUS [1]. A model of a chemical process involving delays can be found in RAY-SOLIMAN [1]. It is typical for many chemical technological processes. More generally, chemical plants with transportation lags can be modelled by sets of coupled ordinary and partial differential equations which in some cases can be reduced to differential-difference equations (cf. HIRATSUKA-ICHIKAWA [1]). A highly simplified model of a metal rolling control system can be found in R.A. JOHNSON [1].

* This research was supported by National Research Council of Canada under Grants A-8730 and A-9240 and in part by a FCAC Grant from the Quebec Ministry of Education.

In this example we obtain nonlinear equations with a state dependent delay. Such equations are also encountered in some population models (K.L. COOKE [1]), and in the two-body problem of classical electrodynamics (R. DRIVER [1]). Nonlinear functional differential equations have also been used to describe dynamics of nuclear reactors (W.K. ERGEN [1], ERGEN-NOHEL [1], H.B. SMETS [1]). Extensive study of such models for reactors can be found in the mathematical literature (LEVIN-NOHEL [1], J.A. NOHEL [1]).

In several papers, R.K. BRAYTON [1], BRAYTON-MIRANKER [1], W.L. MIRANKER [1] and COOKE-KRUMME [1] have discussed certain nonlinear mixed initial boundary value problems for partial differential equations arising from transmission line theory. They have shown that for certain hyperbolic systems the boundary problem can be replaced by an initial value problem for an associated neutral differential-difference equation. Likewise, G.A. KENT [1] has shown how such hyperbolic partial differential equations with boundary controls reduce to control problems involving neutral functional differential equations. The replacement of a mixed initial-boundary problem for a partial differential system by a pure initial value problem for a differential-difference system has important theoretical and practical consequences. For instance it provides effective means for numerical integration, for investigations of stability and oscillations (M. SLEMROD [1]) and for calculation of optimal boundary controls.

In biomedical applications, the differential-difference equations have been used in a mathematical model of a human respiratory control system (MILHORN-BENTON-ROSS-GUYTON [1]). Another model of this type, involving 14 differential equations with five different time lags, studied by BUELL and GRODINS, is mentioned in K.L. COOKE [1]. For examples of modeling and control in the biomedical sciences, the reader is referred to H.T. BANKS [1], [2], [3].

Hereditary models have also appeared in several studies of growth of biological populations (COOKE-YORKE [1], A.J. LOTKA [1], [2], LOTKA-SHARPE [1], WANGERSKY-CUNNINGHAM [1], K.L. COOKE [1], COOKE-KRUMME [1] and G.E. HUTCHINSON [1]), and in studies of growth of two competing populations, that is prey-predator models, (V. VOLTERRA [1], H.H. BUEHLER [1], C.E. MUELLER [1]). Potential applications of these models and of their optimal control include areas such as control of pests, fish ressources etc.

Differential-difference and functional-differential equations have been often used in the modeling of diseases in the population (J.A. YORKE [1], COOKE-YORKE [1], HOPPENSTEADT-WALTMAN [1], P. WALTMAN [1]). Models of controlled epidemics have been studied in N.K. GUPTA [1] and GUPTA-RINK [1].

Another important class of systems which exhibits delays between the decisions and their effect are economic systems. A pioneering step in modeling the influence of these delays on the dynamics of an economic system has been done by M. KALECKI [1], [2], [3]. More recently, delays have played an important role in the macroeconomical models of the Forrester type. For instance in the known book "The limit to growth" (MEADOWS-MEADOWS-RANDERS-BEHRENS [1]) we can find that the time delays are present in nearly all the interlocking feedback loops, that constitute the aggregated model of the world system. These are natural delays that cannot be controlled by technological means. They include for example the delay between the time a pollutant is released into the environment and the time it has a measurable influence on human health. Other delays occur because capital cannot be transferred instantly from one sector to another to meet changing demands. These delays in a dynamic system have serious effects if the system itself is undergoing rapid changes, which is the case of the fast economical growth in last two decades. One can expect that mathematical modelling of economical and social systems will be subject to intensive studies in coming years, and that models of hereditary type will be quite often used in these studies.

1.2. The linear theory of hereditary differential systems (HDS) of the retarded type. Perhaps the most useful part of optimal control theory for ordinary differential equations is the theory of optimal control of linear differential systems with a quadratic cost criterion. This theory is also the most complete, both for systems evolving in a finite-time interval as well as over an infinite-time interval. It is well known that in the finite-time case the optimal control can be expressed in linear feedback form, where the "feedback gains" satisfy a matrix differential equation of Riccati type. In the infinite-time case by using the theory of controllability and observability, the asymptotic behavior of the controlled system can be studied and a rather complete solution to the problem is available.

Systems with delays only constitute a small subclass of the larger family of hereditary systems whose future behavior depends essentially on the events of the past. In such systems, the rate of change of present state may depend on past states, or on past state change rates, or on past controls.

In this paper we shall only report on the linear theory of hereditary differential systems (HDS) of the type:

$$(1.1)\quad \begin{cases} \dot{x}(t) = \sum_{i=0}^{N} A_i x(t+\theta_i) + \int_{-b}^{0} A_{01}(\theta)x(t+\theta)d\theta + Bu(t), & t \geq 0, \\ x(\theta) = \phi(\theta) \text{ in } [-b,0], \end{cases}$$

where $N \geq 0$ is an integer and $a > 0$, $-a = \theta_N < \ldots < \theta_{i+1} < \theta_i < \ldots < \theta_0 = 0$ and $b \geq a$ are real numbers. We shall also assume observations of the form

$$(1.2)\qquad y(t) = Cx(t).$$

At this stage and in the hilbertian product space formulation the linear-quadratic optimal control and filtering problems are almost complete together with the relevant system theoretic concepts of stabilizability, detectability, controllability and observability. A fairly up to date bibliography of the latest results is also included in the list of references. It is hoped that the now available results will find their way into the applications and that their use will be eventually reported in the literature.

Notation and terminology. Let $\mathbb{R}$ (resp. $\mathbb{C}$) be the field of all real (resp. complex) numbers. Let $X = \mathbb{R}^n$, $U = \mathbb{R}^m$ and $Y = \mathbb{R}^k$ for some integers n, m and k greater or equal to one. Given two Hilbert spaces H and K we denote by $\mathcal{L}(H,K)$ the Banach space of all continuous linear maps $T : H \to K$. When H=K, we shall use the notation $\mathcal{L}(H)$. The dual operator of T in $\mathcal{L}(H,K)$ is an element of $\mathcal{L}(K',H')$ denoted by T^*, where H' and K' are the respective topological duals of H and K. Given $a < b$, $C(a,b;H)$ will denote the Banach space of all bounded continuous maps $[a,b] \to H$, $C^1(a,b;H)$ the space of continuous map with a bounded continuous derivative, $L^2(a,b;H)$ the Hilbert space of all equivalence classes of Lebesgue measurable maps $[a,b] \to H$ which are square integrable, $H^1(a,b;H)$ the Sobolev space of all maps x in $L^2(a,b;H)$ with a distributional derivative Dx in $L^2(a,b;H)$ which in this case coincides with the usual derivative almost everywhere on $[a,b]$. The derivative of a map x will be denoted $\dot{x}$.

2. Linear autonomous HDS. In this section we summarize known facts about the representation of linear autonomous HDS, and we introduce a certain "hereditary operator" F which will play a central role in our development.

2.1. The system (S). Let (S) denote the following controlled HDS

$$(2.1)\quad \begin{cases} \dot{x}(t) = \sum_{i=0}^{N} A_i x(t+\theta_i) + \int_{-b}^{0} A_{01}(\theta)x(t+\theta)d\theta + Bu(t), \quad t \geq 0, \ u \in L^2_{loc}(0,\infty;U), \\ x(0) = \phi^0, \ x(\theta) = \phi^1(\theta), \text{ a.e. in } [-b,0[, \ \phi = (\phi^0,\phi^1) \in M^2 \triangleq X \times L^2(-b,0;X), \end{cases}$$

where $N \geq 0$ is an integer, $a > 0$, $-a = \theta_N < \ldots < \theta_{i+1} < \theta_i < \ldots < \theta_0 = 0$ and $b \geq a$ are real numbers, $A_0,\ldots,A_N$ are elements of $\mathcal{L}(X)$, A_{01} of $L^2(-b,0;\mathcal{L}(X))$ and B of $\mathcal{L}(U,X)$. The space M^2 is a Hilbert space endowed with the following inner product and norm

$$(2.2)\quad ((\phi,\psi)) = (\phi^0,\psi^0)_X + \int_{-b}^{0} (\phi^1(\theta),\psi^1(\theta))_X d\theta, \quad \|\phi\| = ((\phi,\phi))^{\frac{1}{2}}.$$

We associate with system (S) the following "hereditary operator" F in $\mathcal{L}(M^2)$:

$$(2.3)\quad [F\phi]^0 = \phi^0, \ [F\phi]^1(\alpha) = \sum_{i=1}^{N} A_i \chi_i(\alpha)\phi^1(\theta_i-\alpha) + \int_{-b}^{\alpha} A_{01}(\theta)\phi^1(\theta-\alpha)d\theta,$$

where χ_i is the characteristic function of the interval $[\theta_i,0]$. This operator will serve as an important tool in the analysis of duality.

Remark 2.1. If u=0 in (2.1), then $\{x(t) = 0 \ \forall\, t \geq 0\} \Leftrightarrow \{F\phi = 0\}$.

2.2. The system (S^+). Let (S^+) denote the following (dual) controlled HDS

$$(2.4)\quad \begin{cases} \dot{p}(t) = \sum_{i=0}^{N} A_i^* p(t+\theta_i) + \int_{-b}^{0} A_{01}^*(\theta)p(t+\theta)d\theta + C^*y(t), \quad t \geq 0, \\ p(0) = \psi^0, \ p(\theta) = \psi^1(\theta) \text{ a.e. in } [-b,0[, \ \psi = (\psi^0,\psi^1) \in M^2, \ y \in L^2_{loc}(0,\infty;Y), \end{cases}$$

where C belongs to $\mathcal{L}(X,Y)$. With this equation we associate the operator F^*, which will have the form given by (2.3) with all the matrices A_i, $A_{01}(\theta)$ replaced by their respective transposed A_i^*, $A_{01}(\theta)^*$. A very important fact is that F* is the dual operator of F in the usual sense; this can be checked by direct calculation.

2.3. The state equation $(\tilde{S})$ and the co-state equation $(\tilde{S}^+)$. As is well known, by using the theory of strongly continuous semigroups, both $(\tilde{S})$ and $(\tilde{S}^+)$ can, under some standard regularity conditions on ϕ, ψ, u and y be written as abstract differential equations in the Hilbert space M^2. Define the state $\tilde{x}(t)$ at time t as

(2.5) $\tilde{x}(t) = (\tilde{x}(t)^0, \tilde{x}(t)^1)$, $\tilde{x}(t)^0 = x(t)$, $\tilde{x}(t)^1(\theta) = x(t+\theta)$, a.e. in $[-b,0]$,

and the co-state $\tilde{p}(t)$ at time t as

(2.6) $\tilde{p}(t) = (\tilde{p}(t)^0, \tilde{p}(t)^1)$, $\tilde{p}(t)^0 = p(t)$, $\tilde{p}(t)^1(\theta) = p(t+\theta)$, a.e. in $[-b,0]$.

Let V denote the subset $\{(\phi(0),\phi) : \phi \in H^1(-b,0;X)\}$ of M^2, and $\Lambda : V \to M^2$ the (dense) injection of V into M^2. Then, (S) is equivalent to the state equation $(\tilde{S})$

(2.7) $$\dot{\tilde{x}}(t) = \tilde{A}\tilde{x}(t) + \tilde{B}u(t), \quad t \geq 0, \qquad \tilde{x}(0) = \phi;$$

(S^+) is equivalent to the co-state equation $(\tilde{S}^+)$

(2.8) $$\dot{\tilde{p}}(t) = \tilde{A}^+p(t) + \tilde{C}^*y(t), \quad t \geq 0, \qquad \tilde{p}(0) = \psi.$$

The domains $\mathcal{D}(\tilde{A}) = \mathcal{D}(\tilde{A}^+) = V$, and

(2.9) $$\tilde{A}\phi = \Big(\sum_{i=0}^{N} A_i\phi(\theta_i) + \int_{-b}^{0} A_{01}(\theta)\phi(\theta)d\theta, \dot{\phi}\Big), \quad \tilde{B}u = (Bu,0)$$

(2.10) $$\tilde{A}^+\psi = \Big(\sum_{i=0}^{N} A_i^*\psi(\theta_i) + \int_{-b}^{0} A_{01}(\theta)^*\psi(\theta)d\theta, \dot{\phi}\Big), \quad \tilde{C}^*y = (Cy,0).$$

$\tilde{A}$ (resp. $\tilde{A}^+$) generates a strongly continuous semigroup S(t) (resp. $S^+(t)$), $t \geq 0$, in M^2. Note that $(\tilde{S}^+)$ simply corresponds to transposed state equation with $\tilde{B}u$ replaced by $\tilde{C}^*y$. The solution of $(\tilde{S})$ is given by (the integration is in Bochner sense)

(2.11) $$\tilde{x}(t) = S(t)\phi + \int_0^t S(t-\tau)\tilde{B}u(\tau)d\tau, \quad t \geq 0.$$

An analogous formula holds for $\tilde{p}$. The regularity conditions mentioned above can be relaxed if (2.11) is used instead of (2.7): $\tilde{x}(t)$ is defined for all ϕ in M^2 and all v in $L^2(0,T;U)$.

2.4. The adjoint state equations $(\tilde{S}^*)$ and $(\tilde{S}^{+*})$. Consider the adjoint semigroup $S(t)^*$ (resp. $S^+(t)^*$), $t \geq 0$, of S(t) (resp. $S^+(t)$). The infinitesimal generator $\tilde{A}^*$ of $S(t)^*$ is characterized as follows

(2.12) $$\mathcal{D}(\tilde{A}^*) = \{\psi : \psi^1 = g + [F\psi^0]^1 \text{ for some g in } H^1(-b,0;X),\ g(-b) = 0\}$$

$$[\tilde{A}^*\psi]^0 = A_0^*\psi^0 + \psi^1(0), \quad [\tilde{A}^*\psi]^1 = \dot{g}.$$

For ψ in $\mathcal{D}(\tilde{A}^*)$ and y in $C^1(0,T;Y)$, define the adjoint state equation $(\tilde{S}^*)$

(2.14) $$\dot{q}(t) = \tilde{A}^*q(t) + \tilde{C}^*y(t), \quad t \text{ in } [0,T], \quad q(0) = \psi.$$

There is an interesting relationship between the adjoint state equation $(\tilde{S}^*)$ and the co-state equation $(\tilde{S}^+)$, namely the semigroups $S^+(t)$ and $S^*(t)$ are related to each other through the operator F^* as follows.

Proposition 2.1. (i) $S^*(t)F^* = F^*S^+(t)$ for all $t \geq 0$, (ii) $\tilde{A}^*F^*\phi = F^*\tilde{A}^+\phi$ for all ϕ in $\mathcal{D}(\tilde{A}^+)$, (iii) $\text{Im } S(t)^* \subset \text{Im } F^*$ for all $t \geq b$, (iv) $q(t) = F^*\tilde{p}(t)$ for all $t \geq 0 \Leftrightarrow q(0) = F^*\tilde{p}(0)$.

Proof. Cf. BERNIER-MANITIUS [1] and DELFOUR-MANITIUS [1]. □

Remark 2.2. $\{(\psi^0,0): \psi^0 \in X\} \subset \{\psi \in M^2: \psi = F^*\psi\}$.

Analogous relations hold between $S(t)$ and $S^+(t)^*$, with F^* replaced by F. Consequently almost all relevant properties of $(\tilde{S}^*)$ are provided by $(\tilde{S}^+)$ and F^*. This seems to be a specific property of HDS as opposed to many other infinite dimensional systems which do not have simple substitutes for their adjoint semigroup $S(t)^*$.

Remark 2.3. An analog of the variation-of-constants formula (2.11) holds for each of the four systems discussed above, with appropriate replacements of $S(t)$ and $\tilde{B}u$.

3. The linear quadratic optimal control problem. Consider the cost functional to be minimized

$$(3.1) \qquad J(u) = (x(T),Zx(T))_X + \int_0^T[(x(t),C^*Cx(t))_X+(u(t),Nu(t))_U]dt,$$

where Z (resp. N) are self-adjoint positive semi-definite (resp. definite) elements of $\mathcal{L}(X)$ (resp. $\mathcal{L}(U)$) and C was defined in sec. 2.3.

Complete theoretical results have been obtained for the linear quadratic optimal control problem and the filtering problem associated with system (S) both over a finite time horizon $[0,T]$, $T > 0$, as well as over an infinite time horizon. For the finite time optimal control problem the reader is referred to A. MANITIUS [3], ELLER-AGGARWAL-BANKS [1], KUSHNER-BARNEA [1], ALEKAL-BRUNOVSKY-CHYUNG-LEE [1], C.E. MUELLER [1], DELFOUR-MITTER [3] and M.C. DELFOUR [1]. The last two papers use the state space approach; for the infinite time horizon problem, the reader is referred to N.N. KRASOVSKII [1], [2], ROSS-FLÜGGE-LOTZ [1], [2] and DELFOUR-McCALLA-MITTER [1]. A rather complete survey of those results is contained in A. MANITIUS [5]. For the related filtering problem the reader is referred to H. KWAKERNAAK [1], A. BENSOUSSAN [1], BENSOUSSAN-DELFOUR-MITTER [2], [7], A. LINDQUIST [1], [2], R.B. VINTER [2], R.T. CURTAIN [1], MITTER-VINTER [1], R.H. KWONG [1], [2], KWONG-WILLSKY [1].

For the case of practical interest ($Z=0$ and $T \to \infty$), it was shown that if the optimal control u exists it is given by

$$(3.2) \qquad u(t) = -N^{-1}\tilde{B}^*\Pi\tilde{x}(t), \quad t \geq 0,$$

where Π in $\mathcal{L}(M^2)$ is a solution of the following operational "algebraic" (as opposed to "differential") Riccati equation

$$(3.3) \qquad \Lambda^*\Pi\tilde{A} + \tilde{A}^*\Pi\Lambda + \Lambda^*[\tilde{Q}-\Pi\tilde{R}\Pi]\Lambda = 0 \text{ in } \mathcal{L}(V,V'),$$

where $\tilde{Q} = \tilde{C}^*\tilde{C}$, $\tilde{R} = \tilde{B}N^{-1}\tilde{B}^*$ and Λ is defined in sec. 2.3 (cf. DELFOUR-McCALLA-MITTER [1], BENSOUSSAN-DELFOUR-MITTER [3]). In the general context of an arbitrary semigroup of class C_0, J. ZABCZYK [1] studied Eq. (3.3). He stated that there exists a solution to Eq. (3.3) when the pair $(\tilde{A},\tilde{B})$ is stabilizable; moreover this solution is unique and the closed loop system $(\tilde{A}-\tilde{B}N^{-1}\tilde{B}^*\Pi)$ is stable when, in addition, the pair $(\tilde{A},\tilde{C})$ is detectable (see below).

Definition 3.1. (i) The pair $(\tilde{A},\tilde{B})$ is said to be stabilizable if there exists an operator K in $\mathcal{L}(M^2,U)$ such that the operator $\tilde{A}+\tilde{B}K$ generates a stable semigroup.
(ii) The pair $(\tilde{A},\tilde{C})$ is said to be detectable if there exists an operator L in $\mathcal{L}(Y,M^2)$ such that the operator $\tilde{A}+L\tilde{C}$ generates a stable semigroup. □

Remark 3.1. The pair $(\tilde{A},\tilde{C})$ is detectable if and only if the pair $(\tilde{A}^*,\tilde{C}^*)$ is stabizable (cf. BHAT-WONHAM [1]).

The more concrete verifiable conditions for stabilizability and detectability for linear HDS and their relationship with controllability were for some time a missing link in the whole theory. Our sections 4 and 5 summarize recent developments that have eventually provided this missing link.

By using a purely algebraic approach E.W. KAMEN [1], [2] has obtained new important results for the stabilization problem by feedback. Our approach is different but the final results seem to converge with those of Kamen.

Before proceeding further, we wish to emphasize that efficient numerical techniques have recently become available for solving the Riccati equation in the case $T < \infty$ (as well as $T=\infty$). These are reported by M.C. DELFOUR [2][3][4][5][7]. The numerical techniques of the linear-quadratic problem were also investigated by BANKS-MANITIUS [1], BANKS-BURNS [1], [2], C.E. MUELLER [1], ELLER-AGGARWAL-BANKS [1], LEE-MANITIUS [1], by using two different projection techniques associated with the semigroup S(t). One of them, the spectral projection method, investigated previously by BANKS-MANITIUS [1] in the context of space C, has been recently investigated within the framework of space M^2 (cf. DELFOUR-MANITIUS [1] and also BANKS-BURNS [3]), where some new insight is gained. This constitutes a theme of the next section.

4. Spectral decomposition. In this section we summarize the main results on the spectral theory of linear HDS which will be useful in this paper. A more detailed development is given in DELFOUR-MANITIUS [1]. It will be convenient to define the "exponential map" E_λ associated with λ in $\mathbb{C}$ as an element of $\mathcal{L}(X,H)$:

(4.1) $$[E_\lambda x]^0 = x, \quad [E_\lambda x]^1(\theta) = e^{\lambda\theta}x.$$

All previously real spaces are now to be interpreted as their complex extension. The adjoint map E_λ^* of E_λ is given by

(4.2) $$E_\lambda^*\phi = \phi^0 + \int_{-b}^{0} e^{\bar{\lambda}\theta}\phi^1(\theta)d\theta \quad (\bar{\lambda}, \text{ the conjugate of } \lambda \text{ in } \mathbb{C}).$$

The spectrum $\sigma(\tilde{A})$ of $\tilde{A}$ is a point spectrum which is characterized by

(4.3) $$\sigma(\tilde{A}) = \{\lambda \in \mathbb{C}: \det \Delta(\lambda) = 0\}$$

where $\det \Delta(\lambda)$ is the determinant of $\Delta(\lambda)$ defined as

$$\Delta(\lambda) = I\lambda - \sum_{i=0}^{N} A_i e^{\lambda\theta_i} - \int_{-b}^{0} A_{01}(\theta)e^{\lambda\theta}d\theta. \tag{4.4}$$

The complement of $\sigma(\tilde{A})$ is denoted by $\rho(\tilde{A})$. The operators F and E_λ enable us to represent the resolvent operator $R(\lambda,\tilde{A})$ of $\tilde{A}$ in a very simple way.

Proposition 4.1. For all λ in $\rho(\tilde{A})$, the resolvent of $\tilde{A}$ is given by

$$R(\lambda,\tilde{A}) = (I\lambda-\tilde{A})^{-1} = E_\lambda\Delta(\lambda)^{-1}E_\lambda^* F + T_\lambda, \tag{4.5}$$

where

$$[T_\lambda\phi]^0 = 0, \quad [T_\lambda\phi]^1(\theta) = \int_\theta^0 e^{\lambda(\theta-\alpha)}\phi^1(\alpha)d\alpha. \quad \Box \tag{4.6}$$

Let λ in $\sigma(\tilde{A})$ be a pole of order m of $R(\lambda,\tilde{A})$ and let $M_\lambda = \mathrm{Ker}(I\lambda-\tilde{A})^m$, $R_\lambda = \mathrm{Im}(I\lambda-\tilde{A})^m$. Define the operator

$$P_\lambda\phi = \frac{1}{2\pi i}\oint_{\Gamma_\lambda} R(\mu,\tilde{A})\phi d\mu, \tag{4.7}$$

where Γ_λ is a closed rectifiable curve containing λ inside and all the other spectral points outside. One has (cf. A.E. TAYLOR [1])

$$P_\lambda^2 = P_\lambda, \quad \mathrm{Im}\, P_\lambda = M_\lambda, \quad \mathrm{Ker}\, P_\lambda = R_\lambda, \tag{4.8}$$

so that P_λ is a projection operator ("spectral projection") that decomposes M^2, that is $M^2 = M_\lambda \oplus R_\lambda$. From (4.5) and (4.7)

$$P_\lambda = \mathcal{E}_\lambda F, \quad \mathcal{E}_\lambda = \frac{1}{2\pi i}\oint_{\Gamma_\lambda} E_\lambda\Delta(\lambda)^{-1}E_\lambda^* d\lambda; \tag{4.9}$$

the integral of the term T_λ is zero since it is an entire function.

Remark 4.1. For all λ in $\sigma(\tilde{A})$, $\mathrm{Ker}\, F \subset \mathrm{Ker}\, P_\lambda$.

Since R_λ is closed, one has $R_\lambda = [\mathrm{Ker}(I\lambda-\tilde{A}^*)^m]^\perp$. On the other hand it can be proved (cf. DELFOUR-MANITIUS [1]) that

$$M_\lambda^* \triangleq \mathrm{Ker}(I\lambda-\tilde{A}^*)^m = F^*\mathrm{Ker}(I\lambda-\tilde{A}^+)^m. \tag{4.10}$$

Hence

$$\mathrm{Ker}\, P_\lambda = \{\phi: (\!(F^*\psi,\phi)\!) = 0, \quad \forall\ \psi \text{ in } \mathrm{Ker}(I\lambda-\tilde{A}^+)^m\}. \tag{4.11}$$

Consequently, introducing the basis $\phi_1,\ldots,\phi_d$ of M_λ and a basis $\psi_1,\ldots,\psi_d$ of $\mathrm{Ker}(I\lambda-\tilde{A}^+)^m$ such that $(\!(F^*\psi_i,\phi_j)\!) = \delta_{ij}$, and defining

$$\hat{P}_\lambda\phi = \sum_{i=1}^{d} \phi_i(\!(F^*\psi_i,\phi)\!), \tag{4.12}$$

one has that $\hat{P}_\lambda \equiv P_\lambda$. Formulas (4.9) and (4.11) are just alternative (and computationally different) expressions for the spectral projection P_λ. An important fact about the spectral projection P_λ is that the state equation $(\tilde{S})$ projected onto M_λ becomes an ordinary differential equation; e.g. if m=1, then $\xi(t) \triangleq P_\lambda\tilde{x}(t)$ is governed by

(4.13) $$\dot{\xi}(t) = \lambda\xi(t) + ku(t),$$

where $k = ⟪F^*\psi_1, \tilde{B}⟫$.

Definition 4.2. The system $(\tilde{S})$ is said to be spectrally controllable if all the spectral projections of $(\tilde{S})$ are controllable. □

In particular if all the spectral projections of $(\tilde{S})$ are simple (all m=1), the spectral controllability of $(\tilde{S})$ means that all the coefficients k in (4.13) corresponding to all λ in $\sigma(\tilde{A})$ are nonzero. Spectral controllability is important because it implies that the system $(\tilde{S})$ can be made exponentially stable by a linear feedback (cf. sec. 5), with an arbitrary prefixed exponential decay rate. Criteria for spectral controllability have recently become available (cf. L. PANDOLFI [1], BHAT-KOIVO [1], BHAT-WONHAM [1], MANITIUS-TRIGGIANI [1]). One of them is

(4.14) $$\operatorname{rank}[\Delta(\lambda), B] = n, \text{ for all } \lambda \text{ in } \sigma(\tilde{A}).$$

This criterion, although simple, is not always very practical as the computation of eigenvalues of $\tilde{A}$ is quite difficult. This motivates a search for other controllability concepts that would be easier to verify (cf. sec. 5).

Another important feature of M_λ and P_λ is that under some conditions on $(\tilde{S})$ one can have

(4.15) $$\overline{\operatorname{span}}\{M_\lambda : \lambda \in \sigma(\tilde{A})\} = M^2,$$

and for some ϕ and some $(\tilde{S})$

(4.16) $$\sum_{\lambda\in\sigma(\tilde{A})} P_\lambda\phi = \phi.$$

Detailed answers to these convergence questions are given in DELFOUR-MANITIUS [1]. Here we only point out that a sufficient condition for (4.15) to be true is $\theta_N = -b$, $\det A_N \neq 0$; if, in addition ϕ satisfies some regularity conditions (e.g. $\phi \in \mathcal{D}(\tilde{A}^2)$), then (4.16) also holds.

Definition 4.3. The system of generalized eigenfunctions of $\tilde{A}$ is said to be F-complete (resp. M^2-complete) if

(4.17) $$\overline{F(\operatorname{span}\{M_\lambda : \lambda \in \sigma(\tilde{A})\})} = \overline{\operatorname{Im} F} \text{ (resp. (4.15) holds).} \quad \square$$

The class of systems $(\tilde{S})$ satisfying F-completeness property is obviously larger than of those satisfying (4.15); more importantly, it includes finite dimensional systems without delays. Criteria and examples are given in DELFOUR-MANITIUS [1].

Most of these considerations can be extended to the system $(\tilde{S}^*)$. For example, the resolvent of $\tilde{A}^*$ is (for λ in $\rho(\tilde{A}^*) = \rho(\tilde{A})$)

(4.18) $$R(\lambda,\tilde{A}^*) = R(\bar{\lambda},\tilde{A})^* = (E_{\bar{\lambda}}\Delta(\bar{\lambda})^{-1}E^*_{\bar{\lambda}}F+T_{\bar{\lambda}})^* = F^*E_\lambda\Delta^*(\lambda)^{-1}E^*_{\bar{\lambda}} + T^*_{\bar{\lambda}},$$

where

(4.19) $$[T^*_{\bar{\lambda}}\psi]^0 = 0, \quad [T^*_{\bar{\lambda}}\psi]^1(\theta) = \int_{-b}^{\theta} e^{\lambda(\alpha-\theta)}\psi^1(\alpha)\,d\alpha.$$

Likewise, an analog of P_λ is

(4.20) $$P^*_\lambda = F^*\mathcal{E}^*_\lambda, \quad \mathcal{E}^*_\lambda = \frac{1}{2\pi i}\oint_{\Gamma_\lambda} E_\lambda \Delta^*(\lambda)^{-1} E^*_\lambda d\lambda.$$

5. Controllability, observability and duality. In this section we introduce the new concepts of F-controllability and F-observability and show how they are related to stabilizability and detectability. A complete duality is also shown between systems $(\tilde{S})$ and $(\tilde{S}^{+}*)$ and $(\tilde{S}*)$ and $(\tilde{S}^{+})$.

5.1. M^2-controllability, F-controllability and spectral controllability. We denote by K_t the set of all reachable states of $(\tilde{S})$ at time t

(5.1) $$K_t = \{\int_0^t S(t-s)\tilde{B}u(s)ds: u \text{ in } L^2(0,t;U)\}, \quad K_\infty = \cup\{K_t: t > 0\}.$$

By Definition 4.2, the pair $(\tilde{A},\tilde{B})$ is spectrally controllable if

(5.2) $$\operatorname{span}\{M_\lambda: \lambda \in \sigma(\tilde{A})\} \subset K_\infty.$$

Definition 5.1. We say that the pair $(\tilde{A},\tilde{B})$ is F-controllable (resp. M^2-controllable) if

(5.3) $$\overline{FK_\infty} = \overline{\operatorname{Im} F} \quad (\text{resp. } \overline{K_\infty} = M^2). \quad \square$$

Theorem 5.2. (i) M^2-controllability ⇒ F-controllability.

(ii) F-controllability ⇒ spectral controllability.

(iii) Spectral controllability ⇏ stabilizability.

Proof. (i) Cf. MANITIUS-TRIGGIANI [1]. (ii) Cf. A. MANITIUS [2]. (iii) Cf. Y.S. OSIPOV [1], R. TRIGGIANI [1]. □

The concept of F-controllability which was first introduced in the above form by A. MANITIUS [2] is weaker than that of M^2-controllability. Criteria for M^2-controllability and F-controllability have been extensively investigated by MANITIUS-TRIGGIANI [1][2][3][4]. For systems with one delay and $A_{01}(\theta) \equiv 0$, complete algebraic tests exist. For instance it was shown that the simple conditions

$$\operatorname{rank}[B, A_1B, \dots, A_1^{n-1}B] = n \text{ and } \operatorname{Im} A_0A_1^jB \subset \sum_{i=0}^{j} \operatorname{Im} A_1^iB, \quad j=0,\dots,n-1$$

guarantee together the M_2-controllability (for more results of this type see MANITIUS-TRIGGIANI [1][2][3][4] and MANITIUS [4]). Similar techniques apply to F-controllability. Therefore, even though our subsequent discussion will remain at the abstract level, we strongly emphasize that most of the concepts discussed below can be translated into simple language of linear algebra and Laplace transforms (at a cost of loosing somewhat the simplicity of notation).

In view of Proposition 2.1 applied to $(\tilde{S})$ and $(\tilde{S}^{+}*)$ we can easily check that the attainable set $K^+_\infty*$ of $(\tilde{S}^{+}*)$ and the attainable set K_∞ of $(\tilde{S})$ are related as follows

(5.4) $$K^+_\infty* = FK_\infty.$$

Thus it is natural to extend the concept of F-controllability to $(\tilde{S}^{+}*)$.

Definition 5.3. We say that the pair $(\tilde{A}^{+*},\tilde{B})$ is F-controllable if

(5.5) $$\overline{K_\infty^{+*}} = \overline{\text{Im } F}. \quad \square$$

The concept of F-controllability for the pair $(\tilde{A},\tilde{B})$ can also be interpreted by introducing the quotient space $M^2/\text{Ker } F$ and the canonical surjection $\varphi: M^2 \to M^2/\text{Ker } F$. Then

(5.6) $$\overline{FK_\infty} = \overline{\text{Im } F} \Leftrightarrow \overline{\varphi K_\infty} = M^2/\text{Ker } F.$$

Remark 5.1. In the "degenerate case" without delays, that is $A_i = 0$, $i = 1,\dots,N$ and $A_{01} = 0$, $\text{Im } F = X \times \{0\}$ and the concept of F-controllability exactly reduces to the usual one for systems without delays! This is not the case of M^2-controllability or other function space controllability concepts. Thus it is a natural extension of the classical concept.

F-controllability is also the right concept for the stabilizability of the pair $(\tilde{A},\tilde{B})$. An interesting open problem is whether the converse of Theorem 5.2 (ii) is true. A. MANITIUS [2] has shown that it is true under the hypothesis of F-completeness (cf. Definition 4.3). However it is possible to construct examples where $(\tilde{S})$ is not F-complete and yet the pair $(\tilde{A},\tilde{B})$ is M^2-controllable, F-controllable and spectrally controllable (cf. A. MANITIUS [2]).

5.2. F-observability, F*-controllability and duality. We now turn to a concept of observability which will imply detectability of the pair $(\tilde{A},\tilde{C})$, or equivalently (cf. Remark 3.1) the stabilizability of the pair $(\tilde{A}^*,\tilde{C}^*)$. Referring to system $(\tilde{S}^*)$, Eq. (2.14) and the analog of formula (2.11), define the attainable set

(5.7) $$K_t^* = \{\int_0^t S^*(t-s)\tilde{C}^*y(s)ds: y \text{ in } L^2(0,t;Y)\}, \quad K_\infty^* = \cup\{K_t^*: t > 0\}.$$

By Proposition 2.1 and Remark 2.2 we have that for all $t \geq 0$

(5.8) $$q(t) = \int_0^t S^*(t-s)\tilde{C}^*y(s)ds = F^* \int_0^t S^+(t-s)\tilde{C}^*y(s)ds \in \text{Im } F^*.$$

Thus K_∞^* is at most $\text{Im } F^*$.

Definition 5.4. (i) The system $(\tilde{S}^*)$ is said to be spectrally controllable if

(5.9) $$\text{span}\{M_\lambda^*: \lambda \text{ in } \sigma(\tilde{A}^*)\} \subset K_\infty^*.$$

(ii) We say that the pair $(\tilde{A}^*,\tilde{C}^*)$ is F*-controllable (resp. M^2-controllable) if

(5.10) $$\overline{K_\infty^*} = \overline{\text{Im } F^*} \quad (\text{resp. } \overline{K_\infty^*} = M^2). \quad \square$$

Theorem 5.5. (i) M^2-controllability ⇒ F*-controllability.

(ii) F*-controllability ⇒ spectral controllability.

(iii) Spectral controllability ⇒ stabilizability.

Proof. Similar to proof of Theorem 5.2. □

Again it is natural to extend the concept of F*-controllability to $(\tilde{S}^+)$ by noting that $K_t^* = F^*K_t^+$ (cf. Eq. (5.8)) where K_t^+ is the attainable set of $(\tilde{S}^+)$ corresponding to the pair $(\tilde{A}^+,\tilde{C}^*)$.

Definition 5.6. We say that the pair (A^+,C^*) is F*-controllable if

(5.11) $$\overline{F^*K_\infty^+} = \overline{\operatorname{Im} F^*}. \quad \square$$

Again the concept of F*-controllability for the pair $(\tilde{A}^+,\tilde{C}^*)$ can be interpreted by introducing the quotient space $M^2/\operatorname{Ker} F^*$ and the canonical surjection $\varphi^*: M^2 \to M^2/\operatorname{Ker} F^*$. Then

(5.12) $$\overline{F^*K_\infty^+} = \overline{\operatorname{Im} F^*} \iff \overline{\varphi^*K_\infty^+} = M^2/\operatorname{Ker} F^*.$$

Calculating the dual operator of (5.8) we find that it is a mapping $\phi \to y: M^2 \to L^2_{loc}(0,\infty;Y)$ defined by

(5.13) $$y(t) = \tilde{C}S(t)\phi = \tilde{C}S^+(t)^*F\phi, \quad t \geq 0,$$

(we have used the analog of Proposition 2.1 (iv) for $(\tilde{S})$ and $(\tilde{S}^{+}*)$). To say that $(\tilde{A}^*_+,\tilde{C}^*)$ is F*-controllable is equivalent to say that the mapping

(5.14) $$\phi \to y: M^2/\operatorname{Ker} F \to L^2_{loc}(0,\infty;Y)$$

is injective, or equivalently the mapping

(5.15) $$\phi \to \bar{y}: \overline{\operatorname{Im} F} \to L^2_{loc}(0,\infty;Y)$$

is injective, where

(5.16) $$\bar{y}(t) = \tilde{C} \quad S^+(t)^*\phi, \quad t \geq 0.$$

This very naturally suggests the following two equivalent definitions of F-observability.

Definition 5.7. (i) The pair $(\tilde{A},\tilde{C})$ is said to be F-observable if the mapping (5.14) is injective.

(ii) The pair $(\tilde{A}^+*,\tilde{C})$ is said F-observable if the mapping (5.15) is injective. $\square$

Proposition 5.8. The following statements are equivalent:

(i) $(\tilde{A},\tilde{C})$ is F-observable;

(ii) $y(t) = 0,\ t \geq 0$ in (5.13) $\Rightarrow F\phi = 0$;

(iii) $y(t) = 0,\ t \geq 0$ in (5.13) $\Rightarrow x(t) = [S(t)\phi]^0 = 0,\ t \geq 0$. $\square$

The second statement has been used in the literature on HDS (cf. R.H. KWONG [1], E.B. LEE [1] and A.W. OLBROT [1]).

It is important to note that

1) the observability in the sense of Proposition 5.8 (ii) was investigated by A.W. OLBROT [1], who, for systems with one delay, using the method of steps gave some computable criteria based on augmented matrices and their exponentials. Therefore, at least for these systems, F-controllability and F-observability can be practically tested,

2) this type of observability along with stabilizability guarantees the asymptotic stability of the optimal filter, even in the case of delays in the observations (cf. R.H. KWONG [1]).

Concluding this section we note that there is a complete duality between the controllability and observability concepts discussed above, which can be summarized in the following diagram

$$\begin{array}{ccc} (\tilde{A},\tilde{C}) \text{ F-observable} & \Longleftrightarrow & (\tilde{A}^*,\tilde{C}^*) \text{ F*-controllable } (\overline{K^*_\infty} = \overline{\text{Im } F^*}) \\ \Updownarrow & & \Updownarrow \\ (\tilde{A}^{+*},\tilde{C}) \text{ F-observable} & \Longleftrightarrow & (\tilde{A}^{+},\tilde{C}^*) \text{ F*-controllable } (\overline{F^*K^+_\infty} = \overline{\text{Im } F^*}). \end{array}$$

6. Concluding remarks. As seen in previous sections, the use of the abstract differential equation in the space M^2 along with the operator F makes it possible to complete the linear theory of HDS in a way which is a natural extension of the finite dimensional theory, and which contains the latter as a special case, when operator $F = (I,0)$. Many other new insights into previous work can be gained by giving appropriate interpretations to the operator Π of the Riccati equation (3.3) using the representations involving F. For instance it can be shown that the operator Π of Eq. (3.3) satisfies $\Pi = F^*P = P^*F$ for some P in $\mathcal{L}(M^2)$. This gives a new interpretations of the presence of discontinuities in the integral kernels representing the feedback $u(t) = -N^{-1}\tilde{B}^*\Pi\tilde{x}(t) = -N^{-1}\tilde{B}^*P^*F\tilde{x}(t)$ in the examples computed numerically by M.C. DELFOUR [2].

Other observations of this type seem to be possible, which would lead to substantial simplifications of the existing theory.

A special case which needs further investigation and is important from the point of view of applications is the one with delays in the control and/or observations. Here it seems that the extensions of the present controllability theory based on the resolvent operator $R(\lambda,\tilde{A})$ should permit to obtain complete solutions as well.

This coupled with efficient numerical algorithms for computation of feedback controllers will hopefully make the present theory a useful tool in applications.

References

Y. ALEKAL, P. BRUNOVSKY, D.H. CHYUNG and E.B. LEE [1], The quadratic problem for systems with time delays, IEEE Trans. on Automatic Control AC-16 (1971), 673-688.

H.T. BANKS [1], Modeling and control in the biomedical sciences, Springer Lecture Notes in Biomath., Vol. 6, 1975.
[2], Delay systems in biological models: approximation techniques, Proc. International Conference on Nonlinear Systems and Applications, July 1976, Arlington, Texas.
[3], Modeling of control and dynamical systems in the life sciences, in "Optimal control theory and its applications", Part II, B.J. Kirby, ed., pp. 1-112, Springer-Verlag, New York, 1974.

H.T. BANKS and J.A. BURNS [1], An abstract framework for approximate solutions to optimal control problems governed by hereditary systems, Proc. International Conference on Differential Equations, H.A. Antosiewicz, ed., pp. 10-25, Academic Press, New York, 1975.
[2], Hereditary control problems: numerical methods based on averaging approximations, Report, Lefschetz Center for Dynamical Systems, Division of Applied Mathematics, Brown University, Providence, R.I., 1976.
[3], Eigenmanifold decomposition for retarded functional differential equations in Hilbert space, to appear.

H.T. BANKS and A. MANITIUS [1], Projection series for retarded functional differential equations with applications to optimal control problems, J. Differential Equations 18 (1975), 296-332.
[2], Application of abstract variational theory to hereditary systems - a survey, IEEE Trans. Automatic Control AC-19 (1974), 524-533.

A. BENSOUSSAN [1], Filtrage des systèmes linéaires avec retard, IRIA Report INF 7118/71027, oct. 1971.

A. BENSOUSSAN, M.C. DELFOUR and S.K. MITTER [1], Representation theory for linear infinite dimensional continuous time systems, in "Mathematical Systems Theory", G. Marchesini and S.K. Mitter, eds., pp. 204-225, Springer-Verlag, Berlin, 1976.
[2], Optimal filtering for linear stochastic hereditary differential systems, Proceedings of the 1972 IEEE Conference on Decision and Control and 11th Symposium on Adaptive Processes, pp. 378-380, New York 1972.
[3], The linear quadratic optimal control problem for infinite dimensional systems over an infinite horizon: survey and examples, Proc. 1976 IEEE Conference on Decision and Control, 1976.
[4], Representation and control of infinite dimensional system, Reports ESL-P-602, 603 and 604, Electronic Systems Laboratory, Massachusetts Institute of Technology, June 1975.

C. BERNIER et A. MANITIUS [1], L'étude des semi-groupes d'opérateurs associés aux équations linéaires retardées, Rapport CRM-623, Université de Montréal, mai 1976.

K.P.M. BHAT and H.N. KOIVO [1], Modal characterizations of controllability and observability for time-delay systems, IEEE Trans. on Automatic Control AC-21 (1976), 292-293.

K.P.M. BHAT and W.M. WONHAM [1], Stabilizability and detectability for evolution systems on Banach spaces, Report, Dept. of Electrical Engineering, University of Toronto, 1976.

J.G. BORISOVIC and A.S. TURBABIN [1], On the Cauchy problem for linear non-homogeneous differential equations with retarded argument, Solviet Math. Doklady 10 (1969), 401-405.

R.K. BRAYTON [1], Nonlinear oscillations in a distributed network, Quant. Appl. Math. 24 (1966/67), 289-301.

R.K. BRAYTON and W.L. MIRANKER [1], A stability theory for nonlinear mixed initial boundary value problem, Arch. Rational Mech. Anal. 17 (1964), 358-376.

H.H. BUEHLER [1], Applications of a general theory of extremals to optimal control problems with functional differential equations, Ph.D. dissertation, Univ. Southern California, June 1971.

K.L. COOKE [1], Functional differential equations: some models and perturbation problems, in "Differential equations and dynamical systems", J.K. Hale and J.P. La Salle, eds., pp. 167-183, Academic Press, New York, 1967.

K.L. COOKE and D.W. KRUMME [1], Differential-difference equations and nonlinear initial-boundary value problems for linear hyperbolic partial differential equations, J. Math. Anal. Appl. 24 (1968), 372-387.

K.L. COOKE and J.A. YORKE [1], Equations modelling population growth, economic growth, and gonorrhea epidemiology, in "Ordinary differential equations", L. Weiss, ed., pp. 35-55, Academic Press, New York, 1972.

R.T. CURTAIN [1], A Kalman-Bucy theory for affine hereditary differential equations, in "Control theory, numerical methods and computer systems modelling", eds. A. Bensoussan and J.L. Lions, Springer-Verlag, New York 1975, 22-43.

M.C. DELFOUR [1], State theory of linear hereditary differential systems, J. Math. Anal. and Appl., to appear.
[2], The linear quadratic optimal control problem for hereditary differential systems: theory and numerical solution, J. Applied Mathematics and Optimization, to appear.

[3], Solution numérique de l'équation différentielle de Riccati rencontrée en théorie de la commande optimale des systèmes héréditaires linéaires, in "Control Theory, Numerical Methods and Computer Systems Modelling", A. Bensoussan and J.L. Lions, eds., pp. 362-383, Springer-Verlag, New York, 1975.
[4], Numerical solution of the operational Riccati differential equation in the optimal control theory of linear hereditary differential systems with a linear-quadratic cost function, Proceedings 1974 IEEE Conference on Decision and Control, pp. 784-790, New York 1974.
[5], Numerical solution of the operator Riccati equation for the filtering of linear stochastic hereditary differential systems, in "Optimization techniques, modelling and optimization in the service of man", Part 2, J. Cea, ed., pp. 700-719, Springer-Verlag, New York 1976.
[6], Linear hereditary differential systems and their control, in "Optimal Control and its Applications", Part II, B.J. Kirby, ed., pp. 92-154, Springer-Verlag, New York 1974.
[7], Filtering of linear stochastic hereditary differential systems: numerical solution, Proc. 14th Allerton conference on circuit and system theory, 1976.

M.C. DELFOUR and A. MANITIUS [1], Report CRM-658 (to appear).

M.C. DELFOUR and S.K. MITTER [1], Hereditary differential systems with constant delays, I - General case, J. Differential Equations, 12 (1972), 213-235.
[2], Hereditary differential systems with constant delays, II - A class of affine systems and the adjoint problem, J. Differential Equations, 18 (1975), 18-28.
[3], Controllability, observability and optimal feedback control of affine hereditary differential systems, SIAM J. Control 10 (1972), 298-328.
[4], Controllability and observability for infinite dimensional systems, SIAM J. Control 10 (1972), 329-333.

M.C. DELFOUR, C. McCALLA and S.K. MITTER [1], Stability and the infinite-time quadratic cost problem for linear hereditary differential systems, SIAM J. Control 13 (1975), 48-88.

M.C. DELFOUR and F. TROCHU [1], Discontinuous finite element methods for the approximation of optimal control problems governed by hereditary differential systems, Proceedings IFIP Working Conference on Distributed Parameter Systems: Modelling and Identification, Springer-Verlag, to appear, 1976.

R. DRIVER [1], A two-body problem of classical electrodynamics: the one-dimensional case, Ann. Phys. 21 (1963), 122-142.

D.H. ELLER, J.K. AGGARWAL and H.T. BANKS [1], Optimal control of linear time-delay systems, IEEE Trans. on Automatic Control AC-14 (1969), 678-687.

W.K. ERGEN [1], Kinetics of the circulating-fuel nuclear reactor, J. Appl. Physics, 15 (1954), 702-711.

W.K. ERGEN and J.A. NOHEL [1], Stability of a continuous-medium reactor, J. Nucl. Energy, Part A: Reactor Science, 10 (1959), 14-18.

W.K. ERGEN, H.J. LIPKIN and J.A. NOHEL [1], Application of Lyapunov's second method in reactor dynamics, J. Math. and Phys., 36 (1957), 36-48.

H. GORECKI [1], Control systems with delays (Polish), Wydawnictwa Naukowo-Techniczne, Warszawa, 1972.

N.K. GUPTA [1], Modelling and optimum control of epidemics, Ph.D. thesis, Univ. of Alberta, Edmonton, Canada, 1972.

N.K. GUPTA and R.E. RINK [1], A model for communicable disease control, in Proc. 24th Annual Conf. Eng. in Medecine and Biology, Las Vagas, Nevada, p. 296, 1971.

J.K. HALE [1], Functional differential equations, Springer-Verlag, New York 1971.

S. HIRATSUKA and A. ICHIKAWA [1], Optimal control of systems with transportation lags, IEEE Trans. on Automatic Control, AC-14 (1969), 237-247.

F. HOPPENSTEADT and P. WALTMAN [1], A problem in the theory of epidemics I, II, Math. Biosciences 9 (1970), 71-91; 12 (1971), 133-145.

G.E. HUTCHINSON [1], Circular causal systems in ecology, Annals of New York Academy of Science, 50 (1948), 221-246.

R.A. JOHNSON [1], Functional equations, approximations, and dynamic response of systems with variable time delay, IEEE Trans. on Automatic Control, AC-17 (1972), 398-401.

M. KALECKI [1], A macrodynamic theory of business cycles, Econometrica 3 (1935), 327-344.
[2], Studies in economic dynamics, Allen and Unwin, 1943.
[3], Theory of Economic Dynamics, Allen and Unwin, 1954.

E.W. KAMEN [1], Module structure of infinite-dimensional systems with applications to controllability, SIAM J. Control and Optimization 14 (1976), 389-408.
[2], State and input feedback in systems containing time delays, Proc. 14th Allerton conference on circuit and system theory, 1976.

G.A. KENT [1], Optimal control of functional differential equations of neutral type, Ph.D. Thesis, Brown University, June 1971.

H. KOİVO and E.B. LEE [1], Controller synthesis for linear systems with retarded state and control variables and quadratic cost, Automatica 8 (1972), 203-208.

N.N. KRASOVSKII [1], On the analytic construction of an optimal control in a system with time lags, Prikl. Mat. Mekh. 26 (1962), 39-51 (English transl. J. Appl. Math. Mech. (1962), 50-67).
[2], Optimal processes in systems with time lag, Proc. Second IFAC Congress [in Russian], Vol. I, Izd-vo "Nauka" (1964).

H.J. KUSHNER and D.I. BARNEA [1], On the control of a linear functional differential equation with quadratic cost, SIAM J. Control 8 (1970), 257-272.

H. KWAKERNAAK [1], Optimal filtering in linear systems with time delay, IEEE Trans. on Automatic Control 12 (1967), 169-173.

R.H. KWONG [1], Structural properties and estimation of delay systems, doctoral dissertation, Massachusetts Institute of Technology, Cambridge, Mass. 02139, September 1975 (also report ESL-R-614, M.I.T., Sept. 1975).
[2], The linear quadratic Gaussian problem for systems with delays in the state, control, and observation, Proc. 14th Allerton conference on circuit and system theory, 1976.

R.H. KWONG and A.S. WILLSKY [1], Estimation and filter stability of stochastic delay systems, CRM-Report 613, Université de Montréal, 1976.

E.B. LEE [1], Linear hereditary control systems, in "Calculus of Variations and Control Theory", pp. 47-72, Academic Press Inc., New York, 1976.

E.B. LEE and A. MANITIUS [1], Computational approaches to synthesis of feedback controllers for multivariable systems with delays, Proc. 1974 IEEE Conference on Decision and Control, pp. 791-792, IEEE, New York, 1974.

J.J. LEVIN and J. NOHEL [1], On a nonlinear delay equation, J. Math. Anal. Appl. 8 (1964), 31-44.

N. LEVINSON and C. McCALLA [1], Completeness and independence of the exponential solutions of some functional differential equations, Studies in Applied Math. 53 (1974), 1-15.

A. LINDQUIST [1], A theorem on duality between estimation and control for linear stochastic systems with time delay, J. Math. Anal. Appl. 37 (1972), 516-536.
[2], Optimal control of linear stochastic systems with applications to time lag systems, Information Science 5 (1973), 81-126.

A.J. LOTKA [1], Studies on the mode of growth of material aggregates, Amer. J. Science 24 (1907), 199-216.
[2], A problem in age distribution, Philosophical Magazine, Ser. 6, 21 (1911), 435-438.

A.J. LOTKA and F.R. SHARPE [1], Contributions to the analysis of malaria epidemiology, Am. J. Hygiene 3 (1923), January Supplement, 1-121.

A. MANITIUS [1], Mathematical models of hereditary systems, Report CRM-462, Centre de Recherches Mathématiques, Université de Montréal
[2], Controllability, observability and stabilizability of retarded systems, Proc. 1976 IEEE Conference on Decision and Control, December 1-3, 1976.
[3], Optimal control of time-lag systems with quadratic performance indexes, Proc. Fourth IFAC Congress, Warsaw 1969.
[4], Function space controllability of retarded systems: some new algebraic conditions, Proc. 14th Allerton conference on circuit and system theory, 1976.
[5], Optimal Control of Hereditary Systems (lecture notes), in Control Theory and Topics in Functional Analysis, Vol. III, pp. 43-178, International Atomic Energy Agency, Vienna 1976.

A. MANITIUS and R. TRIGGIANI [1], Function space controllability of linear retarded systems: a derivation from abstract operator conditions, Internal report CRM-605, Centre de Recherches Mathématiques, Université de Montréal, Canada, March 1976.
[2], New results on functional controllability of time-delay systems, Proc. 1976 Conference on Information Sciences and Systems, The John Hopkins University, Baltimore, Maryland (1976), 401-405.
[3], Function space controllability of retarded systems: a derivation from abstract operator conditions (announcement), Proceedings of International Conference on Dynamical Systems, Univ. of Florida, Gainesville, Florida, 24-26 March 1976, Academic Press (to appear).
[4], Sufficient conditions for function space controllability and feedback stabilizability of linear retarded systems, Proc. 1976 IEEE Conference on Decision and Control, Dec. 1-3, 1976.

D.H. MEADOWS, D.L. MEADOWS, J. RANDERS and W.H. BEHRENS [1], The limits to growth, Universe Books Publishers, New York, 1971.

H.T. MILHORN, Jr., R. BENTON, R. ROSS and A.C. GUYTON [1], A mathematical model of the human respiratory control system, Biophysical Journal 5 (1965), 27-46.

W.L. MIRANKER [1], The wave equation with a nonlinear interface condition, IBM J. Res. Development 5 (1961), 2-24.

S.K. MITTER and R. VINTER [1], Filtering for linear stochastic hereditary differential systems, in "Control theory, numerical methods and computer systems modelling", A. Bensoussan and J.L. Lions, eds., pp. 1-21, Springer-Verlag, New York 1975.

C.E. MUELLER [1], Optimal feedback control of hereditary processes, Ph.D. Dissertation, Univ. of Minnesota, Minneapolis, March 1971.

J.A. NOHEL [1], A class of nonlinear delay differential equations, J. Math. and Phys. 38 (1960), 295-311.

A.W. OLBROT [1], On the existence of stabilizing control of linear systems with delays in control, Archivum Autom. i Telem. 17 (1972), 133-147.

Yu. S. OSIPOV [1], The stabilization of controlled systems with time lag, Differentsial'nye Uravneniya, 1, No. 5 (1965), 605-618.

L. PANDOLFI [1], On feedback stabilization of functional differential equations, Bolletino U.M.I. 4, 11, Supplemento al fascicolo 3, Giugno 1975, Serie IV, Vol. XI, 626-635.

W.H. RAY and M.A. SOLIMAN [1], The optimal control of processes containing pure time delays - I, Necessary conditions for an optimum, Chem. Eng. Sci. 25 (1970), 1911-1925.

D.W. ROSS and I. FLÜGGE-LOTZ [1], Optimal control of systems described by differential-difference equations, Division of Engineering Mechanics, Stanford University, Technical Report no. 177, 1967.
[2], An optimal control problem for systems with differential-difference equation dynamics, SIAM J. Control 7 (1969), 609-623.

H. SASAI and T. FUKUDA [1], Consideration of linear delay-differential systems by approximation systems, Trans. Soc. Instrument Control Engr. 10 (1974), 298-303.

M. SLEMROD [1], Nonexistence of oscillations in a nonlinear distributed network, J. Math. Anal. Appl. 11 (1971).

H.B. SMETS [1], On the effect of delayed neutrons in reactor dynamics, Nuclear Sci. and Engineering 25 (1966), 236-241.

E.D. SONTAG [1], Linear systems over commutative rings: a survey, Ricerche di Automatica, to appear.

A.E. TAYLOR [1], Functional analysis, John Wiley and Sons, New York, 1958.

R. TRIGGIANI [1], On the stabilizability problem in Banach space, J. Math. Anal. and Appl. 52 (1975), 383-403.

R.B. VINTER [1], On the evolution of the state of a linear differential delay equation in M^2: properties of the generator, Report ESL-R-541, Electronic Systems Laboratory, Massachusetts Institute of Technology, Cambridge, Mass. 02139, U.S.A.
[2], A representation of solutions to stochastic delay equations, Imperial College of Science and Technology, internal report, 1975.

V. VOLTERRA [1], Variazioni e fluttuzaioni del numero d'individui in specie animali conbiventi, Mem. Accad. Lin. cei 2 (1926), 31-113.

P. WALTMAN [1], A deterministic model of the spread of an infection between two populations, in "Delay and Functional Differential Equations and Their Applications", K. Schmitt, ed., pp. 281-291, Academic Press, New York 1972.

P.J. WANGERSKY and W.J. CUNNINGHAM [1], Time lag in population models, in Cold Spring Harbor Symposia on Quantitative Biology, 22 (1957), 329-338.

J.A. YORKE [1], Selected topics in differential-delay equations, in "Lecture Notes in Mathematics", #243, pp. 16-28, Springer-Verlag, Berlin-New York 1971.

J. ZABCZYK [1], Remarks on the algebraic Riccati equation in Hilbert space, J. Applied Math. and Optimization 2 (1976), 251-258.

APPLICATIONS DE LA THEORIE DU CONTROLE DANS LES ACIERIES

I.D. LANDAU Maître de Recherches L.A.G. - I.N.P.G. GRENOBLE.

B. COURTIOL
A. FRANCON
L. MULLER
Ingénieurs. Département d'Automatique et d'Electronique.
Direction des Recherches ALSTHOM - ATLANTIQUE. GRENOBLE.

Résumé.

On illustre l'utilisation des théories modernes de l'automatique à l'affinage de l'acier par la méthode du convertisseur à oxygène (Basic Oxygen Furnace) et à la coulée continue de l'acier. La présente communication essaye de dégager quelques situations typiques qui se rencontrent en pratique lors de l'application de méthodes modernes de contrôle.

I. Introduction.

L'utilisation de ce qu'on apelle théorie moderne du contrôle (ou de l'automatique) concerne essentiellement les méthodes qui ont été développées à partir de 1960 (variables d'état, (commande optimale, stabilité des systèmes non linéaires, filtrage, identification, commande adaptative).

L'intêret de l'application de ces méthodes peut-être vu sous deux angles.

a) elles apportent des solutions pour des problèmes de contrôle qui ne peuvent pas être traités par les méthodes dites "classiques".

b) tester le potentiel d'applicabilité de ces théories, comprendre leur mode d'utilisation, compléter les recherches méthodologiques si besoin, et définir éventuellement les domaines d'application.

Bien que le deuxième aspect présente un très grand intêret surtout pour guider les recherches méthodologiques, l'application dans les acieries des méthodes modernes, s'inscrit dans le cas a.

Dans le cas des applications de la théorie pour réaliser des schémas de conduite de processus, à haute performance , on distingue deux situations :

1) le processus technologique fonctionne et on souhaite améliorer ses performances par l'utilisation d'une méthode de conduite plus élaborées.

2) le schéma de commande, et l'outil de production (le processus) sont concus simultanément.

La deuxième solution est la seule qui permet à notre avis, de rééllement tirer tous les avantages concernant l'utilisation de l'automatique moderne. Néanmoins, la mise au point de l'ensemble "commande + processus" est relativement longue et donc coûteuse. Elle comporte aussi des risques d'échec.

Cette situation est celle rencontrée, par exemple, dans la régulation de niveau en lingotière pour la coulée continue de l'acier.
Dans le premier cas, bien que les risques soient moindres, les résultats obtenus sont la plupart du temps loin de l'optimum. En général, l'amélioration de la conduite n'est considérée que pour la phase ou la zone critique du processus. En fait, les performances du système dépendent de la reconsidération de l'ensemble du système de conduite ; ce qui en pratique, n'est que rarement possible à cause des investissements que cette reconsidération comporte. Cette situation apparait par exemple dans la conduite des réacteurs à oxygène.
Dans le cadre de nos propres expériences, les techniques suivantes ont été réellement implantées dans les acieries :

- -le régulateur à variable d'état,
- -l'observateur,
- -l'identification en ligne avec modèle,
- -les systèmes adaptatifs avec modèle.

Par ailleurs, on a utilisé comme autres techniques :

- -la compensation des caractéristiques non linéaires statiques,
- -le modèle de prédiction pour compensation des retards de mesure et commande,
- -la linéarisation.

Deux autres techniques ont été utilisées en phase d'étude et ont été abandonnées :

- -filtre de KALMAN étendu (mauvaises performances),
- -filtrage non linéaire (quantité de calcul très grande pour des performances moyennes).

Il faut aussi remarquer que dans les deux cas (réacteur à oxygène et coulée continue de l'acier) le pré-traitement dynamique et statique des données des capteurs est fondamental. Cette opération fait intervenir déjà des techniques de l'automatique, et pour certains processus, la conception des capteurs doit, à notre avis, se faire en directe collaboration entre le spécialiste des mesures sur le processus et l'automaticien.

II. Description des procédés et des schémas de conduite.

II. a) Convertisseurs à oxygène.(B O F)

Le schéma de principe d'un convertisseur à oxygène pour la production de l'acier est indiqué dans la figure 1. La réduction du carbone dans le bain est obtenue par un soufflage d'oxygène , presque pur, à travers une lance. Le carbone entre en réaction avec l'oxygène produisant du CO et CO_2. La dynamique du processus de décarburation dépend de la hauteur de la lance par rapport au bain, et du débit d'oxygène. Actuellement, la méthode de conduite consiste à souffler l'oxygène au débit maximum, et pour une hauteur fixe de lance (nous considérons que cette approche est loin d'être optimale). L'objectif de la conduite est de déterminer le temps auquel le pourcentage désiré du carbone dans le bain d'acier est obtenu. Une évolution typique de la courbe de vitesse de décarburation dans le cas des réactions se déroulant normalement, est représentée dans la figure 2.

On distingue trois phases, la troisième phase étant la phase critique pendant la quelle le processus doit être arrêté. Pour cette dernière phase, les métallurgistes ont établi divers modèles reliant la vitesse de décarburation à la teneur en carbone du

$$\frac{dC}{dt} = \frac{1}{B + \frac{A'}{C^2}} \qquad (1)$$

ou

$\frac{dC}{dt}$ = vitesse de décarburation

C = teneur en carbone

$\frac{dC}{dt}$ se mesure avec un certain retard (15 - 25 sec) en utilisant un analyseur de gaz

et des mesures de débit sur les gaz sortant du bain.

Néanmoins les paramètres A' et B varient d'une charge à l'autre, en tenant compte du retard de la mesure, et de la commande d'arrêt, pour pouvoir commander correctement le processus ; il faut que l'on dispose d'un modèle dynamique d'évolution de $\frac{dC}{dt}$.

Par simple dérivation de l'équation (1) on obtient :

$$\dot{x} = -A\left[x\,(1 - B\,x)\right]^{3/2}$$

ou

$$x = \frac{dC}{dt} \qquad A = \frac{2}{\sqrt{A'}} \qquad (2)$$

Pour utiliser ce modéle en prédiction, il faut en plus d'identifier en ligne les paramètres A et B. Connaissant A et B et le contenu final en carbone étant donné Cf on détermine la valeur finale de $\left(\frac{dC}{dt}\right)_f$ A l'aide du modèle de prédiction donné par l'équation (2), on détermine à quel instant $\frac{dC}{dt}$ = x atteint la valeur désirée $\left(\frac{dC}{dt}\right)_f$

En pratique, tant pour l'identification de A et B que pour la prédiction, on utilise le modèle échantilloné :

$$x_{k+I} = x_k - T\,A\left[x_k\,(I - B\,x_k)\right]^{3/2}$$

Pour identifier ce modèle, on utilise les techniques des systèmes adaptatifs avec modèle avec un algorithme d'adaptation à gain décroissant. Le modèle d'estimation est de type parallèle pour la partie linéaire, et série parallèle pour la partie non-linéaire et à la forme.

$$Y_{k+I} = Y_k - T\hat{A}(k+I)\left\{x_k\left[I - \hat{B}(k+I)\, x_k\right]^{3/2}\right\} + a\varepsilon_{k+I} \qquad (3)$$

où

Y_k = valeur estimée de la vitesse de décarburation.

et

$$\varepsilon_k = x_k - Y_k \qquad (4)$$

a dans l'équation (3) est une constante introduite pour des considérations de stabilité (le processus a un pôle à l'origine).
La méthodologie de prédiction est la suivante :

On identifie les paramètres A et B sur la première partie de la courbe, on valide le modèle obtenu, on fait une première estimation du temps final. Cette opération est reprise à l'arrivée des nouveaux points de mesure. Néanmoins l'application pratique de l'algorithme suppose tout d'abord une reconnaissance du début de la dernière phase. Ceci est obtenu par une estimation de la dérivée seconde de la courbe de décarburation, en utilisant une régression linéaire. Cette technique a été utilisée à une acierie USINOR de DUNKERQUE . Les résultats obtenus sur 65 charges ont montré que la méthode préconisée donne d'excellents résultats quant à l'estimation du carbone final obtenu par l'arrêt à un certain moment. En effet, l'erreur quadratique moyenne est de $1.92.10^{-3}$ % pour une valeur moyenne de carbone réalisé de 66.10^{-3} %. Par contre, l'utilisation de cette approche pour la prédiction du temps final d'arrêt n'a pas apporté en moyenne l'amélioration escomptée par rapport à une méthode basée sur l'utilisation des paramètres A et B identifiés hors ligne, sur la charge antérieure. Une étude détaillée des courbes de décarburation a permis de donner l'explication. En effet, si la phase 2 se poursuit normalement, c'est-à-dire que $\frac{dC}{dt}$ est approximativement constant (voir figure 2), le modèle de la troisième phase donné par l'équation (1) est bon, et son identifiaction correcte se fait relativement vite. Par contre, si $\frac{dC}{dt}$ dans la phase 2, n'est pas constant (des oscillations importantes peuvent apparaîtrent) ceci a comme effet une oxidation non uniforme du bain et des accroissements de $\frac{dC}{dt}$ tout à la fin du processus apparaissent. Dans ces conditions le processus ne peut plus être modèlisé par l'équation (1). Ceci nous amène donc à conclure que l'utilisation d'une méthode performante de prédiction nécessite une régulation de $\frac{dC}{dt}$ dans la deuxième phase (pour modification de la hauteur de la lance) afin d'assurer la validité de la structure du modèle utilisé pour la prédiction.

II. b) Coulée Continue de l'Acier;

La méthode moderne pour couler de l'acier consiste à utiliser le procédé dit "Coulée Continue" pour la fabrication des ronds d'acier d'un diamètre de 120 à 210 mm qu'on coupe à des longueurs de l'ordre de 10 m. On utilise le procédé dit "Coulée Continue centrifuge".
Le schéma simplifié du procédé de coulée continue centrifuge au niveau de la génération de la barre est illustré dans la figure 3. L'acier liquide est placé dans le "tendish". La quenouille obstrue la "busette" et commande le débit acier coulant dans la lingotière. La lingotière tourne sur elle-même et oscille dans l'axe vertical à fréquence et amplitude variable afin de donner une surface correcte au rond d'acier. L'objectif de la régulation est de maintenir constant le niveau de l'acier liquide dans la lingotière par rapport à la terre. Ce niveau doit être tenu constant pour plusieurs raisons, mais entre autre pour assurer une certaine géométrie de la coulée d'acier liquide, afin d'éviter le perçage des parois du rond à cause de la pression de l'acier liquide et pour des raisons de qualité métallurgique du produit. La mesure de niveau se fait à partir d'un capteur utilisant une source radioactive et un scintillomètre placés dès la construction dans le corps de la lingotière. Le problème de mesure de niveau est rendu particulièrement difficile par les oscillations dans l'axe vertical de la lingotière et par le niveau de bruit propre au principe du capteur. Les mesures effectuées font apparaître des variations importantes du gain dynamique du processus pour une même dimension de rond, comme l'illustre la figure 4. Ces variations sont dûes à l'usure de la busette et de la quenouille, aux variations des caractéristiques de l'acier et au caractére non linéaire des lois d'écoulement. En moyenne, le gain dynamique varie du simple au double, mais des situations correspondant à des variations plus importantes peuvent apparaître.

L'expèrience a montré que l'utilisation d'un régulateur linéaire à variables d'états dont les paramètres sont modifiés en fonction de la dimension du rond permet d'obtenir une commande robuste avec des performances satisfaisantes. Les variables d'état inacessibles ont été obtenues à l'aide d'un observateur. Les performances présentent une régularité remarquable (+ 5 mm de variation de niveau) par rapport à la régulation manuelle (± 20 mm). La régulation permet en même temps d'améliorer les conditions de travail, car le poste de quenouilleur est extrèmement pénible. Quatre installations de ce type fonctionnent en exploitation courante à VALLOUREC - SAINT -SAULVE.

III. Conclusion.

Les théories modernes de l'automatique permettent de résoudre les problèmes difficiles de commande. Néanmoins, leur application avec succès ne peut se faire sans une connaissance approfondie du processus et sans considérer l'automatisation et l'instrumentation de l'ensemble du processus dès la phase de conception du procédé.

Références.

I. I.D. LANDAU. L. MULLER G.DOLLE G. BIANCHI.
' A new method for carbon control in basic oxygen furnace".

Proc. Znd I F A C Symp on automation in mining mineral and metal processing 07.1976. JOHANNESBURG.

II. B. COURTIOL. C. FRANCON. S. NEGOESCO.
Régulation de niveau d'acier en lingotière.

Notice technique ALSTHOM - ATLANTIQUE 1976.

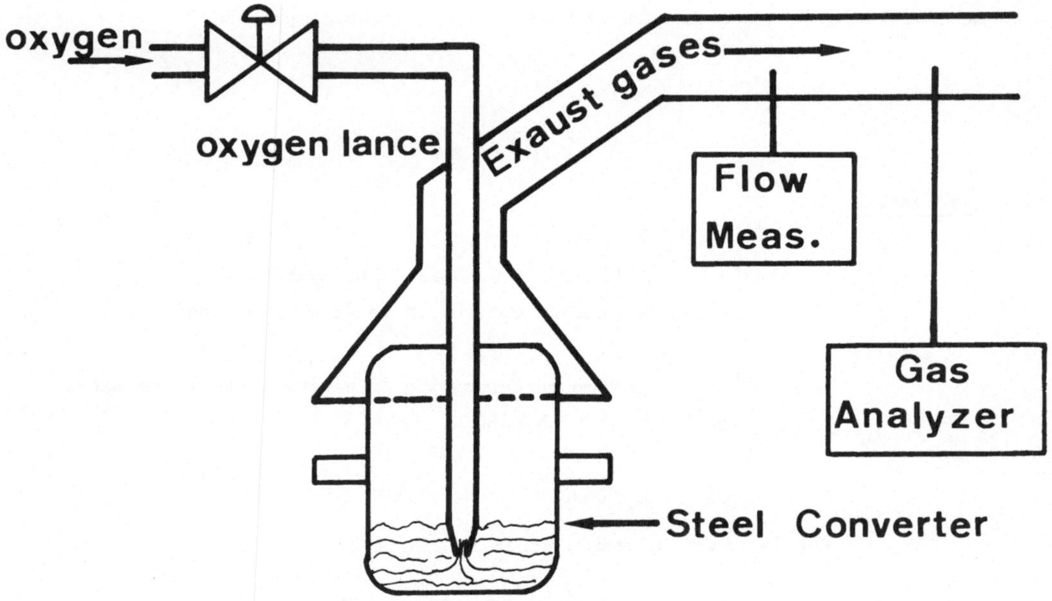

Fig 1. Schéma de principe du convertisseur à oxygène (Basic Oxygen Furnace).

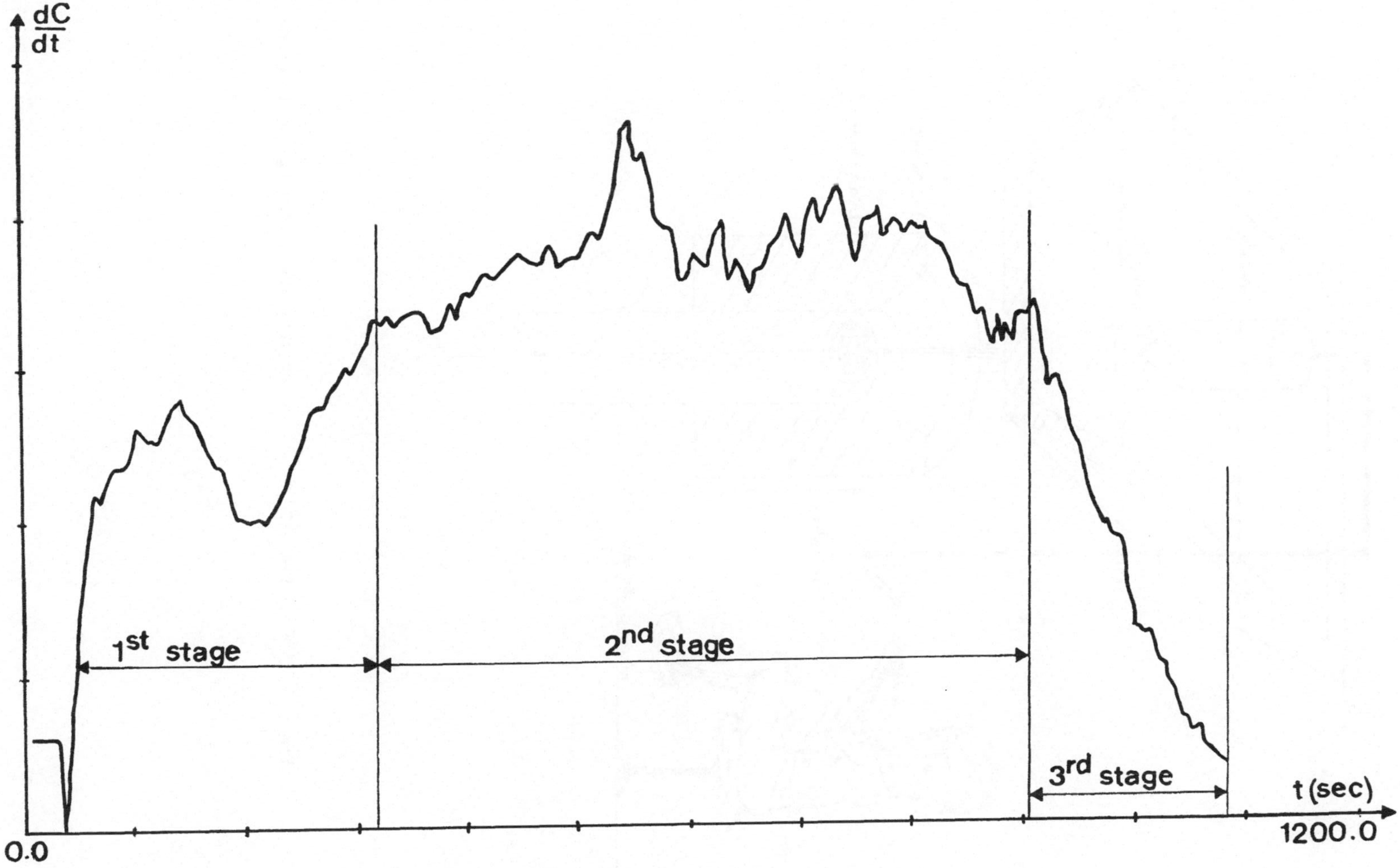

<u>Fig</u> 2. Evolution de la vitesse de décarburation pendant une charge.

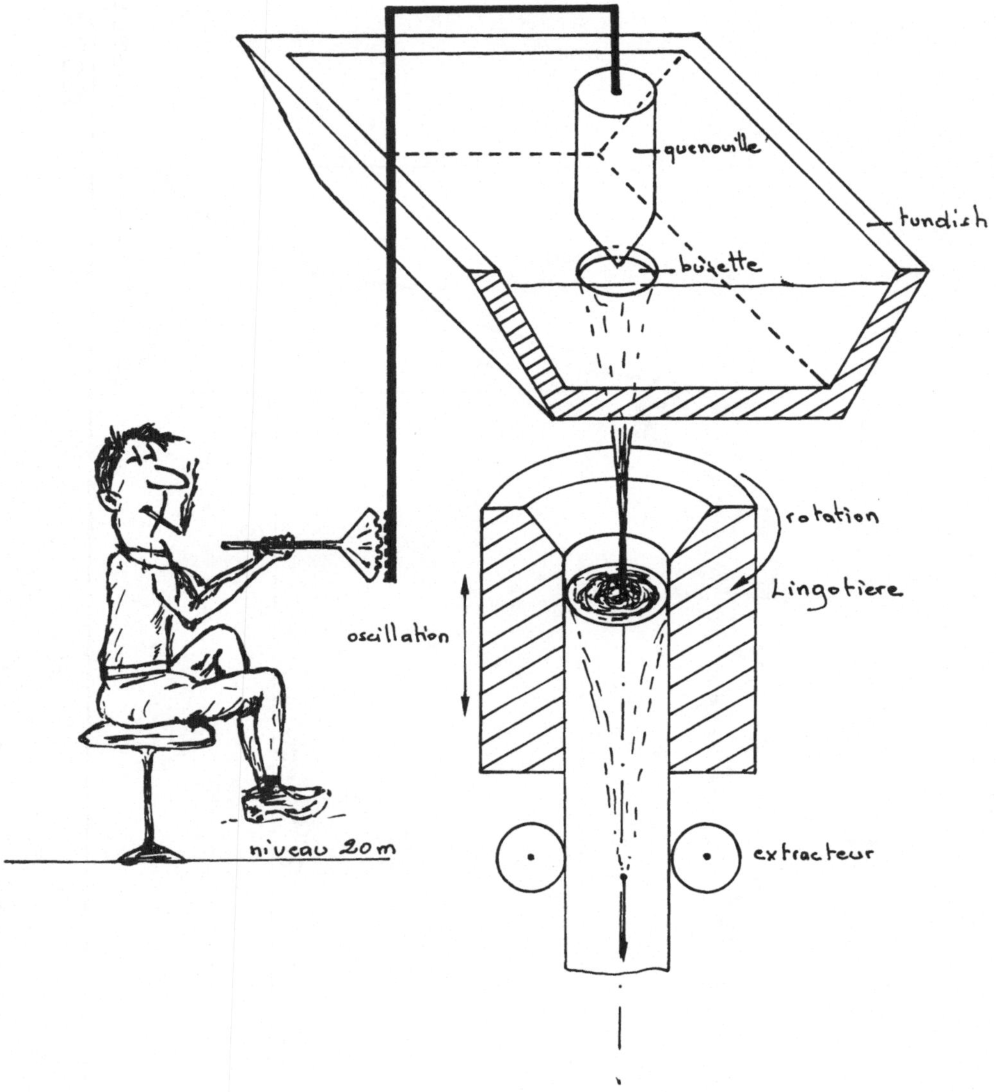

Fig 3. Schéma de principe de la coulée continue centrifuge de l'acier.

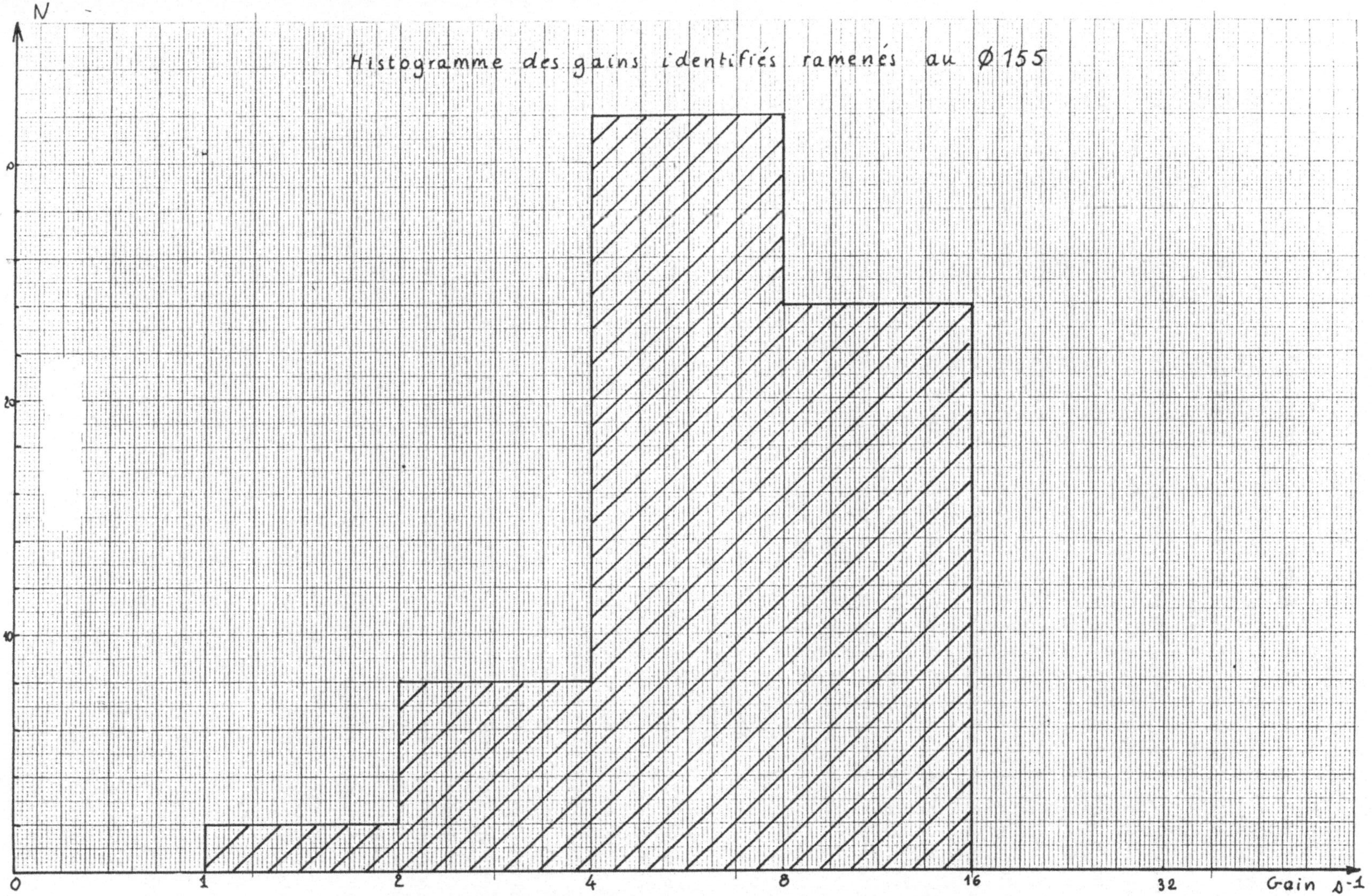

<u>Fig</u> 4. Histogramme des gains identifiés ramenés au diamètre 155.

MULTILEVEL STRUCTURES FOR CONTROL SYSTEMS

W. Findeisen
Institute of Automatic Control
Technical University of Warsaw
00-665 Warszawa, Poland

Abstract. This paper is a survey rather than a detailed contribution. It presents several of the possible multilevel structures for control of complex systems. Steady-state optimization structures using measured outputs or inputs as feedback information are considered first. Various methods of coordination (direct, penalty function and price) are presented and discussed for this kind of problems. Then dynamic on-line coordination is introduced and the essential differences explained. Dynamic prices are shown to be one of the adequate coordination instruments. Other possibilities making use of the feedback gain concept and of the conjugate variables are mentioned.

1. Introduction and the problem considered

In this paper we shall be concerned with "on-line" or "current" control of complex systems. The following will be essential:

- we assume the system under control to be in actual operation and to be influenced by disturbances,
- some kind of current information about the system behavior or about the disturbances is available and can be used to improve the control decisions.

These two features will make our study differ from problems of planning, scheduling, etc., where the only data we can use in determining a control or a policy is an a priori model, that is the description of the system. The accuracy of results would therefore heavily depend on the exactness of the models and cannot reach beyond it. Planning problems would be solved by a direct use of optimization methods or mathematical programming; as opposed to it, in control systems the success that is the performance obtained depends not only on the models available, but also on the structure in which we use the feedback information.

A "complex system" will be an arrangement of some elements interconnected between their outputs and inputs, as it happens for example in an industrial plant. If we draw it in an orderly way introducing an input-output interconnection matrix H we obtain a scheme as in Fig. 1.

We are now interested in control of system like Fig. 1 by use of some special structures, referred to as "multilevel". The multilevel concept in hierarchical control systems has been inspired by decomposition and coordination methods developed for mathematical programming or for solving other kinds of formally specified problems. We should well note, however, that the "Mathematical Programming" decomposition can be applied directly only as open-loop control (as a rule - with model adaptation), as shown in Fig. 2. But here in fact any method of solving the optimization problem can be used and the results achieved will be all the same - depending on model accuracy. Nevertheless, structuring the optimization algorithm in Fig. 2 as multi-level may be desirable for the reasons of software (computational economy) as well as hardware (multi-computer arrangement) considerations.

In the sequel we shall be paying much more attention to those multilevel structures of control where feedback information from the real system is used to improve control decisions.

It will be essential to distinguish local decision makers (local problems) and also a coordinator, whose aim it will be to influence the local decision makers in such a way as to provide for achievement of an overall goal.

Several questions will arise:

- what kind of coordination instruments will the coordinator be allowed to use and how will his decisions enter into the local problems,
- will the feedback information be available to the coordinator or to local decision makers or to both levels,
- what procedures (algorithms) could be used at each level, respectively, in determining the coordinating decisions and the control decisions (control actions) to be applied to the real system,
- how will the whole of the structure perform when disturbances appear,
- what would be the impact of limited information that can be transmitted between the levels or of the cost of it, etc.

Before we get to work any further on our subject it might be worth mentioning that the purpose of studying hierarchical control systems may be twofold: we may be interested in design of such systems for industrial or organizational applications, or we may want to know how a hierarchical control system behaves, providing it is already in existence. The second case applies to macroeconomical systems, for example. The two cases differ very much in the focus of attention, permissible simplifications and assumptions that can be made in the investigation.

Let us describe the system of Fig. 2 and the control problem more carefully. We will consider:

<u>system elements (subsystems)</u>, having input vectors u_i, output vectors y_i and control vectors c_i, so that

(1) $y_i = f_i(c_i,u_i), \qquad i = 1,\ldots,N$

<u>system interconnections</u>, consisting in each of the input vector component u_{ik} being equal to a specified component of an output vector y_{jl}. This is described for input u_i and for the whole system, respectively, by

(2) $u_i = H_i y$, and $u = Hy$

where $u = (u_1,\ldots,u_N)$, $y = (y_1,\ldots,y_N)$, H interconnection matrix.

<u>system resource constraint</u>

(3) $\sum_{i=1}^{N} r_i(c_i,u_i) \leq r$

where $r_i(\cdot)$ is the amount of common system resources used by subsystem No. i.

<u>subsystem (local) constraints</u>

(4) $(c_i,u_i) \in CU_i, \qquad i = 1,\ldots,N$

We assume that a <u>local performance index</u> $Q_i(c_i,u_i)$ is associated with each subsystem and the local decision maker would tend to extremize it.

The task of coordination will be to influence the local decision makers in such a way, that:

- system constraints will be preserved,
- overall optimum will be achieved.

We define the global optimum by introducing a <u>global performance index</u> Q:

$$Q = \psi(Q_1,\ldots,Q_N)$$

where ψ is a strictly order-preserving function.

Note that the global and local performances may result from two practical cases. It might be that there were some local decision makers already in existence and we decided to set up an overall Q to provide for some harmony in their actions. But it also might be that we had overall Q first and we then decided to distribute the decision making among the lower level units.

2. <u>Coordination by direct method</u>

The simplest way to present direct coordination (also called primal or parametric coordination) is to assume that the coordinator would prescribe the outputs y_i, demanding an equality $y_i = y_{di}$. If a resource constraint is present, coordinator would also allocate a value r_{di} to each local problem.

A local decision problem would become

$$\text{maximize } Q_i(c_i,u_i)$$

subject to

$$u_i = H_i y_d$$

$$f_i(c_i,u_i) = y_{di}$$

$$(c_i,u_i) \in CU_i$$

$$r_i(c_i,u_i) \leq r_{di}$$

When this problem is solved, results depend upon (y_d,r_{di}). We may denote the local results as $\hat{c}_i(y_d,r_{di})$ and $\hat{Q}_i(y_d,r_{di})$.

The coordination instruments y_d, r_d can be adjusted to an optimum by solving the problem

$$\underset{(y_d,r_d)}{\text{maximize}}\ Q = \psi(\hat{Q}_1(y_d,r_{d1}),\ldots,\hat{Q}_N(y_d,r_{dN}))$$

subject to

$$r_{d1} + r_{d2} + \ldots + r_{dN} \leq r$$

Main difficulty of the method lies in the fact that a local problem may have no solution for some (y_d,r_d) because of its inequality constraints (an output value may be not achievable and/or the allocated resources inadequate). Therefore the values (y_d,r_d) set by the coordinator must be such as to keep the local problems feasible

$$(y_d,r_d) \in YR$$

The set YR cannot be easily determined. Moreover, the boundaries of set YR are affected by the system uncertainty or by the disturbances. This has the implication that the "coordinator" would have to keep his decisions (y_d,r_d) in a "safe" region of YR, where "safe" would relate to the worst case of system uncertainties. Apart from the difficulty to define the safe region we of course realize that the worst case approach may give the result that this region is very small or even empty.

3. Penalty functions in direct coordination

We can propose an iterative procedure to be used at the coordination level such that the feasible set YR would not have to be known. The main idea is to use penalty functions in the local problems while imposing there the coordinator's demands. The local problem will get the form:

$$\text{maximize } Q'_i = Q_i(c_i,u_i) - K_i(y_i-y_{di})$$

with the substitutions

$$u_i = H_i y_d$$

$$y_i = f_i(c_i, u_i)$$

and subject to constraints

$$(c_i, u_i) \in CU_i$$

$$r_i(c_i, u_i) \leq r_{di}$$

As can be seen we used penalty function for the condition $y_i = y_{di}$. The resource constraint could also be dealt with by a penalty term, if necessary.

The result of using penalty formulation is that solution to the local problem would exist even for a non-feasible y_{di}. The demand would simply not be met.

We must now have a mechanism to let the coordinator know that he is demanding something impossible. We let his optimization become:

$$\text{maximize } Q' = \psi[(\hat{Q}_1(y_d, r_{d1}) - K_1(\hat{y}_1 - y_{d1})), \ldots, (\hat{Q}_N(\cdot) - K_N(\cdot))]$$

where the clue is that we introduce local performances <u>less</u> the penalty terms. Hence, the coordination iterations will try to adjust y_d so as to reduce the values of penalty terms, whereby the local problems do the same on their part, acting on y_i.

It has been shown elsewhere [Tatjewski 1975] that when the iterations reach their limit where penalty terms vanish, the values y_d obtained there are both feasible and strictly optimal.

4. <u>A mechanistic system or a human decision making hierarchy</u>?

The reader of the previous text may get confused as to what do our considerations really apply. Let us clarify it as follows.

(i) First, we can obviously think of coordination used in off-line, model-based solving of a set of local problems. This would be "decomposition and coordination in mathematical programming" and it is quite appropriate there to discuss, for example, whether gradient procedures can be used or not. Should we apply the solution of optimization problem, that is the finally obtained control values $\hat{c}_i$ to a real system, feasibility of the result with respect to the real system (differing from the models) must be considered. The problem of "generating feasible controls" will arise. From the control point of view we would have an open-loop structure. Hence, the approach would apply to both static and dynamic problems.

(ii) Second, we can consider the coordination level as acting on local decision makers who control the real system elements trying to comply with the coordinator's demands. Here we may not even know what is the local decision making process. Let us look at the situation by assuming that the coordinator works by iteration as he actually must act in the penalty function method. For each step of this iteration the local decision makers "do their best" with respect to the real system outputs. Would we know the algorithm which the local decision maker is using, a discussion of time-behavior of the system from one coordination step to another could be done. Let us only state that the behavior may be unstable due to many separate decision makers acting on the same system. If a steady-state is achieved, the coordinator may make his next step, trying to improve the value of his performance function (whether in the penalty form or without it). Note that in the case where no penalty terms are used the direct coordination can in principle be achieved in one step: the coordinator sets values (y_d, r_d) which should optimize the system according to his best knowledge (i.e., according to the model of the system) and then the local decision makers do their job by achieving $y_i = y_{di}$ and complying with the resources constraint. It is in this case, however, that y_{di} should be feasible for the real system, otherwise the expectations of the coordinator may be considerably unfulfilled.

It is important to note that "iterations of the coordinator on the real system" can essentially be done in static optimization only (we come back to this remark in the next section).

(iii) We can also consider, and this has been done quite extensively, a mechanistic decision-making hierarchy of control, where we attribute certain formal algorithms to decision making at the local level. In that case we may use the measured value of the real outputs y_{*i} in essentially two ways: in the local algorithm and in the coordination algorithm. Only the second possibility has been satisfactorily explored [Woźniak 1976] leading to coordination algorithms which:

- end in a point non-violating real system constraints (provided they are of the form $(c_i, u_i) \varepsilon CU_i$ and $y \varepsilon Y$),
- provide for a value of overall performance which is superior to the result of open-loop control (this was shown by examples only).

5. Coordination by price methods

Let us recall the problem formulation of Section 1, that is consider the complex system of Fig. 1, its constraints and the local decision makers.

Price coordination consists in letting the coordinator prescribe prices on inputs, outputs and resources and then permitting the local decision makers to define their own choices of the values of these variables. The system is coordinated when the local choices cause the interconnection equation (2) to be satisfied and the global constraint (3) to be non-violated. The prices which effect this state of coordination can be termed equilibrium prices, since satisfaction of (2) means equilibrium.

Price coordination brings about overall system optimum if the global performance index is a sum of local ones

$$Q = \sum_{i=1}^{N} Q_i$$

It is worth remembering, that direct and penalty function coordination methods presented in Sections 2 and 3 admitted more general form of global performance.

The discussion of price coordination in this section will omit the resource constraint (3), thus focusing on interconnections (2). Suitable extensions will be mentioned.

Interaction balance and "tatônnement" procedures

Price coordination has been known in economic systems for a long time. The prices were called upon to cause equilibrium of production and demand, that is equality of the corresponding outputs and inputs. In terms of the system description, the aim of price adjustment will be to provide for satisfaction of the interconnection equation (2).

Let us look at this in some detail. The local problems i.e., problems associated with the individual system elements can be formulated as follows:

(5) minimize $Q_{i\ mod} = Q_i(c_i,u_i) + \langle p_i,u_i\rangle - \langle q_i,f_i(c_i,u_i)\rangle$

subject to

$$(c_i,u_i) \in CU_i$$

with the results $\hat{c}_i(p)$, $\hat{u}_i(p)$, $\hat{y}_i(p) = f_i(\hat{c}_i(p),\hat{u}_i(p))$.

If (5) is related to a finite-dimensional problem, then the scalar product $\langle p_i,u_i\rangle$ means $\sum_j p_{ij}u_{ij}$.

In the problem (5) we assumed coordination by a price vector p, composed of prices on inputs u in the whole system. Hence p_i are prices on u_i, and prices q_i on output y_i are defined as well by virtue of (2), namely

$$q_i = \sum_{j=1}^{N} H_{ji}^{T} p_j$$

It is therefore right to say that the results of (5) are all dependent on vector p.

The "interaction balance" or "equilibrium" prices $\hat{p}$ will be defined as

(6) $p = \hat{p} : \hat{u}(p) - H\,\hat{y}(p) = 0$

where $\hat{y}(p) = f(\hat{c}(p), \hat{u}(p))$.

Providing for the condition (6) to be satisfied is the task of the coordinator. In the classical economics this would be assigned to a "tatônnement" procedure at the stock exchange: a person outside the negotiating parties would vary the price p, watch the responses $\hat{u}(p)$ and $\hat{y}(p)$, and stop the procedure at $p = \hat{p}$.

Essentially the same idea has been brought up in the study of multilevel control systems, started by Mesarović. Several questions have been raised in those more formalized studies, for example:

- existence of $\hat{p}$,
- system optimality with control $\hat{c}(\hat{p})$,
- procedures to obtain $\hat{p}$.

The exact answers can be found elsewhere [Mesarović 1970] [Malinowski 1975, 1976].

They are based on discussions of the Lagrangian function

$$\phi(p) = \sum_{i=1}^{N} Q_i(\hat{c}_i(p), \hat{u}_i(p)) + \langle p, \hat{u}(p) - Hf(\hat{c}(p), \hat{u}(p))\rangle$$

for which we require that it has a maximum at $p = \hat{p}$:

$$\phi(\hat{p}) = \max_p \phi(p)$$

If $\hat{p}$ so defined exists, its further use to determine contol $\hat{c}$ is practically restricted to the case where $(\hat{c}, \hat{u})$ are single-valued functions of p. This requirement appears to be vital. Unfortunately we know sufficient conditions only: $(\hat{c}, \hat{u})$ are single-valued if the functions $Q_i(\cdot)$ are strictly convex and the mappings $f_i(\cdot)$ are linear.

With $p = \hat{p}$ the solutions $(\hat{c}, \hat{u})$ are optimal.

Let us now turn to the question of what procedures could be used at the coordination level in the search for $\hat{p}$. It has been shown elsewhere that if $Q_i(\cdot)$ are continuous and $f_i(\cdot)$ are continuous then gradient procedures for p can be used, provided we find a way to deal with the points where the $(\hat{c}, \hat{u})$ are not unique and where the gradient is not defined (subgradients can be considered there). In the regions of p-space where $(\hat{c},\hat{u})$ are unique the following formula holds for the (weak) derivative of $\phi(p)$:

$$\nabla\phi(p) = \hat{u}(p) - Hf(\hat{c}(p),\hat{u}(p))$$

Note that this is exactly the input-output difference in the system.

The second derivative, $\nabla^2\phi(p)$, does not exist in the general case.

Note that the equilibrium condition (6) as a goal to be achieved in the search for $\hat{p}$ can obviously be used on models only. In the already operating system the interconnection equation is satisfied for any control and we could never see if p has been correct.

We should mention that the interaction balance coordination just described can be applied to both static and dynamic problems, as we are dealing only with models. It is therefore a computational concept rather than a control structure. We could use the concept for open-loop control of a system by applying the computed $\hat{c}(\hat{p})$ to a reality, with a result depending strongly on the accuracy of the models.

Let us come back for a while to the resource constraint

$$r_1(c_1,u_1) + \ldots + r_N(c_N,u_N) \leq r$$

This additive form of a global constraint can be incorporated in the price coordination scheme by using an additional price vector ψ (the resource price) and adding to each local problem a value

$$\langle\psi,r_i(c_i,u_i)\rangle$$

By varying ψ the coordinator would change the resource requirements of the local problems so as to satisfy the overall constraint. In the Lagrangian terminology, ψ would be a Kuhn-Tucker multiplier.

The next subsections will show some other ideas of price coordination, where feedback from the real operating system will be used to improve the control.

Coordination in steady-state with feedback to coordinator

We shall now consider the optimization problem to be in the finite-dimensional space, i.e., to be a problem of non-linear programming. In terms of control it means optimization of steady-state in a complex system. It should be mentioned that steady-state optimization is an appropriate technique if the optimal state trajectory of a dynamic system is slow enough. We will have to distinguish the model-based problem

$$\text{miminize } Q = \sum_{i=1}^{N} Q_i(c_i,u_i)$$

subject to

$$y_i = f_i(c_i,u_i), \qquad i = 1,\dots,N$$
$$u = H\,y$$
$$(c_i,u_i) \in CU_i, \qquad i = 1,\dots,N$$

with its solution providing for model-based control $\hat{c}$, and the following real problem:

$$\text{minimize } Q = \sum_{i=1}^{N} Q_i(c_i,u_i)$$

subject to

$$y_i = f_{*i}(c_i,u_i), \qquad i = 1,\dots,N$$
$$u = H\,y$$
$$(c_i,u_i) \in CU_i, \qquad i = 1,\dots,N$$

We should notice that the only difference between model and reality is considered to exist in the system element equations.

It must be stressed, however, that differences might exist also in performance function and the constraint set.

Solution to the real problem will be termed real-optimal control $\hat{c}_*$. It is not obtainable by definition since reality is not known. We can only look for a structure which would yield control better than purely model-based $\hat{c}$. In principle it is bound to be inferior than $\hat{c}_*$.

One of the possible structures is price coordination with feedback to the coordinator, shown schematically in Fig. 3.

The local problems are exactly the same as in the interaction balance method of the preceding subsection, that is:

$$\text{minimize } Q_i(c_i,u_i) + \langle p_i,u_i\rangle - \langle q_i,f_i(c_i,u_i)\rangle$$

subject to

$$(c_i,u_i) \in CU_i$$

The controls $\hat{c}_i(p)$ determined by this problem for the current value of p are applied to the real system, resulting in some u_* and y_*. The coordination concept consists in the following upper-level problem:

(7) find $p = \tilde{p} : \hat{u}(p) - u_*(\hat{c}(p)) = 0$

Condition (7) is an equality of model-based solution for the input $\hat{u}(p)$ and of the inputs u_*, measured in the real system and caused by control $\hat{c}(p)$.

Solution $\tilde{p}$ exists, if solution $\hat{p}$ of the usual interaction balance method exists for all s-shifted systems [Malinowski 1975]:

$$u = H\,f(c,u) + s$$

where $s \in S$, and S is the set of all possible values of the model-reality difference

$$H f_*(c,u) - H f(c,u) = s$$

with $(c,u) \in CU = CU_1 \times \dots \times CU_N$.

When the models do not differ from reality, $\hat{c}(\hat{p})$ is strictly optimal control and $\tilde{p}$ equals equilibrium prices $\hat{p}$ which would be obtained by solving the problem by the interaction balance method of the previous section. When models differ from reality, control based on (7) is in the first approximation always non-inferior to the one based on open-loop value $\hat{p}$. In the particular case where

$$f_{*i}(c_i,u_i) = f_i(c_i,u_i) + \beta_i \qquad i = 1,\dots,N$$

that is the model-reality difference consists in a shift, control based on (7) is strictly real-optimal.

A most important feature of control based upon (7) is its property to keep to the constraints in the real system. This happens because real c_* equals model c for any p, and for $p = \tilde{p}$ also $u_* = \hat{u}$. Since the model will keep $(\hat{c}_i,\hat{u}_i) \in CU_i$, $i = 1,\dots,N$, the same will be kept in the real system, at $p = \tilde{p}$. Note that the open-loop control $\hat{c}(\hat{p})$ may violate these constraints in the real system, because at $p = \hat{p}$ it will in general be $u_* \neq \hat{u}$.

As far as the procedures to find $\tilde{p}$ are concerned, iterations have to be done at a rate acceptable by the real system, i.e., permitting new values u_* to establish themselves after a change of p. Unfortunately, the expression

(8) $F(p) = \hat{u}(p) - u_*(\hat{c}(p))$

which has to be brought to zero is not a derivative of any function, as it was in the case of interaction balance method. The value $\tilde{p}$ has to be found by equation-solving methods, $F(p) = 0$. It should be stressed that if there are inequality constraints in the local problems, F(p) will in general be non-differentiable. Suitable numerical methods to find $\tilde{p}$ have been proposed elsewhere [Malinowski, Ruszczynski 1975] [Szymanowski et. al., 1976].

We must justify discussion of steady-state control here as opposed to more general problem formulation in the previous subsection. The reason is the practical field of application of coordination principle (6): it must be iteratively done on the real system. This can be performed in steady-state optimization, but not in a dynamical one. The only exception would be iterative optimization of batch or cyclic processes, the iteration in time-function space being performed from one batch to another.

Decentralized control with price coordination

The structure of Fig. 3, however proved to be effective and superior to open-loop model-based control, may be criticized; the information about real system u_* is made available to the coordinator only. The local problems base on models and calculate their imaginative $\hat{u}$ for each p, "knowing" that reality is different. The scheme of Fig. 3 is therefore a structure suitable for a mechanistic control system, but does not reflect the situation which would be established if the local problems were confined to some free decision makers.

In that case the local decision maker would tend to use real value u_{*i} in his problem, that is he would perform

(9) minimize $Q_i(c_i,u_{*i}) + \langle p_i,u_{*i}\rangle - \langle q_i,f_i(c_i,u_{*i})\rangle$

subject to

$$(c_i,u_{*i}) \in CU_i$$

Schematically this is presented in Fig. 4 as feeding u_{*i} to the corresponding local problem. Even with fixed p the control exercised by local decision makers on the system as a whole remains to some extent coordinated, since the value of p will influence the control decisions. However, since u_{*i} are used locally, we may call the structure of Fig. 4 decentralized control.

A problem for itself is system stability or the convergence of iterations made by local optimizers while trying to achieve their goals. It is obvious that all the iteration loops in the system are interdependent, since any u_{*i} will depend on all decisions $c = (c_1,\ldots,c_N)$ in the previous stage.

If the iterations converge, steady values $\hat{c}(p)$, $\hat{u}_*(p)$ and $\hat{y}_*(p)$ will be obtained for the given price vector p.

We should look for some way to iterate on prices p in the system of Fig. 4. A possibility might be

(10) minimize $Q_i = \sum_{i=1}^{N} Q_i(\hat{c}_i(p),\hat{u}_{*i}(p))$

which simply means to find a price p such, that the overall result of local controls be optimized.

6. Multilevel structures in dynamic optimization

Introduction

Structures of on-line dynamic control using decomposition present difficulties unknown to static systems. In steady-state control it could be enough to use feedback in form of measured inputs u or outputs y and to provide for extremum of a current or "instantaneous" performance index. The dynamic optimization needs considering at time t all the future behavior of the system, which depends on both control and the initial state. This means that if we wish to have a control structure with feedback from the reality this feedback must contain information on the state $x(t)$.

We should not be misled by the possibility to obtain dynamic optimization by iterations on the real system, for example determining the best price trajectories $\hat{p}(t)$, $t \in (0,T)$, using a search procedure. Although this could apply to consecutive runs of a batch process, we would still be interested in having a feedback control structure in the course of a single run of the process.

Dynamic price coordination

One of the possible structures for dynamic optimal control using both decomposition and feedback is the use of prices on inputs and on outputs of the system elements.

Assume the optimal control problem of an interconnected system to be as follows

(11) minimize $Q = \sum_{i=1}^{N} \int_0^{t_f} f_{oi}(x_i, m_i, u_i)\,dt$

subject to

$\dot{x}_i = f_i(x_i, m_i, u_i)$, $i = 1,\ldots,N$ (state equations)

$y_i = g_i(x_i, m_i, u_i)$, $i = 1,\ldots,N$ (output equations)

$u = Hy$ (interconnections)

with $x(0)$ given, $x(t_f)$ free or specified.

Consider that in solving the problem we incorporate the interaction equation into the following Lagrangian:

$$L = \sum_{i=1}^{N} \int_0^{t_f} f_{oi}(x_i, m_i, u_i)\,dt + \int_0^{t_f} \langle p, u - Hy\rangle\,dt$$

where $\langle p, u-Hy\rangle$ means $\sum_{j=1}^{\dim u} p_j (u-Hy)_j$

Assume the solution to the global problem using this Lagrangian has been found and it has provided for

$\hat{x}_i$, $i = 1,\ldots,N$ - optimal state trajectories

$\hat{m}_i$, $i = 1,\ldots,N$ - optimal controls

$\hat{u}_i$, $i = 1,\ldots,N$ - optimal inputs

$\hat{y}_i$, $i = 1,\ldots,N$ - optimal outputs

$\hat{p}$ - solving value of Lagrangian multipliers

Note now that our Lagrangian can be split into additive parts, thus allowing to form a kind of local problems:

(12) minimize $Q_i = \int_0^{t_f} [f_{oi}(x_i,m_i,u_i) + \langle\hat{p}_i,u_i\rangle - \langle\hat{q}_i,y_i\rangle]dt$

where $y_i = g_i(x_i,m_i,u_i)$ and optimization is subject to

$\dot{x}_i = f_i(x_i,m_i,u_i)$

$x_i(0)$ given, $x_i(t_f)$ free or specified as in the original problem.

In the local problem the price vector $\hat{p}_i$ is an appropriate part of $\hat{p}$ and $\hat{q}_i$ is also determined by $\hat{p}$.

Notice that we have put optimal value of price vector $\hat{p}$ into the local problems, which means we have solved the global problem before. Thanks to it the solutions of local problems will be strictly optimal. There is little sense, however, in solving the local problems if the global was solved before, because the global solution would provide not only $\hat{p}$ but also $\hat{x},\hat{m}$ for the whole system.

To make the thing practical let us try to shorten the local horizons and to use feedback there. Problem (12) will now become

(13) minimize $Q_i = \int_0^{t'_f} [f_{oi}(x_i,m_i,u_i) + \langle\hat{p}_i,u_i\rangle - \langle\hat{q}_i,y_i\rangle]dt$

with $x_i(0)$ given as before, but the target state taken from the global long-horizon solution, $x_i(t'_f) = \hat{x}_i(t'_f)$.

The short horizon formulation (13) will pay off if we will have to repeat the solving of (13) many times as opposed to solving the global problem once only. Consult now Fig. 5, where the principle of the proposed control structure is presented.

Feedback at the local level consists in solving the short-horizon local problems at some intervals $T_1 < t'_f$ and using the actual value of measured state $x_{*i}(kT_1)$ as new initial value for each repetition of the optimization problem.

This brings a new quality; we now have a truly on-line control structure and can expect, in appropriate cases, to get results better then those dependent on the models only. Note that the often repeated local problems are low-dimension and short-horizon.

The feedback introduced so far cannot compensate for the errors done by the coordination level in setting the prices p. Another repetitive feedback can be introduced to overcome this shortage, for example bringing to the coordinator actual values x_{*i} at time t'_f, $2\ t'_f$, ... and asking the global problem to be resolved for each new initial value, as presented in Fig. 5.

A doubt may exist whether the feedback to the coordinator shown in Fig. 5 makes sense, because the lower level problems have to achieve $x_i(t'_f) = \hat{x}_i(t'_f)$ as their goal and already use feedback to secure it. It should be remembered, however, that the model-based target value $x_i(t'_f)$ is not optimal for the real system and asking the local decision making to achieve exactly $x_{*i}(t'_f) = \hat{x}_i(t'_f)$ may be not advisable or even not feasible.

The coincidence of feedback to coordination level with times t'_f, $2t'_f$ is not essential.

The length of the global problem horizon t_f has to be matched to the slowest system element dynamics and the slowest of the disturbances. It may then happen that the dynamics of a particular system element are fast enough to be neglected in its local optimization problem within the horizon t'_f. This means, in other words, that this local optimization will be a static problem.

In the described structure of on-line dynamic coordination we have made no use till now of the possibility of having a simplified model in the global problem which is being solved at the coordination level at times 0, t'_f, $2\,t'_f$ etc.

The global problem may be simplified for at least two reasons: the solution of the full problem may be too expensive to be done, and the data on the real system, in particular prediction of disturbances, may be too inaccurate to justify computation based on an exact model.

Simplification may concern dimension of state vector (introduce aggregated x^c instead ot x), dimension of control vector (m^c instead of m) and dimensions of inputs and output ($u^c=H^c y^c$ instead of $u = H\,y$). Appropriate linking of the global problem to the local ones would have to be designed. For example, p^c would be "group prices" and full price vector p is to be generated.

The system interconnections in Fig. 5 were stiff, that is an output was assumed to be connected to an input in a permanent way. The dynamic problem formulation gives an opportunity to consider another type of interconnection, a "soft" constraint of integral type:

$$\int_{kt_b}^{(k+1)t_b} (u_{ij} - y_{lr})\,dt = 0$$

which corresponds to taking input u_{ij} from a store, with an output y_{lr} connected to the same store. Asking for integral over $[kt_b,(k+1)t_b]$ to be zero means that supply and drain have to be in balance over each balancing period t_b.

A store may be supplied by several outputs and drained by more than one subsystem input. There may also be many stores, for example for different products. If we assume the same balancing period for all of them the integral constraint becomes

$$\int_{kt_b}^{(k+1)t_b} (Pu_w - My_w)dt = 0$$

where u_w, y_w are parts of u, y connected to the stores. Matrices P,M show the way by which u_w, y_w are connected to various stores. A state vector w of the inventories can also be introduced

$$w(kt_b + t) = w(kt_b) + \int_{kt_b}^{kt_b+t} (Pu_w - My_w)d\tau$$

With both stiff and soft interconnections present in the system, the global problem Lagrangian becomes

$$L = \sum_{i=1}^{N} \int_0^{t_f} f_{oi}(x_i,m_i,u_i)dt + \int_0^{t_f} <p,u_s - Hy_s>dt + \sum_{k=0}^{k=\frac{t_f}{t_b}-1} <\psi^k, \int_{kt_b}^{(k+1)t_b} (Pu_w - My_w)dt>$$

and we of course continue to consider

$$\dot{x}_i = f_i(x_i,m_i,u_i), \quad i = 1,\dots,N$$

$$y_i = g_i(x_i,m_i,u_i), \quad i = 1,\dots,N$$

$x_i(0)$ given, $x_i(t_f)$ free or specified, $i = 1,\dots,N$.

In comparison with the previous Lagrangian a new term has now appeared, reflecting the new constraint. Note that prices ψ^k associated with the integral constraint are constant over periods t_b.

With two kinds of interconnections the local problems also change correspondingly and they become

$$\text{(14) minimize } Q_i = \int_0^{t_f} [f_{oi}(x_i,m_i,u_i) + <\hat{p}_i,u_{si}> - <\hat{q}_i,y_{si}>]dt + \sum_{k=0}^{k=\frac{t_f}{t_b}-1} <\psi^k, \int_0^{t_b} (P_i u_{wi} - M_i y_{wi})dt>$$

where $y_{si} = g_{si}(x_i,m_i,u_i)$, $y_{wi} = g_{wi}(x_i,m_i,u_i)$ and optimization is subject to

$$\dot{x}_i = f_i(x_i,m_i,u_i)$$

$x_i(0)$ given, $x_i(t_f)$ free or specified

A new quality has appeared in problem (14) in comparison with (13): the inputs u_{wi} taken from the stores are now free control variables and can be shaped by the local decision maker, who previously had only m_i in his hand. The local decisions will be under the influence of prices $\hat{p}$ and $\hat{\psi} = (\hat{\psi}^o, \hat{\psi}^1, \ldots)$, where both $\hat{p}$ and $\hat{\psi}$ have to be set by the solution of the global problem.

The local problem (14) has no practical meaning yet; it will make sense when we introduce local feedback and shorten the horizon, like it was in the previous stiff-interconnection case.

We shall omit the details and show it only as a control scheme, Fig. 6.

Thinking about how to improve action of the coordinator we made previously a proposal to feed actual $x_*(t_f')$ to his level. We have now additional state variables, the inventories w. If the price $\hat{\psi}^k$ is wrong, the stores will not balance over $[kt_b, (k+1)t_b]$. It is almost obvious that we can catch-up by influencing the price for the next period $\hat{\psi}^{k+1}$ and that we should condition the change on the difference $\hat{w}((k+1)t_b) - w_*((k+1)t_b)$, where $w_*(\cdot)$ is a value measured in the real system. This kind of feedback is also shown in Fig. 6.

Multilevel control based upon state-feedback concept

Optimal control theory has paid considerable attention to the structure where the control at time t, that is m(t), would be determined as a given function of current state x(t). Comprehensive solutions exist for the linear system and quadratic performance case, where

$$m(t) = R(t)\ x(t)$$

and R(t) is in general a time-varying matrix.

Trying to apply this approach to the complex system we might implement for each local problem

(15) $m_i(t) = R_{ii}(t)\ x_i(t)$

where R_{ii} is one of the diagonal blocks in the matrix R.

The result of such local controls, although all state of the system is measured and used, is not optimal, since we should rather make $m_i(t)$ dependent on the whole state x(t).

We can compensate for the error committed in (15) by adding a computed correction signal

(16) $m_i(t) = R_{ii}(t)x_i(t) + \hat{v}_i(t)$

The exact way to get $\hat{v}_i(t)$ would be to generate it continuously basing upon the whole x(t). This would, however, be equivalent to implementing state feedback for the whole system directly, with no advantage in having separated the local problems.

Exactness has to be sacrificed. With this in mind we may propose various solutions, for example (see also Fig. 7):

(i) $\hat{v}_i$ will be generated at $t = 0$ for the whole optimization horizon t_f' (open-loop compensation)

(ii) $\hat{v}_i$ will be generated at $t = 0$ as before but will be re-computed at $t = t_f' < t_f$, using actual $x(t_f')$, etc. (repetitive compensation)

(iii) $\hat{v}_i$ will not be generated at all, but we implement instead in the local problems

(17) $m_i(t) = \tilde{R}_{ii}(t)x_i(t)$

where $\tilde{R}_{ii}$ is adjusted so as to approach optimality.

It may be worthwhile to mention that local decision making based upon (15), (16), or (17) makes more sense for a mechanistic implementation than for a hierarchy of human operators, where the previous approach based on "maximization of local performance subject to imposed prices" seems to be more adequate to what really happens in the system.

Structures using conjugate variables

It is conceivable to base on-line dynamic control upon maximization of the current value of the Hamiltonian, thus making a direct use of the Maximum Principle and of conjugate variables.

For the complex system described as (11) the Hamiltonian would be

$$\mathcal{H} = - \sum_{i=1}^{N} f_{oi}(x_i, m_i, u_i) + \langle\psi, f(x,m,u)\rangle$$

The interconnection equation

$$y - Hy = u - Hg(x,m,u) = 0$$

provides for u to be a function of (x,m) in the interconnected system

$$u = \phi(x,m)$$

Therefore

$$\mathcal{H} = - \sum_{i=1}^{N} f_{oi}(x_i, m_i, \phi_i(x,m)) + \langle\psi, f(x,m,\phi(x,m))\rangle$$

Assume the global problem has been solved (model-based) using the Hamiltonian and hence the optimal trajectories of conjugate variables $\hat{\psi}$ are known. We are going to use these values in local problems.

First let us note that having $\hat{\psi}$ we could re-determine optimal control m by performing at the current time t

(18) maximize $\mathcal{H} = - \sum_{i=1}^{N} f_{oi}(x_i, m_i, \phi_i(x,m)) + \langle\hat{\psi}, f(x,m,\phi(x,m))\rangle$

where the problem is an "instantaneous maximization" and needs no consideration of final state and future disturbances.

Problem (18) is static optimization, not a dynamic one. We would now like to divide it into subproblems. It can be done if we come back to treating $u - Hy = 0$ as a side condition and solve (18) by using the Lagrangian

$$(19)\quad L = -\sum_{i=1}^{N} f_{oi}(x_i,m_i,u_i) + \langle\hat{\psi},f(x,m,u)\rangle + \langle p,u-Hy\rangle$$

where $y = g(x,m,u)$,

We should note the difference with respect to dynamic price coordination presented so extensively before, where the Lagrangian was used for the original dynamic problem.

In the present case there are no integrals in $L(\cdot)$ and the dynamics are taken care of by the values of conjugate variables $\hat{\psi}$.

Assume we have solved problem (19), using system models i.e., by computation and we have the current optimal value of price p, that is $\hat{p}(t)$. We can then form the following static local problems to be solved at time t

$$(20)\quad \underset{m_i,u_i}{\text{maximize}}\ L_i = - f_{oi}(x_i,m_i,u_i) + \langle\hat{\psi}_i,f_i(x_i,m_i,u_i)\rangle + \langle\hat{p}_i,u_i\rangle - \langle\hat{q}_i,y_i\rangle$$

These goals could be used in a structure of decentralized control, see Fig. 8. The local decision makers are asked here to maximize $L_i(\cdot)$ in a model-based fashion and apply control $\hat{m}_i$ to the system elements. Current value x_i is needed in performing the task. The coordination level would supply $\hat{\psi}_i$ and the prices $\hat{p}_i,\hat{q}_i$ for the local problem. They would be different for each t.

Fig. 8 would first imply that the local model-based problems are solved immediately with no lag or delay. We can therefore assume, conceptually, that the local decision making is nothing else but implementation of a state feedback loop, relating control $\hat{m}_i(t)$ to the measured $x_i(t)$ (the feedback decision rule).

Now let us think about feedback to the coordinator. We might decide to have him know the state of the system at some time intervals t_f', that is $x(kt_f')$. On this he could base his solution $\hat{\psi}$ for all $t \geq kt_f'$ and also the prices $\hat{p}$ for next interval $[kt_f',(k+1)t_f']$.

The main feature in using conjugate variables is that the local problems are static. However, the local goals are slightly less natural, as they involve $<\hat{\psi}_i, \hat{x}_i>$ that is a value of the trend. This would be difficult to explain economically and hence difficult to implement in a human decision making hierarchy.

7. Concluding Remarks

It is beyond doubt that hierarchical control systems exist in many applications. Some of them involve human decision makers only, other may be hierarchies of control computers, or mixed systems. Hierarchical control theory is developing rather rapidly, with the following goals in mind:

- we want to explain behavior of an existing system, for example find out the reasons for some phenomena which occur (usually some failures, like instability),
- we want to design a new system structure, for example determine what decisions are to be made at each level, what coordination instruments are to be used, etc.,
- we want to implement computer-based decision making in the system.

In the first two cases a qualitative theory may be sufficient, whereby the models or the description of the actual system do not have to be very precise. The available hierarchical control theory seems to be quite relevant for this kind of applications, and can help in drawing conclusions as well as in making system design decisions.

The third case calls for having relatively exact models of the system to be controlled (although suitable feedback structures relax the requirements) and calls also for having appropriate decision-making algorithms, which would have to be programmed into the control computers. The existing theory and above all the existing experience are rather scarce in this area.

REFERENCES

F. N. Bailey: Decision Processes in Organizations, in "Large Scale Systems", R. Saeks, Ed., Western, Los Angeles, 1976

A. Bensoussan, J. L. Lions, R. Teman: Decomposition des problèmes d'optimisation, Cahier de l'IRIA No. 11, 1972

A. Benveniste, P. Bernhard, G. Cohen: On the Decomposition of Stochastic Control Problems, Invited paper, IFAC Symposium on Large Scale Systems Theory and Applications, Udine, 1976

M. Brdyś: Methods of Feasible Control Generation for Complex Systems. Bull. Pol. Acad. Sci., Vol. XXIII, No. 12, 1975

C. Y. Chong, M. Athans: On the Periodic Coordination of Linear Stochastic Systems. IFAC Congress, Boston (Proceedings Pt 3), 1975

W. Findeisen: Multilevel Control Systems. PWN, Warszawa 1974 (in Polish)

W. Findeisen: A Structure for On-Line Dynamic Coordination. Bull. Pol. Acad. Sci., Vol. XXIII, No. 9, 1975

W. Findeisen, K. Malinowski: A Structure for On-Line Dynamic Coordination. IFAC Symposium on Large Scale Systems Theory and Applications, Udine, 1976

A. Heescher, K. Reinisch, R. Schmitt: On Multilevel Optimization of Nonconvex Static Problems-Application to Water Distribution of a River System. IFAC Congress, Boston (Proceedings Pt 3), 1975

R. Kulikowski, L. Kruś, K. Mańczak, A. Straszak: Optimization and Control Problems in Large Scale Systems. IFAC Congress, Boston (Proceedings Pt 3), 1975

I. Lefkowitz: Systems Control of Chemical and Related Process Systems. IFAC Congress, Boston (Proceedings Pt 2), 1975

K. Malinowski: Properties of Two Balance Methods of Coordination. Bull. Pol. Acad. Sci., Vol. XXIII, No. 9, 1975

M. D. Mesarovic, D. Macko, Y. Takahara: Theory of Hierarchical, Multilevel Systems. Academic Press, New York, 1970

N. R. Sandell, P. Varaiya, M. Athans: A Survey of Decentralized Control Methods for Large Scale Systems. IFAC Symposium on Large Scale Systems Theory and Applications, Udine, 1976

D. D. Siljak: Competitive Economic Systems: Stability, Decomposition, and Aggregation. IEEE Trans. on Aut. Contr., Vol. AC-21, pp. 149-160, 1976

M. G. Singh, S. Drew, J. F. Coales: Comparisons of Practical Hierarchical Control Methods for Interconnected Dynamical Systems. Automatica, Vol. 11, pp. 331-350, 1975

M. G. Singh, M. F. Hassan, A. Titli: Multilevel Feedback Control for Interconnected Dynamical Systems Using the Prediction Principle. IEEE Trans. Syst., Man, Cybern., Vol. SMC-6, pp. 233-239, 1976

J. Szymanowski, M. Brdyś, A. Ruszczyński: An Algorithm for Real Process Coordination. IFAC Symposium on Large Scale Systems Theory and Applications, Udine, 1976

P. Tatjewski: Coordination by Penalty Function Methods. Proceedings, Workshop Discussion on Multilevel Control. Institute of Automatic Control, Technical University of Warsaw, 1975

A. Woźniak: Parametric Method of Coordination Using Feedback from the Real Process. IFAC Symposium on Large Scale Systems Theory and Applications, Udine, 1976

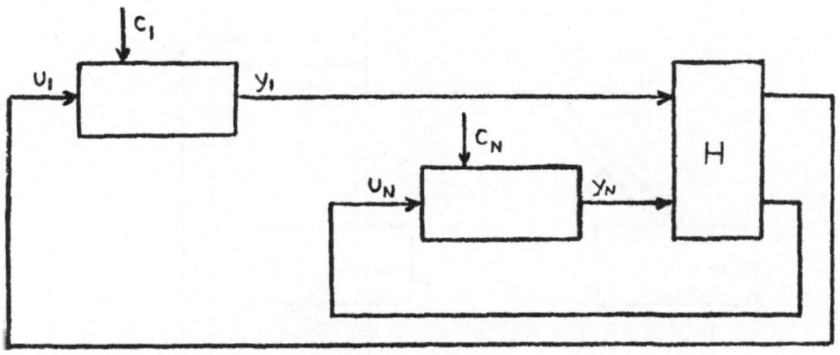

Fig. 1. Schematic presentation of a complex system

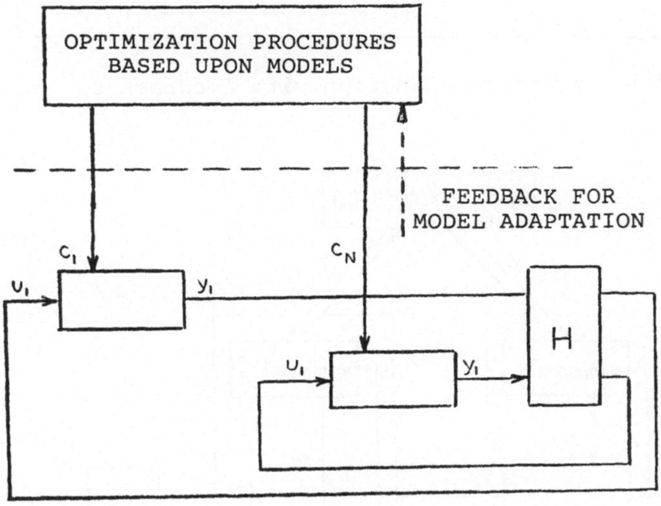

Fig. 2. Open-loop control of a complex system

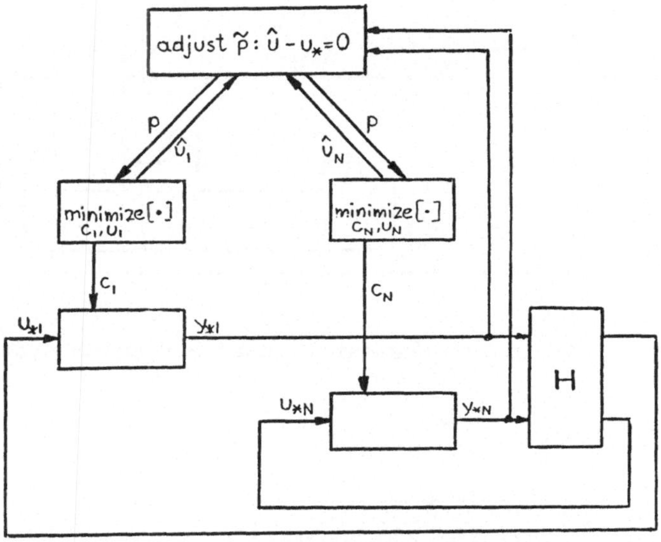

Fig. 3. Iterative price coordination with feedback to the coordinator

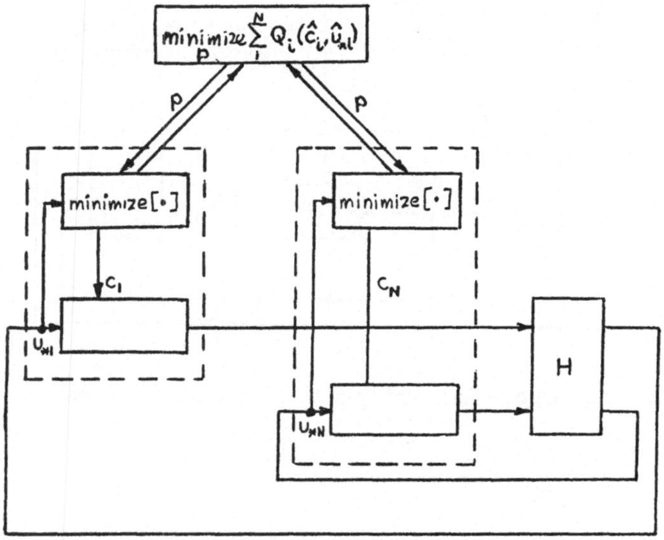

Fig. 4. Decentralized control with on-line price coordination

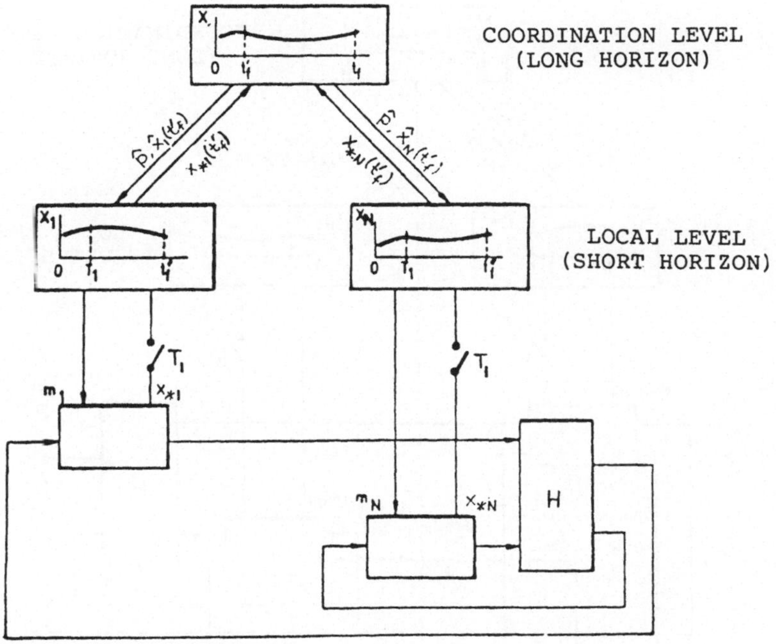

Fig. 5. Structure of on-line dynamic price coordination

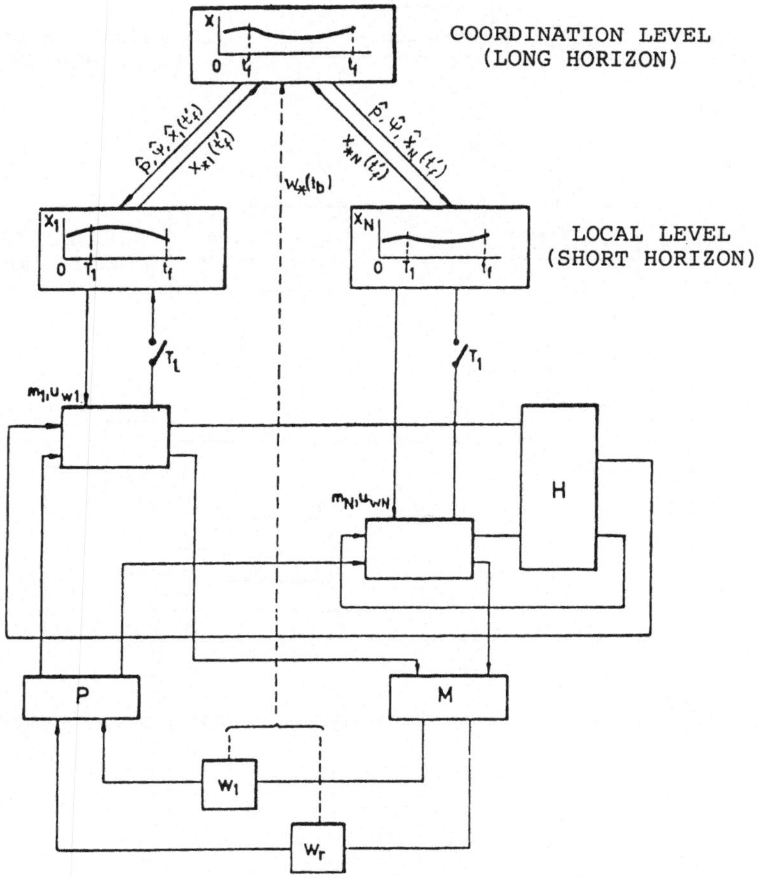

Fig. 6. On-line dynamic price coordination in a system containing stores in the interconnections

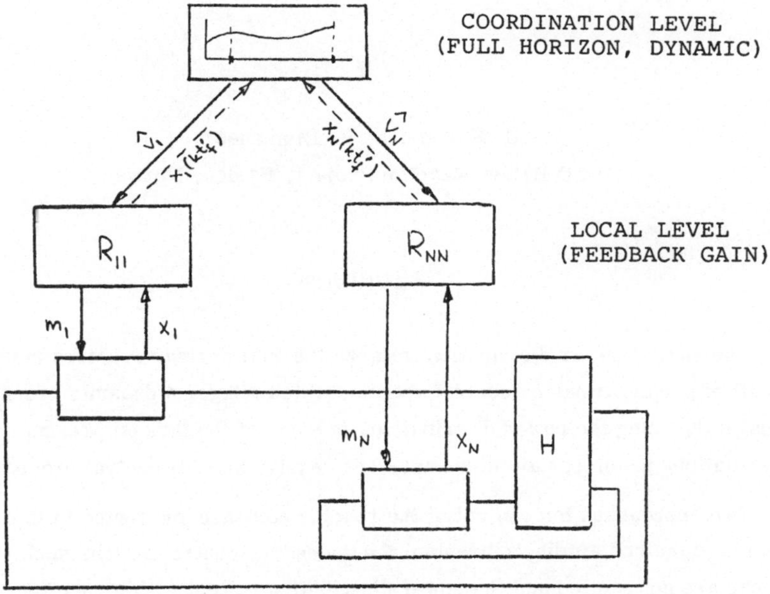

Fig. 7. Dynamic multilevel control based on feedback gain concept

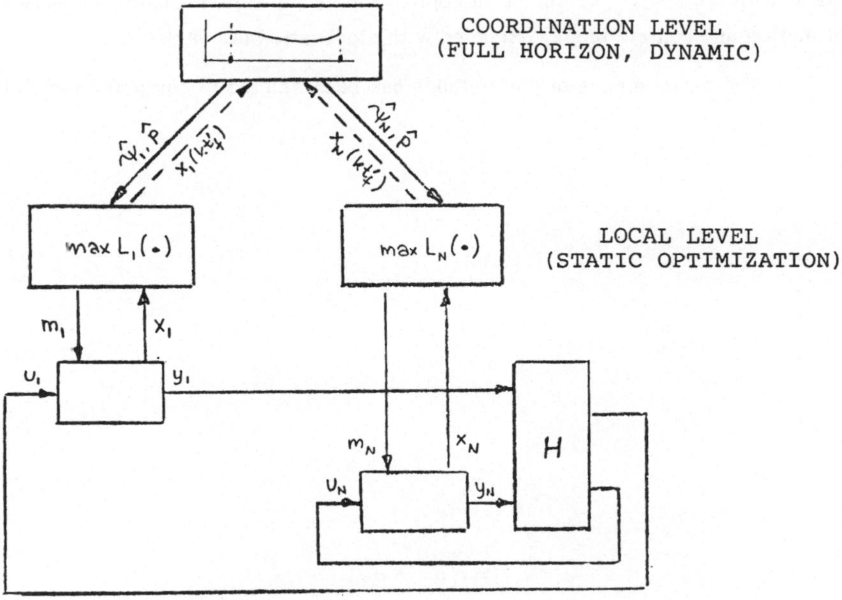

Fig. 8. Dynamic multilevel control using conjugate variables

AN APPLICATION OF OPTIMIZATION METHODS TO SPATIAL CONTROL OF NUCLEAR REACTOR CORES

by

J. Karppinen, B. Blomsnes
OECD Halden Reactor Project, Halden, Norway

ABSTRACT

The spatial power distribution in large thermal nuclear reactors may oscillate as a result of perturbations or control actions, which trigger a dynamic process (Xe-I dynamics) influencing the power distribution. In some of the largest present day reactors these oscillations under certain circumstances require special control procedures.

Two approaches for control of the reactor core are presented in this paper. One is a predictive method aiming to preplan the necessary control actions such that the oscillations are not excited and the power distribution is kept within specified bounds. It is formulated with a linearized discrete-time reactor core model, quadratic performance criterion and a linear constraint set. The resulting optimization problem is solved with quadratic programming. The other approach is intended for damping of the oscillations with a feedback controller and is an application of the Linear-Quadratic-Gaussian optimal estimation and control theory extended with stochastic bias variables.

The performance of the methods has been studied in computer simulations.

1. INTRODUCTION

Mathematical methods for predicting the dynamical behaviour of large thermal nuclear reactors are well developed, but they tend to be far too complex to be used as system models for optimization methods. The heterogeneous structure of reactor cores leads to spatially complicated, distributed parameter systems. They are converted by standard reactor physics methods to very high order lumped parameter systems with several feedback loops, which must be solved iteratively.

The increasing reactor core sizes together with growing demand for load following operation make the spatial effects and core power distribution control important for reliable and flexible operation. Fairly many methods applying optimization methods have been proposed for solving the arising problems, but the practical realization has been inhibited mainly by computational difficulties. Two new concepts are presented in this paper. The aim has been to approach a realizable optimal spatial control system.

The control problem is discussed in chapter two, where particulary the sections on the xenon-iodine dynamics and excitation of the core dynamics are central. The new developments are presented in chapter three, where the simplified control models are derived and the control concepts are presented. The simulation results in chapter four are obtained with simplified reactor core simulation models.

2. THE CONTROL PROBLEM

The description here applies mainly to the most common reactor type, the pressurized light water reactor (PWR), where the spatial effects are fairly strong and which has been modelled for the simulations.

2.1. Fundamental PWR Core Characteristics

The energy is released in neutron induced fissions, in which the fissionable atoms split into fission products i.e. other atoms. The released energy heats up the fuel pins , which are cooled by water under high pressure. The water also acts as neutron moderator, slowing down the speed of the neutrons born in the fission to speeds where they are more effective in caucing new fissions. The migration and absorption of neutrons depends on the atomic composition and temperatures in the core, which change continuously during power operation of the reactor.

The fuel pins (4 m high, 1 cm diameter) are assembled together to form fuel elements. There are about 200 pins in each element and about 200 elements in the whole core. The coolant flows along the fuel pins from the bottom of the core upwards. In certain fuel elements some of the fuel pins are replaced by tubes, in which strongly neutron absorbing material can be entered from above into the core. These absorber pins form control rods, which are moved syncronized in control rod banks such that all rods in one bank are equally deeply inserted in the core. The control rods reduce the power generation in their surroundings and can thus be used for changing both the total power and the power distribution in the core. Another type of power controller is the soluble boric acid (a strong neutron absorber) concentration in the coolant. It has an almost homogeneous distribution and uniform effect on the power. The control rod banks can be operated quickly, but the changing of the soluble boron concentration is fairly slow.

The reactor is normally equipped with neutron detectors in and outside the core and thermocouples in the core. The power distribution in the core can be inferred from these measurements.

2.2. Nuclear Reactor Core Dynamics.

The dynamical phenomena are normally treated in four different time scales ranging from milliseconds to months. The neutron population is basically a stochastic variable as a result of the stochastic nature of the fission process itself and thermal-hydraulic processes. The resulting noise is treated with filtering.

The dynamics of interest in the time scale of seconds are caused by the so called delayed neutrons, which are not born directly from fission but from decay of delayed neutron precursors, thermal hydraulic transients and fast power feedback effects. The core is designed to be self-stabilizing with respect to these effects. However, if too large perturbations would occur, a fast responding protection system would be automatically activated.

Assuming the above effects stationary, the neutron distribution in core wide calculations can with sufficient accuracy be described by the two neutron speed group diffusion equations:

$$\frac{1}{v_1}\frac{d\phi_1}{dt} = \nabla D_1 \nabla \phi_1 - \Sigma_1 \phi_1 + \nu_1 \Sigma_{f1} \phi_1 + \nu_2 \Sigma_{f2} \phi_2 \qquad /1/$$

$$\frac{1}{v_2}\frac{d\phi_2}{dt} = \nabla D_2 \nabla \phi_2 - \Sigma_2 \phi_2 + p_1 \Sigma_1 \phi_1 \qquad /2/$$

where

ϕ_i is the neutron flux of fast (i = 1) and slow (i = 2) neutrons

v_i is the neutron velocity in the fast (i = 1) and slow(i = 2) groups

D_i, Σ_i, Σ_{fi}, p_i are space and time dependent parameters obtained by averaging over the speed variable. The reaction rates between the neutrons and atoms in the core are expressed as the product of the neutron flux and a macroscopic cross section (Σ). The equations /1/ and /2/ are the conservation laws for neutrons, and the different terms have the following interpretations:

$\Sigma_i \phi_i$ rate of neutrons lost from group i through absorption or change in speed.

$\nu_i \ \Sigma_{fi} \ \emptyset_i$	rate of neutrons born in fissions caused by fast (i=1) and slow (i = 2) neutrons.
$\nabla D_i \nabla \emptyset_i$	leakage rate of neutrons into the differential volume considered
$p_i \ \Sigma_i \ \emptyset_i$	rate of neutrons slowing down to the slow group from the fast group

The cross sections and other parameters change due to the changes in the material composition and temperatures in the core caused by the burn-up of the fuel, thermal-hydraulic changes and control actions changing the control poison distribution (control rod positions and concentration of boric acid in the cooling water).

In the long term the isotope composition of the core change slowly over the whole refueling period, which is about one year. This effect is treated in so called burn-up calculations, when all the faster effects are assumed to be in equilibrium. The slow changes of the parameters can thereby be predicted.

Xenon - Iodine Dynamics

The dynamics in the time scale of hours-days is caused by one of the atoms generated through the decay of the fission products. This atom, xenon, has an extremely large absorption cross section for slow neutrons. In those parts of the core, where the Xe concentration is high, many of the neutrons are absorbed by Xe atoms and the power generation is therefore reduced. The formation of Xe is illustrated in Fig. 1. and the whole xenon-iodine dynamics is governed by the following equations:

$$\frac{dX}{dt} = -(\lambda_x + \sigma_x \emptyset_2)X + \lambda_I I + \gamma_x S \qquad /3/$$

$$\frac{dI}{dt} = -\lambda_I I + \gamma_I S \qquad /4/$$

where

X, I	are the xenon and iodine concentrations
$\gamma_x, \ \gamma_I$	are Xe and I yields from fission
$\lambda_x, \ \lambda_I$	are Xe and I decay constants
$S = \Sigma_{f1} \emptyset_1 + \Sigma_{f2} \emptyset_2$	fission rate
$\sigma_x X \emptyset_2$	slow neutron absorption rate in Xe

Xe is mainly formed from the decay of I^{135} with a half-life of 6,7 h. In that time scale I can be considered to come directly from fission. Xe is removed through decay (half life 9,2 h) and absorption. The instantaneous Xe concentration thus depends upon the neutron flux history over the last 30 h or so through iodine and upon the present neutron flux through the absorption. In a modern light water reactor core the Xe absorption term and decay term are close to each other in magnitude leading to the possibility of Xe induced power osçillations.

If the power for some reason or other would decrease from an equilibrum state, the Xe-concentration would start increasing, because the Xe production through iodine decay would continue with only slowly decreasing rate and the removal of xenon through absorption would decrease. The increasing xenon would mean more neutron absorption into xenon instead of fissions and thus a further decrease in the power. Gradually decreasing power would lead to a low iodine concentration and decay and thus to a small xenon production. The xenon concentration would then pass a peak value and start decreasing. The decreasing xenon would lead to a diminishing absorption, growing power and growing iodine production. The power, xenon iodine would thus start oscillating with typically a 20 to 30 h period. The power and xenon would have about opposite phases, peak power at the time of minimum xenon concentration, while the iodine would follow the power with about 15 degree phase shift.

The effect of xenon in the neutron balance equations /1/ and /2/ occurs in the slow group absorption cross section:

$$\Sigma_2 = \Sigma_2^{o} + \sigma_x X \qquad /5/$$

where Σ_2^{o} is the absorption cross section without xenon.

The neutron balance and Xe-I dynamics equations are thus coupled through the fission rate S and the non-linear term($\sigma_x X \phi_2$)

The coupled neutron flux - Xe-I equations form an extremely stiff system, because the time constants of the flux equation are several orders of magnitude smaller than those of the Xe-I dynamics. Physically that can be interpreted so that the neutron flux very quickly, compared to the Xe-I dynamics, comes to new equilibrium with changing xenon. It is therefore customary when considering Xe-induced effects to eliminate the flux time derivatives by introducing an artifical eigenvalue by which the fission source is multiplied. The eqs. /1/ and /2/ are then transformed to an algebraic eigenvalue problem. If the slow flux is then formally solved from the new form of eq. /2/ and substituted to eq. /1/ and some simplifications are made, one has:

$$-M^2 \nabla^2 \phi_1 + \phi_1 = \frac{k_\infty}{k} \phi_1 \qquad /6/$$

where M^2 and k_∞ depend on all the parameters of eqs. /1/ and /2/ and k is the introduced eigenvalue. The simplifications were with respect to the spatial dependence operator and require the spatial dependence of the parameters and variables to be sufficiently weak. Physically the approximations are justified by the fact that the overall flux shape is primarily determined by the fast neutrons, which migrate over much larger distrances than the slow neutrons.

Criticality Control.

If the eigenvalue k of eq. /6/ is equal to 1 with the given parameters, the solution is a real stationary state of the reactor and the reactor is said to be critical. If $k < 1$ the real flux would be decreasing with time (the source term was multiplied by $1/k$) and the reactor is said to be subcritical. If $k > 1$ the flux time derivatives would be positive and the reactor supercritical.

The criticality control of the reactor means that k (the largest eigenvalue) is controlled to be equal to one. In practice that is done by changing the amount of control absorbers i.e. control rod banks and boron concentration in the core. Computationally it is simulated by changing the absorption cross sections Σ_1 and Σ_2 and thereby the parameters M and k_∞ of eq. /6/, such that the largest eigenvalue becomes equal to 1.

Fast Responding Power Feedback Effects.

The power density is proportional to the fission rate:

$$P = E_{eff} (\Sigma_{f1}\phi_1 + \Sigma_{f2}\phi_2) \qquad /7/$$

The slow flux ϕ_2 can approximately be solved from the time independent form of eq. /2/ by neglecting the leakage term as:

$$\phi_2 \approx \frac{\Sigma_2}{p\,\Sigma_1}\,\phi_1 \qquad /8/$$

Eq. /6/ can now be written in terms of the power density.

The parameters of eq. /6/ also depend on the power density. Physically one of the feedback effects is due to the fuel temperature and the other due to the coolant temperature. The fuel temperature can be assumed directly proportional to the local power while the coolant temperature also depends on the coolant flow. In order to take into account the coolant temperature effects, the core thermo-hydraulics must be modelled. Both effects have time constants which are much smaller than those of the Xe-I dynamics, and can therefore be treated with their equilibrium values.

The core is designed such that the fuel temperature feedback has a negative feedback coefficient i.e. it tends to diminish the changes in power and has thus a stabilizing effect.

The coolant temperature may have a positive or a negative feedback coefficient changing normally to more negative over the core life. The physical mechanism works through the coolant density, which affects the neutron migration and the absorption to soluble boron in the coolant.

These feedback effects also have some interaction.

2.3 Spatially Dependent Core Models and Spatial Stability

The time and neutron speed dependence of the neutron diffusion equation were treated in the previous sections. The spatial dependence is complicated because of the strong heterogeneity of the core and boundary value problems.

In order to obtain the parameters (called group constants) of /1/ and /2/ (or /6/) for the core wide calculations, so-called homogenization calculations must be performed. The core is therefore divided into homogenization regions within which very detailed computations are done. More accurate methods than the diffusion theory are used and many neutron speed groups and a fine spatial mesh are used. The space and speed dependent neutron flux is then used for weighting the space and speed dependent parameters to obtain the group constants. Thereafter the reactor core is assumed regionwise homogeneous, i.e. the parameters constant within the regions.

A straight forward spatial discretization of the resulting three dimensional equations /1/ and /2/ would, however, require about $7 \cdot 10^6$ spatial meshpoints (1). With special methods the number of spatial unknowns can be reduced by several orders of magnitude. The reactor core is divided into subvolumes or nodes, within which the neutron flux is approximated with analytical functions. The average nodal fluxes (or power densities) will then be the unknowns. The number of nodes required is in the order of magnitude of 10^3.

The neutron diffusion equation /6/ can be written in the form

$$\underline{L}\bar{P} = \frac{1}{k}\,\underline{M}\bar{P} \qquad /9/$$

where $\bar{P}$ is a vector of the nodal power densities, $\underline{L}$ and $\underline{M}$ are the neutron destruction and production operators, respectively. For a certain core configuration, nodal division and spatial discretization method the operators $\underline{L}$ and $\underline{M}$ can finally be evaluated as numerical matrices. The dimension of $\bar{P}$ will be the number of nodes N, and there will be N solutions for the eigenvalue problem:

$$\underline{L}\,\bar{\Psi}_i = \frac{1}{\lambda_i}\,\underline{M}\,\bar{\Psi}_i \qquad i=0,\,1,\,\dots,\,N-1 \qquad /10/$$

Spatial Stability

It is illustrative for understanding of the current problem to look at the shapes of the eigenfunctions Ψ_i. If they are assumed spatially separable with respect to the axial (z) and radial-azimuthal (r, φ) variables in cylindrical geometry:

$$\Psi_i = \Psi_j(z)\;\Psi_{k,l}(r,\varphi)$$

they look like those in Fig. 2. The $\Psi_0 = \Psi_0(z)\,\Psi_{00}(r,\varphi)$ function corresponding to the largest eigenvalue, is the fundalmental mode solution giving the steady state power distribution. In

Fig. 2 it is a cosine shape for the z-direction, flattered cosine in r, and azimuthally constant.

The higher modes (i=1,..., N-1) are exited, if the equilibrium is perturbed. The deviation from the equilibrium

$$\delta\bar{p}(\bar{r},t) = \bar{P}(\bar{r},t) - \bar{P}_{eq}(\bar{r})$$

can be expressed in terms of the mode functions

$$\delta\bar{p}(\bar{r},t) = \sum_{l=0}^{N-1} a_l(t)\,\Psi_l(\bar{r})$$

Depending on the initial perturbation, a certain number of modes is exited, i.e. their amplitude factors $a_l(t)$ are different from zero. In a linear stability analysis each mode can be assigned its own exponential time behaviour

$$a_l(t) = a^o{}_l\, e^{\alpha_l t}$$

Depending on the sign of the real part of α_l, each mode can be said to be unstable ($Re\{\alpha_l\} > 0$), neutral or stable. In the case of xenon oscillations the α_l's are complex so that oscillatory solutions occur. The non-linearities of the problem limit the maximum amplitude such that $a_l(t)$ will have a maximum value (limit cycle oscillation).

The stability of different modes depends primarily on the eigenvalue separation (2):

$$\frac{1}{\lambda_i} - \frac{1}{\lambda_{i-1}}$$

The larger the eigenvalue separation, the more stable the mode in question.

The eigenvalue separation decreases and the reactor becomes less stable, with e.g. increasing spatial dimensions and flattening of the fundamental mode power distribution, both of which are current trends in reactor design. They are advantageous features in other respects, but make the control more difficult. In the current design PWR's only the fundamental mode and the first axial overtone mode are unstable. The first azimuthal overtone is close to the stability threshold, but still stable. In future designs, when the cores get larger, new unstable modes may occur.

2.4 Excitation of the Dynamics

The core dynamics is particularly strongly excited always when the total power of the core is changed. The increasing share of nuclear plants in an electrical grid will make it necessary for them to follow the daily load variations and perhaps also shorter term variations to stabilize the grid. As the time constants of the Xe-I dynamics are in the same time range, they will play a very important role in the daily operation.

For power level changes both the control rod banks and the boron control are used. Spatially the effects could roughly be divided into three types . First the average power, xenon and iodine levels in the core change. Secondly the global distribution change and thirdly the fine structure of the distributions change particularly strongly there where the control rods are moved. In terms of the oscillation modes the level changes mean exitation of the fundamental mode oscillation amplitudes, global distribution changes excite the first overtone oscillations and local distribution changes induce the higher oscillation modes.

Even if only the boron control would be used for power level changes, the first overtone oscillations would be excited primarily as a result of thermal hydraulic effects and the non-linear dependence of the xenon on power. If the modes were unstable special control actions were necessary. However, usually the control rod banks are used and therefore also the higher modes are excited. Also the marginally stable modes are undesirable, because they hardly have time to die out before they are exited again. Also the normal procedures used for going up and down in power have an enhancing not a compensating effect on the power distribution oscillations. There may also exist a certain degree of coupling between the different modes of oscillation, i.e. certain modes excite and amplify each other.

3. APPLICATION OF OPTIMIZATION METHODS

Basically, the spatial reactor core dynamics is governed by three dimensional, non-linear, distributed parameter partial differential equations. With standard reactor physics methods they can be reduced to a system of non-linear, lumped parameter ordinary differential equations, which must be solved numerically. The application of most optimization methods is therefore very complicated, if not computationally impractical.

The main approximations in the previous chapter were with respect to the spatial dependence. The distributed system parameters were lumped by forming homogeneous regions, which again were divided into subvolumes or nodes. The dynamics is then described by the following equations:

$$\underline{L}\bar{P} = \frac{1}{k}\underline{M}\bar{P} \qquad \text{(N equations)} \qquad /11/$$

$$\frac{dX_i}{dt} = -\lambda_x X_i - \Gamma_i X_i P_i + \lambda_I I_i + \gamma_x^* P_i \qquad /12/$$

$$\frac{dI_i}{dt} = -\lambda_I I_i + \gamma_I^* P_i \qquad /13/$$

$$i = 1, \ldots, N$$

where

N is the number of nodes

and the other symbols are as in /3/, /4/ and /6/. The equations are coupled through the power distribution ($\bar{P}$) and non-linear because of the coupling term $X_i P_i$ in /12/ and the dependence of the operators $\underline{M}$ and $\underline{L}$ on the xenon distribution ($\bar{X}$). They also depend on the power distribution through the power feedback effects. The eigenvalue problem is therefore solved iteratively and for a critical core (k=1). The dependence of $\underline{L}$ on the control variables is used to maintain criticality. The control variables are still implicit in the $\underline{L}$ and $\underline{M}$

matrices. They will influence the power $\overline{P}$ and through the power the xenon and iodine distributions $\overline{X}$ and $\overline{I}$, which cannot be directly influenced.

The system is thus of the order 2 · N with a non-linear algebraic feedback constraint. For proper three dimensional reactor core description the value of N should be of the order of magnitude of thousand.

3.1 Control Models

The system model is further simplified with respect to the non-linearity and the system order. Two control models are derived, the one is a linearization of the problem while the other makes more use of the specific problem structure with some non-linear features.

Linearization

The $\underline{L}$ matrix is diagonal and the diagonal elements consist of two parts, one describing the absorption of neutrons in each node and the other the leakage of neutrons from the node. The first part depends on the state variables $\overline{P}$ and $\overline{X}$ (through the system parameters) and control inputs (control absorption) in a fairly linear relation. The second part depends on the same variables, but in a much more complicated way. The dependence is not only on the local (nodal) variable, but also on the variables in the adjacent nodes and the dependence is non-linear.

The $\underline{M}$ matrix is a band matrix representing the fission source and the diffusion of the neutrons from one node to another. The diffusion parts again depend on the state variables and control inputs in a non-linear fashion.

The leakage and diffusion describe the coupling of the nodes, i.e. the dependence of the power in one node on the power in another node. Mathematically it is described by a so-called spatial coupling coefficient matrix.

Differentiating /11/with respect to time gives:

$$\dot{\underline{L}}\,\overline{P} + \underline{L}\,\dot{\overline{P}} = \frac{1}{k}\,(\dot{\underline{M}}\,\overline{P} + \underline{M}\,\dot{\overline{P}}) \qquad /14/$$

Neglecting the changes in the spatial coupling coefficient matrix and taking into account only the above mentioned dependencies of the $\underline{L}$ matrix on the absorption, one has formally:

$$\dot{\underline{M}} = 0$$

$$\dot{\underline{L}} = \frac{\delta\,\underline{L}}{\delta\,\overline{X}}\,\dot{\underline{X}} + \frac{\delta\,\underline{L}}{\delta\,\overline{C}}\,\dot{\underline{C}} + \frac{\delta\,\underline{L}}{\delta\,\overline{P}}\,\dot{\underline{P}} \qquad /15/$$

where the $\dot{\overline{P}}$, $\dot{\overline{X}}$ and $\dot{\overline{C}}$ vectors are written as diagonal matrices and the partial derivatives $\delta\,\underline{L}/\delta\overline{Y}$ will be diagonal matrices with diagonal elements $\delta\,L_i/\delta\,Y_i$. The equation /14/ reads now:

$$(\underline{L} - \frac{1}{k}\,\underline{M} + \frac{\delta\,\underline{L}}{\delta\,\overline{P}}\,\overline{P})\,\dot{\overline{P}} = -\frac{\delta\,\underline{L}}{\delta\,\overline{X}}\,\underline{P}\dot{\overline{X}} - \frac{\delta\,\underline{L}}{\delta\,\overline{C}}\,\underline{P}\dot{\overline{C}} \qquad /16/$$

This is the first step in the linearization of the problem. The dependence of the problem parameters on the state variables through the spatial coupling coefficient matrix is neglected. If that would be taken into account, the matrices $\delta \underline{L}/\delta \overline{Y}$ would be more complicated and not diagonal, and also $\dot{\underline{M}} \neq \underline{0}$.

In the above equations /15/ and /16/ the $\dot{\overline{C}}$ vector gives the change in the absorption properties of the nodes due to the controllers, i.e. the control rods and soluble poison. Because the rods are not present in all of the N nodes, the change in the nodal control absorption caused by the rod movements, is described by a projection matrix $\underline{D}$:

$$\dot{\overline{C}} = \underline{D}\,\dot{\overline{U}} \qquad /17/$$

where $\dot{\overline{U}}$ is a vector of the controller speeds introducing the control inputs explicitly.

/16/ can further be written as:

$$\dot{\overline{P}} = -\underline{A}_{11}^{-1}\,\underline{A}_{12}\underline{P}\dot{\overline{X}} - \underline{A}_{11}^{-1}\,\underline{A}_{14}\underline{P}\dot{\overline{U}} \qquad /18/$$

where:

$$\underline{A}_{11}^{-1} = \left[\underline{L} - \frac{1}{k}\,\underline{M} + \frac{\delta\,\underline{L}}{\delta\,\overline{P}}\,\underline{P}\right]^{-1} \qquad /19/$$

and $\underline{A}_{12}$ and $\underline{A}_{14}$ are defined through /16/ and /17/. The critical point now is the existence of the inverse of the $\underline{A}_{11}$ matrix. Without the feedback term $\delta\,\underline{L}/\delta\,\overline{P}$ the matrix would be singular. However, the feedback terms are large enough to make the matrix invertable.

Linear Control Model

The reactor state is now described by a state vector

$$\overline{Y}^T(t) = [\,\overline{P}^T(t)\,\overline{X}^T(t)\,\overline{I}^T(t)\,\overline{U}^T(t)\,] \qquad /20/$$

which has the dimension $3 \cdot N + R$ if R is the number of the controllers. A perturbation model is derived around a state $\overline{Y}_o$:

$$\overline{Y}(t) = \overline{Y}_o + \overline{y}(t) \qquad /21/$$

Substitution of /21/ into /12/, /13/ and /18/ and use of lower case letters for the deviations from Y_o gives:

$$\dot{\overline{p}} = \underline{B}_{11}\,\dot{\underline{X}}_o\,\overline{p} + \underline{B}_{12}\,\underline{P}_o\,\dot{\overline{x}} + \underline{B}_{14}\,\underline{P}_o\,\dot{\overline{u}} \qquad /22/$$

$$\begin{bmatrix} \dot{\overline{x}} \\ \dot{\overline{i}} \end{bmatrix} = \begin{bmatrix} \underline{B}_{22} - \underline{\Gamma}\,\underline{P}_o & \underline{B}_{23} \\ \underline{0} & \underline{B}_{33} \end{bmatrix} \begin{bmatrix} \overline{x} \\ \overline{i} \end{bmatrix} + \begin{bmatrix} \underline{B}_{21} + \underline{\Gamma}\underline{X}_o \\ \underline{B}_{31} \end{bmatrix} \overline{p} + \begin{bmatrix} \dot{\overline{X}}_o \\ \dot{\overline{I}}_o \end{bmatrix} \qquad /23/$$

where the B matrix definitions are obvious from the original equations.

The terms $\dot{\overline{X}}_o$, $\dot{\overline{I}}_o$ and $\underline{B}_{11}\,\dot{\underline{X}}_o\,\overline{p}$ appear if the state $\overline{Y}_o$ is not an equilibrium state. If the last term is, however, neglected, the equation /22/ can be integrated to give an algebraic feedback relation:

$$\overline{p}(t) = \underline{B}_{12}\,\underline{P}_o\,\overline{x}(t) + \underline{B}_{14}\,\underline{P}_o\,\overline{u}(t) \qquad /24/$$

Substitution of /24/ into /23/ leads to linearized system dynamics:

$$\begin{bmatrix} \dot{\bar{x}} \\ \dot{\bar{i}} \end{bmatrix} = \begin{bmatrix} \underline{A}_{xx} & \underline{A}_{xi} \\ \underline{A}_{ix} & \underline{A}_{ii} \end{bmatrix} \begin{bmatrix} \bar{x} \\ \bar{i} \end{bmatrix} + \begin{bmatrix} \underline{C}_x \underline{P}_o \\ \underline{C}_i \underline{P}_o \end{bmatrix} \bar{u} + \begin{bmatrix} \dot{\bar{X}}_o \\ \dot{\bar{I}}_o \end{bmatrix} \qquad /25/$$

All the system matrices will depend on $\underline{A}_{11}^{-1}$.

Equations /25/ form a suitable model of the system dynamics for control purposes. The power, which is of the main interest, can be obtained by using eq. /24/.

Control Model with some Non-Linearity

In variable load operation of the reactor both the power, xenon and iodine levels and their distributions change and the changes are coupled. They can, however, be partly separated by the following technique, which also introduces some non-linearity into the control model.

The state vector $\bar{Y}(t)$ is written as a product of level factors and normalized distribution vectors

$$\bar{Y}(t) = \underline{Y}_l(t)\, \bar{y}_n(t) \qquad /26/$$

where $\underline{Y}_l$ is a diagonal matrix with N first diagonal elements equal to the core averaged power level, and the following elements equal to the xenon and iodine levels. For control vector the level factor is equal to one.

The deviation from the linearization point $\underline{Y}_o$ can be written:

$$\bar{y}(t) = \bar{Y}(t) - \bar{Y}_o = \underline{Y}_l\, y_n - \underline{Y}_l^o\, \bar{y}_n^o = \underline{Y}_l\, \Delta\bar{y}_n + \Delta\underline{Y}_l \bar{y}_n^o \qquad /27/$$

where

$$\Delta\bar{y}_n = \bar{y}_n - \bar{y}_n^o$$

$$\Delta\underline{Y}_l = \underline{Y}_l - \underline{Y}_l^o$$

i.e. $\Delta\bar{y}_n$ gives the change in the normalized distributions and $\Delta\underline{Y}_l$ in the bulk levels.

Substitution of the xenon and iodine parts of /27/ into /25/ gives:

$$\frac{d}{dt}\left(\underline{Y}_l\, \Delta\bar{y} + \Delta\underline{Y}_l \bar{y}_n^o\right) = \underline{A}\left(\underline{Y}_l\, \Delta\bar{y}_n + \Delta\underline{Y}_l\, \bar{y}_n^o\right) + \underline{C}\underline{P}_o\bar{u}$$

where a compact notation with $\underline{A}$, $\underline{C}$ and $\bar{d}$ is adopted for the system parameters. Rearranging gives:

$$\Delta\dot{\bar{y}}_n(t) = \underline{A}^\star(t)\,\Delta\bar{y}_n(t) + \underline{C}^\star(t)\,\bar{u}(t) + \bar{f}^\star(t) \qquad /28/$$

where

$$\underline{A}^\star(t) = \underline{A} - \underline{Y}_l^{-1}(t)\,\dot{\underline{Y}}_l(t)$$

$$\underline{C}^\star(t) = \underline{Y}_l^{-1}(t)\,\underline{C}\,\underline{P}_o$$

$$\bar{f}^\star(t) = \underline{Y}_l^{-1}(t)((\underline{A}\Delta\underline{Y}_l(t) - \Delta\dot{\underline{Y}}_l(t))\,\bar{y}_n{}^o + \bar{d})$$

The system dynamics is now described in terms of the normalized distributions, but the system parameters depend on the bulk level factors.

A model for the bulk level changes, called a point model, is obtained by weighting the eqs. /12/ and /13/ by the node volumes and summing over the whole reactor core:

$$\dot{X}_l = -\lambda_x X_l - \langle \Gamma x_n(t) \rangle X_l P_l + \lambda_I I_l + \langle \gamma_x^\star p_n(t) \rangle P_l \qquad /29/$$

$$\dot{I}_l = -\lambda_I I_l + \langle \gamma_I^\star p_n(t) \rangle P_l \qquad /30/$$

where P_l, X_l and I_l are the power, Xe and I level factors, the bracket terms represent the distribution weighted model parameters and the distribution time derivatives are neglected. The coupling between the distribution model (eq. /28/) and the point model can be reduced to a one way coupling only by using the linearization point distributions for weighting the parameters. The point model can be integrated if $P_l(t)$ is known, which assumes the load demand to be known for some time in advance.

The derived model is linear with respect to the normalized distributions, but non-linear with respect to the bulk levels. Compared to the first model the present one has the merit that it is linearized just with respect to normalized distributions, which change less than the absolute distributions during variable load operation.

Another variant of this model is obtained if $\underline{Y}_l \Delta\bar{y}_n$ is chosen as the computational state variable instead of $\Delta\bar{y}_n$. The eq. /28/ then reads:

$$\frac{d}{dt}(\underline{Y}_l \Delta\bar{y}_n) = \underline{A}(\underline{Y}_l \Delta\bar{y}_n) + \underline{C}\,\underline{P}_o\,\bar{u} + \bar{f}^1(t), \qquad /31/$$

where:

$$\bar{f}^1(t) = (\underline{A}\,\Delta\,\underline{Y}_l(t) - \Delta\dot{\underline{Y}}_l(t))\,\bar{y}_n{}^o + \bar{d}$$

The model matrices do not depend on the level factors in this case. The bulk levels obtained from the point model enter only the vector $\bar{f}^1$. A drawback is that the bulk levels are not any more calculated entirely by the non-linear point model, but partly by the linearized model. Therefore the xenon and iodine levels obtained from the state vector $(\underline{Y}_1 \Delta \bar{y}_n)$ will be slightly different from those predicted by the point model, which are used in the $\bar{f}^1$ vector.

3.2. Reduction of the System Order

The system order is 2N, with N the number of nodes. For accurate three dimensional reactor physical description that would mean a state vector with several thousand elements. However, for control model purposes the requirements with respect to spatial detail and accuracy are generally not that high.

For present day reactors only oscillations in the axial direction are unstable and the control problems essentially one-dimensional, which of course reduces the system order drastically. For large future reactors three dimensional effects may become so important that three dimensional control models are necessary. Also control systems, divided into two sub-systems, one for the axial direction (one dimensional) and another for the planar directions (two dimensional) could be considered. The success of such a system would depend on the amount of modal coupling between the oscillation modes as such and through the control actions.

The oscillation modes are the more stable the higher mode (i.e. the more peaks it has) is in question. From that point of view fairly little spatial detail is needed in a control model, because the modes of interest are spatially fairly smooth. Assume that the control system could be designed such that the control actions do not cause undesirable local transients leading to strong peaks or rapid changes in the local power.

Then it would be enough to describe the global distribution effects with the control model. On the other hand the accuracy of the model for describing the global effects decreases if the number of nodes is reduced.

One solution still would be to increase the node size of present methods until the acceptable accuracy limit is reached. The way chosen here is to choose two different spatial meshes, one with normal size nodes and another with considerably larger nodes, called control zones. One control zone will thus consist of several nodes.

The procedure for obtaining the control model is the following. First a high accuracy calculation with a reactor physics programme is made. The solution is obtained from the eigenvalue problem of eq. /20/. The matrices $\underline{L}$ and $\underline{M}$ correspond then to the normal node spatial mesh. With a special procedure the equations are then collapsed to correspond to the spatial structure of the large control zones. The matrices $\underline{L}$ and $\underline{M}$ and other necessary parameters are calculated for the control zones.

The dimensions of the $\underline{A}_{11}^{-1}$ matrix (eq. /19/), which essentially describes the neutronics of the system, is thereby reduced to a practical level. From then on the distributions within the control zones are frosen to those at the linearization point and only the zonal averaged values of the variables are considered. At the linearization state the low order control zone model is consistent with the nodal model. The number of control zones should for computational reasons be below one hundred.

3.3. Optimal Control

Based on the time discretized form of the above derived control models two optimal control methods are applied to the control problem. The first one is an application of the Linear - Quadratic - Gaussion (LQG) theory. It results in a state variable feedback control law. The other one uses Quadratic Programming (QP) for sloving a multi-stage, feedforward control problem with constraints.

3.3.1. State Variable Feedback Control

In this approach the state vector of eq. /25/ is extended with the control vector $\bar{u}$ and a bias vector $\bar{\xi}$. Noise vectors $\bar{\eta}$ are also included to describe the process noise, which is assumed to be zero-mean, non-correlated white gaussion noise. The same assumptions are made about the measurement noise later. The system is now described by the following equations:

$$\begin{bmatrix} \dot{\bar{y}} \\ \dot{\bar{\xi}} \end{bmatrix} = \begin{bmatrix} \underline{A} & \underline{D} \\ \underline{0} & \underline{0} \end{bmatrix} \begin{bmatrix} \bar{y} \\ \bar{\xi} \end{bmatrix} + \begin{bmatrix} \underline{C} \\ \underline{0} \end{bmatrix} \bar{u} + \begin{bmatrix} \bar{\eta}_y \\ \bar{\eta}_\xi \end{bmatrix} \qquad /32/$$

where the $\underline{D}$ matrix describes the effect of the bias vector $\bar{\xi}$ on the xenon and iodine parts of the state vector. Actually the bias variable is added to the power equation (compare with eq. /22/):

$$\dot{\bar{p}} = \underline{A}_{px}\dot{\bar{x}} + \underline{C}_p \dot{\bar{u}} + \bar{\xi} + \bar{\eta}_p$$

$$\dot{\bar{\xi}} = \bar{\eta}_\xi$$

and the dimension of $\bar{\xi}$ will the same as the dimension of $\bar{p}$. When $\bar{p}$ is eliminated from the system equations, $\bar{\xi}$ and also $\bar{\eta}_p$ enter the xenon and iodine dynamics. Therefore also the power noise covariance has to be taken into account.

The measurement relation is

$$\bar{m} = [\,\underline{M}\,\underline{O}\,] \begin{bmatrix} \bar{y} \\ \bar{\xi} \end{bmatrix} + \bar{\omega} \qquad /33/$$

where $\bar{\omega}$ is the measurement noise vector. The real measurements in the reactor give only the neutron flux at certain positions in the core. The dependence of the zonal power densities on these is fairly complicated, but it is reasonable to assume that a system for performing this conversion exists on the plant. Therefore the zonal powers are assumed measurable and the measurement relation is actually the equation /24/ appended with the noise vector.

The state vector augmented with the bias variable is estimated with a Kalman filter based on the discrete time versions of the state equation /32/ and the measurement relation /33/:

$$\tilde{z}(k) = \underline{G}\,\hat{z}\,(k-1) + \underline{C}\,\bar{v}\,(k-1)$$
$$\hat{z}\,(k) = \tilde{z}\,(k) + \underline{K}\,(\bar{m} - \underline{M}\,\bar{y}\,(k)) \qquad /34/$$

with a constant gain matrix $\underline{K}$, because the asymptotic solution is used. The matrix $\underline{K}$ will depend on the covariance matrices of the process and measurement noise. The filter will produce estimates of the non-measurable xenon and iodine distributions and of the bias variable

The basic objective of the control system is to prevent the power distribution oscillations. They are mainly excited by the control actions necessary for the criticality or total power control. Since the criticality and power distribution control are so tightly coupled, both aspects are included into the objective function to be minimized:

$$J = \sum_{k=1}^{\infty} [\,(P\,(k) - P_{set})^2 + W_1\,(P_1\,(k) - P_{1\,set})^2 + W_2\,(P_2\,(k) - P_{2\,set})^2 + \bar{u}^T(k)\,\underline{W}_3\,\bar{u}(k) + \bar{v}^T(k)\,\underline{W}_4\,\bar{v}\,(k)\,] \qquad /35/$$

where

$P(k)$	is the total power
$P_i(k)$	is the power of subvolume i
$\bar{v}(k)$	is the vector of controller speeds
W_i	are weighting factors or matrices

The power distribution control is realized by specifying setpoint values for the power generated in certain parts of the core. If P_1 is for example the power in the lower half of the core, the first axial overtone is suppressed, if P_1 is kept at setpoint. Similarly, P_2 can be the power in the left half of the core and control of that would suppress the first azimuthal overtone oscillations. Because no hard constraints are used, it is necessary to include the controller positions and speeds into the objective function in order to avoid unrealistic control inputs.

The power in any subvolume of the core can be expressed as a linear combination of the zonal powers and by using /24/ the objective function can be expressed in terms of the state vector.

The state vector is still augmented with the setpoints so that it will be:

$$\bar{z}^T = [\bar{x}^T\,\bar{i}^T\,\bar{u}^T\,\bar{\xi}^T\;P_{set}\,P_{1\,set}\,P_{2\,set}]$$

The control problem is thus formulated as a standard LQG control problem and can be solved with standard methods. Using the asymptotic solution of the matrix Riccati equation, the optimal control is obtained in the state variable feedback law form

$$\underline{u} = \underline{F}\,\hat{z}$$

where the optimal estimate $\hat{z}$ is obtained with the Kalman filter.

The control will also depend on the estimates of the bias variable $\hat{\xi}$, which are intended to compensate for modelling inaccuracies and biased disturbances. They actually represent a very simple form of on-line parameter identification. The bias variable will have an integrating effect on the control and thus counteract steady state offsets.

Because the setpoints are included in the state vector, they can also be changed in the operational use of the feedback law, but for obvious reasons they should not be to far from the linearization state.

3.3.2 Constrained Multi-Stage Control

This control approach aims at predictive calculation of the control for several time steps ahead. The control period could be for example 10 hours long and consist of about 10 steps.

The control models are derived from the linearized model of /31/ used together with the non-linear point model. This form is chosen instead of the obviously more accurate combination of /28/ with the point model, because of computational reasons. In both cases the discretized model parameters can be calculated without knowing the level factors and the parameters will be analytical function of the level factors. In the latter case all the system matrices will depend on the level factors, while in the chosen technique only a driving term-type vector will depend on the level factors. In the optimization phase, when the discretized models are used, the memory space and computational requirements are therefore smaller. The discretized models are of the form:

$$\bar{z}(k) = \underline{G}(k)\,\bar{z}(k-1) + \underline{C}(k)\,\bar{v}(k) + \bar{f}(k) \qquad /36/$$

$$k=1,\ldots,K$$

The state vector $\bar{z}(k)$ is defined as:

$$\bar{z}(k) = \bar{Y}(k) - \underline{Y}_1(k)\,\bar{y}_n^{o,k}$$

where the notation is the same as in /20/ and /28/. $\bar{y}_n^{o,k}$ gives the normalized distributions at the linearization point used for time step k. The power distribution is in the state vector for convenience, although it is not really a state variable, only an auxiliary variable. As in the previous section, the power part of system equations represent the measurement relation. Therefore the form of the $\underline{G}(k)$ matrix is:

$$\underline{G}(k) = \begin{bmatrix} \underline{o} & \underline{G}_{px} & \underline{G}_{pi} & \underline{G}_{pu} \\ \underline{o} & \underline{G}_{xx} & \underline{G}_{xi} & \underline{G}_{xu} \\ \underline{o} & \underline{G}_{ix} & \underline{G}_{ii} & \underline{G}_{iu} \\ \underline{o} & \underline{o} & \underline{o} & \underline{I} \end{bmatrix}$$

The matrices $\underline{G}_{pu}$, $\underline{G}_{xu}$, $\underline{G}_{iu}$ as well as the corresponding submatrices of $\underline{C}$, will depend on the power level, because P(t) is used instead of P_o (/31/).

The controller speeds $\bar{v}$ are used as the control inputs. The $\bar{f}$ vector contains the level factor effects and other known disturbances to the system:

$$\bar{f}(k) = \Delta \underline{Y}_1(k)\,\bar{f}_1 + \Delta \underline{Y}_1(k-1)\,\bar{f}_2 + \underline{F}_1\,\bar{g}(k) + \underline{F}_2\,\bar{g}(k-1) + \dot{\bar{Y}}_o(k) \qquad /37/$$

where

$\bar{f}_i$, $\underline{F}_i$ are precalculated system parameter vectors and matrices
$\bar{g}(k)$ known disturbance vector

The $\bar{g}$ vector may contain effects like known (power level dependent) changes in the input temperature, and the estimated bias variable $\bar{\xi}$. They must, however, be known for all the future time steps k=1,...K.

The control model will thus have two features introducing some non-linearity: The power level dependent control transmission matrices and the level factor etc. dependent driving term $\bar{f}(k)$.

Control Objectives and Solution

The objective function to be minimized is:

$$J_K = \sum_{k=1}^{K} [(\bar{y}_n(k) - \bar{y}_{n,d}(k))^T\,\underline{W}(k)\,(\bar{y}_n(k) - \bar{y}_{n,d}(k)) + \bar{v}^T(k)\,\underline{R}(k)\,\bar{v}(k)\,]$$

where

$\bar{y}_n(k)$ are vectors of the normalized power, xenon and iodine distribution and controller positions

$\bar{y}_{n,d}(k)$ desired distribution vectors
$\underline{W}(k)$, $\underline{R}(k)$ diagonal weighting matrices

Equilibrium distributions at different power levels can be used as desired distributions. The fuel cycle optimization also leads to some desired burn-up distributions, which require certain power distributions. The control of the power distribution is the primary concern, but the xenon and iodine distributions in the objective function can be utilized to effectively stabilize the core.

The criticality control is taken care of by a total power constraint.

$$P_{tot}(k) = P_{tot,set}(k) \qquad k=1,\dots K \qquad /38/$$

and also a number of other constraints can be used:

$$\bar{v}_{min}(k) \leq \bar{v}(k) \leq \bar{v}_{max}(k) \qquad /39/$$

$$\bar{U}_{min}(k) \leq \bar{U}(k) \leq U_{max}(k) \qquad /40/$$

$$\bar{P}(k) \leq \bar{P}_{max}(k) \qquad /41/$$

$$\dot{\bar{P}}(k) \leq \dot{\bar{P}}_{max}(k) \qquad /42/$$

$$q^l_{min}(k) \leq \sum_{i=1}^{N} a^l_i(k) \cdot P_i(k) \leq q^l_{max}(k) \qquad /43/$$

The two first constraints limit the controller speeds and positions. The basic aim of the control is to deliver the demanded power while keeping the power distribution and its time rate of change within operational limits. The constraints /38/, /41/ and /42/ can be used for that purpose within the accuracy of the linearized models.

These constrains are, however, very costly in terms of the computational problem size. If the power distribution perturbations are fairly smooth, like the first overtone oscillations, constraints on integral measures of the power distribution may suffice. Constraints of the type /43/ can then be used. By appropriate choice of the coefficients a_i^l, for example the difference between the power generation in the upper and lower halves of the core can be limited. This type of constraints are computationally much more economical. In general the constraints can be any linear combination of the state variables.

By recursive use of the state equation /36/, any state $\bar{z}(k)$ can be expressed as a function of the initial state $\bar{z}(o)$ and the control sequence:

$$\bar{z}(k) = \sum_{l=1}^{k} \left(\prod_{i=l+1}^{k} \underline{G}(i)\right) \underline{C}(l)\, \bar{v}(l) + \left(\prod_{i=1}^{k} \underline{G}(i)\right) \bar{z}(o) + \sum_{l=1}^{k} \left(\prod_{i=l+1}^{k} \underline{G}(i)\right) \bar{f}(l) \qquad /44/$$

Using the above relation, the control problem can be transferred to the standard form of quadratic programming:

$$\text{Min!} \quad J = \bar{c}^T \bar{X} + \tfrac{1}{2} \bar{X}^T \underline{Q} \bar{X} \qquad /45/$$

subject to

$$\underline{A} \bar{X} \geq \bar{b} \qquad /46/$$

where

$$\bar{X}^T = [\, \bar{v}^T(1) \; \dots \; \bar{v}^T(k) \; \dots \; \bar{v}^T(K) \,]$$

The number of unknowns is K·R, i.e. the number of control inputs. The dimension of the constraint set depends on the constraints chosen to be used. If local constraints are used in certain parts of the core, it also depends on the number of zones.

The solution of the control problem is summarized in Fig. 3. In the iterative loop the solution is improved by updating the linearized model control matrices ($\underline{C}$) along the solution trajectory as predicted by the linear models.

Operational Use

The proposed operational use of the control method is outlined in Fig. 4. The reactor state is estimated with a Kalman filter or by other methods. The parameters for a number of control models in different operational situations, like at various power levels, have been generated off-line by a reactor physics programme and another programme, which performs the time discretization. These models form a library for the on-line computations. Based on the present reactor state and anticipated future load demand the control problem is set up.

That procedure would include the automatical choice of the number and length of time steps, linearized models, objective function parameters and constraints to be used. A different linear model can be used for each time step. The choice must be based on the predicted load demand, which is also used for calculation of the power, Xe and I level factors. The optimization calculation then gives the control sequence for the next few hours. If the real load demand would differ from the predicted one, or if the control would not perform as predicted, a new control calculation would be initiated already before the end of the current control period.

In off-line control studies an outer iteration loop could be established (dashed line to the left of Fig. 4), where the control sequence would be simulated with the non-linear reactor physics simulator and new linearized models could be generated along the solution trajectory. The optimization could then be repeated with the new control models.

The use of reactor simulators based on physics models on future nuclear power plants as an operational aid, has been proposed. Such simulators could also solve the estimation problem and be used for testing out control procedures as indicated by the dotted lines in Fig. 4.

Feedback Control with Estimated State

The numerical solution of the QP problem gives as a result the controller speeds for the next K time steps leading to an open-loop control for that period. Some feedback is introduced by comparing the real reactor behaviour with the predicted one and recalculating the control if necessary. However, it is possible to interprete the solution of some QP algorithms as a kind of feedback control law. The theory is outlined below.

In the complementary pivot algorithm by Lemke (3), the QP problem is transformed by using the Kuhn -Tucker conditions into a set of linear equations, which is solved with a LP like pivoting algorithm. The solution is obtained in a form

$$\bar{X} = \underline{B}\,\bar{q} \qquad /47/$$

where the $\underline{B}$ matrix is calculated by the algorithm and the $\bar{q}$ vector originally depends on the initial system state and the constraint limit values, although it is modified in the cource of the solution. The $\underline{B}$ matrix depends on the control model and objective function parameters. The original $\underline{q}$ vector can thus be expressed as a linear function of the state trajectory $\bar{z}$:

$$\bar{q}^{o} = \underline{M}^{o}\,\bar{z} + \bar{r}^{o} \qquad /48/$$

where

$$\bar{z}^{T} = [\,\bar{z}^{T}(1)\,\ldots\,\bar{z}^{T}(k)\,\ldots\,\bar{z}^{T}(K)\,]$$

and the $\underline{M}$ matrix depends on the constraint matrix and control models. If the relation /48/ is updated during the QP problem solution process, we have at the optimum:

$$\bar{q}_{opt} = \underline{M}\,\bar{z}_{opt} + \bar{r} \qquad /49/$$

where $\bar{z}_{opt}$ is the optimal state trajectory as predicted by the control models. Substitution of /49/ into /47/ yields:

$$\bar{x}_{opt} = \underline{B}\,\underline{M}\,\bar{z}_{opt} + \bar{s}_{opt}$$

If the calculated state trajectory $\bar{z}_{opt}$ is now replaced by an estimated trajectory $\hat{\bar{z}}$, a kind of feedback control low is obtained, with the $\underline{B}\ \underline{M}$ matrix as the feedback matrix. The $\bar{s}$ vector will depend on the numerical values of the problem parameters and variables.

If the bias variable $\bar{\xi}$ is also estimated, its effect on the control could also be extracted from the solution and the estimated values used in the feedback form of the control.

The resulting control would not satisfy the constraints exactly, but because there is anyway a certain discrepancy between the real process and the control models, that would perhaps not be such a big disadvantage in all cases. The big advantage would be that the control would all the time be based on the (estimated) process behaviour.

4. SIMULATION RESULTS

In the computer simulations the same non-linear reactor simulator was used for simulating the reactor core and for generating the basic data for the control models. The simulator model was simplified with respect to spatial description such that the simulator nodes were identical with the control zones.

First some one dimensional, axial studies with a 13 node core model (26'th order system) were made. Uncontrolled the simulator exhibited unstable oscillations. A linear stability analysis showed that the model was unstable with respect to the fundamental mode, marginally stable with respect to the first axial overtone and stable with respect to higher modes.

In the case of Fig. 5 the core power has to go down to 88% of full power in one minute and after 6 hours back to full power again. Three controllers are available, two control rod banks of different strength and the soluble boron control system. From the power distribution point of view it would be desirable to use the boron control system for power level changes, but it is not technically possible because the boron system is too slow. Realistic constraints are therefore specified on the boron control speeds. Other constraints applied are the controller position and speed constraints and the total power constraint. The initial state vector is assumed measureable and the control is obtained from one optimization calculation over the time period from 0 to 10 hours. The control rods are run exactly according to the solution, but small adjustments are allowed in the boron concentration to maintain criticality. The equilibrium distributions at full power with the stronger rod bank 40 cm inserted and the other bank out of core are specified as the desired distributions. Most weight in the objective function is put on the reactor state after return to full power.

The thin lines in Fig. 5 represent the optimal control and the stronger lines a conventional control solution . In the latter case return to full power takes place one hour later for better resolution of the curves. In the optimal control case the desired state is achieved right after return to full power as a consequence of the feedforward action of the control system, activated by the load demand change and resulting in preconditioning of the core at reduced power. In the conventional control case the distribution control is finished after return to full power and only boron is used to maintain criticality. The maximum peaking is defined as the maximum local (zonal) power normalized to the core average. In the optimal control case a fairly strong peak occurs right before return to full power. That is due to the anticipatory control actions, but it happens at reduced power and can be tolerated. At full power the peaking is smaller for the optimal control case than for the conventional control.

Fig. 6 shows steady-state control results for a three dimensional case with 36 zones (72'th order system). The core model is unstable with respect to the fundamental mode, the first axial overtone and two symmetrical azimuthal first overtone oscillation modes. The dotted lines show the core response to an inital perturbation. The axial offset describes the imbalance in the power distribution between the top and bottom of the core and the planar peaking factors describe the oscillations in the side-to-side direction in the plane perpendicular to the core axis. Four control rod banks (1...4, individual rod positions belonging to different banks in the plane indicated in the figure) and boron are used as controllers. The desired state is the equilibrium with only bank 1 somewhat in the core and all other rods out. Therefore the rod position constraints play an active role in this case. The banks 2,3 and 4 are entered into the core in an optimal manner to damp simultaneously both the axial and azimuthal oscillations. The solid lines show the damping of the oscillations when the optimal control is applied.

In both of the above cases the state vector was assumed measurable. Results for the state-variable feedback control are shown in Figs. 7 and 8. In these cases, however, the linear control model was used also as the simulation model in stead of the nonlinear simulator, which was used in the previous cases. The core model was the one-dimensional core described above, except that only one control rod bank and boron were used as controllers.

Figure 7 shows steady-state control after an initial perturbation. The state vector was estimated with the constant gain Kalman filter from power distribution measurements contaminated with measurement and process noise. The total power is kept fairly constant and the power axial offset is controlled effectively to the desired value. The dotted line represents the uncontrolled (constant power) oscillation.

In the case of Fig. 8 the state vector was assumed measureable. The control objective was to increase the total power by 5% from the linearization point value and at the same time reduce the power in the lower core half by 5%. Both goals are rapidly reached and continuous rod movement and boron adjustment is necessary to maintain the desired state.

5. CONCLUSIONS

The problem of controlling the total power and power distribution of a nuclear reactor is characterized by its high-order, strong coupling and non-linearity. It has been formulated as a LQG feedback control problem and as a constrained quadratic programming problem.

The simulation results with the latter method show that the linearized control model with some non-linear features is accurate enough also in three spatial dimensions. Studies with respect to the necessary order of the control model have to be conducted. The practical control problem fairly strongly suggests the use of constraints both on the control variables and on the state variables. That is possible with the QP formulation. On the other hand the strong non-linearity of the problem in certain operation modes (load cycling and following) reduces the applicability range of the control models and constraints are needed to obtain realistic solutions. The method is presently studied on a large scientific computer and its use on a process computer would require fairly advanced system in terms of memory space and accuracy. Because the process dynamics arefairly slow, the computing time would not be so critical.

The LQG approach results in an efficient on-line feedback algorithm and is computationally easily realizable. However, it can not handle constraints and does not possess the effective feedforward feature of the QP concept.

However, in practical use on a nuclear reactor the methods could complement each other and be used in different operational situations.

For both methods the estimation of the non measurable parts of the state vector requires furtherwork.

The practical need of this kind of optimal control systems depends on the design and operation of future nuclear reactors, which in the light of current trends seems to lead to increasing spatial control problems.

REFERENCES

1. R. Fröhlich: Review of Current Problems for Multidimensional Reactor Statics Calculations. Kernforschungzentrum Karlsruhe, Report KFK 1821 (1973).

2. W.M. Stacey: Space-Time Nuclear Reactor Kinetics. Academic Press, New York and London (1969).

3. C.E. Lemke, J.T. Howson Jr.: J. Soc. Indust. Appl. Math. 12 (1964).

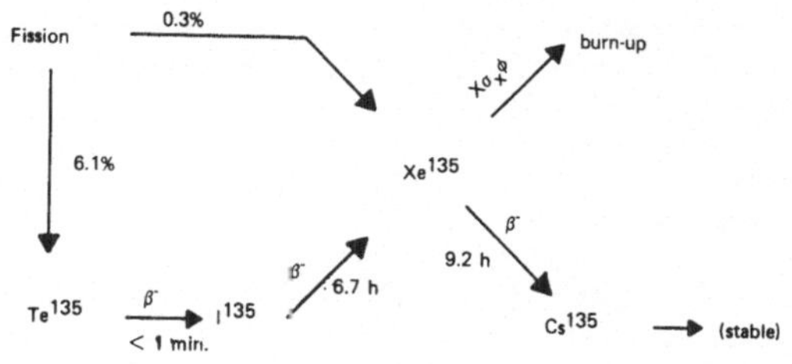

Fig. 1 Production of Xe^{135} from fission and by decay of I^{135} and destruction by burn-up and decay

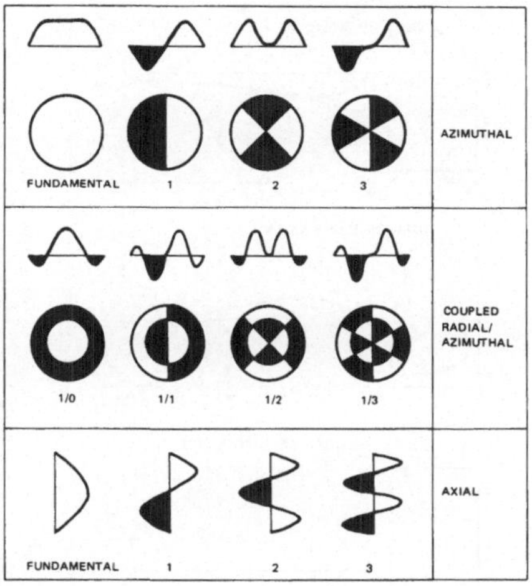

Fig. 2 Spatial oscillation modes of an idealized cylindrical reactor core

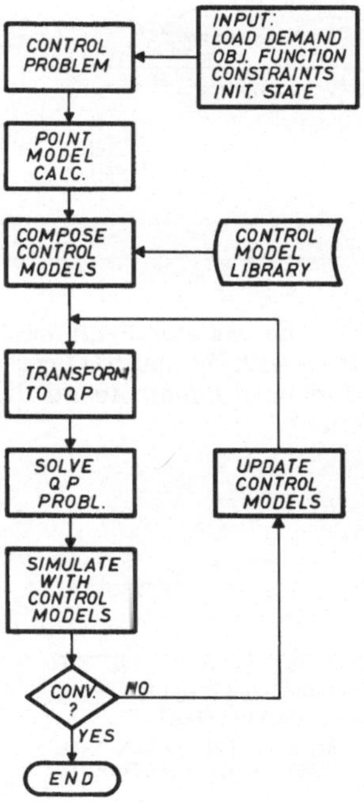

Fig. 3 Computational flow in the constrained multi-stage control method. (QP = Quadratic Programming)

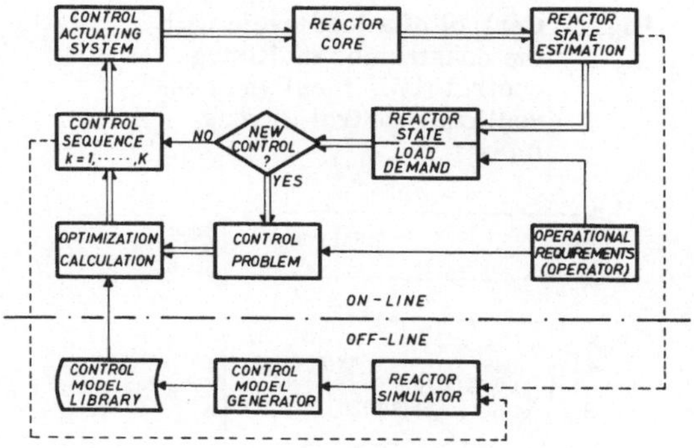

Fig. 4 Proposed operational use of the constrained multi-stage control

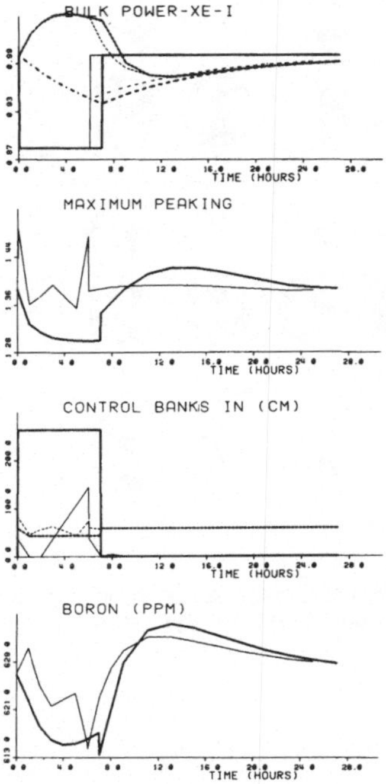

Fig. 5 Control of a load cycle with the constrained multistage control (thin lines) and conventional control (strong lines)

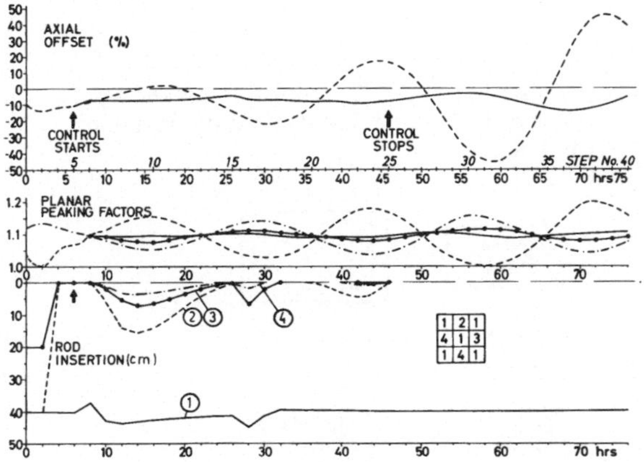

Fig. 6 Control of an unstable 3-dimensional oscillation with the multi-stage control method (dashed lines: uncontrolled oscillation)

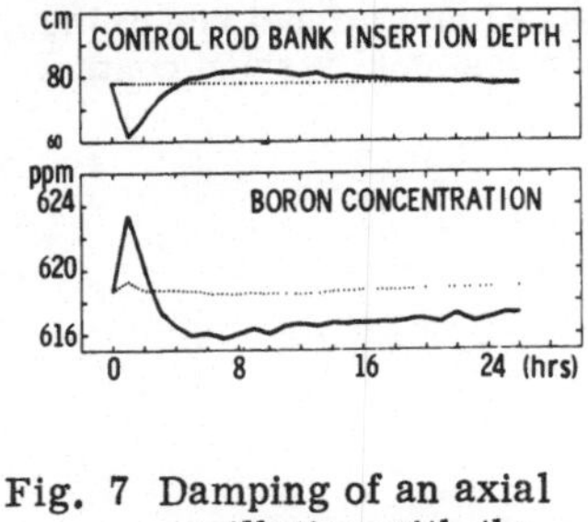

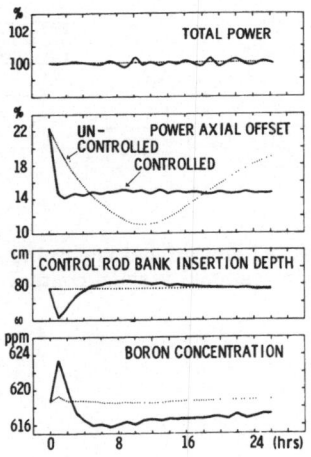

Fig. 7 Damping of an axial oscillation with the state variable feedback method

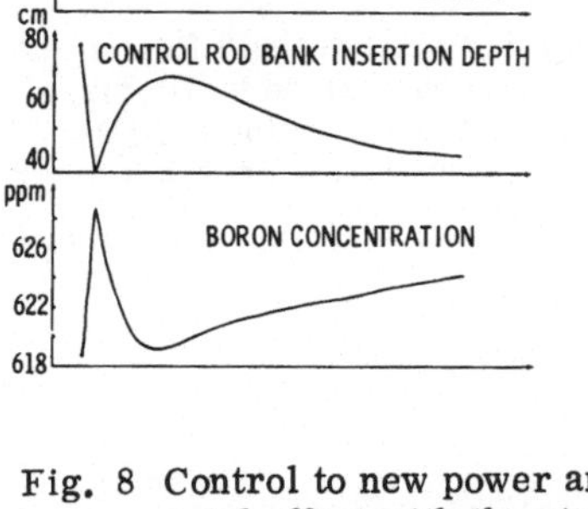

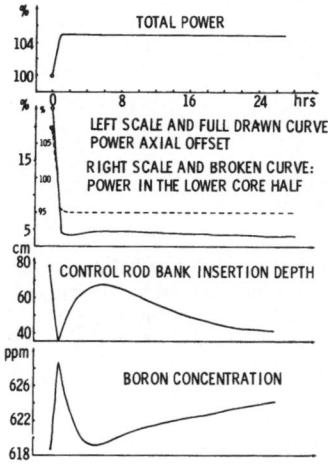

Fig. 8 Control to new power and axial offset with the state variable feedback method

FREE BOUNDARY PROBLEMS IN OPTIMAL CONTROL

J.A. Bather
Mathematics Division
University of Sussex
Brighton, Sussex.

1. Introduction.

This paper is an attempt to illustrate a range of optimisation problems by giving a few examples and a sketch of the methods which have been developed. The common feature in these problems is that, in spite of the wide variety of their origins, they can all be expressed as decision problems for a gambler who aims to maximise his expected gains or minimise his losses by choosing sequentially between specified alternative actions. Often the choice is simply whether to terminate a given sequence of gambles or not. In this case, the decision problem reduces to finding the critical "free" boundary between the optimal stopping and continuation regions in an appropriate state space. This kind of problem has been studied quite thoroughly in recent years, but much less progress has been made towards understanding games where the gambler has more than two effective alternatives at each stage. Even in the case of three alternatives the free boundary problem associated with locating the optimal decision regions is formidable.

2. Discrete stopping problems.

The first example involves coin tossing. Consider a game in which the player is allowed to toss a balanced coin as often as he likes at unit cost for each toss. His reward, when he finally decides to stop, is $\lambda|j|$, where $\lambda > 0$ is a given constant and j is the difference between the number of heads and the number of tails he has obtained. It is convenient to imagine that he plays on credit and then his net return at the end of the game is represented by the reward function r :

$$(2.1) \qquad r_j = \lambda|j| - j^2 , \qquad (j = 0, \pm1, \dots) .$$

Initially $j = 0$, but we can define for each possible state of play, the maximum expected reward f_j which can be attained by starting at j and using an optimal policy for continuing the game from that state. Obviously

$$(2.2) \qquad f_j \geq r_j ,$$

because the player always has the option of stopping immediately. The other possible action at j is to toss the coin, which leads to state $j + 1$ or $j - 1$ with equal probabilities. It follows that, in general,

$$(2.3) \qquad f_j \geq \tfrac{1}{2}(f_{j+1} + f_{j-1}) .$$

In fact, f can be characterised as the smallest function which satisfies both the above inequalities. This is an application of a general result first established by Dynkin [11] through the study of excessive functions for a Markov process. It is not difficult to determine f by noting that, for each j, one of the two alternative actions must be chosen and equality must hold in either (2.2) or (2.3). Thus,

$$(2.4) \qquad f_j = \max \left\{ r_j , \tfrac{1}{2}(f_{j+1} + f_{j-1}) \right\} .$$

Let $k \geq 0$ be the integer defined by : $\frac{1}{2}(\lambda - 1) < k \leq \frac{1}{2}(\lambda + 1)$. Then $f_j = r_j$ for $|j| \geq k$ and $f_j = r_k$ for $|j| < k$. This solution of (2.4) specifies an optimal policy by indicating which of the two terms on the right of the equation is appropriate. Hence, the player should terminate the game as soon as he reaches a state with $|j| \geq k$.

Of course, the effective value of the game to the player is $f_0 = r_k$ and this suggests the level of entrance fee which might be charged in order to make the game "fair" to the banker. With this modification, it could be profitable to a casino, since players may not use an optimal policy.

A concise introduction to the theory of optimal stopping can be found in the books by Dynkin and Yushkevich [12]. They also describe an interesting application which has become known as the "marriage problem" or "secretary problem". However, let us turn to a different type of illustration which, at first sight, has little connection with games of chance.

A recent paper by Cohen [9] gives two different examples of stopping problems originating in the field of elasticity. Imagine a horizontal net or hammock with strings intersecting at points (i, j). The edges of the hammock form a fixed rectangle, but the interior nodes are free to move vertically provided that the displacement function f satisfies the constraint

$$(2.5) \qquad f_{ij} \leq c_{ij} , \qquad (0 < i < a, \quad 0 < j < b) .$$

Here, the function c prescribes an upper bound which represents a roof over the hammock. Now let us imagine that forces of equal magnitude μ are applied in the upward direction at each interior node and that all the strings have the same tension τ. For small displacements, the conditions of equilibrium for a node are as follows:

$$(2.6) \qquad f_{ij} = \frac{\mu}{4\tau} + \tfrac{1}{4}(f_{i+1,j} + f_{i-1,j} + f_{i,j+1} + f_{i,j-1})$$

whenever $f_{ij} < c_{ij}$ and

(2.7) $$f_{ij} \leq \frac{\mu}{4\tau} + \frac{1}{4}(f_{i+1,j} + f_{i-1,j} + f_{i,j+1} + f_{i,j-1})$$

if $f_{ij} = c_{ij}$.

These conditions are equivalent to

(2.8) $$f_{ij} = \min \left\{ c_{ij} \, , \frac{\mu}{4\tau} + \frac{1}{4}(f_{i+1,j} + f_{i-1,j} + f_{i,j+1} + f_{i,j-1}) \right\} .$$

The last equation is a two-dimensional version of (2.4) and we can now recognise an optimal stopping problem. In this case, the random process involves jumps from a state (i, j) to any of its four nearest neighbours, with equal probabilities, and there is a constant cost $\mu/4\tau$ for each transition. The cost of stopping instead of allowing another transition is c_{ij} and f_{ij} is the minimum expected cost, starting at (i, j). The optimal stopping region can be determined by solving (2.8) subject to the condition that $f_{ij} = 0$ on the boundary of the rectangle. This region corresponds to the set of nodes pressed up against the roof in the original problem.

The paper [9] also discusses a continuous model of the hammock which leads to a stopping problem for Brownian motion. We shall consider such processes in the next section. Cohen's second example is concerned with plastic-elastic torsion of a cylindrical bar and, in this case, the optimal stopping and continuation sets correspond precisely with the regions of plastic and elastic deformation in a cross section of the bar.

3. Optimal stopping of Brownian motion.

One of the attractions of mathematical models with continuous variables is the possibility of using the techniques of differential calculus. Brownian motion is a continuous version of the discrete random processes mentioned previously. The theory of optimal stopping for continuous trajectories is more complicated, but also more revealing. The following paragraphs give a brief summary of the general results established in [3].

The mathematical representation of Brownian motion is usually called a Wiener process. It can be defined in the following way. Let $\{X(t), 0 \leq t < \infty\}$ be an m-dimensional random process with mutually independent components. Each component $\{X_i(t)\}$ has independent, normally distributed increments and $X_i(0) = 0$, $E\{X_i(t)\} = 0$, $E\{(X_i(t_1) - X_i(t_2))^2\} = |t_1 - t_2|$, $i = 1,2,\ldots, m$, where E is the expectation operator. Further, it may be assumed that almost every trajectory is continuous. A stopping time T is a non-negative random variable which depends, without anticipation, on this process.

We introduce the following notation. Let $z = (u_1, u_2, \ldots, u_m, v)$, or simply $z = (u, v)$, be a point of Euclidean $(m + 1)$-space and let S denote the open half-space where $v > 0$. We suppose given a non-negative function $c(z)$ which determines the stopping cost on the closure of S. For simplicity, let us assume that $c(z)$ is continuous for $v \geq 0$. Consider the process $\{Z(t)\}$ with initial point $z \in S$, defined by

$$(3.1) \qquad Z(t) = (u + X(t), \ v - t), \qquad (0 \leq t \leq v) .$$

Then, for any stopping time $T \leq v$, the process stops at the point $Z(T)$ and the cost is $c(Z(T))$. We are mainly interested in the corresponding expectation, denoted by $E\{c(Z(T)) \mid z\}$, and its dependence on the initial point z. Suitable restrictions on the asymptotic magnitude of the given cost function will ensure that such expectations are finite : see Section 4 of [3]. For each $z \in S$, we seek an optimal stopping time which attains the minimum :

$$(3.2) \qquad f(z) = \inf_{T \leq v} E\{c(Z(T)) \mid z\} .$$

Fortunately, it turns out that the only stopping times we need consider are those defined by reference to an open subset of the space S. Let $A \subset S$ be open and consider, for each initial point $z \in A$, the random point Z_A where the process (3.1) first hits the boundary of A. The corresponding expectation is

$$(3.3) \qquad f_A(z) = E\{c(Z_A) \mid z\}$$

and we can extend the definition by setting $f_A(z) = c(z)$ for $z \notin A$. This function has the property that

$$(3.4) \qquad \frac{1}{2} \sum \frac{\partial^2 f_A}{\partial u_i^2} = \frac{\partial f_A}{\partial v} , \qquad (z \in A) ,$$

which is a consequence of the fundamental relation between Brownian motion and the classical heat equation : see Doob [10].

Returning to the minimum expected cost, it can be shown that $f(z)$ is continuous in z and hence, that $B = \{z \in S : f(z) < c(z)\}$ is an open set. By the definition of $f(z)$, there is a stopping time for the initial point z, which is preferable to stopping immediately, if and only if $z \in B$. This suggests that B is the optimal stopping region, but it is not obvious that

$$(3.5) \qquad f_B(z) = f(z) .$$

The proof of this result in [3] is quite long and technical, but it is worth commenting on one of the main ideas. The stopping rule associated with any open set A can be improved by reducing it to the subset $A^* = \{z \in A : f_A(z) < c(z)\}$. In fact,

$$(3.6) \qquad f_{A^*}(z) = \min \{ f_A(z), \; c(z)\} .$$

Further, it can be shown that when two modified open sets A_1^* and A_2^* are combined,

$$(3.7) \qquad f_{A_1^* \cup A_2^*}(z) \leq \min \left\{ f_{A_1^*}(z), \; f_{A_2^*}(z) \right\} .$$

This argument leads eventually to the identity :

$$(3.8) \qquad f_{\cup A^*}(z) = \inf_{A \subset S} \{ f_A(z)\} ,$$

where the union includes every modified open subset of S. It remains to establish that the infimum here is equivalent to that in (3.2) and also that $B = \cup A^*$.

The representation of the optimal continuation region B as a union of open sets is interesting, but the properties of the function f may be more useful. In view of (3.4) and (3.5), we know that

$$(3.9) \qquad \frac{1}{2} \sum \frac{\partial^2 f}{\partial u_i^2} = \frac{\partial f}{\partial v} , \qquad (z \in B) .$$

One of the boundary conditions for this equation follows from the continuity of f and the fact that $f(z) = c(z)$ for $z \notin B$. However, the boundary is not specified in advance and we need further information in order to locate it. A second, necessary condition involves continuity of the first partial derivatives of f on the boundary of B. This holds provided that the given cost function c has continuous derivatives there. Thus, we have a free boundary problem specified by equation (3.9), together with the boundary conditions :

$$(3.10) \qquad f(z) = c(z), \; \frac{\partial f}{\partial u_i} = \frac{\partial c}{\partial u_i} , \; \frac{\partial f}{\partial v} = \frac{\partial c}{\partial v} , \quad (i = 1,2,\ldots, m).$$

Strictly speaking, the conditions on first derivatives may not hold at certain irregular points on the boundary, but these form a set of probability measure zero with respect to the Brownian motion. In any case, the last qualification is less serious than the fact that the minimum expected cost function may not be the only solution to the free boundary problem.

Many special solutions of (3.9) and (3.10) and approximations have been described in the literature of probability and statistics. Indeed, several of the ideas underlying the general results we have described first emerged during the investigation of a statistical problem by Chernoff and others : for example, see [7]. A review of this investigation and further examples of free boundary problems can be found in [8].

More recently, a different approach to optimal control problems, including optimal stopping, has been developed by Bensoussan and Lions using methods in functional analysis, rather than probability. A summary of their results, based on the study of variational inequalities, is contained in [6]. It will be interesting to see whether further progress can be made by combining these methods of analysis with the tools of probability.

4. Further developments.

The results described so far are supported by a well-established theory, but this does not extend to more complicated problems of optimal stochastic control. Nevertheless, a pattern is beginning to emerge from the ad-hoc methods which have been used to investigate special cases. This section is concerned with particular examples, but it is also intended to indicate some of the ideas which appear to be more generally applicable.

The first example is fully explained in [2] and also mentioned in [8]. Briefly, the aim is to construct an optimal policy for controlling the path of a space-ship as it moves towards its target. This leads to a sequential decision problem specified in terms of three variables: a quantity which summarises the available information and gives a prediction of the final distance from the target, the time to go and the amount of fuel remaining. The predictor variable behaves like Brownian motion, except that it can be modified impulsively by using fuel in order to change the direction of motion. As in the case of stopping problems, there are two possible actions at each point of the state space, but the associated free boundary problem is more complicated because of the behaviour of the controlled stochastic process near the critical boundary. It turns out that the heat equation must be solved, subject to boundary conditions on both first and second partial derivatives. The main results of [2] are in the form of bounds on the optimal decision regions. However, the calculations depend on an interesting, but unproven conjecture about the effect of a hypothetical tax on the use of fuel.

Of course, there are many decision problems which cannot be reduced to a simple choice between two alternative actions at each point of the state space. For discrete models, formulated as Markovian decision processes, there are many results and computational techniques available for dealing with finite or denumerable state and action spaces. However, the advantage of using continuous variables is that sometimes a more explicit description of the optimal decision regions is possible and hence, a clearer understanding of the structure of the optimal policy. There is also a price to pay in terms of the analytical difficulties encountered. In particular, the inductive technique of dynamic programming needs to be applied more carefully when the induction parameter is replaced by a continuous variable.

A general feature of deterministic and stochastic control problems is that, when the minimum expected cost function is finite, it can be expressed as an extreme member of a class of functions defined by a set of inequalities. This is the point of view adopted by Dynkin, as explained in Section 2. The results about optimal stopping of Brownian motion can also be interpreted in the same way. More precisely, the function f defined by (3.2) can be characterised as the maximal element in the class of functions determined by the inequalities:

$$(4.1) \qquad g(z) \le c(z) \ , \qquad \tfrac{1}{2}\sum \frac{\partial^2 g}{\partial u_i^2} \ge \frac{\partial g}{\partial v} \ .$$

Strictly speaking, f need not satisfy the second of these at every point in the state space, but $f(z) \ge g(z)$ uniformly in z for all such g : see Section 6 of [3]. The general feature is that each inequality is obtained by considering the effect of a single action at an arbitrary point in the state space. This kind of characterisation of the minimum expected cost function suggests few clues how to determine the function and its associated policy, but there is a related idea which often helps. Roughly speaking, if there is a well defined policy π which determines an expected cost function g_π and if this function satisfies all the relevant inequalities, then $g_\pi = f$ and π is optimal.

Illustrations of the above ideas for problems with three alternative actions can be found in [4] and [5]. In both cases, the results depend on the construction and interpretation of special solutions of three basic inequalities. However, we shall discuss a less complicated, but rather isolated example which has an explicit solution.

Our final illustration is taken from a recent paper by Balmer [1], and it relates to a stopping problem with the extra facility that statistical information can be obtained at a prescribed cost before reaching a decision to stop. Consider a simple stochastic process $\{\theta(t)\}$ with a single transition from 0 to 1 at a random time which cannot be observed directly. A-priori, $P(\theta(t) = 0) = e^{-\lambda t}$ and $P(\theta(t) = 1) = 1 - e^{-\lambda t}$ for any $t \ge 0$, where $\lambda > 0$ is prescribed. The costs associated with the process before termination are $a_1 + a_2\theta(t) + b$ or $a_1 + a_2\,\theta(t)$ per unit time, according to whether information is being collected or not; the cost of termination is $c_1 - c_2\theta(t)$, where a_1, a_2, b, c_1 and c_2 are positive constants. The idea is that the random transition to $\theta(t) = 1$ represents the arrival of a disturbance which should be detected as soon as possible and nullified by the action of stopping the process. It will not be necessary for us to study the structure of the statistical information. The possible actions by the decision maker can be expressed in terms of a single state variable $w \geq 0$, where $w(t) = p(t)/(1 - p(t))$ and $p(t)$ is the conditional probability that $\theta(t) = 1$, given any information which may have been collected during the period $[0, t]$.

Let $w(t) = w$ and consider the alternatives (a) wait until $t + \delta t$, (b) collect information until $t + \delta t$ and (c) stop the process. Each of these actions incurs an immediate cost and has a different effect on the state w. For example, the minimum expected cost $f(w)$ must satisfy the following condition:

$$f(w) \leq \left\{ \frac{a_1(1 + w) + a_2 w}{1 + w} \right\} \partial t + E\{f(w + \delta w)\} + o(\delta t) \tag{4.2}$$

as $\delta t \downarrow 0$. The first term on the right is the immediate cost of action (a) and the second is the expected future cost calculated with respect to the known distribution of the increment δw for this action. The condition simply states than an optimal choice must be at least as good as action (a). A suitable expansion of $f(w + \delta w)$ and evaluation of the expectation up to terms of order δt leads to the inequality

$$\lambda(1 + w)^2 f'(w) + a_1(1 + w) + a_2 w \geq 0 . \tag{4.3}$$

A similar analysis of the effect of action (b) shows that

$$\tfrac{1}{2}w^2(1+w) f''(w) + \{\lambda(1+w)^2 + w^2\}f'(w) + (a_1+b)(1+w) + a_2 w \geq 0 . \tag{4.4}$$

Finally, $f(w)$ cannot exceed the expected cost of stopping, so we have

$$f(w) \leq c_1 - c_2 w/(1 + w) . \tag{4.5}$$

The same kind of argument shows that, in the optimal decision region A where (a) is appropriate, f must satisfy the equation obtained by removing the strict inequality from (4.3). Similarly, (4.4) and (4.5) lead to equations for f in the corresponding regions denoted by B and C.

There is a detailed analysis of the necessary boundary conditions in [1], leading to the free boundary problem specified as follows : determine f and a partition of the state space $[0, \infty)$ into regions A, B and C so that f

satisfies the equations obtained from (4.3), (4.4) and (4.5), each in the corresponding region, f and f' are continuous at every boundary point and f'' is continuous on the boundary between A and B.

By carefully fitting together solutions of the equations according to the stated boundary conditions, Balmer succeeded in proving that there is exactly one function f which also satisfies the three basic inequalities at every point $w \geq 0$. The optimal policy is uniquely determined and each of the following configurations of the optimal decision regions is possible, for suitable values of the model parameters : either $C = [0, \infty)$,

or A is a bounded interval on the left of C and B is empty,

or A, B and C are intervals with A on the left of B and C is unbounded.

References.

[1] Balmer, D.W. (1975) On a quickest detection problem with costly information, J. Appl. Prcb. 12, 87-97.

[2] Bather, J.A. and Chernoff, H. (1967) Sequential decisions in the control of a space-ship, J. Appl. Prob. 4, 584-604.

[3] Bather, J.A. (1970) Optimal stopping problems for Brownian motion, Adv. Appl. Prob. 2, 259-286.

[4] Bather, J.A. (1973) An optimal stopping problem with costly information, Bulletin of the I.S.I. Vol XLV, Book 3, 9-24.

[5] Bather, J.A. (1976) A control chart model and a generalised stopping problem for Brownian motion, to appear in Mathematics of Operations Research.

[6] Bensoussan, A. and Lions, J.L. (1974) On certain questions related to optimal control, Russian Math. Surveys 29, 79-87.

[7] Chernoff, H. (1965) Sequential tests for the mean of a normal distribution III and IV, Ann. Math. Statist. 36, 28-68.

[8] Chernoff, H. (1968) Optimal stochastic control, Sankhya 30, 221-252.

[9] Cohen, J.W. (1975) Plastic-elastic torsion, optimal stopping and free boundaries, J. Engineering Math. 9, 219-226.

[10] Doob, J.L. (1955) A probability approach to the heat equation, Trans. Amer. Math. Soc. 80, 216-280.

[11] Dynkin, E.B. (1963) Optimal selection of stopping time for a Markov process, Dokl. Akad. Nauk. USSR 150, 238-240.

[12] Dynkin, E.B. & Yushkevich, A.A. (1969) Markov processes, Plenum, New York.

A SELECTION PROBLEM ASSOCIATED TO A RENEWAL PROCESS

J. Zabczyk
Institute of Mathematics
Polish Academy of Sciences
Sniadeckich 8, 00-950 Warszawa
Poland

1. Introduction

Let $\{X_1, X_2, \ldots\}$ and $\{\xi_1, \xi_2, \ldots\}$ be two sequences of real valued random variables. Let us assume that X_i, ξ_i have distributions, respectively F and G, that the random variables ξ_i are non-negative and that $X_i, \xi_j, i,j = 1,2,\ldots$ are mutually independent. We shall interpret X_i as the absolute values of offers made to a man at the epochs $\tau_i = \xi_1 + \xi_2 + \ldots + \xi_i$, $i = 1,2,\ldots$ A man has been allowed a time T in which to accept an offer. At any epoch $\tau_i \leq T$ the offer arises, he has either to accept it and then the selection procedure ends, or reject it and wait for the next offer. The man's objective is to maximise the chance of accepting the best offer from those (if any) available in the interval $[0, T]$. We distinguish two cases:

Case I: Complete Information Case

The man observes the sequence $X_1, X_2, \ldots$, and at the epoch τ_k he knows the value of the kth offer and all preceding ones.

Case II: Incomplete Information Case

The man does not observe the sequence $X_1, X_2, \ldots$. At the epoch τ_k he is only able to rank a given offer amongst all those considered to date.

It is assumed, in both cases, that the distribution G, as well as for any t all moments $\tau_i \leq t$, are known to the man. In the Case I he knows also the distribution F which we assume has no atoms. Let us remark that the situation described in the Case II can be equivalently stated as follows:- the man observes consecutively $X_1, X_2, \ldots$, but he does not know the distribution F.

The natural assumption is that T is a fixed number. Other possibilities will be discussed in Section 6. If in addition ξ_i are also deterministic variables, $\xi_i = \alpha$ say, $i = 1,2,\ldots$, then the Case I was solved, using a heuristic argument, in [1], a precise solution is given in the report [2]. The Case II is equivalent, (See Remark 1 in Section 2, to the so-called "secretary problem" and the solution can be found in [3], [4] and [5]. In this note we report the solutions of the Case I and Case II obtained in [2], [6] and [7] under, probably, the most natural assumptions, that offers occur at the epochs of a stationary Poisson process of intensity λ. Preliminary results together with precise, mathematical formulation of the problems are given in Section 2. Method of solving such problems are described in Section 3. Case I is treated in Section 4 and Case II in Section 5. Possible generalizations are in Section 6.

2. Preliminaries

2.1 Markov chains associated with selection problems

We start from Proposition 1 and Proposition 2 below which enables us to formulate selection problems as optimal stopping time problems for Markov chains.

Proposition 1 Let $X_1, X_2, \dots$, be independent real valued random variables with non-atomic common distribution F. Define: $T_1 \equiv 1$ and $T_{k+1} = \inf\{l > T_k, X_l \geq X_{T_k}\}, k=1,2,\dots$

Then

1) The sequence $(T_k)_{k=1,2,\dots}$ is a Markov chain on the state set $N=\{1,2,\dots\}$ with transition probabilities:

$$p(k,l) = \begin{cases} \dfrac{k}{l(l-1)} , & \text{for } l > k \\ 0 & \text{otherwise} \end{cases}$$

2) The sequence $Y_k = (X_{T_k})_{k=1,2,\dots}$ is a Markov chain on the state space R, with transition function

$$q(u;(-\infty,v)) = \begin{cases} \dfrac{F(v)-F(u)}{1-F(u)} , & \text{if } v \geq u \\ 0 , & \text{otherwise} \end{cases}$$

Proof

Let $(l_i)_{i=1,2,\dots}$ be a strictly increasing sequence of natural numbers, $l_1 = 1$. We show first that

(1) $$P\{T_1 = l_1,\dots,T_n = l_n\} = \frac{1}{(l_2-1)(l_3-1)\cdot\ldots\cdot(l_n-1)\,l_n}$$

By the very definition:

$$P\{T_1 = l_1,\dots,T_n = l_n\} = P\{X_{l_1} \leq X_{l_2} \leq \dots \leq X_{l_n} \text{ and for } i=1,2,\dots,n-1$$
$$\max(X_{l_i+1},\dots,X_{l_{i+1}-1}) < X_{l_i}\}.$$

Consequently

$$P\{T_1 = l_1,\dots,T_n = l_n\} = \int_{\Delta_n} (F(x_1))^{l_2-l_1-1}\cdot\ldots\cdot(F(x_{n-1}))^{l_n-l_{n-1}-1}F(dx_1)\dots F(dx_n),$$

where $\Delta_n = \{(x_1,\dots,x_n) \in R^n;\ x_1 \leq x_2 \leq \dots \leq x_n\}$

Taking into account that for the non-atomic distribution F, all $x \in R$ and all $p = 0,1,2,\dots$

$$\int_{-\infty}^{x} (F(s))^p F(ds) = \frac{1}{p+1}(F(x))^{p+1}$$

we easily prove by induction that (1) holds. It follows from (1) that

$$P\{T_{n+1}=\ell \mid T_1=1, T_2=\ell_2, \dots, T_n=\ell_n\} = \frac{\ell_n}{\ell(\ell-1)}$$

provided $1<\ell_2<\ell_3<\dots<\ell_n<\ell$. Thus the proof of 1) is completed. The proof of 2) follows from the definitions, see [2].

Remark 1

Markov chain $(T_k)_{k=1,2,\dots}$ restricted to the state set $\{1,2,\dots,m\}$, with a slightly different interpretation, appeared in the solution of the classical "secretary"problem" in [3] and [5].

Remark 2

The sequence $Y_k=(X_{T_k})_{k=1,2,\dots}$ is a Markov chain under the weaker assumption that $(X_k)_{k=1,2,\dots}$ is a Markov chain. This is not true as far as $(T_k)_{k=1,2,\dots}$ is concerned. The sequence $(T_k)_{k=1,2,\dots}$ is a Markov chain if, for instance, $(X_k)_{k=1,2,\dots}$ is a random walk. A constructive description of those Markov processes $(X_k)_{k=1,2,\dots}$ for which $(T_k)_{k=1,2,\dots}$ is a Markov process as well, is unknown to the author.

If now the random variables ξ_i are exponentially distributed: $P\{\xi_i \le x\}=e^{-\lambda x}$, $x \ge 0$, $i=1,2,\dots$, then Proposition 1 and some standard calculations imply:

Proposition 2

Under the same assumption as in Proposition 1:

(1) The sequence . $Z_k=(\xi_1+\dots+\xi_{T_k}, T_k)$, $k=1,2,\dots$

$Z_0=(0,0)$ is a Markov chain on the state space $([0,+\infty)\times N)\cup\{(0,0)\}$ with the transition density

$$P((x,\ell),(y,m))=\begin{cases}\lambda e^{-\lambda y} & \text{if } x=0,\ \ell=0,\ m=1\\ \lambda e^{-\lambda(y-x)}\dfrac{(\lambda(y-x))^{m-\ell-1}}{(m-\ell-1)!}\dfrac{\ell}{m(m-1)} & \text{if } y\ge x,\ m>\ell\\ 0 & \text{otherwise}\end{cases}$$

(2) The sequence $V_k=(\xi_1+\dots+\xi_{T_k}, X_{T_k})_{k=1,2,\dots}$

$V_0=(0,-\infty)$ is a Markov chain on the state space $([0,+\infty)\times R)\cup\{(0,-\infty)\}$ with the transition probability:

$$Q((x,u), y\times(-\infty,v))=\begin{cases}\lambda e^{-\lambda y}F(v) & \text{if } x=0,\ u=-\infty\\ \lambda e^{-\lambda(y-x)(1-F(u))}(F(v)-F(u)) & \text{if } y\ge x>0,\ v\ge u\\ 0 & \text{otherwise}\end{cases}$$

In the paper [7], random variables $\xi_1 + \xi_2 + \dots + \xi_{T_i}$, $i = 1,2,\dots$ were called serious epochs because all non-trivial decisions occur only at them. This is because non-trivial decisions take place when the submitted offer is the best of those to date. Thus our Markov chains (Z_n), (V_n) change state whenever a serious epoch occurs and remains in that state until the next serious epoch.

2.2 Reward functions associated with selection problems

As was stated in the Introduction the objective of selection procedures is to maximise the chance of accepting the best offer from those available in the interval $[0,T]$. Thus the corresponding cost functional is of the "all-or-nothing" type: it is equal 1 if we accept the best offer from those available in the interval $[0,T]$ and is equal o otherwise. If, in Case I, we accept the kth offer which is of absolute value u and arises at the serious epoch $x \leq T$ then the conditional probability that we accepted the best one is equal to:

$$g(x,u) = \begin{cases} Q((x,u),(T,+\infty) \times R) & \text{if} \quad 0 < x \leq T \\ 0 & \text{otherwise} \end{cases}$$

Similarly, in Case II, if we accept the kth offer which arises at the serious epoch $x \leq T$, then the conditional probability that we accepted the best one is equal to

$$h(x,l) = \begin{cases} P((x,l),(T,+\infty) \times N) & \text{if} \quad 0 < x \leq T \\ 0 & \text{otherwise} \end{cases}$$

Straightforward calculations yield:

$$g(x,u) = e^{-\lambda(T-x)(1-F(u))} \qquad 0 < x \leq T$$

$$h(x,l) = e^{-\lambda(T-x)} \sum_{n=0}^{+\infty} \frac{(\lambda(T-x))^n}{n!} \cdot \frac{l}{n+l} \qquad , 0 < x \leq T$$

2.3 Selection problems as optimal stopping time problems

Selection problems can now be formulated as follows:

Case I Find a Markov time S relative to the Markov chain $(V_n)_{n=0,1,\dots}$ which maximises the expectation:

$$Eg(V_S) \ .$$

Case II Find a Markov time S relative to the Markov chain $(Z_n)_{n=0,1,\dots}$ which maximises the expectation:

$$Eh(Z_S) \ .$$

3. Method of solving selection problems. Basic lemma

Selection problems were formulated in 2.3 as stopping time problems for some Markov chains. There exists a well developed theory of optimal stopping, which can be found in monographs [8] and [9]. But only in special cases is it possible to find explicit expressions for optimal solutions. In the Case I and Case II the situation is complicated since the state spaces are infinite and transition probabilities as well as reward functions h, g are defined through not very simple expressions. Nevertheless the following lemma, see [6] and [7], allows us to solve selection problems.

Lemma 1

Let f be a nonnegative, bounded, measurable function on a measurable space $(E,\mathcal{E})$ and let $\mathcal{P}(\cdot\,,\cdot)$ be a transition function defined on $E\times\mathcal{E}$. Define $G=\{x\in E;\ \mathcal{P}f(x)\leq f(x)\}$ and $\tau_G=\inf\{k,\ X_k\in G\}$, where (X_k) is a Markov chain associated with $\mathcal{P}$. If

1) $\mathcal{P}(x,G)=1$ for $x\in G$

2) $P(X_k\in G$ for some $k\,|\,X_0=x)=1$ for all $x\in E$,

then
$$E(f(X_\tau)|X_0=x)\leq E(f(X_{\tau_G})|X_0=x),$$
for any Markov time τ and any initial state $x\in E$.

Remark 2

Lemma 1 was proved in [7]. It may also be deduced from Theorem 3.3 of [9]. Its formulation is especially well suited for selection problems. It expresses what "the monotone case" means in the Markov case.

4. Solution of the selection problem, Case I

To find the optimal selection rule we apply Lemma 1 taking f equals g and P equals Q. It is not difficult to calculate that

$$Qg(x,u) = \begin{cases} e^{-\lambda(T-x)(1-F(u))}\int_0^{\lambda(T-x)(1-F(u))} \frac{1}{v}(e^{v}-1)\,dv, & 0 \leq x \leq T \\ 0 & \text{otherwise} \end{cases}$$

Let us introduce a function φ:

$$\varphi(s) = \int_0^s \frac{1}{v}(e^{v}-1)\,dv, \quad s \geq 0.$$

Obviously, there exists exactly one number γ such that

(2) $$\varphi(\gamma) = 1, \quad \gamma > 0.$$

Consequently, in the considered case, the set G is given by the formula:

$$G = \{(x,u);\ \lambda(T-x)(1-F(u)) \leq \gamma \text{ and } 0 < x \leq T \text{ or } x \geq T\}$$

Since the Markov chain (V_n) reaches the set $\{(x,u);\ x \geq T\}$ with probability 1 starting from any initial state, the condition 2) of Lemma 1 is satisfied. But the condition 1) is also satisfied. This is because the chain (V_n) "goes to the right and upwards" and if $(x,u) \in G$ then every point (x', u') such that $x' \geq x$, $u' \geq u$ also belongs to G. Thus the optimal Markov time is exactly τ_G. Therefore the following theorem, see [2], is true.

Theorem 1

Let γ be the unique solution of the equation (2). In Case I the following selection rule is optimal:

> Accept the first offer which arises at a serious epoch $x \leq T$ and is of a value u satisfying the inequality
> $$\lambda(T-x) \leq \frac{\gamma}{1-F(u)}$$

Remark 3

The proof of Theorem 1 sketched here is a simplification of that given in [2].

Remark 4

The numerical value of $\gamma = 0.8043\ldots$

Example 1

If $\lambda T \leq \gamma$ then the best rule is to accept the first offer.

5. Solution of the selection problem, Case II

We proceed as in Section 4. By direct computation we obtain

$$Ph(x,l) = \begin{cases} e^{-\lambda T} & , x=l=0 \\ e^{-\lambda(T-x)} \sum_{n=1}^{+\infty} \frac{(\lambda(T-x))^n}{n!} \cdot \frac{l}{l+n}\left(\frac{1}{l}+\dots+\frac{1}{l+n-1}\right) & , x\le T, l\ge 1 \\ 0 & , x\ge T \end{cases}$$

Consequently $(x, l) \in G$ if and only if $x \geq T$ or

$$\sum_{n=1}^{+\infty} \frac{(\lambda(T-x))^n}{n!} \frac{1}{l+n}\left(\frac{1}{l}+\dots+\frac{1}{l+n-1}\right) \leq \sum_{n=0}^{+\infty} \frac{(\lambda(T-x))^n}{n!} \frac{1}{l+n} \quad , l \geq 1$$

The set G satisfies the condition 1) of the Lemma 1. To prove that the condition 2) is satisfied we need the following Lemma 2, see [6] and [7].

Lemma 2

For every $l = 1,2,\dots$ the equation

$$\text{(3)} \qquad \sum_{n=1}^{+\infty} \frac{y^n}{n!} \cdot \frac{1}{l+n}\left(\frac{1}{l}+\dots+\frac{1}{l+n-1}\right) = \sum_{n=0}^{+\infty} \frac{y^n}{n!} \cdot \frac{1}{l+n} \quad , y>0$$

has exactly one positive solution y_l. Moreover the sequence $(y_l)_{l=1,2,\dots}$ is strictly increasing and

$$0 < \underline{\lim}_{l\to+\infty} \frac{y_l}{l} \leq \overline{\lim}_{l\to+\infty} \frac{y_l}{l} < +\infty$$

If now $(x,l) \in G$ and $x' \geq x$, $l' \geq l$ then, because of emma 2, $(x', l') \in G$ Since the chain $(Z_n)_{n=0,1,\dots}$ also "goes to the right and upwards" therefore we can conclude that in the Case II, the Markov time τ_G is optimal too. Thus the following theorem holds, see [6] and [7].

Theorem 2

Let the numbers y_k, $k=1,2,\dots$ be the unique, positive, solutions of the equation (3). In case II the following selection rule is optimal

Accept the first offer which arises at a serious epoch $x \leq T$ and which index k satisfies the inequality

$$\lambda(T-x) \leq y_k$$

We recall that the offers are numbered in the order they arise, thus the index of the kth offer is the number k.

The numbers y_k, $k=1,2,$ were partially tabulated in [7]. Computations of the sequence $\left(\frac{y_k}{k}\right)_{k=1,2,\dots}$ suggest that $\frac{y_k}{k}$ approaches the number $e-1$.

6. Generalisations

We indicate now some extensions of the obtained results as well as possible directions of further investigations.

a) Sequence (X_k). We have assumed independence of the random variables $X_1, X_2, \ldots$. If we assume only that $(X_k)_{k=1,2,\ldots}$ is a Markov chain, then the Case I can be treated as in Section 4, but to apply Lemma 1 we obviously need some more specific assumptions. A particular case of random walk $(X_k)_{k=1,2,\ldots}$ was discussed in [10]. To solve Case II we have first to answer the question: is the sequence $(T_k)_{k=1,2,\ldots}$ a Markov chain as well?

b) Cost functionals. Different cost functionals than the "all-or-nothing" are of some theoretical and practical interest. For instance a "satisfaction function" can be equal 1 if we accept the best offer or the second best and 0 otherwise. It may also depend on the absolute value of the selected offer and so on.

c) Random variable T We considered only the case of fixed time interval $[0,T]$ If T is exponentially distributed then some results have been obtained in [7].

d) Moments $\tau_i = \xi_1 + \ldots + \xi_i$ at which the offers arise
A natural assumption is that $(\tau_i)_{i=1,2,\ldots}$ is a general renewal process. The set G was described in [7] but it is not known under which assumptions Lemma 1 can be applied.

References

[1] J. Gilbert and F. Mosteller, Recognising the maximum of a sequence, Amer. Stat. Assoc. Jour. 61, 1966.

[2] T. Bojdecki, On optimal stopping of a sequence of independent random variables. Probability maximizing approach, preprint, 1976.

[3] E.B. Dynkin, The optimal choice of stopping time for Markov processes, Doklacly AN USSR, 150, 2(1963), 238-240, (in Russian).

[4] Y. Chow, S. Moriguti, H. Robbins, S. Samuels, Optimal selection based on relative rank ("the secretary problem"), Jsr. Journ. Math, 2, 2(1964), 81-90.

[5] E.B. Dynkin and A.A. Yushkevich, Markov processes. Theorems and problems. Plenum Press, New York, 1969.

[6] R. Cowan and J. Zabczyk, A new version of the best choice problem, Bull. Pol. Acad. Sc., Serie Math., 1976 (to appear).

[7] R. Cowan and J. Zabczyk, An optimal selection problem associated with the Poisson process, submitted to Theory of Probability and Applications, 1976.

[8] A.N. Shiriajev, Statistical Sequential Analysis, Nauka, Moscow, 1969 (in Russian)

[9] Y.S. Chow, H. Robbins and D. Siegmund, Great Expectation, the theory of optimal stopping. Houghton Mifflin Co., Boston, 1971.

[10] T. Bojdecki, A note on optimal stopping of sums of independent random variables, Bull. Pol. Acad. Sc. Serie Math., 1976 (to appear).

EXISTENCE AND UNIQUENESS OF STATIONARY DISTRIBUTIONS IN A MODEL OF ROLL-BACK RECOVERY+)

Erol Gelenbe

Département de Mathématiques
Université Paris-Nord
Avenue J.-B. Clément
93 Villetaneuse

0 - Summary

In this paper we consider a mathematical model of a transaction oriented computing system (airline reservation system, file system, data-base system, etc.) operating in the presence of intermittent failures, and with a checkpoint and roll-back recovery scheme built-in to preserve system integrity. An arbitrary distribution of inter-checkpoint times is assumed. A condition on the traffic intensity of transaction requests is established which insures that the system will not saturate. This condition is essential if meaningful simulation studies of these complex systems are to be conducted. In probabilistic terms, this is the necessary and sufficient condition for the existence of the stationary probability distribution associated with the non-Markovian queueing process representing the backlog of requets to the computer system.

The model which we study and the results obtained are also new in the context of reliability theory. We are dealing with a queue with service interruptions for maintenance and for repairs of failures. The time for repair of a failure is assumed to be a function of the age of the failure with respect to the most recent maintenance epoch.

+) Work supported by an IRIA-SESORI research contract to Université Paris-Nord.

1 - Introduction

The model we analyze in this paper arises in the context of reliability theory in general. Our motivation is due to the fact that it appears in the study of reliable data-base systems and transaction oriented computer systems.

Consider a data-base system (the server) which executes transactions (the customers) arriving to it in first-come-first-served order. In such systems it is essential to be able to reconstitute the contents of the primary memory to its correct state after a failure occurs which invalidates memory contents. To this effect each transaction is stored in the audit trail ; a checkpoint is established from time to time, and after a failure all transactions stored in the audit trail since the most recent checkpoint are executed once again. A checkpoint is established by copying the contents of primary (which can be affected by failures) into some safe secondary memory device (disk or tape). After a failure, and before all the transactions on the audit trail can be re-executed, the contents of the checkpoint have to be copied back into primary memory. In [Gelenbe 76a], this system has been modelled as a queue whose server can be in one of three states ; the server state is controlled by a Markov chain. In [Gelenbe 76b] the case of multiple types of failures and checkpoints has been considered. [Chandy 75] presents a survey of earlier work on the subject ; in particular, a simple model which does not take into account the queueing delays is used to optimize the availability of the system. In [Robin 77] an optimization problem related to our model is considered. The main optimization problem in this context is the optimal placement of the checkpoints. It is clear that the time necessary for recovery from a failure will depend on the time separating the instant of failure from the most recent checkpoint, and in particular on the total number of transactions processed in this interval.

A similar model arises in reliability studies. Consider a server which goes through maintenance at predetermined instants of time, and which is subject to failures. Suppose that during maintenance periods and while failures are being repaired, the server cannot serve customers. We assume that the time necessary to repair a failure is a function of the age of the failure with respect to the most recent maintenance epoch. Also suppose that customers are served in their order of arrival. This is precisely the model which is being considered in this paper.

The formulation of our problem is contained in Sections 2, 3. The model corresponds to a queue with Poisson arrivals and exponential service times. Maintenance epochs (the checkpoints) are represented by a renewal process. Failures occur at instants described by a Poisson process independent of the arrivals, services and of maintenances. Repairs take an amount of time which is a function of the age of the failure with respect to the most recent maintenance. Service is interrupted during maintenance and repair.

2 - The roll-back recovery process

The service rendered to customers depends on the "state" of the server X_t, $t \geq 0$, which is

$$(2.1) \qquad X_t = \begin{cases} 2 & \text{if the system is creating a checkpoint} \\ 1 & \text{if it is recovering from a failure} \\ 0 & \text{if it is operating normally} \end{cases}$$

Service to requests for transaction processing is rendered only in state 0. $\{X_t, t \geq 0\}$ is a stochastic point process with the following properties :

(i) The total time spent in state 0 between two consecutive transitions to state 2 is a random variable independent of the past history of the process with general distribution function $F(y)$ and density $f(y)$. That is, during this time the server is available for serving customers which are in queue. Let $E\,Y \triangleq \int_0^\infty y dF(y) < \infty$.

(ii) When the process enters state 2 it remains there for a random epoch, independent of past history, of general distribution function $C(y)$. At the end of this time it returns to state 0. This is the time it takes to create a checkpoint. We suppose that $E \triangleq \int_0^\infty y dC(y) < \infty$.

(iii) During epochs when the system is in state 0, instants of transition to state 1 are defined by a Poisson process of parameter γ. γ is the failure rate of the server.

(iv) When a transition into state 1 occurs, the time spent by the server in that state until its return to state 0 is defined as follows. Let $h : R^+ \to R^+$ be a measurable function. For a failure (transition from state 0 to 1) taking place at time t, let

$$t' = \sup\{\sigma : \sigma < t \text{ and } 1_2(\sigma) = 1\}$$

Let the random variable Y_t be defined by

$$(2.2) \qquad Y_t = \begin{cases} \int_{t'}^{t} 1_0(\tau)d\tau & \text{if } X_t = 0 \text{ or } 1 \\ 0 & \text{otherwise} \end{cases}$$

That is, Y_t is the total time spent by the server in state 0 in the interval $[t', t]$ where t' is the most recent time before t at which the server was in state 2. Then the server remains in state 1 (after a failure which occurred at time t) for a time of duration $h(Y_t)$.

Thus the recovery time of the server is a function of the age Y_t of the server with respect to the most recent checkpoint.

Formally speaking, let (Ω, A, P) be a probability space, and let X_n, T_n, $n \in N$, be random variables defined on such that

$$X_n = \Omega \rightarrow F, \; T_n : \Omega \rightarrow R^+, \; T_n \leq T_{n+1}$$

where F is a finite set. Then for all $j \in F$, $n \in N$, $t \in R^+$ we assume that

$$(2.3) \qquad P[X_{n+1} = j, T_{n+1} - T_n \leq t \mid X_i, T_i, 0 \leq i \leq n]$$

$$= P[X_{n+1} = j, T_{n+1} - T_n \leq t \mid X_n, T_n - T_{n-1}]$$

$$\neq P[X_{n+1} = j, T_{n+1} - T_n \leq t \mid X_n]$$

The process (X, T) is clearly not a Markov-renewal process [Çinlar 76] because of the above non-equality.

Consider now the random variable

$$A_n = T_n - T_{n-1}, \; n \geq 0$$

and the process $\{X_n, Z_n, T_n, n \geq 1\}$; it may be viewed as a Markov renewal process with state space $F \times R^+$. We associate with it the process $(X, \hat{A}) = \{X_t, \hat{A}_t, t \geq 0\}$ such that

$$X_t = X_n \quad \text{for } t \in [T_{n-1}, T_n[$$

$$\hat{A}_t = t - T_n \quad \text{for } t \in [T_{n-1}, T_n[$$

The queueing system we analyze in the following section is controlled by a process of the form $(X, \hat{A})$.

Returning now more specifically to the stochastic process $(X) = \{X_t, t \geq 0\}$ defined by (1), (i) to (iv), and (2), we are interested in the stationary (equilibrium) probabilities associated with it :

$$\Pi_j \triangleq \lim_{t \to \infty} Pr[X_t = j], \; j = 0, 1, 2$$

Since the process is not Markovian, or Markov renewal, we cannot call upon classical results in order to obtain them. We can, however, proceed using an elementary approach.

For $t \geq 0$, define

$$Z_t = \begin{cases} 1 & \text{if } X_t \in \{0, 1\} \quad , \quad t \geq 0 \\ 0 & \text{otherwise} \end{cases}$$

and notice that

$$\Pr[X_t = 1] = \Pr[X_t = 1 \mid Z_t = 1] \Pr[Z_t = 1]$$

$(Z) \triangleq \{Z_t, t \geq 0\}$ is an alternating renewal process. Therefore we can use its properties to compute Π_0.

Consider an epoch between two successive checkpoints such that the total time spent in state $X_t = 0$ is y. Since failures occur according to a Poisson process, conditioned on n occurrences of failures the instants of occurrence of the n failures are independent and each is uniformly distributed of density 1/y in the interval ; this follows from well-known properties of the Poisson process (cf. [Cox 66], pp. 27-28). Thus the expected value of the total time spent in state 1 of (Z) is

$$y + \sum_{n=0}^{\infty} n\frac{(\gamma y)^n}{n!} e^{-\gamma y} \int_0^y (h(x)/y)dx = y[1 + \gamma \int_0^y (h(x)/y)dx]$$

for given y, and its expectation over all values of y is

$$\text{(2.4)} \qquad EY + \gamma \int_0^\infty dy\ f(y) \int_0^y h(x)\ dx$$

and therefore

$$\text{(2.5)} \qquad \lim_{t\to\infty} \Pr[Z_t = 1] = \frac{EY + \gamma \int_0^\infty dyf(y) \int_0^y h(x)dx}{EC + EY + \gamma \int_0^\infty dyf(y) \int_0^y h\ (x)dx}$$

using a standard result for alternating renewal processes. [Cox 62].

Notice that

$$\Pi_0 = \lim_{t\to\infty} \Pr[X_t = 0 \mid X_t = 0 \vee 1] \cdot \lim_{t\to\infty} \Pr[Z_t = 1]$$

It is derived using an argument for which I am indebted to I. MITRANI. Let a(x) be the probability density function of the <u>total time</u> between successive checkpoints, and let b(x) the expectation of total time during which the state for the server is 0 in an interval between two successive checkpoints given that the length $\mathcal{L}$ of this interval is x. Given x, notice (using the properties of the "random observer", see for instance [Takacs 62] pp. 10-11) that

$$\lim_{t\to\infty} \Pr[X_t = 0 \mid X_t = 0 \vee 1, \mathcal{L} = x] = \frac{b(x)}{x}$$

because the instant t will be uniformly distributed in

$$\Pi_0 = \int_0^\infty \frac{b(x)}{x} \cdot \frac{xa(x)\,dx}{\int_0^\infty xa(x)dx} = \frac{\int_0^\infty b(x)\,a(x)dx}{\int_0^\infty xa(x)\,dx}$$

because $[xa(x)dx/\int_0^\infty xa(x)dx]$ is the probability that the random observer falls within an interval of length $\mathcal{L} = x$ (again using [Takacs 62] pp. 10-11). But

$$\int_0^\infty b(x)a(x)dx = EY$$

The expected value of the total time spent in state 0 between two successive check-points $\int_0^\infty xa(x)dx$ is given by (2.4). Therefore we have

Theorem 1 : The stationary probabilities associated with $\{X_t,\ t \geq 0\}$ are

$$\Pi_0 = EY/(EC + EY + \gamma \int_0^\infty dyf(y) \int_0^y h(x)dx) \tag{2.6}$$

$$\Pi_1 = \frac{\gamma \int_0^\infty dyf(y) \int_0^y h(x)dx}{EC + EY + \gamma \int_0^\infty dyf(y) \int_0^y h(x)dx} \tag{2.7}$$

and $\Pi_2 = 1 - \Pi_0 - \Pi_1$.

Since Π_0 is the stationary probability that the server is available for service, we shall call it the availability of the server. In the following section, it will reappear in the ergodicity conditions for the queue length process. We write it in the more convenient form :

$$\Pi_0 = [1 + EC/EY + (\gamma/EY) \int_0^\infty h(y)(1-F(y))dy]^{-1} \tag{2.8}$$

3 - Analysis of the queue

In this section we analyze the queueing process representing the number of transactions awaiting processing and the state of the server. Our purpose is to determine measures of performance such as the utilization of the server (i.e. the steady-state probability that the queue length is not zero), the saturation condition (i.e. the value of the arrival rate λ of transaction requests beyond which stationary queue length will be infinite) and the distribution of the number of customers in queue. Of interest to us is the stochastic process

$(N, X, Y) \triangleq \{N_t, X_t, Y_t, t \geq 0\}$ where N_t and X_t are the number of customers in queue and the state of the server, respectively, at time t ; Y_t is defined in (2.2).

Intuitively speaking, the random variable Y_t allows us to compute the amount of time $h(Y_t)$ which is necessary for recovery from a failure which occurs at time t when the server is in state 0.

The analysis of the queueing system is undertaken under the following assumptions. Requests for transactions arrive according to a Poisson process of parameter λ, and are served in first-come-first-served order when the server is in state 0. No service is rendered in states 1 and 2 of the server. The service time distribution for a transaction is exponentially distributed of parameter μ.

Our study begins with the conditional process $(N, Y \mid X = 0) \triangleq \{N_t, Y_t \mid X_t = 0, t \geq 0\}$.

3.1 - The conditional process $(N, Y \mid X = 0)$

Let $p(n, y, t) = P[N_t = n, Y_t = y \mid X_t = 0]$[1], and let us introduce the following notations :

$$(3.1) \qquad \eta(y) = f(y)/(1 - F(y))$$

$$r_y(j) = \frac{(\lambda h(y))^j}{j!} \exp(-\lambda h(y)), \quad j \geq 0$$

Clearly $\eta(y)dy$ is the probability that a checkpoint is established in the interval $[t, t + dy[$ given that $X_t = 0$ and $Y_t = y$. $r_y(j)$ is the probability that j arrivals occur during a recovery from a failure which took place at time t when $X_t = 0$ and $Y_t = y$.

The following equations are obtained in the usual manner. For $y \geq 0$, $n > 0$:

$$(3.2) \qquad \left(\frac{\partial}{\partial t} + \frac{\partial}{\partial y}\right) p(n, y, t) = -(\lambda + \mu + \eta(y) + \gamma)\, p(n, y, t) + \lambda p(n-1, y, t) + \mu p(n+1, y, t) + \gamma \sum_{j=0}^{n} r_y(j)\, p(n-j, y, t)$$

and for $y \geq 0$, $n = 0$:

$$(3.3) \qquad \left(\frac{\partial}{\partial t} + \frac{\partial}{\partial y}\right) p(0, y, t) = -(\lambda + \eta(y) + \gamma)\, p(0, y, t) + \mu p(1, y, t) + \gamma r_y(0)\, p(0, y, t)$$

1) We mean that $p(n, y, t)dy = P[N_t = n, y \leq Y_t < y + dy \mid X_t = 0]$ at $t \geq 0$.

For $y = 0$ we have for $n \geq 0$:

(3.4) $$p(n, 0, t) = \int_0^\infty \sum_{j=0}^{n} c(j)\, p(n-j, y, t)\, \eta(y)dy$$

where

(3.5) $$c(j) = \int_0^\infty \frac{(\lambda z)^j}{j!} e^{-\lambda z} dC(z) \quad , \quad j \geq 0$$

is the probability of j arrivals during the establishment of a checkpoint (see (ii) of section 2).

In the sequel we study the stationary probability distribution for the process $(N, Y \mid X = 0)$.

Theorem 2 : The stationary solution of (3.2), (3.3), (3.4) exists if and only if $(\lambda/\mu) < [1 + EC/EY + (\gamma/EY) \int_0^\infty h(y)\, (1 - F(y))dy]^{-1}$

Proof : "Only if" part (necessary condition).

Set $(\partial/\partial t) = 0$ in (3.2), (3.3). Let

$$p^*(n, s) = \int_0^\infty e^{-sy}\, p(n, y)dy$$

where we have dropped the dependence on t. Denote

$$G_y(x) = \sum_0^\infty x^n\, p(n, y), \quad G^*(s, x) = \int_0^\infty G_y(x)e^{-sy}dy$$

We obtain for $n > 0$,

(3.6) $$\begin{aligned} sp^*(n, s) - p(n, 0) = &-(\lambda + \mu + \gamma)p^*(n, s) + \mu p^*(n+1, s) \\ &+ \lambda p^*(n-1, s) - \int_0^\infty e^{-sy}\, \eta(y)\, p(n, y)dy \\ &+ \sum_{j=0}^{n} \gamma \int_0^\infty r_y(j)\, p(n-j, y)e^{-sy}dy \end{aligned}$$

and $$\begin{aligned} sp^*(0, s) - p(0, 0) = &-(\lambda+\gamma)\, p^*(0, s) + \mu p^*(1, s) \\ &- \int_0^\infty \eta(y)e^{-sy}p(0, y)dy \\ &+ \gamma \int_0^\infty r_y(0)\, p(0, y)e^{-sy}dy \end{aligned}$$

yielding

$$(3.7)\qquad G^*(s, x)\,[s + \lambda(1-x) + \mu(1 - 1/x) + \gamma] - G_0(x)$$

$$= p^*(0, s)\,\mu(1 - 1/x) + \gamma\, H^*(s, x)$$

$$- \int_0^\infty \eta(y)\, G_y(x) e^{-sy} dy$$

where

$$H^*(s, x) = \int_0^\infty e^{-sy}\, e^{-\lambda(1-x)h(y)}\, G_y(x) dy$$

We use (3.4) to obtain

$$(3.8)\qquad G_0(x) = C^*(\lambda(1-x)) \int_0^\infty \eta(y)\, G_y(x) dy$$

where

$$C^*(\lambda(1-x)) = \int_0^\infty e^{-\lambda(1-x)z} dC(z)$$

From (3.7) we remain with

$$(3.9)\qquad G^*(s, x) = \frac{p^*(0, s)\,\mu(1 - 1/x) - \int_0^\infty \eta(y)\, G_y(x) e^{-sy} dy + G_0(x)}{s + \lambda(1-x) + \mu(1 - 1/x)}$$

$$+ \frac{\gamma[H^*(s, x) - G^*(s, x)]}{s + \lambda(1-x) + \mu(1 - 1/x)}$$

where $G_0(x)$ is given by (3.8). It is clear that if the stationary distribution $\{p(n, y)\ ,\ n \geq 0,\ y \geq 0\}$ exists we must have

$$\lim_{x\to1} \lim_{s\to0} G^*(s, x) = 1$$

Taking the limits in (3.9), we have an indeterminate form in both terms on the right-hand side. Therefore take first

$$(3.10)\qquad \lim_{s\to0} G^*(s, x) = \frac{p^*(0, 0)\,\mu(1 - 1/x) + [C^*(\lambda(x-1)) - 1] \int_0^\infty \eta(y)\, G_y(x) dy}{\lambda(1-x) + \mu(1 - 1/x)}$$

$$+ \frac{\gamma[H^*(0, x) - G^*(0, x)]}{\lambda(1-x) + \mu(1 - 1/x)}$$

and now apply l'Hôpital's rule using

$$\lim_{x\to1} \frac{d}{dx}\, C^*(\lambda(1-x)) = \lambda\, E\, C$$

$$\lim_{x\to 1} C^*(\lambda(1-x)) = 1$$

$$\lim_{x\to 1} \frac{d}{dx} H^*(0, x) = \lim_{x\to 1} \frac{d}{dx} G^*(0, x) + \int_0^\infty \lambda h(y)\, G_y(1)dy$$

so that

$$\lim_{x\to 1} \lim_{s\to 0} G^*(s, x) = \frac{\mu p^*(0, 0) + \lambda EC \int_0^\infty \eta(y)G_y(1)dy + \lambda\Upsilon \int_0^\infty h(y)G_y(1)dy}{-\lambda + \mu} \tag{3.11}$$

To complete the proof, we shall call upon the following lemma.

<u>Lemma 3</u> : $G_y(1) = \lim_{t\to\infty} \sum_{n=0}^{\infty} p(n, y, t)$ is given by

$$G_y(1) = (1 - F(y))/EY$$

<u>Proof</u> : This is again a consequence of the well-know result([Takacs 62], pp. 10, 11) concerning renewal processes. Write

$$K(y, t) = \int_0^\infty p(n, z, t)dz$$

so that

$$\lim_{t\to\infty} K(y, t) = \int_0^y G_z(1)dz$$

Then

$$K(y, t) = \sum_{k=1}^{\infty} P[t < \sigma_k \leq t+y < \sigma_{k+1}] \tag{3.12}$$

where (since we are dealing with the conditional process $(N, Y \mid X = 0)$) any instant of time t is relative to epochs during which the state of server is 0 ; that is t corresponds to the "real" time t' (in process time of (N, Y, X)) where

$$t = \int_0^{t'} 1_0(\tau)d\tau$$

In (3.12) $\sigma_1 < \ldots < \sigma_k < \sigma_{k+1} < \ldots$ are defined by $Y_{\sigma_i} = 0$. Clearly the $(\sigma_{k+1} - \sigma_k)$ are independent and identically distributed of probability distribution function F(y). Thus

$$\lim_{t\to\infty} K(y, t) = \int_0^y [1 - F(x)]dx/EY \tag{3.13}$$

and the lemma is established.

Now returning to (3.11) and the proof of Theorem 2, we see that

$$\int_0^\infty \eta(y)\ G_y(1)dy = \int_0^\infty [dF(y)/(1 - F(y))][1 - F(y)]/EY$$
$$= 1/EY$$

Therefore

$$(3.14) \qquad p^*(0,\ 0) = 1 - (\tfrac{\lambda}{\mu})\ [EC/EY + \gamma \int_0^\infty dyh(y)\ (1 - F(y))/EY]$$

if the stationary solution to (3.2), (3.3), (3.4) exists. But we must have $p^*(0,\ 0) = \int_0^\infty p(0,\ y)dy > 0$, completing the **first** of the proof.

<u>"If" part (sufficient condition)</u>

To prove that the condition is sufficient consider the instants σ_i^+ just <u>after</u> the instants σ_i when $Y_{\sigma_i} = 0$ in the process time of $(N,\ Y \mid X = 0)$. The process

$$(\hat{N} | X = 0) \equiv \{N_{\sigma_i^+}\ ,\ i \geq 1 \mid X_t = 0,\ t \geq 0\}$$

is a discrete time Markov chain, and it is easy to see that it is aperiodic and irreducible. We first prove that is ergodic under the condition of the Theorem by applying a lemma of [Pakes 69] which we recall below.

<u>Lemma</u> : Let $\{B_i,\ i \geq 1\}$ be an aperiodic irreducible Markov chain. It is ergodic if the following conditions are satisfied :

$$|E[B_{i+1} - B_i \mid B_i - j]| < \infty \text{ for all } j$$

$$\limsup_{j \to \infty} E[B_{i+1} - B_i \mid B_i = j] < 0$$

Let $\alpha = \sigma_{i+1} - \sigma_i$; in the sequel all events are conditioned on $N_{\sigma_i^+} = j$. Let T be the total time in the interval $[\sigma_i^+,\ \sigma_{i+1}^+[$ during which the queue is non-empty. Clearly $T \leq \alpha$. Let $D(\alpha)$ be the number of departures from the queue in the interval $[\sigma_i^+,\ \sigma_{i+1}^+[$.

$$1 \geq P[T = \alpha] \geq P[D(\alpha) < j]$$

But $$P[D(\alpha) < j] \geq \int_0^\infty dF(\tau)\ \Sigma_0^{j-1}\ (\tfrac{\mu\tau}{\ell!})^\ell\ e^{-\mu\tau}$$

since the event $[D(\alpha) < j]$ implies the event [(the number of departures in a busy period of length α) $< j$]. Therefore

$$(3.15) \qquad \limsup_{j \to \infty} P[T = \alpha] = 1$$

Now consider

$$E[N_{\sigma_{i-1}^+} - N_{\sigma_i^+} \mid N_{\sigma_i^+} = j] = E[D(\alpha) - A(\alpha)]$$

where $A(\alpha)$ is the number of arrivals in $[\sigma_i^+, \sigma_{i+1}^+[$. Clearly

$$E[A(\alpha)] = \lambda EY + EC + \gamma\mu \int_0^\infty h(y)(1 - F(y))dy$$

Also $E[D(\alpha)] = \mu E[T]$; however

$$\limsup_{j \to \infty} E[T] = EY$$

Therefore, if the condition of the Theorem is satisfied then both conditions of Pakes' Lemma are satisfied by $(\hat{N}|X = 0)$ so that this Markov chain is ergodic. Let $\{\Pi_n, n \geq 0\}$ be the stationary probability distribution associated with this chain, which has just been shown to exist. It is easily seen that $p(n, y)$ also exists.

As an immediate consequence we have

<u>Theorem 4</u> : Under the conditions of Theorem 2, the stationary probability distribution for the process $(N \mid X = 0)$ exists and its generating function $G(x) \triangleq \lim_{s\to 0} G^*(s, x)$ satisfies :

$$G(x) = \frac{\gamma H^*(0, x) + p^*(0, 0)\mu(1 - 1/x) + (C^*(\lambda(x-1)) - 1)\int_0^\infty \eta(y)G_y(x)dy}{\gamma + \lambda(1 - x) + \mu(1 - 1/x)}$$

<u>3.2 - The process (N)</u>

Let the (unconditional) queue length process be denoted $(N) \triangleq \{N_t, t \geq 0\}$.

In this section we extend the results of Sections 2 and 3.1 to (N). The remaining work is largely technical.

Let us introduce the following notations for $t \geq 0$:

$$a(n, u, t) \triangleq P[N_t = n, U_t = u, X_t = 2]$$

where for $X_t = 2$:

$$t - U_t \triangleq \sup\{\tau = \tau < t \wedge X_\tau = 0\}$$

$$b(n, y, v, t) = \begin{cases} 0 & \text{if } v > h(y) \\ P[N_t = n, Y_t = y, V_t = v, X_t = 1], & \text{otherwise} \end{cases}$$

where for $X_t = 1$:

$$t - V_t \triangleq \sup\{\tau : \tau < t \wedge X_\tau = 0\}$$

Let $a(n, u)$, $b(n, y, v)$ be the corresponding quantities obtained by taking $\lim t \to \infty$, if they exist.

Remark 1 : $a(n, u) = \Pi_0.(1 - C(u)) \sum_{j=0}^{n} \frac{(\lambda u)^j}{j!} e^{-\lambda m} \int_0^\infty p(n-j, y).\eta(y)dy$

Remark 2 : $b(n, y, v) = \Pi_0 \gamma \sum_{j=0}^{n} \frac{(\lambda v)^j}{j!} e^{-\lambda v} p(n-j, y)$

Theorem 5 : $a(n, u)$, $b(n, y, v)$ exist for all $n \geq 0$, $y \geq 0$ and $y \geq 0$ such that $0 \leq v \leq h(y)$, if and only if $p(n, y)$ exists for all $n \geq o$, $y \geq 0$.

4 - Conclusion

In this paper we have considered a complex queueing model encountered in reliability theory and in the modelling of roll-back recovery procedures in computer systems. Necessary and sufficient conditions have been estaablished for the existence of the stationary probability distribution of the model.

A complete analytical solution of the model is probably impossible to obtain in the general case. Therefore this condition is of particular interest if a study of this model via simulation is to be conducted, because a simulation study of the non-stationary system would be very costly to conduct.

The condition derived in this paper has been used in the simulation experiments reported in [Flamand 76].

REFERENCES

[Cox 62] D.R. Cox - "Renewal Theory" - Methuen - London - 1962.

[Cox 66] D.R. Cox, P.A.W. Lewis - "The Statistical Analysis of Series of Events" - Methuen - London - 1966.

[Takacs 62] L. Takacs - "Introduction to the Theory of Queues" - Oxford University Press - New York - 1962.

[Loynes 62] R.M. Loynes - "The stability of a queue with non-independent inter-arrival and service times" - Proc. Cambridge Philos. Soc. 58 - 497-520 - 1962.

[Çinlar 75] E. Çinlar - "Introduction to Stochastic Processes" - Prentice Hall - New York - 1975.

[Borovkov 76] A.A. Borovkov - "Stochastic Processes in Queueing Theory" - Springer - New York - 1976

[Gelenbe 76a] E. Gelenbe, D. Derochette - "On the stochastic behaviour of a computer system under Intermittent failures" - in Modelling and Performance Evaluation of Computer Systems - H. Beilner and E. Gelenbe eds. - North-Holland - 1976.

[Gelenbe 76b] E. Gelenbe - "On roll-back recovery with multiple checkpoints" - Proc. 2nd International Symposium on Software Engineering (IEEE Press) - San Francisco - Oct. 1976.

[Chandy 75] K.M. Chandy - "A survey of analytic models of roll-back and recovery strategies" - IEEE Computer 8, n° 5 - 40-47 - 1975.

[Robin 77] M. Robin - To appear.

[Pakes 69] A.G. Pakes - "Some conditions for ergodicity and recurrence of Markov chains" - Operations Research 17, 1058-1061 - 1969.

[Flamand 76] J. Flamand, E. Gelenbe - "Simulation of roll-back recovery in a data-base system" - To appear.

CONTROL OF ECONOMICS SYSTEMS

CONTROLE DES SYSTÈMES ÉCONOMIQUES

SOME APPLICATION OF CONTROL AND SYSTEM THEORY IN A MODEL OF DYNAMIC OPEN ECONOMY

Masanao Aoki
Department of System Science
School of Engineering and Applied Science
University of California
Los Angeles, California 90024

1. Introduction

We hold the view that control and system theory is important in analysis of dynamic systems [1,2,8]. Concepts and techniques of control and system theory, unfortunately, is yet to find their wide spread application in socio-economic problem areas. There are several reasons for this, but we shall not speculate on them here. See for example, [6,11]. Instead we shall describe one potential application area in dynamic economic analysis in the hope that it will accelerate the process of the information dissemination.

In economics, one of the natural and important problem areas is found in analysis of open economies. Control and system theory is, of course, relevant in dynamic analysis of closed economies. As a matter of fact, some applications of control theory has already been made in policy analysis and forecast of states of economies, for example, by means of large scale econometric models [9,12]. The reason for singling out potential application to dynamic analysis of open economies is that this problem area offers some new questions that require genuine dynamic analysis. Recent events since the demise of the Bretton Woods agreement renewed some economists' interest in flexible exchange rate regimes and initiated re-examinations of questions related to autonomies of national governments' policy actions. For example, in open economies, it is very important to identify areas of potential policy conflicts between the home government and foreign government, and transmission paths of foreign disturbances as a preliminary step to policy coordination negotiations. Besides, questions related to decentralized policy decisions really make sense only in international context.

We shall use a two country model of the world economy as a vehicle of illustration to show how two countries can jointly affect the equilibrium dynamics of the world economy. For example, growth of capital stocks of the two countries can be divorced from the balance of payment considerations if the two governments so choose to coordinate their monetary and fiscal policy instruments. We shall also indicate how impact and short-run multipliers of the home governments' policy instruments can be used to illustrate interdependence of the two governments' decision.

2. Model

The model is the same as the one used in [4,5]. Each country's economy is composed of the asset market for domestic and foreign monies and bond-equities and the real sector which produces a composite good which is a nonperfect subsitute for the foreign composite good. Domestic private and government bond-equities are regarded as perfect substitutes. Foreign bond-equities are, however, imperfect substitutes for domestic bond-equities. In real economies, asset markets will equilibrate very fast. After the asset markets, the real sectors reach equilibrium. Then the capital stocks will change according to the investments carried out in each countries. There is another source of dynamics from (flow variable) constraints imposed on the government instruments. This is dynamics for instruments (control variable) generation. This, together with the capital accumulation dynamics determines the dynamics of the total system. In this paper, we assume that asset markets and the real markets are always in equilibrium so that algebraic equilibrium conditions are always maintained. Therefore, the model is the one for equilibrium growth. The models are all specified in log-linear terms. Foreign variables are starred.

We employ the approximation that

$$b = y - b_o i$$

$$b^* = y^* - b_o(i^* + \epsilon)$$

where b is the logarithm of the real value of the private bond-equity, y is the logarithm of the real domestic output, i is the domestic interest rate (not its logarithm) and ϵ is the expected rate of the exchange rate change. e is the logarithm of the exchange rate.

Let $d = b_g - b_{g^*}$ and $d^* = b^*_{g^*} - b^*_g$, where b_g is the logarithm of the supply of the home governments' bond held by domestic government, b_{g^*} is the logarithm of the home government bond held by the foreign government as international reserves. $b^*_{g^*}$ then is the logarithm of the foreign government bond held by the foreign government. m is the logarithm of the domestic money stock. p is the logarithm of the domestic price index.

Asset Sector

The asset sector equilibrium conditions are:

$$d = -b_1 y + b_2 y^* + b_3 i - b_4 i^* - b_6 \varepsilon \tag{1}$$

$$m - p = m_1 y + m_2 y^* - m_3 i - m_4 i^* - m_6 \varepsilon \tag{2}$$

$$d^* - p + p^* + e = b^*_1 y - b^*_2 y - b^*_3 i + b^*_4 i^* + b^*_6 \varepsilon \tag{3}$$

where b's , m's and b^*'s are positive scalars (elasticities).

Define two-dimensional vectors.

$$\underset{\sim}{i} = \begin{bmatrix} i \\ i^* \end{bmatrix}, \quad \underset{\sim}{p} = \begin{bmatrix} p \\ p^* \end{bmatrix}, \text{ etc.}$$

Solve (1) and (2) for i and i^* .

$$\underset{\sim}{i} = -I_1 m + I_2 d + I_3 \underset{\sim}{p} - I_4 \varepsilon + I_5(\underset{\sim}{k}) \tag{4}$$

where $I_5(k)$ depends on k . Other coefficient vectors I_1 , I_2 and I_4 and the matrix I_3 do not depend on k . See Appendix for their expressions.

Solve (3) for e . After substituting (4) for $\underset{\sim}{i}$, it is given by

$$e = e_1 m - e_2 d - d^* - e_3 \underset{\sim}{p} + e_4 \varepsilon - e_5(\underset{\sim}{k}) \tag{5}$$

where $\underset{\sim}{k}$ appears only in e_5 . See Appendix for their expressions.

The Real Sector

The supply vector of the goods $\underset{\sim}{y}_s$ is taken to be

$$\underset{\sim}{y}_s = S_1 \underset{\sim}{k} + S_2(\underset{\sim}{p} - \underset{\sim}{w}) .$$

The demand vector $\underset{\sim}{y}_d$ is, in its partially reduced form

$$D_3 \underset{\sim}{y}_d = D_1 \underset{\sim}{g} - D_2(\underset{\sim}{i} - \underset{\sim}{\pi}) - D_4 \underset{\sim}{p} + \underset{\sim}{\delta} e$$

where

$$D_i = \mathrm{diag}(d_i, d^*_i) , \quad i = 1,2$$

$$D_3 = \begin{bmatrix} 1 & d_3 \\ -d_3^* & 1 \end{bmatrix} , \quad D_4 = \underset{\sim}{\delta}(1 -1) , \quad \underset{\sim}{\delta} = \begin{bmatrix} d_4 \\ -d^*_4 \end{bmatrix}$$

and where $-D_4 \underset{\sim}{p} + \underset{\sim}{\delta} e$ expresses the effect of the terms of the trade i.e., $d_4(p-p^*-e)$ and $-d_4^*(p-p^*-e)$ appear y_d and y_d^* respectively. The inflation expectations are expressed by $\underset{\sim}{\pi}$. In most parts of the paper $\underset{\sim}{\pi}$ is assumed to be exogenously given and fixed. We assume $\underset{\sim}{y}_s = \underset{\sim}{y}_d$ in our analysis and eliminate $\underset{\sim}{y}$ to express $\underset{\sim}{p}$ in terms of $\underset{\sim}{i}$, e and $\underset{\sim}{k}$. After (4) and (5) are substituted for $\underset{\sim}{i}$ and e , we obtain the prices which prevail in the flow equilibria in the goods sectors

$$\underset{\sim}{p} = \pi_o \underset{\sim}{g} + \pi_1 m - \pi_2 d - \pi_3 d^* + \pi_4 \varepsilon + \pi_5(\underset{\sim}{k}) . \tag{6}$$

See Appendix for the expression of the coefficients.

Short-Run Equilibrium

When (6) is substituted into $\underset{\sim}{p}$ that appears in (4) and (5), we obtain the expression for the short-run equilibrium values of $\underset{\sim}{i}$ and e . They are

$$\underset{\sim}{i} = \rho_o \underset{\sim}{g} - \rho_1 m + \rho_2 d - \rho_3 d^* + \rho_4 \varepsilon + \rho_5(\underset{\sim}{k}) \tag{7}$$

where

$$\rho_o = I_3 \pi_o , \quad \rho_1 = I_1 - I_3 \pi_1 , \quad \rho_2 = I_2 - I_3 \pi_2 , \quad \rho_3 = I_3 \pi_3$$

$$\rho_4 = -I_4 + I_3 \pi_4 , \quad \rho_5 = I_3 \pi_5 + I_5 \quad \text{where only } \rho_5 \text{ depends on } \underset{\sim}{k},$$

and

$$e = -R_o \underset{\sim}{g} + R_1 m - R_2 d - R_3 d^* + R_4 \varepsilon - R_5(\underset{\sim}{k}) \tag{8}$$

where

$$R_o = e_3\pi_o$$

$$R_1 = e_1 - e_3\pi_1 \qquad R_2 = e_2 - e_3\pi_2$$

$$R_3 = 1 - e_3\pi_3 \qquad R_4 = e_4 - e_3\pi_4$$

$$R_5 = e_5 + e_3\pi_5 \ .$$

Only R_5 depends on $\underset{\sim}{k}$.

Growth

The growth of the capital stocks is governed by

$$\dot{\underset{\sim}{k}} = -F(\underset{\sim}{i}-\underset{\sim}{\pi})-\underset{\sim}{\lambda} \tag{9}$$

where

$$F = \text{diag}(f,f^*) \ .$$

A little more realistic expression involving the real rate of return to the capital stock is possible but we use this simpler version for illustrative purposes.

After $\underset{\sim}{i}$ of (7) is substituted in (9) the differential equation for $\underset{\sim}{k}$ is obtained. We need an equation for ε to complete the specification of the model. We adopt the perfect foresight assumption as a benchmark case. We therefore assume

$$\varepsilon = \dot{e} \ .$$

Then (8) and (9), together with stock and flow government instrument constraints to be specified shortly, determine the dynamic behavior of the endogenous variables completely.

The state equation for $\begin{bmatrix} e \\ \underset{\sim}{k} \end{bmatrix}$ is

$$\frac{d}{dt}\begin{bmatrix} e \\ \underset{\sim}{k} \end{bmatrix} = \Phi \begin{bmatrix} e \\ \underset{\sim}{k} \end{bmatrix} + \overline{G}\begin{bmatrix} \underset{\sim}{g} \\ m \\ d \\ d^* \end{bmatrix} + \underset{\sim}{\nu} \tag{10}$$

where

$$\Phi = \begin{bmatrix} R_4^{-1} & R_4^{-1}R_6 \\ -\underset{\sim}{h}R_4^{-1} \ , & -\underset{\sim}{h}R_4^{-1}R_6 - F\rho_6 \end{bmatrix}$$

$$\overline{G} = \begin{bmatrix} 1 & 0 \\ -\underset{\sim}{h} & I \end{bmatrix}\begin{bmatrix} R_4^{-1} & 0 \\ 0 & F \end{bmatrix}\begin{bmatrix} R_o - R_1 R_2 R_3 \\ -\rho_o - \rho_1 \rho_2 - \rho_3 \end{bmatrix}$$

$$\underset{\sim}{\nu} = \begin{bmatrix} -R_4^{-1}R_7 \\ \underset{\sim}{h}R_4^{-1}R_7 - \underset{\sim}{\lambda} + F(\underset{\sim}{\pi} - \rho_7) \end{bmatrix}$$

$$\underset{\sim}{h} = F\rho_4$$

where we write

$$\rho_5(\underset{\sim}{k}) = \rho_6\underset{\sim}{k} + \rho_7$$

and

$$R_5(\underset{\sim}{k}) = R_6\underset{\sim}{k} + R_7 \ .$$

See Appendix for the expressions.

We note that the elements of Φ are related by

$$\phi_{21} = -h\phi_{11}$$

$$\phi_{22} = -F\rho_6 - h\phi_{12} \ . \tag{11}$$

Furthermore, if we let

$$u = R_4^{-1}\left[(-R_1, R_2, R_3)\begin{bmatrix} m \\ d \\ d^* \end{bmatrix} + R_o\underset{\sim}{g}\right] \tag{11'}$$

$$\underset{\sim}{v} = F(\rho_1, -\rho_2\ \rho_3)\begin{bmatrix} m \\ d \\ d^* \end{bmatrix} - F\rho_o\underset{\sim}{g}$$

then

$$\bar{G}\begin{bmatrix} \underset{\sim}{g} \\ m \\ d \\ d^* \end{bmatrix} = G\begin{bmatrix} u \\ \underset{\sim}{v} \end{bmatrix}$$

where

$$G = \begin{bmatrix} 1 & 0 \\ -\underset{\sim}{h} & I \end{bmatrix} \ .$$

In other words, the monetary and fiscal instruments of both countries appear only through u and $\underset{\sim}{v}$ in their effects on the rate of change of e and the growth rate of $\underset{\sim}{k}$.

Fixed Exchange Regime

In the fixed exchange regime u , which is a linear combination of g , m , d and d^* , must be manipulated to maintain $e = o$, i.e., a constraint is imposed on m , d and d^* by

$$u = -\phi_{12}\underset{\sim}{k} - \nu_1 \tag{12}$$

With u specified by (12), the growth equation becomes

$$\dot{\underset{\sim}{k}} = \phi_{22}\underset{\sim}{k} - \underset{\sim}{h}u + \underset{\sim}{v} + \underset{\sim}{\nu}_2$$

$$= (\phi_{22} + \underset{\sim}{h}\phi_{12})\underset{\sim}{k} + \underset{\sim}{v} + \underset{\sim}{\nu}_2 + \underset{\sim}{h}\nu_1$$

Here from (11), we note that

$$\phi_{22} + \underset{\sim}{h}\phi_{12} = F\rho_6 \ .$$

This shows that the term $-F\rho_6$ in (11) is associated with the growth dynamics of $\underset{\sim}{k}$ under the fixed exchange rate regime. We can therefore identify the term $-\underset{\sim}{h}\phi_{12}$ being the influence on $\dot{\underset{\sim}{k}}$ of the flexible exchange rate.

Approximate Dynamic Equation

Casual observation of the exchange rate changes seem to indicate that the exchange rate dynamics appears to be much faster in response, compared with the process of capital stock accumulation. This becomes apparent from (8) if we assume m_6 b_6 and b_6^* in (1) and (3) are small. (See Appendix for R_4 expressed in terms of m_6, b_6 and b_6^*). We assume that $|R_4|$ is very small.

Under this assumption, we shall treat $R_4\dot{e}$ by the singular perturbation technique [10]. We have, letting $R_5 = R_6\underset{\sim}{k} + R_7$ in (8)

$$R_4\dot{e} = e + R_6\underset{\sim}{k} + x + R_7$$

where

$$x = R_o g - R_1 m + R_2 d + R_3 d^* \ .$$

To the first order of approximation, then e is approximated by $\bar{e}$

$$\bar{e} = -R_6\underset{\sim}{k} - x - R_7 \tag{13}$$

Introduce a new variable η by

$$\eta = e + R_6\underset{\sim}{k} + R_7 + R_4 n\underset{\sim}{k} \tag{14}$$

where n is a row vector to be chosen to separate η dynamics from $\underset{\sim}{k}$. See Appendix for derivation.

We obtain

$$R_4\eta = \mu\eta + \phi'(\hat{\underset{\sim}{\nu}}_2 + \underset{\sim}{v}) + \mu x \tag{15}$$

where

$$\phi' = R_4(R_6 + R_4 n) \ , \ \hat{\underset{\sim}{\nu}}_2 = -\underset{\sim}{\lambda} + F\underset{\sim}{\pi} - F\rho_7 \ , \text{ and}$$

where n is a row vector given in Appendix. Replacing e by η in (14), $\dot{\underset{\sim}{k}}$ of (10) becomes

$$\dot{\underset{\sim}{k}} = -F(\rho_6 - \rho_4 n)\underset{\sim}{k} - \frac{F\rho_4}{R_4}\eta + \underset{\sim}{\nu}_2 + \underset{\sim}{v} - \frac{F\rho_4}{R_4}x \ .$$

Let $\tau = t/|R_4|$. This changes the real time t to the stretched time τ. If $R_4 < 0$, (15) becomes then

$$\frac{d\eta}{d\tau} = -\mu\eta-\phi'\underset{\sim}{v}-\mu x-\phi'\hat{\underset{\sim}{\nu}}_2 \ .$$

For any $t > 0$, the corresponding τ is large. Assuming $\mu < 0$, we let $\tau \to \infty$ and approximate

$$\eta \simeq \eta_\infty = \frac{-1}{\mu} (\phi'\underset{\sim}{v} + x_t + \phi'\hat{\underset{\sim}{\nu}}_2) \ .$$

We obtain an approximation for e by

$$e_t \simeq \bar{e}_t + x_t + \eta_\infty - R_4 n\underset{\sim}{k}_t$$

or

$$e_t = \bar{e}_t - \frac{\phi'}{\mu}(\underset{\sim}{v}_t + \hat{\underset{\sim}{\nu}}_2) - R_4 n\underset{\sim}{k}_t = \bar{e}_y + O(|R_4|) \ . \tag{16}$$

By replacing η with η_∞ , the dynamics for $\underset{\sim}{k}$ becomes approximately

$$\dot{\underset{\sim}{k}} = -F(\rho_6-\rho_4 n)\underset{\sim}{k} + \underset{\sim}{\nu}_2-\underset{\sim}{v}- \frac{F\rho_4}{R_4} x$$

$$= -F(\rho_6-\rho_4 n)\underset{\sim}{k} + (I + \frac{F\rho_4\phi'}{R_4})(\underset{\sim}{\nu}_2-\underset{\sim}{v}) \ . \tag{17}$$

From (16) and (17), we can state that to the first order in R_4, e is primarily influenced by x while $\underset{\sim}{k}$ is affected by $\underset{\sim}{v}$.

From (8), (5) and (6)

$$x = -e_s + e_3\underset{\sim}{p} + R_4\epsilon - e_5(\underset{\sim}{k}) - e_3\pi_5(\underset{\sim}{k})$$

where e_s is the short-run equilibrium value of e when the real sector equilibrates. Suppose that in response to Δx and $\Delta\underset{\sim}{v}$, we have $\Delta\underset{\sim}{k} = 0$ and $R_4\Delta\epsilon \approx 0$. Then

$$\Delta x \simeq -\Delta e_s + e_3\Delta\underset{\sim}{p} \ .$$

From (13) and (16)

$$\Delta\bar{e} = -\Delta x$$

$$\Delta e = \Delta\bar{e} + \frac{1}{\mu}\phi'\Delta\underset{\sim}{v}$$

$$\simeq \Delta e_s - e_3\underset{\sim}{p} + O(R_4) \ .$$

The last two terms express therefore the dynamic effect of the capital stock growth on the changes in the exchange rate.

From (6)

$$e_3\Delta\underset{\sim}{p} \simeq e_3(\pi_0\Delta g + \pi_1\Delta m - \pi_2\Delta d - \rho_3\Delta d^*) \ .$$

This equation can be used to assess short-run or impact effects of policy instrument changes on e .

3. Policy Coordination

Having derived the state equation of the dynamics, we discuss several aspects of policy coordination problems as illustrations of the way such a model may be analyzed to draw out dynamic implications of the interdependence of decision-makings by the two governments coupled together through trade in goods and capital transactions.

Modifications of Dynamics

It is possible to isolate the growth of the capital stocks from the balance of payment considerations if both countries coordinate their policy instruments.

As an illustration, consider

$$\begin{bmatrix} u \\ \underset{\sim}{v} \end{bmatrix} = L \begin{bmatrix} e \\ \underset{\sim}{k} \end{bmatrix} + \begin{bmatrix} \omega_1 \\ \underset{\sim}{\omega}_2 \end{bmatrix} \tag{18}$$

where

$$L = \begin{bmatrix} \ell_1 & L_2 \\ L_3 & L_4 \end{bmatrix} .$$

In (18), the instruments are therefore composed of the automatic rule and the discretionary part $\begin{bmatrix} \omega_1 \\ \underset{\sim}{\omega}_2 \end{bmatrix}$.

With (18), the dynamics given by (10) becomes

$$\frac{d}{dt} \begin{bmatrix} e \\ k \end{bmatrix} = (\Phi + GL) \begin{bmatrix} e \\ k \end{bmatrix} + G \begin{bmatrix} w_1 \\ \underset{\sim}{w}_1 \end{bmatrix} .$$

The problem of choosing the feedback matrix L to give a desired dynamic behavior to the economy has not been addressed in the economic literature. For example, L may be chosen to induce a desired growth rate of $\underset{\sim}{k}$ and stable e behavior. Or, since

$$(\Phi + GL)_{21} = \phi_{21} - \ell_1 \underset{\sim}{h} + L_3$$

the governments may adopt $L_3 = -\phi_{21} + \ell_1 \underset{\sim}{h}$ to make $(\Phi + GL)_{21}$ zero. In other words, this choice of L_3 would insulate the dynamics of the growth paths of the two countries from balance of payments considerations. This would require that both governments agree on a time path for e and k which specifies u and $\underset{\sim}{v}$, which in turn determines the time paths individual government instruments must follow. Choices of elements in G are not independent. For example, L_3 depends on ℓ_1 in the above. ℓ_1 may be chosen to stabilize e dynamics, i.e., to make $\phi_{11} + \ell_1 < o$. Alternately, the governments may choose to make $(\Phi + GL)_{12}$ zero or $L_2 = -\phi_{12}$ to isolate the exchange rate dynamics from the effects of the real sectors. The stability of the growth rates then is determined by that of $\phi_{22} -hL_2-L_4$. There are many possibilities of stabilizing e and/or k dynamics separately or in a decoupled manner, or jointly for that matter if the governments coordinate their instruments.

Without coordination decentralized stabilizability by the home government must be examined. We shall not pursue this topic in this paper.

Perfect Output Controllability

It is important for policy-makers to be able to maintain stable price levels, interest rates and to let output and capital stocks grow at some desired rates in both countries. These requirements shall not be met if the system does not possess reproducibility or perfect output controllability. See [1,3] for additional arguments and necessary and sufficient conditions for it.

To maintain certain price levels, interest rates, and/or to maintain some desired growth rate in output require that u and $\underset{\sim}{v}$ are made to follow certain time paths. To illustrate, to the first order of approximation, to maintain a desired rate of growth $\underset{\sim}{\kappa}$ requires that

$$\underset{\sim}{\kappa} = K\underset{\sim}{k} + \underset{\sim}{\nu}_2 - \underset{\sim}{v} .$$

Define $\underset{\sim}{v}^d$ by

$$\underset{\sim}{v}^d - \underset{\sim}{\nu}_2 - K\underset{\sim}{k} - \underset{\sim}{\kappa} = \begin{bmatrix} v_d \\ v_d^* \end{bmatrix} .$$

In words, to keep $\dot{\underset{\sim}{k}} = \underset{\sim}{\kappa}$ requires that the time-path of $\underset{\sim}{v}$ follow $\underset{\sim}{v}^d$. From its definition (11'),

$$\underset{\sim}{v} = -F\rho_o \underset{\sim}{g} + \begin{bmatrix} \gamma_1 & \gamma_2 & \gamma_3 \\ \gamma_1^* & \gamma_2^* & \gamma_3^* \end{bmatrix} \begin{bmatrix} m \\ d \\ d^* \end{bmatrix}$$

where we define

$$\begin{bmatrix} \gamma_1 & \gamma_2 & \gamma_3 \\ \gamma_1^* & \gamma_2^* & \gamma_3^* \end{bmatrix} = F(-\rho_1 \rho_2 - \rho_3) .$$

Recalling our definition of d and d* , we have

$$\underset{\sim}{v} = -F\rho_o g + \begin{bmatrix} \gamma_1 , & \gamma_2 - \gamma_3 \\ \gamma_1^* & \gamma_2^* - \gamma_3^* \end{bmatrix} \begin{bmatrix} m \\ b_g \\ b_g^* \end{bmatrix} + \begin{bmatrix} \gamma_3 , & -\gamma_2 \\ \gamma_3^* , & -\gamma_2^* \end{bmatrix} \begin{bmatrix} b_{g^*}^* \\ b_{g^*} \end{bmatrix} .$$

Aside from g which are constrained by the flow variable constraints of the government instruments, the need for policy instrument coordination is clearly seen from this equation. Without knowing the other governments' instrument time paths, v cannot be made to follow v_d nor v^* can be made to follow v_d^* , since each governments' instruments affect both components of $\underset{\sim}{v}$.

Discussion

If we drop the assumption that $\underset{\sim}{\pi}$ is constant and/or the assumption that $\varepsilon = \dot{e}$, the dynamics of the system will naturally be altered. We shall leave this aspect for another paper in which the effects on stability of rational expectation anc adaptive expectation schemes are explored. In addition to policy coordination question, we can use the model developed in this paper to examine transmission of foreign disturbsnces to the home economy since they affect I_5 , ρ_7 and R_7 , for example.

Another topic that we have not discussed is that of decentralized or centralized stabilization question. See for example [7] for some special results. For application of decoupling, see [1].

Equations (4) through (8) can be used to perform impact and short-run studies of policy changes and evaluations of foreign disturbances on i , e and/or p . This has not been done in this paper.

Appendix

The coefficients in (4) are after substituting $y = s_1k - s_2w + s_2p$

$$I_1 = \frac{1}{D}\begin{bmatrix} b_4 \\ b_3 \end{bmatrix} , \quad I_2 = \frac{1}{D}\begin{bmatrix} m_4 \\ -m_3 \end{bmatrix}$$

where

$$D = b_3m_4 + b_4m_3$$

$$I_3 = I_1\alpha_6' + I_2\alpha_4'$$

where

$$\alpha_4' = (b_1s_2, -b_2s_2^*) , \quad \alpha_6' = (1 + m_1s_2, m_2s_2^*)$$

$$I_4 = m_6I_1 + b_6I_2 \tag{A.1}$$

$$I_5 = \{I_1(m_1,m_2) + I_2(b_1,-b_2)\}(S_1\underset{\sim}{k} - S_2\underset{\sim}{w})$$

where

$$S_1 = \mathrm{diag}(s_1, s_1^*) , \quad i = 1,2 .$$

In (5), the coefficients are:

$$e_1 = (b_3^*b_4 - b_3b_4^*)/D , \quad e_2 = (b_3^*m_4 + b_4^*m_3)/D$$

$$e_3 = e_1\alpha_6' + e_2\alpha_4' - \alpha_2' \tag{A.2}$$

where

$$\alpha_2' = (1 + b_1^*s_2, -1 - b_2^*s_2^*)$$

$$e_4 = e_1m_6 + e_2b_6 + b_6^* \tag{A.3}$$

$$e_5 = \{e_1(m_1,m_2) + e_2(b_1,-b_2) - (b_1^*,-b_2^*)\}(S_1\underset{\sim}{k} - S_2\underset{\sim}{w}) .$$

In (6),

$$\pi_o = (D_3S_2 + D_4 + D_2I_3 + \underset{\sim}{\delta}e_3)^{-1}D_1$$

$$\pi_1 = \pi_oD_1^{-1}(D_1I_2 + e_1\underset{\sim}{\delta})$$

$$\pi_2 = \pi_oD_1^{-1}(D_2I_2 + e_2\underset{\sim}{\delta})$$

$$\pi_3 = \pi_oD_1^{-1}\underset{\sim}{\delta}$$

$$\pi_4 = \pi_oD_1^{-1}(D_2I_4 + e_4\underset{\sim}{\delta})$$

$$\pi_5 = \pi_oD_1^{-1}\{-D_2I_5 - e_5\underset{\sim}{\delta} + D_2\underset{\sim}{\pi} - D_3(S_1\underset{\sim}{k} - S_2\underset{\sim}{w})\} .$$

Define $I_5 = \hat{I}_1(m_1,m_2) + I_2(b_1,-b_2)$,

$$\hat{e}_5 = e_1(m_1,m_2) + e_2(b_1,-b_2)-(b_1^*,-b_2^*)$$

$$\hat{\pi}_5 = -\pi_o D_1^{-1}(D_2\hat{I}_5 + \underset{\sim}{\delta}\hat{e}_5 + D_3) \ .$$

Then

$$\pi_5 = \hat{\pi}_5(s_1\underset{\sim}{k}-s_2\underset{\sim}{w}) + \pi_3 D_1^{-1}D_2\underset{\sim}{\pi}$$

$$\rho_6 = (I_3\hat{\pi}_5 + \hat{I}_5)S_1 \ , \ \rho_7 = I_3\pi_3 D_1^{-1}D_2\ \pi-(I_3\hat{\pi}_5 + \hat{I}_5)S_2\ w$$

$$R_6 = (\hat{e}_5 + e_3\hat{\pi}_5)S_1 \ , \ R_7 = -(\hat{e}_5 + e_3\hat{\pi}_5)S_2\underset{\sim}{w} + e_3\pi_3 D_1^{-1}D_2\underset{\sim}{\pi}$$

From (8) in the main body of the paper and from (A.1), (A.2) and (A.4), we see that R_4 is

$$R_4 = e_4-e_3\pi_4 = [1-(e_1\alpha_6' + e_2\alpha_4')\pi_o D_1^{-1}\underset{\sim}{\delta}]e_4$$

$$-(e_1\alpha_6' + e_2\alpha_4'-\alpha_4')\pi_o D_1^{-1}D_2(m_6 I_1 + b_6 I_2)$$

where e_4 is given by (A.3). We see that R_4 is of the same order of smallness as m_6 , b_6 and b_6^* .

Constraints

Policy instruments are subject to stock and flow constraints.

Home Government

flow: $P(G-T) + EP^*\dot{B}_g^* = \dot{M} + P\dot{B}_g$

stock: $\Delta M + P\Delta B_g = EP^*\Delta B_g^*$

Foreign Government

flow: $P^*(G^*-T^*) + \frac{PB_{g^*}}{E} = M^* + P^*B^*_{g^*}$

stock: $M^* + P^*\ B^*_{g^*} = \frac{P\Delta B_{g^*}}{E}$.

Singular Perturbation Analysis of the Exchange Rate Dynamics

Change the variable form e to η by

$$\eta = e + R_6\underset{\sim}{k} + R_7 + R_4 n\underset{\sim}{k}$$

$$= e + R_7 + (R_6 + R_4 n)\underset{\sim}{k}$$

where n shall be chosen next to decouple η dynamics from $\underset{\sim}{k}$. The dynamic equation for η is given, letting $\sigma = R_4$

$$\sigma\dot{\eta} = \sigma\dot{e} + \sigma(R_6 + \sigma n)(\underset{\sim}{\hat{v}}_2-F\rho_6\underset{\sim}{k} + \underset{\sim}{v})$$

$$-\sigma(R_6 + \sigma n)F\rho_4\dot{e}$$

$$= [1-(R_6 + \sigma n)F\rho_4](\eta - \sigma n\underset{\sim}{k} + x)$$

$$+ \sigma(R_6 + \sigma n)(\underset{\sim}{\hat{\nu}}_2 - F\rho_6\underset{\sim}{k} + \underset{\sim}{v})$$

$$= \{1-(R_6 + \sigma n)F\rho_4\}\eta + \sigma(R_6 + \sigma n)(\underset{\sim}{\hat{\nu}}_2 + F\underset{\sim}{v})$$

$$+ \{1-(R_6 + \sigma n)F\rho_4\}x$$

if n is chosen to satisfy

$$R_6F\rho_6 + n(1-R_6F\rho_4 + \sigma F\rho_6) - \sigma n\rho_4'Fn' = 0 \ .$$

Substituting (7) for i in (9), k-dynamics is

$$\dot{\underset{\sim}{k}} = \underset{\sim}{\hat{\nu}}_2 - F\rho_6 k + \underset{\sim}{v} - F\rho_4\dot{e}$$

where

$$\underset{\sim}{\hat{\nu}}_2 = -\underset{\sim}{\lambda} + F\underset{\sim}{\pi} - F\rho_7 \ .$$

Replacing $\dot{e}$,

$$\dot{\underset{\sim}{k}} = -(F\rho_6 - F\rho_4 n)\underset{\sim}{k} + \underset{\sim}{v} + \underset{\sim}{\hat{\nu}}_2$$

$$- \frac{F\rho_4}{R_4}(\eta + x) \ .$$

References

1. Aoki, M., Optimal Control and System Theory in Dynamic Economic Analysis, North Holland/American Elsevier, New York, 1976.

2. Aoki, M., "Stochastic Control in Economic Theory and Economic System", IEEE Trans. Auto. Control AC-21, 213-110, April, 1976.

3. Aoki, M., "On a Generalization of Tinbergen's Condition in the Theory of Policy to Dynamic Models", Rev. Econ. Stud. 42, 293-296, April, 1975.

4. Aoki, M. and Canzoneri, M., "A Dynamic Model of Canadian-American Economic Relations". Presented at Canadian Econ. Assoc. Meeting, Quebec City, May, 1976.

5. Aoki, M. and Canzoneri, M., "On Short-Run Policy Impacts in a Dynamic Two Country Model". Presented at the North American Meeting of the Econometric Society, Atlantic City, Sept., 1976.

6. Aoki, M. and Lejonhufvud, A., "Cybernetics and Macroeconomics: A Comment Economic Inquiry 14, 251-258, June, 1976.

7. Aoki, M., "On Decentralized Stabilization Policies and Dynamic Assignment Problems", J. International Economics 6, 143-171, 1976.

8. Athans, M. and Kendrick, D., "Control Theory and Economics: A Survey, Forecast, and Speculations", IEEE Trans. Auto. Control AC-19, 518-524, Oct., 1974.

9. Garbade, K. D., Discretionary Control of Aggregate Economic Activity, Lexington Books, March, 1975.

10. O'Malley, R. E., Jr., Introduction to Singular Perturbations, Academic Press, New York, 1974.

11. Peterson, D. W., "Transferring Ideas from Engineering to the Social Sciences", Proc. IEEE 63, 354-359, March, 1975.

12. Pindyck, R., "An Application of the Linear Quadratic Tracking Problem to Economic Stabilization", IEEE Trans, Auto. Control AC-17, 287-300, June, 1972.

SYSTEMES CYBERNETIQUES ET PROBLEMES DE LA GESTION DES PROCESSUS ECONOMIQUES

N. MOISSEEV
Steklow Institute of the USSR Academy of Science
Moscow - U.S.S.R.

INTRODUCTION

Dès sa création la science économique cherchait à connaître les lois objectives les plus générales qui dirigent la forme essentielle de l'activité humaine, l'activité de production. C'est au milieu du XIXe siècle qu'a été conçue la théorie de la production élargie qui a couronné la création de la base conceptuelle de l'économie politique classique. Il est à noter que cette science étudiait les processus économiques comme dynamiques, se développant dans le temps.

Pourtant, vers la fin du XIXe siècle on voit apparaître un nouvel accent dans les intérêts des chercheurs. La production, tout en se développant, annonce beaucoup de problèmes concrets et en premier, les problèmes de la gestion rationnelle de l'économie, de la meilleure utilisation des investissements des capitaux et de la main-d'oeuvre. La théorie de l'utilité limite surgit.

Les problèmes concrets de l'économie ont relégué au deuxième plan une quantité de questions de caractère conceptuel. Les recherches de ce type ont stimulé le développement des méthodes économiques mathématiques, la mise en pratique des idées et de la technique des calculs d'optimisation. En même temps, l'objet de recherche devenait de plus en plus limité et les facteurs sociaux déterminants les motifs de prise de décisions, ainsi que la recherche elle-même des fonctions de but décrivant les buts du fonctionnement de la sociéte, se trouvaient à l'écart de la science économique. Les problèmes statiques ont commencé à attirer une attention toujours plus grande. Les idées de l'équilibre se répandaient largement bien que le développement de l'économie et son progrès soient liés avant tout à l'absence de l'équilibre.

Il me semble que maintenant, à la fin du XXe siècle ce sont les problèmes généraux d'un caractère conceptuel qui deviennent surtout actuels et non pas la solution des problèmes d'optimisation isolés. Je crois qu'il faut retourner aux conceptions dynamiques générales de la reproduction. Il faut étudier la perspective générale de l'évolution des processus économiques. Il y a beaucoup de raisons pour faire de telles affirmations. La raison principale est un grand accroissement de la puissance de l'homme et l'existence du danger de la prise de décisions basées sur une information insuffisante.

Dans les années d'après guerre surgit un grand nombre de problèmes auxquels la science économique actuelle n'a pas encore de solution.

La capacité de l'homme d'influencer l'environnement nous fait envisager son activité productive comme une composante naturelle des processus écologiques généraux. L'homme n'est pas contre la biotope, mais avec la biotope ce principe-là doit être d'une grande importance dans les recherches économiques.

Cependant, sa réalisation exige non seulement une grande extention des recherches économiques, mais aussi une transformation essentielle de nos conceptions concernant le contenu, les buts et l'instrument des recherches économiques.

Puis, l'unité de l'organisme de la Planette commune se fait sentir de plus en plus. L'influence mutuelle des processus économiques ayant lieu aux différents latitudes et méridiens devient de plus en plus un facteur déterminant de l'évolution de la société humaine. Ainsi surgissent les problèmes globaux de la gestion des ressources et de l'activité humaine. Les problèmes de la coexistance doivent recevoir une base conceptuelle de l'analyse scientifique aussi bien que les méthodes de recherches des solutions rationnelles collectives.

La science s'est trouvée incapable d'expliquer et de prévoir les plus importants phénomènes de l'actualité; elle n'a pas su comprendre les causes de l'inflation et trouver des moyens de lutter contre celle-ci. La destruction du marché monétaire unique et le développement des corporations internationales, le mercantilisme qui réapparaît sur une base nouvelle, posent des problèmes qu'on pourrait croire insolubles si on considère comme objectif d'une science non pas la description d'une situation, mais la création des méthodes de l'analyse permettant de prévoir les résultats des décisions prises.

En parlant de l'économie actuelle Galbraith [1], affirme "Elle conduit aux conclusions qui arrangent les grandes corporations mais qui presentent des inconvénients pour la société. Il en résulte les convictions et la conduite exigées par les intérêts économiques de ces corporations". On pourrait bien continuer à citer des problèmes identiques. Et par la suite on est convaicu de faire de profondes recherches fondamentales et non pas des principes généraux. On a besoin aussi d'un appareil de recherches. Une multitude de causes, de conséquences de liaisons, les flux d'information compliquent l'analyse mathématique traditionnelle. On a besoin d'approches et de méthodes plus générales qui permettraient de prévoir les tendances et les possibilités générales dans le chaos des faits. Mais pour cela tout d'abord, on a besoin d'un langage qui permette d'avoir la description unique des divers processus où l'homme participe, un langage qui rende avant tout le caractère dynamique des processus économiques.

C'est à la discussion du problème d'une telle description et aux certaines idées sur les méthodes de l'analyse que cet exposé est consacré. Les exemples cités ne prétendent pas à l'originalité de l'analyse économique. Ils sont choisis de facon à rendre plus claires les idées de l'auteur sans compliquer l'exposé.

1. Les Systèmes Cybernétiques

Nous parlerons des systèmes dont la position est décrite uniquement par le vecteur de dimension finie x, ses composantes $x^j (j = 1, 2 - N)$ sont fonctions du temps (t) et d'une variable spatiale (r). Le changement de la position est dû aux forces aléatoires dont la description statique est connue aux actions $\eta(t, r)$ appartenant à un ensemble G_η

$$\eta(t, r) \in G_\eta(t) \; \forall \; t, r \quad , \tag{1,1}$$

et aux contrôles

$$u_i (i = 1, 2 \ldots K) \quad .$$

Nous dirons que le système est décrit cybernétiquement si on peut construire l'opérateur A qui permet de déterminer la position du système à tout point t, $t \in [t_o \; T \; (t_o)]$ selon les valeurs du vecteur x(t) donné à un intervalle $[t_1; t_o]$, à condition que toutes les actions et tous les contrôles soient fixés

$$x(t) = A\left(x(\tau) \; \xi, \; \eta, \; u\right) \quad . \tag{1,2}$$

Remarque:

Ainsi, dans le cas général, la variable de phase sera un processus aléatoire. C'est pourquoi il est mieux parfois de considérer comme position de phase non pas la grandeur x, mais sa distribution.

Les systèmes cybernétiques, dont le contrôle est une fonction de phase, des perturbations ou du temps, sont appelés les systèmes réflexes. Si le contrôle u (x, t) est choisi selon la condition de la maximisation de l'unique fonctionnelle $\gamma(u)$, ce système est toujours réflexe.

Tous les systèmes techniques sont réflexes. Les systèmes biologiques contrôlés par des réflexes sont aussi des systèmes réflexes.

Donc, on appelle réflexes tous les systèmes au contrôle strictement programmé.

Contrairement aux systèmes techniques et biologiques, tous les systèmes économiques ou sociaux ne sont pas réflexes. A ces systèmes participent les gens et les organisations de gens qui ont la liberté de prendre une décision. Ces gens-là seront appelés sujet du système.

Dans le cas général des systèmes non-réflexes, les contrôles u_i sont à la disposition des sujets et leur choix est déterminé par l'ambition de réaliser certains objectifs qui, sans limiter la communauté, peuvent être décrits comme ambitions à la maximisation des certaines fonctionnelles I_i (i = 1, 2...K).

Remarque:

Ces fonctionnelles sont décrites habituellement par des paramètres et des coordonnées de phase. Mais, puisque ces dernières sont les représentations d'un ensemble de contrôles, les fonctionnelles I sans limiter la communauté, peuvent être considérées comme déterminées dans l'espace de contrôle.

On appelle description subjective du système Σ, la description du point de vue d'un sujet isolé. Pour trouver leur propre contrôle à eux, tous les sujets doivent avoir certaines hypothèses convernant le choix de contrôles des autres sujets. On exprime ces hypothèses en termes d'appartenance

$$u_i \in G_{ij} \quad . \tag{1,3}$$

C'est-à-dire, le contrôle du sujet du numéro i, selon le sujet du numéro j, appartiendra à la classe G_{ij}. L'étude des systèmes cybernétiques se fait toujours à partir d'un sujet déterminé et, est basée sur ses buts et la compréhension de la situation.

Les intérêts exprimés par les fonctionnelles I, peuvent être connus exactement, "plus ou moins connus", d'après la terminologie de Zadeh [2]. Ils peuvent être aussi inconnus. Mais ils existent toujours objectivement dans les systèmes non-réflexes. La reconnaissance de ce fait est une pierre angulaire de la théorie.

Les systèmes cybernétiques sont appelés systèmes de Hermaier [3], si les intérêts du sujet du numéro i, à la disposition duquel se trouve le contrôle u_i, sont exprimés par la maximisation de la fonctionnelle I_i ayant la forme suivante

$$I_i = \psi \; [\; f_i(U_i),\; F(U_1, \ldots U_k)] \quad , \tag{1,4}$$

où

ψ est une certaine contraction d'un critère vectoriel consistant des composantes f_i et F. Par exemple

$$I_i = \min \{f_i(U_i) \; ; \; \lambda_i \; F(U_1 \ldots U_k)\} \quad , \tag{1,4}$$

$$I_i = f_i(U_i) + \mu_i F(U_1 \ldots U_k) \quad , \tag{1,4}$$

où

λ_i, μ_i sont des coefficients de pondération dans les contractions correspondantes des critères.

On appelle statique, un système cybernétique s'il ne dépend pas du temps.

2. Les Problèmes de la Théorie des Systèmes Cybernétiques

Pour les systèmes cybernétiques du type du système de Hermaier, on peut formaliser la notion de l'homéostasie. On appelle limite de l'homéostasie dans l'espace des variables, la surface

$$F(U_i \ldots U_k = F_o = cst \quad . \qquad (2,1)$$

qui détermine dans cet espace le domaine de l'existence (de l'homéostasie, de la stabilité) du système. Convenons que les valeurs d'une fonctionnelle dépassant F_o correspondent au domaine de l'homéostasie. Ainsi, la maximisation de la fonctionnelle F donne la description formelle de l'ambition du sujet de se trouver dans une position aussi stable que possible.

Le problème principal de la théorie des systèmes de Hermaier est la détermination du domaine de l'homéostasie.

Remarque:

La détermination de la constante F_o n'est bien sûr pas le problème d'une analyse mathématique de même que l'expression du critère F lui-même. Mais, si la grandeur F_o et la forme du critère sont connus, le problème obtient un sens mathématique exact. On appelle problème général de la stabilité, le problème de la détermination de l'ensemble des fonctions U_i dans l'espace des contrôles satisfaisants à la condition

$$F(U_i, \ldots U_k) > F_o \quad . \qquad (2,2)$$

On appelle problème particulier de stabilité (homéostasie), le problème de la détermination des points isolés du domaine de l'homéostasie.

Les systèmes dynamiques aux fonctions libres sont un cas particulier important des systèmes cybernétiques. Pour ces systèmes-là, le problème de la détermination du domaine de l'homéostasie peut être reformulé en termes de domaines d'accessibilité. Pour réaliser une telle réduction, il ne faut que construire la représentation de l'ensemble des contrôles dans l'espace des positions.

Le choix des contrôles est un acte de prise de décisions collectives et, par la suite, l'élaboration des principes de la prise de décisions collectives est un des plus importants problèmes de la théorie. Comme il est connu, il n'y a pas beaucoup de principes de prise de décisions collectives et pour le cas général des systèmes cybernétiques, ce problème-là est pratiquement insoluble. Cependant, les systèmes de Hermaier sont une exception à cet égard.

Pour les systèmes statiques de Hermaier, le théorème suivant de Hermaier-Vatel [3] est valable si les critères des sujets ont l'expression (1,4) où F $(U_1 \ldots U_k)$, $f_i(U_i)$ relativement des fonctionnelles monotones croissantes et monotones décroissantes de leurs arguments, il existe alors des solutions stables (les points de l'équilibre par Nash) parmi lesquelles au moins une solution est effective (c'est-à-dire appartenant à l'ensemble de Paréto).

S'il se trouve que ce théorème-là est valable pour le cas général des systèmes de Hermaier, c'est évident qu'il soit pratique de prendre comme principe de la prise de décision, celui du choix d'une solution stable de Paréto.

Ainsi, la détermination des conditions (nécessaires et suffisantes) auxquelles l'opérateur doit satisfaire pour que le théorème de Hermaier-Vatel soit encore valable, est un des problèmes fondamentaux de la théorie.

3. Paramétrisation: les Trajectoires de Base, le Dialogue Homme-Machine

La description cybernétique est toujours une description approximative de modèles. Au cours de recherches on est obligé de simplifier des modèles isolés, les remplacer parfois par des liaisons finies. Ce processus est appelé paramétrisation.

Les idées de la paramétrisation sont utilisées souvent dans la physique. Par exemple, le modèle compliqué d'interaction de molécules du gaz peut être remplacé, après la paramétrisation, par la relation finie, c'est-à-dire par l'équation de l'état. La régularisation des problèmes non corrects est un autre exemple de la paramétrisation. Enfin, l'idée générale du petit paramètre de H. Poincaré fournit encore une classe de méthodes de paramétrisation qui peut être la plus importante, etc.

Le problème de paramétrisation consiste à construire une description simplifiée qui puisse assurer l'approximation des problèmes à résoudre pour une description simplifiée et initiale. La notion d'approximation est comprise dans le sens de telles ou telles métriques faibles qui sont déterminées par des critères d'un problème. Ainsi, par exemple, la paramétrisation du modèle de Navier-Storce par le modèle d'une couche limite donne une topologie des lignes différentes du courant, mais en même temps elle garantie l'approximation des valeurs de la fonctionnelle exprimant la résistance totale.

Contrairement aux systèmes physiques où les méthodes de la paramétrisation sont utilisées par les mathématiciens depuis longtemps dans les systèmes cybernétiques, les méthodes de leur analyse sont pratiquement absentes. Il est normal que les systèmes cybernétiques, construits pour les recherches de situations réelles, soient très compliqués et exigent la création de méthodes numériques spéciales. Cependant, la recherche numérique elle-même, est souvent difficile et doit être précédée d'une analyse qualitative.

Les recherches des méthodes de paramétrisation des systèmes controlés présentent encore une étape initiale. A proprement parler, les problèmes de paramétrisation dans la théorie des systèmes contrôlés ne sont pas encore transformés en problèmes mathématiques rigoureusement posés.

Parmi les divers moyens de recevoir des estimations approximatives un rôle particulier appartient aux différentes variantes de la théorie des perturbations.

Mais pour les construire, il faut savoir déterminer certaines trajectoires d'appui.

Dans la théorie du contrôle pour une analyse des systèmes stochastiques compliqués, on utilise aussi la (soi-disant) méthode d'optimisation à deux étapes.

Expliquons cette méthode à l'aide d'un simple exemple du système dynamique. Supposons que l'évolution du système est décrite par l'équation

$$x = f(x, u, \xi) \quad , \qquad (3,1)$$

où

$u \in G_n$ est le contrôle,
ξ^n est le processus aléatoire.

Le choix $u = u(x, t)$ est contraint par deux critères. J_1 et J_2. L'un d'eux aura le sens d'énergie

$$J_1(x) \Rightarrow \min . \qquad (3,2)$$

Si l'on traite l'ensemble des trajectoires possibles $x(t)$ comme celui des trajectoires de l'appareil qui atteignent l'orbite fixée, la condition (3,2) signifie l'atteinte de l'orbite fixée avec des dépenses minimales du combustible.

Soit le deuxième critère d'une dispersion,

$$J_2 = (x_1 - \hat{x})^2 \Rightarrow \min \quad , \tag{3,3}$$

on peut traiter ce critère comme caractéristique de l'exactitude de l'atteinte du résultat désiré.

Puisque x(t) sera un certain processus aléatoire, la fonctionnelle qui caractérise l'atteinte du but fixé doit avoir une forme semblable à (3,3). Ainsi, le problème consiste à choisir un contrôle et par conséquent une trajectoire de manière à pouvoir atteindre le but du contrôle aux dépenses minimales. Pour transformer ce problème en problème mathématique, if faut faire encore une analyse non formelle pour la contraction de ces critères.

Il se trouve qu'à certaines conditions de l'analyse de cette situation conflictuelle, on peut utiliser la théorie des perturbations.

Supposons que $\xi \equiv 0$. Au lieu du critère J_2 considérons le critère

$$J_2' = \begin{cases} \infty, & \text{si } x \neq \hat{x} \\ 0, & \text{si } x = \hat{x} \end{cases} \tag{3,4}$$

où x est la position terminale du système. Le problème aux critères (3,2) et (3,4) est déjà soluble. Désignons sa solution par $\hat{x}(t)$ et $\hat{u}(t)$, et supposons que

$$x = \hat{x}(t) + y(t) \; ,$$
$$u = \hat{u}(t) + v(y, t) \quad . \tag{3,5}$$

Ayant linéarisé ce problème par rapport à y, v et ξ on arrive au problème suivant:

$$\overline{Y_t^2} \Rightarrow \min \quad .$$
$$\dot{Y} = By + Cv + D\xi \quad . \tag{3,6}$$

où B, C et D sont certaines matrices.

Le problème (3,6) est un problème de synthèse optimale. Sa solution est une fonction aléatoire $V = V(y, t)$.

A certaines limitations sur le processus aléatoire $\xi(t)$ une telle optimisation par étape est valable et fournit une solution approximative pour toute contradiction linéaire des critères J_1 et J_2

$$J = c_1 J_1 + C_2 J_2 \quad , \qquad (3,7)$$

c'est-à-dire pour tout coefficient de ce procédé, dans le cas général des systèmes non réflexes n'est pas trivial du tout, mais tout progrès promet des perspectives intéressantes pour l'analyse numérique et qualitative des situations conflictuelles.

Il est évident que dans ce cas-là le problème principal est celui du choix de la solution de base.

Leur choix erroné peut donner des résultats incorrects. Citons un exemple pour illustrer cette affirmation. Supposons qu'on veuille étudier le caractère des mouvements oscillatoires d'un pivot sur lequel est appliquée la force p. C'est le problème classique de Eiler. On sait que si $p < p^*$ est la force critique, l'unique position d'équilibre est la forme horizontale et cette position est stable. L'expérience numérique avec un modèle linéarisé (linéariser est une des variantes de la théorie des perturbations) donne un tableau d'oscillations amorties. La position limite du pivot qui est déterminée à partir des calculs, sera naturellement horizontale. Supposons, maintenant que $p > p^*$. Dans ce cas-là il existe à l'état stable une autre position d'équilibre $x^*(s)$ à laquelle viendra la forme du pivot. Cependant, l'expérience numérique avec le modèle précédent donnera

$$\lim_{t \to \infty} x(s, t) = \infty \quad , \qquad (3,8)$$

Pour utiliser la technique de la théorie des perturbations nous devons faire la linéarisation par rapport à $x - x^*$.

Nous avons donné l'exemple relativement simple du système physique. Dans les systèmes cybernétiques tous ces problèmes se trouvent beaucoup plus compliqués mais concervent leur sens. Le problème de recherches des solutions de base aussi bien que dans les systèmes physiques, reste un des éléments les plus importants de l'analyse qualitative.

Malgré l'absence pratiquement complète des recherches théoriques, on commence à utiliser la théorie des perturbations en choisissant comme trajectoire de base les solutions aux problèmes statiques correspondants qui sont les résultats d'une analyse des problèmes des jeux spécialement posés.

Les problèmes qui surgissent dans la pratique ont habituellement une telle dimension qu'il est impossible d'obtenir un résultat exact à l'aide de M.C.E. de puissance hypothétique. Dans ce cas-là l'unique moyen est d'utiliser le dialogue à l'aide d'un système d'imitation. Cette approche est justifiée parce que les problèmes réels ne peuvent pas être posés assez exactement. Dans leur position et par conséquent dans leurs résultats, il y a un élément de "vague" si l'on utilise la terminologie de Zadeh.

La méthode d'imitation est au fond un moyen d'analyser des variantes avec l'estimation du résultat par un expert. Pourtant, l'organisation des processus d'un dialogue n'est jamais triviale et exige des recherches spéciales.

Un dialogue est aussi en soi un certain algorithme d'optimisation où il y a un procédé du calcul des grandeurs qui caractérisent la fonction de but, bien que la fonction elle-même soit inconnue. L'estimation du résultat du calcul aussi bien que le choix de la variante suivante sont effectués par un expert. Malgré le grand rôle des différentes considérations euristiques, on arrive souvent à réduire ce système de procédés à une forme qui détermine le nombre des variantes examinées.

4. Quelques Remarques Sur Les Systèmes Ecologiques Economiques

Une des classes les plus importantes des systèmes non-réflexes, dont l'étude devient de plus en plus importante sont les systèmes qui décrivent l'influence mutuelle des processus écologiques et de production. En principe, ils sont extrêmement compliqués et sont décrits par des modèles aux caractères différents.

Pratiquement, tout système d'interaction de l'homme et de l'environnement a la structure indiquée sur la Figure 1. Si l'on exclut les modèles de l'activité humaine, le système représenté sur la Figure 1 se trouve réflexe. Quoique ce système soit compliqué, son étude peut être possible à l'aide des méthodes des sciences naturelles. Les difficultés de son analyse sont avant tout d'un caractère non-formel et sont liées au caractère non-réflexe du bloc d'activité humaine.

C'est pour cela que je crois que l'analyse quantitative des problèmes de la pratique concrète doit être orientée dès le début vers l'utilisation des méthodes d'imitation. La formalisation totale du problème est évidemment possible seulement dans les cas particulièrement simples.

Mais si nous pouvions même surmonter les difficultés de la formalisation, l'analyse des systèmes dans chaque cas concret resterait assez difficile.

Les prémisses fondamentales de la simplification de l'analyse consistent en la différence de leurs échelles de temps caractéristiques. Le temps caractéristique du changement des conditions climatiques T_k, par exemple, est beaucoup plus grand que ceux des autres processus. Voilà pourquoi on a la possibilité d'étudier les 3 modèles cités ci-dessus, indépendamment des modèles du climat. L'inverse est naturellement impossible, parce que les effets antropogènes sur le climat présentent le problème de l'analyse.

Ensuite, les processus dans la biotope et les processus au cycle des matières dans la nature sont réflexes d'après nature et par conséquent nous pouvons formuler le résultat de l'influence de l'homme sur l'environnement à l'aide de certaines fonctionnelles qui caractérisent la qualité du milieu. De la même façon, on peut paramétriser dans les cas les plus simples les modèles de la biotope lorsqu'on veut concentrer l'attention sur l'analyse des modèles de l'activité humaine, et inversement, quand on étudie les processus dans la biotope, il faut essayer de paramétriser les modèles de l'activité humaine. La condition de l'homéostasie peut être parfois formulée en termes d'indices qualitatifs du milieu. Pourtant les possibilités de cette approches-là ne sont pas évidemment universelles parce que l'efficacité de l'influence humaine sur l'environnement accroît très vite. L'humanité constitue une partie de la biotope qui doit trouver sa place dans la structure du modèle. D'après un mathématicien, l'analyse des modèles de l'activité humaine est la plus difficile. Ce sont ces modèles-là qui font tout le système non-réflexe.

Cependant, le système en tout représenté par la Figure 1, est toujours le système de Hermaier.

En effet, la perte d'équilibre de la biotope, ou le changement irreversible de climat, tirera toute l'humanité du domaine de l'homéostasie. Par conséquent, quel que soit l'ensemble du sujet du système cybernétique considéré parmi les critères, déterminant les solutions subjectives, il y a toujours un critère commun pour tous les sujets, c'est-à-dire le critère de type $F(U_1, \ldots U_n)$.

Comme à l'heure actuelle il'est normal de postuler la thèse de l'académicien Vernadski, "aucune espèce vivante ne peut exister dans un milieu formé par ses déchets", nous n'allons donc pas discuter les possibilités de la création d'un milieu artificiel pour y habiter. Ainsi, nous devons postuler le désir de sauvegarder la stabilité de l'environnement, sauvegarder l'homéostasie comme à tous les sujets du système cybernétique, qui decrivent le fonctionnement de l'homme et de la biosphère". Mais, si c'est un système de Hermaier, il est raisonnable de considérer pour celui-ci les problèmes de recherche des solutions stables et collectives appartenant à l'ensemble de Paréto.

Ainsi, le système des raisonnements décrit donne certains fondements pour créer une théorie permettant d'étudier les types des solutions admissibles dans les processus de l'interactions de l'activité humaine et de l'environnement. Au fur et à mesure de son évolution, une telle théorie peut se trouver utile à résoudre beaucoup de problèmes de gestion des ressources, de l'activité de production dûs à la nécessité de la coexistance.

5. Simple Exemple d'Analyse d'un Système Cybernétique Non-Réflexe

Considérons maintenant quelques problèmes se rapportant au bloc de l'activité humaine.

Les recherches du problème de la construction des systèmes cybernétiques décrivant les relations entre l'homme et l'environnement montrent l'utilité de l'application de la théorie de reproduction et de l'instrument des fonctions de production. Avant tout ils fournissent un langage universel pour décrire les processus de production aussi bien que les processus ayant lieu en biotope.

Remarque:

Le choix d'un tel langage peut être argumenté non seulement pragmatiquement, mais aussi philosophiquement. Les processus de reproduction dont les recherches ont été commencées par Kené au XVIIIe siècle encore, et 100 ans plus tard, continuées par K. Marx avec une profondeur surpenante, sont en principe la base de tous les processus de la biotope. Le fonctionnement de toute substance vivante est avant tout la transformation d'une substance dans une autre. Et l'homme n'est qu'une partie de la biotope. Ainsi, le retour aux traditions dans le domaine philosophique souligne l'unité de la nature vivante et de notre planète et l'unité de l'homme et du reste de la biotope.

Le modèle le plus simple de l'activité de production, est un modèle universel. Il peut être utilisé pour beaucoup de problèmes pratiquement importants, mais il ne permet pas de décrire la particularité de la repartition des biens. C'est pourquoi pour illustrer ces idées on utilise le modèle de l'économie bisectorielle. Introduisons les désignations suivantes:

Φ_i le volume des fonds dans la section du numéro i,
L_i le nombre d'hommes occupés dans le processus de production,
w le "niveau de vie",
K_i les coefficients d'amortissement,
Y_i les investissements,
P_i le flux de produit,
Q_1 les réserves.

Les équations du modèle seront:

$$\dot{\phi}_i = Y_i - K_i\Phi_i \quad , \quad i = 1, 2 \quad ,$$

$$Q_i = P_1 - Y_1 - Y_2 \quad ,$$

$$Q_2 = P_2 - w(L_1 + L_2) \quad ,$$

$$P_i = F_i\ (\phi_i, L_i) \quad , i = 1, 2 \quad . \qquad (5,1)$$

Ici F_1 sont les fonctions de production. Toutes les grandeurs de l'équation (5,1) ne sont pas négatives.

Outre les variables de phase ϕ_i et Q_i, l'équation comprend les grandeurs Y_i, L_i et w qui dans le cadre de ce modèle doivent être considérés comme contrôles. En réalité, elles sont liées au fonctionnement des autres modèles, celui de repartition et d'investissement. Leur choix reflète les intérêts et les buts de l'état et de la société, en particulier les intérêts intégrés des consommateurs et des producteurs. Pour les décrire il faut ajouter encore une quantité de modèles et avant tout ceux du fonctionnement de l'argent, sans lequel la description des processus de répartition des biens n'est pas possible. Les équations qui décrivent l'activité de production sont les lois de la conservation. Elles ne dépendent pas de la nature sociale de la société. Quant aux autres modèles, ils ne sont pas standardisés et sont liés au fonctionnement du mécanisme social. Dans l'économie du marché, ils seront différents de ceux utilisés dans l'économie planifiée.

Ainsi, pour faire une analyse complète même d'un modèle bisectoriel de l'économie, il faut utiliser beaucoup d'autres modèles. Un schéma approximatif des modèles est représenté sur la Figure 2.

Ainsi, même dans des cas primitifs, on est obligé de considérer le système cybernétique d'une grande dimension. C'est pourquoi, si nous voulons étudier en détail un bloc de reproduction, nous devons paramétriser ces modèles d'une façon ou d'une autre. La paramétrisation permet à ce niveau une description agrégée des mécanismes qui fonctionnent dans l'organisme économique étudié.

Remarque:

En paramétrisant tel ou tel modèle, comme règle, nous ne l'écrivons même pas. C'est pourquoi l'élément important de l'analyse est un problème inverse de la paramétrisation, c'est-à-dire, trouver l'ensemble des modèles auxquels répond la paramétrisation décrite.

Le caractère d'une paramétrisation doit permettre d'étudier telles ou telles particularités du modèle de reproduction, trouver les possibilités essentielles des mécanismes virtuels théoriquement admissibles.

Remarque:

Une telle analyse ne présente pas qu'un intérêt théorique. Dans l'économie centralisée des pays socialistes, la science économique doit avoir pour objet, non seulement les mécanismes de planification mais aussi tout autre type de relations inverses. C'est un premier pas important dans la description des mécanismes du fonctionnement de l'organisme économique.

Considérons, par exemple, les capacités de la politique d'investissements. Dans cette situation il est normal de considérer comme donnée, le niveau de vie, $w = w(t)$.

Le choix de la relation $w = w(t)$ est en réalité la paramétrisation d'un système de modèles qui dans cet ouvrage est inclus dans le bloc unique du fond social contenant à son tour d'autres modèles. La grandeur w peut être le résultat d'un conflit entre les syndicats et les patrons où la conception du relèvement du niveau de vie dans l'économie planifiée etc.

Le nombre total des travailleurs,

$$L_1 + L_2 = L(t) \quad , \tag{5,2}$$

et le rapport,

$$\lambda = \frac{L_2}{L_1} \quad . \tag{5,3}$$

Convenons aussi de les considérer comme données.

Le pas suivant de l'analyse, est le choix d'une trajectoire de base. Supposons qu'il s'agisse de l'économie du marché. Alors, nous devons naturellement considérer comme trajectoire de base, un certain régime d'équilibre, celui de la prospérité sociale maximale. Quant à la condition de l'emploi complet, il faut évidemment la considérée comme appartenant aux conditions qui déterminent ce régime-là. Outre cela, ce régime sera caractérisé par une certaine croissance donnée par la consommation $w(t)$. Bien sûr, la fixation de la grandeur $w(t)$, c'est aussi le résultat de l'analyse d'une situation conflictuelle décrite par l'interaction du travail et du capital, c'est-à-dire un certain système des modèles de la conduite sociale.

Au régime d'équilibre à la croissance de la consommation donnée $w = w(t)$, il faut évidemment prendre $Q_i = 0$. En effet, les réserves croissantes ou décroissantes deviendront un stimulant supplémentaire à l'activité humaine et mettront en marche les mécanismes différents qui existent dans la société. Ainsi, la deuxième équation par rapport à Q_2 donne

$$F_2 \, (\tilde{\phi}_2 \, L_2) = wL(t) \quad , \tag{5,4}$$

c'est-à-dire qu'elle permettra de déterminer le volume nécessaire des fonds $\tilde{\phi}_2$ dans la deuxième section. Mais alors, on détermine univoquement l'investissement $\tilde{Y}_2$ à la deuxième section.

$$\tilde{Y}_2 = \dot{\tilde{\phi}}_2 + K_2 \, \tilde{\phi}_2 \quad . \tag{5,5}$$

Après cela, la première équation par rapport aux réserves donne

$$\tilde{Y}_1 = F_1(\tilde{\phi}_1 L_1) - \tilde{Y}_2 \quad ,$$

et on arrive à l'équation différentielle suivante par rapport aux fonds ϕ,

$$\tilde{\phi}_1 = F_1(\tilde{\phi}_1 L_1) - \tilde{Y}_2 - K_1 \tilde{\phi}_1 \quad . \qquad (5,6)$$

Ainsi, on peut prendre n'importe quelle solution au problème de Coshy pour l'équation (5,6) comme trajectoire de base.

Ensuite, on construit la théorie des perturbations. Dans le cas décrit, on linéarise le problème par rapport à la trajectoire d'équilibre de base

$$\phi_i = \tilde{\phi}_i + \rho_i \quad ,$$

$$Y_i = \tilde{Y} + y_i \quad ,$$

$$Q_i = \tilde{Q}_i + q_i \quad .$$

Finalement, on arrive à un système de 4 équations de premier ordre. Si nous admettons que $w = w(\varepsilon t)$, $L = L(\varepsilon,t)$, $\lambda = \lambda(\varepsilon t)$ c'est-à-dire que toutes les grandeurs exogènes sont des fonctions de temps qui varient lentement, alors que le système perturbé sera un système linéaire aux coefficients variables et ses grandeurs y_1 et y_2 seront des fonctions libres.

Ces grandeurs doivent réaliser les relations inverses selon les paramètres envisagés du systèmes. S'il s'agit de l'économie du marché, les paramètres envisagés ne sont que le surplus ou le manque de la marchandise au marché, c'est-à-dire les grandeurs q_1 et q_2. C'est pourquoi dans le cas décrit, il est normal de prendre

$$y_1 = c_1 q_1 , \quad y_2 = -c_2 q_2 \quad .$$

où c_i sont certains coefficients positifs des efforts.

<u>Remarque</u>:

Ainsi on a paramétrisé le mécanisme du marché sous forme de relation inverse négative. Dans le cadre du schéma donné, il est impossible de déterminer la valeur de C_1. Dans ce but on a besoin d'une analyse plus détaillée du modèle d'investissement. De toute façon, la relation inverse (5,7) qualitativement négative correspond au désir des producteurs de maximaliser le profit attendu. Ayant pris y_1 et y_2 en forme de (5,7), on reçoit un système fermé des équations. Pour ce système on peut démontrer l'affirmation suivante.

La solution de n'importe quel problème de Coshy aux valeurs initiales non-négatives pour l'équation (5,6), si $w(\varepsilon t)$ et $L(\varepsilon t)$ sont croissants monotone, n'est pas stable et avec cela les variables caractérisant la deuxième section sont d'un caractère oscillatoire et les variables caractérisant la première section sont oscillatoirement instable à la croissance exponentielle de l'amplitude.

Ce résultat est d'une grande importance politique et économique. Il montre qu'aux conditions de l'économie du marché à la croissance simultanée de la consommation et de la conservation de l'empoi, la stabilisation de croissance due aux changements d'investissements n'est pas possible.

Dans l'économie planifiée, on doit prendre comme trajectoire de base celle qui peut réaliser une certaine conception de développement de la production. Dans plusieurs ouvrages, cette conception est formulée comme une maximisation de la consommation, par exemple, de la façon suivante:

$$J(Y_1Y_2) = \int_0^t w(t)\, L(t)\, dt \Rightarrow \max \qquad (5,8)$$

Sans discuter profondément de telles conceptions, notons qu'elles aboutissent toutes aux problèmes mathématiques dont la solution ne peut probablement pas être acceptée par les économistes. En effet, à cause de la linéarité des problèmes par rapport aux contrôles, les contrôles optimaux sont toujours d'un caractère de relais.

$$\begin{aligned} Y_1 &= F_1 & \forall t < t^* \\ Y_2 &= 0 & \forall t > t^* \\ Y_2 &= 0 & \forall t < t^* \\ Y_2 &= F_1 & \forall t > t^* \end{aligned} \qquad (5,9)$$

où la valeur de t^* dépend de l'intervalle de la planification T.

L'économie n'aime pas les changements brusques et les solutions du type (5,9) ne peuvent pas être utilisées dans la pratique. De plus, elles ne peuvent probablement pas être réalisées. Le défaut d'une telle analyse consiste en ce que la formulation du problème (5,8) ne tient pas compte de la variété des critères, l'un desquels exige une minimisation des modifications structurales. Ce fait peut être formalisé de la manière suivante: au lieu de Y_i on introduit un nouveau contrôle u:

$$Y_1 = u\, F_1 \quad , \quad Y_2 = (1-u)\, F_2 \quad , \quad u \,\varepsilon\, (01) \quad .$$

Alors la minimisation de la modification peut être formalisée de la facon suivante

$$J^*(u) = \int_o^t (u-u_o)^2 \, dt \Rightarrow \min \qquad (5,10)$$

où u_o est la répartition des investissements au cours de la dernière année de la période du plan précédent.

Il en résulte que la trajectoire de base est la solution d'un problème de conflit aux fonctionnelles (5,9) et (5,10), c'est-à-dire que son choix, outre la solution d'une série de problèmes d'optimisation (nécessaire pour la construction de l'ensemble de Paréto), exige encore une analyse non-formelle.

En effet, une analyse formelle peut donner seulement la dépendance J(J*) et pas plus. Cette dépendance est représentée sur la Figure 3. Quel point de cette courbe peut-on prendre, c'est-à-dire, lequel des contrôles optimaux représentés sur la Figure 4, faut-il prendre comme celui de base? A cette question il est impossible de répondre à l'aide d'une théorie formelle dans le cadre du modèle décrit.

Après avoir fait l'étape des considérations non-formelles et ayant choisi la trajectoire de base, on peut de nouveau linéariser le problème et commencer à étudier les mécanismes des relations inverses. Notamment on a la possibilité d'utiliser les relations inverses linéaires du type (5,7). Il en résulte que l'analyse ultérieure du fonctionnement du modèle peut être faite suivant le schéma de ce paragraphe; ajoutons aux conditions de l'économie socialiste centralisée, les fonds appartiennent aussi aux paramètres envisagés. C'est pourquoi, en principe, on peut créer des mécanismes de stabilisation du type des relations inverses linéaires seulement à l'aide des investissements.

6. Modèle de la Mise à l'Amende pour la Pollution de l'Environnement

Encore un exemple instructif d'un système cybernétique aux plusieurs sujets qui est donné par les problèmes du fonctionnement d'une région où se trouvent les entreprises polluant l'environnement (l'eau, par exemple).

Désignons par ϕ_i (i = 1, 2...N) les fonds de ces entreprises. Convenons de décrire les changements de fonds par les équations suivantes

$$\dot{\phi} = Y_i - K_i \phi_i \quad . \qquad (6.1)$$

où

Y_i investissement,
K_i coefficients d'amortissement.

Chaque entreprise produit par unité de temps la production P_i

$$P_i = F_i(\phi_i) \quad . \tag{6,2}$$

où

F_i fonction de production.

Les entreprises produisent non seulement un produit utile, mais aussi un produit insalubre. Désignons par Π_i le vecteur du flux des substances encrassantes.

$$\Pi_i = f_i(P_i, V_i) \quad . \tag{6,3}$$

où

V_i dépenses de l'entreprise au perfectionnement des technologies ou à la purification dans les conditions d'usine.

On va considérer la situation quand dans la région outre les producteurs il existe encore un sujet du système cybernétique, c'est-à-dire le contrôle régional. Il a le droit de mettre à l'amende les autres sujets.

$$w_i = C\Pi_i \quad , \tag{6,4}$$

et dispose des composantes du vecteur C suivant certains buts. On en parlera plus tard. Tous les autres contrôles Y_i et V_i sont à la disposition des producteurs.

Pour ne pas compliquer l'exposé, convenons que l'investissement s'effectue seulement à partir des ressources intérieures des entreprises et tous les capitaux libres sont dispensés aux investissements. Cela signifie qu'on a des relations de balance suivantes

$$F_i(\phi_i) = Y_i + V_i + w_i \quad . \tag{6,5}$$

Considérons la description subjective du système du point de vue du sujet que nous avons appelé contrôle régional.

Pour prendre telle ou telle décision, le sujet doit faire certaines hypothèses sur la conduite des autres sujets. Il est normal d'adopter l'hypothèse suivante. Le choix des grandeurs V_i et w_i est déterminé par la condition

$$J_i = V_i + w_i \Rightarrow \min \tag{6,6}$$

Puisque "le contrôle régional" a le droit de faire le premier pas, c'est-à-dire qu'il peut faire savoir d'avance aux autres sujets la valeur de l'amende, l'hypothèse (6,6) permettra de déterminer le réflexe des producteurs. En effet, puisqu'on a

$$J_i = V_i + C\Pi_i = V_i + Cf_i(F_i\phi_i)\ V_i \quad ,$$

la condition (6,6) permettra de déterminer le volume d'investissement au perfectionnement des technologies et à la purification à l'intérieur de l'usine

$$V_i = \Psi_i(c_1\ \phi_i) \qquad (6,7)$$

Introduisons encore, pour simplifier, quelques suppositions: toutes les ressources reçue par le contrôle régional à l'aide des amendes sont dépensées à la purification centralisée de la sphère. Outre cela, limitons-nous au cas où Π_i sont des ckolaires. L'équation qui caractérise le changement du niveau de la pollution du milieu, peut être écrite de la façon suivante:

$$x = \sum \Pi_i - f(x) - w(\sum w_i) \quad , \qquad (6,8)$$

où w est la quantité des déchets insalubres qui sont exterminés à l'aide de la purification centralisée

$$w = \mu \sum w_i \quad ,$$

et la fonction f(x) est la purification naturelle.

En supposant que les producteurs sauront sa politique des amendes, le contrôle régional selon l'analyse effectuée doit admettre que

$$w_i = cf_i[F_i\ (\phi_i),\ \psi[c_1\phi_i)] = cf_i^*\ (c_1\phi_i) \quad .$$

Alors on récrit l'équation (6,8) de la façon suivante

$$x = \sum f_i^*\ (c_1\phi_i)\ (1-\mu c) - f(x) \quad . \qquad (6,9)$$

Il est temps de discuter des motifs dont le contrôle régional doit tenir compte avant de mettre à l'amende.

Avant tout, le contrôle régional doit avoir pour but la condition que la qualité de l'environnement ne s'altère pas; c'est-à-dire pour que

$$\dot{x} \leqslant 0 \qquad (6.10)$$

Cette condition signifie qu'il s'agit de la maximisation d'un certain critère, qui peut être formalisé par exemple, de la façon suivante:

$$J^1 = \begin{array}{l} I,\ \text{si}\ \dot{x} \leqslant 0 \\ 0,\ \text{si}\ \dot{x} > 0 \end{array}$$

Mais le critère (6,10), dont le contrôle régional doit tenir compte, n'est pas unique. Il est intéressé encore au développement industrial de la région. Ce critère peut être formalisé de manières différentes, par exemple on peut admettre que le contrôle régional cherche à avoir une trajectoire stable de croissance continue

$$\frac{d\phi_\Sigma}{dt} = \delta \tag{6,11}$$

où

$\phi_\Sigma = \sum \phi_i$

δ un certain paramètre qui doit être le plus grand possible du point de vue du contrôle régional, c'est-à-dire δ est un critère de plus.

Ainsi, ayant pris certaines hypothèse concernant les réactions possibles des producteurs dues aux valeurs des amendes, nous n'avons pas encore fait tout le système entièrement réflexe.

L'étape suivante, tout comme au problème précédent, c'est le choix d'une trajectoire de base.

La condition (6,11)

$$\Sigma Y_i - \Sigma K_i\phi_i \equiv \Sigma F_i(\phi_i) - \Sigma\psi_i(c_1\phi_i) - c\Sigma f_i^*(c_1\phi_i) - \Sigma K_i\phi_i = 0$$

nous permettra de déterminer C

$$C = C(\phi_1,\ \phi_2,\ldots.\phi_N,\ \varepsilon)\quad ,$$

après qui l'équation (6,9) aura l'expression suivante

$$x = X(\phi_1,\ \phi_2,\ldots\phi_N,\varepsilon) - f(x) \tag{6,12}$$

et l'équation dynamique (6,1) peut être récrite de la façon suivante

$$\dot{\phi}_i = Z_i\ (\phi_1,\ \phi_2,\ldots..\phi_N,\ \varepsilon) \tag{6,13}$$

Maintenant le chercheur a à résoudre le problème suivant: il faut vérifier que le problème de Coshy

$$x(t_o) = x_o$$
$$\phi_i(t_o) = \phi_{io} \tag{6,14}$$

pour le système (6,12) - (6,13) détermine les trajectoires satisfaisantes au critère (6,10).

Ici deux situations différentes peuvent surgir. Premièrement, il peut se trouver qu'il existe tout un intervalle E pour lequel la condition (6,10) est valable, on a besoin de nouveau de faire une analyse non-formelle. En effet, les méthodes formelles peuvent fournir la dépendance suivante

$$\dot{x} = \dot{x}(\phi_1, \phi_2, \ldots \phi_N, \varepsilon) \quad , \qquad (6,15)$$

et finalement elles permettront de calculer

$$\lim_{t \to \infty} x(t) = x^\infty(\varepsilon) \quad . \qquad (6,16)$$

Deuxièmement, il peut arriver qu'il n'existe pas d'intervalle auquel la réalisation de la condition (6,10) soit possible. Dans ce cas-là on est hors du domaine de l'utilisation du modèle. Il est impossible de garantir à la fois le rythme positif d'accroissement et la diminution de ses influences nuisibles, si on utilise comme contrôle seulement les amendes. L'analyse dans ce cas exige un modèle plus précis.

Revenons maintenant au premier cas. Supposons qu'on ait choisi un certain $\varepsilon = \varepsilon^*$. Les conditions (6,4) déterminent alors la trajectoire unique ϕ_i^*. Il nous reste à étudier sa stabilité. S'il se trouve qu'elle est stable, l'analyse est finie à ce point-là.

Supposons qu'elle soit instable. Alors, il faut construire un certain mécanisme de relations inverses. Il est convenu de considérer que les grandeurs mesurées sont des volumes de production. Alors il faut poser que

$$c = c^* + \delta c \quad ,$$

et construire le mécanisme sous une forme suivante

$$\delta c = \delta c \quad (\phi - \phi^*) \quad .$$

Le système considéré n'a pas été celui de Hermaier. Il appartenait à un cas particulier du système hiérarchique décrit dans [3]. Nous sommes partis de la supposition que tous les producteurs sont intéressés seulement à une chose, c'est-à-dire à la minimisation de leurs dépenses pour éliminer la pollution. Cependant, dans le cas général, il n'en est pas de même. Le fait-même de l'existance du "contrôle régional" montre que les producteurs ont certains intérêts communs. C'est pourquoi en faisant une analyse plus approfondie, il faut considérer que les intérêts des producteurs doivent être formulés sous une forme suivante

$$J_i = V_i + w_i + \lambda_i R(x) \Rightarrow \min \qquad (6,17)$$

où

λ_i coefficients de pondération

R^i fonction du niveau de pollution, c'est-à- ce la grandeur qui dépend des actions simultanées de tous les producteurs.

L'introduction des fonctionnelles du type (6,17) ne change pas la nature hiérarchique du système. Ainsi on est arrivé aux systèmes hiérarchiques du type de Hermaier, c'est-à-dire à une classe de systèmes pratiquement inétudiés.

7. Modèle Minimal Pour l'Analyse des Processus Economiques Ecologiques

En parlant des processus économiques écologiques, on a en vue une analyse aux intervalles de temps assez larges comptant des dixaines d'années. Cela produit plusieurs limitations à la structure des modèles faisant partie du bloc de l'activité humaine (voir Figure 1.). C'est pourquoi il est raisonnable d'introduire la notion d'un modèle minimal de ce bloc, c'est-à-dire énumérer les facteurs principaux dont l'ignorance peut défigurer qualitativement le caractère de l'évolution des valeurs étudiées.

Pour l'analyse des processus d'interaction de l'homme et de la biosphère ayant en vue l'aspect perspectif, il faut avant tout tenir compte des facteurs du progrès scientifique et technique. En effet, c'est le progrès scientifique et technique qui sert de cause essentielle à l'intensification de l'activité de production et par la suite de tous les processus de l'interaction de l'homme avec l'environnement. Comment donc peut-on calculer ce facteur tellement indéfini et l'introduire dans le modèle.

Le progrès scientifique et technique déforme avant tout les fonctions de production. Il existe beaucoup de diverses conceptions pour décrire leurs changements, mais la caractéristique principale généralement admis c'est l'augmentation de intensification des fonds. Ce dernier signifie qu'aux mêmes fonds et au même nombre de travailleurs le flux de produits augmente avec le développement du progrès scientifique et technique

$$P_i = F_i(\phi_i, L_i, \partial_i) \qquad (7,1)$$

où

∂_i signifie le facteur d'efficacité.

Dans un simple cas linéaire cette dépendance a la forme suivante

$$P_i = \partial_i F_i(\phi_i, L_i, 1) \qquad (7,2)$$

où

$F_i(\phi_i, L_i, 1)$ coïncide avec la fonction considérée dans le paragraphe précédent.

On peut prendre des formes plus compliquées pour tenir compte de l'effet du progrès scientifique et technique. Ainsi, par exemple, la quantité des fonds de la première section, rapportée à l'unité du produit de la deuxième section est une caractéristique très importante du niveau technique de l'économie. La description détaillée n'est pas le but de ce rapport-là. Pour illustrer les structures d'un simple modèle nous prenons l'écriture sous les formes (7,1) - (7,2).

La variation ∂_i dépend des investissements au progrès scientifique et technique et l'efficacité acquise des fonds:

$$\dot{\partial}_i = \delta_i(y_i^*, \partial_i) \quad , \qquad (7,3)$$

où y_i^* est l'investissement correspondant.

La représentation sous forme (7,2) - (7,3) est évidemment une simple paramétrisation du progrès sciencitifique et technique. Il est certain que dans les conditions actuelles le progrès scientifique et technique se transforme en branche entière, mais la paramétrisation du type (7,2) - (7,3) permet d'utiliser effectivement l'information existante.

Aux conditions actuelles, il est nécessaire aussi de tenir compte des changements des ressources. Comme l'extraction des ressources attire de jour en jour plus de force et de moyens à la mesure de leur épuisement, les ressources doivent être choisies dans une branche à part.

Il existe plusieurs conceptions pour tenir compte de la restriction des ressources. Je crois qu'il est mieux d'utiliser la supposition que la structure des fonctions de production des branches d'extraction à la forme suivante

$$P = P(\phi_1 \; Q) \quad , \qquad (7,4)$$

où Q est la quantité des ressources déjà extraites. La fonction (7,4) est la fonction décroissante Q, et il est à noter qu'à la valeur donnée P la courbe intégrale de l'équation

$$\dot{Q} = P(\phi_1 \; Q) \quad ,$$

a au certain t^* final une asymptote verticale.

Le plus compliqué et discutable c'est le choix de la description des blocs biothiques d'un modèle économique. Je crois que les biocénoses exploitées, c'est-à-dire les cénoses de bois, agrocénoses, dynamique des populations des poissons doivent finalement être décrites à l'aide de l'instrument des fonctions de production et doivent être considérées comme une certaine branche.

Quant aux autres processus, ayant lieu dans la biosphère il faut les apprécier dans un modèle minimal à l'aide de certaines fonctionnelles $J(P_1,\ldots P_K)$, qui dépendent du volume du produit de la production $P_1\ldots.P_K$.

Ainsi, un minimal système cybernétique pour la description de l'interaction de l'homme et de la biosphère représente un certain système dynamique contrôlé dans lequel on utilise comme variables de phase les fonds des branches différentes, les objets existants des produits, les volumes des ressources extraites et des intensifications des fonds. Nous pouvons représenter ce système sous une forme suivante

$$\dot{x} = f(x, \xi, \eta, u_1,\ldots u_K) \qquad (7,5)$$

où U_j sont des contrôles qui sont à la disposition du système du numéro j et qui sont les investissements, les volumes des productions etc. Les intérêts des sujets sont différents. Chacun d'eux a ses propres buts que nous allons formaliser comme désir de maximiser les fonctionnelles $J_j(u_j)$. Enfin, il y a un système des fonctionnelles

$$I_s = I_s(U_1,\ldots U_K) \quad , \quad s = 1, 2\ldots S \quad , \qquad (7,6)$$

dont les valeurs critiques déterminent dans cet espace des fonctionnelles, le domaine de la homéostasie

$$I_s > I_j^* \quad .$$

Les grandeurs I_s^* désignent les caractéristiques limites, admissibles du milieu extérieur (par exemple des diverses pollutions la qualité de l'oxygène produit, etc.).

Soit la fonction $F(U_1,\ldots U_K)$ décrit la distance de la surface (7,6) par exemple

$$F = \min_s \frac{Is}{Is^*} \qquad (7,7)$$

Il est évident que chacun des sujets est intéressé à maximiser cette fonction. Outre cela, à la condition de la homéostasie doit contenir une certaine condition de type de stabilité de la trajectoire du système économique. On écrit cette condition sous forme de

$$I_o \Rightarrow \max$$

où

$$I_o = \begin{cases} 0, & \text{si le système stable} \\ -\infty, & \text{si le système instable.} \end{cases} \qquad (7,8)$$

Ainsi, les intérêts de chacun des sujets peut être écrit sous forme de w_i=>max, où

$$w_i = \psi_i\{J_i(u_i),\ Io\ (U_1,\ldots U_K),\ F(U_1,\ldots U_K)\} \qquad (7,9)$$

ψ_i est une certaine contraction des critères décrits.

A la fonctionnelle w_i, on a tenu compte des intérêts personnels du sujet et des intérêts "commun pour tout système". Si le système est instable, on a $Io = -\infty$ et le système ne peut pas exister. C'est pourquoi, au lieu de fonctionnelle (7,8) il faut considérer la fonctionnelle où toutes les variables où tous u_i appartiennent à un ensemble pour lequel

$$Io = 0\ . \qquad (7,10)$$

Ainsi, le système minimal est un système de Hermaier d'une forme speciale.

CONCLUSION

Comme il a déjà été mentionné dans l'introduction, le but de l'ouvrage est de tracer les voies de la création d'un langage de la description du fonctionnement des systèmes non-réflexes et notamment des systèmes économiques et de proposer quelques conceptions initiales d'une description formelle et de présenter dans ce contexte le contenu et le rôle des richesses mathématiques. Il me semble que la formalisation proposée est très universelle. Elle décrit aussi la situation qui surgit à l'appréciation des plans perspectifs à long terme du développement régional et à la solution des divers problèmes de la coopération économique internationale. Le dernier fait est surtout important parce que la description proposée met peut être la base pour construire une théorie mathématique de coexistance. Il permet aussi d'inclure dans un système unique les processus ayant lieu dans la biotope et dans un organisme économique.

En exposant les idées d'un caractère méthodique, nous avons cité quelques exemples. Ils illustrent une circonstance très importante.

L'analyse des systèmes non-réflexes est impossible si on ne s'oriente qu'aux méthodes formelles. Il est indispensable d'utiliser des approches euristiques. Même la réduction du système initial non-réflexe à un système réflexe est impossible sans hypothèses supplémentaires, c'est-à-dire sans description subjective.

Cela veut dire que l'analyse de l'évolution du système et les processus de la prise des décisions exigent un dialogue homme-machine.

Il existe une opinion (apparue tout d'abord aux USA) que le dialogue homme-machine décharge les mathématiciens de plusieurs obligations et simplifie les méthodes mathématiques utilisées. Je n'accepte absolument pas cette idée. Le dialogue homme-machine ne simplifie pas, mais complique l'instrument des recherches nécessaires. Il déplace ces recherches dans une autre sphère.

Le dialogue est aussi un algorithme ~~qui~~ enlève l'incertitude met en évidence les intérêts objectifs et les représentations objectives en raison desquels finalement on prend des décisions. Le but de l'organisation d'un dialogue est de faire correspondre le mieux possible les décisions à ces intérêts dont la formulation exacte n'est pas possible.

L'homme ne peut répondre qu'aux questions relativement simples. Donc la tâche d'un mathématicien est de faire l'analyse de telle manière pour qu'un expert puisse donner seulement des réponses univoques. Si on n'y arrive pas, cela signifie que le modèle exige d'être développé et de tenir compte des nouveaux facteurs ou bien, que l'instrument utilisé pour l'analyse du modèle est insuffisant aux buts qui sont posés par un chercheur.

Références:

[1] Galbraith, J.K., *Economics and the Public Purpose*, Mifflin, Boston 1973.

[2] Zadeh, L., *Concept d'une Variable Linguistique et de son Utilisation pour une Prise de Décision Approximative*, Mir, Moscou 1976.

[3] Hermaier, Yu.B. et I.A. Vatel, *Jeux de Fonctions Objectives avec Vector Hiérarchique*, Izvestia de l'Académie des Sciences de l'URSS, Cybernétique Technique, No. 1974.

[4] Moiseev, N.N., *Eléments de Contrôle Optimal de la Théorie des Systèmes*, Nauka, 1975.

Plan Principal d'Interactions
Homme - Environnement

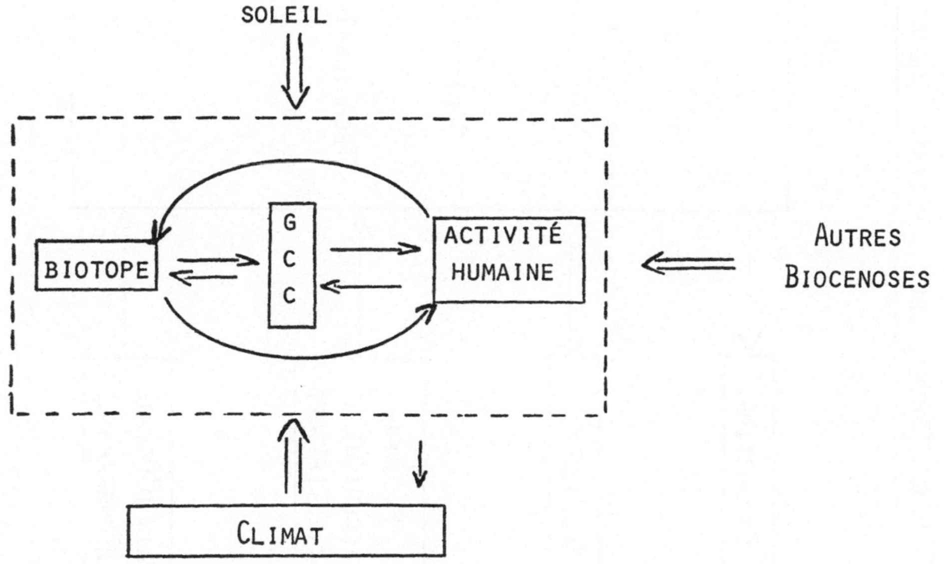

T CLIMAT >> T

Figure 1. Groupes de cénoses étant exploités (forêts, agrocénoses, etc.) peuvent être inclus dans l'activité humaine.

PLAN GÉNÉRAL DE L'ACTIVITÉ HUMAINE

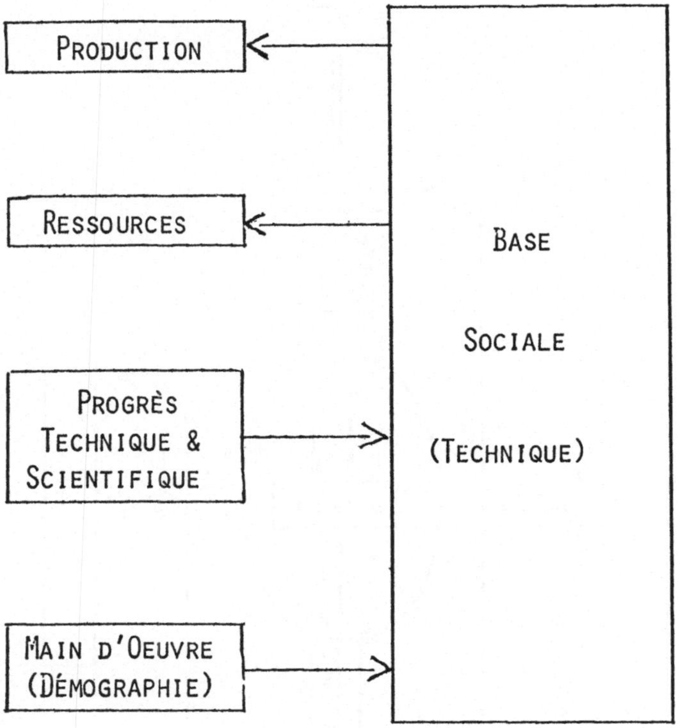

Figure 2.

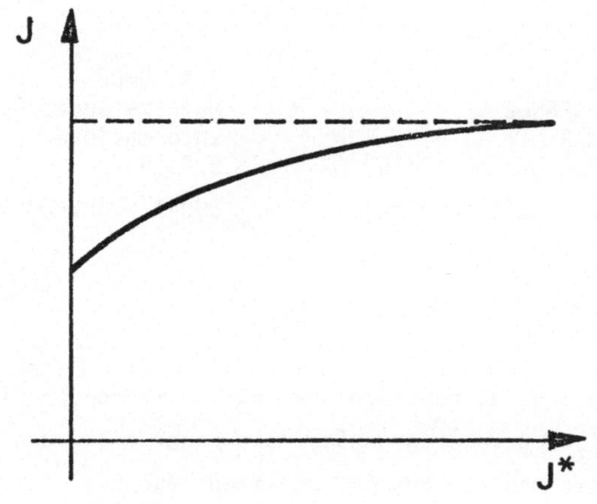

FIGURE:3

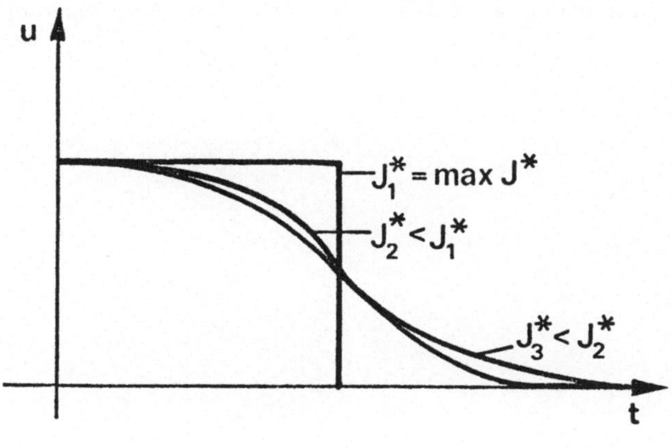

FIGURE: 4

L'APPLICATION DU CONTROLE AUX MODELES MACROECONOMIQUES FRANCAIS : EXPERIENCES ET PERSPECTIVES D'AVENIR

M. DELEAU
P. MALGRANGE
CEPREMAP
142, Rue du Chevaleret
75013 - PARIS (France)

B.A. OUDET
Mathématiques Appliquées
Informatique
B.P. 53
38041 - GRENOBLE Cedex (France)

1. INTRODUCTION

L'application des techniques du contrôle aux modèles macroéconomiques s'est particulièrement développée ces dernières années. Des congrès lui sont consacrés régulièrement(1) et plusieurs manuels ont été récemment publiés(2).

Les études réalisées en France même dans ce domaine sont toutefois restées, à ce jour, peu nombreuses. Il semble qu'il faille chercher une raison de ce moindre développement dans les conditions de construction et d'utilisation des modèles spécifiques à notre pays. A cet égard, il convient de souligner une caractéristique importante du processus de modélisation macroéconomique français. Dans leur quasi-totalité, les modèles existants de l'économie française ont été conçus pour servir des processus administratifs particuliers et ont été, pour la plupart, élaborés par l'administration elle-même. Le tableau 1 en donne les caractéristiques essentielles.

---

(1) - Ces congrès sont organisés par le National Bureau of Economic Research chaque année (une sélection des communications est publiée dans Annals of Economic and Social Measurement) et par IFAC/IFORS (Congrès de Warwick 73, et Vienne 77).

(2) - Voir Chow [1975], Aoki [1976].

Modèle	Base Temporelle	Nombre d'équations	Référence	Organisme Constructeur	Type et Période d'utilisation
ZOGOL	Annuel	107	HERZOG, OLIVE (1966)	Direction de la Prévision	Préparation des budgets économiques (67-68)
DECA	Annuel	300	BILLAUDOT (1971)	Direction de la Prévision	Préparation des budgets économiques (69-73)
FIFI	Annuel (moyen terme)	1500 (app.)	AGLIETTA et al. (1973) BUSSERY et al. (1975)	INSEE	Préparation du Plan (68)
STAR	Annuel	120	BOULLE et al. (1974)	Direction de la Prévision	Préparation des budgets économiques (74-)
METRIC	Trimestriel	250 (app.)	DE MENIL, NASSE (1976)	INSEE Direction de la Prévision	Prévision à court terme
D.M.S.	Annuel	1300 (app.)	FOUQUET et al. (1976)	INSEE	Préparation du Plan
REGINA	Annuel (moyen terme)	n.d. (plusieurs milliers)	COURBIS, PRAGER (1974)	GAMA	Planification régionale

Tableau 1 - Modèles économiques d'ensemble de l'économie française

Les modèles macroéconomiques français sont ainsi destinés, dans leur ensemble, à fournir des projections susceptibles d'éclairer la préparation de la politique économique de l'Etat, de court ou de moyen terme, par la révélation des tensions existantes et l'évaluation quantitative de mesures alternatives. Les travaux correspondants sont des travaux techniques largement internes à l'administration, effectués de manière discrétionnaire en fonction des demandes de celle-ci. La subordination de l'activité modélisatrice à des processus administratifs spécifiques implique par ailleurs une absence de "concurrence" entre modèles. Chaque modèle a sa vocation propre, liée en particulier au champ temporel couvert, et qu'il satisfait de manière exclusive (jusqu'à son remplacement éventuel par une autre structure). On mesure ainsi les différences existant en matière de modélisation macroéconomique entre la situation française, plus centralisée et administrative mais aussi directement tournée vers l'opératoire, et la situation américaine, par exemple, où la construction et l'utilisation de modèles s'effectuent en particulier dans des centres universitaires, de manière plus concurrentielle et publique, mais aussi plus "académique" en un sens.

Ces différences expliquent assez largement le moindre développement en France de l'application des méthodes d'optimisation aux modèles[(1)], ces méthodes n'offrant aux yeux des utilisateurs administratifs que peu d'intérêt en tant qu'instruments de gestion des modèles (caractère discrétionnaire du processus d'utilisation) et la priorité accordée aux préoccupations opératoires reléguant au second plan la poursuite de recherches jugées plus "gratuites". Les expériences mêmes de contrôle réalisées jusqu'à présent et présentées ci-dessous doivent certains de leurs traits à la situation qui vient d'être décrite. Elles se sont en effet déroulées dans une double direction. Les méthodes d'optimisation ont tout d'abord été utilisées dans une optique "*théorie de la politique économique*" (TINBERGEN (1952), THEIL (1964)) pour éclairer méthodologiquement un problème concret lié à la préparation des décisions publiques et atteindre certaines conclusions quantitatives. Il en a été ainsi dans l'opération Optimix, où l'on a recouru à un schéma classique d'optimisation pour donner un traitement formalisé de la liaison entre politique économique de moyen terme et politique économique de court terme, entre Plan et Budget. Cette opération, ses caractéristiques, ses résultats sont présentés et discutés dans la partie 2. Par ailleurs, les méthodes d'optimisation ont été utilisées en tant que *techniques d'analyse des modèles*. Une préoccupation croissante s'est faite jour, en effet, pour la réalisation d'études visant à fournir une "évaluation" des modèles auxquels l'administration a recours et, par là, à en accroître la fiabilité. Il est apparu que les méthodes d'optimisation étaient pour ce faire des techniques efficaces, largement complémentaires d'autres approches. Divers travaux correspondant à ce second mode

(1) - Il faut noter également que le retard initial de la France en matière de modélisation - le processus n'ayant démarré avec ampleur qu'à partir des années 65- se retrouve mécaniquement au niveau des applications du contrôle.

d'utilisation des méthodes du contrôle sont présentés dans la partie 3. Enfin, la conclusion envisage des perspectives possibles d'avenir pour la poursuite de telles études en France.

2. APPLICATION DES METHODES D'OPTIMISATION AUX PROBLEMES DE POLITIQUE ECONOMIQUE : L'OPERATION OPTIMIX(1)

Les travaux réunis sous le vocable d'Optimix constituent une application du formalisme et des techniques de l'optimisation à un problème économique spécifique : la liaison entre Plan et Budget. Nous décrirons brièvement les conditions dans lesquelles se pose ce problème (i), pour traiter ensuite de la formalisation retenue (ii) et des travaux numériques effectués (iii). On conclut sur les enseignements qui peuvent être tirés de cette opération (iv).

i) On sait que le Plan Français est un plan dit de moyen terme qui porte sur une période de cinq ans. Les choix macroéconomiques qu'il fixe sont principalement discutés à partir de *projections relatives à l'année terminale et déterminées en fonction de l'information disponible au début du Plan*. Ces projections n'appréhendent donc pas explicitement ni le problème du "cheminement" de l'économie entre année de départ et année terminale, ni celui des "accidents de parcours" susceptibles de contredire les hypothèses retenues. Il s'ensuit que le plan est largement silencieux sur les modalités ponctuelles, année par année, de la réalisation de ses options.

D'où la signification ambigüe du Plan pour la définition de la politique économique annuelle telle qu'elle s'inscrit dans le Budget de l'Etat. Deux difficultés peuvent se cumuler en effet. D'une part, si les conditions de départ sont excessivement "heurtées" (exemple : VIIe Plan), la référence au cheminement moyen "régulier" associable au Plan (exemple : croissance à x % sur les cinq années du Plan), est tout à fait illusoire. D'autre part, la survenance d'aléas majeurs en cours de Plan, internes (Mai 68 pour le Ve Plan) ou externes (crise du pétrole pour le VIe Plan), peut rendre totalement caduques les hypothèses initiales et donc, dans une large mesure, les choix qui leur sont associés. La conception traditionnelle d'un "Plan-cible", spécifié en termes atemporels et rigides, paraît ainsi inadéquate aux conditions économiques actuelles et laisse irrésolu le problème des implications du Plan pour la politique économique annuelle.

(1) - La plupart des travaux afférents à l'opération Optimix ont été réalisés par des chercheurs du CEPREMAP. Ils se sont échelonnés sur la période 68-70 (préparation du VIe Plan). L'exposé donné ci-après s'inspire largement de la présentation plus complète figurant dans l'article de DELEAU, GUESNERIE, MALGRANGE (1973) (voir aussi id. (1972)).

ii) La formalisation de ce problème retenue dans l'opération Optimix se fonde sur l'altération de trois éléments fondamentaux du schéma français de planification :

- considération de trajectoires au lieu de points terminaux, et donc référence à un *modèle dynamique* et non plus statique ;
- passage d'une spécification d'objectifs rigides ("à la Tinbergen") à la définition d'une *fonction objectif* ;
- prise en compte explicite des éléments "risqués" conduisant à une *conception stratégique* du Plan.

Cette formalisation utilise donc tous les éléments d'un schéma décisionnel classique, l'originalité essentielle en étant la recherche d'une cohérence avec les caractéristiques concrètes du VIème Plan. Nous décrirons brièvement chacun des éléments constitutifs.

Le modèle utilisé pour l'opération a été DECA, modèle dynamique annuel de 300 équations environ, servant à l'époque à la Direction de la Prévision pour des projections à deux-trois ans (tableau 1). Le modèle a été simulé dans l'opération Optimix sur la période du VIème Plan (71-75). On a pu prendre en compte trois instruments :

- dépenses publiques,
- transferts aux ménages,
- transferts aux entreprises.

La politique correspondante est donc exclusivement budgétaire et fiscale, sans composante monétaire ou financière, ce qui traduit une limitation de DECA (modèle non intégré).

La définition d'une fonction objectif a constitué une partie très importante de l'opération (voir GUESNERIE, MALGRANGE (1972)). En effet, contrairement à d'autres recherches où cette fonction joue un rôle quasi-technique ou expérimental, il était essentiel dans le cas étudié qu'elle puisse être considérée comme véritablement *"associée" au VIème Plan*. La méthode de détermination suivie a consisté en l'usage combiné d'interviews et de techniques d'optimum inverse. Les objectifs annuels retenus étant au nombre de sept (consommation des ménages, consommation collective, chômage, pression fiscale, capacité de financement des administrations, stock de devises, investissement) et l'aspect intertemporel soulevant des problèmes spécifiques de valorisation (variables de fin de période).

Enfin, dernier point de la spécification, les éléments de risque et la manière dont ils conduisent à une conception stratégique de la planification.

Deux aléas reconnus comme majeurs ont pu être transcrits dans les termes du modèle. Le premier, d'ordre interne, porte sur la croissance des salaires et a été identifié à la variable résiduelle de la relation de PHILLIPS. L'autre aléa, externe, affecte la croissance de la demande extérieure, donnée exogène dans DECA. Notons que l'on a supposé par ailleurs une absence d'incertitude sur les coefficients structurels du modèle. Les aléas ont été pris indépendants entre eux et de période à période, leur variance étant estimée économétriquement.

La reconnaissance explicite de ces aléas conduit évidemment à substituer à l'énoncé d'une action fixée une fois pour toutes, la recherche d'une *règle d'action* qui précise des valeurs alternatives pour les instruments retenus en fonction de l'information (progressivement) acquise sur les aléas. Il a paru à cet égard particulièrement pertinent de faire jouer un rôle important à la *structure d'information* retenue (MARSCHACK, RADNER (1972)) qui spécifie les "évènements" pris en compte pour la fixation à chaque date des divers instruments. On a pu ainsi faire correspondre certains schémas types de planification (révision périodique par exemple) avec des structures d'information spécifiques.

iii) Deux types de travaux d'optimisation ont été conduits sur le schéma ainsi défini et pour la période du VIème Plan (cinq ans : 71-75). On a réalisé d'une part des travaux d'*optimisation déterministe* sur le schéma complet, donc non linéaire, pour des aléas ramenés à leur valeur moyenne, aucune contrainte n'étant imposée sur la variation des variables de commande[(1)]. Le cheminement résultant peut être, en un sens, interprété comme "cheminement optimal moyen" associé au Plan, si du moins l'on considère que l'incertitude n'est pas "trop grande" ni les non linéarités "trop importantes" (ce qui paraît vérifié pour le cas d'Optimix). Par ailleurs, des calculs de *stratégies contraléatoires* ont été effectués sur une approximation linéaire quadratique du schéma complet. Les calculs ont été conduits sur la forme finale du modèle (TREIL (1971)) en ayant recours à des formules analytiques du type "théorie des équipes" (voir MARSCHAK, RADNER (1972), DELEAU, MALGRANGE (1972)). On a en particulier calculé les stratégies optimales correspondantes à diverses structures d'information caractéristiques (révision périodique, oubli, affectation instrument-aléa ...)[(2)].

iv) Quelques mots pour conclure sur le bilan qui peut être fait de l'opération Optimix, et par là de l'approche en termes d'optimisation vis à vis du problème concret étudié.

---

(1) - L'algorithme utilisé consistait en une méthode de gradient, l'ampleur du déplacement le long du gradient à chaque itération étant calculée par référence à une approximation quadratique.

(2) - Pour plus de détails, voir DELEAU, MALGRANGE (1972 ou 1974).

D'un point de vue méthodologique et technique, le bilan est sans conteste positif. Les concepts et le formalisme de l'optimisation ont permis une structuration éclairante du problème en distinguant les éléments constitutifs essentiels et en fournissant des réponses précises. Par ailleurs, l'opération a démontré l'applicabilité technique de cette approche à un problème "grandeur nature" directement lié, qualitativement et quantitativement, aux travaux de planification.

La pertinence économique des résultats dépend, quant à elle, assez largement de la fiabilité du modèle retenu. On peut considérer de ce point de vue que le modèle DECA présentait certains défauts (absence de mécanismes auto-régulateurs pour l'investissement en particulier) et que les résultats numériques associés n'étaient donc pas entièrement fiables.

Enfin, c'est surtout au plan politique et institutionnel que la transcription de l'approche retenue dans la pratique planificatrice soulève les plus sérieux problèmes. Il faut être bien conscient du fait que la référence au cadre précédent, qui peut apparaître "classique" d'un point de vue technique, conduit à une altération très notable du processus de planification existant. Le passage d'un raisonnement en termes statiques à un raisonnement en termes dynamiques est sans doute la modification qui soulève les moindres difficultés. Mentionnons d'ailleurs qu'un modèle dynamique, DMS (tableau 1), doit être désormais utilisé dans les travaux de planification. La référence exclusive à une "fonction objectif du plan" et à la conception stratégique associée semble par contre plus difficilement conciliable avec le souci de maintenir un processus de planification relativement "transparent" et d'afficher un projet clair. Une solution moins radicale pourrait être recherchée dans la direction suivante. Le processus de préparation du plan aurait pour objet de définir un "cheminement du plan". A ce stade, aucune optimisation explicite ne serait effectuée, le choix final résultant de la procédure itérative habituelle. Par contre, au niveau du "suivi" du Plan - c'est-à-dire de l'examen chaque année de son exécution-phase essentiellement technique, on pourrait avoir recours à une procédure d'optimisation pour démontrer dans quelle mesure le cheminement du plan peut être "respecté". La fonction objectif utilisée étant alors conçue comme instrument de pénalisation des écarts. Les vertus techniques inhérentes aux procédures d'optimisation, à savoir l'automaticité et l' "efficacité" des réponses données (cf. CHOW (1976)) comme la possibilité d'explorer le domaine des stabilisations possibles par variation des poids retenus, trouveraient là, sans doute, un domaine d'application privilégié.

3. L'APPLICATION DU CONTROLE DANS L'ETUDE DE LA DYNAMIQUE DES MODELES MACROECONOMIQUES : L'EXEMPLE DE STAR

Les travaux présentés dans ce paragraphe [1976a] [1976b] [1976c] ont été menés par une équipe d'automaticiens et d'économistes de Grenoble. Leurs originalités tiennent à l'application des techniques du contrôle pour l'étude systématique de la dynamique des modèles macroéconomiques non linéaires.

L'objectif ainsi fixé a guidé le choix du schéma de contrôle retenu : celui-ci en effet doit être d'application facile et apporter le maximum d'information sur la dynamique du modèle. En revanche, il n'a pas besoin de permettre le calcul de la commande "optimale" pour les contraintes non linéaires. Le schéma de contrôle proposé et appliqué à STAR est dérivé du schéma classique de commande en deux niveaux : calcul des matrices de bouclage et des vecteurs d'anticipation sur une approximation linéaire en variables d'état, et application de ces fonctions dans le calcul des commandes lors de simulations sur le modèle non linéaire.

Nous présentons brièvement ce schéma de commande (i) avant de donner un aperçu des informations sur la dynamique de STAR qu'il a permis de mettre en évidence (ii).

(i) L'approche proposée pour le contrôle du modèle macroéconomique non linéaire comprend quatre étapes. La liste des variables d'état (X), de sortie (Y) et de contrôle (U) est tout d'abord établie. Le vecteur d'état est obtenu simplement : à la liste des variables endogènes (expliquées par le modèle) est ajouté un état pour chaque variable décalée de plus d'une période[(1)] ; les sorties sont les variables objectifs du modèle qui sont fonction des états de la même période. Une trajectoire de référence est ensuite calculée par le modèle non linéaire. Un modèle linéaire en variables d'état implicite dans le modèle non linéaire est ensuite estimé par les moindres carrés. Le contrôle en deux niveaux est enfin appliqué dans la dernière étape. Il consiste à résoudre le modèle non linéaire pour les variables exogènes non commandables (les entrées) de la trajectoire de référence et les commandes

(1) $U(k) = U^*(k) + \Delta U(k) + G(k)$ avec

(2) $\Delta U(k) = -L(k)\,[X(k) - X^*(k)]$

où U^*, X^* sont les états et les commandes de la trajectoire de référence, L(k) et G(k) les matrices et les vecteurs calculés pour minimiser sous les contraintes linéaires du modèle en variables d'état :

---

(1) - Le vecteur d'état ainsi obtenu n'est pas de dimension minimale. Il a cependant l'avantage déterminant pour l'étude de ne comprendre que des variables du modèle original.

$$(3) \quad J = \sum_{K=0}^{T-1} [(\Delta Y(k)-\Delta Y^D(k))'Q(\Delta Y(k)-\Delta Y^D(k))+(\Delta U(k)-\Delta U^D(k))'R(\Delta U(k)-\Delta U^D(k))] + (\Delta Y(T)-\Delta Y^D(T))'F(\Delta Y(T)-\Delta Y^D(T))$$

avec ΔY^D, ΔU^D les écarts désirés de la trajectoire de référence.

La seconde innovation de cette approche est l'estimation des matrices A et B de la représentation d'état par la méthode des moindres carrés. Chaque ligne des matrices est déterminée par une régression par pas, les observations sur les variables indépendantes étant les écarts sur les états et les commandes à t, les observations sur les variables dépendantes, les écarts résultants calculés par le modèle non linéaire. Les régressions par pas ont l'avantage de classer les états et les commandes suivant leur influence sur les variations des états de la période suivante. Elles servent à éliminer des matrices A et B des coefficients sans importance et isoler au contraire ceux qui sont cruciaux dans la dynamique du système.

(ii) L'application du modèle STAR illustre bien les informations qu'il est possible de retirer d'un tel schéma. La version du modèle STAR étudiée a été publiée dans BOULLE et al. [1974]. La partie centrale du modèle est non linéaire. Elle comprend 78 équations ; 24 de ces équations ont donné lieu à des estimations économétriques, 7 sont des équations solde ; les équations restantes définissent des variables (prix, taux d'accroissement). La représentation d'état de STAR comprend 10 variables de commande, 32 états et une sortie. L'étude de la variation des coefficients de l'approximation linéaire en fonction du point de linéarisation a permis de conclure, dès le premier stade de l'étude, à un comportement quasi linéaire du modèle autour de la trajectoire de référence sur un horizon de cinq ans (72-76). Sur cette base, une approximation linéaire à *coefficients constants* a été retenue.

Les informations retirées de l'application du schéma portent sur les propriétés de stabilité et de commandabilité du modèle.

Stabilité du modèle

STAR est un modèle présentant des instabilités. Treize des modules des valeurs propres de la matrice A sont égaux ou supérieurs à un(1). Les causes de la divergence ont été établies à partir de l'examen d'une matrice A simplifiée.

---

(1) - L'instabilité de STAR a été vérifiée par simulation. Notons néanmoins qu'elle n'est pas gênante pour l'usage habituel du modèle (projection à deux-trois ans), les effets des mécanismes divergents n'étant vraiment sensibles qu'à partir de cinq-six ans.

A chaque coefficient a_{ij} de la matrice est associé un pourcentage r_{ij} d'explication de la variation de l'état i à t par l'état j à t-1. L'annulation de tous les coefficients ayant un pourcentage d'explication inférieur à 1 % a permis de simplifier considérablement la matrice A : dix coefficients en moyenne par ligne restent différents de zéro.

Les causes de la divergence sont facilement localisées sur cette matrice simplifiée : dix éléments diagonaux de A aux indices r_{ii} élevés sont égaux ou supérieurs à un. L'annulation de ces éléments diagonaux, puis le recalcul des valeurs propres confirment le rôle de ces coefficients : la totalité des modules est alors inférieure à un.

L'étude des équations de STAR qui décrivent l'évolution de ces états révèle immédiatement une caractéristique commune à ces équations : leurs variables, lors de l'estimation,sont soit des taux d'accroissement, soit des différentes premières. Les divergences associées à STAR paraissent ainsi d'ordre essentiellement mécanique, résultant de la spécification des variables retenue pour l'estimation du modèle. Quatre genres de spécifications coexistent : différences premières, taux d'accroissement, rapports de deux variables en niveau, variables en niveau. Les deux premiers sont à l'origine de la divergence.

Commandabilité du modèle

L'étude de l'instabilité de STAR illustre bien les informations que l'on peut retirer du simple passage de la forme structurelle, employée par les économistes lors de l'estimation, à la représentation d'état. L'étude de la commandabilité demande d'aller plus loin que le passage en variables d'état. L'application des critères classiques est en effet insuffisante : la trajectoire peut n'être atteinte que par des variations irréalistes des variables de commande et des états (augmentation "intolérable" de la pression fiscale, dépenses négatives de l'Etat par exemple). Le modèle est dans ce cas "non commandable pour l'économiste". La possibilité d'atteindre effectivement la trajectoire désirée ne peut être établie que par simulation de la commande.

L'approximation linéaire de STAR vérifie le critère de commandabilité. La simulation de commandes en deux niveaux indique cependant que certaines trajectoires des variables objectifs ne sont atteintes que par des évolutions irréalistes des états. C'est le cas par exemple d'une trajectoire de taux de croissance plus élevée et d'une balance commerciale équilibrée : la trajectoire n'est obtenue que par une baisse totale des prix (34 % sur la période !) et de la consommation en volume.

Les résultats pratiques de l'étude sur STAR

L'étude ainsi menée a d'une part permis de mettre en évidence certaines instabilités du modèle STAR. Ces instabilités tiennent principalement au mélange de différentes catégories de variables (taux de croissance, différences premières, niveaux). Il en résulte des dynamiques divergentes non souhaitées par les modélisateurs. Notons que leur élimination ne demande que de légères reformulations du modèle ; elle laisse inchangées les relations du coeur du modèle. Ainsi une telle étude menée dès la construction de la première version d'un modèle devrait permettre d'en améliorer à peu de frais la fiabilité.

Par ailleurs, les travaux d'optimisation ont révélé, à peu de frais, certaines caractéristiques fondamentales d'un modèle. Ainsi, une trajectoire de croissance plus élevée entraîne un déficit accru du commerce extérieur. La réduction du déficit conduit à une baisse du taux de croissance. Le rapprochement d'une cible, avec à la fois plus de croissance et moins de déficit, n'est possible qu'à travers une évolution irréaliste des prix et une pénalisation de la consommation au profit de l'investissement. Ces trajectoires illustrent bien l'apport des méthodes d'optimisation plus efficaces et plus systématiques par rapport aux techniques de simulation.

4. CONCLUSION

On voit donc que le recours aux méthodes d'optimisation n'a fait l'objet jusqu'à présent, en France, que d'un petit nombre d'expériences.

Des deux grandes voies d'application possibles, celle qui consiste à employer ces méthodes comme instruments d'*utilisation* des modèles ne donnera probablement pas lieu à des développements très rapides dans un futur proche. Si de telles expériences ne sont pas à exclure, elles ne joueront probablement encore, pendant plusieurs années, qu'un rôle assez marginal par rapport aux modes de gestion discrétionnaires traditionnels. Par contre, l'application des techniques d'optimisation à l'étude des modèles peut se développer beaucoup plus rapidement. Ces techniques permettent en effet de répondre de manière efficace à de nombreuses questions posées par les économistes. Par exemple, y a-t-il des conflits entre plusieurs objectifs ? Certaines commandes sont-elles plus efficaces que d'autres ? Peut-on associer une commande à un objectif donné ? Sur quels indicateurs faut-il baser le choix de la politique économique ? Une politique fondée sur deux ou trois indicateurs est-elle loin de l'optimum ? La réponse à ces questions, puis la confrontation aux connaissances acquises par ailleurs, est une démarche de validation d'un modèle qui complète le recours à d'autres techniques (simulations, calcul de multiplicateurs, analyse explicative, etc ... (DELEAU, MALGRANGE [1975a] [1975b]).Cet objectif d'étude de modèles fixé aux applications du contrôle semble bien perçu et désiré par les constructeurs et les utilisateurs de modèles et devrait donner lieu à plusieurs développements dans les années qui viennent[(1)].

---

(1) - Un groupe de travail regroupant des constructeurs de modèles (D.M.S., Metric-Tableau 1) et des chercheurs "extérieurs" (CEPREMAP, IRIA, Universités de Lyon et Grenoble) doit se consacrer en partie à ce type d'études (parmi les travaux envisagés : applications sur les nouveaux modèles de techniques précédemment utilisées sur STAR, analyse de décomposition, poursuites de recherche sur les méthodes de résolution et d'optimisation).

REFERENCES

AGLIETTA M., COURBIS R., SEIDEL C. (1973)
Le modèle physico-financier,
Collections de l'INSEE, Série C, n° 22.

AOKI M. (1976)
Optimal Control and System theory in dynamic economic analysis,
North Holland, Amsterdam.

BILLAUDOT B. (1971)
Le modèle DECA.
Statistiques et Etudes Financières, Série Orange, n° 1.

BOULLE J., BOYER R., MAZIER J., OLIVE G. (1974)
Le modèle STAR.
Statistiques et Etudes Financières, Série Orange n° 15.

BUSSERY H., COURBIS R., SEIBEL C. (1975)
Le modèle Fifi : les équations.
Collections de l'INSEE, Série C n° 37/38.

CHOW G.C. (1975)
Analysis and control of dynamic economic systems, John Wiley, New York.

CHOW G.C. (1976)
Control methods for macroeconomic policy analysis, American Economic Review Papers and proceedings, Vol. 66, n° 2.

COURBIS R., PRAGER (1974)
Analyse régionale et planification nationale : le projet de modèle Régina,
Collections de l'INSEE, Série R n° 12.

DELEAU M., GUESNERIE R., MALGRANGE P. (1972)
Planning uncertainty and economic policy : the Optimix study,
Economics of Planning, Vol. 12 n° 1-2.

DELEAU M., GUESNERIE R., MALGRANGE P. (1973)
Planification, incertitude et politique économique : l'opération Optimix,
Revue Economique, Vol. 24, n° 5-6.

DELEAU M., MALGRANGE P. (1972)
Information et politiques dynamiques contraléatoires,
Annales de l'INSEE, n° 9.

DELEAU M., MALGRANGE P. (1974)
Information and contrastochastic dynamic economic policies,
European Economic Review, Vol. 5, n° 2.

DELEAU M., MALGRANGE P. (1975a)
Les Méthodes d'analyse des modèles empiriques.
Annales de l'INSEE, n° 20.

DELEAU M., MALGRANGE P. (1975b)
Etude des mécanismes du modèle STAR,
Annales de l'INSEE, n° 20.

FOUQUET D., CHARPIN J.M., GUILLAUME H., MUET P.A., VALLET D. (1976)
DMS, modèle de prévision à moyen terme, Economie et Statistique, n° 79.

GUESNERIE R., MALGRANGE P. (1972)
Formalisation des objectifs à moyen terme. Application au VIème Plan,
Revue Economique, Vol. 23, n° 3.

HERZOG P., OLIVE G. (1966)
Le modèle de projection à court terme Zogol I,
Note INSEE-DP, ronéo.

MARSCHAK J., RADNER R. (1972)
Economic theory of teams, Yale University Press, New Haven.

de MENIL G., NASSE P. (1976)
Metric : a progress report on the structure and the specification of a quarterly model of the French economy,
Note INSEE, ronéo.

OUDET B.A. (1976a)
Etude de la dynamique déterministe à court terme des modèles macroéconomiques : application au modèle STAR,
Thèse de Sciences Economiques.

OUDET B.A. (1976b)
Use of the linear quadratic approach to study the dynamic policy responses of a nonlinear model of the French economy, Annals of Economic and Social Measurement, Vol. 5, n° 2.

OUDET B.A. (1976c)
La dynamic à court terme des modèles macroéconomiques : application à STAR, Annales de l'INSEE, n° 20.

THEIL H. (1964)
Optimal decision rules for government and industry, North Holland, Amsterdam.

THEIL H. (1971)
Principles of econometrics, John Wiley, New York.

TINBERGEN J. (1952)
On the theory of economic policy, North Holland, Amsterdam.

AN EXPERIMENT ON CONTROLLING A NATIONAL ECONOMY

J. H. Westcott
Department of Computing and Control
Imperial College, London

Abstract

The work described in this paper was carried out as part of the Programme of Research in Econometric Methods (PREM), a programme for investigating whether modern control theory can be applied to improve the control of a national economy. The development of a simple linear econometric model is described which is specifically motivated towards representing the dynamics of the economic system accurately from a control point of view. This is described in terms of four sectors, each sector having up to six dynamic behavioural equations expressed in rational structural form. A method for simultaneously estimating equation parameters within sectors is indicated and seen to result in simplification of equations which provide the basis for the design of optimal controls.

In order to employ known results from optimal control theory the system has first to be transformed into state vector form and techniques for achieving this are indicated. A quadratic criterion function is adopted leading to much simplification in the work. Explanations are given as to how such a quadratic criterion function may be applied in an unobjectionable manner.

To demonstrate the likely performance of controls derived in this fashion from a control model when employed on the actual economy it is proposed to use them to drive one of the large forecasting models in closed-loop fashion. Methods of matching the controls to the large model are described which avoid the necessity for complicated 'observers' in deriving the appropriate feedback.

A novel technique is then described whereby automatic modification of the weights attaching to terms of the quadratic performance function can be obtained directly from the modification to outputs desired by a policy-maker. This new method appears to go a long way towards removing rigidities in the use of the quadratic criterion function to which exception has previously been taken. A simple example of its use is given in the paper.

Introduction

There is now a very well established body of control theory. Certainly in its more simple forms it has been very successfully and widely applied to the control of technical systems. In its more esoteric forms it has been applied to very complex industrial processes often with dramatically improved results but in these cases there are pitfalls for the unwary and the application has to be treated with discretion and skill. It has been established that when properly applied these methods can yield markedly improved performance allowing greater versatility in the control strategy. The purpose of the experiment described in this paper is to attempt to extend the scope of these achievements into the economic field. It has to be admitted that the assumption of linear continuous dynamics that underlies so much that is successful in the application of control theory will strike many economists as a very limiting set of assumptions on which to base improvement in control of the economy. However the same was also thought to be the case for many industrial processes of great complexity which nevertheless have responded to careful exploitation of these known techniques. There seems therefore to be a sufficient justification for making a determined effort to establish the extent to which control theory can be applied to the solution of the difficult problem of controlling the economy.

There are however a number of special difficulties that apply in the field of economics. Central to control theory lies the acceptance of a causal mechanism, namely, that response follows action and cannot precede it. With market operators taking a view on events yet to happen it might be thought that in the field of economics this is not invariably the case. Again there is a body of Economic Theory, details of which are hotly disputed between professional economists to the confusion of outsiders. Econometricians claim that they can only work on the basis of received economic theory; for control engineers to do otherwise would be fraught with dangers of criticism from economists on the grounds of lack of realism. Engineers would much prefer the 'black box' approach with very lengthy signals in and out enabling a precise identification of the system. Both are denied in the case of a national economy, in the first place due to the brevity of reliable records and in the second place by the guardian officials of the Treasury who will not hear of such an outrageous suggestion as imposing test signals on the economy. Identification of the system is further confused by the 'adjustments' to the system by officials in their attempts to control it, so that it is never clearly an open-loop one. Furthermore, responses of the system as experienced could be likened to those of a quivering jelly so one concludes that the system is loosely restrained and unusually affected by random fluctuations.

Modelling the Physical System

The starting point in seeking to apply control to a system is to formulate a set of equations describing as accurately as possible the dynamic behaviour of the system. For this, of course, a detailed understanding of the physical mechanisms underlying the process is necessary; an awkward point in the case of the economy where underlying mechanisms are rather obscure. Fortunately much work along these lines has been done in connection with the large forecasting models that have been produced; for the U.K. economy a good example is the London Business School model which has about 350 non-linear equations and represents the measurable quantities in the economy to a fair degree of detail. As so often at this stage the equations look quite unmanageable from the point of view of designing a control system. Such is indeed very frequently the case with the equations formulated to describe the physical mechanism of industrial processes.

Complicated as these equations are they are utilised as the basis for development of the reduced model required for control. This process of condensing down the equations is started by drawing out simple relationship from the complete set that are relevant to the operations of controlling the system. The larger set have to be wrestled with to bring them into explicit forms in which essential cross-couplings and interdependencies between key outputs are faithfully retained. This is a skilled business, an art rather than a science and requires both the collaboration of those who understand the mechanisms and a good deal of experience. It is necessary as far as possible to choose as basic and simple a structure as possible for the reduced model without doing grave injustice to underlying mechanisms. It must be emphasised that this reduced model is totally orientated towards control performance of the system - its faithfulness of representation in other areas of interest (such as, for example, in forecasting) are irrelevant to this exercise as is explained later.

Thus this procedure will generate a structure capable of representing control essentials. It is then necessary from given data to estimate the parameters of this model. In the case of a national economy the time duration of available data is extremely restricted; for the U.K. to about 80 quarterly readings. Two conclusions are immediate; first, the "black-box" approach is not feasible and two, even with very sophisticated estimation procedures the variance of the estimates will be large.

Specification of the Model

The model is to be chosen to accurately reflect the dynamic relationships between variables but particularly between selected control variables (instruments) and relevant outputs. Thus the model is an econometric one and the basic purpose in the choice of this model is its use as a vehicle to apply modern control methods to improvement in control of the economy. The Government mainly controls the economy through the use of two types of measures, that is, fiscal measures which are normally promulgated once a year at the time of the budget, and monetary measures which act on interest rates and can be adjusted at any time. The monetary controls are of a rather subtle and indirect kind and control of the money supply is not considered. With the return into favour of the monetarist viewpoint in economics this is unsatisfactory and some thought has been given to including monetary variables as is mentioned later.

The fiscal controls in the hands of the Government are essentially taxes, both direct and indirect, but both of these while powerful controls tend to be delayed in their action. Most Governments have found it necessary to have a more swift acting form of control through control of credit. Of course, Governments do also have a very powerful influence on the internal economy through the system of Government grants at their disposal. Finally, as far as trade with the rest of the world is concerned they have resort to the Exchange Rate. These then are the five ways in which Governments can influence the course of a National Economy.

The next consideration is to specify the essential output variables that Governments seek to influence through the use of these controls. Two of the controls, namely direct taxes and Government grants, have an influence on the distribution of wealth and so the model should have representation of variables in a Distribution Sector of the economy. On the other hand, indirect taxes on expenditure and control of credit have their effect in what may be described as the Expenditure Sector. Finally exchange rate has its influence in matters of overseas trade and so the Trade Sector. In seeking to specify a simple model of the economy it will be convenient to think in terms of these three sectors. As has been mentioned the addition of a fourth, a Monetary Sector, is under discussion.

The initial specification will be of a very simple economic structure but it should be sufficiently realistic to allow something to be said about the key problems of control experienced in the real economy. In the case of U.K., policy-makers are confronted particularly with problems of controlling price stability, unemployment, balance of payments and economic growth generally and these should be represented in the model.

As a starting point the essential economic equilibrium is the instantaneous equating of aggregate supply and demand in volume terms. On the supply side of the equation is Gross Domestic Product to which is added the volume of Imports. This is equated to demand in the following way:-

$$\begin{aligned}\text{GDP} + \text{Imports} = {} & \text{Consumption} + \text{Gross Investment} + \text{Stockbuilding} + \text{Government} \\ & \text{Expenditure} + \text{Factor Cost Adjustment} + \text{Exports} \qquad -(1)\end{aligned}$$

thus giving the relationship for Gross Domestic Product which is the one used in almost all macro-econometric models. Each of the seven components of this expression for GDP is itself a candidate output variable for a behavioural equation. This however proves to be too simple an approach; for Consumption needs to be decomposed into durable and non-durable and Investment into private residential and non-residential, making ten equations in all already:-

GDP + Imports = Consumption (durables) + Consumption (non-durables)
+ Investment (private residential) + Investment (non-residential)
+ Stockbuilding + Government Expenditure + Factor Cost Adjustment
+ Exports -(2)

In an economy with growth, data recorded for these variables in Government statistics form a non-stationary time series. The highly developed estimation techniques for stationary time series could not be used on these directly. On the other hand economic growth itself is a factor of significant interest in this study and both objectives could be secured, namely of studying growth in the economy and dealing in stationary time series by expressing all variables in growth terms. This is achieved by expressing the % change of each variable in the GDP equation in relation to GDP itself as the normalising quantity. Other advantages are also found to flow from this choice in that the remanent unaccounted for in the estimated behavioural equations tend to be more nearly purely random fluctuations and furthermore the representation of dynamic relations themselves prove to be more simple. All these factors suggest the advantage of working entirely in growth variable terms for purposes of designing controls and when necessary recovering the levels of variables from these. For the parameters of these growth equations to be constant requires the assumption therefore that the relative proportion of GDP in each component also remains constant.

The behavioural equations representing output variables are constituted from a number of input variables selected on the weight of economic and empirical evidence, strongly influenced by the statistical confidence generated by the estimation procedures for their inclusion. The dynamic relationships between variables comes entirely from statistical evidence and the complexity of relationship is decided by what is statistically justified on the evidence of the official records available. The process of selection of terms to be included in any one expression is thus an iterative procedure involving much discussion and computation.

Expenditure Sector

Leaving aside for the moment Imports and Exports and also Factor Cost Adjustment and regarding Government Expenditure as a control we are left with six other output variables all of which could be said to be concerned with the Expenditure Sector of the economy. In Fig. 1 the output variables associated with the Expenditure Sector are detailed (together with these for two other sectors). There are two exogenous variables (right hand column) Current Government Expenditure and Public Investment which have to be regarded as independently specified variables in the model. In projecting control actions forward in time the handling of these variables represents one of the trickiest points of techniques, since poor assumptions as to their likely behaviour can result in an ineffective control performance. It will be noted that three accounting type identities (second column in Fig. 1) occur in this sector which in themselves consist of sums of variables appearing elsewhere in the model. These are algebraic statements of component variables without dynamic relationships as such. As the small degree of decomposition of these gross aggregates found necessary in the interests of an accurate representation of dynamics proceeds, more and more of these accounting type relationships prove necessary and although they do not contain dynamic relationships themselves they do, due to the coupling between variables, nevertheless influence dynamic response. In the current version of the model a total of 13 of these identities are necessary and are expressed in growth rate terms and linearised about the fourth quarter of 1973 as shown in Appendix I.

Trade Sector

Imports and Exports as part of the Trade Sector are recorded in money terms but as is evident since the model is based on the volume of goods flowing it is essential to associate with these variables a price index in each case; furthermore these indices will have a dependency on foreign exchange rates. Two further behavioural equations relating to import and export prices are involved here to give a total of four equations for the sector. Clearly World Indices of Trade, Value Added and Commodity Prices are exogenous variables here over which no internal control can be exerted.

Distribution Sector

The remaining sector which may be called the Distribution Sector is the one that brings in the question of Employment and Earnings and also, closely related to these, the question of Trading Profits of Companies but also Consumer Durable Price Index and Factor Cost Adjustment. Perhaps of even greater significance than total employment is the question of the number that fail to become employed. Thus Unemployment is regarded as a separate variable and found to have different determinants from total Employment. Furthermore as is explained below the question of a suitable tax control leads to the need for a further equation defining the Total Tax Yield. Thus the sector has seven outputs with behavioural equations corresponding to each, but owing to the complexity of interconnections between these quantities the majority of identities (number nine in all) occur in this sector. Exogenous variables here are Other Income and Average Hours Worked. It is this sector that plays a central role in the issue of inflation.

Monetary Sector

However with inflation in mind there is one sector of importance which is not represented in the model. This comes about through concentration on volume of goods to the exclusion of monetary features which are now an important factor when significant inflation occurs. Clearly a monetary sector needs to be included but first attempts to do so by concentrating on the terms contributing to money supply ramified among existing equations to such an extent as to cause the model to enlarge alarmingly. This approach has been abandoned in favour of a much more simplified structure which connects the Minimum Lending Rate as monetary control instrument interrelated by means of three new behavioural equations to the money supply itself (M3 version). This has the great advantage of calling for the restructuring of only two of the previous behavioural equations and work is continuing in estimating and perfecting these relationships which are not included for the present.

Matching Structures

Up to this point the evolution of the model informed by economic theory and guided by the quality of parameter estimates has tended to be of an unavoidable character in the sense that nothing has been introduced that could rationally be avoided. Every new element has been a necessary addition and this is true although the model remains very much an aggregated one. A much greater degree of disaggregation could of course be readily achieved if necessary and would need to be if the objective were a good forecast of variables. For control purposes this may not be justified and this must be tested. The objective here is by means of skilful manipulaton of control variables to ensure that target trajectories selected for output variables which are relevant in the four well-defined areas of policy that have been noted should be followed as closely as possible. Thus the methodology of control theory is to be drawn upon to design a control strategy that can be demonstrated to be effective in these areas of policy. The success of such an objective can only be judged by the improvements in control performance that result from following the recommended strategy and given that making experiments on the actual economy will be strenuously resisted, then some form of simulation of the true economy has to be resorted to for the usefulness of the experiment to be evaluated.

Very fortunately finely detailed models of the U.K. economy do exist and we have been fortunate in interesting the team working on one of the most successful of these at the London Business School (ref. 7) in allowing the use of their model for the conduct of such a control experiment. This large model has approximately 150 output variables. The small set of 17 used in the model developed here are of course very highly aggregated by comparison with these but it is not a difficult matter to decide which groups of variables in the larger model need to be merged in order to have a reasonable mapping on the one of the other. A significant factor is that one is matching output variables expressed as levels with ones put into growth form but this also involves no serious difficulty.

It is in matching the controls that difficult considerations arise. Much compromise and refitting proves to be necessary involving extensive re-estimation of equations in order to get the most realistic controls that are representable in both models and which will remain effective in controlling the economy. In the Expenditure Sector it has been found necessary to separate Consumption into durable and non-durable. Correspondingly the tax control in this sector needs also to be divided into control of tax for durable and non-durable goods separately (u_4 and u_5 in Fig. 1).

A much trickier issue arises in the Distribution Sector in connection with control via direct taxes. The most powerful of these is that on incomes, but as is (too) well known this is a sharply progressive tax and not easily represented by linear relationships. This is resolved after much trial and error by separating out as a new output variable the total personal tax yield with an associated behavioural equation (Appendix I, equation 17) containing two controls the one, u_6, being the basic tax rate and the other, u_7, representing the aggregate effect of the system of personal allowances. A further control in this sector was still necessary and national insurance contributions were chosen, u_8, which has an effect on real disposable income (z_1) and also on Gross Trading Profits of Companies (see Appendix I, equation 10).

The number of controls has increased by a further three to make eight in all; a list of them is shown in the third column of Fig. 1 where it will be observed that they are reasonably distributed between sectors as is to be expected if they are to be effective. The difficult sector is the important Trade Sector where Exchange Rate is perhaps a control of rather doubtful availability. This is where the need for a monetary sector exerts itself, in the meantime Exchange Rate remains the only lever to hand.

Equation Structure and Parameter Estimation Procedures

Reference has been made to the manner in which the composition of each of the behaviourly equations is arrived at by a combination of economic arguments and statistical evidence. The equations are considered in the following linear structural form familiar to econometricians:-

$$A(z^{-1})\ y(k) = B(z^{-1})\ u(k) + C(z^{-1})\ w(k) \qquad -(3)$$

where A, B and C are polynomials in the backward shift operator z^{-1}; y is the vector of outputs, u the control instruments and w the random residuals. The estimation procedure that is used is a dynamic generalisation of the method of full information maximum likelihood estimation. Under the assumption that the vector of residuals, w, form a series of independent jointly normal processes it is possible to form the joint density function of the outputs y, inputs u, and the computed lagged residuals. This allows a simultaneous estimation of the parameters in the complete set of equations yielding certain advantages. It is convenient for the numerical work to take the natural logarithm of a loss function which relates to the conditional observed y's rather than the unobserved w's and to minimise this with respect to the unknown elements of the coefficient matrices. Further detail of the procedure together with a numerical example is given in ref. 1. Computer programs have been prepared for undertaking the numerical computation. Since the computation is fairly heavy going it has been the practice to derive simultaneous estimates of this sort across sectors of the model or even sub-sectors rather than across the whole set. Where the coupling across equations is thought to be significant it is important to estimate simultaneously for the best results and it is interesting that the resulting set of equations is often more simple in the number of components and their dynamic complexity than would otherwise be the case.

This estimation procedure while quite sophisticated depends for its full justification on two factors; stationarity of time series and constancy of parameters. The first requirement has been provided for by use of growth variables, the second remains an assumption and one upon which recent data casts increasing doubt. Much work has recently been done on study of estimation for time-varying parameters; ref. 8 is an interesting example. In control theory the well-known Kalman-Bucy filter lends itself to extension in this direction as has been attempted in ref 4. For the present these possibilities have yet to be fully explored in the context of the modelling exercise described.

In Appendix I are given the complete set (17 in all) of estimated behavioural equations together with the variances of the estimates for each coefficient. Where the estimates have been derived simultaneously this is indicated and the identity of the coefficients is given in Fig. 1. There follows then the set of 13 identities expressed also in growth terms linearised about 1973 IV; symbols are again identified in Fig. 1.

Optimal Control

Having obtained the model, albeit a parsimonious one as econometric models go, it is now necessary to design the best control system possible with this as a basis. Control theory provides an answer to this in optimal control given only that the problem can be case into a format to which the theory applies. The linear form of the equation is satisfactory but the polynomial structural form is not. It is necessary to transform this into a linear state space representation. A quadratic criterion function is adopted here; its use is justified below. Other unsymmetrical measures for the criterion function are feasible but more onerous and restricting to apply. A new method is introduced which allows great flexibility in the choice of the weights that are to be associated with the individual terms of a quadratic performance measure.

The transformations to state space realisations have already been established. An interesting discussion of the issues involved in given in ref. 2 where a realisation procedure specially suited to econometric problems is worked out by producing an observable canonical realisation for each equation. The resulting set preserves the original structural information. The result in the present case yields a model of the following form:-

$$x_{k+1} = Fx_k + Gu_k + G_1e_k + G_2z_k + G_3w_k$$

$$my_k = Hx_k + Du_k + D_1e_k + D_2z_k + D_3w_k \qquad - (4)$$

$$z_k = J_1y_k + J_2u_k + J_3e_k + J_4z_k$$

where x is the state-vector and w the random residuals and the remaining variables are as in Fig. 1.

Eliminating the identities z and rearranging gives the more familiar form:-

$$x_{k+1} = Fx_k + Gu_k + G_1e_k + G_3w_k$$
$$\qquad - (5)$$
$$y_k = Hx_k + Du_k + D_1e_k + D_3w_k$$

The solution to the optimal control problem in this form is given in detail in ref. 3 Appendix A. The optimal control is shown there to be of the form:-

$$u^*_k = L_kx_k + h_k \qquad - (6)$$

where L_k and h_k are the control and tracking gains respectively. One important step remains in attempting to make use of this optimal result. In the large-scale simulation of the economy that it is proposed to control by using these control instrument values u^*_k there is no natural appearance of state variables x_k which are an essential component for deriving u^*_k. In ref. 5 it is shown that on certain assumptions the initial state x_1 may be calculated precisely and w_k in equations (5) eliminated so that a simple algorithm allows the state variables x_k to be recovered exactly from the given output sequence y_k which are available. Furthermore the algorithm is simple to apply and allows recovery of the states x_k without recourse to complicated 'observers' or estimations. Its use is illustrated in Fig. 2 which shows the interconnection between the simulated economy and the controller, derived in this way from the control model, together with the relationships between the parameters in equations (5) and those in the controller.

The Quadratic Criterion Function

There has been much discussion about the usefulness and validity of working with the quadratic criterion function. As to whether it is seriously objectionable or not depends very much on the detail of how it is employed. As it is used here its exact form is not a dominant consideration since it is being employed as a means to impose varying trade-offs between the accuracy with which particular desired trajectories are to be followed. This is elaborated below.

There are selected desired trajectories varying with time for a set of target output variables. To achieve these trajectories corresponding values of control instruments would need to be imposed. The performance criterion is set up to take into account the quadratic departure of target variables from their desired paths. In order to use optimal control these are translated into equivalent state variable forms using the transformations of the state space realisations already mentioned. To this are added quadratic measures of control instrument variables that are in a sense "costly" to the economic system. As between these components of performance a set of weights has to be decided which expresses the importance to be attached to each in the total which is then to be minimised overall. In fact once the weights have been assigned then the optimal system response that gives the minimum overall is the restraint deciding what control instrument values are to be imposed. The decisive elements in this are the choice of a) the desired trajectories for the relevant outputs and then b) the allocation of relative weights to each component of the performance criterion function. The role of the quadratic measure is as a restraining force to hold the balance between the set of desirable results. Where something has to "give" it allows this to happen in the least damaging manner in terms of the criterion function.

When the role of the Performance Index is viewed in this way it can be seen that the requirement is placed on the policy-maker to select politically acceptable paths for target variable and the optimal calculations will then generate values for the control instruments to drive the output variables as near to these target paths as is technically possible judged by the quadratic criterion and in the light of the relative weights assigned to each control instrument and to the output variables.

In ref. 3 a number of simple numerical examples are given illustrating how this works in practice. It will be appreciated that while the policy-maker finds no special difficulty with the choice of target trajectories of output variables it is considerably more difficult for him to decide on the relative weights to attach to particular controls. He would much rather decide this on the evidence of their effects on outputs. With this in mind a new method has been devised whereby the respecification of the weighting matrix necessary can be derived directly from the desired changes in target trajectories of output variables so as to yield optimal output responses more nearly approximating to the output desired. The procedure is an interactive one and very precise optimal approximations to the desired ones can in due course be obtained. Full discussion of the method together with mathematical proof of the convergence characteristics of the algorithm is given in ref. 6.

An Example of Respecification of a Weighting Matrix

A simple example of the application of the method follows, and is taken from an earlier version of the model discussed in this paper. To simplify the work the example is in terms of desired changes to control instrument values only, but the method applies equally for desired changes in output variables. The relationships are then more indirect and the computations more complicated but the technique is essentially the same. A total of six control instruments are involved whose associated weighting matrix G is as follows:

$$G = \begin{bmatrix} 10 & & & & & \\ & 10 & & & & \\ & & 250 & & & \\ & & & 2.5 & & \\ & & & & 2.5 & \\ & & & & & 2.5 \end{bmatrix}$$

The optimal trajectories of six control variables are shown in Fig. 3a). We assume the policy-maker was dissatisfied with the first free values (the initial values are fixed) of the first two of these variables and felt that these values should be markedly reduced. Let us assume these can be reduced to zero. Then the change desired in the set of these values of the six control variables will be:-

$$\delta = - \begin{bmatrix} 3.1769 \\ 1.2197 \\ 0 \\ 0 \\ 0 \\ 0 \end{bmatrix}$$

We now use an update formula which is derived in ref. 6 as follows:-

$$G_{new} = G - \frac{G\underline{\delta}(G\delta)^T}{\underline{\delta}^T G\underline{\delta}}$$

where $\underline{\delta}$ is the desired change in output $\underline{y}$ and G is the original control weighting matrix.

Using this yields:

$$G_{new} = \begin{bmatrix} 1.285 & -3.346 & & & & \\ -3.346 & 8.715 & & & & \\ & & 250 & & & \\ & & & 2.5 & & \\ & & & & 2.5 & \\ & & & & & 2.5 \end{bmatrix}$$

The resulting values of the six optimal control variables are given in Fig. 3b) where it will be noted that the two initial values of the first two variables have been substantially reduced, but also that there are repercussions in the values of the other variables as well. If these are in unfavourable directions then iterations with further changes can be considered and the policy-maker can soon obtain a 'feel' for the latitude that an optimal policy still allows. This new technique helps to remove many of the rigidities when using a quadratic criterion function to which objection has been raised in the past.

Discussion and Conclusions

The derivation of a control model of a National Economy has been outlined in detail to illustrate how concentration on the control aspects of the situation can lead to a simple economic model in relation to a selected number of important policy issues. On the basis of this simple linearised model optimal controls are calculated, using an agreed quadratic criterion function, which are ideal for the model. The analysis can be cast into a form that allows the optimal controls to be realised through the medium of a linear feedback controller. This has the advantage of yielding the well-known benefits of feedback control in reducing the perturbations due to disturbances and in giving very tolerable results even when the system being controlled departs quite substantially from the simplifying assumptions as to its complexity and from the assumptions of linearity.

Thus the point of interest is not so much how good is this controller on the simple model itself, but how good is it on the real economy. Understandably it is not possible to take this step directly. However it is felt that useful insights will be gained by using the technique to improve control performance on large-scale simulations of a national economy. For a given national economy there are often a number of these, differing in accuracy of detail and emphasising differing policy issues in the economy. Inevitably these differences of emphasis have an effect on the control model that is needed.

A particular large-scale simulation of the U.K. economy has been considered in the paper and the manner in which this affects the choice of both controls and behavioural equations has been described. The difficulty with a monetary sector illustrates how a control model for such a particular case can require radical changes not easily resolved, but the point is clear that no single control model can be made to work for the differing policy emphasis of every large-scale simulation. Each case has to be the subject of discussions over the important underlying mechanisms, followed by restructuring of equations and re-estimation of parameters and so by an iterative procedure converge on an appropriate matching of the control model to the large-scale simulation.

The final proof of the merit of the controller so arrived at has to be in terms of achieved control performance. In the case of the present experiment it is hoped shortly to be able to report on first results.

ACKNOWLEDGEMENTS

The work described here was carried out as part of the Programme of Research in Econometric Methods (PREM). The financial support of the Social Science Research Council is gratefully acknowledged. The author would also like to record his appreciation of the contributions of members of the PREM team, in particular to Dr. Sean Holly as resident econometrician and to Berc Rustem and Dr. Martin Zarrop as mathematician engineers who have attended to the rigour of the analytical results.

REFERENCES

1. Wall,K.D. and Westcott,J.H.: "Macro-Economic Modelling for Control", IEEE Transactions on Automatic Control, Vol. AC-19, No. 6, December 1974, pp. 862-873.
2. Preston,A.J. and Wall,K.D.: "Some Aspects of the Use of State Space Models in Econometrics", Proceedings of IFAC/IFORS International Conference on Dynamic Modelling of National Economies, Warwick, England, July 1973.
3. Wall,K.D. and Westcott,J.H.: "Policy Optimisation Studies with a Simple Control Model of the U.K. Economy", Vol. 4, Proceedings of the IFAC/75 Congress, Boston, Massachusetts, August 1975.
4. Rustem,B., Velupillai,K. and Westcott,J.H.: "Recursive Parameter Estimation using the Kalman Filter: An Application to Analyse Time-Varying Model Parameters and Structural Change". Paper presented at the European Meeting of the Econometric Society, Helsinki, 23-27 August 1976.
5. Zarrop,M.B.: PREM Working Paper MBZ-01, January 1976.
6. Rustem,B., Velupillai,K. and Westcott,J.H.: "A Method for Respecifying the Weighting Matrix of the Quadratic Cost Function", to be read at the IFAC/IFORS/IIASA 2nd International Conference on Dynamic Modelling and Control of National Economies, Vienna, January 1977.
7. London Business School Quarterly Econometric Model.
8. Wall,K.D.: "Time-Varying Models in Econometrics: Identification and Estimation", Conference Paper.

Sector	Outputs	Identities	Controls	Exogenous
Expenditure	(y_2) Private Investment less Dwellings (y_3) Stockbuilding as % of GDP (y_5) Private Residential Investment (y_6) Consumer non-durable Expenditure (y_7) Consumer durable Expenditure (y_{16}) GDP at factor cost (Dynamic Identity)	(z_8) Total Consumer Spending (z_9) Total Final Sales excl.Stockbuilding (z_{10}) Total Fixed Investment	(u_2) Minimum Deposit Rate for h.p. (u_4) Expenditure Tax on non-durables (u_5) Expenditure Tax on durables	(e_4) Govt. Current Expenditure (e_5) Public Investment
Distribution	(y_1) Wholly Unemployed excl.school-leavers (y_4) Employment (Total) (y_8) Consumer Durable Price Index (y_9) Earnings (y_{10}) Gross Trading Profits of Companies (y_{15}) Factor Cost Adjustment (y_{17}) Personal tax yield (Total)	(z_1) Real Personal Disposable Income (z_2) Wages Bill (z_3) Deductions from taxable income (z_4) Personal Income (z_5) Personal Disposable Income (z_6) Non-Durable Consumer Prices (z_{11}) Unit Labour Costs (z_{12}) Consumer Price Index (z_{13}) Real Value of Govt. Grants to personal sector	(u_1) Govt. current grants to personal sector (u_6) Basic tax rate (u_7) Aggregated allowances (u_8) National Insurance contributions	(e_2) 'Other' Personal Income (e_8) Average Hours Worked
Trade	(y11) Exports of Goods and Services (y_{12}) Imports of Goods and Services (y_{13}) Export Price Index (y_{14}) Import Price Index	(z_7) Terms of Trade	(u_3) Index of weighted Exchange Rate	(e_3) World Trade Index (e_6) World Value Added Index (e_7) World Primary Commodity Prices
Other				(e_1) Productivity

Fig. 1: Classification of Variables

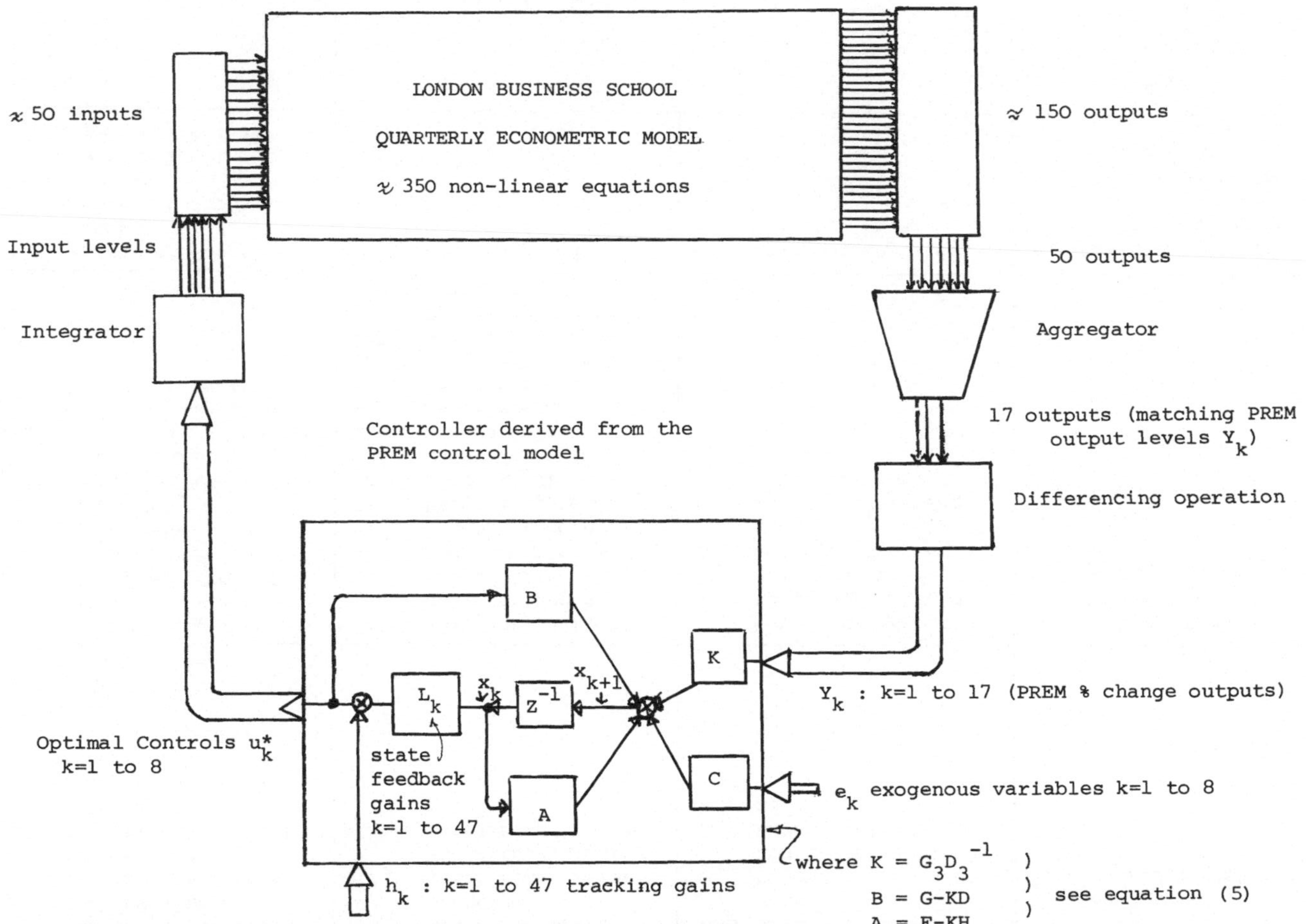

Fig. 2: Optimal Controller from PREM Model 2.3a) used to control the U.K. Economy represented by the L.B.S. Quarterly Econometric Model

3a) Optimal Controls expressed as % change on the Basis of Original Weighting Matrix G

Quarter	Tax as % of Income (1)	Tax as % of GDP (2)	Social Expenditure (3)	Private Borrowing as % of Income (4)	Public Investment (5)	Exchange Rate (6)
0	-0.2782	-0.0264	0.3383	-1.4749	-9.6812	-0.6631
1	3.1769	1.2197	6.0341	-0.0818	3.5624	-7.9876
2	2.5064	0.7859	1.7306	-0.0604	2.8682	-3.4551
3	1.8554	0.2920	0.3415	-0.0444	2.7615	-1.0542
4	1.4113	0.0382	0.0820	-0.0305	2.8376	0.1475
5	0.9405	-0.3071	0.4200	-0.0223	3.0115	0.6440
6	0.6435	-0.4554	0.6969	-0.0184	3.1346	0.7795
7	0.4878	-0.4992	0.8032	-0.0173	3.1913	0.7232
8	0.4268	-0.4560	0.8014	-0.0178	3.2049	0.5702
9	0.4229	-0.3785	0.7528	-0.0190	3.1958	0.3815

3b) Optimal Controls expressed as % change on the Basis of a New Weighting Matrix G_{new}

Quarter	(1)	(2)	(3)	(4)	(5)	(6)
0	-0.2782	-0.0264	0.3383	-1.4749	-9.6812	-0.6631
1	2.0230	1.0729	4.6798	-0.1070	3.1389	-9.0710
2	1.6368	0.7024	0.6400	-0.0781	2.5216	-4.1327
3	1.2576	0.2331	-0.4273	-0.0558	2.5120	-1.4158
4	0.9643	-0.0329	-0.4221	-0.0372	2.6724	0.0123
5	0.6901	-0.3624	0.0992	-0.0262	2.9085	0.6492
6	0.5040	-0.5066	0.4719	-0.0207	3.0682	0.8546
7	0.3961	-0.5546	0.6259	-0.0191	3.1460	0.8134
8	0.3421	-0.5157	0.6321	-0.0196	3.1671	0.6410
9	0.3247	-0.4430	0.5708	-0.0213	3.1571	0.4148

Fig. 3: Respecification of Weighting Matrix of Controls, G.

APPENDIX I

A.1

The Model Equations of PREM Model 2.3a)

Behavioural Equations (Stochastic Equations)

1. Rt. of gr. of unemployment

$$y_1(k) = \frac{\overset{(.981)}{-\,1.995}}{(1 - \underset{(.315)}{1.345}B + \underset{(.265)}{.521}B^2)}\; y_{16}(k) + (1 + \overset{(.094)}{.367}B)\; w_1(k)$$

$$R^2 = .54$$

2. Rt. of gr. of private fixed non-residential investment

$$y_2(k) = \frac{(\overset{(.241)}{.720} - \overset{(.248)}{.622}B)}{(1 - \underset{(.072)}{1.643}B + \underset{(.073)}{.820}B^2)}\; y_{16}(k-3) + (1 - \overset{(.132)}{.640}B)\; w_2(k)$$

$$R^2 = .28$$

3. Gr. in stockbuilding as % of GDP

$$y_3(k) = \frac{\overset{(.067)}{.415}}{(1 - \underset{(.041)}{.876}B)}\; y_{16}(k) + \frac{w_3(k)}{(1 - \underset{(.119)}{.245}B)}$$

$$R^2 = .52$$

4. Gr. in Employment

$$y_4(k) = \frac{\overset{(.028)}{-\,.085}}{(1 - .428B + .652B^2)}\; y_9(k-5) + \frac{w_4(k)}{(1 - \underset{(.109)}{.488}B^2)}$$

$$R^2 = .25$$

1. ~ 4. estimated simultaneously

5. Gr. rate for private res. investment

$$y_5(k) = \frac{\overset{(.1523)}{-\,.3926}}{(1 - \underset{(.1704)}{.8272}B)}\; y_2(k-3) + (1 + \overset{(.1259)}{.5899}B^3)\; w_5(k)$$

$$R^2 = .80$$

Single estimation due to paucity of data

6. Gr. rate for consumer non-durable expenditure

$$y_6(k) = \underset{(.059)}{.347} z_1(k) + .073\, z_{13}(k) + \frac{w_6(k)}{(1 + \underset{(.210}{.684B} + \underset{(.17)}{.263B^2})}$$

$R^2 = .43$

7. Gr. rate for consumer durable expenditure

$$y_7(k) = \underset{(.419)}{1.897}\, z_1(k) - \underset{(.168)}{.836}\, u_2(k) + \frac{w_7(k)}{(1 + \underset{(.126)}{.481B} + \underset{(.127)}{.596B^2}}$$

$R^2 = .52$

6. - 7. estimated simultaneously

8. Gr. rate for consumer durable price index

$$y_8(k) = \underset{(.109)}{.678}\, y_9(k-3) + (\underset{(.061)}{.298} + \underset{(.073)}{.151B}) y_{14}(k) + (\underset{(.191)}{.404} + \underset{(.189)}{.410B}) u_5(k-1)$$

$$+ \frac{w_8(k)}{(1 - \underset{(.170)}{.563B} + \underset{(.198)}{.336B^2}}$$

$R^2 = .48$

9. Gr. rate of hourly wage rate (ch. in earnings rate)

$$y_9(k) = \underset{(.222)}{.737}\, z_{12}(k-1) + \underset{(.084)}{.214}\, e_1(k-2) - \underset{(.016)}{.028}\, y_1(k-1)$$

$$+ (1 + \underset{(.133)}{.418B^3})\, w_9(k)$$

$R^2 = .32$

8. - 9. estimated simultaneously

10. Gr. rate of Company Gross Trading Profits

$$y_{10}(k) = \underset{(.600)}{3.012}\, z_{12}(k) + \underset{(.354)}{3.078}\, z_1(k) - \underset{(.348)}{3.358}\, y_9(k) + (1 - \underset{(.125)}{.359B})\, w_{10}(k)$$

$R^2 = .63$

11. Gr. rate of Export of Goods and Services

$$y_{11}(k) = \underset{(.234)}{-.401}\, z_7(k) - \frac{\overset{(.044)}{.149}}{(1 - \underset{(.042)}{.865}B)}\, u_3(k) + \overset{(.153)}{.30}e_3(k)$$

$$+ (1 - \underset{(.128)}{.260}B - \underset{(.124)}{.407}B^2)\, w_{11}(k)$$

$$R^2 = .28$$

12. Gr. rate of Imports of Goods and Services

$$y_{12}(k) = \overset{(.33)}{1.702}\, z_9(k) + (1 - \overset{(.172)}{.444}B)\, w_{12}(k)$$

13. Gr. rate of Export Price Index

$$y_{13}(k) = \overset{(.081)}{.671}\, y_{14}(k) + \overset{(.059)}{.212}\, z_{11}(k-2) + (1 - \overset{(.114)}{.459}B)\, w_{13}(k)$$

14. Gr. rate of Import Price Index

$$y_{14}(k) = \frac{\overset{(.082)}{-.396}}{(1 - \underset{(.116)}{.496}B)}\, u_3(k) + \overset{(.226)}{.378}e_6(k) + \overset{(.087)}{.185}e_7(k-1) = w_{14}(k)$$

15. Gr. rate of Factor Cost Adjustment

$$y_{15}(k) = \overset{(.158)}{1.428}\, z_8(k) + \overset{(.069)}{.099}\, y_{11}(k) + \overset{(.056)}{.111}\, z_{10}(k) + (1 - \overset{(.092)}{.577}B)\, w_{15}(k)$$

$$R^2 = .608$$

Dynamic Identity treated as a behavioural equation with zero noise

16. GDP (Dynamic Identity)

$$y_{16}(k) = (1 - 1.0B)\, y_3(k) + .763\, z_8(k) + .293\, y_{11}(k) + .215\, z_{10}(k)$$

$$- .300\, y_{12}(k) + .216e_4(k) - .191\, y_{15}(k)$$

17. Rate of Growth of Personal Tax Yield

$$y_{17}(k) = \overset{(.2149)}{1.3687}\, z_4(k) + \overset{(.1743)}{.8134}\, u_6(k) - \overset{(.113)}{.6144}\, u_7(k) + (1 - \overset{(.1418)}{.4244}B + \overset{(.214)}{.5697}B^4)\, w_{17}(k)$$

$$R^2 = .684$$

<u>Identities (Gr. Rates linearised about 1973 IV)</u>

1. $z_1(k) = z_5(k) - z_{12}(k)$

2. $z_2(k) = y_9(k) + e_8(k) + y_7(k)$

3. $z_3(k) = .664\, y_{17}(k) + .336\, u_8(k)$

4. $z_4(k) = .689\, z_2(k) + .102\, u_1(k) + .208\, e_2(k)$

5. $z_5(k) = 1.399\, z_4(k) - .2588\, z_3(k) - .1398\, u_1(k)$

6. $z_6(k) = 1.1009\, \{z_8(k) + z_{12}(k) + u_4(k)\} - .099\, \{y_7(k) + y_8(k) + u_4(k)\}$

7. $z_7(k) = y_{13}(k) - y_{14}(k)$

8. $z_8(k) = .903 y_6(k) + .097\, y_7(k)$

9. $z_9(k) = .513\, z_8(k) + .144\, z_{10}(k) + .197\, y_{11}(k) + .145\, e_4(k)$

10. $z_{10}(k) = .502\, y_2(k) + .107\, y_5(k) + .391\, e_5(k)$

11. $z_{11}(k) = z_2(k) - y_{16}(k)$

12. $z_{12}(k) = .072\, y_6 - .018\, y_7(k) + .972\, z_6(k) + .072\, y_8(k)$

13. $z_{13}(k) = u_1(k) - z_{12}(k)$

TIME-VARYING MODELS IN ECONOMETRICS: IDENTIFIABILITY AND ESTIMATION

Kent D. Wall
Systems Control, Inc.
Palo Alto, CA., USA

INTRODUCTION

One of the principal concerns of econometrics is the acquisition of precise information about the structure of economic relationships. This has led to a wealth of theory concerning the estimation of constant parameter models. Examples of the extent and depth of this theory are given by the textbooks of Johnston [1963], Malinvand [1966], Dhrymes [1970], and Theil [1971]. Associated with this development has been the evolution of a theory of identification (identifiability as it is known in control theory). While this theory is more often expounded in the econometric journals, one textbook has been written solely on identification (see Fisher [1966]. The theories of identification and estimation have reached a mature level in econometrics.

Recently, however, attention has been shifting towards the estimation of models with nonconstant or time-varying parameters (TVP). There are several reasons for this shift, the most notable being: (1) the realization that misspecification of relationships leads to sequential variation in coefficients; and (2) the development of economic theory which stipulates a temporal variation in economic structures. Allied with these reasons is the desire to estimate models which explicitly contain expectational variables such as price expectations. These variables are themselves inaccessible for measurement, likely to change over time, and must be estimated along with the unknown coefficients.

Naturally, the econometric literature has begun to reflect this trend (see for example the October 1973 Special Issue of the Annals of Economic and Social Measurement) with an increasing number of papers being published on TVP estimation. The development has, no doubt, been facilitated by the many similarities between the econometric TVP problem and the filtering problem in control theory. The extensive results of the latter have served to aid the development of a theory for the former. It seems odd then, that there should be an almost total lack of identifiability results for the TVP problem: If econometrics can relate to filtering theory, why has it not seized upon the existing identifiability results of control theory?

The answer to this question serves as the motivation for this paper. The identifiability results of control theory are viewed in the context of econometrics, and, unlike the filtering results, are found to require some modification to be relevant. A different approach is then taken in order to establish identifiability conditions for the econometric problem.

THE ECONOMETRIC PROBLEM

The basic TVP model of econometrics can best be characterized by a single regression equation whose coefficients evolve in time as autoregressive stochastic processes. The regression equation itself is represented as

$$y_t = X_t \beta_t + e_t \qquad (1)$$

where y_t is the single dependent variable (scalar output), X_t a 1xK matrix of explanatory variables, and β_t a Kx1 vector of time dependent parameters. There is an additive random error term e_t which is assumed to constitute a sequentially independent, identically distributed (normal) stochastic process with zero mean and variance σ^2, i.e., $e_t \sim \mathcal{N}(0,\sigma^2)$. Each element of the β_t vector is assumed to follow an autoregressive process of order $n_k (1 \leq k \leq K)$,

$$\beta_{kt} = \phi_{k1} \beta_{k,t-1} + \ldots + \phi_{kn_k} \beta_{k,t-n_k} + \eta_{kt-1},$$

where $\phi_{kn_k} \neq 0$ and η_{kt} is another independent identically (normal) distributed stochastic process with zero mean and $\mathcal{E}\{\eta_{kt}\, \eta_{\ell t}\} = q_{k\ell}$. Moreover $\mathcal{E}\{e_t\, \eta_t'\} = 0$. The complete model can be described compactly by (1) together with a state space representation for the β_t vector:

$$\beta_t = Hz_t \qquad (2)$$

and,

$$z_t = \Phi z_{t-1} + \Lambda \eta_{t-1} \qquad (3)$$

The vector z_t plays the role of the state and is defined by

$$z_t = \left[(z_t^1 \,\vdots\, (z_t^2)' \,\vdots\, \ldots \,\vdots\, (z_t^K)'\right]'$$

with z_t^k containing the n_k state variables associated with the difference equation describing β_{kt}. H is a Kxn ($n = \Sigma n_k$) matrix of the form

$$H = \left[h_1 \,\vdots\, h_2 \,\vdots\, \ldots \,\vdots\, h_K\right]'$$

with h_k a column vector of zeros except for unity in the $1 + n_1 + \ldots + n_{k-1}$ row. The nxK matrix Λ is defined as H'. The state transition matrix Φ is therefore of the following structure

$$\Phi = \begin{bmatrix} \Phi_{11} & \Phi_{12} \cdots \Phi_{1K} \\ \Phi_{21} & \Phi_{22} \cdots \Phi_{2K} \\ \vdots & \vdots \quad \vdots \\ \Phi_{K1} & \Phi_{K2} \cdots \Phi_{KK} \end{bmatrix}$$

where

$$\Phi_{kk} = \left[\begin{array}{c|c} \multicolumn{2}{c}{\phi_k'} \\ \hline I_{n_k-1} & 0 \end{array}\right]$$

$$\phi_k' = [\phi_{k1}\ \phi_{k2}\cdots\phi_{kn_k}]$$

The assumed form of the Φ_{kk} is a natural one given the autoregressive representation of the process governing each β_{kt}. Although the original description implies $\Phi_{k\ell} = 0$ for $k \neq \ell$, it is possible that economic theory may call for some form of interparameter coupling. Therefore, the $\Phi_{k\ell}$ submatrices will not necessarily be assumed zero.

To further simplify the discussion of estimation and identifiability the covariance structure of the η_t is explicitly incorporated in the state equations by replacing $\Lambda\eta_t$ with a related term Γu_t such that

$$\mathscr{E}\{u_t\} = \mathscr{E}\{\eta_t\} = 0\ ,\ \mathscr{E}\{u_t u_t'\} = I$$

and

$$\mathscr{E}\{\eta_t\eta_t'\} = \mathscr{E}\{(H\Lambda\eta_t)(H\Lambda\eta_t)'\} = Q = \mathscr{E}\{(H\Gamma u_t)(H\Gamma u_t)\}.$$

Γ is an nxK matrix of the same structure as Λ except that the nonzero rows contain the corresponding rows of the unique lower triangular factorization of Q. Henceforth Γu_t will replace $\Lambda\eta_t$ in (3).

The complete econometric TVP problem can now be stated as two related problems:
(A) <u>Identification Problem</u>. Given the model (1) - (3). Under what conditions are $(\Phi, \Gamma, z_o, \sigma^2)$ identified. That is, what constitutes a unique specification in the sense that, given an infinitely long data set, one can uniquely estimate the unknown elements in Φ, Γ, z_o, and σ^2?

(B) <u>Estimation Problem</u>. Given the identification of (1) - (3). How can one estimate $(\Phi, \Gamma, z_o, \sigma^2)$ and thus $\{\beta_t\}$ $1\leq t\leq T$?

The estimation of $\{\beta_t\}$ $1\leq t\leq T$ given Φ, Γ, z_o, and σ^2 requires nothing more than a straightforward application of the Kalman filter. The associated identifiability problem reduces to the observability of z_t (and hence β_t) and is solved through application of the concept of Uniform Complete Observability. More often, however, the econometrician does not have <u>a priori</u> knowledge of Φ, Γ, or a proper prior for β_o (and therefore z_o) - all these quantities are completely unknown. In this environment both problems (A) and (B) become quite difficult. Partial solutions do exist in the control literature, but a complete transfer of results is not possible. This is due to the slight, but critical, differences in the structure of the model used in the control literature.

COMPARISON WITH THE CONTROL MODEL

The control literature dealing with identifiability and estimation has centered on a system description employing two constant coefficient equations:

$$y_t = Cz_t + e_t \tag{4}$$

$$z_t = Az_{t-1} + Bu_{t-1}. \tag{5}$$

Identification and estimation of the model (4) - (5) has been extensively treated in the control literature, first for scalar outputs (Lee [1964], Aoki and Yue [1970], Mehra [1970, 1971]; and then more recently for multivariable systems (Tse and Anton [1972], Tse and Weinert [1973, 1976]). The principle idea involved in all the approaches was that of the canonical form or the invariants of the system description (see Popov [1972], or Kalman [1971]. This approach is rich in its algebraic content and makes much of the theory surrounding the equivalence relation in state space models. Although, in principle, it is possible to extend such theory to nonautonomous systems, this has not been done. Nonconstant models are the rule rather than the exception in econometrics.

Substitution of (2) into (1) gives the econometric equivalent of (4) - (5):

$$y_t = \tilde{X}_t z_t + e_t$$

$$z_t = \Phi z_{t-1} + u_t.$$

The elements of $\tilde{X}_t = X_t H$, corresponding to C, are not only time-varying but also are observed realizations of random processes (as well as deterministic or constant functions). Any theory relying on equivalence transformations becomes burdensome. Furthermore, the very nature of econometrics requires that (1) - (3) be identified and estimated and not an equivalent innovations representation. Indeed, it is often the sole purpose in econometrics to estimate the structural model (i.e., Φ and two distinct disturbances characterized by Γ and σ^2) and not a reduced form (i.e., the innovations representation with cannonical A and just one disturbance characterized by the steady-state filter gain). Finally note that even with just scalar y_t the econometric problem demands that Φ be decomposable into distinct blocks with corresponding substate vectors. In control theory a one output problem is automatically associated with just one canonical nxn block in A. In terms of companion canonical structures, the control theory concerns itself with identifying and estimating a Φ matrix with only unknown elements in the first row, whereas the econometric problem demands identification and estimation of Φ with K companion blocks on the diagonal.

The estimation theory associated with (4) - (5) is more flexible than the identification theory (identifiability theory). Given identification of (1) - (3), the many practically useful techniques of nonlinear extended Kalman filters can be employed. Even the problem of improper, or diffuse priors, for β_o has been solved in the control literature by the use of information form filters. Of particular importance are the smoothing techniques using forwards-and-backwards filters (see Fraser and Potter [1969]. If the forward filter is also in information form then a complete smoothing solution ideally suited to econometrics is obtained (see Cooley and Wall [1976] for a derivation). The solution of the related nonlinear estimation problem is then well established and practical results from control theory have been employed in econometrics. The identifiability problem is, however, another matter. The particular nonstationary structure of the econometric model appears to require a different approach than that found in the existing control literature. The remainder of this paper addresses this problem.

The identification problem will not be completely solved since it is assumed that σ^2 has been specified as some arbitrary positive constant. Thus the problem of determining what constitutes a unique specification for Φ, Γ, and z_o will be considered instead of the unique specification of Φ, Γ, z_o, and σ^2.

IDENTIFIABILITY THEORY

The identifiability of the unknown stochastic specification parameters Φ, Γ, and z_o can be determined through an investigation of the Classical Information Matrix of R. A. Fisher. This approach has two main advantages: First, it permits the identification problem to be studied within the general framework of statistical information theory - a point well emphasized by Bowden [1973]. Second, it provides a useful connection between certain concepts in control systems theory and mathematical statistics.

The Information Matrix of R. A. Fisher is defined as (see Rothenberg [1971] or Bowden [1973]:

$$\mathscr{I}(\psi) = -\mathscr{E}\left\{\left(\frac{\partial \ell np}{\partial \psi}\right)\left(\frac{\partial \ell np}{\partial \psi}\right)'\Bigg|_{\psi=\psi^o}\right\} \tag{6}$$

where ψ is the Nx1 vector of unknown parameters with true value ψ^o, and ℓnp is the natural logarithm of the density function for the jointly observed outputs over the interval $1 \le t \le T$.

The density function for the jointly observed outputs follows from (1) - (3) and the fact that e_t is normally distributed for each t. Repeated substitution of (3) into (2) and (1) yields

$$Y = \tilde{X}\, G(\psi) + E$$

where $Y' = [y_1, y_2, \ldots, y_T]$, $E' = [e_1, e_2, \ldots, e_T]$, and $U' = [u_1' \,|\, u_2' \,|\, \ldots \,|\, u_T']$.

In addition, $G(\psi)$ is defined as

$$G(\psi) = A(\Phi)z_o + B(\emptyset)C(\gamma)U \quad : nTx1$$

$$A(\Phi) = [\Phi' \mid (\Phi^2)' \mid (\Phi^3)' \mid \ldots \mid (\Phi^T)'] \quad : nTxn$$

$$B(\Phi) = \underbrace{\begin{bmatrix} I & 0 & \cdots & 0 \\ \Phi & I & \cdots & 0 \\ \cdot & \cdot & \ddots & \cdot \\ \cdot & \cdot & & \cdot \\ \cdot & \cdot & & \cdot \\ \Phi^{T-1} & \Phi^{T-2} & & I \end{bmatrix}}_{nTxnT} \qquad C(\gamma) = \underbrace{\begin{bmatrix} \Gamma & & & & \\ & \Gamma & & & \\ & & \ddots & & \\ & & & & \Gamma \end{bmatrix}}_{nTxnK}$$

The composite parameter vector ψ is made up of ϕ, γ, and z_o, i.e., $\psi = [\phi' \mid \gamma' \mid z_o']'$ where ϕ:N1x1 represents all unknowns in Φ and γ:N2x1 represents the unknowns in Γ. In the most general case $N1 = n^2$ and $N2 = K(K+1)/2$. $\tilde{X}$ is a TxnT block diagonal matrix with $X_t H$ on the diagonal. Since E is jointly normal,

$$\ell np(Y|\tilde{X},\psi) = \text{const.} - \frac{1}{2\sigma^2} [Y - \tilde{X}G(\psi)]'[Y - \tilde{X}G(\psi)] \tag{7}$$

Defining the gradient of $G(\psi)$ with respect to ψ as (see the Appendix)

$$\frac{\partial}{\partial\psi}\left\{G'(\psi)\right\} = \left[\frac{\partial G}{\partial\psi_1} \,\middle|\, \frac{\partial G}{\partial\psi_2} \,\middle|\, \cdots \,\middle|\, \frac{\partial G}{\partial\psi_N}\right]'$$

we can write

$$\frac{\partial \ell np}{\partial\psi} = -\frac{1}{\sigma^2} \frac{\partial}{\partial\psi}\left\{G'(\psi)\right\} \tilde{X}'[Y - \tilde{X}G(\psi)].$$

Inserting this expression into (6), evaluating ψ at ψ^o, and completing the expectation operation yields

$$\mathscr{I}(\psi) = -\frac{1}{\sigma^2}\left[L'L + \sum_{i=1}^{TK} P_i' P_i\right] \tag{8}$$

where

$$L = [\tilde{M} \mid 0 \mid \tilde{A}] \tag{8a}$$

$$P_i = \left[\frac{\partial\tilde{B}'}{\partial\phi} Ce_i \,\middle|\, \tilde{B} \frac{\partial C'}{\partial\gamma} e_i \,\middle|\, 0\right] \tag{8b}$$

$$\tilde{M} = [\tilde{X}A_1 z_o \mid \tilde{X}A_2 z_o \mid \ldots \mid \tilde{X}A_{N1} z_o] \tag{8c}$$

$$\tilde{A} = \tilde{X}A(\phi). \tag{8d}$$

The details of this derivation are relegated to the Appendix. They are, on the whole, straightforward but tedious and not central to the following discussion.

The complete identification of the parameterization embodied in the specification of $\{\Phi,\Gamma,z_o\}$ obtains if and only if the Information Matrix is negative definite. This leads to the rather obvious, but no less fundamental, result:

Proposition 1. Given the model (1) - (3) with $\sigma^2>0$. Then Φ,Γ, and z_o are completely identified if and only if $[L'L + \sum P_i'P_i]>0$.

Practical application of the above identification condition does not appear likely owing to the complex nature of L and P_i, and the way in which these two factors interact. Indeed, reference to (A.9) reveals the complete coupling of the problem: The identifiability of Φ is related to that of z_o through the $\tilde{M}'\tilde{A}$ term, and the identifiability of Γ is related to that of Φ through the $\mathscr{P}$ matrix. A closer examination of this interaction does, however, yield some interesting insights and some simpler sufficient conditions.

If both Φ and Γ are known, then identifiability of z_o is the only concern. In such a situation, $\mathscr{I}(z_o)<0$ if and only if $\tilde{A}'(\phi)\tilde{A}(\phi)>0$ and this obtains whenever rank $\tilde{A} = n$. It is obvious from the definition that this requirement is nothing more than a condition for the Uniform Complete Observability (UCO) of (1) - (3). Hence identifiability of z_o is equivalent to observability!

Next consider the case where (Φ, z_o) are unknown, but Γ and σ^2 are given. The necessary and sufficient condition for the identification of (Φ, z_o) is that

$$\text{rank } [\tilde{M}\,|\,\tilde{A}] = N1+n. \tag{9}$$

From (8c) the striking similarity of this requirement to that of n-identifiability (given by Lee [1964, p 94 - 96]) is evident. Whereas in the deterministic problem z_o must be such that it excites all the modes of Φ, the stochastic problem considered here requires that z_o excite all the modes of the partial derivatives of the powers of Φ. Explicitly, we must have

$$\text{rank } \tilde{M} = \text{rank}\left\{\tilde{X}[A_1z_o\,|\,A_2z_o\,|\cdots|\,A_{N1}z_o]\right\} = N1$$

which casts A_i in the role of Φ.

The case where σ^2 and z_o are given reduces identifiability to that of (Φ,Γ). A sufficient condition for this to obtain is that

$$\left[\begin{array}{c|c} \mathscr{Q} & \mathscr{P} \\ \hline \mathscr{P}' & \mathscr{R} \end{array}\right] = \sum_{i=1}^{TK} P_i' \, P_i > 0$$

irrespective of any rank condition on $\tilde{M}$. Since P_i involve $\Gamma\,\Phi^t$ and their partials, this condition is remarkably similar to a requirement that the "true" system be Uniformly Completely Controllable (UCC) with respect to the u_t.

In the case where Φ and z_o are known, but γ is unknown the Information Matrix reduces to

$$\mathscr{I}(\gamma) = -\frac{1}{\sigma^2}\mathscr{R} = -\frac{1}{\sigma^2}\sum_{i=1}^{KT}\begin{bmatrix} e_i' C_1' \tilde{B}' \\ e_i' C_2' \tilde{B}' \\ \vdots \\ e_i' C_{N2}' \tilde{B}' \end{bmatrix}\left[\tilde{B}\, C_1 e_i \,\Big|\, \cdots \,\Big|\, \tilde{B}\, C_{N2} e_i\right].$$

$$= -\frac{1}{\sigma^2}\sum_{t=1}^{T}\begin{bmatrix} tr(\Gamma_1' W_t \Gamma_1) & tr(\Gamma_1' W_t \Gamma_2) \cdots \\ tr(\Gamma_2' W_t \Gamma_1) & tr(\Gamma_2 W_t \Gamma_2) \cdots \\ \vdots & \vdots \quad \vdots \\ tr(\Gamma_{N2}' W_t \Gamma_1) & tr(\Gamma_{N2} W_t \Gamma_2) \cdots \end{bmatrix}$$

where $W_t = \sum_{\tau=t}^{T}(\Phi^{\tau-t})' H' X_t' X_t H \Phi^{\tau-t}$ (i.e. the traditional observatibility matrix of control-theory) and $\Gamma_j = \partial\Gamma/\partial\gamma_j$. Note that $\Gamma_j \Gamma_i' = 0$ for all γ_j and γ_i that do not lie in the same column of Γ. Likewise $\Gamma_j \Gamma_i' = E_{pq}$ (the nxn unit matrix) when γ_j and γ_i lie in row p and row q, respectively, of the same column of Γ. Therefore $\mathscr{I}(\gamma)$ reduces to the sum of T matrices, each N2xN2, which dislay the following pattern in their nonzero elements.

$$\begin{bmatrix} w_{11} & w_{s_1,1} & 0 & w_{s_2,1} & 0 & 0 \cdots \\ w_{1,s_1} & w_{s_1,s_1} & 0 & w_{s_2,s_1} & 0 & 0 \cdots \\ 0 & 0 & w_{s_1,s_1} & 0 & w_{s_2,s_1} & 0 \cdots \\ w_{1,s_2} & w_{s_1,s_2} & 0 & w_{s_2,s_2} & 0 & 0 \cdots \\ 0 & 0 & w_{s_1,s_2} & 0 & w_{s_2,s_2} & 0 \cdots \\ 0 & 0 & 0 & 0 & 0 & w_{s_2,s_2} \\ \vdots & \vdots & \vdots & \vdots & \vdots & \ddots \end{bmatrix}$$

where the subscript t has been suppressed for clarity and $s_\ell = 1 + \sum_{i=1}^{\ell} n_i$. For every t, the above matrix is equivalent to one with the following structure (obtained from the above by simple elementary row and column exchanges):

$$\begin{bmatrix} \underline{W}_t(K) & & & & \\ & \underline{W}_t(K-1) & & & \\ & & \cdot & & \\ & & & \cdot & \\ & & & & \cdot \\ & & & & \underline{W}_t(1) \end{bmatrix}$$

Each $\underline{W}_t(k)$ is a kxk matrix obtained from W_t via a sequence of singular transformations (such as the zeroing of a row or column), thus $\underline{W}_t(K) = Z\, W_t(K)\, Z'$ where Z is an nxn elementary (singular) transformation matrix of rank K. In addition, $\underline{W}_t(k-1)$ is obtained from $\underline{W}_t(k)$ by deleting its first row and column. Therefore the rank of $\mathscr{I}(\gamma)$ can at most be K, and this gives the following

Proposition 2. Given the model (1) - (3). Γ, and hence Q, is never completely identified. At most K linear combinations of the $K(K+1)/2$ elements of Γ can be identified.

It is interesting to note how this result agrees with the conclusion of Mehra [1970, 1971] concerning the underidentification of Q in the time invariant case. He concludes that only nxr linear combinations of the elements of Q can be uniquely estimated. In the case considered in this paper $r=1$ (the dimension of y_t in (1)) and Proposition 2 yields the same conclusion regarding the identifiability of Q.

Finally, consider the special case in which each β_{kt} of (3) obeys a first order autoregressive process, i.e., $n_k = 1$ for all $1 \le k \le K$. Also, let there be no dynamic coupling between any two β_{kt} so that Φ and Q are diagonal. In such a situation it is quite easy to establish identifiability of the $N = N1 + NR + n = 3n$ unknown parameters. First examine $\tilde{M}$: As long as each element the "true" z_o is nonzero, $\tilde{M}$ will be an nTxn matrix of T nxn diagonal blocks and thus will always have rank n so long as each regressor is not identically zero. Second, note that $H = I$ in (2) and thus rank $[A(\phi)] = n$ automatically. Third, $\mathscr{R}$ will be a diagonal matrix with each element on the diagonal positive since (Φ,Γ) is a completely controllable structure. Thus rank $[L] = 2n$, $\mathscr{R}>0$, and identifiability obtains:

Proposition 3. Given the model (1) - (3) with Φ and Q diagonal but unknown (i.e. $n_k = 1$ for $1 \le k \le K$). If $X_t \neq 0$ and no element of z_o is zero then (1) - (3) is completely identified.

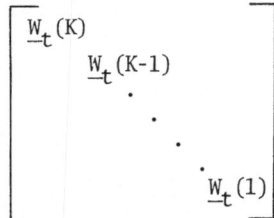

This result, which might seem somewhat obvious, is still of interest both from a practical and a theoretical standpoint. Econometric models are very often specified with $n_k = 1$ $(1 \le k \le K)$ so that the result in Proposition 3 will be quite useful in applications. Conceptually speaking, Proposition 3 demonstrates that even given a scalar output, it is still possible to uniquely estimate a non canonical form structure. In control theory, the scalar output case is automatically associated with an observable canonical form with all the unknown elements of Φ lying in a single row or column. Here we find it possible to associate one unknown element of Φ with each row of Φ. In other words, canonical forms are not necessary for establishing identifiability - they are merely a conceptual antifact for establishing a sufficient condition!

CONCLUSIONS

The extension of economic theory to time-varying structures has opened up a whole new area for the application of control systems theory. Indeed, recent publications in the econometric literature clearly indicate the utility of filtering and smoothing theory in the analysis of nonstationary economic phenomena. Little attention, however, has been paid to the important problem of identifiability - even though a fairly complete solution to this problem now exists in control-theory. A brief comparison of the TVP estimation problem in each discipline reveals subtle differences which result in a more complicated situation within the econometric framework. The identifiability results in control theory are not entirely applicable and a different approach is required.

One alternate method of investigating identifiability relys on an analysis of the Information Matrix, and as such, may be considered more direct than recourse to the theory of canonical forms and invariants. Such a procedure leads to a representation of the Information Matrix which is helpful in developing a general necessary and sufficient condition for complete identifiability. Although complicated, the condition stated in Proposition 1 can be used to establish complete identifiability in certain special structures. This has been done for a diagonal structure. It is open to conjecture whether, using a similar train of thought, one can also establish the complete identifiability of the various canonical forms of control theory. Nonetheless, the representation (8) has proved instructive by revealing how identifiability relates to earlier results (Lee [1964]) and the concepts of complete observability and complete controllability.

APPENDIX

The derivation of the Information Matrix defined by (6) makes extensive use of several definitions involving the representation of matrix gradients; these are stated first to facilitate understanding: Let $F = F(x)$ be a pxq matrix, x an $nx1$ vector, and y a $qx1$ vector, then

$$\frac{\partial F}{\partial x} = \left[\frac{\partial F}{\partial x_1} \,\Big|\, \frac{\partial F}{\partial x_2} \,\Big|\, \cdots \,\Big|\, \frac{\partial F}{\partial x_n}\right]' \tag{A.1}$$

$$\left[\frac{\partial F}{\partial x}\right]' y = \left[\frac{\partial F}{\partial x_1} y \,\Big|\, \frac{\partial F}{\partial x_2} y \,\Big|\, \cdots \,\Big|\, \frac{\partial F}{\partial x_n} y\right] \tag{A.2}$$

$$y' \left[\frac{\partial F}{\partial x}\right] = \left[\left(\frac{\partial F}{\partial x}\right)' y\right]' \tag{A.3}$$

If D is some rxq matrix, then $D[\partial F/\partial x]$ is defined as the partitioned matrix $[\partial F/\partial x_1 D' \mid \partial F/\partial x_2 D' \mid \cdots \mid \partial F/\partial x_n D']'$.

Substitution of (7) into (6), with $\partial G/\partial\psi$ defined by (A.1), yields

$$\mathscr{I}(\psi) = -\frac{1}{\sigma^4}\mathscr{E}\left\{\begin{bmatrix}\frac{\partial G'}{\partial\phi} \\ \frac{\partial G'}{\partial\gamma} \\ \frac{\partial G'}{\partial z_o}\end{bmatrix}\tilde{X}' E E' \tilde{X}\left[\frac{\partial G}{\partial\phi} \,\Big|\, \frac{\partial G}{\partial\gamma} \,\Big|\, \frac{\partial G}{\gamma z_o}\right]\Bigg|_{\psi = \psi^o}\right\}$$

$$\mathscr{I}(\psi) = -\frac{1}{\sigma^4}\begin{bmatrix}\mathscr{E}\left\{\frac{\partial G'}{\partial\phi}V\frac{\partial G}{\partial\phi}\right\} & \mathscr{E}\left\{\frac{\partial G'}{\partial\phi}V\frac{\partial G}{\partial\gamma}\right\} & \mathscr{E}\left\{\frac{\partial G'}{\partial\phi}V\frac{\partial G}{\partial z_o}\right\} \\ \mathscr{E}\left\{\frac{\partial G'}{\partial\gamma}V\frac{\partial G}{\partial\phi}\right\} & \mathscr{E}\left\{\frac{\partial G'}{\partial\gamma}V\frac{\partial G}{\partial\gamma}\right\} & \mathscr{E}\left\{\frac{\partial G'}{\partial\gamma}V\frac{\partial G}{\partial z_o}\right\} \\ \mathscr{E}\left\{\frac{\partial G'}{\partial z_o}V\frac{\partial G}{\partial\phi}\right\} & \mathscr{E}\left\{\frac{\partial G'}{\partial z_o}V\frac{\partial G}{\partial\gamma}\right\} & \mathscr{E}\left\{\frac{\partial G'}{\partial z_o}V\frac{\partial G}{\partial z_o}\right\}\end{bmatrix}$$

where $V = \tilde{X}' E E' \tilde{X}$. Now, using (A.2) & (A.3) we find:

$$\frac{\partial G}{\partial\phi} = z_o' \frac{\partial A}{\partial\phi} + U'C' \frac{\partial B}{\partial\phi}$$

$$\frac{\partial G}{\partial\gamma} = U' \frac{\partial C}{\partial\gamma} B'$$

$$\frac{\partial G}{\partial z_o} = A(\phi).$$

The above matrix gradient expressions can now be substituted into $\mathscr{I}(\psi)$ and the expectations evaluated on a block-by-block basis:

$$\mathscr{E}\left\{\frac{\partial G'}{\partial\phi} V \frac{\partial G}{\partial\phi}\right\} = \mathscr{E}\left\{\left[z_o' \frac{\partial A}{\partial\phi} + U'C' \frac{\partial B}{\partial\phi}\right] \tilde{X}' E E' \tilde{X} \left[\frac{\partial A'}{\partial\phi} z_o + \frac{\partial B'}{\partial\phi} C U\right]\right\}$$

$$= \mathscr{E}\left\{z_o' \frac{\partial A}{\partial\phi} \tilde{X}' E E \tilde{X} \frac{\partial A'}{\partial\phi} z_o + U'C' \frac{\partial B}{\partial\phi} \tilde{X}' E E' \tilde{X} \frac{\partial A}{\partial\phi} C U\right.$$

$$\left. + U'C' \frac{\partial B}{\partial\phi} \tilde{X}' E E' \tilde{X} \frac{\partial B'}{\partial\phi} C U + z_o' \frac{\partial A}{\partial\phi} \tilde{X}' E E' \tilde{X} \frac{\partial B'}{\partial\phi} C U\right\}$$

$$= \sigma^2\left(z_o' \frac{\partial A}{\partial\phi} \tilde{X}' \tilde{X} \frac{\partial A'}{\partial\phi} z_o\right) + \mathscr{E}\left\{U'C' \frac{\partial B}{\partial\phi} \tilde{X}' E E' \tilde{X} \frac{\partial B'}{\partial\phi} C U\right\}$$

Since U and E are zero mean and independent of each other, the second term above can be easily evaluated on an element-by-element basis using the representation for the expectation of the fourth moment of a Gaussian random variable (see Parzen [1962, pg. 93]). The result of this computation produces a matrix $\sigma^2\mathscr{Q}$ with its $(i,j)^{th}$ element defined by $tr(C'[\partial B'/\partial\phi_i]\tilde{X}'\tilde{X}[\partial B/\partial\phi_j]C)$. Thus,

$$\mathscr{E}\left\{\frac{\partial G'}{\partial\phi} V \frac{\partial G}{\partial\phi}\right\} = \sigma^2 \ [\tilde{M}'\tilde{M} + \mathscr{Q}] \tag{A.4}$$

where $\tilde{M} = [\tilde{A}_1 z_o \mid \tilde{A}_2 z_o \mid \dots \mid \tilde{A}_{N1} z_o]$ and $\tilde{A}_i = \partial\tilde{X}A/\partial\phi_i$. Similarly, with $\tilde{B}_i = \partial B\tilde{X}/\partial\phi_i$ and $C_j = \partial C/\partial\gamma_j$, it can be shown that

$$\mathscr{E}\left\{\frac{\partial G'}{\partial\phi} V \frac{\partial G}{\partial\gamma}\right\} = \sigma^2 \mathscr{P}, \tag{A.5}$$

where $\mathscr{P}$ is an N1xN2 matrix with its $(i,j)^{th}$ element defined by $tr(C'\tilde{B}_i'\tilde{B}C_j)$. In much the same manner,

$$\mathscr{E}\left\{\frac{\partial G'}{\partial\phi} V \frac{\partial G}{\partial z_o}\right\} = \sigma^2\left[z_o \frac{\partial\tilde{A}}{\partial\phi} \tilde{A}(\phi)\right] \tag{A.6}$$

$$\mathscr{E}\left\{\frac{\partial G'}{\partial\gamma} V \frac{\partial G}{\partial z_o}\right\} = \mathscr{E}\left\{u' \frac{\partial C}{\partial\gamma} \tilde{B}' E E' \tilde{A} (\phi) = \right\} 0 \tag{A.7}$$

$$\mathscr{E}\left\{\frac{\partial G'}{\partial\gamma} V \frac{\partial G}{\partial\gamma}\right\} = \sigma^2 \mathscr{R}, \tag{A.8}$$

where $\mathscr{R}$ is an N2xN2 matrix with its $(i,j)^{th}$ element given by $tr(C_i' \tilde{B}' \tilde{B} C_j)$.

Substitution of (A.4) - (A.8) in $\mathscr{I}(\psi)$ gives

$$\mathscr{I}(\psi) = -\frac{1}{\sigma^2}\left[\begin{array}{c|c|c} \tilde{M}'\tilde{M} & 0 & \tilde{M}'\tilde{A} \\ \hline 0 & 0 & 0 \\ \hline \tilde{A}'\tilde{M} & 0 & \tilde{A}'\tilde{A} \end{array}\right] - \frac{1}{\sigma^2}\left[\begin{array}{c|c|c} \mathscr{Q} & \mathscr{P} & 0 \\ \hline \mathscr{P}' & \mathscr{R} & 0 \\ \hline 0 & 0 & 0 \end{array}\right], \qquad (A.9)$$

and, since $tr(S) = \sum_{i=1}^{n} e_i' S e_i$ for any nxn matrix S (where e_i denotes the ith unit vector of the usual Euclidean n-dimensional orthonormal basis),

$$\mathscr{I}(\psi) = -\frac{1}{\sigma^2}\left[L'L + \sum_{i=1}^{TK} P_i' P_i\right] \qquad (A.10)$$

$$L = [\tilde{M} \mid 0 \mid \tilde{A}] \qquad (A.11)$$

$$P_i = \left[\frac{\partial \tilde{B}'}{\partial \phi} Ce_i \;\middle|\; \tilde{B}\frac{\partial C'}{\partial \gamma} e_i \;\middle|\; 0\right]. \qquad (A.12)$$

REFERENCES

Aoki, M. and Yue, P. C. [1970] "On Certain Convergence Questions in System Identification," SIAM Jour. Control, vol. 8, no. 2 pp.239-256.

Bowden, R. [1973] "The Theory of Parametric Identification," Econometrica, vol. 41, no. 6, pp. 1069-1074.

Cooley, T. F. and Wall, K. D. [1976] "A Note on Optimal Smoothing for Time-Varying Coefficient Problems," NBER Working Paper No. 128, May 1976.

Dhrymes, P. H. [1970] Econometrics, New York: Harper & Row, Inc.

Fisher, F. M. [1966] The Identification Problem in Economics, New York: Mc-Graw-Hill, Inc.

Fraser, D. C. and Potter, J. E. [1969] "The Optimum Linear Smoother as a Combination of Two Optimum Linear Filters" IEEE Trans. Auto. Control, vol. AC-14, no. 4, (August) pp. 387-390.

Johnson, J. [1963] Econometric Methods (2nd Ed.), New York: McGraw-Hill

Kalman, R. E. [1971] "Knonecker Invariants and Feedback," Proc. Conference on Ordinary Differential Equations (Mathematics Research Center, Madison, Wis., 1971). Naval Research Lab., Washington, D.C.

Lee, R. C. K. [1964] Optimal, Estimation, Identification, and Control, Cambridge, Mass.: MIT Press.

Malinvand, E. [1966] Statistical Methods of Econometrics, Paris: North Holland.

Mehra, R. [1970] "On the Identification of Variances and Adaptive Kalman Filtering," IEEE Trans. Auto. Control, vol. AC-15, no. 2, pp. 175-184 (April).

Mehra, R. [1971] "Online Identification of Linear Dynamic Systems with Applications to Kalman Filtering," IEEE Trans. Auto. Control, vol. AC-16, no. 1, pp. 12-21 (February).

Parzen, E. [1962] Stochastic Processes, San Francisco: Holden Day.

Popov, V. M. [1972] "Invariant Description of Linear, Time-Invariant Controllable Systems" SIAM Jour. Control, vol. 10, no. 2, pp. 252-264.

Rothenberg, T. J. [1971] "Identification in Parametric Models," Econometrica, vol. 39, no. 3, pp. 577-591 (May).

Theil, H. [1971] Principles of Econometrics, New York: Wiley & Sons, Inc.

Tse, E. and Anton, J. [1972] "On the Identifiability of Parameters," IEEE Trans. Auto. Control, vol. AC-17, no. 5, pp. 637-645. (October).

Tse, E. and Weinert, H. [1973] "Correction and Extension of 'On the Identifiability of Parameters'" IEEE Trans. Auto. Control, vol. AC-18, no. 6, pp. 687-688 (December).

Tse, E. and Weinert, H. [1975] "Structure Determination on Parameter Identification for Multivariable Stochastic Linear Systems," IEEE Trans. Auto. Control, vol. AC-20, no. 5, pp. 603-612 (October).

METHODES D'OPTIMISATION ADAPTEES AUX MODELES MACROECONOMIQUES

P. NEPOMIASTCHY

IRIA-LABORIA
78150 - Rocquencourt (France)

Résumé.

En choisissant comme test un modèle monétaire français, nous avons entrepris de faire une étude comparative de diverses méthodes d'optimisation de modèles macro-économiques.

Le modèle retenu est déterministe, dynamique (36 périodes), fortement non linéaire, il contient des retards allant jusqu'au 4ème ordre, il est petit (14 variables endogènes dynamiques) mais le nombre de variables de décision indépendantes est assez élevé (144).

Les méthodes d'optimisation retenues sont, d'une part, la méthode séquentielle (sans calcul de dérivées) et, d'autre part, la méthode du gradient conjugué pour laquelle le gradient du critère est calculé soit par différences finies (méthode classique), soit par la méthode de l'état-adjoint.

Les essais numériques effectués montrent la très nette supériorité des méthodes d'optimisation adaptées à la structure des modèles macroéconomiques par rapport à l'utilisation de programmes standards de recherche opérationnelle.

1. Introduction.

En choisissant comme test un modèle monétaire français [1], nous avons entrepris de faire une étude comparative de diverses méthodes de résolution et d'optimisation de modèles macroéconomiques. Le but recherché dans cette étude est de mettre en évidence le gain considérable par rapport à l'utilisation mécanique de sous-programmes bibliothèques (ou de langage de simulation comme TROLL) que l'on obtient en adaptant les techniques de résolution et d'optimisation à la structure particulière des modèles macroéconomiques.

Dans [2], nous avions proposé une méthode de résolution du modèle basée sur la méthode de Newton et tenant compte des particularités du modèle décrit dans [1], en particulier du fait que sur les 14 variables endogènes, 2 seulement sont implicites (*). Les essais numériques effectués récemment par B. Oudet ont montré que cette technique de résolution est environ trois fois plus rapide que l'utilisation du système TROLL (cf. [3]).

Dans [2], nous avions également proposé une méthode d'optimisation (la méthode séquentielle) qui s'était avérée être plus performante que les méthodes habituelles, au moins dans le cas d'un critère non régulier. La meilleure méthode retenue pour la comparaison a été le gradient conjugué, le gradient étant calculé par différences finies comme c'est l'usage en économétrie [4]. Cette méthode était "battue" par la méthode séquentielle parce que le calcul du gradient par différences finies coûte très cher; en effet, chaque calcul du gradient nécessite un nombre de résolutions du modèle égal à la dimension du contrôle (**). Nous proposons ici une nouvelle technique de calcul du gradient qui est l'adaptation aux modèles économétriques de la méthode de l'état adjoint bien connue en théorie du contrôle optimal. Cette technique, réduisant très considérablement le temps de calcul du gradient, permet d'obtenir un programme beaucoup plus performant que celui décrit dans [2] et, a fortiori, que ceux des bibliothèques de programmes.

Nous pensons que les raisons qui rendent ce programme compétitif ne sont pas spécifiques au modèle étudié et nous espérons dans l'avenir réussir à utiliser les idées générales développées dans [2] et ici pour résoudre et optimiser des modèles plus importants, comme ceux de l'INSEE.

(*) ce qui a l'air assez fréquent en économétrie; dans le modèle STAR de l'INSEE, par exemple, sur 74 variables 3 seulement sont implicites.

(**) i.e. 144 résolutions du modèle par calcul du gradient pour le modèle étudié ici.

2. Le modèle monétaire.

Le modèle monétaire trimestriel PIMPON a été développé et estimé par A. Coutière de la Direction de la Prévision [1].

équations de comportement.

(1) $$TXPA_t = 0.7\ TXPA_{t-1} + 0.3\ TXP_t$$

(2) $$IB_t = a_1\ IB_{t-1} + a_2\ IO_t + a_3$$

(3) $$\mathrm{Log}(L_t/P_t) = a_4 TXPA_t + a_5 TXPA_{t-1} + a_6 TXPA_{t-2} + a_7 TXPA_{t-3} + a_8 TXPA_{t-4} + a_9 IB_t + a_{10} IB_{t-1} + a_{11} IB_{t-2} + a_{12} IB_{t-3} + a_{13} IB_{t-4} + b_t^1$$

(4) $$\mathrm{Log}(CB_t/P_t) = a_{14} IO_t + a_{15} IO_{t-1} + a_{16} IO_{t-2} + a_{17} IO_{t-3} + a_{18} IO_{t-4} + a_{19} TXPA_t + a_{20} TXPA_{t-1} + a_{21} TXPA_{t-2} + a_{22} TXPA_{t-3} + a_{23} TXPA_{t-4} + b_t^2$$

(5) $$\mathrm{Log}(D_t) = a_{24}\ \mathrm{Log}(L_t) + b_t^3$$

(6) $$\mathrm{Log}(CE_t) = a_{25}\ \mathrm{Log}(L_t) + b_t^4$$

(7) $$\mathrm{Log}(TRE_t) = a_{26}\ \mathrm{Log}(L_t) + b_t^5$$

(8) $$\mathrm{Log}(RF_t) = a_{27}\ \rho_t + a_{28}\ \rho_{t-1} + a_{29}\ \rho_{t-2} + a_{30}\ \mathrm{Log}(RO_t) + b_t^6$$

relations de définition.

(9) $$TXP_t = 100\ \frac{P_t - P_{t-1}}{P_{t-1}}$$

(10) $$RO_t = \lambda_t\ D_t + \mu_t\ CB_t$$

(11) $$\rho_t = IO_t - I1_t\ \frac{RF_t}{CB_t}$$

identités.

(12) $$L_t = E_t + D_t + CE_t + TRE_t$$

(13) $$RF_t = E_t + RO_t + \alpha_t\ CE_t + b_t^7$$

(14) $$RF_t + D_t = RO_t + CB_t$$

variables endogènes :

P : niveau général des prix
TXP : taux de croissance du prix
L : ensemble des liquidités
IB : taux des obligations
CE : épargne des Caisses d'Epargne
E : billets
RF : refinancement bancaire
IO : condition des banques
TXPA : taux d'inflation anticipé
CB : crédit bancaire
D : dépôts bancaires
TRE : liquidités du Trésor
RO : réserves obligatoires
ρ : taux de rentabilité bancaire

variables de contrôle :

λ : coef. de réserve sur les dépôts
I1 : taux du marché monétaire
μ : coef. de réserve sur les crédits.
α : taux de liquidité de la CDC.

Les variables exogènes du modèle initial [1] ont été inclues dans les vecteurs $b^1,\ldots,b^7$.

3. La méthode de l'état-adjoint.

Cette méthode de calcul du gradient est bien connue et très utilisée en théorie du contrôle optimal (cf. , par exemple, [5]). Toutefois en contrôle optimal on considère généralement le cas ou l'équation d'état est une équation différentielle résolue par rapport à $\frac{dx}{dt}$ et ne comprenant pas de retards ; ceci correspond, en temps discret, à un système d'équations explicites et des retards n'excédant pas l'unité, ce qui ne correspond pas à la réalité des modèles macroéconomiques ; c'est peut-être la raison pour laquelle cette méthode ne semble pas avoir été utilisée en économétrie. Nous allons montrer comment cette méthode s'applique ici, puis nous montrerons au paragraphe suivant qu'elle est beaucoup moins coûteuse que la méthode des différences finies.

Nous allons d'abord introduire 10 variables endogènes fictives définies par 10 équations de comportement supplémentaires :

(15)
$$TXPA_t^1 = TXPA_{t-1}\ ;\ TXPA_t^2 = TXPA_{t-1}^1\ ;\ TXPA_t^3 = TXPA_{t-1}^2$$
$$IB_t^1 = IB_{t-1}\ ;\ IB_t^2 = IB_{t-1}^1\ ;\ IB_t^3 = IB_{t-1}^2$$
$$IO_t^1 = IO_{t-1}\ ;\ IO_t^2 = IO_{t-1}^1\ ;\ IO_t^3 = IO_{t-1}^2$$

$$\rho_t^1 = \rho_{t-1}$$

On notera que (15) implique, par exemple, que $TXPA_{t-2} = TXPA^1_{t-1}$, $TXPA_{t-3} = TXPA^2_{t-1}$ et $TXPA_{t-4} = TXPA^3_{t-1}$; on peut donc à l'aide de (15) et en faisant passer le nombre d'équations du modèle de 14 à 24, éliminer du modèle les retards supérieurs à l'unité.

Nous appellerons x_t le vecteur de dimension n (ici n=24) représentant les variables endogènes (y compris les fictives) à la période t ; nous appellerons x le vecteur $x = \{x_1,\ldots,x_t,\ldots,x_T\}$ de dimension $N = nT$, où T est le nombre de périodes (ici T=36, d'où N = 864). De même, nous appellerons u_t le vecteur $\{I1_t,\lambda_t,\mu_t,\alpha_t\}$ de dimension r (ici r=4) représentant le contrôle à la période t et u le vecteur $\{u_1,\ldots,u_t,\ldots,u_T\}$ de dimension $R = rT$ représentant la politique de contrôle.

A l'aide de (15) et de ces notations, les équations de modèle (y compris les 10 équations supplémentaires) prennent maintenant la forme compacte :

(16a) $$f_{it}(x_t\ ,\ x_{t-1}\ ,\ u_t) = 0\ ,\quad i=1,\ldots,n\ ,\ t=1,\ldots,T$$

(16b) x_o donné

On notera que pour que le modèle (1)-(14) soit résoluble, il faut, par exemple, pour la variable TXPA, connaître les valeurs de $TXPA_o$, $TXPA_{-1}$, $TXPA_{-2}$ et $TXPA_{-3}$; mais, à cause de (15), cela revient à connaître $TXPA_o$, $TXPA^1_o$, $TXPA^2_o$ et $TXPA^3_o$, d'où (16b).

Nous supposerons que le contrôle u pour lequel nous cherchons à calculer le gradient est une politique de contrôle raisonnable. Plus précisément, nous supposerons l'existence d'un nombre strictement positif c et d'un voisinage U de u tels que pour tout $v \in U$ la solution du modèle correspondante existe et soit non inférieure à c au moins pour toutes ses composantes intervenant dans le modèle par leur logarithme. Il est alors clair que dans ce voisinage de u, les fonctions f_{it} de (16) sont continûment différentiables. Pour tout v de U, nous noterons x(v) la trajectoire correspondante.

Nous supposerons que le critère à minimiser est de la forme très générale suivante :

(17) $$j(x,u) = \sum_{t=1}^{T} j_t(x_t,\ x_{t-1},\ u_t,\ u_{t-1})$$

On supposera que pour tout contrôle appartenant au voisinage U et pour sa trajectoire correspondante, la fonction j_t est continûment différentiable. On pose :

(18) $$J(v) = j[x(v),v] \quad , \quad \forall\ v \in U$$

Alors, le gradient $J'(u)$ du critère J en u est, par définition, le vecteur de R^R qui vérifie :

(19) $$\lim_{\varepsilon\to 0} \frac{J(u+\varepsilon v) - J(u)}{\varepsilon} = (J'(u),v)_R \quad , \quad \forall\ v \in R^R$$

où $(x,y)_R$ désigne le produit scalaire de R^R. Pour simplifier les notations ultérieures, nous poserons d'abord :

(20) $$u_\varepsilon = u+\varepsilon v \ ; \ x_\varepsilon = \frac{1}{\varepsilon}[x(u_\varepsilon)-x(u)] \ ; \ \Delta_\varepsilon = \frac{1}{\varepsilon}[J(u_\varepsilon)-J(u)]$$

puis nous noterons F_t, G_t et H_t les matrices de dimensions respectives (n,n), $(n;n)$ et (n,r) dont les éléments sont respectivement $\partial f_{it}/\partial x_{jt}$, $\partial f_{it}/\partial x_{j,t-1}$ et $\partial f_{it}/\partial u_{jt}$ pris au point u.

Il est clair que $u_\varepsilon \to u$ lorsque $\varepsilon \to 0$, donc il est clair que, U étant un voisinage de u, on a $u_\varepsilon \in U$ pour tout ε assez petit, ce qui entraîne la différentiabilité des f_{it} et, par conséquent, la correction de trajectoire x_ε est la solution de :

(21a) $$F_t\, x_{\varepsilon t} + G_t\, x_{\varepsilon,t-1} + H_t\, v_t = O(\varepsilon) \quad , \quad t=1,\dots,T$$

(21b) $$x_{\varepsilon o} = 0$$

au moins pour ε assez petit. Enfin, on pose :

(22a) $$y_{it} = \frac{\partial j_t}{\partial x_{it}} + \frac{\partial j_{t+1}}{\partial x_{it}} \quad , \quad i=1,\dots,n \quad , \quad t=1,\dots,T-1$$

(22b) $$y_{it} = \frac{\partial j_t}{\partial x_{it}} \quad , \quad i=1,\dots,n \quad , \quad t=T$$

(22c) $$w_{it} = \frac{\partial j_t}{\partial u_{it}} + \frac{\partial j_{t+1}}{\partial u_{it}} \quad , \quad i=1,\dots,r \quad , \quad t=1,\dots,T-1$$

(22d) $$w_{it} = \frac{\partial j_t}{\partial u_{it}} \quad , \quad i=1,\dots,r$$

En notant $(x,y)_n$ et $(x,y)_r$ les produits scalaires respectifs de R^n et de R^r, en utilisant (17), (18), (20), $x_{\varepsilon o} = v_o = 0$ et les notations (22), on vérifiera que l'on a :

(23) $$\Delta_\varepsilon = \sum_{t=1}^{T} [y_t,x_{\varepsilon t})_n + (w_t,v_t)_r] + O(\varepsilon)$$

pour tout ε assez petit.

Soit enfin Ψ le vecteur $\{\Psi_1,\ldots,\Psi_t,\ldots,\Psi_T\}$ de R^N, i.e. on a $\Psi_t \in R^n$ pour tout t, que l'on appelle état adjoint et qui est la solution du système :

(24a) $$G_{t+1}^* \Psi_{t+1} + F_t^* \Psi_t + y_t = 0 \quad , \quad t=1,\ldots,T-1$$

(24b) $$F_t^* \Psi_t + y_t = 0 \quad , \quad t=T$$

où G_{t+1}^* et F_t^* désignent les matrices transposées de G_{t+1} et F_t. De (24) on déduit :

(25a) $$(y_t,x_{\varepsilon t})_n = -(G_{t+1}\, x_{\varepsilon t}, \Psi_{t+1})_n - (F_t\, x_{\varepsilon t}, \Psi_t)_n \quad , \quad t=1,\ldots,T-1$$

(25b) $$(y_t,x_{\varepsilon t})_n = -(F_t x_{\varepsilon t}\, , \Psi_t)_n \quad , \quad t=T$$

Combinant (21a) et (25), on obtient :

(26a) $$(y_t,x_{\varepsilon t})_n = -(G_{t+1}\, x_{\varepsilon t}, \Psi_{t+1}) + (G_t\, x_{\varepsilon,t-1}, \Psi_t)_n + (H_t v_t,\Psi_t)_n + O(\varepsilon) \; ,$$

$$t = 1,\ldots,T-1$$

(26b) $$(y_t, x_{\varepsilon t})_n = (G_t\, x_{\varepsilon,t-1}\, , \Psi_t)_n + (H_t v_t, \Psi_t)_n + O(\varepsilon) \quad , \quad t=T$$

En sommant les équations (26) et en tenant compte de $x_{\varepsilon o} = 0$, on trouve, à l'aide de (23) :

(27) $$\Delta_\varepsilon = \sum_{t=1}^{T} [(H_t v_t, \Psi_t)_n + (w_t,v_t)_r] + O(\varepsilon)$$

pour tout ε assez petit ; de la définition (20) de Δ_ε et de la définition (19) de $J'(u)$ on déduit alors le résultat final :

(28) $$J'_t(u) = H_t^* \Psi_t + w_t \quad , \quad t=1,\ldots,T .$$

4. Application de la méthode de l'état-adjoint au modèle PIMPON.

La seule difficulté pour appliquer la méthode de l'état-adjoint est la résolution du système (24), système que l'on résout pour t = T, T-1, T-2, etc. Pour chaque t, on calcule Ψ_t connaissant Ψ_{t+1}, on doit donc résoudre un système linéaire de n équations à n inconnues, système que nous noterons simplement $A\Psi_t = b$.

Il faut noter que, si l'on appelle n_1 le nombre de variables endogènes du modèle initial et n_2 le nombre de variables fictives ajoutées pour éliminer les retards (on a $n = n_1 + n_2$ et, pour PIMPON, $n_1 = 14$ et $n_2 = 10$) alors on déduit aisément de (15) et (24) que les n_2 dernières équations du système $A\Psi_t = b$ s'écrivent simplement $\Psi_{it} = b_i$, $i = n_1+1,\ldots,n$. Par conséquent, la dimension du système linéaire à résoudre est seulement n_1 (ici 14 et non 24). Il est clair d'ailleurs que cette réduction de la dimension du système n'est pas caractéristique du modèle PIMPON et s'applique chaque fois que les retards sont éliminés par des formules telles que (15).

En ce qui concerne le système linéaire de dimension 14 à résoudre pour PIMPON, nous avons constaté que sur ses 196 coefficients seulement 43 n'étaient pas nuls, ce qui nous a permis de résoudre ce système analytiquement. Les essais numériques décrits ci-dessous montrent le gain de temps machine que représente cette résolution analytique par rapport à une résolution numérique. Reconnaissons cependant que cette résolution analytique n'est envisageable que pour les petits modèles.

Nous avons retenu pour tester la méthode deux critères :

$$J_1 = \sum_{t=1}^{T} \left| \frac{L_t - L_{t-1}}{L_{t-1}} - \frac{Y_t - Y_{t-1}}{Y_{t-1}} \right| + k \text{ DERIV} \tag{29}$$

avec

$$\text{DERIV} = \sum_{t=1}^{T} \left[\left| I1_t - I1_{t-1} \right| + \left| \lambda_t - \lambda_{t-1} \right| + \left| \mu_t - \mu_{t-1} \right| + \left| \alpha_t - \alpha_{t-1} \right| \right] \tag{30}$$

d'une part, et :

$$J_2 = \sum_{t=1}^{T} \left[\frac{L_t - L_{t-1}}{L_{t-1}} - \frac{Y_t - Y_{t-1}}{Y_{t-1}} \right]^2 \tag{31}$$

d'autre part. Le critère J_1 est celui que nous avions choisi dans [2] ; la variable exogène Y_t étant le PNB en volume, ce critère exprime la politique monétariste qui tend à ramener le taux de croissance de la masse monétaire (L_t) au niveau du taux de croissance du PNB en volume; la partie DERIV du critère J_1 est un stabilisateur de la politique de contrôle. Le critère J_1 n'étant pas différentiable, l'application de la méthode de l'état-adjoint décrite au paragraphe précédent entraîne une certaine erreur sur le gradient. Ceci explique qu'au bout d'un certain nombre d'itérations, le gradient approché cesse d'être une direction de descente et l'algorithme du gradient conjugué se bloque.

Nous avons choisi pour J_2 un critère différentiable pour bien montrer la différence.

5. Résultats numériques.

Pour la minimisation du critère J_1, nous avons retenu trois méthodes basées sur l'algorithme du gradient conjugué (Fletcher - Reeves) et différant seulement par la technique de calcul du gradient. Pour ce calcul, la méthode 3 utilise la méthode classique des différences finies (cf. [2]) et les deux premières méthodes utilisent la méthode de l'état-adjoint décrite au paragraphe 3. Pour la méthode 1, le système linéaire (24) permettant le calcul de Ψ est résolu analytiquement et pour la méthode 2 il est résolu numériquement à l'aide de la méthode de Gauss. La méthode séquentielle (ou méthode des variations locales) décrite en [2], et qui s'est montrée être particulièrement adaptée à la minimisation des critères non différentiables, est compétitive pour la minimisation du critère J_1 et est donnée ici à titre de comparaison. La table 1 indique, pour chaque méthode, la valeur du critère atteinte au bout de T secondes d'unité centrale d'un ordinateur IBM 370-168.

T	méth.1	méth.2	méth.3	méth.4
5	2.538	2.604	2.813	2.217
10	2.073	2.370	2.624	1.990
15	1.499	1.938	2.609	1.832
20	1.236	1.638	2.606	1.674
25	1.161	1.391		1.491
30		1.170		1.421
40		1.161		1.378
50				1.336
60				
70				

Table 1

Pour ce critère non différentiable, la méthode classique des différence finies, qui se bloque au bout de 20 secondes (le gradient cesse d'être une direction de descente), se trouve être la plus mauvaise des quatre méthodes testées. La méthode séquentielle, qui n'utilise pas les dérivées, est la meilleure des quatre pendant les 10 premières secondes de calcul, mais le meilleur résultat est obtenu à l'aide de la méthode de l'état-adjoint, qui converge en 81 itérations avec un temps de calcul de 25,83 sec. pour la méthode 1 et de 38,15 sec. pour la méthode 2.

Pour la minimisation du critère J_2, qui est différentiable, la méthode séquentielle cesse d'être compétitive et la table 2 montre les résultats des trois premières méthodes.

T	méth.1	méth.2	méth.3
5	2.701	3.562	11.205
10	1.940	2.701	10.917
15	1.262	2.662	10.355
20	1.214	1.881	9.508
25		1.694	8.845
30		1.544	7.815
40		1.214	6.329
60			4.769
80			3.882
100			3.720
120			3.217
140			3.051
160			2.964

Table 2

On constate là encore la très nette supériorité de la méthode de l'état-adjoint qui converge en 151 itérations et avec un temps de calcul de 16.55 sec. pour la méthode 1 et de 39.91 pour la méthode 2 vers une solution meilleure que celle atteinte par la méthode 3 au bout de 160 secondes.

La conclusion de notre étude ne peut être que très partielle puisque cette étude ne porte pour l'instant que sur un seul modèle. Cependant, les résultats obtenus avec ce (petit) modèle sont suffisamment nets pour motiver des études complémentaires sur l'efficacité de la méthode de l'état-adjoint appliquée à l'optimisation des modèles macroéconométriques.

6. Bibliographie.

[1] Coutière A.; "Un modèle du système monétaire français", INSEE, Statistiques et études financières. 1975/17.

[2] Népomiastchy P.; Oudet B.; "Comparison of Optimization Techniques for a French Monetary Model", Publ. IRIA et Univ. Grenoble, présenté à la "Stochastic Control Conference" Palo Alto, 26-28 Mai 1976.

[3] TROLL ; "An Introduction and Demonstration" Publ. D0083, NBER (1974).

[4] Fair R.C.; "On the Solution of Optimal Problems as Maximization Problems", Annals of Economic and Social Measurement , V.3, n°1, Janv. 1974, pp 135-154.

[5] Népomiastchy P.; "Méthode de pénalisation et applications", Doc. Travail 75-28, IERESM (Bruxelles), Juillet 1975.

ENVIRONMENT AND POLLUTION

ENVIRONNEMENT ET POLLUTION

A DECISION MAKING MODEL FOR ENVIRONMENTAL MANAGEMENT SYSTEMS

Y. Sawaragi, K. Inoue
Faculty of Engineering, Kyoto University
Kyoto, Japan
and
H. Nakayama
Faculty of Science, Kohnan University
Kobe, Japan

1. Introduction

The material civilization has advanced to the highest degree for the past one or two decades, while it produced not a few harmful influences for the human society and its environment. Above all, the environmental pollution and destruction has been a serious social problem since about 1970. Because its causes and effects are very complex and cover a wide range, environmental problems should be resolved by an interdisciplinary treatment including politics, economics, sociology, medical science and engineering, etc. Moreover, we recently recognize the multiplicity of value judgement in the human society. Therefore, it is necessary to consider the environmental problem as a total system with multiple conflicting objectives including related other problems, for example, social welfare, medical service, education, trafic etc. On the wholistic standpoint like this, environmental management systems aim to decide a long range and drastic policy for environmental problems. In this regard, it finally becomes a decision making problem with multiple conflicting objectives that we have to solve. One procedure solving it is as in Fig. 1.

In the following, we shall discuss each phase in more detail.

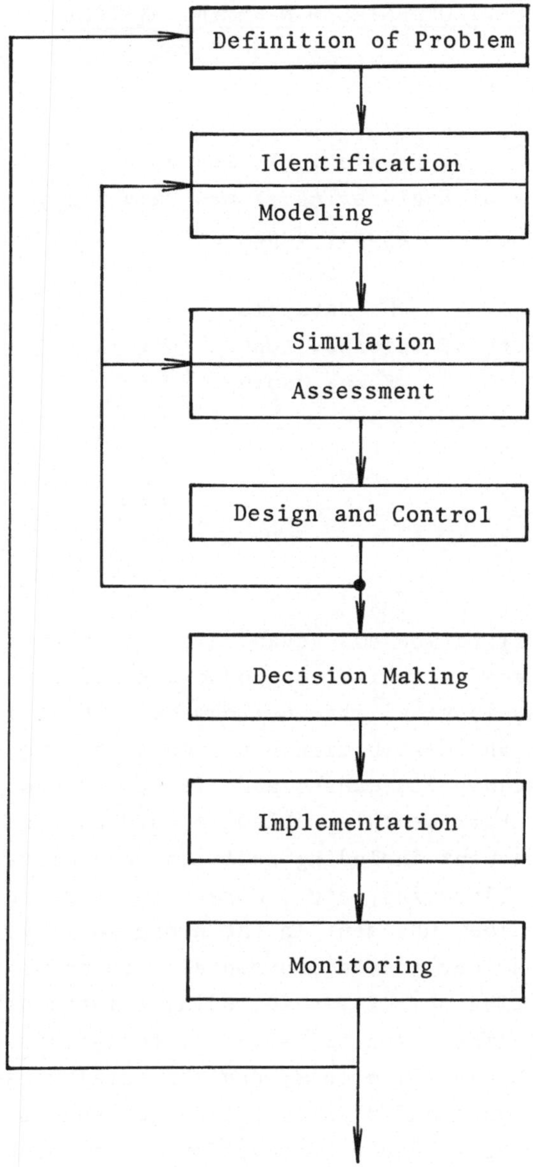

Fig. 1 Decision making model for environmental management systems

2. Perception of Environmental Pollution Problematique

The environmental pollution problem itself is a collection of complexly interelated problems such as air pollution, water pollution, solid waste discharge, noise and vibration problems, and so on. Furthermore, since from wider view point the environmental pollution problem is closely related to problems involved in environmental administration, industrial activities, energy, economy, society, transportation, etc., then it is easily recognized that the true solution to the problem cannot be obtained no matter how deeply the problem alone is pursuited.

The collection of the interrelated problems in the center of which is of course the environmental pollution problem is called a "environmental pollution problematique". By analysing this problematique, that is, by making clear the interrelationships, hierarchical structure and importance ranking between various problems included in the problematique, it is expected that we can obtain very useful information to solve the environmental pollution problem. This is a new trend in systems approach to the environmental problems /8/.

In order to understand the structure of the complexly interrelated environmental pollution problematique, we at first have to establish each relation between each pair of the problems. To this end, it is necessary and important to consult those who bear collective responsibility, for example, statemen, leaders of opinion, scientists, philosophers, etc., because in the identification of such a very complex problem as the environmental pollution problematique where any experiment may not be allowed, the maximum use of the rich experience and insight of the human beings is the first attempt towards the understanding of the problematique.

As a communication procedure with these influencing persons, a method of questionnaire-and-answer together with interviews can be effectively used /5/. For example, an influencial person is asked to answer how each of the problems is directly related in both directions and intensities with the other problems. The analysis of the questionaires is performed to make clear the direct and indirect relations among the problems. For this purpose, mainly methods extracted from the graph theory; the weighted digraph and its matrix representation together with some matrix manipulation, is introduced /4/.

As a result of the analysis of the questionaires, we can get classification of problems according to their importance and urgency, a hierarchy of problems according to their interrelations and the intensity of such interrelations, and graphs showing the hierarchy and interrelations. The interpretation of these results gives us insight into the "objectives" set up by influencing persons for the environmental pollution problematique, the "key problems" to be solved for achieving the intended objectives, and the meaningful relations for the definition of sub-systems and a better knowledge of the functioning of society.

Through this kind of global analysis of such an interdisciplinary and complex problem as the environmental pollution problematique will give us better understanding of the problem itself and will give us possible solution strategies to the problem.

3. Environmental Assessment

3.1. Methodologies

In the field of environmental assessment, the impact analysis of an "action" on the value of the environment which surrounds the action has been a focal issue. An action, which is often called as an "alternative" means any kind of decision concerned with planning, design, construction or manipulation of an environmental system. In this class of problems, it is well and widely recognized that an action or alternative should be assessed from a multi-objective viewpoint.

The process of the approach usually used for environmental assessment has five distinctive steps;

(1) goal definition
(2) decomposition of the goal into objectives
(3) structuring and weighting of objectives
(4) rating of alternatives
(5) ranking of alternatives.

The first three steps (1), (2) and (3) are concerned with the analysis of the goal and the objectives and also concerned with the interrelationship analysis of complexly related objectives, the process of which we discuss in this section. The other steps (4) and (5) are concerned with the numerical evaluation of each alternatives and the selection of the best.

Additionally, we try to do quantitative modeling of the system as well as the qualitative ones. Though there are several well known quantitative modeling methods, here we refer only to GMDH (Group Method of Data Handling) /9/. GMDH is a kind of data fitting method in terms of multi-variable polynomial doing self-organization based on comparatively few data. It seems to be most prominent among other existing identification techniques especially for nonlinear complex systems because it does not require so many input/output data and so much computing effort, and moreover its algorithm is stable. It has been applied for actual problems, for example, the estimation of the quantity of a river water, and its efficiency is proved /7/.

What we have to do next is to assess alternatives. Assessment itself depends on the decision maker's view of value, and therefore alternatives are evaluated on the basis of decision maker's value judgement. First of all, a hierachical structure of the objectives should be identified in order to grasp the value structure of the system. ISM (Interpretive Structural Modeling) suggested by Warfield /17/ may be available for this purpose. Multi-attribute utility theory seems to provide a most efficient tool for assessment of alternatives; above all, the multi-attribute utility function suggested by Keeney /10/ is most attractive because it is based on assumptions which are easily inspected even in actual problems. In order to hold those assumptions (utility indepence and preferential independence), the hierarchical structure of objectives should be a so-called single sink digraph tree. In general, however, such a single sink tree can not always be obtained because of interrelations among objectives. By using ISM, we can grasp not only the hierarchical structure of objectives but also causes violating single sink tree, say, cycles in the digraph and plural paths from a objective to a objective at higher levels. Farris and Sage have suggested a method obtaining a single sink tree of objectives by cutting the interrelation with the help of ISM /3/.

However, there are several methods of assessment considering the interrelationship among objectives at the highter levels explicitly. In the following, we shall discuss one of the methods in some detail.

3.2. Interrelationship Analysis of Objectives

Generally, certain of the objectives are more "important" than the others in determining the goal satisfaction of alternatives. This importance is expressed by the assignment of a weight to each objective. The weight is used to indicate relative improtance between objectives.

The relative importance of an objective is determined on the basis of the following two distinctively different judgement. The first is subjective judgement or preference judgement on how important is an alternative itself in the stated goal, disussin of which is out of the scope of this section. The second is a measure of importance of an alternative judged on the basis of its relationship to the other objectives. A certain objective may be more important than the other in the sense that the achievement of the objective makes more contribution to the achievement of all other objectives.

		Objectives Influenced					
		g_1	g_2	...	g_j	....	g_n
Objectives Influencing	g_1	\	a_{12}		a_{1j}		a_{1n}
	g_2	a_{21}	\		a_{2j}		a_{2n}
	......						
	g_i	a_{i1}	a_{i2}		a_{ij}		a_{in}
	...						
	g_n	a_{n1}	a_{n2}		a_{nj}		\

Fig. 2 Objectives cross-support matrix A

In the field of Technology Assessment, the interrelationships among objectives are commonly determined by a cross-support analysis or similar ones called matrix approaches /2/. Fig. 2 shows an objectives cross-support matrix $A = [a_{ij}]$, where g_i $(i=1,2,\ldots,n)$ stands for the i-th objective and a_{ij} $(i,j = 1,2,\ldots,n)$ represents the degree of contribution of the objective g_i to the objective g_j. The total degree of contribution G_i, of the objective g_i to all the other objectives is given by

$$G_i = \sum_{j=1}^{n} a_{ij} \qquad (i \neq j) \tag{3-1}$$

Specialists assess the degree of each contribution a_{ij} by associating numeric values to an adjectival scale, as follows;

major contribution	$a_{ij} = 8$
considerable contribution	$a_{ij} = 4$
some contribution	$a_{ij} = 2$
negligible contribution	$a_{ij} = 0.$

If the effects are negative, then the same scale can be used with negative signs.

The logarithmic scale is often chosen as opposed to the arithmetic one, since experience has shown that several physiological processes or functions tend to be logarithmic in nature.

The weight V_i defined by

$$V_i = \frac{G_i}{\sum_{i=1}^{n} G_i} \tag{3-2}$$

reflects the relative importance of the objective g_i judged on the basis of its relationship to the other objectives.

This matrix approach often used in the field of Technology Assessment has a drawback that it does not take the "feedback" or "indirect" effects among objectives into account /15/. The total degree of contribution G_i given by (3-1) reflects only the direct influence of the objective g_i to all the others. Suppose g_i contributes to g_j and then g_j contributes to g_k, then it is true from experiences to consider that g_i contributes to g_k indirectly through g_j. That is, it is natural to consider that the law of transitivity holds in many cases.

Although a method to evaluate these indirect effects has been proposed /15/, a more general and computationally more effective method similar to the graph-matrix method used in the DEMATEL project by Battell /4,5/ is described here.

We define a direct influence matrix D by

$$D = \begin{bmatrix} d_{11}, & d_{12}, \ldots, & d_{1n} \\ d_{21}, & d_{22}, \ldots, & d_{2n} \\ \ldots & \ldots & \ldots \\ d_{n1}, & d_{n2}, \ldots, & d_{nn} \end{bmatrix} \tag{3-3}$$

where

$$d_{ij} = s \cdot a_{ij}, \qquad s>0 \qquad (i,j = 1,2,\ldots,n) \tag{3-4}$$

or equivalenty,

$$D = sA \tag{3-5}$$

and a_{ij} is the degree of direct contribution of the objective g_i to the objective g_j which are shown in Fig. 2 and s is a sealing factor which is to be discussed later.

It should be noted that a row sum of the matrix D,

$$d_{is} = \sum_{j=1}^{n} d_{ij} \qquad (3\text{-}6)$$

shows the total degree of scaled direct influence to give of the objective g_i on all the others, similarly a colum sum

$$d_{sj} = \sum_{i=1}^{n} d_{ij} \qquad (3\text{-}7)$$

represeuts the total degree of scaled direct influence received of the objective g_j from all the others.

Let the (i,j)-element of D^2 by $d_{ij}^{(2)}$, then

$$d_{ij}^{(2)} = \sum_{k=1}^{n} d_{ik} \cdot d_{kj}. \qquad (3\text{-}8)$$

One can easily see that $d_{ij}^{(2)}$ of D^2 shows the degree of the 2-step influeuce from g_i to g_j through all the other objectives (k = 1,2,..., n), provided that the indirect influence with 2 steps can be represented by the product of the two direct influences, that is, by $d_{ik} \cdot d_{kj}$, which seems natural in practice. Similarly $d_{ij}^{(m)}$ of D^m shows the degree of the m-step or m-th order indirect influence from g_i to g_j. Thus

$$D + D^2 + \ldots + D^m = \sum_{i=1}^{m} D^i \qquad (3\text{-}9)$$

shows the sum of the direct and indirect influence up to the order m.

If D^m tends to zero as m goes to infinity, then we have

$$F = \sum_{i=1}^{\infty} D^i = D(I - D)^{-1} \qquad (3\text{-}10)$$

where I is the unit matrix. F is called a direct and indirect influence matrix which measures the direct and indirect effects between objectives.

The matrix H given by

$$H = \sum_{i=2}^{\infty} D^i = D^2(I - D)^{-1} \qquad (3\text{-}11)$$

gives the measure of the indirect effects only between the objectives.

The i-th row sum of the direct and indirect matrix $F = [f_{ij}]$,

$$f_{is} = \sum_{j=1}^{n} f_{ij} \qquad (3\text{-}12)$$

gives the total of the direct and indirect influence to give of the objective gi onto all the others, similarly

$$f_{sj} = \sum_{i=1}^{n} f_{ij} \tag{3-13}$$

gives the measure of the total of the direct and indirect influence received of the objective g_i from all the others.

Thus W_i defined by

$$W_i = \frac{f_{is}}{\sum_{i=1}^{n} f_{is}} \tag{3-14}$$

gives the normalized weight of the objective g_i viewed from the direct and indirect influence to give, and

$$Y_j = \frac{f_{sj}}{\sum_{j=1}^{n} f_{sj}} \tag{3-15}$$

gives the normalized weight of the objective g_j viewed from the direct and indirect influence received.

The assumption that D^m tends to zero as m increases to the infinity corresponds to the emprically proofed assumption that the indirect effects vanish as the chain of cause-consequence becomes longer. This assumption gives information how to select the scaling factor s of the matrix D from the matrix A.

A theorem in the matrix theory says that if and only if $\rho(D) < 1$, then the series F converges to $D(I - D)^{-1}$, where $\rho(D)$ is the spectral radius of the matrix D. A rough estimate on the upper bound of $\rho(D)$ is simply given by /16/

$$\rho(D) \le \max_{1 \le i \le n} \sum_{j=1}^{n} |d_{ij}| = \max_{1 \le i \le n} s\sum_{j=1}^{n} |a_{ij}| \tag{3-16}$$

or

$$\rho(D) \le \max_{1 \le j \le n} \sum_{i=1}^{n} |d_{ij}| = \max_{1 \le j \le n} s\sum_{i=1}^{n} |a_{ij}| \tag{3-17}$$

A better estimate is given by

$$\rho(D) \le \min\{ \max_{1 \le i \le n} \frac{1}{x_i} \sum_{j=1}^{n} |d_{ij}| x_j, \max_{1 \le j \le n} x_j \sum_{i=1}^{n} \frac{|d_{ij}|}{x_i} \}$$

$$= \min\{ \max_{1\le i\le n} \frac{s}{x_i} \sum_{j=1}^{n} |a_{ij}| x_j, \max_{1\le j\le n} x_j s \Sigma \frac{|a_{ij}|}{x_i} \} \quad (3\text{-}18)$$

where $x_1, x_2, \ldots, x_n$ and arbitrary chosen n positive real numbers.

These estimates on the upper bound of $\rho(D)$ suggest that the scaling factor s should be selected from the region

$$0 < s < s_{ub}$$

where

$$s_{ub} = \frac{1}{\max_{1\le i\le n} \sum_{j=1}^{n} |a_{ij}|} \quad (3\text{-}19)$$

or

$$s_{ub} = \frac{1}{\max_{1\le j\le n} \sum_{i=1}^{n} |a_{ij}|} \quad (3\text{-}20)$$

so that the series F to converge.

By adjusting s, we can control the degree of transitivity, or the degree of the indirect effects. If the smaller value of s is selected, the direct effects are more conspicuous than the indirect effects.

4. Design and Control

As was stated above, multi-attribute utility functions represent the global preference structure of the decision maker. The optimal strategy, in general, is selected as one which affords a maximum to the expected utility. However, it is not always necessary to identify the global utility function, if our aim is only to find out an optimal solution among the set of alternatives. Especially when we consider deterministic cases, in which one consequence certainly occurs by performing one alternative, we can make use of interactive programming methods. That is, in the case where the utitity function of the decision maker is not previously assessed explicitly, the partial information about the preference attitude of the decision maker may be extracted through the interaction with him. The optimal policy can be decided based upon those informations. Although several attractive methods have recently been developed, we shall, in the following, make a brief introduction of a method which was suggested by the authors/13/.

Let X be the set of alternatives, and let $f=(f_1 \ldots f_n)$ be the criterion to be minimized. The preference of the decision maker may be represented as follows:

$$x^1 \; P \; x^2, \quad x^1, x^2 \in X \Longleftrightarrow y^1 \prec_D y^2, \quad y^i = f(x^i) \qquad (4\text{-}1)$$

where $x^1 \; P \; x^2$ means that x^1 is preferred to x^2, and $\prec_D$ is the preference ordering among the feasible region $f(X)$ in the criterion space. Our aim is to find out an optimal solution $x^* \in X$ such that

$$x^* \; P \; x \quad \text{for every} \quad x \in X \qquad (4\text{-}2)$$

or equivalently

$$y^* \prec_D y \quad \text{for every} \quad y \in Y \qquad (4\text{-}3)$$

where $y^* = f(x^*)$ and $Y = f(X)$. If $\prec_D$ is a weak order, the optimal solution y^* is well defined under some appropriate assumptions, for example, the continuity of $\prec_D$ and compactness of Y. Even though it is the case, it is not so easy to find out the optimal solution as long as the preference structure is not known a priori. In this situation, it is very useful to reduce the set of alternatives by some appropriate value judgement. Pareto's unanimity rule is an example of such a weak value judgement which may be recognized by everybody. That is, the ordering $\prec_P$ such that

$$y^1 \prec_P y^2 \overset{\Delta}{\Longleftrightarrow} y^1 - y^2 \in R^n_- \qquad (4\text{-}4)$$

admits the following inclusion

$$(Y, \prec_P) \subset (Y, \prec_D) \qquad (4\text{-}5)$$

Therefore, according to /18/ we have

$$M[Y, \prec_P] \supset M[Y, \prec_D] \qquad (4\text{-}6)$$

where $M[Y, \prec]$ denotes the minimal set of the ordered set Y with a binary relation $\prec$. This implies that each Pareto solution of the set $M[Y, \prec_P]$ is a candidate of the optimal solution with respect to the preference of the decision maker.

Under the assumption of smoothness of the criterion $f=(f_1 \ldots f_n)$, the Pareto solution set $M[Y, \prec_P]$ defines an $(n-1)$-dimensional surface, often called trade-off surface, in the criterion space R^n. When the criterion f is of at most 3-dimensional, the trade-off surface actually can be visualized. With the help of that illustration, the decision maker easily makes his decision.

Multiplier method /12/ seems most prominent for obtaining such a visible trade-off surface, because it provides not only Pareto solutions but also the direction ratio of the normal of the trade-off surface, often called trade-off ratio. However, in the case when the criterion is of more than 3-dimensional, we have to invoke to other methods since this visualization becomes impossible.

We denote by M_{ij} the marginal rate of substitution which implies the increment of Y_j in compensation for loss of the marginal unit of Y_i. In this event, the preference structure of the decision maker can be defined by the level of the critreion f and the vector of the marginal rate of substitution $M = (M_1, M_2, \ldots, M_{n-1}, 1)$ where $M_i = M_{in}$. That is, the preference attitude of the decision maker can be represented as the vector field (R^n, M). For example, the indifference surface may be defined as a differential equation in terms of the marginal rate of substitution:

$$M_1 dy_1 + \ldots + M_{n-1} dy_{n-1} + dy_n = 0, \qquad M_i = M_{in} \tag{4-7}$$

Since it is in general difficult to identify the form of $M_i(y)$, the differential equation (4-7) can be resolved in no more than restricted cases. However, if our aim is only to find out the optimal solution, there is no need to solve the differential equation. According to the well known Lagrangian rule, we have the following at the optimal solution y^0:

$$y^0 \in G, \quad M_{ij}(y^0) = T_{ij}(y^0) \qquad (i,j = 1,\ldots,n) \tag{4-8}$$

where G denotes the trade-off surface and T_{ij} denotes the trade-off ratio. Because of the so-called chain rule, the equation (4-8) can be reduced to

$$y^0 \in G, \quad M_i(y^0) = T_i(y^0) \qquad (i=1,\ldots,n-1) \tag{4-9}$$

Note that it is very easy for the decision maker to judge whether his marginal rate of substitution at a point y, $M_i(y)$, is more or less than the trade-off ratio $T_i(y)$.

Making use of this fact yields the following computation algorithm: For brevity of illustration, it is assumed that the utility function can be represented by $U(y_1, y_2, \ldots, y_n)$ and the trade-off surface by $G(y_1, y_2, \ldots, y_n) = 0$. If we have $y_n = F(y_1, \ldots, y_{n-1})$ by solving $G(y_1, y_2, \ldots, y_n) = 0$, the marginal rate of substitution restricted on the trade-off surface, $\tilde{U}_i (= [\partial U/\partial y_i]_G)$, can be given by

$$\tilde{U}_i = U_i + U_n F_i \qquad (i=1,\ldots,n-1) \qquad (4\text{-}10)$$

where $U_i = \partial U/\partial y_i$, $F_i = \partial F/\partial y_i$. On the other hand, on the trade-off surface G we have

$$G_i + G_n F_i = 0 \qquad (i=1,\ldots,n-1) \qquad (4\text{-}11)$$

where $G_i = \partial G/\partial y_i$. Therefore, making use of the fact that

$$M_{in} = U_i/U_n, \qquad T_{in} = G_i/G_n, \qquad (4\text{-}12)$$

we have

$$\tilde{U}_i \gtreqless 0 \qquad M_{in} \gtreqless T_{in} \qquad (i=1,\ldots,n-1) \qquad (4\text{-}13)$$

Consequently, transforming the minimization of the utility restricted on the surface G into that of the function $U(x_1, \ldots, x_{n-1}, F(x_1, \ldots, x_{n-1}))$ on the space R^{n-1}, the optimal solution could be easily obtained by searching in the direction of the co-ordinate axis changed cyclically.

Bisectioning method, for example, may be employed for the search in each axis direction.

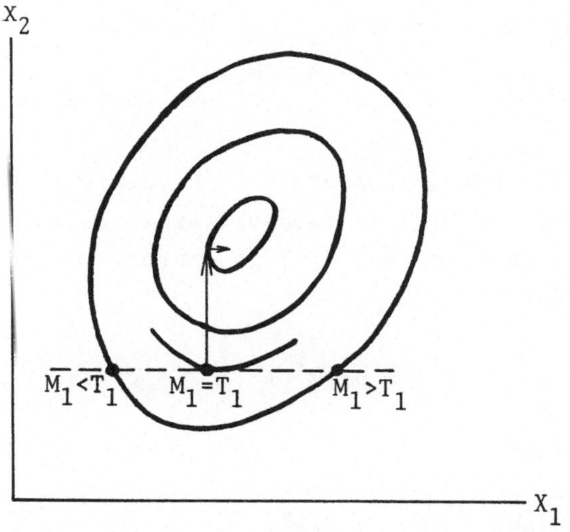

Fig. 3. Interactive coordinatewise searching method

This method seems very attractive because it requires the decision maker only to judge whether his marginal rate of substitution at some points on the trade-off surface is more or less than the trade-off ratio. We have the following lemma in regard to convergence of the method:

[Lemma]

Let X be a convex set and let $f_i(x)$ $(i=1,\ldots, n)$ be convex functions. If the utility function $U(y_1,\ldots,y_n)$ is quasi-convex (pseudo-convex or convex), then the function $\tilde{U}(y_1,\ldots, y_{n-1}) \equiv U(y_1,\ldots, y_{n-1}, F(y_1,\ldots, y_{n-1}))$ is also quasi-convex (pseudo-convex or convex, respectively).

(proof) As to quasi-convexity, the proof is the same as /6/ and therefore omitted.

In the case when

$$\tilde{U}^1_{\tilde{y}}(\tilde{y}^2 - \tilde{y}^1) \equiv U^1_{\tilde{y}}(\tilde{y}^2 - \tilde{y}^1) + U^1_{y_n} \cdot F^1_{\tilde{y}}(\tilde{y}^2 - \tilde{y}^1) \geqq 0 \tag{4-14}$$

where $\tilde{y} = (y_1,\ldots,y_{n-1})$ and $U^1_{\tilde{y}} = U_{\tilde{y}}(\tilde{y}^1)$, etc., we have

$$\begin{aligned} U^1_y(y^2 - y^1) &\equiv U^1_{\tilde{y}}(\tilde{y}^2 - \tilde{y}^1) + U^1_{y_n}(y^2_n - y^1_n) \\ &\geqq U^1_{\tilde{y}}(\tilde{y}^2 - \tilde{y}^1) + U^1_{y_n} \cdot F^1_{\tilde{y}}(\tilde{y}^2 - \tilde{y}^1) \\ &\geqq 0 \end{aligned} \tag{4-15}$$

because $F(\tilde{y})$ is convex under the convexity assumption of $f_i(x)$ $(i=1,\ldots n)$ and X. Therefore, we obtain that

$$\tilde{U}(\tilde{y}^2) - \tilde{U}(\tilde{y}^1) \geqq 0 \quad \text{if} \quad \tilde{U}^1_{\tilde{y}}(\tilde{y}^2 - \tilde{y}^1) \geqq 0 \tag{4-16}$$

by virtue of the pseudo-convexity of $U(y_1\ldots y_n)$. (4-16) means $\tilde{U}(\tilde{y})$ is pseudo-convex if $U(y)$ is pseudo-convex, as was to be proved.

Similarly in case that $U(y)$ is convex, we conclude that $\tilde{U}(\tilde{y})$ is convex because

$$\begin{aligned} \tilde{U}(\theta\tilde{y}^1 + (1 - \theta)\tilde{y}^2) &\equiv U(\theta\tilde{y}^1 + (1 - \theta)\tilde{y}^2, F(\theta\tilde{y}^1 + (1 - \theta)\tilde{y}^2)) \\ &\leq U(\theta\tilde{y}^1 + (1 - \theta)\tilde{y}^2, \theta F(\tilde{y}^1) + (1 - \theta)F(\tilde{y}^2)) \\ &\leq \theta\tilde{U}(\tilde{y}^1) + (1 - \theta)\tilde{U}(\tilde{y}^2), \qquad 0 \leq \theta \leq 1 \end{aligned} \tag{4-17}$$

Here, we made use of the monotonicity of U in the first inequality and the convexity of U in the second inequality. This completes the proof.

With the help of the above lemma, the convergence of the interactive coordinatewise searching method is guaranteed when X is convex and $f_i(x)$ (i=1,...,n) are convex. Even though the convexity assumption of X and f_i is violated, we can obtain the local convergence property of the method since the function $\tilde{U}(\tilde{y})$ is convex in a neighbourhood of the optimal solution $\tilde{y}^0$.

Since the interactive coordinatewise searching method make use of the trade-off ratio, it requires f_i to be smooth and alternatives to be infinitely divisable. Although this fact implies that the method is slightly restrictive for application, it seems most prominent among the existing interactive methods because it needs to extract only partial informations about his preference attitude, which are most easily obtained, from the decision maker. The following simple example, which was firstly introduced by Reid-Vemuri, shows well the effectiveness of our method. The problem is to decide an optimal storage capacity of a multi-purpose dam subject to a specified set of release rules. Let us denote by x_1 total man hours devoted to building the dam and by x_2 the mean radius of the lake impounded in some fashion. Criteria to be minimized are as follows;

$$f_1(x_1, x_2) = 1 / V(x_1, x_2) = e^{-0.005x_1} (x_1)^{0.01} (x_2)^{-2} \qquad (4\text{-}18)$$

where V represents the total volume capacity of the dam. As to the water loss (volume/year) due to evaporation,

$$f_2(x_2) = (1/2)(x_2)^2. \qquad (4\text{-}19)$$

The last ctiterion is the capital cost of the project;

$$f_3(x_1, x_2) = e^{0.01x_1} (x_1)^{0.02} (x_2)^2. \qquad (4\text{-}20)$$

The result of our numerical experiment by using the interactive coordinatewise searching method is depicted in Fig.4.

Although the model is simplified too much to represent actual problems, the numerical experiment proves the effectiveness of our method sufficiently. We are now applying this method to a water resource problem of Kinki area in Japan.

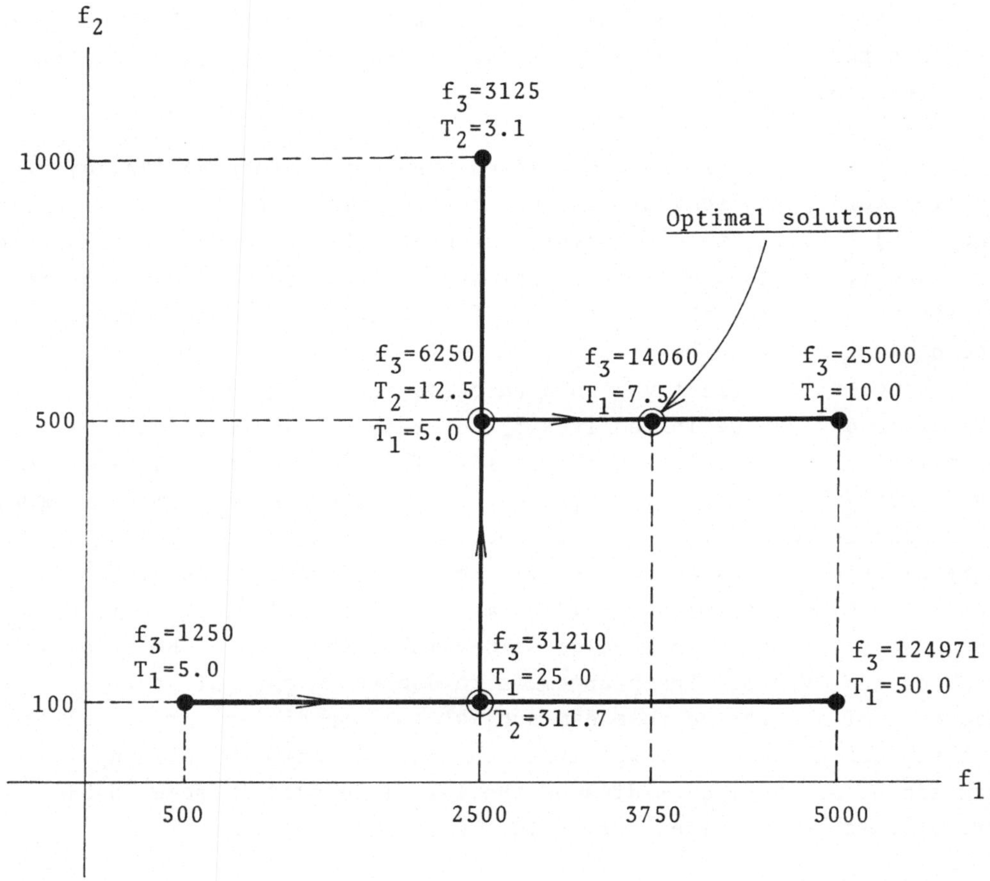

Fig. 4 Simple numerical experiment by using the interactive coordinatewise searching method

5. Concluding remarks

In this paper, we surveyed several new types of systems-analytical methods for environmental management systems. Especially, we illustrated in detail two methods, that is, a graph-matrix method in environmental assessment and an interactive programming method in the design and control phase. The stated graph-matrix method is valid for making the complex interrelation among the objectives clear. One of the advantages of the method over the conventional ones is in its feature that not only direct or obvious dependencies among objectives but also indirect or hidden dependencies can be easily evaluated. The simplicity of computer implementation is another advantage of the method. The interactive programming method described in the section 4 may be available when our aim is only to find out an optimal policy. The method does not need any complete information about the preference attitude of the decision maker; it requires the decision maker only to judge whether his marginal rate of substitution is more or less than the trade-off ratio. This is the reason that the method is most prominent among existing interactive programming methods. The method, however, may be unsuitable for decision making under uncertain circumstances because the decision maker's attitude toward risks can not be evaluated by the method. On the other hand, the multi-attribute utility function, considering the decision maker's attitude toward risks, may be employed as an assessment technique for a wide range of actual problems.

The discussion in this paper was restricted to a case of one decision maker. However, in many social problems, from environmental problems down, we encounter difficult problems of group decision making: how should people find themselves out in agreement? As is well known, Arrow's general impossibility theorem /1/ shows that it is impossible in a general sense (under Arrow's five axioms) to construct a social utility function from individual ordinal utility functions. The multi-attribute utility function as a cardinal utility, however, provides the comparability between individual utilities and makes it possible to construct a social welfare function from individual utility functions. In fact, Keeney has recently presented a representation of a type of cardinal social utility function on the basis of his multi-attribute utility function /11/.

Methodology resolving such social problems as environmental ones based on mutual understanding with other people will undoubtedly become more and more important in the future.

REFERENCES

[1] Arrow, K.J., "A Difficulty in the Concept of Social Welfare", in "Readings in Welfare Economics" ed. by K.J. Arrow & T. Scitovsky, R.D.Irwin, Inc. (1969)

[2] Cetron, M.J. and B. Bartocha, "The Methodology of Technology Assessement", Gordon and Breach Science Pub., 1972.

[3] Farris, D.R. & A.P.Sage, "On the Use of Interpretive Structural Modeling for Worth Assessment", Computer & Electrical Engineering,

Vol. 2, pp. 149-174, 1975.

[4] Fontela, E., "Perceptions of the World Preblematique, Report No. 2", DEMATEL 1973 Reports, Battelle, Geneva, Oct., 1973.

[5] Gabus, A., "Perceptions of the World Problematique, Report No. 1", DEMATEL 1973 Reports, Battelle, Geneva, Nov., 1973.

[6] Geoffrion, A.M., "Solving Bicriterion Mathematical Problems", Operations Research, Vol. 15, No. 1, 1967.

[7] Ikeda, S. and Y. Sawaragi, "GMDH (Heuristic Self-Organization) Applying to Identification and Estimation for Complex Systems", Transactions of Society of Instrument and Control Engineers, Vol. 14, No. 2, pp. 185-195, 1975 (in Japanese).

[8] Inoue, K. and K. Matsumoto, "A Method of Budgetary Allocation for Environmental Protection," Report No. 4, Monitoring and Control of Environmental Pollution, Feb., 1975 (in Japanese).

[9] Ivakhnenko, A.G., "Heuristic Self-Organization in Problems of Engineering Cybernetics, Automatica, Vol. 6, pp. 207-219, 1970

[10] Keeney, R.L., "Multiplicative Utility Functions", Operations Research, Vol. 22, pp. 22-34, 1974.

[11] Keeney, R.L., "Group Decision Making Using Cardinal Social Welfare Functions", Management Science, Vol. 22, No. 4, 1975.

[12] Nakayama, H., H. Sayama and Y. Sawaragi, "A Generalized Lagrangian Function and Multiplier Method", Journal of Optimization Theory and Applications, Vol. 17, No. 3/4, 1975.

[13] Nakayama, H. and Y. Sawaragi, "Decisions with Multiple Objectives and Applications", Systems and Control, Vol. 20, No. 10, pp.511-520, 1976 (in Japanese).

[14] Reid, R.W. and V. Vemuri, "On the Noninferior Index Approach to Large-Scale Multi-Criteria Systems," Journal of the Franklin Institute, Vol. 291, No. 4, 1971.

[15] Takamatsu, T. and I. Hashimoto, "An Approach to Technology Assessment", Proc. HESC Meeting, Kyoto, Japan, 1975 (to appear)

[16] Varga, R.S.,"Matix Iterative Analysis", Prentice-Hall Inc., 1962.

[17] Warfield, J.N.,"Forward Interpretation of Complex Structural Models", IEEE Transactions on Systems, Man and Cybernetics, Vol. SMC-4, No. 5, 1974.

[18] Yu, P.L., "Cone Convexity, Cone Extreme Points and Nondominated Solutions in Decision Problems with Multi-objective", Journal of Optimization Theory and Applications, Vol. 15, No. 3, 1974.

INTEGRATED MODEL FOR PREDICTING THE REGIONAL POLLUTION FOR THE LOCAL GOVERNMENTS

AKIRA MURAMATSU TAKAKUNI WATANABE HITOSHI AKAIKE
Systems Development Laboratory
Hitachi, Ltd.
Totsuka, Yokohama, Japan

INTRODUCTION The environmental pollution monitering system has recently become popular and set up in many regions in Japan. This system has usually three subsystems;the environment telemeter subsystem gathers and communicates information of the environment,the emission telemeter subsystem which is settled near the emission sources monitors the emitted pollutants, and the data processing subsystem receives these data and processes them.

This system which monitors environment and issues a warning when the concentration of a pollutant exceeds its standard is thought as an element of a feedback system. Since there is usually a time lag as in any other feedback systems, the people in the region might be exposed to intensive pollution for several hours.

Recently, the idea of feedforward control was brought in this area and the on-line forecasting model of air pollution has been developed. It can certainly be said that such a system is an evolution of the monitering system. But this type of system is imperfect to control the environmental pollution in the region because it does not deal with the long range problems.

We have placed our REgional Pollution Predicting model(REPP model) in the extent line of this evolution. This model is expected to support the planning of long(medium) range environmental policies with the environmental data bank which we have also been developing. (Fig. 1)

The purpose of this research is to establish the standard structure of the long range predicting model of the environmental pollution for the local governments.

The REPP model

The purpose of this section is to provide an overview of the regional pollution predicting model, a complex set of computer programs to predict the future state of the economy and the environment.

In the description of the environmental pollution, it is possible to view it from the hierarchical standpoint. Various pollutions are originally caused by human economic activities and also observed as the material

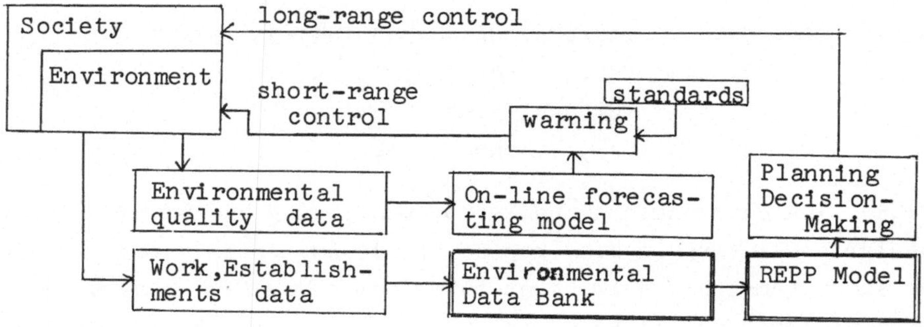

Fig. 1 A concept of the Environmental Information System

flows in various processes or as the physico-chemical reactions in various environments. Therefore, we can grasp the phenomena of the environmental pollutions on at least three strata: Economic, Process and Physicochemical. Fig.2 shows this idea.

The hierarchical structuring of the process of pollution is useful because it offers us a standpoint from where we can view various aspects of the problem of pollution without omission.

To determine the structure of our REPP model, we also considered the use of the models which had been made in different sections of the local government. It is often said that the most appropriate way to construct a large-scale model is to build various submodel carefully and then combine them into comprehensive whole. Here we call such a large-scale model "Integrated Model". In practical sense, the methodology is significant because there are usually various well-known and well-established models of economics or population or land useetc.

Fig.3 shows the structure of REPP model. From this, we can recognize that our REPP model is a hierarchical and integrated model and there are one exogenous(main) and four satellite models. An exogenous model ---- Economic submodel --- is used to project the information such as gross regional products, regional expenditure, regional income etc. on satellite models.

ECONOMIC SUBMODEL

This is an econometric model with four blocks ---- production, distribution, expenditure and labor. This submodel predicts each final demand which is used as the input to the production submodel. It also predicts

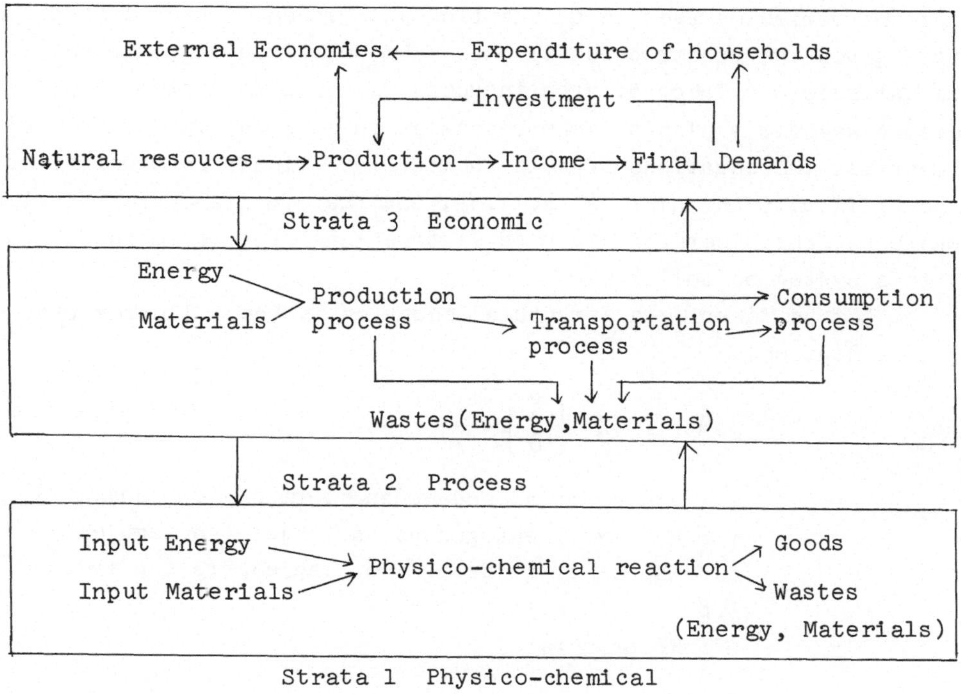

Fig. 2 Three strata of Environmental pollution

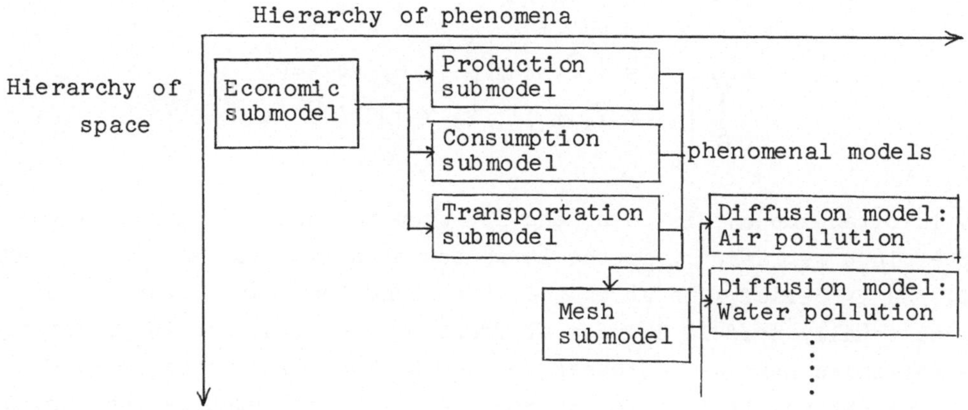

Fig. 3 Structure of REPP Model

some of the variables used in Consumption and Transportation submodel.

Fig.4 gives the construction tf this submodel. Population is an exogenous variable and labor of each industry is calculated from this. This is because we have a plan to make a population submodel in the future.

almost all the equations of this submodel are linear in order to avoide the difficulty in numerical soltion, and they form a system of simultaneous equations. Therefore we used 2 stage least squares method to identify this system as follows:-

Let us describe a structural equation in the following representation.

$$y = (Y, X) \begin{bmatrix} \gamma \\ \beta \end{bmatrix} + e$$

y ; Vector of an endogenous variable (n samples)

Y : Matrix of endogenous variables (n samples)

X : Matrix of predetermined regressors (n samples)

γ, β : Coefficients of Y, X

e : Error term

In 2 stage least square method, we make Y regress to X and get the estimated value Y of Y . Then we use Y in stead of Y to do ordinary least squares estimation.

1st step $Y = X\Pi + V \xrightarrow{\text{estimation}} \hat{Y} \doteq X\hat{\Pi}$

$\hat{\Pi} = (X'X)^{-1}X'Y$

2nd step From $y = (\hat{Y}, X) \begin{bmatrix} \gamma \\ \beta \end{bmatrix} + e$, we get

$$\begin{bmatrix} \hat{\gamma} \\ \hat{\beta} \end{bmatrix} = [(\hat{Y}, X)'(\hat{Y}, X)]^{-1}(\hat{Y}, X)'y$$

It is often impossible to do the 1st step because the number of the predetermined regressor X is too large compared with sample size. In our model, the number of X is 28,on the other hand,the sample size is 15. Since we usually need 10 degrees of freedom of estimation, 28 predetermined variables must be decreased to 5 or 6. There is another reason to do so. The muticollinearity of regressers which is caused by the strong correlation among the 28 variables must exist. It usually makes estimate inaccurate. In order to solve these problems, we used the principal component analysis to decreas the number of the predetermined variables. The principal components are orthogonal to each other, then there is also no trouble about the multicollinearity.

For this purpose, we may use only the principal components vector Z in stead of X as follows.

$$Y = Z\hat{\Pi} = Z(Z'Z)^{-1}Z'Y$$

The economic submodel was identified using the data from the statistical yearbook of the region which is published every year by all the local governments in Japan.

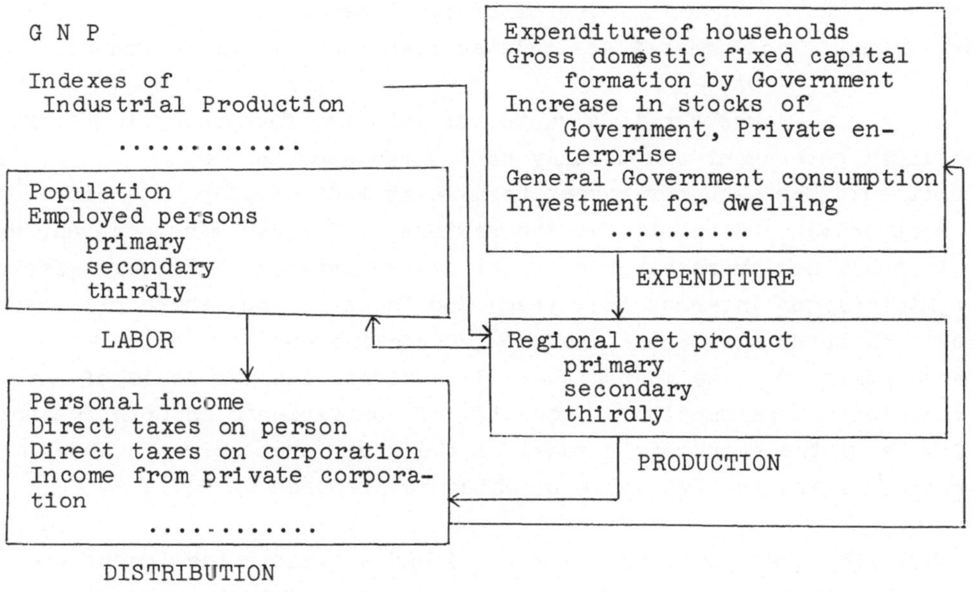

Fig. 4 Economic submodel

PRODUCTION SUBMODEL

This submodel predicts the amount of various pollutants emitted from industries in the region. We may also analyze the relation between the economical construction of the region and the emission of these pollutants.

We used the Input/Output Table and the emission factors of each industry to make up this submodel. The emission factor is originally defined on each of the facilities. Since all industries are different in emission factors, it is better to classify them into as many industries as possible. But, the more industries, the more difficulties in predicting their activities. Then, we used the 43 sectors I/O table to classify them. This table is made at regular intervals(5 years) in all 9 zones of Japan by Government: Hokkaido,Tohoku,Kanto,Tokai,Hokuriku,Kinki,Chugoku, Shikoku and Kyushu.

In this submodel, the outputs of industries X are shown described as follows.

$$X = (I - A - M)^{-1}F$$

where I is a unit matrix, A is a I/O coefficients matrix, M is a diagonal matrix of import coefficients and F is a vector of final demands.

The amount of pollutant is calculated from the following product.

$$pX$$

where p is a vector of emission factors by industry.

The local government has usually no I/O table of the region and it is very difficult for each government to make it individually. Therefore, it is most convenient to utilize the regional I/O table mentioned above, which is published by research and statistics division, Minister's Secretariat,Ministry of International Trade and Industry. But there are some difficulties to do so because the two I/O coefficients are different from each other. Then we must either (1) estimate the I/O table of the prefecture on the assumption of equality of coefficients in both regions or (2) make up the econometric model of the wider area which includes the prefecture and the I/O table of which is prepared by MITI.

In this model, we selected the way (1) and estimated the import coefficients by iteration. We also prepared the way of making the wider regional econometris model by the analysis of covariance.

CONSUMPTION SUBMODEL

This submodel has three blocks : Home sewege, Urban wastes and Consumer durable goods.

(1) Home sewege block

This block predicts the amount of urine and sewege from the domestic life. After analysing the statistical data of them, we assumed that the proportion of urine and sewege to population is unchangable in the future and used this proportion in calculation.

(2)Urban wastes block

The amount of urban wastes depends on the consumer's behavior, the activities of recycling and the contents of goods----especially, containers and packages. But there are usually few data of these factors and we can not estimate statistically the relation among them.

In our case, we made some assumptions and used the method of System Dynamics to test their validity by simulation. Fig. 5 shows the main structure of this block.

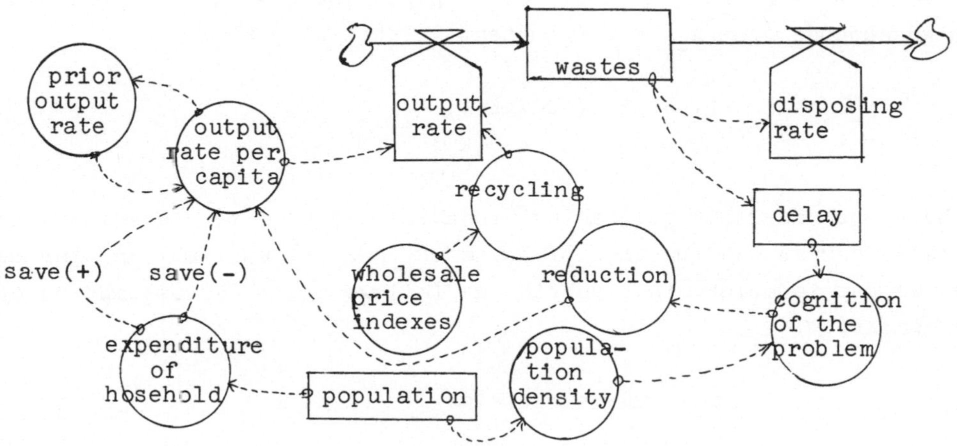

Fig. 5 Main structure of Urban wastes block

The output rate of waste is defined as the amount of wastes per capita. And we assumed the following equation;

The output rate = The prior output rate
× The increase rate of household income × The saving multiplier
× The reduction multiplier

where the saving multiplier is used to show the intensity of saving in accordance with the increase rate of income. The reduction multiplier shows the activities such as domestic management of wastes (Home incineration), home recycling, home storage of dusts, etc..

(3) Consumer durable goods block

The consumer durable goods are kept in a house for several years and then dumped. If we know the purchasing amount of them and their life span, then we can predict the amount of such trashes from the material balance equation.

There are some researches available on the life spans of various consumer durable goods in Japan. We could use them for building this model.

It is widely known that the distribution processes of these goods depend on the demonstration effect. We made use of this idea as follows.

The impact against i th consumer R_i by j th consumer's expenditure C_j is written as $R_i = a_{ij}C_j$. a_{ij} shows the relative frequency of contact of i th consumer with j th consumer. If we consider only one commodity, we may normalyze C_j (to 1) and get the relation $R_i = a_{ij}$. Then, the total of such impacts of i th consumer in the mass of K people is represented as $R_i = \sum_j a_{ij}$. If there are X people possessing the commodity and we suppose that a_{ij} = a (constant), then we get

$$\begin{aligned} R_i &= aX \quad (0<X<K) \\ &= 0 \quad (X = 0,K) \end{aligned}$$

Next, consider the purchasing probabilities of i th cosumer p_i. As p_i is of course the function of R_i and R_i has its supremum and infimum, then we can formulate the function as follows under the assumption of its linearity:

$$p_i = bR_i = baX = cX \qquad (0 \; p_i \; 1)$$

If there are X ownersof the commodity, then there are (K - X) non owners and

$$X = p_i(K-X) = cX(K-X)$$

people will purchase these commodities. As continuous approximation,we get the following equations.

$$\frac{dX}{dt} = cX(K-X)$$

This is a logistic equation and we expressed the purchasing process of consumer durable goods by this equation. Fig.6 shows the purchasing and dumping processes of a part of this block.

TRANSPORTATION SUBMODEL

This submodel has three blocks: to predict the number of cars in the region, to estimate the traffic and to calculate the exhausted gasses.

Fig.7 shows the relation among these blocks.

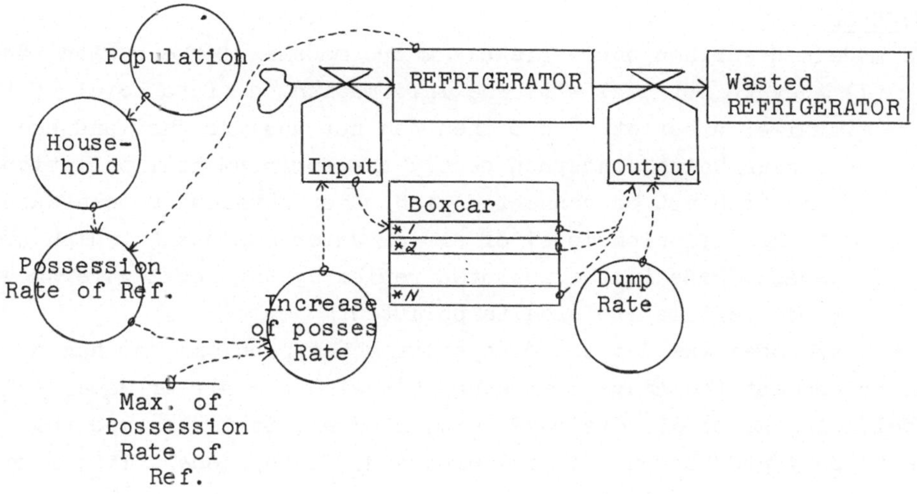

Fig.6 Purchasing & Dumping of refrigerator

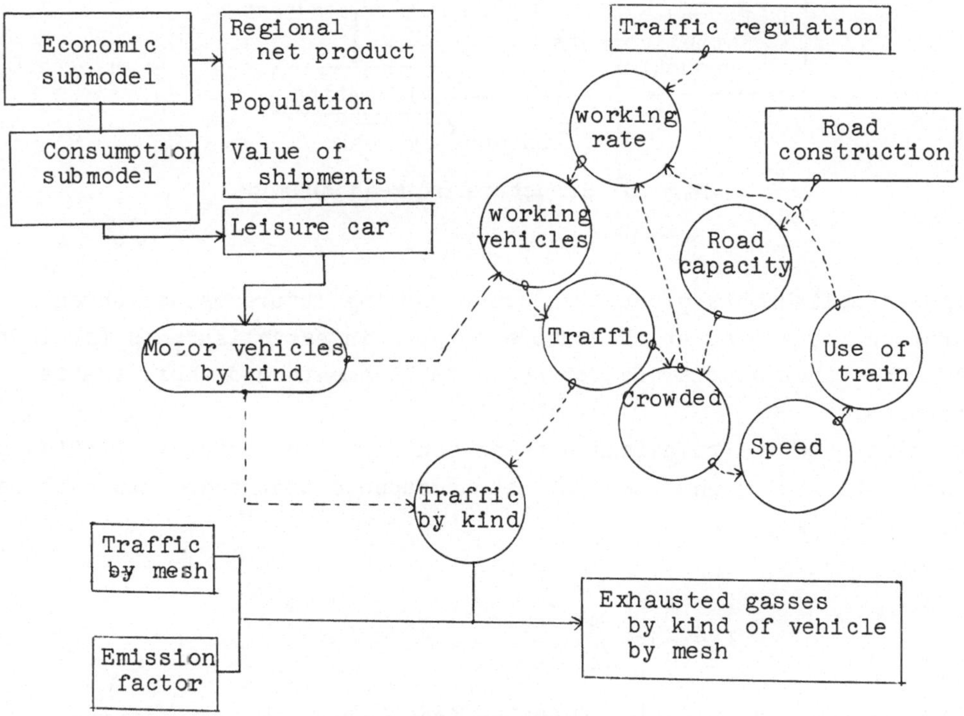

Fig.7 Framework of TRANSPORTATION SUBMODEL

MESH SUBMODEL

These models described above are all macro models of the region, and

(1) they do not deal with the information on micro level,of the smaller areas etc., and then can not analyze the land use problem which concerned deeply the environmental pollution,

(2) they can not be connected with other physical models such as the diffusion model of air or water pollutants,which are usually made in the polluted region by the local government whose legislative area is polluted.

The mesh submodel was developed to solve these problems and has a function to connect the above four submodels with the air or water pollution model. In the model developed here, however, it is assumed that it connects only production submodel with a diffusion model. This model has five blocks as shown in Fig.8.

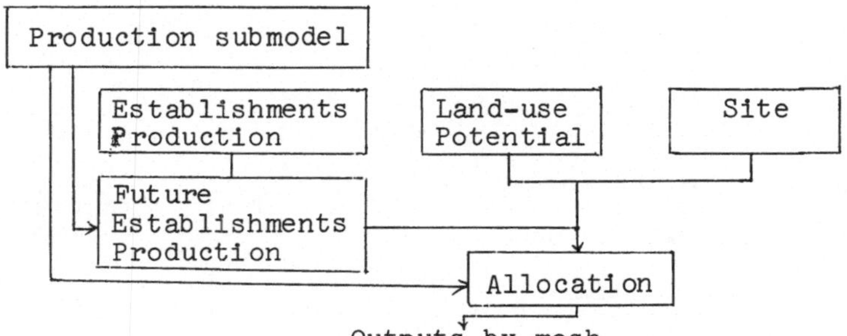

Fig. 8 Structure of Mesh submodel

The establishments production block and the future establishments production block predict the future outputs in establishments (by industry). The other blocks predict new establishments and their spatial allocation.

Consider now the relations between space of industrial facilities and inputs----Capital K and Labor L. Let us suppose that there are such relations as follows:

$$K = aS^{b}$$
$$L = eS^{d}$$

Then,we get the following equation from Cobb-Douglas function:

$$X = \alpha K^{\beta} L^{\gamma}$$

$$= \alpha (aS^b)^\beta (eS^d)^\gamma$$
$$= \delta S^\varepsilon$$

where X is output and $\delta = \alpha a^\beta c^\gamma$, $\varepsilon = b\beta + d\gamma$.

These parameters can be identified from the data in Census Manufactures. We estimated their future parameters by calculating its elasticity.

Next, we have to get the present distribution of the scales of establishments by industry to predict the number and the scale of the future establishments which are newly build. Then, we select at random a scale of establishments and calculate its output from the above equation. we repeat this procedure untill the total of outputs reach the output predicted by Production submodel.

The land use potential block represents the potential for siting of industries in each mesh. We used the discriminant function which is calculated by the mesh data bank in this block to estimate the potential.

However, there are many land use regulations and existing buildings in these meshes so that we can not select a site only according to the potential. The site block derivers the room for siting from the area of existing buildings and of the planned district for manufacturing. If there is no room for siting after calculation, the model selects it from the area for agriculture or forestry or reclaim.

The allocation block finally integrates the results of three blocks to get the outputs by mesh by industry. At first, the siting potential of each mesh is converted into the virtual siting probability. Then the meshes in which establishments can newly be build are selected by Monte-Carlo method.

The room for siting of these meshes are calculated if the area of new establishments is smaller than that of the room, then this mesh is accepted and the room of it is calculated again. If not so, the mesh is rejected. The allocation block repeats above procedure till all new establishments are completely allocated.

The mesh data banks of some local governments in Japan have been prepared to assist in land use planning and economic analysis. Among the other prefectures, there are many plans to build the mesh data banks under the guidance of Bureau of Statistics, Office of the prime minister.

Some of the mesh data we used are as follows:

area of the district for factories, housing, business, agriculture and forestry; time distance from the central town of the region; density of roads; time distance from railway station or highway ramp;

above the sea; relief; slant; some land use regulations; etc.

SUMMARY AND CONCLUSION

The modeling of environmental systems is a theme of current importance which is considerably difficult to be treated in the local government because,

the legislative area of a local government is geographically and economically open,

the phenomena of environmental pollution have various sides both macro-scopic and micro-scopic,

there are usually the poorer data than on the national level,

there are usually only a few budget for the modeling.

In this paper, we represented the framework of REPP model as the standard structure of long range predicting model for the local governments. At the same time, we presented the way of use of the standard statistics such as:

The regional Input/Output Table
The national income statistics
The regional income statistics
Census of manufactures
The statistical yearbook of the region
Mesh data bank

Under the circumstances described above, we expect that the construction of this model is useful and guidable for the local government It is also feasible to use REPP model for assessment of present or new environmental programs.

REFERENCES

(1) B. Harris, "Quantitative models of urban development: Their role in metrppolitan policy-making," Issues in Urban Economics, H.S.Perloff and L. Wingo, Jr., Eds. Baltimore, Md.: Johns Hopkins Press, 1968
(2) Kneese & Bwer: Environmental Quality Analysis, Resources for the future,Inc. 1972
(3) Walter Isard: Ecologic-Economic Analysis for Regional Development, Free Press 1972
(4) Roland Artle & Pravin P. Varaiya: Economic theories and Empirical models of Location choice and Land use; A survey, Proceedings of the IEEE ,63,3, 421-430 1975
(5) Ivaras Gutmanis: Input-Output Models in Economic and Environmental Policy Analysis, ibid. 1975
(6) Environmental Protection Agency of U.S.A.: Draft of Strategic Environmental Assessment System, 1975
(7) Proceedings of International Symposium "Environmental Disruption", Asahi Evening News 1970
(8) Economic Planning Agency of Japan: Basic Economic and Social Plan,1973

Environmental Potential Survey by Remote Sensing

J. Iisaka

Tokyo Scientific Center
IBM, Japan Ltd.
Tokyo, Japan

1. Introduction

This paper describes some results of remote sensing obtained in Japan. Remote sensing is the measurement of electromagnetic radiation reflected, emitted, or absorbed by the earth's surface, as measured from air or space vehicles for the purpose of evaluating resources and monitoring the environment. Therefore, it is a very useful technique for gathering environmental information widely and timely.

Developed countries of today are consuming quite a large amount of resources like oil, water, minerals and so on. When the amount of the consumption was low, resource supplies were considered to be un-limited and the amount of waste to be very small. Therefore, environmental impacts due to development, wasted matter, and so on looked negligible and were overlooked. Even if they caused some environmental impacts, such problems could be solved, say, by moving to another place.

That is, space was also another un-limited environmental resource. The current problems concerning the environment are considered to have been caused due to violation of these preconditions. The areas relevant to the current environmental problems are widely spread, and it is very difficult to assess them, for example, by setting an experimental test site. On the other hand, the environmental conditions should not always be conserved. For example, a progress of social activities, or economic growth makes some impacts to the previous conditions of the environment.

Prepared for the presentation at the international symposium on "New Trends in System Analysis," Rue de la Chancellerie, Versailles, December 13-17, 1976.

Therefore, we are forced to know the potentialities of our environment.

How these environment potentials can be identified, is a basic consideration to this subject. Here, a common procedure for this purpose is illustrated in Fig. 1.

The environmental information should be gathered widely and on time. The carriers of this information are physical ones. This information is to be stored and accumulated for later use, like temporal change analysis, dynamic studies, or dissemination of data.

If the information could be gathered periodically, it would be very useful for environment monitoring. By accumulating such information, some dynamic patterns can be generated and can be built into a model of environment change or impact dynamics. The menu of environmental potentialities derived from the current state of environment and the models are expected to be verv useful for impact assessment.

In this sense, remote sensing is a powerful technique for those studies.

In section 2, an example of sea water pollution analysis will be shown, and in section 3, thermal energy emission from an urban area is treated. An agricultural application of remote sensing is discussed in section 4.

2. Sea Water Pollution Analysis

In this section, sea water pollution is examined based upon LANDSAT MSS data. This kind of water pollution is considered as typical problem which reflects the ecological impact of industrial waste loads.

The area which was examined by this study is the Seto-inland Sea where many industrial sites are located along the coast of this inland sea.

A lot of industrial waste water and sewage flow into this inland-sea.

As Fig. 2 shows the trends of sea water pollution like red tide occurence in this sea vs economic growth, sea water pollution is very serious in this area. The band widths of the LANDSAT MSS are selected mainly for the substances on a land but, as shown in Fig. 3, the spectral transparency of water provides information of the substance resolved in the water.

If the number of solutant types is very large, due to the complexity of waste materials, it is difficult to estimate the quantity of the contents of the water, and to identify the types of solutants, campared to the case of water mixed with a single substance.

Therefore, we made an attempt to find the correlation between observed MSS data and sea water qualities which were tested by samples.

MSS data used for this study is recorded on CCT (Computer Compatible Tape) of Scene ID: 1093-0106000, and the date of survey was Oct. 24, 1972. So far as data as sea truth is concerned, we referred to the data which was collected by the Environmental Agency of Japan for the project of the Seto inland sea water pollution survey. The sampling points of this survey are shown in Fig. 4.

It is natural that the sea truth survey should be done coincidentally to the satelite survey. But the data of sea truth survey was done 10 days later than satelite observation survey. The observed data is listed in Table I the left-most column mean the sampled points which correspond to the location number in Fig. 4. The items tested are turbidity limpidness, PH, BOD and COD.

The procedure used in this study is as follows.

1) to extract the spectral data from the same location where the sea truth data was sampled. The spectral characteristics of the sea water are shown in Fig. 5a-c.

2) to find the correlation between sea water spectral data and sea truth data. As is shown in Fig. 6, a good correlation between spectral responce and water qualities was obtained.

3) based upon the spectral model, to contour the sea water qualities.

Three test areas were selected: one is Harima-nada, rather center part of Seto Inland Sea: another is Kiisuido, facing rather the ocean and the last is the Osaka bay along Osaka city.

Fig. 7 shows classified results where the sea water qualities are divided into several classes. Each color corresponds to the respective class. Computer time to generate this output was 4 minutes by IBM S/360-M195.

Issues: It can be concluded that the state of sea water pollution might be classified based upon the spectral response of sea water. So, it is possible to introduce spectral indexes which show the water qualities, instead of conventional variables like BOD, COD, Transparency, ... etc.

3. Thermal Energy Emission from Urban Area

3-1. Thermal energy emission survey and a model for thermal flow

Since the mankind came to use "fire", the energy which is reserved in various materials like oil or coal which originally has stored the sun energies, is being converted as thermal energy. This trend is growing very rapidly. Heat un balances in nature make winds or sea currents, and form natural environment changes. To use fire gives some impact on environment, and this impact becomes very serious when we see the present status of industrialized societies.

This section describes a survey result obtained by estimating the thermal emission against the land use difference by using remote sensing techniques.

By remote sensing techniques, we determine the current figure of thermal emission against land-use type. A thermal channel (8.5-12.0 μ) of aircraft MSS is useful for this application. By flying over a training area where typical land-use types are involved, the parameters for the models are estimated.

As a training area, Tokyo is selected and we found the fact that the temperature range in the center of Tokyo is very wide, that there is some temperature difference depending on the directions of roads because of sun illumination angles, and that there is also temperature difference between green park and other area, of about 5°C.

The equation of the heat balance on the ground surface is expressed as:

$$S + I - R + G - \varepsilon\sigma T^4 = \pm N = \pm B \pm V \pm LE \pm A \pm P = N \pm HE$$

Here S: Sun radiation energy

I: Radiation energy from sky

R: Reflected energy from surface

G: Thermal energy from sky

$\varepsilon\sigma T^4$: Thermal radiation from surface

D: Total radiation

R: Heat transfer to soils, roads, buildings

V: Heat transfer between surface and atmosphere

LE: Latent energy transfer

A: Heat transfer by air

P: Energy transfer by photosynthesis

N: Heat transfer absorbed by rain fall

HE: Artificial heat energy (fire etc ...) (see Fig. 8)

After establishing a heat transfer model for each land-use category using observed data, some thermal flow maps were generated, which are shown in Fig. 9. Each color means thermal flow as a unit $Kcal/m^2h$.

Level	Color	Thermal Flow ($Kcal/m^2.h$)
0	Black	-8 - 16
1	Gray	- 40
2	Dark Brown	- 64
3	Dark Blue	- 88
4	Olive	- 112
5	Dark Violet	- 137
6	Green	- 161
7	Blue	- 185
8	Light Brown	- 209
9	Light Green	- 233
10	Light Violet	- 257
11	Light Blue	- 281
12	Yellow	- 305
13	Red	- 330
14	Light Gray	- 354
15	White	- 376

3-2. Land Cover Classification

In the course of the simulation for thermal energy flows as described in 3-1, it is required to know more accurately the substantial ground cover types. These kinds of survey can also be done by remote sensing techniques. In this section, by using aircraft remote sensing data, an example of the land cover type of an urban area is shown.

Remote sensing can detect not only visible changes in urban development such as increases in man-made objects--houses, roads and buildings--but also invisible changes including energy emission and its impact to environment as well as city amenity resulting from decreases in greenery.

In applying the remote sensing technology to the high-density city of Tokyo which represents urban problems in Japan, there are some points that must be taken into consideration.

In the first place, each resolution element comprising Japanese cities is comparatively small in measurement. For instance, the average measurement for individual estates in residential areas is 150 to 200 square meters (15 by 15 meters). The width of most roads in Tokyo is less than 10 meters in the exception of express ways which are more than 50 meters wide.

Secondly, topographical complexity is very high. In other words, many different objects exist in a resolution element. Even in the case of the neighboring elements, different objects are mixed together, rather than continuation of the same objects.

Data was gathered on one of urban development areas in the out-skirts of Tokyo called Tama New Town.

11 channel MSS digital data by an aircraft survey is used for this analysis. The model of MSS is DS-1250 manufactured by Deadlus Corporation. The wave length of the MSS covers from 0.38 μ to 1.1 μ for the first 10 channels and from 8.0 μ to 14.0 μ for the 11th channel. The six channels used for this analysis are:

Channel 1	0.38 - 0.42 μ
Channel 2	0.45 - 0.50 μ
Channel 3	0.55 - 0.60 μ
Channel 4	0.65 - 0.69 μ
Channel 5	0.80 - 0.89 μ
Channel 6	8.00 - 14.00 μ

In this analysis, the conventional most-likelihood decision scheme was tried. Spectral characteristics reflect most of substantial properties. Therefore, the correlation between spectral categories and the conventional concept of land-use should be checked. For this purpose, we selected 15 categories from training fields. As described before, the size of a field of the same class is so small that the training fields were carefully selected by unsupervised clustering techniques.

Generally, a canal consists of a water stream, concrete banks, grass and so on. Therefore, if we select the training field as a canal, variance of that spectrum is very large.

We concluded the following categories could be classified.

A. Residential area

* Concrete multi-storey apartment complexes:
* Lawn around apartment houses:
* Single housing units:

* Estate houses:

B. Agricultural fields, forests and paddy fields
   * Paddy fields:
   * Agriculture fields:
   * Forests:

C. Roads, Canals and rail roads
   * Roads:
   * Other roads:
   * Rail roads:

An Example of land cover classification is shown in Fig. 10.

4. Agricultural Potentials and Sun Energy

The potential for food resource supplies is the most important thing for the mankind. There are so many factors which determine the potentialities for agricultured yields: they are i.g. soil conditions, soil moisture states, water supplies, climate, manure supply and its timing, soil temperature, planting conditions and so on. But in this section, an attempt of using remote sensing for agricultural application by LANDSAT data is described.

Here, we like to consider the meaning of the observed data which was reflected by vegetation. The schematic diagram is shown in Fig. 11. Suppose a situation where a vegetation is growing under some conditions of the soil, water supply, and other environmental conditions. The sun light illuminate the earth ground carrying energy which is described as the sun illumination model. The sun light is absorbed or scattered by the atmosphere and some of the energy which illuminates the vegetable are absorbed by a photo-synthetic process and some others are transmitted, and the rest is reflected to the air. In short, some amount of sun energy are reserved in a material produced by the photo-synthesis process. Generally, the growth model is not directly related to the yields of crops by time sequence reflectance measurements, which are used to build a time-dependent reflectance model.

The data observed from air or space simply carries the information about the kind of bio-chemical process and its stage, and class about effective reflectance which changes depending on the actual setting of vegetables. Vegetables require, while growing, some amount of light energy supply of narrow bands which are specific for specific vegetables.

Where the yield is concerned, it depends on wether the sun illuminated the vegetable enough at its growth stage.

If the sequential remote sensing data is available, it is very useful for yield prediction, site selection of the equal potential for that plant or alternative plants. In this section, simply application of LANDSAT data to the agricultural potential survey is illustrated.

The place examined is Tokachi district, which is located in Hokkaido, north part of Japan. Taking this district as an example, soil type classification and discrimination of pasture growth were investigated.

The reason why Tokachi district was selected is that the size of the field is quite large compared with that in the main land of Japan. Therefore, in spite of the current size of resolution elements of LANDSAT data, it is expected to be applicable to our studies.

Classification has been done by most-likelihood decision rules.

A resultant map displayed on color CRT is shown in Fig. 13. Color codes displayed on CRT are

1. Volcanic ashey soil (Black) (Thick) or wet, or organic
2. " (Thin)
3. Volcanic ashey soil (Brown)/dry
4. Allurial soil
5. Tree
6. Timothy (2nd year for harvest)
7. Timothy (1st year for harvest)
8. Red clover (1st year)
9. Orchard (1st year)
10. Rye (partly wheat)

According to this result, a difference between 1st year timothy and 2nd year timothy, was identified which reflects the yield difference.

Difference of soil types was also classified. Seeing those results, the idea will be raised that remote sensing can be useful for making a planting plan where historical cultivation is taken into account.

In Fig. 14, the spectral of each ground cover type is shown.

Conclusion

As illustrated above, remote sensing techniques are very useful for survey of various environmental potentials especially for a large scale area, and the results of the survey by remote sensing are obtained very quickly. Surveyed information itself reflects the state of an objective area, but if temporal data are available, it is very easy to see the changing behavior of the states. The presented examples are based upon the rather visible light and near infra-red wave, but the sensor range for remote sensing is increasing very rapidly. Already, it covers up to a longer wave-length range like a mirowave and so on. Thus, we can expect wide varieties of potentialities. Of course, it requires more discussion and other verifications to reach the final goals to make environment potential menues.

But the following problems are important to fill the gap between the remote sensing area and the people.

1. Availability of data with reasonable cost
2. Cycle of survey
3. Ground data gathering and integration
4. Availability of base data like digital map, etc.
5. How to establish the useful model based upon R/S data

and the last one is one of the most important problems, for instance, to establish a crop yield model.

From the view point of system analysis, how to cook these hugh amount of data still remains.

Acknowledgements

The author is grateful to Y. Sawaragi (Kyoto Univ.) Y. Emori (Chiba Univ.) for their suggestions contributing to the report. He is also indebt to M. Fukuhara (Hokkaido National Agricultural Experiment Station), Y. Yasuda (Chiba Univ.) and Y. Henmi (IBM Japan) for preparing data and discussions

Referrence

1. H. Nishimura, "On the Development of Industrial Ecology model for soil & water," Proc. 6th IBM Computer Science Symposium on Social System, 1972, IBM Japan Tokyo.

2. E.O. Hulbert, "Optics of Disbilled and Natural Water," J. Optical Society of America, 5 (1945), p698.

3. J. Iisaka, et al Tokyo Scientific Center Report, "On the thermal flow map of Kanto Area," GE318-0018 (1973) Tokyo.

4. Wilfrid Bach, "An Urban Circulation Model," Arch. Met. Geoph. Biokl., Ser. B, 15, p158-168 (1970).

5. J. Iisaka, et al "On the Data Processing of Aircraft MSS and its Application to the Change Detection of Urban Area," Presented at US-JAPAN Seminor on Image Processing for Remote Sensing Washington, 1976.

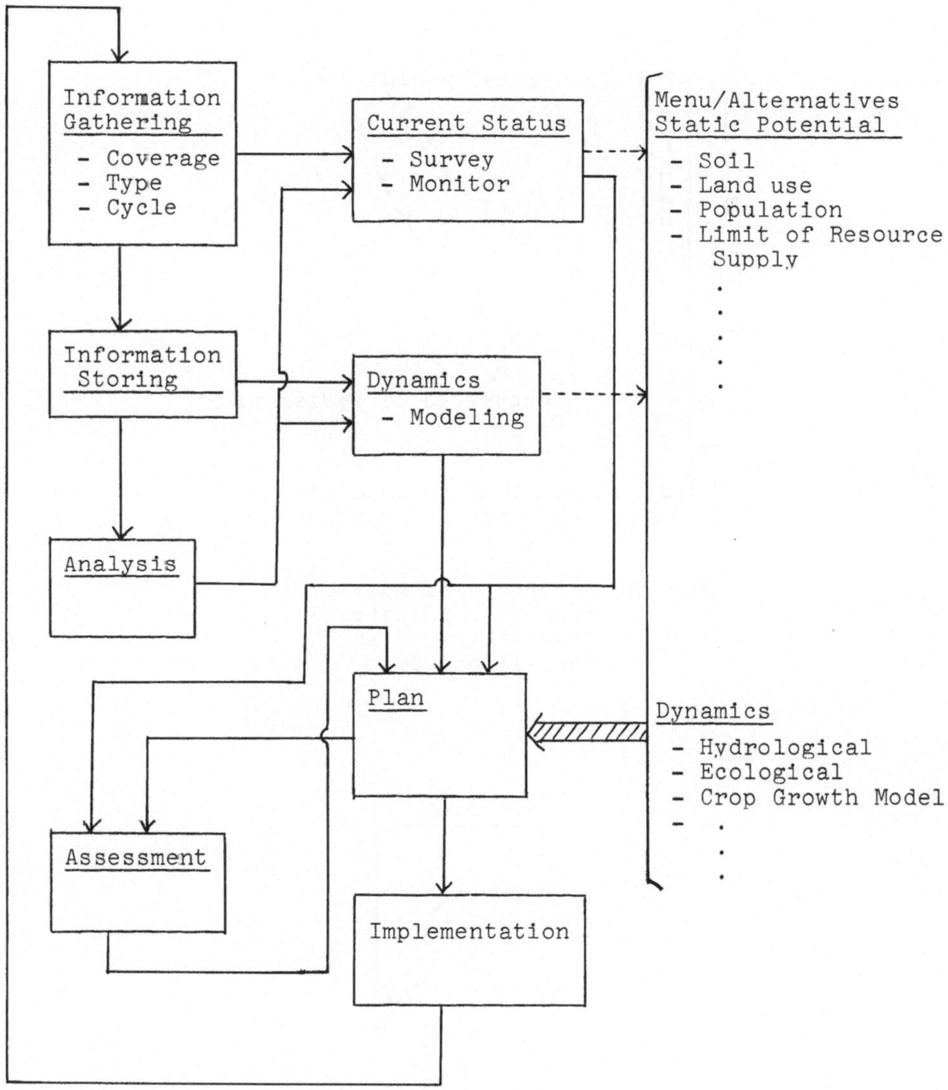

Fig. 1 Flow of Environmental Potential Survey

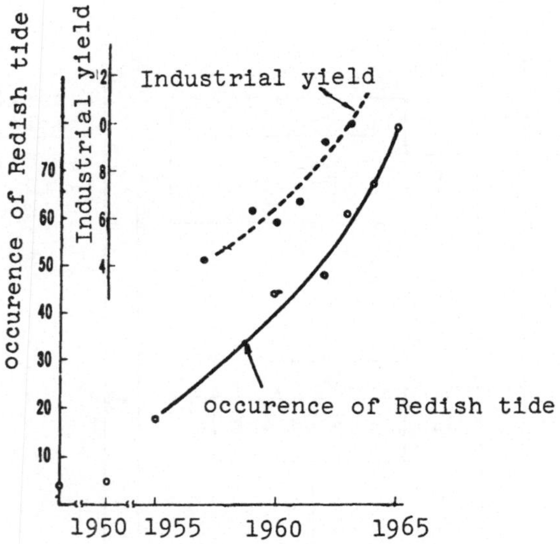

Fig. 2 Occurence of Redish tide v.s. industrial product growth in Seto Inland Sea

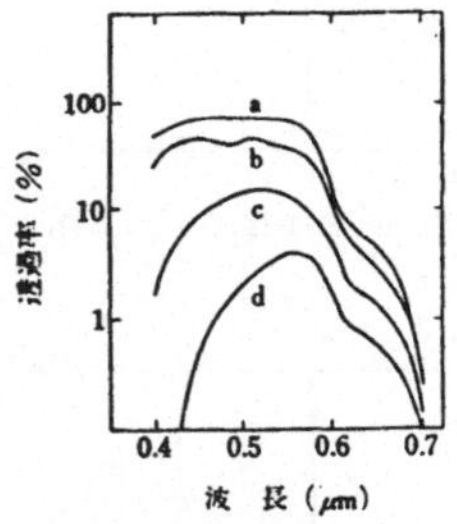

a) distiled sea water
b) oceanic sea water
c) coastal sea water
d) inner sea water

Fig. 3 Spectral transparancy

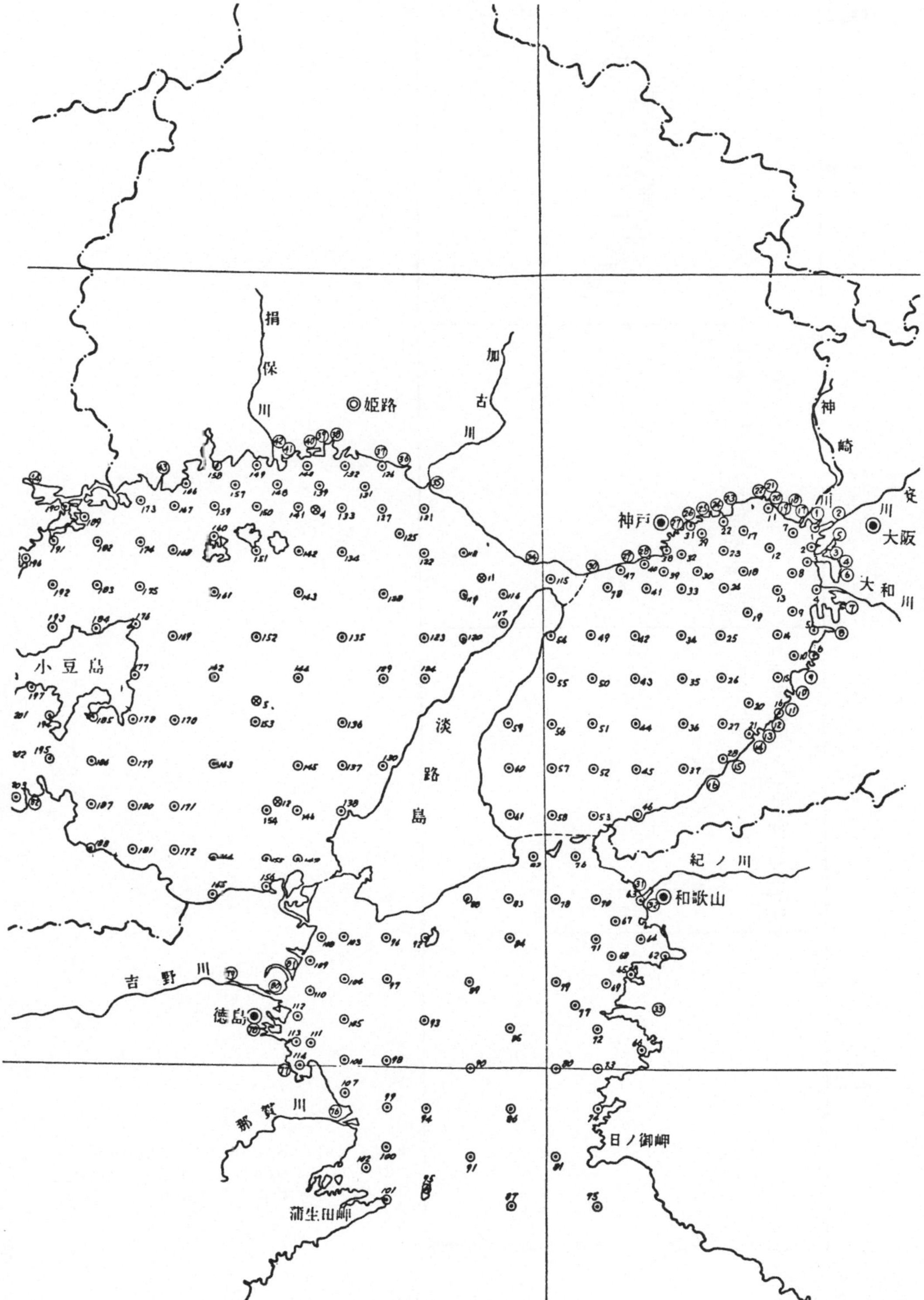

Fig. 4 Sea truth sampled point for Seto Inland Sea

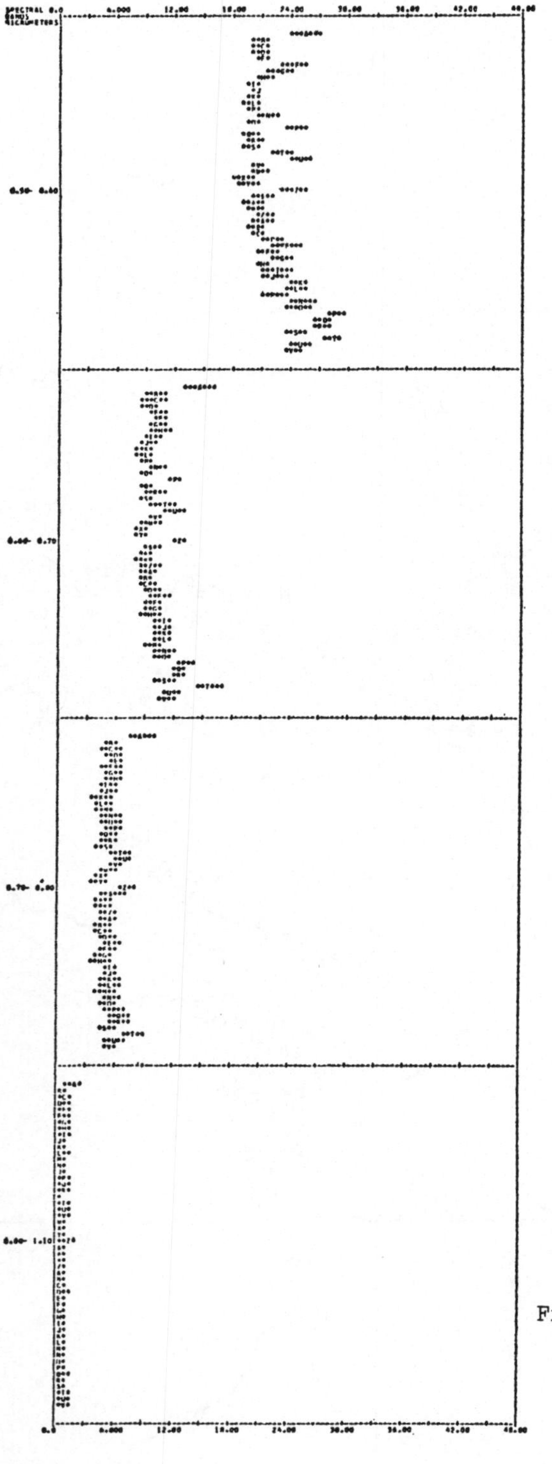

Fig. 5-a Spectral Responce of Inland Sea Water: Kii-channel

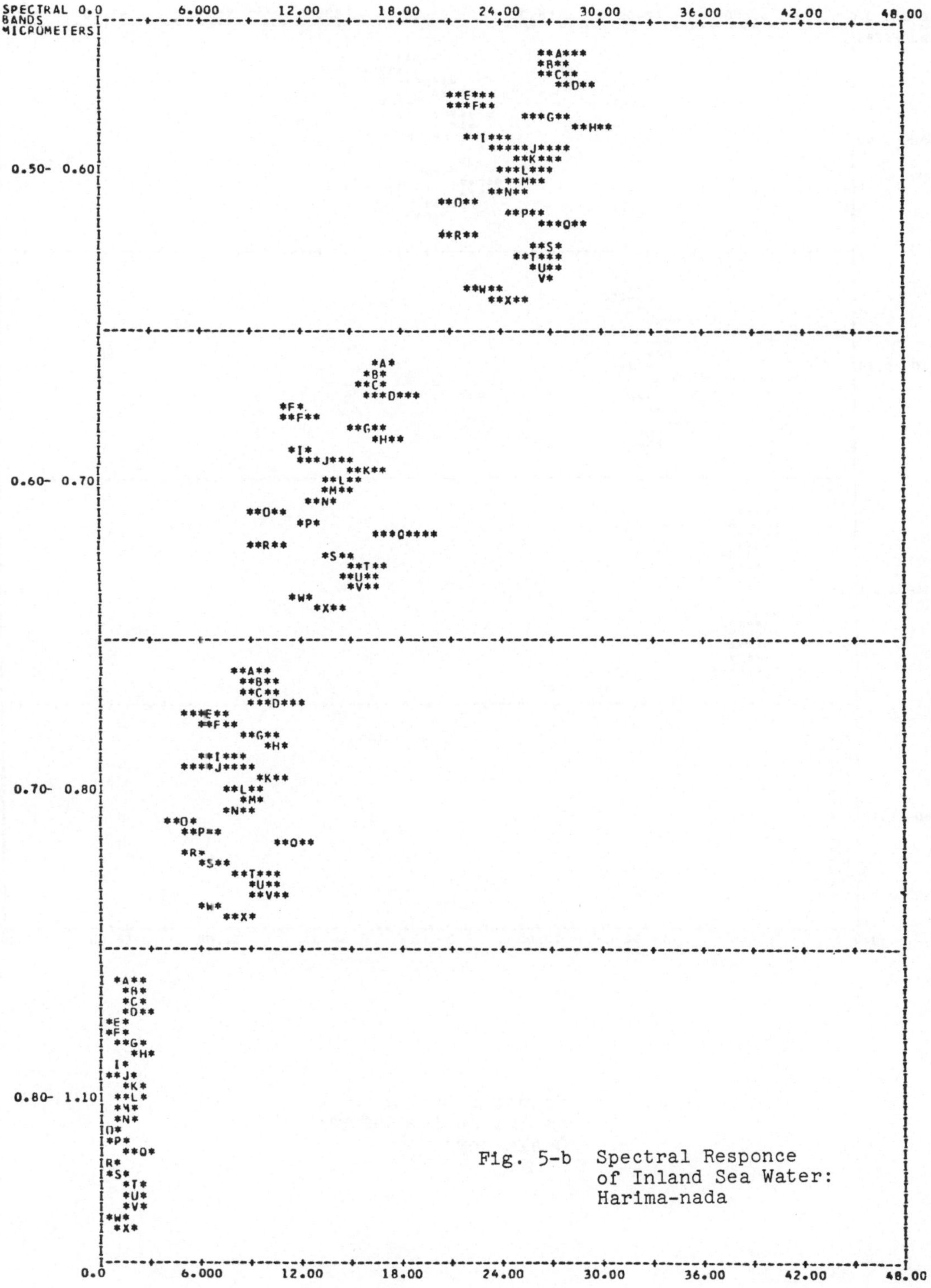

Fig. 5-b Spectral Responce of Inland Sea Water: Harima-nada

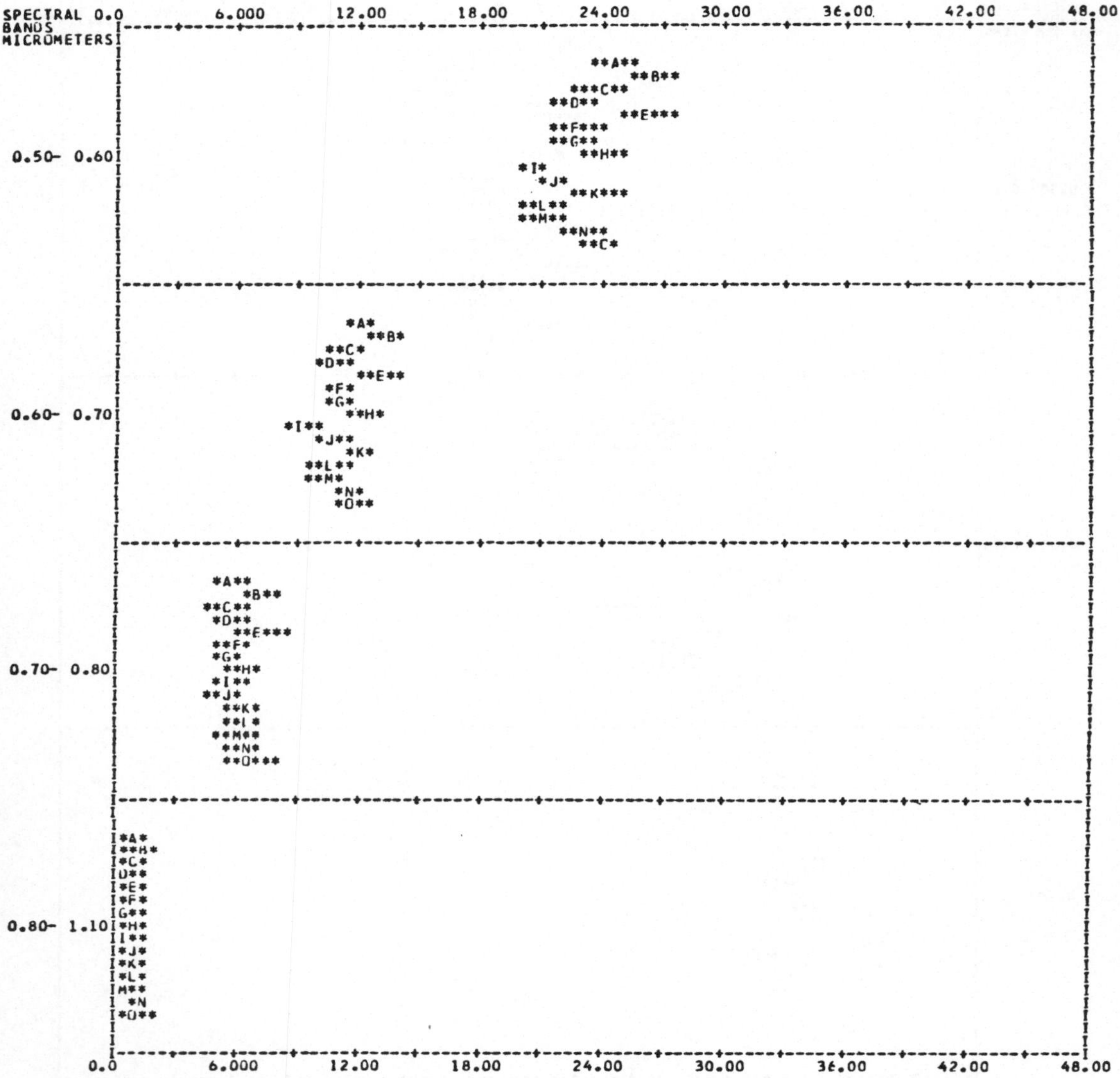

Fig. 5-c Spectral Responce of Inland Sea Water: Osaka-bey

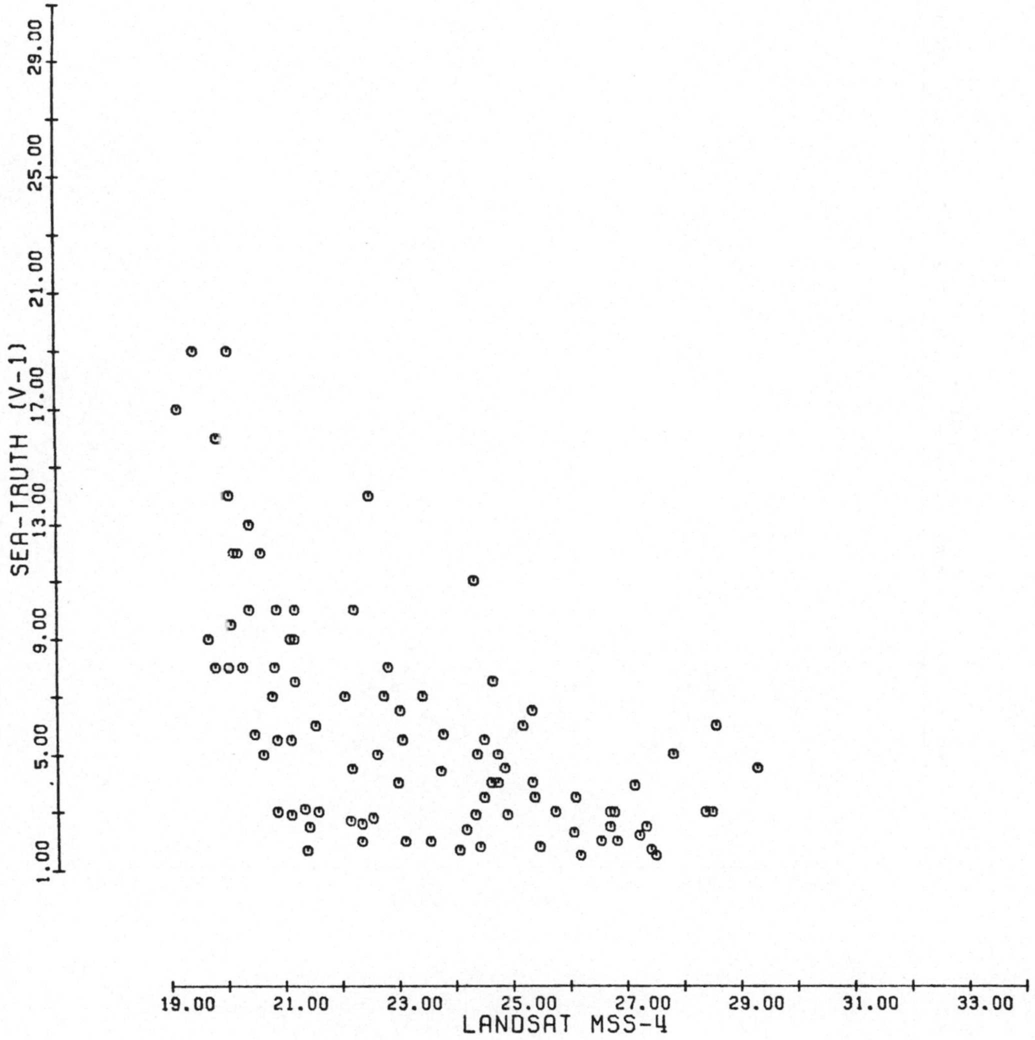

Fig. 6-a An Illustration of Correlation between Spectral Responce & Sea Water Quality

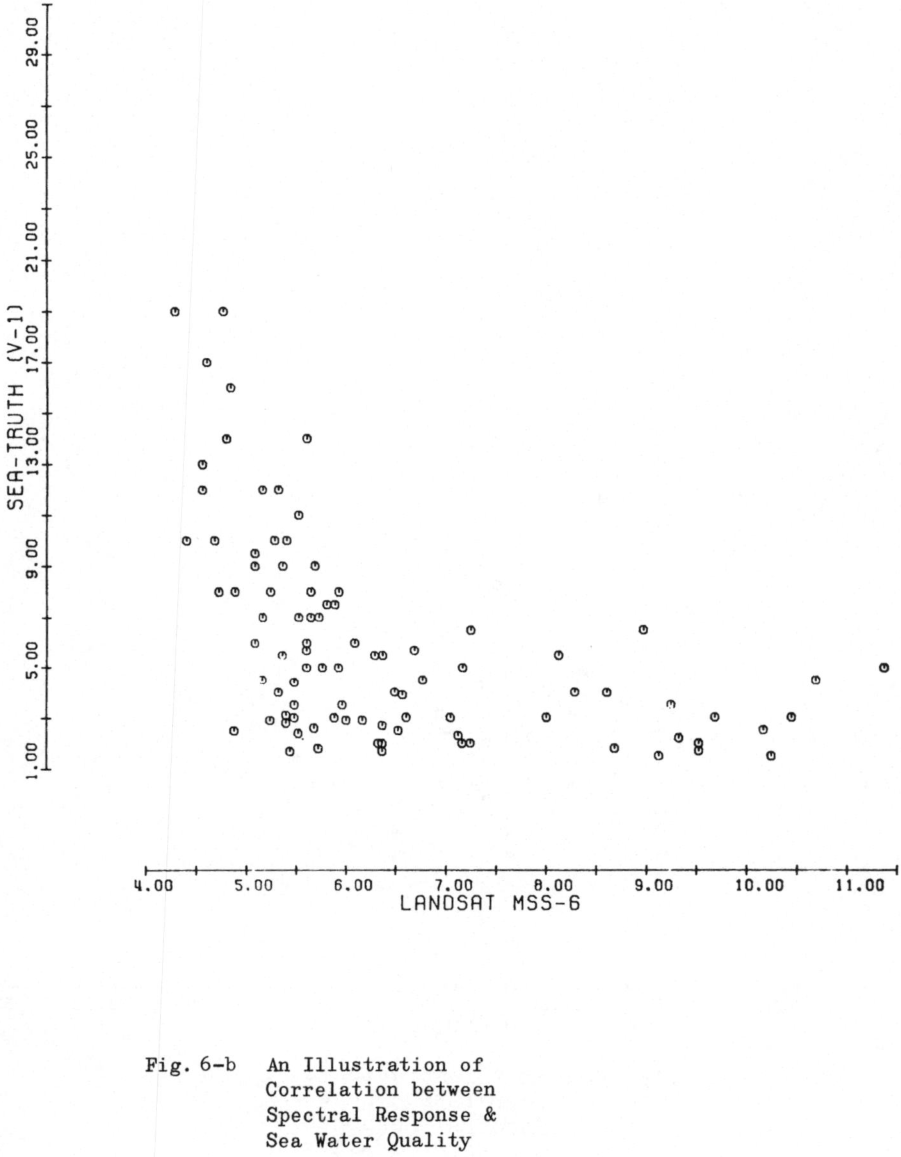

Fig. 6-b An Illustration of Correlation between Spectral Response & Sea Water Quality

Harima-nada

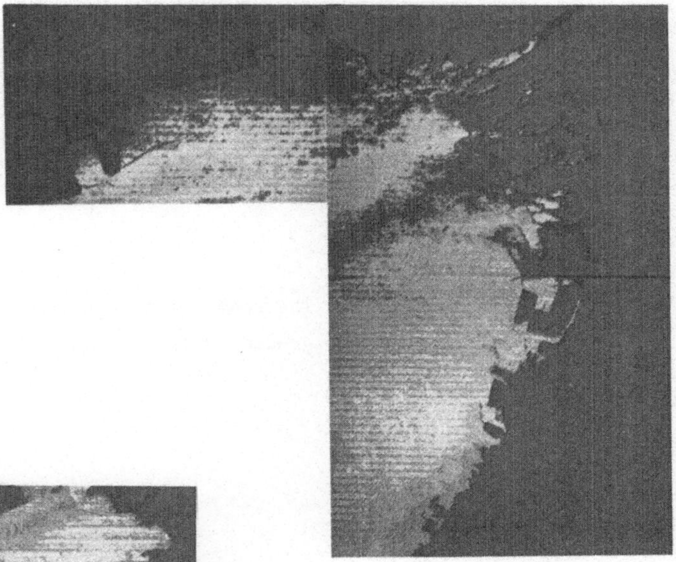

Osaka Bay

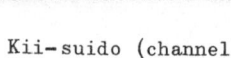

Kii-suido (channel)

Fig. 7 Classification of sea water quality based upon LANDSAT data

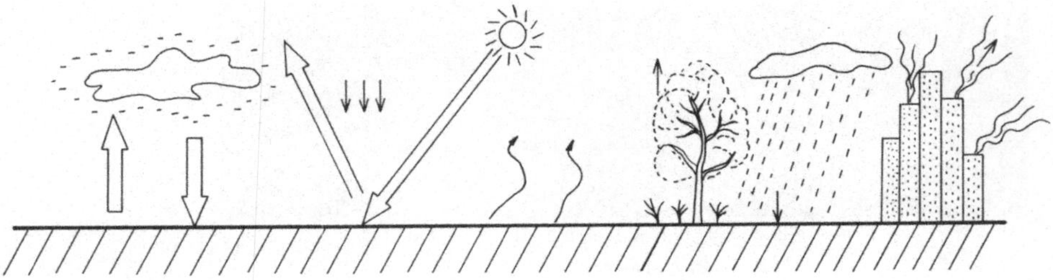

Fig. 8 The heat balance on the ground surface

15:00

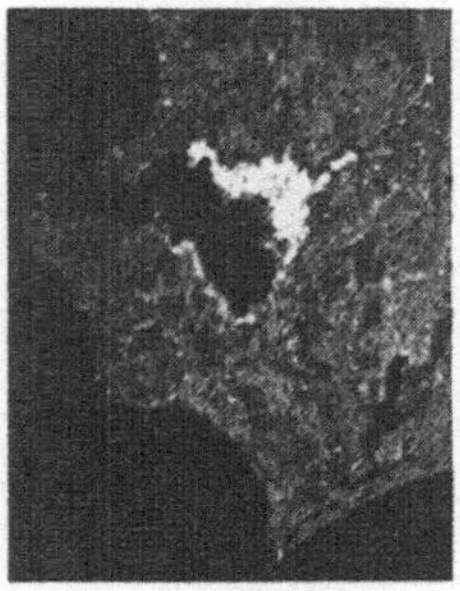

18:00

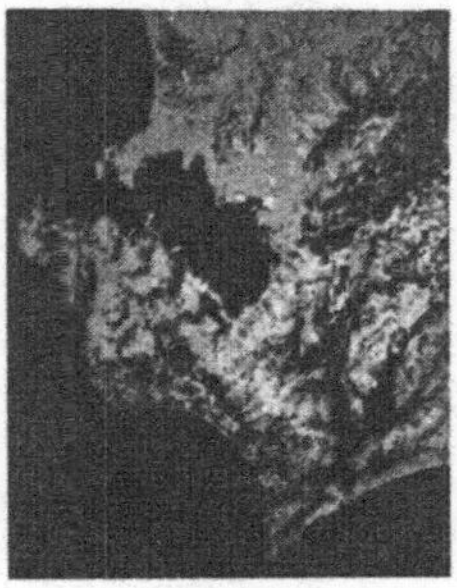

21:00

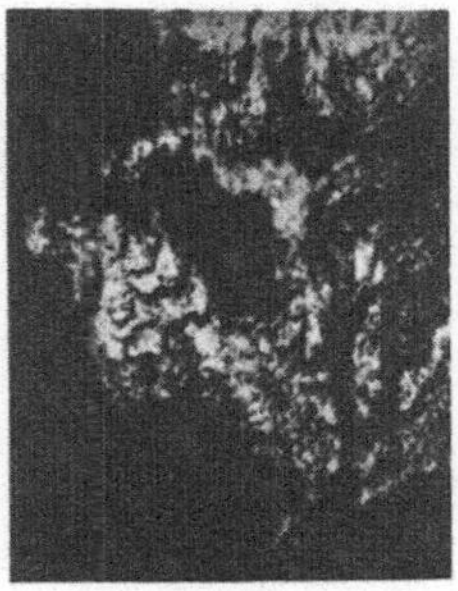

3:00

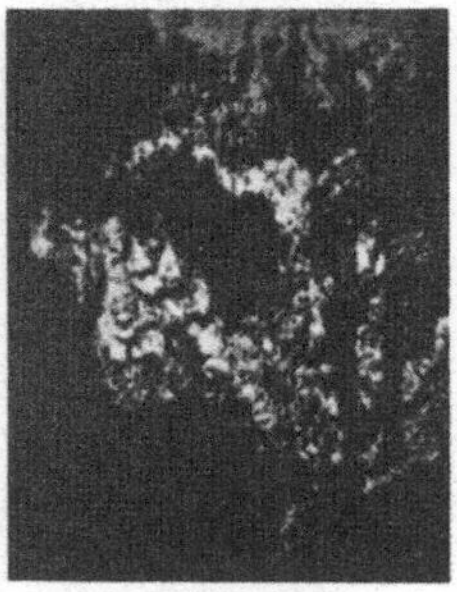

6:00

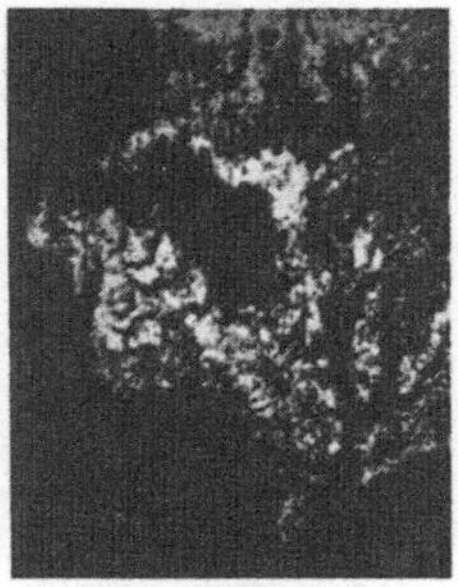

9:00

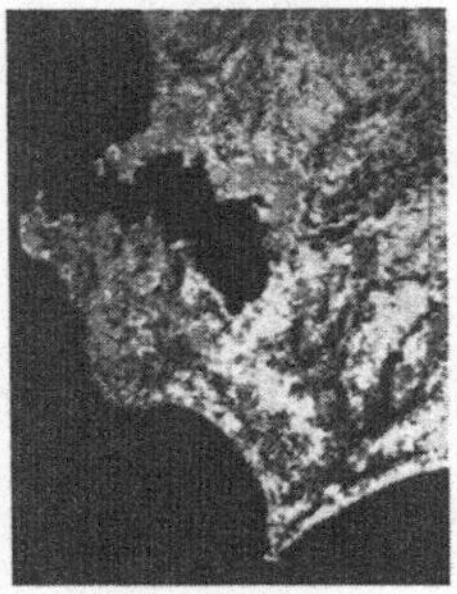

12:00

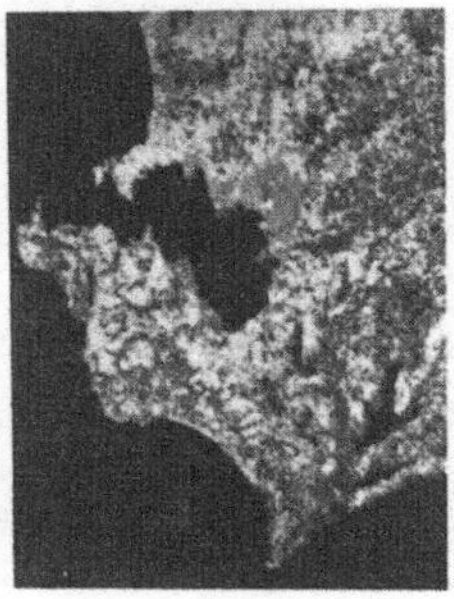

Fig. 9 Thermal emission v.s. time in a day in the Kanto districts

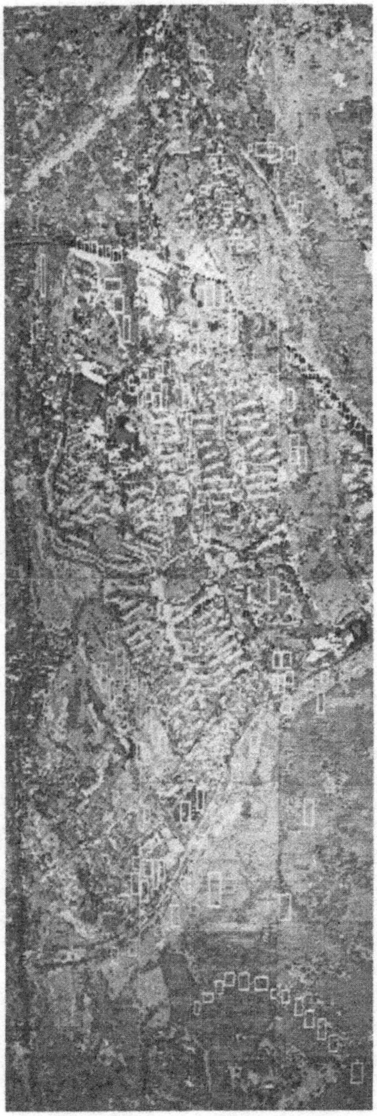

Fig. 10 Land cover type mapping by aircraft remote sensing

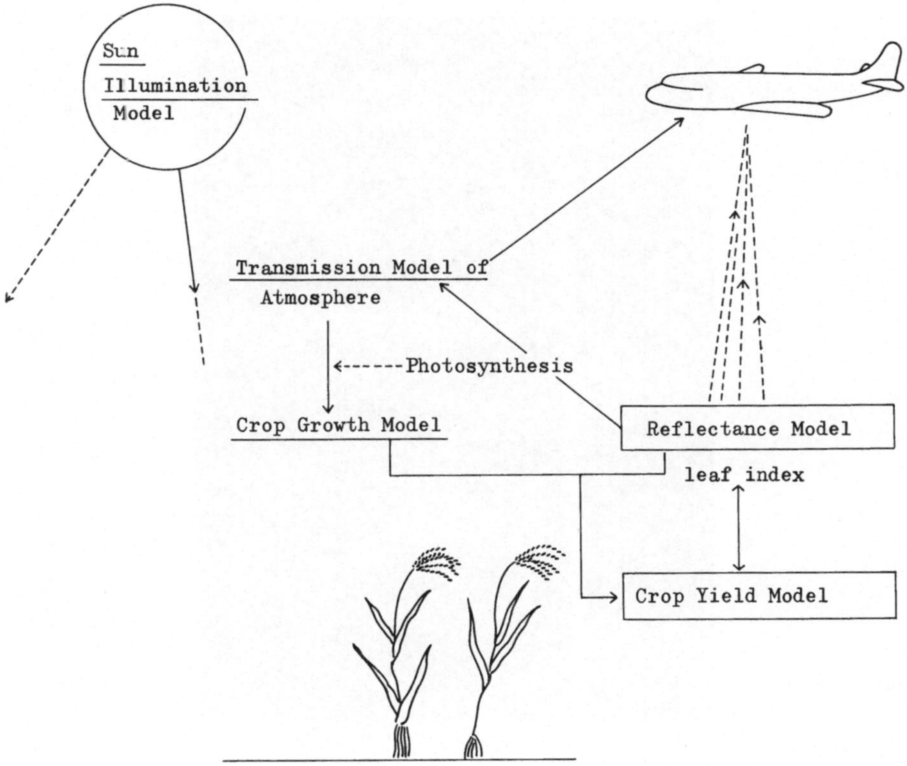

- Soil Condition: Soil Type: Soil Temperature
  : Soil Moisture

- Water Supply

Fig. 11 Sun Energy Illumination and a Reflectance Model

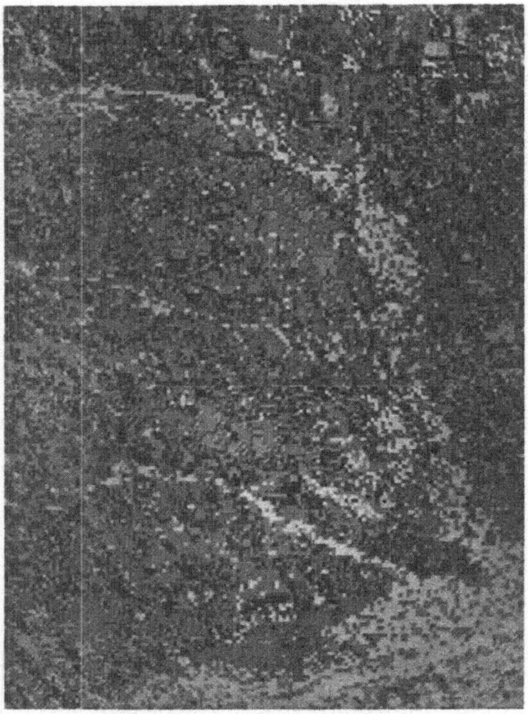

Fig. 12 Land cover type classification for Tokachi district

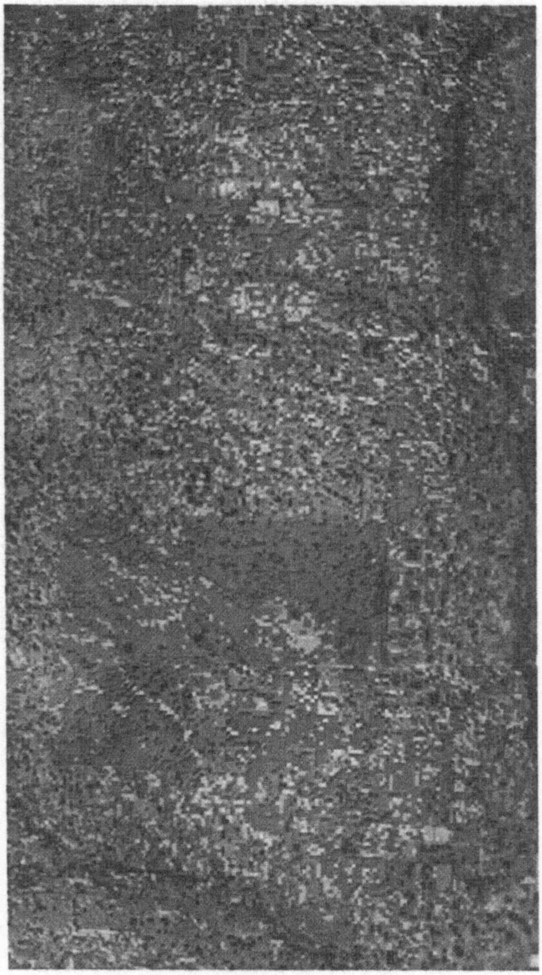

Fig. 13 Land cover type classification for Tokachi district

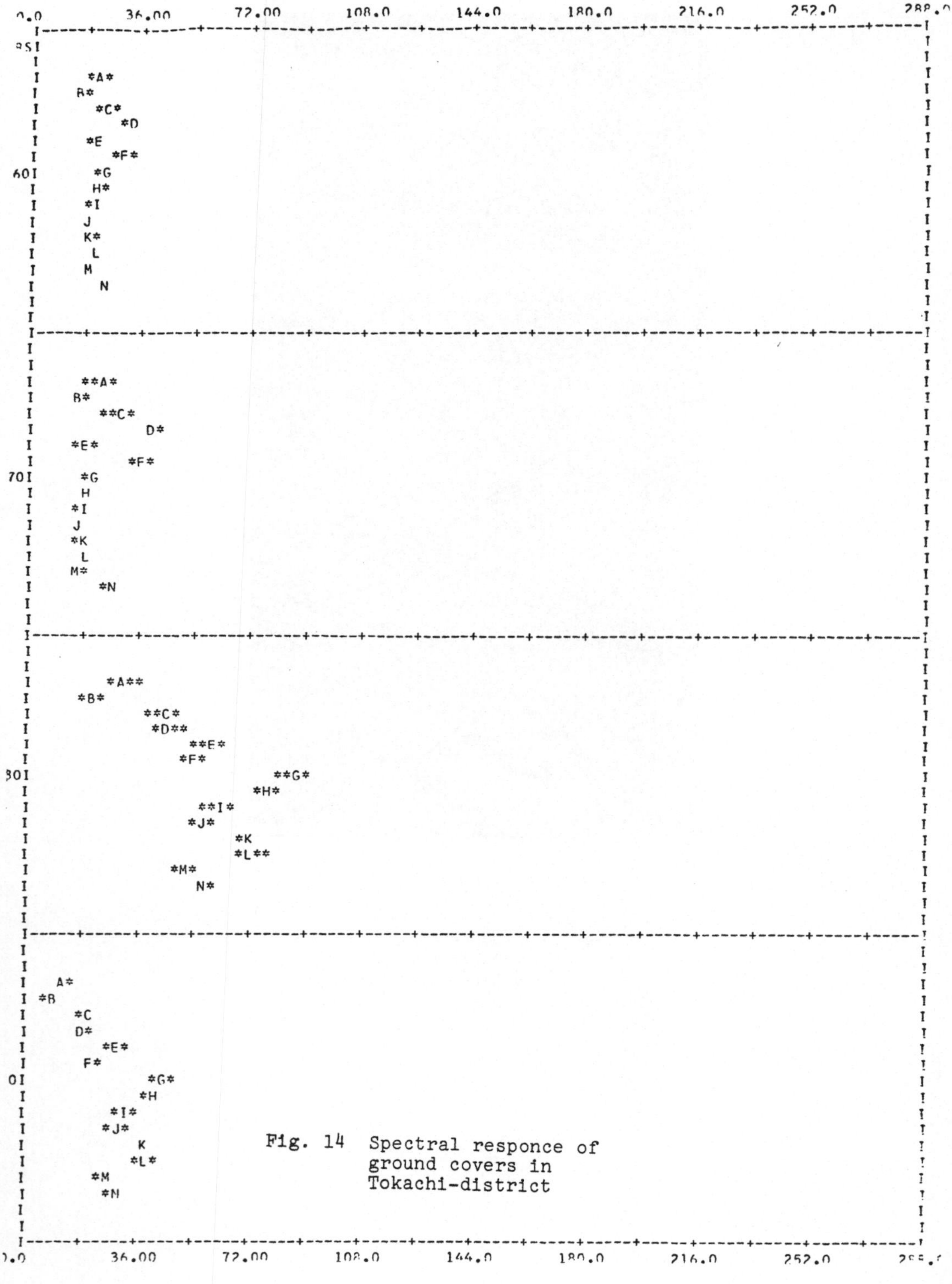

Fig. 14 Spectral responce of ground covers in Tokachi-district

Sampled Point Number		Turbidity	Limpidness	PH	BOD	cl	COD_{AC}	$COD_{AL.}$	Area
S121	6	1.8	3.0	8.5	6.14	16.50	1.81	1.58	HARIMA-NADA
S126	7	2.0	2.2	8.05	6.78	16.65	3.19	1.25	HARIMA-NADA
S127	3	4.4	2.0	8.32	6.25	16.65	1.81	1.64	HARIMA-NADA
S131	4	2.6	1.9	8.18	8.37	16.50	2.01	1.83	HARIMA-NADA
S132	8	2.3	2.2	8.03	6.37	16.72	2.50	1.60	HARIMA-NADA
S133	2	5.0	2.0	8.32	8.27	16.72	1.93	1.65	HARIMA-NADA
S139	4	2.8	0.8	8.22	8.89	16.50	2.62	1.81	HARIMA-NADA
S140	6	1.7	2.1	7.99	6.49	16.39	2.78	1.98	HARIMA-NADA
S141	2	5.7	1.0	8.15	6.97	16.77	0.87	1.46	HARIMA-NADA
S148	4	3.1	0.8	8.19	8.53	16.55	2.48	1.75	HARIMA-NADA
S147	5	2.0	1.4	8.15	7.79	16.66	2.52	1.77	HARIMA-NADA
S150	2	5.5	1.1	8.11	6.98	16.83	1.16	1.50	HARIMA-NADA
S157	3	2.9	0.7	8.17	8.29	16.50	3.29	1.75	HARIMA-NADA
S158	5	2.0	1.4	8.12	7.69	16.50	3.21	1.89	HARIMA-NADA
S159	4	5.7	0.5	8.12	7.64	16.77	1.87	1.49	HARIMA-NADA
S063	8	1.8	3.4	7.99	6.73	12.79	3.1		KII-SUIDO
S064	1	7.0	0.5	8.19	7.04	17.76	0.63		KII-SUIDO
S065	1	5.5	0.7	8.16	7.03	17.75	1.57		KII-SUIDO
S066	1	8.0	0.6	8.17	9.33	17.68	1.49		KII-SUIDO
S067	2	3.0	1.3	8.03	5.34	17.45	1.7		KII-SUIDO
S068	1	11.0	0.7	8.20	6.95	17.75	0.92		KII-SUIDO
S069	1	7.0	0.5	8.16	7.21	17.93	1.64		KII-SUIDO
S070	1	7.5	3.4	8.12	6.94	17.78	1.0		KII-SUIDO
S071	1	9.5	0.7	8.15	6.99	17.73	0.63		KII-SUIDO
S072	2	8.0	0.6	8.13	7.13	17.80	1.05		KII-SUIDO
S073	1	12.0	0.3	8.17	7.35	17.96	1.28		KII-SUIDO
S074	1	3.0	0.7	8.10	7.47	18.01	1.02		KII-SUIDO
S075	1	14.0	0.7	8.22	7.03	19.51	0.69		KII-SUIDO
S076	3	3.0	1.7	8.18	6.24	18.02	1.2		KII-SUIDO
S077	1	8.0	0.7	8.15	6.99	17.69	1.16		KII-SUIDO
S078	4	7.5	0.7	8.16	6.81	17.66	1.1		KII-SUIDO
S079	1	9.0	0.7	8.19	6.96	17.66	0.9		KII-SUIDO
S080	1	12.0	0.6	8.17	7.57	17.75	1.63		KII-SUIDO
S081	1	16.0	0.6	8.19	7.11	18.31	0.80		KII-SUIDO
S082	4	5.5	0.5	8.16	6.79	17.66	1.4		KII-SUIDO
S083	6	4.5	2.8	8.07	6.06	17.27	1.4		KII-SUIDO
S084	2	5.0	2.6	8.19	6.56	18.03	1.2		KII-SUIDO
S085	1	12.0	1.9	8.15	8.04	17.91	0.9		KII-SUIDO
S086	1	17.	0.5	8.17	7.53	17.86	1.21		KII-SUIDO
S087	1	19.	0.3	8.20	6.90	18.40	0.52		KII-SUIDO
S088	5	5.	1.0	8.16	6.59	17.96	6.58		KII-SUIDO
S089	1	9.	0.7	8.17	7.01	17.74	0.78		KII-SUIDO
S090	2	8.	0.3	8.16	7.65	17.86	1.02		KII-SUIDO
S091	1	17.	0.3	8.17	7.20	17.96	1.1		KII-SUIDO
S092	1	9.	1.5	8.00	7.0		0.7		KII-SUIDO
S093	2	10.	2.5	8.1	6.6		0.7		KII-SUIDO
S094	1	10.	2.0	8.1	7.1		1.0		KII-SUIDO
S095	1	13.	2.5	8.1	7.2		0.5		KII-SUIDO
S096	2	7.	2.0	8.0	6.6		0.6		KII-SUIDO
S097	2	7.	2.5	8.0	4.5		0.59	0.17	KII-SUIDO
S098	2	6.	2.0	8.0	7.0		1.0		KII-SUIDO
S099	3	8.	2.5	8.0	6.9		0.78	0.20	KII-SUIDO
S100	1	10.	1.0	8.0	6.8		0.8		KII-SUIDO
S101	2	14.	2.5	8.1	6.9		0.5		KII-SUIDO
S102	4	10.	2.0	8.0	7.1		0.6		KII-SUIDO
S103	7	5.	3.0	8.1	6.6		1.0		KII-SUIDO
S104	5	3.5	3.5	8.0	6.9		0.6		KII-SUIDO
S105	4	4.5	1.5	8.0	7.3		0.8		KII-SUIDO
S106	6	6.0	1.5	8.0	7.2		0.8		KII-SUIDO
S107	7	4.0	2.5	8.0	7.2		0.7		KII-SUIDO
S108	7	6.0	1.5	8.1	6.8		1.4		KII-SUIDO
S109	7	2.5	2.9	8.1	7.1		1.2		KII-SUIDO
S110	7	3.9	3.5	8.1	7.3		1.2		KII-SUIDO
S111	5	2.9	3.0	8.0	7.7		1.0		KII-SUIDO
S112	8	3.0	3.5	8.0	7.3		0.6		KII-SUIDO
S113	6	2.9	3.0	8.0	7.6		1.2		KII-SUIDO
S114	5	2.4	5.0	8.0	7.5		0.7		KII-SUIDO
S001	9	1.5	5.1	7.5	3.3	15.35	3.6		OSAKA-WAN
S002	9	2.2	1.9	7.6	3.5	13.63	2.5		OSAKA-WAN
S003	9	1.7	2.5	7.5	3.1	12.28	2.5		OSAKA-WAN
S004	9	3.0	1.9	8.2	8.2	15.89	3.4		OSAKA-WAN
S005	5	2.7	1.9	8.1	6.4	17.25	3.5		OSAKA-WAN
S006	4	2.0	2.3	8.0	5.9	16.93	7.0		OSAKA-WAN
S007	8	2.0	2.0	7.9	5.2		2.7	1.0	OSAKA-WAN
S008	9	4.5	1.9	7.9	4.7	15.44	2.4	0.8	OSAKA-WAN
S009	5	6.5	1.3	8.1	6.4	16.39	3.9		OSAKA-WAN
S010	5	3.0	1.7	8.4	9.7	17.18	2.6		OSAKA-WAN
S011	9	1.5	5.0	7.8	4.7		2.7	1.0	OSAKA-WAN
S012	9	4.0		8.2	7.2		2.5	0.6	OSAKA-WAN
S013	8	6.5	1.1	8.0	6.3	16.36	2.8		OSAKA-WAN
S014	5	5.5	1.3	8.2	7.0	16.75	2.7		OSAKA-WAN
S015	4	2.5	2.3	8.4	7.5	17.19	3.9		OSAKA-WAN
S016	7	3.5	2.3	8.4	9.1	17.23	2.4		OSAKA-WAN
S017	9	5.0		8.2	8.2		2.1	0.7	OSAKA-WAN
S020	2	1.7	4.1	8.2	8.5	16.74	1.8		OSAKA-WAN
S021	7	3.0	2.3	8.4	8.4	17.29	3.1		OSAKA-WAN
S022	9	3.5	2.0	8.1	7.7		1.9	0.8	OSAKA-WAN
S027	8	3.0		8.1	6.7		1.4	1.0	OSAKA-WAN
S031	9	2.5	3.0	8.1	3.4		2.0	0.6	OSAKA-WAN
S032	4	4.0		8.2	7.5		2.3	0.9	OSAKA-WAN
S033	5	4.0	[illegible]	8.1	3.3		1.4	1.3	OSAKA-WAN

Table I Sampled data of sea water qualities in Seto Inland Sea

LONG TERM POLICY ASSESSMENT OF ENERGY/ENVIRONMENT FUTURES: A SYSTEMS APPROACH

W.K. Foell, J. Buehring, W. Buehring, R. Dennis, K. Ito*,
R. Keeney**, and B. Lapillonne

International Institute for Applied Systems Analysis
2361 Laxenburg
Austria

November, 1976

Prepared for the International Symposium on New Trends in Systems Analysis, Institute de Recherche D'Informatique et D'Automatique, Le Chesnay, France; 13-17 December, 1976

Current Affiliation:

*Osaka University, Faculty of Engineering, Osaka, Japan

**Woodward-Clyde Consultants, San Francisco, California, USA

ACKNOWLEDGEMENTS

The authors wish to acknowledge the research contributions of the following individuals:

IIASA: J. Bigelow, J.-P. Charpentier, A. Hoelzl, H. Stehfest, J. Weingart, and R. Yorque.

Institut fuer Energetik, Leipzig GDR: W. Haetscher, P. Hedrich W. Kluge, and D. Ufer.

Institut Economique et Juridique de l'Energie, Grenoble France: B. Chateau, D. Finon, and J.-M. Martin.

University of Wisconsin-Madison: M. Hanson, J. Mitchell, and J. Pappas.

ABSTRACT

A research program on "Management of Regional Energy/Environment Systems" has been conducted at IIASA for the past 18 months. The study, designed to integrate energy and environment considerations from a system perspective, has four primary objectives:

1) To describe and analyze existing patterns of regional energy use and supply, and to gain an insight into their relationships to socio-economic patterns;
2) To analyze and compare alternative methodologies for regional energy and environmental forecasting, planning and policy design;
3) To develop new concepts and methodologies for energy/environment system management and policy design;
4) To use these methodologies to examine alternative energy policies and strategies for test regions, to explore their environmental implications from various perspectives using sets of indicators related to environmental impacts, energy-use efficienceis, etc., and to investigate whether these strategies represent a viable choice for the society in which they are being considered.

This paper provides an overview description of the methodology and selected results for three case studies within this research program, namely, the state of Wisconsin (U.S.A), the German Democratic Republic, and Rhone-Alpes (France).

LONG TERM POLICY ASSESSMENT OF ENERGY/ENVIRONMENT FUTURES: A SYSTEMS APPROACH

W.K. Foell, J. Buehring, W. Buehring, R. Dennis, K. Ito, R. Keeney, and B. Lapillonne

A research program on "Management of Regional Energy/Environment Systems" had been conducted at IIASA for the past 18 months [1]. The study, designed to integrate energy and environment considerations from a system perspective, has four primary objectives:

1) To describe and analyze existing patterns of regional energy use and supply, and to gain an insight into their relationships to socio-economic patterns;
2) To analyze and compare alternative methodologies for regional energy and environmental forecasting, planning and policy design;
3) To develop new concepts and methodologies for energy/environment system management and policy design;
4) To use these methodologies to examine alternative energy policies and strategies for test regions, to explore their environmental implications from various perspectives using sets of indicators related to environmental impacts, energy-use efficiencies, etc., and to investigate whether these strategies represent a viable choice for the society in which they are being considered.

This paper describes the methodological framework within which the study has been conducted and presents some representative results.

One of IIASA's strengths is its access to research institutions and scientists throughout the world and its mandate to interact with them in applied and policy-oriented research. To take advantage of this capability and as a vehicle to sharpen the research, the Energy/Environment study was organized on a comparative basis, with three distinct geographical regions being chosen as the first case studies: The German Democratic Republic (GDR), the Rhone-Alpes region in southern France, and the state of Wisconsin in the U.S.A. The regions were chosen in part because of their greatly differing characteristics--socio-economic and political structures, technological base, geographic and ecological properties, and institutional approaches to environmental and energy planning management--and partly because of the presence in each region of a collaborating institution with a policy-oriented research program, examining energy/environment systems from a broad resource-management perspective.

The research activities can be broken down into five components:

- Description of the energy/environment systems of each region: past and current energy use, energy supply modes and flows, environmental quality indices (air, land, water, etc.), economic activity, demography, human settlement patterns, and so on;
- Description and comparison of institutional and organizational structures within which energy and environment planning, management, and policy design are conducted;
- Comparison of energy/environment modelling tools used in each region, according to methodology, domains of policy and planning applications, relation to the decision-making structure, transferability to other regions, etc;
- Development of alternative futures (scenarios) for each region as a tool to examine alternate energy and environmental policies and strategies;
- Development of methods and concepts for communicating and evaluating energy/environment strategies and options.

The remainder of this paper focuses on the fourth and fifth components above. Section II gives an overview of the quantitative tools used for scenario building. Section III presents some of the alternative futures studies, followed in Section IV by a description of an approach to evaluation and communication, based upon decision analysis techniques.

II. MODELS AND METHODOLOGY

The main quantitative tool used for scenario building is a large-scale simulation model, originally developed at the University of Wisconsin and extended at IIASA to treat regional energy/environment systems with characteristics differing from Wisconsin. For each region, the model was driven by alternative socio-economic patterns provided by the collaborating institute in that region. For example the Institut fuer Energetik in Leipzig provided extensive economic input based upon their preparation of the GDR long-term energy plan.

The WISconsin Regional Energy Model (WISE) is a computerized simulation model designed to describe the technological-economic-environmental interactions in a regional energy system [2]. It is built of a hierarchy of submodels. Its simulation structure provides considerable flexibility in both the modeling process and the application; it makes possible the modification of selected components without the necessity to rework the entire model, and the focusing of attention on specific system areas as well as on the entire system. Although there are numerous ways to describe the overall structure of the WISE model, one of the more revealing is by component subsystems (Figure 1). Within this scheme, the model can be conveniently subdivided into five major components:

1) Socio-Economic Activity

   This component includes population and demographic characteristics, economic activity, and the geographic distribution within the region. Most of the inputs to these components are exogenous and were derived from other macroeconomic regional or national models of studies.

2) Sources of Primary Energy

   This component contains information on fuel sources within and external to the region, according to origin, composition, energy content, price, availability, etc.

3) End-Use Energy Demand

   Demand is modelled according to various sets of energy use categories; the specific choice of these categories depends upon the application of the model. The sets include class of use according to economic sector, physical process, fuel type, location within the region, and time period when use takes place.

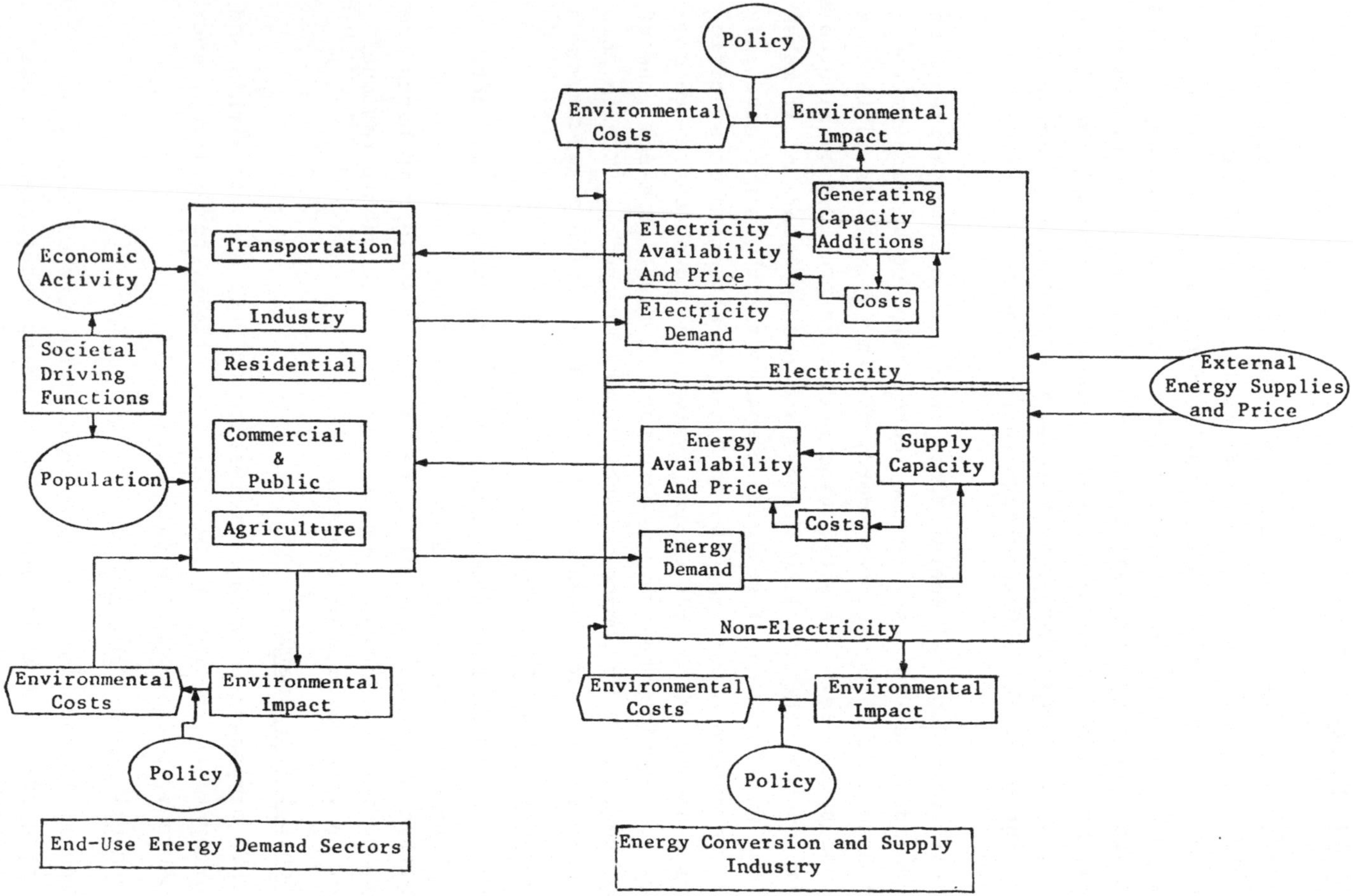

Figure 1: The WISconsin Regional Energy Model (WISE)

4) Energy Conversion and Supply

This component treats the conversion of primary fuels into intermediate or final forms of energy for end use. The two main groups of submodels treat electrical and non-electrical energy.

5) Environmental Impact

This component simulates on a year-to-year basis the "quantified" environmental impacts resulting from a region's energy use and the associated energy supply and conversion system [3]. As an example of the information contained in the impact models, Fig. 2 illustrates the impact pathways which the model associates with electricity use in a region. The calculation of quantified impacts from electricity use in an energy system in a particular year is based upon impact factors that relate impacts to a unit of electricity generation for a reference plant in the specified year. The impacts are classified into the general categories of land, air, water, human health and safety, and fuel resource use.

The flow of information in the model begins with the exogenous specification of population, human settlement patterns, and economic activity. These variables provide a basis for calculating end-use energy demand. A second group of models calculates characteristics of supply systems necessary to meet that demand, including supply capacities, primary energy, etc. The environmental impact models use population and human settlement data, as well as outputs of the energy demand and supply models, to calculate environmental impacts (indicators), including human health and safety. A growing literature exists on the structure and applications of the WISE model, [e.g. 4,5] and on the IIASA extensions.

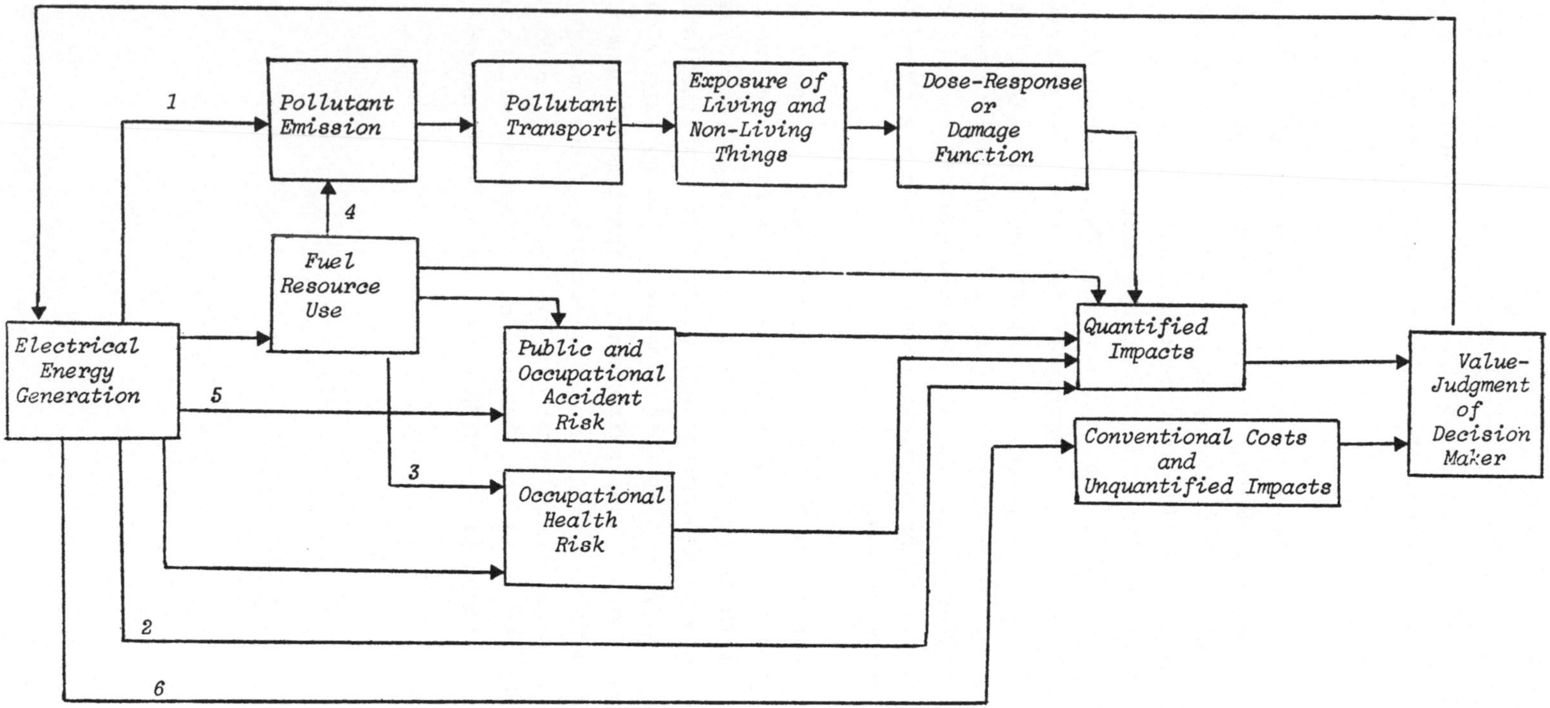

Figure 2: Electrical Energy Impact Pathways

III. SCENARIOS

A. Definition

As described earlier, scenario building was employed as a device for analyzing alternative energy and environment policies and strategies in the regions. They were constructed for Wisconsin, Rhone-Alpes, and a composite region ("Bezirk X"), typical of the heavily industrialized southeastern GDR. The resulting scenarios were not developed as predictions. They are intended to help test and compare the consequences of different policy choices. It is obvious that each of the regions has many alternate energy futures open to it; the scenarios chosen for the research highlight only three of them in order to improve our understanding of energy and environmental management.

It should be emphasized here that the assumptions underlying the scenarios were not chosen arbitrarily by the IIASA research team. They were developed after lengthy and repeated interactions with collaborating specialists in the respective regions; in some cases exogenous inputs to the scenrios were supplied directly by the collaborating institutions. Whenever possible these were tested by reference to other economic or technical studies, e.g. the Ford Foundation Energy Policy Study [6], the GDR Long Term Energy Plan [7], and national energy assessments in France [8]. Where feasible, the Wisconsin Energy Model was used to construct sectoral energy demand descriptions, based upon data and parameters from the respective regions. However the 50 year time span of the scenarios clearly introduces major uncertainty into many of the underlying assumptions and parameters.

As pointed out earlier, regional rather than national scenarios were studied because of the former's value in addressing environmental issues--often regional in nature. However, because none of the regions are institutionally or economically autonomous, it is not possible to discuss regional scenarios while ignoring the evolution of the national systems. The scenarios were based upon policies which could be implemented, albeit in varying degrees, both nationally and regionally, the resulting contrasting energy patterns and environmental consequences were then evaluated for the regions.

The policy areas explicitly addressed in the scenarios are:

- o Urban Form
- o Energy-Use Technology
- o Transportation
- o Energy Supply
- o Environmental Control

Contrasting policy alternatives were formulated in each of these areas. These alternatives formed the basis for the three scenarios, chosen to correspond to a consistent rationale.

The scenario characteristics are summarized by the following:

<u>Scenario S1</u>: The "Base Case"

- No dramatic changes in the current policies (e.g. in the GDR, it follows objectives of the 20 year plan); this therefore represents a continuation of current socio-economic trends.

<u>Scenario S2</u>:

- Results from combinations of policies favoring higher growth in energy use than in S1;
- Based on presumption of low or moderate energy costs and few or no special incentives for improved efficiency of energy use.

<u>Scenario S3:</u>

- Based on presumption of high cost of energy and on desirability of implementation of energy-saving measures;
- Emphasis is placed on conservation of energy resources, leading to development of solar energy.
- Pollution control is stressed.

As an example, Table 1 shows the policy set for the three Wisconsin scenarios. The building of the scenarios within the policy frameworks enabled us to systematically examine the energy and environmental consequences. In addition several sensitivity studies, in which only a single parameter is varied, were carried out.

A most important similarity among the three scenarios for a given region is that they are all based on essentially the same overall economic and population growth rates. Macro-economic studies of the Ford Foundation Energy Policy Project indicated that for the U.S., within the range of the above policy frameworks, the coupling between energy use and economic growth rate is loose, although there can be significant

	SCENARIO		
	S1	S2	S3
URBAN FORM	o Suburban extension o 25% apartments	o Exurban dispersal o 50% apartments	o Small Compact cities o 50% apartments
TECHNICAL	o Almost constant energy use per unit value-added in service & industry	o Increasing energy use per unit value-added o Emphasis on electricity	o Declining energy use per unit value-added o Conservation measures
TRANSPORTATION	o Auto efficiency gain	o No auto efficiency gain	o Large auto efficiency gain
ENERGY SUPPLY	o Synthetic fuel from coal o Mix of coal & nuclear for electricity	o Synthetic fuel from coal o Mostly nuclear for electricity	o Solar for electricity & heating
ENVIRONMENT	o Present trends of increasing controls for SO_2 and particulates	o Low controls of SO_2 and particulates	o Stringent controls of SO_2 & particulates

Table 1: Policies for Wisconsin Scenarios, 1970-2025.

sectoral interactions. We have followed this approach in our studies. The population and overall economic growth developments, as provided by the collaborating institutions, are discussed in detail in Reference [9].

B. Selected Results

Space limitations permit the presentation here of only a few results of the scenarios. Because of the focus of this conference, environmental impact is emphasized; energy demand and supply consequences are given elsewhere (9).

A wide range of environmental indicators is used to characterize the environmental implications. Some environmental indicators used were associated with "quantified" human health and safety impacts. Quantified here refers only to those impacts explicitly included in the Environmental Impact Models, [e.g.3, 10, 11] used in this research. The choice of this set of impacts is to some extent subjective; in addition, some degree of uncertainty (and perhaps controversy) is associated with some of the impact factors. There are also many indicators which are recognized but remain unquantified; there are others that are unrecognized and hence unquantified. An approach to coping with this uncertainty and subjectivity is described in Section IV. The impacts described below are only a fraction of those studied with the methodology described in Reference [3]. Emphasis is given here to a cross-regional comparison of the impacts.

1. Carbon Dioxide Emissions

Carbon dioxide emissions are of concern on a global scale since the atmospheric concentration of CO_2 affects average global temperature [12, 13, 14]. Burning of fossil fuels has produced enormous quantities of CO_2, e.g. about 10,800 million metric tons in 1960 [12], for which there are three main reservoirs: the oceans, the biosphere (defined as the mass of living and nonliving organic matter), and the atmosphere. About half of the CO_2 liberated by fossil fuel combustion has remained in the atmosphere [12, 13]. Calculations have shown that CO_2 concentration in the atmosphere may increase from about 320 parts per million (ppm) by volume in 1970 to 370-380 ppm in 2000; the resulting global temperature increase may be nearly one degree Celsius. Global temperature changes of this magnitude may have serious implications for agriculture, global sea level, and global precipitation patterns. Thus, CO_2 emissions that result from burning of fossil fuels may involve a significant long-term risk to future generations.

The per capita CO_2 emissions in the year 2025 for the three scenarios in each region are shown in Figure 3 along with the 1970 emission levels. All three regions have greater CO_2 emissions in 2025 for all three scenarios than they had in 1970. The total CO_2 emissions in Wisconsin in 2025 for Scenario S1 are more than a factor of five greater than the 1970 emissions (population increases by about 50 percent over this period). Bezirk X relies on coal for a large fraction of its energy in all scenarios; the total emissions for the high energy scenario (S2) in the Bezirk are nearly five times greater than the 1970 emissions. In Rhone-Alpes the availability of fossil fuels is more limited and a significant factor of the energy comes from other sources, such as hydro or nuclear.

The emissions resulting from Wisconsin's energy use in 2025 are approximately four percent of the total emissions for the world in 1960. If all regions of the world were to increase their CO_2 emissions as in these scenarios, methods for reducing CO_2 emissions to the atmosphere, e.g. Marchetti's disposal method [15], or even CO_2 removal from the atmosphere, may be required, or the fossil fuel option might be unacceptable.

Other potential long-term problems such as radioactive waste production and nuclear safeguards, must also be considered in the evaluation of alternative energy futures. These types of impacts are in contrast to the usual localized impacts; cooperation among nations will be needed to avoid "the tragedy of the commons [16] on a global scale.

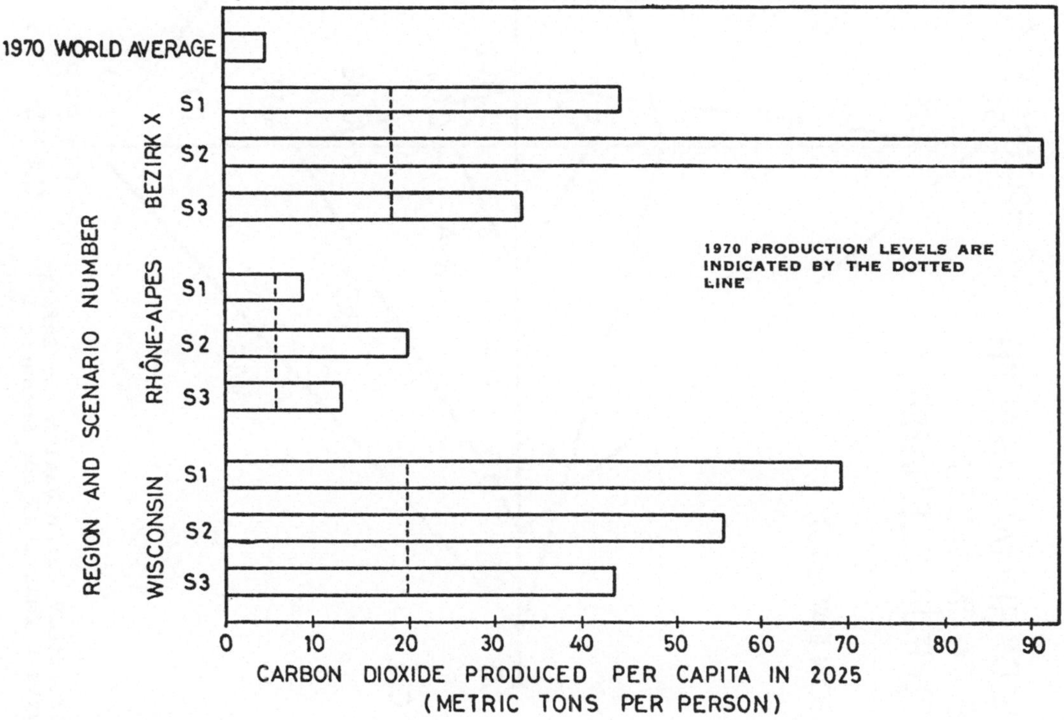

Figure 3: Carbon Dioxide Production Per Capita in 1970 and 2025

2. Human Health and Safety

The total "quantified" human health and safety impacts in the year 2025 for Scenario S1 are shown in Figure 4, which is similar in

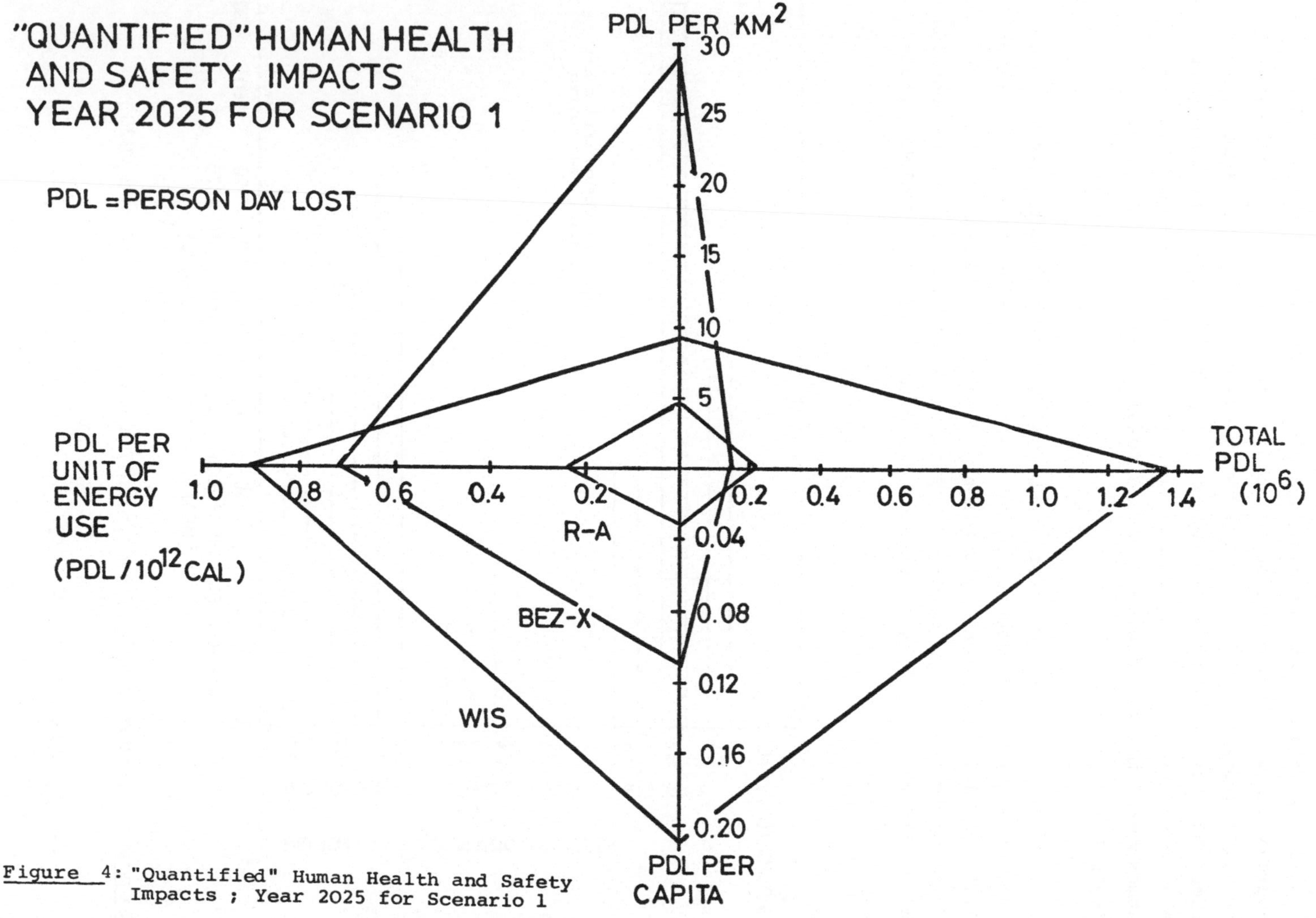

<u>Figure 4</u>: "Quantified" Human Health and Safety Impacts ; Year 2025 for Scenario 1

format to the previous figure. Person days lost (PDL) are used to combine the effects of mortality and morbidity. The quantified totals shown in the figure include health and accidental impacts on the general public and those people employed throughout the energy system, from resource extraction to waste disposal. In contrast to SO_2 emissions, Bezirk X has the largest impact only on the scale showing PDL per unit area. On the other three scales Wisconsin has the greatest impact. Quantified impacts of air pollution are a major share of the total PDL for Wisconsin.

To provide some perspective on these numbers, let us compare the PDL per capita in Figure 4 with the PDL per capita that result from all accidental fatalities in the U.S. The risk of fatality from all accidents (autos, falls, burns, drowning, firearms, etc.) was 49 per 100,000 in the U.S. in 1974 (Source: 1974 U.S. Statistical Abstract, Bureau of Census). This is equivalent to 2.9 PDL per person per year.* The quantified PDL per capita in 2025 that result from Wisconsin energy use are about seven percent of the PDL per capita from all fatal accidents at current incidence levels.

The quantified health and safety impacts are not spread evenly over all population groups. For example, nearly 30 percent of the quantified PDL in 2025 for Wisconsin Scenario S1 are imposed on less than one percent of the total population, namely, 53,000 elderly people who live in the industrialized Milwaukee area and have preexisting heart or lung disease.

The total PDL per 1000 population in the region are displayed in Figure 5 for the years 1970 and 2025 for all scenarios. It is interesting to note that there is at least one scenario in each region that has fewer PDL per capita in 2025 than occurred in 1970. Also, it is clear from the figure that a significant fraction of the total PDL are imposed in regions other than where the energy is consumed. Impacts in other regions result from consuming fuels that must be mined elsewhere and transported into the region, or from the expected global health effects from radioactive releases, etc. The quantified health impacts of air pollution are an important consideration in all scenarios considered.

---

*One accidental fatality is equivalent to 6,000 PDL in this accounting system [17].

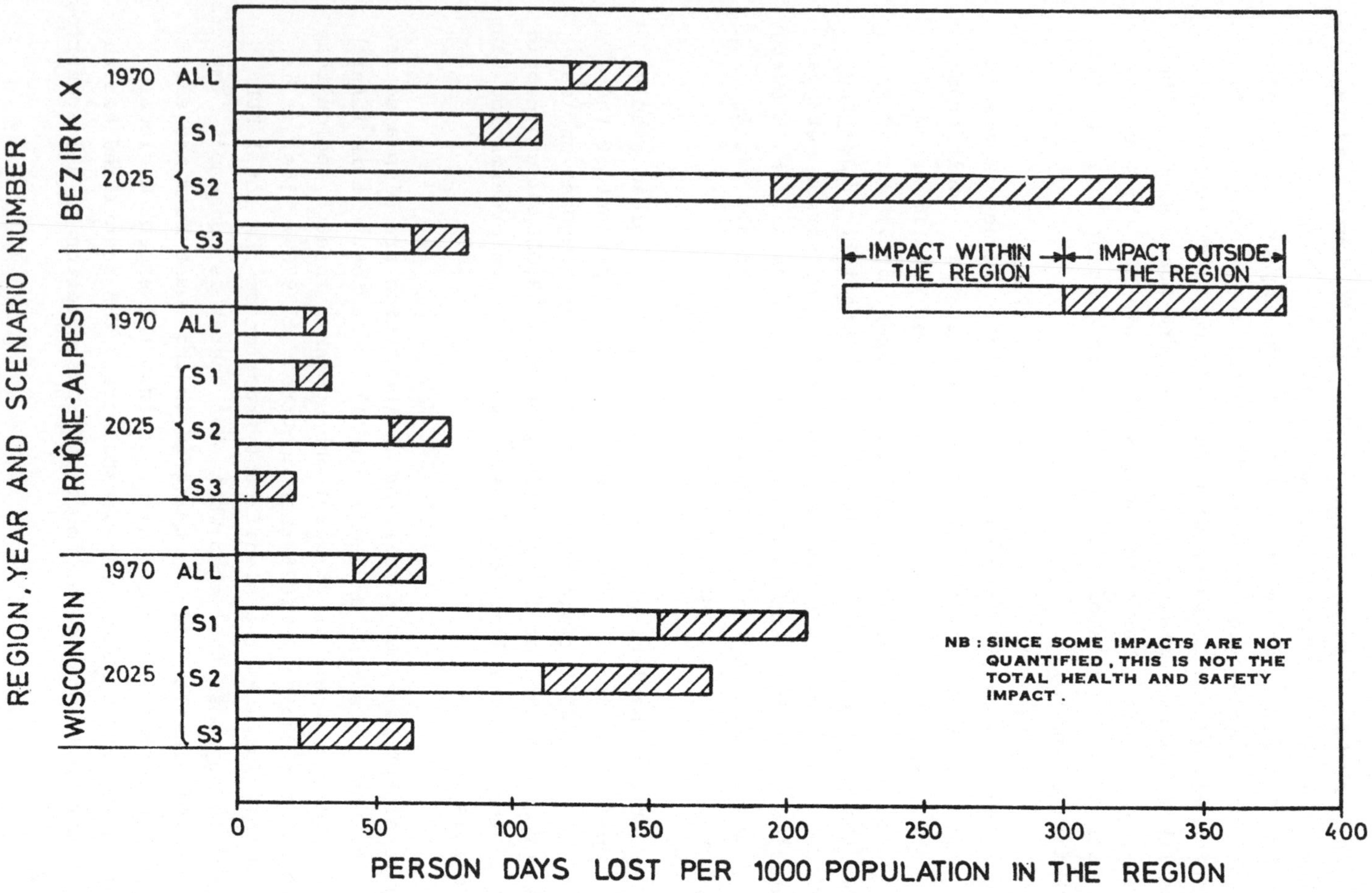

Figure 5: Cross-Regional Comparison of Quantified Human Health Impacts.

3. Land Use

The low energy scenario (S3) for Wisconsin has greater impacts in some categories than the other scenarios. For example, land distrubed per unit of primary energy is considerably greater in S3 because of the solar electrical generation plants. The land shown in Figure 6 is the sum of all land disturbed, except for electricity transmission, in order to produce the energy in the year shown; this includes land used for sites for power plants and fuel system facilities, for mining, and for storage of various waste products. The land use in 2025 for Scenarios S2 and S3 is about 0.3 percent of the area of Wisconsin; however, not all land use shown here is in Wisconsin. The solar land use by 2025 in S3 is 240 km^2; solar electrical generation accounts for 30 percent of the total in that year. The annual land use in S2 is slightly greater than for S3; however, the primary energy requirements is approximately twice as large for S2 as for S3.

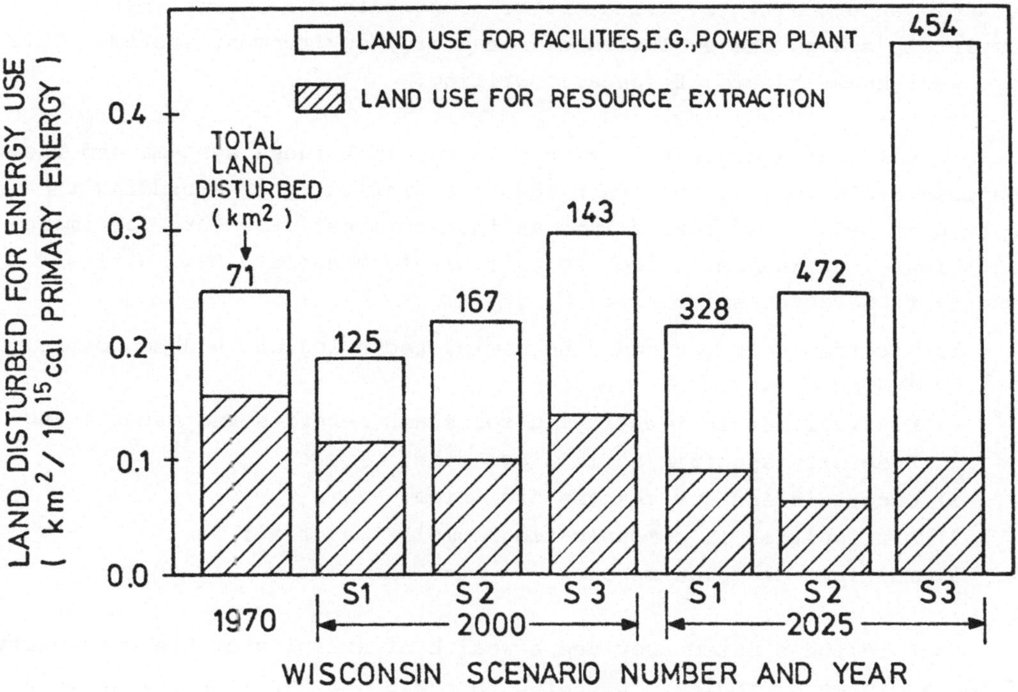

Figure 6: Land Disturbed Per Unit of Primary Energy for the Wisconsin Scenarios.

IV. EVALUATION OF OPTIONS AND STRATEGIES

It has been pointed out that scenario writing in no way represents a forecasting or prediction procedure. The scenarios are meant to stimulate discussion and to provide a better basis for evaluating alternative futures. The success of their use in design or management depends on feedback between the scenario builders and the managers and designers of the energy/environment systems. Feedback in scenario writing is similar to the mechanism by which man's knowledge grows. In that sense, the cycling is a process that rarely stops for long; new knowledge evolves continuously. Time also affects feedback, to the extent that hypothetical future events as laid out in the scenarios either do or do not occur.

From the methodological description in this paper, it is obvious that no formal method has been applied for including uncertainty in the procedure. Rather, the uncertainties must be judged subjectively by scrutinizing the scenarios and the sensitivity studies. Clearly there is ample opportunity to exclude major components and events that can completely change the evolution of the energy/environment system. This is a well-known hazard of scenario writing.

It has been a major task simply to describe these systems and their possible evolution. If one then adds the difficulty of embedding the descriptive and prescriptive into an institutional structure for implementation, the management problem is truly formidable. Some of its important characteristics are:

1) Interdependencies among economic, technological and ecological characteristics of a region;
2) Difficulties in identifying costs and benefits and associating them with specific societal groups;
3) Uncertainties and changes over time;
4) Difficulties in communicating complex material;
5) Multiple decision makers.

Each region studied provides a wealth of examples of the complexity of the management problem. Decision analysis has been applied in this study as one approach to the evaluation and communication of alternative policy designs. The method used was based upon multiattribute utility theory [18]. In this approach, a so-called preference model is introduced into the evaluation process. The relationship between the energy/

environment impact model and the preference model is illustrated in Figure 7. The outputs of the impact model are impact levels of the attributes, i.e. the altered system states. Examples are the sets of environmental impacts associated with the various regional scenarios. To the extent possible, impact models are meant to be objective and to exclude value-judgment content. The construction of the preference model for a decision maker requires the assessment of a utility function for each attribute.

Assessment requires personal interaction with the decision maker, since his utility function is a formalization of his subjective preferences for the attributes (impacts). One of the advantages of this evaluation framework is that recognized but unquantified impacts can be identified and included in the analysis by determining an appropriate proxy variable that can be measured. The overall preference model, based on the measured utility function for a particular individual, allows the calculation of the individual's expected utility associated with the combined impacts of a given policy (scenario). The expected utility calculated for an alternative is a measure of the relative desirability of that alternative for the assessed individual.

This application of this technique to the three-region study was based upon a set of policies related to the choice of electricity generation systems for Wisconsin [19]. Because of space limitations, only a highly simplified version is presented here as an example. The Electricity Impact Model was used to generate the following four attributes (shown in Table 2) of a set of scenarios based upon alternative policies. The ranges are representative of the cumulative impacts

ATTRIBUTES	UNITS	RANGE
X_1 = Total Quantified Fatalities	Deaths	100-700
X_2 = SO_2 Pollution	10^6 Tons	5-8
X_3 = Radioactive Waste	Metric Tons	0-200
X_4 = Electricity Generated	10^{12}kWh	0.5-3.0

Table 2: Attributes and Ranges Used for Utility Measurements

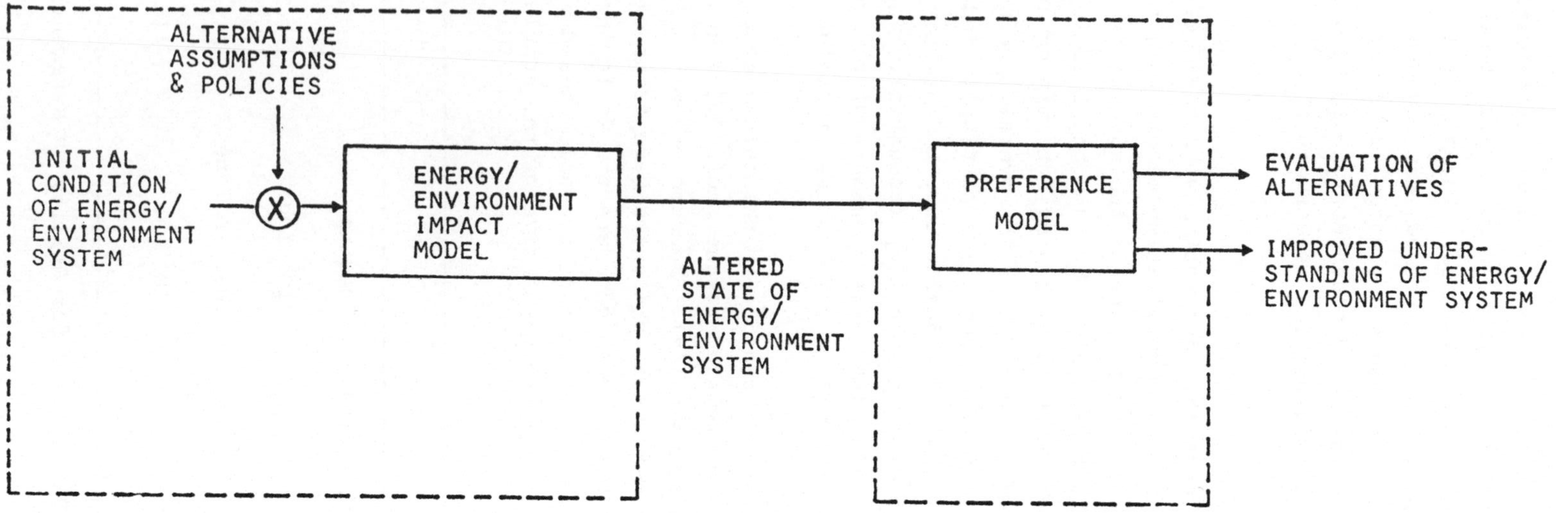

Figure 7: Relationship Between Impact Model and Preference Model.

and electrical generation that may occur for a variety of Wisconsin scenarios over the period 1970 through 2000. The set of scenarios is not identical but similar to the set S1, S2, and S3. Preliminary utility assessments were completed for five individuals from Rhone-Alpes, the GDR, and Wisconsin. The group included a mixture of decision makers and energy/environment specialists; the non-Wisconsin individuals were familiarized with current trends in Wisconsin electricity use so that they would understand the ranges of the attributes. The assessments formed the basis of a preference model for each of the individuals.

A utility function u_i over attribute X_i is set equal to zero at the least desirable level of X_i in the range and set equal to one at the most desirable level of X_i in the range. The results for one of the assessed individuals are shown in Fig. 8. The assessments also provided scaling constants for each of the attributes shown in Figure 8; comparison of these scaling constants for an individual indicates the relative importance of each of the attributes for the specified ranges. Total quantified fatalities had either the largest or second largest scaling constant for all five individuals.

The functions $u_i(x_i)$ and the scaling factors specify completely the multiattribute utility function $u(x_1, x_2, x_3, x_4)$. These five preliminary utility functions were used to evaluate expected utilities associated with the set of alternative policies for electrical generation in Wisconsin. The levels of the four attributes and the expected utilities for each of the individuals are listed in Table 3. If it is assumed that the individuals expressed their true preferences and that they act in a logically consistent manner, the expected utilities can be used to indicate their overall preferences. Under these conditions Table 3 shows that all five individuals should prefer one or more of the other policies to policy 3. This is primarily the result of the large number of fatalities expected for policy 3 and the relatively high scaling factor each of the individuals placed on fatalities.

In applying this technique to an actual policy study, the attribute list must be expanded to include other impacts and conventional costs (eleven impacts have been used in another Wisconsin study [20]. Clearly, considerations other than environment play a major role in the policy design. Our initial efforts with this approach have convinced us that the <u>process</u> of assessing the utility function has many benefits in itself. It can be a substantial aid in identifying and

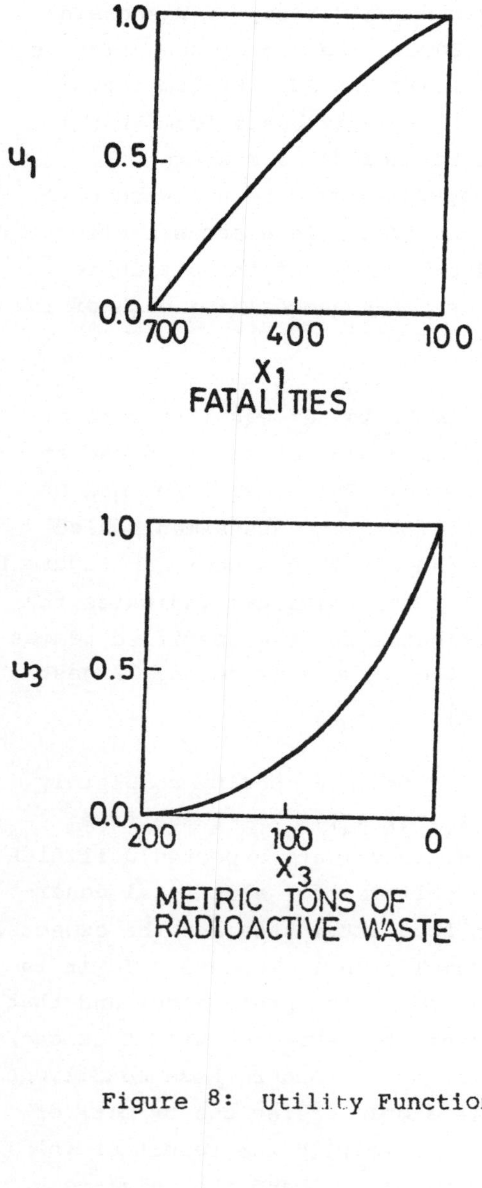

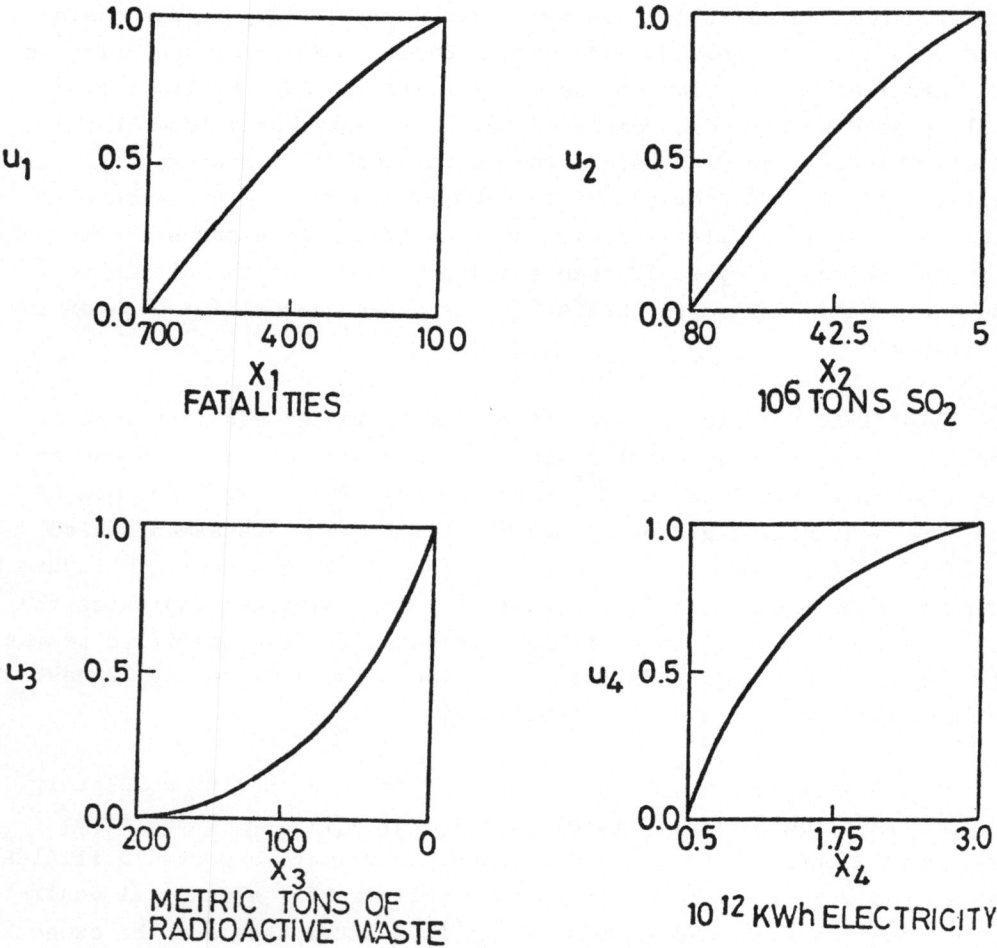

Figure 8: Utility Functions for One Individual

Table 3: Expected utilities for five individuals for several policies.

Attributes and Expected Utilities		Reference Case: Attributes at Extreme Levels	Policy 1: Mostly Coal, Good Pollution Control	Policy 2: Mostly Nuclear	Policy 3: Low Sulfur Coal from Distant Mines & Some Nuclear	Policy 4: Mostly Coal with Less Electricity
Total quantified fatalities		100	380	240	680	280
SO_2 pollution (10^6 tons)		5.0	12	8.0	8.6	9.5
Radioactive waste (metric tons)		0.0	61	160	110	54
Electricity generated (10^{12} kWh(e))		3.0	1.7	1.7	1.7	1.3
Expected utility for individual	A	1.00	0.53	0.66	0.14	0.65
	B	1.00	0.56	0.63	0.14	0.65
	C	1.00	0.76	0.83	0.64	0.41
	D	0.92	0.62	0.66	0.24	0.73
	E	1.00	0.65	0.72	0.31	0.74

sensitizing individuals to important issues, generating and evaluating alternatives, isolating and resolving conflicts of judgment and preference among members of the decision making team, communicating among the several decision makers, and identifying improvements needed in the impact model. Because of these and other benefits experienced during the initial use of this approach we are incorporating it into our future energy/environment research both at IIASA and at the University of Wisconsin.

V. CONCLUSIONS AND SUMMARY

This paper has presented some methodological components and a few selected results of a research program on long-term policy assessment of regional energy/environment systems. Some results and conclusions of the study to date are:

1) A quantitative description and comparison of energy/environment systems has been developed for the three regions; the comparative descriptions have provided insight into the relationships between energy and the regional socio-economic patterns.

2) Alternative energy/environment scenarios were written for the three regions as a vehicle for analysis of selected long-term policy issues; indications are that these scenarios are playing a role in energy/environment planning in the regions.

3) A significant socio-technical interaction of specialists and decision makers from the regions took place at an IIASA workshop in 1975 during which the energy/environment scenarios were discussed and analyzed.

4) A set of energy/environment models were tested for their relevance and validity by application to the greatly differing regions.

5) A decision analysis approach was developed and applied to energy/environment policy analysis.

6) A significant transfer of models and analytic methodology occurred among the collaborating institutions in the three region study.

V. FUTURE WORK

One of the most important outputs of the research has been the creation of a network of research institutions coordinated by IIASA. This has provided IIASA with encouragement in its role as a catalyst and coordinator of policy-oriented research in the international scientific community. The three collaborating institutions will continue to puruse research during 1976, and in addition IIASA will extend the studies to other regions, again with very different socio-economic, geographic, and institutional characteristics. Specifically, one of them will be located in a less industrialized country to allow the IIASA team to further generalize their models and methodologies. Although we realize that there can never be a universal energy/environment model, our long-range goal is generalization of the approaches into a coherent and sound process for resource management in all regions of the world.

References

[1] Foell, W.K., The IIASA Research Program on Management of Regional Energy/Environment Systems, RM-76-40, International Institute for Applied Systems Analysis, Laxenburg, Austria, 1976.

[2] Foell, W.K., J.W. Mitchell, and J.L. Pappas, The Wisconsin Regional Energy Model: A Systems Approach to Regional Energy Analysis, University of Wisconsin-Madison, Institute for Environmental Studies, Report 56, Sept. 1975.

[3] Buehring, W.A., and W.K. Foell, Environmental Impact of Electrical Generation: A Systemwide Approach, RR-76-13, International Institute for Applied Systems Analysis, Laxenburg, Austria, 1976.

[4] Mitchell, H.W. and D.A. Jacobsen, Implications of Commercial Building Codes for Energy Conservation, University of Wisconsin-Madison, Institute for Environmental Studies, Report 42, December 1974.

[5] Hanson, M.E. and J.W. Mitchell, A Model of Transportation Energy Use in Wisconsin: Demographic Considerations and Alternative Scenarios, University of Wisconsin-Madison, Institute for Environmental Studies, Report 57, December 1975.

[6] Energy Policy of the Ford Foundation, A Time to Choose: America's Energy Future, Ballinger, Cambridge, Mass., 1974.

[7] Personal Communication, Institut fuer Energetik, Leipzig, German Democratic Republic, 1975.

[8] Chateau, B., and B. Lapillonne, Previsions a Long Terme de la Consommation d'Energie: pour une Nouvelle Approche Methodologique, Synthetical Report, 74 p., IEJE, Grenoble, 1976.

[9] Proceedings of a Workshop on Integrated Management of Regional Energy/Environment Systems held November 10-14, 1975. International Institute for Applied Systems Analysis, Laxenburg, Austria, forthcoming.

[10] Dennis, R.L., Regional Air Pollution Impact: A Dispersion Methodology Developed and Applied to Energy Systems, RM-76-22, International Institute for Applied Systems Analysis, Laxenburg, Austria, 1976.

[11] Buehring, W.A. and R.L. Dennis, Evaluation of Health Effects from Sulfur Dioxide Emission for a Reference Coal-Fired Power Plant, RM-76-23, International Institute for Applied Systems Analysis, Laxenburg, Austria, 1976.

[12] Matthews, W.H., W.W. Kellogg, and G.D. Robinson, eds., Man's Impact on the Climate, MIT Press, Cambridge, Mass, 1971.

[13] Broecker, W.A., "Climate Change: Are We on the Brink of a Pronounced Global Warming?" Science, 189 (1975), pp. 460-463.

[14] Niehaus, Friedrich, A Nonlinear Eight Level Tandem Model to Calculate the Future CO_2 and C-14 Burden to the Atmosphere, RM-76-35, International Institute for Applied Systems Analysis, Laxenburg, Austria, 1976.

[15] Marchetti, Cesare, On Geoengineering and the CO_2 Problem, RM-76-17, International Institute for Applied Systems Analysis, Laxenburg, Austria, 1976.

References (ctd)

[16] Hardin, Garrett, "The Tragedy of the Commons", Science, Vol. 162, pp. 1243-1248.

[17] American National Standards Institute, "The American National Standard Method of Recording and Measuring Work Injury Experience", ANSI Z16.1 - 1967.

[18] Keeney, R.L. and H. Raiffa, Decision Analysis with Multiple Conflicting Objectives: Preferences and Value Trade-offs, Wiley, New York, (in press).

[19] Buehring, W.A., W.K. Foell and R.L. Keeney, Energy/Environment Management: Application of Decision Analysis, RR-76-14, International Institute for Applied Systems Analysis, Laxenburg, Austria, 1976.

[20] Buehring, W.A., "A Model of Environmental Impacts from Electrical Generation in Wisconsin", Unpublished Ph.D. dissertation, Department of Nuclear Engineering and Institute of Environmental Studies, University of Wisconsin, Madison, 1975.

List of Figures

List of Tables

A MATHEMATICAL MODEL FOR FINDING COMPROMISES FOR SITING OF INDUSTRIAL PLANTS

G. Halbritter

Nuclear Research Center Karlsruhe
Karlsruhe, Germany

1. INTRODUCTION

The example of the conflict between the two objectives of industrializing on the one hand and preserving of ecological qualities on the other hand is meant to present a systems analytical approach and its effectiveness to solve this very conflict.

The problem to be solved is the siting of large technical facilities which will possibly have a strong impact on the natural environment. When tackling the problem of siting various and even opposing aspects, among them technological, economical and ecological ones have to be taken into account.

A systems analytical approach is presented which combines a method providing a compromise solution for dissimilar conflicting objectives with a method allowing to compute atmospheric diffusion. Two techniques were selected to reach such compromise solutions:

(1) maximization of the sum of goal achievements of the individual objectives and

(2) maximization of a common minimum goal achievement for all objectives.

With the help of considerations on scaling it is examined, which method will give the more appropriate compromise solutions as far as the practical problem treated here is concerned.

2. ALGORITHM FOR FINDING COMPROMISE SOLUTIONS FOR DIFFERING OBJECTIVE CONCEPTS

The scalar valued optimization yielding an optimum value for an objective concept formulated as an objective function has proved its efficiency in a variety of problems of microeconomy and technical process control. In other fields of microeconomy and in almost every macroeconomical field problems have been raised requiring several objective concepts to be considered. Because of the orientation towards one single goal, scalar valued optimization does not yield a satisfactory solution for such problems. If orientation for a multitude of objective concepts is demanded, an unambiguously "optimum" solution cannot be expected; only so-called Pareto-optimum solutions will rather be obtained, none of which clearly preferable to the others. The related amount of strategies bringing about such solutions will then correspond to the Pareto-optimum amount of solutions.

The problem known as the vector maximum problem can be represented as follows:

Def. 1:
$$\left\{ \begin{matrix} c_1 & (\underline{x}) \\ c_2 & (\underline{x}) \\ \vdots & \\ c_k & (\underline{x}) \end{matrix} \;\middle|\; \underline{x} \varepsilon X \right\} \qquad k = 1, \ldots, K$$

with $X = \{\underline{x} | A \cdot \underline{x} \leq \underline{b}, \underline{x} \geq \dot{0}\}$ convex polyhedron in R^n

$$\underline{x} = \begin{pmatrix} x_1 \\ \vdots \\ x_n \end{pmatrix} \qquad \text{vector of strategies}$$

$c_1(\underline{x})$, $c_2(\underline{x})$ ..., $c_k(\underline{x})$ objective functions

The elements a_{ij} (i=1, ..., m; j=1,..., n) of the matrix A denote the consequence of an action j on the state of a variable i while the components of the vector $\underline{b}$ denote the limits of the space in which the variable of state i is available. We search for the components of the vector $\underline{x}$, the so-called vector of strategies, which maximizes the K objective functions at the same time. In the general case of conflicting objectives no vector of strategies $\underline{x}$ will be found reaching all goals at the same time. Therefore, so-called efficient objective vectors $\underline{c}(\underline{x})$ will be searched, these objective vectors being Pareto-optimum meaning that for a transition from $\underline{c}(\underline{x})$ to another admissible objective vector $\underline{c}(\underline{x}')$ never holds $\underline{c}(\underline{x}') \geq \underline{c}(\underline{x})$ in other words, starting from an efficient objective vector, no higher level can be attained, for all objective functions at the same time. The amount of Pareto-optimum solutions (amount of efficient objective vectors) is correlated by the corresponding amount of strategies leading to these solutions. Vectors of strategies $\underline{x}$ yielding the efficient objective vectors are called functionally efficient which means that there is no vector x' having the property $\underline{c}(\underline{x}') \geq \underline{c}(\underline{x})$. The amount of all functionally efficient vectors of a vector maximum problem is called the complete solution of the vector maximum problem /DINKELBACH (1969)/. For practical problems the complete solution of the vector maximum problem can mostly not be determined. For the given problem, i.e., the siting of large-scale technical facilities, two methods were used in order to obtain efficient solutions:

1) The approach by /JÜTTLER (1969)/ and /KÖRTH (1969)/ maximizes a minimum goal achievement for all objective functions. This approach corresponds to a game-theoretical concept of solution with the minimum goal achievement being identical with the game value of a two-person zero sum game.

2) The approach by /ALLGAIER (1974)/ maximizes the sum of the individual goal achievements of the objective functions. In addition to the exact indication of the individual goal achievements for all objective functions, this approach allows to take into account exogenous preferences. This is done by the inclusion of the minimum goal achievements for the individual objective functions into the system of constraints.

Both approaches call for the establishment of scales on which the goal achievements for the objective functions can be found.

3. APPLICATION OF VECTOR VALUED OPTIMIZATION TO SITING PROBLEMS

The occupation vector $\underline{x}$ must be found for a given site grid, i.e., the number of standardized facilities (e.g. 100 MWe power stations) at given grid points with the best possible achievement of the following objective concepts:

1) minimum costs for the facilities,

2) minimum impact by pollutants to the population.

These objective concepts shall be optimized subject to the following constraints:

a) The environmental standards (long-term and short-term standards) have to be observed at all points of the region,

b) a minimum production level, e.g., of energy generation in the region, must be maintained.

Thus, two alternative goals form the conflicting objective for which vector valued optimization is to yield the compromise occupation vectors.

Models are presented which take into account the single objective concepts indicated above and then models for finding compromise solutions will be described.

Cost Minimization Model (1. Model)

Minimum costs shall be achieved for the siting. In a first approximation the following costs can be considered as site specific:

1) Costs for secondary energy transport systems to the nearest centers of consumption (e.g., transmission lines, distant heat transport lines, pipelines).

2) Costs for a cooling water transport system to the nearest main canal.

As to power stations and heating power stations, respectively, the costs under 1) can be broken down into cost fractions for

- the current transport by transmission lines, and
- the transport of the waste heat produced in power stations,

each of them up to the nearest center of consumption. There will be a degressive development of costs for increasing power installed, both with respect to the secondary energy and the cooling water transport systems. Consequently, we are faced with a non-linear optimization problem. The non-linear cost objective function has to be minimized while environmental and energy supply constraints have to be fulfilled. Therefore, the following problem arises:

$$\min \left\{ \sum_{l=1}^{P} \sum_{j=1}^{n} D_{lj} f_1(x_j) + \sum_{j=1}^{n} E_j f_2(x_j) \right\}$$

subject to the constraints

$$\sum_{j=1}^{n} T_{ij} \cdot x_j \leq b_i \qquad i = 1,\dots, m$$

$$\sum_{j=1}^{n} T1_{lj} \cdot x_j \geq b1_l \qquad l = 1,\dots, p$$

$$x_j \geq 0 \qquad j = 1,\dots, n$$

where

x_j occupation number of the source point j by standard power stations and standard heating power stations, respectively

$f_1(x_j)$ cost function for the secondary energy transport per unit distance of the site j with x_j standard units installed

$f_2(x_j)$ cost function for cooling water transport per unit distance of the site j with x_j standard units installed

D_{lj} matrix element expressing the distance from the location of energy generation j to the center of consumption l (l=1,..., p; j=1,..., n)

E_j vector component expressing the distance of the point of energy generation j from the nearest main canal (j=1,..., n)

T_{ij} element of the environmental transfer matrix T(m x n), describing the influence of a specific emission (emission per occupation number x_j) at the point j on the outdoor pollutant concentration at the field point i

$T1_{lj}$ element of the technical transfer matrix T1(p x n) describing the possible contribution of a standard power station and standard heating power station, respectively, to the total supply of electricity and heat, respectively, of the center of consumption l

b_i environmental quality standard to be observed at the field point i

$b1_l$ minimum production of electricity and heat, respectively, for the center of consumption l.

The site-specific costs for the site j are obtained by multiplication of the cost function per unit distance $f_1(x_j)$ and $f_2(x_j)$, respectively, by the respective distance from the nearest center of consumption (cost fraction 1) and the nearest main canal (cost fraction 2), respectively.

The first m constraints ensure compliance with the environmental quality standards. The following p constraints ensure the minimum energy generation for the p centers of consumption in terms of electric current and heat. The environmental transfer matrix T is determined by means of diffusion calculations. The elements T_{ij} of this transfer matrix describe the influence of a standard source at the point j of the source point grid on the point i of the field point grid.

The elements of the technical transfer matrix Tl_{lj} describe the contribution of a standard power station and a standard heating power station, respectively, at the point j of the source point grid to the current and heat generation, respectively, of the center of consumption l.

The environmental transfer matrix T is established by means of a statistical diffusion model. This model calculates the pollutant concentration in a preestablished field point grid, regarding the meteorological statistics obtained from different wind directions, different wind velocities and different stability classes of the atmospheric stratification. Dependent on the frequency of occurence, each meteorological combination contributes to the concentration at the field points. The resulting concentration distribution for each point of the field grid can be evaluated with a view to the expectation value (=long term concentration) and with a view to a higher fractile value (for instance 95% fractile = short term concentration). The concentration is calculated from the famous douple exponential formula for turbulent atmospheric diffusion /PASQUILL (1962), SLADE (1968)/.

We search for the lowest costs distribution of power station units and heating power station units, respectively, in the source point grid. The degressive development of costs raises a problem of non-linear programming. When the cost function is broken down into linear subtotals, the problem can be solved by "separable" programming /HADLEY (1969)/. It should be noted in this context that the solution of concave objective functions in a convex space of solutions does not lead to an unambiguous global optimum. In the previous calculations only linear development of costs has been considered. This simplification allowed to use familiar methods of linear programming.

Minimum Impact to Population Model (2. model)

In this model the siting should achieve a minimization of the weighted pollutant concentrations $p_i \cdot x_i$ at the field points i of the region while complying with the environmental standards b_i and with a minimum production level bl_l in the subregion l. Weighting is done proportional to the density of population. The minimization of the impact to population in addition to compliance with the environmental standards can be justified as follows: Although in the environmental standards the findings of industrial medicine are considered, these standards are, on the whole, the result of political privisions in which also economical requirements play a role. Environmental standards are no threshold for the non-occurence of damage. Therefore, besides the observation of standards for individual persons, minimizing of the total risk for the population should be achieved.

The following problem arises:

$$\min \left(\sum_{i=1}^{m} p_i \cdot x_i \right)$$

$$x_i = \sum_{j=1}^{n} T_{ij} \cdot x_j$$

thus

$$\min \left(\sum_{i=1}^{m} p_i \cdot \sum_{j=1}^{n} T_{ij} \cdot x_j \right)$$

or written as a matrix

$$\min \quad p^T \cdot T \cdot \underline{x}$$

subject to the following constraints

$$\sum_{j=1}^{n} T_{ij} \cdot x_j \leq b_i \qquad \text{for all values } i = 1,\ldots, m$$

$$\sum_{j=1}^{n} T1_{lj} \cdot x_j \geq b1_l \qquad \text{for all values } l = 1,\ldots, p$$

$$x_j \geq 0 \qquad \text{for all values } j = 1,\ldots, n$$

where

p_i weighting of the field point i according to the density of population

x_i outdoor pollutant concentration at the field point i.

We search for the occupations by power stations and heating power stations, respectively, in the given source point grid, which involves the lowest impact to the population. Since both the objective function and the constraints are linear expressions, optimization can be performed using the known Simplex algorithm.

Model for Calculating Compromise Solutions

The occupation vector $\underline{x}$ has to be found for a given site grid, which complies with the following objective concept:

- minimum costs for the facilities,
- minimum impact by pollutants to the population.

These are two alternative goals described by models 1 and 2. The requirements of fulfilling these objectives simultaneously creates a conflicting objective. This conflicting objective is not solved by a uniform model but by the following single steps using the models already described.

1) Determination of scaling for goal achievement by the individual objectives in the space of solutions.

2) Determination of compromise solutions for goal achievement by the individual objectives using different approaches.

3) Evaluation of compromise results obtained.

Scaling (single step 1)) results from the determination of the most favorable and most unfavorable solutions for each objective function in the space of solutions defined by the system of constraints. The solutions of the problems of minimization described in models 1 and 2 yield the most favorable solutions, the so-called scalar maxima $c_1(\underline{x}^*) = f^{01}$ and $c_2(\underline{x}^*) = f^{02}$.

Model 1.

$$\min \{D \cdot f_1(\underline{x}) + \underline{E}^T \cdot f_2(\underline{x})\} = c_1(\underline{x}^*)$$

Model 2.

$$\min \{p^T \cdot T \cdot \underline{x}\} = c_2(\underline{x}^*)$$

where

$$\underline{x} \in X, \quad X = \{\underline{x}\ T \cdot x \leq \underline{b} \wedge T1 \cdot \underline{x} \geq \underline{b1} \wedge \underline{x} \geq 0\}$$

The most unfavorable solutions, the so-called scalar minima $c_1(\bar{\underline{x}}_1) = f_{01}$ and $c_2(\bar{\underline{x}}_2) = f_{02}$ are obtained from the respective maximum problems of models 1 and 2. The differences between the scalar maximum and the scalar minimum are mapped to the interval /0, 1/ and the goal achievements for each solution can be found on the scales so obtained.

The second single step comprises application of the procedures allowing to find compromise solutions. The selected procedures are:

(1) Maximization of the sum of goal achievements for the individual objective functions.

(2) Maximization of a common minimum goal achievement for both objective functions.

Method (2) yields the greatest possible goal achievement which can be obtained simultaneously for both objective concepts. This minimum goal achievement will be exactly applicable, at least for one objective concept, and can be exceeded for further objective concepts. Thus, the method (2) is an achievement of individual goals having equal weights. The following expressions are obtained for the problem of siting:

(1) $\max\ (v_1 + v_2)$

subject to the following constraints

$$c_1(\underline{x}) - (c_1(\underline{x}_1^*) - c_1(\bar{\underline{x}})) \cdot v_1 \le c_1(\bar{\underline{x}}_1)$$

$$c_2(\underline{x}) - (c_2(\underline{x}_2^*) - c_2(\bar{\underline{x}})) \cdot v_2 \le c_1(\bar{\underline{x}}_2)$$

$\underline{v} = (v_1, v_2)^T$ vector of individual goal achievements

(2) $\max\ v$

subject to the following constraints

$$c_1(\underline{x}) - (c_1(\underline{x}^*) - c_1(\bar{\underline{x}})) \cdot v \le c_1(\bar{\underline{x}}_1)$$

$$c_2(\underline{x}) - (c_2(\underline{x}^*) - c_2(\bar{\underline{x}})) \cdot v \le c_2(\bar{\underline{x}}_2)$$

$\underline{v}$ minimum goal achievement

where

$$\underline{x} \in X, \quad X = \{\underline{x} \mid T \cdot \underline{x} \le \underline{b} \wedge T1 \cdot \underline{x} \ge \underline{b1} \wedge \underline{x} \ge \underline{0} \wedge v \text{ bzw. } \underline{v} \ge 0\}$$

In the first lines of (1) and (2) the individual goal achievements and the common minimum goal achievement, respectively, are maximized. The constraints always ensure that the individual goal achievement and the common minimum goal achievement, respectively, are at least attained. The other constraints determine the space of solutions already defined for the scalar valued problems.

4. COMPROMISE SOLUTION FOR SITING

The calculations for siting were done for the Northern Upper Rhine region, i.e. the Upper Rhine Valley from Mannheim to Kehl. It is assumed that the energy is generated by means of fossil fuels implying the emission of the sulphur dioxide (SO_2). The pollutant concentrations caused by the emission sources are considered in a field point grid extending 60 km in the west-east and 120 km in the north-south directions. The field point grid has a mesh size of 5 km - 12 base stations in the west-east directions and 24 km in the north-south directions which means a total of 288 field points. The source point grid, containing the eligible, preestablished sites, lies within the field point grid. There are 108 source points. Care was taken that the main regions exposed to pollutant concentration from sources located at the periphery of the source point grid do not lie outside the field point grid. The elements T_{ij} of the environmental transfer matrix T describe the effect of a standard source at the point j of the source point grid on the point i of the field point grid. This effect is calculated by a diffusion model and stored in the matrix T (288, 108). A standard power station unit of 100 MWe is taken as a basis. The assumption that the burnt fuel oil (S) contains 2 wt.% of sulphur yields a sulphur dioxide (SO_2) emission of about 0.9 t/h and a heat emission from the stack of about 3 x 10^3kcal/sec. The stack height is taken to be 150 m. A total energy of 5 GWe is to be generated within the region. The environmental standard for normal areas is 140 μg SO_2/m^3 in the FRG, this standard is to be observed.

Scaling

To solve the conflicting objective of minimum costs versus minimum impact to the population, it is attempted to reach compromise solutions for siting. Such compromise solutions always include evaluations of the individual objective concepts. The special problems associated with such evaluations are attributable to the differing subjective appraisals. In these calculations a pragmatic approach was chosen and the attempt was made to present quantitative evaluations. This implies a double problem of evaluation because different goal achievements must be evaluated for the individual objectives and, in addition, the individual goals must be aggregated.

The first part of the evaluation problem is solved by setting up evaluation scales for the goal achievements by the individual objectives. Within the system of constraints the most favorable and most unfavorable solutions can be calculated for each objective. Using these solutions scales are defined. To be able to compare goal achievements on these scales, they are standardized which means that the scales are mapped to the interval /0, 1/. The scale value 1 is always correlated by the most favorable and the scale value 0 by the most unfavorable value of solution. A linear benefit curve is assumed on these scales.

Figs. 1 to 4 show the most favorable and most unfavorable sites whose cost and impact values fix the two scales. The solution which is most favorable in terms of costs (Fig. 1) yields power station sites in the vicinity of rivers. By contrast, the most adverse case in terms of costs (Fig. 2) would be sites very much distant from rivers. In both cases accumulations of 100 MWe power units are obtained. Figs. 3 and 4 show the results of calculations in case of the most favorable and most unfavorable impact to the population from pollutant concentration. It is characteristic of the most favorable impact that the eastern column of the source point grid is preferred (Fig. 3). In case of the most unfavorable burden the sites are located south-west of the regions more densely populated (Fig. 4). These sites are determined by the main wind direction which is from south-west. In both cases accumulations of 100 MWe nuclear power units are again obtained.

Figs. 5 and 6 show the outdoor pollutant concentration for the cases of the most favorable cost and the most favorable impact solution. The improvement of the impact for the densely populated area of MANNHEIM can be seen in Fig. 6 compared with the impact of the best cost solution in Fig. 5.

Results for Compromise Solutions

Scaling permitted to map objective concepts to standardized scales on which goal achievements and benefit functions, respectively, can be defined. Aggregation of such benefit functions which express the relative weighting of the individual objective concepts, is the second part of the evaluation problem. Since no statements have been made on the relative appraisal of the two objective concepts, it seems to be acceptable to consider them as equal. Now compromise solutions must be searched which guarantee this equality. Two methods were selected in order to reach these solutions:

1) Maximization of the sum of individual goal achievements.
2) Maximization of the common minimum goal achievement for both objective functions.

Method 1 corresponds to an equal weight addition of both utility functions (single goal achievements) to form a common benefit function. However, the criterion of optimality does not ensure that very different single goal achievements might be obtained. The advantage of this method consists in the possibility of directly indicating the weighting of the original objective functions.

Method 2 does not correspond to a direct aggregation of individual objectives. The approach according to the theory of games - choice of strategy without knowing the strategies of the opponent-guarantees equal consideration of individual objective concepts.

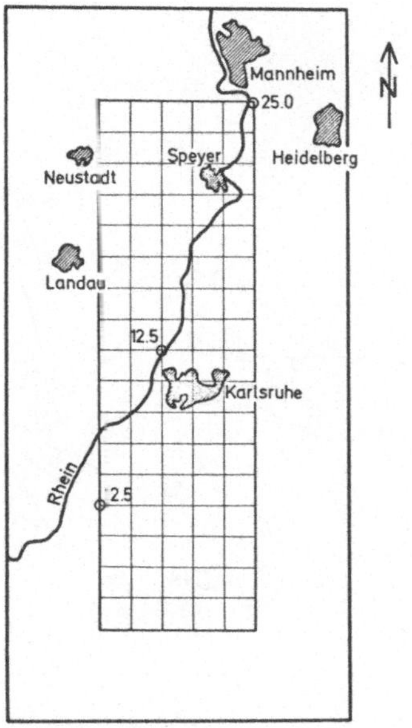

Fig.1: Distribution of occupation-numbers for 100 MWe-power stations in the source-point grid for minimum costs.

Energy generation capacity: 5 GWe
Environmental standard: 140 µg SO_2/m^3

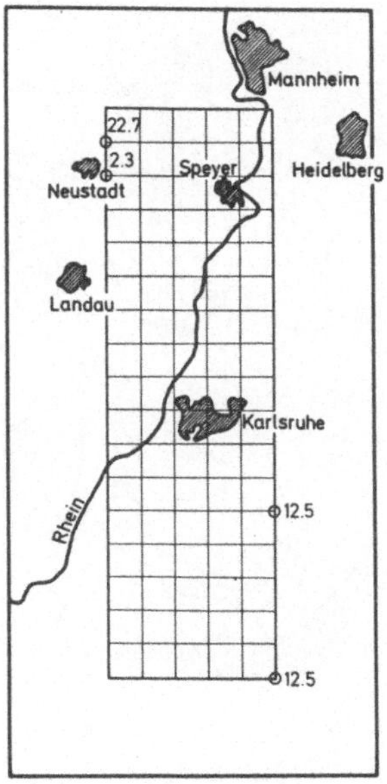

Fig.2: Distribution of occupation-numbers for 100 MWe-power stations in the source-point grid for maximum costs.

Energy generation capacity: 5 GWe
Environmental standard: 140 µg SO_2/m^3

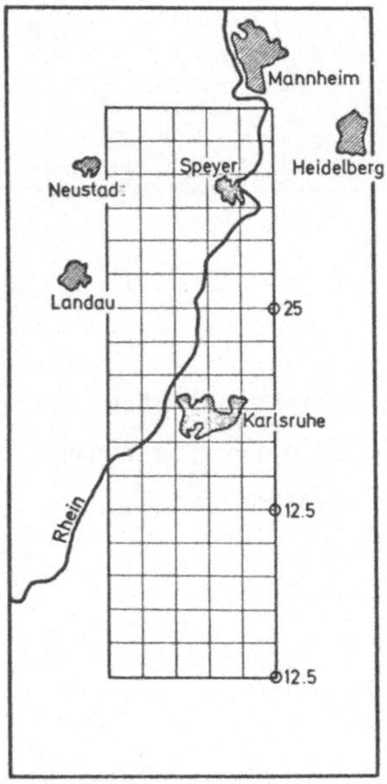

Fig.3: Distribution of occupation-numbers for 100 MWe-power stations in the source-point grid for minimum impact on the population.
Energy generation capacity: 5 GWe
Environmental standard: 140 µg/SO_2/m^3

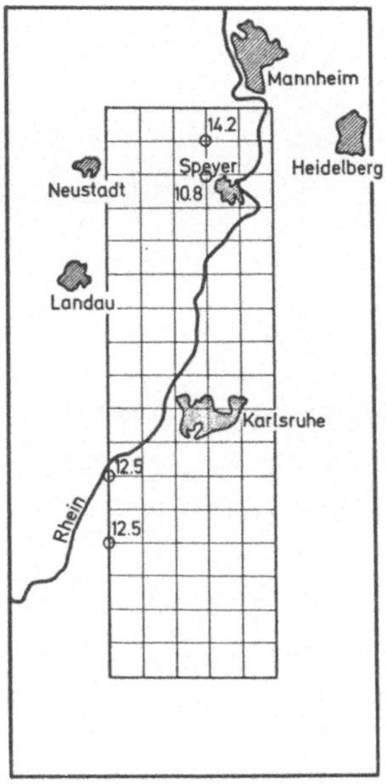

Fig.4: Distribution of occupation-numbers for 100 MWe-power stations in the source-point grid for maximum impact on the population

Energy generation capacity: 5 GWe
Environmental standard: 140 µg SO_2/m^3

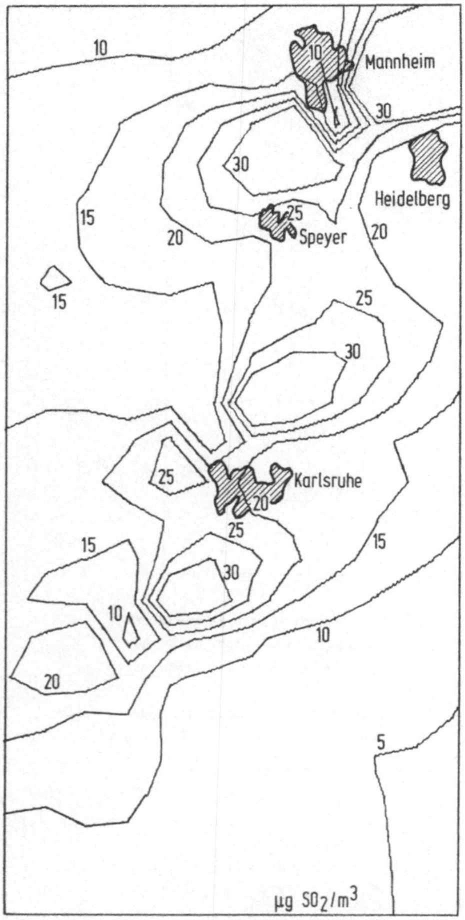

Fig.5: Ambient pollutant concentration (SO_2) for the minimum costs solution (Fig.1)

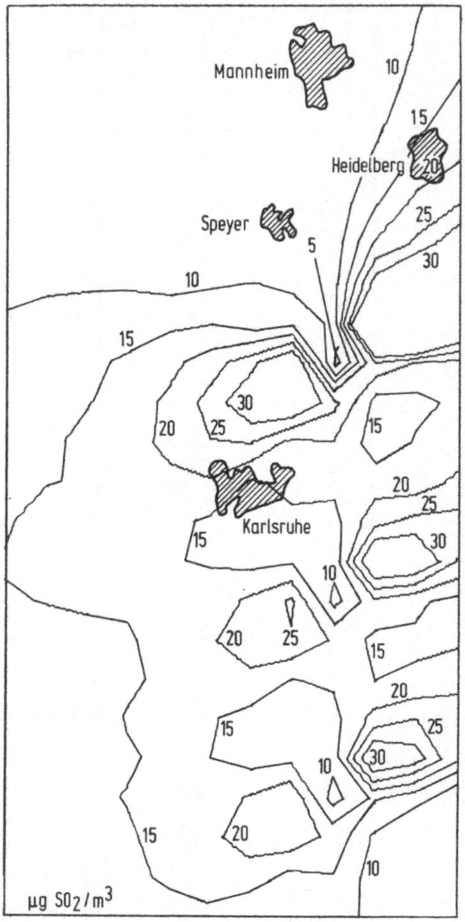

Fig.6: Ambient pollutant concentration (SO_2) for the minimum impact solution (Fiq.2)

Figs. 7 and 8 show results of the compromise calculations. In the case of maximization of the sum of individual goal achievements a site distribution is obtained which is very similar to the most favorable cost solution (Fig. 7). Accordingly, the values for the goal achievement are 89% on the scale of cost values and 47% on the scale of values indicating the impact to the population. These differing goal achievements are not satisfactory for a compromise solution.

In the case of maximization of the common minimum goal achievement for the individual objectives only some of the sites are located near the main canal (Fig. 8). No sites can be found in the northern part of the source point grid so that the burden to the population is kept particularly low in the northern region. Very unfavorable solutions in terms of costs are obtained for the southern sites (far distance from the main canal) which, however, entails a lower impact to the population in the central region of the field point grid. A common minimum goal achievement of 67% in total is obtained for both objective functions.

Comparison of Results Obtained

The result of method 1 - maximization of the sum of individual goal achievements - shows that under this method the goal achievement of cost values is improved at the expense of a deterioration of the goal achievement of the impact values. This confirms the critical comments already experessed with respect to this approach. The result obtained can be determined both by the special form of the space of solutions and , in addition, by the difference in the development of objective functions within the space of solutions. Although equal weights have been considered for the benefit functions obtained for the objective concepts, a compromise solution according to the method 1 does not ensure equality with respect to the benefit values derived for the objective concepts in the possible spaces of solutions. The compromise results obtained for the problem - site selection for large-scale technical facilities - is quite unsatisfactory.

If exogenous preferences for individual objective concepts, i.e., minimum goal achievements are given in the system of constraints, which implies a modification of method 1, too great preference of one objective concept over another can be avoided. If data about exogenous preferences are available, a modified method 1 might offer an acceptable compromise solution for the problem of siting for technical-scale facilities.

However, in the modified method 1 the advantage proper of the method 1 is given up, i.e., the possibility of indicating weight factors for the overriding objective function of the parameter optimization problem (addition of the single objective functions) equivalent to the vector maximum problem. These factors can be calculated from the reciprocal values of the differential amounts between scalar

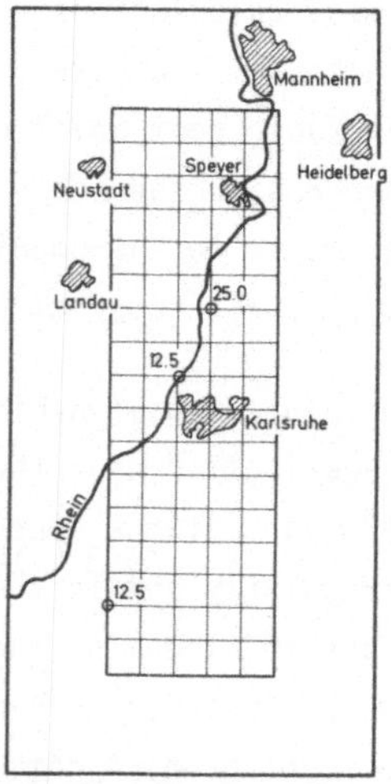

Fig.7: Distribution of occupation-numbers for 100 MWe-power stations in the source-point grid for maximal sum of objective attainments (objective attainment best costs: 89 %; objective attainment best impact: 47 %)
Energy generation capacity: 5 GWe
Environmental standard: 140 μg SO_2/m^3

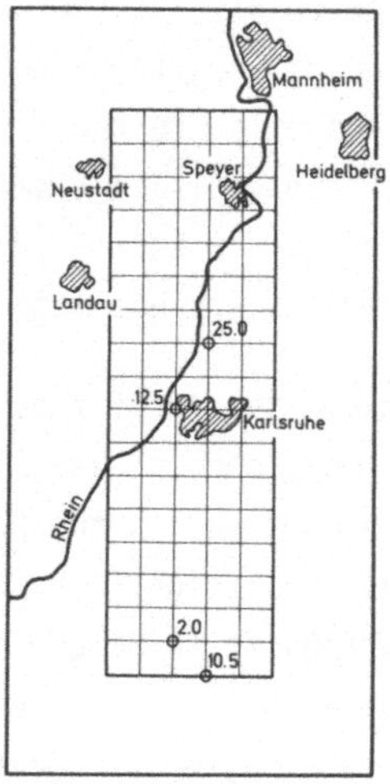

Fig.8: Distribution of occupation-numbers for 100 MWe-power stations in the source-point grid for best minimum objective attainment (minimum objective attainment: 67 %).

Energy generation capacity: 5 GWe
Environmental standard: 140 μg SO_2/m^3

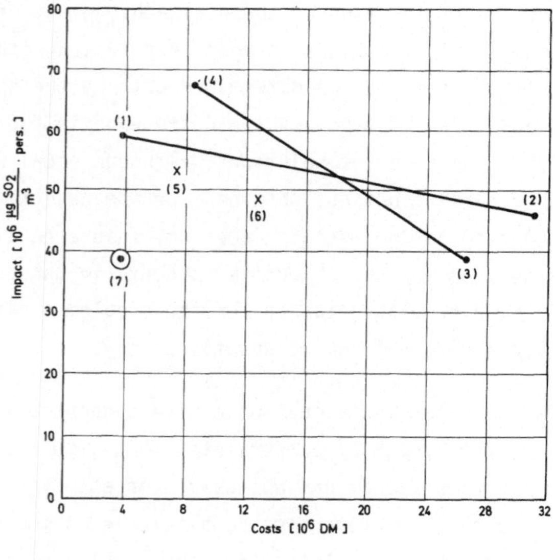

(1) minimum costs solution

(2) maximum costs solution

(3) minimum impact solution

(4) maximum impact solution

(5) compromise solution - maximal sum of objective attainments

(6) compromise solution - best minimum objective attainment

(7) ideal solution

Fig.9 Values of objective functions

maxima and scalar minima.

Regarding the sites according to method 1 the following values are obtained for the weight factors of individual objective functions:

Costs objective function:	0.51
Population impact objective function:	0.49

This almost equal weight addition of the two objective functions in the parameter optimization problem is obtained from the scaling selected. The scalar maximum minus scalar minimum difference yields for both objective concepts values of the same order (about 30 mill): for the minimum cost objective function units of DM and for the minimum population impact function units of ($\mu g\ SO_2/m^3$ x persons). A change of units, e.g. ($mg\ SO_2/m^3$ x persons) instead of ($\mu g\ SO_2/m^3$ x persons) or substitution by other reference systems, e.g., total capital costs during the period of depreciation instead of annual costs, produces a considerable shift of the weight factors for the same result applicable to siting. If equal units are used for the minimum impact objective function, but if the total capital costs during the period of depreciation are taken into account instead of annual costs for the minimum costs objective function, the following values are calculated for the weight factors:

Costs objective function:	0.06
Population impact objective function:	0.94.

This result makes very clear that the vector maximum problem cannot be solved in a satisfactory manner by direct weighting of the objective functions.

In conclusion it can be stated that with respect to the practical problem of siting for technical-scale facilities and considering the lack of knowledge of exogenous preferences for single objective concepts, the method 2 - maximization of a common minimum goal achievement for both goals - leads to appropriate compromise solutions. Equal weight additions of the single goal achievements for the objective functions (method 1) does not ensure an equal result for the goal achievement. This is clear from Fig. 9 which represents the objective function values from all scaling computations and from all vector valued optimization calculations within the space mapped of both objective functions. The so-called efficient borderline of possible objective function values will lie between the points (1) - best cost solution - and (3) - best solution for the impact to the population. All values on this borderline are characterized by Pareto optimality. In most of the practical calculations the full course of this borderline will remain unknown and only some points can be obtained. These results will not always offer a satisfactory solution, despite Pareto optimality. Therefore, it is necessary to fix, either by appropriate solution finding procedures or by further constraints imposed by external preferences, the possible solutions in such a way that the minimum level of aspiration is attained. The exclusive guarantee that functionally efficient solutions are obtained is not sufficient to solve the problem under consideration. This limitation will aply to the majority of practical problems.

REFERENCES

ALLGAIER, R. (1974), Zur Lösung von Zielkonflikten, Dissert., TU Karlsruhe.

DINKELBACH, W. (1969), Entscheidungen bei mehrfacher Zielsetzung und die Problematik der Zielgewichtung
In: BUSSE v. COLBE, W., MEYER-DOHM, P., Unternehmerische Planung und Entscheidung, Bertelsmann Universitätsverlag, Bielefeld.

HADLEY, G. (1969), Nichtlineare und dynamische Programmierung, Physica Würzburg-Wien.

JÜTTLER, H. (1968), Ein Modell zur Berücksichtigung mehrerer Zielfunktionen bei Aufgabenstellungen der mathematischen Optimierung.
In: Math. Modelle und Verfahren der Unternehmensforschung, Köln, S. 11-31.

KÖRTH, H. (1969), Zur Berücksichtigung mehrerer Zielfunktionen bei der Optimierung von Produktionsplänen.
In: Mathematik und Wirtschaft, Band 6, Berlin, S. 184-201.

PASQUILL, F. (1962), Atmospheric Diffusion. D. van NOSTRAND Company Ltd.

SLADE, D.H. (1968), Meteorology and Atomic Energy. U.S. Atomic Energy Commission, Division of Technical Information

ON TEMPORAL AND SPATIAL STRUCTURE IN MODEL SYSTEMS AND APPLICATION TO ECOLOGICAL PATCHINESS

Daniel M. DUBOIS*
University of LIEGE
Institute of Mathematics
Depts. of Applied Statistics
and Operations Research
15, avenue des Tilleuls
B-4000 LIEGE - BELGIUM.

Conceptual subdivision of a real system into interacting sub-systems is subjective and is always made with the purpose of explaining a particular phenomenon.

A model system can be represented by a set of partial differential equations the solutions of which simulating self-sustained oscillations and spontaneous spatial structure (morphogenesis).

A class of such model systems, presented in the literature, represents in fact forced temporal and spatial structures due to symmetry breaking of boundary condition.

The general problem dealing with non-homogeneous spatial pattern (patchiness effect) is of great interest in ecological populations in interaction with their stochastic environment. Attention was focused on the mathematical modelling of the mechanism of patches emergence occuring in diffusive predator-prey ecosystems.

---

* Maître de Conférences (Biomathématique).

1. MODELLING OF ECOSYSTEMS.

An ecological system can be defined as a system for which a flow of energy and matter from its environment is a necessary condition to the maintenance of its functionality.

Contrary to classical physical systems which are described in the energy space, ecological systems must be described, not only in the energy-space, but also in the energy and matter flows-space.

At the level of energy, a structural stability will be defined, while at the level of energy and matter flows a functional stability will be studied. The flows-space will be the supplementary dimension for describing the logics of living systems in the purpose of the understanding of their functionality.

Emergence of structural and functional properties of ecological system will be the consequence of exchanges of energy and matter between the components of the system and between the system and its environment. In the real world, the dynamics of phenomena depends on a so large number of variables and parameters at all spatial and temporal scales that the observer is unable to obtain a global view of the reality. For describing, quantitatively, the evolution of an open system, the observer will build a mathematical model of energetic processes occuring in the system.

For that, the observer will subdivide the system into a certain number of components. In these conditions, the mathematical model will be only a particular representation of the reality, resulting from the projection of this reality into the human brain by the intermediate of captors collecting data. Thus, necessarily, an uncertainty on the exact knowledge of the real world will exist for the observer.

From experimental data, the observer subdivides a system into interacting sub-systems. This subdivision process leads to a rather subjective understanding of the reality, the subjectivity depending on captors and human brain properties. The observer will then define emettors, receptors and communication channels of energy and matter inside the system and between the system and its environment.

After this step, the observer will build a particular model with a purpose in his mind : the explanation of mechanisms dealing with the studied system.

2. ON MATHEMATICAL MODELLING.

From a very general point of view, let us consider a system of volume V enclosed by a surface of area A. If the concentration of any component i par unit volume at a point inside the system is denoted by c_i, the local flow vector $\underline{J}_i$ may be defined by

$$\underline{J}_i = c_i \underline{V}_i \tag{1}$$

where $\underline{V}_i$ is the geometrical translation of the ith component represented by its velocity at the given point.

For characterizing the behavior of the flow, Gauss introduced the notion of divergence of the flow :

$$\text{div } \underline{J}_i \equiv \nabla . J_i = \frac{\partial J_i(x)}{\partial x} + \frac{\partial J_i(y)}{\partial y} + \frac{\partial J_i(z)}{\partial z}$$

where $J_i(x)$, $J_i(y)$ and $J_i(z)$ are the projections of the flow $\underline{J}_i$ on the three spatial cartesian axis and x,y and z the spatial coordinates.

The physical meaning of div $\underline{J}_i$ is the following : a positive divergence means that at the point under consideration there is a net outflow of the ith species, or, in more descriptive language, the point of positive divergence is a "source" of species i. On the other hand, a negative divergence indicates a net inflow of the ith species; the point under consideration is a "sink". At points where div J_i = o, there is neither accumulation nor removal of material.

Gauss demonstrated that the integral of the divergence over the volume is equal to the total flow of the ith species through the surface bounding the volume :

$$\int_V \nabla . \underline{J}_i dV = \int_A \underline{J}_i d\underline{A}$$

The concept of divergence is very useful in the consideration of local conservation laws at all points of a system.

It can be show that for non-conservative continuous systems, the local conservation law of c_i is given by

$$\frac{\partial c_i}{\partial t} = I_i - \nabla . \underline{J}_i$$

where I_i is the local expression for the transformation or formation of species i as a consequence of chemical, biological or ecological interactions with other species.

The difficulty is to find the best mathematical formulation for both flow and interaction terms.

Theoretical study on partial differential equations becomes more and more important (e.g. GOLDSTEIN, 1975).

3. METHODOLOGIC ASPECTS IN MATHEMATICAL MODELLING TEMPORAL AND SPATIAL STRUCTURE.

VOLTERRA (1931) introduced the set of equations

$$\frac{dN_1}{dt} = k_1 N_1 - k_2 N_1 N_2 \tag{3}$$

$$\frac{dN_2}{dt} = - k_3 N_2 + k_2 N_1 N_2 \tag{4}$$

for describing self-oscillations in a predator (N_2)-prey(N_1) system. The growth rate of the prey k_1 is considered as constant. It means that the nutrient (N) concentration is maintained constant

$$k_1 = k_1' N = \text{constant}$$

It is well-known that the solutions of this model are given by a time periodic behavior which are represented by closed trajectories or orbits in the phase space (orbital stability). After any perturbation, the system will follow an other trajectory. This system enters the class of conservative systems which exhibit a constant of motion. This constant depends on initial conditions, the value of which changing after each perturbation. This system is structurally unstable.

Let us show that the fact of maintaining the nutrient (N) concentration constant involves a temporally dependent rate of input of the nutrient concentration thus shifting the oscillations from being a spontaneous property of the system (self-oscillations) to being an externally forced property.

Indeed, let us write explicitly the equation for the nutrient

$$\frac{dN}{dt} = - k_1' N N_1 + \frac{d_e N}{dt} \tag{5}$$

where the consumption of N is continually compensated by an external flux of N, noted by d_eN/dt. As the nutrient concentration is maintained constant, its time derivative is zero ($dN/dt = o$) and then the input of N is governed by the equation

$$\frac{d_eN}{dt} = k_1'NN_1$$

At the stationary state, $N_1 = N_{10}$ is constant and the input flux of N is constant

$$\frac{d_eN}{dt} = k_1'NN_{10} = \text{constant} \tag{6}$$

When the system exhibits oscillations $N_1 = N_1(t)$, the input flux of N must oscillate exactly like $N_1(t)$,

$$\frac{d_eN}{dt} = k_1'NN_1(t) \tag{7}$$

Thus, sustained oscillations will exist only if an adequate oscillating input flux of nutrient is performed. These sustained oscillations are then forced oscillations and not self-oscillations.

These conclusions are also true for the LOTKA (1925) model system of the irreversible autocatalytic chemical reactions

$$B + X \xrightarrow{k_1} 2X$$

$$X + Y \xrightarrow{k_2} 2Y$$

$$Y \xrightarrow{k_3} C$$

described by the equations

$$\frac{dX}{dt} = k_1BX - k_2XY$$

$$\frac{dY}{dt} = - k_3Y + k_2XY$$

where the input species B is maintained constant. This set of equations is formally identical to the Volterra one and the same conclusions hold.

In Appendix A, general conclusions about the origin of temporal and spatial structure in chemical model systems are given (in collaboration with Morowitz). In these model systems, the *symmetry breaking* corresponding to a spatial structure is no more a spontaneous phenomenon depending on the intrinsic properties of the system but is the reflect of the symmetry breaking in the boundary condition; indeed the input flux B is no more a constant but becomes a function of space and time (eq. A5).

4. PATCHES EMERGENCE BY DIFFUSIVE INSTABILITY.

The general problem dealing with non-homogeneous spatial pattern is of great interest in many fields. On one hand, morphogenesis related to structural stability was studied by THOM (1972, 1974). On the other hand, morphogenesis in relation with diffusive instability was firstly developped by TURING (1952) and largely applied by others (e.g. GLANDSDORFF and PRIGOGINE, 1974). A recent review on populations dynamics in heterogeneous environment was made by LEVIN (1976).

We will focuse our attention on the mathematical modelling of the mechanism of patches emergence occuring in the marine planktonic ecosystem. Details about the dynamics of the plankton ecosystem can be found elsewhere (DUBOIS and MAYZAUD, 1976 and DUBOIS and CLOSSET, 1976).

The spatial repartitions of phytoplankton and herbivorous zooplankton are heterogeneous under the form of patches (patchiness effect). The phytoplankton is the prey and the herbivorous zooplankton the predator. The diffusivity of seawater is not constant but increases with the diameter $\emptyset$ of the seawater mass. If diameters (which are estimated by the variances of the spatial distributions of populations) of phytoplankton and herbivorous zooplankton patches are given by $\emptyset_1$ and $\emptyset_2$, respectively, their diffusivity coefficients will be given by

$$K_1 = K(\emptyset_1) \tag{8}$$

and

$$K_2 = K(\emptyset_2) \tag{9}$$

The mechanism of patches emergence by diffusive instability is similar to the spatial structuration in chemical model systems given by TURING (1952). But here we consider the diffusivity coefficients as functions of diameters of patches.

In this paper we consider only the influence of diffusion. Model systems including advective currents are given elsewhere (DUBOIS, 1975; DUBOIS and ADAM, 1976).

A general mathematical model is written :

$$\frac{\partial N_1}{\partial t} = f_1(N_1)N_1 - f_2(N_1)N_1N_2 + \nabla.(K(\emptyset_1)\nabla N_1) \qquad (10)$$

$$\frac{\partial N_2}{\partial t} = - f_3(N_2)N_2 + f_4(N_1)N_1N_2 + \nabla.(K(\emptyset_2)\nabla N_2) \qquad (11)$$

where N_1 and N_2 represent the prey and the predator concentrations, respectively.

In this study only horizontal variability will be taken into account.

We are interested by the following spatially homogeneous steady state ($\partial N_1/\partial t = \partial N_2/\partial t = o$)

$$N_{10} = \frac{f_3(N_{20})}{f_4(N_{10})} \qquad (12)$$

$$N_{20} = \frac{f_1(N_{10})}{f_2(N_{10})} \qquad (13)$$

which give the classical non-trivial spatially homogeneous steady state (e.g. DUBOIS, 1976) $N_{10} = k_3/k_4$ and $N_{20} = k_1/k_2$ in the classical Lotka-Volterra predator-prey model.

Under certain conditions, the spatially homogeneous steady state can be unstable for some well-defined spatial perturbations. This local instability is due to non-equal diffusivities of the prey and predator populations leading to the emergence of patches with well-defined diameters.

The physical mechanism of the spatial emergence of plankton patches can be explained as follows.

Let us consider the spatially homogeneous steady state. The ecosystem will be stable locally if spatial heterogeneities created by random perturbations around the spatial homogeneous steady state regress with time.

For values of the wavelength of perturbations belonging to a certain range around a critical wavelength λ_c these perturbations will amplify.

For some conditions of non-linear ecological interactions between the activator and the inhibitor, due to the faster diffusion of the predator (inhibitor), the prey (activator) will amplify its activating effect leading to the formation of a prey patch. With a certain time lag, an inhomogeneity will appear in the predator spatial repartition and we will then assist to the spatial structuration of the patch.

The horizontal pattern of the patches repartition will be given by an *hexagonal symmetry* in ideal conditions, i.e. without environmental large disturbances like advection currents. This hexagonal repartition is logic from the point of view of the optimization of the spatial occupancy. Moreover, patches can differ from each other in their species content : it should exist a *competitive exclusion principle between patches* which then would play the role of *ecological niches*.

Let us consider small perturbations n_1 and n_2 around the homogeneous steady state (eqs. (12) and (13))

$$N_1 = N_{10} + n_1 \tag{14}$$

$$N_2 = N_{20} + n_2 \tag{15}$$

Substitution into 10 and 11 leads to, after linearization, ($f_j(N_{io}+n_i) \simeq f_j(N_{io}) + (\partial f_j/\partial N_i)_o n_i$; j=1,2,3,4 and i=1,2) :

$$\frac{\partial n_1}{\partial t} = a_{11}n_1 + a_{12}n_2 + K(\emptyset_1)\nabla^2 n_1 \tag{16}$$

$$\frac{\partial n_2}{\partial t} = a_{21}n_1 + a_{22}n_2 + K(\emptyset_2)\nabla^2 n_2 \tag{17}$$

where diameters (which are estimated by the variances of the spatial distributions of populations) of prey and predator patches are fixed and given by $\emptyset_1$ and $\emptyset_2$ (this assumption is correct during the first phase of the patches emergence). The coefficients a_{ij} are given by ($f_j \equiv f_j(N_{io})$, $f_j' \equiv (\partial f_j/\partial N_i)_o$) :

$$a_{11} = f_1 - f_2N_{20} - f_2'N_{10}N_{20} + f_1'N_{10} \tag{18}$$

$$a_{22} = f_4N_{10} - f_3 - f_3'N_{20} \tag{19}$$

$$a_{12} = - f_2N_{10} \tag{20}$$

$$a_{21} = f_4N_{20} + f_4'N_{10}N_{20} \tag{21}$$

To know whether the homogeneous steady state is stable it is sufficient to study the behavior of solutions of eqs. (16) and (17) which have the form (Fourier's analysis).

$$n_i(x,y,t) = \tilde{n}_i \cos(\underline{k}.\underline{r} + \phi)\exp(\sigma t) \quad (i=1,2) \tag{22}$$

where $\tilde{n}_i$, $\underline{k}$, ϕ and σ are constants. Stability is assured if and only if all these solutions decay with time, i.e. if and only if σ has a negative real part. It will take place if and only if the two following conditions hold

$$(a_{11} - K(\emptyset_1)k^2) + (a_{22} - K(\emptyset_2)k^2) < o \tag{23}$$

$$(a_{11} - K(\emptyset_1)k^2) + (a_{22} - K(\emptyset_2)k^2) - a_{12}a_{21} > o \tag{24}$$

For having diffusive instability (TURING, 1952), perturbations of zero wavenumber are required to be stable. For $k = o$, eqs. (23) and (24) give necessary conditions for diffusive instability,

$$a_{11} + a_{22} < o \tag{25}$$

$$a_{11}a_{22} - a_{12}a_{21} > o \tag{26}$$

From inspection of eqs. (18) to (21), it can be seen that we could have

$a_{11} > o$ (the prey is an activator)

$a_{22} < o$ (the predator is an inhibitor)

$a_{12} < o$

$a_{21} > o$

Eq. (23) is always verified for all positive values of k^2, meanwhile eq. (24) can be violated for finite positive real values of k^2. The roots k^2 solutions of eq. (24) equal to zero,

$$(a_{11}-K(\emptyset_1)k^2)(a_{22}-K(\emptyset_2)k^2) - a_{12}a_{21} = o \tag{27}$$

are given by

$$k^2=\frac{a_{11}K(\emptyset_2)+a_{22}K(\emptyset_1)\pm\sqrt{(a_{11}K(\emptyset_2)+a_{22}K(\emptyset_1)^2)-4K(\emptyset_1)K(\emptyset_2)(a_{11}a_{22}-a_{12}a_{21})}}{2K(\emptyset_1)K(\emptyset_2)} \tag{28}$$

For values of k^2 between these two roots, eq. (27) is negative thus stability condition (24) is violated, with the conditions

$$a_{11}K(\emptyset_2) + a_{22}K(\emptyset_1) > o \tag{29}$$

and

$$(a_{11}K(\emptyset_2) + a_{22}K(\emptyset_1))^2 \geq 4K(\emptyset_1)K(\emptyset_2)(a_{11}a_{22}-a_{12}a_{21}) \tag{30}$$

for having real and positive values of k^2. When equality occurs in the condition 30, we obtain a double root. In this case, only one wavenumber corresponding to a critical wavelength λ_c is unstable

$$\lambda_c = \frac{2\pi}{k_c} = 2\pi\sqrt{\frac{2K(\emptyset_1)K(\emptyset_2)}{a_{11}K(\emptyset_2)+a_{22}K(\emptyset_1)}} \tag{31}$$

LITERATURE CITED.

[1] DUBOIS, D.M. (1975), "A model of patchiness for prey-predator plankton populations", Ecological Modeling, 1:67-80.

[2] DUBOIS, D.M. (1976), "Modelling and simulation of the mesoscale mosaic structure of the lower marine trophic levels", Lecture Notes in Computer Science, Springer-Verlag, 40:407-418.

[3] DUBOIS, D.M. and Y. ADAM (1976), "Spatial structuration of diffusive prey-predator biological populations : simulation of the horizontal distribution of plankton in the North Sea", System Simulation in Water Resources, Ed. G.C. Vansteenkiste, North-Holland, 343-356.

[4] DUBOIS, D.M. and P.L. CLOSSET (1976), "Patchiness in primary and secondary production in the Southern Bight : a mathematical theory", 10th European Symposium on Marine Biology, Ostend, Belgium, September 17-23, 1975, p. 000-000.

[5] DUBOIS, D.M. and P. MAYZAUD (1976), "Experimental and theoretical approach of the production and transformation of organic matter in a semi-enclosed basin", 10th European Symposium on Marine Biology, Ostend, Belgium, September 17-23, p. 000-000.

[6] GOLDSTEIN, J.A. (Editor) (1975), "Partial differential equations and related topics", Lecture Notes in Mathematics, Springer-Verlag, n° 446, 389 p.

[7] GLANSDORFF, P., and PRIGOGINE, I. (1974), "Thermodynamic theory of structure, stability and fluctuations", Wiley Interscience, 306 p.

[8] LEVIN, S.A. (1976), "Population dynamic models in heterogeneous environments", Annu. Rev. Ecol. Syst., 7:000-000.

[9] LOTKA, A.J. (1925), "Elements of physical biology, William and Wilkins, Baltimore.

[10] THOM, R. (1972), "Structural stability and morphogenesis", Ediscience, Paris, Benjamin, Reading, Mass.

[11] THOM, R. (1974), "Modèles mathématiques de la morphogénèse", Collection 10/18, UGE, Paris.

[12] TURING, A.M. (1952), "The chemical basis of morphogenesis", Proc. Royal Society, London, B 237:37-72.

[13] VOLTERRA, V. (1931), "Leçons sur la théorie mathématique de la lutte pour la vie", Gauthier-Villars, Paris, 214 p.

APPENDIX A

ON THE ORIGIN OF SPATIAL STRUCTURE AND TEMPORAL OSCILLATION IN CHEMICAL MODEL SYSTEMS

D.M. DUBOIS and H.J. MOROWITZ *

A large number of studies have been carried out on chemical systems in which spatial or temporal structure is developped as a consequence of a kinetic argument. These studies have recently been reviewed (1,2). A general feature of such models is that one of the input species is maintained constant in space or time as a boundary condition of the problem. In this note we shall show that in many cases the process of maintaining the boundary value constant is not a passive one but involves a spatially or temporally dependent rate of input of the constant species thus shifting the structure from being a spontaneous property of the system to being an externally forced property.

The general class of systems we wish to examine involves an irreversible interaction of the constant input species with one of the variable species of the system. Thus,

$$B + X \xrightarrow{k_1} \text{products} \qquad \text{(A1)}$$

where B is the constant and X the variable species. When the full problem is solved, X turns out to vary with space or time.

B is consumed by the reaction and is supplied by an external source so that we may write :

$$\frac{dB}{dt} = - k_1 BX + \frac{d_e B}{dt} \qquad \text{(A2)}$$

The term $d_e B/dt$ gives the rate at which B is supplied from an external (e) source.

Consider first the spatial variation so that in one dimension

* Molecular Biophysics and Biochemistry, Yale University, New Haven, CT 06520 U.S.A.

X may be written as X(x) where x is the spatial coordinate. For a steady state system dB/dt is zero and since B was assumed to be a spatially maintained constant, B_o, we can write

$$\frac{d_e B}{dt} = k_1 B_o X(x) \tag{A3}$$

The rate at which B is added is dependent on x and the structure thus becomes a consequence of the forcing of this system by a spatially structured input.

Examples of such cases are the TURING (3) model and the BRUSSELATOR (4) where morphogenetic structure is supposed to arise from chemical processes, but instead results from external structure in rate of nutrient supply.

An analogous situation arises in the time dependent homogeneous case, where X is shown to be X(t) and B is held constant. Here equation (A2) becomes

$$\frac{d_e B}{dt} = k_1 B_o X(t) \tag{A4}$$

and the temporal behavior, believed to be a property of the system, results, in fact, from a temporal forcing of the input. Examples of such cases are VOLTERRA (5) - LOTKA (6) oscillators.

For both spatial and temporal structure, X = X(x,t), such as travelling waves, the input rate at which B is added is dependent on x and t and equation (A2) is now written :

$$\frac{d_e B}{dt} = k_1 B_o X(x,t) \tag{A5}$$

and the behavior results from a space-time forcing of the input.

In a more detailed study we have investigated what happens when purely passive input protocols are used; and have found that in general they lead to a disappearance of spatial and temporal structure (7).

<u>LITERATURE CITED</u>.

(1) NICOLIS, G. and PORTNOW, J., 1973, Chem. Rev., <u>73</u>, 265.

(2) NOYES, R.M., and FIELD, R.J., 1974, A; Rev. Phys. Chem., <u>25</u>, 95.

(3) TURING, A.M., 1952, Philos. Trans. R. Soc. London, <u>B237</u>, 37.

(4) GLANSDORFF, P. and I. PRIGOGINE, 1971, "Thermodynamic theory of structure, stability and fluctuations", Wiley Interscience, New-York, NY.

(5) VOLTERRA, V., 1931, "Leçons sur la théorie mathématique de la lutte pour la vie", Gauthier-Villars, Paris.

(6) LOTKA, A.J., 1920, J. Am. Chem. Soc., <u>42</u>, 1595.

(7) Unpublished studies.

Lecture Notes in Economics and Mathematical Systems

For information about Vols. 1–95 please contact your bookseller or Springer-Verlag

Vol. 96: O. Moeschlin, Zur Theorie von Neumannscher Wachstumsmodelle. XI, 115 Seiten. 1974.

Vol. 97: G. Schmidt, Über die Stabilität des einfachen Bedienungskanals. VII, 147 Seiten. 1974.

Vol. 98: Mathematical Methods in Queueing Theory. Proceedings 1973. Edited by A. B. Clarke. VII, 374 pages. 1974.

Vol. 99: Production Theory. Edited by W. Eichhorn, R. Henn, O. Opitz, and R. W. Shephard. VIII, 386 pages. 1974.

Vol. 100: B. S. Duran and P. L. Odell, Cluster Analysis. A Survey. VI, 137 pages. 1974.

Vol. 101: W. M. Wonham, Linear Multivariable Control. A Geometric Approach. X, 344 pages. 1974.

Vol. 102: Analyse Convexe et Ses Applications. Comptes Rendus, Janvier 1974. Edited by J.-P. Aubin. IV, 244 pages. 1974.

Vol. 103: D. E. Boyce, A. Farhi, R. Weischedel, Optimal Subset Selection. Multiple Regression, Interdependence and Optimal Network Algorithms. XIII, 187 pages. 1974.

Vol. 104: S. Fujino, A Neo-Keynesian Theory of Inflation and Economic Growth. V, 96 pages. 1974.

Vol. 105: Optimal Control Theory and its Applications. Part I. Proceedings 1973. Edited by B. J. Kirby. VI, 425 pages. 1974.

Vol. 106: Optimal Control Theory and its Applications. Part II. Proceedings 1973. Edited by B. J. Kirby. VI, 403 pages. 1974.

Vol. 107: Control Theory, Numerical Methods and Computer Systems Modeling. International Symposium, Rocquencourt, June 17–21, 1974. Edited by A. Bensoussan and J. L. Lions. VIII, 757 pages. 1975.

Vol. 108: F. Bauer et al., Supercritical Wing Sections II. A Handbook. V, 296 pages. 1975.

Vol. 109: R. von Randow, Introduction to the Theory of Matroids. IX, 102 pages. 1975.

Vol. 110: C. Striebel, Optimal Control of Discrete Time Stochastic Systems. III. 208 pages. 1975.

Vol. 111: Variable Structure Systems with Application to Economics and Biology. Proceedings 1974. Edited by A. Ruberti and R. R. Mohler. VI, 321 pages. 1975.

Vol. 112: J. Wilhlem, Objectives and Multi-Objective Decision Making Under Uncertainty. IV, 111 pages. 1975.

Vol. 113: G. A. Aschinger, Stabilitätsaussagen über Klassen von Matrizen mit verschwindenden Zeilensummen. V, 102 Seiten. 1975.

Vol. 114: G. Uebe, Produktionstheorie. XVII, 301 Seiten. 1976.

Vol. 115: Anderson et al., Foundations of System Theory: Finitary and Infinitary Conditions. VII, 93 pages. 1976

Vol. 116: K. Miyazawa, Input-Output Analysis and the Structure of Income Distribution. IX, 135 pages. 1976.

Vol. 117: Optimization and Operations Research. Proceedings 1975. Edited by W. Oettli and K. Ritter. IV, 316 pages. 1976.

Vol. 118: Traffic Equilibrium Methods, Proceedings 1974. Edited by M. A. Florian. XXIII, 432 pages. 1976.

Vol. 119: Inflation in Small Countries. Proceedings 1974. Edited by H. Frisch. VI, 356 pages. 1976.

Vol. 120: G. Hasenkamp, Specification and Estimation of Multiple-Output Production Functions. VII, 151 pages. 1976.

Vol. 121: J. W. Cohen, On Regenerative Processes in Queueing Theory. IX, 93 pages. 1976.

Vol. 122: M. S. Bazaraa, and C. M. Shetty, Foundations of Optimization VI. 193 pages. 1976

Vol. 123: Multiple Criteria Decision Making. Kyoto 1975. Edited by M. Zeleny. XXVII, 345 pages. 1976.

Vol. 124: M. J. Todd. The Computation of Fixed Points and Applications. VII, 129 pages. 1976.

Vol. 125: Karl C. Mosler. Optimale Transportnetze. Zur Bestimmung ihres kostengünstigsten Standorts bei gegebener Nachfrage. VI, 142 Seiten. 1976.

Vol. 126: Energy, Regional Science and Public Policy. Energy and Environment I. Proceedings 1975. Edited by M. Chatterji and P. Van Rompuy. VIII, 316 pages. 1976.

Vol. 127: Environment, Regional Science and Interregional Modeling. Energy and Environment II. Proceedings 1975. Edited by M. Chatterji and P. Van Rompuy. IX, 211 pages. 1976.

Vol. 128: Integer Programming and Related Areas. A Classified Bibliography. Edited by C. Kastning. XII, 495 pages. 1976.

Vol. 129: H.-J. Lüthi, Komplementaritäts- und Fixpunktalgorithmen in der mathematischen Programmierung. Spieltheorie und Ökonomie. VII, 145 Seiten. 1976.

Vol. 130: Multiple Criteria Decision Making, Jouy-en-Josas, France. Proceedings 1975. Edited by H. Thiriez and S. Zionts. VI, 409 pages. 1976.

Vol. 131: Mathematical Systems Theory. Proceedings 1975. Edited by G. Marchesini and S. K. Mitter. X, 408 pages. 1976.

Vol. 132: U. H. Funke, Mathematical Models in Marketing. A Collection of Abstracts. XX, 514 pages. 1976.

Vol. 133: Warsaw Fall Seminars in Mathematical Economics 1975. Edited by M. W. Loś, J. Loś, and A. Wieczorek. V. 159 pages. 1976.

Vol. 134: Computing Methods in Applied Sciences and Engineering. Proceedings 1975. VIII, 390 pages. 1976.

Vol. 135: H. Haga, A Disequilibrium – Equilibrium Model with Money and Bonds. A Keynesian – Walrasian Synthesis. VI, 119 pages. 1976.

Vol. 136: E. Kofler und G. Menges, Entscheidungen bei unvollständiger Information. XII, 357 Seiten. 1976.

Vol. 137: R. Wets, Grundlagen Konvexer Optimierung. VI, 146 Seiten. 1976.

Vol. 138: K. Okuguchi, Expectations and Stability in Oligopoly Models. VI, 103 pages. 1976.

Vol. 139: Production Theory and Its Applications. Proceedings. Edited by H. Albach and G. Bergendahl. VIII, 193 pages. 1977.

Vol. 140: W. Eichhorn and J. Voeller, Theory of the Price Index. Fisher's Test Approach and Generalizations. VII, 95 pages. 1976.

Vol. 141: Mathematical Economics and Game Theory. Essays in Honor of Oskar Morgenstern. Edited by R. Henn and O. Moeschlin. XIV, 703 pages. 1977.

Vol. 142: J. S. Lane, On Optimal Population Paths. V, 123 pages. 1977.

Vol. 143: B. Näslund, An Analysis of Economic Size Distributions. XV, 100 pages. 1977.

Vol. 144: Convex Analysis and Its Applications. Proceedings 1976. Edited by A. Auslender. VI, 219 pages. 1977.

Vol. 145: J. Rosenmüller, Extreme Games and Their Solutions. IV, 126 pages. 1977